THE ROUTLEDGE COMPANION TO MEDIA DISINFORMATION AND POPULISM

This *Companion* brings together a diverse set of concepts used to analyse dimensions of media disinformation and populism globally.

The Routledge Companion to Media Disinformation and Populism explores how recent transformations in the architecture of public communication and particular attributes of the digital media ecology are conducive to the kind of polarised, anti-rational, post-fact, post-truth communication championed by populism. It is both interdisciplinary and multidisciplinary, consisting of contributions from leading and emerging scholars analysing aspects of misinformation, disinformation, and populism across countries, political systems, and media systems. A global, comparative approach to the study of misinformation and populism is important in identifying common elements and characteristics, and these individual chapters cover a wide range of topics and themes, including fake news, mediatisation, propaganda, alternative media, immigration, science, and law-making, to name a few.

This *Companion* is a key resource for academics, researchers, and policymakers as well as undergraduate and postgraduate students in the fields of political communication, journalism, law, sociology, cultural studies, international politics, and international relations.

Howard Tumber is Professor in the Department of Journalism at City, University of London, UK. He is a founder and editor of *Journalism: Theory, Practice and Criticism*. He has published widely on the sociology of media and journalism.

Silvio Waisbord is Director of and Professor in the School of Media and Public Affairs at George Washington University, USA. He was the editor-in-chief of the *Journal of Communication*, and he has published widely about news, politics, and social change.

THE ROUTLEDGE COMPANION TO MEDIA DISINFORMATION AND POPULISM

Edited by Howard Tumber and Silvio Waisbord

Routledge
Taylor & Francis Group

LONDON AND NEW YORK

First published 2021
by Routledge
2 Park Square, Milton Park, Abingdon, Oxon OX14 4RN

and by Routledge
52 Vanderbilt Avenue, New York, NY 10017

Routledge is an imprint of the Taylor & Francis Group, an informa business

British Library Cataloguing-in-Publication Data
A catalogue record for this book is available from the British Library

Library of Congress Cataloging-in-Publication Data
A catalog record for this book has been requested

ISBN: 978-0-367-43576-9 (hbk)
ISBN: 978-0-367-70491-9 (pbk)
ISBN: 978-1-003-00443-1 (ebk)

Typeset in Bembo
by Apex CoVantage, LLC

CONTENTS

Contents

FIGURES

TABLES

CONTRIBUTORS

Rachel Armitage is a PhD candidate in the Online Civic Culture Centre at Loughborough University. Her research aims to identify the political and social psychological roots of misinformation and disinformation and to explore how different interventions on social media might reduce individuals' propensity to share such content. Rachel holds a BA in political science from the University of Birmingham and is a 2016 Nottingham Roosevelt Memorial Travelling Scholar. She has worked in both community engagement and local government, with a specific focus on promoting democratic participation.

Babak Bahador is Associate Research Professor at the School of Media and Public Affairs (SMPA) at George Washington University and a senior fellow at the University of Canterbury in New Zealand. He holds a PhD in international relations from the London School of Economics. His research focuses on the overlap of media and politics/international relations, with primary focus on peacebuilding. At GW, Babak directs the Media and Peacebuilding Project, which aims to bridge the gap between academic research and peacebuilding practice. He is also a faculty member at GW's Institute for Data, Democracy and Politics.

Catherine R. Baker is a PhD researcher in the Online Civic Culture Centre (O3C) at Loughborough University. Her research focuses on infrastructures of meaning, identity, and rhetoric within the online misogynist incel movement. Catherine holds a first-class honours degree in psychology from Trinity College Dublin, where she also worked as a research assistant in the Trinity Institute of Neuroscience.

Sarah Banet-Weiser is Professor of Media and Communications at the London School of Economics. She is the author of *The Most Beautiful Girl in the World: Beauty Pageants and National Identity* (1999), *Kids Rule! Nickelodeon and Consumer Citizenship* (2007), *Authentic™: The Politics of Ambivalence in a Brand Culture* (2012), and *Empowered: Popular Feminism and Popular Misogyny* (2018). She is the co-editor of *Cable Visions: Television Beyond Broadcasting* (2007), *Commodity Activism: Cultural Resistance in Neoliberal Times* (2012), and *Racism PostRace* (2019) and has published in journals such as *Social Media and Society*, *International Journal of Communication*, *American Quarterly*, *Critical Studies in Media Communication*, *Feminist Theory*, and *Cultural Studies*.

Robin Bayes is a PhD candidate in political science at Northwestern University. Her research focuses on the political communication and political psychology of science-related policy issues, particularly the environment, sustainability, and climate change. In recent projects, she has investigated the motivational dynamics behind partisan-motivated reasoning, the need for publicly available data sources regarding science literacy and attitudes in the American public, and the future of climate change consensus messaging research.

Leticia Bode is a provost's distinguished Associate Professor in the Communication, Culture, and Technology master's programme at Georgetown University. She researches the intersection of communication, technology, and political behaviour, emphasising the role communication and information technologies may play in the acquisition, use, effects, and implications of political information.

Svetlana S. Bodrunova is habilitated Doctor of Political Science and Professor at the School of Journalism and Mass Communications, St. Petersburg State University, Russia. She has led five research projects and published two books, several chapters, and over 80 research papers in Russian and English on Russian and European journalism, media and politics, social media, and automated methods of media research. She leads the Center for International Media Research in her university. Her works have appeared in *Journalism, International Journal of Communication, Media and Communication*, and *Journalism Practice*. She is a co-creator and host of CMSTW, an annual conference on comparative media studies.

Toby Bolsen is Associate Professor of Political Science and Faculty Affiliate at the Urban Studies Institute, Georgia State University. He studies public opinion, political behaviour, science and political communication, and experimental methods.

Carolina Carazo is Professor of Media and Political Communication in the School of Communication at the University of Costa Rica. She obtained her PhD in sociology from Universidad Nacional de Educación a Distancia (Spain) and holds a master's degree in political communication (Emerson College, Boston, MA). She is a researcher at the Communication Research Center at University of Costa Rica and has published articles on media, journalism, and political communication.

Andrew Chadwick is Professor of Political Communication in the Department of Communication and Media at Loughborough University, where he is also director of the Online Civic Culture Centre (O3C).

Precious N. Chatterje-Doody is Lecturer in Politics and International Studies at Open University, UK. Her multidisciplinary research interests centre on questions of communication, soft power, identity, and security, particularly in relation to Russia. She has published articles in *Politics, Critical Studies on Security,* and *Media and Communication*, and her monographs, 'The Russian Identity riddle: Unwrapping Russia's Security Policy' and 'Russia Today and Conspiracy Theory' (with Dr. Ilya Yablokov, Leeds University) are due to be published by Routledge in 2021.

Nicole Cooke is the Augusta Baker Endowed Chair and Associate Professor at the University of South Carolina. Her research and teaching interests include human information behaviour, critical cultural information studies, and diversity and social justice in librarianship. She was the 2019 ALISE Excellence in Teaching Award recipient, and she has edited and authored several books, including *Information Services to Diverse Populations* and *Fake News and Alternative Facts: Information Literacy in a Post-truth Era*.

Glenda Cooper (PhD) is Senior Lecturer in journalism at City, University of London. She is the author of *Reporting Humanitarian Disasters in a Social Media Age* (Routledge, 2018) and co-editor of *Humanitarianism, Communications and Change* (Peter Lang, 2015). Prior to City, she was the 14th Guardian Research Fellow at Nuffield College, Oxford, and has worked as a staff reporter and editor at *The Independent*, the *Sunday Times*, the *Washington Post*, the *Daily Telegraph*, and BBC Radio 4.

Rhys Crilley is a Leverhulme Early Career Fellow in the Department of Politics and International Relations at the University of Glasgow, Scotland. His current research explores the politics of nuclear weapons through an attention to narratives and emotions in policies of deterrence and strategies for disarmament. Rhys has published on the intersections of popular culture, social media, and war in several journal articles, and he is currently working on writing his first monograph.

Eileen Culloty is Post-doctoral Researcher at the Dublin City University Institute for Future Media and Journalism, where she leads research on countering disinformation as part of the H2020 project Provenance (grant no. 825227).

Stephen Cushion is Professor at Cardiff University's School of Journalism, Media and Culture. He has written three sole-authored books, *News and Politics: The Rise of Live and Interpretive Journalism* (2015, Routledge), *The Democratic Value of News: Why Public Service Media Matter* (2012, Palgrave), and *Television Journalism* (2012, Sage), and one co-authored book, *Reporting Elections: Rethinking the Logic of Campaign Coverage* (2018, Polity Press, and co-edited *The Future of 24-Hour News* (2016, Peter Lang) and *The Rise of 24-Hour News* (2010, Peter Lang). He has published over 70 journal articles, book chapters, and reports on issues related to news, politics, and journalism.

James Deane is Director of Policy and Research at BBC Media Action, the BBC's international media support charity. He is also the principal author of a feasibility study to create a new international fund for public interest media. James is a founding member and former executive director of the Panos Institute, founded in 1986 to inform and improve developing country–driven public debate on environment and development issues. He is also chair of the Board of Global Voices, a citizens' journalism network. He is the author and commissioner of multiple briefings and publications on the role of media in international development.

Carlos de la Torre is Professor and Director of the Center for Latin American Studies at the University of Florida. He has been a fellow at the Simon Guggenheim Foundation and the Woodrow Wilson Center for Scholars. He is the editor of *The Routledge Handbook of Global Populism* (2019); *The Promise and Perils of Populism* (2015); and *Latin American Populism of the Twenty-First Century*, co-edited with Cynthia Arnson (2013). He is the author of *Populisms: A Quick Immersion* and *Populist Seduction in Latin America*.

Claes de Vreese is Professor and Chair of Political Communication in the Amsterdam School of Communication Research (ASCoR), University of Amsterdam (UvA). He is the founding director of the Center for Politics and Communication. His research interests include technology and democracy; comparative journalism research; the effects of news, public opinion, and European integration; and the effects of information and campaigning on elections, referendums, and direct democracy.

Leen d'Haenens is Professor in Communication Science at the Institute for Media Studies of the Faculty of Social Sciences in KU Leuven, where she teaches Analysis of Media Texts and European Media Policy at the BA level and Media, Audiences and Identity at the MA level. Her research interests touch upon the topic of young people and (social) media use, with a focus on vulnerable youth. She combines quantitative and qualitative methods; multi-site comparisons; and, in recent years, 'small data' with 'big data' methods. She is co-editor of *Communications: the European Journal of Communication Research* and associate editor of *The International Communication Gazette*. She is a member of the Euromedia Research Group.

James N. Druckman is the Payson S. Wild Professor of Political Science and a faculty fellow at the Institute for Policy Research, Northwestern University. He studies public opinion, science and political communication, and experimental methods.

Anthony Dudo (PhD, University of Wisconsin-Madison) is Associate Professor at the Stan Richards School of Advertising and Public Relations at the University of Texas at Austin and the programme director for science communication in the Center for Media Engagement. Anthony researches the intersection of science, media, and society. He is particularly interested in scientists' public engagement activities, media representations of science and environmental issues, and the contributions of informational and entertainment media to public perceptions of science. His recent work has examined factors influencing scientists' likelihood to engage in public communication, scientists' goals for public engagement, and the growing community of science communication trainers.

Johanna Dunaway is Associate Professor at Texas A&M University. Her research focuses on political communication and media effects on political learning, attitudes, and behavior. Her current research examines the political impact of the changing contemporary media environment. Her work appears in journals such as *The American Journal of Political Science*; *Information, Communication & Society*; *The Journal of Computer-Mediated Communication*; *The Journal of Communication*; *The Journal of Politics*; *Journalism Studies*; *PLoS One*; *Political Communication*; *Political Research Quarterly*; *Political Behavior*; *Public Opinion Quarterly*; and *Social Science Quarterly*. She also co-authored the 9th and 10th editions of *Mass Media and American Politics*.

William H. Dutton is Emeritus Professor at the University of Southern California; an Oxford Martin Fellow, supporting the Global Cyber Security Capacity Centre at the University of Oxford's Department of Computer Science; a senior fellow at the Oxford Internet Institute (OII); and a visiting professor in media and communication at the University of Leeds. Until 2018, Bill was the James H. Quello Professor of Media and Information Policy at Michigan State University, where he was the director of the Quello Center. Prior to that, he was the OII's founding director and the first professor of internet studies at Oxford University.

Jennifer Earl is Professor of Sociology and Government and Public Policy at the University of Arizona. Her research focuses on social movements, information technologies, and the sociology of law, with research emphases on internet activism, social movement repression, youth activism, and legal change. She is the recipient of a National Science Foundation CAREER Award for research from 2006 to 2011 on web activism, was a member of the MacArthur Research Network on Youth and Participatory Politics, and co-authored (with Katrina Kimport) *Digitally Enabled Social Change*.

Jana Laura Egelhofer is a PhD candidate at the Department of Communication, University of Vienna. Her research interests include fake news and disinformation, media criticism, political journalism, and media perceptions. Her work has been published in international journals such as *Annals of the International Communication Association* and *Journalism Studies*.

Simon Faulkner is Senior Lecturer in art history and visual culture at Manchester Metropolitan University. His research is concerned with the political uses and meanings of images, with a particular emphasis on conflict, activism, and protest. Since 2007, this research has been particularly concerned with relationships between visual practices and the Israeli occupation. He is also the co-director of the Visual Social Media Lab and has a strong interest in the development of methods relevant to the analysis of images circulated on social media.

Kevin Foster is the head of the School of Languages, Literatures, Cultures and Linguistics at Monash University in Melbourne. He is the author of *Fighting Fictions: War, Narrative and National Identity* (1999), *Lost Worlds: Latin America and the Imagining of Empire* (2009), and *Don't Mention the War: The Australian Defence Force, the Media and the Afghan Conflict* (2013). He edited *What Are We Doing in Afghanistan? The Military and the Media at War* (2009) and *The Information Battlefield: Representing Australians at War* (2011). His new book, *Anti-Social Media: Conventional Militaries in the Digital Battlespace*, will be published in 2021.

Des Freedman is Professor of Media and Communications at Goldsmiths, University of London, and co-director of the Goldsmiths Leverhulme Media Research Centre. He is the author of *The Contradictions of Media Power* (Bloomsbury, 2014) and *The Politics of Media Policy* (Polity, 2008) and co-author (with James Curran and Natalie Fenton) of *Misunderstanding the Internet* (Routledge, 2016). He has edited a number of volumes on broadcasting, media reform, liberalism, terrorism, and the politics of higher education and is one of the founder members and former chair of the UK Media Reform Coalition.

Thomas Frissen is Assistant Professor in Digital Technology and Society at the Faculty of Arts and Social Sciences, Maastricht University. His research centres around questions concerning the influences of digital media and technologies in radicalisation, extremism, and terrorism. Specifically, his research aims to advance a better understanding of various 'dark' online cultures, ranging from Salafi-jihadism, and right-wing extremism, to communities of non-suicidal self-injurious behavior. His current research concentrates on the spread dynamics of (extreme) conspiracy theories, fake news, and memes in the online information ecosystem. Thomas uses a research toolbox that consists of both classical and digital social scientific research methods.

Daniel Funke is a staff writer covering online mis- and disinformation for PolitiFact, a Pulitzer Prize–winning fact-checking website based at the Poynter Institute for Media Studies. He has been writing about fact-checking, technology, misinformation, and politics since 2017, when he joined the International Fact-Checking Network as a reporter. Funke is a former recipient of the Google News Lab Fellowship and has worked for several news outlets in the United States, including the *Los Angeles Times*, *USA Today*, and the *Atlanta Journal-Constitution*. He is a graduate of the Grady College of Journalism and Mass Communication at the University of Georgia.

Cherian George is Professor of media studies at Hong Kong Baptist University. He researches media freedom, censorship, and hate propaganda. His 2016 monograph, *Hate Spin: The Manufacture of Religious Offense and its Threat to Democracy* (MIT Press), was named one of the 100 best books of the year by *Publishers Weekly*. His other recent books include *Media and Power in Southeast Asia* (with Gayathry Venkiteswaran; Cambridge University Press, 2019).

His graphic book on cartoon censorship, *Red Lines: Political Cartoons and the Struggle against Censorship* (with Sonny Liew), will be published by MIT Press in 2021.

Eva Haifa Giraud is Senior Lecturer in Media at Keele University, her research focuses on frictions and affinities between non-anthropocentric theories and activist practice. Her monograph on these themes, *What Comes After Entanglement? Activism, Anthropocentrism and an Ethics of Exclusion* (Duke University Press), was published in 2019 and she has also published articles in journals including *Theory, Culture & Society*, *Social Studies of Science*, *New Media & Society*, and *The Sociological Review*. She is currently reviews editor for *Cultural Politics*.

Shawn Goh is a research assistant at the Institute of Policy Studies at the Lee Kuan Yew School of Public Policy, National University of Singapore. His research focuses on the social and policy implications of digital media and the internet: specifically in the areas of misinformation and disinformation, internet governance, digital inclusion, and government communications. In 2018, he was invited by the Singapore Parliamentary Select Committee on Deliberate Online Falsehoods as an expert witness to present his research on tackling online falsehoods. His recent publications on the topic include a conference paper presented at the 69th annual International Communication Association Conference and a peer-reviewed journal article on governing the information ecosystem in Southeast Asia that was published in *Public Integrity* in 2019.

Lucas Graves is Associate Professor in the School of Journalism and Mass Communication at the University of Wisconsin-Madison. He has been at the forefront of research on the global fact-checking movement and is the author of *Deciding What's True: The Rise of Political Fact-Checking in American Journalism* (Columbia University Press, 2016). His work has appeared in the *New York Times*, *The Columbia Journalism Review*, *The Nieman Journalism Lab*, and many scholarly journals. From 2017 to 2019, he was Senior Research Fellow and acting Research Director at the Reuters Institute for the Study of Journalism at Oxford University.

Hannah Guy is a PhD student at Manchester Metropolitan University, examining the role of images in the spread of disinformation on social media. This project is funded through an Economic and Social Research Council (ESRC) Collaborative Doctoral Award and is in partnership with First Draft. She is also a member of the Visual Social Media Lab, where her current projects explore images shared on Twitter during the emergence of the Black Lives Matter movement and digital literacy in the context of the COVID-19 pandemic.

Daniel C. Hallin is Distinguished Professor of Communication at the University of California, San Diego, and is a fellow of the International Communication Association. His books include *The "Uncensored War": The Media and Vietnam*; *"We Keep America on Top of the World": Television News and the Public Sphere*; *Comparing Media Systems: Three Models of Media and Politics*; and *Making Health Public: How News Coverage Is Remaking Media, Medicine and Contemporary Life*. He is currently doing research on media systems in Latin America.

Michael Hameleers (PhD, University of Amsterdam, 2017) is Assistant Professor in Political Communication at the Amsterdam School of Communication Research (ASCoR), Amsterdam, The Netherlands. His research interests include corrective information, disinformation, populism, framing, (affective) polarisation, and the role of social identity in media effects.

Jaron Harambam is an interdisciplinary sociologist working on conspiracy theories, (social) media, and AI (content moderation, search/recommender systems). He is Marie Sklodowska-Curie Individual Fellowship holder at the Institute for Media Studies (KU Leuven,

Belgium) and held a post-doctoral research position at the Institute for Information Law (University of Amsterdam). His monograph "Contemporary Conspiracy Culture: Truth and Knowledge in an Era of Epistemic Instability" is out at Routledge and won the Best Dissertation 2017–19 Award of the Dutch Sociology Association (NSV). He is editor-in-chief of the open-access Dutch peer-reviewed journal www.TijdschriftSociologie.eu and a member of the European network of scholars working on conspiracy theories, COST COMPACT.

Alison Harcourt is Professor of Public Policy at the Department of Politics at the University of Exeter. She is also Director of the Centre for European Governance. Alison specialises in regulatory change in digital markets and is interested in solutions to regulatory problems based around the citizen/consumer and/or civil society voice. She has written on the regulation of traditional and new media markets and internet governance at EU and international levels contributing to the literature on agenda-setting, regulatory competition, soft governance, Europeanisation, and policy convergence.

Jonathan Hardy is Professor of Communications and Media at the University of the Arts, London, and teaches media political economy at Goldsmiths College, London. He writes and comments on media industries, media and advertising, communications regulation, and international media systems. His books include *Critical Political Economy of the Media* (2014), *Cross-Media Promotion* (2010), and *Western Media Systems* (2008). He is co-editor of *The Advertising Handbook* (2018) and series editor of Routledge Critical Advertising Studies. He is a member of the editorial boards of *Digital Journalism* (Taylor and Francis), *Political Economy of Communication*, and *Triple C: Communication, Capitalism & Critique*.

George Hawley is Associate Professor of political science at the University of Alabama. His research interests include electoral behaviour, politics and religion, conservatism in the US, and right-wing radicalism. He is the author of six books, including *Making Sense of the Alt-Right* and *Right-Wing Critics of American Conservatism*.

Alfred Hermida (PhD) is Professor at the School of Journalism, Writing, and Media at the University of British Columbia and co-founder of The Conversation Canada. With his more than two decades of experience in digital journalism, his research addresses the transformation of media, emergent news practices, media innovation, social media, and data journalism. He is the author of *Tell Everyone: Why We Share and Why It Matters* (Doubleday, 2014), winner of the 2015 National Business Book Award, as well as co-author of *Data Journalism and the Regeneration of News* (Routledge, 2019) and *Participatory Journalism: Guarding Open Gates at Online Newspapers* (Wiley Blackwell, 2011). Hermida was a BBC TV, radio, and online journalist for 16 years, including 4 in North Africa and the Middle East, before going on to be a founding news editor of the BBC News website in 1997.

Karina Horsti (PhD) is a media and migration scholar whose work focuses on refugees, migration, memory, racism, and nationalist populist movements. She is Senior Lecturer in Cultural Policy at the University of Jyväskylä, Finland. She works across disciplines and collaborates with artists, activists, and refugees. She has directed multiple research projects, including Post-Truth Public Stories in the Transnational Hybrid Media Space (2017–2018) and two Nordic research networks – Borderscapes, Memory and Migration (2016–2017) and Nordic Research Network for Media, Migration and Society (2007–2010). She is the editor of *The Politics of Public Memories of Forced Migration and Bordering in Europe* (2019).

Rina James is a doctoral candidate in sociology at the University of Arizona, specialising in technology, culture, and inequality. They are currently engaged in two strands of research.

The first is concerned with economic impacts of disparities in digital skills; the second focuses on the production and spread of gender-essentialist, anti-feminist ideology on social media.

Maria Kyriakidou is Senior Lecturer in the School of Journalism, Media and Culture at Cardiff University. Her research addresses the relationship between media and globalisation, with a particular focus on the mediation of distant suffering and global crises. She has published work on audience engagement with distant disasters, the media coverage of the Euro crisis, and global media events.

Matthew Lease (PhD, Brown University) is Associate Professor and computer scientist in the School of Information and a faculty research associate for the Center for Media Engagement, University of Texas at Austin. His research spans crowdsourcing, information retrieval, and natural language processing. His lab received recent paper awards at the 2019 European Conference for Information Retrieval and the 2016 Association for the Advancement of Artificial Intelligence Human Computation and Crowdsourcing conference. Lease is currently helping lead Good Systems, an eight-year, university-wide Grand Challenge Initiative at UT Austin to design AI technologies that maximally benefit society.

Sophie Lecheler is Professor of Political Communication at the Department of Communication Science, University of Vienna. Her research focuses on political journalism, digitalisation of news, emotions, and experimental methods. She previously worked at the Amsterdam School of Communication Research (ASCoR) and the LSE's Department of Government. Her work has been published in a wide range of international journals, such as *Political Communication*, *Political Psychology*, *Communication Research*, *Journal of Communication*, and *New Media & Society*. She is currently Associate Editor of the *International Journal of Press/Politics* and editorial board member of several high-ranking journals.

Eun-Ju Lee (PhD Stanford University) is Professor in the Department of Communication at Seoul National University, Republic of Korea. Her research has focused on social cognition and social influence in computer-mediated communication and human-computer interaction. She co-edited *Media Psychology* and is the current editor-in-chief of *Human Communication Research*. She is an ICA Fellow.

Jeremy Levy is a PhD candidate in Northwestern's Department of Political Science. He studies public opinion, political communications and political psychology, belief systems, and public policy. His current project focuses on conceptual issues in defining misinformation and what this means for our understanding of misinformation prevalence, difficulty in correction, and normative implications. Before coming to Northwestern, he worked at the Urban Institute and received his Masters of Public Policy from the University of California, Berkeley.

Jianing Li is a PhD student and a Knight Scholar of Communications and Civic Renewal the School of Journalism and Mass Communication at the University of Wisconsin-Madison. Her research centres on misinformation, misperception, and fact-checking in new communication ecologies. Using experimental, computational, and social neuroscience methods, her work examines citizens' knowledge in contested political and public health issues, psychological and contextual mechanisms contributing to misperceptions, dissemination of and discourse around misinformation in digital media environments, and effective corrective messages that facilitate belief and attitude updating.

Gina M. Masullo (PhD, Syracuse University) is the associate director of the Center for Media Engagement and Associate Professor in the School of Journalism and Media at the

University of Texas at Austin. Her research focuses on how the digital space both connects and divides people and how that influences society, individuals, and journalism. She is co-editor of *Scandal in a Digital Age* and author of *Online Incivility and Public Debate: Nasty Talk* and *The New Town Hall: Why We Engage Personally with Politicians*, is forthcoming in 2020.

Declan McDowell-Naylor is a research associate in the Cardiff School of Journalism, Media and Culture at Cardiff University. His research focuses on digital politics, political communication, science and technology development, and democracy. Alongside Professor Stephen Cushion and Dr Richard Thomas, he is a researcher on the ESRC-funded project titled 'Beyond the MSM: Understanding the Rise of Alternative Online Political Media'. He has been published in *Journalism* and contributed chapters to the edited editions of *Political Communication in Britain* (Palgrave Macmillan, 2019) and *A Research Agenda for Digital Politics* (Edward Elgar, 2020).

Judith Möller is tenured Assistant Professor in political communication at the Department of Communication Science at the University of Amsterdam. In her research, she focuses on the effects of political communication: in particular, social media and digital media.

Bruce Mutsvairo is Professor of Journalism at Auburn University in the US. His research focuses on the development of journalism and democracy in the global South. He is the author/ editor or editor of eight books published by Palgrave Macmillan, Amsterdam University Press, and Rowman and Littlefield. His ninth book, *Decolonizing Political Communication in Africa*, is due in early 2021 from Routledge. He is a visiting research fellow at the University of Free State in South Africa.

Sarah Oates is Professor and Senior Scholar at the Phillip Merrill College of Journalism at the University of Maryland, College Park. Her work focuses on political communication and democratisation. Her most recent book, *Revolution Stalled: The Political Limits of the Internet in the Post-Soviet Sphere* (Oxford University Press), found a faint hope for online mobilisation in Russia. Her current work examines how political messages travel through media ecosystems, including a study of how Russian propaganda narratives gain traction in US media.

Michaël Opgenhaffen is Associate Professor at the Institute for Media Studies (KU Leuven, Belgium). He is director of the master's in journalism programme at the KU Leuven and visiting professor at the University of Leiden, The Netherlands. His research focuses on the production and consumption of social media news. In this context, he studies disinformation on social media platforms. He is co-founder of a fact-checking website in Belgium that uses artificial intelligence to detect fake news.

Christian Staal Bruun Overgaard (MSc, University of Southern Denmark) is a Knight Research Associate at the Center for Media Engagement and a doctoral student at the School of Journalism and Media at the University of Texas at Austin. He holds a BSc and an MSc in economics and business administration from the University of Southern Denmark. His research focuses on the psychological and behavioural effects of news media and the societal and political ramifications of these effects.

Reece Peck is Associate Professor at the Department of Media Culture at the College of Staten Island, CUNY. He is the author of *Fox Populism: Branding Conservatism as Working Class* (Cambridge, 2019). His research engages the media dimension of the American political right and specifically examines how conservative news outlets have used tabloid media styles and populist political rhetoric to reconfigure the meaning of social class in the United States. He also provides commentary on television and politics for news outlets such as the *Washington Post, The Columbia Journalism Review* and *New York Magazine.*

Elizabeth Poole is Professor of media at Keele University. Her work focuses on the production, representation, and reception of Muslims in the media, and she has written widely on this subject including Reporting Islam (I. B. Tauris, 2002), Muslims and the News Media (I.B. Tauris, 2006), and Media Portrayals of Religion and the Secular Sacred (Ashgate, 2013). She has recently been working in the area of digital activism and Islamophobic hate speech online (British Academy, AHRC). She is an executive member of MECCSA, the UK's Media, Communication and Cultural Studies Association.

Elliot Ramo is a first-year PhD student at the University of Arizona School of Sociology. They received their Bachelor of Arts degree in 2012 from the University of Mary Washington. Their research agenda intersects law and society, technology, stratification, and power. Elliot is currently using a mixed-methods approach to investigate how online legal research tools (e.g. the Westlaw database) shape legal knowledge. Prior to graduate school, Elliot worked in the insurance and technology sectors as an analyst and project manager.

Jeannine E. Relly is Professor in the School of Journalism at the University of Arizona. She holds a courtesy appointment with the School of Government and Public Policy and is affiliated with the university's Center for Latin American Studies, Center for Middle Eastern Studies, and Center for Digital Society and Data Studies. Her research focus includes global influences on news media systems. Other research focuses on factors influencing democratic institutions, such as public information access, online disinformation, and various forms of insecurity. She is a research fellow with Columbia University's Tow Center for Digital Journalism.

Craig T. Robertson (PhD, Michigan State University) is a postdoctoral research fellow at the Reuters Institute for the Study of Journalism at the University of Oxford. Craig's research focuses on news audiences, with particular emphasis on audience attitudes and beliefs with respect to journalism, as well as their news consumption behaviors. Key interests are around news trust and credibility, individuals' epistemological beliefs with respect to journalism, audience verification practices, and how people interact with misinformation.

Alex Rochefort is a doctoral student in the Division of Emerging Media Studies at Boston University's College of Communication. His research agenda focuses on platform governance, communication policy, content moderation, and the political uses of misinformation. His 2020 article 'Regulating Social Media Platforms: A Comparative Policy Analysis' appeared in *Communication Law & Policy*. He has also contributed to the 2019 and 2020 editions of Freedom on the Net, a report by Freedom House, where he was a 2019 Google Public Policy Fellow.

Susana Salgado (PhD, 2007) is Research Fellow at the Institute of Social Sciences, University of Lisbon, Portugal. Her most recent publications include the book *Mediated Campaigns and Populism in Europe* (editor; Palgrave, 2019,) and the articles 'Never Say Never . . . Or the Value of Context in Political Communication Research' (*Political Communication*, 2019), 'Interpretive Journalism' (*Oxford Bibliographies in Communication*, 2019), and 'Online Media Impact on Politics: Views on Post-truth Politics and Post-postmodernism', (*International Journal of Media and Cultural Politics*, 2018). Susana is PI of the research project Hate: Streams of Hate and Untruth, funded by the Foundation for Science and Technology (PTDC/CPO-CPO/28495/2017).

Tuija Saresma (PhD) is a senior researcher in the Research Centre for Contemporary Culture at the University of Jyväskylä, Finland. Saresma is a co-director of the research consortium Crossing Borders and is currently working on two projects: *Mainstreaming Populism* and *Crises Redefined*. She has published academic and popular texts on affects, hate speech, mobility, populism, and social media. She is the chair of the Finnish Association of Gender Studies, SUNS; the treasurer of the Association for Cultural Studies; the former chair of the Finnish Association of Cultural Studies; and the former editor-in-chief of the Finnish Cultural Studies journal *Kulttuurintutkimus*.

Sam Scovill is a fourth-year PhD candidate in the School of Sociology at the University of Arizona. They received their bachelor's degree from Smith College in 2015. Their research centres around social movements, communication and new technology, and feminist theory. They've done projects centred on how news media impacts how young people choose to participate politically and how perceptions of news media's impact on people influences movement mobilisation, demobilisation, and countermovement mobilisation.

Soo Yun Shin (PhD, Michigan State University) is Assistant Professor in the Department of Communicology at the University of Hawaii at Manoa. Her research topics include how people process information online to form impressions and make decisions in various contexts, including social media, e-commerce websites, and virtual teams.

Ignacio Siles is Professor of Media and Technology Studies in the School of Communication at the University of Costa Rica. He holds a PhD in media, technology, and society (Northwestern University) and a master's degree in communications (Université de Montréal). He is the editor of *Democracia en Digital: Facebook, Comunicación y Política en Costa Rica* (CICOM, 2020) and the author of *A Transnational History of the Internet in Central America, 1985–2000* (Palgrave Macmillan, 2020) and *Networked Selves: Trajectories of Blogging in the United States and France* (Peter Lang, 2017), along with several articles on the relationship between technology, communication, and society.

Carol Soon (PhD) is a Senior Research Fellow at the Institute of Policy Studies at the Lee Kuan Yew School of Public Policy, National University of Singapore. Her research focuses on media regulation, digital inclusion, new media and activism, and public engagement. Her research has been published in *The Journal of Computer-Mediated Communication*, *The Asian Journal of Communication*, and *Public Integrity*. In 2018, she made a written submission to the Select Committee on Deliberate Online Falsehoods. Carol is also Associate Director of the Asia Journalism Fellowship and the vice chair of Singapore's Media Literacy Council. In 2012, she received the Australian Endeavour Award. Her paper on political blogging in Singapore won the Best Paper Award at the Conference for E-Democracy and Open Government in 2013.

Natalie Jomini Stroud (PhD, University of Pennsylvania) is the founding and current director of the Center for Media Engagement and Professor of Communication studies and journalism at the University of Texas at Austin. Her research on the uses and effects of political news has received numerous national and international awards, including the Outstanding Book Award from the International Communication Association for her book *Niche News: The Politics of News Choice*.

Scott R. Stroud (PhD, Temple University) is Associate Professor in the Department of Communication Studies at the University of Texas at Austin. He is the founding director of the Media Ethics Initiative and the program director of media ethics at the Center for Media Engagement at the University of Texas at Austin. Dr. Stroud's work specialises in the intersection between communication and culture. His books include *John Dewey and the Artful Life* and *Kant and the Promise of Rhetoric*.

Jane Suiter is Associate Professor in the School of Communications at Dublin City University and director of the Institute for Future Media and Journalism. She is the coordinator of H2020 Provenance on countering disinformation and the Marie Sklodowska Curie project JOLT on advancing digital and data technology for journalism.

Edson C. Tandoc Jr. (PhD, University of Missouri) is Associate Professor at the Wee Kim Wee School of Communication and Information at Nanyang Technological University in Singapore. His research focuses on the sociology of message construction in the context of digital journalism. He has conducted studies on the construction of news and social media messages. His studies about influences on journalists have focused on the impact of journalistic roles, new technologies, and audience feedback on the various stages of the news gatekeeping process. This stream of research has led him to study journalism from the perspective of news consumers as well, investigating how readers make sense of critical incidents in journalism and take part in reconsidering journalistic norms and how changing news consumption patterns facilitate the spread of fake news.

Richard Thomas is Senior Lecturer in journalism and Programme Director at Swansea University. His research centres on the news coverage of the key issues shaping the twenty-first century, such as politics, elections, inequality, economic growth, and conflict. He has published many articles in leading journals and, with Professor Stephen Cushion, wrote *Reporting Elections: Rethinking the Logic of Campaign Coverage*. He is also the co-investigator on the ESRC-funded project titled 'Beyond the MSM: Understanding the Rise of Alternative Online Political Media', working alongside Professor Cushion and Dr Declan McDowell-Naylor.

Emily Thorson is Assistant Professor of political science at Syracuse University. Emily's research traces how political information and misinformation reaches citizens (through traditional and new forms of media) and how this information shapes their attitudes and behavior. She co-edited *Misinformation and Mass Audiences* (University of Texas Press), and her book *The Invented State: Systematic Policy Misperceptions in the American Public* is forthcoming from Oxford University Press. She received a dual PhD in communications and political science at the Annenberg School of Communication and at the Department of Political Science at the University of Pennsylvania.

Larissa Tristán is Associate Professor of Media and Social Communication in the School of Communication at the University of Costa Rica (UCR). She has a PhD and a master's degree in social communication (both from Universitat Pompeu Fabra, Catalonia). She is a researcher at the Communication Research Center (CICOM) at UCR and has published articles on discourse analysis, migration, urban studies, and political communication.

Dariya Tsyrenzhapova is a doctoral student in the School of Journalism and Media at the University of Texas at Austin. She is a current graduate research assistant with the Propaganda Research Team at UT's Center for Media Engagement. Her research focuses on public opinion polarisation, big data, and computational science. Prior to starting her Ph.D., Tsyrenzhapova worked on NPR's Investigations Desk in Washington, D.C., was a Dow Jones Data Fellow at the Investigative Reporting Workshop at American University, and a country manager for the Media Program at the Open Society Foundations (OSF) in Almaty, Kazakhstan.

Melissa Tully (PhD, University of Wisconsin-Madison) is Associate Professor in the School of Journalism and Mass Communication at the University of Iowa. Her research interests include news literacy, misinformation, civic and political participation, and global media studies. She has published widely in the area of news literacy and perceptions and responses to (mis) information in journals like *Mass Communication and Society, Communication Research, Information, Communication and Society*, and *Journalism*, among others.

Cristian Vaccari (PhD, IULM University, Milan, 2006) is Professor of Political Communication and Co-director of the Centre for Research in Communication and Culture at Loughborough University and a research associate of the Center for Social Media and Politics at New York University. He studies political communication by elites and citizens in comparative perspective, with a particular focus on digital and social media. He is the editor-in-chief of the *International Journal of Press/Politics* and a member of the Committee of Experts on Freedom of Expression and Digital Technologies of the Council of Europe.

Farida Vis is Director of the Visual Social Media Lab (VSML) and Professor of Digital Media at Manchester Metropolitan University. The VSML brings together interdisciplinary researchers from academia and across sectors interested in better understanding social media images. Her academic and data journalism work focuses on developing methods for analysing social media images, the spread of mis- and disinformation online, and developing novel visual media literacy approaches to combat this. She has served on the World Economic Forum's Global Agenda Council on Social Media (2013–2016) and the Global Future Council for Information and Entertainment (2016–2019) and is a director at Open Data Manchester.

Emily K. Vraga is Associate Professor at the Hubbard School of Journalism and Mass Communication at the University of Minnesota, where she holds the Don and Carole Larson Professorship in Health Communication. Her research examines methods to correct health misinformation on social media, to limit biased processing of news content, and to encourage attention to more diverse political content online.

Chris Wells is Associate Professor in the Division of Emerging Media Studies and the Department of Journalism at Boston University. He is a scholar of political communication, currently studying how the attention economy shapes media production and social media sharing, how hybrid media flows create the depictions of politics that citizens experience, and how social and political identity influence individuals' interpretations of political communications and political engagement. He is the author of *The Civic Organization and the Digital Citizen* (Oxford University Press, 2015) and recipient of the Young Scholar Award from the International Communication Association (2018).

Oscar Westlund is Professor at the Department of Journalism and Media Studies at Oslo Metropolitan University, where he leads the OsloMet Digital Journalism Research Group. He holds secondary appointments at Volda University College and the University of Gothenburg. He is the editor-in-chief of *Digital Journalism*. He leads The Epistemologies of Digital News Production, a research project funded by the Swedish Foundation for Humanities and Social Sciences. He is a project member of the international research project Source Criticism and Mediated Disinformation (2020–2024). His most recent book is *What Is Digital Journalism Studies?* (Routledge, 2020), co-authored with Steen Steensen.

Samuel C. Woolley (PhD, University of Washington) is Assistant Professor in the School of Journalism and Media at the University of Texas at Austin. He studies computational propaganda: how automated online tools are used to enable both democracy and civic control. He is the author of *The Reality Game* (PublicAffairs, 2020) and co-editor (with Phil Howard) of *Computational Propaganda* (Oxford, 2018). Woolley is the former director of research of the Computational Propaganda Project at Oxford. He is a former Belfer Fellow at the Anti-Defamation League and former research fellow at the German Marshall Fund, Google Jigsaw, and the tech policy lab at the University of Washington.

Bilge Yesil is Associate Professor of Media Culture at the College of Staten Island and on the doctoral faculty of Middle Eastern Studies at the Graduate Center, City University of New York. Her research interest is in global media and communication, with a particular focus on Turkey and the Middle East, global internet policies, online surveillance, and censorship. She is the author of *Video Surveillance: Power and Privacy in Everyday Life* (2009) and *Media in New Turkey: The Origins of an Authoritarian Neoliberal State* (2016). Yesil's current project, *Talking Back to the West: Muslim Turkish Voices in the Global Public Sphere*, explores Turkey's global media and communication projects in relation to geopolitics, history, and religion.

INTRODUCTION

Howard Tumber and Silvio Waisbord

The premise of this *Companion* is that recent transformations in the architecture of public communication and particular attributes of the digital media ecology are conducive to the kind of polarised, anti-rational, post-fact, post-truth communication championed by populism. The rise of populist parties, politicians, and movements around the world is grounded in multiple causes. It is no coincidence that the resurgence of populism has been taking place alongside new forms of disinformation and misinformation.

The purpose of this *Companion* is to bring together in one volume contemporary analyses of various dimensions of dis/misinformation and populism and to understand the linkages between media and journalistic practices and political processes in different countries and cultures.

The relation between populism and mis/disinformation is at the centre of recent research in journalism studies, political communication, and media studies. The guiding question is whether new forms of disinformation and misinformation are connected to populism. Although populism lacks a single definition, we understand it to be a political movement that both reflects the crisis of liberal democracy and challenges core democratic premises, including freedom of the press, freedom of speech, government accountability, and tolerance of difference.

While we recognise that the rise of populist parties, politicians, and movements around the world is grounded in multiple causes, our interest in this *Companion* is exploring whether and how recent transformations in the spaces of public communication and particular attributes of the digital media ecology are conducive to populism. Just as right-wing populism has ascended in many countries in the past years, notably in Brazil, Britain, Hungary, India, the Philippines, Poland, Russia, and the United States, irrationalism in public communication is on the rise too. The latter is represented by post-fact, post-truth communication, as illustrated by the spread of fake information, conspiracy beliefs, and propaganda – issues that have received significant attention and raised justifiable concerns worldwide in recent years. Irrationalism comprises both disinformation and misinformation. Disinformation refers to deliberate attempts to sow confusion and misinformation among the public, with the purpose of political gain by a range of public, private, and social actors. Misinformation alludes to the existence of false information around a range of issues relevant to public life, including political, historical, health, social, and environmental matters, in the public.

We believe it is necessary to audit existing knowledge to map out the dynamics of mis/disinformation globally and their linkages to the current 'populist moment'. While on the surface there seems to be a connection between communication and political trends, it is not immediately obvious that dis/misinformation is necessarily conducive to the kind of illiberal politics represented and championed by populism. To flesh out the relationship between developments in public communication and political dynamics, we think it is necessary to understand the multiple dimensions and the new aspects of mis/disinformation; to study the unique aspects of contemporary populism in relation to media, journalism, and public communication; and to examine plausible and demonstrable connections between these developments. In Chapter 1 we attempt, as editors, to highlight and contextualise the key themes, questions, and debates relevant to media, mis/disinformation, and populism. We set the 'scene' and map key processes and questions for the *Companion*. We outline the principal aims and objectives. In conceptual terms, we discuss the intellectual formation of media, misinformation, and populism; definitions and models; and introduce key interdisciplinary debates about misinformation and the reporting of various aspects of populism.

To explore these issues and the relationship between communication/informational trends and populism, we asked contributors to produce in-depth analyses of key concepts in the literature and to discuss linkages to specific aspects of populist politics, including new empirical work. With this goal in mind, we requested that contributors consider several questions. Are media, disinformation, and populist politics connected; if so, how; and what is the nature of these connections? What specific media changes foster disinformation? What is new about current forms of disinformation, and how are they linked to political strategies and movements? Finally is populism both a cause and effect of deep transformations in media and information?

This introduction explains the rationale for the selection of parts and topics and provides an overview of each chapter.

The *Routledge Companion to Media Disinformation and Populism* is divided into five parts:

Part I Key Concepts
Part II Media Misinformation and Disinformation
Part III The Politics of Misinformation and Disinformation
Part IV Media and Populism
Part V Responses to Misinformation, Disinformation and Populism

Key concepts (Part I)

The first part of the *Companion* comprises chapters on key concepts in the study of misinformation, disinformation and populism. They provide important and valuable insights for building and refining theory in these areas. Misinformation, disinformation and populism are rich subjects of inquiry in many disciplines, and the place of media provides an opportunity both to examine and to deploy broad concepts and theories to understand the dynamics between them.

Carlos de la Torre (Chapter 2) opens this part by asking 'What do we mean by populism?' He identifies four conceptualisations which are prominent nowadays: namely, a set of ideas, a political strategy, a political style, and a political logic. He traces the history of the way sociologists and historians have adopted both the concept and the ideal types with accompanying attributes. He discusses the strategies used by populists to gain and maintain power and then examines their use and abuse of media, demonstrating how some populist leaders are media innovators. Rachel Armitage and Cristian Vaccari (Chapter 3) provide an insight into media use by populists and others by presenting an overview of the main debates about misinformation and disinformation within a political communication context. They demonstrate how mis/disinformation has gained prominence in public discourse, together with the denigration of experts and independent journalists; all this at the expense of evidence-based debate and a subsequent decline in trust of the mainstream media and news organisations. All these developments have been accelerated by social media. They presage the chapters in Part V of the *Companion* by briefly discussing some of the possible solutions to counteract the phenomena of mis/disinformation. Daniel C. Hallin (Chapter 4) continues the theme of populist leaders use of the media. He argues that mediatisation requires a rethink as contemporary mediatised populist politics as exhibited by Donald Trump does not fit well into the traditional narrative about the mediatisation of politics. Hallin argues that we need to think comparatively about its varying, changing forms. He concludes the chapter by providing five points regarding the reconceptualisation of mediatisation. Jonathan Hardy (Chapter 5) analyses how misinformation provides what he terms 'a form of stress testing of media systems analysis'. He focuses on nation-centrism, digital communications, and normativity, all elements in questioning features of 'system-ness' as areas of critique most relevant to the analysis of misinformation. Hardy shows how misinformation poses various challenges to media systems analysis: namely, 'the handling of transnational and transcultural, the range and complexity of digital communications, the multiplicity of actors and processes'.

Sarah Oates (Chapter 6) examines how another 'old' concept – in this case, propaganda – can be located in the digital age. She shows 'how the democratizing effect of online information to create informed citizens is outmatched by the internet's ability to leverage misinformation in the service of populist propaganda'. Using the cases of Trump's election and Russian interference in the campaign, Oates argues that free speech and fairness are put at a disadvantage in the online 'rewired' propaganda war, giving populist actors more success than traditional political parties. Cherian George (Chapter 7) maintains the propaganda theme by analysing the use of hate propaganda. He shows how hate studies have a long pedigree and hate propaganda, sometimes called hate speech, has been around a lot longer 'than the digitally-assisted misinformation that has triggered concern in recent years'. Hate propagandists, whether repressive governments or organised hate groups, are able to dodge attempts at censorship and regulation on social media, thereby stifling the voices of their ideological enemies. He argues that it is important to understand (and, therefore, to counter the fact) that hate campaigns are layered, distributed, and strategic. Judith Moller (Chapter 8) traces the history and meaning of the terms *filter bubble* and *echo chamber*, emphasising that the concepts describe a state rather than a process. While both are described as enclosed spaces, 'the metaphor of the echo chamber focuses on the nature of what is inside this space while the metaphor of the filter bubbles emphasises what constitutes its boundaries: the filtering algorithms'. Moller illustrates the mismatch of theoretical and empirical research on these subjects, suggesting this may be due to the lack of normative research and hence pointing to directions for future research. Susana Salgado (Chapter 9) assesses the major conceptual debates regarding post-truth politics. By interpreting post-truth politics in the context of post-post-modernism, she shows how populism reshapes boundaries in political discourse. In contrast digital media and technologies create favourable conditions for the spread of all kinds of alternative narratives. To combat mis/disinformation Salgado calls for action to ensure social media are compatible with democratic values. The theme of post-truth is continued by Edson C. Tandoc (Chapter 10), who looks at the phenomenon of fake news. He shows how its resurgence as a term arose in the 2016 US presidential election, with subsequent scholarly attention. There are two main components of the term defined in communication studies – namely, the level of facticity and the main intention behind the message. Whilst fake news may be categorised as a form of disinformation, its subsequent spread via social media may be unintentional. Whilst fake news can spread like a virus and continue to evolve, the means to counteract it becomes ever more difficult.

Media misinformation and disinformation (Part II)

The chapters in this part analyse the role of media and journalism platforms in misinformation and disinformation. They examine the way digital technologies have introduced new forms for the expression of misinformation and populist discourse. Dariya Tsyrenzhapova and Samuel C. Woolley (Chapter 11) open this part by examining the digital interference by Russia in the 2016 US presidential election to analyse computational propaganda campaigns on social media. They draw on the literatures from propaganda studies, reflexive control theory, and information diffusion to conceptualise how false news messages, constructed with the specific intention to engender social disagreement, can be utilised in order to mobilise social movements around the world. Johanna Dunaway (Chapter 12) shows how some of the key concepts discussed in Part 1 of the Companion – echo chambers, filter bubbles – are sometimes blamed for polarisation in the era of post-truth. In reviewing the literature, she posits the argument that 'cognitive biases, affective polarisation, and sorting are as much to blame for susceptibility to misinformation and the development of misperceptions' rather than the media and information environment facilitating the dissemination and exposure of misinformation. Dunaway goes on to say that research on misinformation should concentrate on looking at the conditions under which the exposure to misinformation occurs and with what effects. The focus on the epistemology and practice of data journalism is the subject discussed by Oscar Westlund and Alfred Hermida (Chapter 13). They show how data is political – affecting its collection; its availability; the choice of who is included and excluded; and the way it is processed, analysed, and presented. Despite these shortcomings in the data, Westlund and Hermida point out the flaws by showing how journalists repeatedly make authoritative and definitive knowledge claims, instead of indicating the level of credibility present in the data. In the following chapter (14), George Hawley examines the major forms of alt-right media and outlines how the alt-right differed from earlier iterations of the white nationalist movement. He argues that over its relatively short history, the alt-right has relied on different forms of online media to disseminate its message and has effectively used social media to spread its content to a wider audience. In this regard podcasts are an especially important medium for the alt-right. The phenomenon of Fox News is the subject discussed by Reece Peck (Chapter 15). He argues that the resonance of Fox News lies in the populist style of television news that the network innovated rather than an attraction to its conservative ideological orientation as many scholars have posited. Peck explains the components of Fox's populist epistemological framework, arguing that Fox's challenge to expert knowledge and technocratic authority is not simply tied to a profit motive but is a representational choice that is directly connected to Fox's larger populist branding strategy, which interlocks with and is reflective of the ongoing hegemonic project of the American post-war conservative movement.

Declan McDowell-Naylor, Richard Thomas, and Stephen Cushion in Chapter 16 take a contrasting look away from Fox by looking at alternative online political media (AOPM) and asking whether it challenges or exacerbates populism and mis/disinformation or represents just a continuation of partisan news. They discuss whether AOPM provides a corrective role to the mainstream media and remain ambiguous as to whether there is conclusive empirical evidence to link AOPM with contributing to or challenging mis/disinformation or, indeed, contributing to support populist politics. The possible threat from AOPM to the public sphere is left tantalisingly open to future research. Jeannine E. Relly (Chapter 17) is in no doubt about the dangers to the public sphere of online harassment of journalists coming as a direct consequence of populism, mis/disinformation, and impunity. She shows how populist governments frequently disparage news coverage and encourage social media users to attack journalists, particularly women reporters. Anonymous online abusers unleash bots and troll armies to harass and spread disinformation about journalists that inevitably puts them in danger. Around the world, impunity becomes the norm when journalists are killed, populist leaders encourage or create a fertile environment for the attacks, and perpetrators cannot be identified to redress online attackers. Lucas Graves (Chapter 18) uses the questions raised by the 'infodemic' of fake news as a platform to articulate several heuristics for thinking about how mediated misinformation matters in public life today – namely, that there's no such thing as 'online misinformation'. Misinformation (like information) works by allusion, not reason. Misinformation is an index of political incentive structures; just don't call it an echo chamber. Each of these reminders is based on gaps or caveats that are often acknowledged, though only rarely addressed, in the growing literature on misinformation. Taken together, he argues, they may help illuminate new priorities for scholars working in this area. Considering how much of both social media and manipulated content is visual, Simon Faulkner, Hannah Guy, and Farida Vis (Chapter 19), in the final piece of Part II, argue that analysing the role of news images may be a better way to understand misinformation and disinformation. Images and photographs are predominantly examined through a journalistic lens, with a focus on verifying whether an image is 'true' or 'false', whereas Faulkner, Guy, and Vis consider the socio-political context, which they say is fundamental to comprehending how images maybe used for mis/disinformation purposes.

The politics of misinformation and disinformation (Part III)

The chapters in Part III analyse the politics of misinformation by examining transformations in public communication: namely, facticity and deception in relation to a range of contemporary topics and public debates. Many of the chapters define the problems of mis/disinformation and its misperceptions, discuss the causes, and then review potential antidotes. In the opening piece, Sarah Banet-Weiser (Chapter 20) analyses the relationship between misinformation and misogyny and shows how misogyny is often at the core of misinformation campaigns in which women become direct targets of attack. She argues that misogynistic information is similar to racism in being profitable for search engines as they both generate large amounts of web traffic. 'Misogynistic misinformation campaigns do not represent a disruption or a crisis in everyday lives; rather, they represent the centrality and normalization of misogyny as a central part of that everyday life'. Eileen Culloty and Jane Suiter (Chapter 21) show how anti-immigrant disinformation has a long and worldwide history and how a diverse network of actors push anti-immigrant disinformation, bolstering and promoting anti-immigrant attitudes among the wider public. They argue that anti-immigrant disinformation can be viewed as part of a culture war in which an increasing transnational matrix of far-right, alt-right, populist, and conservative groups reinforce a common opposition to a pluralist worldview. Jeremy Levy, Robin Bayes, Toby Bolsen, and Jamie Druckman (Chapter 22) summarise the research on scientific mis/disinformation and the challenges this poses for science communicators seeking to disseminate knowledge and for the implementation of government policies. They argue that the politicisation of science results in public distrust of scientific evidence and conspiratorial thinking (see also Chapters 28 and 29), especially when consensus information contradicts existing beliefs or positions on an issue. They show the possible corrections to misinformation and science politicisation, in order to enhance the positive impact that science can have on societies.

The following two chapters examine the ways in which governments and the military use disinformation to enhance their policies. Rhys Crilley and Precious N. Chatterje-Doody (Chapter 23) trace the recent historical development and thinking around government mis/disinformation in war and its connection with the development of new communication technologies such as the printing press, photography, cinema, television, the internet, and social media. They argue that new developments allow states to bypass the traditional gatekeepers of news and information. Crilley and Chatterje-Doody also show how concepts of propaganda, framing and strategic narratives, and discourse can be adopted to comprehend government disinformation during conflict. Kevin Foster (Chapter 24) discusses the changes in military disinformation from the second world war to the recent conflicts in Iraq and Afghanistan. Strategies have constantly changed in response to previous conflicts. Lessons supposedly learned are found wanting when new media developments scupper tactics previously deployed. Foster shows how disinformation is a key weapon used by the military and governments not only to fight their adversaries but also to win over and maintain the hearts and minds of their domestic audiences. Thomas Frissen, Leen d'Haenens, and Michaël Opgenhaffen (Chapter 25) provide an overview of research on information disorders (e.g. fake news and conspiracy theories – see also Chapters 10 and 28) and examine how extreme right actors have weaponised disinformation. They reflect upon and conceptually develop how the media ecosystem is instrumentalised by examining both social contagion and the algorithmic architecture of online communities that spread and mainstream their extreme-right worldviews, including those on anti-Semitism and white supremacy. The theme of information disorder is taken up by Svetlana Bodrunova (Chapter 26). Using propaganda as a case study, she examines the practices implemented in and by contemporary Russia. She argues that the practices are multi-faceted, with systemic misinformation targeted at internal audiences for populist purposes and outside Russia for international policy goals. These duel goals are a reflection of the complexities of the Russian media ecosystem, where troll activity and misinformation via mainstream media operate for both internal and external audiences. Jennifer Earl, Rina James, Elliot Ramo, and Sam Scovill (Chapter 27) show how social movements and protest have a long relationship with misinformation and disinformation, tracing them back to early theories of collective behaviour and pointing out the changes in the prevalence, patterns of production, spread, and consumption. They introduce five theoretical lenses for false information and social movements – false information as movement catalyst, disinformation and propaganda as repressive tools, false information as a weaponisation of free speech, false information as a commodity, and misinformation resulting from journalistic norms applied to protest.

Jaron Harambam (Chapter 28) poses the question of whether conspiracy theories are the result of a misinformed public or one wittingly believing false information. He asks how they are circulated in the media eco-system and why people follow forms of information often embraced by populists – distrust of institutions, distrust of knowledge/official truth, worldview/ideology. Who are the people who share and endorse these ideas? And should something be done to counter them – is debunking necessary? (See also Chapter 42.) Research on conspiracy theories is mostly rather serious business. It features the causes and consequences of a cultural phenomenon that is generally regarded a societal problem, and hence focuses too much on its dangers. This, he argues, obscures the affective and playful dimensions that are just as much part of conspiracy theories and points to this as a possible direction for future research. Conspiracy theory is one of the themes touched on by Catherine Baker and Andrew Chadwick (Chapter 29). They examine post-truth identities online by providing a conceptual framework for empirical research on the ideology of post-truth movements such as anti-vaxxers, flat-Earthers, and involuntary celibates. They argue that while cognitive biases, conspiracy mentalities, and the decline of trust in institutions are important roots of post-truth identities, digital and social media have played a role in enabling the construction and visibility of these identities and have made it easier for their adherents to connect with each other and sustain their knowledge, norms, and values. The final piece in Part III looks at the consumption of mis/disinformation.

Sophie Lecheler and Jana Egelhofer (Chapter 30) identify two dimensions of the consumption of misinformation and disinformation: namely, 'real' and 'perceived'. The first is the result of the consequences of the consumption of misinformation for citizen attitudes, behaviors, and emotions in various contexts. The second concerns public worries about a 'disinformation crisis' causing widespread perceived consumption effects. Citizens are concerned about being manipulated by what they perceive as disinformation. Consequently, they change their news media diet. This perceived consumption effect is aided by frequent uses of the 'fake news' and 'disinformation' labels by populist politicians when describing legacy news media.

Media and populism (Part IV)

Part IV presents a selection of studies that explore the linkages between media and populism around news coverage of particular political events in different contexts. How do the news media report within a populist milieu in different cultures, and how accurate and consistent is the coverage? The part begins with Bruce Mutsvairo and Susana Salgado (Chapter 31), who look at the rise of populism in Africa, highlighting its initial linkages to anti-colonial politics and its later manifestation as a response to governments that had become detached from the population. They examine four cases in which political leaders have emerged using populist rhetoric and the discourse of the logic of the enemy of the people to gain power. This is often followed by creating or maintaining repressive media laws and regulations to dispel dissent and counter alternative voices who may threaten their power and status. The focus shifts to North America, where Chris Wells and Alex Rochefort (Chapter 32) demonstrate that the tendencies towards populism and susceptibility to misinformation are long-standing characteristic aspects of American political culture. They show that the US is especially susceptible to populist currents. It assumes prominence in contexts in which democratic legitimacy is called into question. The growth in social media in relentlessly re-articulating underlying resentments and supplying end-less resentful interpretations of current events is a permutation of misinformation the US has not seen before, and, they argue, it poses a grave threat to democratic culture. Ignacio Siles, Larissa Tristán, and Carolina Carazo (Chapter 33) examine the role of social media platforms in shaping populism and issues of misinformation in Latin America. They argue that a consideration of the 'elective affinity' between post-truth and populism in the case of Latin America requires assessing the significance of religion and its associated forms of polarisation and messianic authority. Framing religion helps explain the particular manifestations that this link has acquired in Latin America over the past years. Recent presidential campaigns in various countries show how this tripartite affinity has manifested in the parallel dissemination of particular kinds of content, served as a platform for the rise of populist political/religious figures, and shaped the outcome of electoral processes.

The following three chapters look at the media and populism in Europe. Michael Hameleers and Claes deVreese (Chapter 34) provide a conceptualisation and evidence from a study of ten European countries. They argue that it is crucial to explore the extent to which news consumers actually trust the media and whether they perceive a crisis of accuracy and honesty in the news to which they are exposed. Mis/disinformation may thus correspond to societal developments beyond the lack of facticity and honesty of information and can spill over into demand-side evaluations of the media's accuracy and honesty. From their analysis, they confirm that most citizens can distinguish misinformation from disinformation. However, there is strong between-country variation, with news consumers in Western and Northern European countries more likely to trust the accuracy of journalistic reporting and less likely to doubt the honesty of the media elites. In contrast citizens in Eastern and Southern European countries are more likely to have strong perceptions of mis- and disinformation. Karina Horsti and Tuija Saresma (Chapter 35), using the case of Finland, examine the role of social media in the emergence of a right-wing populist movement and its transformation into a political force. They emphasise how the new multi-platform media ecology, together with its decentralised anonymous online spaces, enables political mobilisation to flourish as a precursor to electoral success for right-wing populist parties. Alongside this media system of 'connectivities', the emergence of transnationally widely spread ideologies of Islamophobia and misogyny (see also Chapters 19, 20, and 21) helps to cement the populist movement. In a similar vein, Bilge Yesil (Chapter 36) considers Turkey as a case study to explore the linkages between the structural conditions of the Turkish media system and the governing Justice and Development Party's (AKP) manipulation of social media through the proliferating of falsehoods and conspiracies. She shows how social media, like the mainstream media, is partisan and polarised as groups affiliated with the AKP harass and silence dissent on Twitter and Facebook, overwhelming these sites with government narratives. The ruling party's digital surveillance schemes and heavy use of legal provisions to prosecute its critics make social media sites especially vulnerable to the effects mis/disinformation campaigns. The possibility of Turkey joining the European Union became an important disinformation issue in the United Kingdom Brexit referendum. Glenda Cooper (Chapter 37) examines how populist rhetoric and media manipulation was incorporated into the 2016 campaign. Whilst research on referenda is very limited, with an emphasis on whether the media reporting is balanced and fair, she argues that if news media follow the populist narrative, even while challenging and debunking misinformation, this can end up shaping public reaction. Turkey became a useful conduit to combine EU migration and the refugee crisis in voters' minds. The Leave campaign's use of populist rhetoric, unchallenged for many years, combined with misinformation, managed to overcome the supposed advantage of Remain.

Des Freedman (Chapter 38) reflects on the implication for media systems of conceptions of populism as a threat to reason and social order as well as to consensual and 'objective' journalism. He argues that from the perspective of traditional liberal democratic politics, populism and its mediated forms can be seen as examples of 'policy failure', four of which he identifies: namely, failure to tackle concentrated ownership, to regulate tech companies, to safeguard an effective fourth estate, and to nurture independent public service media. He concludes that existing liberal democratic approaches to media policy have fostered highly unequal and distorted communication systems that have been exploited by forces on the far right. In the final piece in this part, William H. Dutton and Craig T. Robertson (Chapter 39) present the results of their surveys of internet users in seven developed nations indicating that populism is indeed prominent as conventionally defined, making it difficult to view these beliefs as extreme in the contemporary digital age. Interestingly they find that those who hold populist attitudes are no more likely to be trapped in filter bubbles or echo chambers than are other internet users. Instead, they are more politically engaged and actively seek out sources of information about politics. The results lead Dutton and Robertson to speculate on alternative perspectives on populism, such as the rise of a sense of citizen empowerment and the polarisation of political communication in the digital age.

Responses to misinformation, disinformation and populism (Part V)

Part V looks at the responses to misinformation and disinformation, particularly in areas of freedom of speech, human rights, and the diminishing of public trust and journalistic legitimacy and authority. It examines political and social efforts to address the causes and the consequences of mis/disinformation, through mitigating the effects of fake news and other inaccuracies.

The first three pieces in this part examine legal and regulatory responses to mis/disinformation. Alison Harcourt (Chapter 40) explains the current legislative response by the European Union whilst also examining case studies on the UK's, Germany's, and France's responses. Germany introduced a law in 2017 which polices social media websites following a number of high-profile national court cases concerning fake news and the spread of racist material. France passed a law in 2018 which similarly obliges social media networks to take down content upon request from a judge. The UK took a more self-regulative approach after a UK Commons committee investigation into fake news (2017) concluded that Facebook's Mark Zuckerberg failed to show 'leadership or personal responsibility' over fake news. Daniel Funke (Chapter 41) follows Alison Harcourt's analysis of the EU by looking at worldwide actions in restricting the flow of falsehoods on the internet, particularly during elections and other political events. Funke shows that at least 50 countries took some form of action against online mis/disinformation. These range from hard regulations, such as internet shutdowns, to soft regulations, such as media literacy initiatives (see Chapters 44 and 45) and task forces. The effectiveness of these actions is hard to assess since many were only implemented recently. Critics of 'hard' actions see them as having the potential to censor citizens whilst those of 'soft' regulations see little meaningful change being elicited. Shawn Goh Ze Song and Carol Soon (Chapter 42) explore the possibility that Singapore's resilience against rising populism in other parts of the world and the onslaught of populist-fuelled disinformation stems from a balance between the government's using strong-handed regulation to protect national interests and remaining hyper-responsive to public opinion and public demands in order to maintain popular support. They look at how the Protection from Online Falsehoods and Manipulation Act (POFMA) was scoped and communicated to the public and how the government responded to the concerns of civil society, academics, and the wider public regarding potential legislative overreach and censorship. Eun-Ju Lee and Soo Yun Shin (Chapter 43), in discussing debunking misinformation, show that at its core, it entails exposing falsehood and inaccuracies in verifiable information, thereby correcting misbeliefs. They suggest that although the challenges associated with debunking misinformation are well known, such as the continued influence of misinformation, recent meta-analyses suggest that corrective messages can attenuate the influence of misinformation to varying degrees, depending on message content and audience-related factors.

The next two chapters focus on literacy as a possible response to mis/disinformation. Because of the wide variety of different media and their roles in our lives, Melissa Tully (Chapter 44) argues that news literacy requires its own definitions and scholarly attention because the knowledge and skills – fact-checking, verifying, and correcting – required to identify news are similar to those needed to identify (and possibly reject) misinformation. She proposes and defines five domains – context, creation, content, circulation, and consumption – that make up news literacy. Nicole A. Cooke (Chapter 45) adds a third category to misinformation and disinformation: namely, malinformation, which is genuine information shared to cause harm, such as revenge porn. Media and information literacies have long been taught in libraries and classrooms to educate consumers about the perils of false information. However there are gaps that do not reach audiences. Part of the solution, she suggests, is the need for a critical information literacy to comprehend the underlying power structures that shape information and media. Cooke also argues for a critical cultural literacy, which can aid in verifying and refuting false information and can question and investigate cultural contexts of the information. The following three chapters look at ways of countering mis/disinformation. Firstly Leticia Bode and Emily Vraga (Chapter 46) show that the correction of misinformation on social media can take several forms, including coming from platforms themselves or from other users on the platforms. As a consequence of what they see as the limitations of various responses to mis/disinformation, Bode and Vraga propose observational correction, in which people update their own attitudes after seeing someone else being corrected on social media. They argue that

> observational correction represents a flexible, robust, and community solution to misinformation on social media that appeals to populist ideals. Rather than depending on elites to combat the problem of misinformation, motivating ordinary users to respond to misinformation not only provides the scalable response needed but one that can appeal to people regardless of their position or beliefs.

Babak Bahador (Chapter 47) offers a critical assessment of the counterspeech approach to hate speech (see also Chapter 7). He presents a model of five dimensions of counterspeech: the targeted audiences, including the public, the vulnerable, hate-group members, and violent extremists; the goals of those engaging in counterspeech efforts, which often vary by target audience; the tactics employed to reach different audiences, both online and offline; the messaging which reviews the different content typologies used to try and influence audiences; and the effects in which the findings from different evaluation studies on counterspeech are assessed.

Eva Giraud and Elizabeth Poole (Chapter 48) map out how digital counter-narratives can be constructed to contest and respond to disinformation and online hate speech circulated by right-wing populists. While they point out the limitations of new media platforms for mediated activism, they show through specific case studies how social media such as Twitter can be harnessed for anti-racist and anti-Islamophobic strategies. They conclude that while digital spaces offer marginalised communities some opportunities to claim social power, they are located in socio-political systems in which the distribution of power is unequal; hence, structural inequalities tend to be reproduced online. Maria Kyriakidou and Stephen Cushion (Chapter 49) detail some of journalism's response to counter mis/disinformation such as 'independent' fact-checking by public service broadcasters and specialist education and training. Establishing the veracity of an event or issue and accurately informing the public about it are deeply ingrained in the 'fourth-estate role' of journalism in holding power to account and exposing abuses of authority. However, attempts to manipulate information and deceive the public are more sophisticated, renewing the urgency of the demands placed on journalists to retain legitimacy and trust. James Deane (Chapter 50) takes this response further by summarising the strategies that BBC Media Action, the BBC's international media support charity, adopts to combat mis/disinformation. Their approach is heavily informed by BBC values believing

> that improving the character and quality of the information and communication environment – privileging the availability and access to trustworthy information, increasing societal capacity for debate and dialogue across societal divides, enabling a diversity of voices to be heard – makes societies more resilient to (although certainly not immune to) populism as well as authoritarianism.

In the penultimate piece, Emily Thorson and Jianing Li (Chapter 51) focus on a slightly different question: what happens after a person receives a correction to a piece of misinformation? When are corrections successful, and when do they fail? Can misinformation continue to affect attitudes even after it is successfully corrected? They conclude that on average, corrections are successful at moving people closer to the truth. However it is often only some people who change their beliefs, and this can be a problem with information on vaccines, for example. They conclude that corrections work better when they come from a trusted source; offer the reader (either with visuals or with narrative) a clear, compelling story; and are met with curiosity, desire for accuracy, and the ability to navigate the increasingly complex media environment. The final piece in this part, by Christian Staal, Bruun Overgaard, Anthony Dudo, Matthew Lease, Gina M. Masullo, Natalie Jomini Stroud, Scott R. Stroud, and Samuel C. Woolley (Chapter 52), tackles polarisation, another escalating international issue, with its democratic consequences and its intertwinement with the spread of misinformation. They suggest that the spread of false or manipulative messages is connected to polarisation amongst a number of social entities: political parties, religious denominations, issue publics, social classes, racial groups, and others. They map out empirically sound and theoretically rigourous solutions to the problem of polarisation. The authors argue that these solutions are integral to building what they term a new 'connective democracy' in a world now defined by digital communication and the promises and perils of networked life.

The *Companion* is the first collection to examine all these issues in one volume. The distinctiveness of the *Companion* is that it encompasses a variety of subject areas: political communication, journalism, law, sociology, cultural studies, international politics, and international relations. Thus, it will be of great benefit to undergraduate and postgraduate students pursuing degrees and joint degrees in these disciplines. Considering that populism is a subject of interest across disciplines and fields of study and practice, the book will appeal to students and academics working and teaching in these various subject areas. The book is theoretically and methodologically comprehensive and features various historical and critical approaches to provide a full understanding of media, disinformation, and populism. The *Companion* is therefore both interdisciplinary and multidisciplinary. The companion consists of 52 contributions from scholars based in different regions of the world whose work deals with aspects of misinformation and populism across countries, political systems, and media systems. We feel that a global, comparative approach to the study of misinformation and populism is also necessary to identify common elements and particular characteristics.

We are especially grateful to everyone for accepting our invitation to participate in this project. What no one could have anticipated when we began to plan out the *Companion* was the outbreak of a worldwide pandemic, COVID-19, that occurred halfway through the writing of the book. Despite having to cope with changes to workload patterns, moving to online teaching, home schooling for those with children, and the constant worries about infection, everyone did their utmost to keep to the deadlines. Not only that, but many of the authors included both explicit and nuanced discussion about the effects of the virus in their chapters. It makes for a more relevant and insightful *Companion* about the media, disinformation, and populism than we could ever have imagined.

We are grateful to Margaret Farrelly, Editor of Media and Journalism Studies at Routledge, for her generous encouragement and support in initiating the project and seeing it to completion. At Routledge, we are also thankful to Priscille Biehlmann, Editorial Assistant for Journalism and Media Studies, and Jennifer Vennall, Senior Editorial Assistant Media and Cultural

Studies, for their efficiency and support whilst working closely with us during the length of the project. Thanks are also due to the production staff at Routledge who assisted in the preparation of the manuscript. Thank you to Ramachandran Vijayaragavan, project manager, for the production of the book and to copyeditor Lisa A. Bannick. We are also grateful to Sarah Dicioccio for her assistance in preparing the manuscript.

We hope that readers will enjoy and be challenged by the *Companion*.

Howard Tumber
City, University of London

Silvio Waisbord
George Washington University
Autumn 2020

1

MEDIA, DISINFORMATION, AND POPULISM

Problems and responses

Howard Tumber and Silvio Waisbord

Current research and debates in media, disinformation, and populism are issues central to contemporary societies and polities as well as to multidisciplinary research agendas. Media, disinformation, and populism have attracted a great deal of attention in past years. The reasons are self-evident. The digital revolution has upended old media orders, technologies, industries, access, distribution, and uses. New and sophisticated forms of disinformation flooded the global public sphere with falsehood at the same time that populist politics gained citizens' support worldwide. The global pandemic of COVID-19 has only added to the plethora of misinformation and disinformation bombarding the public with conspiracy theories, falsehoods, and rumours propagating by the day.

As these distortions of public communication are central issues in contemporary societies, they are approached from multiple disciplinary and theoretical positions. We are interested in the way these concepts and related themes are approached by scholars who work at the intersection of journalism studies, media studies, information studies, media sociology, and political communication.

Our goal is not only to provide an overview of fundamental concepts, debates, findings, and arguments but also to foster discussions about the relationships among concepts and phenomena. Various literatures provide valuable insights about the core themes of the scope and consequences of media transformations; the scale, strategies, and effects of disinformation and misinformation; and the causes and the characteristics of populism. Despite the growing literature, lines of inquiry generally run in parallel. Few studies explore how and why media, disinformation, and populism are connected. In this chapter we seek out and discuss points of intersection.

Media

In light of the transformations in communication and political processes, it is important to revisit the conceptual scaffolding used to study media, disinformation, and populism. These concepts have long been the subject of semantic disputes. Technological and social innovations, as well as political developments, therefore make it imperative to reassess their validity and to determine whether new concepts are required to comprehend emergent phenomena.

'Media' is a notoriously ambiguous, fluid concept. It was and is commonly used to refer to technologies, industries, and institutions that 'mediate' social interaction – that 'assemble' (Latour 2005) the social through symbolic exchanges. The digital revolution adds layers of conceptual complexity as it profoundly unsettles media technologies, institutions, and industries. Because contemporary life is mediated like never before in human history, 'the media' is a more flexible, dynamic notion.

'The media' are not limited to the legacy industries and technologies of the golden era of the mass media and mass society in the past century. If 'the media' refers to what 'mediates' communication and interaction, then it is self-evident that the types of media are substantially broader than in the past. Among other developments, the proliferation of portable technologies and applications, the encroachment of digital media in social life, and the Internet of things reshuffled the meanings of 'the media'. 'The media' are understood as technologies, processes, and institutions that connect individuals, organisations, and groups in multiple ways in the network society. 'The media' are not unitary, homogenous, or centralised.

Conceptual pruning and clarification are essential to map the media industries, media systems, and media content, which are constantly proliferating and evolving.

'Media industries' is a concept in flux, due in part to the dilution of traditional boundaries between technology and content companies. Contemporary media industries include hundreds of digital companies, together with the foundational technologies of modern society – newspapers/press, radio, film, television. A diversity of internet companies, including hardware and software companies, populate the ever-expanding media universe. Media industries encompass a larger universe than just the familiar UK's Fleet Street, the US's Hollywood, and Silicon Valley and other geographical metonyms.

'Media systems' are also more diffused and multi-layered than in the past. The geographical-political boundaries of 'national' media systems are destabilising due to unprecedented technological and economic globalisation. New and hybrid actors populate 'media systems': state, public, commercial, and 'public/private' platforms; civil society; radical, alternative, and open/closed media. There is no single 'media logic'. Consequently, multiple 'media logics' may be a better concept to capture the unique aspects of media platforms and institutions. Similarly, the concept of 'media content' includes ever-multiplying forms of expression – from memes to movies, from instant messaging to social media postings. Likewise, 'mediatisation' is not simply a coherent, one-way process by which unique aspects of media technologies, industries, and institutions encroach upon society.

Contemporary disinformation tactics attest to the shapeshifting nature of media (Chadwick, Vaccari, & O'Loughlin 2018; Gorwa & Guilbeault 2020). In recent years, studies examined automated bots, trolls, troll farms, fake news, deepfakes, news feeds, 'backstaging', filter bubbles, echo chambers, synthetic media, algorithms, far/alt-right media, doxing, swatting, and other phenomena. We note here that hardly any new concepts refer to these developments as something to embrace; rather, they present a depressing picture of gloom and doom for society. This demoralising vocabulary is not only revelatory about troubling developments for public life and democracy but is also symptomatic of previous gaps in the analytical toolkit. Media and communication studies lacked the terminology to understand a slew of new media platforms and practices. Given constant media innovations, conceptual updates and repurposing become inevitable.

The lesson of the evolution of 'media' as a concept is twofold. Existing concepts should be approached cautiously to determine their semantic validity and analytical usefulness in new scenarios. Secondly an open attitude is essential to generate concepts that capture novel initiatives and developments.

Dis/misinformation

Unlike the concept of 'media', disinformation and misinformation possess clearer meanings. They refer to different phenomena, even though sometimes, they are carelessly and interchangeably used. Disinformation is the deliberate dissemination of false information for political, economic, and other benefits. Misinformation refers to unintentional dissemination of incorrect information (Wardle & Derakhshan 2018). Whereas disinformation agents know that they disseminate false information in their attempts to deceive others, misinformed citizens are largely unaware that they consume and share false content.

The recent spike in scholarly and popular attention to both concepts reflects empirical developments: namely, the presence of new, insidious forms of disinformation by states and other actors, especially in the aftermath of the 2016 US presidential election and the 2016 UK Brexit referendum, as well as novel disinformation practices on digital platforms.

Neither dis/misinformation nor the phenomena they refer to are strictly new. Disinformation is conceptually close to propaganda. Both refer to spreading information and ideas linked to the exercise of power. However, there is an important distinction. Whereas disinformation emphasises deliberate deception through fabrications, propaganda may consist of disseminating selective ideas that are not necessarily demonstrably false. Praising the nation, publicising half-truths, leaving out inconvenient facts, inculcating dogmas, and puffery are typical of propaganda by states, corporations, and other powerful actors. They are part of the arsenal used to confuse public opinion, gain political support, and draw economic benefits. But these actions do not exclusively spread outright falsehoods in the same manner of disinformation campaigns. Propaganda blends exaggerations, one-sided arguments, and false/pseudo facts.

Governments are renewing propaganda strategies by taking advantage of digital affordances. Propaganda is no longer centralised, controlled, and activated at the top by state agencies. Instead, it is designed to engage both aware and distracted publics through networked technologies. The 'rewiring' of propaganda (Oates 2021) transforms old communication dynamics and muddles the identity of the original perpetrators. Citizens are now both willing and unwilling actors as recipients of dis/misinformation. Digital propaganda resorts to sophisticated techniques of data production and analysis to shape public opinion.

What is new? Despite obvious continuities with pre-digital forms of propaganda, contemporary disinformation makes it possible to target and distribute false information to billions of citizens who, in turn, can easily redistribute and replicate these deceptions. Everyone potentially can be a willing or unwilling participant, as receiver and distributor, in disinformation campaigns.

Novel forms of dis/misinformation spawn and reinvigorate interest in buzzword concepts such as 'post-truth'. Post-truth refers to the current situation of confusion and pervasive lies. Due to the configurations of the contemporary information (dis)order, it is harder to disentangle truths from lies, to erect a single truth as dominant, and to persuade others about objective truths. Communication and information abundance make it possible to challenge any claims to truth in public.

Attaching 'post' implies a new condition supposedly different from a past of 'truth'. To state the obvious, a congenial state of concord over truth was not exactly common or dominant in pre-digital times. Truths always existed in plural, no matter how much realists and objectivists insisted. Truths are partial, contested, doubted, even when opportunities to challenge truths in public were significantly more limited than today. Of course, political truths clashed with philosophical truths, as Hannan Arendt (2017) memorably argued.

So the question to ask is what, if anything, is different about present conditions and justifies the usage of 'post-truth'? It is a matter of the structures and the dynamics of truth-telling: the ability of citizens and institutions to dispute any claim to truth and reality through personalised and mass communication. In contemporary media ecologies, anyone's truth can be publicly challenged through rigourous methods, new facts, simple opinions, falsehoods, and disinformation.

Media abundance is a boon and a bane for dis/information. It opens new possibilities for communication grounded in democratic principles. It acts as a catalyst for citizen empowerment and the affirmation of human rights. However, the lowering of barriers to public communication presents deleterious consequences. It facilitates staggering opportunities for dis/misinformation. Powerful actors, especially governments, intelligence services, and the military, are uniquely positioned to take advantage of networked communication to pump falsehoods into the public sphere.

The severity of dis/information and its consequences are under dispute. Categorical generalisations are elusive because many factors affect the scale of disinformation and its effects on public affairs: namely, psychological processes, political context, affective polarisation, and media systems. Generally, the literature ranges from 'strong' to 'minimal' effects in ways that, unsurprisingly, echo similar positions in classic debates about media effects. Parsimonious arguments are required about when and why disinformation affects selected publics with negative consequences for democracy. Cross-national, cross-thematic studies may assist us in discerning whether, indeed, disinformation profoundly pollutes public communication on a range of issues such as politics, health, science, and the environment.

Populism

Populism is a conceptual chestnut of sociology, political science, and economics. Understandably, it remains a notoriously ambiguous concept (de la Torre 2018). Under the umbrella of 'populism', various forms of political traditions, parties, and movements are carelessly bandied about. Renewed global academic and journalistic interest in contemporary populism is not settling semantic debates. Despite the availability of compelling and comprehensive definitions (Cohen 2019; Müller 2017), populism remains analytically porous and open-ended. It is a conceptual Rorschach test of political, economic, and sociological interpretations.

Lately, populism is associated with dozens of contemporary leaders (such as Bolsonaro, Chavez, Correa, Duda, Duterte, Erdogan, Johnson, LePen, Maduro, Modi, Orban, Ortega, Putin, Salvi, Trump, van Grieken) and political parties and movements on the right and the left (Mounk & Kyle 2018). What do they all have in common? Do they a share a lingua franca, a political style, and a policy blueprint? If a leader constantly praises the virtue of 'the common person' and excoriates 'the elites', is it enough to call him (generally, it is 'him') and the movement 'populist'? Is charismatic leadership a necessary condition of populism? Is populism the expression of cultural backlash and/or socio-economic penuries (Norris & Inglehart 2019)? Like ice cream, populists come in different varieties.

From a perspective interested in the media and communication aspects of populism, it is important to emphasise shared characteristics.

Populism refers to a style of discourse that presents a binary view of politics as neatly and essentially divided in two camps – the popular and the elites/anti-popular. Populism draws arbitrary and firm distinctions between these two camps and presents itself as the true representation of 'the people'. It is ideologically empty, flexible, and omnivorous. It sponges up right-wing and left-wing ideologies plus myriad narratives and policies along the ideological spectrum.

Because populism favours a view of politics as pure and permanent conflict, it has no need for communication values and practices such as dialogue, tolerance, compromise, respect for difference, and listening. It dismisses dissident, critical, and independent voices. Worse, as the fractious history of populism in power shows, it actively seeks to suppress institutions, including the media, that hold it accountable. Its intolerance of criticism and tendency to ignore and disable accountability mechanisms attest to populism's dangerous and unstable relationship with democracy.

This is a feature of populism. It is grounded in its grandiose, authoritarian claim to represent 'the people' as a singular actor and to portray the leader as the true plebeian hero who can do no wrong. Anyone who criticises the leader and the movement is condemned as a member of the elite, not the people – the legitimate political community. Neither criticism nor accountability are priorities for populism.

Therefore, populism eschews the use of the legal edifice of political liberalism, such as equality of rights and a system of checks and balances (Galston 2017). It deems them unnecessary and fundamentally mistaken for it believes that political sovereignty resides in 'the people' and 'the movement' that it purports to represent. This also explains why populist leaders have a tendency to strengthen executive power, reshape the political order in their image, and demand reverence and submission. Populism's propensity to go down the authoritarian path is embedded in its political DNA.

Because populism is ideologically empty, it is parasitic on other ideologies. Populists typically rummage through the ideologies of political parties, social movements, and economic proposals. Devoid of distinctive ideological traditions, populism borrows ideas and policies from fellow travellers and tactical allies. The existence of right-wing and left-wing versions shows this unique quality of populism.

Recent cases in Latin America and Southern Europe show how left-wing populism selectively adopted ideas from socialism and communism as well as nationalist, anti-capitalist, and anti-imperialist movements. In its attempt to build movements against neoliberalism and construct a self-glorying rhetoric, it tapped into anti-capitalist ideologies and a range of social movements – human rights, environmental, peasants, feminist, unions (Waisbord 2014). This is the kind of radical, populist coalition that Ernesto Laclau (2005) theorised in his defence of populism. Populism is viewed as the catalyst of revolutionary processes that deepen major social and political rifts in late capitalism and lead to the formation of counter-hegemonic alliances and a new order.

Right-wing populism also borrows ideologies and forms strategic alliances with different groups and movements. Contemporary right-wing populism in the Americas, Europe, and Asia finds ideological inspiration and justification in social and political expressions with one element in common: staunch opposition to radicalism, progressivism, and liberalism. These ideologies are represented by a range of rights-based movements: women's rights, multiculturalism, anti-racist, immigrants' rights, LGBTI, and others. Tactical allies of right-wing populism include hate groups (racists, Islamophobic, anti-Semites), misogynist movements, anti-science advocates, xenophobic forces, and religious conservatives.

Seemingly divergent populists such as Modi in India and Erdogan in Turkey, potential rivals in a clash of civilisations, are pursuing political projects that are mirror images. 'Both are champions of a brand of politics that seeks to fuse religion, the nation and the leader. Both lead countries with secular constitutions but want to place religion back at the heart of the nation and state' (Rachman 2020, 21)

Although right-wing populism presents variations, common elements can be identified. They are reactionary movements that wish to turn back the political clock to a time when a range of people lacked legal and social equality based on their gender, sexuality, race, religion, or ethnicity. Contemporary right-wing populism is defined by its rabid opposition to progressive parties and human rights movements. However, it has different levels of organisation and mobilisation. Whereas some rely on the backbone of bricks-and-mortar organisations like evangelical churches, others echo fundamentally online phenomena such as the alt-right, xenophobic groups, and the manosphere.

Finally, populism's binary view of politics potentially leads to polarised politics. If politics is viewed essentially as a constant conflict between two enemies, then polarisation is not only inevitable but also necessary for populism to succeed. Populism thrives on affective polarisation, plebiscitary politics, and elections as referenda on leaders (Schulze, Mauk, & Linde 2020).

Intersections

What are the connective threads then among media, disinformation, and populism? We break down these relationships into two separate questions.

Media and populism

Populism always sees the media as essential political instruments to drum up support and reaffirm boundaries between 'the people' and 'the elites'. Contemporary populist parties and leaders maintain close relations with public and private media and regularly clash with and threaten critical media organisations. For populism, ensuring regular and unopposed media access is required for spreading messages and narratives adjusted to the views of leaders and supporters. In turn, media organisations tend to support populism based on ideological communion, economic benefits, and/or political calculations.

Does populism have an affinity with certain media? Do specific media cultivate populist politics given their target audiences, style, and formats? Do citizens who support populism have a distinctive media diet? What is the role of mainstream media in the rise and the consolidation of populism?

Despite scores of valuable national and comparative studies, there are no clear answers to these questions. There is no straightforward relation between populism and the media because there is neither a single form of populism nor a single media order. Real populisms have different relations with the media. Massive, unprecedented changes affect the relationship between populism and the media. 'The media' is not a seamless whole anywhere but, rather, a multilayered, crowded, and chaotic environment. Populist style, discourse, communication strategies, and policies map differently across the vast constellation of media organisations and digital spaces.

On these issues, the literature features various lines of research.

One set of studies pays attention to populism's relationship with like-minded media organisations on the right and the left. Partisan news media offer receptive, supportive coverage which fits populism's triumphant narratives and tirades against opponents. They also contribute to populism's ideological content and legitimacy. Finally, these media generously provide leaders with constant acclaim and comfort. Such connections are visible in the relation between right-wing tabloids (e.g. the *Daily Mail* and the *Sun* in the UK) and populism in Europe and the ties between Fox News and Donald Trump in the United States. Recent studies also show the conservative media's role in sowing confusion about the effects of the coronavirus: [T]hey paint a picture of a media ecosystem that amplifies misinformation, entertains conspiracy theories and discourages audiences from taking concrete steps to protect themselves and others.

(Ingraham 2020)

Such alliances also matter because, arguably, populism thrives in endogamic media and communicative spaces where like-minded citizens find others who reaffirm their views (Gerbaudo 2018). Populism is antithetical to anything resembling communication in difference – exposure to ideas that differ and contradict official discourses. Instead, it exhibits an affinity for communication homophily. The importance of these spaces does not mean that citizens with populist preferences are sequestered in ideologically homogeneous bubbles.

Populism's chain of supportive media goes beyond legacy news organisations, including newspapers, radio, and television stations. It includes state-owned media that populism in power tightly controls as propaganda machines, as shown in the cases of Duda in Poland, Orban in Hungary, Duterte in the Philippines, Maduro in Venezuela, and Ortega in Nicaragua. Propaganda networks also includes partisan and alternative platforms. These media platforms may not be as visible to the public eye as prominent legacy media, yet they are part of populism's communication texture and resources. In the case of right-wing populism, this includes a string of far-right, white supremacy, anti-science, anti-Semitic, Islamophobic, and misogynist online sites (Haller, Holt, & de La Brosse 2019; Heft, Mayerhöffer, Reinhardt, & Knüpfer 2020).

These media provide populism not only with ideological content and legitimacy but also with platforms for reaching sympathetic audiences. They are conduits for populism's constant attacks on opponents. Unpaid and paid trolls and operatives who harass critics become accessories to the politics of fostering conflicts and intimating adversaries. In some countries, populism bankrolls both media and supportive operatives through networks of patronage and favouritism.

Further attention should also be paid to populism's relation to social media platforms and corporations. First, the significance of specific platforms whose technological affordances fit populism's trademark communication style: leader-centred messages, personalistic appeals, the illusion of unobstructed interaction between leaders and citizens, and avoiding the press. Unquestionably, Twitter is a good match, fitting perfectly with populism's long-standing preferences for top-down, one-way public communication (Waisbord & Amado 2017). Second, social media, such as Facebook and YouTube, are central for right-wing media. Legacy news organisations such as Fox News draw significant audiences from Facebook. Also, YouTube and other platforms serves as channels for far-right and other extreme groups. Twitter makes it possible for right-wing influencers and trolls to reach large audiences and spread their messages.

A further issue to consider is populism's relation with legacy mainstream media that are not editorially aligned with its politics. This includes public service corporations and private companies that remain bounded by journalistic ideals of fairness and even-handedness. At face value, populism generally has tense and difficult relations with mainstream news organisations. Populism is permanently locked in a state of conflict with 'the media'. Not uncommonly, populist leaders actively provoke such conflicts when they purport to get negative coverage. They are fond of accusing media critics of being producers of 'fake news', acting as 'enemies of the people' and as 'traitors'. Difficult relations with the mainstream media are not unique to populism. Yet populism is a particular case, given its anti-democratic bent.

Underlying the tense relationship is populism's suspicion of, if not outright contempt for, speech rights and freedom of the press. Populism and democratic communication are at loggerheads. Populism's position on media, journalism, and public communication is grounded in its distrust of liberal principles. It is predisposed against the right to speech and protections of public speech from government intervention as well as progressive principles of communication such as dialogue, pluralism, empathy, and tolerance.

Populism tends to be particularly sensitive and impatient with media reports that challenge its self-serving narratives. Leaders legitimise anti-mainstream media sentiments among ideological allies in government, business, media, and universities. Tapping into prejudice, hate, and conspiracies, they dismiss critical news as the deeds of anti-popular, anti-national interests and call on their supporters to punish media companies. In some cases, populist leaders try to weaken critical media by pressuring their owners and editors into compliance with a mix of legal and economic sticks and carrots.

It would be mistaken, however, to see the relations between populism and mainstream media in purely antagonistic terms, as populist leaders often contend. Because populism is a mass phenomenon, it requires coverage by the mainstream media (Boczkowski & Papacharissi 2018). Populism constantly craves media attention to reinforce the dominant public positions of its leaders, amplify messages, and gain visibility. Any media pulpit is critical for populist leaders. Media with large audiences are useful to reach various constituencies, win elections, and cement power.

By providing massive coverage, mainstream media are central to the ascent of populist leaders and movements. With their oversize personas, discursive styles, and colourful histories, typical populist leaders align with media interest in personalities, drama, and entertainment. Populists' penchant for ceaseless conflict and polarisation is enormously attractive for news organisations focused on controversy, loud voices, and scandal. Populists' frequent news-making spats with 'the mainstream press' might be considered shrewd ruses to reel in media attention. These present opportunities for populist leaders to dominate news cycles but also to show that the 'elite/ establishment media' are the enemies of the people. They function as performative instances of populism's narrative about 'evil media' and popular leaders committed to scolding 'the media' and their allies.

Although some private media adopt critical positions vis-à-vis populism, it is not unreasonable to suggest that commercial media systems possess built-in tendencies that favour certain aspects of populism. Clearly, they do not make populism inevitable. However, some aspects of hyper-commercialised media may lay the ground for populist ideas. Widespread lack of trust in media (Park, Fisher, Flew, & Dulleck 2020) mirrors populism's frequent tirades against media companies. Certain news biases favour populist messages – distrust of elites and experts; focus on conflict; negative portrayal of governments, politics, and politicians. Even shining examples of investigative journalism, which expose corruption and spawn scandals, may unintendedly foster anti-politics sentiments that dovetail with populism's cynical view of democracy.

Populism, media, and disinformation

What, then, are the connections among populism, media, and disinformation?

Populism is not the only political movement that resorts to disinformation. The history of propaganda shows that governments and the powerful have tried to manipulate consciousness through disinformation. The temporal concurrence of populism and new forms of disinformation should not lead us to simplistic causal explanations.

What is truly novel? Are populism and disinformation interlocked in unique ways? Populism has an affinity with disinformation even though it is not the only political movement that resorts to disinformation.

Populism generally concentrates power in leaders who are deemed infallible. The tendency to build a leadership cult easily devolves into narratives that liberally blend facts, faux facts, proven lies, and absolute fantasies. Populism utilises disinformation because distinguishing between truth and lies is not exactly a priority. And at the same time, populism's demagogic leaders are fond of making appeals that validate existing beliefs, identities, and prejudice in order to cement popular support. Since populism believes that enemies constantly plot to bring leaders and movements down, it resorts to disinformation as a legitimate means to fight opponents. Populism tries to remain in power without regard for democratic rules and norms, contesting elections using all means possible. Erasing the distinctions between truth and fabrications and flooding public opinion with disinformation then become essential for political perpetuation. As elections are construed as vital to the future prospects of the leader, the fatherland, and the people, disinformation tactics are justified to secure victories.

In this regard, contemporary populism, especially its right-wing variant, displays a close affinity with communicative spaces and alternative media filled with disinformation and misinformation. These platforms cover and discus hot-button issues, such as immigration, white supremacy, nativism, and climate change denialism, which are at the heart of populist identities and are closely identified with right-wing and far-right groups. Conspiracy theories, absolute lies, fake news, 'alternative' facts, and similar informational aberrations are a common presence on these outlets. Whereas social media regularly circulate away from the attention of legacy media, they gain enormous visibility in specific circumstances, such as when powerful newsmakers spread and legitimise disinformation and hate, when sympathetic influential news organisations offer positive coverage, and when high-profile hate crimes receive broad political and media attention.

In this regard populism possesses an affinity with post-truth (Waisbord 2018). Media abundance offers an endless menu of possible information adjusted to people's convictions and desires. Mediating institutions, including the press, which, because of their dominance, were the arbiters of 'Truth' for the rest of society, do not occupy the same position in today's chaotic, multi-layered media ecologies.

Truth necessitates social agreements on methods and facts to demonstrate the veracity of claims. It demands trust in the way that facts are produced, examined, and discussed. Populism, however, embraces and legitimises a state of epistemological fracture by pushing a binary view of politics, with truth belonging to its leaders and followers. In a similar vein, truth is fractured by political identities. Populism uncritically accepts the 'truths' of allies while it disparages the enemies as liars. 'Our' truths are the antipode of 'their' lies. Truth encompasses 'popular' beliefs, no matter how or whether they are proven. Populism eschews demonstrable facts and scientific rigour to reach truth. Loyalty to the leader and their policies is often sufficient to determine the truthfulness of any claim.

Populism's claims to owning the truth lead to embracing disinformation and legitimising post-truth. It supports beliefs regardless of whether they are grounded in quality, factual, proven information. It perpetuates communities of belief that feed off and reinforce information dynamics that teem with falsehoods. It weaponises cognitive biases in support of disinformation and hate.

Responses

The preceding discussion illustrates a formidable set of media, information, and political problems. With the tacit complicity of citizens and allies, governments and rogue actors are responsible for large-scale disinformation campaigns in a complex web of domestic politics and geopolitical competition. Misinformed citizens consume and distribute false information and are generally unaware of their ignorance. Populism disfigures democracy. It tends to ignore speech rights, flout norms of civility and tolerance, and persecute and suppress critics. It represents and legitimises various forms of hate speech. Deep, epistemic fractures make it difficult, if not impossible, for the existence of public agreement over ways to determine veracity and truth. All together, the combination of these problems results in multi-faceted threats to public life and communicative spaces.

One can reasonably argue that these problems are as old as public communication and politics. Yet now they present novel and complex forms in chaotic and dynamic media and information ecologies. They are contrary to optimum communicative conditions in multicultural democracies: namely, facticity, quality information, truth-telling, tolerance, difference, consensus, understanding, empathy, inclusion, and dialogue.

As communication and media scholars, we should not just be concerned with understanding the scope and the causes of the problems. We also need to identify and assess effective actions to respond to the challenges. The complexities of this scenario present important variations of solutions by country and region. Not all societies may be similarly susceptible to dis/misinformation or correspondingly equipped to respond.

The causes of dis/misinformation are located in three levels: individual, group, and systemic/ structural, and societies require multipronged actions to combat these threats (Koulolias, Jonathan, Fernandez, & Sotirchos 2018).

One set of responses focuses on equipping individuals and groups with critical media/news literacy skills to assist them in navigating the current information landscape. In this case the focus is on citizens rather than on the sources of disinformation and misinformation. The premise is that citizens should be aware and smart when they consume and share information. Today, more than ever, a citizen requires the skills to constantly hone their communication and informational competencies.

The challenges for implementing successful media literacies are vast. It is difficult to promote and to implement media/news literacy programmes at scale because of the logistical and funding challenges. Media systems heavily tilted in favour of commercial interests are antithetical to actions aimed at cultivating critical learning skills. Systems with strong public service media grounded in truly public ideals are seemingly better equipped to confront the challenges of dis/ misinformation.

Changing the way publics interact with information entails addressing significant behavioural and social obstacles, as the mixed record of interventions suggest (Tully, Vraga, & Bode 2020). Well-known cognitive processes, such as motivated reasoning, confirmation bias, and selective exposure/perception, as well as strong, affective identities, present significant demands. 'Incorrect' opinions and vulnerability to misinformation are often grounded in partisan and ideological identities. Therefore, offering counter-information may be insufficient to reduce hateful attitudes and behaviours, especially when confronting hard beliefs and strong resistance. Dis/misinformation is not simply a problem of groups who happen to hold incorrect knowledge due to poor media literacy skills, nor is it the failure of news providers to separate the wheat of information from the chaff of disinformation. Toxic identity politics that embrace dogmatic thinking, loyalty to leaders, and hate are significant obstacles.

Another set of responses focuses on systemic issues. Unsurprisingly, here the challenges are significant as well.

One type of intervention spotlights improving information ecologies by adding quality information. Notably, scores of programmes concentrate on producing fact-based information to debunk lies and to counter deception campaigns. Just as rogue actors aim to flood digital media with mis/disinformation to sow confusion, journalism, non-government organisations, scientific organisations, think tanks, and university centres try to infuse the public sphere with demonstrable, evidence-based facts to achieve the opposite. What brings these initiatives together is the hope that multiplying 'healthy' information options may arm societies with more resources and contribute to turning the tide of dis/misinformation.

The challenges are multi-fold, involving taking fact-checking actions to scale, targeting publics who are particularly vulnerable to falsehoods and harder to reach, avoiding boomerang effects, and providing timely corrections to torrents of dis/misinformation. Fact-checking organisations rarely occupy towering positions in disjointed and multi-layered communication infrastructures. Gone are the days of firm pyramidal, hierarchical communication with a limited number of journalistic/media, informational, and scientific institutions atop. Furthermore, uneven and divided public trust in these media institutions across countries affect their position and credibility.

A different set of responses target social media and other digital corporations on the basis that they are major culprits in the current plight. Governments and civic organisations insist that those companies should be held accountable to the public for polluting the public sphere with toxic content. The call to arms comprises demands for transparency, consistent enforcement of their own guidelines, curbs on harmful content in their platforms, and legal action. Amid public pressure and outcry and advocacy campaigns, corporate responses to recurrent public relations crises are ad hoc, halfhearted, scattered, uneven, self-interested, and opaque. For example, Facebook and Twitter, in response to the flood of coronavirus disinformation on their platforms, are constantly updating their policies regarding conspiracy theories and fake news. They do this by flagging up disinformation using labels or warnings to highlight disputed, unverified, or misleading posts and tweets. As Claire Wardle, director of First Draft, quoted on NBC News, commented, 'They trumpet these transparency initiatives, but they're marking their own homework' (Zadrozny 2020).

The decision to prioritise content by 'trustworthy' legacy news organisations or to de-platform postings and actors hardly amounts to a coherent set of policies in the public interest. None of these actions are sufficient or convincing.

Certainly, policy and regulatory tools remain important to address the symptoms and the deep-seated causes of dis/misinformation. Options are wide ranging. Eliminating or making access to misinformation difficult may be effective, inadequate, or problematic, depending on the various legal traditions and ethical issues in each country and whether they are public or private spaces. Legislation to regulate and shut down 'fake news' raises a host of problems, especially in countries with a strong history and tradition of governments clamping down on dissident speech.

Finally, it is important to develop responses to political and media elites who foster and perpetuate dis/misinformation, hate speech, and other forms of dangerous communication. Priority actions and targets should be mindful of deep power asymmetries in disinformation structures and dynamics. Not all disinformation institutions and agents carry similar responsibility in disseminating dis/misinformation at scale. Political elites and media corporations and funders wield significantly more power than scattered, ordinary citizens who consume and share falsehoods. Unfortunately, media and communication scholarship pays insufficient attention to effective responses to populism. Boycotting media companies that traffic in lies and deception and discouraging the use of digital platforms teeming with mis/disinformation are important steps, but they are hardly sufficient to break vicious cycles of disinformation and populist politics.

The belief there are easy-to-implement, one-shot, off-the-shelves solutions should be avoided. As the problems are complex, there is no single 'magic bullet'. Some responses to disinformation show promise. However, none has proved to be stunningly effective to curb misinformation in a whack-a-mole scenario in which lies and deception constantly pop up.

Responses should be part of systematic, evidence-driven, flexible, and localised approaches. Reactive and haphazard interventions are unlikely to tackle fundamental problems or to produce sustainable results. Successful responses at individual, group, and systemic levels may provide valuable insights for future action. Comparative analysis can help work out ways to reach out to and engage with various populations in the battle against disinformation, misinformation, and hate. Just as exposure to dis/misinformation takes place in different circumstances, attitudes and beliefs about politics, health, education, climate, and other issues vary too. Also, responses should take context into consideration, whether it is domestic politics, legal traditions, media systems, social trends, or combinations thereof. What may be viable and effective in certain settings does not necessarily apply elsewhere.

Ultimately, it is necessary to recognise that the challenges are daunting. If we are living in a time of 'disrupted public spheres' (Bennett & Pfetsch 2018), then where should societies focus attention and resources? How can societies reconstruct their information ecologies to support democracy and public life? Amid fractured publics and polarisation, how are shared actions feasible? Answers to these questions are necessary to re-imagine common paths to implement successful actions.

References

Arendt, H. (2017). *The Origins of Totalitarianism*. London: Penguin.

Bennett, W. L., & Pfetsch, B. (2018). Rethinking political communication in a time of disrupted public spheres. *Journal of Communication*, 68(2), 243–253.

Boczkowski, P. J., & Papacharissi, Z. (Eds.). (2018). *Trump and the Media*. Cambridge, MA: MIT Press.

Chadwick, A., Vaccari, C., & O'Loughlin, B. (2018). Do tabloids poison the well of social media? Explaining democratically dysfunctional news sharing. *New Media & Society*, 20(11), 4255–4274.

Cohen, J. L. (2019). Hollow parties and their movement-ization: The populist conundrum. *Philosophy & Social Criticism*, 45(9–10), 1084–1105.

De la Torre, C. (2018). Global populism: Histories, trajectories, problems, and challenges. In C. de la Torre Ed., *Routledge Handbook of Global Populism*, 1–28. New York: Routledge.

Galston, W. A. (2017). *Anti-Pluralism: The Populist Threat to Liberal Democracy*. New Haven, CT: Yale University Press.

Gerbaudo, P. (2018). Social media and populism: An elective affinity? *Media, Culture & Society*, 40(5), 745–753.

Gorwa, R., & Guilbeault, D. (2020). Unpacking the social media bot: A typology to guide research and policy. *Policy & Internet*, 12(2), 225–248.

Haller, A., Holt, K., & de La Brosse, R. (2019). The 'other' alternatives: Political right-wing alternative media. *Journal of Alternative and Community Media*, 4(1), 1–6.

Heft, A., Mayerhöffer, E., Reinhardt, S., & Knüpfer, C. (2020). Beyond Breitbart: Comparing right-wing digital news infrastructures in six western democracies. *Policy & Internet*, 12(1), 20–45.

Ingraham, C. (2020). New research explores how conservative media misinformation may have intensified the severity of the pandemic. *Washington Post*. www.washingtonpost.com/business/2020/06/25/fox-news-hannity-coronavirus-misinformation/, accessed 19 August 2020.

Koulolias, V., Jonathan, G. M., Fernandez, M., & Sotirchos, D. (2018). *Combating Misinformation: An Ecosystem in Co-Creation*. Paris: OECD Publishing.

Laclau, E. (2005). *On Populist Reason*. London: Verso.

Latour, B. (2005). *Reassembling the Social*. New York: Oxford University Press.

Mounk, Y., & Kyle, J. (2018). What populists do to democracies. *The Atlantic*, December 26. www.theatlantic.com/ideas/archive/2018/12/hard-data-populism-bolsonaro-trump/578878/.

Müller, J. W. (2017). *What Is Populism?* London: Penguin.

Norris, P., & Inglehart, R. (2019). *Cultural Backlash: Trump, Brexit, and Authoritarian Populism*. Cambridge: Cambridge University Press.

Oates, S. (2021). Rewired propaganda: Propaganda, misinformation, and populism in the digital age. In H. Tumber & S. Waisbord Eds., *Routledge Companion to Media, Misinformation and Populism*. London: Routledge.

Park, S., Fisher, C., Flew, T., & Dulleck, U. (2020). Global mistrust in news: The impact of social media on trust. *International Journal on Media Management*, 1–14.

Rachman, G. (2020). Erdogan and Modi thrive on divisive politics. *Financial Times*, August 11, p. 21.

Schulze, H., Mauk, M., & Linde, J. (2020). How populism and polarization affect Europe's liberal democracies. *Politics and Governance*, 8(3), 1–5.

Tully, M., Vraga, E. K., & Bode, L. (2020). Designing and testing news literacy messages for social media. *Mass Communication and Society*, 23(1), 22–46.

Waisbord, S. (2014). *Vox Populista: Medios, Periodismo, Democracia*. Buenos Aires: Gedisa.

Waisbord, S. (2018). Truth is what happens to news: On journalism, fake news, and post-truth. *Journalism Studies*, 19(13), 1866–1878.

Waisbord, S., & Amado, A. (2017). Populist communication by digital means: Presidential Twitter in Latin America. *Information, Communication & Society*, 20(9), 1330–1346.

Wardle, C., & Derakhshan, H. (2018). Thinking about 'information disorder': Formats of misinformation, disinformation, and mal-information. In C. Ireton & J. Posetti Eds., *Journalism, 'Fake News' & Disinformation*, 43–54. Paris: UNESCO.

Zadrozny, B. (2020). These disinformation researchers saw the coronavirus 'infodemic' coming. *NBC News*. www.nbcnews.com/tech/social-media/these-disinformation-researchers-saw-coronavirus-infodemic-coming-n1206911, accessed 19 August 2020.

PART I

Key concepts

2

WHAT DO WE MEAN BY POPULISM?

Carlos de la Torre

In the first major publication on global populism, Ghita Ionescu and Ernest Gellner (1969, 1) wrote 'there can at present, be no doubt about the *importance* of populism. But no one is quite clear just what it *is*' (emphasis in original). Peter Wiles (1969, 166) corroborated their assessment when he wrote in the same volume, 'to each his own definition of populism, according to the academic axis he grinds'. For the next fifty years or so, scholars engaged in conceptual debates. Four broad conceptualisations of populism are prominent nowadays: a set of ideas, a political strategy, a political style, and a political logic. Interestingly, and despite the fact that advocates of these concepts present theirs as the most useful, scholars continue to combine concepts or to develop their own definition of populism. For instance several contributors to three handbooks of populism combine different conceptual perspectives or develop their own (Heinisch and Mazzoleni 2017; Rovira Kaltwasser, Taggart, Ochoa Espejo and Ostiguy, 2017; de la Torre 2019).

The first section of this chapter briefly maps out what scholars say populism is. Then their different conceptualisation strategies are analysed. The third follows Nadia Urbinati's (2019) suggestion that since it would be very difficult to find an agreement on the genus of populism, scholars should focus instead on what it does when seeking power and once in government. The last section focuses on how populists use the media.

Searching for the right concept

Sociologists and historians first used the concept of populism to describe a particular phase or stage in the modernisation process linked to the transition from an agrarian to an industrial and urban society. Richard Hofstadter in *The Age of Reform* argued that the US Populist Party of the 1890s was the product of an agrarian crisis and a transitional stage in the history of agrarian capitalism. Its base of support was those sectors of society that had attained a low level of education, whose access to information was poor, and who were so completely shut out from access to the centres of power that they felt themselves completely deprived of self-defence and subjected to unlimited manipulation by those who wielded power (1955, 71). Populists aimed to restore a golden age, and their utopia 'was in the past and not in the future' (1955, 62).

Sociologist Gino Germani (1978) viewed populism as a transitional stage provoked by the modernisation of society. Relying on modernisation and mass society theories, he argued that abrupt processes of modernisation such as urbanisation and industrialisation produced masses in a state of anomie that became available for top-down mobilisation. The social base of Peronism was the new working class, made up of recent migrants who were not socialised into working-class culture and therefore could be mobilised from the top by a charismatic leader.

These pioneer studies reduced class interest to the alleged irrationality of rural dwellers and recent migrants. Germani critics showed that the working class supported Perón because, as secretary of labor, he addressed many of their demands for better working conditions and salaries and the right to win strikes. Similarly, historians showed that the US Populist Party 'resembled a type of reformist and evolutionary social democracy' (Postel 2016, 119) and that populist followers were not irrational masses.

Germani critics used dependency theory and Marxism to argue that populism was a multi-class alliance between the industrial bourgeoisie, the working class, and the middle class that supported industrialisation via state intervention in the economy (Ianni 1973). Import substitution industrialisation was a response to the Great Depression and was based on nationalist policies: the redistribution of income to create an internal market, tariffs, and other state protections and incentives to create local industries. When this strategy of development failed in the 1970s and was replaced by neoliberal models that minimised the role of the state in the economy and opened markets to globalisation, it was assumed that populism had run its course. The military dictatorships of the 1970s put an end to democracy, repressed workers, and dismantled unions, thus abolishing what many sociologists argued were the social bases of populism.

Yet in the 1980s, populism reemerged with democratisation. A new brand of populists continued to use populist rhetoric and styles to appeal to the poor and the excluded. Alberto Fujimori, president of Peru (1990–2000), and Carlos Menem (1989–1999) in Argentina abandoned state protectionism and tariffs and advocated for open markets, globalisation, and a minimal and lean state. To make sense of populism as a political phenomenon not reduced to economics policies or a particular class base, scholars studied it as a political style, a strategy, an ideology, or a political logic.

Populism is a style of doing politics that appeals to what elites consider 'bad manners' (Moffit 2016; Ostiguy 2017). If elites appropriate for themselves what are considered good manners – refined, sophisticated tastes and styles; technocratic and rational discourses – populists use words and performances that shock elites as vulgar, distasteful, low, and unlearned. Populism is a form of cultural resistance. Instead of proposing to educate the low into the good, sophisticated, and rational manners of the rich and refined, they challenge their claims to cultural superiority.

Populism can also be conceptualised as a political strategy to get power and to govern (Weyland 2001). Leaders appeal directly to their constituencies, bypassing traditional mediating institutions like parties and unions. If the focus of the previous approach was on the leaders' performances, those who identify it a strategy study the resources that populists mobilised to get to power and their tactics to stay in office. Populist leaders, they argue, are more pragmatic than ideological, and their main goal is to get to and to stay in power. When institutions are fragile, populism in power often leads to competitive authoritarianism (Levitsky and Loxton 2019). By competitive authoritarianism, they mean regimes that use elections that take place on skewed playing fields that make it very difficult for the opposition to win them. Using the term *competitive authoritarianism* means that these regimes are no longer diminished forms of democracy. They have become autocracies.

Populism has been characterised as a set of ideas about politics. Cas Mudde (2004, 543) defined populism as 'an ideology that considers society to be ultimately separated into two homogeneous and antagonistic groups, "the pure people" versus "the corrupt elite", and which argues that politics should be an expression of the *volonté générale* (general will) of the people'. In *Populism in Europe and the Americas*, he and his coauthor Cristóbal Rovira-Kaltwasser (2012, 8–9) argued that

> populism is in essence a form of moral politics, as the distinction between 'the elite' and 'the people' is first and foremost moral (i.e. pure vs. corrupt), not situational (e.g. position of power), socio-cultural (e.g. ethnicity, religion), or socioeconomic (e.g. class).

Accordingly populists construct politics as a Manichaean struggle between the forces of good and evil. If populism is a set of ideas about politics, it encompasses political parties and horizontal social movements like Occupy Wall Street or the Indignados in Spain and Greece that do not have leaders.

When populism is analysed as a political practice, the focus is not on the content of its ideology, policies, or class base; rather, it is on its formal logic (Laclau 2005). Populism aims to rupture existing institutional systems, build enemies, and reduce all political and social conflict to the confrontation between two antagonistic camps. Populism creates strong identities of the people by constructing them as antagonistic to a series of enemies. The name of the leader gives unity to all demands for change and renewal.

Laclau contrasts everyday mundane and administrative politics with those exceptional moments of a populist rupture that, according to him, constitute 'the political'. He argues that the division of society into two antagonistic camps is required to put an end to exclusionary institutional systems and to forge an alternative order. In order to create strong, emotional popular identities, an enemy need to be built. Politics becomes an antagonistic confrontation between two camps: the people versus the oligarchy. The logic of populism is anti-institutional; it is based on the construction of a political frontier and in a logic that could lead to the rupture of the system. The name of the leader becomes the symbol that unites all the demands for change.

Conceptual strategies

Historians and interpretative social scientists acknowledge that the complexity of populism cannot be reduced to one main attribute or to a generic and universal definition. Hence, they use accumulative concepts of populism or ideal types that list a series of attributes. For instance, Jean Cohen (2019, 13–14) lists ten criteria to identify a movement, leader, or party as more or less populist:

1   Appeal to 'the people' and 'popular sovereignty' – empty signifiers deployed to unify heterogeneous demands and grievances.
2   *Pars pro toto* logic that extracts the 'authentic people' from the rest of the population via a logic of equivalences by which a set of demands are constructed into a substantive particular identity that stands for the whole.
3   Discourse that pits the people against elites – the political-economic, cultural 'establishment' cast as usurpers who corrupt, ignore, or distort the 'authentic' people's will.
4   Construction of a frontier of antagonism along the lines of a Schmittian friend/enemy conception of the political that identifies alien others who violate the people's values and whom elites unfairly coddle.

5 Unification, typically through strong identification with a leader (or, more rarely, a unified leadership group) claiming to embody the authentic people's will and voice, incarnating their unity and identity.

6 Focus on the symbolic and authorisation dimensions of political representation.

7 Performative style of leadership that mimics the habitus (dress, speech, manners) of the authentic people.

8 Dramatic and rhetorical forms of argumentation linking talk about making the nation great again to discourses about the restoration of honor, centrality, and political influence to the authentic people.

9 Focus on alleged crises, national decline, and an orientation to the extraordinary dimensions of politics.

10 Dependence on a host ideology for content and moral substance.

Positivist-oriented scholars argue that cumulative concepts do not allow for the accumulation of knowledge. They argue that enumerating a series of attributes to define populism results in conceptual stretching that lumps 'together under the same conceptual roof dissimilar political parties' (Pappas 2019, 29). They are uneasy with gradations and, hence, opt to define populism in contrast with what it is not. The goal of positivists is to produce a generic definition of populism that can travel and explain experiences in different historical times and places. Their first task is to designate the field of populism. Kurt Weyland (2001) argues that the domain of populism is politics understood as strategic struggles over power. Takis Pappas (2019, 33–35) locates it in the domain of democratic politics; he defines populism as 'democratic illiberalism'. Cas Mudde and Cristóbal Rovira Kaltwasser (2012) argue that its domain is morality and that populism is, hence, a form of Manichaean politics. While for Weyland and Pappas, the role of the leader is crucial, Mudde and Rovira Kaltwasser do not define the leader as central and broaden the populist camp to attitudes, movements, and parties.

The concept of populism hence refers to a vague ideology that the people use to challenge the elites, a strategy and a style to get to power and to govern, and political practices that produce popular identities antagonistic to the power bloc. The concept can be constructed as an ideal type with multiple traits or as a minimal concept. Given these profound epistemological differences, scholars regularly argue for abandoning the concept of populism altogether. Historian Enzo Traverso (2019, 16) contends that the concept of populism is an 'empty shell, which can be filled by the most disparate political contents'. Yet despite his call to abolish this term from the vocabulary of the social sciences, he uses it to describe Trump as a 'populist politician' for example (Traverso 2019, 20).

Instead of abandoning populism, it might be more productive to acknowledge that it is an irreplaceable and inescapable part of our political and social vocabulary. Populism is 'a basic concept deployed in the public languages in which political controversy was conducted' (Ritcher 2005, 227). As such, it does not carry a single indisputable meaning, and a variety of conflicting constituencies passionately struggle to make their definitions 'authoritative and compelling' (Baehr 2008, 12).

What populism does

Instead of trying to resolve endless disputes about what populism is, perhaps it is more fruitful to focus on what it does. Nadia Urbinati (2019) argues that regardless of how leaders and parties are defined, there are a series of actions, words, and performances through which we can see populists in action.

Creating enemies

Populists do not face political rivals with whom one could disagree. They transform rivals into existential and symbolic enemies. Differently from fascists, who physically eliminate their enemies, populists do not kill them. Instead they depict them as the dangerous other. In a different way from a rival that one tries to convince about ones point of view in an argument, an enemy needs to be contained because it is an existential threat. Populists are constantly manufacturing enemies. When seeking power, their enemy is broadly cast as the establishment. Once in power, their enemies become particular political, economic, and cultural elites who supposedly hold the real power.

Populists differ on whom they construct as the enemies of the people. Right-wing populists often face two types of enemies: cosmopolitan elites above and dependents of colour bellow. The enemies of European right-wing populists are the global elites of the European community, their cronies at home, and immigrants who do not work and live off the hard-earned money of taxpayers. Similarly, the Tea Party and Donald Trump struggle against dependents of colour below, who allegedly live off welfare paid by white producers, and cosmopolitan liberal elites, who tax middle-class makers above.

Racist arguments are used to cast whole populations not just as inferior but as inherently culturally different and inassimilable. The other is imagined as a plague, a virus, or a disease that could contaminate the purity of the people. Their culture and/or their religion is not just different; it is the opposite of the good values and morals of the host ethnic population. Right-wing populists hence politicise emotions such as fear to the different, dangerous, and treacherous other. They argue that citizens cannot be complicit with cosmopolitan elites who allow for the massive entrance of the dangerous other to European or American neighbourhoods and schools.

The other becomes dehumanised. In Europe the Muslim immigrant, for instance, is perceived as an 'infection agent' (Traverso 2019, 75), whereas in America the illegal Mexican immigrant, a term that encompasses populations of Latin American origins, is seen as the source of evil. Because 'Mexican' immigrants were previously cast as the subhuman other who is willing to do any trick in order to enter into the US, even renting children or putting them at risk in rivers and deserts, they needed to be punished. Families were separated, and 'Mexican' children and babies were put in cages in immigrant detention centres. Fear leads to lack of empathy, dehumanisation, and perhaps to extreme measures of containment such as mass detention and deportation.

The enemies of left-wing populists are the economic and political elites of the establishment, the 1 percent, the oligarchy, or the caste. For the most part, leftists do not use xenophobic and racist arguments. If the right politicises fears to the danger of contamination of culture, religion, and race, the left focuses on the angers produce by socioeconomic and political exclusions and by systemic inequalities. They politicise anger, indignation, and envy. These emotions could lead to mobilisation against those who are at the top because of oligarchic privileges or corruption.

Populism's *pars pro toto* dynamic and the leader as the embodiment of the true people

Populists do not aim to give power back to all the population. They do not appeal to Rousseau general will either. They aim to empower only a section of the population, those excluded who represent the right and truthful people. The rest are depicted as the oligarchy, the caste, or those sectors of the population who are not part of the sincere and good people. The *pars pro toto* dynamic of populism is inherently exclusionary. When ethnic and religious criteria are used to name the real or authentic people, these constructs attempt against modern and plural civil societies. However it could be argued that casting the 1 percent or the oligarchy as not part of the people is not such a terrible problem; after all, the hyper-rich and powerful live from the work of the poor. The problem is that even in left-wing populism, the *pars por toto* dynamic excludes the organisations of the poor that do not uncritically support the leader. The exclusionary dynamic of left-wing populism is not only used against class enemies but also and fundamentally against political enemies. After all, the leader is the person who names those who belong to the good people, and his enemies could become former members of the populist coalition or anybody critical of the leader's claim to embody the people.

For populism to be successful, it needs a leader; otherwise it remains at the margins of the political system. A leader is built as the authentic and truthful representative of the right people. Even when populists are inclusionary, it is on the condition of accepting the leadership of the wise leader.

Populists challenging power, populists in power, and populist regimes

Populists attempting to get to power, populists in office, and populist regimes are not the same. When challenging power, populists politicise issues that other politicians ignore or do not address. They show the failures of democracies and protest against inequalities. However for populism to develop into a new 'ism', it has to get to power (Finchelstein 2017). Once in office, populists show their true colours and characteristics. Populists are not regular politicians elected for a set period of time. They have the mission of liberating their people. Elections are not just regular democratic contestations for power. They become gargantuan battles between the past of oppression and the liberation to come. Populists rule as if they have the urgency to transform all democratic disputes into existential battles between antagonistic camps. They confront and manufacture enemies. Traditional political elites, media elites, or the leaders of social movements and non-governmental organisations could become enemies of the leader, the people, and the nation.

When in power, populists follow a similar playbook. Steven Levitsky and Daniel Ziblat (2018, 78–96) show how in nations as different as Venezuela, Hungary, Poland, Turkey, and the US, populists followed similar strategies to consolidate their rule. (1) Capturing the referees such as the judicial system, law enforcement, intelligence agencies, tax authorities, regulatory agencies, and institutions in charge of horizontal accountability. (2) Silencing opponents by buying or bribing them. Using the law instrumentally to try to quiet critics by fining newspapers or suing journalists. Regulating the activities of organisations of civil society like non-governmental organisations (NGOs). In some cases weakening independent social movements by creating alternative organisations from the top. Silencing businesspeople using tax authorities and hushing important cultural figures. (3) Changing the rules of the game by reforming the constitution and changing electoral rules. (4) Fabricating or taking advantage of crises to concentrate power and crack down on the opposition.

Populists pretend to follow the rule of law; hence, it is imperative for them to control the legal system to use laws to punish critics and, in some cases, to stay indefinitely in power. When populists are able to change constitutions and to regulate the public sphere, control civil society, and change the educational system, they become regimes. Populist regimes combine a democratic commitment to elections as the only legitimate tool to elect and remove politicians with undemocratic views of political rivals as enemies and conceptions of the people as unitary actors and, in some cases, of the political theologies of the leader as the savior of the people.

Analysing populists as particular regimes better captures their autocratic and inclusionary practices than branding them competitive authoritarian. Characterising populist regimes as competitive authoritarian misses the inclusionary processes provoked by some populist regimes. From Perón to Chávez, populists distributed income and, to a lesser extent, wealth; reduced poverty; and valued the worth of common and non-white citizens, while simultaneously transforming a person into the redeemer of a unitary people. Populists acted in the name of democracy, and their projects were to improve not to destroy it. Moreover, because elections gave legitimacy to these regimes, they aimed to control and regulate but not to destroy the institutional framework of democracy, fundamental liberties, autonomous civil societies, and an independent public sphere.

Differentiating populisms

Not all populisms are the same. Right-wing populists like Donald Trump, Rodrigo Duterte, and Jair Bolsonaro are nostalgic and backward looking. They do not propose to radicalise democracy. On the contrary their projects aim to limit rights in order to strengthen law and order. Other right-wing populists aim to preserve European welfare states by excluding non-natives. Differently Hugo Chávez and other left-wing populists promised to include the excluded, to improve the quality of democratic participation, and even to create utopias. Chávez proposed socialism of the twentieth-first century as an alternative to neoliberalism and communism, and Rafael Correa and Evo Morales proposed alternative relations between humans, nature, and development.

Populists don't only differ across the right and left axis. Light and full-blown populism should be differentiated. By light populism, I refer to political parties and politicians who occasionally use populist tropes and discourses but do not aim to rupture existing institutions. Under this criterion, Bernie Sanders, who did not break with the Democratic Party to create a third party in 2016 nor in 2020, is a light populist. Full-blown populists aim to rupture existing institutions by polarising society and the polity into two camps of enemies and constructing a leader as the symbol of all the demands for change and renewal. Light populists are almost indistinguishable from other politicians in contemporary democracies who appeal to trust in their personas and use the mass media to bypass traditional parties. Full-blown populists often use democratic institutional mechanisms and mass mobilisation to try to bring change. When seeking power, full-blown populists appeal to constituencies that the elites despise or ignore. They use discourses and performances to shock and disturb the limits of the permissible and to confront conventions.

Populism and the media

Populists are media innovators. Eva Perón in the 1940s and 50s made use of the radio to directly communicate with her followers. In the 1990s populists such as Silvio Berlusconi used television to bypass parties. In the twenty-first century, the Five Star Movement and Podemos use the web to organise and mobilise followers. When seeking power populists often raise important questions about how democratic the media is. They often challenge media monopolies and the authority of cultural elites to claim to be public opinion. Yet the populist critique of the media needs to be distinguished from the populist solutions and their practices in office.

When in power the body of the populist leader – which is no other than the body of the people struggling for its liberation – becomes omnipresent. For seven years Eva Perón was present everywhere. Her face was on millions of billboards in streets and in stores, the state radio broadcast her speeches daily, and she had a prominent role in the weekly news shown in all Argentinean movie theaters (Sebreli 2008). Hugo Chávez and Rafael Correa put their images or slogans from their regimes in visible spots along highways and cities. They used mandatory TV and radio messages to constantly broadcast their images and to be seen in newspapers, on television, and on social media, as they were constantly on Twitter and Facebook. They had weekly television and radio shows on which Chávez talked for about six hours and Correa for about three. They marked the news agenda because, in addition to entertaining their audiences they announced important policies.

Similarly, Donald Trump's image is everywhere at all times. Pundits are constantly discussing and analysing his latest tweet. The obsessive need of television for politics as entertainment meets the compulsive need of the populist to become a permanent feature in citizens' everyday lives. He occupies the centre stage of media discussions, transforming politics into melodrama and sheer emotional entertainment. For some his image produces pleasure and enjoyment as his attacks on political correctness and his racist, homophobic, xenophobic, and misogynist remarks appear to be sincere expressions of libidinal energy repressed by social conventions. For others his words produce fear, anguish, disgust, and even nausea. The strong emotions that his body and words provoke put him at the centre of conversations in the public and private spheres.

Populists as diverse as Donald Trump, Viktor Orbán, and Rafael Correa have embarked on wars against the media. These leaders devalue truth and the practices of professional journalism. Whereas Orbán and Trump favour particular private media venues, control and regulation of the media by the state was at the centre of the leftist populist struggle for hegemony (Waisbord 2013). Chávez and Correa enacted laws to regulate the content the media could publish; the state took away radio and television frequencies from critics, becoming the main communicator in these nations.

Conclusion

Focusing on what populists do allows us to avoid endless conceptual debates. Instead of continuing to search for the right concept, this move to practice helps explain the commonalities and differences between varieties of populism. Some politicise fears of cosmopolitanism using race, ethnicity, and culture to mark the boundaries of inclusion to the people and the nation. Other populists give meanings to feelings and emotions of exclusion and anger at economic and political elites who pretend that neoliberalism is the only technically acceptable economic policy. We need to differentiate populists seeking office, populists in power, and populist regimes. Light and full-blown populists are not the same.

When Ionesco and Gellner published their work, populism was absent from Europe. In 2018 'the governments of eight countries of the European Union (Austria, Belgium, Denmark, Finland, Italy, Poland, Hungary, and Slovakia) were led by far-right nationalist, and xenophobic parties' (Traverso 2019, 3). Populism is here to stay. Our task as citizens, students, and scholars is to understand its complexities without demonising it. We have to comprehend why these parties mobilise citizens without using stereotypes that label followers as irrational. The populist critique needs to be taken seriously, yet we have to ask if their solutions will actually return power to the people or lead to the disfigurement of democracy (Urbinati 2014) or, even worse, to its slow death.

References

Baehr, Peter. 2008. *Caesarism, Charisma and Fate: Historical Sources and Modern Resonances in the Work of Max Weber*, New Brunswick, NJ: Transaction Press.

Cohen, Jean L. 2019. "Populism and the Politics of Resentment" *Jus Cogens* 1, 5–39.

de la Torre, Carlos, ed. 2019. *The Routledge International Handbook of Global Populism*, New York: Routledge.

Finchelstein, Federico. 2017. *From Fascism to Populism in History*, Oakland, CA: The University of California Press.

Germani, Gino. 1978. *Authoritarianism, Fascism, and National Populism*, New Brunswick, NJ: Transaction Books.

Henisch, Holtz-Bacha and Oscar Mazzoleni. 2017. *Political Populism: A Handbook*, Baden-Baden: Nomos.

Hofstadter, Richard. 1955. *The Age of Reform*, New York: Alfred A. Knopf.

Ianni, Octavio. 1973. "Populismo y Contradicciones de Clase" in *Populismo y contradicciones de clase en Latinoamérica*, edited by Octavio Ianni, México: Era, 83–150.

Ionescu, Ghita and Ernest Gellner. 1969. "Introduction" in *Populism: Its Meanings and National Characteristics*, London: The Macmillan Press, 1–5.

Laclau, Ernesto. 2005. *On Populist Reason*, London: Verso.

Levitsky, Steven and James Loxton. 2019. "Populism and Competitive Authoritarianism in Latin America" in *The Routledge International Handbook of Global Populism*, edited by Carlos de la Torre, New York: Routledge, 334–351.

Levitsky, Steven and Daniel Ziblatt. 2018. *How Democracies Die*, New York: Crown.

Moffitt, Benjamin. 2016. *The Global Rise of Populism: Performance, Political Style, Representation*, Stanford, CA: Stanford University Press.

Mudde, Cas. 2004. "The Populist Zeitgeist" *Government and Opposition* 39(4), 541–563.

Mudde, Cas and Cristóbal Rovira Kaltwasser. 2012. *Populism in Europe and the Americas*, Cambridge: Cambridge University Press.

Ostiguy, Pierre. 2017. "Populism a Socio-Cultural Approach" in *The Oxford Handbook of Populism*, edited by Cristóbal Rovira Kaltwasser, Paul Taggart, Paulina Ochoa Espejo and Pierre Ostiguy, Oxford: Oxford University Press.

Pappas, Takis. 2019. *Populism and Liberal Democracy: A Comparative and Theoretical Analysis*, Oxford: Oxford University Press.

Postel, Charles. 2016. "The American Populist and Anti-Populist Legacy" in *Transformations of Populism in Europe and the Americas History and Recent Tendencies*, edited by J. Abromeit, B. Cherston, G. Marotta and N. York, London: Bloomsbury Press, 105–116.

Ritcher, Melvin. 2005. "A Family of Political Concepts Tyranny, Despotism, Bonapartism, Caesarism, Dictatorship, 1750–1917" *European Journal of Political Theory* 4(3), 221–248.

Rovira Kaltwasser, Cristóbal, Paul Taggart, Paulina Ochoa Espejo and Pierre Ostiguy. 2017. *The Oxford Handbook of Populism*, Oxford: Oxford University Press.

Sebreli, Juan José. 2008. *Comediantes y Mártires: Ensayos contra los Mitos*, Buenos Aires: Editorial Debate.

Traverso, Enzo. 2019. *The New Faces of Fascism: Populism and the Far Right*, London: Verso.

Urbinati, Nadia. 2014. *Democracy Disfigured: Opinion, Truth, and the People*, Cambridge, MA: Harvard University Press.

Urbinati, Nadia. 2019. *Me the People: How Populism Transforms Democracy*, Cambridge, MA: Harvard University Press.

Waisbord, Silvio. 2013. *Vox Populista, Medios, Periodismo, Democracia*, Buenos Aires: Gedisa.

Weyland, Kurt. 2001. "Clarifying a Contested Concept" *Comparative Politics* 34(1), 1–22.

Wiles, Peter. 1969. "A Syndrome Not a Doctrine" in *Populism: Its Meanings and National Characteristics*, London: The Macmillan Press, 166–180.

3

MISINFORMATION AND DISINFORMATION

Rachel Armitage and Cristian Vaccari

Introduction

This chapter will provide an overview of the debates surrounding misinformation and disinformation in political communication. After defining the key terms, we will contextualise this discussion, connecting recent concern about mis/disinformation with the growth of populism, declining trust in the media, and the role of digital platforms. We will then examine the key political, psychological, technological, and contextual factors that make people susceptible to mis/disinformation, before assessing current efforts to identify and tackle factually problematic content online. We conclude with broad recommendations for future efforts in this field.

Defining the key terms

Descriptors of problematic information range from general catch-all terms to specific references, competing in disputed hierarchies that change across people, context, and time. Terms including 'junk news' (Narayanan et al. 2018) and 'fake news' (Lazer et al. 2018) have variously been employed to represent manipulated, fabricated, extremist, satirical, sensationalist, parody, propagandist, and conspiratorial content (Tandoc, Lim & Ling 2018). This lack of definitional consistency potentially underlies conflicting academic findings (Tucker et al. 2018), illustrating how terminology can influence both the perception of the problem and its solution.

The most commonly accepted distinction between types of problematic information is misinformation and disinformation. Both terms refer to the sharing of incorrect, inaccurate, or misleading content, but they are separated by intentionality. While misinformation entails accidentally sharing inaccurate content, disinformation constitutes deliberate deception, often based on outright fabrications (Jack 2017). Difficult as it may be to determine the intentions of mis/disinformation sharers – especially when they are ordinary social media users – this distinction captures an important normative as well as empirical difference.

Some authors have suggested additional terms to cover conceptual space bordering mis/disinformation, including 'xisinformation', in which it is hard to parse a sharer's intent (Jack 2017, 16), and 'mal-information' to describe intentionally harmful sharing of accurate information (Wardle & Derakhshan 2017, 5). However, this ongoing semantic discussion may distract from the need to tackle such problematic information (Weeks & Gil de Zúñiga 2019). Any such efforts must start from a comprehensive understanding of the contextual factors that enable mis/disinformation to take root.

Contextualising the challenge of mis/disinformation

Whilst misleading information is not a new phenomenon, increasing concern about global mis/disinformation has revealed contemporary catalysts behind such problematic content (Lazer et al. 2018). One contributing factor is the rise of populism in political systems around the world. Populist leaders often attack experts and independent journalists, alleging bias in response to any negative media coverage (Newman et al. 2019). This is particularly effective in an increasingly polarised context, where populist supporters and detractors are ever less willing to engage with one another (Mason 2018). As a result, mis/disinformation has gained a stronger foothold in public discourse, reducing the space for evidence-based debate (Nyhan 2018). Political actors themselves often bear responsibility for spreading disinformation, especially during election campaigns. Prior to the United Kingdom's 2016 referendum to leave or remain in the European Union (EU), there was a preponderance of misleading content favouring the Leave campaign on Twitter, with problematic assertions by the campaign itself achieving greater traction than disinformation efforts by outside groups (Gorrell et al. 2019). Similar activity was decried during the 2019 UK general election, with politicians accused of 'playing fast and loose with the facts, avoiding journalistic scrutiny, and denigrating the media' (Newman 2020, 12).

Accordingly, populism and political polarisation have contributed to the decline of trust in mainstream media and news organisations. In the UK, trust in news has been falling since 2015, and even the BBC is now seen as having an agenda, especially regarding divisive issues such as Brexit (Newman et al. 2019). Populist supporters are particularly likely to distrust independent news media, which they see as part of despised elites (Fawzi 2019), limiting the ability of the established media to authoritatively correct mis/disinformation. One possible outcome is the cultivation of an 'anything-goes' mentality among social media users (Chadwick & Vaccari 2019), who may become less vigilant about the quality of news they share as online social norms are eroded, and establishing the truth becomes increasingly difficult and contested.

Indeed, the broad proliferation of mis/disinformation has arguably been accelerated by social media (Wardle & Derakhshan 2017). Social networking sites have challenged the role of traditional media as information gatekeeper (Resnick, Ovadya & Gilchrist 2018), lowering the cost of entry to the production and distribution of news and thereby vastly increasing the quantity (but not necessarily the quality) of available content (Lazer et al. 2018). This has allowed politicians – especially those who can afford mass-scale digital advertising – to communicate directly with the public, devoid of the restrictions normally accompanying journalistic mediation (Siegel 2018). Social media has further facilitated the artificial inflation of problematic content via bots (automated accounts) and cyborgs (hybrid human/automated accounts), as well as empowering average citizens – including partisan activists – to quickly create and widely disseminate material of varying veracity (Cook, Ecker & Lewandowsky 2015), often using content from news organisations as a resource to influence others (Chadwick, Vaccari & O'Loughlin 2018). Mobile messaging apps (such as WhatsApp, Snapchat, Facebook Messenger, and Vine) pose distinctive challenges, facilitating private informal discussions between small, strong-tie networks that may be less guarded against mis/disinformation (Valeriani & Vaccari 2018). However, users are more likely to both issue and receive corrections when they share mis/disinformation on WhatsApp than they are on Facebook, possibly because they are less fearful of suffering backlash for challenging members of their strong-tie networks than they are when they engage with their weak ties on the more open social media platforms (Rossini et al. 2019).

Susceptibility to mis/disinformation

Exposure to mis/disinformation is widespread online. A survey of UK social media users found that as many as 57 percent believed they had seen inaccurate news on social media in the previous month, and another one-fifth of respondents could not tell whether they had or not (Chadwick & Vaccari 2019). During the COVID-19 pandemic, between half and one-quarter of the British public, depending on the period, reported coming across false or misleading news about the virus and an additional one-quarter was not sure (Ofcom 2020). Hence, it becomes important to identify factors that make individuals susceptible to mis/disinformation.

Political and social psychological factors

Humans respond to the uncertainty in our world through 'shared sensemaking', including sharing rumours and doubtful information (DiFonzo 2008, 10), which now occurs predominantly via social media and mobile messaging apps. Importantly, the framing of information under uncertainty can influence how we perceive a situation (Tversky & Kahneman 1986), as can our affinity for, or aversion to, uncertainty (Sorrentino & Roney 2000). Individuals favouring the familiar are likely to seek out certainty in societal groups (Lane 1962) that define their social identities (Hogg et al. 2007). Uncertainty reinforces feelings of in-group belonging and out-group enmity, creating inflated perceptions of differences between groups (Sherman et al. 2009). This is exacerbated if intergroup competition is seen as a zero-sum game, in which gains for one group become losses for the other (Mason 2018).

Such intergroup conflict is arguably characteristic of party politics, particularly in majoritarian two-party systems in which there is little hope of cooperation across the aisle. To this end, exposure to messages reinforcing inter-party differences can stoke divisions and increase polarisation (Vaccari 2018), feeding into the creation of opposing shared realities (DiFonzo 2008). Indeed, as political groups are perceived as ever more disparate, they are simultaneously viewed by in-group members as ever more clearly defined (Sherman et al. 2009). In many political systems, personal identities and political affiliations have become increasingly aligned (Arceneaux & Vander Wielen 2017), creating socially homogenous parties with ever more intolerant members (Mason 2018), thus reinforcing feelings of ingroup belonging that validate one's worldviews (Hogg et al. 2007).

Worldviews provide the basis for political ideologies, or the rationalised beliefs of a group employed by members in countering their opponents (Lane 1962). Individuals' group identities therefore inevitably affect their political judgments, making it unlikely that they self-correct erroneous out-group beliefs for fear of undermining their worldview (Mason 2018). Instead people use heuristics, or stereotypes, concurrent with their worldview to cue their decisions (Lane 1962). Accordingly, messages alluding to group stereotypes can encourage acceptance of misleading information about political out-groups (Vaccari 2018; Nyhan 2018), discouraging critical reflection. Indeed, the term 'political sectarianism' has recently been proposed to more precisely capture the moralized nature of partisan identifications (Finkel et al. 2020). When political identities combine othering, aversion, and moral repulse towards other political groups, partisans become more willing to intentionally discount information that does not support their views and are even prepared to accept the use of anti-democratic tactics from their side if they can secure victory against opponents seen as immoral.

To this end, understanding the world mainly from a group perspective can contribute to social polarisation, or action based in prejudice and emotional volatility. People emotionally invest in the maintenance of their group identity even when this is irrational because questioning an affiliation incorporating core aspects of one's identity risks increasing uncertainty. In this vein, scholars contend that decision-making unavoidably begins with unconscious emotional intuition (Arceneaux & Vander Wielen 2017). Indeed, existing affect can prevent the rational processing of new information (Redlawsk 2002), and emotions are often the main catalyst for rumour transmission, overriding concerns for veracity (DiFonzo 2008; Lewandowsky et al. 2012). Individuals motivated to experience strong emotions need only to *feel* that they are accurate, forming strong opinions from gut reactions and failing to interrogate their intuition, and are thus particularly susceptible to believing and sharing mis/disinformation (Anspach, Jennings & Arceneaux 2019). While the mechanisms described here have existed for a long time, recent technological changes have arguably magnified their impact and implications.

Technological factors

The affordances of digital media exacerbate susceptibility to worldview-congruent mis/disinformation as they tend to facilitate instantaneous, uncritical behaviour based on little cognitive consideration (Bartlett 2018). Indeed, social media platforms design and constantly update their affordances to retain users' attention, mainly by providing content they are more likely to interact with (Bucher 2018). Whilst users do have capacity to curate the content they see online, giving rise to concerns about echo chambers (Lewandowsky et al. 2012), research suggests that only a minority of users consistently avoid political content they disagree with (Vaccari & Valeriani forthcoming). Indeed, most social media users have ideologically diverse online networks and are therefore indirectly exposed to unfamiliar perspectives (Dubois & Blank 2018), although such exposure may reinforce rather than challenge users' pre-existing beliefs (Bail et al. 2018) and has been associated with the sharing of mis/disinformation (Rossini et al. 2019).

The online environment is also attractive to nefarious actors running propaganda and disinformation campaigns (Narayanan et al. 2018), who take advantage of social media business models prioritising clicks and data capture over content quality. Such campaigns employ computational propaganda techniques, manipulating algorithms, cluttering conversations, and hijacking public spaces (such as hashtags) to reach users with inauthentic content (Sanovich & Stukal 2018). They further utilise microtargeting to tap into users' identities, preferences, and prejudices, thus making it harder for users to recognise and reject mis/disinformation consistent with their beliefs (Bartlett 2018). Another concern is the rapid evolution of technologies that can distort audio-visual content, particularly in the creation of so-called deepfakes: synthetic videos generated to appear real by artificial intelligence software, increasingly available in open-source format and trained with publicly available data. Recent research suggests that even if individuals may not be misled by deepfakes, many react to them with uncertainty, reducing trust in all news encountered on social media as a result (Vaccari & Chadwick 2020).

Contextual factors

Political and media institutions can also affect the production, circulation, and impact of mis/disinformation. According to Humprecht, Esser & Van Aelst (2020), disinformation-resilient countries feature both an infrastructure that protects most citizens from exposure to false information (including strong public service broadcasters) and a citizenry less likely to believe and disseminate, and more likely to challenge, poor quality information. In an assessment of 18 Western democracies, the researchers found countries in Northern Europe (including Denmark, Finland, and The Netherlands) to be the most disinformation resilient, whilst Southern

European countries (including Italy, Spain, and Greece) and the United States were found to be particularly susceptible. This is confirmed by survey results showing greater concern about online mis/disinformation from citizens in South America (Brazil), the US, and the UK than from respondents in Germany and The Netherlands (Newman et al. 2019).

A nation's resilience to mis/disinformation also depends on the type of social media platform favoured by its citizens. Notably, large WhatsApp and Facebook groups have become popular means of sharing and discussing news in non-Western countries such as Brazil, Malaysia, and Turkey. WhatsApp groups were exploited in both the 2018 Brazilian presidential election (Machado et al. 2019) and the 2019 Indian general election (Narayanan et al. 2019) to distribute misleading and divisive political content. Notably, information flows on mobile messaging apps are encrypted and generally private, making it hard for news organisations and digital platforms themselves to observe, correct, and limit the spread of inaccurate content via this medium.

Solutions to the problem of mis/disinformation

In light of the very real threat posed by mis/disinformation to democratic governance and the unprecedented scale at which digital media enable it to spread, efforts to effectively identify, limit, and correct it have become increasingly important.

Identifying mis/disinformation

To date, most work has focused on the development of automatic detection techniques to identify problematic content (Cook, Ecker & Lewandowsky 2015). These include classifiers to determine who might share misinformation online (Ghenai & Mejova 2018) and computational tools to detect clickbait, rumours, and bots. Whilst such tools can efficiently filter vast amounts of online content, the machine learning necessary to develop them can be prohibitively time and resource intensive (Tucker et al. 2018). Moreover, their effectiveness is limited by restricted access to social media data, as well as by increasingly effective automation that makes bots difficult to distinguish from real accounts. Even where detection is successful, bot developers soon adapt, and many bot accounts will never be discovered (Sanovich & Stukal 2018). Importantly, computational classifiers are not a replacement for human experts, who must intermittently retrain such tools and be on hand to mitigate any inadvertent discrimination classifiers may perpetuate (Ghenai & Mejova 2018). To this end, there is a risk that such tools will be more effective and precise in countries and on topics that digital platforms prioritise for investment.

Another approach in identifying mis/disinformation online is human content moderation. These efforts are conducted by large teams, employed by social media platforms to monitor and review content in line with their terms of service or community standards (Gillespie 2018). However, such work comes replete with associated mental health difficulties (Chen 2014), blowback from angry users (Newton 2019), and concerns about poor remuneration and the massive volume of content to be checked. Often moderators act based on user reporting, despite users' tendency to rely on partisanship and ideology when identifying misleading content (boyd 2017) or, indeed, failing to challenge it at all (Chadwick & Vaccari 2019). Finally, the often implicit assumptions underlying content moderation threaten to undermine the key democratic value of freedom of information (Kaye 2019). That any politically relevant but untrue speech should be censored and that such determinations should be made by quasi-monopolistic private companies arguably raises more problems than it solves.

Tackling mis/disinformation

Despite the difficulties inherent in isolating problematic content, further decisions must be taken about dealing with mis/disinformation when it is identified. Perhaps the easiest approach for platforms is to take down, downrank, or label such content, adjusting algorithms to promote reliable information, indicating source quality and story veracity, banning offending accounts, and removing harmful bot activity (Lazer et al. 2018). However, this kind of moderation risks bias or error such that legitimate content is accidentally removed, opening platforms up to censorship accusations (Sanovich & Stukal 2018). Moreover, previous attempts at algorithm change have counter-intuitively increased the prevalence of divisive topics (NewsWhip 2019), and there is no guarantee that algorithms cannot be gamed by bad actors. There is also the issue of what to do when disinformation is spread by popular political actors, including incumbent presidents, whom platforms have been more reluctant to police than ordinary users.

Another popular approach in tackling mis/disinformation is fact-checking. However, creating effective fact-checks is resource intensive, and their efficacy can be limited (Marwick 2018). The fractured nature of the online environment makes it difficult for corrections to reach those exposed to mis/disinformation, with problematic content going an average of 10 to 20 hours before fact-checking catches up (Shao et al. 2016). Where corrections do reach their desired audiences, repetition of mis/disinformation as part of the corrective effort merely increases its cognitive fluency – 'the experience of ease or difficulty associated with completing a mental task' (Oppenheimer 2008, 237) – paradoxically making acceptance of the misleading information more likely (Lazer et al. 2018). Indeed, if mis/disinformation is congruent with one's worldview, belief in such content is especially likely to persist in the face of corrections (Cook, Ecker & Lewandowsky 2015). Moreover, problematic content often continues to influence attitudes even after corrections have been cognitively accepted (Thorson 2016). Nevertheless, various techniques can increase the effectiveness of correction, including an emphasis on facts (Lewandowsky et al. 2012), avoiding repetition of the mis/disinformation, issuing corrections as soon as possible, avoiding negation, reducing ideological or partisan cues, citing credible sources, using graphics (Nyhan & Reifler 2012), and providing causal alternatives (Thorson 2016). However, even such carefully crafted corrections have a greater chance of success if they are congruent with their target's worldview (Lewandowsky et al. 2012). Accordingly, misleading political content is particularly difficult to correct (Walter & Murphy 2018), with journalists finding that their fact-checks are failing to impact large portions of the public (Newman 2020).

An alternative tool in the fight against mis/disinformation is legislation. In Britain, recent high-level reports have called for the independent regulation of social media companies, with legal and financial consequences for failing to protect users against harmful content (Digital, Culture, Media & Sport Committee 2019; Cairncross et al. 2019), although other expert groups have recommended against such measures (Council of Europe 2018; European Commission 2018; Nielsen et al. 2019). There is a fine line between controlling problematic information and compromising free speech, with any government regulation efforts potentially facing criticism for censorship or partiality. The lack of an agreed definition for problematic content (boyd 2017) and, perhaps more importantly, of a shared understanding of the problem across the political spectrum also constitute major obstacles to regulatory solutions.

Other efforts to tackle mis/disinformation have focused on changing journalistic practice. A key concern here is the decline of resources among news organisations, which has led many outlets, especially at the local level, to close or substantially downscale newsrooms. However, many journalists feel their industry should make greater efforts to challenge misleading information (Newman 2020) and attempt to re-establish their reputations – possibly with some help from civil society organisations that are developing training programmes on source verification and responsible reporting (First Draft n.d.). However, efforts to restore public trust in the media may demand more financial and editorial resources than are available (Jukes 2018), and continued efforts to fact check will be perpetually undermined or ignored by partisan actors – without whose self-restraint journalists will always be facing an uphill battle.

Approaches focused on news consumers are also relevant, with civic and digital education efforts seeking to equip social media users against online mis/disinformation. Research suggests that young people are often unable to tell real from misleading news content on social media (McGrew et al. 2017) and that media literacy strategies – for instance, teaching users how to employ fact-checking techniques – could help address this (Wineburg & McGrew 2017). Attempts to inoculate users against mis/disinformation have also shown promise, as 'fake news' games have often improved identification of, and resistance to, misleading content (Roozenbeek & van der Linden 2019). Nevertheless, there are concerns that media literacy techniques may be ineffectual (Marwick 2018), with questions about the long-term maintenance of skills and the risk of such efforts reducing trust in news altogether (Lazer et al. 2018). Media literacy is also time and resource intensive and is unlikely to reach or affect all users who need it.

Finally, changes in the way social media works may also be helpful. For instance, creating more friction in the user experience may reduce users' inclination to mindlessly accept and share mis/disinformation that fits with their worldview. Research suggests that inducing social media users to think about accuracy, or to think critically, can reduce the likelihood that users trust, like, or share problematic information online (Pennycook et al. 2019). Requiring defence of a decision can trigger accuracy motivations (Kunda 1990), and this in turn encourages successful processing of worldview-incongruent information (Redlawsk 2002). Moreover, simply introducing elements of difficulty or 'disfluency' (unease) to a task can interrupt and correct reasoning based on partisan cues (Alter et al. 2007). Indeed, interventions based on disfluency have been found to increase analytic thinking and to reduce belief in conspiracy theories (Swami et al. 2014). If such friction can be introduced into the social media environment, it might reduce users' propensity to believe and share mis/disinformation, although the question of how to achieve this in practice remains to be answered. This is a momentous task, as the success of social media platforms has largely depended on encouraging fluency, ease of use, and 'stickiness' – the 'ability to attract users, to get them to stay longer, and to make them return again and again' (Hindman 2018, 2).

Conclusion

This chapter has sought to define, contextualise, and explain susceptibility to online mis/disinformation and to discuss solutions to the problem. These phenomena are rooted in psychological, political, technological, and contextual factors that are unlikely to change substantially in the future, and there is no single effective approach that might limit or reverse this course. Thwarting the capability of disinformation campaigns – whether run by mainstream political actors, outside groups, or foreign governments – to exploit a continually changing online landscape and to employ social media users as their (knowing or unknowing) foot soldiers in spreading problematic content will be no easy task.

Whilst there is no apparent 'silver bullet' solution to mis/disinformation, such content relies on exposure to and engagement by average social media users to be effective. Therefore, whilst it is undoubtedly important to continue developing tools and techniques that take on the production and distribution of misleading information, there is surely a key, long-term role to be played by approaches seeking to equip citizens with the tools to recognise, challenge, and reject mis/disinformation. However, even this might prove insufficient if the underlying political and technological catalysts for such content cannot be remedied.

Bibliography

Alter, A. L., Oppenheimer, D. M., Epley, N. & Eyre, R. N. (2007) Overcoming intuition: Metacognitive difficulty activates analytic reasoning. *Journal of Experimental Psychology: General, 136* (4), 569–576. doi:10.1037/0096-3445.136.4.569

Anspach, N. M., Jennings, J. T. & Arceneaux, K. (2019) A little bit of self knowledge: Facebook's news feed and self-perceptions of knowledge. *Research & Politics, 6* (1), 1–9. doi:10.1177/2053168018816189

Arceneaux, K. & Vander Wielen, R. J. (2017) *Taming intuition: How reflection minimizes partisan reasoning and promotes democratic accountability.* Cambridge: Cambridge University Press.

Bail, C. A., Argyle, L. P., Brown, T. W., Bumpus, J. P., Chen, H., Fallin Hunzaker, M. B., . . . Volfovsky, A. (2018) Exposure to opposing views on social media can increase political polarization. *Proceedings of the National Academy of Sciences, 115* (37), 9216–9221. doi:10.1073/pnas.1804840115

Bartlett, J. (2018) *The people vs tech: How the internet is killing democracy (and how we save it).* London: Ebury Press.

boyd, d. (2017, March 27) Google and Facebook can't just make fake news disappear. *WIRED.* Retrieved from: www.wired.com/2017/03/google-and-facebook-cant-just-make-fake-news-disappear/

Bucher, T. (2018) *If . . . then: Algorithmic power and politics.* Oxford: Oxford University Press.

Cairncross, F., Adetunji, J., Allinson, G., Azhar, A., Curtis, P., Highfield, A., . . . Wright, P. (2019) *The Cairncross review: A sustainable future for journalism.* Retrieved from: https://assets.publishing. service.gov.uk/government/uploads/system/uploads/attachment_data/file/779882/021919_DCMS_ Cairncross_Review_.pdf

Chadwick, A. & Vaccari, C. (2019) *News sharing on UK social media: Misinformation, disinformation, and correction.* Retrieved from: www.lboro.ac.uk/media/media/research/o3c/Chadwick%20Vaccari%20 O3C-1%20News%20Sharing%20on%20UK%20Social%20Media.pdf

Chadwick, A., Vaccari, C. & O'Loughlin, B. (2018) Do tabloids poison the well of social media? Explaining democratically dysfunctional news sharing. *New Media & Society, 20* (11), 4255–4274. doi:10.1177/1461444818769689

Chen, A. (2014, October 23) The laborers who keep dick pics and beheadings out of your Facebook feed. *WIRED.* Retrieved from: www.wired.com/2014/10/content-moderation/

Cook, J., Ecker, U. & Lewandowsky, S. (2015) Misinformation and how to correct it. *Emerging Trends in the Social and Behavioral Sciences.* doi:10.1002/9781118900772.etrds0222

Council of Europe. (2018) *Recommendation CM/Rec(2018)2 of the committee of ministers to member states on the roles and responsibilities of internet intermediaries.* Retrieved from: https://search.coe.int/cm/Pages/ result_details.aspx?ObjectID=0900001680790e14

DiFonzo, N. (2008) *The watercooler effect: An indispensable guide to understanding and harnessing the power of rumors.* New York: Avery.

Digital, Culture, Media and Sport Committee. (2019) *Disinformation and 'fake news': Final report* (HC 2017–19 (1791)). Retrieved from: https://publications.parliament.uk/pa/cm201719/cmselect/cmcu-meds/1791/1791.pdf

Dubois, E. & Blank, G. (2018) The echo chamber is overstated: The moderating effect of political interest and diverse media. *Information, Communication & Society, 21* (5), 729–745.

European Commission. (2018) *Final report of the high level expert group on fake news and online disinforma-tion.* Retrieved from: https://ec.europa.eu/digital-single-market/en/news/final-report-high-level-expert-group-fake-news-and-online-disinformation

Fawzi, N. (2019) Untrustworthy news and the media as 'enemy of the people'? How a populist worldview shapes recipients' attitudes toward the media. *The International Journal of Press/Politics, 24* (2), 146–164.

Finkel, E. J., Bail, C. A., Cikara, M., Ditto, P. H., Iyengar, S., Klar, S., . . . Druckman, J. N. (2020) Political sectarianism in America. *Science, 370,* 533–536.

First Draft. (n.d.) *Training and resources for journalists in an age of disinformation.* Retrieved from: https:// firstdraftnews.org/training/

Ghenai, A. & Mejova, Y. (2018) Fake cures: User-centric modeling of health misinformation in social media. *Proceedings of the ACM on Human-Computer Interaction, 2,* 58:1–58:20. doi:10.1145/3274327

Gillespie, T. (2018) *Custodians of the internet: Platforms, content moderation, and the hidden decisions that shape social media*. New Haven, CT: Yale University Press.

Gorrell, G., Bakir, M. E., Roberts, I., Greenwood, M. A., Iavarone, B. & Bontcheva, K. (2019) Partisanship, propaganda & post-truth politics: Quantifying impact in online debate. *Journal of Web Science, 7*, 1–14.

Hindman, M. (2018) *The Internet trap: How the digital economy builds monopolies and undermines democracy*. Princeton, NJ: Princeton University Press.

Hogg, M. A., Sherman, D. K., Dierselhuis, J., Maitner, A. T. & Moffitt, G. (2007) Uncertainty, entitativity, and group identification. *Journal of Experimental Social Psychology, 43* (1), 135–142. doi:10.1016/j.jesp.2005.12.008

Humprecht, E., Esser, F. & Van Aelst, P. (2020) Resilience to online disinformation: A framework for cross-national comparative research. *The International Journal of Press/Politics*. doi:10.1177/1940161219900126

Jack, C. (2017) *Lexicon of lies: Terms for problematic information*. Data & Society Website. Retrieved from: https://datasociety.net/pubs/oh/DataAndSociety_LexiconofLies.pdf

Jukes, S. (2018) Back to the future: How UK-based news organisations are rediscovering objectivity. *Journalism Practice, 12* (8), 1029–1038. doi:10.1080/17512786.2018.1494512

Kaye, D. (2019) *Speech police: The global struggle to govern The Internet*. New York: Columbia Global Reports.

Kunda, Z. (1990) The case for motivated reasoning. *Psychological Bulletin, 108* (3), 480–498.

Lane, R. E. (1962) *Political ideology: Why the American common man believes what he does*. New York: The Free Press.

Lazer, D. M. J., Baum, M. A., Benkler, Y., Berinsky, A. J., Greenhill, K. M., Menczer, F., . . . Zittrain, J. L. (2018) The science of fake news. *Science, 359* (6380), 1094–1096. doi:10.1126/science.aao2998

Lewandowsky, S., Ecker, U., Seifert, C., Schwarz, N. & Cook, J. (2012) Misinformation and its correction: Continued influence and successful debiasing. *Psychological Science in the Public Interest, 13* (3), 106–131. doi:10.1177/1529100612451018

Machado, C., Kira, B., Narayanan, V., Kollanyi, B. & Howard, P. N. (2019) A study of misinformation in WhatsApp groups with a focus on the Brazilian presidential elections. *Companion Proceedings of the 2019 World Wide Web Conference*, 1013–1019. doi:10.1145/3308560.3316738

Marwick, A. E. (2018) Why do people share fake news? A sociotechnical model of media effects. *Georgetown Technology Law Review, 474*.

Mason, L. (2018) *Uncivil agreement: How politics became our identity*. Chicago: University of Chicago Press.

McGrew, S., Ortega, T., Breakstone, J. & Wineburg, S. (2017) The challenge that's bigger than fake news: Civic reasoning in a social media environment. *American Educator*. Retrieved from: www.aft.org/sites/default/files/periodicals/ae_fall2017_mcgrew.pdf

Narayanan, V., Barash, V., Kelly, J., Kollanyi, B., Neudert, L. M. & Howard, P. N. (2018) *Polarization, partisanship and junk news consumption over social media in the US*. COMPROP Data Memo 2018.1. Retrieved from: https://comprop.oii.ox.ac.uk/research/polarization-partisanship-and-junk-news/

Narayanan, V., Kollanyi, B., Hajela, R., Barthwal, A., Marchal, N. & Howard, P.N. (2019) *News and information over Facebook and WhatsApp during the Indian election campaign*. COMPROP Data Memo 2019.2. Retrieved from: http://comprop.oii.ox.ac.uk/wp-content/uploads/sites/93/2019/05/India-memo.pdf

Newman, N. (2020) *Journalism, media, and technology trends and predictions 2020*. Retrieved from: https://reutersinstitute.politics.ox.ac.uk/sites/default/files/2020-01/Newman_Journalism_and_Media_Predictions_2020_Final.pdf

Newman, N., Fletcher, R., Kalogeropoulos, A. & Kleis Nielsen, R. (2019) *Reuters institute digital news report 2019*. Retrieved from: https://reutersinstitute.politics.ox.ac.uk/sites/default/files/2019-06/DNR_2019_FINAL_0.pdf

NewsWhip. (2019) *2019 guide to publishing on Facebook*. Retrieved from: https://go.newswhip.com/rs/647-QQK-704/images/Facebook%20Publishing%202019_Final.pdf

Newton, C. (2019, February 25) The trauma floor: The secret lives of Facebook moderators in America. *The Verge*. Retrieved from: www.theverge.com/2019/2/25/18229714/cognizant-facebook-content-moderator-interviews-trauma-working-conditions-arizona

Nielsen, R. K., Gorwa, R. & de Cock Buning, M. (2019) *What can be done? Digital media policy options for strengthening European democracy*. Retrieved from: https://reutersinstitute.politics.ox.ac.uk/sites/default/files/2019-11/What_Can_Be_Done_FINAL.pdf

Nyhan, B. (2018) How misinformation and polarization affect American democracy. In J. A. Tucker et al. (Eds.), *Social media, political polarization, and political disinformation: A review of the scientific literature* (pp. 49–53). Menlo Park, CA: William and Flora Hewlett Foundation. doi:10.2139/ssrn.3144139

Nyhan, B. & Reifler, J. (2012) *Misinformation and fact-checking: Research findings from social science.* New America Foundation Media Policy Initiative Research Paper. Retrieved from: http://www-personal. umich.edu/~bnyhan/Misinformation_and_Fact-checking.pdf

Ofcom (2020) *Covid-19 news and information: Summary of views about misinformation.* Retrieved from: https://www.ofcom.org.uk/__data/assets/pdf_file/0017/203318/covid-19-news-consumption-week-twenty-five-misinformation-deep-dive.pdf

Oppenheimer, D. M. (2008). The secret life of fluency. *Trends in Cognitive Sciences, 12* (6), 237–241.

Pennycook, G., Epstein, Z., Mosleh, M., Arechar, A. A., Eckles, D. & Rand, D. G. (2019) Understanding and reducing the spread of misinformation online. *PsyArXiv Preprint.* doi:10.31234/osf.io/3n9u8

Redlawsk, D. P. (2002) Hot cognition or cool consideration? Testing the effects of motivated reasoning on political decision making. *The Journal of Politics, 64* (4), 1021–1044. doi:10.1111/1468-2508.00161

Resnick, P., Ovadya, A. & Gilchrist, G. (2018) *Iffy quotient: A platform health metric for misinformation.* Retrieved from: http://umsi.info/iffy-quotient-whitepaper

Roozenbeek, J. & van der Linden, S. (2019) Fake news game confers psychological resistance against online misinformation. *Palgrave Communications, 5* (65). doi:10.1057/s41599-019-0279-9

Rossini, P., Stromer-Galley, J., Oliveira, V. V. & Baptista, E. A. (2019, September 16–17). *The era of mobile misinformation? How citizens engage with online misinformation on WhatsApp and Facebook in Brazil.* Fifth Conference of the International Journal of Press/Politics, Loughborough.

Sanovich, S. & Stukal, D. (2018) Strategies and tactics of spreading disinformation through online platforms. In J. A. Tucker et al. (Eds.), *Social media, political polarization, and political disinformation: A review of the scientific literature* (pp. 30–39). Menlo Park, CA: William and Flora Hewlett Foundation. doi:10.2139/ssrn.3144139

Shao, C., Ciampaglia, G. L., Flammini, A. & Menczer, F. (2016) Hoaxy: A platform for tracking online misinformation. *Companion Proceedings of the 25th International Conference Companion on World Wide Web,* 745–750. doi:10.1145/2872518.2890098

Sherman, D. K., Hogg, M. A. & Maitner, A. T. (2009) Perceived polarization: Reconciling ingroup and intergroup perceptions under uncertainty. *Group Processes & Intergroup Relations, 12* (1), 95–109. doi:10.1177/1368430208098779

Siegel, A. (2018) Producers of disinformation. In J. A. Tucker et al. (Eds.), *Social media, political polarization, and political disinformation: A review of the scientific literature* (pp. 22–29). Menlo Park, CA: William and Flora Hewlett Foundation. doi:10.2139/ssrn.3144139

Sorrentino, R. M. & Roney, C. J. R. (2000) *The uncertain mind: Individual differences in facing the unknown.* Philadelphia, PA: Psychology Press.

Swami, V., Voracek, M., Stieger, S., Tran, U. S. & Furnham, A. (2014) Analytic thinking reduces belief in conspiracy theories. *Cognition, 133* (3), 572–585. doi:10.1016/j.cognition.2014.08.006

Tandoc, E. C., Lim, Z. W. & Ling, R. (2018) Defining 'fake news': A typology of scholarly definitions. *Digital Journalism, 6* (2), 137–153. doi:10.1080/21670811.2017.1360143

Thorson, E. (2016) Belief echoes: The persistent effects of corrected misinformation. *Political Communication, 33* (3), 460–480. doi:10.1080/10584609.2015.1102187

Tucker, J. A., Guess, A., Barberá, P., Vaccari, C., Siegel, A. Sanovich, S., . . . Nyhan, B. (2018) *Social media, political polarization, and political disinformation: A review of the scientific literature.* Menlo Park, CA: William and Flora Hewlett Foundation. doi:10.2139/ssrn.3144139

Tversky, A. & Kahneman, D. (1986) Rational choice and the framing of decisions. *The Journal of Business, 59* (4), S251–S278. doi:10.1086/296365

Vaccari, C. (2018) Online content and political polarization. In J. A. Tucker et al. (Eds.), *Social media, political polarization, and political disinformation: A review of the scientific literature* (pp. 40–48). Menlo Park, CA: William and Flora Hewlett Foundation. doi:10.2139/ssrn.3144139

Vaccari, C. & Chadwick, A. (2020) Deepfakes and disinformation: Exploring the impact of synthetic political video on deception, uncertainty, and trust in news. *Social Media + Society.* doi:10.1177/2056305120903408

Vaccari, C. & Valeriani, A. (forthcoming) *Outside the bubble: Social media and political participation in Western democracies.* Oxford: Oxford University Press.

Valeriani, A. & Vaccari, C. (2018). Political talk on mobile instant messaging services: A comparative analysis of Germany, Italy, and the UK. *Information, Communication & Society, 21* (11), 1715–1731.

Walter, N. & Murphy, S. T. (2018) How to unring the bell: A meta-analytic approach to correction of misinformation. *Communication Monographs, 85* (3), 423–441. doi:10.1080/03637751.2018.1467564

Wardle, C. & Derakhshan, H. (2017) *Information disorder: Toward and interdisciplinary framework for research and policy making.* Council of Europe Report DGI(2017)09. Retrieved from: https://firstdraftnews.org/wp-content/uploads/2017/11/PREMS-162317-GBR-2018-Report-de%CC%81sinformation-1.pdf?x80491

Weeks, B. E. & Gil de Zúñiga, H. (2019) What's next? Six observations for the future of political misinformation research. *American Behavioral Scientist,* 1–13, Online First. doi:10.1177/0002764219878236

Wineburg, S. & McGrew, S. (2017) *Lateral reading: Reading less and learning more when evaluating digital information.* Report, Stanford History Education Group. doi:10.2139/ssrn.3048994

4

RETHINKING MEDIATISATION

Populism and the mediatisation of politics

Daniel C. Hallin

The presidency of Donald Trump is surely the most highly mediatised presidency that has ever existed in the United States. Trump became a public figure as a reality TV star and tabloid media celebrity. Like many populists, he was an outsider without support from the organisational structures of a political party and had little in the way of a traditional campaign organisation, but was able to mobilise popular support by stealing the media spotlight and by exploiting social media, particularly Twitter. As president, he spends huge parts of his day watching television and tweeting, relies more on television for information than on intelligence agencies and other expert sources, relies heavily on the advice of media personalities, and is far more concerned with political theatre than with details of policy. Trump has 'always scripted his presidency like a reality show', as one news article put it in the context of reporting on Trump's briefings during the coronavirus crisis, where he insisted on taking the central role more often delegated to public health officials (Karni 2020).

Trump's rise to power can be seen as a step forward in the process of the 'mediatisation of politics', which has been an important focus of scholarship since the turn of the century. This is true in general of populist leaders and movements: that they depend centrally on the media to obtain and to exercise power. In this sense, the rise of populist politics in much of the world can be seen as reflecting a 'radicalising [of] the mediatisation of politics and political communication' (Mazzoleni 2014, 44).

Yet Trump, like most populist leaders, is constantly at war with established media institutions, and his rise is often seen as reflecting and threatening to deepen their decline from a central place in the communication process. Mediatised populist politics does not fit well into the traditional narrative about the mediatisation of politics, and in order to make sense of it, we need to rethink mediatisation in important ways. We need to make the concept more complex and also to historicise it and to make it comparative. We should move away, that is, from thinking of mediatisation as a kind of unitary, homogeneous process, like the old concept of modernisation, and to think comparatively about its varying and changing forms, including, specifically, forms of mediatisation of politics. Recent literature, to which I will return in the concluding section, has already moved in the direction of rethinking the concept, and the case of populist politics underscores the importance of the issues raised in that literature. I will develop this argument here, working from the case of Donald Trump in the United States but bringing in numerous other examples as well, including, particularly, from Latin America, which has a long history of populist politics on which there is a large body of scholarship.

The mediatisation of politics

Stig Hjarvard (2013, 3) defines the concept of mediatisation in this way, in one classic conceptualisation:

> The media acquire greater authority to define social reality and condition patterns of interaction . . . Media have become an integral part of other institutions' operations, while also achieving a degree of self-determination and autonomy which forces other institutions . . . to submit to their logic.

The classic literature on the mediatisation of politics (Mazzoleni 1987; Mazzoleni & Schulz 1999; Meyer & Hinchman 2002; Strömbäck 2008), which is probably the most strongly developed domain of mediatisation literature, is based mainly on the history of Europe in the 1960s, 70s, and 80s. In this period the commercial press and television grew in power, displacing the party press that was once central to political communication. New forms of critical professionalism in journalism developed, which assigned to the journalist a more active role in reporting and interpreting the news. One manifestation of this change, which was central in my own work on US television news (Hallin 1992a), was the shrinking of the average soundbite in television over a 20-year period. This represented a broad change from an era when television news transmitted the words of political leaders with little editing or interpretation to one in which they cut those words up to weave them into narratives and interpretive frameworks, which they would articulate for their audiences. Forms of marketing based on the use of the emerging media became increasingly central to politics.

These new practices displaced to a significant extent the forms of politics centred around the political party, trade unions, and other social groups and their base organisations, producing a shift, as Manin (1997) put it, from 'party democracy' to 'audience democracy', in which personalisation, dramatisation, and image were increasingly central, and politics centred increasingly on the marketing of particular leaders to a mass public rather than on negotiation among parties representing social groups, interests, and ideologies.

Populist politics

Central to most analyses of populism is the idea that populism articulates the world of politics around a polar opposition between the people and an elite or power bloc that is seen as blocking popular sovereignty. In some versions this elite is seen as aligned with an out-group – immigrants, for example, or a minority ethnic group – which is also understood as hostile to the values and interests of the people; this is partly what distinguishes right-wing from left-wing populism. In Laclau's classic discussion of populism (2005), populist politics arises when ordinary politics based on negotiation among diverse interests in society – based on what he calls the 'logic of difference' corresponding, in one form at least, to Manin's party democracy – breaks down, and parties and other institutions are no longer able to satisfy popular demands. Politics then shifts to the 'logic of equivalence', in which diverse grievances and demands come to be seen as all equivalently representing the oppression of the people by the elite.

Because these grievances and demands are diverse, populist movements rely heavily on 'empty signifiers', in Lacalu's terms (see also Yilmaz 2016), symbols that lack particular referents and thus can represent the diversity of specific demands and of 'the people' as a whole. Very often, this symbolic role is served above all by the figure of the personalised leader. Personalised, charismatic leadership may not be characteristic of populist politics in all cases; we can probably say that certain social movements – Occupy Wall Street, for example – are populist movements without any such leader. Nevertheless, populist movements that persist and that come to power typically are organised around a leader who is seen as representing 'the people'. These leaders typically are outsiders, not connected with the established political parties and without a history of participation in the process of bargaining among elites (Levitsky & Loxton 2013), though again there is some variation, as, for example, established political leaders may sometimes adopt elements of the populist style of politics. Populist movements therefore depend heavily on the ability of the leader to maintain a direct connection with the mass public that represents the base of the movement, and for this the media are essential.

Populism and mediatisation

Trump got elected. But TV became president.

James Poniewozic (2019, 240)

Berlusconi is not just the owner of television channels, he is television.

Paolo Mancini (2011, 21)

Up to a point, the standard narrative about the mediatisation of politics certainly applies to the rise of populist leaders like Trump. Trump rose to power, despite the hostility of the existing organisation of the Republican Party, by building a relationship with voters through the media. He became a public figure as a media celebrity, building his public presence by cultivating a relationship with tabloid newspapers in New York and with television, becoming the star of the reality television programme, *The Apprentice*, and a regular on Fox News. During the primaries, he succeeded by dominating the media agenda, hogging the spotlight to push past a large field of more traditional Republican politicians; then, during the general election campaign, he constantly drew attention to himself with controversial statements which not only made him the centre of the story even on media generally hostile to him (Mahler 2017; Watts & Rothschild 2017) but also had the important effect of focusing coverage in the traditional media on the primary issues around which Trump's appeal was based, particularly immigration and conflicts with Islam/Muslims (Faris et al. 2017). This pattern is seen widely with other successful populist leaders: they rise to power to a significant extent by attracting media attention, performing well in front of television cameras; know how to create a persona that resonates with codes of popular culture; speak colloquial language and identify themselves with the aspirations of ordinary people; understand the importance of symbolism; and understand what draws audience attention, which often involves transgressive behavior and the generation of conflict. The ability to grab media attention is almost always an element in the rise of populist leaders, across a wide range of global contexts. Mancini's (2011) account of Berlusconi's rise in Italy; Peri's (2004) of the rise of Netanyahu in Israel; and accounts of the rise of Hugo Chávez in Venezuela, who agreed to give up a coup attempt in 1992 in return for the right to make a television address to the nation, tell closely parallel stories of mastery of the idiom of popular media, particularly of television.

In a broader sense, we could also say that media, particularly but not exclusively commercial television, played a key role in preparing the cultural ground for the emergence of populist leaders (Manucci 2017). News media have become more 'populist', in a loose sense of the word, over the years, emphasising the point of view of ordinary people more extensively, presenting themselves, as Djerff-Pierre (2000, 257) shows for the (relatively restrained) case of Swedish television, as a 'representative/ombudsman of the public' against elites and institutions; personalising and emphasising subjectivity and emotion; and blurring boundaries between news and popular culture (Baym 2010). They have also taken a more adversarial stance towards elites and presented both those elites and established institutions in more negative terms.

Some media advanced much more specifically populist agendas, in the sense of the term that is usually used in discussing politics: that is, they have articulated a view of the world centred around, as Klein (2000) puts it in relation to the German *Bild-Zeitung* (see also Krämer 2014), a narrative of the people versus the power bloc. In the US case, Trump's populist appeal can be traced back as far as the 1960s New York *Daily News* (Pressman 2019) and was really articulated in its present form by Fox News before Trump came along and rode it into political office – but we will have to come back to the role of Fox, because it is in part there that we have to begin to confront some of the contradictions of applying the traditional understanding of the mediatisation of politics to populism. In the case of Venezuela, years before Hugo Chávez came to power,

> the media began to echo the frustrations of the population, becoming more active in the reporting of denuncias of corruption. The majority of media corporations assumed an open position to all kinds of information, denuncias [roughly, accusations] or analyses that confronted [the political] leadership, marking the beginning of a battle that pitted the media against the government, the institutions of the state, the political parties, and ultimately the ruling class.
>
> (Tulio Hernández, quoted in Samet 2019, 125)

Poniewozic (2019), in his account of Trump and television, makes a broader argument about the way in which television, not merely through news reporting but in its entertainment programming, prepared the way for rise of Trump as a transgressive character.

Contradictions

Other aspects of populist political communication, however, do not fit so easily into the standard narrative. Most obviously, while the standard narrative of the mediatisation of politics focused on the growing importance of centralised mass media organisations and of an increasingly autonomous profession of journalism, populist leaders typically attack these institutions, challenge their legitimacy, and exploit new forms of media – today, above all, social media (for Trump, it is Twitter; for Bolsonaro in Brazil and Modi in India, often WhatsApp) – to circumvent them. These patterns have long histories in populist politics. Juan Perón, the Argentine populist of the 1940s–1950s, wrote (*Conducción Política*, quoted in Ruíz 2014, 262):

> When we carry out a civic act, it is enough for us to speak to the whole country by radio and not a single Argentine will remain unaware of what we have to say. Before this was impossible. Today we do it in a minute. Before, it required six, eight months, a year. . . . Thus it was that we defeated our adversaries clinging to the old forms of committees and of transmission through intermediaries, who were the political *caudillos*.

In the U.S. case, immediately after Trump's election, there was a lot of speculation that the age of the professionalised legacy media was, finally, over. That turned out to be exaggerated, as many legacy media enjoyed a revival after Trump took office, both in terms of audience and in terms of their centrality to the flow of information. *The New York Times*, *The Washington Post*, *The Wall Street Journal*, CNN, and other prominent media organisations have enjoyed growing audiences and been full of investigative reports and inside accounts of the Trump administration. Clearly, they are still seen as the place to go for those who want to get a message into the public sphere. Nevertheless, Trump does not depend on them to reach his base, and in this respect, the emphasis in the classic literature on the mediatisation of politics on the growing autonomy and power of media institutions seems not to capture much of what is going on in this new form of mediatisation.

A second and, of course, related issue with applying the standard narrative about the mediatistion of politics to populist politics has to do with the politicisation of media and the role of partisan media. An important part of Manin's (1997) argument about the shift from 'party democracy' to 'audience democracy' in the 1960s through the 1980s had to do with the rise of 'catch-all' media, whose audiences crossed political party lines and thus made it possible for political leaders to market themselves to individual voters without regard to party. Laclau (2005), at the same time, argues that one of the things populism does, for better or for worse, is to revive politics. And certainly in the US case, one of the most important developments of the Trump era is a significant repoliticisation of the media. Trump's relationship with his base depends not only on social media but also, probably even more importantly, on a new set of right-wing populist media organisations which defend him, give him a platform, and help to mobilise his supporters, the most important of which is Fox News. Partisan media have also emerged on the left, though much of the legacy media have tried to maintain their identity as non-partisan. Nevertheless, patterns of media use and trust in media have definitely become politicised in the US in ways they were not for many decades, from about the mid-twentieth century (DiCamillo 2017; Pew Research Center 2014). This, again, is very common, in different forms, in populist politics; in the Latin American case, periods of populist rule are typically characterised by '*Guerras mediaticas*': media wars in which all of the media are essentially divided into political camps, for and against the populist leader (Avila & Kitzberger, 2020).

In some cases, we might interpret populism as a reimposition of political influence over the media. And, in this sense, populism could be said actually to reverse the mediatisation of politics, even if populist leaders may make heavy use of media channels to reach the public. This interpretation is persuasive particularly in cases in which a populist leader is able to consolidate power and to win the '*guerra mediatica*', as Hugo Chávez eventually did in Venezuela, Viktor Orbán did in Hungary, and Recep Tayyip Erdoğan did in Turkey (Yesil 2016).

Donald Trump has not been able to impose control over most of the media, though he has strained their ability to stand apart from partisan alignments. It is worth looking more closely, however, at his relationship with Fox News because this raises interesting questions about how to conceptualise the new forms of mediatisation that are emerging in the context of populist politics, including questions about the key concepts of 'political logic' and 'media logic'.

Jane Mayer (2019) closed a widely read popular article on Trump and Fox by writing that Trump 'has something no other President in American history ever had at his disposal – a servile propaganda operation'. Although it is widely known that there are tensions within Fox News often between the journalists who produce the news broadcasts and the commentators whose shows are the core of Fox's audience appeal, by most accounts, Fox's content does revolve mainly around the defence of Trump. Its fortunes and Trump's seem inextricably tied at this point. In this sense Fox does look like a form of state TV and could be seen as a case of the reimposition of political control over an important part of the media. But Mayer's article isn't really consistent in supporting this 'state TV' interpretation; in many cases, it seems to suggest that the direction of influence actually goes the other way: that we have in Trump more of a TV state than state TV. Much of the reporting on the Trump presidency suggests as much; this is partly what Poniewozic means in writing that 'TV became president'. Trump relies heavily on Fox and its commentators for both information and advice. (He once said, appearing on the morning programme *Fox and Friends* and explaining how he knew his lawyer's payments to women for their silence were not criminal acts, 'I watch a lot of shows. Sometimes you get pretty good information watching shows'(23 April 2018)). Many have noted that Trump's tweets seem driven much of the time by what he is watching on Fox News. Often his policy decisions seem to be as well. One of the most dramatic cases was during the government shutdown of 2018–2019, when he had made a deal to reopen the government, only to back out when it was criticised on Fox and in other right-wing media. At a deeper level, it was largely Fox News that created the particular populist discourse that Trump then appropriated. 'Fox news programs', as Peck (2019, 90) puts it, 'have helped articulate the various political positions and identity groups of the conservative movement onto what Laclau terms a "chain of equivalence"'. It did this, Peck argues, by reinterpreting social class in cultural terms, presenting itself as the champion of the 'working class' by embracing cultural identifications seen as anti-elite and connecting this cultural identity to a set of conservative policy positions and political antagonisms – anti-immigrant and anti-Muslim sentiment, resentment of minorities and multiculturalism, economic and political nationalism, hostility to government regulation, and a pro-business 'producerist' economic ideology.

So maybe the role of Fox is an example of mediatisation after all. But is Fox News really a media institution, or is it a political actor? This brings us to a key conceptual issue. The literature on mediatisation has always depended on drawing a distinction between media logic – an idea first articulated by Altheide and Snow (1979) – and the logics of kinds of institutions which, in classic formulations of the concept of mediatisation, are obligated to 'submit' to media logic. As Strömbäck and Esser (2014) point out, however, there has always been considerable ambiguity in defining both of them. It seems clear that in the case of Fox News, they are really fused into a kind of hybrid logic that cannot be understood either as the imposition of a separate 'media logic' onto politics or the other way around. Roger Ailes, the original president of Fox News, was a television producer who managed Richard Nixon's 1968 presidential campaign. That was a clear sign of mediatisation: the fact that Nixon hired a television producer to run his campaign, rather than a traditional party politician. But Roger Ailes always had a political agenda and was as much a political entrepreneur as a media one. And Fox News, in Peck's account, succeeded by combining innovations in the aesthetics of television news, including tabloid style and an emphasis on opinion, with political innovations in the form of the populist discourse described earlier; it was simultaneously a form of media marketing, building a market niche through political identity, and a form of political action, remaking the American political right.

Media logics and political logics have historically been closely related. Balzac once described *press* as 'the word adopted to express everything which is published periodically in politics and literature, and where one judges the works both of those who govern and of those who write, two ways of leading men' (quoted in Ferenczi 1993, 28). Max Weber described the journalist as a 'type of professional politician' (Gerth & Mills 1946, 99); this was in the context of making an argument in 'Politics as a Vocation', about politics as leadership of public opinion, taking public stands, and trying to create majorities around particular visions of where society should go. Media logics (they have definitely always been plural, reflecting differences in media systems, genres of media, and tensions between professionalism and commercialism) became significantly differentiated from political logics in much of the West, especially, during the late twentieth century, in the 'high modernist' period (Hallin 1992b). But in many other cases, they are merged. The relation of Fox News to Trump may be unique in many ways. Probably there have been few political leaders so heavily influenced by information and advice from a particular media outlet. But media organisations that are activist in character, that intervene in the world of politics, are common in much of the world. This is a common pattern in Latin America, for example, and Chakravartty and Roy's (2017, 4082) discussion of mediated populisms in Asia stresses the role of new media elites, rooted in emerging commercial media, as 'vanguard and champions' of market-based 'economic reform'. Where activist media are strong, as Fox News is in the United States in the current period, this suggests a form of mediatisation significantly different from the form built around non-aligned, professionalised journalism, which was theorised by the first generation of scholarship on the mediatisation of politics.

Conclusion: rethinking mediatisation

Populist politics is clearly mediatised politics. But its forms of mediatisation, even if they may have roots in an earlier history of mediatisation of politics, are quite distinct in many ways from those conceptualised in earlier scholarship, and they require us to think about mediatiaisation in more complex ways. I would like to conclude by making five points about this reconceptualistion. None of these is a new idea; recent literature on mediatisation in general, and the mediatisation of politics specifically, has already moved considerably towards more complex conceptualisations in all these ways. Reflecting on populist politics, in the specific case of Donald Trump and more generally, helps to demonstrate the importance of this rethinking.

First, and most generally, we need to make the concept of mediatisation comparative and historical. De Beus (2011), in an application of Manin's analysis of the shift from party democracy to audience democracy, cites as examples of the kinds of political leaders produced by mediatised politics such figures as Tony Blair and Bill Clinton. But a conceptualisation that is so broad as to apply to Blair and Clinton and equally to Trump or to Jair Bolsonaro clearly explains too much. We need to move away from treating the mediatisation of politics as a general, unilinear process to conceptualise different forms of mediatisation which exist in different historical periods and in different contexts, varying according to the nature of the political and media system and sometimes also by the particular situation or conjuncture (Strömbäck & Esser 2014).

Second, zero-sum conceptualisations of mediatisation involving the 'colonisation' of other social fields or institutions by the media or an imposition of media logics onto those fields, a process in which media gain in power and autonomy while other institutions decline correspondingly, are clearly inadequate. Marcinkowski and Steiner (2014; also Marcinkowski 2014) have made one particularly well-articulated statement of this position, arguing that mediatisation often involves other institutions appropriating media technologies and logics to serve their own purposes and that institutions do not necessarily lose either power or their coherence as distinct institutions by becoming mediatised. Looking back at the mediatisation of politics in the period described in the first generation of scholarship, the zero-sum conceptualisation is too simplistic even for that era. In the case of my own work on television soundbites, for example, a key element of the story is the Nixon campaign in 1968, in which Roger Ailes produced campaign events as television shows, excluding journalists from the set and using the technology of television to bypass the established news media. Television journalists responded to new forms of image-making and media manipulation, initiated in the political sphere, by moving in the direction of more active and often critical reporting of campaigns. But it is not self-evident that political parties lost their power either to reach voters or to shape political discourse; they learned to use the new practices of television news production to their advantage. Clearly, populist leaders often build highly effective political movements through both the appropriation of media logics and the exploitation of new media technologies and practices.

This leads directly to three related points. One, our third point overall, is that, though it may seem paradoxical at first glance, we need to move away from mediacentric conceptualisations of mediatisation. That is to say, in order to understand the mediatisation of politics or of any other social field, we cannot assume that whatever changes are taking place in that field are purely the product of what is going on in the media field. We need to understand how the dynamics of other social fields drive their interaction with the media and shape the changes that result.[1] The shift from party democracy to new, more mediated forms of politics is influenced by the rise of television and of commercial media generally. But it is also rooted in changes in political economy and public policy, including the rise of the consumer society and the shift away from the growth of the welfare state. And the rise of what Panebianco (1988) called the 'electoral-professional party', which turned to new forms of political communication and new types of leadership, was no doubt driven by internal developments within political party institutions as much as by outside pressure from the media system. The growth of political polarisation which is one of the hallmarks of Trump-era American politics is certainly connected to the shift to multi-channel media that is part of the move towards the 'third era of political communication' (Blumler & Kavanaugh 1999). But it is also something that political scientists in the US have traced back to political developments in the 1970s, long before those changes in media took place (Jacobson 2001).

Fourth, it is essential to disaggregate our conceptualisation of mediatisation to distinguish its different forms, including, particularly, the distinction between the effects of media institutions and the effects of media technologies. The classic literature on the mediatisation of politics focused primarily on media institutions – organisations like television networks and the shared practices developed as they competed with one another, as well as journalism as an institution. Populist politics, however, draws our attention to the importance of considering also the possibility that other actors may be able to appropriate media technologies in ways that disrupt established institutions of political communication, both on the side of media and on the side of the political system. Media technologies are understood here in the broad sense since something like social media, for example, is obviously not simply a kind of hardware, but a set of communicative practices afforded by the infrastructure of networked digital communication.

Finally, we need to move away from conceptualisations of mediatisation that assume clear boundaries between media and political (or other) institutions and clear separation of their logics. If we take seriously both the idea that other social fields and institutions incorporate media technologies, personnel, and practices into their own structures, what Strömbäck (2008) called 'premediatisation' and Couldry and Hepp (2016) have further conceptualised as deep mediatisation, and the idea that other social fields may not so much submit to media logics as appropriate them, then we are likely to encounter many actors and practices that are hybrid in character and, like Fox or Trump or Berlusconi, can actually be media and politics simultaneously.

Note

1 This point is developed in another context in Briggs and Hallin (2016), looking at the mediatisation of health and medicine in relation to the literature in sociology and anthropology of medicine on the process of 'biomedicalisation'.

References

Altheide, D. L. and Snow, R. P. (1979). *Media logic.* Beverly Hills, CA: Sage.

Avila, C. and Kitzberger, P. (2020). Populist communication and media wars in Latin America. In B. Krämer & C. Holts-Bacha, eds., *Perspectives on populism and the media.* Baden-Baden: Nomos pp. 145–160.

Baym, G. (2010). *From Cronkite to Colbert: the evolution of broadcast news.* Boulder, CO: Paradigm.

Blumler, J. G. and Kavanaugh, D. (1999). The third age of political communication: influences and features. *Political Communication,* 16(3), 209–230.

Briggs, C. L. and Hallin, D. C. (2016). *Making health public: how news coverage is remaking media, medicine and contemporary life.* London: Routledge.

Chakravartty, P. and Roy, S. (2017). Mediated populisms: inter-Asian lineages. *International Journal of Communication,* 11, 4073–4092.

Couldry, N. and Hepp, A. (2016). *The mediated construction of reality.* London: Polity.

de Beus, J. (2011). Audience democracy: an emerging pattern in post-modern political communication. In K. Brants and K. Voltmer, eds., *Political communication in postmodern democracy: challenging the primacy of politics.* New York: Palgrave Macmillan, pp. 19–38.

DiCamillo, M. (2017). *Partisanship colors voter opinions of the way the media cover the news.* Berkeley: Institute of Governmental Studies, Release #2017–06.

Djerf-Pierre, M. (2000). Squaring the circle: public service and commercial news on Swedish television 1956–99. *Journalism Studies,* 1(2), 239–260.

Faris, R., Roberts, H., Etling, B., Bourassa, N., Zuckerman, E. and Benkler, Y. (2017). *Partisanship, propaganda, and disinformation: online media and the 2016 U.S. presidential election.* Cambridge, MA: Berkman-Klein Center for Internet and Society. https://cyber.harvard.edu/publications/2017/08/mediacloud

Ferenczi, T. (1993). *L'Invention du journalisme en France.* Paris: Librairie Plon.

Gerth, H. H. and Mills, C. W., eds. (1946). *From Max Weber: essays in sociology.* New York: Oxford University Press.

Hallin, D. C. (1992a). Sound bite news: television coverage of elections, 1968–1988. *Journal of Communication,* 42(2), 5–24.

Hallin, D. C. (1992b). The passing of the "high modernism" of American journalism. *Journal of Communication,* 42(3), 14–25.

Hjavard, S. (2013). *The mediatisation of culture and society.* London: Routledge.

Jacobson, G. (2001). A house and senate divided: the Clinton legacy and the congressional elections of 2000. *Political Science Quarterly,* 116, 5–27.

Karni, A. (2020). Rallies cancelled, Trump moves stage to the briefing room. *The New York Times,* March 24, p. A8.

Klein, U. (2000). Tabloidised political coverage in the German *Bild-Zeitung.* In C. Sparks and J. Tulloch, eds., *Tabloid tales: global debates over media standards.* Lanham, MD: Rowman & Littlefield, pp. 177–193.

Krämer, B. (2014). Media populism: a conceptual clarification and some theses on its effects. *Communication Theory,* 24, 42–60.

Laclau, E. (2005). *On populist reason.* London: Verso.

Levitsky, S. and Loxton, J. (2013). Populism and competitive authoritarianism in the Andes. *Democratisation,* 20(1), 107–136.

Mahler, J. (2017). "That is great television": inside the strange symbiosis between the CNN president Jeff Zucker and Donald Trump. *New York Times Magazine,* April 9, pp. 40–47, 67–69.

Mancini, P. (2011). *Between commodification and lifestyle politics: does Silvio Berlusconi provide a new model of politics for the twenty-first century?* Oxford: Reuters Institute for the Study of Journalism.

Manin, B. (1997). *The principles of representative government.* New York: Cambridge University Press.

Manucci, L. (2017). Populism and the media. In C. R. Kaltwasser, P. Taggart, P. Ochoa Espejo and P. Ostiguy, eds., *The Oxford handbook of populism.* Oxford: Oxford University Press, pp. 467–488.

Marcinkowski, F. (2014). Mediatisation of politics: reflections on the state of the concept. *Javnost – The Public,* 21(2), 5–22.

Marcinkowski, F. and Steiner, A. (2014). Mediatisation and political autonomy: a systems approach. In F. Esser and J. Strömbäck, eds., *Mediatisation of politics: understanding the transformation of Western democracies.* Basingstoke: Palgrave MacMillan, pp. 74–92.

Mazzoleni, G. (1987). Media logic and party logic in campaign coverage: the Italian general election of 1983. *European Journal of Communication,* 2(1), 81–103.

Mazzoleni, G. (2014). Mediatisation and political populism. In F. Esser and J. Strömbäck, eds., *Mediatisation of politics: understanding the transformation of Western democracies*. Basingstoke: Palgrave Macmillan, pp. 42–56.

Mazzoleni, G. and Schulz, W. (1999). "Mediatisation" of politics: a challenge for democracy? *Political Communication*, 16(3), 247–261.

Mayer, J. (2019). The making of the Fox News White House. *The New Yorker*, March 4.

Meyer, T. and Hinchman, L. P. (2002). *Media democracy: how the media colonize politics*. Cambridge: Polity.

Panebianco, A. (1988). *Political parties: organisation and power*. Cambridge: Cambridge University Press.

Peck, R. (2019). *Fox populism: branding conservatism as working class*. New York: Cambridge University Press.

Peri, Y. (2004). *Telepopulism: media and politics in Israel*. Stanford, CA: Stanford University Press.

Pew Research Center. (2014). *Political polarisation & media habits: from Fox News to Facebook, how liberals and conservatives keep up with politics*. Washington, DC: Pew Research Center.

Poniewozic, J. (2019). *Audience of one: Donald Trump, television, and the fracturing of America*. New York: Liveright Publishing.

Pressman, M. (2019). America's biggest newspaper 70 years ago sounded a lot like Trump today: the New York *Daily News* helped fashion a brand of right-wing populism that the president eventually rode to power. *The Atlantic*, May 10. www.theatlantic.com/ideas/archive/2019/05/new-york-daily-news-sounded-just-like-trump/589009/

Ruíz, F. J. (2014). *Guerras mediáticas: las grandes batallas periodísticas desde la révolución de mayo hasta la actualidad*. Buenos Aires: Sudamérica.

Samet, R. (2019). *Deadline: populism and the press in Venesuela*. Chicago: University of Chicago Press.

Strömbäck, J. (2008). Four phases of mediatisation: an analysis of the mediatisation of politics. *International Journal of Press/Politics*, 13(3), 228–246.

Strömbäck, J. and Esser, F. (2014). Mediatisation of politics: towards a theoretical framework. In F. Esser and J. Strömbäck, eds., *Mediatisation of politics: understanding the transformation of Western democracies*. Basingstoke: Palgrave Macmillan, pp. 3–24.

Watts, D. and Rothschild, D. M. (2017). Don't blame the election on fake news. blame it on the media. *Columbia Journalism Review*, December 5. www.cjr.org/analysis/fake-news-media-election-trump.php

Yesil, B. (2016). *Media in new Turkey: the origins of an authoritarian neoliberal state*. Urbana: University of Illinois Press.

Yilmaz, F. (2016). *How the workers became Muslims: immigration, culture and hegemonic transformation in Europe*. Ann Arbor: University of Michigan Press.

5

MEDIA SYSTEMS AND MISINFORMATION

Jonathan Hardy

There has been significant advancement of scholarship on media systems over the last two decades. This provides resources to map and integrate media misinformation with studies of the evolution and configuration of media within countries and regions. However, bringing together misinformation and media systems also poses a series of challenges. Misinformation is enabled by digital media, engages transnational and transcultural flows, and involves a diverse range of actors and processes in its creation, circulation, and use, all of which are areas in which media systems scholarship has been found wanting. Misinformation thus provides a form of stress testing of media systems analysis, one which can help to identify more integrative and forward-facing approaches.

Media systems

The analysis of media systems began as a mid-twentieth-century approach whose deficiencies were recognised and at least partly tackled in the early twenty-first century. The key change was to privilege empirical comparative analysis, as advanced by Hallin and Mancini (2004), over the previously heavily normative framework of Siebert et al.'s (1956) *Four Theories of the Press* (FTP). Hallin and Mancini proposed an analysis of the evolution and development of media in countries and regions, drawing upon existing historical studies. In a pivotal argument, they stated that the available data was insufficient for causal analysis, instead proposing to map the 'co-presence' of variables to identify the 'characteristic patterns of relationship between system characteristics', (Hallin and Mancini 2004, 11). They examined four main media system variables:

1   The development of the media market (especially newspapers).
2   Political parallelism (alignment of media to political divisions).
3   Journalistic professionalism.
4   The degree and nature of state intervention in the media system.

They argued that the pattern of correspondences supported the identification of three different 'models' of Western media systems: a Mediterranean or polarised pluralist model, a North/Central European or democratic corporatist model, and a North Atlantic or liberal model. These were most distinctive in their historical formation, up to a high point of differentiation in the 1970s, and were now undergoing a gradual convergence, towards the liberal model of a predominantly commercial market media, with 'low' state involvement.

Both the book and its adoption have been subject to extensive review and critique (Humphreys 2012; Hardy 2012; Flew and Waisbord 2015). Here, the focus is on three areas of critique most relevant for misinformation analysis: nation-centrism and transnational/transcultural features, digital communications, and normativity. These are all elements in a broader questioning of the features of system-ness, claims for what constitutes media systems, and the choices of what to measure and how to assess their constituent parts. One powerful critique challenges the 'methodological nationalism' and 'container thinking' (Beck 2000) that posits the territorially bound nation-state as explanatory unit at the expense of processes of globalisation, transnational interaction, and transcultural flows (Couldry and Hepp 2012). Taking 'media system' as the primary unit of comparative research is challenged as methodologically flawed, inappropriate in aligning media cultures to nation-states and advancing an inexact analytical unit (see Flew and Waisbord 2015, 622). This overlaps with the second main problem area: digitalisation.

Although it was published a decade after internetisation, the digital barely features in Hallin and Mancini (2004). More significantly, the analysis is anchored around the formation and organisation of newspapers. Hardy (2008, 2012) argues the models must be revised if broadcasting is made the anchor since the public service media (PSM) systems of the UK, Canada, and Ireland are too divergent from those of the US, with its much lower investment and reach (Benson and Powers 2011). Yet satisfactorily addressing digital communications poses even greater challenges. Newspapers, radio, and television maintain strong 'vertical' linkages within nation-states, from jurisdiction to media production and primary audiences. These media have also always been transnational and transcultural, from the carriage and consumption of physical objects to the transfer of technologies, forms, and practices. Yet the ways mass media were organised and shaped at national and sub-national levels provided coherence for claims underpinning 'media systems' analysis. Both the increasing globalisation of electronic media from the mid-twentieth century and internetisation, challenge that framework by moving the 'horizontal' dimension of transcultural media flows from periphery to centre. Instead of remaining within either a nation-centric or 'strong globalisation' framing, a third approach emphasises both the continuing relevance and transformation of the national level within processes of global-local interaction (Flew and Waisbord 2015).

The third critical issue is normativity. This is the critique that Hallin and Mancini's work partly disguises its structuring normativity. Their account of the US as a market liberal, pluralist media system is challenged for its disavowal of state-directed information management by an informal empire (Curran 2011). While dethroning US-centricity, their account privileges features of media professionalism and 'independence' associated with commercial media. Legacies of Western imperialism and cultural exchange are neglected. Instead, Zhao (2012, 145) calls for analysis of the 'world's media systems in their structural relationships – not simply in comparative terms, which tend to flatten asymmetric power relations between the systems under comparison'.

To address these challenges, comparative media systems research should aim to integrate vertical dimensions (focused on political and media institutions within nations) with horizontal dimensions (incorporating cultural flows and exchanges of media forms, ideas, and practices). Hardy (2012) advocates expanding the scope of the media system variables outlined by Hallin and Mancini and adding two new ones. Their first variable, 'the development of media markets', is most amenable for extension to include the range of historical and contemporary communications. Both political parallelism and journalist professionalism need to be examined beyond their 'mass/professional' media presumptions to engage with contemporary and historical forms of citizens'/community media, citizen journalism, and professional/amateur hybridisations. A new, fifth variable is geocultural, to address the patterns of transcultural exchanges and factors shaping media markets and cultures, including geolinguistic and cultural affinities, diasporas, regionalism, and religion. A sixth category is media and civil society, inviting consideration of a broader range of social actors beyond organised politics. While certainly not exhaustive, these additions seek to balance the intended parsimony of the original variables with two interlinked 'dimensions' that incorporate the horizontal and transnational aspects of communications, cultural production, and exchange.

Misinformation

Misinformation has several connected aspects that are especially pertinent to the discussion of media systems analysis. There are a variety and complex co-mingling of actors, multiplicity of communication channels, and multiplication of misinformation opportunities in the digital age. Even the most state-directed disinformation today usually involves a complex mix of state actors, para-state actors, and supporting actors whose directedness may be attenuated to untraceability or be 'self-generated' in motivation. According to the EU Stratcomm Taskforce's (Medium 2017) analysis of Russian propaganda:

> Not only (are) big media outlets like Russia Today or Sputnik . . . deployed, but also seemingly marginal sources, like fringe websites, blog sites and Facebook pages. Trolls are deployed not only to amplify disinformation messages but to bully those . . . brave enough to oppose them. And the network goes wider: NGOs and "GONGOs" (government organised NGOs); Russian government representatives; and other pro-Kremlin mouthpieces in Europe, often on the far-right and far left. In all, literally thousands of channels are used to spread pro-Kremlin dis-information, all creating an impression of seemingly independent sources confirming each other's message.

Silverman (2015, 15) describes a misinformation ecosystem with three key actors: official sources of propaganda, fake news websites, and individual hoaxters. To these can be added the full range of human and non-human intermediaries acting between communication sources and those accessing communications. This includes public relations and marketing agencies, lobbyists, and overt or covert campaigners, all illustrated by the disgraced, and subsequently disbanded, Bell Pottinger's disinformation campaign to foment racial polarisation in South Africa on behalf of the Gupta business family. It also includes the non-human actants arising from human-computer interaction, from automated buying and selling of programmatic advertising to social bots creating the illusion of popularity for social media content, to the algorithms shaping the selection, presentation, and ordering of circulating stories (Bayer 2019, 33–34). The range of actors and their interconnections makes for a more complex mapping of political actors and communications than is common in media systems analyses. Yet government agencies and political parties remain key actors, with one study of computational propaganda finding these actors were using social media to manipulate public opinion domestically in 48 countries studied, across democracies and dictatorships alike (Bradshaw and Howard 2018).

Misinformation fits well with some core elements of media systems analysis. There are significant 'vertical' dimensions linking the national political sphere, regulation, media, and publics. Much political 'information disorder' is designed to influence electorates, those with voting rights in respect of a territorially defined authority. There are strong links between voters and national media. A range of individual and institutional actors seek to influence national policies or are stakeholders whose actions or attitudes may influence policies. Finally, non-national actors with agendas to influence domestic politics provide much of the recent policy and research focus, including Russian and Chinese state and para-state misinformation and cyber-attacks (Bayer 2019).

Misinformation involves both 'vertical' and 'horizontal' processes and flows; it occurs in the gaps identified by critiques of media systems analyses. However, while those critiques provide useful resources, they have rarely offered explicit strategies to reincorporate misinformation. In fact, misinformation has not been a strong theme across media systems analysis. While that may be explained, in part, by the rapid growth in attention to 'fake news' phenomena from 2016, the neglect of the longer histories of information disorder in the service of power is a more significant and revealing omission. While communication and power are major themes for Hallin and Mancini (2004), there is no index entry on misinformation or related terms. It is therefore necessary to draw on resources beyond those that more commonly populate media systems analysis.

Misinformation and media systems: approaches and resources

Non-governmental organisations

The first key resource emanates from beyond academia, in the work of non-governmental organisations measuring freedom of expression, the treatment of journalists, media plurality, and other metrics. These offer a global ranking of countries and commonly identify laws and policies affecting reporting, media ownership and plurality indicators, and forms of 'interference' in media autonomy by state, political actors, media owners, and commercial interests. Various NGOs offer indexes of media freedom, inflected by normative values, such as the US-headquartered Freedom House, which traditionally privileged commercial non-state media. Others include Reporters sans Frontières (France), Article 19, and Index on Censorship (UK), as well as trade union groupings such as the International Federation of Journalists. Reporters sans Frontières' (2020) World Press Freedom index ranks lowest states such as North Korea, China, the Philippines, Egypt, and Iraq, which denied the extent of the COVID-19 outbreak amongst their populations, harassed journalists, and suppressed scientific information.

References to these well-established NGO resources is surprisingly rare across media systems literature. However, there are limitations to these resources too. Their focus is on contemporary actions and not historical dimensions, they concentrate on state agency, and their contestable criteria produce reductive labels such as Freedom House's tripartite classification of free, partly free, and not free. Such rankings tend to exonerate those marked 'free', to a degree that critical media scholars challenge (Curran 2011; Hardy 2014), and condemn those found wanting, yet in doing so, risk smoothing over the complexity and contradictions in performance. While many would agree on the qualities assessed, based on core human rights principles and values and the importance for policy action of doing so, there are many contexts in which policy action is aided by narrower comparability. Finally, the normativity that shapes all such measurements, while valuable and defensible, also needs to be subjected to much greater reflexivity and review. Media systems analysis can seek to examine broader interconnections than media freedom indexes and do so across synchronic and diachronic axes.

Supranational and intergovernmental organisations

Supranational governmental organisations provide another rich source of data and analysis. These include the UN and its agencies such as UNESCO, supranational regulatory bodies like the ITU, intergovernmental authorities such as the European Union and SADEC, and political and human rights bodies like the Council of Europe. These organisations have varying forms of regulatory power but have in common a policy orientation so their relevant work on misinformation tends to combine data collection, research, legal-regulatory analysis, and policy proposals (Bayer 2019). For example, the EU's high-level expert group on fake news and online misinformation (European Commission 2018) made proposals concerning transparency, media literacy, empowering users and journalists, safeguarding European news, and promoting research.

Academic research

Livingstone (2012, 421) draws on Kohn's (1989) framework identifying four types of cross-national comparative research: ideographic, hypothesis-testing, system-sensitive, and transnational. The first three focus on the nation-state as unit; the fourth, transnational, treats countries as the locus for global trends. To date, comparative studies of misinformation fall mainly into ideographic and transnational categories. An example of the latter is Vosoughi et al.'s (2018, 1146) study finding false news stories on Twitter 'diffused significantly farther, faster, deeper, and more broadly' than true stories. There has been some development of hypothesis-testing but negligible system-sensitive, 'media systems' research to observe and explain 'how and why nations vary systematically' (Livingstone 2012, 419).

The vast majority of studies have been ideographic, single country studies, mostly of the US, providing resources for comparability and system analysis but not explicitly combining both. A recent study noted that outside the US, 'we lack even the most basic information about the scale of the problem in almost every country' Fletcher et al. 2018, 1). This is being remedied by an increasing number of cross-national studies, but most focus on discrete phenomena for the purposes of comparison. For instance, Fletcher et al. (2018, 7) examine false news websites in France and Italy, finding that 'false news has more limited reach than is sometimes assumed, in line with US research'. Yet this short study does not compare the findings cross-country, much less relate these to system-level features.

A comparative study of fact-checking does incorporate hypothesis testing: namely, that high-source transparency will correspond to high journalistic professionalism and that countries with low trust in media will have fact-checkers who provide comparatively 'higher levels of source transparency'. The study concludes (Humprecht 2019, 14):

> Although online disinformation is a global phenomenon, practices of correction still seem to be shaped by national news cultures – in newsrooms as well as in independent organizations. Consequently, from a user's perspective, the possibility of coming across transparent, professional fact-checking depends on the country in which one lives.

More commonly, misinformation is addressed in relation to discrete aspects of media performance, politics, or policies and usually with a focus on two of those three domains, although with recognition of their interconnectedness. Here, misinformation fits within research specialisms, such as news coverage, journalistic practices and cultures, and the relationship between media structures and content and the public affairs knowledge of citizens (Aalberg and Curran, 2012; Esser et al. 2012). More recent studies examine how the production and circulation of misinformation is shaped by the economic drivers of platformisation and the challenge and opportunities of monetisation across online publishing and social media. This includes studies of the commercial dynamics driving politically oriented misinformation, whereby 'political disinformation succeeds because it follows the structural logic, benefits from the products, and perfects the strategies of the broader digital advertising market' (Ghosh and Scott 2018). The digital advertising model has rewarded maximising clicks and undermined the value and resources for quality reporting while social media gateways have disaggregated news content from suppliers and retained advertising revenues. Misinformation has been aided by the growth of programmatic advertising, automating ad buying, and placement processes (Bakir and McStay 2018). In addition, political marketers have used behavioural advertising and micro-targeting, with studies (Bayer 2019, 33) showing

> many UK political parties use third-party digital campaigning platforms (such as NationBuilder), which enables parties to match voters' contact information with the data on Facebook and Twitter. . . [while] political micro-targeting was also reported in Italy, Germany and the Netherlands, although to a lesser degree.

While media systems research has closest affinities with studies of media institutions and production, misinformation analysis includes rich resources comparing users' communication activities. WhatsApp is used more widely across Southern than Northern countries: with nearly 60 percent in Brazil in discussion groups with strangers and nearly a fifth discussing politics, compared to 2 percent in the UK (Newman et al. 2019, 2020). More broadly, studies of misinformation examine digital materialities, socio-cultural and psycho-cognitive aspects that are expanding areas of comparative communication research but barely incorporated into 'media systems' literature. Disinformation is often intentionally affective and thrives on the generation of feelings of superiority, fear, and anger (Wardle and Derakhshan 2017; Bakir and McStay 2018). Those are mobilised by a mix of loosely affiliated or tightly structured networks, such as across the alt-right (Lewis 2018) to sustain racism and racial violence, misogyny, and other forms of hate speech. This makes studies of gender, sexuality, race, and the communicative resources used by or against all minorities of vital importance. Again, that is reflected across comparative communication research (Esser and Hanitzsch 2012) but not yet integrated into 'system sensitive' media systems analysis.

Greater advance has been made examining the relationship between misinformation flows and key variables concerning the political system; patterns of media and information availability; levels of trust across politics, media and sources of authority; and user profiles, including demographics, access, education levels, literacy, and usage patterns across legacy media, social media, and search. For instance, studies suggest that ideologically motivated disinformation is more prevalent in polarised societies with low trust in media (Humprecht 2019). Audience research conducted across the US, the UK, Spain, and Finland found low trust in media was common but varied (Nielsen and Graves 2017, 6):

> [L]ess than half of online news users in the US and the UK think you can trust most of the news most of the time. While the figures are higher in Spain and in Finland, very large parts of the population still have limited trust in news in general, and – strikingly – only somewhat higher trust in the news that they themselves use.

Trust illustrates the significance of another key resource. Commercial sector data analysis or large-scale surveys usually exceed the capacity available through university-funded research. The Edelman (2020) Trust Barometer has charted falling trust in media worldwide, although with differences between countries and among media vehicles and platforms and class position, finding a widening gap in trust levels between the more affluent and general populations. This is also an example of integration, with Edelman's research widely cited by academics. In the US, overall positive trust in media was only around half (53 percent) in 1997, yet had fallen to less than a third (16 percent) in 2016 (Newman and Fletcher 2017, 7). In research conducted by the Reuters Institute for the Study of Journalism, a corporate-sponsored academic research centre, Denmark, Germany, Ireland, and Spain were at the higher end of trust in media, and the US, France, and Greece had comparatively low trust scores, with Australia and the UK in between. Newman and Fletcher (2017, 26) conclude, '[t]he reasons for lack of trust in the media are remarkably consistent across countries. Bias and agendas are rife and are perceived to have worsened with the advent of the internet'.

Trust and confidence in journalistic processes are associated with journalism that supports claims with evidence, conducts and highlights fact-checking, and is transparent about sources. There is evidence of growing distrust in the commercial bias in news. Newman and Fletcher (2017, 24) report that '[a]nother reason for mistrust identified by our respondents is the belief that media companies are distorting or exaggerating the news to make money'.

The reshaping of news for commercial agendas, including brand-sponsored content, native advertising, content recommendation, and clickbait, is being examined, yet there is a need for integrative studies encompassing sources of misinformation across political and commercial speech, one of many key tasks for future research.

Future directions: integrating misinformation and media systems

There has been much debate on the merits of pursuing media system typologies or instead focusing on comparing the characteristics of similar institutions and inter-institutional relations (Humphreys 2012; Flew and Waisbord 2015). For misinformation, the latter course appears to have been favoured, although with a focus on transcultural processes and transnational institutions. The case for a media systems approach is well-made by Flew and Waisbord (2015, 632):

> Media systems are points of convergence of political, economic, social, and cultural forces grounded in the local, the national, and the global.
> They should be seen neither as self-contained entities nor as extensions or epiphenomena of global developments. Instead, we should think of 'media systems' as analytical units to understand how and where multiple dynamics intersect as well as the comparative weight of actors and institutions in shaping the media.

The ambition for a more effective analysis of misinformation and media systems will be to enhance dialogue across work centred on both, within a broader, revising approach. Here, three key areas are discussed: actors and processes, governance, and comparative normativity.

Actors and processes

Media systems research draws heavily on political science and the study of governing institutions, political actors, and parties. This is indispensable for analysis of states' activities, from engineering and directing to combatting misinformation. The mapping of COVID responses, discussed earlier, illustrates the range well. Authoritarian-populist governments (Brazil, Turkey, Russia, Hungary) have weakened non-compliant media institutions, alongside the undermining of civil society, but have been countered more effectively in pluralist democracies (US, UK, India). More authoritarian systems have exercised command and control (Saudi Arabia, Iran, China), while corporatist democratic systems in Western Europe have exercised information management. However, for misinformation, it is vital to accommodate a much wider field of action. Around each of the main actor categories that have shaped conventional political sociology there are a plurality of actor-types and increasing blurring and hybridisation, which a synthesising media system analysis must address, including AI-generated content from private and state-sponsored bot accounts. Agencies of control over communications that need to be encompassed are state; para state actors; state media; public service media; private media publishers; platform owners and operators; civil society media/radical-alternative media; pro-am publishers; open, 'public' social communications; and intergroup 'private' communications.

Governance

In expanded form, media systems analysis is best placed to pursue connections between regulation, the role of the state, the organisation of markets, and the ever-changing institutional arrangements of media and their performance. Those are all matters that are addressed by contemporary governance analysis, conceived as encompassing 'all the collective and organizational rules that govern the organization of media systems' (de'Haenans et al. 2010, 132). Media governance is 'a framework of practices, rules and institutions that set limits and give incentives for the performance of the media' (Puppis 2010). While governance has been adopted to broaden media policy analysis, it offers a means to integrate analysis of media practices, performance, and policy. In its contemporary form, governance analysis highlights the importance of more informal processes of rule-making such as amongst professionals in networks and the 'house rules' of firms or teams, as well as those shaped by interacting agencies from service users to protestors and by non-human actants.

Ginosar (2013) advances the case to use governance as 'an analytical framework for the classification and typology of communication systems' and proposes 'a continuum on which different such systems are placed according to their governance types'. He identifies forms of 'social control' from liberal to authoritarian in political systems and corresponding levels of protection afforded to the 'independence' of journalism, acknowledging that '[b]etween these two distinct types, there is a variety of social control forms (governance types) that enable the existence of many types of communication systems'. However, this system-level typology risks reproducing problems of reification that were the legacy of FTP. Rather than identify media systems with macrolevel features of governance alone, it is preferable to analyse the multidimensional forms of governance of communications and how these relate to forms of governance within the political economic system overall. Reducing governance to a singularity risks smoothing out the internal complexity and contradictions that often are the focus of critical scholarship, such as the co-existence in 'liberal' systems of both high 'rational legal authority' in regulatory proceduralism and high policy influence from commercial interests and lobbyists. Governance analysis can help bridge the national/transnational division by inviting consideration of the multiple agencies, processes, and modes of rule-making across contemporary communications.

Governmental action on misinformation is intelligible across the political system spectrum of authoritarian to democratic, subdivided into neoliberal and regulated economic systems (Curran and Park 2000). Authoritarian governments have legislated against 'fake news' to shore up information control, especially where media are instruments of state. Germany's Network Enforcement Act 2017, requiring social media platforms to block 'fake news', hate-inciting, or illegal content, illustrates action by democratic governments within a human rights legal framework. Several authoritarian populist governments have used various tools to attempt to discipline media that operate within more pluralist and formally democratic legal-regulatory systems, such as Bolsanaro in Brazil and Orbán in Hungary.

The arguments made so far identify the need for an expansive political economic analysis conducted to incorporate socio-cultural, historical, and psycho-social dimensions. More comparative data gathering is needed before synthesising 'system sensitive' perspectives can be advanced, but that must be a guiding aspiration. Misinformation is most common in polarised political systems; is most prevalent among domestic political actors and supporters during electoral campaigning; and correlates with high public concern about misinformation, low trust in media, significant bypassing of professional news, and unreliable news circulation via social media (Bradshaw and Howard 2018; Fletcher et al. 2018). The key reason to integrate misinformation into media systems analysis is that identifying interconnections across 'system' variables is vital for analysis, evaluation, and policy proposals. That interconnectedness is demonstrated by questions concerning the degree to which resources to counter misinformation are present and effective alongside those that generate it. How is the discursive space for misinformation ordered across different systems in relation to different media channels and spaces? How is the performance of those channels shaped by governance arrangements, practices, and cultures?

In countries with strong PSM, researchers have found positive 'spill over' effects on private sector news journalism (Aalberg and Curran 2012). For misinformation, such interconnections need to be explored throughout communications resources and activities, within and across media systems. In a six-country study of online news diversity, Humprecht and Esser (2018) find that the UK, Germany, and France showed the greatest diversity, while the US achieved the lowest rates. They conclude that 'media systems that financially support strong public service-oriented news outlets are most likely to create media discourses that meet the normative goal of diversity in voices, backgrounds, and perspectives' Humprecht and Esser (2018, 1841). Yet PSM generally face falling audiences and revenue and calls from right-wing populist movements to scrap license fees.

Following Sen's (1999) powerful linking of media, democratic rule, and the cultivation of capabilities, a compound hypothesis is that the more democratic is a media system, the more resources are available for challenging information disorder. However, to proceed, both clarity in measurement and a comparative normative approach are needed. The media systems conceptual apparatus is strongly rooted in Western liberal discourses of state 'intervention', media 'independence', and so on. The challenges include building an architecture in which normativities can be espoused yet scrutinised for their particularities and application to create a critical, reflexive discursive space that is more capable of engaging subaltern understandings (Zhao 2012). That is especially important as so much misinformation cultivates stories of imperialism and nationhood, identity, and religion and mobilises cleavages of class, race, gender, sexuality, age, political affiliation, and cultural values. Media systems analysis needs to connect with feminist, critical race, postcolonialist, and other perspectives whose insights have rarely been foregrounded, again part of the 'stress test' that misinformation provides.

Integrating misinformation and media systems can be organised into the six media system variables discussed earlier.

1   Media markets

Analysis of all communication channels; plurality of supply, exposure diversity, usage.
Media publishers, marketing communications, platforms, communication intermediaries, fact-checking services, automation across communications.

2   Political parallelism

Political system variables; political-media relations; political communication and information management.

3   Professionalisation (Media governance 1)

Industry regulation (self/co); professional and trade body standards; informal rule-making and behaviours across communication services and users.

4   Role of the state [Media governance 2]

Laws and policies affecting information and communications.

5   Geocultural

Platforms; circuits of communication across affiliated communities; diasporic communications; transnational and transcultural flows; regional dynamics (supranational and subnational).

6   Media and civil society

Civic communications; protest action; education and media literacy; fact-checking.

Conclusions

This chapter argues that misinformation and media systems should be integrated but that the latter must adapt to do so. The value of a 'media systems' approach is not to advance a reified and reductive account of selected features for the purpose of creating taxonomies but to create a framework for examining the connections between aspects of communications within and across territories. 'A system is not an entity with a fixed set of characteristics, but a pattern of variation' (Hallin and Mancini 2017, 167). The value of system-ness is in pursuing analysis of how elements interact. Generalisation at the level of system is a heuristic, part of a necessary tension between the ideographic (historical, institutional, cultural) and classificatory (system) that continually interact and correct each other. Media systems analysis pursues, and privileges, sets of connections between politics, public media, and governance, within the wider arena of comparative analysis. This chapter argues that misinformation poses, in acute form, various underlying challenges to media systems analysis: the handling of the transnational and transcultural, the range and complexity of digital communications, the multiplicity of actors and processes. Misinformation stress tests media systems analysis. This chapter also suggests how these may be incorporated both within and beyond the schema of variables advanced by Hallin and Mancini and by expanding governance analysis and comparative normative evaluation. The reconfigurations arising from bringing together misinformation and media systems research can hopefully strengthen how this vital, synthesising work is pursued.

References

Aalberg, T. and Curran, J. (eds) (2012) *How media inform democracy: A comparative approach*. London: Routledge.

Bakir, V. and McStay, A. (2018) 'Fake news and the economy of emotions', *Digital Journalism*, 6(2), 154–175.

Bayer, J. (ed) (2019) *Disinformation and propaganda – impact on the functioning of the rule of law in the EU and its member states*. Report for European Parliament's Committee on Civil Liberties, Justice and Home Affairs (LIBE). www.europarl.europa.eu/supporting-analyses.

Beck, U. (2000) *What is globalization?* Oxford and Cambridge: Blackwell.

Benson, R. and Powers, M. (2011) *Public media and political independence: Lessons for the future of journalism from around the world*. New York: Free Press.

Bradshaw, S. and Howard, P. (2018) *Challenging truth and trust: A global inventory of organized social media manipulation.* Oxford: Oxford Internet Institute.

Couldry, N. and Hepp, A. (2012) 'Comparing media cultures', in Frank Esser and Thomas Hanitzsch (eds) *Handbook of comparative communication research.* New York: Routledge, pp. 249–261.

Curran, J. (2011) 'Questioning a new orthodoxy', in J. Curran (ed) *Media and democracy.* Abingdon: Routledge.

Curran, J. and Park, M. J. (eds) (2000) 'Beyond globalization theory', in J. Curran and M.-J. Park (eds) *De-Westernising media studies.* London: Routledge.

De'Haenans, L., Mansell, R. and Sarikakis, K. (2010) 'Editor's introduction', *Communication, Culture & Critique,* 3(2), 131–133.

Edelman. (2020) *2020 Edelman trust barometer.* www.edelman.com/trustbarometer

Esser, F., de Vreese, C., Strömbäck, J., et al. (2012) 'Political information opportunities in Europe: A longitudinal and comparative study of 13 television systems'. *International Journal of Press/Politics,* 17(3), 247–274.

Esser, F. and Hanitzsch, T. (eds) (2012) *Handbook of comparative communication research.* New York: Routledge.

European Commission. (2018) *A multi-dimensional approach to disinformation: Report of the independent high level group on fake news and online disinformation.* Brussels: European Commission.

Fletcher, R., Cornia, A., Graves, L. and Nielsen, R. A. (2018) *Measuring the reach of "fake news" and online disinformation in Europe.* Factsheet February. Oxford: Reuters Institute for the Study of Journalism.

Newman, N. and Fletcher, R. (2017) *Bias, bullshit and lies: Audience perspectives on low trust in the media.* Oxford: Reuters Institute for the Study of Journalism.

Flew, T. and Waisbord, S. (2015) 'The ongoing significance of national media systems in the context of media globalization', *Media, Culture & Society,* 37(4), 620–636.

Ghosh, D. and Scott, B. (2018) *#Digitaldeceit: The technologies behind precision propaganda and the Internet,* p. 4. Harvard Kennedy School, January. https://d1y8sb8igg2f8e.cloudfront.net/documents/digital-deceit-final-v3.pdf.

Ginosar, A. (2013) 'Media governance: A conceptual framework or merely a buzz word?' *Communication Theory,* 23, 356–374.

Hallin, D. and Mancini, P. (2004) *Comparing media systems: Three models of media and politics.* Cambridge: Cambridge University Press.

———. (2017) 'Ten years after comparing media systems: What have we learned?' *Political Communication,* 34, 155–171.

Hardy, J. (2008) *Western media systems.* London: Routledge.

———. (2012) 'Comparing media systems', in Frank Esser and Thomas Hanitzsch (eds) *Handbook of comparative communication research.* New York: Routledge, pp. 185–206.

———. (2014) *Critical political economy of the media: An introduction.* Abingdon: Routledge.

Humphreys, P. (2012) 'A political scientist's contribution to the comparative study of media and politics in Europe: A response to Hallin and Mancini', in N. Just and M. Puppis (eds) *Trends in communication policy research: New theories, methods and subjects.* Bristol: Intellect, pp. 157–176.

Humprecht, E. (2019) 'How do they debunk "fake news"? A cross-national comparison of transparency in fact checks', *Digital Journalism.* DOI:10.1080/21670811.2019.1691031

Humprecht, E. and Esser, F. (2018) 'Diversity in online news: On the importance of ownership types and media system types', *Journalism Studies,* 19(12), 1825–1847.

Kohn, M. L. (ed) (1989) *Cross-national research in sociology.* Newbury Park, CA: Sage.

Lewis, R. (2018) 'Alternative influence: Broadcasting the reactionary right on YouTube', *Data & Society.* https://datasociety.net/library/alternative-influence/

Livingstone, S. (2012) 'Challenges to comparative research in a globalizing media landscape', in Frank Esser and Thomas Hanitzsch (eds) *Handbook of comparative communication research.* New York: Routledge, pp. 415–429.

Medium. (2017) *How disinformation campaigns are threatening the EU,* June 21. https://medium.com/eu-security-and-defence-in-a-volatile-world/how-disinformation-campaigns-are-threatening-the-eu-a45d86b1c35e

Newman, N. et al. (2019) *Reuters institute digital news report 2019.* Oxford: Reuters Institute.

———. (2020) *Reuters institute digital news report 2020.* Oxford: Reuters Institute.

Nielsen, R. and Graves, L. (2017) *"News you don't believe": Audience perspectives on fake news.* Factsheet October. Oxford: Reuters Institute for the Study of Journalism.

Puppis, M. (2010) 'Media governance: A new concept for the analysis of media policy and regulation', *Communication, Culture & Critique*, 3(2), 134–149.

Reporters sans Frontières. (2020) *World press freedom index.* https://rsf.org/en/ranking#

Sen, A. (1999) *Development as freedom.* Oxford: Oxford University Press.

Siebert, F. S., Peterson, T. and Schramm, W. L. (1963) [1956] *Four theories of the press.* Champaign: University of Illinois Press.

Silverman, C. (2015) *Lies, damn lies and viral content.* New York: Tow Centre for Digital Journalism. www.towcenter.org/research/lies-damn-lies-and-viral-content/

Vousoughi, S., Roy, D. and Aral, S. (2018) 'The spread of true and false news online', *Social Science*, 359, March 9. Massachusetts Institute of Technology.

Wardle, C. and Derakhshan, H. (2017) *Information disorder: Toward an interdisciplinary framework for research and policymaking.* Strasbourg: Council of Europe.

Zhao, Y. (2012) 'Understanding China's media system in a world historical context', in D. Hallin and P. Mancini (eds) *Comparing media systems beyond the Western world.* Cambridge: Cambridge University Press.

6

REWIRED PROPAGANDA

Propaganda, misinformation, and populism in the digital age

Sarah Oates

Introduction

This chapter aims to synthesise a working definition of propaganda in the digital age. The term *propaganda* often evokes a simplistic and overt attempt to persuade, such as the glorification of the Soviet worker on posters or an image of the American spokesman 'Uncle Sam' marketing bonds in World War II. While this chapter addresses the classic definition of propaganda, it also expands the definition into a concept of 'rewired propaganda' that demonstrates the utility of the term in understanding the interplay of misinformation and populism in the digital age. In particular, an awareness of the classic concept of propaganda allows us to see how the democratising effect of online information to create informed citizens is outmatched by the internet's ability to leverage misinformation in the service of populist propaganda. In other words, propaganda can now 'hide in plain sight' as it is so difficult to disentangle from the broad range of information in the digital sphere. At the same time, those who adhere to principles of free speech and fairness are at a significant disadvantage both domestically and internationally in the sphere of rewired propaganda that lends itself more to the success of populist movements than traditional party politics.

Propaganda and media models

The classic definition of *propaganda* is 'the spreading of ideas, information, or rumor for the purpose of helping or injuring an institution, a cause, or a person', as well as 'ideas, facts, or allegations spread deliberately to further one's cause or to damage an opposing cause' (Merriam-Webster online dictionary www.merriam-webster.com/dictionary/propaganda). The key element that is often overlooked in these definitions is that propaganda is not, in and of itself, a negative communication tool. Rather, the term is defined by its ends rather than its means: you do not have to tell falsehoods in order to propagandise nor do you have to 'dupe' or fool people. This is reflected in the way that Russians, for example, have traditionally labelled propaganda as either 'white' or 'black'. Propaganda can attempt to persuade through positive messaging, or it can attack and undermine through lies, half-truths, rumour, innuendo, or even fakery. Certainly, people may be propagandised into actions that do not reflect their core beliefs, but often people embrace propaganda that echoes their own values and desires.

71

That being said, propaganda has a justifiably negative connation in the contemporary media sphere that reflects a deep and enduring debate about the role of media in society in general. The media is supposed to function as the 'fourth estate' in the United States, a further balance against excess of power by the legislative, judicial, and executive branches of the government. More broadly, freedom of the press allows for a constant watchdog on powerful elites, meaning that the press work in the service of the citizens, telling 'truth to power'. While the notion of an objective media is more an aspiration than a reality (Hearns-Branaman 2014), the notion of the media as the critical 'voice of the people' is the central organising ideal for journalists in democracies, in the same way that the 'first do no harm' principle in the Hippocratic oath is the touchstone of the medical profession.

Siebert et al. (1956) address the operationalisation of media freedom in their classic work about models of the press, highlighting the varying roles that the media is expected to play in different societies by analysing how the media functions in different countries. They developed a libertarian (or commercial) model of the media from the United States system, in which the press meet consumer demand for information in a commercialised setting with little interference from the state. From the United Kingdom, Siebert et al. articulated the social-responsibility model of the media, which suggests that media function as arbiters of political norms and respect state needs more closely than in the libertarian model. Thus, one could find better justification for the persuasive elements of propaganda more clearly in the social-responsibility model than in the libertarian model. However, as Herman and Chomsky (1988) argue, the libertarian media system is particularly vulnerable to manipulation by commercial interests.

For authoritarian regimes, Siebert et al. suggested that the concepts of media and propaganda are fused. In the case of the 'Soviet Communist' model, Siebert et al. found that the media's primary purpose in the former Soviet Union was to propagandise the citizens about ideals of communism. Practically, this also took the form of censoring a great deal of information on international and domestic opposition to communism. In their fourth and final model from their 1956 volume, Siebert et al. suggested that the authoritarian model placed the press in the role of promoter of a dictator and his oligarchic circle. Again, in practice, this meant a great deal of censorship and control of the mass media.

Thus, propaganda would have been a normal and expected element of non-free media systems. Overt propaganda, except during wartime, was much less acceptable in the libertarian and social-responsibility systems of the media in the twentieth century.[1] This is what has made the concurrent rise of online communication, populism, and misinformation particularly jarring in the US media sphere. The following sections will discuss two case studies about this synergistic relationship in both a domestic and global setting: the election of Donald Trump as US president in 2016 and ongoing Russian propaganda delivered via the US media system.

Trump: populism's perfect storm

Trump ran a campaign almost devoid of traditional policy statements or even a definable political ideology. A study of campaign messages found that Trump did not post clear issue statements on his website during the critical period of the 2016 primary campaign, although his main Democratic contender, Hillary Clinton, did (Oates and Moe, 2017, p. 213). The Oates and Moe study also found that Trump rarely tweeted specifically about policy, although he and his supporters tweeted in large volume about non-policy-specific ideas that could be considered populism, especially around Trump's vow to 'build a wall' to control immigration. It was clear from both the nature of Trump's tweets and those who tweeted about the candidate that his campaign followed the central tenet of populism as 'a political approach that strives to appeal to ordinary people who feel that their concerns are disregarded by established elite groups' (www.lexico.com/en/definition/populism).

It's important here to note that Trump's campaign went beyond merely striving to appeal to people on a populist issue, in that Trump also routinely used misinformation in his campaign. For example, despite extensive evidence to the contrary, he characterised immigrants as lawless individuals who were stealing jobs from American citizens. Paradoxically, his tactics gave him an unprecedented amount of media coverage as the US media not only reported the misinformation but also attempted to correct it (Patterson 2016). Clinton, pursuing a policy-based rather than a populist campaign, struggled to gain the same attention as Trump. Perversely, her perceived misdeeds were amplified, even when evidence later suggested that her leaked emails in the final moments of the campaign came from foreign adversaries (Patterson 2016; Jamieson 2018). By running a populist campaign with a misinformation playbook, Trump garnered far more coverage and less serious criticism than Clinton.

There are two elements here that suggest Trump's victory could rewrite the rules of US campaigns in terms of how candidates fight for office and how their messages are amplified in the traditional and social media. In the first place, can a rational, policy-based candidate have the same appeal as a populist candidate who tailors his message to what an audience would like to hear (rather than suggesting realistic policies)? The second issue is that both traditional and social media engaged more with the misinformation than with a rational discussion of policies and respect for facts. It is not surprising that this was the issue on social media, where a lack of moderation as well as design that favours sensation over information have been well documented by analysts such as Vaidhyanathan (2018).

The libertarian media system was not effective at averting an election campaign from being overwhelmed by a propaganda campaign rife with misinformation in 2020 in the United States. The libertarian media system dictates that media should provide the consumers with the news they will find most interesting and engaging. It is a system that relies heavily on the ability of the citizen, rather than the journalists, to filter news. The US media system failed particularly to stem populism overwhelming an informed campaign and electorate on two major fronts. First, traditional journalists did not provide equal coverage to the two candidates. According to Patterson, the media consistently gave Trump both more coverage and less criticism than Clinton. At the same time, by the 2016 election, those who were inclined to support Trump's populism over more traditional policymaking and ideology were likely to be alienated from traditional, fact-based journalism. According to a study by Benkler et al. (2018), a right-wing media bubble was firmly established by the 2016 elections. Interestingly, while Clinton supporters still consumed news across a range of media sites, Trump supporters were increasingly isolated in an echo chamber anchored by news sites such as Fox News, Infowars, and Breitbart. Many of the news sites used by Trump supporters were likely to combine support for Trump with misinformation about his opponents.

This far-right alternative sphere was further isolated and strengthened by social media information algorithms, which encourage users to consume like-minded media content. Benkler et al. argue that information communication technology needs to be understood both within the context of political institutions and through change over time. By analysing the linkages between online news sources and Twitter, they found that Trump supporters isolated themselves within self-reinforcing information bubbles and rejected traditional journalistic content characterised by objectivity, lack of bias, truthfulness, and verification. Benkler et al. see this as the culmination of decades of media changes and political development in the Republican Party, accelerated by the affordances of the online sphere. Their analysis is useful evidence of the need to consider the role of information communication technology within political contexts. If the changes in the media environment wrought by technology had a set effect on information consumption, we would expect the changes to be essentially the same across both the right and the left. However, as Benkler et al. demonstrate, populism only became entrenched and powerful on the right in the United States.

Although Trump's election based on misinformation-fuelled propaganda may have appeared to change campaign norms in the United States, there are important caveats. Trump actually lost the popular vote in 2016, winning because his pattern of support gave him the majority of Electoral College votes. In addition, there were several factors aside from propaganda that significantly helped Trump to victory. First, Clinton was surprisingly unpopular as a grudging compromise candidate who had endured a grueling primary battle with the more liberal and charismatic Senator Bernie Sanders. Her long history as first lady and secretary of state left opponents – and even possible supporters – with plenty of complaints about perceived or real failures of personality or character. At the same time, Trump's campaign was more aggressive at exploiting the features of social media that could target undecided voters in key states. Finally, given that most of the media and many pundits did not seriously believe that Trump could win, particularly given his racist and sexist comments as well as his complete lack of political experience, many unenthusiastic Democrats didn't bother to vote.

Yet overall, there was a significant underestimation of the power of Trump's combination of populism and misinformation to inspire voters to 'Make American Great Again'. Trump's victory is a compelling example of how populism and misinformation can craft an intoxicating form of 'rewired' propaganda. After 2016, the question is whether this has permanently altered the terms of engagement for political campaigning in the United States. Given the attraction of desire over reason in Trump's campaign, does this signal the end of policy-based campaigning in the United States and the start of an era of electoral propaganda?

Russia and digital disinformation

As noted earlier, media systems used to parallel national borders closely, a point underlined by Siebert et al. and more recent studies of the way in which media systems reflect national political systems (Hallin and Mancini 2004). While there were extensive attempts at foreign propaganda throughout the twentieth century, they were of limited reach and success due to the ability of national systems to control their key information outlets. The online sphere offers a way for governments to produce and distribute foreign propaganda far more effectively. The twin forces of populism and misinformation, delivered through a US system made vulnerable to populist propaganda through the 2016 elections, give an unprecedented opportunity for foreign media manipulation.

Russia has received a great deal of attention for its propaganda campaign in the 2016 US elections, particularly after congressional investigations and hearings revealed the nature and extent of the campaigns. Although the campaign was initially dismissed as relatively small, later evidence suggested that the Russians had succeeded in disseminating a fairly wide range of content in the 2016 election (Jamieson 2018). The material created and disseminated on social media by the Internet Research Agency in Russia was designed to look like it was produced by Americans. The goal of the content was to spark political action, in particular to organise rallies and protests. This was met with very limited success (Jamieson 2018), although the Russians identified and worked to motivate groups on both sides of the political spectrum through wedge issues such as immigration, gay rights, et cetera.

As Jamieson acknowledges in her detailed study of the 2016 Russian disinformation campaign, it is impossible to establish with any precision the effect of the messaging. In part, this is due to the fact that the Russian content aimed at the right was difficult to disentangle from Trump's campaign messages. It is never possible to gauge the effect of a particular ad, although Jamieson and others have noted that Trump's higher spending on late television ads, his more tactical approach to social media deployment, and his efforts in swing states were important.

What is significant about Russian propaganda in the 2016 US elections is that it demonstrated the realm of possibilities for manipulation for authoritarian states in democratic media systems. This gives an asymmetric advantage to non-free states in terms of propaganda and misinformation. As social media companies continued to (slowly) wrestle with the problem, the extension of the libertarian principles into the online sphere – freedom of speech as paramount, virtually no regulation of content – has left open a clear channel for propaganda from foreign states. At the same time, democracies have a much harder time penetrating the more closed online or traditional media systems in non-free states.

Rewired propaganda

These two case studies of Trump's election and the Russian interference in 2016 lead to a consideration of 'rewired' propaganda. Propaganda has been a part of society and media systems for a long time. Yet propaganda has been bounded in US elections by the history and tradition of political campaigning. As the two political parties control the nomination system, candidates are expected to generate ideologies and policies that resonate with the core party constituencies. The Republican Party has experienced significant changes in the past decade, in particular as moderates and conservatives have pulled further apart. Trump could be considered the fruition of a long shift away from policy-based or even ideological argument to populism in the United States, which is a departure from the form and calculus of party politics. At the same time, as Benkler et al. point out, the US media system has become notably more polarised, with a separate right-wing echo system that preferences propaganda over information.

Thus, the political system in the United States has demonstrated that populism can win the biggest election of them all, albeit in a contest with a surprisingly untraditional contender. However, it should be noted that Trump had an enormous, unprecedented media advantage. His constant stream of misinformation and populist messages led to more, rather than less, uncritical coverage than was given to his more traditional opponent (Patterson 2016). Nor were the traditional media connected with all of the American electorate. The media sphere itself was 'rewired' into two separate sectors (Benkler et al. 2018): Clinton supporters consumed a range of more fact-based media while many Trump supporters preferred content that leaned more towards propaganda than news. This was then reinforced by social media patterns of consuming information. In this sense, the media system itself is 'rewired' in that the traditional bastions of political influence – the parties and the mass media – are essentially sidelined for many in the digital world.

In earlier work, I defined *rewired propaganda* in Russia as "a commitment to disinformation and manipulation, when coupled with the affordances of the new digital age, give particular advantages to a repressive regime that can proactively shape the media narrative" (Oates 2016, p. 399). In other words, we needed to move beyond the 'Soviet Communist' (Siebert et al. 1956) concept of censorship and heavy-handed state manipulation to understand that an attractive narrative that resonated with citizens was a far more effective means of persuasion in the contemporary media sphere. Often – indeed, almost inevitably – one will need misinformation or even disinformation to maintain a plausible propaganda narrative. An additional important element of the notion of 'rewired' propaganda, beyond a discussion of the transition from Soviet to Russian propaganda, is that the media system has shifted globally. It has moved from a top-down model in which information was controlled and preferenced by key media outlets to a far more audience-driven and algorithmic model in which stories circulate among networks.

The concept of 'rewired propaganda' is suggested as way of understanding a communicative method that leverages misinformation, campaign tactics, and the way both traditional and social media functioned in the 2016 US elections. When populism replaces party-based politics rooted in ideology and articulated policies, rewired propaganda becomes as powerful in democracies as it has been in non-free states such as Russia.

At the same time that there are comparisons of systems in Russia and the United States in 2016 in terms of populist propaganda, there is the specific issue of Russian propaganda in the 2016 US elections. Historically, effective propaganda has tended to be bonded within state systems and certainly within national media systems. While there were many well-documented attempts at foreign influence, the opportunity for international mass propaganda was limited by several factors. Notably, although foreign actors could either run open propaganda outlets or attempt to subvert existing media outlets or journalists, it remained a complex and cumbersome task. For example, in one well-documented case of classic propaganda, the Soviet Union planted a story in an Indian newspaper that AIDS had been developed in an American laboratory (Boghardt 2009). By then using that story as a source, the Soviet media repeated and amplified the claim. However, it took an immense effort and years to give the story any traction at all.

In 2016, foreign interference rode a populist wave in a media environment that was ripe for manipulation. Especially when isolated from competing information in the ring-wing information sphere in the United States, populist messages flourished, given that citizens have little trust in sources that do not resonate with their worldview. This raises many complex questions about media audiences: namely, is the system design or the individual citizen ultimately responsible for consuming populist misinformation rather than democratic knowledge? Much of the popularity of Trump stems from his ability to identify unmet grievances of American citizens, resentments that are often based in grim economic realities. Yet how long will citizens continue to blame Democrats, rather than deeper and broader economic forces, for their particular challenges? To what extent are a significant segment of Americans accepting of the racism and sexism as voiced by their president? A populist president is new in the United States and currently dealing with one of the most significant global challenges to health and the economy to date. This will provide a significant challenge to a populist ruler as citizens are much more demanding of effective action in a crisis.

Rewired propaganda in the digital age

One of the most powerful ways in which the online sphere differs from traditional media systems is in its global reach. Within countries, traditional media outlets had enormous power to set the agenda and disseminate information (considered to be news in democracies and propaganda in non-free states). The internet initially challenged this information hegemony through the creation of alternative information sources: namely, digital native media, blogs, and forums. With the creation and explosive growth of social media, the distribution channel for news and information metamorphosed into a different system, one that Benkler et al. assert fostered 'network propaganda'.

Wardle and Derakhshan (2017) write that 'the emergence of the internet and social technology have brought about fundamental changes to the way information is produced, communicated and distributed' (p. 11). These characteristics include 'widely accessible, cheap and sophisticated' publishing technology that makes is possible for virtually anyone to create and distribute content; making private consumption patterns visible and public; the speed at which information is disseminated; and the fact that information is now passed in 'real time between trusted peers, and any piece of information is less likely to be challenged' (11–12). They cite Frederic Filloux in highlighting how Moore's law has fostered the spread of misinformation as the exponential growth of available technology drastically lowers the cost of creating, disseminating, and acquiring information.

Technology itself, however, cannot account for the rise of propaganda and populism. Technology is value neutral, and the features outlined by Wardle and Derakhshan are available to essentially all sides in political debates. Indeed, most of the original conception of how the internet would reshape the global communication space suggested that the internet would level information hierarchies, tell truth to power, and create more freedom of speech. While scholars and analysts had become increasingly more cynical after the failure of the Arab Spring to bring enduring democratic change to most of the Middle East, it was the election of Donald Trump in 2016 that caused a significant switch in the debate from 'cyberoptimism' to 'cyberpessimism'.

Certainly, the internet, especially social media, brought great changes to the consumption, production, and distribution of information. Yet an often-overlooked aspect of the digital sphere is the way in which it challenges national information hegemony. While there are still powerful media outlets and information sources within countries, information boundaries are increasingly porous and opaque. This allows foreign actors who wish to try to influence domestic audiences in other countries new and more promising opportunities, such as those shown by Russian actors in the 2016 US presidential election. For example, Russia has an extensive network of foreign-language websites, such as RT (formerly Russia Today), that blend news and misinformation to promote particular strategic narratives for the Russian state. It should be noted that Russia is not alone in these tactics, but democracies are more limited in how they can promote information to authoritarian states. One could also argue that Russians have been more proactive and creative in their information warfare strategies than their Western counterparts.

If we consider the misinformation and propaganda opportunities surrounding the COVID-19 pandemic, it is easy to see the opportunities afforded by the contemporary media system combined with misinformation creating an environment in which propaganda can thrive. US media consumers have experienced a large amount of misinformation and even disinformation emerging from the White House, which has highlighted the difficulty of informed policymaking and citizen action in a national crisis. It is interesting to note that while Trump was skilled at populist messages during the 2016 election, by late April 2020, he was still struggling to find a populist rhetoric to address the pandemic. The structure of the US traditional and social media system itself, divided and divisive, not only created a challenge to crafting a national response but also left a void into which both domestic and foreign misinformation could push propaganda narratives. A comparison of the painstaking planting of the AIDS virus story by Russians in the 1980s and the ease with which foreign propaganda can accuse the Americans of having created COVID-19 in a lab as a bioweapon showcases the power of rewired propaganda.

The relationship of propaganda to populism

This volume is focused on the broad sweep of populism and its relationship to propaganda, a synergistic partnership that is discussed in detail throughout the book. For the purposes of this chapter, it's important to consider how propaganda, misinformation, and the digital age create such a promising environment for populism. Indeed, this is a particularly important question because there was so much earlier focus by analysts on the exact opposite: how the internet would foster genuine debate and stronger democracies.

As noted in the introduction to this volume, populism can be considered to be 'a political movement that both reflects the crisis of liberal democracy and challenges core democratic premises' and has flourished in environments with the 'spread of fake information, conspiracy beliefs, and propaganda'. Although populist movements are typically grounded in genuine grievances, these grievances are often magnified or distorted in ways that make it easier for politicians to manipulate the masses. This is in opposition to the notion of a democracy founded on informed debate and rational voters.

The success of populist movements around the world from the United States to Russia to Brazil suggests that propaganda is a better pair with populism than with traditional democracy. This chapter has discussed how populism, particularly in the 2016 US elections, can be fuelled by propaganda and misinformation. In addition to the features outlined by Wardle and Derakhshan, the new media ecosystem allows malicious actors, both foreign and domestic, to 'hide in plain sight' by posing as media outlets or (in the case of social media) as trusted fellow citizens.

This leaves us with two significant challenges to traditional US democracy. First, political actors can now see the power of populism. Even if your goal is not to undermine democracy, it is very tempting to use propaganda and misinformation, rather than informed debate and traditional party politics, in order to win elections. At the same time, the current US media ecosystem asymmetrically favours populist propaganda over informed debate. Not only did many citizens preference misinformation and propaganda over real news in the 2016 campaign, but there is also a growing body of evidence that social media actively misinforms the public by its very nature. The dilemma that remains is whether the global rise of populism, as well as the new media environment engendered by the digital age, will permanently disadvantage responsible journalism and democratic elections. There is a pervasive power in rewired propaganda, the modernisation of classic propaganda infused with misinformation that is supported by the nature of traditional and social media. It remains to be seen if rewired propaganda will outpace the democratic function of the media in democracies such as the United States.

Note

1 This leaves aside the issue of democratic states that broadcast propaganda in foreign countries.

References

Benkler, Yochai, Robert Faris and Hal Roberts. 2018. *Network Propaganda: Manipulation, Disinformation, and Radicalization in American Politics*. New York: Oxford University Press.

Boghardt, Thomas. 2009. Operation INFEKTION: Soviet Bloc Intelligence and Its AIDS Disinformation Campaign. *Studies in Intelligence* 53(4): 1–25.

Hallin, Daniel C. and Paulo Mancini. 2004. *Comparing Media Systems: Three Models of Media and Politics*. New York: Cambridge University Press.

Hearns-Branaman, Jesse Owen. 2014. Journalistic Professionalism as Indirect Control and Fetishistic Disavowal. *Journalism* 14(1): 21–36.

Herman, Edward S. and Noam Chomsky. 1988. *Manufacturing Consent: The Political Economy of the Mass Media*. New York: Pantheon Books.

Jamieson, Kathleen Hall. 2018. *Cyber War: How Russian Hackers Helped Elect a President – What We Don't, Can't, and Do Know*. New York: Oxford University Press.

Oates, Sarah. 2016. Russian Media in the Digital Age: Propaganda Rewired. *Russian Politics* 1: 398–417.

Oates, Sarah and Wendy W. Moe. 2017. Donald Trump and the "Oxygen of Publicity": Branding, Social Media, and Traditional Media. In Dan Schill and John Allen Hendricks (eds.) *The Presidency and Social Media: Discourse, Disruption, and Digital Democracy in the 2016 Presidential Election*. 1st edition. New York: Routledge.

Patterson, Thomas E. 2016. *News Coverage of the 2016 General Election: How the Press Failed the Voters*. Cambridge, MA: Harvard Kennedy School Faculty Research Working Paper Series.

Siebert, Fred, Theodore Peterson and Wilbur Schramm. 1956. *Four Theories of the Press: The Authoritarian, Libertarian, Social Responsibility, and Soviet Communist Concepts of What the Press Should Be and Do*. Chicago: University of Illinois Press.

Vaidhyanathan, Siva. 2018. *Antisocial Media: How Facebook Disconnects Us and Undermines Democracy*. New York: Oxford University Press.

Wardle, Claire and Hossein Derakhshan. 2017. *Information Disorder: Toward an Interdisciplinary Framework for Research and Policy Making*. Strasbourg: Council of Europe.

7
HATE PROPAGANDA

Cherian George

Until recently, scholars of political communication in stable democracies treated hate speech as a marginal phenomenon. That changed with the entry of various anti-establishment and anti-pluralist tendencies into the mainstream electoral politics of the United States and Western Europe. In 2016, Donald Trump's election and the Brexit referendum jolted dominant paradigms in communication studies, reordering research priorities and challenging assumptions about normal democratic discourse. Information disorders, ranging from individual-level 'post-truth' preferences to the distortions wrought by computational propaganda, are now central to the field's concerns. Hate speech is a key constituent of this basket of deplorables.

As suggested by the title, this chapter focuses on organised campaigns that promote hate to achieve larger political objectives. Examples abound from contemporary politics. In India, false rumours of forced marriage, cow slaughter, and child abductions are used to unleash violence against minorities, terrorising their communities into submitting to majoritarian domination (Harsh 2020). In South Africa, the Gupta oligarchs bankrolled a disinformation campaign to shift attention away from allegations of state capture. Designed by the public relations multinational Bell Pottinger, the covert programme involved stoking racial hatred with a narrative of 'white monopoly capital' (Wasserman 2020). In Europe, the far right has amplified reports of sexual harassment by people of colour into a 'rapefugee' crisis, riding on the #MeToo movement to grow support for their xenophobic and nativist agenda (Sorce 2018).

Hate propaganda has a history measurable in millennia, considerably longer than the digitally assisted misinformation that has triggered concern in recent years. Hate studies, similarly, have a long pedigree. The well-established study of hate can benefit from dialogue with the flurry of new research into online misinformation – and vice versa. Much of the recent research on online misinformation makes only cursory reference to the rich literature on how hate agents work. This chapter tries to engage in such a conversation.

Hate speech

Hate speech is the vilification of an identifiable group in order to stigmatise its members and cause them harm. The group in question could be distinguished by race, ethnicity, religion, nationality, immigrant status, gender, sexual orientation, or any other feature that is applied in an unfairly discriminatory manner (Parekh 2012). United Nations bodies fighting racial discrimination treat hate speech as 'a form of other-directed speech which rejects the core human rights principles of human dignity and equality and seeks to degrade the standing of individuals and groups in the estimation of society' (CERD 2013, 4). Hate speech can hurt its targets directly by inflicting emotional distress (Matsuda 1989) or causing them to retreat fearfully from public life (Fiss 1996). But it is most harmful when it incites others to discriminate or inflict violence against the target group. Hate speech has been harnessed by state and non-state actors to whip up hostility against enemies while uniting followers and allies. Such propagandistic use of hate speech has facilitated all the major atrocities that peoples have inflicted on one another in modern times, from slavery to imperial rule, land dispossession, war crimes, ethnic cleansings, and genocides (Gahman 2020; Meisenhelder 2003; Said 1979; Thompson 2007; Tsesis 2002).

The term hate speech straddles such a wide spectrum of harms – from the diminution of self-esteem to the decimation of a people – that many scholars have proposed more precise terminology. Benesch (2012), for example, uses 'dangerous speech' to refer to expression that increases the risk that its audience will support or perpetrate violence against another group. Observing Europe's Roma being routinely subjected to a 'language of negation, destruction and erasure', Townsend (2014, 9) suggests the term 'genocidal discourse'. Most legislation sidesteps the term hate speech entirely. Laws refer to explicit calls to action as incitement. Others make reference to insult, offence, or the wounding of religious or racial feelings, for example – categories that liberal jurisdictions tend not to criminalise.

The hate speech that attracts the most attention and regulatory or societal intervention tends to be expression that is shocking in and of itself, such as when President Donald Trump tweeted that certain progressive Democratic congresswomen – referring to four women of colour, three of whom were born in the United States – should 'go back' to the countries where they 'originally' came from (Coe & Griffin 2020; Rothe & Collins 2019). But hate campaigns can be much more indirect. They do not have to be fuelled by foul language or ethnic slurs. Some of their most effective work has been pseudoscientific (such as nineteenth-century physiognomy, which stratified different races based on their outward resemblance to apes) or critically acclaimed for its artistic merit (like Rudyard Kipling's 1899 poem 'The White Man's Burden', justifying American imperial rule over the Philippines). Holocaust denial was dressed in scholarly garb, though it is now obvious to most that it served no purpose other than to normalise anti-Semitic negationism. Many other examples of disguised hate propaganda have wider sway. Tactics include inserting Islamophobic talking points into the formal public sphere, through referenda and legislative proceedings ostensibly to fight non-existent threats such as minaret building in Europe (Cheng 2015) and religious law in the United States (Lemons & Chambers-Letson 2014).

Therefore, the individual hateful message, no matter how incendiary, is not the most illuminating unit of analysis for students of hate propaganda. Scholars have learned more by studying long-running campaigns. For example, Whillock (1995) focused on hate appeals systematically inserted as talking points woven into an election campaign. Hamelink (2011) takes an even longer view, showing how the aggressor's calls to action count on historical prejudices and deep anxieties within the groups being mobilised.

Full-blown hate campaigns start with an us/them framing of collective identity. Enlarging and intensifying in-group commitments is often the hate agents' main strategic objective, constructing an out-group being just the other side of the coin. The process involves the essentialising of identity: a set of arbitrary attributes is reified as definitive of the group (Gahman 2020; Said 1979). While the in-group is essentialised as exceptionally noble and civilised, the out-group's members are caricatured as barbaric, alien, or bestial, thus suggesting that they are not fully entitled to equal citizenship or human rights. Next, hate agents scapegoat the Other (Tsesis 2002). They blame the in-group's genuine grievances and anxieties on the out-group. In its most advanced form, scapegoating becomes 'accusation in a mirror' (Marcus 2012; Kiper 2015). A term associated with the Rwandan genocide, this refers to the technique of depicting the out-group as the real aggressor. In-group members come to believe that pre-emptively eliminating this threat to themselves and their families would be nothing more than an act of self-defence. This helps explain why ordinary people are prepared to inflict violence on a weaker community when leaders flag off war crimes, pogroms, and genocides, let alone lesser evils such as separating children from immigrant parents. The final step is the call to action. This often follows a trigger event, such as news of an attack on in-group members or some other intolerable provocation. Leaders opportunistically transform the event into an 'injustice symbol' (Olesen 2015), framing it the ultimate outrage that requires now-or-never retaliation.

Every stage in what Hamelink (2011, 21) calls a 'spiral of conflict escalation' involves deception and manipulation. The us/them binary is deceptive because everyone actually has plural identities. Portraying a single identity as supreme and exclusive (one's religion or race, for example) while discounting all others (including species) promotes a myth of 'choiceless singularity of human identity' (Sen 2006, 16). As for essentialising the out-group, this is a form of 'epistemic violence' (Spivak 1988). Scapegoating and accusation in a mirror, similarly, invariably involve messages that mislead. Anti-Semitic propaganda paving the way for the Holocaust included the publication of *The Protocols of the Elders of Zion*, an elaborate hoax intended to add weight to the conspiracy theory about a Jewish plan for global domination. Contemporary hate merchants carry on the tradition. India's Hindu nationalists have constructed a 'love jihad' conspiracy theory about Muslim population growth (Rao 2011). Muslim hardliners in Indonesia, meanwhile, have strengthened their hand by reviving the communist bogey, as well as stoking fears of domination by the small minority of ethnic Chinese and Christians (Miller 2018).

Finally, the triggering injustice symbols may be partly or wholly fabricated. In Indonesia, the 2016 demonstrations leading to the prosecution and ouster of Jakarta's Christian, ethnic Chinese governor were provoked by viral videos misquoting him as claiming that the Quran was lying to Muslims (Peterson 2020). Hate campaigns do not necessarily depend on pants-on-fire lies. The European 'rapefugee' myth, for example, can be sustained through the selective highlighting of factual news reports of sexual offences involving a suspect with a foreign-sounding name, supported by centuries of stereotypes concerning brown and black men (Sanos 2018). Nonetheless, the campaigns in their totality are maliciously deceptive. Hate propaganda is thus a trick or 'stratagem', says Whillock (1995). Tsesis (2002, 1) builds this observation into his definition of hate speech, calling it 'misinformation that is disseminated with the express purpose of persecuting targeted minorities'.

Digital hate

Not surprisingly, most of the research into hate propaganda over the past two decades has focused on the internet. The exponential growth in online tools and spaces has helped hate groups organise, mobilise, and spread their messages to new audiences (Levin 2002; Caiani & Parenti 2016). The salience of digital hate and incivility means that researchers are less likely to underestimate the internet's role than to exaggerate it. It is not obvious from most of the evidence presented whether the internet has multiplied the incidence and intensity of hate speech or just its styles and visibility. It is certainly not the case that the internet is indispensable for hate agents. Ethnographic studies of intolerant movements and case studies of their campaigns show that most are technologically promiscuous. They are 'innovation opportunists', adept at 'finding openings in the latest technologies' but not wedded to any particular medium (Daniels 2018, 62). They embrace the internet alongside other modes of communication, from radio and television talk shows to sermons in places of worship.

These caveats aside, it is clear that the internet has added several new dimensions to the communication of hate. First, there is the digital revolution's impact on the wider information ecosystem. The digital revolution has weakened traditional hierarchies that, at their best, used to maintain a common civic space and help keep toxic expression on the fringes. The decline of public service media in Europe is part of this trend (Schroeder 2019). Furthermore, the platformisation of online interactions and lowered barriers to entry mean that toxic content gets showcased alongside more trustworthy material as 'equal residing members of the inter-connected digital culture' (Klein 2017, 12). Through this process of 'information laundering', Klein says, 'false information and counterfeit movements can be washed clean by a system of advantageous associations' (2017, 26). A related concern is the normalisation or mainstreaming of extremist rhetoric both directly through social media (Govil & Baihsya 2018) and indirectly through subsequent mainstream media coverage (Phillips 2018).

Long before the arrival of 'deepfake' technologies, the ready access to internet platforms, web design templates, and innocuous domain names was making it easy disguise extreme content as mainstream. For example, the website with the address 'martinlutherking.org' was launched in 1999, not by supporters of the American civil rights leader but by the founder of the pioneering white supremacist site Stormfront (Daniels 2018).

Just as a hate movement can use digital technologies to bypass traditional media gatekeepers, it can also circumvent established political parties that may have moderated the impact of more extreme elements. Govil and Baihsya (2018) cite this factor as a reason for the right-wing-populist shift of India's Hindu nationalist Bharatiya Janata Party (BJP). Digital tools helped BJP leader Narendra Modi roll out a national marketing strategy, 'India Shining', which reduced his reliance on the powerful local party bosses and other brokers who used to control access to grassroots vote banks. Personalised text messages and the Narendra Modi app gave citizens the sense that they had a direct and immediate connection with the leader. Thus, the authors argue, 'digital social networking has given absolutist charismatic fascists new ways of engaging the masses' (p. 69).

Second, both the production and consumption of hate propaganda have undergone a pathological form of democratisation. The internet allows the creation and circulation of hate messages to be crowdsourced and encourages lone actors to take up cudgels and Kalashnikovs for the cause. One should not exaggerate the novelty of these dynamics. Nazi Germany's propaganda did not depend only on the centralised efforts of Josef Goebbels and Julius Streicher but was also built on decades of creative work by unknown artists, writers, and small businesses that produced cheaply produced anti-Semitic stickers, for example (Enzenbach 2012). The internet did not create the (misleadingly named) phenomenon of the 'lone-wolf' terrorist – embedded in a networked, communal ideology but acting with a high degree of autonomy (Schuurman et al. 2019; Berntzen & Sandberg 2014). Nathuram Godse, who assassinated Mahatma Gandhi in 1948, probably fit that description (Debs 2013).

What is clear is that the new, more open digital environment brings into play many new kinds of loosely coordinated actors. Modi's Hindu nationalist propaganda machine comprises top-level ideologues generating talking points, a professionally managed information technology (IT) cell, and perhaps 100,000 online volunteers at home and abroad, not to mention millions of other acolytes who cheer their leaders and troll critics (Govil & Baihsya 2018). When it occurs alongside violence in the real world, trolling can have a chilling effect on the target's speech (Bradshaw & Howard 2019). Many participants may be treating such online engagement as fun entertainment, resulting in a banalisation of hate (Udupa et al. 2020). Much of this activity resembles 'slacktivism' – low-energy work of seemingly negligible practical impact – but its sheer volume on social media can drown out and intimidate minorities and their spokesmen. The size of the mob can be multiplied with fake online identities or 'sock-puppets', automated accounts, and bots (Delwiche 2019). The outsourcing of propaganda work to internet brigades has not made central coordination redundant. Political consultancies and professional public relations and marketing firms are intimately involved in designing hate campaigns (Ong & Cabañes 2019). Despite the aforementioned Bell Pottinger scandal in South Africa, these industries remain under-regulated and under-studied.

Third, data analytic capabilities give hate agents unprecedented power to go far upstream in the process of dividing society. While earlier studies of online hate focused on the digital production and dissemination of messages, the more insidious threat probably lies in the datafi-cation of subject formation. The digital advertising infrastructures built into internet platforms enable the algorithmic construction of identity groups that can be manipulated by influence campaigns. This involves mass surveillance of internet users' behaviour patterns in fine detail, the data-driven construction of detailed profiles without their knowledge, identifying their cognitive and psychological dispositions, and then micro-targeting them with messages designed to exploit their vulnerabilities (Crain & Nadler 2019; Woolley & Howard 2016). The 'networked subject', argue Boler and Davis (2018, 83), is thus 'fed personalized findings which functionally determine one's windows on the infoworld'. Hate agents can, for example, heighten a target demographic's sense of victimhood and vulnerability to make them more open to the scape-goating of minorities by authoritarian populists. Since it is difficult of keep track of which Face-book demographics are receiving which content and why, much of this propaganda work can be done surreptitiously. Counterspeech – liberalism's recommended antidote for bad speech – is rendered impotent since it is not possible to counter what we don't know is being spoken or to whom.

Regulatory dilemmas

The concept of hate speech within political theory, moral philosophy, and law has evolved with the emergence of human rights doctrine over the past century. Traditional societies – including today's liberal democracies until fairly recently, as well as many contemporary illiberal regimes – protect the powerful from disparagement by the weak. The laws of seditious libel and lese-majeste, for example, are intended to preserve the special veneration that rulers claim they are due. Blasphemy law serves the same purpose for dominant religions and their clerics. The modern human rights standard, however, turns the tables on the powerful, enshrining the right to freedom of expression, including in particular the right to offend society's most dominant individuals, institutions, and beliefs. As for hate speech, the human rights approach aims to protect the people who are most vulnerable, rather than those with the means to insulate themselves from the harms caused by speech.

International jurisprudence on hate speech is anchored in the International Covenant on Civil and Political Rights (ICCPR), the United Nations' core human rights treaty. Article 19 of the ICCPR, which establishes the right to freedom of expression, states that governments may restrict this right to protect the rights of others. Article 20 goes further, requiring states to prohibit by law the 'advocacy of national, racial or religious hatred that constitutes incitement to discrimination, hostility or violence'. Hate speech is thus unique among the various types of disorder under the 'misinformation' umbrella – from voter suppression hoaxes to fake science – in that it is the only one that international human rights law requires states to prohibit.

The European Convention on Human Rights contains similar language. Racist hate speech is treated even more stringently under the International Convention on the Elimination of All Forms of Racial Discrimination (ICERD). Article 4 of ICERD requires states to declare as an offence punishable by law not only incitement but also 'all dissemination of ideas based on racial superiority or hatred'. Organisations and activities engaged in racist propaganda must also be prohibited, ICERD says.

The laws of most liberal democracies are generally aligned with Article 20 of ICERD. The US is an outlier, applying a much higher threshold for state intervention in speech: most hate speech that occurs in public discourse is constitutionally protected; courts will only permit government to interfere if the speech directly incites imminent violence (Abrams 2012). When the US ratified ICCPR and ICERD, it did so with the proviso that the treaties' Article 19 and Article 4, respectively, would not trump its own free speech guarantees. The difference in European and American approaches is a major theme in the literature on hate speech law (Hare 2009; Post 2009; Rosenfeld 2012). It has long been a source of frustration among European anti-hate groups who see neo-Nazis from their continent taking shelter in American cyberspace (Breckheimer II 2001; Posner 2014). With Europeans' online experience now largely mediated by a handful of American platforms such as Google, Facebook, and YouTube, critics argue that the internet's hospitability to hate is more a product of America's idiosyncratic commercial and libertarian ethos than of universal values (van Dijck 2019).

The differences in norms among jurisdictions within the liberal West should not obscure their more fundamental similarities. They, along with international treaties, concur that laws should restrict hate speech only if it can be objectively shown to cause harm. They differ mainly in what threshold of harm to apply. But if it amounts to nothing more than subjective offence, the liberal consensus is that society's response should take non-legal form: opinion shapers can engage in counterspeech while news media can behave ethically by choosing not to spread the offensive content, for example (Garton Ash 2016). The line that liberal democracies draw between harm and offence distinguishes them sharply from illiberal regimes, most of which have laws that punish various kinds of insult and offence. The Indian Penal Code, for example, criminalises the intentional wounding of religious feelings (Section 298). Pakistan's notorious blasphemy law (Section 295C of its Penal Code) threatens capital punishment or life imprisonment for defiling the Prophet's name, whether in words or images, directly or indirectly.

The stark difference in attitudes towards offensive expression is a key source of international friction in transborder cultural flows. The quintessential case is the 2005–2006 controversy over a Danish newspaper's deliberately provocative publication of cartoons of the Prophet Mohammed (Klausen 2009). The Danish government's refusal to offer even an expression of regret provoked the Organisation of Islamic Cooperation (OIC) to intensify its diplomatic efforts at the United Nations to get 'defamation of religions' recognised in international law as a legitimate justification for restricting freedom of expression (Langer 2014; McLaughlin 2010). Muslim governments argued that free speech was being abused to fuel Islamophobia and discrimination against Muslim minorities. Notably, several non–OIC members, such as the Philippines, Singapore and Thailand, voted in favour of a 2009 'defamation of religions' resolution at the General Assembly. India, Jamaica, and many other states abstained, supporting the idea of revising UN standards but arguing that this should be done on behalf of all religions, not just one. Though ultimately unsuccessful, the OIC campaign exposed an as-yet-unresolved concern that the liberal approach is enabling harmful hate propaganda to go unchecked (Appiah 2012; Hafez 2014).

Free speech theory's harm/offence distinction – especially the First Amendment doctrine's extremely high harm threshold – has also been challenged from within the liberal democratic fraternity. Critics argue that the prevailing standard is lopsided in its treatment of democracy's twin pillars, favouring liberty over equality at the expense of society's weakest communities (Waldron 2012; Cohen-Almagor 2019; Demaske 2019; Wilson & Kiper 2020). Scholars working within the paradigm of critical race theory say that any assessment of harm must take into account prevailing structural inequalities. Expression that seems only mildly provocative or innocently humourous to members of a privileged community can trigger psychological distress and add to a hostile climate for people already struggling under the weight of historical prejudice and disadvantage (Delgado & Stefancic 2018; Matsuda 1989; Schauer 1995). Although these 'microaggressions' have long-term cumulative effects, they may not even be recognised by the victim at the time (Sue 2010). Other scholars continue to defend the liberal standard, arguing that it is too dangerous to give states more powers to police harms that are too hard to verify independently (Heinze 2016; Strossen 2018). Furthermore, in societies where equal rights are not already well protected, communities do not enjoy equal access to the supposed protection that offence laws provide. These laws, such as those against blasphemy, end up being used by dominant groups to punish minorities who are deemed to have caused offence through their speech and conduct (George 2016a; Marshall & Shea 2011).

While critical race theory and related challenges have had little impact on hate speech laws, they have influenced the behaviour of Western media organisations, internet intermediaries, universities, and other cultural institutions. For example, news organisations have over the decades updated their ethical guidelines against stereotyping women and minorities and on how to report extremist newsmakers. But despair at unending injustice and the rise of white nationalism have sharpened activists' demands for greater sensitivity in speech. In the US and other liberal democracies, activists have mobilised outrage on college campuses and social media, occasionally resulting in the 'de-platforming' of speakers, boycotting of celebrities, and self-censorship by media (Hughes 2010; Kessler 2018). Ironically, the mobilisation of righteous indignation by progressives has parallels with the opportunistic offence-taking that many hate groups and intolerant movements have adopted alongside, or in lieu of, traditional hate speech (George 2016a). Predictably, even as it mocks the 'political correctness' of 'social justice warriors', the right occasionally appropriates the cultural left's anti-hate language and tactics against its opponents. The most sophisticated examples from recent years are the 'anti-Semitic' labels deployed by Israel's right-wing government and its supporters against critics of the country's racist policies and practices, including liberal-secular Jews (Davidson 2018). Philo et al. (2019) have exposed as an elaborate disinformation campaign the damaging allegations of anti-Semitism against the British Labour Party and its leader Jeremy Corbyn.

Hate propagandists are also adept at making censorship and regulation backfire. Social media platforms have been developing mechanisms for removing hate speech and other inappropriate content, but online operatives of repressive governments, intolerant movements, and hate groups have been gaming these systems to stifle the voices of their ideological opponents, including human rights activists, progressive cartoonists, and feminist writers. Exploiting the fact that the platforms' reporting systems are mostly automated, malevolent actors submit complaints en masse, triggering the temporary or permanent take-down of non-harmful content or accounts. This false-positives problem is one of the key challenges facing researchers and technologists who are trying to harness artificial intelligence to detect and counter digital hate (see, for example, Carter & Kondor 2020; Di Nicola et al. 2020; Oriola & Kotzé 2020; Vidgen & Yasseri 2020). A more fundamental problem is that algorithms can only deal with individual messages containing extreme or uncivil expression, rather than large-scale online campaigns, most of whose individual messages may be unobjectionable.

Gaps and future directions

Most of the public debate and scholarly work on misinformation and hate propaganda focuses on the veracity and civility of individual posts, tweets, and other utterances, examining how toxic messages can be identified and then subject to legal prosecution, administrative orders, removal by media and platforms, correction by fact-checkers, and other interventions. Such research and policy interventions implicitly apply a 'toxic bullet' model of hate propaganda, even as every introductory media effects course debunks the 'magic bullet' theory of persuasion. A policy and research agenda informed by decades of hate research would instead recognise hate campaigns as layered, distributed, and strategic (George 2017).

First, they are layered in the sense that they are composed of multiple messages, motifs, and narratives delivered over years or even centuries. The vast majority of these are not problematic in isolation and may even have been put to positive, prosocial use. Patriotic narratives, for example, can inspire great acts of self-sacrifice as well as war crimes. In some of the examples cited earlier, the skill of the hate propagandist lies in the creative combination of a community's treasured repertoire of stories and symbols, together with carefully curated news from the recent past, topped off with more pointed observations about current events. To believe that social media moderators and algorithms checking for inappropriate language and fake news can make much difference is to grossly underestimate how the most pernicious hate campaigns actually work.

Second, the work is distributed, with a movement-style division of labour. Different actors take responsibility for the campaign's different layers. While fringe organisations have no compunctions about using flagrantly racist language, national leaders tend to rely on dog whistles. Or they confine themselves to grand themes like 'India Shining' or 'Make America Great Again' to help promote an essentialised in-group identity without spelling out their exclusionary intent. The most emphatic statements of Modi and Trump are delivered in silence: by refusing to condemn allies guilty of hate speech and hate crimes, they express their sympathies unequivocally. Think tanks and outward-facing websites try to sound reasonable in order to attract converts (Meddaugh & Kay 2009). Their efforts also help members who need to rationalise their prejudice. Norwegian white supremacist Anders Behring Breivik, who killed 77 in a shooting spree in 2011, cited American ideologue Robert Spencer and his Jihad Watch blog 162 times in his manifesto.

Third, the most sophisticated hate propaganda is strategic: the communication is designed to achieve goals that go deeper than its superficial intent. In many cases, the strategy factors in the likelihood of pushback. Taking a leaf from how progressive civil disobedience campaigners make censorship backfire (Jansen & Martin 2003), hate groups turn legal and regulatory obstacles into opportunities for generating sympathy and mobilising support. For example, campaigners who purchased advertising space in American metro systems for anti-Muslim billboards expected to be censored; they could then mount First Amendment challenges that would generate news coverage (George 2016b). When white supremacists adopted Pepe the Frog as an icon, it was added to the Anti-Defamation League's database of online hate symbols and deplored by media and politicians, but the reaction was built into the campaign's design as 'a prank with a big attention payoff' (Daniels 2018, 64; Phillips 2018). In Europe, attempts by governments and internet platforms to rein in anti-immigrant hate speech have been exploited by nativists as evidence that establishment institutions obsessed with multiculturalism and political correctness are silencing people's grievances – hence, the need to support the far right (Nortio et al. 2020; van Noorloos 2014).

Hate studies have benefited from the recent surge in scholarly interest in Western democracies' problems with misinformation and populism. But this is a mixed blessing. It trains the spotlight on a limited number of narrow, message-centric questions, such as what social media companies can do about 'fake news'. Shifting the focus to actor-centric questions would be more revealing of the ingenuity with which hate campaigns are rolled out. Also lacking are demand-side investigations to understand why people are susceptible to hate appeals in the first place and why these seem to be growing. Communication studies as a field is well positioned to investigate the symptoms of this trend. But it should also take an interest in underlying causes. Beneath the surge in intolerance and hate may be resentments arising from the exhaustion of the modern idea of progress, with its deep injustices and inequalities. The claims of populist leaders that they possess humane answers to their societies' problems is the mother of all disinformation campaigns. But until those who care about questions of justice and equality emerge with better answers themselves, we can expect hate propaganda to continue figuring prominently throughout the world.

References

Abrams F. (2012) On American Hate Speech Law. In: Herz M. and Molnar P. (eds) *The Content and Context of Hate Speech: Rethinking Regulation and Responses*. New York: Cambridge University Press, pp. 116–126.

Appiah K.A. (2012) What's Wrong with Defamation of Religion? In: Herz M. and Molnár P. (eds) *The Content and Context of Hate Speech: Rethinking Regulation and Responses*. New York: Cambridge University Press.

Benesch S. (2012) Words as Weapons. *World Policy Journal* 29(1): 7–12.

Berntzen L.E. and Sandberg S. (2014) The Collective Nature of Lone Wolf Terrorism: Anders Behring Breivik and the Anti-Islamic Social Movement. *Terrorism and Political Violence* 26(5): 759–779. DOI:10.1080/09546553.2013.767245.

Boler M. and Davis E. (2018) The Affective Politics of the "Post-Truth" Era: Feeling Rules and Networked Subjectivity. *Emotion, Space and Society* 27: 75–85. DOI:10.1016/j.emospa.2018.03.002.

Bradshaw S. and Howard P.N. (2019) *The Global Disinformation Order: 2019 Global Inventory of Organised Social Media Manipulation*. Computational Propaganda Research Project. Oxford: Oxford University Press.

Breckheimer II P.J. (2001) A Haven for Hate: The Foreign and Domestic Implications of Protecting Internet Hate Speech Under the First Amendment. *Southern California Law Review* 75: 1493.

Caiani M. and Parenti L. (2016) *European and American Extreme Right Groups and the Internet*. Abingdon, Oxford: Routledge.

Carter P. and Kondor K. (2020) Researching the Radical Right: Making Use of the Digital Space and Its Challenges. In: Littler M. and Lee B. (eds) *Digital Extremisms: Readings in Violence, Radicalisation and Extremism in the Online Space*. Palgrave Studies in Cybercrime and Cybersecurity. Cham: Springer International Publishing, pp. 223–252. DOI:10.1007/978-3-030-30138-5_11.

CERD. (2013) *General Recommendation No. 35: Combating Racist Hate Speech*. UN Committee on the Elimination of Racial Discrimination CERD/C/GC/35, 26 September. Available at: www.refworld.org/docid/53f457db4.html (accessed 30 March 2020).

Cheng J.E. (2015) Islamophobia, Muslimophobia or Racism? Parliamentary Discourses on Islam and Muslims in Debates on the Minaret Ban in Switzerland. *Discourse & Society* 26(5): 562–586. DOI:10.1177/0957926515581157.

Coe K. and Griffin R.A. (2020) Marginalized Identity Invocation Online: The Case of President Donald Trump on Twitter. *Social Media + Society* 6(1): 1–12. DOI:10.1177/2056305120913979.

Cohen-Almagor R. (2019) Racism and Hate Speech – A Critique of Scanlon's Contractual Theory. *First Amendment Studies* 53(1–2): 41–66. DOI:10.1080/21689725.2019.1601579.

Crain M. and Nadler A. (2019) Political Manipulation and Internet Advertising Infrastructure. *Journal of Information Policy* 9: 370–410. DOI:10.5325/jinfopoli.9.2019.0370.

Daniels J. (2018) The Algorithmic Rise of the "Alt-Right". *Contexts*: 60–65. DOI:10.1177/1536504218766547.

Davidson L. (2018) On the "New Anti-Semitism" and Its Political and Religious Consequences. *Journal of Holy Land and Palestine Studies* 17(2): 221–234. DOI:10.3366/hlps.2018.0192.

Debs M. (2013) Using Cultural Trauma: Gandhi's Assassination, Partition and Secular Nationalism in Post-Independence India. *Nations and Nationalism* 19(4): 635–653. DOI:10.1111/nana.12038.

Delgado R. and Stefancic J. (2018) *Must We Defend Nazis? Why the First Amendment Should Not Protect Hate Speech and White Supremacy.* New York: New York University Press.

Delwiche A. (2019) Computational Propaganda and the Rise of the Fake Audience. In: Baines P., O'Shaughnessy N. and Snow N. (eds) *The Sage Handbook of Propaganda.* London: Sage.

Demaske C. (2019) Social Justice, Recognition Theory and the First Amendment: A New Approach to Hate Speech Restriction. *Communication Law and Policy* 24(3): 347–401. DOI:10.1080/10811680.2019.1627800.

Di Nicola A., Andreatta D., Martini E., et al. (2020) Hatemeter: Hate Speech Tool for Monitoring, Analysing and Tackling Anti-Muslim Hatred Online. *eCrime Research Reports*: 6. Available at: https://research.tees.ac.uk/en/publications/hatemeter-hate-speech-tool-for-monitoring-analysing-and-tackling (accessed 15 March 2020).

Enzenbach I. (2012) Stamps, Stickers and Stigmata: A Social Practice of Antisemitism Presented in a Slide-Show. *Quest: Issues in Contemporary Jewish History*: 3. Available at: www.quest-cdecjournal.it/focus.php?id=307 (accessed 27 March 2020).

Fiss O.M. (1996) *The Irony of Free Speech.* Cambridge, MA: Harvard University Press.

Gahman L. (2020) *Land, God, and Guns: Settler Colonialism and Masculinity in the American Heartland.* London: Zed Books Ltd.

Garton Ash T. (2016) *Free Speech: Ten Principles for a Connected World.* New Haven, CT: Yale University Press.

George C. (2016a) *Hate Spin: The Manufacture of Religious Offense and Its Threat to Democracy.* Boston: MIT Press.

George C. (2016b) Regulating "Hate Spin": The Limits of Law in Managing Religious Incitement and Offense. *International Journal of Communication* 10: 2955–2972.

George C. (2017) Hate Spin: The Twin Political Strategies of Religious Incitement and Offense-Taking. *Communication Theory* 27(2): 156–175. Oxford Academic. DOI:10.1111/comt.12111.

Govil N. and Baishya A.K. (2018) The Bully in the Pulpit: Autocracy, Digital Social Media, and Right-Wing Populist Technoculture. *Communication, Culture and Critique* 11(1): 67–84. DOI:10.1093/ccc/tcx001.

Hafez F. (2014) Shifting Borders: Islamophobia as Common Ground for Building Pan-European Right-Wing Unity. *Patterns of Prejudice* 48(5): 479–499.

Hamelink C.J. (2011) *Media and Conflict: Escalating Evil.* Boulder, CO: Paradigm Publishers.

Hare I. (2009) Extreme Speech Under International and Regional Human Rights Standards. In: Hare I. and Weinstein J. (eds) *Extreme Speech and Democracy.* Oxford: Oxford University Press, pp. 62–80.

Harsh M. (2020) India's Lynchings: Ordinary Crimes, Rough Justice or Command Hate Crimes? In: Malreddy P.K., Purakayastha A.S. and Heidemann B. (eds) *Violence in South Asia: Contemporary Perspectives.* Abingdon, Oxford: Routledge.

Heinze E. (2016) *Hate Speech and Democratic Citizenship.* Oxford, New York: Oxford University Press.

Hughes G. (2010) *Political Correctness: A History of Semantics and Culture.* Chichester: John Wiley & Sons.

Jansen S.C. and Martin B. (2003) Making Censorship Backfire. *Counterpoise* 7(3): 5–15.

Kessler M.J. (2018) The Difference Between Being Offended and Taking Offense. In: Downs D.A. and Suprenant C.W. (eds) *The Value and Limits of Academic Speech: Philosophical, Political, and Legal Perspectives.* New York: Routledge.

Kiper J. (2015) War Propaganda, War Crimes, and Post-Conflict Justice in Serbia: An Ethnographic Account. *The International Journal of Human Rights* 19(5): 572–591. DOI:10.1080/13642987.2014.992882.

Klausen J. (2009) *The Cartoons That Shook the World.* New Haven, CT: Yale University Press.

Klein A. (2017) *Fanaticism, Racism, and Rage Online: Corrupting the Digital Sphere.* Cham, Switzerland: Palgrave Macmillan. DOI:10.1007/978-3-319-51424-6.

Langer L. (2014) *Religious Offence and Human Rights: The Implications of Defamation of Religions.* Cambridge, New York: Cambridge University Press.

Lemons K. and Chambers-Letson J.T. (2014) Rule of Law: Sharia Panic and the US Constitution in the House of Representatives. *Cultural Studies* 28(5–6): 1048–1077.

Levin B. (2002) Cyberhate: A Legal and Historical Analysis of Extremists' Use of Computer Networks in America. *American Behavioral Scientist* 45(6): 958–988. DOI:10.1177/0002764202045006004.

Marcus K.L. (2012) Accusation in a Mirror. *Loyola University Chicago Law Journal* 43(2): 357–393.

Marshall P. and Shea N. (2011) *Silenced: How Apostasy and Blasphemy Codes Are Choking Freedom Worldwide.* New York: Oxford University Press.

Matsuda M.J. (1989) Public Response to Racist Speech: Considering the Victim's Story. *Michigan Law Review* 87(8): 2320–2381.

McLaughlin N. (2010) Spectrum of Defamation of Religion Laws and the Possibility of a Universal International Standard. *Loyola of Los Angeles International and Comparative Law Review* 32: 395–426.

Meddaugh P.M. and Kay J. (2009) Hate Speech or "Reasonable Racism?" The Other in Stormfront. *Journal of Mass Media Ethics* 24(4): 251–268.

Meisenhelder T. (2003) African Bodies: "Othering" the African in Precolonial Europe. *Race, Gender & Class* 10(3): 100–113.

Miller S. (2018) Zombie Anti-Communism? Democratization and the Demons of Suharto-Era Politics in Contemporary Indonesia. In: McGregor K., Melvin J. and Pohlman A. (eds) *The Indonesian Genocide of 1965.* Cham, Switzerland: Palgrave Macmillan, pp. 287–310. DOI:10.1007/978-3-319-71455-4_15.

Nortio E., Niska M., Renvik T. A., et al. (2020) "The nightmare of multiculturalism": Interpreting and deploying anti-immigration rhetoric in social media. *New Media & Society.* DOI:10.1177/1461444819899624.

Olesen T. (2015) *Global Injustice Symbols and Social Movements.* New York: Palgrave Macmillan.

Ong J.C. and Cabañes J.V.A. (2019) When Disinformation Studies Meets Production Studies: Social Identities and Moral Justifications in the Political Trolling Industry. *International Journal of Communication*: 13.

Oriola O. and Kotzé E. (2020) Evaluating Machine Learning Techniques for Detecting Offensive and Hate Speech in South African Tweets. *IEEE Access* 8: 21496–21509. DOI:10.1109/ACCESS.2020.2968173.

Parekh B. (2012) Is There a Case for Banning Hate Speech? In: Herz M. and Molnar P. (eds) *The Content and Context of Hate Speech: Rethinking Regulation and Responses.* New York: Cambridge University Press, pp. 37–56.

Peterson D. (2020) *Islam, Blasphemy, and Human Rights in Indonesia: The Trial of Ahok.* New York: Routledge.

Phillips W. (2018) *The Oxygen of Amplification: Better Practices for Reporting on Extremists, Antagonists, and Manipulators.* Data & Society Research Institute. Available at: https://datasociety.net/library/oxygen-of-amplification/ (accessed 14 March 2020).

Philo G., Miller D., Berry M., et al. (2019) *Bad News for Labour: Antisemitism, the Party and Public Belief.* London: Pluto Press.

Posner E. (2014) *The Twilight of Human Rights Law.* Oxford and New York: Oxford University Press.

Post R. (2009) Hate Speech. In: Hare I. and Weinstein J. (eds) *Extreme Speech and Democracy.* Oxford: Oxford University Press, pp. 123–138.

Rao M. (2011) Love Jihad and Demographic Fears. *Indian Journal of Gender Studies* 18(3): 425–430. DOI:10.1177/097152151101800307.

Rosenfeld M. (2012) Hate Speech in Constitutional Jurisprudence: A Comparative Analysis. In: Herz M. and Molnar P. (eds) *The Content and Context of Hate Speech.* New York: Cambridge University Press, pp. 242–289.

Rothe D.L. and Collins V.E. (2019) Turning Back the Clock? Violence Against Women and the Trump Administration. *Victims & Offenders* 14(8): 965–978. DOI:10.1080/15564886.2019.1671284.

Said E.W. (1979) *Orientalism.* New York: Vintage.

Sanos S. (2018) The Sex and Race of Satire: Charlie Hebdo and the Politics of Representation in Contemporary France. *Jewish History* 32(1): 33–63. DOI:10.1007/s10835-018-9308-2.

Schauer F. (1995) Uncoupling Free Speech. In: Lederer L. and Delgado R. (eds) *The Price We Pay: The Case Against Racist Speech, Hate Propaganda, and Pornography.* New York: Farrar, Straus and Giroux, pp. 259–265.

Schroeder R. (2019) Digital Media and the Entrenchment of Right-Wing Populist Agendas: *Social Media + Society.* DOI:10.1177/2056305119885328.

Schuurman B., Lindekilde L., Malthaner S., et al. (2019) End of the Lone Wolf: The Typology That Should Not Have Been. *Studies in Conflict & Terrorism* 42(8): 771–778. Routledge. DOI:10.1080/1057610X.2017.1419554.

Sen A. (2006) *Identity and Violence: The Illusion of Destiny.* New York: W. W. Norton.

Sorce G. (2018) Sounding the Alarm for Right-Wing #MeToo: "120 Dezibel" in Germany. *Feminist Media Studies* 18(6): 1123–1126. DOI:10.1080/14680777.2018.1532146.

Spivak G.C. (1988) Can the Subaltern Speak? In: Nelson C. and Grossberg L. (eds) *Marxism and the Interpretation of Culture*. Chicago: University of Illinois Press, pp. 271–313.

Strossen N. (2018) *Hate: Why We Should Resist It With Free Speech, Not Censorship*. New York: Oxford University Press.

Sue D.W. (2010) *Microaggressions and Marginality: Manifestation, Dynamics, and Impact*. Hoboken, NJ: John Wiley & Sons.

Thompson A. (ed.) (2007) *The Media and the Rwanda Genocide*. Ottawa: International Development Research Centre.

Townsend E. (2014) Hate Speech or Genocidal Discourse? An Examination of Anti-Roma Sentiment in Contemporary Europe. *Journal of Multidisciplinary International Studies* 11(1). DOI:10.5130/portal.v11i1.3287.

Tsesis A. (2002) *Destructive Messages: How Hate Speech Paves the Way For Harmful Social Movements*. New York: New York University Press.

Udupa S., Gagliardone I., Deem A., et al. (2020) *Hate Speech, Information Disorder, and Conflict*. SSRC Research Review. Available at: https://www.en.ethnologie.uni-muenchen.de/aktuelles/network_research_review/index.html.

van Dijck J. (2019) Governing Digital Societies: Private Platforms, Public Values. *Computer Law & Security Review*. DOI:10.1016/j.clsr.2019.105377.

van Noorloos M. (2014) The Politicisation of Hate Speech Bans in the Twenty-First-Century Netherlands: Law in a Changing Context. *Journal of Ethnic and Migration Studies* 40(2): 249–265. DOI:10.1080/1369183X.2013.851474.

Vidgen B. and Yasseri T. (2020) Detecting Weak and Strong Islamophobic Hate Speech on Social Media. *Journal of Information Technology & Politics* 17(1): 66–78. DOI:10.1080/19331681.2019.1702607.

Waldron J. (2012) *The Harm in Hate Speech*. Cambridge, MA: Harvard University Press.

Wasserman H. (2020) Fake News from Africa: Panics, Politics and Paradigms. *Journalism* 21(1): 3–16. DOI:10.1177/1464884917746861.

Whillock R.K. (1995) The Use of Hate as a Stratagem for Achieving Social and political Goals. In: Whillock R.K. and Slayden D. (eds) *Hate Speech*. Thousand Oaks, CA: Sage Publications, pp. 28–54.

Wislon R.A. and Kiper J. (2020) Incitement in an Era of Populism: Updating Brandenburg After Charlottesville. *University of Pennsylvania Journal of Law & Public Affairs* 5(2): 56–120.

Woolley S.C. and Howard P.N. (2016) Automation, Algorithms, and Politics| Political Communication, Computational Propaganda, and Autonomous Agents — Introduction. *International Journal of Communication* 10: 4882–4890.

8

FILTER BUBBLES AND DIGITAL ECHO CHAMBERS[1]

Judith Möller

Are filter bubbles and echo chambers two names for the same phenomenon?

Filter bubbles and echo chambers are often named as key drivers of political polarisation and societal fragmentation (Pariser 2011; Sunstein 2001). Both concepts are based on the notion that people are excluded from information that is different from what they already believe. Very often, they refer to a partisan divide in ideological camps. The core argument here is that individuals on the political left are exclusively exposed to information that is leaning to the ideological left, and the same is true for those who identify as politically right. Inherent in the concepts is a notion of strong effects of information and technology. Both Sunstein (2001) and Pariser (2011) argue that it is due to the biased information environment that people lose sight of different perspectives and topics, which leads to increased polarisation across partisan lines, decreasing tolerance and understanding of minorities and resulting in a public debate that becomes ever more fragmented (Zuiderveen-Borgesius et al. 2016). Some commentators even explain the surprise outcomes of the 2016 presidential election and the Brexit referendum as direct results of echo chambers and filter bubbles (Groshek and Koc-Michalska 2017).

The original meaning of the term *echo chamber* refers to hollow enclosures used to create reverberation of sound: for example, in churches, cathedrals, and recording studios. Sunstein (2001) introduced the term to describe enclosed spaces of communication. Originally, he directly linked the concept to the presence of filtering systems online, inspired by Negroponte's (1996) idea of the 'daily me'. Yet, in the meantime, the concept has become popular to describe fragmented and isolated audiences in general. As Dubois and Blank put it, 'The idea of an "echo chamber" in politics is a metaphorical way to describe a situation where only certain ideas, information and beliefs are shared. . . . People inside this setting will only encounter things they already agree with' (2018: 729).

The term *filter bubble* was coined by internet activist Eli Pariser (2011) nearly a decade later. He describes a filter bubble as a 'personal ecosystem of information that's been catered by these algorithms to who they think you are'.[2] Like the echo chamber, the filter bubble is defined as an enclosed space, but whereas the metaphor of the echo chamber focuses on the nature of what is inside this space, the metaphor of the filter bubbles emphasises what constitutes its boundaries: the filtering algorithms. It is important to note that both concepts describe a state rather than a process. Individuals are already excluded from challenging information, yet both arguments imply that the isolation from information that is counter-attitudinal happens gradually over time.

The conceptualisation of echo chambers and filter bubbles and their relationship is still subject to an ongoing academic debate (see, for example, Bruns 2019). However, a consensus on some of the key differentiating characteristics is slowly emerging. First, they can be distinguished by the argument of why people are excluded from counter-attitudinal information. For echo chambers the agency of the selection lies with humans: either a person is self-selecting an information diet that is a perpetual echo of their own thoughts (Stroud 2010), or the social network of an individual spreads primarily information that is in consonance with the belief system and norms of that group (Dubois and Blank 2018). In the original filter bubble argument, the agency lies with the algorithms employed to select information for online news feeds. Following the filter bubble argument, these algorithms are detecting user preferences in an opaque and unobtrusive way and subsequently offer users more of the same content. Inherit in this argument is that this a strong sense of technological determinism. It is important to note that filter bubbles can distort the perception of public opinion. The neutral architecture of online news feeds might create the impression that users see the same content as everybody else while they are really receiving a highly personalised and biased news feed (Zuiderveen-Borgesius et al. 2016).

The underlying mechanism

The reason individuals are exclusively exposed to information that does not challenge their belief system is rooted in the same social-psychological mechanisms for both concepts: selective exposure and homophily. Selective exposure theory suggests that individuals prefer to expose themselves to content that confirms their belief systems because dissonant information can cause cognitive stress they would rather avoid (Festinger 1957). This process is also often called confirmation bias and has been studied and discussed extensively in social psychology and beyond (Oswald and Grosjean 2004). Homophily suggests that we are attracted to others who are similar to us, online and offline. Shared norms, ideology, and ideas are among the most important characteristics when forming relationships (Lazarsfeld and Merton 1954). That means we are frequently talking to others who are likely to agree with us. Our like-minded friends are likely to introduce us to new information that is aligned with shared perspectives and interests. Hence, both mechanisms, selective exposure and homophily, suggest that individuals are motivated to surround themselves with information that aligns with their belief systems while avoiding dissonant information (Stroud 2010).

In fact, we saw such an alignment of political ideology and information environment in the beginning of the twentieth century. During this time, most European citizens were clearly segmented in groups like the working class, liberals, or the Catholics in their respective countries (for example, pillarisation in the Netherlands; Steininger 1977). Back then, group members were associating primarily with each other and consulting only dedicated newspapers and broadcasting stations. Over the past decades, this clear segmentation of the population has become much less pronounced. Today, partisans still prefer news outlets that are aligned with their belief systems but generally no longer avoid counter-attitudinal information (Weeks, Ksiazek, and Holbert 2016). Yet to this day, this kind of political parallelism (Hallin and Mancini 2004) can be observed in many European countries. Hence, the observation that we surround ourselves with voices that agree with us is nothing new or inherently connected to the emergence of the internet. The larger question that Sunstein (2001) in particular has put forward is whether the affordances of online communication amplify those tendencies. On the theoretical level, the two concepts, echo chambers and filter bubbles, differ in this point.

For echo chambers, the constituting affordances of online communication mainly pertain to online social networks. Sunstein argued that the possibility of engaging in online communities and easily sharing information causes increased fragmentation of the public debate as 'unsought, unanticipated and even unwanted exposure to diverse topics, people, and ideas' is not afforded in the 'gated communities' online (Sunstein 2001: 2). For the filter bubble, the technical affordances are more complex. Algorithmic filtering is a process in which content is sorted and prioritised by certain principles to optimise specific key performance indicators (KPIs). The sorting principles are often a combination of different algorithms: for example, collaborative filtering or content-based filtering (Bozdag 2013). To sort all available information to fill a personalised news feed using collaborative filtering, the recommender engine compares user signals such as past behaviour or location with other users and recommends new content these other users have engaged with. A content-based filtering algorithm identifies content in the pool that shares content characteristics with the content a user already engaged with. Both these principles imply that if a user has a clear preference, this preference is likely to be amplified to increase the likelihood that the user clicks on the content: that is, if it is true that all users prefer content that is an echo of their thoughts. The majority of empirical evidence so far, however, points in a different direction.

Empirical inquiry into filter bubbles and echo chambers

According to a range of empirical studies, users of online information seek out diverse information. This is associated with less rather than more political polarisation. Empirical evidence stemming from large-scale panel studies demonstrates that social networks of users online are often quite diverse, which leads to engagement with a larger variety of news sources (Beam et al. 2018; Beam, Hutchens, and Hmielowski 2018). This finding is in line with a comparative study by Fletcher and Nielsen (2018) in Italy, Australia, the UK, and the US, which finds that social media users who are incidentally exposed to news consult a wider range of sources than those who do not use social media, based on self-reports collected as part of the Reuters Digital News Survey. Recent work by Yang and colleagues (2020), based on a combination of digital tracking data and survey data collected over a five-year time frame, demonstrates that exposure to cross-cutting information even exceeds self-reported exposure to diverse sources.

These large-scale, multi-platform studies all show that the prevalence of filter bubble and echo chamber effects among the majority of the population is low. However, as most of those studies are based on self-reported media use measures, they cannot distinguish whether this is a consequence of social curation and self-selection (echo chamber) or a result of an algorithmic filter system (filter bubble). Even if they are combined with digital trace data of clicks outside social media (Yang et al. 2020), it is still unclear how diverse the news feed that was offered to an individual user was. Therefore, in the following, studies that focus on the different technical affordances of echo chambers and filter bubbles are discussed.

Echo chambers

Several studies focus specifically on the influence of network composition without an additional layer of algorithmic filtering. The 'gated communities' that are core to the echo chamber argument were famously illustrated by Adamic and Glance (2005) based on interlinkage analysis of political bloggers in the 2004 presidential election. They find a clear division of the red and the blue blogosphere, although both spheres remained connected. These findings were later replicated for political hashtag communities on Twitter (Williams et al. 2015; Garimella et al. 2018). The division along partisan lines online, characteristic of the US political systems, can be understood as an extension of the polarised media system offline. Combining online and offline data, Stroud showed that partisanship predicts the kind of a media diet people follow offline as well as online (2010). This finding is important to keep in mind when thinking about the potential effects of echo chambers because they illustrate two points: first, individual preferences as an expression of interests and political leaning are among the most important determinants of news selection; second, in order to assess whether individuals are locked in echo chambers and excluded from anything but the reverberance of their own thoughts, information intake needs to be studied across all sources. For example, Vaccari and colleagues (2016) find that the structure of offline discussion networks reflects their discussion networks online; those who prefer to discuss politics with those supporting their positions often do so online and offline.

It should be noted that, while it is not necessary that the members of online echo chambers have personal relationships, they matter when it comes to news selection. Anspach (2017) found in a survey experiment in a small student sample that recommendations by friends and family positively influence the likelihood of engaging with the items, even if they are counter-attitudinal.

Filter bubbles

Studying the difference between social curation and algorithmic filtering is notoriously difficult (Kitchin 2017). First, the algorithms employed by social media companies are considered trade secrets. That means the algorithms that are supposedly constructing filter bubbles are beyond reach for academic inquiry (Bruns 2019). Studying automatically scraped user timelines to accurately and reliably measure exposure to diverse information online is currently also considered a violation of the terms of service of these platforms (Walker, Mercea, and Bastos 2019). Moreover, social curation and algorithmic curation are inherently connected and part of a larger system that shapes news curation (Thorson et al. 2019). Hence, a research design that is able to combine detailed news exposure and news consumption, both online and offline, as would be required to understand whether it was an algorithm, social curation, or self-selection that potentially limited a users' access to diverse information, is currently not possible. Having said this, there are a number of studies that can shed light on certain aspects of the process, although they are often limited to one platform or lack external validity because they are based on in vitro experiments that emulate social media news feeds.

There are a number of studies that investigated the effect of algorithmic filter systems on singular platforms: for example Facebook (Bakshy, Messing, and Adamic 2015), Google and Google news (Haim, Graefe, and Brosius 2018; Puschmann 2019; Nechushtai and Lewis 2019), or a news website (Möller et al. 2018). These studies focus on specific affordances that influence the process of algorithmic filtering. For example, Bashky and colleagues (2015) studied the effect of ideological homophily in friend networks compared to algorithmic filtering. They found that the composition of the network reduces the chance of being exposed to cross-cutting content, in particular for conservatives, to a much higher degree than the algorithmic sorting. For Google searches, Haim, Graefe, and Brosius (2018) used a method of agent-based testing to assess whether variation in the signals used for algorithmic filtering affected the diversity of the results in Germany. They found that in contrast to the usage of search terms, the algorithmic selection did not reduce the diversity of the results. In line with this finding, Puschmann reported a high overlap in search results for equal search terms related to politics in donated data from 4,379 users. Nechushtai and Lewis (2019) came to a similar conclusion for Google News in the US context. Focusing on differences in specific algorithms used, we found that the diversity of algorithmic selection can be even higher than the diversity of human editorial choice for a news website in the Netherlands (Moeller et al. 2016). It should be noted, however, that it mattered how the algorithm was designed. Content-based filters did reduce the diversity in topics while collaborative filtering did not. Collectively these studies indicate that the potential of algorithmic filter systems to exclude users from information that might challenge their extant belief systems has not been realised.

However, should this change in the future, it could lead to increased polarisation. In an experiment focused on the effects of biased, personalised news feeds, Dylko and colleagues (2017) presented 93 university students with personalisation technology with varying possibilities to exercise control. They found that if participants were presented with fewer counter-attitudinal items, it resulted in less engagement with those items. If the participants customised the news feeds themselves, the selective engagement with news was still present, although less pronounced. This implies that even though algorithmic filter systems might not actively reduce diversity through the automatic selection, their user interfaces influence selective exposure.

Bubbles at the fringes

While most research indicates that the specific affordances of online communication do not contribute to the formation of echo chambers and filter bubbles among the majority of the population, several studies suggest that these affordances matter for small-scale bubbles at the fringes of the mainstream. For example, Quattrociocchi, Scala, and Sunstein (2016) studied the emergence of conspiracy-related and science-related bubbles on Facebook, focusing on 1,105 Facebook group pages in Italy and the US. They found that highly engaged users in these communities interacted primarily with those sharing their beliefs and actively sought out information in accordance with their belief systems. Smith and Graham (2019) came to a similar conclusion studying anti-vaccination networks on Facebook. They note that while the movement itself is global, the network among them is dense, and sub-networks appear to be 'small worlds', shielded from counter-attitudinal information.

Conclusion and future directions

All in all, it seems that there is a mismatch between the strong theoretical assumptions of filter bubbles and echo chambers and their empirical manifestations. It is not wrong that people seek out information that confirms their attitudes and beliefs, but they do so online and offline. If anything, the reality of social media and algorithmic filter systems today seems to be that they inject diversity rather than reducing it. A notable exception to this conclusion are highly polarised or radicalised individuals who seek out online communities to connect with like-minded users on a global level. Does that mean we should stop researching echo chambers and filter bubbles? To some extent the answer is yes. As Helberger (2019) and Bruns (2019) point out, the imaginary of filter bubbles distracts from a different, more important discourse on how intermediaries and platforms shape information ecologies. However, the lack of large effects at the moment does not mean that these cannot occur in the future. It is not clear yet whether the formation of fringe bubbles is an exception to the rule or a harbinger of a larger development (Benkler, Faris, and Roberts 2018). From this perspective, there are several avenues for future research.

Towards a spiral of noise

First, we need to gain a better understanding of how choice architecture afforded by social media biases the perception of public opinion (Wojcieszak 2011; Wojcieszak and Price 2009), especially in cloistered online information environments in which users with radical viewpoints feel surrounded by like-minded peers (Schulz and Roessler 2012). Experiencing a virtual majority on a specific platform agreeing with fringe bubble inhabitants could bolster their confidence to reach outside the bubble. As citizens who inhabit fringe bubbles grow more vocal, their favoured issues seep into the general public sphere.

It can be argued that ideas and attitudes expressed in fringe bubbles hold higher news value because of their novelty and extremity (Harcup and O'Neill 2017). This means that once they have overcome a critical threshold, their issues start to gain visibility in legacy media. In this final step, formerly marginalised issues are amplified in public far beyond their support in the population, which in turn can affect the broader climate of opinion (Benkler et al. 2018). Accordingly, we should observe that the spiral of silence (Noelle-Neumann 1974) is essentially reversed. Rather than being muted, fringe voices are amplified into a spiral of noise.

New vulnerabilities

Second, several recent studies (Thorson et al. 2019; Kümpel 2020; Möller et al. 2019) indicate that media use on social media and through algorithmic filter systems creates new digital inequalities. Hence, the most important echo chamber might not be a left- or right-leaning chamber, but a chamber of those interested in current affairs and politics while others are excluded from much of this information. Through automatic profiling and collaborative filtering, those who are already engaged with politics are likely to see more of that, creating substantial knowledge gaps among those who do not. This is especially concerning since this is also the group of people most vulnerable to attempts to be strategically persuaded through tailored, personalised strategic (dis)information (Zuiderveen Borgesius et al. 2018).

A broader conception of diversity

Third, in the review of literature on filter bubbles and echo chambers, it became clear that both concepts are frequently operationalised as ideological bubbles. The notion of diversity is thus reduced to sorting into exactly two political camps: the liberals and the conservatives. While this is an important question, in particular in electoral systems that favour a two-party system, it falls short in accounting for the multi-faceted role information diversity plays in democratic societies (Helberger 2019). For example, the structure of social networks can contribute to communities around certain topics (Bruns, Burgess, and Highfield 2014; Moeller et al. 2016). So far, very little is known about how these issue publics afforded by social media affect the processes of agenda-setting and the formation of public opinion. Similarly, there is a gap in research on diversity in journalistic genre and style users of social media and algorithmic filter systems encounter. In the future we need to learn more about the informational quality of items exchanged in online communities or prioritised by algorithms for individual users. Do these present a mix of long and short formats, opinion and factual reporting? Do they together give an accurate reflection of the diversity in arguments and actors involved in a specific issue?

Finally, the mismatch of theoretical work and empirical work on echo chambers and filters bubbles might also be a manifestation of a lack of explicit normative research in the field. As the impact of technology on opinion formation and political behaviour is either dreaded or not, the concepts are evaluated from an implicit normative framework about how democracy is supposed to be. To move forward, we need to make this discussion explicit and develop answers to the question of which role social networks and filtering technology should play. This might lead to a more useful answer to the question of whether or the role these technologies are playing at the moment is problematic or not.

Acknowledgment

This work was supported by the Dutch Research Council (NWO) grant nr. VI.Veni.191S.089.

Note

1 This work was supported by the Dutch Research Council (NWO) grant nr. VI.Veni.191S.089.
2 As quoted in an interview with Lynn Parramore in *The Atlantic*. Accessed at www.theatlantic.com/daily-dish/archive/2010/10/the-filter-bubble/181427 (28 April 2020).

References

Adamic, Lada A., and Natalie Glance. 2005. "The Political Blogosphere and the 2004 U.S. Election." *05: Proceedings of the 3rd International Workshop on Link Discovery*: 36–43. https://doi.org/10.1145/1134271.1134277.

Anspach, Nicolas M. 2017. "The New Personal Influence: How Our Facebook Friends Influence the News We Read." *Political Communication* 34 (4): 590–606. https://doi.org/10.1080/10584609.2017.1316329.

Bakshy, Eytan, Solomon Messing, and Lada A. Adamic. 2015. "Exposure to Ideologically Diverse News and Opinion on Facebook." *Science* 348 (6239): 1130–1132. https://doi.org/10.1126/science.aaa1160.

Beam, Michael A., Jeffrey T. Child, Myiah J. Hutchens, and Jay D. Hmielowski. 2018. "Context Collapse and Privacy Management: Diversity in Facebook Friends Increases Online News Reading and Sharing." *New Media & Society* 20 (7): 2296–2314. https://doi.org/10.1177/1461444817714790.

Beam, Michael A., Myiah J. Hutchens, and Jay D. Hmielowski. 2018. "Facebook News and (de)Polarization: Reinforcing Spirals in the 2016 US Election." *Information, Communication & Society* 21 (7): 940–958. https://doi.org/10.1080/1369118X.2018.1444783.

Benkler, Yochai, Robert Faris, and Hal Roberts. 2018. *Network Propaganda: Manipulation, Disinformation, and Radicalization in American Politics*. Oxford: Oxford University Press.

Bozdag, Engin. 2013. "Bias in Algorithmic Filtering and Personalization." *Ethics and Information Technology* 15 (3): 209–227. https://doi.org/10.1007/s10676-013-9321-6.

Bruns, Axel. 2019. *Are Filter Bubbles Real?* 1st edition. Medford, MA: Polity.

Bruns, Axel, Jean Burgess, and Tim Highfield. 2014. "A 'Big Data' Approach to Mapping the Australian Twittersphere." In *Advancing Digital Humanities: Research, Methods, Theories*, edited by Paul Longley Arthur and Katherine Bode, 113–129. London: Palgrave Macmillan. https://doi.org/10.1057/9781137337016_8.

Dubois, Elizabeth, and Grant Blank. 2018. "The Echo Chamber Is Overstated: The Moderating Effect of Political Interest and Diverse Media." *Information, Communication & Society* 21 (5): 729–745. https://doi.org/10.1080/1369118X.2018.1428656.

Dylko, Ivan, Igor Dolgov, William Hoffman, Nicholas Eckhart, Maria Molina, and Omar Aaziz. 2017. "The Dark Side of Technology: An Experimental Investigation of the Influence of Customizability Technology on Online Political Selective Exposure." *Computers in Human Behavior* 73: 181–190, August. https://doi.org/10.1016/j.chb.2017.03.031.

Festinger, Leon. 1957. *A Theory of Cognitive Dissonance*. Stanford, CA: Stanford University Press.

Fletcher, Richard, and Rasmus Kleis Nielsen. 2018. "Are People Incidentally Exposed to News on Social Media? A Comparative Analysis." *New Media & Society* 20 (7): 2450–2468. https://doi.org/10.1177/1461444817724170.

Garimella, Kiran, Gianmarco De Francisci Morales, Aristides Gionis, and Michael Mathioudakis. 2018. "Political Discourse on Social Media: Echo Chambers, Gatekeepers, and the Price of Bipartisanship." *ArXiv:1801.01665 [Cs]*, February. http://arxiv.org/abs/1801.01665.

Groshek, Jacob, and Karolina Koc-Michalska. 2017. "Helping Populism Win? Social Media Use, Filter Bubbles, and Support for Populist Presidential Candidates in the 2016 US Election Campaign." *Information, Communication & Society* 20 (9): 1389–1407. https://doi.org/10.1080/13691 18X.2017.1329334.

Haim, Mario, Andreas Graefe, and Hans-Bernd Brosius. 2018. "Burst of the Filter Bubble?" *Digital Journalism* 6 (3): 330–343. https://doi.org/10.1080/21670811.2017.1338145.

Hallin, Daniel C., and Paolo Mancini. 2004. *Comparing Media Systems: Three Models of Media and Politics*. Cambridge: Cambridge University Press.

Harcup, Tony, and Deirdre O'Neill. 2017. "What Is News?" *Journalism Studies* 18 (12): 1470–1488. https://doi.org/10.1080/1461670X.2016.1150193.

Helberger, Natali. 2019. "On the Democratic Role of News Recommenders." *Digital Journalism* 7 (8): 993–1012. https://doi.org/10.1080/21670811.2019.1623700.

Kitchin, Rob. 2017. "Thinking Critically About and Researching Algorithms." *Information, Communication & Society* 20 (1): 14–29. https://doi.org/10.1080/1369118X.2016.1154087.

Kümpel, Anna Sophie. 2020. "The Matthew Effect in Social Media News Use: Assessing Inequalities in News Exposure and News Engagement on Social Network Sites (SNS)." *Journalism*, April. https://doi.org/10.1177/1464884920915374.

Lazarsfeld, Paul F., and Robert K. Merton. 1954. "Friendship as Social Process: A Substantive and Methodological Analysis." In: M. Berger, T. Abel, and C.H. Page (Hrsg.), *Freedom and Control in Modern Society*. Toronto, New York and London: Van Nostrand, 18–66.

Moeller, Judith, Damian Trilling, Natali Helberger, Kristina Irion, and Claes De Vreese. 2016. "Shrinking Core? Exploring the Differential Agenda Setting Power of Traditional and Personalized News Media." *Info* 18 (6): 26–41. https://doi.org/10.1108/info-05-2016-0020.

Möller, Judith, Robbert Nicolai van de Velde, Lisa Merten, and Cornelius Puschmann. 2019. "Explaining Online News Engagement Based on Browsing Behavior: Creatures of Habit?" *Social Science Computer Review*, February. https://doi.org/10.1177/0894439319828012.

Möller, Judith, Damian Trilling, Natali Helberger, and Bram van Es. 2018. "Do Not Blame It on the Algorithm: An Empirical Assessment of Multiple Recommender Systems and Their Impact on Content Diversity." *Information, Communication & Society* 21 (7): 959–977. https://doi.org/10.1080/13691 18X.2018.1444076.

Nechushtai, Efrat, and Seth C. Lewis. 2019. "What Kind of News Gatekeepers Do We Want Machines to Be? Filter Bubbles, Fragmentation, and the Normative Dimensions of Algorithmic Recommendations." *Computers in Human Behavior* 90: 298–307, January. https://doi.org/10.1016/j.chb.2018.07.043.

Negroponte, Nicholas. 1996. *Being Digital*. New York: Vintage.

Noelle-Neumann, Elisabeth. 1974. "The Spiral of Silence a Theory of Public Opinion." *Journal of Communication* 24 (2): 43–51. https://doi.org/10.1111/j.1460-2466.1974.tb00367.x.

Oswald, M. E., and S. Grosjean. 2004. "Confirmation Bias." *Cognitive Illusions: A Handbook on Fallacies and Biases in Thinking, Judgement and Memory*: 79.

Pariser, Eli. 2011. *The Filter Bubble: What the Internet Is Hiding from You*. New York: Penguin Books.

Puschmann, Cornelius. 2019. "Beyond the Bubble: Assessing the Diversity of Political Search Results." *Digital Journalism* 7 (6): 824–843. https://doi.org/10.1080/21670811.2018.1539626.

Quattrociocchi, Walter, Antonio Scala, and Cass R. Sunstein. 2016. *Echo Chambers on Facebook*. SSRN Scholarly Paper ID 2795110. Rochester, NY: Social Science Research Network. https://papers.ssrn.com/abstract=2795110.

Schulz, Anne, and Patrick Roessler. 2012. "The Spiral of Silence and the Internet: Selection of Online Content and the Perception of the Public Opinion Climate in Computer-Mediated Communication Environments." *International Journal of Public Opinion Research* 24 (3): 346–367. https://doi.org/10.1093/ijpor/eds022.

Smith, Naomi, and Tim Graham. 2019. "Mapping the Anti-Vaccination Movement on Facebook." *Information, Communication & Society* 22 (9): 1310–1327. https://doi.org/10.1080/1369118X.2017.1418406.

Steininger, Rudolf. 1977. "Pillarization (Verzuiling) and Political Parties." *Sociologische Gids* 24 (4): 242–257.

Stroud, Natalie Jomini. 2010. "Polarization and Partisan Selective Exposure." *Journal of Communication* 60 (3): 556–576. https://doi.org/10.1111/j.1460-2466.2010.01497.x.

Sunstein, Cass R. 2001. *Republic.Com*. Princeton, NJ: Princeton University Press.

Thorson, Kjerstin, Kelley Cotter, Mel Medeiros, and Chankyung Pak. 2019. "Algorithmic Inference, Political Interest, and Exposure to News and Politics on Facebook." *Information, Communication & Society*: 1–18. https://doi.org/10.1080/1369118X.2019.1642934.

Vaccari, Cristian, Augusto Valeriani, Pablo Barberá, John T. Jost, Jonathan Nagler, and Joshua A. Tucker. 2016. "Of Echo Chambers and Contrarian Clubs: Exposure to Political Disagreement Among German and Italian Users of Twitter." *Social Media + Society* 2 (3). https://doi.org/10.1177/2056305116664221.

Walker, S., D. Mercea, and M. T. Bastos. 2019. "The Disinformation Landscape and the Lockdown of Social Platforms." *Information, Communication and Society* 22 (11): 1531–1543. https://doi.org/10.1080/1369118X.2019.1648536.

Weeks, Brian E., Thomas B. Ksiazek, and R. Lance Holbert. 2016. "Partisan Enclaves or Shared Media Experiences? A Network Approach to Understanding Citizens' Political News Environments." *Journal of Broadcasting & Electronic Media* 60 (2): 248–268. https://doi.org/10.1080/08838151.2016.1164170.

Williams, Hywel T. P., James R. McMurray, Tim Kurz, and F. Hugo Lambert. 2015. "Network Analysis Reveals Open Forums and Echo Chambers in Social Media Discussions of Climate Change." *Global Environmental Change* 32: 126–138, May. https://doi.org/10.1016/j.gloenvcha.2015.03.006.

Wojcieszak, Magdalena Elzbieta. 2011. "Computer-Mediated False Consensus: Radical Online Groups, Social Networks and News Media." *Mass Communication and Society* 14 (4): 527–546. https://doi.org/10.1080/15205436.2010.513795.

Wojcieszak, Magdalena Elzbieta, and Vincent Price. 2009. "What Underlies the False Consensus Effect? How Personal Opinion and Disagreement Affect Perception of Public Opinion." *International Journal of Public Opinion Research* 21 (1): 25–46. https://doi.org/10.1093/ijpor/edp001.

Yang, Tian, Silvia Majo-Vazquez, Rasmus Kleis Nielsen, and Sandra González-Bailón. 2020. *Exposure to News Grows Less Fragmented with Increase in Mobile Access*. SSRN Scholarly Paper ID 3564826. Rochester, NY: Social Science Research Network. https://doi.org/10.2139/ssrn.3564826.

Zuiderveen Borgesius, Frederik, Judith Moeller, Sanne Kruikemeier, Ronan Ó Fathaigh, Kristina Irion, Tom Dobber, Balázs Bodó, and Claes H. de Vreese. 2018. *Online Political Microtargeting: Promises and Threats for Democracy*. SSRN Scholarly Paper ID 3128787. Rochester, NY: Social Science Research Network. https://papers.ssrn.com/abstract=3128787.

Zuiderveen-Borgesius, Frederik, Damian Trilling, Judith Möller, Balázs Bodó, Claes H. de Vreese, and Natali Helberger. 2016. "Should We Worry About Filter Bubbles?" *Internet Policy Review*, March. https://policyreview.info/articles/analysis/should-we-worry-about-filter-bubbles.

9

DISPUTES OVER OR AGAINST REALITY?

Fine-graining the textures of post-truth politics

Susana Salgado

What if...?

Imagine a (not-so-far) dystopian world where relativism was so prevalent that any consensus about facts and policy, and thus accountability, was virtually impossible. Now, add to that unlimited means and freedom of expression. Everyone could say absolutely anything without any filter or barrier. One of the consequences of the impossibility of distinguishing between reliable and fake information could be rampant levels of disconnection and apathy, which would certainly compromise a functional democracy. By the same token, debates would not make any sense as everyone would primarily follow their own beliefs rather than negotiating the expression of thoughts to a common ground of understanding problems and facts. Such a scenario would result, in practice, in the impossibility of democracy, due to absolute freedom of expression and lack of shared norms and a common ground of reality to stand on. The organisation of these societies would be based on a system that discouraged the idea of control and would thus be closer to an actual anarchy where no one would ever trust anyone who had any kind of expertise, particularly if it would mean contradicting previous beliefs. The absence of a value assigned to authoritative sources of information or to other symbolic control rules would ultimately translate into a state of institutionalised disorder, which would render virtually impossible any shared ground of perception, experience, or understanding.

The description of this imaginary situation also exposes one of the many paradoxes of democracy: are we all really equal? Here, that is to ask if uninformed and misinformed opinions should count the same as the ones from (more) informed citizens. If so, who gets to decide what is good or bad information and who is informed or misinformed in a world with outright relativism? And, more importantly, would such selection even be democratic? These considerations relate closely with what is known as the "elitist view of democracy" (e.g. Schubert, Dye and Zeigler 2015), which upholds fundamental differences between the common citizen and the elites in terms of capacity to rule and, at an elemental level, even to understand the democratic political processes. This could then lead to situations in which voters would prefer those political leaders who presented themselves as part of the people and displayed anti-system views of politics: in sum, those with a stated disparagement of traditional structures.

All this underlines the fact that, without mechanisms to ensure common basic references for the significance of and procedures for gathering and reporting information that relies on

101

fact-based, accurate reports rather than on fabricated and deceptive accounts of reality, the practice of democracy would become unsustainable. What would follow in that extreme situation is left to an exercise of our greater or lesser imagination, but the current state of affairs already provides some clues. An intensification of the present-day pervasiveness of social media platforms as information tools and of the rising levels of relativism in post-modern societies, both in terms of prevalence and toleration, could actually lead to the dystopian reality just described. It is not for nothing that the term *post-truth* has been put forward to describe the current era.

Post-truth: what it is (and what it entails)

Post-truth era (e.g. Keyes 2004; Levitin 2017; McIntyre 2018; Farkas and Schou 2020) is one of a number of expressions that have been used to characterise the current state of affairs; examples of other relevant terms include 'post-truth order' (Harsin 2015), 'the misinformation age' (e.g. O'Connor and Weatherall 2019), 'post-factual democracies' (e.g. Hendricks and Vestergaard 2019), 'ersatz reality' (Pomerantsev 2019), and 'infocalypse' (Schick 2020), among other close variations. The underlying meaning is very similar as these terms all draw attention to the idea that we live in a time in which facts seem to matter less than opinions and in which traditional authoritative sources seem to have lost most of their importance in the face of the democratisation of access to online publication tools, such as social media. The *Oxford Dictionary*'s word of the year in 2016 was *post-truth*, and for Dictionary.com, the word of the year in 2018 was *misinformation*. The first term highlights that objective facts have become less influential in shaping public opinion than appeals to emotion and personal belief while the second term refers to the increasing prevalence of false information that is spread, regardless of whether there is intent to mislead. Public discourse is influenced by a plethora of information (including biased, fake, offensive, etc.) that, despite of the different status and credibility of sources, is usually treated as equivalent in online environments. Moreover, how content spreads has gone through drastic transformations with the rise of social media. It spreads faster than ever.

Attempts to distort the truth and facts are by no means a new phenomenon in history, including in the history of democracy, but coupled with rising relativism and technological development, they have become more sophisticated and harder to detect and are being undertaken by an unprecedented number of actors. The credibility of facts has been increasingly under pressure due not just to the pervasive relativism of our post-modern times but also to media environments that are increasingly being defined by the logics of social media and algorithms that give users more of their preferences, prioritise shocking and polarising content, and function as content accelerators. Conditions such as these propitiate and magnify the dissemination of propaganda, fake news, and disinformation in general. Additionally, technologies used to distort reality (e.g. deepfakes) are evolving at a fast pace and substantially faster than the capacity to understand and control their effects on politics and society.

Even though intents to deceive in politics are not especially new and have been around ever since there have been attempts to persuade others, the technological setup favours new actors to take advantage of these conditions. And the impact on democracy of such a combination of elements has already proved to be particularly unsettling. A non-exhaustive list of examples that have already occurred include unauthorised access to users' private information to develop targeted misinformation campaigns or meddle in elections, computational propaganda, and fake political activism. Some of these campaigns aim at influencing and polarising opinions; a common strategy is to change the environment in which those opinions are formed, and decisions are made: hence, the relevance of the wide spread of misinformation.

What 'post-truth era' and other analogous terms thus describe is a time when (more than ever before) we are regularly exposed to all sorts of sensationalised, misleading, and false content, such as fake news, conspiracy theories, bogus claims, rumours, computational propaganda, disinformation campaigns assisted by trolls, targeted misinformation campaigns, fake political activism, synthetic media, et cetera. This kind of information environment downgrades the value of the truth and erodes authenticity and the integrity of reliable content and sources. There are disputes over the validity of almost everything (including proven scientific facts and the actual occurrence of events in history). But more than that, there is a constant battle to define reality that is often supported in this type of content.

The blurring of facts and fiction caused by the manipulation of discourses, images, and sounds is now carried out not only by humans directly but also through efficient artificial intelligence devices. Already materialised examples include fictitious videos with statements by political leaders that never happened or with details about an event that never took place (to influence domestic or foreign policy or to discredit an opponent, for example). AI-powered bots can now also compete with humans to influence agendas and decisions. These new, increasingly sophisticated technological tools have already proved their efficacy in creating climates of opinion, manipulating perceptions, stretching the boundaries of online behaviours and discourses, and falsifying reality. Just the knowledge that this type of technology exists and can be used is already enough to cast doubt on everything, including on what is real. In itself this also contributes to eroding the integrity of facts and, hence, the truth.

The traditional sources of information also have had their authority further undermined in this media environment. In fact, although it is not the only cause of deepening distrust, it has lowered considerably trust in what used to once be respected sources of factual information (e.g. Kavanagh and Rich 2018; Marietta and Barker 2019). Authoritative sources (in all areas of knowledge and expertise) have an important role as benchmarks for what is reality, for the identification of problems and solutions for those problems. Journalists, elected politicians, scientists, and other experts, for example, have taken this role in democracy and have framed issues and guided democratic debates. However, media and audience developments, in particular those related to social media platforms' use for access to information, allow for calling everything into question by circulating large amounts of conflicting information.

On social media, the views and news postings of family, friends, and even acquaintances now have more potential to be influential than the statements of journalists or pundits (Bode and Vraga 2018). By prioritising individual opinions and content posted by the users' friends and family over professional news outlets (with the justification that this is what people really want to see), some social media platforms have, in fact, contributed directly to this state of things. With such logic, principles, and procedures, they are reiterating distrust of authoritative, informational sources and thus also indirectly undermining the journalism industry's business model. Journalism has had historically an important role in the construction of the common ground for public debate. However, this role is influenced by commercial goals, as well as by media effects, such as agenda-setting, priming, and framing, all of which have often led to questioning the true mission and value of journalists. Uscinski (2014) posits that news has become a commodity bought and sold on the market; journalists report certain issues over others in response to ratings, polls, and audience demographics and not necessarily because audiences need to know them or need to be informed about them to ensure democratic values.

Mainstream news media outlets have also been accused of being too close to power and too remote from the citizens' concerns (for example, the well-known attacks on journalism by populists, among others) (e.g. Bennett and Pfetsch 2018), which has caused some to predict the revival of local news sources (e.g. Fowler-Watt and Jukes 2019; Sullivan 2020) as a response to this lack of proximity to citizens and as an effort to suppress fake news. Despite the social media logic and the fact that some politicians have exploited distrust of the media to actively undermine the role of journalism in democracy, it cannot be ignored that a commonly agreed set of facts (reported by independent journalism) was and continues to be the foundation of a functioning, healthy democracy. As Pickard (2019) explains, without a viable, strong news media system, democracy is reduced to an unattainable ideal. Additionally, downgrading authoritative informational sources paves the way for the spread of uninformed accounts and all kinds of misinformation (e.g. Bennett and Livingstone 2018).

In this type of environment, misleading narratives frequently become the basis for debate and political opinion formation. Moreover, and according to Edelman (2001), public discourses of democracy tend to be populistic, as typical problem definitions and solutions do not usually encourage popular understanding or involvement in politics. The deepening distrust of all kind of authorities relates closely to populism. Much has already been written about populism in recent years, and the purpose here is not to revisit this prolific literature; however, it makes sense to briefly ascertain how populism interacts with misinformation and post-truth environments.

In a book of essays about 'backward phenomena', Umberto Eco (2014) identifies cases of revolutionary and reactionary populism but sees an extraordinary resemblance between the two types: populism 'is a method that plays on the visceral attraction of what are believed to be the most deeply entrenched opinions or prejudices of the masses' (2014, 146). Such interpretation of populism opens the way to the acknowledgement of its varied (sometimes even contradictory) current forms and its fluid connection with ideology, but obliquely, it also underlines the appeal to emotions, such as the resurgence of old polemics that had been resolved long ago (e.g. the anti-Darwinian stance or the anti-vaxxer movement) and the open expression of attitudes that fall outside political correctness norms (e.g. racist, xenophobic, and misogynous attitudes). But most importantly, this links to the aforementioned decreasing trust in authorities, coupled with a mindset that encourages convincing others by any means, even if that entails bending the facts to extract a predetermined meaning.

This is close to what Frankfurt (2005) defines as 'bullshit', which in itself is slightly different from lying, according to him. 'Bullshitters' do not care about what is true and false in their assertions. They use ideas to suit their purposes. They seek to convey a certain image, and this goal justifies distorting reality and not being concerned about whether anything at all is true. While here any claims about truth and falsehood are completely irrelevant, the liar, by lying, at least acknowledges the existence of the truth. Green (2019) explored the connections between populism and the rhetoric of bullshit and identified different performative values in the use of this type of rhetoric in populism. The exclusivity of the populists' claim to popular representation means that they overlook evidence and thus tend to bullshit whenever confronted with what is contradictory. Hendricks and Vestergaard (2019) clarify how isolated facts and news may be cherry-picked to support a populist argument and that if facts run counter the core narrative, they are left out or reasoned away as not valid (e.g. statistics are rejected whenever they contradict claims or agendas), and conspiracy theories are presented to explain that the facts are being manipulated.

Populism and conspiracy theories do seem to resonate well with each other. Haranovitch (2011) shows how a conspiracy theory is often populist: namely, when it suggests that actions were undertaken by an elite against the people. Actually, most conspiracy theories tend to fit populist narratives very well because they accuse elites and posit Manichean views in which political competitors are considered enemies of the people (Uscinski 2020). The ideas that political elites ignore the interests of the people in favour of their own and that the establishment is corrupt and inefficient are commonplaces in populism and in conspiracy theories. New forms of conspiracism even avoid the burden of explanation and simply impose their own reality through repetition (Muirhead and Rosenblum 2019). Both the conspiracy and populist rhetoric appeal to a similar logic: the manipulation of misconceptions. And the fact that populist political leaders circumvent all kinds of mediation and prefer to communicate directly with the people means that their views can spread without any type of verification of the narratives put forward and then shared. Political motivations are thus accelerating the post-truth era. In fact, populism blends well with most of the noted 'communication disorders'.

Why this state of things?

Even though political motivations have been at the core of the erosion of truth in our societies, the post-truth era is not simply a by-product of populism (Salgado 2018). It is impossible to attribute these developments to one single reason. Instead, a number of factors have contributed to the decline of the importance of the truth and to an increased emphasis on duelling fact perceptions driven by emotions and misinformation. Lewandowsky, Ecker, and Cook (2017) see the post-truth era as a result of societal mega-trends, such as a decline in social capital, growing economic inequality, increased polarisation, declining trust in science, and an increasingly fractionated media landscape.

This is an era in which emotions seem increasingly to matter more than facts. Objective facts are often less influential in shaping opinions than appeals to emotions and beliefs (e.g. in different types of populist discourse, in which the resort to emotions, such as the exploitation of fear and resentment, always outweighs reasoned arguments). In this sense, we could say that post-truth politics is more a symptom of the current social and political status of the truth than it is their cause (Salgado 2018).

The current changes to the status of the truth are partly explained by the relativism of the post-modern age that emerged as a response to the unified, definite meanings and universal truths of the modern age (see, e.g. Foucault [1969] 2002 or Lyotard [1979] 1991). Post-modernism questions these ideas and values of modernism and proposes a relativism of the truth (and facts) that lies deep in intersubjectivity and in upholding diversity as an aim in itself. 'The difference between modernity and post-modernity lies precisely in the proposal of an ontology of reality versus a construction of reality, that is, if reality pre-exists to be discovered or if it is instead constructed through subjective discourse and interpretation' (Salgado 2018, 321).

In the post-modern world, reality does not pre-exist its interpretation; reality is the negotiation of meaning in each individual that results from the interplay of different factors, including identity, personal experience and beliefs, and type of media exposure and use. Reality is thus developed in relation to a specific context and to individual features and assessments. Consequently, not only moral norms (good and bad, right and wrong, etc.) but also what is considered truth and untruth depends on the context and is subject to diverse, often competing interpretations and meanings. This ultimately means that there is no absolute or definite truth and that knowledge and values are constructed through discourse and experience (see, e.g. Rorty 1991).

Such an ethos spurs and gives rise to the co-existence of a wide range of (often contradictory) interpretations of reality and values, which ultimately make the entire search for the truth a meaningless process as there are several truths and not just one truth. In this respect, post-modernism perfectly accounts for the post-truth mindset. This approach to reality and knowledge affects the value of the truth and the perception of facts and also has a decisive impact on democratic politics. There have always been different ideological and partisan positions in democratic politics, but they would proceed from a shared basis in fact. A society in which there is no agreed body of facts renders democratic decision-making virtually impossible.

These are changes that are still unfolding in time, and, in some cases, elements of modernity subsist in post-modernity (see, e.g. Giddens 1990), but there is nevertheless a noticeable change in contemporary Western societies that adheres to growing levels of relativism in different aspects of life, including politics. We are now very likely to find cases in which knowledge and belief and truth and falsehood are completely blurred.

Before the so-called post-truth era, there was the belief that the truth was out there to be found and that there were mechanisms based on factual objectivity (e.g. scientific method, journalistic procedures) to assist those interested in that pursuit. Now, underpinned by technological advancements, the notions of relativism and subjectivity have been expanded to all domains, including facts and information. The growing relativism of the truth (and facts) in our societies could thus lead to situations in which there is no common understanding of basic facts as their meaning results from the negotiable expression of identities, experiences, opinions, and preferences. This shift in paradigm and the ensuing consequences for information could lead to information ecosystems in which diversity (diversity here does not necessarily mean plurality) is valued and enhanced, but quality does not need to be necessarily part of the equation, particularly if it is achieved at the expense of diversity.

Implications are also noted for moral and ethics standards because they are interpreted according to context and thus become relative to specific points of view. There is much more flexibility in the meaning that is attributed to virtually everything, which is also what Bauman (2007) refers to as 'liquid' times. This applies to discourses about scientific facts as well (e.g. global warming and climate change, vaccination) and to politics, which may pose important ethical dilemmas, particularly when it impacts not only on political discourses but also on ways of governing and political action in general.

Much of what is considered post-truth politics is thus explained by the post-modern cultural ethos, but it is also related to known features of politics and political propaganda that have been amplified by technology, in particular social media (Salgado 2018). The internet and the digital culture have caused and intensification and amplification of some of the main features of post-modernism, and the pace of change has accelerated significantly, which has led some scholars to suggest new terms to designate the era in which we currently live in (e.g. Nealon's [2012] notion of post-post-modernism). In politics, several of post-truth's most notable features are actually old attributes. There are important political precedents behind the post-truth era: lies, rumours, deceits, and manipulation tactics have been used to shape public opinion throughout history (Salgado 2005).

There is even a long-standing debate on whether deception is good or bad for politics. Particularly for those sceptical of democracy, deception is seen as an inherent part of politics; it is not only fully justifiable but also necessary (Robinson et al. 2018). But even the most enthusiastic democrat recognises, once in a while, the necessity of governments and political leaders lying and using deception in specific circumstances. Election campaigns (and other situations of political competition) are moments in democracy that are commonly noted for stretching the boundaries of truth and facts as political candidates usually go the extra mile to convince voters, but crises, in foreign affairs or domestic politics, are deemed to justify the use of deception by governments.

The work of spin doctors and other political communication professionals is specifically related to conveying favourable interpretations of events to the media and the public (e.g. Louw 2010; Salgado 2014). Shaping the information environment and preparing the climate of opinion for the announcement of decisions often mean resorting to tactics that are not transparent and based on authenticity, or even to deception. The use of these tactics entails the selection and framing of information that is presented in ways that are meant to be, first and foremost, convincing and appealing. Notwithstanding the excesses that tend to occur due to loose interpretations of what the limits should be, such strategies are considered part of the normal functioning of democracy in today's societies. Robinson et al. (2018) refer to 'organised political communication' and to the use of deception by lying, omission, distortion, or misdirection.

While politicians produce strategically advantageous interpretations of reality, citizens' perceptions are also shaped by their choice of medium (Logan 2004) and political preferences (e.g. Bartels 2002; Jerit and Barabas 2012; Hochschild and Einstein 2015). Biased political communication with the purpose of promoting a specific position – that is to say, hypes and propaganda – acts upon the individuals' pre-existent political preferences (e.g. political interest and sophistication, ideology, partisan attachment) and psychological mechanisms that are known to affect perceptions and attitudes. It is, for example, the case of selective attention, prior-belief bias, affective bias, and motivated reasoning processes. By choosing content that confirms their beliefs while avoiding and denying what is divergent and conflicting, individuals tend to expose themselves to, process, and evaluate information in a biased manner. Selective attention is a well-known mechanism in cognitive psychology that basically explains that because individuals cannot focus on everything all the time, they focus on what matters the most to them (e.g. Graf and Aday 2008). Motivated reasoning basically means that people's goals and predispositions influence how they interpret information (Kunda 1990; Petersen et al. 2013; Stanley et al. 2020). Perceptual biases are shortcuts that individuals use to make sense of the world. Because they are shortcuts, they only provide a partial understanding and may thus be misleading. For example, politically motivated reasoning makes individuals view politics through the narrow lenses of ideology and partisanship. In a polarised context (among others), people are likely to see their choices as right and good and to evaluate the choices that are different from theirs as wrong and bad. On the demand side, these shortcuts influence information exposure when individuals seek information that supports their beliefs and preference, while on the supply side, resources are devoted to shaping the information environment.

And what now?

In his essays, Eco (2014) suggests that history got tired of leaping forward and has been trying to catch its breath, contemplating the 'splendours of tradition'. This could be an interesting image of the consequences of introducing dramatic changes in the media too quickly into society. In fact, most accelerated disruptions that have occurred throughout history have immediately triggered opposite, strong reactions against them. This becomes the perfect breeding ground for the rise of polarised views, which tend to rely on relativism and misinformation to assert the value of their positions. As Lewandowsky et al. explain, 'the framing of the current post-truth malaise as "misinformation" that can be corrected or debunked fails to capture the full scope of the problem' (2017, 4).

The use of online media to spread fake information as a deliberate strategy to gain advantage in political conflicts or to reinforce beliefs and polarise opinions is closely related to post-truth politics. The same holds true for disseminating emotional, confrontational, highly charged political discourse. All this is propelled by the distrust of facts presented by authorities and a growing structural relativism that leads to facts being treated as matters of opinion. The immediate outcome is that it becomes more difficult to share and rely on common understandings of reality.

Given that new forms of producing, spreading, and organising information and of connecting individuals have precipitated much of what is now known as the post-truth era, not to mention that (for commercial reasons) online platforms are organised in ways that favour sensationalist, misleading, and polarising information, it seems natural (and pressing) to reflect on the effects of the particulars of these media landscapes on democracy in order in devise possible ways forward.

We have just started to experience the disruptive social and political effects of the internet and of the social media platforms in particular. While the internet has made spreading any idea easier than ever before, different forms of harmful content and misinformation have become rather common in online environments. Sophisticated computer algorithms curate the information available in specific, purposeful ways, but they also collect and analyse data about users that is then exploited in various ways to influence those same users.

Consequently, social media platforms have been facing growing pressure from governments and from users to address the problems, in particular those related to hate speech and fake news. Censorship and surveillance of online environments have been put forward as possible means to tackle these problems, but this type of solution is not generally supported in democratic countries as it would resemble the practice of an authoritarian state and would collide with the fundamental right of freedom of expression in particular. Nevertheless, action must be taken to ensure that the internet and social media platforms are compatible with all the other democratic values.

References

Bartels, L.M. (2002) Beyond the Running Tally: Partisan Bias in Political Perceptions. *Political Behavior* 24: 117–150.

Bauman, Z. (2007) *Liquid Times: Living in an Age of Uncertainty*. Cambridge: Polity Press.

Bennett, W.L., and Livingstone, S. (2018) The Disinformation Order: Disruptive Communication and the Decline of Democratic Institutions. *European Journal of Communication*, 33(2): 122–139.

Bennett, W.L., and Pfetsch, B. (2018) Rethinking Political Communication in a Time of Disrupted Public Spheres. *Journal of Communication*, 68(2): 243–253.

Bode, L., and Vraga, E.K. (2018) Studying Politics Across Media. *Political Communication* 35(1): 1–7.

Eco, U. (2014) *Turning Back the Clock: Hot Wars and Media Populism*. New York: Random House.

Edelman, M. (2001) *The Politics of Misinformation*. Cambridge: Cambridge University Press.

Farkas, J., and Schou, J. (2020) *Post-Truth, Fake News and Democracy: Mapping the Politics of Falsehood*. New York and Oxon: Routledge.

Foucault, M. ([1969] 2002) *Archeology of Knowledge*. Oxon: Routledge.

Fowler-Watt, K., and Jukes, S. (2019) *New Journalisms: Rethinking Practice, Theory and Pedagogy*. London and New York: Routledge.

Frankfurt, H.G. (2005) *On Bullshit*. Princeton, NJ: Princeton University Press.

Giddens, A. (1990) *The Consequences of Modernity*. Stanford, CA: Stanford University Press.

Graf, J., and Aday, S. (2008) Selective Attention to Online Political Information. *Journal of Broadcasting & Electronic Media*, 52(1): 86–100.

Green, A. (2019) *Speaking Bullshit to Power: Populism and the Rhetoric of Bullshit*. SSRN. http://dx.doi.org/10.2139/ssrn.3382161.

Haronovitch, D. (2011) *Voodoo Histories: The Role of Conspiracy Theory in Shaping Modern History*. New York: Riverhead.

Harsin, J. (2015) Regimes of Posttruth, Postpolitics, and Attention Economies. *Communication, Culture & Critique*, 8(2): 327–333.

Hendricks, V.F., and Vestergaard, M. (2019) *Reality Lost: Markets of Attention, Misinformation and Manipulation*. Cham: Springer.

Hochschild, J.L., and Einstein, K.L. (2015) *Do Facts Matter? Information and Misinformation in American Politics*. Norman: University of Oklahoma Press.

Jerit, J., and Barabas, J. (2012) Partisan Perceptual Bias and the Information Environment. *The Journal of Politics*, 74(3): 672–684.

Kavanagh, J., and Rich, M.D. (2018) *Truth Decay: An Initial Exploration of the Diminishing Role of Facts and Analysis in American Public Life*. Santa Monica, CA: RAND Corporation.

Keyes, R. (2004) *The Post-Truth Era: Dishonesty and Deception in Contemporary Life*. New York: St. Martin's Press.

Kunda, Z. (1990) The Case for Motivated Reasoning. *Psychological Bulletin*, 108(3): 480–498.

Levitin, D.J. (2017) *Weaponized Lies: How to Think Critically in the Post-Truth Era*. New York: Dutton.

Lewandowsky, S., Ecker, U.K.H., and Cook, J. (2017) Beyond Misinformation: Understanding and Coping with the "Post-Truth" Era. *Journal of Applied Research in Memory and Cognition*, 6(4): 353–369. https://doi.org/10.1016/j.jarmac.2017.07.008

Logan, R.K. (2004) *The Sixth Language: Learning a Living in the Internet Age*. Caldwell, NJ: Blackburn Press.

Louw, E. (2010) *The Media and Political Process*, 2nd edition. London and Thousand Oaks, CA: Sage.

Lyotard, J.-F. ([1979] 1991) *The Post-Modern Condition: A Report on Knowledge*. Minneapolis: University of Minnesota Press.

Marietta, M., and Barker, D.C. (2019) *One Nation, Two Realities: Dueling Facts in American Democracy*. Oxford and New York: Oxford University Press.

McIntyre, L. (2018) *Post-Truth*. Cambridge, MA: The MIT Press.

Muirhead, R. and Rosenblum, N. (2019) *A Lot of People Are Saying: The New Conspiracism and the Assault on Democracy*. Princeton, NJ: Princeton University Press.

Nealon, J.T. (2012) *Post-Postmodernism: Or, The Cultural Logic of Just-in-Time Capitalism*. Stanford, CA: Stanford University Press.

O'Connor, C., and Weatherall, J.O. (2019) *The Misinformation Age: How False Beliefs Spread*. New Haven and London: Yale University Press.

Petersen, M.B., Skov, M., Serritzlew, S., and Ramsoy, T. (2013) Motivated Reasoning and Political Parties: Evidence for Increased Processing in the Face of Party Cues. *Political Behavior*, 35: 831–854. https://doi.org/10.1007/s11109-012-9213-1

Pickard, V. (2019) *Democracy Without Journalism? Confronting the Misinformation Society*. New York: Oxford University Press.

Pomerantsev, P. (2019) *This Is Not Propaganda: Adventures in the War Against Reality*. New York: PublicAffairs.

Robinson, P., Miller, D. Herring, E., and Bakir, V. (2018) Lying and Deception in Politics. In J. Meibauer (Ed.), *The Oxford Handbook of Lying*. Oxford Handbooks Online. www.oxfordhandbooks.com/view/10.1093/oxfordhb/9780198736578.001.0001/oxfordhb-9780198736578-e-42?print

Rorty, R. (1991) *Objectivity, Relativism, and Truth*. Cambridge: Cambridge University Press.

Salgado, S. (2005) O poder da comunicação ou a comunicação do poder (The Power of Communication or the Communication of Power). *Media & Jornalismo*, 7: 79–94.

Salgado, S. (2014) The Media of Political Communication. In C. Reinemann (Ed.), *Political Communication Volume of the Handbook of Communication Sciences (HOCS)*. Berlin: De Gruyter Mouton Pub. 269–288.

Salgado, S. (2018) Online Media Impact on Politics: Views on Post-Truth Politics and Post-Postmodernism. *International Journal of Media and Cultural Politics*, 14(3): 317–331.

Schick, N. (2020) *Deep Fakes and the Infocalypse: What you Urgently Need to Know*. London: Monoray.

Schubert, L., Dye, T.R., and Zeigler, H. (2015) *The Irony of Democracy: An Uncommon Introduction to American Politics*, 17th edition. Wadsworth: Cengage Learning.

Stanley, M.L., Henne, P., Yang, B.W., and De Brigard, F. (2020) Resistance to Position Change, Motivated Reasoning, and Polarization. *Political Behavior*, 42, 891–913. https://doi.org/10.1007/s11109-019-09526-z

Sullivan, M. (2020) *Ghosting the News: Local Journalism and the Crisis of American Democracy*. New York: Columbia Global Reports.

Uscinski, J.E. (2014) *The People's News: Media, Politics, and the Demands of Capitalism*. New York and London: New York University Press.

Uscinski, J.E. (2020) *Conspiracy Theories: A Primer*. Lanham: Rowman & Littlefield.

10

FAKE NEWS

Edson C. Tandoc Jr.

Fake news has attracted a lot of scholarly attention. A quick search for the term on Google Scholar yields more than 30,000 results published between 2016 and 2019, with most studies examining how fake news is characterised, created, circulated, and countered (Bente 2018). Fake news articles range from something as harmless as reporting that an 83-year-old woman had trained 65 cats to steal valuable items from her neighbours (Palma 2017) to something as serious as spreading false information about kidnappers descending on small villages in India, which triggered a spate of mob killings perpetrated by angry residents (Frayer 2018). Social media companies, which have borne much of the blame for the spread of fake news through their platforms, have taken actions, such as limiting how often a message can be forwarded, deleting accounts that share fake news, and partnering with third-party fact-checkers to debunk fake news (Dixit 2019; Frenkel 2018). Governments around the world have also passed legislation to combat the spread of fake news (Funke 2018). For example, Singapore passed a law empowering ministers to require individuals, social media companies, and even internet service providers to correct or take down fake news posts that threaten public interest (Singapore 2019). But what, to begin with, is fake news?

Defining fake news

Fake news is not a new term. Studies in the past used the term to label a range of messages, such as news satires and parodies. For example, studies had labelled political satires on television, such as *The Daily Show*, which rose to popularity in the early 2000s, as fake news programmes. These programmes engage in political commentary based on facts, often delivered with humour or exaggeration, using formats and techniques associated with real television news programmes, such as using a news anchor and doing live reports. However, some scholars questioned early on whether this was an appropriate label for such programmes. In an analysis of *The Daily Show*, Baym (2005, 268) argued that the combination of comedy and political commentary in the programme constituted instead 'a new form of critical journalism, one which uses satire to achieve that which the mainstream press is no longer willing to pursue'. Others also used the term to refer to news parodies, such as *The Onion*, a popular website that publishes mostly fictitious entries written in news formats. In parodying news, these sites call attention to the excesses of real news organisations, such as engaging in sensationalism and clickbaiting. Thus,

Berkowitz and Schwartz (2016, 13) argued that 'fake-news organizations have come to serve as a Fifth Estate watching over the mainstream journalism institution'.

The 2016 United States presidential election saw a resurgence of the 'fake news' term but applied to a different set of messages. A quick look at Google Trends, which tracks how frequently a search term is sought via its search engine in comparison to the total search volume within a particular span of time, shows that searches for 'fake news' started to increase in October 2016, when the United States presidential campaign was in full swing. News reports documented cases of viral social media posts about the campaign, propagating lies while disguising themselves as real news articles. A famous example is a fake news article that wrongly reported that Pope Francis, the leader of the Catholic church, had endorsed then-candidate Donald Trump (Silverman 2016). Not all fake news posts are political. Others are downright ridiculous. For example, one of the most viral fake news posts in 2016 was about a woman who supposedly defecated on her boss's desk after she won the lottery (Silverman 2016).

Contemporary use of the term *fake news* applies it to falsehoods packaged to look like news to deceive people. For example, Allcott and Gentzkow (2017, 213) defined fake news as 'news articles that are intentionally and verifiably false, and could mislead readers' while Rochlin (2017, 388) defined it as 'a knowingly false headline and story [that] is written and published on a website that is designed to look like a real news site, and is spread via social media'. Tandoc et al. (2017) reviewed the different ways the term has been used in communication studies and identified two main components of fake news definitions: the level of facticity and the main intention behind the message. Facticity refers to 'the degree to which fake news relies on facts' while intention refers to 'the degree to which the creator of fake news intends to mislead' (Tandoc et al. 2017, 147). For example, in terms of facticity, political satires tend to be high while news parodies tend to be low; both, however, have low levels of intention to deceive. Satires and parodies depend on the audiences' acknowledgement of their news formats being fake for the humour to work; they also often come with disclaimers that they do not produce real news (Tandoc et al. 2017; Rashkin et al. 2017). Thus, Tandoc et al. (2017) argued that satires and parodies do not fall under the contemporary definition of fake news, echoing earlier questions about the use of the term to refer to these messages (Baym 2005; Berkowitz and Schwartz 2016).

Situating fake news

The rise of fake news is also marked by several related terms, such as *misinformation* and *disinformation*. Singapore's anti–fake news law refers to 'online falsehoods and manipulation' (Singapore 2019).

Wardle (2017) distinguished between misinformation and disinformation. While these two terms both refer to the dissemination of false information, *misinformation* refers to inadvertent sharing while *disinformation* refers to intentional dissemination of false information (Wardle 2017). Such distinction makes the role of intentionality particularly salient. For example, studies on fake news identified two main types of intention: financial and ideological. The now-infamous teens in a small town in Macedonia who operated websites that pushed fake news stories were motivated by making money from the ad revenues their websites were getting from pushing out outrageous and false content online (Subramanian 2017). Writing fake stories required no legwork and, hence, no substantial operational costs. Other creators of fake news were clearly motivated by ideological reasons, such as influencing voting decisions and, hence, electoral outcomes (Albright 2016).

It is important, however, to distinguish between motivations for creating fake news stories on one hand and sharing fake news stories on the other. Studies have documented that some people share fake news not primarily to deceive others. Some people share fake news to humour friends, warn loved ones, or show others they care, without necessarily realising they were sharing something that was false; others share fake news hoping someone will confirm or debunk it for them (Tandoc et al. 2018). Therefore, while a piece of fake news can be categorised as a form of disinformation – intentionally created with the main purpose of deceiving others either for profit or for propaganda – based on the intention behind its production, its subsequent spread through social media users might be unintentional.

Fake news is just one type of online falsehood, and a way to distinguish it from other types is through its format (see Figure 10.1). Fake news takes some of its power to deceive from being able to masquerade as real news through the use of formats associated with real news, such as the use of an inverted-pyramid style, a headline, and a byline (Tandoc 2019). For example, Waisbord (2018, 1866) referred to fake news as 'fabricated information that astutely mimics news and taps into existing public beliefs to influence electoral behaviour'. The news format functions as a heuristic that affects online readers' credibility assessments (Sundar 2008). Such mimicry is not only limited to the article; fake news producers also create websites that mimic the layout of real news sites and, in some cases, even mimic the URLs of legitimate news sites, just changing a letter or a word. Furthermore, the fake news ecosystem also seems to mimic that of real news. Equipped with bots, fake news creators create a synthetic network of fake news websites so that when a user searches online a piece of fake news she had come across, the user is bound to find the same fake news reported elsewhere, mimicking widespread news coverage of real events (Albright 2016).

But *fake news* as a term has also been weaponised by some political actors to use against real journalists. Numerous cases have been documented of politicians around the world labelling a legitimate article they disagree with or that paints them in a negative light as fake news and the news outlet and journalists behind the article as fake news producers (Holan 2017; Farhall et al. 2019; Tandoc, Jenkins et al. 2019). Thus, Egelhofer and Lecheler (2019, 97) also distinguished between fake news as a genre, which refers to 'the deliberate creation of pseudojournalistic disinformation', and fake news as a label, which refers to 'the political instrumentalization of the term to delegitimize news media'. Because of this politicised used of the label, others have proposed other terms to replace 'fake news', such as 'junk news' (Howard et al. 2017). In October 2018, the UK government also banned the use of 'fake news' in policy documents and official communication, arguing that it is 'a poorly-defined and misleading term that conflates a variety of false information, from genuine error through to foreign interference in democratic processes' (Murphy 2018, para. 2).

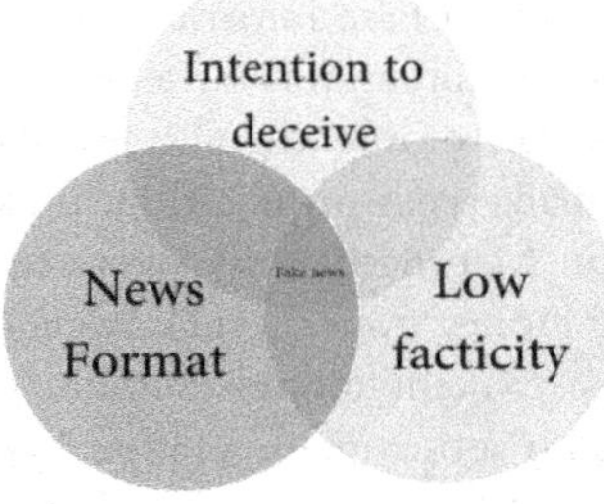

Figure 10.1 Elements of 'fake news'

Others, however, argued that the term *fake news* has conceptual utility and refers to a form of falsehood that is distinct based on its mimicry of an artifact imbued with social legitimacy (see, for example, Mourão and Robertson 2019). While it has been misused by political actors with vested interests, *fake news* as a term has conceptual use: first, it is a term now routinely used in normal conversations and therefore has implications on how different stakeholders understand the phenomenon it supposedly denotes; second, it refers to a specific type of online falsehood that leeches on a journalistic format and therefore might require specific responses and interventions; and third, it also makes the problem more salient for journalists, who now find themselves revisiting assumptions and conventions that have dominated traditional news-works (and their potential vulnerabilities) (Carlson 2020; Tandoc, Jenkins et al. 2019). We cannot drop a term that clearly refers to a particular phenomenon just because a few actors have misused it.

What is fake?

An online dictionary defines *fake news* as a noun that refers to 'false stories that appear to be news, spread on the internet or using other media, usually created to influence political views or as a joke' (Cambridge 2020b). Combining two words, *fake news* as a term is an oxymoron (Tandoc et al. 2017). While news is normatively based on truth, the *Cambridge Dictionary* defines *fake* as a noun that refers to 'an object that is made to look real or valuable in order to deceive people' (Cambridge 2020a). Online resources list the following synonyms: *counterfeit*, *forgery*, and *sham*, among others. Thus, a 'fake' requires a referent, one that is 'real' or 'authentic'. For example, the huge illegal industry of counterfeit products that mimic luxury items, such as expensive bags and watches, depends on the existence of the authentic goods. How good a fake Louis Vuitton bag is, for example, depends heavily on how closely it resembles the authentic bag. Its 'quality' as a fake item depends on how able it is to closely resemble the original.

Embedded in the definition of what constitutes a 'fake' is intentionality. A fake Louis Vuitton bag is not a product of a manufacturing process gone wrong. It is a product of a thoughtful, intentional, and usually meticulous copying of its authentic, original counterpart. Thus, a piece of information might be wrong but not necessarily fake. News outlets routinely get their accounts of events wrong, especially when an event is still developing. But a news report about the novel coronavirus originating in bats, only to be debunked by a later scientific discovery, is not copying an authentic counterpart.

Intentionality is, of course, challenging to study empirically. For example, Egelhofer and Lecheler (2019, 101) argued: 'While we consider the intention to deceive as inherently given in regard to pseudojournalistic fake news websites, we suggest that determining this intentionality for journalistic sources is a crucial challenge for future research'. Establishing intentionality requires confirming the motivation of fake news producers, but as websites producing fake news rarely carry real names or contact details, doing so is a big challenge. Despite such difficulty, it is important to recognise that intentionality is an important element in the conceptualisation of what counts as 'fake'. This, however, is made more complex by how some fake news sites see their blending of real and fake news as not morally wrong – the main intention is to advocate for their ideological causes, and mixing truths and falsehoods is just one tool to achieve this goal. For example, an analysis of how websites that routinely publish fake news – as well as some real news – in the United States present themselves in their About pages found that these sites 'sought to provide alternative interpretations, rejecting objectivity in favour of approaches to "truth-seeking" rooted in personal and political values' (Robertson and Mourão 2020, 16). These actors do not see themselves as engaging in deception; they believe in their own lies.

What is news?

The word *fake* in the term *fake news* acts as a modifier of the word *news*. A ubiquitous word, *news* is a complex concept. Such complexity explains the multitude of ways it has been defined in newswriting textbooks and journalism studies handbooks. It is said that journalists know news when they see it, or what Rogers (2004) called the 'news sense', but will find it difficult to define what news really is. Some texts define *news* as referring to an account of a recent, interesting, significant, and extraordinary event (Patterson 1993; Berner 1992; Harriss et al. 1981; Kershner 2005) while other sources identify instead factors that journalists look for in an event or issue to consider it as newsworthy. These factors are sometimes referred to as 'news values' that guide editorial decisions, such as timeliness, proximity, eliteness, impact, conflict, and novelty, among others (Galtung and Ruge 1965; Harcup and O'Neill 2016). A fundamental assumption across these various definitions is that news is something based on truth (Kovach and Rosenstiel 2001).

News, therefore, is more than just the event or issue that is reported about; it is also how such reports are socially constructed. News production is characterised by layers of processes to ensure accuracy and is guided by numerous rules, such as ensuring accountability. For example, in a study of fake news websites in the United States, Mourão and Robertson (2019, 2080) argued that fake news, while packaged like real news, 'is not subjected to traditional news norms as ascribed by the Western liberal model of professional journalism: it is not – although it possibly never aspired to be – factual, objective, neutral, and informational'. Real news, therefore, is defined not only by the output per se but also by the processes involved in its production. However, while this is instructive for scholars who study mediated messages, it is challenging for individuals exposed to both real and fake news who might not know what really goes into news production.

This is where media literacy as an important intervention to combat the spread of fake news comes in, but it is also important to understand how different stakeholders define 'news', for this has implications for how nuanced our understanding of the fake news problem and its potential solution becomes. As news consumption patterns change, especially in terms of how and when people get their news, it is plausible that what news means to people is also changing. For example, news has always been regarded as an important conversation starter and can bring people together (Lasswell 1948), but this is now even more true on social media, where news seems to be valued more for its social than its informational utility (Tandoc et al. 2020). The spread of fake news might be emblematic not only of people's changing news behaviour but also of their changing valuation and definition of news. For example, in some of the focus group discussions we conducted in Singapore, we asked participants to define what they consider to be news. While many referred to outputs by traditional news outlets, some elderly participants referred to health tips they come across on Facebook, as well as WhatsApp messages forwarded to them by friends, as constituting news.

Such dynamic definitions of what counts as news have implications on how we define fake news as well as on how we design interventions to combat its spread. If we go by the traditional definition of what news is and take traditional news formats as part of that definition, this might be inconsistent with discourses about fake news spreading via messaging apps and Twitter, where 'fake news' comes in the form of short messages. Changing news distribution and consumption patterns might have also changed audience expectations of what news is and should be. For example, as news outlets and journalists embraced Twitter as a platform to disseminate breaking news, audiences might be considering 280-character messages as a legitimate news format. Indeed, Mourão and Robertson (2019) argued that the definition of 'fake news' is relational: first, it is in relation to what is 'real', and second, that the 'news' it mimics also depends on cultural contexts (see also Wasserman 2017). This might also be true in relation to temporal context as the definitions of news and, consequently, fake news, evolve over time. This is something that future studies should explore.

Impact of fake news

The popularity of fake news as a research topic is partly based on its assumed negative impact on numerous aspects of social life. News reports and personal anecdotes abound that detail different types of real harm caused by fake news. However, compared with the scholarly attention devoted to studying how fake news is characterised, created, circulated, and countered (Bente 2018), fewer studies have examined the consequences of fake news. A study in the United States concluded that 'the fake news audience is small and comprises a subset of the Internet's heaviest users' (Nelson and Taneja 2018, 3732). The experience of many other countries, however, might be different, given the various levels of social media and messaging app penetration rates around the world, on top of differences in political systems and cultural contexts. Furthermore, tracking the actual spread of fake news is challenging, especially as more and more information exchanges occur on closed messaging apps, such as WhatsApp, that third-party observers and researchers cannot easily track.

Some have expressed concern about the use of fake news as a form of foreign interference, with external actors sowing tensions and perceptions of chaos in a particular community to achieve political ends, such as influencing electoral outcomes or sabotaging economies (Jayakumar 2018; Allcott and Gentzkow 2017). Thus, fake news has also been weaponised to weaken trust in social institutions, including science, politics, and journalism (Egelhofer and Lecheler 2019). Others have also explored the impact of fake news on the reputation of organisations. For example, a study found that appearing next to a piece of fake news can affect an online advertisement's perceived trustworthiness (Visentin et al. 2019). Fake news websites might also exert some agenda-setting effects on a few partisan news sites (Guo and Vargo 2018). A study also found that discourse around fake news can also increase scepticism towards real news (Van Duyn and Collier 2019). These are a few examples of social and organisational implications. But how does fake news affect interpersonal relationships? Understanding the impact of fake news on interpersonal relationships as well as on personal, day-to-day decision-making can help reveal mechanisms that facilitate, if not encourage, the sharing of information regardless of its veracity (see Cabañes 2020). It can also help explain how individuals respond to fake news and why. For example, a survey conducted in Singapore found that most participants ignore fake news when they come across it on social media, instead of taking steps to correct or report it (Tandoc, Lim et al. 2019).

Conclusion

Fake news has attracted much scholarly attention and rightfully so. It is a problem facilitated by communication technologies and channels that millions routinely use, involves the mimicry of a social artifact imbued with history and legitimacy, and betrays a fundamental virtue that holds communities together: truth. The multitude of studies conducted after fake news rose again to buzzword status in late 2016 has provided us some understanding of the kind of problem we are facing – and yet there are still many things we don't fully understand.

The spread of the novel coronavirus around the world in 2020 demonstrated there is still a lot of work to do. A church in South Korea, taking its cue from viral messages that claimed gargling saltwater could kill the virus that causes COVID-19, sprayed salt water into the mouths of its followers, infecting dozens of people (Park 2020). A spokesperson for the Philippine government echoed in a public broadcast viral social media messages that wrongly claimed eating bananas can protect people from COVID-19 (Luna 2020). In the United States, President Trump mentioned in a televised press briefing injecting disinfectants into people to kill the virus – this was followed by a few cases of Americans ingesting disinfectants (Slotkin 2020). Fake news provides one channel for falsehoods to enter public consciousness, but mainstream news coverage also provides another pathway as falsehoods now also come from political leaders whose voices dominate real news.

Fake news spreads like a virus – all it takes is one vulnerable host to spread it to others. Online and offline communities are still in need of being disinfected. As information technologies develop and people's communication needs, habits, and values change, the phenomenon of fake news will also continue to evolve.

References

Albright J. (2016) The #election 2016 micro-propaganda machine. *Medium* (accessed April 1, 2017).

Allcott H. and Gentzkow M. (2017) Social media and fake news in the 2016 election. *Journal of Economic Perspectives* 31(2): 211–236.

Baym G. (2005) The daily show: Discursive integration and the reinvention of political journalism. *Political Communication* 22(3): 259–276.

Bente K. (2018) Fake news. *Oxford Research Encyclopedia of Communication* (accessed April 13, 2020).

Berkowitz D. and Schwartz A. (2016) Miley, CNN and the onion. *Journalism Practice* 10(1): 1–17.

Berner R.T. (1992) *The Process of Writing News*. Boston: Allyn and Bacon.

Cabañes J.V.A. (2020) Digital disinformation and the imaginative dimension of communication. *Journalism & Mass Communication Quarterly* 97(1).

Cambridge. (2020a) Fake. In: *Cambridge Academic Content Dictionary*. Cambridge: Cambridge University Press.

Cambridge. (2020b) Fake news. In: *Cambridge Advanced Learner's Dictionary & Thesaurus*. Cambridge: Cambridge University Press.

Carlson M. (2020) Fake news as an informational moral panic: The symbolic deviancy of social media during the 2016 US presidential election. *Information, Communication & Society* 23(3): 374–388.

Dixit P. (2019) WhatsApp is now letting users know when a message has been forwarded too many times. *BuzzFeed News* (accessed November 1, 2019).

Egelhofer J.L. and Lecheler S. (2019) Fake news as a two-dimensional phenomenon: A framework and research agenda. *Annals of the International Communication Association* 43(2): 97–116.

Farhall K., Carson A., Wright S., et al. (2019) Political elites' use of fake news discourse across communications platforms. *International Journal of Communication* 13: 4353–4375.

Frayer L. (2018) Viral WhatsApp messages are triggering mob killings in India. *NPR* (accessed August 29, 2018).

Frenkel S. (2018) Facebook says it deleted 865 million posts, mostly spam. *The New York Times* (accessed August 29, 2018).

Funke D. (2018) A guide to anti-misinformation actions around the world. *Poynter* (accessed August 29, 2018).

Galtung J. and Ruge M.H. (1965) The structure of foreign news. *Journal of Peace Research* 2(1): 64–91.

Guo L. and Vargo C. (2018) "Fake news" and emerging online media ecosystem: An integrated intermedia agenda-setting analysis of the 2016 U.S. presidential election. *Communication Research* 47(2): 178–200.

Harcup T. and O'Neill D. (2016) What is news? News values revisited (again). *Journalism Studies*: 1–19.

Harriss J., Leiter K. and Johnson S. (1981) *The Complete Reporter: Fundamentals of News Gathering, Writing, and Editing, Complete with Exercises*. New York: Palgrave Macmillan.

Holan A. (2017) The media's definition of fake news vs. Donald Trump's. *PolitiFact* (accessed October 29, 2017).

Howard P.N., Bolsover G., Kollanyi B., et al. (2017) *Junk News and Bots During the US Election: What Were Michigan Voters Sharing Over Twitter*. Oxford: Project on Computational Propaganda.

Jayakumar S. (2018) Elections integrity in fake news era: Who protects, and how? *RSIS Commentaries* (accessed April 27, 2020).

Kershner J.W. (2005) *The Elements of News Writing*. Boston: Pearson Allyn and Bacon.

Kovach B. and Rosenstiel T. (2001) *The Elements of Journalism: What Newspeople Should Know and the Public Should Expect*. New York: Three Rivers Press.

Lasswell H. (1948) The structure and function of communication in society. In: Bryson L. (ed) *The Communication of Ideas*. New York: Harper and Brothers.

Luna F. (2020) Fact check: Panelo says Korea did total lockdown; eating bananas and gargling prevent COVID-19. *Philippine Star Online* (accessed April 28, 2020).

Mourão R.R. and Robertson C.T. (2019) Fake news as discursive integration: An analysis of sites that publish false, misleading, hyperpartisan and sensational information. *Journalism Studies* 20(14): 2077–2095.

Murphy M. (2018) Government bans phrase "fake news". *The Telegraph* (accessed October 30, 2018).

Nelson J.L. and Taneja H. (2018) The small, disloyal fake news audience: The role of audience availability in fake news consumption. *New Media & Society* 20(10): 3720–3737.

Palma B. (2017) Did an elderly woman train 65 cats to steal from her neighbors? *Snopes* (accessed April 22, 2020).

Park C.-K. (2020) Coronavirus: Saltwater spray infects 46 Church-goers in South Korea. *South China Morning Post* (accessed April 6, 2020).

Patterson T.E. (1993) *Out of Order*. New York: Random House.

Rashkin H., Choi E., Jang J.Y., et al. (2017) Truth of varying shades: Analyzing language in fake news and political fact-checking. In: *2017 Conference on Empirical Methods in Natural Language Processing*. Copenhagen, Denmark: Association for Computational Linguistics, 2921–2927.

Robertson C.T. and Mourão R.R. (2020) Faking alternative journalism? An analysis of self-presentations of "fake news" sites. *Digital Journalism*: 1–19.

Rochlin N. (2017) Fake news: Belief in post-truth. *Library Hi Tech* 35(3): 386–392.

Rogers T. (2004) *Newswriting on Deadline*. Boston: Pearson.

Silverman C. (2016) Here are 50 of the biggest fake news hits on Facebook from 2016. *BuzzFeed* (accessed March 4, 2017).

Singapore. (2019) *Protection from Online Falsehoods and Manipulation Act 2019*. Bill No. 10/2019. Singapore, 1–81. https://www.parliament.gov.sg/docs/default-source/default-document-library/protection-from-online-falsehoods-and-manipulation-bill10-2019.pdf.

Slotkin J. (2020) NYC poison control sees uptick in calls after Trump's disinfectant comments. *NPR* (accessed April 27, 2020).

Subramanian S. (2017) Inside the Macedonian fake-news complex. *Wired* (accessed April 19).

Sundar S.S. (2008) The main model: A heuristic approach to understanding technology effects on credibility. In: Metzger M.J. and Flanagin A.J. (eds) *Digital Media, Youth, and Credibility*. Cambridge, MA: The MIT Press, 73–100.

Tandoc E. (2019) The facts of fake news: A research review. *Sociology Compass* 13(9): 1–9.

Tandoc E., Huang A., Duffy A., et al. (2020) To share is to receive: News as social currency for social media reciprocity. *Journal of Applied Journalism & Media Studies* 9(1): 3–20.

Tandoc E., Jenkins J. and Craft S. (2019) Fake news as a critical incident in journalism. *Journalism Practice* 13(6): 673–689.

Tandoc E., Lim D. and Ling R. (2019) Diffusion of disinformation: How social media users respond to fake news and why. *Journalism* 6(2). doi:10.11771464884919868325.

Tandoc E., Lim Z.W. and Ling R. (2017) Defining "fake news": A typology of scholarly definitions. *Digital Journalism* 6(2): 137–153.

Tandoc E., Ling R., Westlund O., et al. (2018) Audiences' acts of authentication in the age of fake news: A conceptual framework. *New Media & Society* 20(8): 2745–2763.

Van Duyn E. and Collier J. (2019) Priming and fake news: The effects of elite discourse on evaluations of news media. *Mass Communication and Society* 22(1): 29–48.

Visentin M., Pizzi G. and Pichierri M. (2019) Fake news, real problems for brands: The impact of content truthfulness and source credibility on consumers' behavioral intentions toward the advertised brands. *Journal of Interactive Marketing* 45: 99–112.

Waisbord S. (2018) Truth is what happens to news. *Journalism Studies* 19(13): 1866–1878.

Wardle C. (2017) Fake news. *It's Complicated* (accessed April 1, 2017).

Wasserman H. (2017) Fake news from Africa: Panics, politics and paradigms. *Journalism* 21(1): 3–16.

PART II

Media misinformation and disinformation

11
THE EVOLUTION OF COMPUTATIONAL PROPAGANDA

Theories, debates, and innovation of the Russian model

Dariya Tsyrenzhapova and Samuel C. Woolley

Acknowledgements

For their help and feedback, the authors would like to acknowledge colleagues in the School of Journalism and Media and the Center for Media Engagement (CME), both at the University of Texas at Austin. For their generous support of the Propaganda Research Team at CME, we would like to thank the Beneficial Technology team at Omidyar Network, the Open Society Foundations-US, and the Knight Foundation. Any opinions, findings, and conclusions or recommendations expressed in this material are those of the authors and do not necessarily reflect the views of these funders. Please direct correspondence to the School of Journalism and Media, Belo Center for Media, 300 W Dean Keeton St, Austin, TX 78712.

Introduction

Russia's digital interference during the 2016 US presidential election and the UK Brexit referendum helped catalyse broadscale international debates about the global spread of political manipulation online (Mueller 2019; U.S. Senate Foreign Relations Committee 2018). During the Arab Spring protests, Facebook and Twitter were celebrated for their power to mobilise crowds for social movements (Tufekci and Wilson 2012). The recent outbreak of dis/misinformation and inorganic political communication campaigns has, however, led many to argue that social media are now vessels for 'new and powerful forms of disguised propaganda' (Farkas 2018, 6), as well as channels for 'organized and coordinated' public opinion manipulation (Bradshaw and Howard 2017, 4).

But computational propaganda campaigns on social media are not simply powerful and organised; they are massive, far-reaching, and international. The people who wage them make use of legitimate advertising tools on sites like Facebook as well as illicit tactics, including fake profiles and social media bots – pieces of software algorithmically programmed to spread propaganda messages (Woolley and Howard 2016). Russian efforts during the 2016 US election underscore these features.

During the investigation of US special counsel Robert S. Mueller III, Twitter identified nearly 4,000 accounts associated with Russia's Internet Research Agency (IRA) and over 50,000 automated accounts linked to the Russian government (Mueller 2019). All told, in the ten weeks prior to the 2016 US election, 1.4 million people directly engaged with these tweets by acts of quoting, liking, replying, or following (Twitter Public Policy 2018). In a similar effort, Facebook disabled 5.8 million fake accounts. This included purging 120 IRA-linked pages, which posted 80,000 pieces of content between June 2015 and August 2017, according to Facebook general counsel Colin Stretch. Facebook also discovered that the IRA had disseminated more than 3,500 ads through a number of groups: 'Stop All Immigrants', 'Black Matters', 'LGBT United', 'United Muslims of America', etc. These ad campaigns cost the IRA as little as $100,000 (Mueller 2019), only a tiny fraction of its $125 million monthly budget in the run-up to the US election, (*United States of America v Internet Research Agency LLC* 2018) and reached almost one in three Americans, or 126 million US-based users (U.S. Senate Committee on Crime and Terrorism 2017).

The Russian propaganda machine has been successful in harnessing social media as platforms for stimulating social and political unrest – particularly in pushing polarisation, apathy, and disbelief both online (Bastos and Farkas 2019; Bessi and Ferrara 2016) and offline (Allbright 2017). The government in Moscow and many other powerful political actors well understand Manuel Castells's premise surrounding information warfare in a network society: 'torturing bodies is less effective than shaping minds' (Castells 2007, 238).

In this chapter we focus on the global diffusion of the Russian computational propaganda model in order to highlight broader changes in the use of social media in attempts to deceptively alter the flow of information during high-stakes political events. Drawing on literature from propaganda studies, reflexive control theory (RC), and information diffusion, we conceptualise how false news messages, built with the intention of igniting the flame of social disagreement, can be harnessed in order to mobilise social movements globally.

There is a clear and continued need for more effects-driven research in computational propaganda. We point to several pieces of work that provide theoretical insight into how behavioural changes may occur as a result of an audience's exposure to disinformation online. As Bernhardt, Krasa and Polborn (2008) note, the residual effects of this manipulation can include affective polarisation and media bias, which lead to electoral mistakes. In response to targeted criticisms about the lack of demonstrable effects of computational propaganda on behavior at the voting booth (Metaxas, Mustafaraj and Gayo-Avello 2011), we include a preliminary discussion on the difficulties of measuring first-order (direct) socio-political effects in the era of digital dis/misinformation. We join other scholars in calling for more computational propaganda and digital dis/misinformation research exploring the measurement of second-order (indirect) behavioural changes.

A historical overview of propaganda

The rise of organised social media campaigns in recent years led scholars to advocate for the continued relevance of propaganda studies (Jack 2019; Woolley and Howard 2016), which may inform the current debates on the propagating scale of information warfare. Classical scholarship defines propaganda as a form of deliberately organised manipulation of public opinion. It primarily manifests a small group of institutional actors exerting power over a larger populace, striving to 'activate people', 'arouse questions', and 'lead to critical reactions' (Hemánus 1974, 215).

In manipulating public opinion, propagandists aim to convert suggestions into 'strong active beliefs', triggered and reinforced through past memories (Moscovici 1993, 73). Through the 'manipulation of symbols' (Hemánus 1974, 215), propaganda shapes people's thoughts, beliefs, and actions by creating 'pictures in our heads' or igniting stereotypes (Lippmann 1922). Propaganda escalates emotions of 'hope or fear', which lead audiences to internalise information without scrutiny and deliberation (Lee 1952, 62). If the persuasion is successful, Ellul (1973, 166) contends that the suggested notions seamlessly transform into 'prejudices and beliefs, as well as objective justifications', representing new notions of reality. Therefore, classic scholarship suggests that propaganda does not just manipulate the mind; it can also cause other forms of distress as it alienates those who spread and consume it – subtly and slowly making them give up beliefs and integrity to obey someone else (Ellul 1973).

Media (and therefore, uses of propaganda) have changed rapidly over the past century since Lasswell's (1927) pioneering scholarship in the fields of political communication and media studies. As of 2019, 43 percent of US adults consumed news via Facebook while 12 percent relied on Twitter (Pew Research Center 2019). The networked architecture of social media commands the information flow, algorithmically warranting certain messages wider exposure and exhibiting potential for new and hyper-specific types of audience engagement (Van Dijck 2012). Jack (2019) accounts for the uncertainty of how today's active audiences, imbued with the power of social sharing, may inadvertently be contributing to a wider spread of dis/misinformation online. By introducing a framework of 'wicked content', Jack (2019) calls for treating propaganda as 'a sensitizing concept', which also includes fake news (448). She suggests that the complementary concept will retain room for 'ambiguities of meaning, identity, and motivation, along with unintentional amplification and inadvertent legitimization' of problematic digital content circulating in an ever-more-complex media ecosystem (449).

Computational propaganda: a global overview

Computational propaganda employs automated and algorithmic methods to spread and amplify messages on social media coupled with the overt propaganda tactics of ideological control and manipulation (Woolley and Howard 2018). Unlike early information systems for propaganda, discussed by pioneer researchers (Ellul 1973; Lee 1952), the current form operates via 'the assemblage of social media platforms, autonomous agents, and big data' (Woolley and Howard 2016, 4886). It can rely upon political bots or automated computer code built to mimic human users and push out targeted political messages. Content that begins with bots is often immediately spread across a wide network of high-volume users, including politicians, influencers, and pundits (Woolley and Guilbeault 2017).

Computational propaganda is an international phenomenon. Russian global digital machinations well display this. Brexit was 'a petri dish' used to test and gear up for digital information campaigns during the 2016 US election (Mayer 2019). There is a growing body of research detailing the ways in which computational propaganda was strategically leveraged across several government types: by oppressive political regimes, including in China (Yang 2017), Hong Kong (Zhong, Meyers Lee and Wu 2019), Iran (FireEye Intelligence 2018), Saudi Arabia (Benner et al. 2018), Venezuela (Forelle et al. 2015) and by embattled democracies such as Brazil (Arnaudo 2017), Turkey (Akin Unver 2019), and the Philippines (Bengali and Halper 2019).

Political groups in the United States and other Western democracies, many of which face issues of growing polarisation and illiberalism, have employed similar digital tactics in efforts to shape public opinion in their favour. Various studies on Twitter traffic and the 2016 US election indicate that bots have accounted for anywhere from 8 to 14 percent of active accounts (at a given time), and they were responsible for generating from nearly one-fifth to one-third of the overall Twitter traffic surrounding the event (Shao et al. 2018; Bessi and Ferrara 2016). In Italy, bots have been used to deliberately target influencers during political events by enticing them to share misleading information (Stella, Ferrara and De Domenico 2018). Respected media outlets in Western democracies are also targets of digital disinformation campaigns, many amplified by bots. Lukito et al. (2018) found that a total of 116 stories from 32 major news outlets, including *The Washington Post*, National Public Radio, *USA Today*, *The New York Times*, and other major outlets embedded at least one IRA tweet as a source, often showcasing an account expressing strong partisan beliefs. Bots, largely, spread and amplify messages from low-credibility sources (Shao et al. 2018), and their conversations rarely leave the confines of social media platforms; thus, being quoted by the mainstream media could be attributed to second-order indirect effects, influencing public opinion.

Consequences of computational propaganda

The first documented instance of using social bots and 'astroturf' campaigning in political communication on social media dates back to the 2010 US midterm elections (Ratkiewicz et al. 2011). However, researchers are still working to determine concrete societal and electoral effects of political bot communication more narrowly and dis/misinformation and propaganda on social media more broadly. To date, scholarship studying fake news and bot-driven content has devoted considerable attention to highlighting the role automated social media accounts play in disseminating low-credibility content, including false news reports, hoaxes, clickbait headlines, etc. (Shao et al. 2018; Bastos and Farkas 2019). But knowing that many people saw or shared this sort of problematic political content, as Lazer et al. (2018) note, is not the same as knowing if digital disinformation affected users' behavior.

New work in computational propaganda suggests that bots were successful in amplifying negative and inflammatory stories and sentiments during the 2017–2018 anti-government protests in Iran (Thieltges et al. 2018) and the 2017 Catalan referendum in Spain (Stella, Ferrara and De Domenico 2018). Researchers found that this amplification then resulted in increased polarisation amongst dissenting voices. Political polarisation, according to Bernhardt, Krasa, and Polborn (2008), ultimately causes important information to be lost due to media bias. This, in turn, can lead to voters lacking quality information when they go to the polls; thus, making electoral mistakes becomes more likely.

Scholarship exploring audience engagement with fake news during the 2016 US election suggests that the anticipated effects are 'less than you think' (Guess, Nagler and Tucker 2019) because 'persuasion is really hard' (Little 2018, 50). When evaluating the success of the computational propaganda campaigns during elections, it is important to note that effects may not always be obvious or linear. Second-order effects may be easier to track than first-order ones, indirect ones more viable then those that are direct. Importantly, many bots and other groups working to amplify disinformation do not work to communicate directly with people on social media – they are constructed to trick trending algorithms and journalists into re-curating content to users via existing 'trusted' sources (Woolley and Guilbeault 2017).

While there has been a consistent effort to study the quantitative breadth of computational propaganda campaigns (Stukal et al. 2019; Ruck et al. 2019; Spangher et al. 2020; Bessi and Ferrara 2016; Shao et al. 2018; Badawy, Ferrara and Lerman 2018), much research still has to be done to examine the persuasive qualities of the groups who generate such campaigns and the consumer demand for those messages.

Theorising the diffusion of propaganda over social media

The rise of social media as crucial tools for information sharing has disrupted the traditional pathways information used to follow while travelling to its intended audience. This inherently changes the way public opinion is formed today. Recent studies detailing news-sharing practices emphasise Twitter's 'crowd phenomenon' (Kim, Newth and Christen 2014), which makes it a conducive news diffusion space, facilitating immediate and wide audience exposure to information. As Hummel and Huntress (1952) note, this is exactly what propaganda aims for: if it does not reach its intended audience by making people 'listen, or read, or watch', it ultimately fails (51).

For the past decade, communications scholars have made a concerted effort to study what makes messages go viral on Twitter (Stieglitz and Dang-Xuan, 2013; Hansen et al. 2011), but until recently, there has not been a holistic approach to explaining why emotionally charged and politically polarised messages diffuse at a higher rate and scale in digital arenas. The mediated skewed diffusion of issues information theory (MSDII), however, works to bridge this gap (McEwan, Carpenter and Hopke 2018).

MSDII provides an alternative theoretical perspective to well-known theories concerning echo chambers (Jamieson and Cappella 2008) and filter bubbles (Pariser 2011). Using exposure as a key metric to determining message diffusion, MSDII suggests that predisposed views (or personal ego involvement with an issue), message quality (the shorter it is, the more factual, less biased and of stronger argument quality it is perceived), and user's social network ecosystem (the larger the following, the more likely it is to encounter opposing views) each contribute to wider information sharing on social media (McEwan, Carpenter and Hopke 2018).

Ego involvement, or individuals' determination to express views dear to them while also seeking out and sharing information that supports personal beliefs, is conceptually similar to individuals' decisions to practice selective exposure in response to like-minded information and selective avoidance when encountering ideologically conflicting views (Stroud 2011). This practice solidifies a 'web of belief', as discussed by Quine and Ullian (1978), which allows people to reject or dismiss information based on how well it fits with their social group conventions. MSDII contends, despite the fact that a social media news feed provides opportunities for users to receive 'attitude-consistent and attitude-inconsistent messages', ego involvement with an issue still can make it difficult for the networked communities of strong-tied users to 'accurately access' the quality of divergent arguments regardless of positive message attributes (McEwan, Carpenter and Hopke 2018, 2). With this in mind, mere exposure to like-minded information only strengthens ideological beliefs and attitudes and has little to do with actually changing them. Increased presence on social media, combined with connections to like-minded individuals, solidifies one's views and perceptions, turning the cognitive process into a 'cyclical feedback loop, (McEwan, Carpenter and Hopke 2018, 9), intensified over time through repeated exposure and engagement.

Crucially, MSDII needs further empirical testing of its key propositions. It does, however, provide new insights into how social media, given their technological affordances and embedded network ties, facilitate and extend the reach of computational propaganda once it hits a like-minded audience. It holds exciting potential to contribute to our understanding of why those exposed to computational propaganda could be susceptible to 'biased argument processing' (McEwan, Carpenter and Hopke 2018, 4) that contributes to 'affective and behavioral divide' across party lines – a phenomenon Iyengar et al. (2019) define as 'affective polarization' (134).

The progression of the Russian model

The Russian government puts great emphasis on directing information operations – an umbrella term for propaganda efforts that today include computational propaganda. Their use of online manipulation strategies highlights the broader international phenomenon of computational propaganda. They primarily see information operations generally as 'a decisive tool' for maintaining social control rather than just 'a supporting element of state power' (Allen and Moore 2018, 61). This explains their government-sponsored attempts to mold public opinion through a diverse network of agents and channels, tracking and targeting audiences at home (Yapparova 2019) as well as abroad (MacFarquhar 2020). In scholarly debates, Russia's propaganda efforts have been interpreted through the lens of the reflexive control theory (RC) (Thomas 2004; Bjola 2018; Till 2020; Kowalewski 2017). Developed in the wake of the Cold War by the Russian military, this elaborate form of propaganda is still seen by scholars as 'an empirical black box' (Bjola 2018, 23).

Russian attempts at reflexive control played out prominently during the 2016 US election. The IRA leveraged an army of roughly 400 human curators who used bots and other digital tools in disseminating content (Chen 2015). Till (2020) described this group as 'fully employed "agents of influence"' used in an opaque digital form of Russian 'statecraft' (7). As a part of a minimum daily quota, each 'agent' was expected to post comments on 50 articles, run six Facebook accounts, post three posts on each Facebook account, hold two discussions on Facebook, and manage ten Twitter accounts, populating those with at least 50 tweets a day (Singer and Brooking 2018),

Conceptually, the goal behind RC is to control the reflex of the opponent by finding 'the weak links' (for example, racial tensions) and further exploiting them to 'sharpen ideological polarisation, maximize political disunity and weaken democratic institutions' (Bjola 2018, 22). Walker and Ludwig (2017) call this form of deliberate manipulation 'sharp power', which acts like 'the tip of [the] dagger', aiming to 'pierce, penetrate, or perforate' the media system of targeted countries. Bjola (2018) states that manipulation is accomplished through 'cognitive mapping' and 'micro-targeting' of the intended audiences (22).

The rise of advanced computation and big data has opened up a wide range of possibilities for novel reflexive control tactics, used by Russia and a variety of other powerful political actors. Specifically, these innovations allow for new means of 'exploiting moral, psychological . . . as well as personal characteristics' in the form of 'biographical data, habits, and psychological deficiencies' to acquire 'the highest degree of reflex', which maximises the chances of defeating the opponent by covertly influencing the other's perception of reality (Thomas 2004, 241–242).

The sheer size of the global digital audience, with 3.8 billion users now present on social media (Kemp 2020), simplifies the task of orchestrating computational propaganda campaigns: the audience is vast, and exposure to a message is immediate. Moreover, automated technology used on Twitter and other social media sites is increasingly cheap and easy to obtain. An investigation from *The Daily Beast* found that a social bot account could be purchased online for less than five cents (Cox 2017). The fact that the Russian government inundated important political conversations with bots to tilt public opinion in its favour exemplifies a shrewd strategy of solving an essential dilemma between either selectively censoring problematic content or blocking Facebook and Twitter within Russia entirely (Sanovich 2019). Given the present power of social media in the global information infrastructure, neither of these measures would have been possible without causing a public outcry. In launching computational propaganda via reflexive control, Russia made a power move internally and externally by turning an old worry into a boon.

Early news coverage surrounding the 2020 US election suggest that the Russian propaganda machine made efforts to gear up for a more sophisticated and abstruse 'reflexive control' operation aimed at influencing the general public. A CNN investigation run in collaboration with researchers at Clemson University, Facebook, and Twitter found a network of more than 200 accounts stirring up racial tensions amongst the Black Lives Matter community, drawing thousands of shares and reactions. Masquerading as US-based users, those accounts turned out to be run by trolls based in Ghana and Nigeria (Ward et al. 2020). Facebook later deemed these accounts to be perpetuating 'coordinated inauthentic behavior' and linked their activities to the Russian IRA (Gleicher 2020).

Russian attempts to control US public opinion aren't just occurring over social media. Another arm of the Russian government propaganda – Radio Sputnik (formerly the Voice of Russia and RIA Novosti) recently opened for business on US soil. Radio Sputnik now plays at 104.7 FM in Kansas City, Missouri. Acting through a broker in Florida, the Russian government prepaid the Missouri-based Alpine Broadcasting Corporation $324,000 for three years' worth of news programming at an hourly rate of $49.27 (MacFarquhar 2020).

Conclusion

Computational propaganda, as exemplified by the Russian model, rapidly evolves to satisfy current demands and a changing informational environment. During the 2016 US election, Russia enjoyed modest levels of success in leveraging digital dis/misinformation campaigns in order to encourage digital polarisation and offline protest. They, and other governments around the world, have leveraged computational propaganda in efforts to exert reflexive control over their opposition – internally and abroad. They and others will continue to deploy bots and other mechanisms of computational propaganda in attempts to manipulate public opinion.

Classic literature from media and propaganda studies, paired with more recent work on computational propaganda, information operations, and political communication helps in formulating theorical understandings of the current and ever-changing state of digital political manipulation. Reflexive control theory and the recent developments in theories of news diffusion offer a comprehensive explanation for why computational propaganda from Russia and other political actors works to spread and take hold.

There is a marked need for concerted and continued empirical work on computational propaganda in order to discern the behavioral effects – and cultural impact – of this relatively new problem. These efforts should be compared and combined with broader efforts on disinformation and polarisation, issues closely tied to research on computational propaganda. While first-order behavioural effects may prove difficult to track, second-order ones may be more possible to discern. Computational propaganda has been established as a phenomenon; now the scholarly community needs to work to figure out what this phenomenon does to peoples' behaviour.

References

Akin Unver, H 2019, 'Russia has won information war in Turkey', *Foreign Diplomacy*, 21 April. Available at: https://foreignpolicy.com/2019/04/21/russia-has-won-the-information-war-in-turkey-rt-sputnik-putin-erdogan-disinformation/

Allbright, C 2017, 'A Russian Facebook page organized a protest in Texas: A different Russian page launched a counterprotest', *The Texas Tribune*, 1 November. Available at: www.texastribune.org/2017/11/01/russian-facebook-page-organized-protest-texas-different-russian-page-1/

Allen, TS and Moore, AJ 2018, 'Victory without casualties: Russia's information operations', *Parameters*, *48*(1), pp. 59–71.

Arnaudo, D 2017, 'Computational propaganda in Brazil: Social bots during elections', *The Computational Propaganda Research Project*, *8*, pp. 1–39.

Badawy, A, Ferrara, E and Lerman, K, 2018, 'Analyzing the digital traces of political manipulation: The 2016 Russian interference Twitter campaign', Proceedings of the 2018 IEEE/ACM International Conference on Advances in Social Networks Analysis and Mining (ASONAM), Barcelona, Spain, 28–31 August, pp. 258–265.

Bastos, M and Farkas, J 2019, '"Donald Trump is my president!" The Internet Research Agency propaganda machine', *Social Media + Society*, *5*(3), pp. 1–13.

Bengali, S and Halper, E 2019, 'Troll armies, a growth industry in the Philippines, may soon be coming to an election near you', *The Los Angeles Times*, 19 November. Available at: www.latimes.com/politics/story/2019-11-19/troll-armies-routine-in-philippine-politics-coming-here-next

Benner, K, Mazzetti, M, Hubbard, B and Isaac, M 2018, 'Saudis' image makers: A troll army and a Twitter insider', *The New York Times*, 20 October. Available at: www.nytimes.com/2018/10/20/us/politics/saudi-image-campaign-twitter.html

Bernhardt, D, Krasa, S and Polborn, M 2008, 'Political polarization and the electoral effects of media bias', *Journal of Public Economics*, *92*(5–6), pp. 1092–1104.

Bessi, A and Ferrara, E 2016, 'Social bots distort the 2016 U.S. presidential election online discussion', *First Monday*, *21*(11–17), pp. 1–14.

Bjola, C 2018, 'Propaganda as reflexive control: The digital dimension', in Bjola, C and Pamment, J (eds.) *Countering online propaganda and extremism: The dark side of digital diplomacy*. London: Routledge, pp. 11–27.

Bradshaw, S and Howard, PN 2017, 'Troops, trolls and troublemakers: A global inventory of organized social media manipulation', *The Computational Propaganda Research Project*, *2017*(12), pp. 1–36.

Castells, M 2007, 'Communication, power and counter-power in the network society', *International Journal of Communication*, *1*, pp. 238–266.

Chen, A 2015, 'The agency', *The New York Times Magazine*, 2 June. Available at: https://nytimes.com/2015/06/07/magazine/the-agency.html

Cox, J 2017, 'I bought a Russian bot army for under $100', *Daily Beast*, 13 September. Available at: www.thedailybeast.com/i-bought-a-russian-bot-army-for-under-dollar100

Ellul, J 1973, *Propaganda: The formation of men's attitudes*. New York: Vintage Books.

Farkas, J 2018, 'Disguised propaganda on social media: Addressing democratic dangers and solutions', *Brown Journal of World Affairs*, *1*, pp. 1–16.

FireEye Intelligence 2018, 'Suspected Iranian influence operation leveraging inauthentic news sites and social media aimed at U.S., U.K., other audiences'. Available at: www.fireeye.com/content/dam/fireeye-www/current-threats/pdfs/rpt-FireEye-Iranian-IO.pdf

Forelle, M, Howard, P, Monroy-Hernández, A and Savage, S 2015, 'Political bots and the manipulation of public opinion in Venezuela', *arXiv preprint arXiv:1507.07109*. Available at: https://arxiv.org/abs/1507.07109

Gleicher, N 2020, 'Removing coordinated inauthentic behavior from Russia', *Facebook Newsroom*, 12 March. Available at: https://about.fb.com/news/2020/03/removing-coordinated-inauthentic-behavior-from-russia/

Guess, A, Nagler, J and Tucker, J 2019, 'Less than you think: Prevalence and predictors of fake news dissemination on Facebook', *Science Advances*, *5*(1), pp. 1–8. https://doi.org/10.1126/sciadv.aau4586

Hansen, LK, Arvidsson, A, Nielsen, FA, Colleoni, E and Etter, M 2011, 'Good friends, bad news – affect and virality in Twitter', in Park JJ., Yang LT and Lee C (eds.) *Future information technology*. Communications in Computer and Information Science, vol 185. Berlin and Heidelberg: Springer, pp. 34–43.

Hemánus, P 1974, 'Propaganda and indoctrination; a tentative concept analysis', *Gazette* (Leiden, Netherlands), *20*(4), pp. 215–223. https://doi.org/10.1177/001654927402000402

Hummel, WC and Huntress, KG 1952, *The analysis of propaganda*. New York: The Dryden Press.

Iyengar, S, Lelkes, Y, Levendusky, M, Malhotra, N and Westwood, SJ 2019, 'The origins and consequences of affective polarization in the United States', *Annual Review of Political Science*, *22*, pp. 129–146. https://doi.org/10.1146/annurev-polisci-051117-073034

Jack, C, 2019, 'Wicked content', *Communication, Culture and Critique*, *12*, pp. 435–454. https://doi.org/10.1093/ccc/tcz043

Jamieson, K and Cappella, J 2008, *Echo chamber: Rush Limbaugh and the conservative media establishment*. London: Oxford University Press.

Kemp, S 2020, 'Digital 2020: 3.8 billion people use social media', *WeAreSocial*, 30 January. Available at: https://wearesocial.com/blog/2020/01/digital-2020-3-8-billion-people-use-social-media

Kim, M, Newth, D and Christen, P 2014, 'Trends of news diffusion in social media based on crowd phenomena', Proceedings of the 23rd International Conference on World Wide Web, ACM Press, Seoul, Korea, pp. 753–758. https://doi.org/10.1145/2567948.2579325

Kowalewski, A 2017, 'Disinformation and reflexive control: The new cold war', *Georgetown Security Studies Review*, 1 February. Available at: https://georgetownsecuritystudiesreview.org/2017/02/01/disinformation-and-reflexive-control-the-new-cold-war/

Lasswell, HD 1927, *Propaganda technique in the world war*. Cambridge: Ravenio Books.

Lazer, DM, Baum, MA, Benkler, Y, Berinsky, AJ, Greenhill, KM, Menczer, F, Metzger, MJ, Nyhan, B, Pennycook, G, Rothschild, D and Schudson, M 2018, 'The science of fake news', *Science, 359*(6380), pp. 1094–1096.

Lee, AM 1952, *How to understand propaganda*. New York: Rinehart.

Lippmann, W 1922, *The world outside and the pictures in our heads*. New York: Penguin.

Little, AT 2018, 'Fake news, propaganda, and lies can be pervasive even if they aren't persuasive', *Critique, 11*(1), pp. 21–34.

Lukito, J, Wells, C, Zhang, Y, Doroshenko, L, Kim, SJ, Su, MH and Freelon, D 2018, 'The Twitter exploit: How Russian propaganda infiltrated US news', *University of Wisconsin-Madison Computational Methods Group, February*. Available at: https://mcrc.journalism.wisc.edu/files/2018/05/Twitter Exploit.pdf

MacFarquhar, N 2020, 'Playing on Kansas city radio: Russian propaganda', *The New York Times*, 13 February. Available at: www.nytimes.com/2020/02/13/us/russian-propaganda-radio.html

Mayer, J 2019, 'New evidence emerges of Steve Bannon and Cambridge analytica's role in Brexit', *The New Yorker*, 17 November. Available at: www.newyorker.com/news/news-desk/new-evidence-emerges-of-steve-bannon-and-cambridge-analyticas-role-in-brexit

McEwan, B, Carpenter, CJ and Hopke, JE 2018, 'Mediated skewed diffusion of issues information: A theory', *Social Media + Society, 4*(3), pp. 1–14. https://doi.org/10.1177/2056305118800319

Metaxas, PT, Mustafaraj, E and Gayo-Avello, D 2011, 'How (not) to predict elections', Proceedings of the 2011 IEEE Third international conference on privacy, security, risk and trust and 2011 IEEE third international conference on social computing, Boston, MA, 9–11 October, pp. 165–171.

Moscovici, S 1993, 'The return of the unconscious', *Social Research, 60*(1), pp. 39–93. Available at: www.jstor.org/stable/40970728?seq=1&cid=pdf-reference#references_tab_contents

Mueller III, RS 2019, 'Report on the investigation into Russian interference in the 2016 presidential election', vol. I (Redacted version of 18 April 2019). Available at: www.justice.gov/storage/report.pdf

Pariser, E 2011, *The filter bubble: How the new personalized web is changing what we read and how we think*. New York: Penguin.

Pew Research Center 2019, '10 facts about Americans and Facebook', 16 May. Available at: www.pewresearch.org/fact-tank/2019/05/16/facts-about-americans-and-facebook/

Quine, WVO and Ullian, JS 1978, *The web of belief*, vol. 2. New York: Random House.

Ratkiewicz, J, Conover, MD, Meiss, M, Gonçalves, B, Flammini, A and Menczer, FM 2011, 'Detecting and tracking political abuse in social media', Proceedings of the Fifth International AAAI Conference on Weblogs and Social Media, Barcelona, Spain, 17–21 July.

Ruck, DJ, Rice, NM, Borycz, J and Bentley, RA 2019, 'Internet research agency Twitter activity predicted 2016 U.S. election polls', *First Monday, 24*. https://doi.org/10.5210/fm.v24i7.10107

Sanovich, S 2019, 'Russia: The origins of digital misinformation', in Woolley, SC and Howard, PN (eds.) *Computational propaganda: Political parties, politicians, and political manipulation on social media*. New York: Oxford University Press, pp. 21–40.

Shao, C, Ciampaglia, GL, Varol, O, Yang, K, Flammini, A and Menczer, F 2018, 'The spread of low-credibility content by social bots', *Nature Communications, 9*(1), pp. 1–9. https://doi.org/10.1038/s41467-018-06930-7

Singer, PW and Brooking, ET 2018, *Like war: Weaponization of social media*. Boston: Eamon Dolan Books.

Spangher, A, Ranade, G, Nushi, B, Fourney, A and Horvitz, E 2020, 'Characterizing search-engine traffic to Internet research agency web properties', WWW'20, Taipei, Taiwan, 20–24 April. https://doi.org/10.1145/3366423.3380290

Stella, M, Ferrara, E and De Domenico, M 2018, 'Bots increase exposure to negative and inflammatory content in online social systems', *Proceedings of the National Academy of Sciences*, *115*(49), pp. 12435–12440.

Stieglitz, S and Dang-Xuan, L 2013, 'Emotions and information diffusion in social media – sentiment of microblogs and sharing behavior', *Journal of Management Information Systems*, *29*(4), pp. 217–248. https://doi.org/10.2753/MIS0742-1222290408

Stroud, NJ 2011, *Niche news: The politics of news choice*. Oxford: Oxford University Press on Demand.

Stukal, D, Sanovich, S, Tucker, JA and Bonneau, R 2019, 'For whom the bot tolls: A neural networks approach to measuring political orientation of Twitter bots in Russia', *Sage Open*, *9*(2), pp. 1–16. https://doi.org/10.1177/2158244019827715

Thieltges, A, Papakyriakopoulos, O, Serrano, JCM and Hegelich, S 2018, 'Effects of social bots in the Iran-debate on Twitter', *arXiv preprint arXiv:1805.10105*. Available at: https://arxiv.org/pdf/1805.10105.pdf

Thomas, T 2004, 'Russia's reflexive control theory and the military', *The Journal of Slavic Military Studies*, *17*(2), pp. 237–256. https://doi.org/10.1080/13518040490450529

Till, C 2020, 'Propaganda through "reflexive control" and the mediated construction of reality', *New Media & Society*, pp. 1–17. https://doi.org/10.1177/1461444820902446

Tufekci, Z and Wilson, C 2012, 'Social media and the decision to participate in political protest: Observations from Tahrir square', *Journal of Communication*, *62*(2), pp. 363–379.

Twitter Public Policy 2018, 'Update on Twitter's review of the 2016 US election', *Twitter Blog*, 19 January. Available at: https://blog.twitter.com/en_us/topics/company/2018/2016-election-update.html

United States of America v Internet Research Agency LLC (2018) 18 U.S.C. §§ 2, 371, 1349, 1028A.

U.S. Senate Committee on Crime and Terrorism 2017, *Extremist content and Russian disinformation online: Working with Tech to find solutions*. Testimony of Colin Stretch, General Counsel, Facebook. Washington, DC: Hart Senate Office Building 216. Available at: www.judiciary.senate.gov/imo/media/doc/10-31-17%20Stretch%20Testimony.pdf

U.S. Senate Foreign Relations Committee 2018, *Putin's asymmetric assault on democracy in Russia and Europe: Implications for US national security* (S. Rpt. 115–121). Washington, DC: Government Publishing Office. Available at: www.foreign.senate.gov/imo/media/doc/FinalRR.pdf

Van Dijck, J 2012, 'Facebook and the engineering of connectivity: A multi-layered approach to social media platforms', *Convergence*, *19*(2), pp. 141–155.

Walker, C and Ludwig, J 2017, 'The meaning of sharp power: How authoritarian states project influence', *Foreign Affairs*, 16 November. Available at: https://foreignaffairs.com/articles/china/2017-11-16/meaning-sharp-power

Ward, C, Polglase, K, Shukla, S, Mezzofiore, G. and Lister, T 2020, 'Russian election meddling is back – via Ghana and Nigeria – and in your feeds', *CNN*, 13 March. Available at: www.cnn.com/2020/03/12/world/russia-ghana-troll-farms-2020-ward/index.html

Woolley, SC and Guilbeault, DR 2017, 'Computational propaganda in the United States of America: Manufacturing consensus online', *The Computational Propaganda Research Project*, *2017*(5), pp. 1–29.

Woolley, SC and Howard, PN 2016, 'Political communication, computational propaganda, and autonomous agents', *International Journal of Communication*, *10*, pp. 4882–4890.

Woolley, SC and Howard, PN 2018. *Computational propaganda: Political parties, politicians, and political manipulation on social media*. Oxford: Oxford University Press.

Yang, Y 2017, 'China's Communist Party raises army of nationalist trolls', *Financial Times*, 29 December. Available at: www.ft.com/content/9ef9f592-e2bd-11e7-97e2-916d4fbac0da

Yapparova, L 2019, 'The information nation: A Kremlin-managed research center is selling services that can deanonymize anyone in Russia', *Meduza*, 20 September. Available at: https://meduza.io/en/feature/2019/09/20/the-information-nation?fbclid=IwAR0FhXlp36V9HhaBXD6zxiqeInk1nEmbWkjwRnX0TTP1bUgUuZ6r1BEBovY

Zhong, R, Meyers Lee, S and Wu, J 2019, 'How China unleashed Twitter trolls to discredit Hing Kong's protesters', *The New York Times*, 18 September. Available at: www.nytimes.com/interactive/2019/09/18/world/asia/hk-twitter.html

12

POLARISATION AND MISINFORMATION

Johanna Dunaway

Introduction

Media choice, echo chambers, filter bubbles, and other characteristics of the communication environment are often blamed for political polarisation and a post-truth era (Sunstein 2017; Weeks 2018). It is reasonable; expanding media choice and rising polarisation incentivise media selectivity and fact avoidance while increasing vulnerability to misinformation. The potential consequences are troubling amidst rising populism, in which elites utilise mass media to employ polarising communication strategies divorced from fact (Waisbord 2018). Yet existing evidence emphasises the centrality of predispositions in motivating information seeking and processing, cognitive biases, and the relative unimportance of facts in belief formation (Kunda 1990; Lodge and Taber 2013; Swire et al. 2017a). These perspectives suggest political misperceptions are a product of cognitive and affective processes that operate independently from or in tandem with exposure to misinformation (Thorson et al. 2018).

A review of the literature suggests that rather than remaining fixated on how the information environment facilitates misinformation's dissemination and exposure, we should more carefully consider whether and how cognitive biases, motivated reasoning, and affective polarisation foster permissiveness towards misinformation, as well as its processing, acceptance, and endorsement. The central argument in this chapter is that despite the media ecology's potential for heightening misinformation exposure (Allcott and Gentzkow 2017), cognitive biases, affective polarisation, and sorting are as much to blame for susceptibility to misinformation and the development of misperceptions as structural changes to the media.

Literature review

There is ample evidence for enduring, widely held misperceptions in the US (Kuklinski et al. 2000; Lazer et al. 2018; Jerit and Zhao 2020). Misperceptions persist across several domains, including policy (Jerit and Barabas 2012), the evaluation of politicians (Nyhan and Reifler 2010; Miller et al. 2016), and even parties and partisans (Ahler and Sood 2018). Misperceptions plague citizens of both parties when supporting of their political predispositions (Jerit and Barabas 2012). Because misperceptions are often characterised as being on the rise and correlated with changes to media and rising polarisation (Sunstein 2017; Weeks 2018), both are blamed for the spread and effects of misinformation. Recent Russian interference in the 2016 US presidential election and rising populism exacerbate these concerns, making it easy to understand references to an 'epidemic of misinformation' and a surge in related research.

Yet neither political misinformation nor misperceptions are new (Waisbord 2018). Misinformation has been around as long as politics, and researchers have been explaining why Americans cannot articulate coherent policy preferences since the 1950s (Converse 1964; Zaller and Feldman 1992; Deli Carpini and Keeter 1996). Nevertheless, both are often characterised as on the rise, enabled by digital media, and capable of affecting citizen beliefs and judgments (Weeks 2018).

Media-structural explanations

Most explanations for misinformation spread and misperceptions are based on changing media structures or cognitive and affective processes. Media explanations focus on two structural aspects of the digital media environment: those allowing for ideological segregation through media selectivity and algorithmic filtering and those facilitating massive and rapid exposure to misinformation.

High choice, selectivity, and filtering

Media-based accounts depict exposure to misinformation as both a cause and a consequence of polarisation, where polarisation facilitates selective exposure in a high-choice context, and the misinformation is persuasive because it comes from like-minded sources. Assuming that much misinformation comes from biased sources of partisan information, high choice encourages exposure by allowing for partisan media selectivity and through algorithmic filtering and homogeneous social networks (Sunstein 2017). Under this view, echo chambers and filter bubbles are harmful contexts for misinformation because attitude-consistent information is viewed as credible and is more likely to be accepted and shared, especially within networks (Bakshy et al. 2015).

But evidence for ideological segregation is mixed (e.g. Weeks et al. 2017), as is evidence about its effects (Flaxman et al. 2016; Peterson et al. 2018). Some studies link digital media to ideological segregation (Sunstein 2017); others find that high choice and networks facilitate exposure diversity (e.g. Gil de Zúñiga et al. 2017). Cross-ideology exposure is frequent (Bakshy et al. 2015), attributable to the 'social' nature of cross-ideology network ties and endorsements (Messing and Westwood 2014). Additionally, media audiences are highly concentrated on neutral mainstream sites (Hindman 2018; Flaxman et al. 2016). When echo chambers are found, there is little evidence of attitudinal or behavioural effects (Peterson et al. 2018). Despite evidence of echo chambers, they are not impenetrable; their potential to intensify exposure to misinformation and misperceptions may be overstated, especially amidst polarisation.

Rapid information sharing and network structures

A defining feature of the digital media environment is its ability to concentrate attention even while fragmented (Hindman 2018). Thus, some concerns about misinformation are related to digital media's vast and instantaneous reach. Low reproduction costs, network structures, and peer-to-peer sharing capabilities facilitate rapid information dissemination and information cascades, allowing the opportunity for intense exposure to misinformation (Vosoughi et al. 2018). The digital media environment lacks the gatekeeping infrastructure of traditional media, making it amenable to misinformation spread (Rojecki and Meraz 2016). Elites have an advantage for spreading rumours online and spurring informational cascades (Bakshy et al. 2011) and are known to enlist digital media to spread persuasive and divisive misinformation to encourage polarisation and mistrust (Engesser et al. 2017; Ernst et al. 2017; de Vreese et al. 2018).

Yet concerns about the persuasive power of mass misinformation exposure are reflective of now-debunked theories of massive media impact from the earliest phases of media effects research, which was motivated by fears about elites' use of mass media to disseminate powerful and persuasive propaganda (Iyengar 2017). Given what we have since learned about active and selective audiences (Prior 2007; Bennett and Iyengar 2008; Arceneaux and Johnson 2013), the power of predispositions (Kunda 1990; Zaller 1992), and competing demands on the attention of modern audiences (Hindman 2018), we should not necessarily expect persuasion from misinformation except under narrow conditions. Though polarised audiences may be exposed to more misinformation through media choice and personalisation, its potential to significantly change attitudes and behavior is unknown.

However, digital and social media may compound the effects of misinformation in ways other than through persuasion. One is by increasing familiarity. Repeated information exposure increases perceived accuracy even when false (Swire et al. 2017b; Pennycook et al. 2018). When misinformation is disseminated widely and continually circulates within networks, it increases familiarity (Weaver et al. 2007), cognitive accessibility (e.g. DiFonzo et al. 2016), ease of processing (e.g. Schwarz et al. 2016), and perceptions of consensus (e.g. Leviston et al. 2013), all of which influence judgments about accuracy. Thus, even allowing for the limited circumstances under which misinformation should persuade (Zaller 1992; Bennett and Iyengar 2008), the information environment's amenability to disseminating and recirculating misinformation prompts concerns that repeated exposure will increase its perceived accuracy.

The effects of even highly intense doses of misinformation should, however, be dependent on the message, political context, and individual-level characteristics like political awareness and predispositions (Zaller 1992; Bennett and Iyengar 2008). These factors and high polarisation may help explain why, despite the proliferation of misinformation on social media, there is little direct evidence that it promotes misperceptions (e.g. Allcott and Gentzkow 2017; Garrett 2019).

Cognitive and affective processes

Cognitive and affective explanations portray media environment as more handmaiden than driver of misperceptions; instead, they point to the importance of polarisation in terms of how it affects misinformation processing upon exposure (Flynn et al. 2017; Weeks and Garrett 2014). Some downplay the role of misinformation entirely, highlighting processes that operate independently of exposure (e.g. Thorson et al. 2018; Reedy et al. 2014). Similarly, evidence from research on affective polarisation and partisan sorting (e.g. Iyengar et al. 2012; Iyengar and Westwood 2015; Mason 2015, 2016) and expressive responding (e.g. Bullock et al. 2013; Schaffner and Luks 2018) questions a causal role for the media environment.

Motivated reasoning

Motivated reasoning depicts information seeking and processing as goal directed. Accuracy goals produce information seeking and processing aimed at coming to an informed decision. Directional goals are concerned with finding and processing information to support an attitude-consistent conclusion. With political information, directional goals are presumed to be heavily guided by partisanship (Druckman et al. 2013; Lodge and Taber 2013). This reasoning is particularly important for understanding misinformation in the high-choice media environment (Jerit and Zhao 2020).

Because directional motives are presumed common with respect to political information, motivated reasoning is considered a primary cause of misperceptions (Jerit and Zhao 2020) under the logic that misinformation – like information – is processed to yield attitude-consistent conclusions. There is evidence to this effect. Americans interpret economic information in ways that defend their partisan identities, regardless of accuracy (Schaffner and Roche 2016). Predispositions also predict which conspiracies partisans endorse (Miller et al. 2016). Similarly, when misinformation is corrected or retracted, partisans are reluctant to dismiss it when it reinforces their pre-existing attitudes.

However, it is important to recall that under motivated reasoning, exposure to counter-attitudinal misinformation is unlikely to alter preferences and predispositions because it is consistent with out-group arguments. Rather than persuading, exposure to counter-attitudinal information increases the salience of one's in-group identity, prompting counter-arguments as part of a defensive strategy (Kunda 1990). Directional motivated reasoning goals should dictate the extent to which congenial misinformation is accepted and disagreeable misinformation is resisted. In short, attitudes and identities determine partisans' willingness to accept misinformation as fact more than exposure to misinformation shapes their attitudes (Thorson 2016; Nyhan and Reifler 2010). This is especially important in contexts with rising affective polarisation and sorting.

Affective polarisation and sorting

Affective polarisation is sharply rising in America (Iyengar et al. 2012; Iyengar and Krupenkin 2018; Mason and Wronski 2018), and political identities are becoming more coherent through a process called partisan-ideological sorting, in which party becomes more entwined with worldview and social and cultural identity, strengthening partisan identities (Mason 2015, 2016). Sorted partisans have stronger emotional reactions to political information than weaker partisans (Huddy et al. 2015; Iyengar and Krupenkin 2018), and as partisan affect intensifies, it increasingly reflects in-group favouritism and out-group dislike (Iyengar and Krupenkin 2018; Mason and Wronski 2018).

These changes should only exacerbate the influence of cognitive and affective biases upon exposure to misinformation. More sorted and affect-driven partisans seek out and process information as highly motivated reasoners, and counter-attitudinal misinformation will be ignored or processed in ways that reinforce beliefs; the same will be true for attitude-consistent misinformation (Lewandowsky et al. 2005; Gaines et al. 2007; Nyhan and Reifler 2010; Leviston et al. 2013).

Research on misperceptions confirms the importance of political identity. When misinformation is worldview consistent, it is more likely to be accepted as fact (Flynn et al. 2017; Weeks and Garrett 2014; Marsh and Yang 2018). Misinformation is used to support existing positions (Reedy et al. 2014), and those with strong political identities accept political misinformation to support in-party evaluations (e.g. Garrett et al. 2016) and embrace misperceptions (e.g. Gaines et al. 2007; Schaffner and Roche 2016), questioning whether misperceptions reflect beliefs about facts or fact bending.

Research on expressive responding questions whether political misperceptions reflect beliefs at all and posits that they instead reflect partisan cheerleading, expression (Bullock et al. 2013; Khanna and Sood 2018; Schaffner and Luks 2018), or the effort to bait researchers (e.g. Lopez and Hillygus 2018). Evidence for expressive responding is mixed, however (Berinsky 2018; Jerit and Zhao 2020). Related work questions misperceptions on measurement (Cor and Sood 2016; Jerit and Zhao 2020), asserting that survey responses reflect guesses or top-of-the-head responses instead of misperceptions, consistent with early work on survey response instability (Zaller and Feldman 1992).

Assessing the state of knowledge

Researchers are keenly interested in how polarisation and misinformation contribute to misperceptions (e.g. DiFonzo et al. 2016; Flynn et al. 2017; Leviston et al. 2013; Pennycook et al. 2018; Thorson et al. 2018). The fact that the digital media environment is thought to facilitate both polarisation and misinformation exposure makes it a natural place to look for causal explanations. Evidence suggests there is more to the story. Cognitive accounts suggest misinformation effects should be highly conditional on predispositions, motivations, and context. Causal effects from affective polarization are just as much about how misinformation is processed as they are about dictating exposure to misinformation.

While the digital media environment provides ample opportunity for misinformation exposure, beliefs drive information consumption and processing more than they are shaped by them. And as demonstrated by the US – a context of growing affective and elite polarisation – motivated reasoning is only likely to increase the influence of existing beliefs. If partisan identity is so rigidly in place as to drive even the evaluation of information upon exposure, the likelihood that misinformation about politics and issues has much potential for persuasive effects among out-partisans should be minimal in polarised contexts.

Yet whether there are important behavioral effects from exposure remains an open question. We know that exposure to misinformation can make people more likely to endorse or embrace attitude-congruent misinformation, even when aware of inaccuracies (Gaines et al. 2007; Garrett et al. 2016; Schaffner and Luks 2018; Schaffner and Roche 2016). Even though evidence suggests direct persuasive effects of factual misinformation should be minimal – or, at the very least, conditional – despite high rates of mass exposure, this conclusion depends on several unanswered questions.

First, what effects are of most concern? Misinformation studies focus largely on direct persuasive effects, but what about indirect effects? Given the role strong partisans play as opinion leaders (Holbert et al. 2010), their vulnerability to attitude-consistent misinformation may have harmful indirect effects as they feel emboldened to endorse and/or share misinformation (Garrett et al. 2016; Messing and Westwood 2014). If there is a two-step flow in the digital media environment, and at least some evidence suggests there is (e.g. Feezell 2018), there may be cause for concern, especially considering that facts do not matter for what gets shared online (Weng et al. 2012; Vosoughi et al. 2018; Van Duyn and Collier 2019). If misperceptions are more about expressive responding or strategic endorsement than belief, should we be any less concerned? Or are the downstream effects just as troubling?

It could be that there are effects from the media environment, but the mechanisms through which they operate might be different than commonly articulated. Misinformation promotes the expression or endorsement of political misperceptions but not through persuasion with incorrect facts. Instead, misperceptions are embraced as partisans feel emboldened to endorse inaccurate but attitude-consistent beliefs (e.g. Garrett et al. 2016). In-network cheerleading and repetition might persuade those without strong political predispositions by enhancing familiarity, accessibility, and perceptions of accuracy (Weaver et al. 2007; DiFonzo et al. 2016; Schwarz et al. 2016; Leviston et al. 2013), but among partisans, it just reinforces willingness to accept false information and embrace misperceptions in service to identity (e.g. Garrett et al. 2016). In the context of trying to understand how digital media stoke populism, this kind of indirect process seems just as troublesome. Still, it is important that we do not mischaracterise the causal relationships.

Second, what kinds of attitudinal changes and behavioural outcomes should we be most concerned about? Currently, misinformation studies are primarily interested in persuasive effects producing attitude change or misperceptions, primarily regarding voting behavior. This is ironic given the difficult time researchers had demonstrating persuasive media effects (Iyengar 2017), and the bar is much higher to change minds and sides than to undermine and discourage.

Evidence from recent elections underscores the point, showing the intent behind recent misinformation tactics – including recent Russian disinformation campaigns – was to use false-hoods to demobilise and discourage/ rather than persuade (Lewandowsky et al. 2017; Kim et al. 2018).[1] The facts are not relevant, and neither is attitude change. Rather, the relevant outcomes reflect disengagement with politics, such as declining participation among targeted groups, or related precursors, like apathy, efficacy, and cynicism (Lewandowsky et al. 2017). Few studies of misinformation focus on these outcomes; the literature provides few answers about behavioural effects (Lazer et al. 2018).

However, what we do know supports insights from cognitive explanations. Misperceptions are irrelevant for vote choice, more evidence downplaying the importance of facts (Swire et al. 2017a). Yet when the aim is to mobilise or demobilise, emotional appeals and divisive issues are often successful (Krupnikov 2011). Research on recent Facebook misinformation tactics reflects this, revealing effective strategies aimed at casting doubt and causing confusion (Kim et al. 2018). If the point is more to discourage and dissuade than to change hearts and minds, we should look at participatory outcomes or their precursors as opposed to vote choice or factual political questions. While the conditions for persuasive misinformation effects might be narrow, the potential for mobilisation and demobilisation seems profound (Lewandowsky et al. 2017).

Relatedly, what kinds of misinformation are most important? There is conceptual opacity across the literature on misinformation and misperceptions (Flynn et al. 2017; Jerit and Zhao 2020). Kuklinski and colleagues define political misinformation as when someone 'holds the wrong information' (2000, 792). Allcott and Gentzkow define fake news as 'news articles that are intentionally and verifiably false and could mislead readers' (2017, 213). Lazer and colleagues define it as 'fabricated information that mimics news media content in form but not in organizational process or intent' (2018, 1094). Slippage aside, these are all reasonable conceptualisations. Political misinformation exists in many forms and overlaps heavily with a range of variants from unintentionally erroneous information to purposefully misleading information to all-out fabrication. All of these are found in news, elite rhetoric, and other political communication. Yet recent evidence (e.g. Kim et al. 2018) suggests that these definitions miss the mark, either because they fail to capture outcomes intended by actors spreading misinformation or because they do not capture the tactics being employed with respect to message or source. If the aim is to divide, distract, or discourage, indicators based on facts tell only part of the story. Similarly, isolating studies to fake news might miss important paid media strategies like those used by stealth groups on Facebook (Kim et al. 2018). And limiting research to those messages that are demonstrably false rather than purposefully but only slightly misleading (Rojecki and Meraz 2016) may do the same.

Another underexplored question asks which targets of misinformation are most important to consider. Electoral misinformation tactics are targeted on the basis of class and race and use wedge issues to divide (Kim et al. 2018). This strategy is troubling because it appeals to populist sentiments and may be effective, further exacerbating racial, ethnic, and socio-economic divides. Partisanship provides one route for motivated reasoning; targeting other-group divides may be equally effective. According to the literature on media effects (e.g. Zaller 1992), if paid media allow for strategies based on intense, micro-targeted messaging, we should be most concerned about misinformation targeting citizens of low political interest and knowledge (Miller et al. 2016), with affective appeals meant to distract, obscure, and demobilise.

Conclusion

An underlying theme in this chapter is that misinformation is information – albeit an especially problematic type – which means we already know a lot about its effects. Some research characterises misinformation as a new problem, implying the potential for more powerful effects on attitudes and behaviour, which, according to literature on media effects, is unlikely. We need to reconcile what we know about media effects – they are real but indirect and limited at best, and possibly minimal (e.g. Bennett and Iyengar 2008) – with alarm over misinformation. Misinformation might be rampant and exposure widespread (but see Guess et al. 2019), but the persuasive effects of that information should be limited to particular individuals in particular informational and political conditions (Zaller 1992). That said, we know so little about misinformation effects across varying political, institutional, and cultural contexts, it is difficult to draw conclusions about the severity of the problem absent more cross-national comparative research, especially with respect to the roles misinformation and polarisation play in rising populism around the globe.

Nevertheless, we should not mischaracterise the nature of the causal relationships between polarisation, the media environment, exposure to misinformation, and misperceptions. Some accounts suggest the process is that people will be more exposed to misinformation or develop misperceptions because of decisions they make about what kinds of information to attend – especially popular accounts. Other accounts seem preoccupied with exposure because of digital media potential for mass exposure – and network and filtering effects that allow for echo chambers – based on the expectation that such mass exposure will further partisan extremity and polarisation. But an argument more consistent with psychological models is that polarisation – especially the affective form – makes people more susceptible to misinformation once exposed, such that causal influence from polarisation is less about how it dictates selections and exposure and more about how it affects processing upon exposure.

Building on literatures from information processing, motivated reasoning, and media effects, misinformation research should be more focused on the conditions under which three distinct types of exposure to misinformation occurs – motivated, incidental, and targeted – and whether and how that misinformation is processed upon exposure and with what effects. It could be that the current information environment allows for very high rates of motivated exposure to misinformation, which result in processing and acceptance, but little attitudinal or behavioural change due to ceiling effects, though motivated information seekers may publicly endorse misinformation with indirect downstream effects. Similarly, rates of incidental exposure may be high, especially on some platforms, but not sufficiently high to prompt message acceptance or behavioural change among low-interest citizens. If misinformation strategists target groups with high-message intensity and identity-base appeals (e.g. Kim et al. 2018), these messages may permeate enough to induce processing, acceptance, and even attitude change even among those with low political interest. We do not know. It may be more important to consider what cultural, political, and institutional processes have produced the strengthening of political identities and increased affective polarisation in the first place. Doing this properly will require more cross-national comparative research.

It is also worth considering whether studies of misinformation need better partitions between politics and health, science, and public safety, despite the fact that these can never be fully separated from politics. This review questions the relevance of facts to political misperceptions. But this is not to say that facts are unimportant – their importance in health, science, and safety has never been clearer than now amidst the COVID-19 crisis. But, however unfortunate, the relevance of facts is domain specific, and politics is different. If we want to understand the conditions under which elites – populist or otherwise – effectively use misinformation tactics to mobilise support, our research questions and designs should reflect the fact that political battles are not fought or won on the basis of facts. At least under conditions of low media and government trust, elite polarisation, and mass social polarisation, facts do not win hearts and minds; political support is affective (Iyengar et al. 2012). The digital media ecology is an effective handmaiden to misinformation tactics, but it will only be effective in the context of existing structural and political trends that foster post-truth culture (Waisbord 2018) characterised by permissiveness towards misinformation and a disregard for facts.

Note

1 For anecdotal accounts (see Lewandowsky et al. 2017): www.washingtonpost.com/graphics/politics/trump-claims/; http://bangordailynews.com/2017/01/23/opinion/editorials/there-are-not-alternative-facts-just-truth-and-lies/.

References

Ahler, D.J. and Sood, G., 2018. The parties in our heads: Misperceptions about party composition and their consequences. *The Journal of Politics*, *80*(3), pp. 964–981.

Allcott, H. and Gentzkow, M., 2017. Social media and fake news in the 2016 election. *Journal of Economic Perspectives*, *31*(2), pp. 211–236.

Arceneaux, K. and Johnson, M., 2013. *Changing minds or changing channels? Partisan news in an age of choice*. Chicago: University of Chicago Press.

Bakshy, E., Hofman, J.M., Mason, W.A. and Watts, D.J., 2011, February. Everyone's an influencer: Quantifying influence on twitter. In *Proceedings of the fourth ACM international conference on Web search and data mining* (pp. 65–74). https://dl.acm.org/doi/10.1145/1935826.1935845

Bakshy, E., Messing, S. and Adamic, L.A., 2015. Exposure to ideologically diverse news and opinion on Facebook. *Science*, *348*(6239), pp. 1130–1132.

Bennett, W.L. and Iyengar, S., 2008. A new era of minimal effects? The changing foundations of political communication. *Journal of Communication*, *58*(4), pp. 707–731.

Berinsky, A.J. 2018. Telling the truth about believing the lies? Evidence for the limited prevalence of expressive survey responding. *Journal of Politics*, *80*, pp. 211–224.

Bullock, J.G., Gerber, A.S., Hill, S.J. and Huber, G.A., 2013. Partisan bias in factual beliefs about politics. *Quarterly Journal of Political Science*, *10*, pp. 519–578.

Carpini, M.X.D. and Keeter, S., 1996. *What Americans know about politics and why it matters*. New Haven, CT: Yale University Press.

Converse, P.E., 1964. The nature of belief systems in mass publics: Ideology and discontent. *Ideology and Discontent*, pp. 206–261.

Cor, M.K. and Sood, G., 2016. Guessing and forgetting: A latent class model for measuring learning. *Political Analysis*, pp. 226–242.

De Vreese, C.H., Esser, F., Aalberg, T., Reinemann, C. and Stanyer, J., 2018. Populism as an expression of political communication content and style: A new perspective. *The International Journal of Press/Politics*, *23*(4), pp. 423–438.

DiFonzo, N., Beckstead, J.W., Stupak, N. and Walders, K., 2016. Validity judgments of rumors heard multiple times: The shape of the truth effect. *Social Influence*, *11*(1), pp. 22–39.

Druckman, J.N., Peterson, E. and Slothuus, R., 2013. How elite partisan polarization affects public opinion formation. *American Political Science Review*, *107*(1), pp. 57–79.

Engesser, S., Ernst, N., Esser, F. and Büchel, F., 2017. Populism and social media: How politicians spread a fragmented ideology. *Information, Communication & Society*, *20*(8), pp. 1109–1126.

Ernst, N., Engesser, S., Büchel, F., Blassnig, S. and Esser, F., 2017. Extreme parties and populism: An analysis of Facebook and Twitter across six countries. *Information, Communication & Society*, *20*(9), pp. 1347–1364.

Feezell, J.T., 2018. Agenda setting through social media: The importance of incidental news exposure and social filtering in the digital era. *Political Research Quarterly*, *71*(2), pp. 482–494.

Flaxman, S., Goel, S. and Rao, J.M., 2016. Filter bubbles, echo chambers, and online news consumption. *Public Opinion Quarterly*, *80*(S1), pp. 298–320.

Flynn, D.J., Nyhan, B. and Reifler, J., 2017. The nature and origins of misperceptions: Understanding false and unsupported beliefs about politics. *Political Psychology*, *38*, pp. 127–150.

Gaines, B.J., Kuklinski, J.H., Quirk, P.J., Peyton, B. and Verkuilen, J., 2007. Same facts, different interpretations: Partisan motivation and opinion on Iraq. *The Journal of Politics*, *69*(4), pp. 957–974.

Garrett, R.K., 2019. Social media's contribution to political misperceptions in US presidential elections. *PLoS One*, *14*(3).

Garrett, R.K., Weeks, B.E. and Neo, R.L., 2016. Driving a wedge between evidence and beliefs: How online ideological news exposure promotes political misperceptions. *Journal of Computer-Mediated Communication*, *21*(5), pp. 331–348.

Gil de Zúñiga, H., Weeks, B. and Ardèvol-Abreu, A., 2017. Effects of the news-finds-me perception in communication: Social media use implications for news seeking and learning about politics. *Journal of Computer-Mediated Communication*, *22*(3), pp. 105–123.

Guess, A., Nagler, J. and Tucker, J., 2019. Less than you think: Prevalence and predictors of fake news dissemination on Facebook. *Science Advances*, *5*(1), p.eaau4586.

Hindman, M., 2018. The Internet trap: How the digital economy builds monopolies and undermines democracy. Princeton, NJ: Princeton University Press.

Holbert, R.L., Garrett, R.K. and Gleason, L.S., 2010. A new era of minimal effects? A response to Bennett and Iyengar. *Journal of Communication*, *60*(1), pp. 15–34.

Huddy, L., Mason, L. and Aarøe, L., 2015. Expressive partisanship: Campaign involvement, political emotion, and partisan identity. *American Political Science Review*, *109*(1), pp. 1–17.

Iyengar, S., 2017. *A typology of media effects* (pp. 59–68). New York: Oxford University Press.

Iyengar, S. and Krupenkin, M., 2018. The strengthening of partisan affect. *Political Psychology*, *39*, pp. 201–218.

Iyengar, S., Sood, G. and Lelkes, Y., 2012. Affect, not ideology a social identity perspective on polarization. *Public Opinion Quarterly*, *76*(3), pp. 405–431.

Iyengar, S. and Westwood, S.J., 2015. Fear and loathing across party lines: New evidence on group polarization. *American Journal of Political Science*, *59*(3), pp. 690–707.

Jerit, J. and Barabas, J., 2012. Partisan perceptual bias and the information environment. *The Journal of Politics*, *74*(3), pp. 672–684.

Jerit, J. and Zhao, Y., 2020. Political misinformation. *Annual Review of Political Science*, *23*.

Khanna, K. and Sood, G., 2018. Motivated responding in studies of factual learning. *Political Behavior*, *40*(1), pp. 79–101.

Kim, Y.M., Hsu, J., Neiman, D., Kou, C., Bankston, L., Kim, S.Y., Heinrich, R., Baragwanath, R. and Raskutti, G., 2018. The stealth media? Groups and targets behind divisive issue campaigns on Facebook. *Political Communication*, *35*(4), pp. 515–541.

Krupnikov, Y., 2011. When does negativity demobilize? Tracing the conditional effect of negative campaigning on voter turnout. *American Journal of Political Science*, *55*(4), pp. 797–813.

Kuklinski, J.H., Quirk, P.J., Jerit, J., Schwieder, D. and Rich, R.F., 2000. Misinformation and the currency of democratic citizenship. *Journal of Politics*, *62*(3), pp. 790–816.

Kunda, Z., 1990. The case for motivated reasoning. *Psychological Bulletin*, *108*(3), p. 480.

Lazer, D.M., Baum, M.A., Benkler, Y., Berinsky, A.J., Greenhill, K.M., Menczer, F., Metzger, M.J., Nyhan, B., Pennycook, G., Rothschild, D. and Schudson, M., 2018. The science of fake news. *Science*, *359*(6380), pp. 1094–1096.

Leviston, Z., Walker, I. and Morwinski, S., 2013. Your opinion on climate change might not be as common as you think. *Nature Climate Change*, *3*(4), pp. 334–337.

Lewandowsky, S., Ecker, U.K. and Cook, J., 2017. Beyond misinformation: Understanding and coping with the "post-truth" era. *Journal of Applied Research in Memory and Cognition*, *6*(4), pp. 353–369.

Lewandowsky S., Oberauer K. and Morales M., 2005. Memory for fact, fiction, and misinformation: The Iraq War 2003. *Psychological Sciences, 16*, pp. 190–195.

Lodge, M. and Taber, C.S., 2013. *The rationalizing voter.* Cambridge: Cambridge University Press.

Lopez, J. and Hillygus, D.S., 2018. *Why so serious? Survey trolls and misinformation.* https://ssrn.com/abstract=3131087 or http://dx.doi.org/10.2139/ssrn.3131087

Marsh, E.J. and Yang, B.W., 2018. Believing things that are not true: A cognitive science perspective on misinformation. *Misinformation and Mass Audiences*, pp. 15–34.

Mason, L., 2015. "I disrespectfully agree": The differential effects of partisan sorting on social and issue polarization. *American Journal of Political Science, 59*(1), pp. 128–145.

Mason, L., 2016. A cross-cutting calm: How social sorting drives affective polarization. *Public Opinion Quarterly, 80*(S1), pp. 351–377.

Mason, L. and Wronski, J., 2018. One tribe to bind them all: How our social group attachments strengthen partisanship. *Political Psychology, 39*, pp. 257–277.

Messing, S. and Westwood, S.J., 2014. Selective exposure in the age of social media: Endorsements trump partisan source affiliation when selecting news online. *Communication Research, 41*(8), pp. 1042–1063.

Miller, J.M., Saunders, K.L. and Farhart, C.E., 2016. Conspiracy endorsement as motivated reasoning: The moderating roles of political knowledge and trust. *American Journal of Political Science, 60*(4), pp. 824–844.

Nyhan, B. and Reifler, J., 2010. When corrections fail: The persistence of political misperceptions. *Political Behavior, 32*(2), pp. 303–330.

Pennycook, G., Cannon, T.D. and Rand, D.G., 2018. Prior exposure increases perceived accuracy of fake news. *Journal of Experimental Psychology: General, 147*(12), p. 1865.

Peterson, E., Goel, S. and Iyengar, S., 2018. *Echo chambers and partisan polarization: Evidence from the 2016 presidential campaign.* Unpublished manuscript. https://5harad.com/papers/selecfive-exposure.pdf.

Prior, M., 2007. *Post-broadcast democracy: How media choice increases inequality in political involvement and polarizes elections.* Cambridge: Cambridge University Press.

Reedy, J., Wells, C. and Gastil, J., 2014. How voters become misinformed: An investigation of the emergence and consequences of false factual beliefs. *Social Science Quarterly, 95*(5), pp. 1399–1418.

Rojecki, A. and Meraz, S., 2016. Rumors and factitious informational blends: The role of the web in speculative politics. *New Media and Society, 18*(1), pp. 25–43.

Schaffner, B.F. and Luks, S., 2018. Misinformation or expressive responding? What an inauguration crowd can tell us about the source of political misinformation in surveys. *Public Opinion Quarterly, 82*(1), pp. 135–147.

Schaffner, B.F. and Roche, C., 2016. Misinformation and motivated reasoning: Responses to economic news in a politicized environment. *Public Opinion Quarterly, 81*(1), pp. 86–110.

Schwarz, N., Newman, E. and Leach, W., 2016. Making the truth stick and the myths fade: Lessons from cognitive psychology. *Behavioral Science and Policy, 2*(1), pp. 85–95.

Sunstein, C.R., 2017. *#Republic: Divided democracy in the age of social media.* Princeton, NJ: Princeton University Press.

Swire, B., Berinsky, A.J., Lewandowsky, S. and Ecker, U.K., 2017a. Processing political misinformation: Comprehending the Trump phenomenon. *Royal Society Open Science, 4*(3), p. 160802.

Swire, B., Ecker, U.K. and Lewandowsky, S., 2017b. The role of familiarity in correcting inaccurate information. *Journal of Experimental Psychology: Learning, Memory, and Cognition, 43*(12), p. 1948.

Thorson, E.A., 2016. Belief echoes: The persistent effects of corrected misinformation. *Political Communication, 33*, pp. 460–480.

Thorson, E.A., Shelbe, L. and Southwell, B.G., 2018. An agenda for misinformation research. In B.G. Southwell, E. A. Thorson, & L. Sheble (Eds.), *Misinformation and mass audiences* (pp. 289–293). Austin: University of Texas Press.

Van Duyn, E. and Collier, J., 2019. Priming and fake news: The effects of elite discourse on evaluations of news media. *Mass Communication and Society, 22*(1), pp. 29–48.

Vosoughi, S., Roy, D. and Aral, S., 2018. The spread of true and false news online. *Science, 359*(6380), pp. 1146–1151.

Waisbord, S., 2018. The elective affinity between post-truth communication and populist politics. *Communication Research and Practice, 4*(1), pp. 17–34.

Weaver, K., Garcia, S. M., Schwarz, N. and Miller, D. T. 2007. Inferring the popularity of an opinion from its familiarity: A repetitive voice can sound like a chorus. *Journal of Personality and Social Psychology, 92*, pp. 821–833.

Weeks, B.E., 2018. Media and political misperceptions. *Misinformation and Mass Audiences*, pp. 140–156.

Weeks, B.E. and Garrett, R.K., 2014. Electoral consequences of political rumors: Motivated reasoning, candidate rumors, and vote choice during the 2008 US presidential election. *International Journal of Public Opinion Research*, 26(4), pp. 401–422.

Weeks, B.E., Lane, D.S., Kim, D.H., Lee, S.S., and Kwak, N., 2017. Incidental exposure, selective exposure, and political information sharing: Integrating online exposure patterns and expression on social media. *Journal of Computer-Mediated Communication*, 22(6), pp. 363–379.

Weng, L., Flammini, A., Vespignani, A. and Menczer, F., 2012. Competition among memes in a world with limited attention. *Scientific Reports*, 2, p. 335.

Zaller, J.R., 1992. *The nature and origins of mass opinion*. Cambridge: Cambridge University Press.

Zaller, J.R. and Feldman, S., 1992. A simple theory of the survey response: Answering questions versus revealing preferences. *American Journal of Political Science*, pp. 579–616.

13

DATA JOURNALISM AND MISINFORMATION

Oscar Westlund and Alfred Hermida

Introduction

Journalism, news publishers, and journalists are often perceived as having essential roles in society and for democracy. Journalists are assumed to provide verified knowledge daily about public affairs and current events (Carlson 2017). In many countries, there is freedom of speech and freedom of the press, with journalists and news publishers having significant autonomy and professional routines for news production. Journalism maintains a position as one of the most influential knowledge-producing institutions in society, though its role clearly varies substantially around the world. In some countries, journalism is well resourced and able to scrutinise those in power, whereas in others, the authorities exert a substantial degree of control and censorship. News publishers engage in various epistemologies of journalism, involving the production of written news stories, live blogging, and broadcasting, as well as turning to data to identify and report on important patterns and developments. Amid the growing significance of platforms there is an overall process of dislocation, where news is separated from journalism (Ekström & Westlund, 2019a).

This chapter focuses on the intersection of data journalism and misinformation by discussing research into epistemic practices for finding and working with data as well as how data is used to make claims about events and public affairs. Data journalism, computer-assisted reporting, and computational journalism are various conceptualisations used to track the quantitative turns in journalism over time (Coddington 2015). Behind these terms is an epistemology of the evidential forte of data-driven journalism, with journalists as 'apostles of certainty' (Anderson 2018). Data journalism draws on fields such as information visualisation, computer science, and statistics to convey news through the analysis and representation of quantitative, computer-processed data. Data journalism has continuously expanded around the world and to the global South (Mutsvairo, Bebawi & Borges-Rey 2019).

In traditional news journalism, journalists have often relied on established networks of sources that are mainly composed of known institutions and elites (Ettema, James & Glasser 1987). While journalists have often been content as long as they selected and reported the opinions of seemingly reliable sources (and in contrast to each other when needed), their claims to the truth sometimes go no further than assuring 'he says' versus 'she says' among seemingly reliable sources. This is obviously incredibly problematic as it means journalists offer prominent exposure to presidents and prime ministers who repeatedly articulate false claims, whether misinformation or disinformation. Fortunately, there is not just one universal form of journalism but several genres and epistemologies of (digital) journalism (Ekström & Westlund 2019b), taking a more distinct form in the case of, for example, live blogging compared to traditional news journalism (Matheson & Wahl-Jorgensen 2020; Thorsen & Jackson 2018). Ekström and Westlund (2019b) write that 'epistemology is the study of knowledge: what we know, how we know, and how knowledge is justified' (1), referring to the standards, norms, and methods that journalists use when deciding when information is reliable and truthful and when it is not.

While data journalism has been envisioned to advance solid ways of knowledge in society, it is contingent on factors such as access to datasets, reliable and representative data, and individuals (journalists) with the skills to understand and analyse the data (Cairo 2015). In the best case, data journalists can employ data to reveal and visualise complex phenomena in ways that advance journalism practice and spread important knowledge. In the worst case, journalists and news publishers end up publishing data journalism that skews information and spreads misinformation.

Misinformation is produced and shared by a great number of actors (Napoli 2020; Quandt 2018; Tandoc, Lim & Ling 2018) and is published and shared across digital platforms. This connects with alternative news media that situated themselves as a counter to established news publishers gaining ground (Boberg, Quandt, Schatto-Eckrodt & Frischlich 2020; Figenschou & Ihlebæk 2019; Holt, Ustad Figenschou & Frischlich 2019). There are outright 'fake news' producers that imitate some journalistic practices and the style of news content (Robertson & Mourão 2020) and use bots to fuel programmatic advertising revenues (Braun & Eklund 2019). Moreover, to political leaders and the public, 'fake news' is also a label used to delegitimise others, including, but not limited to, the institutions of journalism (Egelhofer & Lecheler 2019). 'Disinformation' refers to situations in which actors deliberately, driven by political and/or economic interests, produce and distribute information intended to disinform for their own ends. 'Misinformation' refers to information that is inaccurate and/or false but where there is no intention to mislead. The category of misinformation extends to the public, authorities, academics, and journalists who unintentionally produce and/or spread misleading, inaccurate, or false information. Journalists obviously are expected to seek out and verify important claims with different reliable sources, but that does not mean they always succeed. Scholars have long since questioned whether journalists actually can achieve fundamental levels of 'accuracy' (Compton & Benedetti 2010; Shapiro, Brin, Bédard-Brûlé & Mychajlowycz 2013).

The next section focuses on two main epistemological dimensions at the intersection of data journalism and misinformation. First, what do (data) journalists know, and how do they know it, in the context of their norms, practices, and routines? Second, how are knowledge claims made in, and in relation to, data journalism materials? This chapter will draw on examples of data journalism and misinformation related to the COVID-19 pandemic.

The epistemology of data journalism amid challenges of misinformation

There is a significant body of literature in (digital) journalism studies focusing on the developments in data journalism over time as well as current practices, challenges, and outcomes (Appelgren, Lindén, & van Dalen 2019; Hermida & Young 2019; Lewis 2015). Data journalism is associated with computer science and statistics, involving the use of computers and software programmes to process and analyse quantitative data to build new knowledge, and the publication of the results through information visualisation. The term *data journalism* is used to capture the multiple and fluid forms of data-driven journalism (Fink and Anderson 2015; Hermida and Young 2019; Mutsvairo 2019).

In the best of worlds, data journalists and other social actors can employ data to examine, reveal, and visualise complex phenomena in ways that advance journalism practice and offer important, accurate, and verified knowledge. In the worst-case scenario, journalists and news publishers end up publishing data journalism that skews information and ends up misinforming the public (Coddington 2015; Lewis & Westlund 2015). Raw, objective, and completely unbiased data is a fantasy rather than a reality. Even in countries where public authorities have ambitious intentions for collecting and compiling reliable datasets, analyses of such data can result in drawing inappropriate data visualisations and conclusions, resulting in readily available misinformation that can be shared by the public.

In the course of writing this chapter, the COVID-19 pandemic has changed society and life as we know it. Many nations enforced lockdown measures in an attempt to prevent the virus from spreading, with unprecedented consequences for macroeconomics and climate, as well as daily life. COVID-19 has resulted in packed hospitals and depleted stocks of medical equipment, panic buying by citizens, armed demonstrations against lockdown measures, and everyday acts of kindness such as coordinated live music performances across balconies. Napoli (2020) points out that amid COVID-19, a convergence is taking place between health misinformation and political misinformation.

COVID-19 has resulted in millions of news articles and news broadcasts by journalists. Then there have been the countless pictures, videos, and observations by the public. There is a sort of mechanical objectivity in the nature of pictures (Carlson 2019), showing the world 'as it is'. Nevertheless, photos of empty shelves in grocery stores can misinform, even more so when it comes to the status of the supply chains. Data journalists can identify and report on the supply chains to grocery stores, such as from toilet paper factories, in order to debunk misinformation about perceived shortages. During such a pandemic, data journalists can play a significant role in gathering, analysing, and publishing data journalism of crucial importance alongside other journalists, authorities, the public, and various stakeholders. In the next two sections, we explore two key aspects integral to the epistemology of data journalism and problematise these in relation to misinformation and COVID-19.

What (data) journalists know and how they know it

Producing reliable information and knowledge through data journalism depends on a range of conditioning factors, including, but not limited to, (1) access, (2) expertise, and (3) coordinating practices.

First, news publishers and journalists must have access to relevant and reliable datasets, which is not the case for several areas of inquiry and varies in different countries (Lewis & Nashmi 2019; Porlezza & Splendore 2019a, 2019b). Journalists can also turn to international and accessible sources to extract data and reveal patterns in specific countries: for example, by using satellite images and data to track a multitude of aspects relating to climate change. In relation to this, journalists have been developing online sourcing to include satellite images to detect and analyse activities relating to news events that may contrast with misleading official accounts (Seo 2020).

Second, news publishers and related social actors must have relevant expertise to process, analyse, interpret, and present the data. Specifically, social actors must have fundamental or advanced knowledge of statistics and handling statistics software to process the data in appropriate ways (Coddington 2015; Lewis & Westlund 2015). In analysing and interpreting datasets, they should be sensitive to the strengths and weaknesses of the data and, ideally, be transparent about these. Data journalism may require expertise in how to develop algorithms to automatically collect large amounts of data from authorities and international organisations, such as the World Health Organization and the United Nations, and from social media platforms, such as Twitter. There is the additional step of presenting the data to the public, often through data visualisations that may offer some interactivity (Young, Hermida & Fulda 2018).

Third, data journalism is a specialised expertise that not all journalists have, and thus, coordinating practices can be critical for advancing and integrating tacit and explicit knowledge amongst members of the news organisation. Inside some news organisations, journalists collaborate with technologists towards shared goals by building on each other's tacit and explicit knowledge (Hermida & Young 2019; Lewis & Westlund 2015; Usher 2016). Some of the most well-known data journalism efforts, such as the Panama Papers, resulted from cross-cultural coordination among journalists who shared resources and efforts during the investigation. Data journalists may also have to coordinate their practices with actors outside journalism, such as civic technologists (Cheruiyot, Baack & Ferrer-Conill 2019).

Now let's turn to what data journalists know and how they know it in the salient case of COVID-19. In their reporting, news publishers can follow updates and access data collected and assembled by entities such as the WHO, Johns Hopkins University, national governments, et cetera. Data from the WHO about new cases, active cases, recovered cases, deaths, total cases, and so forth allows comparison across countries and over time. However, such comparisons depend on individual countries reporting accurately and regularly and using the same methods to count the number of cases and fatalities. Despite many inconsistencies, such figures have become a feature of daily reporting. Take *The Guardian* and its daily "Coronavirus latest: at a glance" report as an example. On 6 April 2020, it reported:

> Italy registered 525 new coronavirus deaths on Sunday, the lowest daily rate since 19 March, while Spain recorded 674 deaths in the past 24 hours – the lowest daily death toll reported since 26 March. In France, 357 people died from COVID-19 in hospitals.

Do *The Guardian* and other news publishers producing similar news materials inform or misinform when reporting this data? The reporting on figures and developments depends on the reliability of the databases. For each country to produce reliable and comparable data, there must be systematic procedures of reporting diagnosed cases, the number of patients in treatment, recoveries, and deaths. There is good reason to assume the actual number of those infected is far higher than the number of reported diagnosed cases, which depend on the scale of testing conducted in each country. Researchers reported that even in the early stages of the spread of the coronavirus, the number of undiagnosed cases was high (Li et al. 2020).

Journalists, authorities, and publics are acting on publicly accessible data, despite such data being problematic and seemingly unstandardised. How some countries track infections and deaths has changed over time. For example, at the end of April 2020, the UK government changed how it reported deaths related to COVID-19 to include fatalities outside hospitals. The result was news stories about the UK being the 'worst-hit European country', outstripping Italy to have the highest number of coronavirus deaths in Europe (Campbell, Perraudin, Davis & Weaver 2020). Whether this was true is hard to ascertain as Italy used a different method to count cases, and the actual figures in both countries might be higher due to missed cases or delays in reporting. Some countries report all deaths and not only COVID-19-related deaths, which results in a higher number. Other countries only report deaths as being caused by

COVID-19 when there has been a confirmed test. Thus, official figures are open to manipulation and/or misrepresentation.

At the end of April 2020, as COVID-19 deaths were rising in the UK, the government added a new graph to its news briefing. The slide offered a comparison of global deaths per million population, suggesting that the death rate in the UK was below those in Belgium, Italy, and Spain (Doyle 2020). The visuals told a politically convenient story, even if the small print acknowledged differences in fatalities attributed to COVID-19. Politicians and authorities elsewhere have adopted similar approaches to shape the communication of COVID-19 data. Moreover, a shortage of testing kits has meant testing the dead has been a low priority (Dupree, Hauslohner, Dalton & Sun 2020). Not only are there problems with testing accuracy and the availability of testing equipment; in some countries political leaders have questioned and/or seemingly downplayed the prevalence of the virus altogether.

The problems with accessing and reporting reliable data for COVID-19 also extend to hospital beds, ventilators, masks, and so forth. Alternative news media and citizens across the globe have published and shared materials for digital media, some with videos, discussing immediate shortages at grocery stores and hospitals. This has fuelled fear, panic buying, hoarding, demonstrations, and violence. Journalists, authorities, and fact-checkers, as well as platform companies and citizens, play important roles in critically examining information and disinformation. Platform companies continuously moderate illegal content as well as misinformation (Gillespie 2018), and companies such as Facebook have ramped up these efforts during COVID-19.

Since institutions of journalism play an authoritative role in pursuing truthfulness and typically verify information with different and reliable sources (Carlson 2017), professional fact-checkers have been working on debunking misinformation in most countries. However, fact-checkers in Austria, Germany, the UK, and the US demonstrate substantially different approaches to transparency (Humprecht 2020), despite arguments about the need for transparent practices to gain trust. A study from Brazil found that people are not very receptive to debunking misinformation relating to new and unfamiliar diseases such as Zika, compared to more familiar diseases such as yellow fever (Carey, Chi, Flynn, Nyhan & Zeitzoff 2020).

Journalists can, of course, interview and quote reliable sources discussing inventory while data journalists seek to access datasets and visualise developments in real time as well as over time. Data journalists reporting about COVID-19 should have expertise in examining the strengths and weaknesses in such data and do their best to report in transparent ways as the pandemic evolves. In the rush to cover all aspects of the coronavirus pandemic, many news outlets have reassigned reporters and editors with no background or expertise in science or health communication to the story. Aside from getting to grips with the terminology, methodologies, and research on viruses and pandemics, there is the additional challenge of interpreting data such as national fatalities. Given the limitations of daily death rates, a more reliable approach advocated by health experts is to compare the number of deaths with the expected numbers – the excess mortality. To their credit, some news publishers such as the BBC, *The Economist*, *The Financial Times*, and the *New York Times* have been reporting excess mortality rates. Integrating information from different datasets can produce more reliable information and help debunk misinformation. Expertise as well as coordinating practices are important for achieving this.

Knowledge claims associated with data journalism

The allure of 'big data' is that 'it is unencumbered by the conventional thinking and inherent biases implicit in the theories of a specific field' (Mayer-Schönberger & Cukier 2013, 71). Despite critical questions (boyd & Crawford 2012), the news industry has been optimistic about new possibilities for producing information with a strong knowledge claim as it aligns with journalism's assumed authoritative role in society to provide verified facts (Carlson 2017; Karlsson, Clerwall & Nord 2017). In traditional news reporting, journalists articulate knowledge claims in their text and the language of news in the way they present sources, the subject, and themselves in text, talk, and visual representations. Visuals create a feeling of 'out-thereness' (Montgomery 2007), resulting in a sort of mechanical objectivity associated with visuals and other forms of photojournalism. While there is a long history of data being visually represented, there has been renewed interest in the digital possibilities of data visualisation and interactivity (Young, Hermida & Fulda 2018). Data visualisations present a visible argument for a story and can be more persuasive than words and figures alone as they 'look and feel objective, precise, and, as a consequence, seductive and convincing' (Cairo 2015, p. 7). Yet choices of scale, form, colour, and hue all shape the narrative and impact of a visualisation (Munzner 2014).

In data journalism, descriptions of sources and epistemic truth claims made on the basis of the data are important. Following processes of computer-supported analyses of quantitative datasets, data journalists publish findings in the form of data visualisations, interactive representations, and/or textual storytelling (possibly with accessible datasets). The data journalist extracts or simply shares findings from the dataset used for the visualisations and/or interactives, based on an epistemic process of producing knowledge about a phenomenon. Statistics are repeatedly presented and interpreted as objective 'facts'. However, any statistician knows data is not objective as its characteristics and shortcomings can lead to misinformation or even be manipulated for disinformation. Gitelman (2013) problematises this in discussions of raw data being an oxymoron. Ultimately it is important to ask if data journalism and the findings produced are presented as 'facts' or with descriptions of the biases and limitations of the data.

In terms of knowledge claims, there are multiple questions that data journalists can ask and provide answers to if they access and analyse reliable datasets. Ongoing research at the Swedish public service broadcaster Sveriges Television (SVT) by one of the authors find that in their COVID-19 data journalism, the SVT data journalism team has systematically sought to be transparent about the data used, how these are analysed, and its shortcomings. The *New York Times* addressed the fundamental question of how the virus got out using data to show how hundreds of millions of people travelled out of Wuhan in China in the early days of the virus (Wu, Cai, Watkins & Glanz 2020). In the analysis, the journalists used not only reported data about confirmed cases but also rough estimates of total cases at the time provided by scholars from two US universities. They also accessed data from technology giant Baidu and telecom operators, reporting that a million citizens left Wuhan for other cities on 1 January 2020, with another seven million travelling in the following three weeks. The storytelling also combines data from the airline industry, reports on diagnosed cases from China, and diverse estimates by US scholars. The headline of the story authoritatively states, 'How the virus got out'. The overarching narrative is marked by robust knowledge claims on how Wuhan citizens travelled and spread the coronavirus across China and elsewhere in the world for multiple weeks before travel restrictions came into force. The piece concludes, 'But by then, the virus had a secure foothold. It continued to spread locally throughout parts of Seattle, New York City and across the country, once again outpacing efforts to stop it'. In the weeks that followed, the number of cases and deaths in the US grew exponentially. While data journalists are clear and transparent about sourcing, the only cues about uncertainty in the data and findings are phrases such as 'estimates of'. Ultimately, the news piece takes an authoritative voice, masking uncertainties about the data. Other sources have reported on COVID-19 emerging from elsewhere than China, with the UN launching a well-resourced investigation into its origin and spread in May 2020.

Concluding discussion

This chapter has focused on the epistemology and practice of data journalism. While there is significant potential for uncovering important and valuable information and news, making authoritative knowledge claims based on data is inexorably imperfect. Clearly, the notion of letting the data speak for itself (cf Benzécri 1973) is deeply flawed. Data is political, affecting what is collected, who is included and excluded, how it is processed and analysed, and how it is presented. Access to, availability of, and restrictions on data shape the agenda for data journalists, with major implications for what the journalists know. Despite inherent shortcomings in the data itself, journalists are repeatedly making authoritative and definitive knowledge claims when they could well be more transparent and include linguistic markers to indicate levels of certainty and uncertainty. It is challenging for the public to develop adequate media literacy and, more specifically, data literacy to interrogate the work of data journalists. Discourse on media literacy tends to urge citizens to generally adopt a more critical lens, which may result in overly sceptical attitudes and approaches and contribute to the ongoing decline in trust in the news media.

Using examples related to COVID-19, which unarguably is an important topic to report on, we have discussed how divergent standards for data across countries and over time have resulted in many data journalists and news publishers not only informing but also misinforming the public. Together with misinformation produced and shared by other actors readily and efficiently via social media, this has made it increasingly difficult for the public to assess the evolution of the pandemic.

On 15 February 2020, World Health Organization (WHO) director-general Tedros Adhanom Ghebreyesus warned 'we're not just fighting an epidemic; we're fighting an infodemic. Fake news spreads faster and more easily than this virus, and is just as dangerous' (Tedros 2020). COVID-19 has highlighted an acute issue in data journalism and, more generally, in the profession as the complexity of the pandemic demands disciplinary expertise, resources, and time. However, this comes at a time when news publishers are struggling to survive amid substantial losses in advertising revenues not compensated for gains in reader revenues. Addressing the issue of the magnitude of the pandemic necessitates so-called communal news work, an approach in which diverse stakeholders in news as a public good do their part in contributing to its survival (Olsen, Pickard & Westlund 2020).

References

Anderson, C. W. (2018). *Apostles of Certainty: Data Journalism and the Politics of Doubt*. Oxford: Oxford University Press.

Appelgren, E., Lindén, C. G., & van Dalen, A. (2019). Data Journalism Research: Studying a Maturing Field Across Journalistic Cultures, Media Markets and Political Environments. *Digital Journalism*, 7(9), 1191–1199. https://doi.org/10.1080/21670811.2019.1685899

Benzécri, J. P. (1973). *L'analyse des données. Tome II: L'analyse des correspondances*. Paris: Dunod.

Boberg, S., Quandt, T., Schatto-Eckrodt, T., & Frischlich, L. (2020). *Pandemic Populism: Facebook Pages of Alernative News Media and the Corona Crisis – A Computational Content Analysis (Muenster Online Research (MOR) Working Paper No. 1/2020*. Munester. Retrieved from: https://arxiv.org/abs/2004.02566

boyd, d., & Crawford, K. (2012). Critical Questions for Big Data. *Information, Communication & Society*, 15(5), 662–679. https://doi.org/10.1080/1369118X.2012.678878

Braun, J. A., & Eklund, J. L. (2019). Fake News, Real Money: Ad Tech Platforms, Profit-Driven Hoaxes, and the Business of Journalism. *Digital Journalism*, 7(1), 1–21. https://doi.org/10.1080/21670811.2018.1556314

Cairo, A. (2015). Graphics Lies, Misleading Visuals. In *New Challenges for Data Design* (pp. 103–116). London: Springer.

Campbell, D., Perraudin, F., Davis, N., & Weaver, M. (2020). Calls for Inquiry as UK Reports Highest COVID-19 Death Toll in Europe. *The Guardian*, May 5. Retrieved from: www.theguardian.com/world/2020/may/05/uk-coronavirus-death-toll-rises-above-32000-to-highest-in-europe

Carey, J. M., Chi, V., Flynn, D. J., Nyhan, B., & Zeitzoff, T. (2020). The effects of corrective information about disease epidemics and outbreaks: Evidence from Zika and yellow fever in Brazil. *Science Advances*, 6(5), eaaw7449. https://doi.org/10.1126/sciadv.aaw7449

Carlson, M. (2017). *Journalistic Authority: Legitimating News in the Digital Era*. New York: Columbia University Press.

Carlson, M. (2019). News Algorithms, Photojournalism and the Assumption of Mechanical Objectivity in Journalism. *Digital Journalism*, 7(8), 1117–1133. https://doi.org/10.1080/21670811.2019.1601577

Cheruiyot, D., Baack, S., & Ferrer-Conill, R. (2019). Data Journalism Beyond Legacy Media: The Case of African and European Civic Technology Organizations. *Digital Journalism*, 1–15. https://doi.org/10.1080/21670811.2019.1591166

Coddington, M. (2015). Clarifying Journalism's Quantitative Turn: A Typology for Evaluating Data Journalism, Computational Journalism, and Computer-Assisted Reporting. *Digital Journalism*, 3(3), 331–348. https://doi.org/10.1080/21670811.2014.976400

Compton, J. R., & Benedetti, P. (2010). Labour, New Media and the Institutional Restructuring of Journalism. *Journalism Studies*, 11(4), 487–499. https://doi.org/10.1080/14616701003638350

Doyle, Y. (2020). *Slides and Datasets to Accompany Coronavirus Press Conference: April 29th 2020*. Prime Minister's Office, 10 Downing Street. Retrieved from: www.gov.uk/government/publications/slides-and-datasets-to-accompany-coronavirus-press-conference-29-april-2020

Dupree, J., Hauslohner, A., Dalton, B., & Sun, L. H. (2020). Coronavirus Death Toll: Americans Are Almost Certainly Dying of Covid-19 but Being Left Out of the Official Count. *The Washington Post*, April 5. Retrieved from: www.washingtonpost.com/investigations/coronavirus-death-toll-americans-are-almost-certainly-dying-of-covid-19-but-being-left-out-of-the-official-count/2020/04/05/71d67982–747e–11ea-87da-77a8136c1a6d_story.html?fbclid=IwAR1lpYlcW8JZvkoKK997u78qZUNa

Egelhofer, J. L., & Lecheler, S. (2019). Fake News as a Two-Dimensional Phenomenon: A Framework and Research Agenda. *Annals of the International Communication Association*, 43(2), 97–116. https://doi.org/10.1080/23808985.2019.1602782

Ekström, M., & Westlund, O. (2019a). The Dislocation of News Journalism: A Conceptual Framework for the Study of Epistemologies of Digital Journalism. *Media and Communication*, 7(1), 259. https://doi.org/10.17645/mac.v7i1.1763

Ekström, M., & Westlund, O. (2019b). Epistemology and Journalism. In *Oxford Encyclopedia of Journalism Studies*. Oxford: Oxford University Press. http://dx.doi.org/10.1093/acrefore/9780190228613.013.806

Ettema, J., & Glasser, T. (1987). On the Epistemology of Investigative Journalism. In M. Gurevtich & M. Levy (Eds.), *Mass Communication Yearbook*. London: Sage.

Figenschou, T. U., & Ihlebæk, K. A. (2019). Challenging Journalistic Authority. *Journalism Studies*, 20(9), 1221–1237. https://doi.org/10.1080/1461670X.2018.1500868

Fink, K., & Anderson, C. W. (2015). Data Journalism in the United States: Beyond the "Usual Suspects". *Journalism Studies*, 16(4), 467–481. https://doi.org/10.1080/1461670X.2014.939852

Gillespie, T. (2018). *Custodians of the Internet*. Retrieved from: http://custodiansoftheinternet.org/application/files/8915/6839/9761/Gillespie_CUSTODIANS_print.pdf

Gitelman, L. (2013). *Raw Data Is an Oxymoron*. Cambridge: MIT Press. Retrieved from: https://mitpress.mit.edu/books/raw-data-oxymoron

Hermida, A., & Young, M. L. (2019). *Data Journalism and the Regeneration of News*. Abingdon, Oxon: Routledge.

Holt, K., Ustad Figenschou, T., & Frischlich, L. (2019). Key Dimensions of Alternative News Media. *Digital Journalism*, 1–10. https://doi.org/10.1080/21670811.2019.1625715

Humprecht, E. (2020). How Do They Debunk "Fake News"? A Cross-National Comparison of Transparency in Fact Checks. *Digital Journalism*, 8(3), 310–327. https://doi.org/10.1080/21670811.2019.1691031

Karlsson, M., Clerwall, C., & Nord, L. (2017). The Public Doesn't Miss the Public: Views from the People: Why News by the People? *Journalism*. https://doi.org/10.1177/1464884917694399

Lewis, N. P., & Nashmi, E. Al. (2019). Data Journalism in the Arab Region: Role Conflict Exposed. *Digital Journalism*, 1–15. https://doi.org/10.1080/21670811.2019.1617041

Lewis, S. C. (2015). Journalism in an Era of Big Data. *Digital Journalism*, *3*(3), 321–330. https://doi.org/1 0.1080/21670811.2014.976399

Lewis, S. C., & Westlund, O. (2015). Big Data and Journalism: Epistemology, Expertise, Economics, and Ethics. *Digital Journalism*, *3*(3). https://doi.org/10.1080/21670811.2014.976418

Li, R., Pei, S., Chen, B., Song, Y., Zhang, T., Yang, W., & Shaman, J. (2020). Substantial Undocumented Infection Facilitates the Rapid Dissemination of Novel Coronavirus (SARS-CoV2). *Science (New York, N.Y.)*. https://doi.org/10.1126/science.abb3221

Matheson, D., & Wahl-Jorgensen, K. (2020). The Epistemology of Live Blogging. *New Media & Society*, *22*(2), 300–316. https://doi.org/10.1177/1461444819856926

Mayer-Schönberger, V., & Cukier, K. (2013). *Big Data: A Revolution That Will Transform How We Live, Work and Think*. Boston, MA: Houghton Mifflin Harcourt.

Montgomery, M. (2007). *The Discourse of Broadcast News: A Linguistic Approach*. London: Routledge.

Munzner, T. (2014). *Visualization Analysis and Design*. Boca Raton, FL: CRC Press.

Mutsvairo, B. (2019). Challenges Facing Development of Data Journalism in Non-Western Societies. *Digital Journalism*, *7*(9), 1289–1294. https://doi.org/10.1080/21670811.2019.1691927

Mutsvairo, B., Bebawi, S., & Borges-Rey, E. (Eds.). (2019). *Data Journalism in the Global South*. Cham: Springer International Publishing. https://doi.org/10.1007/978-3-030-25177-2

Napoli, P. M. (2020). Connecting Journalism and Public Policy: New Concerns and Continuing Challenges, *Digital Journalism*, *8*(6).

Olsen, R. K., Pickard, V., & Westlund, O. ; (2020). Communal News Work: Covid-19 Calls for Diverse Approaches to Collective Funding of Journalism. *Digital Journalism*. https://doi.org/10.1080/216708 11.2020.1763186

Porlezza, C., & Splendore, S. (2019a). From Open Journalism to Closed Data: Data Journalism in Italy. *Digital Journalism*, *7*(9), 1230–1252. https://doi.org/10.1080/21670811.2019.1657778

Porlezza, C., & Splendore, S. (2019b). From Open Journalism to Closed Data: Data Journalism in Italy. *Digital Journalism*. https://doi.org/10.1080/21670811.2019.1657778

Quandt, T. (2018). Dark Participation. *Media and Communication*, *6*(4), 36. https://doi.org/10.17645/mac. v6i4.1519

Robertson, C. T., & Mourão, R. R. (2020). Faking Alternative Journalism? An Analysis of Self-Presentations of "Fake News" Sites. *Digital Journalism*, 1–19. https://doi.org/10.1080/21670811.2020.1743193

Seo, S. (2020). "We See More Because We Are Not There": Sourcing Norms and Routines in Covering Iran and North Korea. *New Media & Society*, *22*(2), 283–299. https://doi.org/10.1177/1461444819856927

Shapiro, I., Brin, C., Bédard-Brûlé, I., & Mychajlowycz, K. (2013). Verification as a Strategic Ritual. *Journalism Practice*, *7*(6), 657–673. https://doi.org/10.1080/17512786.2013.765638

Tandoc, E. C., Lim, Z. W., & Ling, R. (2018). Defining "Fake News": A Typology of Scholarly Definitions. In *Digital Journalism*. London: Routledge. https://doi.org/10.1080/21670811.2017.1360143

Tedros, A. G. (2020). *Munich Security Conference: World Health Organization,* February 15. Retrieved from: www.who.int/dg/speeches/detail/munich-security-conference

Thorsen, E., & Jackson, D. (2018). Seven Characteristics Defining Online News Formats. *Digital Journalism*, *6*(7), 847–868. https://doi.org/10.1080/21670811.2018.1468722

Usher, N. (2016). *Interactive Journalism: Hackers, Data, and Code*. Urbana: University of Ilinois Press.

Westlund, O., & Ekström, M. (2019). News Organizations and Routines. In K. Wahl-Jorgensen & T. Hanitzsch (Eds.), *Handbook of Journalism Studies*. London: Routledge.

Wu, J., Cai, W., Watkins, D., & Glanz, J. (2020). How the Virus Got Out. *The New York Times*, March 22. Retrieved from: www.nytimes.com/interactive/2020/03/22/world/coronavirus-spread.html

Young, M. L., Hermida, A., & Fulda, J. (2018). What Makes for Great Data Journalism?: A Content Analysis of Data Journalism Awards Finalists 2012–2015. *Journalism Practice*, *12*(1), 115–135. https://doi.org/10.1080/17512786.2016.1270171

14
MEDIA AND THE 'ALT-RIGHT'

George Hawley

The American extreme right has long been on the cutting edge of media technology. This was largely driven by necessity. Following the civil rights era, explicit expressions of racial prejudice became increasingly taboo. More traditional, mainstream media venues – including conservative venues – began shutting out open racists and anti-Semites (Hawley 2016). Thus, the racist right has had to be creative when it comes to spreading its message. The so-called alt-right, short for 'alternative right' and a recent manifestation of the American white nationalist movement, was, for a time, unusually effective in its media strategy. When it came to spreading its message and gaining attention, the alt-right punched well above its weight, given its small size and limited resources. In the pages ahead, I will describe the alt-right's media strategy, noting how it evolved in the face of new efforts to limit its online presence.

First, however, I must make a few comments about terminology. I vacillate on whether, when discussing the alt-right, it is proper to use the past or present tense. Although the term *alt-right* remains widely known, it is now very rarely used as a self-description. The movement has suffered so many setbacks over the last three years that the label itself is considered toxic. For the first years of the movement's existence, the term was useful precisely because it seemed so anodyne. Now that this is no longer the case, adherents to the ideology have split on whether to use a more explicit term like *white nationalist* or instead try to downplay its racial agenda and blend in with the larger Trumpian populist movement.

Second, although this volume is focused on the phenomenon of populism and the media, I do not consider the alt-right, overall, to have been a populist movement. This is not to say that the alt-right did not have populist elements. However, the alt-right, at its core, did not express a populist worldview. Its main thought leaders were explicit elitists, and contempt for average Americans – including white Americans – was a common theme within the movement.

As Cas Mudde put it,

> Populism as an ideology that considers society to be ultimately separated into two homogeneous and antagonistic groups, 'the pure people' versus 'the corrupt elite', and which argues that politics should be an expression of the volonté générale (general will) of the people.
>
> (2004, 543)

This description does not quite fit the alt-right as it, overall, was much more sceptical of 'the people' than most populist movements, including right-wing populist movements, such as the one that helped propel Donald Trump to the White House. I agree with Richard Marcy (2020a), who argued that the alt-right should be viewed as a vanguard movement', which is qualitatively different from a mass social movement.

We can find movements that promote ideologies analogous to the alt-right in many countries. Some of these movements have borrowed strategies developed by the alt-right and its precursors or even coordinated across national borders (Zúquete 2018). Nonetheless, the alt-right was a primarily American phenomenon, and this analysis will be limited to the United States.

The alt-right's predecessors

Early observers of the alt-right noted that the movement was notable for its use of humour (Gray 2015; Wilson 2017a; Nagel 2017; Hawley 2017). In its internet propaganda, it tended to use the ironic tone common in many online subcultures. To outside observers, it was not always clear when an alt-right voice was being sincere and when it was simply 'trolling' for the nihilistic pleasure of sowing discord. Although the technology they used was up to date, this strategy on the alt-right's part was less novel than many people realised. In many ways, the alt-right simply brought a very old playbook into the twenty-first century.

George Lincoln Rockwell's American Nazi Party, founded in 1959, was one of the most significant extreme-right groups to emerge in the US after World War II (Simonelli 1999). Rockwell, the son of vaudeville actors, deliberately cultivated an outlandish persona. Rather than downplay his racism and try to quietly influence the conservative movement and the Republican Party, as many on the racist right were doing in this era (Lowndes 2008), Rockwell and his supporters flew Nazi flags, marched with weapons, wore Nazi armbands on the sleeves of their brown shirts, and published a magazine called *The Stormtrooper* – and this was an era in which World War II was still a recent memory. This was not an organisation trying to reach out to ordinary, middle-class white Americans, at least not at first. There was a logic to this extremism, however.

Rockwell had an important insight into the American media. He realised that being outlandish was the best strategy for drawing attention to himself. Had he been a run-of-the-mill, middle-class American racist, presenting his views in the most calm and reasonable way he could, he never would have attracted cameras and interviews. He would not have been able to compete with more established right-wing groups in the US. Rockwell understood that the media loves an outrageous story and wild characters, and he provided both. The American Nazi Party created a spectacle. By being outrageous, he became a magnet for reporters. He was interviewed, for example, by Alex Haley in the pages of *Playboy*. His speeches drew curious onlookers. In the long run, Rockwell hoped to turn this fame into real influence. After becoming a household name, Rockwell wanted to drop the Nazi uniform and put on a suit and tie. From there, his influence could grow. Rockwell described his strategy as follows:

> The first phase is to reach the masses: you can do nothing until you've reached the masses. In order to reach them – without money, without status, without a public platform – you have to become a dramatic figure. Now, in order to achieve that, I've had to take a lot of garbage: being called a nut and a monster and everything else. But by hanging up the swastika, I reach the masses. The second phase is to disabuse them

of the false picture they have gotten of me, to educate them about what my real program is. The third phase will be to organize the people I've educated into a political entity. And the fourth phase will be to use that political entity as a machine to win political power.

That's the plan. They all overlap, of course. Right now we're about 50 percent involved in phase two; we're actually beginning to educate people – in interviews like this one, in speaking engagements at colleges and the like. The other 50 percent is still phase one – just raising hell to keep people aware that there's such a thing as the American Nazi Party, not caring what they call us, as long as they call us something.

(Haley 1966, 80)

Whether this could have worked is unknown – Rockwell was murdered by one of his disgruntled former followers in 1967. Rockwell's dramatic demise also set a precedent for the American extreme right. Many subsequent groups were similarly undone by unhinged members within their ranks. Several later white nationalist groups – including groups associated with the alt-right – were eventually ruined when their members engaged in criminal behavior, bringing lawsuits and financial ruin to their organisations, which always operated on shoestring budgets.

There was another element to Rockwell's flamboyance. The theatrical element of the American Nazi Party raised questions about its sincerity. Rockwell and his supporters drove around in a Volkswagen van covered in racial slurs. They dubbed the van 'the hate bus'. He created a small record label called Hatenanny Records. Rockwell also made outrageous predictions. He claimed with absolute certainty that he would shortly be elected president of the United States, for example. The absurd aspects of the American Nazi Party often made it difficult for many people to take it seriously. This created a degree of confusion around the organisation. We saw similar confusion with the alt-right. The distinction between edgy humour and serious radicalism was often blurry. Some alt-right figures, such as Andrew Anglin of the Daily Stormer, specifically cited Rockwell as an inspiration.

As media changed as the twentieth century progressed, white nationalists were typically early adopters of new technology. Tom Metzger, for example, took advantage of public-access television in the 1980s, creating a programme called *Race and Reason*. Metzger was also an early user of the internet, creating a website in the mid-1990s and hosting an online radio show.

Historically, the discussion board Stormfront has been one of the most important white nationalist websites. The site, created by former Ku Klux Klan leader Don Black, went online in the mid-1990s and continues to operate. The site also hosts Black's radio programme. Stormfront includes the political and philosophical content one would expect at a white nationalist forum but also has boards on popular culture and dating. Although Stormfront is the most visited white nationalist forum, many others have been online for many years, such as Vanguard News Network.

Stormfront's influence on the alt-right was surprisingly minimal. There were certainly many people who were involved with Stormfront and created alt-right content, but of the people considered significant figures in the alt-right, I am aware of none who describe Stormfront as a formative influence. There was a more important difference between Stormfront and similar sites and the alt-right at its peak of success. These older white nationalist message boards received a lot of traffic, but they were also insular online communities. If you were not actively seeking out white nationalist material, you could spend massive amounts of time online for many years without even knowing such sites existed.

The alt-right's origin and early media use

When the term *alt-right* was born in 2008, it was not associated with great innovations in media usage. It was entirely online, but its use of the internet was not immediately novel. For its first few years, the alt-right was not a movement of any sort and was instead simply a term associated with a couple of webzines run by Richard Spencer – Taki's Magazine, followed by a site simply called Alternative Right. During its earliest days, the phrase *alternative right* was also not exclusively associated with any specific racial ideas; various right-wing ideologies that dissented from mainstream conservatism fit under the broad umbrella term.

Spencer's websites hosted short blog entries, longer articles, and podcasts. Alternative Right was relatively short lived as Spencer ceased editing the site in 2012 to focus on other projects, especially running the National Policy Institute, a small white nationalist think tank. He shut down the site entirely a year later. It appeared that the term was going to disappear entirely. When it reemerged on social media and sites like 4chan (at that point usually shortened to alt-right) a few years later, it gained new popularity from the ground up, rather than due to any kind of top-down strategy.

It was during this short interim period that the far-right online had an important warm-up before its real breakthrough in 2015 and 2016. So-called Gamergate provided an early demonstration that anonymous online trolls with no formal organisation or leadership could make a real-world impact. It further served to introduce several people who would later be influential in the alt-right to a larger audience.

The details of Gamergate are not important for this chapter. It began as a purported controversy about ethics in video-game journalism. It soon became a misogynistic harassment campaign, as gamers organised on platforms such as 4chan, Twitter, and Reddit. Developers, journalists, and activists who sought to promote a more inclusive gaming community and less misogyny in games were subjected to a barrage of insulting and threatening emails, as were their employers (Parker 2014). Gamergaters also targeted the corporate sponsors of major media venues, leading to a withdrawal of advertising revenue. Their attacks were a key reason the webzine Gawker shut down (Read 2014).

Gamergate was mostly unrelated to race as it focused mostly on gender questions in gaming (Hawley 2019). However, it set an important precedent in online discourse. It revealed the high degree of reactionary sentiment among young men on message boards and social media. People congregating at these online venues expressed shocking hatred towards those they deemed 'social justice warriors', accusing them of injecting 'political correctness' into video games – a form of media that had previously shown little interest in progressive pieties. The alt-right harnessed similar resentments and used similar tactics, on a much larger scale, in the subsequent years.

It was also during this period that websites that eventually became extremely influential within the alt-right were gaining in popularity. There were still sites presenting extreme right-wing arguments in a more traditional manner. After shutting down Alternative Right, Spencer started a new webzine called Radix. The white nationalist publishing company and website Counter Currents had been operating since 2011. Arktos Media began publishing far-right books in 2010 and continues to do so.

The alt-right's recent media use

Given that the alt-right has existed for barely a decade (at least under that label), it may seem strange to divide its history up into different periods. However, internet culture seems to evolve at a breakneck speed. There was a difference between the alt-right's first iteration, when it was a small ideological project led by a small number of writers, and the alt-right during the 2016 presidential election. This first iteration of the alt-right mostly died out when Spencer, its initial originator, decided to drop the label. The subsequent iteration was largely a grassroots phenomenon, driven by trolls working completely anonymously or under one or more pseudonyms.

Richard Marcy (2020b) has argued that, as a modern vanguard movement, the alt-right has a relatively clear division of labor, despite having no top-down organisational structure. He divides the alt-right into 'sensebreakers', 'sensegivers', and 'sensemakers'. Given the fluid and disorganised nature of the alt-right, these are not solid categories, and the same person may perform multiple tasks.

Those in the first category, the sensebreakers, are the face of the movement to the public. They are the ones seeking and gaining significant exposure from the mainstream media. They are the front-line activists leading rallies. They present themselves as uncompromising opponents of the status quo. Marcy argued that Richard Spencer was the most notable person in this category, though he noted that Spencer's influence has waned in recent years. Although there were a few other figures who have sought to play similar roles in the alt-right (such as Patrick Casey and James Allsup), it is unclear if they will experience long-term success.

The sensegivers are the intellectuals associated with the alt-right. Although they are mostly not anonymous, they are not as eager for mainstream media attention as the sensebreakers. Their aim is to give their movement intellectual coherence, a solid ideological foundation that can support the work of others. More educated readers, listeners, and viewers are their target audience. Marcy identified Jared Taylor of the white nationalist group American Renaissance as the alt-right's quintessential sensegiver. Taylor has been a leading voice in the white nationalist movement since the 1990s, but he has been considered an important figure in the alt-right since that term was coined. Taylor and others like him prefer to justify their arguments using peer-reviewed studies and academic language. Alt-right intellectuals tend to be especially interested in reviving 'race science', the idea that race is a biological category, and races have non-trivial biological differences. Other sensegivers also focus on reviving older varieties of right-wing thought, especially fascistic ideas that were popular in Europe in the inter-war period.

Marcy argued that YouTube has been an especially valuable tool for the sensegiving element of the alt-right. The platform has allowed the alt-right to upload high-quality videos, presenting their arguments on their own terms, for free. These videos can receive millions of views. This represents a major change in the use of video media by the far right. In the past, when television was the primary way people viewed video media, the far right was largely locked out of this medium. Their options were public-access television stations (which had a limited reach), VHS tapes (presumably delivered to people who already agreed with their message), and efforts to get mainstream news media to give them coverage (secure in the knowledge that this coverage would be universally hostile). Thanks to YouTube, this method of outreach became widely available to the far right for the first time. Recent scholarship suggests that YouTube has been an important means of online radicalisation (Ribiero et al. 2020).

Within the sensemaker group, Marcy identified two categories: trolls and lurkers. Trolls engage in the least risky form of activism, sharing alt-right ideas or simply attempting to sow racial discord online. They are the ones posting anonymously on social media platforms like Twitter and on image boards like 4chan. Although people in this category may be nothing more than atomised trolls making racist remarks online in their spare time, they nonetheless served a crucial purpose in the alt-right's early days. Their relentless activity on social media and elsewhere was largely responsible for bringing attention to the alt-right.

The lurkers are an even larger number and represent the people consuming alt-right content without creating anything of their own. These people are at various stages of radicalisation. Some already fully agree with every one of the alt-right's major points regarding race, immigration, and Jewish people. Others may lean towards the alt-right but maintain some misgivings. Some lurkers may simply be people who are curious to know what the alt-right or related movements are about and may or may not further engage with its ideas.

The alt-right also demonstrated the importance of podcasts to ideological movements. Most of the major alt-right websites hosted podcasts, on which important figures of the movement conducted interviews and discussed race, gender, popular culture, and current events. Within the alt-right, however, the website The Right Stuff was unquestionably the most influential in terms of podcasting. Its network included its flagship programme called The Daily Shoah (*Shoah* is the Hebrew term for holocaust.) This programme presented radical white nationalist content but did so in an entertaining fashion, modelling itself on radio 'shock jocks' like Howard Stern and Opie and Anthony. The show's creators were serious ideologues, but they sought to gain listeners by presenting their message in a comedic manner, playing parody songs and flouting all conventions of 'political correctness' by infusing their commentary with racist jokes and slurs. This programme, perhaps more than any other, represented the ethos of the alt-right at its peak. The network also included the more serious programme, Fash the Nation. (*Fash* was short for fascism.) This programme provided commentary on current political events from a white nationalist perspective. Before it was banned from SoundCloud, Fash the Nation was that network's most popular 'conservative' podcast (Wilson 2017b).

Gaining mainstream media attention

I mentioned earlier that anonymous trolls were a crucial group when it came to getting the alt-right on the media's radar. Locked out of most mainstream publications – even nativist, race-baiting websites like Breitbart would not openly embrace the alt-right's radicalism – the alt-right needed to manipulate other venues into helping them spread their message. They did so by relentlessly harassing mainstream journalists with large audiences. In some ways, the incessant harassment of media figures was done for its own sake. There was also a larger strategy at work, however. The alt-right wanted to be noticed, and at the time, the best way to do so was to get mainstream journalists and celebrities to speak and write about them. During my interviews with alt-right content creators, one stated this explicitly:

> [Journalists'] lives are lived online on places like Twitter, and so what they see and report on tends to come to life through their articles – at times, it is a self-fulfilling prophecy. Normal people don't live their existence online on places like Twitter, so most people had no idea we existed. We essentially created a false reality for them where they were drowned in responses by our Great Troll Army, to the point where journalists began to become afraid to write anti-white content out of fear of the online backlash. . . . The Alt-Right literally did not have a physical presence until recently; we practically memed ourselves into existence by hijacking the OODA [observe, orient, decide, and act] loop of journalists, getting them to write about this scary, secretive, mean online group, and drawing more and more eyes & converts when people began to tune in and see what our platforms were.
>
> (quoted in Hawley 2017, 89)

This strategy worked quite well for gaining the nation's attention in 2015 and 2016. Although it included a relatively small number of people, the alt-right was able to garner attention from major media by creating an exaggerated picture of its size and reach – creating a sort of digital Potemkin village on journalists' computer screens. The effort eventually led to massive, worldwide recognition, reaching a peak when Hillary Clinton dedicated an entire speech to denouncing the alt-right in August of 2016.

In the long run, however, this strategy proved to also have negative consequences for the movement. When they convinced much of America that they were a large and growing threat to the basic norms of democracy, they started being treated as such. When greater steps were taken to take down the alt-right, the movement proved more brittle than many of its supporters realised.

The alt-right and popular culture

As was the case with twentieth-century white nationalism, the alt-right took a great interest in popular culture. This is because white nationalists have always insisted that forms of entertainment are essential to shaping peoples' worldview (Leonard and King 2014). In fact, many on the far right have long argued that, in the long run, cultural products are more important than partisan political fights. Inspired by the twentieth-century Italian Marxist Antonio Gramsci, many voices on the far right argue that ideological hegemony in the culture must precede permanent political victories. In their view, the left has achieved such astonishing success in recent decades, despite conservative victories at the ballot box, precisely because it controls the culture via popular entertainment – though left-wing dominance in education and the news media is also important.

The alt-right's engagement with popular media predominantly takes the form of critique. A massive number of alt-right podcasts and articles were dedicated to analyses of the messages (explicit and implicit) in major Hollywood films and television shows. A major white nationalist criticism of popular culture is that so many of the leading figures in the movie and music industry are Jewish liberals, and thus, according to the Alt-Right's narrative, they push an anti-white, pro-multiculturalism agenda.

Sometimes, the alt-right deliberately created controversies about popular culture, just to draw attention to itself. For example, some voices in the alt-right declared that they were organising a major boycott of a *Star Wars* film on the basis of a supposed anti-white narrative in the film. The boycott went nowhere, and the movie was a huge success, but they managed to get several mainstream news outlets to report on the story, again giving them free publicity.

For the most part, the alt-right has not sought to create alternative forms of entertainment to compete with the mainstream music and film industry. In some ways, the alt-right has done less in this regard than some of its ideological predecessors. In the 1990s, for example, white power album sales were an important source of revenue for groups like the National Alliance. Given the ease of accessing music for free on the internet, this would likely not be possible today. There are some alt-right content creators who engage in their own artistic endeavors – writing novels, creating parody songs, and posting comedic cartoons online – but this represents a small percentage of the alt-right's overall activity.

Setbacks online

As the alt-right grew in prominence, major online media platforms began to increase their efforts to decrease the movement's presence. The comment sections of major news outlets were once an important venue for extreme right commentators. Any time a story in a major venue touched the issue of race even tangentially, the comment section underneath the story would quickly fill up with extreme right jeremiads (Hawley 2016). This trend actually predated the alt-right. In response to these comments, unmoderated comment sections became less common. To keep out these right-wing trolls, online news sources began moderating their comments, requiring commenters to register, or simply abolishing comment sections entirely.

Other online media platforms have also sought to limit the alt-right's influence. Reddit deleted the popular r/altright subreddit (Weinberger 2017). Twitter has more aggressively enforced its terms of service, kicking people off the platform when they engaged in hate speech or harassment and banning some hateful symbols (Rozsa 2017). There are ways to work around this. As Twitter allows anonymous accounts, someone whose account is deleted can simply create a new one by using a different email address. However, rebuilding an audience and network takes time. A person who once had tens of thousands of followers will need to start from scratch after losing an account and, furthermore, is always at risk of losing the new account.

YouTube has also begun to pursue stronger measures to reduce extreme right content on its platform (Karlins 2019). The site has deleted thousands of videos. YouTube also removed several alt-right channels completely. Some far-right content producers who were not blocked from the site had their channels demonetised, removing their ability to make money from ad revenue.

The alt-right's ability to raise money online has also diminished. Amazon has cancelled the affiliate programme for many alt-right websites, blocking another source of revenue, and it has also begun banning certain alt-right books. PayPal has also deleted the accounts of several alt-right groups and individuals.

The most extreme example of online de-platforming came shortly after the Unite the Right rally in Charlottesville, Virginia. The Daily Stormer, perhaps the most visited extreme-right website, lost its domain registration and DDOS protection. For a time, the site was not visible from ordinary web browsers and could only be accessed from the 'dark web'. The site has since managed to get back online, however.

In response to this, there was a major push within the alt-right to resolve these problems by building their own online infrastructure. The results of these efforts have been mixed. The alt-right's attempt to create alternative online fundraising websites seems to have failed. This is likely because the technical and material challenges of doing so have proved too high.

The effort to create alternatives to Twitter and YouTube have been qualified successes. The social media site Gab and the video-hosting site BitChute function reasonably well. The important thing to remember, however, is that the alt-right's success resulted from its ability to interact with the mainstream. For the most part, ordinary internet users are still using the larger social media platforms, not the alternatives open to alt-right material. Thus, the extreme-right online is increasingly back where it was a decade ago, largely isolated in its own spheres, with less easy access to mainstream venues.

Conclusion

Over its short history, the alt-right has been a predominantly online phenomenon. Although its use of the internet was novel, many of its strategies were lifted (whether they realised it or not) from earlier iterations of the white nationalist movement. The internet is unquestionably where the alt-right achieved its greatest successes. In fact, its efforts to engage in real-world activism have mostly resulted in failure or – especially in the case of the Charlottesville rally – disaster. Their success was largely dependent on their ability to interact with people outside their movement on other major online platforms. Major online media sites have sought to place stronger restrictions on what people can post. This represented a major setback for the alt-right, from which it has not yet recovered. The white nationalist movement has proven resilient, however, and it is not going to just disappear, even if it drops the alt-right label entirely. It remains to be seen how it will regroup and attempt to regain influence in the years ahead.

References

Gray, Rosie. (2015), "How 2015 Fueled the Rise of the Freewheeling, White Nationalist Alt- Movement," *Buzzfeed*, 27 December [online]. Available at: www.buzzfeednews.com/article/rosiegray/how-2015-fueled-the-rise-of-the-freewheeling-white-nationali

Haley, Alex. (1966), "Playboy Interview: George Lincoln Rockwell," *Playboy*, 13 April.

Hawley, George. (2016), *Right-Wing Critics of American Conservatism*, Lawrenceville: University Press of Kansas.

Hawley, George. (2017), *Making Sense of the Alt-Right*, New York: Columbia University Press.

Hawley, George. (2019), *The Alt-Right: What Everyone Needs to Know*, New York: Oxford University Press.

Karlins, Nicole. (2019), "YouTube Says It Will Remove Thousands of Videos Pushing Far-Right Views," *Salon*. 5 June [online]. Available at: www.salon.com/2019/06/05/youtube-says-it-will-remove-thousands-of-videos-pushing-far-right-views/

Leonard, David J. and C. Richard King. (2014), *Beyond Hate: White Power and Popular Culture*, New York: Routledge.

Lowndes, Joseph E. (2008), *From the New Deal to the New Right: Race and the Southern Origins of Modern Conservatism*, New Haven, CT: Yale University Press.

Marcy, Richard. (2020a), "Leadership of Socio-Political Vanguards: A Review and Future Directions," *The Leadership Quarterly*, 31(2), pp. 1–12.

Marcy, Richard. (2020b), "Why the Alt Right Is Not Going Anywhere (Regardless of What We Call It)," in Gottfried, Paul (ed) *The Vanishing Tradition: Perspectives on American Conservatism*, Ithaca, NY: Cornell University Press.

Mudde, Cas. (2004), "The Populist Zeitgeist," *Government and Opposition*, 39(4), pp. 541–563.

Nagel, Angela. (2017), *Kill All Normies: Online Culture Wars from 4chan and Tumblr to Trump and the Alt-Right*, Alresford: Zero Books.

Parker, Simone. (2014), "Gamergate: A Scandal Erupts in the Video-Game Community," *The New Yorker*, 17 October [online]. Available at: www.newyorker.com/tech/annals-of-technology/gamergate-scandal-erupts-video-game-community

Read, Max. (2014), "How We Got Rolled by the Dishonest Fascists of Gamergate," *Gawker*, 22 October [online]. Available at: https://gawker.com/how-we-got-rolled-by-the-dishonest-fascists-of-gamergat-1649496579

Ribiero, Manoel Horta, Virgilio A.F. Almeida, Rapheal Ottoni, Wagner Meira, Jr., Robert West. (2020), "Auditing Radicalization Pathways on YouTube," Proceedings of the 2020 Conference on Fairness, Accountability, and Transparency [online]. Available at: https://dl.acm.org/doi/abs/10.1145/3351095.3372879?download=true

Rozsa, Matthew. (2017), "Twitter Is Starting to Purge Its Alt-Right Users," *Salon*, 18 December [online]. Available at: www.salon.com/2017/12/18/twitter-is-starting-to-purge-its-alt-right-users/

Simonelli, Frederick J. (1999), *American Fuehrer: George Lincoln Rockwell and the American Nazi Party*, Urbana: University of Illinois Press.

Weinberger, Matt. (2017), "Reddit Bans a Major Alt-Right Community – and There May Be a Very Good Reason," *Business Insider*, 2 February [online]. Available at: www.businessinsider.com/why-reddit-banned-alt-right-2017-2

Wilson, Jason. (2017a), "Hiding in Plain Sight: How the 'Alt-right' Is Weaponizing Irony to Spread Fascism," *The Guardian*, 11 July [online]. Available at: www.theguardian.com/technology/2017/may/23/alt-right-online-humor-as-a-weapon-facism

Wilson, Jason. (2017b), "Activists Claim to Unveil Leader of 'Alt-Right' Website the Right Stuff," *The Guardian*, 17 January [online]. Available at: www.theguardian.com/world/2017/jan/17/right-stuff-alt-right-site-mike-enoch-revealed

Zúquete, Pedro. (2018), *The Identitarians: The Movement Against Globalism and Islam in Europe*, Notre Dame, IN: University of Notre Dame Press.

15

'LISTEN TO YOUR GUT'

How Fox News's populist style changed the American public sphere and journalistic truth in the process

Reece Peck

Fox News's famous (or infamous, depending on your politics) slogan, 'Fair & Balanced', had already been previewed in the weeks leading up to the network's launch on October 7, 1996. CEO Roger Ailes had told *USA Today*, 'America needs one fair and balanced news channel and we're going to provide it. The American people believe television is biased to the left . . . and that it's boring' (Lieberman 1996). In this interview, Ailes foreshadowed themes that would define the Fox News brand for decades to come: the mainstream media is liberal and elitist, and Fox News represents 'the people'.

Certainty by the mid-1990s, the technological and economic pieces were in place for a conservative-leaning Fox News to emerge (Prior 2007). Yet the question still remained whether it could ever attain enough journalistic legitimacy to avoid being written off as a hack political operation. Indeed, as soon as Fox aired its first broadcast, the *New York Times* posed the question prevailing among US journalists: 'Will [Fox News] be a vehicle for expressing Mr. Murdoch's conservative political opinions?' (Miffin 1996). Confirming these suspicions would be News Corp. owner Rupert Murdoch himself, who had appointed go-to Republican communications specialist Roger Ailes as Fox's CEO. First making his name as the media wunderkind of Richard Nixon's 1968 presidential campaign, Ailes had gone on to advise the presidential campaigns of Republican presidents Ronald Reagan and George H. Bush in the 1980s (Swint 2008).

Unsurprisingly, Ailes held a deeply political view of journalism, a perspective that attuned him to the contradictions of self-styled professional news outlets. While the dispassionate, 'neutral' approach of network news programmes during the 1950s and 1960s had purported to offer a non-ideological account of the world, Ailes was able to masterfully exploit in his favour the subjective demarcation between 'the balanced centre' and 'the ideological fringe'. 'I don't understand why being balanced is "right of center"', he told the *Washington Post* in 1999, 'unless, the other guys are pretty far left' (Kurtz 1999). Ailes was also quick to lob back at any journalist accusing Fox of having a right-leaning bias, always baiting Fox's competitors into a never-ending contest of bias finger-pointing. The effect would ultimately drain not only the meaning of *bias* but that of *objectivity* itself.

But while Ailes was a talented communicator, we should not attribute too much to his genius. This 'great man' approach obscures the significant degree to which Fox's corporate strategy took advantage of the discursive repertoire of the post-war conservative movement.

Books such as Heather Hendershot's *What's Fair on the Air?* (2011) and Nicole Hemmer's *Messengers of the Right* (2016) illustrate how conservative media activists had been waging critiques against 'liberal media bias' since the 1950s and 1960s. After decades of conservative criticism of the mainstream press, journalism's professional ideology and the 'objectivity regime' that underpinned it had gradually been chipped away.

The 1970s marked the beginning of a concerted effort by conservatives to create a 'counter-intelligentsia' that could take on the 'philanthropic-government-academic-establishment' (O'Connor 2007: 75). Such conservative think tanks as the Heritage Foundation, a research institute George Nash has described as 'the nerve center of the Reagan Revolution' (1998: 335), experienced unprecedented build-ups. With the popularisation of conservative talk radio in the late 1980s and the rise of Fox News in the late 1990s, such 'nerve centers' had become the media weaponry enabling their once-marginal narratives about liberal bias and journalistic elitism to move to the centre of American popular culture.

Having surpassed CNN as the cable ratings leader in 2002, today Fox News dominates US political television and stands as the most profitable asset of Rupert Murdoch's global media empire. According to a recent Pew study, four in ten Americans say they trust Fox for political news (Gramlich 2020). Academic studies on the network have empirically demonstrated how Fox News has affected everything from American voting patterns (DellaVigna and Kaplan 2007) to public knowledge (Cassino 2016) to congressional legislation (Clinton and Enamorado 2014), always in a way that advantages Republicans. More recently, journalistic exposés have revealed the extent to which Fox guides the thinking of President Donald Trump himself (Parker and Costa 2017).

Along with financially profiting from the conservative movement's decades-long crusade against 'liberal media bias', Fox News has also elevated this conservative media criticism tradition to new hegemonic heights, further eroding the public's faith in journalistic objectivity. Yet in contrast to the failed attempts at creating conservative TV before Fox News, Fox offered more than just ideologically congenial programming. It introduced a populist style of conservative news that could break from the middlebrow sensibility of 'first-generation' conservative stars like William F. Buckley (Hemmer 2016) and instead draw talent from such 'low-prestige' public affairs genres as tabloid television and talk radio. In developing such 'anti-anchor' personas (Ricchiardi 2009) in hosts Bill O'Reilly, Shep Smith, and Sean Hannity, Ailes enabled these hosts to derive authority by performatively embodying the cultural-epistemological disposition of those non-college-educated viewers who comprise the demographic majority of Fox's audience.

While the decline in public trust for journalists and 'official sources' had been underway decades before Fox News (Gallup 2016; Schudson 2003: 112), Fox was one of the first major outlets to innovate interpretive news strategies tailor-made for the 'post-modern' media environment of the 1990s, one in which the status of expert authority was weakening (Beck and Giddens 1994), and 'televisual style' was on the rise (Caldwell 1995). The 'Republican Revolution' of the 1994 midterms further defined the political polarisation of the 1990s. In this hyper-politicised media climate, 'facts' were increasingly being evaluated not by the methodological rigour that went in to producing them but rather by the partisan orientation (assumed or actual) of the journalist citing them.

To bolster their interpretations of social reality, Fox's top-rated hosts utilised non-empirical epistemic resources such as lived experience, popular memory, and moral narratives that have been recycled in American political culture for centuries. Unlike formal expertise, these populist bases of authority do not need institutional support to be effective. This chapter explains how Fox's populist mode of address has changed the political logic of the US public sphere and its journalistic standards of truth.

Fox populism versus MSNBC liberalism

'There seems to be in the country . . . a media war', Bill O'Reilly once told his viewers, 'a war between Fox News and talk radio on one side, *The New York Times* and the liberal networks on the other side' (*The O'Reilly Factor*, 18 September 2009). In this narrative, the 'Washington journalistic establishment' (*The O'Reilly Factor*, 30 October 2009) and 'the liberal left-wing elite' (*The O'Reilly Factor*, 11 June 2009) stood on one side while Fox News and the 'hardworking people' of 'middle America' (*Hannity & Colmes*, 27 April 2001) stood on the other. This dichotomous construction of the US news field as consisting of two rival media systems – one for the elite and one for the people – remains intact today, as evidenced by Fox host Tucker Carlson's recent monologues denouncing 'the ruling class' who condescend to 'the rest of us plebes' (Maza 2019).

Meanwhile, taking cues from Fox News's commercial success, MSNBC in the mid-2000s started to counter-programme Fox as the liberal alternative. Emulating Fox's partisan branding strategy and programming formula, MSNBC also prioritised opinion-based shows over 'straight' reporting. Yet even while adopting a partisan brand, MSNBC's conceptualisation of the public sphere still upheld the basic tenets of liberal democratic theory. Their marketing and programming discourse assumed that social tensions and opposing political demands could be managed through reasoned debate and by making politics more informationally sound, receptive, and tolerant.

So while MSNBC's recent Decision 2020 promo declares 'There's power in deciding for ourselves. Even if we don't agree' (NewscastStudio 2020), Fox's contrasting populist imaginary suggests that the national community will only be whole if and when the elite power bloc that corrupts its body politic is confronted and then excised. Fox News's anti-establishment posture brings the conservative coalition together by emphasising its members' common (perceived or real) 'outsider' status away from the elite 'corridors of power' (*The O'Reilly Factor*, 23 October 2009). The communal tie for MSNBC liberalism, on the other hand, is founded on the equal inclusion of all individuals and minoritarian voices in the national discussion.

Political theorist Ernesto Laclau put forth a set of theoretical tools for distinguishing MSNBC's liberal-democratic reasoning from Fox's populist vision, a conceptual divide he describes as one between 'differential logic' and 'equivalential logic' (2005). MSNBC's 'differential logic' is clear in the aforementioned Decision 2020 ad. The promo begins with an American flag graphic, with the narrator saying, 'We all want different things. We all dream different dreams'. At this point, the flag's stripes shoot off in different directions, symbolising the idea that democracy involves a multiplicity of interest groups and demands. 'But', the voice-over reassures, this political diversity is what defines America: 'that's what makes us us'. Democracy 'isn't really about finding common ground', the ad insists. 'It is about finding our footing on *uncommon* ground' (emphasis added).

The progressive community is thus brought together through their common commitment to the right of all citizens to pursue their separate group interests and to express their distinct individual beliefs. MSNBC values the 'politics of difference' above all else, which aligns with the Democratic Party's signature embrace of multiculturalism. Yet not only does MSNBC avoid building a singular political identity for its audience to rally around; it actually rejects the effort to do so as a positive expression of its liberalism.

In contrast, Fox's populist representational strategy is designed to find and perhaps even manufacture 'common ground'. The populist terms Fox uses to address its audience, such as *the folks* and *middle America*, thread and 'articulate' the various political issues of the conservative movement – gun rights, pro-life, deregulation – on what Laclau terms a 'chain of equivalence' (2005). And this is why such populist signifiers are politically useful. In having an 'equivalential logic', Fox can symbolically condense the myriad of factions and interest groups that comprise any given political movement into one unitary bloc.

Still, populist signifiers have no meaning by themselves; their coalescing function only works within an 'us-versus-them' framework. This conflict model is apparent in an *O'Reilly Factor* episode about the conservative Tea Party movement. 'The American media will never embrace the Tea Party. Why? [T]hey look down on the folks. They think you are dumb' (8 February 2010). While part of Fox's strategy is to bombard the audience on a nightly basis with a consistent set of associations between different conservative factions (e.g. libertarian men, religious women, blue-collar workers, wealthy business owners), the central way Fox's programming fuses these constituencies together is by positioning them against a common enemy. Conservatives are one because they are all looked down on by the liberal elite (i.e. 'they think you are dumb').

It is fair to question if, and to what extent, conservatives actually face the kind of marginalisation they claim they do. Indisputable, however, is how this resentment about liberal intellectual condescension has been effectively used to mobilise conservative activists and compel conservative audiences. Working in tandem with a white 'producerist' antagonism against the non-white, 'parasitic' factions below (Peck 2019: Chapter 4), this opposition to the educated elites above is one of the master programming themes of Fox News and of the conservative talk industry writ large. Consequently, this discourse warrants scholarly interrogation and, as A.J. Bauer has stressed, needs to be understood on its own conservative terms (2018: 25).

Cultural populism and the morally 'invested' news style

Like almost all populist speakers, Fox News pundits often deny the fact that they – as wealthy TV personalities – occupy a whole other social stratum than that of their average viewer: 'I'm a regular schlub' (*Glenn Beck*, 20 January 2009). In turn, these personalities frequently assume the 'people's voice' during on-air political debates: ('I think I speak for most Americans', *Hannity & Colmes*, 11 December 2008). In my book *Fox Populism* (2019), I illustrate how Fox programmes have appropriated the discourse of cultural populism, a sub-strain of the broader populist rhetorical tradition. I define *cultural populism* as a political discourse that 'champions the common wisdom, taste, and intellectual capacities of everyday people, and denounces justifications for power based on credentials and elite cultural knowledge' (127). Whereas the left understands class as mostly an economic position, Fox pundits use cultural populism to advance 'an informal theory of class as a cultural identity' (126).

Fox's cultural populist strategy has two main legs. It involves pundits making taste-based appeals to 'lowbrow' cultural forms (e.g. NASCAR), lifestyle practices (e.g. shopping at Walmart), and aesthetics (e.g. hyper-patriotic graphics, bleach-blonde anchors). Secondly, it involves performing an affinity with lay epistemic culture: that is, a non-professional style of truth-telling. 'I am not an expert', Glenn Beck often said on his Fox show. 'I'm an American with an opinion, period. . . . When will we start listening to our own guts, and to common sense?' (4 November 2010). In an episode of *Hannity*, one guest implied that too much education actually hinders a leader's judgment. '[W]ith all the . . . education that President Barack Obama has had, he seems to have trouble making decisions. . . . I think that sometimes it doesn't take a Harvard education to make a good choice' (19 November 2009).

The educated elite has long served as the central class enemy in the conservative movement's populist imaginary. In the 1950s and 1960s, conservative politicians like Joseph McCarthy and George Wallace railed against what they respectively called 'twisted intellectuals' and 'pseudo-intellectuals'. Richard Nixon's 1968 and 1972 presidential campaigns appropriated and refined these themes, pitting the noble, country music–loving 'silent majority' against a 'new class' of knowledge workers, media professionals, and professors.

The conservative animus towards educated elites is as strong today as it was then. According to a 2017 Pew study, 58 percent of Republicans believe higher education is doing more harm than good to American society (Fingerhut 2017). In tune with the Republican base, conservative media figures like Newt Gingrich describe the liberal media as the 'intellectual-yet-idiot' class and, conservative talk radio giant Rush Limbaugh called the expert witnesses at Trump's 2019 impeachment hearing 'professional nerds'. Fox's current top-rated show, *Tucker Carlson Tonight*, features a Campus Craziness segment, in which host Tucker Carlson takes on liberal professors and student activists to expose 'the radical left's' takeover of America's universities. This starts where Carlson's scandalised 8:00 PM predecessor left off. One content study of *The O'Reilly Factor* coded 'academics' as one of Bill O'Reilly's most frequently listed 'villain' groups (Conway et al. 2007).

But direct diatribes against academics and intellectuals is only the most obvious way Fox programming seeks to align conservative policy positions with working-class 'common sense'. What is more interesting and harder to grasp is the way Fox News pundits attempt to embody a lay form of intellectualism I term the 'popular intellect' (Peck 2019: 146–151). Sociologist Pierre Bourdieu has developed a set concepts such as the 'popular gaze' and 'invested disposition' to understand the underlying social logic of working-class culture. These concepts are useful for elucidating how Fox News hosts ventriloquise what they imagine to be a working-class mode of news analysis. According to Bourdieu, the 'popular gaze' of the working class is more utilitarian, evaluating a cultural object or media image in 'reference to the function it fulfils for the person who looks at it or which [such a person] thinks it could fulfil for other classes of beholders' (1984: 42) and, with reference to this invested viewer, the assumed 'interest [behind] the information it conveys' (43).

Mimicking this analytical posture, Fox News hosts purport to cut through the flowery language of the politician and see past the pundit's honorific title, getting to the heart of the matter by exposing who stands to gain or lose in each piece of news information. From this vantage point, providing specific evidence proving political corruption is not always necessary. It can be enough for hosts to simply suggest connections between political and media figures and express what they intuitively 'know' about their intentions. In the end, Chris Peters writes, 'proof is held in [the Fox host's] belief' (2010: 842).

Yet only focusing on the evidentiary inadequacies of Fox's style misses what makes this 'invested' mode of news framing effective. In a media culture deemed minimally objective and maximally political, the traditional anchor's self-presentation of being uninvolved (i.e. 'letting the facts speak for themselves') comes across as insincere or, worse, purposely deceptive. In such a context, the moral agnosticism of the formerly detached professional is less effective than the overtly 'ethical' (Bourdieu 1984: 44–50), emotional performance of the current Fox anchor who fights against 'the powerful' to 'protect the folks' and other innocent groups like 'the kids and the elderly' (*The O'Reilly Factor*, 10 July 2008). '[W]ithin Fox's populist public sphere model, the choice being offered is no longer between disinterested and interested journalism, but between different types of interested analysis' (Peck 2019: 148). As a result, Fox's top opinion hosts strive to demonstrate how 'their news analyses are indeed biased – precisely *because they are invested in the interests of* "the folks"' (151, emphasis in original).

While many liberals view Fox's style as hokey, melodramatic, or just plain dumb, from a political communication standpoint, Fox's populist analytical mode can be shrewdly effective. As cognitive linguist George Lakoff has long argued, within the workings of the political mind, moral reasoning trumps fact-based logic (2004). Moreover, all forms of journalism – partisan and non-partisan alike – rely on narrative structures that themselves carry embedded moral assumptions. It is the inner moral logic of the story form that gives the journalist using it 'cultural authority' (Edy 2006).

Fox producers have demonstrated an acute knowledge of which stories in American culture resonate and which do not, perceiving that US citizens tend to view class and race through non-empirical, normative schemas of social categorisation (Lamont 2000). Hence, Fox News pundits tend to devote more interpretive energy to performing their concern (or outrage) as opposed to their expertise. This allows them to dictate how the policy event will be morally framed as opposed to empirically supported.

During the Nixon era, the conservative movement used populist moral logics to racially stigmatise welfare and to repackage business-class-friendly policies as pro-worker. Fox has shifted the appeal yet again via the 'American populist rhetorical tradition' (Kazin 1998), in which one of the deepest reservoirs of moral themes about politics, wealth, and cultural status is used to re-present Republican partisans as 'the real Americans'. Thus does Fox achieve what Antonio Gramsci long understood: that a 'corporative' political faction can actually be discursively transformed into a commanding 'hegemonic' one (1996).

COVID-19 and the false hope of empirical deliverance

The coronavirus emerged from China's Wuhan province in late December of 2019. A month later the United States would report its first positive case of COVID-19 on 20 January 2020. It took the disease only three months to turn American society upside down. With unprecedented speed, the stay-at-home directives would bring the US economy to a halt, destroying millions of jobs and shuttering thousands of small businesses. From 1 March to 31 March, COVID-19 cases jumped from fewer than a hundred to hundreds of thousands. By 28 April, the virus had claimed over 58,365 American lives, more than were killed in the Vietnam War (Welna 2020).

Yet through the pivotal month of February and well into March, the Trump administration and the president's favourite channel, Fox News, downplayed the severity of the virus, repeatedly suggesting it was no more dangerous than the 'standard flu'. On the 27 February 2020 episode of *Hannity*, Fox's number one show, host Sean Hannity said sarcastically, 'I can report the sky is . . . falling. . . . We're all doomed . . . and it's all President Trump's fault. . . . Or at least that's what the media mob would like you to think' (Wemple 2020).

As someone who has studied Fox's opinion shows for over a decade, I cannot say I was surprised by this response (though *Tucker Carlson Tonight* did, to its credit, take a different tack). From the beginning, the editorial agenda of Fox's primetime shows has been devoted as much to how other outlets cover the news as to the news itself, something Ronald Jacob and Eleanor Townsley term 'media metacommentary' (2011). Fox's opinion hosts have long depicted journalists as a 'villainous' social group (Conway et al. 2007), using rhetoric that dovetails with Trump's repeated casting of the press as 'the enemy of the American people'. And like Trump, Fox hosts endow journalistic interpretations with the capability of determining the nation's destiny (Jamieson and Cappella 2008: 51), a media power so menacing that Fox hosts deemed countering the negative press Trump was receiving for his handling of the crisis more important than the physical threat of the outbreak itself.

It is unclear how this will finally affect Trump's political future, but one can safely predict that the COVID-19 crisis will not end the science wars anytime soon. And yet American liberals continue to hold this hope that the empirical conditions of national crises, if severe enough, will pierce through the 'epistemic closure' of the right-wing media bubble. Rather than challenging the right by advancing an alternative populist narrative or by building a news channel that could surpass Fox in popular appeal and cultural relevance, liberals tend to prefer a more passive-aggressive approach to defeating the conservative opposition.

The liberal strategy seeks to fix the US media's informational culture by reasserting the tenets and practices of professional journalism. This way political disputes can be, once more, decided by facts and third-party experts. In such an ideal media environment, liberal journalists would not need to directly take on the right-wing media ecosystem; it would die off on its own accord as the public comes to view its reporting as erroneous and untrustworthy. By this logic, Fox News, and Sean Hannity in particular, would have to pay a steep reputational price for the misinformation they spread in the critical early stages of the COVID-19 crisis. But, if recent history is any judge, I doubt they will.

Just days before the financial collapse on September 15, 2008, Hannity criticised doomsayer economists and claimed that the fundamentals of the Bush economy were strong (Khanna 2008). Not only did he not face any repercussions for this epically bad take; in April 2009 Hannity and fellow Fox host Glenn Beck helped galvanise the Tea Party movement and successfully redirected public anger away from Wall Street greed towards taxation and 'government tyranny'. The Tea Party's electoral gains in the 2010 midterm elections effectively killed President Obama's progressive economic agenda and skyrocketed Fox's ratings and profits to record levels.

Like the Great Recession, the COVID-19 crisis has exposed the fragility of America's public infrastructure and laid bare the nation's race and class inequalities. While this contemporary crisis should be presenting yet another opportunity for the Democratic left to assert the need for New Deal–style policies and government programmes such as guaranteed health care, unemployment, and living wages. Yet, I do not see many liberals meeting NAACP leader Reverend Barber's call for progressives to forge a 'fusion coalition' around 'a deeper moral language to name the crisis' (Barber 2017, January 30). Instead, as I write this in late April of 2020, we are witnessing a Tea Party–affiliated 'liberty movement' actively trying to drive the political narrative of the COVID-19 crisis (Vogel et al. 2020). These pro-Trump 'liberty' groups are protesting the stay-at-home measures public health officials have instituted to contain the virus, thus baiting leftists to devote their political focus to defending medical expertise as opposed to highlighting and addressing the plight of front-line 'essential workers'.

This layout of rhetorical political positions plays into Fox News's hands in several ways. It assists the network's long-term hegemonic strategy of naturalising the link between political conservatism and working-class counter-knowledge. It also leads the liberal analysts to adopt a limited, informational understanding of Fox's political communication strategies. By only focusing on how Fox deceives its audience with 'bad science' and misinformation, the analyst is distracted from seeing how the network actually derives its cultural authority.

To move the discussion on populism and conservative media forwards, communication and journalism scholars must be able not only to address questions of epistemology and bias but also to think beyond them. More consideration should be given to the persuasive power of moral framing and to the political-identitarian pull of aesthetic style. Otherwise, we risk getting trapped in an endless Ailesian loop wherein a media partisan like Hannity defends his coronavirus coverage by simply counter-charging that it is his academic critics, not him, who live in a world where 'politics trumps truth' (Bond 2020).

References

Barber, W.J. (2017, January 30) These times require a new language and a fusion coalition: The moral crisis we face demands a political pentecost in America today. *Think Progress.* Available at: https://thinkprogress.org/rev-barber-these-times-require-a-new-language-and-a-new-fusion-coalition-c741b9eb1b47/.

Bauer, A.J. (2018) Journalism history and conservative erasure. *American Journalism,* 35(1): 25.

Beck, U. and Giddens, A. (1994) *Reflexive Modernization: Politics, Tradition and Aesthetics in the Modern Social Order.* Stanford, CA: Stanford University Press.

Bond, P. (2020, April 2) Sean Hannity defends Fox News after journalism professors publish critical letter about coronavirus coverage. *Newsweek.* Available at: www.newsweek.com/sean-hannity-defends-fox-news-after-journalism-professors-publish-critical-letter-about-coronavirus-1495880.

Bourdieu, P. (1984) *Distinction: A Social Critique of the Judgment of Taste* (R. Nice, trans.). Cambridge, MA: Harvard University Press: 42–50.

Caldwell, J. (1995) *Televisuality: Style, Crisis, and Authority in American Television.* New Brunswick, NJ: Rutgers University Press.

Cassino, D. (2016) *Fox News and American Politics: How One Channel Shapes American Politics and Society.* Abingdon: Routledge.

Clinton, J. and Enamorado, T. (2014) The national news media's effect on Congress: How Fox News affected elites in Congress. *The Journal of Politics,* 76(4): 928–943.

Conway, M. Maria, E. and Grieves, K. (2007) Villains, victims and the virtuous in Bill O'Reilly's 'no-spin zone.' *Journalism Studies,* 8(2): 197–223.

DellaVigna, S. and Kaplan, E. (2007) The Fox News effect: Media bias and voting. *The Quarterly Journal of Economics,* 122(3): 1187–1234.

Edy, J. (2006) *Troubled Pasts: News and the Collective Memory of Social Unrest.* Philadelphia: Temple University Press.

Fingerhut, H. (2017, July 10) *Sharp Partisan Divisions in Views of National Institutions.* Pew Research Center. Available at: www.people-press.org/2017/07/10/sharp-partisan-divisions-in-views-of-national-institutions/.

Gallup. (2016) *Media Use and Evaluation: Historical Trends.* Available at: www.gallup.com/poll/1663/media-use-evaluation.aspx.

Glenn Beck. (2009, January 20) Fox News Channel.

Glenn Beck. (2010, November 4) Fox News Channel.

Gramlich, J. (2020, April 8) *Five Facts About Fox News.* Pew Research Center. Available at: www.pewresearch.org/fact-tank/2020/04/08/five-facts-about-fox-news/.

Gramsci, A. (1996) *Prison Notebooks* (J. A. Buttigieg, Trans. Vol. 2). New York: Columbia University Press.

Hannity. (2009, November 19) Fox News Channel.

Hannity & Colmes. (2001, April 27) Fox News Channel.

Hannity & Colmes. (2008, December 11) Fox News Channel.

Hemmer, N. (2016) *Messengers of the Right: Conservative Media and the Transformation of American Politics.* Philadelphia: University of Pennsylvania Press.

Hendershot, H. (2011) *What's Fair on the Air?: Cold War Right-Wing Broadcasting and the Public Interest.* Chicago: University of Chicago Press.

Jacobs, R. and Townsley, E. (2011) *The Space of Opinion: Media Intellectuals and the Public Sphere.* Oxford: Oxford University Press.

Jamieson, K. and Cappella, J. (2008) *Echo Chamber: Rush Limbaugh and the Conservative Media Establishment.* Oxford: Oxford University Press: 51.

Kazin, M. (1998) *The Populist Persuasion: an American History* (Revised Edition). Ithaca, NY: Cornell University Press.

Khanna, S. (2008, September 11) Hannity explodes on air, call guest 'fool' and 'idiot,' tells him to get off set. *Think Progress.* Available at: https://thinkprogress.org/hannity-explodes-on-air-calls-guest-fool-and-idiot-tells-him-to-get-off-set-b54bd7c9f217/.

Kurtz, H. (1999, March 26) Crazy like a Fox: Question his news judgment, perhaps, but never underestimate Roger Ailes. *Washington Post.* Available at: www.washingtonpost.com/archive/lifestyle/1999/03/26/crazy-like-a-fox-question-his-news-judgment-perhaps-but-never-underestimate-roger-ailes/a959339f-acaf-4823-8238-27da13eb77be/.

Laclau, E. (2005) *On Populist Reason.* New York: Verso.

Lakoff, G. (2004) *Don't Think of an Elephant!: Know Your Values and Frame the Debate: The Essential Guide for Progressives*. White River Junction, VT: Chelsea Green Publishing Company.

Lamont, M. (2000) *The Dignity of Working Men: Morality and the Boundaries of Race, Class, and Immigration*. Cambridge, MA: Harvard University Press.

Lieberman, D. (1996, September 23). Ailes tackles toughest assignment cable channel battles budget, clock, rivals. *USA Today*.

Maza, C. (2019, April 3) Why Tucker Carlson pretends to hate elites. *Vox*. Available at: www.vox.com/videos/2019/4/3/18294392/tucker-carlson-pretends-hate-elites-populism-false-consciousness.

Miffin, L. (1996, October 7) At the new Fox News Channel, the buzzword is fairness, separating news from bias. *New York Times*.

Nash, G. (1998) *The Conservative Intellectual Movement in America, Since 1945*. Wilmington, DE: Intercollegiate Studies Institute: 335.

NewscastStudio. (2020, February 20) *MSNBC Decision 2020* [Video file]. YouTube. Available at: www.youtube.com/watch?v=bc9oqzXXDy8.

O'Connor, A. (2007) *Social Science for What? Philanthropy and the Social Question in a World Turned Rightside Up*. New York: Russell Sage Foundation: 75.

The O'Reilly Factor. (2008, July 10) Fox News Channel.

The O'Reilly Factor. (2009, June 11) Fox News Channel.

The O'Reilly Factor. (2009, September 18) Fox News Channel.

The O'Reilly Factor. (2009, October 23) Fox News Channel.

The O'Reilly Factor. (2009, October 30) Fox News Channel.

The O'Reilly Factor. (2010, February 8) Fox News Channel.

Parker, A. and Costa, R. (2017, April 23) 'Everyone tunes in': Inside Trump's obsession with cable TV. *Washington Post*. Available at: www.washingtonpost.com/politics/everyone-tunes-in-inside-trumps-obsession-with-cable-tv/2017/04/23/3c52bd6c-25e3-11e7-a1b3-faff0034e2de_story.html?utm_term=.5727eec82e1c.

Peck, R. (2019) *Fox Populism: Branding Conservatism as Working Class*. New York: Cambridge University Press: 126–127, 146–151.

Peters, C. (2010) No-spin zones: The rise of the American cable news magazine and Bill O'Reilly. *Journalism Studies*, 11(6): 842.

Prior, M. (2007) *Post-Broadcast Democracy: How Media Choice Increases Inequality in Political Involvement and Polarizes Elections*. Cambridge: Cambridge University Press.

Ricchiardi, S. (2009) The anti-anchor. *American Journalism Review*, 31(5), 14–22.

Schudson, M. (2003) *The Sociology of News*. New York: W.W. Norton and Co.: 112.

Swint, K. (2008) *Dark Genius: The Influential Career of Legendary Political Operative and Fox News Founder Roger Ailes*. New York: Union Square Press.

Vogel, K., Rutenberg, J. and Lerer, L. (2020, April 21) The quite hand of conservative groups in the anti-lockdown protests. *New York Times*. Available at: www.nytimes.com/2020/04/21/us/politics/coronavirus-protests-trump.html.

Welna, D. (2020, April 28) Coronavirus has now killed more Americans than Vietnam war. *NPR.com*. Available at: www.npr.org/sections/coronavirus-live-updates/2020/04/28/846701304/pandemic-death-toll-in-u-s-now-exceeds-vietnam-wars-u-s-fatalities.

Wemple, E. (2020, March 30) Hannity must go. *Washington Post*. Available at: www.washingtonpost.com/opinions/2020/03/30/hannity-must-go/?outputType=amp.

16

ALTERNATIVE ONLINE POLITICAL MEDIA

Challenging or exacerbating populism and mis/disinformation?

Declan McDowell-Naylor, Richard Thomas, and Stephen Cushion

In this chapter, we examine the rise of new alternative online political media (AOPM) and ask whether these sites challenge or exacerbate the spread of populism and mis/disinformation. We provide a critical overview of the debates within academic literature about alternative media, populism, and mis/disinformation. Overall, we argue that while many of these debates do not represent new phenomena, there is a need to develop different ideas and questions in the context of today's hybrid media system and AOPM's relationship with mainstream media, populism, and mis/disinformation. Informed by relevant literature, we argue that while there are clear connections between AOPM and populism, and some evidence of misinformation, they do not feature the kind of blatant acts of disinformation often found in fake online news sites.

New phenomenon? Alternative online political media, populism, disinformation

Alternative media has long been recognised as important within political communication (Atton 2002; Couldry & Curran 2003). In particular, new social movements, and citizen and independent journalism, have attracted considerable academic attention over recent years. Amid ever-shifting media systems, contemporary forms of alternative media have emerged. These newer forms – which we term AOPM – have attempted to become legitimate sources of news and commentary and, by taking advantage of internet and social media reach, have built up varying levels of influence, sometimes exceeding that of their mainstream counterparts (Waterson 2017). Terms such as 'alternative news media' (Holt, et al. 2019), 'alternative and partisan news websites' (Newman, et al. 2019, 23), and 'right-wing online news sites' (Heft, et al. 2019) have appeared in recent scholarship. However, while 'alternative media' are not new, the wider dissemination of alternative digital news and commentary clearly represents a break from the past.

AOPM are distinguished by their digital-native (Thomas & Cushion 2019) status via websites and social media. They are characterised by strong political editorialisation of news and comment and an explicit self-identification as alternatives to mainstream media (Holt, et al. 2019, 2). Notable global publications include O Antagonista (Brazil), Breitbart News (US), Rebel News (Canada), The Canary (UK), PI News (Germany), Steigan (Norway), and New Matilda (Australia). Despite their novelty, these alternative media still fit many of the broad characteristics defining alternative media as existing outside 'mainstream media institutions and networks', populated by non-professionals seeking to represent marginalised interests and contest media power imbalances (Atton 2007, 18). Such characteristics have evolved, but despite some core similarities, AOPM vary in content, appearance, audience, and reach.

The often-partisan nature of AOBM is exemplified by the US site, Breitbart News. During the 2016 US presidential election for example, it was declared 'the platform for the alt-right' by chairman Steve Bannon (Posner 2016) and grew its audience by focusing on topics such as climate change denial and anti-immigration and anti–Democratic Party rhetoric. During the 2017 UK general election campaign, the left-wing website The Canary also attracted attention by reaching millions of people with content embracing anti-austerity, social justice, and criticism of the Conservative Party and the mainstream media (Waterson 2017).

From different political perspectives, both Breitbart News and The Canary have been accused of promoting populist ideologies and spreading disinformation. Breitbart, for example, became infamous for its propagation of the 'Pizzagate' conspiracy (Robb 2017),[1] while The Canary was admonished for publishing false accusations that BBC political editor Laura Kuenssberg spoke at a Conservative Party conference (BBC News 2017).[2] These debates have been driven by the electoral success of populist political parties across the world and are underpinned by generally low levels of trust in news (Newman, et al. 2019; Fletcher, et al. 2018). Noppari et al. (2019), for example, found that those consuming populist 'counter media' in Finland were motivated by a shared mistrust of legacy journalism. Populism and disinformation are often characteristics associated with concerns about the new digital media environment, raising important questions about their relationships with alternative media. While the evidence is thin, scholars have suggested the rise of alternative media should be seen in conjunction with populist agendas developing global momentum (Heft, et al. 2019, 3–4).

Despite the simultaneous emergence of populist politics and AOPM, the latter should not be regarded as populist without empirical evidence linking the two (Heft, et al. 2019). Similarly, the connection between alternative media and mis/disinformation should also not be assumed but led by evidence (Riebling & Wense 2019). Nonetheless, campaign groups including Stop Funding Fake News and Sleeping Giants have convinced commercial organisations to withdraw advertising from Breitbart and Evolve Politics, on the basis that they promote 'fake news'. Similarly, other alternative media have been dubbed 'false' news producers and 'blacklisted' by fact-checkers and mainstream journalists (Rone 2019).

Measuring the impact of AOPM and their potential role in propagating populism and mis/disinformation is a complex task. Their reach should not be overstated. For example, the weekly use of UK alternative sites ranges from 1 percent to 17 percent,[3] and 'alternative and partisan sites' reached just 6 percent of the 1,711 participants tracked during the 2019 UK general election (Fletcher, et al. 2020). Heft, et al. (2019) found varying levels of website engagement across six western democracies; in the US, four right-wing alternative sites ranked in the top 1,000 most visited websites.

AOPM's reach is perhaps greatest across social media sites. In the UK, for example, Another Angry Voice had over 350,000 Facebook followers as of May 2020, roughly double the total for *The New Statesman* and one-tenth the total of popular tabloid *The Daily Mirror*. An audience study during the 2019 UK general election campaign showed that many alternative media sites significantly increased their social media reach since the previous 2017 general election (Thomas & McDowell-Naylor 2019). Another important measure of impact is the inter-media agenda-setting effects of alt-media sites. For example, journalists such as Ash Sarkar (Novara Media) and Ben Shapiro (Breitbart) often appear on mainstream media, extending their influence beyond alternative media sites.

Conceptualising alternative online political media

There are many long-standing conceptualisations of alternative media (see Holt, et al. 2019). Terms include 'hyper-partisan news outlets' (Marwick & Lewis 2017), 'Facebook-empowered hyperpartisan political clickbait sites' (Faris, et al. 2017, 19), and 'alternative and partisan news websites' (Newman, et al. 2019, 23). Holt et al. (2019, 3) argue that AOPM are characterised by 'a proclaimed and/or (self-)perceived corrective, opposing the overall tendency of public discourse emanating from what is perceived as the dominant mainstream media in a given system'. Additionally, ideological definitions such as 'right-wing online news sites' (Heft, et al. 2019) often refer to anti-immigrant and conservative outlets. Terms such as 'populist counter media' have also been used as it is claimed that they better capture the specifics of alternative media in a national context (Noppari, et al. 2019). The common feature among these definitions is the centrality of digital news and commentary. While alternative media research may have previously encompassed media characterised as 'radical . . . autonomous, activist, independent, participatory and community' (Rauch 2016, 757), contemporary research has more specifically focused on journalism. As a result, conceptual understandings of AOPM are already connected to current debates and concerns about the value and function of journalism (Pickard 2019), of which populism (Hameleers, et al. 2018) and disinformation (Chadwick, et al. 2018) are at the forefront.

Long-standing conceptual debates fundamentally ask how alternative media are understood in relation to legacy/mainstream media. Earlier studies of alternative media applied conceptual frameworks relying on simplistic binary models, but since then, these models have developed into more complicated frameworks embracing hybridity. Within the earlier binary models, for example, alternative media were often understood as progressive and democratic, closely tied to social movements and working in opposition to elitist, monetised, and homogeneous mainstream media (Holt, et al. 2019). However, it has been increasingly recognised that both alternative and mainstream media are more heterogenous than their previous generations. Atton (2002), for example, argues that alternative media are not intrinsically connected to social movements while Harcup (2005, 370) believes that the conceptual relationship between the two can be understood as a continuum on which people, ideas, and practices move bidirectionally.

These conceptual turns to hybridity have carried through to contemporary conceptual thinking. Hackett and Gurleyen (2015), for example, strongly advocate a continuum model while, more recently, Holt, et al. (2019, 3) propose a 'relational, multi-level' model in which content, organisational structure, and the overall function of alternative and mainstream media form multi-layered continuums. Of course, these important developments also fit within broader understanding notions of a hybrid media system (Chadwick 2017). Key changes in alternative media are likely driven by this 'overall hybridisation of media systems' (Holt, et al. 2019, 7; see also Robertson and Mourão 2020, 17).

Finally, criticism of the mainstream media is another defining aspect of AOPM. Indeed, the stated objectives of many sites is to challenge mainstream media orthodoxy. The Canary (2020), for example, propose a 'truly independent and viable alternative' to largely 'conservative' coverage. In Germany, Politically Incorrect News (2020) claim that 'political correctness and goodwill dominate the media everywhere today' and that the 'fundamental right to freedom of expression and information' should be insisted on. Australian site New Matilda (2020) asserts that amid 'shrinking media diversity', 'fewer and fewer outlets' publish 'independent-minded' journalism. Finally, Rebel News (2020) in Canada claims to tell 'the other side of the story', even if it does not align with 'the official narrative of the establishment'.

In this regard, AOPM can be conceptualised as a 'self-perceived corrective' of 'legacy' or 'mainstream' news media (Holt, et al. 2019, 3). This performative role often includes claims that the MSM is lying to defend the establishment or that it is biased against particular politicians. It might also be accompanied by a reframing of events with some form of the 'truth' (Robertson & Mourão 2020, 12). Such conceptual understandings of AOPM's corrective role embrace a more fundamental struggle to define 'the truth' (see Riebling & Wense 2019) and contest general debates about journalistic truth, legitimacy, and trust related to populism and disinformation (Pickard 2019). Studies of alternative media in the UK have shown that the MSM generally and public service media specifically have been the objects of most criticism between 2015 and 2019, with their news reporting under constant surveillance from sites such as Evolve Politics and The Canary (Cushion 2020).

Discussing the evidence base

But what empirical evidence exists to link AOPM with mis/disinformation and populism? Is there evidence of AOPM contributing to – or challenging – mis/disinformation online or supporting populist politics? At present, while there is some evidence that empirically connects AOPM to mis/disinformation or populism, in our view more research is needed to draw clearer conclusions.

For several reasons, many observers consider AOPM sites to be a source of both populist ideologies and disinformation. First, since many AOPM sites are created by non-professionals, there is often an assumption they will not follow professional journalistic standards, such as objectivity. Second, because they are generally partisan, it might be also assumed they promote 'fake news' in pursuit of their editorial/ideological missions. Third, their critiques of mainstream media and the 'establishment at large' echo common populist tropes, which in turn means we may form connections between these critiques and populist politicians such as Donald Trump and Jeremy Corbyn, who have promised to 'take on the establishment'.

These points may have been aided by some of the prominent examples of disinformation previously explored. While often these assumptions may well be correct, as Noppari et al. (2019, 23) caution, populist victories, 'fake news', and the proliferation of alternative media websites have been habitually drawn together under a post-truth narrative. But despite many media commentators regularly making these connections, academic research has yet to establish any causal relationship.

Alternative online political media and mis/disinformation

As Rone (2019) points out, there are few sources of systematic academic evidence directly linking alternative media and mis/disinformation. Where links have been established, they tend to be within larger studies that explore misinformation more generally.

In their extensive report on online disinformation, Marwick and Lewis (2017, 19) describe how online communities are increasingly turning to predominately right-wing, conspiracy-driven news sources (see also Robb 2017). For example, the report identifies Alex Jones, who runs alternative media site Info Wars, and his promotion of the Barack Obama 'birther' conspiracy.[4] This is empirically supported by Starbird (2017), who determined via an analysis of Twitter that the sharing of conspiracy-based narratives online was directly fuelled by sources of alternative media. This was also supported by Buzzfeed's analysis of Facebook (Silverman 2016). Marwick and Lewis (2017) also point out that conspiratorial claims are then covered by the mainstream media, which then perpetuate disinformation.

In looking at how mis/disinformation spreads online, Chadwick, et al. (2018) evidence its production and consumption by examining both media reporting and people's use of it. Using a survey of over 1,000 Twitter users who had shared news sources, researchers investigated the prominence of 'democratically dysfunctional news sharing': what they term the sharing of news sources containing dis/misinformation. There was no evidence that sharing information from UK alternative sites such as Breitbart London, Westmonster, Canary, and Evolve Politics was a predictor of such democratically dysfunctional news sharing (Chadwick, et al. 2018). This was despite these sites featuring prominently in the top 50 most shared news sources in their dataset of those shared by citizens (ibid).

To date, there are no comprehensive studies of AOPM content itself. However, in studying how 'fake news' sites discursively self-present, Roberton and Mourão (2020) link alternative news and mis/disinformation further by compiling a list of 953 websites labelled 'fake news' by third-party experts, activists, and journalists. They find that these sites frequently adopt 'the *discourses* of alternative journalism' and that this suggests a link between the two phenomena, wherein sites create an 'impersonation of alternative journalism, combining its features with false information' (ibid: 16, emphasis in original). Furthermore, there is evidence that AOPM often label mainstream media 'fake news' (Fingenschou & Ihlebæk 2019; Riebling & Wense 2019), complicating the picture further.

The sporadic evidence of links between alternative media and mis/disinformation tends to focus on high-profile incidents, such as Pizzagate or The Canary's false reporting on Laura Kuenssberg. Despite these notable cases, in comparing ten alternative media outlets across Europe, Rone (2019) found limited empirical evidence of mis/disinformation. The study argued that AOPM were characterised by a focus on a narrow set of topics according to their editorial biases and that 'disinformation is only one, and a rather minor, aspect' of alternative media. Moreover, since 'alternative media' can refer to many different groups of already-heterogenous sites across media systems, there is an ontological problem. While some claim to find explicit links between AOPM and disinformation (Faris 2017; Marwick & Lewis 2017), others (Chadwick, et al. 2018; Rone 2019) doubt such assumptions. Viewed another way, many alternative media sites may be spreading the same kind of misinformation that many partisan mainstream media outlets follow. Indeed, the UK editor of The Canary is on record as saying she adopts a kind of 'tabloid styling, tabloid-level language' in order to champion the site's political issues (Chakelian 2017).

Alternative media and populism

Evidence that links alternative media and populism is more substantive than with mis/disinformation, but there are only a limited number of empirical studies exploring this relationship.

Research carried out by Reuters has shown that 'alternative or partisan outlets' are 'often favoured by those with populist views, in addition to having audiences with a heavy left-right skew' (Newman, et al. 2019, 43). In particular, the research highlights both The Canary and Breitbart as those with 'very populist audiences' (ibid, 46). Together with AOPM's reliance on social media, the fact that people with populist attitudes are heavy Facebook News users (Newman, et al. 2019, 42) and research indicating that social media facilitates populist messaging (Engesser, et al. 2016), the synergies are clear to see. Simplified populist discourses that divide society into 'good' and 'bad' groups have shown to be very persuasive (Hameleers, et al. 2018). As Mazzolini and Bracciale argue (2018, 3), social media platforms are suited to the kind of emotional and controversial content shared by populists. The evident adoption of these kinds of discourses by AOPM may be in part what is driving their success, particularly on social media.

Noppari et al. (2019) explored how and why Finnish users consume 'populist counter media'. Based on interviews with a demographically diverse set of their readers, the researchers found they 'made active, affective and conscious choices to consume and engage with material that contradicted the agendas and views of the dominant public sphere and promoted strong ideological stances *expressed via populist address*' (ibid, 33, emphasis added). In particular, Noppari et al. identified a user archetype they termed 'system sceptics' (ibid, 29), whose broadly anti-establishment and legacy media views mirrored typically populist attitudes. These users viewed populist counter media as 'a way to construct and share material that could counter, challenge and bypass the ideological power of the mainstream media' (ibid, 30). However, these valuable qualitative findings come from just one national study.

In the German/Austrian context, Haller and Holt's (2019) study of the populist PEGIDA movement's Facebook page found that alternative media sources were overwhelmingly (99 percent of the time) used to affirm the existing political views of users (ibid, 1674). The researchers suggest this connection relates to the anti-system content of the alternative media observed, supporting Noppari et al.'s interview findings. More recently, Rae (2020) has argued that populism and alternative media such as Breitbart and The Canary share inherent media logics, including 'personalisation', 'emotionalization and simplification', 'polarisation', 'intensification', and 'anti-establishment', which are evidently reflected in the practices of what she terms 'hyper partisan news' (ibid, 4). With respect to personalisation, Marwick and Lewis (2017, 47) observed that 'there is increasing evidence that Trump voters primarily consumed hyper-partisan news, much of which, like Infowars and Breitbart, played a key role in amplifying subcultural messages'.

While there is evidence to suggest a link between AOPM and populism, there are important caveats. For instance, Reuters research shows that people with populist attitudes still prefer television to online as their main source of news (Newman, et al. 2019, 42), meaning claims that AOPM are a primary driver of populist attitudes are overly simplified. Again, due to evidence that AOPM's reach is limited, the accommodation of populism in broadcast and tabloid media is likely to be far more effective.

Considerations for future empirical research

As we have noted, alternative media scholars have been stressing the importance of hybridity for many years. In sum, it is currently easier for 'any online user to establish alternative media and news websites, and to access media material that can be used to construct and support various political and ideological positions' (Noppari, et al. 2019, 24). Consequently, a wider range of news providers could potentially provide more diversity in information and commentary but might also increase the visibility and impact of 'partisan information, disinformation and "fake news"' (Figenschou & Ihlebæk 2019, 1221).

In addition to AOPM sites themselves, social media platforms have been key to populism and disinformation debates. Engesser et al. (2016), for example, showed how European politicians use Twitter and Facebook to spread populist ideologies. Meanwhile, Chadwick et al. (2018) identified a link between social media, tabloid journalism, and the spread of mis/disinformation. This is important since social media environments are central to concerns about spreading disinformation and are crucial to how AOPM disseminate content. According to Newman, et al. (2019, 39), 30 percent of those participating in UK news groups within Facebook or WhatsApp use alternative or partisan brands, compared with just 7 percent for the overall sample.[5]

Moreover, biases can be perpetuated by dominant discourses within commentary and analysis of AOPM. Terms such as *partisan*, for example, are often reserved exclusively for alternative outlets. Indeed, the term *alternative* might simply point to a position 'beyond the mainstream, beyond the pale' (Holt 2018, 52), and such understandings can lead to false accusations. This was the case when three Dutch news outlets were inaccurately labelled as 'fake news' in 2018 (Rone 2019). Moreover, tabloid news outlets are also consistently partisan (Deacon & Wring 2019) and are also a key part of dysfunctional news-sharing behaviour (Chadwick, et al. 2018). In the UK, right-wing partisan outlets such as The Sun, The Daily Mail, and The Telegraph supply the overwhelming majority of digital news (Newman, et al. 2019), emphasising that the impact of partisan-driven mis/disinformation is likely to be much more considerable when it is spread by mainstream media (see Moore 2020).

Conclusion

It is often claimed that the rise of AOPM is associated with populism and mis/disinformation, and that this toxic combination represents a new and more dangerous threat to the public sphere than other media. But, as we have explored in this chapter, the link between AOPM, populism, and mis/disinformation is not always clear cut or straightforward. Moreover, often conclusions about AOPM are based on assumptions lacking evidence and are largely driven by mainstream panics about so-called 'fake news'. In our view, much more research is needed to establish whether AOPM challenge or exacerbate the spread of mis/disinformation or populism. More attention, for example, needs to be paid to the editorial agendas of AOPM, including assessing the accuracy and balance of coverage beyond high-profile stories. As audience research has established (Bursztyn 2020), public confusion with media misinformation is as much a symptom of reporting in some politically biased and opinionated news outlets as it is in new AOPM. This suggests AOPM represent a continuation of partisan news reporting, rather than a new and more dangerous cause of populism or mis/disinformation.

Notes

1 During the 2016 US presidential election, it was claimed by many right-wing actors that Hillary Clinton was sexually abusing children during satanic rituals in the basement of a Washington, DC, pizza restaurant named Comet Ping Pong. A *Rolling Stone* investigative team (Robb 2017) traced the origins of the story through a vast digital network, prominently including Breitbart and Infowars.
2 This did, however, raise questions about her impartiality. The Canary was forced to correct the article and acknowledged it failed to 'take all reasonable steps to ensure accuracy prior to publication' (Hopkins 2017).
3 The Reuters Institute employs YouGov to conduct panel surveys and administer questionnaires on news consumption.
4 The 'birther movement' was formed around a false assertion that Barack Obama was an illegitimate president of the United States because he was not a natural-born citizen of the US, as required by Article Two of the Constitution. The conspiracy theory alleged his birth certificate was fake and that he was born in Kenya, not Hawaii. Donald Trump was among those to perpetuate the conspiracy theory.
5 See note 3.

References

Atton, C. (2002). *Alternative Media*. London: Sage.
Atton, C. (2007). Current issues in alternative media research. *Sociology Compass*, *1*(1), 17–27.
BBC News. (2017). Canary's story about Laura Kuenssberg "breached press code". *BBC News Online*. Retrieved 6 April 2020, from www.bbc.co.uk/news/entertainment-arts-42430083

Bursztyn, A. R., Roth, C., & Yanagizawa-Drott, D. (2020). *Misinformation During a Pandemic*. BFI Working Paper, April 19. Retrieved from https://bfi.uchicago.edu/working-paper/2020-44/

The Canary. (2020). About & FAQ. *The Canary*. Retrieved from www.thecanary.co/about/

Chadwick, A. (2017). *The Hybrid Media System: Politics and Power*. Oxford: Oxford University Press.

Chadwick, A., Vaccari, C., & O'Loughlin, B. (2018). Do tabloids poison the well of social media? Explaining democratically dysfunctional news sharing. *New Media & Society*, *20*(11), 4255–4274.

Chakelian, A. (2017). "Luxury communism now!" The rise of the pro-Corbyn media. *New Statesman*. Retrieved 16 May 2020 from www.newstatesman.com/politics/media/2017/09/luxury-communism-now-rise-pro-corbyn-media

Couldry, N., & Curran, J. (2003). The paradox of media power. In J. P. Curran & N. Couldry (Eds.) *Contesting Media Power: Alternative Media in a Networked World: Alternative Media in a Networked World.* Lanham, MD: Rowman & Littlefield, pp. 3–16.

Cushion. (2020). Six ways alt-left media legitimise their criticism of mainstream media: An analysis of the canary and evolve politics (2015–2019). *Journal of Alternative & Community Media*, Forthcoming.

Deacon, D., & Wring, D. (2019). UK election 2019: Partisan press is pulling out all the stops against labour. *The Conversation*. Retrieved 9 April 2020, from http://theconversation.com/uk-election-2019-partisan-press-is-pulling-out-all-the-stops-against-labour-127133

Engesser, S., Ernst, N., Esser, F., & Büchel, F. (2016). Populism and social media: How politicians spread a fragmented ideology. *Information, Communication & Society*, *20*(8), 1109–1126.

Faris, R., Roberts, H., Etling, B., Bourassa, N., Zuckerman, E., & Benkler, Y. (2017). *Partisanship, Propaganda, and Disinformation: Online Media and the 2016 U.S. Presidential Election*. Cambridge: Berkman Klein Center.

Figenschou, T. U., & Ihlebæk, K. A. (2019). Challenging journalistic authority. *Journalism Studies*, *20*(9), 1221–1237.

Fletcher, R., Cornia, A., Graves, L., & Nielsen, R. K. (2018). *Measuring the Reach of 'Fake News' and Online Disinformation in Europe*. Retrieved 20 February 2020, from https://reutersinstitute.politics.ox.ac.uk/our-research/measuring-reach-fake-news-and-online-disinformation-europe

Fletcher, R., Newman, N., & Schulz, A. (2020). *A mile wide, an inch deep: Online news and media use in the 2019 UK general election*. Digital News Report. Retrieved 6 February 2020, from www.digitalnewsreport.org

Hackett, R. A., & Gurleyen, P. (2015). Beyond the binaries? Alternative media and objective journalism. In C. Atton (Ed.) *The Routledge Companion to Alternative and Community Media*. London: Routledge.

Haller, A., & Holt, K. (2019). Paradoxical populism: How PEGIDA relates to mainstream and alternative media. *Information, Communication & Society*, *22*(12), 1665–1680.

Hameleers, M., Bos, L., Fawzi, N., Reinemann, C., Andreadis, I., Corbu, N., Schemer, C., Schulz, A., Shaefer, T., Aalberg, T., Axelsson, S., Berganza, R., Cremonesi, C., Dahlberg, S., de Vreese, C. H., Hess, A., Kartsounidou, E., Kasprowicz, D., Matthes, J., . . . Weiss-Yaniv, N. (2018). Start spreading the news: A comparative experiment on the effects of populist communication on political engagement in sixteen European countries. *The International Journal of Press/Politics*, *23*(4), 517–538.

Harcup, T. (2005). "I'm doing this to change the world": Journalism in alternative and mainstream media. *Journalism Studies*, *6*(3), 361–374.

Heft, A., Mayerhöffer, E., Reinhardt, S., & Knüpfer, C. (2019). Beyond Breitbart: Comparing right-wing digital news infrastructures in six Western democracies. *Policy & Internet*. https://doi.org/10.1002/poi3.219

Holt, K. (2018). Alternative media and the notion of anti-systemness: Towards an analytical framework. *Media and Communication*, *6*(4), 49–57.

Holt, K., Figenschou, T. U., & Frischlich, L. (2019). Key dimensions of alternative news media. *Digital Journalism*, 1–10. https://doi.org/10.1080/21670811.2019.1625715

Hopkins, S. (2017). The canary makes front page correction over false Laura Kuenssberg Tory conference story. *HuffPost*. Retrieved 6 April 2019, from www.huffingtonpost.co.uk/entry/laura-kuenssberg-the-canary_uk_5a3aa097e4b0b0e5a79f0b4d

Marwick, A., & Lewis, R. (2017). Media manipulation and disinformation online. *Data & Society Research Institute*. Retrieved 6 February 2019, from https://datasociety.net/output/mediamanipulation-and-disinfo-online

Mazzoleni, G., & Bracciale, R. (2018). Socially mediated populism: The communicative strategies of political leaders on Facebook. *Palgrave Communications*, *4*(1), 1–10.

Moore, N. (2020). Study finds more COVID-19 cases among viewers of fox news host who downplayed pandemic. *NPR*. Retrieved 6 February 2019, from www.npr.org/local/309/2020/05/04/849109486/study-finds-more-c-o-v-i-d-19-cases-among-viewers-of-fox-news-host-who-downplayed-pandemic?t=1589382367940&t=1589793762693

Newman, N., Fletcher, R., Kalogeropoulos, & Nielsen, R. K. (2019). *Reuters Institute Digital News Report 2019*. Reuters Institute. Retrieved 6 February 2020, from www.digitalnewsreport.org/survey/2019/overview-key-findings-2019/

New Matilda. (2020). Contact us – about us. *New Matilda*. Retrieved from https://newmatilda.com/about-us/

Noppari, E., Hiltunen, I., & Ahva, L. (2019). User profiles for populist counter-media websites in Finland. *Journal of Alternative and Community Media, 4*(1), 23–37.

Rae, M. (2020). Hyperpartisan news: Rethinking the media for populist politics. *New Media & Society*. https://doi.org/10.1177/1461444820910416

Rauch, J. (2016). Are there still alternatives? Relationships between alternative media and mainstream media in a converged environment. *Sociology Compass, 10*(9), 756–767.

Rebel News. (2020). About rebel news. *Rebel News*. Retrieved from www.rebelnews.com/about

Riebling, J. R., & Wense, I. von der. (2019). Framing the mass media: Exploring 'fake news' as a frame embedded in political discourse. *Journal of Alternative and Community Media, 4*(1), 57–76.

Robb, A. (2017). Anatomy of a fake news scandal. *Rolling Stone Magazine*. Retrieved 6 April 2020, from www.rollingstone.com/politics/politics-news/anatomy-of-a-fake-news-scandal-125877/

Robertson, C. T., & Mourão, R. R. (2020). Faking alternative journalism? An analysis of self-presenta tions of "fake news" sites. *Digital Journalism*, 1–19.

Rone, J. (2019). Why talking about "disinformation" misses the point when considering radical right "alternative" media. *Media@LSE*. Retrieved 6 February 2020, from https://blogs.lse.ac.uk/medialse/2019/01/03/why-talking-about-disinformation-misses-the-point-when-considering-radical-right-alternative-media/

Silverman, C. (2016). This analysis shows how viral fake election news stories outperformed real news on Facebook. *Buzzfeed News*. Retrieved 6 February 2020, from www.buzzfeednews.com/article/craigsilverman/viral-fake-election-news-outperformed-real-news-on-facebook

Starbird, K. (2017). *Examining the Alternative Media Ecosystem Through the Production of Alternative Narratives of Mass Shooting Events on Twitter*. ICWSM. Retrieved from https://www.aaai.org/ocs/index.php/ICWSM/ICWSM17/paper/view/15603

Thomas, R., & Cushion, S. (2019). Towards an institutional news logic of digital native news media? A case study of BuzzFeed's reporting during the 2015 and 2017 UK general election campaigns. *Digital Journalism, 7*(10), 1328–1345.

Thomas, R., & McDowell-Naylor, D. (2019). UK election 2019: How the growing reach of alt-media is shaping the campaign. *The Conversation*. Retrieved 6 February 2020, from http://theconversation.com/uk-election-2019-how-the-growing-reach-of-alt-media-is-shaping-the-campaign-126947

Posner, S. (2016). How Donald Trump's new campaign chief created an online haven for white nation-alists. *Mother Jones*. Retrieved 6 February 2020, from www.motherjones.com/politics/2016/08/stephen-bannon-donald-trump-alt-right-breitbart-news/

Pickard, V. (2019). *Democracy Without Journalism?: Confronting the Misinformation Society*. Oxford: Oxford University Press.

Politically Incorrect News. (2020). Guidelines. *PI News*. Retrieved from www.pi-news.net/leitlinien/

Waterson, J. (2017). The rise of the alt-left British media. *Buzzfeed News*. Retrieved 6 February 2020, from www.buzzfeed.com/jimwaterson/the-rise-of-the-alt-left

17

ONLINE HARASSMENT OF JOURNALISTS AS A CONSEQUENCE OF POPULISM, MIS/DISINFORMATION, AND IMPUNITY

Jeannine E. Relly

Philippine president Rodrigo Duterte dismissed news from the globally recognised investigative journalism site Rappler as 'fake news' (Reporters without Borders 2018a, para. 7). In Ecuador, former president Rafael Correa referred to journalists as 'liars', 'corrupt', and 'cowards' (Waisbord & Amado 2017,1338). Albanian prime minister Edvin 'Edi' Rama often likens journalists to 'rubbish bins' (Selva 2020, 11). US president Donald J. Trump tweeted one month into office, 'The FAKE NEWS media (failing @nytimes, @NBCNews, @ABC, @CBS, @CNN) is not my enemy, it is the enemy of the American People!' and then about three years later on 20 March 2020, 'So much FAKE NEWS!' Though the US likely is an exception to the extent to which mis/disinformation has been absorbed into the national political scene (Bennett & Livingston 2018), all these cases are glimpses of the verbal and social media assaults on journalists as a wave of populist leaders have been elected around the world, harnessing the energy of disenfranchised voters disgusted with the political establishment (Wahl-Jorgensen 2018) in the midst of various crises.

Though the relationship between digital communication and populism has been analysed since the late 1990s (Bimber 1998; Blassnig et al. 2019), this chapter aims to examine additional factors associated with populism, disinformation and online harassment of journalists in an environment of impunity. Though populism has been referenced as a way to bring people together, recent literature largely has linked it to 'demagogy and propaganda' (Kavada 2018, 742), ideology, strategy, discourse, political expression, and political logic that often advances the ideal of a political community fighting a common enemy, including the status quo or political elites, often through provocation and breaking taboos (Bulut & Yörük 2017, 4095; De Vrees et al. 2019; Gerbaudo 2018; Krämer 2018). This popular discourse often constructs various publics as a collective, essentialising and associating the opposition with anti-intellectualism, at times, or conspiracy theories that focus on power structures of privilege and long-held institutional values (Krämer 2014, 44). This onslaught of collective blame and furor has often targeted journalism and other institutions, leading to decreases in trust in the credibility of news media over time (Bennett & Livingston 2018).

Since early in the new millennium, populism largely has been characterised as antagonistic communication, often against journalists based on their coverage (Waisbord & Amado 2017). In fact, populism rejects the public interest model of professional journalism and its core values of independence, and accountability reporting, instead linking it to elite interests and opposition politics (Waisbord 2013, 511), often circumventing mainstream news media and appealing directly to the public. In these fractionalised and polarised political environments around the world where audiences are fragmented and gatekeeping has been stretched (Waisbord 2013), populism has fostered environments of disinformation and misinformation,[1] online and offline. In fact, with populism, institutions and elites are devalued and are bypassed to speak directly to the people using 'an emotional and moralistic style, plainspoken, sometimes aggressive, but appealing to the commonsense' (Krämer 2014, 46). Moreover, the very nature of social media makes it in many ways an ideal vehicle for populist politicians to have maximum visibility, harness a 'mobocratic tendency', and amplify online crowds through the 'network effect', reifying and strengthening nodes in the network to expand the range of connections (Gerbaudo 2018, 750–751).

Though social media has not just been in the province of populists in recent years (Bulut & Yörük 2017), the unmediated format of many social media platforms and the 'gateless' opportunity to offer commentary, announce events, and lob caustic language at political adversaries and others has been at the heart of populist movements gaining momentum (Waisbord & Amado 2017, 1342). Social media allows direct access to various publics, providing unfettered platforms to connect to large networks and develop communities with wide reach, all without 'journalistic interference' (De Vreese et al. 2018, 428). Twitter, specifically, has been strategic in energising publics (Bulut & Yörük 2017). In recent years, political actors messaging on social media, with largely unregulated ecosystems and growth, have galvanised cycles of mis/disinformation production and reproduction, unencumbered by professional ethics or editorial accountability (Crilley & Gillespie 2019). Countries with high social media use are most at risk for disinformation rapidly spreading. It is there, according to Humprecht et al. (2020, 9), that 'it is easier for rumor spreaders to build partisan follower networks'. In democracies in Canada and Western Europe, political systems with consensus orientations marked by low levels of political polarisation have tended to have high resilience to online disinformation and hold high levels of media trust, compared with nations with high political polarisation (Humprecht et al. 2020, 15).

The following sections examine how populist rhetoric has moved towards delegitimising journalism through tactics including disinformation and denigration. The chapter then examines literature on how this environment has led to online harassment of journalists around the world. Studies and media advocacy resources are then analysed to examine how this ecosystem of populism and online harassment has impacted journalists in an environment of impunity. Finally, the chapter considers strategies that have been utilised or suggested to combat online harassment of journalists on the path forward.

Populism, the delegitimisation of journalism, and online mis/disinformation issues

It is not uncommon for sycophant echo chambers or so-called 'populist journalism' to fill a need, like 'necessary journalism' in Venezuela, Nicaragua's 'Sandinista journalism', and other top-down approaches in which state media is re-engineered or advertising is provided based on 'media patrimonialism' (Waisbord & Amado 2017, 1333). Media ecologies that foster populism often have fragmented audiences and political polarisation, which often puts publics at risk for mistaking disinformation for valid information (Waisbord 2018, 21). In addition to politicians and populist media, citizens may engage in populist rhetoric, which often stresses moral divides, in-groups and out-groups, negative stereotypes, uncivil discourse, political tribalism, and points of no compromise (Hameleers et al. 2018; De Vreese et al. 2018). The ideals of truth, fact-producing public-interest journalism run counter to the populist dictum of truth being dismissed as ideological illusion, and as Waisbord (2018, 29–30), noted, populists often advocate that 'the people' do not need mediation or institutional representation from journalists, scientists, universities, or other elites.

The populist perspective on news media is that 'liberal journalism betrays the people and conspires with, or is instrumentalised by, the ruling elite to manipulate the people' (Krämer 2018, 454). On the rise in the last five years have been discreet online methods of drowning out and silencing journalists. Initiatives to distract from journalistic content aim to manipulate information, as well as the flow or dissemination of it, and to bury news content with white noise or other distractions (UNESCO 2019). Many nations, including longtime democracies, are witnessing a rise in the amount of disinformation on social media sites, which masks itself in the format of news (Bennett & Livingston 2018). Scholars have noted that this online spread of mis/disinformation has presented a major issue for democracies, and journalism specifically, as inaccurate information lives alongside journalism and often drowns it out with parallel attacks on journalists as producers of 'fake news', eroding and slowly delegitimising the profession (Balod & Hameleers 2019).

Scholarship has suggested that some public narratives about social media changed after the election of US president Donald J. Trump in 2016. At this critical juncture, concerns were brought forward about 'widespread malfeasance on social media – from "fake news", propaganda, and coordinated disinformation to bot-based media manipulation' (Lewis & Molyneux 2018, 12). A key concern for various publics across democracies as well has been the apparent difficulty in ascertaining the difference between legitimate news and mis/disinformation masked as news (Crilley & Gillespie 2019). Meantime, some political figures harness the rhetoric of xenophobia, racism, and other 'isms' on social media platforms, undermining the trust in and credibility of autonomous news media seeking the truth (Crilley & Gillespie 2019, 174), which has led to a drop in public confidence in the institution of journalism and a crisis of credibility (Lischka 2019). In this environment, online disinformation often is transmitted to pursue political agendas or advance malicious deception (Humprecht et al. 2020).

Online harassment of journalists: the impact and impunity

Attacks on journalists in countries around the world have a long offline history. Media ecosystems that are strong generally can absorb a limited number of official attacks (Bennett & Livingston 2018). However, it is indeed something entirely different when networks of social media spread disinformation continuously and carry out sustained attacks on journalists in longtime democracies (Bennett & Livingston 2018, 125). Thus, in recent times, social media is being re-evaluated for its true social impact, after years of being heralded for its capacity to bridge digital divides, advance digital activism, and provide platforms for democratic uprisings. Online disinformation campaigns have confused voters around the world and contributed to mob killings and myriad forms of online harassment and hate speech (Lewis & Molyneux 2018, 12). Though a majority of social media research has been conducted in just over ten years (Lewis & Molyneux 2018, 17), more recent studies have focused on the role of marginalised and opposition groups' anger in collective actions in social movements online (Wahl-Jorgensen 2018). Social media platforms allow virtually anyone to self-publish and to attack journalists online, offering an ideal venue for populist leaders and their networks to attack, threaten, and denounce the 'pro-establishment bias' of traditional news media (Gerbaudo 2018, 746).

This online harassment has been defined as 'the repeated or severe targeting of an individual or group in an online setting through harmful behaviors' (Vilk 2020, 2). Settings for these acts may vary from email to messaging applications (WhatsApp, Facebook Messenger) to comment sections of news sites to YouTube pages, book reviews, social media platforms (such as Twitter, Instagram, Reddit, and Facebook), and blogs (Pen America 2020). Online abuse tactics include hateful speech, threats, 'dogpiling'[2] 'doxing'[3] online impersonation,[4] 'message bombing',[5] 'Zoom bombing' (crashing a virtual meeting with harassing behavior or images), and distributing non-consensual intimate images, private or manufactured without consent (Vilk 2020). Twitter trolls are utilised to distract from legitimate discourse to provoke or deceive; these trolls are able to create topics that trend and influence the national agenda (Bulut & Yörük 2017). Social media's reach makes it difficult to track or monitor deviant activity (Bennett & Livingston 2018). Thus, impunity — exemption from consequences or punishments for these actions — is the norm in cyberspace. In fact, until recently, the online environment enabled abuse (Article 19 2018).

In this environment, online harassment of journalists has manifest in numerous ways, with rape and death threats, cyberbullying, impersonating accounts, obscene video and images, sexist language, disinformation about news reports, and other antisocial behaviours (International Center for Journalists 2018, para. 3). In the Philippines, journalists have become accustomed to death threats (Balod & Hameleers 2019). There, the well-known online Rappler's editor, Maria Ressa, has received an avalanche of online abuse and has been referred to as 'ugly', 'a dog', and 'a snake' and threatened with rape and murder (Reporters without Borders 2018b, 6).

In 2018, Italian journalist Marilù Mastrogiovanni received some 7,000 death threats through her news outlet email after reporting on organised crime (McCully 2019). A Finnish journalist who was investigating a troll factory and patterns of fake profiles on the social network of a propaganda project was harassed online for four years in a campaign that included tagging her in memes and messages on social media sites and blaming her for deaths in the Ukraine (McCully 2019, 7). Research has primarily focused on the intimidation and harassment of journalists in autocratic and authoritarian nations and emerging democracies (Löfgren Nilsson & Örnebring 2016, 880). These studies show that the ways journalists are harassed online can vary and include name-calling, online trolling through constant internet stalking, threats, and shaming (Löfgren Nilsson & Örnebring 2016, 884).

Online harassment of women journalists has been documented more frequently than of male journalists, who often are attacked because of their coverage (McCully 2019). A study of 19 US on-air journalists found that unwanted sexual advances were the most common form of pervasive online harassment, often daily and frequently multiple times a day (Miller & Lewis 2020). Generally, for men, online harassment surfaced in Facebook comments or on Facebook Messenger while some women journalists received emails with 'repeated requests for dates, solicitations for sex, compliments about the journalist's body, and images of male genitalia' (Miller & Lewis 2020, 11). Media advocacy organisations note that 'female journalists carry the double burden of being attacked as journalists and attacked as women' (McCully 2019, 7). In a study of 75 journalists in five countries,[6] in which online harassment was similar despite geographic differences, researchers found that many women reported frequent sexist comments, criticism, marginalisation, stereotyping, and threats based on their gender or sexuality, with critiques of their work framed in misogynistic attacks and, at times, accompanied by suggestions of sexual violence (Chen et al. 2018, 2). Amnesty International (2017) found in a computational analysis of 778 journalists' tweets that female journalists receive hostile, abusive, or hurtful tweets in one out of fourteen tweets received. In Pakistan, according to one report, 68 percent of journalists have been harassed online (Reporters without Borders 2018b). Across Central and Eastern Europe, among 97 independent journalists responding to a survey about online and offline attacks, nearly two-thirds (64.5 percent) indicated they had been harassed or threatened for their journalistic work and over 8 out of 10 experienced it online (83.3 percent), with 16.7 percent indicating they had experienced being doxed related to their personal information (private life or home address), all posted online (Selva 2020, 13). Almost half indicated that the attacks had gotten worse in the last three years (Selva 2020).

Online harassment has risen in recent years via comment sections under online news articles barraging journalists' emails and social media accounts with defamatory, threatening, demeaning, or even pornographic material. The reason comment sections are targeted by the 'dark participation' of trolls is they are a convenient

> object of manipulation and hate because they basically offer an already established, large audience "for free". . . . And due to the closure of the journalistic process to very limited walled gardens of user debate, the comment sections are often the only way in.
>
> (Quandt 2018, 41)

Journalists who have been harassed online face severe consequences both professionally and personally, not to mention the threat to democratic exchange through disrupting the free flow of information (McCully 2019). This online intimidation also has the potential to place a journalist in physical danger and makes journalists more vulnerable to 'mob' action as well as further targeted attacks (UNESCO 2019). Journalists who are attacked or even murdered often were initially targeted by online abuse (UNESCO 2019, 47). The chilling effect of these online attacks of disinformation, threats, and other forms of harassment may impact news reporting and the role of news media in democracies and, in general, create an uncertain and often hostile media ecosystem (Balod & Hameleers 2019). Ultimately, these environments could impact press freedom (McCully 2019) as impunity, which results in enabling abuses and leaves victims without resolution or protection (Article 19 2018), has become a norm. Online anonymity exacerbates the issue, making it difficult to identify online predators and perpetrators of online violence or to redress it, allowing these cyberstalkers to continue trolling with impunity (International Foundation for Electoral Systems 2019). Online harassment is above all psychologically damaging and can affect journalists' ability to concentrate on work as well as to resist pressures for self-censorship (UNESCO 2019). One cross-country study found that online harassment disrupts routine practices and the extent that women journalists can interact with audiences (Chen et al. 2018). Another study of harassment of journalists – online and offline – found that journalists 'occasionally', 'sometimes', or 'often' avoid covering specific issues (26 percent of the time) or groups/people (30 percent of the time) because of the risk or because of being afraid of threats (49 percent of the time) (Löfgren Nilsson & Örnebring 2016, 888).

In the study of online harassment in the case of 19 US on-air journalists, online criticism in the form of harassment appeared aimed at causing emotional damage (Miller & Lewis 2020). Online harassment, including lobbing criticism at journalists' physical appearance and threatening journalists' physical safety, has led researchers to conclude that while online threats don't involve face-to-face contact, the hateful and sadistic level of the rhetoric can be just as harmful as attacks in person (Miller & Lewis 2020, 11). Unfortunately, harassment of journalists in online environments often is minimised as routine, harmless, or even 'part of the job' (UNESCO 2019, 52). In some contexts, journalists somehow do not support one another in this plight. The survey of journalists in Central and Eastern Europe found there was a lack of solidarity among news organisations and within the industry to 'help journalists and news organizations prevail when their freedoms are under threat' to help them improve the environment (Selva 2020, 21).

Addressing disinformation and online harassment: a way forward

The rise of populist movements that batter 'the messenger' through the onslaught of online harassment via disinformation has led to an erosion in public trust in the institution of the press and a crisis of legitimacy in some journalism communities around the world. Harassment of journalists and news organisations online is not radically different from offline harassment over the years; however, the distances that messages can travel and the capacity of the online multiplier effect is different, as is the veil of protection offered to anonymous perpetrators driven by internet disinhibition; such behaviors often are more radical online than for the same person offline (McCully 2019, 2).

Initiatives are surfacing, albeit slowly, to work towards restoring public legitimacy of the profession when needed and to address the issue of disinformation on social media that has put lives at risk. Some have called on global and national institutions to provide guidance or to regulate social media corporations and to require transparency with political advertisements; others suggest changes that include adjusting algorithms to pull back racist, sexist and other extremist content, calling out disinformation and misinformation in an identifiable way (Crilley & Cillespie 2019, 175). Some social media platforms have tightened rules of engagement in their terms of service, and some jurisdictions have amped up their cyberstalking laws with different interpretations and levels public sector training on protections (Vilk 2020).

There have been some studies that indicate that news outlets' and other entities' corrections to disinformation can reduce the impact of it (Chan et al. 2017; Walter & Murphy 2018). However, other research suggests that initial impressions are most enduring (Karlsson et al. 2017). Among the big-picture strategies: when setting the record straight, journalists should always check the claims, avoid the false equivalency of 'de facto' minority views, and make corrections of disinformation 'in a mater-of-fact way, ideally providing substantial explanations, and using sources that are close to populist positions ideologically' (de Vrees et al. 2019, 244).

Combatting false accusations is another line of defence. One study examined the *New York Times* strategies in their editorial work to address US president Donald Trump's onslaught of accusations of 'fake news' against the organisation. To defend its legitimacy, the *Times* used four delegitimising strategies: moral evaluation, 'negative sarcastic narratives' that challenge President Trump's capacity to govern, quoting authorities (such as academics, experts in politics, journalism thought leaders, the public, and autocratic regimes) to show that accusations about 'fake news' are methods employed by authoritarian regimes to suppress criticism and defend legitimacy (Lischka 2019, 299). Less frequently, the *Times* debunked 'fake news' accusations by demonstrating that the allegations were factually incorrect and describing the president's tactic as 'one of inciting the public against the press' (Lischka 2019, 299).

Globally, most of the responses to online assaults and disinformation to date have been defensive. One study showed that the ways that journalists dealt with being harassed included installing home alarms, finding other forms of protection, limiting social media work, reporting the abuse or threats to law enforcement, blocking email accounts, restricting comments on online content, and closing down accounts (Löfgren Nilsson & Örnebring 2016, 887). Chen et al. (2018, 2) have noted that journalists have developed a variety of strategies for dealing with the abuse, including limiting online posts, changing what is reported, and using technological tools to prevent people from posting offensive words on journalists' public social media pages. Other proactive responses focus on prevention of attacks. Others respond directly to online harassment through investigating. In the Philippines, for example, after the online editor at the Rappler was harassed online, an investigative team of journalists tracked and then exposed the intimidation (UNESCO 2019). In response to hate speech, disinformation, and other forms of harassment, some social media platforms are partnering with journalism organisations and journalists to work on addressing these issues and to launch new safety tools (UNESCO 2019, 48). For example, innovative applications have been designed to document online incidents through uploading attackers' email addresses and social media handles; screenshots of dates, messages, and links; and photos, videos, and any other evidence of the threat for authorities (Nelson 2020). Journalism advocacy and support groups also have provided trainings and materials on digital safety.

There also have been calls for media outlets and journalists to reimagine their relationships with the public related to disinformation campaigns. It has been noted that journalists, by training, tend to be hesitant to advocate for themselves yet those days, many suggest, need to be over as the crisis of delegitimisation and online assault have reached critical levels. Selva (2020, 7) recommends that journalists must 'be prepared [to] talk about the value they provide in society, to convince the public not only to pay for good journalism but to support it when it comes under fire'. Research suggests that going forward, journalists should work to publicly distinguish their role from purveyors of disinformation and combat allegations of disseminating disinformation (Balod & Hameleers 2019, 12). Some news organisation initiatives have included what is now called 'legitimacy management', ways for outlets to 'defend themselves from such accusations' (Lischka 2019, 288). Moreover, there are times when correcting the record through reporting on disinformation is not enough. Selva (2020, 25) offers that journalists should 'talk directly to the public, not just about the stories they cover, but about how and why they do the jobs they do'.

A number of initiatives have been moving on national and transnational levels. Survey research with journalists from Central and Eastern Europe also is instructive for considering ways forward. Intervention measures advocated for include changes in laws to ensure that journalists are protected and receive support from transnational press freedom advocacy organisations, that governments from other nations condemn the attacks and urge countries to act on attacks to reduce impunity, and that assistance be provided to defray legal costs for journalists (Selva 2020, 22). Other goals among those in the region include forming peer-to-peer professional networks to take on the online harassers and disinformation abuse campaigns and developing in-house mental health programmes and tools for newsroom staffs, including 'emotional literacy' programming about trauma and how to deal with it.

The Organization for Security and Cooperation in Europe recommends that countries consider prosecuting the online harassment of journalists through existing harassment laws. This could be accomplished through creating measures that penalise sexual harassment and sexist online harassment, examine laws that address online harassment and amend them when possible to 'capture the phenomenon of online harassment campaigns/"pile on" harassment', and adopt tiered approaches to handling online harassment while ensuring that these legal remedies are compatible with freedom of expression guided by international law (McCully 2019, 38). Moreover, law enforcement and prosecutors should investigate online harassment and abuse of journalists when harm is likely and seek other remedies that would not be as costly to journalists as legal procedures may be (McCully 2019). The United Nations has prescribed a number of actions that governments must take to end these online violations, including training law enforcement, judiciaries, journalists, civil society, and other entities on safety standards for freedom of expression (Article 19 2018). Other recommendations include early-warning programmes and rapid interventions for online harassment cases and developing best-practice approaches to address online harassment coupled with reportage on this major public policy issue of abuse (Reporters without Borders 2018b, 25–27). International organisations as well have been encouraged to urge governments to uphold the same protections of rights online as offline and to monitor, investigate, prosecute, and research abuses against journalists online (Article 19 2018).

In conclusion, rising populism, the growth of mis/disinformation on social media, and impunity around online abuse are growing issues for journalists and the legitimacy of the institution of the press. Journalists, advocacy institutions, civil society organisations, governments, and other entities must take an active role in addressing the issue as it evolves over time. Defensive approaches have their place. However, proactive measures such as developing strategies to directly communicate the value of journalism to the public, as well as ways to filter out the rising and competing white noise of disinformation, are critical to the future of democracies.

Notes

1 The chapter defines *misinformation* as information that is not supported by evidence yet is not necessarily intentionally incorrect (Balod & Hameleers 2019). *Disinformation* in this chapter is strategically disseminated false information that aims to cause harm or has a malicious intent (Humprecht et al. 2020).
2 This is an attack that is coordinated to overwhelm journalists or other victims of abuse with insults, slurs, threats, and numerous other tactics (Vilk 2020, 3).
3 Doxing is when sensitive personal information is published to extort, intimidate, steal an identity, rally, abuse, or other tactics (Vilk 2020, 3).
4 This is a hoax account that has been created to post offensive material or discredit or defame a name (Vilk 2020, 4).
5 This tactic is designed to flood journalists' or other victims' email or phone accounts to block access by others (Vilk 2020, 4).
6 Countries in the study were Germany, India, Taiwan, the United Kingdom, and the United States.

References

Amnesty International (2017) *Troll Patrol Findings: Using Crowdsourcing, Data Science and Machine Learning to Measure Violence and Abuse Against Women on Twitter.* https://decoders.amnesty.org/projects/troll-patrol/findings.

Article 19 (2018, November 2) *Ending impunity for crimes against journalists.* London: Article 19. www.article19.org/resources/ending-impunity-for-crimes-against-journalists/.

Balod HSS and Hameleers M (2019) Fighting for truth? The role perceptions of Filipino journalists in an era of mis-and disinformation. *Journalism,* https://doi.org/10.1177/1464884919865109.

Bennett WL and Livingston S (2018) The disinformation order: Disruptive communication and the decline of democratic institutions. *European Journal of Communication* 33(2): 122–139.

Bimber B (1998) The Internet and political transformation: Populism, community, and accelerated pluralism. *Polity* 31(1): 133–160.

Blassnig S, Ernst N, Büchel F, Engesser S and Esser F (2019) Populism in online election coverage: Analyzing populist statements by politicians, journalists, and readers in three countries. *Journalism Studies* 20(8): 1110–1129.

Bulut E and Yörük E (2017) Digital populism: Trolls and political polarization of Twitter in Turkey. *International Journal of Communication* 11: 4093–4117.

Chan MPS, Jones CR, Hall Jamieson, K and Albarracín D (2017) Debunking: A meta-analysis of the psychological efficacy of messages countering misinformation. *Psychological Science* 28(11): 1531–1546.

Chen GM, Pain P, Chen VY, Mekelburg M, Springer N and Troger F (2018) 'You really have to have a thick skin': A cross-cultural perspective on how online harassment influences female journalists. *Journalism.* https://doi.org/10.1177/1464884918768500.

Crilley R and Gillespie M (2019) What to do about social media? Politics, populism and journalism. *Journalism* 20(1): 173–176.

De Vreese CH, Esser F, Aalberg T, Reinemann C and Stanyer J (2018) Populism as an expression of political communication content and style: A new perspective. *The International Journal of Press/Politics* 23(4): 423–438.

De Vreese CH, Reinemann JS, Esser F and Aalberg T (2019) Adapting to the different shades of populism: Key findings and implications for media, citizens, and politics. In Reinemann C, Stanyer J, Aalberg T, Esser F and de Vreese CH (eds) *Communicating Populism: Comparing Actor Perceptions, Media Coverage, and Effects on Citizens in Europe*. London: Routledge.

Gerbaudo P (2018) Social media and populism: an elective affinity? *Media, Culture & Society* 40(5): 745–753.

Hameleers M, Bos L and de Vreese CH (2018) Selective exposure to populist communication: How attitudinal congruence drives the effects of populist attributions of blame. *Journal of Communication* 68(1): 51–74.

Humprecht E, Esser F and Van Aelst P (2020) Resilience to online disinformation: A framework for cross-national comparative research. *The International Journal of Press/Politics.* https://doi.org/10.1177/1940161219900126.

International Center for Journalists (2018, November 23) *IFJ Global Survey Shows Massive Impact of Online Abuse on Women Journalists.* www.ifj.org/media-centre/news/detail/article/ifj-global-survey-shows-massive-impact-of-online-abuse-on-women-journalists.html.

International Foundation for Electoral Systems (2019, September) *Violence Against Women in Elections Online: A Social Media Analysis Tool.* https://www.ifes.org/sites/default/files/violence_against_women_in_elections_online_a_social_media_analysis_tool.pdf.

Karlsson M, Clerwall C and Nord L (2017) Do not stand corrected: Transparency and users' attitudes to inaccurate news and corrections in online journalism. *Journalism & Mass Communication Quarterly* 94(1): 148–167.

Kavada, A. (2018). Media and the 'populist moment'. *Media, Culture & Society* 40(5): 742–744.

Krämer B (2014) Media populism: A conceptual clarification and some theses on its effects. *Communication Theory* 24(1): 42–60.

Krämer B (2018) Populism, media, and the form of society. *Communication Theory* 28(4): 444–465.

Lewis SC and Molyneux L (2018) A decade of research on social media and journalism: Assumptions, blind spots, and a way forward. *Media and Communication* 6(4): 11–23.

Lischka, JA (2019) A badge of honor? How The New York Times discredits President Trump's fake news accusations. *Journalism Studies* 20(2): 287–304.

Löfgren Nilsson, M and Örnebring H (2016) Journalism under threat: Intimidation and harassment of Swedish journalists. *Journalism Practice* 10(7): 880–890.

McCully J (2019) *Legal Responses to Online Harassment and Abuse of Journalists: Perspectives from Finland, France and Ireland.* Organization for Security & Cooperation in Europe and the International Press Institute. https://www.osce.org/representative-on-freedom-of-media/413552.

Miller KC and Lewis SC (2020) Journalists, harassment, and emotional labor: The case of women in on-air roles at US local television stations. *Journalism.* https://doi.org/10.1177/1464884919899016.

Nelson J (2020, January 28) *JSafe App Empowers Female Journalists to Take Action in Threatening Situations.* Columbia, MO: Donald W. Reynolds Journalism Institute.

Pen America (2020) *Online Harassment Field Guide.* New York: The City University of New York Craig Newmark Graduate School of Journalism. https://onlineharassmentfieldmanual.pen.org/defining-online-harassment-a-glossary-of-terms/.

Quandt T (2018) Dark participation. *Media and Communication* 6(4): 36–48.

Reporters without Borders (2018a, February 21) *Philippine President Duterte Bars Rappler Reporter from Palace.* https://rsf.org/en/news/philippine-president-duterte-bars-rappler-reporter-palace.

Reporters without Borders (2018b) *Online Harassment of Journalists: Attack of the Trolls.* https://rsf.org/sites/default/files/rsf_report_on_online_harassment.pdf.

Selva M (2020) *Fighting Words: Journalism Under Assault in Central and Eastern Europe.* Reuters Institute for the Study of Journalism. https://reutersinstitute.politics.ox.ac.uk/fighting-words-journalism-under-assault-central-and-eastern-europe.

UNESCO (2019) *Intensified Attacks, New Defenses: Developments in the Fight to Protect Journalists and End Impunity.* Paris: UNESCO. https://unesdoc.unesco.org/ark:/48223/pf0000371487.

Vilk V (2020) *Online Abuse Self-Defense Presentation.* New York: Pen America and The City of New York Craig Newmark Graduate School of Journalism.

Wahl-Jorgensen K (2018) Media coverage of shifting emotional regimes: Donald Trump's angry populism. *Media, Culture & Society* 40(5): 766–778.

Waisbord S (2013) Democracy, journalism, and Latin American populism. *Journalism* 14(4): 504–521.

Waisbord S (2018) Why populism is troubling for democratic communication. *Communication Culture & Critique* 11(1): 21–34.

Waisbord S and Amado A (2017) Populist communication by digital means: Presidential Twitter in Latin America. *Information, Communication & Society* 20(9): 1330–1346.

Walter N and Murphy ST (2018) How to unring the bell: A meta-analytic approach to correction of misinformation. *Communication Monographs* 85(3): 423–441.

18

LESSONS FROM AN EXTRAORDINARY YEAR

Four heuristics for studying mediated misinformation in 2020 and beyond

Lucas Graves

In hindsight, 2020 will have been a momentous year to study politics, misinformation, and the media. It may also seem a very disorienting one.

As the year began, a much-needed scholarly course correction was well underway. A raft of studies carried out since 2016 has cast doubt on common assumptions about the influence of echo chambers and so-called 'fake news' on the internet. Growing numbers of scholars recognise that a kind of moral panic around online misinformation – not least among academics – was set off by events like Donald Trump's election and the UK's Brexit vote (Marwick 2018; Carlson 2020), in which alarming statistics about viral Facebook rumours supplied 'a tidy narrative that resonated with concerns about potential online echo chambers' (Nyhan 2019). Repressive new laws from Kenya to Singapore further underscored the risk of 'knee-jerk policy responses' to misinformation (Jiménez Cruz et al. 2018).

At the same time, 2020 has produced extraordinary, unrelenting reminders of the profound and even deadly consequences of misalignment between what Walter Lippmann (1922) called 'the world outside and the pictures in our heads'. In the United States, the year began with the president's acquittal after impeachment hearings that featured top lawmakers citing widely debunked conspiracy theories to defend him. The impeachment had barely faded from headlines when the global COVID-19 pandemic struck, accompanied by what the head of the World Health Organization called an 'infodemic' of 'fake news [that] spreads faster and more easily than this virus, and is just as dangerous' (Ghebreyesus 2020). A tide of misinformation, from bogus cures to conspiracy theories, overwhelmed fact-checkers and alarmed public officials around the world (Brennen et al. 2020). Sensational reports of people killed by consuming dangerous chemicals to fight the disease only hint at much graver questions: how can we measure the human costs of rumours and rhetoric that undermine public health recommendations? What role do the features of different media systems, with varying levels of 'resilience' to misinformation (Humprecht et al. 2020), have in explaining the sharply diverging policy responses and health outcomes seen in different countries?

Events like these offer a reminder that debunking crude assumptions about the effects of false messages is only the first step in understanding how our media shape public discourse in a moment of high polarisation and resurgent populism. This chapter uses the questions raised by the 'infodemic' as a platform to articulate several heuristics for thinking about how mediated misinformation matters in public life today. Each of these reminders is based on gaps or caveats that are often acknowledged, though only rarely addressed, in the growing literature on effects of misinformation, reviewed below. Taken together, they may help illuminate new priorities for scholars working in this area.

The minimal effects of misinformation

Compared to the burgeoning literature on the effectiveness of fact-checking, few studies have systematically explored how misinformation influences political beliefs or behaviour (Li 2020). However, current evidence points to fairly limited direct effects. For example, Guess et al. (2020) find small increases in misperception with exposure to dubious content under experimental conditions as well as in tracking data. Studies around the 2016 US election suggest 'fake news' played a negligible role (but see Gunther et al. 2018): false stories were shared widely but made up a tiny part of most news diets, with heavy use concentrated among extreme partisans who are least persuadable (Allcott and Gentzkow 2017; Guess, Nyhan, et al. 2018; Nelson and Taneja 2018). Interacting with Twitter accounts associated with Russia's Internet Research Agency – which operated massive online disinformation campaigns in 2016 – appears to have had no significant impact on political attitudes or behaviour (Bail et al. 2020). Similarly, Garrett (2019, 3) finds social media use associated with only small increases in partisan misperceptions, suggesting that 'the limited media effects paradigm persists in the face of these new technologies'.

Nothing about the COVID-19 'infodemic' directly refutes this 'limited effects' consensus. Together with evidence that informational 'echo chambers' are less prevalent than has been widely assumed (e.g. Eady et al. 2019), misinformation research shows, yet again, how reluctant we should be to attribute complex social or political phenomena to new media technologies. In hindsight, the current panic about virus-related rumours (though not about the virus itself) may seem excessive. And health-related misinformation can be seen as a special case, both easier to identify and more obviously harmful than 'fake news' about politics. 'False information about COVID-19 can be deadly', Kreps and Nyhan (2020) stress in arguing that social media platforms like Twitter and Facebook should not extend aggressive content moderation rules devised for the pandemic to misleading political speech in general.

However, the line between medical and political misinformation can be difficult to draw in a deeply polarised moment, when the choice to observe or ignore health guidelines itself has become a badge of partisan identity (Clinton et al. 2020). It is one thing to measure the potential influence of an item of 'fake news' as it affects individual health behaviours. But it's something else entirely to ask how patterns of misinformation, as a feature of contemporary landscapes of political communication, are implicated in the divisive politics or incoherent policies around the virus seen in many countries – most notably, in highly populist and partisan environments like Brazil and the United States.

What the pandemic underscores is the narrowness of the paradigmatic approach to misinformation in political communications research, centred on the individual effects of accurate or inaccurate information. The notion of an 'infodemic' itself reflects a model of informed political reasoning that treats bad information as a kind of virus whose effects are false beliefs and poor decisions (Graves and Wells 2019). This continues to be a tremendously productive paradigm; its narrowness and internal rigour are what have allowed easy assumptions about rumour-filled, belief-distorting echo chambers to be tested. But it also sharply limits the ways we think about the relationship between changing media and political systems and the role of misinformation in those shifts – limits that have become more apparent as populist attitudes and leaders come to the fore.

The pandemic raises questions communications scholars too rarely consider in a comprehensive way about the mutually structuring relationship between political culture – especially the shifting norms and practices of elite political actors – and the media environment. These are vital questions at a moment marked by profound political changes, most notably the populist turn, which, while not caused by the media in any simple sense, is profoundly tied to it. The following four heuristics use examples drawn from the pandemic and other events of 2020 to highlight what the 'limited effects' paradigm misses in thinking about how misinformation matters as political discourse.

1 *There's no such thing as 'online misinformation'*

One outcome of rising concern with internet-borne rumours, conspiracy theories, and 'fake news' has been to establish online misinformation as a distinct phenomenon, addressed by a growing research literature of its own. There are some good reasons for this; misleading information spreads in distinctive ways on social networks, and deceptive memes often originate in online subcultures. However, this reification of online misinformation as an object of analysis tends to obscure its active links to elite political rhetoric in general and populist rhetoric in particular. Just as 'fake news' is often crafted to exploit real political divisions, political actors and partisan media outlets continually draw on, amplify, and recontextualise online discourses.

The 'infodemic' around COVID-19 makes these links unusually clear. During the spring of 2020, President Trump promoted numerous coronavirus-related conspiracy theories circulating online and in right-wing media. Often these messages seemed designed to distract from the US response to the pandemic or cast it in a better light – for instance, the claim that officials suppressed the virus's infection rate in order to inflate the mortality rate and 'steal the election' for Democrats, or that China nefariously allowed flights from Wuhan to other countries after restricting internal travel. The US president has also repeatedly endorsed miracle cures trafficked online. Even his shocking, televised musings about the possibility of using disinfectant to treat COVID-19 echoed a long-standing internet discourse promoting dangerous 'bleach cures' for autism and other ailments (Jacobs 2020). There is no way to know whether Trump was directly influenced by such medical hoaxes (conservative promoters of bleach-based Miracle Mineral Solution sought his endorsement). But the effects of the president's suggestion – where it was taken up and what influence it had – can only be understood in the context of those discourses.

The growing research literature on 'fake news' notes its relationship to elite political actors and rhetoric. Marwick and Lewis (2017, 21) stress that politicians and celebrities serve as 'amplification nodes' for online rumours and conspiracy theories by drawing media coverage to outlandish claims which otherwise would receive little attention. Similarly, computational studies suggest 'going viral' is actually a poor metaphor for how information – true or false – spreads on social media, given the crucial role of media and celebrity accounts with many followers (Goel *et al.* 2015). However, these links have been easier to acknowledge than to address in a systematic way, at scale, in studying the influence of online misinformation. One overview identifies this as a key gap in the literature, observing that 'relatively little is known about how politicians and the media help disseminate myths or the process by which they become entrenched in partisan belief systems' (Tucker et al. 2018, 63).

Crucially, understanding how myths become 'entrenched' means seeing politicians and political elites not only as amplifiers, but as contextualisers and meaning-makers, who forge connections between discourses in the crucible of political campaigns and controversies. This gap is especially urgent in the context of populist political actors and rhetoric, whose animating critique of illegitimate elites depends on a notion of hidden facts and agendas ignored by establishment media (Mudde and Kaltwasser 2017; Waisbord 2018). As Müller (2016, 32) writes, 'Conspiracy theories are thus not a curious addition to populist rhetoric; they are rooted in and emerge from the very logic of populism itself'.

2 Misinformation works by allusion, not reason

To understand misinformation as a meaning-making resource requires attention to the role of allusive references in political discourse and identity-building. The question is never just whether a particular unit of misinformation changes belief states or political preferences; true or false, individual political messages generally have small direct effects, particularly in a polarised electorate (e.g. Kalla and Broockman 2017). Rather, the vital question is how characteristic patterns of messages reinforce discourses or narratives that shape identity; affirm affiliations; and, in that way, influence individual or collective behaviour at the margin.

Thinking about the mediated influences that shape our responses to the COVID-19 pandemic brings this difference into sharp relief. Alarm about the 'infodemic' has centred on false medical advice, which can have grave consequences. Cases like that of the Arizona couple who poisoned themselves by drinking fish-tank cleaner containing chloroquine, a drug promoted by President Trump to ward off COVID-19, lend themselves to analysis under a straightforward message-effects model. In such an instance, a specific action can be attributed directly to new information from a specific source or sources on a question about which the recipient likely had no well-formed views. (Of course, political attitudes and personal experiences, perhaps with the medical industry, certainly played a role.) That straight line from bad data to dangerous behaviour helps account for the aggressive responses by social media companies to pandemic-related misinformation (Barrett et al. 2020).

Such instances are relatively rare, however. Vastly more significant patterns of health behaviour cannot be traced to specific messages as cleanly. In the US, for instance, party affiliation has been identified as the primary predictor of both individual attitudes and state-level policies with regard to mask-wearing and social distancing (Clinton et al. 2020; Makridis and Rothwell 2020). That does not mean that party ties predetermine behaviour; rather, an active process of politicisation, informed by elite cues, played out in the news cycle as anti-lockdown demonstrations gave way to a backlash against mask requirements. Rhetoric from media and political figures helped turn public-health choices into ideological ones. One anti-lockdown organiser told a reporter that his pre-existing condition prevented mask-wearing: 'It's called freedom' (Burling 2020). That stance might have been informed by any number of narratives circulating online and promoted by conservative media figures like Sean Hannity and Rush Limbaugh, centring on the view that the virus threat was been exaggerated by Democrats and/or the 'deep state' in order to weaken the economy and hurt Donald Trump's re-election chances.

Understanding how mediated messages inform the decision to wear or not wear a mask means being sensitive to the social and discursive contexts in which people form what social scientists recognise as opinions (Eliasoph 1998; Cramer 2016). It draws attention to 'conventional discourses' (Strauss 2012): patterns of language tied to the shared schemas – what Lippmann called 'stereotypes' – we use to make sense of the world. And it means recognising what Polletta and Callahan (2017) identify as the allusive quality of narrative – the way the moral force of a story about, for instance, 'welfare queens' or 'climate-change deniers' operates by suggestion rather than rational argumentation. As they suggest,

> people's political common sense is shaped by their experience but it is also shaped by stories they read and hear on TV, stories told by friends and acquaintances, stories that

substitute memory for history, stories that make the experience of others seem as if it is their own, and stories whose truth is relatively unimportant to their value.

Scholarly critics have noted that the current moral panic over online misinformation evokes the so-called 'hypodermic' model of early mass communication research that putatively attributed powerful effects to mediated propaganda (Kreiss 2018; Marwick 2018). But as Marwick (2018, 485) observes, studies demonstrating the limited effects of 'fake news' usually share the underlying model of the claims they refute – one that 'prioritizes causal effects on user activity while disregarding the structural influence of problematic patterns in media messaging and representation'. Resisting crude causal assumptions about either media messages or media technologies should not mean being blind to the role that patterns of media use play, especially for political elites and politically active citizens, in sustaining the 'deep stories' (Hochschild 2018) and ideological frameworks that anchor political identity (Kreiss 2018; Peck 2019).

3 Misinformation is an index of political incentive structures

The point that politics is as much about telling allusive stories as making reasoned arguments is hardly new to campaigners, journalists, or scholars. But the kinds of stories told vary depending on the audience and the medium; they also vary in different eras depending on how mediated publics can be assembled and how that alters the calculus of perceived risk and reward in addressing particular audiences in specific ways. The apparent ease with which some politicians traffic in overt falsehood and conspiracy in today's media environment lays bare what Karp (2019) neatly calls the 'load-bearing' myths that have worked to constrain elite behaviour and sustain democratic norms.

The pandemic offers many examples. For instance, President Trump's dismissive, even mocking rhetoric about mask-wearing through the first half of 2020 almost certainly reflected a calculation about how that stance would be presented in conservative outlets; as caseloads surged in mid-summer and Fox News changed the tone of its coverage, the president was forced to follow suit. But a better illustration, because it highlights institutional norms beyond the White House, is the conspiratorial rhetoric that featured in the impeachment proceedings six months earlier. The crudeness of the falsehoods being peddled by Republican lawmakers in such a solemn setting (such as baseless insinuations about Ukrainian interference in the 2016 elections) drew widespread condemnation. One analysis argued, 'Each round of GOP questioning is not meant to interrogate the witnesses . . . but instead to create moments that can be flipped into Fox News segments, shared as bite-size Facebook posts, or dropped into 4chan threads' (Broderick 2019).

A tradition of media scholarship has explored how events like congressional hearings are staged for mediated audiences (Page 1996; Carey 1998). Politicians, like all of us, say things not only for particular audiences but also in specific discursive contexts – a campaign ad, a press conference, a meeting with donors – governed by varying standards of truth. For public figures, the logic of these encounters is sometimes just 'cover': having something to say, an allusion or argument that navigates the moment while advancing, or at least not damaging, strategic aims.

Arguably, then, the conspiracy-laden performance was unusual only in degree.[1] Still, it highlights the fragility of institutional norms such as the expectation that members of Congress observe basic standards of evidence, engage with reasonable arguments, and make a show of appealing broadly to the American public. Norms governing the behaviour of political elites in a democracy depend on the 'democratic myth' (Karpf 2019) or 'regulative fiction' (Nerone 2013) of an attentive, reasoning, and unitary public: what matters is that elites generally *act as if* an abstract public is paying attention and will hold them accountable when lies or abuses are exposed. The power of the press as a democratic watchdog depends on the same reflexive assumption embedded in political culture; it 'resides in the perception of experts and decision makers that the general public is influenced by the mass media' rather than in the media's influence itself (Schudson 1995, 121). That faith in the link from publicity to accountability, in turn, supports the ability of monitory institutions, civil society actors, and political elites to enforce democratic norms on behalf of a wider public (e.g. Page 1996; Schudson 2015).

These useful fictions are harder to sustain in a post-broadcast media environment where even the notion of a broad public tuned in to more or less the same things – never the whole picture – has become not just less accurate, but less natural. Both the moral panic around misinformation and the research refuting it draw attention to underlying realities of electoral politics that, while long understood, may increasingly be common sense. As Karpf (2019) writes, 'Disinformation and propaganda are not dangerous because they effectively trick or misinform otherwise-attentive voters; they are dangerous because they disabuse political elites of some crucial assumptions about the consequences of violating the public trust'.

Related myth-eroding pressures exist within journalism. The self-serving 'audience-image' (Gans 2004) constructed by twentieth-century journalists, with neither means nor motive to know much about their actual readers and viewers, was a mechanism of ideological uniformity, social exclusion, and professional self-justification. But it also helped preserve a space for professional news values to cohere, making it easier to write for an idealised, information-seeking democratic public (Ananny 2018). Conversely, while every news organisation strives to build ties of emotion and identity with its audience, scholars of partisan and populist media emphasise the deeply affective editorial logic that governs their news production (Mazzoleni 2008). Explaining the 'emotional pull' of Fox News's appeal to working-class values, for instance, Peck (2019, 92) points to the 'historical rootedness of the enduring political themes and narratives' that its on-air personalities return to again and again.

4 Just don't call it an echo chamber

The main thrust of the course correction in studying online information and misinformation has been to challenge the received wisdom that the internet traps us in ideological bubbles of news and opinion we agree with. This pervasive notion among academics, policymakers, and journalists – one overview calls it the 'echo chambers about echo chambers' (Guess et al. 2018) – finds little empirical support in large-scale studies of online media habits. Still, the refutation only highlights the need for a better vocabulary to describe the deeply partisan dynamics of the media ecosystem in many countries. As the preceding discussion suggests, a structural view is essential to studying misinformation: where and how it circulates, how it reflects shifting incentives for political elites, and how it becomes a resource for political identity and influences behaviour as a result.

Research on echo chambers and filter bubbles has focused on what might be called the strong version of the hypothesis: that in a high-choice media environment, the preference for congenial information from like-minded sources leads citizens broadly to 'sort themselves into echo chambers of their own design', in Sunstein's (2009, 6) phrase, through selective exposure and/or algorithmic selection. Studies suggest only a small minority of partisans inhabit such bubbles; while evidence is mixed, for most users who do engage with political news online, search engines and social media appear to be a source of diversity (Flaxman et al. 2016; e.g. Dubois and Blank 2018; Fletcher and Nielsen 2018a, 2018b; Eady et al. 2019). An important caveat, though, is that the minority with narrower, ideological news diets also tend to be the most politically engaged (Guess, Lyons, et al. 2018; Tucker et al. 2018). Nyhan (2016) calls this the 'paradox' of echo chambers: 'Few of us live in them, but those who do exercise disproportionate influence over our political system'.

That caveat becomes very important when we consider how misinformation spreads and takes on political valence across discursive networks of media and political actors. For instance, the pandemic offers several cases of flawed research being rapidly 'weaponised' to downplay virus risks in a cascading dynamic across right-wing news outlets, conservative voices on social media, and Republican politicians (Bajak and Howe 2020; Starbird *et al.* 2020). A starker illustration is the perplexing political influence of QAnon, the far-right online subculture and 'conspiracy movement' born in the wake of the 2016 US election. QAnon metastasised during the pandemic, gaining adherents and absorbing COVID-19 conspiracies into its core narrative of a 'deep state' scheming against President Trump (LaFrance 2020). Remarkably, dozens of candidates in 2020 US congressional races endorsed QAnon – some obliquely, others quite openly – in a bid to court Republican primary voters (Rosenberg and Steinhauer 2020). Beliefs cultivated in something like an echo chamber can resonate far beyond it.

Some scholars approach echo chambers in this wider sense: as coordinated, mutually reinforcing patterns of messaging among politicians, partisan media outlets, and outside issue or interest groups (Jamieson and Cappella 2010; Benkler et al. 2018). This is broadly in line with how scholars understand the potential structuring influence of populist or tabloid media, which offer a ready outlet for populist messages, help define an audience for populist politics, and also 'serve as vehicles reflecting people's sentiments back' to populist leaders (Mazzoleni 2008, 54). The question becomes not whether the typical media user is in an ideological bubble that promotes specific attitudes, but how the bubbles that do exist affect political discourse and behaviour more broadly.

Finally, this looser definition of echo chambers raises a thorny question, one that provides a useful cautionary note to conclude this argument for scholarship that looks past individual effects to take a more structural view of mediated misinformation. The question is, what separates harmful echo chambers from the cause- or party-oriented press that forms part of a healthy, pluralistic society? As Nielsen (2020) has observed, 'the women's movement, the labor movement, and the civil rights movement were arguably echo chambers in many ways'. Likewise, contemporary movements like #MeToo and Black Lives Matter take shape across ideological media networks used to share information, develop arguments, and build social ties.

What distinguishes harmful echo chambers from healthy digital activism is, precisely, the extent to which they promote dangerous misinformation like QAnon conspiracy theories. Making this distinction requires judgment and may invite disagreement – but no more so than other normatively freighted categories, such as 'misinformation' and 'populism', which communications scholars employ widely. More important, though, this offers a reminder that the same structural arrangements can and do produce very different outcomes in democratic terms. The challenge is to take seriously how media structures and mediated discourses matter in public life while avoiding the pull of determinism that too often accompanies such perspectives.

Note

1 It certainly fell short of McCarthyite demagoguery during the second red scare – a powerful counter-example to arguments that see only decline from an idealized broadcast era.

Bibliography

Allcott, H. and Gentzkow, M., 2017. Social Media and Fake News in the 2016 Election. *Journal of Economic Perspectives*, 31 (2), 211–236.

Ananny, M., 2018. *Networked Press Freedom: Creating Infrastructures for a Public Right to Hear*. Cambridge, MA: The MIT Press.

Bail, C.A., Guay, B., Maloney, E., Combs, A., Hillygus, D.S., Merhout, F., Freelon, D., and Volfovsky, A., 2020. Assessing the Russian Internet Research Agency's Impact on the Political Attitudes and Behaviors of American Twitter Users in late 2017. *Proceedings of the National Academy of Sciences*, 117 (1), 243–250.

Bajak, A., and Howe, J., 2020. A Study Said Covid Wasn't That Deadly: The Right Seized It. *The New York Times*, 14 May.

Barrett, B., Kreiss, D., and Reddi, M., 2020. *Enforcers of Truth: Social Media Platforms and Misinformation*. Chapel Hill, NC: Center for Information, Technology, and Public Life.

Benkler, Y., Faris, R., and Roberts, H., 2018. *Network Propaganda: Manipulation, Disinformation, and Radicalization in American Politics*. Oxford: Oxford University Press.

Brennen, J.S., Simon, F.M., Howard, P.N., and Nielsen, R.-K., 2020. *Types, sources, and claims of Covid-19 misinformation*. Oxford: Reuters Institute for the Study of Journalism.

Broderick, R., 2019. Republicans' Conspiracy Theory – Ridden Counterprogramming to Impeachment Is Working. *BuzzFeed News*, 20 November.

Burling, S., 2020. Should Coronavirus Lock Down Protesters Waive Their Medical Care? Some Medical Ethicists Think so. *Philadelphia Inquirer*, 22 May.

Carey, J.W., 1998. Political Ritual on Television: Episodes in the History of Shame, Degradation and Excommunication. *In*: T. Liebes and J. Curran, eds. *Media, Ritual, and Identity*. London and New York: Routledge, 42–70.

Carlson, M., 2020. Fake News as an Informational Moral Panic: The Symbolic Deviancy of Social Media During the 2016 US Presidential Election. *Information, Communication & Society*, 23 (3), 374–388.

Clinton, J., Cohen, J., Lapinski, J.S., and Trussler, M., 2020. *Partisan Pandemic: How Partisanship and Public Health Concerns Affect Individuals' Social Distancing During COVID-19*. Rochester, NY: Social Science Research Network, SSRN Scholarly Paper No. ID 3633934.

Cramer, K.J., 2016. *The Politics of Resentment: Rural Consciousness in Wisconsin and the Rise of Scott Walker*. 1 edition. Chicago and London: University of Chicago Press.

Dubois, E., and Blank, G., 2018. The Echo Chamber Is Overstated: The Moderating Effect of Political Interest and Diverse Media. *Information, Communication & Society*, 21 (5), 729–745.

Eady, G., Nagler, J., Guess, A., Zilinsky, J., and Tucker, J.A., 2019. How Many People Live in Political Bubbles on Social Media? Evidence from Linked Survey and Twitter Data. *Sage Open*, 9 (1).

Eliasoph, N., 1998. *Avoiding Politics: How Americans Produce Apathy in Everyday Life*. Cambridge: Cambridge University Press.

Flaxman, S., Goel, S., and Rao, J.M., 2016. Filter Bubbles, Echo Chambers, and Online News Consumption. *Public Opinion Quarterly*, 80 (S1), 298–320.

Fletcher, R., and Nielsen, R.K., 2018a. Automated Serendipity. *Digital Journalism*, 6 (8), 976–989.

Fletcher, R., and Nielsen, R.K., 2018b. Are People Incidentally Exposed to News on Social Media? A Comparative Analysis. *New Media & Society*, 20 (7), 2450–2468.

Gans, H.J., 2004. *Deciding What's News: A Study of CBS Evening News, NBC Nightly News, Newsweek, and Time*. Evanston, IL: Northwestern University Press.

Garrett, R.K., 2019. Social Media's Contribution to Political Misperceptions in U.S. Presidential Elections. *PLoS One*, 14 (3).

Ghebreyesus, T.A., 2020. Speech at Munich Security Conference.

Goel, S., Anderson, A., Hofman, J., and Watts, D.J., 2015. The Structural Virality of Online Diffusion. *Management Science*. Doi:10.1287/mnsc.2015.2158(150722112809007).

Graves, L., and Wells, C., 2019. From Information Availability to Factual Accountability: Reconsidering How Truth Matters for Politicians, Publics, and the News Media. *In*: J.E. Katz and K.K. Mays, eds. *Journalism and Truth in an Age of Social Media*. Oxford: Oxford University Press, 39–57.

Guess, A., Lyons, B., Nyhan, B., and Reifler, J., 2018. *Avoiding the Echo Chamber About Echo Chambers: Why Selective Exposure to Like-Minded Political News Is Less Prevalent Than You Think*. Miami, FL: Knight Foundation.

Guess, A., Nyhan, B., and Reifler, J., 2018. *Selective Exposure to Misinformation: Evidence from the Consumption of Fake News During the 2016 US Presidential Campaign*. Unpublished.

Guess, A.M., Lockett, D., Lyons, B., Montgomery, J.M., Nyhan, B., and Reifler, J., 2020. 'Fake News' May Have Limited Effects Beyond Increasing Beliefs in False Claims. *The Harvard Kennedy School (HKS) Misinformation Review*. https://misinforeview.hks.harvard.edu/article/fake-news-limited-effects-on-political-participation/.

Gunther, R., Nisbet, E.C., and Beck, P., 2018. Trump may owe his 2016 victory to 'fake news,' new study suggests. *The Conversation*.

Hochschild, A.R., 2018. *Strangers in Their Own Land: Anger and Mourning on the American Right*. New York and London: The New Press.

Humprecht, E., Esser, F., and Van Aelst, P., 2020. Resilience to Online Disinformation: A Framework for Cross-National Comparative Research. *The International Journal of Press/Politics*, 25 (3), 493–516.

Jacobs, A., 2020. Trump Disinfectant Remarks Echo Claims by Miracle-Cure Quacks. *The New York Times*, 27 April.

Jamieson, K.H., and Cappella, J.N., 2010. *Echo Chamber: Rush Limbaugh and the Conservative Media Establishment*. New York and Oxford: Oxford University Press.

Jiménez Cruz, C., Mantzarlis, A., Nielsen, R.K., and Wardle, C., 2018. Six Key Points from the EU Commission's New Report on Disinformation. *Medium*.

Kalla, J., and Broockman, D.E., 2017. *The Minimal Persuasive Effects of Campaign Contact in General Elections: Evidence from 49 Field Experiments*. Rochester, NY: Social Science Research Network, SSRN Scholarly Paper No. ID 3042867.

Karpf, D., 2019. On Digital Disinformation and Democratic Myths. *MediaWell, Social Science Research Council*. https://mediawell.ssrc.org/expert-reflections/on-digital-disinformation-and-democratic-myths/.

Kreiss, D., 2018. The Media Are About Identity, not Information. *In*: P.J. Boczkowski and Z. Papacharissi, eds. *Trump and the Media*. Cambridge, MA; London: The MIT Press, 93–101.

Kreps, S., and Nyhan, B., 2020. Coronavirus Fake News Isn't Like Other Fake News. *Foreign Affairs*. https://www.foreignaffairs.com/articles/2020-03-30/coronavirus-fake-news-isnt-other-fake-news.

LaFrance, S.A., 2020. The Prophecies of Q. *The Atlantic*.

Li, J., 2020. Toward a Research Agenda on Political Misinformation and Corrective Information. *Political Communication*, 37 (1), 125–135.

Lippmann, W., 1922. *Public Opinion*. New York: Macmillan.

Makridis, C., and Rothwell, J.T., 2020. *The Real Cost of Political Polarization: Evidence from the COVID-19 Pandemic*. Rochester, NY: Social Science Research Network, SSRN Scholarly Paper No. ID 3638373.

Marwick, A.E., 2018. Why Do People Share Fake News? A Sociotechnical Model of Media Effects. *Georgetown Law Technology Review*, 2 (2), 474–512.

Marwick, A.E., and Lewis, R., 2017. *Media Manipulation and Disinformation Online*. New York: Data & Society Research Institute.

Mazzoleni, G., 2008. Populism and the Media. *In*: D. Albertazzi and D. McDonnell, eds. *Twenty-First Century Populism: The Spectre of Western European Democracy*. Cham: Springer, 49–64.

Mudde, C., and Kaltwasser, C.R., 2017. *Populism: A Very Short Introduction*. 2nd edition. New York: Oxford University Press.

Müller, J.-W., 2016. *What Is Populism?* Philadelphia: University of Pennsylvania Press.

Nelson, J.L., and Taneja, H., 2018. The Small, Disloyal Fake News Audience: The Role of Audience Availability in Fake News Consumption: *New Media & Society*, 20.

Nerone, J., 2013. History, Journalism, and the Problem of Truth. *In*: B. Brennen, ed. *Assessing Evidence in a Postmodern World*. Milwaukee, WI: Marquette University Press, 11–29.

Nielsen, R.K., 2020. *Testimony for Evidence Session on the Future of Journalism*. Reuters Institute for the Study of Journalism, Oxford.

Nyhan, B., 2016. Relatively Few Americans Live in Partisan Media Bubble, but They're Influential. *The New York Times*, 7 September.

Nyhan, B., 2019. Why Fears of Fake News Are Overhyped. *Medium*.

Page, B.I., 1996. *Who Deliberates? Mass Media in Modern Democracy*. Chicago: University of Chicago Press.

Peck, R., 2019. *Fox Populism*. Cambridge and New York: Cambridge University Press.

Polletta, F., and Callahan, J., 2017. Deep Stories, Nostalgia Narratives, and Fake News: Storytelling in the Trump Era. *American Journal of Cultural Sociology*, 5 (3), 392–408.

Rosenberg, M., and Steinhauer, J., 2020. The QAnon Candidates Are Here: Trump Has Paved Their Way. *The New York Times*, 14 July.

Schudson, M., 1995. *The Power of News*. Cambridge, MA: Harvard University Press.

Schudson, M., 2015. *The Rise of the Right to Know: Politics and the Culture of Transparency, 1945–1975.* Cambridge, MA: The Belknap Press of Harvard University Press.

Starbird, K., Spiro, E., and West, J., 2020. This Covid-19 Misinformation Went Viral: Here's What We Learned. *Washington Post*, 8 May.

Strauss, C., 2012. *Making Sense of Public Opinion: American Discourses About Immigration and Social Programs.* Cambridge: Cambridge University Press.

Sunstein, C.R., 2009. *Republic.com 2.0*. Princeton, NJ: Princeton University Press.

Tucker, J.A., Guess, A., Barbera, P., Vaccari, C., Siegel, A., Sanovich, S., Stukal, D., and Nyhan, B., 2018. *Social Media, Political Polarization, and Political Disinformation: A Review of the Scientific Literature*. Rochester, NY: Social Science Research Network, SSRN Scholarly Paper No. ID 3144139.

Waisbord, S., 2018. The Elective Affinity Between Post-Truth Communication and Populist Politics. *Communication Research and Practice*, 4 (1), 17–34.

19

RIGHT-WING POPULISM, VISUAL DISINFORMATION, AND BREXIT

From the UKIP 'Breaking Point' poster to the aftermath of the London Westminster bridge attack

Simon Faulkner, Hannah Guy, and Farida Vis

Introduction

The United Kingdom (UK) experienced significant political turmoil over its relationship with Europe between early 2016 and 2017. This period opened on 22 February 2016, with then–Prime Minister David Cameron calling for a European Union (EU) membership referendum and came to some degree of resolution when the subsequent prime minister Theresa May triggered Article 50 (the first step to start the so-called Brexit process) on 29 March 2017. The EU referendum itself was held on 23 June 2016, in which British citizens were asked to answer the following question: 'should the United Kingdom remain a member of the European Union or leave the European Union?' The referendum resulted in a narrow majority vote to leave the EU. The successful Leave campaign involved a number of organisations. The official campaign, as defined by the electoral commission, was Vote Leave, while their rival organisation was Leave. EU. The latter had links to the longer-standing Eurosceptic UK Independence Party (UKIP), which also ran a campaign. The Leave.EU and UKIP campaigns were both overtly focused on the issue of immigration and mobilised a racialised politics of fear consistent with broader European and international right-wing populist ideas concerning race and nationhood. Our chapter involves two case studies that each analyse a photojournalistic image that gained significant visibility in mainstream and social media during this period. The first image was distributed a week before the EU referendum was held and on the same day that a right-wing extremist murdered British Labour MP Jo Cox (apparently for her pro-EU position and sympathy for migrants). The second was distributed a week before the triggering of Article 50. These images were chosen because they offer rich opportunities to explore the ways in which media manipulation in the UK context has been – in these instances – strongly shaped by populist, racist, anti-immigration, and Islamophobic sentiments.

The first case study examines UKIP's so-called 'Breaking Point' poster, which used a photojournalistic image deriving from the 'refugee crisis' of 2015. This poster was made public on 16 June 2016 at a press conference featuring UKIP leader Nigel Farage, outside the European

Commission's London base in Westminster, as part of the party's campaign for a Leave vote. The poster was also distributed via UKIP's social media accounts and published in a different version in the *Daily Express* newspaper. Photographs and video of the press conference, showing Farage in front of the poster displayed on a mobile billboard, were widely distributed through mainstream and social media (Figure 19.1).

The second case study relates to a terrorist attack that occurred on Westminster Bridge in London on 22 March 2017. This attack involved a single attacker, British Muslim Khalid Masood, who drove a car onto the pavement on Westminster Bridge with the aim of killing pedestrians and then fatally stabbed an unarmed police officer in the grounds of the Palace of Westminster before being shot dead. The attack resulted in the deaths of five other people and the injury of fifty. The case study focuses on how a specific photograph taken of the aftermath of the attack (Figure 19.2) was moved from the mainstream media to social media and then reported as news itself in the mainstream media. It is this journey taken by the image and the multiple reframings and interpretations that took place that are of particular interest here.

The role of news images and images more generally, as a way to better understand mis- and disinformation, has not received the attention it deserves, given how much social media content as well as manipulated content is visual. More than that, when images and photographs are considered, this is often through a journalistic lens, with a focus on verification practices that are essentially aimed at establishing if an image is 'true' or 'false'. Within academic research, work on such images tends to rely on content analysis in order to identify key themes. Our concerns in this chapter go beyond both the verification of photographic images and the identification of themes in order to consider how the examination of socio-political context is fundamental to

Figure 19.1   UK Independence Party Leader (UKIP) Nigel Farage addresses the media during a national poster launch campaign ahead of the EU referendum in London on 16 June 2016

Source: Daniel Leal-Olivas/AFP via Getty Images.

Figure 19.2   Sequence frame showing a woman visibly distressed passing the scene of the terrorist incident on Westminster Bridge, London, 22 March 2017

Source: Jamie Lorriman/Shutterstock.

understanding how images are used for mis- and disinformation purposes. This is particularly true for those images that receive significant coverage and play a key role in shaping public opinion. Thinking about context is particularly important when images are used in ways that reproduce or innovate racial ideas. Examples of mis- and disinformation that mobilise such ideas can be approached through practices of verification, but in the end the racist beliefs that inform such representations cannot be understood in terms of simplistic notions of 'true' or 'false'. Rather, they need to be examined in terms of their ideological content and effects. The overarching goal of this chapter is to help shape this agenda for scholars who are interested in studying these topics and particularly where they intersect. We use these two case studies to start to show how this can be done and why it matters. The focus of the chapter is disinformation. Recognising that there are many competing definitions of *disinformation*, we define it as follows: 'combinations of images and texts, drawing on elements of truthful representations, used to spread misleading, inaccurate or false information designed to cause harm'. In the following sections, we review the existing literature relevant to our subject before discussing the case studies in more detail.

Reviewing the existing literature

Communication on social media is overwhelmingly visual (Faulkner et al. 2018), but this key way in which online disinformation is spread has been overlooked in the emerging research (Wardle & Derakhsan 2017). The lack of focus on images is also a wider issue within social media research (Thelwall et al. 2015; Faulkner et al. 2018). Researchers instead lean towards 'the text-only aspects of online communication', in part because images are considered more complicated to understand and analyse (Highfield & Leaver 2016, 48). This knowledge gap has also been highlighted by Tucker et al. (2018), who identify 'disinformation spread through images and video' (7) as a key gap in research where understanding is 'urgently needed' (61). They note that most disinformation research 'focuses on the textual rather than the visual and audiovisual component of these messages' (47). These sentiments are echoed by other scholars; Fallis (2015) argues that misleading images 'might easily be more epistemically dangerous than misleading words' because images (especially lens-based images) have greater evidentiary value (417). Innes (2020) argues that images are a key component of disinformation and that they are used 'to try and persuade their audiences about the ultimate "truth" of their knowledge claims'. He adds that 'Photographs and videos possess an almost inherent persuasive potency' (13).

More specifically, recontextualised images, in which the original context for the image has been removed and replaced with a falsified context, are identified by several scholars as particularly pervasive. Tucker et al. (2018) explicitly highlight that 'we know very little about' recontextualised images (48). Tandoc et al. (2018) note that 'misappropriated' images are 'an increasingly widespread practice' for spreading disinformation (145). Taken together, these studies suggest that image-based disinformation is potentially more harmful, particularly when involving images taken out of their original context and placed in a false context 'to support a concocted narrative' (Tandoc et al. 2018,145).

A core element of disinformation as pushed by right-wing populists (including the so-called alt-right) is the reshaping of truth and who can be trusted to provide this. Hameleers (2020) has explored common themes of populist disinformation, identifying that crime and immigration are key topics, both intrinsically linked to race. He notes that, from a European right-wing populist perspective, 'Islam is the greatest threat to the Western world', and the mainstream media's supposed 'omittance' of this shows that the media work to protect these ' "dangerous" others' (111). This message is further underpinned by a strong rationale of 'us' versus 'them'. A significant consequence of sharing such divisive disinformation is that it may work to strengthen existing societal divisions and antagonisms; those who align with populist discourse become further entrenched within it, and those who reject it become stronger in their resistance (Hameleers 2020). In a European context Heiss and Matthes (2020) examined populist content on Facebook in Germany and Austria, which was dominated by angry anti-elitist and anti-immigration discourse. The latter 'emerged as the most distinguishing factor' of right-wing populist 'communication on Facebook . . . the unique selling point of right-wing populism' (317). Krzyżanowski's (2020) study of populist rhetoric in Poland since 2015 highlights how pervasive this content is and also that it is not simply limited to social media. This study points out how normalised these discourses have become, resulting in a shift towards more explicit right-wing populist themes in the mainstream media and specifically towards immigration; immigrants, predominantly Muslims, are presented as a dangerous invasion and a threat to European culture and values. These claims are often underpinned by disinformation. This situation allows for the creation of ungrounded arguments, in which disinformation and 'fake news' are accepted as truth 'due to their civil appearance which effectively normalises them in political and media discourse and in both traditional and online public spheres' (25). Overall, however, the research on the content of populist/alt-right disinformation online is still limited, as observed by Panizo-Lledot et al. (2019). Yet even with the limited research into this topic to date, it is evident that anti-immigration and racist rhetoric is a key component of right-wing populist online disinformation.

Discussions about visual disinformation and how to address it continue to be significant within journalism. These discourses around verification practices have also shaped academic thinking on this issue. For journalists, the crux of image verification has focused on establishing if the image is actually what they think it is or others claim it to be. Whilst this continues to be a vital method, the techniques and strategies frequently deployed in mis- and disinformation, across a range of forms of media manipulation, mean it is also key to consider how images are used, how they are shared and by whom, and ultimately what meanings and effects they produce.

In our research we have gone beyond standard forms of journalistic image verification by combining methods from art history with questions designed specifically for mis- and disinformation content (Vis et al. 2020). Our framework, 20 Questions for Interrogating Social Media Images,[1] is an additional tool journalists and others can use when investigating images. It consists of 20 questions for social media images (still image, video, gif, etc.), with an additional 14 questions aimed at different aspects of mis- and disinformation. The questions do not appear in a set order, but these five are central: What is it? What does it show? Who made it? What *did* it mean? What *does* it mean? Whilst these questions significantly take us beyond the standard approaches to verification, especially where they address meaning, it is also important to show how expansive such an exploration into the wider meanings and contexts of an image can be. This chapter aims to do just that. We now turn to our two case studies to explore in more detail examples of image-based right-wing populist disinformation that relate to the wider context of Brexit and themes of immigration and racism.

UKIP's 'Breaking Point' poster, 2016

The UKIP billboard poster (Figure 19.1) that is the focus of our first case study used a cropped version of a photograph taken by the photojournalist Jeff Mitchell (a staff photographer for the picture agency Getty Images) in October 2015. This photograph depicted a large group of predominantly adult male Syrian and Afghan refugees being escorted by Slovenian police from the border between Croatia and Slovenia to the Brezice refugee camp. UKIP purchased a commercial license to use the photograph from Getty Images. The photographic image fills the entire billboard and shows the refugees following a path between fields, from the upper left of the image down to its central foreground, producing a powerful impression of relentless human movement. Over the photographic image were superimposed the slogans 'BREAKING POINT' (in large red block capitals) and 'The EU has failed us all' and 'We must break free of the EU and take back control of our borders' (in smaller white font). This combination of image and text displaced the meaning of the photograph from being about the movement of a specific group of refugees in Slovenia (as described in its caption on the Getty Images website)[2] to being about the purported effect of EU border policies on immigration into the UK. This shift in meaning also involved a shift in the function of the image from being a standard example of photojournalism (and therefore primarily valued for its documentary content) to a political concern to use the image to emphasise connotations of racialised otherness in relation to immigration.

A similar shift in the meaning of Mitchell's photograph also occurred when the right-wing populist Hungarian Fidesz party used the same image for a later anti-immigration poster during the 2018 Hungarian parliamentary elections (Matamoros 2018). This poster presented the photograph with a large red English language stop sign over it. Fidesz and UKIP both used the non-white faces of the refugees depicted in Mitchell's photograph to visually embody their racialised conceptions of immigration. This use of the photograph meant that there was no need to explicitly articulate the racism that underpinned their political viewpoints. Rather, the photographic image did this work for them.[3] This meant that both Fidesz and UKIP could get across their racially charged message while also allowing them a degree of deniability about their populist racist views.

Yet there are also differences between these two posters that are useful to draw out. If the Hungarian poster was not verbally explicit about its racialisation of immigration, it still made its opposition to non-white immigration into Hungary very clear through the use of a simple stop sign over an image of Syrian and Afghan refugees. In contrast to this, the message of UKIP's poster is not so direct, nor is it so univocal. The slogan 'BREAKING POINT' is clearly meant to relate to the refugees shown in Mitchell's photograph in that it frames them as a human force that has brought something to the 'breaking point'. However, it is not exactly clear what is about to break. Is it the EU Schengen border or the UK border that is meant to be breaking? Nigel Farage seemed to answer this question in a radio interview given a number of days after the unveiling of the poster, when he stated that the poster 'was not about Britain'. Rather, 'it was about Schengen, about the fact Schengen is breaking' (quoted in Woodcock 2016). This suggests that UKIP intended the slogan 'BREAKING POINT' to refer to the EU border and for Mitchell's photograph to epitomise the breaking of this border. However, it is apparent that UKIP also intended the poster to be about the UK. This is indicated by the poster's other slogans, in which the people of the UK are referred to as an 'us' who have been 'failed' by the EU and a 'we' who 'must break free of the EU and take back control of our borders'. Consequently, it can be suggested that UKIP intended there to be a duality to the meaning of the slogan 'BREAKING POINT' and to their poster overall. The poster represented the EU border breaking under the weight of non-white immigration, but at the same time, it encouraged a sense of slippage between this framing of the EU border as a border out of control and the UK border. Crucial to this slippage between the EU and UK border was also the visual impact of the poster, in that the refugees it showed were intended to be perceived as moving roughly in the direction of the spectator and thus towards the UK.[4]

This leads us on to thinking more directly about the function of UKIP's poster as disinformation. That the UKIP poster was partly intended to suggest that the refugees it showed were on their way to or even at the UK border means that the poster was disingenuous in its use of a photograph that actually showed refugees in Slovenia, who probably hoped to eventually reach Germany. It was this disingenuousness and the intention to misinform it entailed that Buzzfeed pointed to through their headline: 'These Refugees in UKIP's Anti-EU Poster Are Actually in Slovenia' (Waterson 2016). But this kind of observation should not be the only outcome of a critical analysis of UKIP's poster as disinformation. As emphasised earlier in the chapter, there is also a need to contextualise the poster as an example of disinformation in terms of the racial meanings that it mobilised and was dependent on to have its intended effect. In this sense, the role of the analyst is not that of a journalist simply seeking to verify the 'truthfulness' or 'falseness' of an image they want to publish, but rather of someone who seeks to understand why a particular example of disinformation was produced and had harmful effects under specific socio-political conditions that are, in this instance, significantly defined by racialised notions of nationhood.

Of particular significance when thinking about the ideological context for UKIP's poster is the way that right-wing populist discourses define national belonging. As Wodak notes, populist nationalism in Europe often involves 'a nativist notion of belonging', which is 'linked to a chauvinist and racialized concept of "the people" and "the nation"' (Wodak 2015, 47). Belonging to the nation necessarily means being 'native' and by implication white. This also means that those defined as 'non-natives' are automatically excluded from and constructed as a threat to the national community (Wodak 2015, 66). In line with these ideas, UKIP developed a political position that emphasised immigration as an EU-driven threat to the 'native' population of the

UK in terms of both the free movement of citizens from EU member states and also the supposed openness of EU borders to non-white immigration from beyond Europe. In other words, UKIP understood 'free movement' in the EU as both 'an internal expanse where Eastern and Southern Europeans are alleged to be enjoying excessive access to Britain's economic and social goods' and also 'as a conduit for dark-skinned refugees to march across uninhibited to the sweet fields of England' (Valluvan & Kalva, 2019, 2394). This construction of 'dark-skinned refugees' as a racialised threat to the UK originating from the EU is what UKIP's poster was intended to mobilise and reinforce by giving it a powerful visual form. UKIP did this by using a photograph without concern for what this image depicted in documentary terms. More important for UKIP was what the non-white faces, gender, and number of refugees shown in the photograph could be made to imply within the context of a broader 'Leave' campaign that was 'overdetermined by racism' (Virdee & McGeever 2018, 1804).

Westminster Bridge attack, 2017

Our second case study focuses on a single photograph taken by freelance photojournalist Jamie Lorriman in the aftermath of the Westminster Bridge attack. This photograph shows a Muslim woman wearing hijab walking past a group of people gathered around an injured person on Westminster Bridge. The woman holds her left hand to her face while looking at a mobile phone held in her other hand (Figure 19.2). This photograph was one of a series uploaded by Lorriman to the picture agency Rex Features, which then supplied it to the *New York Daily News* to illustrate its report on the attack. From here the photograph was appropriated for circulation on social media. The case study is specifically concerned with the uploading of this photograph to Twitter by the user @SouthLoneStar, along with the accompanying message: 'Muslim woman pays no mind to the terror attack, casually walks by a dying man while checking phone #Pray ForLondon#Westminster#BanIslam'. This tweet was retweeted thousands of times and widely reported in the UK press. This press coverage reported on the negative responses of other social media users to the Islamophobia of @SouthLoneStar's tweeting of Lorriman's photograph. This coverage was underpinned by the assumption that @SouthLoneStar was the account of an actual North American holding overtly right-wing and Islamophobic views. This assumption was reasonable at the time, given that @SouthLoneStar's profile photograph depicted a young white man wearing a Stetson hat, with an accompanying profile description that stated 'Proud TEXAN and AMERICAN patriot'. However, this matter was complicated in November 2017, when it was revealed that @SouthLoneStar was a fictitious user operated by Russia's Internet Research Agency (IRA) for the purpose of spreading disinformation to Russia's international benefit. This further development in the story of @SouthLoneStar's tweet was itself widely reported in the UK press.

Taken at face value, @SouthLoneStar's tweet of Lorriman's photograph appears to be a straightforward example of racist disinformation. The tweet explicitly directs the viewer to interpret the photograph as showing a Muslim woman's indifference to the violent aftermath of a terrorist attack and to understand that the woman is indifferent because she is a Muslim. @SouthLoneStar's tweet is also easy to identify as intentionally misleading. Lorriman's photographs of the Muslim woman walking past the group of people around a victim on Westminster Bridge on the Rex Features website are all captioned 'Sequence frame showing a woman visibly distressed passing the scene of the terrorist incident on Westminster Bridge, London'.[5] This reveals a clear disjunction between what Lorriman himself presumably wrote about his photograph and what @SouthLoneStar asserts that it shows. However, as with the 'Breaking Point' poster, analysis of @SouthLoneStar's tweet as an example of disinformation should not stop here. There is a need not only to examine how @SouthLoneStar's tweet misrepresented Lorriman's photograph and how this misrepresentation was informed by Islamophobic ideas but also to contextualise the tweet in terms of IRA disinformation practices.

The IRA has operated on Twitter since at least 2012 (Farkas & Bastos 2018), enabling them to develop a sophisticated framework for sowing disinformation, which involves both automated and human-operated accounts (Dawson & Innes 2019). These accounts align with highly partisan beliefs and engage both with genuine users and with each other, simulating fabricated conflict to generate artificial divisions. The IRA targeted the UK especially heavily in 2017 (Howard et al. 2018), with its disinformation campaigns being focused on the series of terrorist attacks that occurred that year, starting with the Westminster Bridge attack. Innes (2020) has observed that IRA accounts specifically targeted the immediate aftermaths of these attacks with 'right-wing, anti-Islam' sentiments with the aim of sowing 'antagonism and anxiety' (12). In relation to this context, Innes also specifically discusses @SouthLoneStar, noting that this account and several others were 'constructed around overtly politically right-wing, Southern state, President Trump supporting' personas (12).

The point about these personas is that they were manufactured out of already-existing right-wing identities and existing chauvinistic and racist discourses. @SouthLoneStar's tweet of Lorriman's photograph in particular tapped into long-standing media tropes about Muslim women that frame them in terms of fundamentalism and terror (Ahmed & Matthes 2017; Bullock & Jafri 2000; Werbner 2007) and identify female Muslim practices of head covering and 'veiling' as forms of 'Islamic aggression' (Perry 2014, 83). The latter is significant because it was the presence of the woman's headscarf in Lorriman's photograph that enabled the image to be reframed in Islamophobic terms. Coming from an IRA-operated account, @SouthLoneStar's tweets were not sincere expressions of an authentic right-wing populist identity. Nevertheless, these tweets mobilised sentiments shared with actual right-wing populists, meaning that they involved a kind of fabricated sincerity that is difficult to distinguish from genuine expressions of a right-wing subjectivity. This fabricated sincerity was essential to the function of @SouthLoneStar's tweet as disinformation and for the IRA's objective of sowing political division. It was this tapping into existing Islamophobic constructions of racial difference and the political antagonisms to which they relate that enabled @SouthLoneStar's tweet to become highly visible on social media and, from there, to gain extensive mainstream media coverage, significantly increasing its reach. It is also important to note the @SouthLoneStar's framing of Lorriman's photograph, and thus the event that it represents, also continues to be highly visible in search engines. It is these multiple reframings and complex online and offline journeys of the image across various mediums that complicate any analysis but are crucial to emphasise before this chapter concludes.

Conclusion

This chapter started by arguing for the need to examine images as a stand-alone type of content in relation to disinformation, given that so much manipulated content is visual. It thus sought to build on the emerging literature in this area with a specific focus on examples of visual disinformation relating to the UK that were informed by racist, anti-immigration, and Islamophobic sentiments. In doing so it has offered a way to analyse visual disinformation that moves beyond verification strategies, originating in journalism, that are underpinned by the ultimate aim of labelling an image as 'true' or 'false'. This approach also goes beyond academic strategies that are overly focused on identifying themes across sets of images, primarily using content analysis. Our approach advocates for research that recognises the significant roles highly visible images – such as the 'Breaking Point' poster and Lorriman's photograph of the aftermath of the Westminster Bridge attack – play within formations of right-wing populism in the UK and beyond. In order to better understand relationships between populism and disinformation, it is crucial to take more seriously the importance of such prominent images as it is clear that their value is recognised by those who hold right-wing populist views. Our case studies highlight the need to address the complexities and nuances of the multiple journeys of these images. This chapter has therefore sought to advocate not simply taking more seriously the role of the visual in disinformation research, but also this multi-layered complexity of how images are used and by whom, how they travel across platforms and mediums, and what effects they have on- and offline. Taking these things seriously necessarily involves exploring the contexts within which visual mis- and disinformation is produced and consumed. In relation to the specific discussion in this chapter, this necessitates examining how examples of visual disinformation connect to well-established right-wing populist ideas in the UK and Europe more widely. The approach laid out in this chapter will contribute to the further development of a research agenda that more closely embraces the study of images as crucial elements of contemporary racist and right-wing populist discourse, specifically focusing on highly visible images that significantly shape public discourse. This approach also adopts a more critical approach to the agents and distributors of manipulated content, including mainstream politicians and parties (in our chapter, Nigel Farage and UKIP) as well as the mainstream media, rather than simply pointing to social media (or indeed foreign interference) as the most significant problem.

Notes

1 The framework can be found here: https://bit.ly/20QuestionsFramework.
2 Getty describes the content of the photograph as follows: 'Migrants are escorted through fields by police as they are walked from the village of Rigonce to Brezice refugee camp on October 23, 2015 in Rigonce, Slovenia'. www.gettyimages.co.uk/detail/news-photo/migrants-are-escorted-through-fields-by-police-as-they-are-news-photo/493896788 (accessed 6 June 2020).
3 The version of UKIP's poster published in *The Daily Express* involved more text than the billboard version, but even here, UKIP avoided explicitly identifying what they intended to communicate as the threat of non-white immigration to the UK. This version of the poster states that 'Net immigration in the UK stands at over 330,000 people a year'. Continuing: 'Just under half of these people are from the EU'. The poster says nothing about who the other non-EU immigrants are, leaving the spectator to surmise this from the appearance of the people in Mitchell's photograph (Farage, 2016).
4 This kind of use of a photograph of a large group of refugees/migrants has precedents in the UK. For example, on 8 May 2003, *The Daily Express* used a similar image of migrants running across a French railyard towards the camera on its front page, with the headline 'WE CAN'T KEEP THEM OUT' (Faulkner 2003).
5 Rex Features (2017) *Major incident at Westminster, London, UK – 22 Mar 2017*. Available at: www.rexfea tures.com/set/8550198.

References

Ahmed, S. & Matthes, J. (2017) "Media representation of Muslims and Islam from 2000 to 2015: A meta-analysis." *The International Communication Gazette* 79(3): 219–244. DOI: 10.1177/174804 8516656305

Bullock, K.H. & Jafri, G.J. (2000) "Media (mis)representations: Muslim women in the Canadian nation." *Canadian Women's Studies* 20(2): 25–40. Available at: https://cws.journals.yorku.ca/index.php/cws/article/view/7607/6738

Dawson, A. & Innes, M. (2019) "How Russia's Internet research agency built its disinformation campaign." *The Political Quarterly* 90(2): 245–256. DOI: 10.1111/1467-923X.12690

Fallis, D. (2015) "What is disinformation?" *Library Trends* 63(3): 401–426. DOI: 10.1353/lib.2015.0014.

Farage, N. (2016) "UKIP advertising sends a message that we are better OUT." *Daily Express*, 15 June. Available at: www.express.co.uk/comment/expresscomment/680296/UKIP-advertising-campaign-vote-leave-Brexit-EU-referendum-Nigel-Farage (Accessed: 28 May 2020)

Farkas, J. & Bastos, M. (2018) "IRA propaganda on Twitter: Stoking antagonism and tweeting local news." In *Proceedings of the International Conference on Social Media & Society*, Copenhagen, Denmark, 18–20 July, pp. 281–285. DOI: 10.1145/3217804.3217929

Faulkner, S. (2003) "Asylum seekers, imagined geography, and visual culture." *Visual Culture in Britain* 5(1): 93–114.

Faulkner, S., Vis, F. & D'Orazio, F. (2018) "Analysing social media images." In Burgess, J., Marwick, A., & Poell, T. (eds.) *The Sage handbook of social media*. London: Sage, pp. 160–178.

Hameleers, M. (2020) "We are right, they are wrong: The antagonistic relationship between populism and discourse of (un)truthfulness". *DisClosure: A Journal of Social Theory* 29(12): 104–120. DOI: 10.13023/disclosure.29.11

Heiss, R. & Matthes, J. (2020) "Stuck in a nativist spiral: Content, selection, and effects of right-wing populists' communication on Facebook." *Political Communication* 37(3): 303–328, DOI: 10.1080/10584609.2019.1661890

Highfield, T. & Leaver, T. (2016) "Instagrammatics and digital methods: Studying visual social media, from selfies and GIFs to memes and emoji." *Communication Research and Practice* 2(1): 47–62. DOI: 10.1080/22041451.2016.1155332

Howard, P. N., Ganesh, B. & Liotsiou, D. (2018). *The IRA, social media and political polarization in the United States, 2012–2018.* Available at: https://comprop.oii.ox.ac.uk/wp-content/uploads/sites/93/2018/12/The-IRA-Social-Media-and-Political-Polarization.pdf (Accessed: 23 May 2020)

Innes, M. (2020) "Techniques of disinformation: Constructing and communicating 'soft facts' after terrorism." *The British Journal of Sociology* 71(2): 284–299. DOI: 10.1111/1468-4446.12735

Krzyżanowski, M. (2020) "Discursive shifts and the normalisation of racism: Imaginaries of immigration, moral panics and the discourse of contemporary right-wing populism." *Social Semiotics*: 1–25. DOI: 10.1080/10350330.2020.1766199

Matamoros, C.A. (2018) "Hungarian government rehashes UKIP anti-migrant poster in new ad." *euronews*, 29 March. Available at: www.euronews.com/2018/03/28/hungary-government-s-new-anti-immigration-ad-copies-ukip-s-controversial-anti-migrant-post (Accessed: 12 August 2020)

Panzio-Lledot, A., Torregrosa, J., Bello-Orgaz, G., Thornburn, J. & Camacho, D. (2019) "Describing alt-right communities and their discourse on Twitter during the 2018 mid-term elections." [PREPRINT]. https://arxiv.org/pdf/1910.03431.pdf

Perry, B. (2014) "Gendered Islamophobia: Hate crime against Muslim women." *Social Identities: Journal for the Study of Race, Nation and Culture* 20(1): 74–89. DOI: 10.1080/13504630.2013.864467

Tandoc, E.C., Lim, Z.W. & Ling, R. (2018) "Defining 'fake news': A typology of scholarly definitions". *Digital Journalism* 6(2): 137–153. DOI: 10.1080/21670811.2017.1360143

Thelwall, M., Goriunova, O., Vis, F., Faulkner, S., Burns, A., Aulich, J., Mas-Bleda, A., Stuart, E. & D'Orazio, F. (2015) "Chatting through pictures? A classification of images tweeted in one week in the UK and USA." *Journal of the Association for Information Science and Technology* 67(11): 2575–2586. DOI: 10.1002/asi.23620

Tucker, J. A., Guess, A., Barbera, P., Vaccari, Cr., Siegel, A., Sanovich, S., Stukal, D. & Nyhan, B. (2018) *Social media, political polarization, and political disinformation: A review of the scientific literature.* Available at: https://papers.ssrn.com/sol3/papers.cfm?abstract_id=3144139; DOI: 10.2139/ssrn.3144139

Valluvan, S. & Kalva, V.S. (2019) "Racial nationalisms: Brexit borders and little Englander contradictions." *Ethnic and Racial Studies* 42(14): 2393–2412. DOI: 10.1080/01419870.2019.1640890

Virdee, S. and McGeever, B. (2018) "Racism, crisis, Brexit." *Ethnic and Racial Studies* 41(10): 1802–1819. DOI: 10.1080/01419870.2017.1361544

Vis, F., Faulkner, S. & Guy, H. (2020) "Verifying and questioning images." In Silverman, C. (ed.) *Verification handbook 3: For disinformation and media manipulation*. Maastricht: European Journalism Centre, Online.

Wardle, C. & Derakhshan, H. (2017) *Information disorder: Toward an interdisciplinary framework for research and policy making*. Strasbourg: Council of Europe. Available at: https://rm.coe.int/information-disorder-toward-an-interdisciplinary-framework-for-researc/168076277c (Accessed 4 September 2019)

Waterson, J. (2016) "These refugees in UKIP's anti-EU poster are actually in Slovenia." *Buzzfeed*, 16 June. Available at: www.buzzfeed.com/jimwaterson/these-refugees-in-ukips-anti-eu-poster-are-actually-in-slove (Accessed 28 May 2020)

Werbner, P. (2007) "Veiled interventions in pure space: Honour, shame, and embodies struggles amongst Muslims in Britain and France." *Theory, Culture & Society* 24(2): 161–186. DOI: 10.1177/0263276407075004

Wodak, R. (2015) *The politics of fear: What right-wing populist discourses mean.* London: Sage.

Woodcock, A. (2016) "Boris Johnson "profoundly unhappy" with controversial Nigel Farage poster." *The Irish News*, 22 June. Available at: www.irishnews.com/news/brexit/2016/06/22/news/boris-johnson-profoundly-unhappy-with-controversial-nigel-farage-poster-574157/ (Accessed 5 June 2020)

PART III

The politics of misinformation and disinformation

20
MISOGYNY AND THE POLITICS OF MISINFORMATION

Sarah Banet-Weiser[1]

In 2016, the *Oxford Dictionary* named *post-truth* the word of the year. In 2017, *Merriam-Webster* named *feminism* the word of the year. Despite their proximity as terms that define the zeitgeist, there is little consideration about how they might intersect and, in fact, constitute one another. Gender is rarely acknowledged as a key context for the very notion of post-truth. The potential connection between feminism and post-truth has not been acknowledged, despite their both reaching fever pitch at the same time in the same political climate, one that gave way to the renaissance of popular feminism as well as the rise of the contemporary crisis of post-truth. They are part of the same cultural ecosystem.

The post-truth 'crisis' is often framed as the downfall of hitherto functional 'rationality' in politics, the decline and waning of expertise and Enlightenment values. 'Democracy' is the normative foundation for this crisis; it is the foundation that needs to be returned to as 'normal'. And, despite the contemporary focus on misinformation and 'post-truth', with scores of books and articles published focusing on this apparently novel 'crisis' (some more historical and critical than others), I think it is crucial to have historical specificity when considering the relationship between gender and misinformation; a historical perspective from the standpoint of gender unseats the assumptions around truth and democracy and urges us to consider alternative futures. The concerns around post-truth – misinformation, disinformation, outright lies – are proclaimed to be a crisis in knowing, in subjectivity, in citizenry; they are seen as affronts to all these ontological and, indeed, scientific claims of being and knowing. Yet this has been the material context for women for centuries, especially for women of colour. In other words, the relationship between misogyny and misinformation is not a new one.

With roots in the Enlightenment and ideas of 'masculine rationality', women were, and continue to be, understood as being governed by their emotions, subjective in their understandings of the world, not even capable of speaking the truth or even having access to the truth because their emotions block the truth. Thus, I argue, they are always already the bearers of 'misinformation'. In this context, in a familiar public/private binary, men are the bearers of public truths while women, at best, are seen as ambassadors of private truths. Men's 'truths' have long been positioned as universal while women's truths have been positioned as incidental, subjective, and unique, even in the most 'rational' corners of the natural sciences (e.g. gender bias in medical research, exclusion of women from drug trials, heart attack symptoms, etc.).

Yet there are specifics of the current moment that mobilise choosing these two cultural and discursive practices – the post-truth and feminism – as words of the year. What were post-truth and feminist discourses responding to in the early aughts? Post-truth characterises a very contemporary cultural moment that responds to increased digital circulation of misinformation about a number of things, from news to health to politics. Contemporary feminism, also in digital circulation, is most often a response to misogyny, though this, too, varies, from resisting online harassment to rape culture to misinformation campaigns. Yet, although feminist theories have long explored the ways in which women's bodies, affects, practices, and ideologies have been framed as subjective compared to the 'objective' masculine spheres and both misogyny and misinformation have been growing concerns in the contemporary digital era, the relationship between these two contemporary discursive practices hasn't been thoroughly explored in scholarship. (There are key exceptions; see Manne 2018; Marwick and Lewis 2015; Jane 2016, and others.)

Again, post-truth and popular feminism each has a foil they are positioning themselves against: misinformation and misogyny. Arguably, both misogyny and misinformation are linked to new forms of digital hate speech. They are both mechanisms of control: misogyny and misinformation control dominant narratives, practices, policies, and bodies; both promote an agenda that is about controlling groups of people. Misinformation is broadly defined as a strategic, deliberate practice of altering the truth or a set of facts as a way to redirect or redefine a narrative (see the introduction to this volume). The digital era has seen misinformation proliferate, in part because of the flexibilities offered by digital media platforms; that is, at the centre of the circulation of current forms of misinformation are digital media and communication platforms which centrally use misinformation to mobilise citizens and communities (Marwick and Lewis 2015). Historically, the public anxiety about truth claims and who can and should be a truth teller has as a core logic the relationship between truth and democracy, as well as the relationship between a rational subject and truth. This relationship is seen to be profoundly disrupted in the current moment. As William Davies, writing in *The Guardian*, put it: 'A sense that the game is rigged now fuels public debate' (Davies 2019). While 'truth' is an often-contested concept, it has nonetheless always depended on the assumption that certain actors tell the truth and that these actors have been authorised with the mantle of veracity in their understandings of the world and of themselves. Yet the idea that the 'game is rigged now fuels public debate' belies a long history, one that suggests that the game is rigged differently at different historical moments and that for women and people of colour, the game has always been rigged.

The current decade is also one in which a networked, digital misogyny has taken hold, described as 'a basic anti-female violent expression that circulates to wide audiences on popular media platforms' (Banet-Weiser and Miltner 2015); the logics and affordances of media platforms allow for an amplification of what philosopher Kate Manne has described as "the system that operates within a patriarchal social order to police and enforce women's subordination and to uphold male dominance" (Manne 2018). The emergence and heightened visibility of networked misogyny, often centred around a space in online culture called the 'manosphere', offer yet another plane in the conjunctural logic of contemporary mechanisms of controlling and disciplining women and have had a central role in the creation and circulation of misinformation (Ging 2017; Jane 2016; Marwick and Lewis 2015).

Misogyny is one of the core common logics in racist, xenophobic, anti-Semitic, and Islamophobic expressions and movements.[2] Thus, I argue here that these two cultural phenomena – misinformation and misogyny – are often mutually constitutive in this historical conjuncture. In the following pages, I explore some of the connections, intersections, and contradictions between misinformation and misogyny and map these connections in two dimensions: (1)

misogyny as a main tactic in the extreme right's misinformation campaigns, mobilised and weaponised against women as a way to secure or 'take back' power and (2) extreme right communities claiming that accusations of misogyny (by feminists, women, and others) are themselves misinformation, thus functioning as a kind of funhouse mirror (Banet-Weiser 2018). I conclude with a discussion of the historical context for these different tactics and point out the long *duree* of the relationship between misogyny and misinformation.

Misogyny as core logic of misinformation campaigns

Extreme-right movements use misogyny as a core logic to their politics and their misinformation campaigns; it is not merely a strategy or tactic, but rather, these movements are frequently based on misogyny as a set of discourses and practices that aim to 'reset' the gender balance back to its 'natural' patriarchal relation (Banet-Weiser 2018). Within these movements, the need for feminist politics (in a similar way as the need to dismantle systemic racism) is positioned as misinformation. While the racist ideologies of the extreme right have often been correctly identified as white nationalism, the extreme right has always also run on an overtly misogynistic agenda; as Matthew Lyons points out, 'Harassing and defaming women isn't just a tactic; it also serves the alt-right's *broader agenda and long-term vision for society'* (2016, para. 8, emphasis added). A key strategy of the extreme right is recuperation: men's rights organisations in digital culture are filled with false campaigns about how women and feminists have not just destroyed society but emasculated it.

The gendered logic of misogynistic misinformation campaigns is that of a zero-sum game: men lose, become invisible, when women win and become more visible. Conservative populist movements take a particular shape in a contemporary crisis in hegemonic masculinity, a crisis brought on by global economic collapse (as men lose their jobs and future security), by more visible efforts to diversify workplaces and cultural spaces (exemplified by a few visible successful women in technology fields), and by increasing popular feminist activism. Within this crisis, some men (particularly white working- and middle-class men) see themselves as losing cultural and political ground, relinquishing patriarchal authority (Rosin 2013; Negra and Tasker 2014; Banet-Weiser 2018). Within the context of this existing sense of injury and loss, feminists' call for more equity is framed as dangerous misinformation. Women, and specifically feminism, are assumed as the reason for this loss and are targets for misinformation campaigns. Consequently, a normalised misogyny is often the price women pay for being visible online, with digital platforms such as Twitter and Facebook doing little to monitor misogynistic misinformation campaigns.

These misinformation campaigns have been directed particularly intensely at black women, as part of what black feminist scholar Moya Bailey has called 'misogynoir', the specific targeting of black women for misogynistic and racist abuse (Bailey 2020). One of the earlier examples of how misinformation was used against black women online came in 2013, when a series of misinformation campaigns were circulated on Twitter (Broderick 2014; Diop 2019; Hampton 2019; Donovan 2019). These Twitter campaigns were initially launched through false hashtags that pretended to come from black women: specifically #EndFathersDay. An elaborate hoax, #EndFathersDay was started by anonymous trolls on 4chan to simulate feminist outrage at the idea of having a national holiday for fathers, claiming that Father's Day was a symbol of patriarchal oppression. As Donovan points out, 'To grab attention, these trolls relied on the social norms of trusted self-identification ("I am a black feminist") alongside feminist support strategies ("listen to women of color")' (Donovan 2019) Not surprisingly, conservative media pundits fell for the hoax, amplifying their critique of feminists, especially black feminists (Hampton

2019). This misinformation campaign was exposed by actual black feminists, particularly Twitter users Shafiqah Hudson and I'Nasah Crockett, who signaled the fabricated tweets with the hashtag "yourslipisshowing" as a way to make others aware that these tweets were intended to pit black women against each other. However, this kind of mimicry can never be complete. The notion that the 'slip is showing' is explicitly about how misinformation will never quite bamboozle those who are in possession of the 'real' information (who know how to hide the proverbial slip). Consequently, it's also a way of calling out the fact that this misinformation campaign does not imagine black women as the recipients at all, but rather white men and women.

#EndFathersDay and other faux black feminist accounts did not receive the kind of international attention that other misinformation campaigns did. As reporter Aremita Diop points out,

> Even before the Russian Internet Research Agency weaponized these tactics for the 2016 election, anonymous 4chan users spread #EndFathersDay through false-flag Twitter accounts, posing as black women to exacerbate fissures between feminists of color and white feminists as well as rile up conservative pundits. But few outside of the online community of black women realized at the time that this was a coordinated operation.
>
> (Diop 2019)

As Ryan Broderick reports, #EndFathersDay was part of a larger Men's Rights Activist effort called 'Operation Lollipop', in which 'the idea is to pose as women of color on Twitter and guide activist hashtags as a way to embarrass the online social justice community' (Broderick 2014). Other early online fake outrage campaigns, such as #WhitesCantBeRaped, also emerged from 4chan (specifically, the site's politically incorrect message board, /pol/), in an effort to outrage feminists and make a mockery out of feminist online campaigns.

But Twitter campaigns of misinformation capitalised on well-established structures of racism and sexism; well before the current preoccupation with the crisis of misinformation in the digital sphere, women and people of colour have been the targets of what could be called misinformation campaigns. In other words, using fake accounts to encourage feminist activists to turn against each other was an early iteration of the relationship between misogyny and misinformation, yet like many other subsequent misinformation campaigns that target women, these faux black feminist accounts did not warrant the same kind of attention that others in the 'post-truth' era have received. Despite the important feminist activism that emerged from the misinformation campaign, exemplified by the #yourslipisshowing campaign, the tactics used by 4chan and other extreme-right online spaces in campaigns such as #EndFathersDay demonstrated the power of such manipulation and provided what media scholar Joan Donovan calls the 'blueprint' for other misogynistic misinformation campaigns (Donovan 2019). They were also quite successful in galvanising right-wing rage online.

One of the most significant misogynistic misinformation campaigns in the digital mediascape was #GamerGate. In August 2014, a relatively small group of mainstream male gamers and social media users began to use the #GamerGate hashtag; their purported purpose was ostensibly legitimate – to register their objection to questionable journalistic ethics. That purpose, however, was a misogynistic ruse for challenging the visibility of women in the gaming world; Gamergaters were primarily concerned with a few increasingly prominent women in this world, whom they labelled social justice warriors: Anita Sarkeesian, Brianna Wu, and Zoe Quinn.

Gamergate began with a misinformation campaign: an aggrieved ex-boyfriend of Zoe Quinn posted a 6,000-word screed, claiming that Quinn, a game developer, slept with gaming journalists in return for good coverage. Though it was quickly demonstrated that this was a false claim, this misinformation, as Charlie Warzel in the *New York Times* puts it,

> spiraled into an online culture war, ensnaring female gaming critics like Anita Sarkeesian and other designers like Brianna Wu who would suffer months of relentless abuse on and offline. What started as a revenge post over a break-up morphed into Gamergate: a leaderless harassment campaign to preserve white male internet culture, disguised as a referendum on journalism ethics and political correctness, which ran amok.
>
> (Warzel 2019)

As several scholars have pointed out, Gamergate functioned as a kind of 'rehearsal' for what is now a normalised online culture of misogynistic harassment based on misinformation. As Warzel continues, Gamergate 'was a rallying cry'. And it achieved its goal, in terms of 'intimidating women, deceiving clueless brands and picking up mainstream coverage taught a once-dormant subculture powerful lessons about manipulating audiences and manufacturing outrage' (Warzel 2019). The idea that Gamergate as a misinformation campaign was a 'rehearsal' for politics is telling as it was, at its core, a misogynistic movement (Marwick and Lewis 2015; Massanari 2017). As Marwick and Lewis explain, ' "Gamergater" has become shorthand for a particular kind of geek masculinity that feels victimized and disenfranchised by mainstream society, particularly popular feminism' (Marwick and Lewis 2105). The ease with which bots, actual individuals, and websites could circulate misinformation about women and feminists within Gamergate reveals the entwined relationship between misogyny and misinformation. The legacy of Gamergate is that it provided a blueprint for how to wage misogynistic misinformation wars, as well as providing guidelines for more general misinformation campaigns mobilised by the extreme right.

Gamergate was successful as a misinformation campaign because it was allowed to proliferate unchecked and unregulated by media platforms, with the masculinist world of tech infrastructure on stand-by as supposedly objective observers. As many scholars have noted, the fact that social media platforms did nothing to curtail or prevent the continued abuse of women in Gamergate set the stage for what is now a broad digital environment that routinely uses misogynistic misinformation campaigns to control and discipline women. And to return to the notion that the current media environment of misinformation is positioned as a 'crisis' of truth, when #EndFathersDay or #GamerGate was happening, and when black women and women in tech called attention to these misogynistic campaigns, media companies either ignored or dismissed them. Misogyny is not seen to be a contemporary 'crisis', perhaps because it has existed as part of the structural environment for centuries; it is often invisible as 'hate speech' because it is so deeply structural.

Numerous other examples of misogynistic misinformation campaigns have occurred in the years since Gamergate. One of the most recent tactics is 'deepfakes', a technology of altering video from the original to a 'fake' copy and passing it off as authentic.[3] Deepfakes, an AI-assisted technology, are important for thinking about the future of misinformation campaigns as deepfakes raise pressing questions about consent and how we consume visual information (Cole 2019). Historically, video has been what reporter Samantha Cole called 'the gold standard of believability', where what one sees on video is taken as what *is*, an authentic and true depiction of something that happened. But this tactic also has misogynistic practices as its origin story; as Cole reminds us, 'When Redditors started using AI to attach celebrities' faces to porn performers' bodies, the media reaction focused on the implications for potential political hoaxes, but we need to focus on the women they harmed' (Cole 2019).

The tactic of deepfakes is seen to have originated in a misogynistic campaign, in which a Reddit user named 'deepfake' imposed actress Gal Gadot's face onto the body of a woman in a pornographic film and then widely circulated the video. Indeed, the original use of deepfakes, and what remains one of its most common uses, involves swapping a cis-gender female celebrity's face onto a porn actress (Paris and Donovan 2019). These kinds of deepfakes remain 'particularly troubling, primarily for its reification of women's bodies as a thing to be visually consumed, here completely circumventing any potential for consent or agency on the part of the face (and bodies) of such altered images'(Wagner and Blewer 2019). These deepfakes are clearly examples of misogynistic campaigns with misinformation and lack of consent as their objectives; indeed, the non-consensual exploitation of the deepfake creators is itself part of the logic of the technology, which works to objectify and use women – indeed, to own women's bodies.

Misogynistic accusations of misinformation

Another dimension of the relationship between misinformation and misogyny distorts the focus of misogynistic misinformation, shifting to men claiming that women's accusations of misogyny (manifest as sexual violence) are fabricated: an elaborate ruse to cast men as villains and criminals. Like a funhouse mirror, the logic here is flipped: alongside the misogynistic misinformation campaigns online directed to women, there are also examples of specific groups (primarily but not exclusively men) claiming that reports of violence against women are themselves misinformation campaigns. As Alice Marwick and Rebecca Lewis point out, narratives of men's rights organisations 'include the idea that men and boys are victimized; that feminists in particular are the perpetrators of such attacks; and that misinformation, political correctness, and the liberal agenda are used to hide the truth from the general public' (Marwick and Lewis 2015).

Another of the rallying cries for contemporary men's rights organisations revolves around the idea that women routinely accuse men of rape falsely, as a way to get revenge for being rejected or as a way to erase a night of regretful sex. The notion that rape accusations are false, put forward by vindictive or spurned women as a way to deflect personal responsibility or as an 'outrageous' claim intended for individual profit, is not a new phenomenon within misogynistic structures: the idea that women fabricate rape as a way to deal with rejection has long been a trope of misogyny, emerging with great visibility in the 1980s and 90s with what Christina Hoff Sommers and Katie Roiphe deemed 'victim feminism' in the context of college date rape awareness (Sommers 1994; Roiphe 1994). This conservative counter to an increasing visibility of rape culture on campus was the claim that college women needed to take accountability and responsibility for their own actions in sexual encounters, rather than claiming that they are victims. This definition of victimhood in the era of social media and online vigilantism, specifically the claim that women capriciously occupy this subject position through routinely and falsely accusing men of rape, has been a newly important justification for white privileged men claiming victimhood.

The idea that feminists are enmeshed in what anti-feminist communities call 'victimology' and are what conservative communities routinely call liberal 'snowflakes' has become a key element of networked misogyny. This networked misogyny has been particularly focused on what men's rights groups label 'false' rape accusations. At least in the United States, the notion that women routinely make false rape accusations as a way to benefit themselves has had a heightened visibility since at least 2014, when men's rights organisations began to shift their attention from fathers and divorcees (where the focus was on paternity and custody rights, as well as domestic violence against men) to the gendered pay gap and young men and rape culture (Banet-Weiser 2018).

Like so much of media culture, men's rights organisations often focus on specific individuals and their crimes as emblematic of an entire demographic or culture. In the early twenty-first century, stories about individual cases on college campuses circulated widely in the media, giving a sense to various publics that false accusations of rape were far more common than actual rapes. In this move, college campuses were highlighted as places where young men's lives were 'ruined' because of the apparently rampant problem of women falsely accusing them of rape. Thus, despite the widely known gap in the numbers of women who have been raped and those of women who falsely accuse men of rape, the few women who have admitted to fabricating a rape become so highly visible in the media that the issue of false accusations becomes over-exaggerated and even normalised.[4] The strategy of amplifying individual cases of misinformation (false rape accusations) works to produce a more broadly ideological form of misinformation that circulates and normalises, shoring up the power that is produced at the intersection of misogyny and misinformation. Men's rights organisations have embraced false rape accusations as one of their major causes; Paul Elam, the founder of what is often considered the flagship website of the men's rights movement, A Voice for Men, stated in 2014 about college rape culture: "We have a problem with feminists hyper-inflating rape statistics, creating a kind of hysteria on campus over a problem that needs due attention from law enforcement" (Matchar 2014). Another men's rights website, The Other McCain, stated that

> campus 'rape culture' [is] hysteria ginned up by the Obama administration and its feminist allies. A major factor in that hysteria was the Department of Education's Office of Civil Rights (OCR) using Title IX to threaten universities for allegedly failing to punish sexual assault. This witch-hunt frenzy resulted in male students being falsely accused of rape and denied their due-process rights in campus kangaroo-court disciplinary proceedings.
>
> (McCain 2017)

The rhetoric of 'hysteria', 'witch-hunts', and 'kangaroo-court' underlies much of the anti-rape culture discourse, often focusing on the apparent fallacy of date rape.[5]

The accusations by men's rights organisations and others that women routinely fabricate claims of being raped typically are levied at white men who have been accused of sexual violence. The exception to this is based on histories of systemic racism: though there is a deep relationship between misogyny and misinformation, it is also the case that some women – white, privileged women – are positioned within misinformation campaigns as truth-tellers, as long as their truths do not disrupt the believability of white men. That is, white women have also enjoyed the status of 'truth-tellers', often with violent consequences for black men and boys. Perhaps most visibly, we see this with the murder of Emmett Till in 1955; in 2017, the white woman who accused Till of harassing her admitted to fabricating her account (Johnson 2017). There is a tension in the dynamic of misinformation, in which the 'believability' of whiteness and the 'unbelievability' of womanhood collide in accusations of criminality and sexual violence made all the more complicated by a long-established discourse that constructs black men as sexual predators and white women as ideal victims. As Martenzie Johnson says, 'We currently live in the world of fake news and alternative facts, but white lies have tangible consequences' (Johnson 2017).

The idea that women falsely accuse men of rape isn't the only misogynistic accusation of misinformation; in May 2020, the president of Mexico, Andrés Manuel López Obrador, when asked about the flood of calls to emergency call centres during the COVID-19 lockdown, when there were more than 26,000 reports of violence against women, said 'Ninety percent of those calls that you're referring to are fake', calling the vast majority of these calls 'pranks' (Kitroeff 2020). The relationship between misogyny and misinformation should be positioned within what I call an 'economy of believability', in which women are seen to be liars and untrustworthy by nature. The idea that rape and domestic violence accusations are 'fake' or 'pranks' for women to profit from relies on this historical and social construction of women as incapable, by nature, of telling the 'truth'.

Misogyny and misinformation: a long-standing relationship

There is an increasing body of work on the crises of misinformation, from post-truth to fake news, but little on the notion that misogyny is often at the core of misinformation campaigns. Yet, as media scholar Safiya Noble points out in her book *Algorithms of Oppression*, search functions in digital media have long peddled in racist terms of reference and images as a way to provide 'information' (Noble 2018). As she argues, those media sites with the most

> titillating, racist, sexist and clickbait kinds of content are often elevated because they generate a lot of web traffic, and that makes money for all search engines. This is why disinformation and racism is so profitable, especially in the United States.
>
> (Noble 2020)

Misogynistic misinformation is similarly profitable, which became quite clear in #GamerGate.

The conception of truth and notions of believability in the West have historically been inextricable from whiteness and masculine subjectivity. The truth has always depended on those who are authorised to define it and make it visible. That is, the concern around post-truth has become urgent when those who have defined the truth historically – primarily white, privileged men – begin to witness their truths being questioned, eroding, when they are potentially not believed. As Occenola points out,

> Disinformation is one of many in the arsenal of weapons used by trolls and propaganda networks to attack and discredit opponents. It can take several forms, such as fabricated headlines, misleading captions, or falsified information. Female targets of disinformation, however, often face direct attacks on their identity as women.
>
> (Occenola 2018)

Within this frame, it is helpful to consider the whole concept of misinformation, which depends on an assumption that the 'information' that the prefix 'mis' qualifies somehow represents the 'truth' or the 'facts'.

Yet the same prefix in misogyny implies a much broader notion: the hatred and control of women. Those misinformation campaigns that directly challenge a dominant understanding of the 'truth' – such as politics, elections, et cetera – garner more public attention than misogyny, perhaps because misogyny is so deeply sedimented in structure, so normalised, that it becomes almost invisible as misinformation. Misogynistic misinformation campaigns do not, that is, represent a disruption or a crisis in everyday lives. They do, however, represent the centrality and normalisation of misogyny as a central part of that everyday life.

Notes

1 I am deeply thankful to Jack Bratich, Inna Arzumanova, and Kat Higgins for their helpful suggestions in writing this chapter.
2 Arguably, misogyny is also frequently part of 'anti-journalism' attacks by conservative groups as female media creators and journalists are often the target for these groups. See, for example, www.politico.com/story/2018/11/09/trump-cnn-white-house-access-980280.
3 The deepfake 'is a prototype of Artificial Intelligence. It is significant to note that a deepfake is more than just two videos that have been merged together to form one video by a person or group using advanced image-editing software (such as Adobe Premiere). Instead, the creation of deepfakes result from feeding information into a computer and allowing that computer to learn from this corpus over time and generate new content' (Wagner and Blewer 2019).
4 According to the National Sexual Violence Research Centre, studies show a lower extreme of 2.1 percent and an upper extreme of 7.1 percent of false reporting. www.nsvrc.org/sites/default/files/Publications_NSVRC_Overview_False-Reporting.pdf.
5 And it is interesting that 'witch hunt' references a specific historical phenomenon in which women were harmed and murdered on the basis of being suspect, unbelievable, untrustworthy, and uncompliant with patriarchal expectations. Discursively, it taps into an anxiety about truth, believability, and authenticity that is deeply gendered.

References

Bailey, M. (2020). "A radical reckoning: A Black woman's racial revenge in Black mirror's Black museum." *Feminist Media Studies*. DOI: 10.1080/14680777.2020.1736120

Banet-Weiser, S. (2018). *Empowered: Popular Feminism and Popular Misogyny*. Durham, NC: Duke University Press.

Banet-Weiser, S. and Miltner, K. M. (2015). "# MasculinitySoFragile: Culture, structure, and networked misogyny." *Feminist Media Studies*, *16*(1), 171–174.

Broderick, R. (17 June 2014). Activists are outing hundreds of Twitter users believed to be 4chan trolls posing as feminists. *Buzzfeed News*. www.buzzfeednews.com/article/ryanhatesthis/your-slip-is-showing-4chan-trolls-operation-lollipop

Cole, S. (19 June 2019). "Deepfakes were created as a way to own women's bodies – we can't forget that." *Vice*. www.vice.com/en_us/article/j5kk9d/deepfakes-were-created-as-a-way-to-own-womens-bodieswe-cant-forget-that-v25n2

Davies, W. (19 September 2019). "Why can't we agree on what's true anymore?" *The Guardian*. www.theguardian.com/media/2019/sep/19/why-cant-we-agree-on-whats-true-anymore

Diop, A. (30 April 2019). "Black feminists on Twitter prove yet again we need to listen to them." https://theoutline.com/post/7374/black-feminists-on-twitter-prove-yet-again-we-need-to-listen-to-them?zd=1&zi=exoynzug

Donovan, J. (2019). "First they came for the black feminists." *New York Times*. https://www.nytimes.com/interactive/2019/08/15/opinion/gamergate-twitter.html#:~:text=First%20They%20Came%20for%20the%20Black%20Feminists.%20The,of%20color.%20By%20JOAN%20DONOVAN%20AUG.%2015%2C%202019

Ging, D. (2017). "Alphas, betas, and incels: Theorizing the masculinities of the manosphere." *Men and Masculinities*. https://journals.sagepub.com/doi/10.1177/1097184X17706401

Hampton, R. (2019). "The black feminists who saw the alt-right threat coming." *Slate*. https://slate.com/technology/2019/04/black-feminists-alt-right-twitter-gamergate.html

Jane, E. (2016). *Misogyny online: A short (and brutish) history*. London: Sage.

Johnson, M. (2017). "Being Black in a world where White lies matter." *The Undefeated*. https://theundefeated.com/features/being-black-in-a-world-where-white-lies-matter/

Kitroeff, N. (31 May 2020). "Mexico's President says most domestic violence calls are 'fake'." *New York Times*. www.nytimes.com/2020/05/31/world/americas/violence-women-mexico-president.html

Lyons, M. (2016). "Alt-right: More misogynistic than many neo-Nazis." https://threewayfight.blogspot.com/2016/12/alt-right-more-misogynistic-than-many.html

Occenola, P. (15 December 2018). "Fake news, real women: Disinformation gone macho." *The Rappler*. www.rappler.com/newsbreak/in-depth/217563-disinformation-gone-macho

Manne, K. (2018). *Down girl: The logic of misogyny*. Oxford: Oxford University Press.

Marwick, A. & Lewis, R. (2015). "Media manipulation and disinformation online." *Data & Society*. https://datasociety.net/pubs/oh/DataAndSociety_MediaManipulationAndDisinformationOnline.pdf

Massanari, A. (2017). "#Gamergate and the fappening: How Reddit's algorithm, governance, and culture support toxic technocultures." *New Media & Society*, *19*(3), 329–346.

Matchar, E. (26 February 2014). " 'Men's rights' activists are trying to redefine the meaning of rape." *New Republic*. https://newrepublic.com/article/116768/latest-target-mens-rights-movement-definition-rape

McCain, R. (17 July 2017). "Feminism's excuse factory: Nikki Yovino, title IX and false rape accusations." *The Other McCain*. http://theothermccain.com/2017/07/17/nikki-yovino-false-rape-accusation-campus-title-ix/

Negra, D. & Tasker, Y. (2014). *Gendering the recession: Media and culture in an age of austerity*. Durham, NC: Duke University Press.

Noble, S. (2018). *Algorithms of Oppression: How Search Engines Reinforce Racism*. New York: New York University Press.

Noble, S. (2020). "A conversation on algorithms and bias." *The Caret*. www.thecaret.co/posts/algorithmic-bias-search-engines-safiya-noble

Paris, B. & Donavan, J. (2019). "DeepFakes and cheap fakes: The manipulation of audio and visual evidence." *Data & Society*. https://datasociety.net/library/deepfakes-and-cheap-fakes/

Roiphe, K. (1994). *The morning after: Sex, fear and feminism*. Boston: Back Bay Books.

Rosin, H. (2013). *The end of men and the rise of women*. New York: Riverhead Books.

Sommers, C. H. (1994). *Who stole feminism: How women have betrayed women*. New York: Simon & Schuster.

Wagner, T. & Blewer, A. (2019). " 'The word real is no longer real': Deepfakes, gender, and the challengers of ai-altered video." *Open Information Science*, *3*, 32–46.

Warzel, C. (15 August 2019). "How an online mob created a playbook for a culture war." *New York Times*. www.nytimes.com/interactive/2019/08/15/opinion/what-is-gamergate.html

21

ANTI-IMMIGRATION DISINFORMATION

Eileen Culloty and Jane Suiter

Introduction

There is a long, global history of anti-immigrant disinformation and such narratives have come to the fore again in recent years. Although this chapter primarily focuses on Europe and the US, anti-immigrant disinformation is not limited to these regions. It also animates populist and far-right discourses in Africa (Kerr et al. 2019), Asia (Ramos 2020), and South America (Saad-Filho and Boffo 2020). Anti-immigrant disinformation is strongly associated with the ideology of exclusion and nativist supremacy that underpin right-wing populism and far-right extremism (Bajomi-Lázár 2019; Mudde 2019). Similarly to these ideologies, definitions of *disinformation* suffer from a lack of conceptual clarity. Populism is typically defined for its 'thin centred' ideology, which sets the homogeneous nation-state against threatening out-groups (Mudde 2019). While a nativist superiority is always implied in populist messaging (Mudde 2019), it is made explicit by far-right actors who denigrate immigrants, and often specific sub-groups of immigrants, as enemies of the nation. Thus, if populism has a 'mercurial nature' (Stanley 2008: 108) so, too, does disinformation.

Current definitions are broad (see Tandoc et al. 2018), encompassing content that is entirely fabricated, decontextualised, or propagandistic in intent (Wardle and Derakhshan 2017). Consequently, while some instances of 'fake news' are absurd and easily disproven, determining what is true or false is not as straightforward in many cases. Social and political issues such as immigration pose particular difficulty because the interpretation of facts is rarely objective or absolute (Coleman 2018: 157). For example, consider debates about the relationship between immigration and crime. This is a topic of long-standing and ongoing academic debate (see Ousey and Kubrin 2018), quite apart from its treatment by sensational media outlets and by populist and far-right actors.

Nevertheless, there is growing evidence that anti-immigrant disinformation plays a central role in 'digital hate culture' (Ganesh 2018). To explain these dynamics, in what follows, we outline anti-immigrant disinformation as a process that may be analysed in terms of actors, platforms, and audiences. So-called bad actors create and push anti-immigrant disinformation, different media platforms facilitate the distribution and promotion of this content, and, finally, the disinformation gains impact by finding receptive audiences who are willing to engage with

221

it. Understanding it in this way, we summarise key trends that drive anti-immigrant disinformation and consider a range of measures that may help to counteract it.

Anti-immigration actors

Those who create disinformation are often called 'bad actors' based on their intention to deceive or manipulate the public. However, the nature of bad actors is multifarious. They may represent individuals, social movements, states, or organisations; their primary motivations may be ideological, social, or financial; their campaigns may be isolated or coordinated; and their target audiences may be specific groups of voters or more general publics. All these factors are at play in anti-immigrant disinformation to varying degrees. In particular, anti-immigrant disinformation is associated with a wide range of right-wing populists, far-right extremists, and alt-right influencers (Hope Not Hate 2019). Although these actors share a common opposition to immigration, they are ideologically diverse in many respects (see Carter 2018; Davey and Ebner 2017; Holt et al. 2020). As a detailed discussion of these ideological differences is beyond the scope of this chapter, we focus here on recent evidence of anti-immigrant disinformation by the far-right, populist politicians, and the alt-right in Europe and the US and on the role of media actors in the promotion of anti-immigrant disinformation.

The advent of the web enabled far-right extremists to develop geographically distant communities (Meddaugh and Kay 2009) while the subsequent development of social media created opportunities for more personal communication strategies (Törnberg and Wahlström 2018). For these far-right communities, anti-immigrant disinformation bolsters community cohesion (Törnberg and Wahlström 2018) and is a means of promoting anti-immigrant attitudes among the wider public (Ekman 2019). In other words, anti-immigrant disinformation serves different functions and is packaged for different audiences across different platforms (see the next section for a detailed discussion).

In recent years, there has been evidence of increased transnational cooperation among these communities (Avaaz 2019; Davey and Ebner 2017). For example, Avaaz (2019) found evidence of transnational coordination among the far-right ahead of national elections in Germany and France. Similarly, there is evidence of a coordinated campaign against the 2018 Global Compact for Safe, Orderly and Regular Migration (GCM). Proponents of this campaign were responsible for almost half the most popular YouTube videos about the GCM and falsely claimed the GCM required states to outlaw criticism of immigration (ISD 2019). In their Twitter analysis of far-right activity in France, Germany, Italy, and the UK, Froio and Ganesh (2018) found that coordination coalesced around the issue of Muslim immigration, which was commonly framed as a threat to Europe's security, economy, and culture. On this basis, the authors concluded that Islamophobia is the 'transnational glue of the far-right' (Froio and Ganesh 2018: 19). More recently, far-right groups have also exploited the COVID-19 crisis to circulate disinformation about immigrants and Muslim immigrants in particular. A recurring theme accuses immigrants of defying isolation measures to reinforce the nativist narrative that migrants do not belong in the nation (Culloty 2020; Parveen 2020).

In many countries, high-profile political actors have normalised anti-immigrant disinformation (Crandall et al. 2018), often in compliance with sympathetic media outlets. For example, Hungary's immigration levels are low, but Prime Minister Viktor Orbán consistently characterises immigrants and pro-immigration 'elites' as major threats to the state (Bajomi-Lázár 2019; Kiss and Szabó 2018). This disinformation campaign has been aided by the government's control over media outlets (Bajomi-Lázár 2019). In the US, Donald Trump's 2016 election campaign generated fears about Mexicans 'swarming' over the southern border and promised to 'build a wall' to protect the integrity of the state. Although Trump's rhetoric was largely directed at Mexicans, media outlets such as Breitbart extended the fear mongering to include Muslims (Benkler, Faris and Roberts 2018; Kamenova and Pingaud 2017). In the UK, pro-Brexit rhetoric focused heavily on immigration from Eastern Europe and the Middle East. Legal EU immigration was frequently confused with asylum-seeking as the Vote Leave campaign stoked fears of an imminent arrival of millions of Turks (Ker-Lindsay 2018) while the right-wing press amplified these views (Holbolt 2016; Morrison 2019). Thus, the emphasis on immigration from predominately Muslim countries provides common ground between the far-right and right-wing populists.

Elements of the news media have long been accused of providing negative coverage of immigration and legitimising anti-immigration political action (Philo et al. 2013). The news media are also predisposed to using fear as a framing device in news stories about immigration (Yadamsuren and Heinström 2011). Consequently, news stories about refugees and immigrants tend to focus on crime, public unrest, and violence resulting in a perpetual flow of 'bad news' about immigrants and refugees (Philo et al. 2013). As a result, the news media provide right-wing populists and the far-right with stories that can be repurposed and de-contextualised to emphasise their own agenda (Ekman 2019).

In terms of promoting false claims about immigration, the so-called 'alt-right' are perhaps more influential on social media, not least because their disinformation tactics and racist messaging are more ambiguous and less overt than those of the far right (Marwick and Lewis 2017). Hartzell (2018: 8) characterises the alt-right as the 'youthful, intellectual, pro-white' faction of the far right, which acts as a bridge between 'mainstream public discourse and white nationalism'. Overall, the diversity of the actors responsible for anti-immigrant disinformation creates different points of exposure for audiences and different rhetorical strategies and tactics through which disinformation is packaged. As Fekete argues (2014), contemporary media facilitate a process of 'cumulative racism' as anti-immigrant disinformation travels from the fringe to the mainstream and back again. Nativist, racist, and xenophobic narratives which were previously marginalised on fringe far-right websites – where people had to actively seek them out – now reach a wider audience on popular social media platforms such as Facebook and Twitter (Ekman 2019; Farkas et al. 2018). It is to these platforms and audiences that we now turn.

Digital platforms and disinformation tactics

The infrastructure of platforms facilitates anti-immigrant disinformation in many ways. Engagement metrics incentivise attention-grabbing, low-quality content, and these metrics can be manipulated by bad actors who piggyback on trending content and use false accounts and automated 'bots' to inflate the popularity of content (Shao et al. 2018). Moreover, micro-targeting services and recommendation algorithms define users by interests with little regard for whether these interests are extremist (Angwin et al. 2017). More generally, platforms enable disinformation to travel at an unprecedented speed and scale. Törnberg and Wahlström (2018) argue that social media provide multiple opportunity mechanisms for anti-immigrant disinformation, including discursive opportunities to exploit topical issues, group dynamic opportunities to strengthen community ties, and coordination opportunities to target different audiences. In this context, some argue that social media platforms have given rise to a digital hate culture (Ganesh 2018) augmented by the coordinated action of anonymous and automated accounts (Phillips 2015; Zannettou et al. 2018).

As noted earlier, the far-right uses different platforms for community building and targeting wider audiences. The segmentation of the far right's online activity is partially a response to pressure from internet service providers (ISPs); as ISPs removed technical support from platforms known to foster extremist ideologies, activity moved to new platforms with strict free speech policies (Zannettou et al. 2018). Consequently, anti-immigrant disinformation campaigns are coordinated on these lesser-known online platforms, and the messages are then disseminated to a wider audience on popular platforms such as Twitter and Facebook (Davey and Ebner 2017; Marwick and Lewis 2017).

Platform affordances also facilitate the online manipulation and disinformation tactics of the far right and the alt-right. These activities broadly revolve around four tactics: appropriating existing hashtags (Jackson and Foucault Welles 2015), decontextualising news stories (Wardle and Derakhshan 2017), the use of memes (Ekman 2019), and automated bots (Avaaz 2019). In a detailed analysis of Twitter activity, Graham (2016) identified key disinformation tactics that enable anti-immigrant actors to direct their messages to a wider, mainstream audience. Actors utilise 'piggybacking' and 'backstaging' manipulation tactics to infiltrate trending topics while the 'narrating' tactic inverts the meaning of trending topics to reframe the original meaning through irony.

This process of appropriating existing hashtags has also been characterised in terms of 'hijacking' (Jackson and Foucault Welles 2015) and the promotion of 'critical counter-narratives' (Poole et al. 2019). For example, during the 2016 US presidential election, far-right activists routinely used the hashtag #StopIslam in conjunction with pro-Trump and anti-Clinton hashtags as part of a broader effort to normalise an anti-immigration narrative and to introduce anti-immigrant disinformation into the election campaign (Poole et al. 2019). Other studies have identified the use of this manipulation tactic in relation to the refugee crisis (Siapera et al. 2018) and Brexit (Green et al. 2016). These hashtag campaigns support the formation of 'affective' (Papacharissi 2015) or 'ad hoc' (Dawes 2017) publics that facilitate the circulation (Groshek and Koc-Michalska 2017) and fermentation (Farkas et al. 2017) of far-right narratives and attitudes. While the ad hoc publics created by hashtag campaigns tend to be short lived (Poole et al. 2019; Dawes 2017), they have a 'liminal' power to disorientate and confuse public debate (Siapera et al. 2018).

Decontextualisation is another simple but effective disinformation tactic (Wardle and Derakhshan 2017). By omitting key explanatory factors, adding textual amendments, or adopting different naming standards, a relatively neutral story can be transformed into one that is imbued with racist or anti-immigrant disinformation (Ekman 2019). In contrast to 'fake news' that is entirely fabricated, these disinformation stories contain nuggets of truth that are corroborated by mainstream news sources. As noted, decontextualisation tactics are challenging in the case of immigration because there is an ongoing dispute about how to establish facts and interpret immigration statistics (Ousey and Kubrin 2018).

To appeal to a broader, younger audience, anti-immigrant actors also make extensive use of memes, music videos, jokes, and irony (Beran 2017; Luke 2016; Marwick and Lewis 2017; Nagle 2017). Ekman (2019) outlines how these manipulation tactics result in the gradual normalisation of previously unacceptable utterances: utterances that dehumanise immigrants and even denigrate them as legitimate targets of violence. The participatory culture of digital media is central to the success of this tactic. For example, Marwick and Lewis (2017: 4) found that memes often function as image macros that are engineered to 'go viral' by conveying far-right ideology through humour.

As with disinformation generally, automated bots and fake accounts are frequently used to inflate the popularity of anti-immigrant disinformation. Avaaz (2019) investigated far-right disinformation on Facebook ahead of the European Parliament elections. In response, Facebook removed 77 pages and 230 accounts from France, Germany, Italy, Poland, Spain, and the

UK. Facebook estimated that this content reached 32 million people and generated 67 million 'interactions' through comments, likes, and shares (Avaaz 2019). Across the countries, fake and duplicate accounts artificially inflated the popularity of anti-immigrant disinformation. In some cases, Facebook pages were deceptively branded as lifestyle content to attract followers and then switched abruptly to a focus on immigration.

While platforms have made some moves to counteract extremist content, the European Commission's Assessment of the Implementation of the Code of Practice on Disinformation[1] in May 2020 found that the platforms' self-regulatory response is beset with a lack of uniform implementation, and, consequently, progress is uneven. It is likely that platforms will come under increasing pressure to address this issue. However, we suggest that addressing disinformation is not simply a matter of targeting the actors who create it and the platforms that facilitate it: audiences are a central part of the equation.

Receptive audiences

Audiences are arguably the most important element of the disinformation process because disinformation only gains impact if people are willing to believe, endorse, and share it. Crucially, repeated exposure to anti-immigrant disinformation can have an impact quite apart from any bias on the part of the individual (Fazio et al. 2015). Thus, reducing overall exposure to anti-immigrant disinformation is a crucial countermeasure. However, as noted earlier, it can sometimes be difficult to distinguish anti-immigrant disinformation from criticism or opposition to immigration more generally. This is further complicated by the fact that certain segments of the public are concerned, rightly or wrongly, about immigration and its implications.

Although it is difficult to make any causal connection between anti-immigrant disinformation and public attitudes towards immigrants, evidence suggests that digital media/digital platforms are key points of exposure to extremist ideas (Hamm and Spaaij 2017; McCauley and Moskalenko 2011). In a study of social media conversations across 28 European countries over a one-year period, Bakamo Social (2018) identified five major immigration narratives. A resounding anti-immigrant stance was evident across the online conversations with varying levels of intensity in individual countries. The humanitarianism narrative (49.9 percent) concerned moral obligations to support refugees, but included arguments for and against humanitarianism. The security narrative (25.9 percent) focused on the threat of immigration in terms of immigrant crime and terror attacks while the identity narrative (15.3 percent) concerned perceived threats to social cohesion and the traditional identity of European countries. Finally, the economic narrative (8 percent) and the demographics narrative (1 percent) focused on issues of sustainability.

At the country level, identity narratives were most prevalent in Germany, The Netherlands, and Slovakia while security narratives dominated in Hungary, Poland, Estonia, and Austria. Identity and security narratives also subverted discussions of humanitarianism. For example, in France, the humanitarian narrative was undermined by those questioning whether refugees were genuinely in need of assistance while in Spain, the humanitarian narrative was subverted by concerns that left-wing politicians would prioritise the needs of migrants over Spaniards. Consequently, those advocating humanitarianism were characterised as a threat to the welfare of European countries (Bakamo Social 2018). Within the national security narrative, anti-immigrant attitudes and disinformation are entangled in broader arguments about multiculturalism and the supposed decline of national identity (Juhász and Szicherle 2017).

In this regard, anti-immigrant attitudes and the appeal of anti-immigrant disinformation have been contextualised in relation to patterns of economic and social change and the decline of traditional party systems (Horgan and Haltinner 2015; Schain 2018). For example, across Europe and North America, the decline of working-class communities is linked to alienation and opposition to immigration (Gusterson 2017; Hobolt 2016; Goodwin and Heath 2016; Inglehart and Norris 2016). In this context, bad actors frame immigration as an economic threat by arguing that immigrants depress wages and increase the tax burden for 'native' citizens (Horgan and Haltinner 2015). In other words, while disinformation and manipulation tactics play a key role in the communication strategies of anti-immigrant actors, it is important to recognise the real or perceived grievances that make these views appealing to segments of the public.

Another key backdrop to these developments is the crisis of legitimacy within democracy (Bennett and Livingston 2018), whereby trust in democratic institutions has declined in tandem with the rise of digital media and the flourishing of alternative information sources. Moreover, the anti-immigration actors identified earlier actively promote distrust in the mainstream media, particularly regarding immigration reporting (Andersson 2017 cited in Ekman 2019). This declining trust reflects growing political polarisation (Suiter and Fletcher 2020) as well as growing use of social media for news (Kalogeropoulos et al. 2019). Consequently, it is important to recognise that a wide range of factors and circumstances overlap to provide fertile ground for actors seeking to exploit public tensions and concerns about immigration. Moreover, addressing these issues extends far beyond the problem of disinformation and how to counter it.

Conclusion

Anti-immigrant disinformation is a complex object of study, given the definitional challenges and the overlap of factors that enable the promotion of disinformation and render audiences receptive to it. The network of actors who push anti-immigrant disinformation is strikingly diverse. In many respects, anti-immigrant disinformation is part of a culture war in which an ecosystem of actors (far right, alt-right, populist, and conservative) reinforces a common opposition to a pluralist worldview. The design of each platform gives rise to distinct forms of participation, which make it difficult to operationalise a consistent set of indicators (Crosset et al. 2019), and the speed of change – with disinformation tactics evolving in response to countermeasures – makes it difficult to develop a reliable method of data collection (Marwick and Lewis 2017).

In terms of counteracting anti-immigrant disinformation, more research is needed to understand what makes different audiences receptive to anti-immigrant messages. Research shows that the negative framing of immigration can affect public attitudes and voting behaviour. However, quite apart from any bias on the part of the individual, repeated exposure can increase perceptions of credibility over time (Fazio et al. 2015). Thus, reducing exposure to disinformation and providing more supports to help audiences evaluate online content appear to be key for mitigating disinformation (Schleicher 2019). Various regulatory, legal, educational, and technological measures have been proposed to counteract disinformation, but to date we know little about the effectiveness of these measures in general and in the context of anti-immigrant disinformation specifically. In this regard, as with social media research generally, researchers are impeded by a lack of quality data from the social media platforms.

Proponents of critical thinking and information literacy highlight the importance of strengthening the capacity of individuals to evaluate content (Schleicher 2019). This is often accompanied by calls for technological approaches that filter out extremist content or flag disinformation. However, research remains limited, and there are contradictory findings about the effectiveness of these approaches. It is likely that countering disinformation and helping audiences evaluate online content will require more systematic action. In this regard, Janda and Víchová (2019) call for a 'whole of society approach' that rests on cooperation between technology companies, governments, civil society organisations, and individuals.

It is clear that the regulatory environment has failed to keep pace with the rapid evolution of digital platforms and their use for political campaigning and propaganda (Jones 2019). However, the regulatory debate is often distorted by far-right activists who claim freedom of expression as a defence for the promotion of extremist agendas (O'Hagan 2018). As Jones (2019: 50) argues, 'freedom of expression does not entail that there must be no restriction of online political content; rather, that any restriction must be properly tailored'. Thus, the major challenge for countering far-right and extremist disinformation rests on the wider issue of establishing normative frameworks for the online environment.

Finally, the proliferation of anti-immigrant disinformation requires attention from mainstream media and politicians in terms of how immigration is discussed and reported. While the online environment is flooded with disinformation, mainstream news media remains highly influential. It is vital that these outlets offer audiences a comprehensive and accurate understanding of issues relating to immigration and avoid platforming extremist views for sensational coverage. In other words, there is no magic bullet to counter anti-immigrant disinformation. It requires a 'whole of society' approach that engages top-down approaches to regulating and monitoring the information and security environments as well as bottom-up approaches to everyday media practices at organisational and individual levels.

Note

1 https://ec.europa.eu/digital-single-market/en/news/study-assessment-implementation-code-practice-disinformation.

References

Andersson, U. (2017), 'Lågt förtroende för rapporteringen om invandring [Low Trust in Immigration Reporting]', In Ulrika Andersson, Anders Ericson, Kristoffer Holt, Bengt Johansson, Michael Karlsson, Torbjörn von Krogh, Edvard Lind, Jesper Strömbäck and Lennart Weibull (eds), *Misstron Mot Medier [The Distrust of Media]*. Stockholm: Institutet för Mediestudier, pp. 17–50.

Angwin, J., Varner, M. and Tobin, A. (2017), 'ProPublica, Facebook Enabled Advertisers to Reach "Jew Haters"'. *ProPublica*, 14 September. www.propublica.org/article/facebook-enabled-advertisers-to-reach-jew-haters

Avaaz (2019), *Far Right Networks of Deception*, London: Avaaz.

Bajomi-Lázár, P. (2019), 'An Anti-Migration Campaign and Its Impact on Public Opinion: The Hungarian Case'. *European Journal of Communication*, 34(6), 619–628.

Bakamo Social (2018), *Migration Narratives in Europe 2017–2018*. London: Bakamo Social.

Benkler, Yochai, Robert Faris and Hal Roberts (2018), *Network Propaganda: Manipulation, Disinformation, and Radicalization in American Politics*. London: Oxford University Press.

Bennett, W. L. and S. Livingston (2018), 'The Disinformation Order: Disruptive Communication and the Decline of Democratic Institutions'. *European Journal of Communication*, 33(2), 122–139.

Beran, D. (2017), '4chan: The Skeleton Key to the Rise of Trump'. *Medium.com*, 14 February, accessed 20 January 2020. https://medium.com/@DaleBeran/4chan-the-skeleton-key-to-the-rise-of-trump-624e7cb798cb.

Carter, E. (2018), 'Right-Wing Extremism/Radicalism: Reconstructing the Concept'. *Journal of Political Ideologies*, 23(2), 157–182.

Coleman, S. (2018). 'The Elusiveness of Political Truth: From the Conceit of Objectivity to Intersubjective Judgement'. *European Journal of Communication*, 33(2), 157–171.

Crandall, C. S., J. M. Miller and M. H. White (2018), 'Changing Norms Following the 2016 U.S. Presidential Election: The Trump Effect on Prejudice'. *Social Psychological and Personality Science*, 9, 186–192.

Crosset, V., S. Tanner and A. Campana (2019), 'Researching Far Right Groups on Twitter: Methodological Challenges 2.0'. *New Media & Society*, 21(4), 939–961.

Culloty, E. (2020), *The Anti-Democratic Narratives Surrounding COVID-19*. Dublin: FuJo Institute. https://fujomedia.eu/the-anti-democratic-narratives-surrounding-covid-19/

Davey, J. and Julia Ebner (2017), *The Fringe Insurgency: Connectivity, Convergence and Mainstreaming of the Extreme Right*. London: Institute for Strategic Dialogue.

Dawes, Simon (2017), '#JeSuisCharlie, #JeNeSuisPasCharlie and Ad Hoc Publics'. In Gavan Titley, Des Freedman, Gholam Khiabany and Aurélien Mondon (eds), *After Charlie Hebdo: Terror, Racism and Free Speech*, London: Zed Books, pp. 180–191.

Ekman, M. (2019), 'Anti-Immigration and Racist Discourse in Social Media'. *European Journal of Communication*, 34(6), 606–618.

Farkas, J., J. Schou and C. Neumayer (2017), 'Cloaked Facebook Pages: Exploring Fake Islamist Propaganda in Social Media'. *New Media & Society*, 20(5), 1850–1867.

Farkas, J, J. Schou and C. Neumayer (2018), 'Platformed Antagonism: Racist Discourses on Fake Muslim Facebook Pages'. *Critical Discourse Studies*, 15(5), 463–480.

Fazio, L. K., M. N. Brashier, B. K. Payne and E. J. Marsh (2015), 'Knowledge Does Not Protect Against Illusory Truth'. *Journal of Experimental Psychology: General*, 144(5), 993–1002.

Fekete L. (2014). 'Anti-Fascism or Anti-Extremism?' *Race & Class*, 55(4), 29–39.

Froio, C. and B. Ganesh (2018), 'The Transnationalisation of Far-Right Discourse on Twitter: Issues and Actors That Cross Borders in Western European Democracies'. *European Societies*, 21(4), 513–539.

Ganesh, B. (2018), 'The Ungovernability of Digital Hate Culture'. *Journal of International Affairs*, 71(2), 30–49.

Goodwin, M. J. and O. Heath (2016), 'The 2016 Referendum, Brexit and the Left Behind: An Aggregate-Level Analysis of the Result'. *The Political Quarterly*, 87(3), 323–332.

Graham, R. (2016), 'Inter-Ideological Mingling: White Extremist Ideology Entering the Mainstream on Twitter'. *Sociological Spectrum*, 36(1), 24–36.

Green, S. F., C. Gregory, M. Reeves, J. K. Cowan, O. Demetriou, I. Koch, M. Carrithers, R. Andersson, A. Gingrich, S. Macdonald and S. C. Açiksöz (2016), 'Brexit Referendum: First Reactions from Anthropology'. *Social Anthropology*, 24(4), 478–502.

Groshek, J. and K. Koc-Michalska (2017), 'Helping Populism Win? Social Media Use, Filter Bubbles, and Support for Populist Presidential Candidates in the 2016 US Election Campaign'. *Information, Communication & Society*, 20(9), 1389–1407.

Gusterson, H. (2017), 'From Brexit to Trump: Anthropology and the Rise of Nationalist Populism'. *American Ethnologist*, 44(2), 209–214.

Hamm, Mark S. and Ramon Spaaij (2017), *The Age of Lone Wolf Terrorism*, New York: Columbia University Press.

Hartzell, S. (2018) '"Alt-White: Conceptualizing the "Alt-Right" as a Rhetorical Bridge Between White Nationalism and Mainstream Public Discourse'. *Journal of Contemporary Rhetoric*, 8(2), 6–25.

Hobolt, S. B. (2016), 'The Brexit Vote: A Divided Nation, a Divided Continent'. *Journal of European Public Policy*, 23(9), 1259–1277.

Hogan, J. and Haltinner, K. (2015), 'Floods, Invaders, and Parasites: Immigration Threat Narratives and Right-Wing Populism in the USA, UK and Australia'. *Journal of Intercultural Studies*, 36(5), 520–543. DOI: 10.1080/07256868.2015.1072907

Holt, T. J., J. D. Freilich and S. M. Chermak (2020), 'Examining the Online Expression of Ideology Among Far-Right Extremist Forum Users', *Terrorism and Political Violence*. DOI: 10.1080/09546553.2019.1701446

Hope Not Hate (2019), *State of Hate 2019*. London: Hope Not Hate.

Inglehart, R. F. and P. Norris (2016), 'Trump, Brexit, and the Rise of Populism: Economic Have-Nots and Cultural Backlash', *HKS Faculty Research Working Paper Series*, RWP16–026, accessed 20 January 2020. www.hks.harvard.edu/publications/trump-brexit-and-rise-populism-economic-have-nots-and-cultural-backlash#citation

Institute for Strategic Dialogue (2019), 'ISD Research Featured in POLITICO About the Trolling of the UN Migration Pact'. Institute for Strategic Dialogue, accessed 20 January 2020. www.isdglobal.org/isd-research-featured-in-politico-surroundingthe-trolling-of-the-un-migration-pact/

Jackson, S. J. and B. Foucault Welles (2015), 'Hijacking #myNYPD: Social Media Dissent and Networked Counterpublics', *Journal of Communication*, 65(6), 932–952.

Janda, J. and V. Víchová (2019), 'What Can We Learn from Russian Hostile Information Operations in Europe?' In Vasu Norman, Jayakumar Shashi and Ang Benjamin (eds), *DRUMS: Distortions, Rumours, Untruths, Misinformation, and Smears*. Singapore: World Scientific, pp. 133–146.

Jones, K. (2019), 'Online Disinformation and Political Discourse: Applying a Human Rights Framework'. *Chatham House International Law Programme*, 6 November, accessed 20 January 2020. www.chathamhouse.org/publication/online-disinformation-and-political-discourse-applying-human-rights-framework

Juhász, Attila and Patrik Szicherle (2017). *The Political Effects of Migration-Related Fake News, Disinformation and Conspiracy Theories in Europe*. Budapest: Friedrich Ebert Stiftung and Political Capital.

Kalogeropoulos, A., J. Suiter and I. Udris (2019), 'News Media and News Consumption: Factors Predicting Trust in News in 35 Countries'. *International Journal of Communication*, 13, 3672–3693.

Kamenova, D. and E. Pingaud (2017), 'Anti-Migration and Islamophobia: Web Populism and Targeting the "Easiest Other"'. In Mojca Pajnik and Birgit Sauer (eds), *Populism and the Web: Communicative Practices of Parties and Movements in Europe*. London: Routledge, pp. 108–121.

Ker-Lindsay, J. (2018), 'Turkey's EU Accession as a Factor in the 2016 Brexit Referendum'. *Turkish Studies*, 19(1), 1–22.

Kerr, P., K. Durrheim and J. Dixon (2019), 'Xenophobic Violence and Struggle Discourse in South Africa'. *Journal of Asian and African Studies*, 54(7), 995–1011.

Kiss, B. and G. Szabó (2018), 'Constructing Political Leadership During the 2015 European Migration Crisis: The Hungarian Case'. *Central European Journal of Communication*, 11(1), 9–24.

Luke, T. W. (2016), 'Overtures for the Triumph of the Tweet: White Power Music and the Alt-Right in 2016'. *New Political Science*, 39(2), 277–282.

Marwick, Alice and Rebecca Lewis (2017), *Media Manipulation and Disinformation Online*. New York: Data & Society Research Institute.

McCauley, Clark and Sophia Moskalenko (2011), *Friction: How Radicalization Happens to Them and Us*. Oxford: Oxford University Press.

Meddaugh, P. M. and J. Kay (2009), '"Hate Speech" or "Reasonable Racism"? The Other in Stormfront'. *Journal of Mass Media Ethics*, 24(4), 251–268.

Morrison, J. (2019). 'Re-Framing Free Movement in the Countdown to Brexit? Shifting UK Press Portrayals of EU Migrants in the Wake of the Referendum'. *The British Journal of Politics and International Relations*, 21(3), 594–611.

Mudde, Cas (2019), *The Far Right Today*. Oxford: Polity.

Nagle, Angela (2017), *Kill All Normies: Online Culture Wars from 4Chan and Tumblr to Trump and the Alt-Right*. Alresford: John Hunt Publishing.

O'Hagan, E. (2018), 'The Far Right Is Rising, and Britain Is Dangerously Complacent About It'. *The Guardian*, 7 May, accessed 20 January 2020. www.theguardian.com/commentisfree/2018/may/07/far-right-britain-freedom-of-speech

Ousey, G. and C. Kubrin (2018), 'Immigration and Crime: Assessing a Contentious Issues'. *Annual Review Criminology*, 1, 63–84.

Papacharissi, Zizi (2015). *Affective Publics: Sentiment, Technology, and Politics*. New York: Oxford University Press.

Parveen, N. (2020), 'Police Investigate UK Far-Right Groups Over Anti-Muslim Coronavirus Claims', *The Guardian*, 5 April. www.theguardian.com/world/2020/apr/05/police-investigate-uk-far-right-groups-over-anti-muslim-coronavirus-claims

Phillips, Whitney (2015), *This Is Why We Can't Have Nice Things: Mapping the Relationship Between Online Trolling and Mainstream Culture*. Cambridge, MA: MIT Press.

Philo, Greg, Emma Briant and Pauline Donald (2013), *Bad News for Refugees*. London: Pluto Press.

Poole, E., E. Giraud and E. de Quincey (2019), 'Contesting #StopIslam: The Dynamics of a Counter-Narrative Against Right-Wing Populism'. *Open Library of Humanities*, 5(1), http://doi.org/10.16995/olh.406.

Ramos, C. G. (2020), 'Change Without Transformation: Social Policy Reforms in the Philippines Under Duterte', *Development and Change*, 51(2), 485–505.

Saad-Filho, A. and Boffo, M. (2020), 'The Corruption of Democracy: Corruption Scandals, Class Alliances, and Political Authoritarianism in Brazil'. *Geoforum*. https://doi.org/10.1016/j.geoforum.2020.02.003

Schain, M. (2018), *Shifting Tides: Radical-Right Populism and Immigration Policy in Europe and the United States*. Washington, DC: Migration Policy Institute.

Schleicher, A. (2019), 'Distinguishing Fact from Fiction in the Modern Age', in Vasu Norman, Jayakumar Shashi and Ang Benjamin (eds), *DRUMS: Distortions, Rumours, Untruths, Misinformation, and Smears*. Singapore: World Scientific, pp. 159–170.

Shao, C., G. L. Ciampaglia, O. Varol, K. C. Yang, A. Flammini and F. Menczer (2018), 'The Spread of Low-Credibility Content by Social Bots'. *Nature Communications*, 9(1), 4787. https://doi.org/10.1038/s41467-018-06930-7. PMID: 30459415; PMCID: PMC6246561

Siapera, E., M. Boudourides, S. Lenis and J. Suiter (2018), 'Refugees and Network Publics on Twitter: Networked Framing, Affect, and Capture'. *Social Media + Society*, 4(1), 1–21.

Stanley, B. (2008), 'The Thin Ideology of Populism'. *Journal of Political Ideologies*, 13(1), 95–110.

Suiter, J. and R. Fletcher (2020), 'Polarisation and Inequality: Key Drivers of Declining Trust in News'. *European Journal of Communication*. In Press.

Tandoc, E. C., Z. W. Lim and R. Ling (2018), 'Defining "Fake News": A Typology of Scholarly Definitions'. *Digital Journalism*, 6(2), 137–153.

Törnberg, A. and M. Wahlström (2018), 'Unveiling the Radical Right Online: Exploring Framing and Identity in an Online Anti-Immigrant Discussion Group'. *Sociologisk Forskning*, 55(2–3), 267–292.

Wardle, Claire and Hossein Derakhshan (2017), *Information Disorder: Toward an Interdisciplinary Framework for Research and Policy Making*. Strasbourg: Council of Europe Report DGI(2017)09.

Yadamsuren, B. and J. Heinström (2011), 'Emotional Reactions to Incidental Exposure to Online News'. *Information Research*, 16(3).

Zannettou, S., B. Bradlyn, E. De Cristofaro, H. Kwak, M. Sirivianos, G. Stringini and J. Blackburn (2018), 'What Is Gab: A Bastion of Free Speech or an Alt-Right Echo Chamber?' In *Companion Proceedings of the Web Conference 2018*. New York: ACM, pp. 1007–1014.

22

SCIENCE AND THE POLITICS OF MISINFORMATION

Jeremy Levy, Robin Bayes, Toby Bolsen, and James N. Druckman

The transformation of the communication environment has been a defining feature of the twenty-first century. The emergence of media choice at the end of the twentieth century (e.g. cable news, the internet) and later social media means we now live in a 'fragmented and polarized media environment' (Iyengar and Massey 2019). This brings a host of positive consequences, such as easier access to information and worldwide connectivity, but it also introduces new challenges, such as echo chambers in which people evade information contrary to their standing beliefs (Sunstein 2001). Perhaps the most troubling consequence is the increased likelihood of misinformation and fake news: there are no longer trusted gatekeepers who curate information for accuracy, so anyone can claim to be an expert while disseminating falsehoods.

Misinformation has become a global problem that affects all aspects of life and garners much attention in the political sphere. This is in part due to the 2016 US election, when the Russian government created fake social media avatars with names like 'Blacktivist' and 'army_of_jesus' to stoke partisan outrage, duping millions of Americans into sharing memes about the turpitude of opposing partisans (e.g. Grinberg et al. 2019). Misinformation about science, however, poses a distinct challenge. Science exists to provide systematic knowledge to improve decision-making (Dietz 2013), but the changed media environment has undermined the privileged cultural authority of science by allowing anyone to claim to be 'scientific'.

There is an urgency to understand and address science misinformation, illuminated most recently by the COVID-19 pandemic. As we write this chapter, the social-scientific community is mobilising to advise political actors about the behavioral challenges posed by COVID-19 (Van Bavel et al. 2020). This includes the major challenge of communicating science to the public. Internationally and within the United States, government leaders differ dramatically in their embrace or disdain of scientific expertise. Early evidence indicates that false information, rumours, and conspiracy theories proliferate through the public. At minimum, this misinformation strains experts' abilities to communicate to the public and coordinate policy; at worst, it leads individuals to make decisions that are downright dangerous.

In this chapter, we summarise research on scientific misinformation and the challenges it poses to the implementation of government policy. Science is certainly valuable for individual decision-making in personal health and other domains. The challenge here is that science in the public sphere often becomes politicised (Oreskes and Conway 2010), with public attitudes and public policies diverging from scientific consensus on topics such as climate change, genetically modified organisms (GMOs), and vaccines (Flynn et al. 2017; Scheufele and Krause 2019). In what follows, we define the problem of science misinformation and misperceptions, discuss its causes, and review potential antidotes.

Contradicting the best available evidence: definitions and nomenclature

One challenge in studying misinformation concerns the proliferation of terms throughout the literature. We thus hope to offer some conceptual clarity. First, we distinguish between communications and beliefs. *Misinformation* refers to a communication that is 'false, misleading, or [based on] unsubstantiated information' (Nyhan and Reifler 2010: 304). This comes in various guises: rumours, defined as misinformation that 'acquire[s its] power through widespread social transmission' (Berinsky 2017: 242–243); fake news, defined as misinformation that 'mimics news media content in form but not in organizational process or intent' (Lazer et al. 2018: 1094); and conspiracy theories attributing events to 'the machinations of powerful people, who attempt to conceal their role' (Sunstein and Vermeule 2009: 205). *Misperceptions*, in contrast, are attitudes – they are 'cases in which people's beliefs about factual matters are not supported by clear evidence and expert opinion – a definition that includes both false and unsubstantiated beliefs about the world' (Nyhan and Reifler 2010: 305).

What, then, does it mean to be 'false' or 'not supported by clear evidence'? This is particularly tricky when it comes to science: the evidentiary standard is ambiguous because the scientific method never allows one to prove a hypothesis is correct. We build on Nyhan and Reifler (2010) and Flynn et al. (2017), who differentiate between information or perceptions that are (1) 'demonstrably false' – that is, contradictory to objective empirical evidence – and (2) 'unsubstantiated' – that is, unsupported by evidence and expert opinion. This distinction may have normative implications as Levy (2020) investigates whether demonstrably false and unsubstantiated misperceptions differ in their prevalence and the extent to which they can be corrected. But when it comes to science, the unsubstantiated standard seems most appropriate, given the impossibility of definitive conclusions. Thus, we define scientific misinformation as a claim made in political communications that is unsupported or contradicted by the scientific community's best available information (Druckman 2015).

Why should we care if people are misinformed about science? First, it undermines the scientific community's ability to provide systematic knowledge to 'help nonscientists make better decisions' (Lupia 2013: 14048). Further, it can be worse for an individual to be misinformed and hold inaccurate beliefs than to be uninformed and hold no factual beliefs on some topic. When individuals form subjective attitudes from misperceptions, their decisions do not occur randomly but become systematically and deleteriously skewed (Kuklinski et al. 2000: 792–793). On the collective level, 'misinformation may form the basis for political and societal decisions that run counter to a society's best interest' (Lewandowsky et al. 2012: 107).

Science misinformation as a public problem

The exact prevalence of misinformation and misperceptions is not entirely clear. What is clear, we think, is that some degree of public concern is warranted. But it is still important to keep in mind certain findings that may temper our alarm about misinformation in general. For example, political misinformation in the 2016 US election

> only reached a small proportion of the public who have the most conservative online information diets [Guess et al. 2020] and who are heavy Internet users (Nelson and Taneja 2018), while those who are exposed to misinformation do not always believe what they read (Allcott and Gentzkow 2017).
>
> (Li 2020: 126)

Yet, given the extent to which science is interwoven into governmental decision-making (Dietz 2013), there may be unique reasons to be concerned when it comes to misperceptions about science. Many of the most prominent misperceptions concern science topics. In a meta-analysis on health-related information, particularly vaccines and infectious diseases, Wang et al. (2019: 8) conclude, 'there is broad consensus that misinformation is highly prevalent on social media and tends to be more popular than accurate information'. In addition, large proportions of the public hold misperceptions about climate change, the safety of GMOs, or a link between vaccines and autism (Flynn et al. 2017). Using 2019 ANES data, Jerit et al. (2020) show that the percent of respondents holding these misperceptions are 25.4 percent, 46.6 percent, and 15.5 percent, respectively. Sixty percent of respondents held at least one misperception, and individuals holding misinformed beliefs were confident in their answers.

A further reason for concern is that people do not invariably update their beliefs when offered information intended to correct or fix misperceptions. For example, in a meta-analysis of 32 experimental studies, Walter and Tukachinsky (2020) find that corrections do not eliminate the effects of misinformation, even though they tend to move attitudes in the intended direction on average. This broad conclusion appears transferable to science misperceptions specifically. Scholars have tested whether individuals, when exposed to corrective information, update their misperceptions concerning vaccines (Nyhan and Reifler 2015; van Stekelenburg et al. 2020), GMOs (Bode and Vraga 2015), climate change (Vraga et al. 2019), food safety (van Stekelenburg et al. 2020), or the size of the federal science budget (Goldfarb and Kriner 2017). The evidence confirms that corrections have a mixed record. As we discuss later, many scholars have sought to better understand the conditions by which corrections lead individuals to update their attitudes.

Why do individuals hold misperceptions about science?

A myriad of individual-level and group-level factors have been theorised to influence the prevalence of misperceptions about science. The former concerns psychological processes following exposure to misinformation, and the latter concerns systemic factors that affect exposure in the first place.

Individual ability and motivation to evaluate science

The likelihood that individuals develop misperceptions about science depends on their ability and motivation to critically evaluate science information and then recognise and reject misinformation. Regarding ability, individuals' limited epistemic knowledge about science constrains their capacity to assess science information. For example, findings from a recent national survey show that 77 percent of respondents could not explain the idea behind a scientific study, and 36 percent had trouble understanding probability, signaling major obstacles to conceptual understanding of the scientific process (Scheufele and Krause 2019).

Individuals also bring motivations to their consumption of science information that affect the likelihood of forming misperceptions, regardless of their abilities. Theories of motivated reasoning posit that people access and evaluate information in ways that fulfil certain goals and motivations (Kunda 1990). Individuals can be driven by accuracy motivation – in which case they are motivated to arrive at accurate conclusions – or they can be driven by directional motivations – in which case they are motivated to arrive at a particular, desired conclusion. For many policy decisions, scientific consensus serves as the most accurate, 'factually competent' information available (Dietz 2013). However, individuals with directional motivations may pursue reasoning strategies that lead them to reject such consensus and develop misperceptions (Pasek 2018).

A common directional goal is one's motivation to defend a prior-standing belief: individuals exposed to scientific information may resist updating their attitudes when the information does not cohere with standing beliefs. For example, Ma et al. (2019) studied the effect of a consensus message concerning human-induced climate change. The results showed a backlash in which people who entered the study sceptical of climate change were unpersuaded by the message and updated their beliefs in the opposite direction. Druckman and Bolsen (2011) similarly show that, once people form opinions about emerging technologies like carbon-nanotubes and GMOs, they cling to those opinions even in the face of contradictory scientific information. Thus, people may maintain science misperceptions due to a motivation to protect their beliefs.

One's defence of group-based identities constitutes another source of directional motivation. Many people want to maintain the beliefs held by their valued groups, regardless of scientific accuracy, to protect against costly social ostracisation. For example, partisans in the US often form beliefs on climate change, fracking, and other scientific issues to align with fellow partisans, regardless of the science (Kahan 2015). Identity-protective motivation does not guarantee misperceptions, but it is likely that individuals will develop misperceptions because their goal is group alignment instead of accuracy. One exception, though, may be if the relevant group are scientists themselves. van der Linden et al. (2018) argue that some individuals see scientists' beliefs as a relevant group norm, which drives them to align their beliefs with the scientific consensus.

Core values can also underlie a directional motivation. In such cases, individuals may only accept science information if it fits their value system. Lewandowsky et al. (2013) find that conservatives and individuals who value free markets reject climate change when the science implies heavier government regulation. In another study, conservatives deny climate science when it is framed in terms of 'fairness' but accept it when it is discussed in terms of the more cherished value of 'sanctity' (Wolsko et al. 2016).

It is worth noting that individuals with accuracy motivation can still develop misperceptions about science. For instance, people who rely on scientific and social consensus as heuristics to help them achieve accuracy may be wrong about the consensus. Scheufele and Krause (2019) cite survey data indicating that a majority of respondents erroneously believe there is no scientific consensus regarding the health effects of GMOs or the proposition that the universe was created in the Big Bang. About one-third erroneously believe there is no scientific consensus on climate change and evolution. People also misestimate social consensus among their peers and the general public, particularly on environmental issues (Schuldt et al. 2019) and human-caused climate change (Mildenberger and Tingley 2019).

Furthermore, accuracy-motivated individuals may still exhibit directional bias regarding the information sources they judge to be accurate: individuals may evaluate scientists as trustworthy sources of information more frequently when science's message is compatible with their standing beliefs (Kahan et al. 2011). As a result, partisan perceptions of source credibility can lead to polarised views on matters of science, despite accuracy motivation (Druckman and McGrath 2019).

Systemic factors that encourage misinformation and misperceptions

While individual-level factors influence susceptibility to misperceptions given exposure to misinformation, systemic factors determine the overall permeation of misinformation into the informational environment in the first place. One important factor is politicisation. The politicisation of science occurs when actors exploit uncertainty in the scientific process to cast doubt on findings (Bolsen and Druckman 2015, 2018a). Unfortunately, the inherent uncertainty of science can be difficult to communicate to the public. Even when certain conclusions constitute a scientific consensus, they are vulnerable to politicisation (Druckman 2017), and misinformation is more likely to spread as various science issues become politicised.

Another closely related factor is partisan polarisation. Growing evidence suggests that enflamed partisan tensions in a more polarised political environment abet the spread of misinformation. In a study of 2,300 American Twitter users, Osmundsen et al. (2020) find that individuals with out-party animus are more likely to share fake news, particularly when they are Republicans. This suggests that polarisation is partly fueling the proliferation of misinformation on the internet. In addition, as political elites polarise on high-profile science issues like climate change, rank-and-file partisans have clearer cues about the 'correct' party position. In such cases, partisans attend more to party endorsements than to substantive information when forming opinions (Druckman et al. 2013). Therefore, a polarised information environment implies both greater exposure to partisan misinformation and higher individual propensities to use party cues, increasing the likelihood that individuals form misperceptions.

Third, the evolved information environment may now be more amenable to spreading misinformation through the rise of bots and trolls on social media platforms, the use of algorithms designed to garner clicks that reward outlandish stories, and the influence of dark money (Lazer et al. 2018; Iyengar and Massey 2019). Researchers hypothesise that structural aspects of technology and digital media facilitate the increased spread of misinformation as a larger interpersonal network size, greater deindividuation, and ability to share or post immediately provide fewer constraints and inhibitions on online behavior (Brady et al. n.d.). Gossiping and the sharing of outrageous content, which would be costly behaviors in physical settings, are less costly online and may even yield rewards in the form of positive social feedback (Crockett 2017).

Given such social feedback incentives, misperceptions can be especially contagious if shared in a morally charged environment. Brady et al. (n.d.)'s MAD model of moral contagion shows how the growing strength of partisan group identity in the American electorate might enhance individual-level motivations. As a result, individuals are likely to share morally charged political messages that attack out-group members and elevate in-group members. The informational value of shared content is secondary to the social status and positive social feedback sharers receive from like-minded partisans in their social network. Thus, content that sparks moral outrage along partisan lines may quickly spread to a large number of viewers, regardless of its accuracy.

While the last quarter century of media and social transformations have had many positive benefits, there have also been negative consequences that can increase the likelihood of scientific misperceptions. Politicised science, polarised parties, social media practices, and the interaction of these forces can lead to the spread of misinformation and the formation of misperceptions.

Misperception antidotes

Next, we turn to antidotes – that is, strategies to combat the formation of scientific misperceptions. Many of these focus on communication strategies aimed at addressing the individual-level psychological drivers of misperceptions. These include inoculation messages, corrections, shifting motivations, and framing. Finally, we also discuss possible interventions to respond to systemic sources of misperceptions.

Inoculation messages

One promising avenue to address misperceptions involves inoculations that warn people that they will be exposed to misinformation (Cook et al. 2017; van der Linden, Leiserowitz, et al. 2017; van der Linden, Maibach, et al. 2017). Inoculation theory (or 'prebunking') posits that this kind of warning – provided through a 'weakened dose' of inaccurate information followed directly by a refutation – can result in resistance to misinformation. The inoculation works to establish an accurate standing belief in the recipient, which they will later 'defend' when they encounter misleading information. For example, Bolsen and Druckman (2015) test inoculation techniques in survey experiments asking respondents about two novel energy technologies. The authors show that warnings are effective in the face of politicised communications. Scientific consensus messages about the benefits of each technology moved opinion for respondents who received a warning prior to receiving a contrary, politicised message. By contrast, respondents who only received a politicised message ignored the scientific consensus. Similarly, van der Linden, Maibach, et al. (2017) warned respondents they would be exposed to belief-threatening information ('some politically motivated groups use misleading tactics to try to convince the public that there is a lot of disagreement among scientists') and then provided a pre-emptive refutation ('there is virtually no disagreement among experts that humans are causing climate change'). As in the earlier experiment, this technique restored the impact of scientific-consensus messages, despite politicisation.

Cook et al. (2017) explore inoculation messages highlighting the argumentation tactics employed in the politicisation of climate science. Such tactics include the presentation of a 'false balance' of evidence and the use of 'fake experts' to manufacture doubt. In one study, they report that an inoculation message was effective at neutralising the impact of a false balance of evidence. However, in a second study, the findings were more mixed: an inoculation message only reduced the effect of politicisation among respondents who valued free markets.

Roozenbeek and van der Linden (2019a, 2019b) investigate whether prompting respondents to actively engage with inoculation messages confers resistance to misinformation. In an initial study, participants were provided facts about an increase in the number of police-related incidents involving Dutch asylum seekers (Roozenbeek and van der Linden 2019a). Small groups of respondents were randomly assigned to produce a fake news article on the topic by role-playing one of four different types of 'characters', including: (1) the denier, (2) the alarmist, (3) the clickbait monger, and, (4) the conspiracy theorist. The results showed that participation in the game increased resistance to political misinformation in a fake news article. In a large follow-up study, participation in the game increased people's ability to detect misinformation and resist it, irrespective of individual-level factors such as political ideology.

Taken together, the results of these studies suggest that pre-emptively refuting science politicisation may be an effective strategy when politicisation can be anticipated. While this is not always possible, the theory and evidence on inoculations do provide one potential route to reducing misperceptions.

Corrections

A large literature explores the extent to which corrections lead individuals to discard factual misperceptions. As mentioned earlier, corrections do not entirely eliminate the effects of misinformation, but evidence suggests that they can be effective under particular conditions. Many findings in this regard follow from psychological concepts such as mental models or fluency. Individuals incorporate misinformation into larger 'mental models of unfolding events' (Lewandowsky et al. 2012: 114) and may 'prefer an incorrect model over an incomplete model' (114). Following, corrections tend to be more effective if they are detailed and provide an explanation of why a misperception is incorrect and less effective if individuals pre-emptively generate reasons supporting the misinformation (Chan et al. 2017). Additionally, individuals may perceive information to be more accurate when they can recall it more easily – the information is characterised by high fluency (Berinsky 2017). As a result, corrections are less effective when misinformation is repeated more often (Walter and Tukachinsky 2020), and many scholars agree that a correction should not repeat the misinformation itself (Cook and Lewandowsky 2011).

While this research has generated insights concerning the conditions for successful corrections, overcoming directional motivations continues to be a fundamental challenge. One can expect corrections to be less effective the more they threaten an individual's worldview or pre-existing attitudes. For instance, Bode and Vraga (2015) find that corrections are more effective for misperceptions concerning GMOs than vaccines. The authors attribute the difference in part to prior-attitude strength. In Bolsen and Druckman (2015), directional motivations account for the findings that corrections were far less effective than inoculations. As discussed previously, directional motivations also interact with individuals' evaluations of information sources. Studies of misinformation corrections are consistent with evidence suggesting that individuals value source trustworthiness more than source knowledge and that directional motivations influence perceived trustworthiness (Jerit and Zhao 2020). This may be troubling in the context of science misperceptions as it suggests that scientific expertise is insufficient for bolstering the effect of corrections. Given the overarching challenge posed by directional motivation in the case of corrections, we now discuss strategies that seek to address individuals' directional motivations and worldviews more directly.

Shifting motivations

One such strategy is to prompt accuracy motivation. As mentioned, such motivation does not ensure accurate beliefs, but it can help. Bolsen and Druckman (2015) find that a correction only works when respondents are primed to pursue an accuracy motivation. Similarly, Pennycook et al. (2019) find that a prompt to think about 'the concept of accuracy' reduces respondents' propensity to share false and misleading news attacking their political opponents.

There are a variety of approaches to stimulating accuracy motivation. One approach involves attenuating the effects of directional motivation by satisfying the underlying goal (see Dunning 2015), which reduces directional rejection of accurate information. For example, Bolsen and Druckman (2018b) show that affirming participants' worldview – even if it involves conspiratorial tendencies – increases their inclination to accept accurate scientific information. Alternatively, encouraging deliberations about science can induce accuracy (Dietz 2013). Finally, highlighting the salience or personal relevance of an issue can temper directional motivations and lead to accuracy since holding inaccurate beliefs may have direct personal consequences. Indeed, this is one possible reason that residents of areas most affected by climate change often accept climate science (Scannell and Gifford 2013). The same has been found with regard to

COVID-19 – in areas with more cases, people were less likely to form opinions about policies based on their partisan leanings (Druckman et al. 2020).

Framing

Another approach to combatting misperceptions is framing, in which messages strategically highlight considerations that may be persuasive for a target audience (Druckman and Lupia 2017). As mentioned earlier, a values-based directional motivation often leads to misperceptions when scientific findings are at odds with strongly held values; reframing seems especially effective for correcting such misperceptions. For example, Campbell and Kay (2014) demonstrated that reframing the need for climate action in free-market-friendly terms allowed proponents of laissez-faire economics to express greater belief in human-induced climate change. Other studies report similar success using moral value frames that appeal to conservatives, such as in-group loyalty, purity, and respect for authority (Feinberg and Willer 2013; Wolsko et al. 2016).

Institutional and techno-cognitive strategies

In addition to social-psychological approaches, scholars are examining the degree to which institutional and 'techno-cognitive' strategies can combat the systemic changes in the information environment, discussed earlier, that exacerbate the spread of scientific misperceptions (Lazer et al. 2018). To address the institutional and financial roots of misinformation spread, a coordinated multidisciplinary effort is necessary to identify groups that finance, produce, and disseminate misinformation and politicisation as a way to confuse the public and protect the policy status quo. Farrell et al. (2019) suggest several interconnected strategies to combat the spread of misinformation that entail (1) academics working more closely with journalists and educators to disseminate inoculations or warnings when possible, (2) the use of lawsuits to defend climate scientists against personal attacks and to identify the most prominent misinformation creators and distributors, and (3) enacting legislation that requires greater financial transparency to eliminate hidden private contributions that shield both individuals and companies who produce fake news.

Another strategy involves using 'technocognition [to] design better information architectures' to suit the 'post-truth era' (Lewandowsky et al. 2017: 362). This approach advocates using technological adaptations to prevent the spread of misinformation, as well as cognitive approaches that might better educate and inform the public. For instance, social media outlets such as Facebook and Twitter can (1) provide feedback to users that allows them to better identify fake news, (2) provide credible sources for different groups that will confirm when a particular story is false, (3) develop and employ algorithms that detect bots and eliminate their ability to spread misinformation, and (4) identify the primary producers of fake news and eliminate their access to social media platforms. Of course, given the contemporary social and informational landscape, technological solutions must be accompanied by serious discussion of political and ethical complications.

Conclusion

Governments and foundations make massive investments in science with the intention of benefitting both individuals and societies. Yet misperceptions among the public can undermine the potential positive impact of science. Concern about scientific misperceptions has increased in the last quarter century due to societal and technological changes, but our understanding of what underlies these misperceptions and possible ways to address them has also advanced. Furthermore, the COVID-19 pandemic is showcasing how quickly misperceptions form and spread, while also showing that social scientists – who quickly offered practical advice – can contribute to limiting that spread.

Perhaps the most substantial hurdle going forward is for researchers to identify interventions that can scale to large populations. This means not only overcoming technological challenges but also finding ways – such as the aforementioned fake news game – to engage individuals. Another obstacle is to determine how research findings concerning inoculation should be incorporated into the communication environment. While inoculations appear to be more effective than corrections, little research has elaborated concrete strategies for targeting inoculation campaigns. This represents a considerable challenge as it is difficult to forecast when misinformation will be widely disseminated. Finally, solutions must consider the interaction of individual psychology, institutional settings, and communication infrastructures. For example, some individuals hold intuitionist worldviews in which they interpret events based on their feelings rather than empirical evidence (Oliver and Wood 2018: 48). Reaching and communicating with intuitive thinkers requires approaches that are quite distinct from those that succeed with more 'rationalist' thinkers. These challenges remind us of the work that still needs to be done to translate research findings into actionable steps for reducing misperceptions and their impact.

References

Allcott, H. and Gentzkow, M., 2017. Social media and fake news in the 2016 election. *Journal of Economic Perspectives, 31*(2), pp. 211–236.

Berinsky, A.J., 2017. Rumors and health care reform: Experiments in political misinformation. *British Journal of Political Science, 47*(2), pp. 241–262.

Bode, L. and Vraga, E.K., 2015. In related news, that was wrong: The correction of misinformation through related stories functionality in social media. *Journal of Communication, 65*(4), pp. 619–638.

Bolsen, T. and Druckman, J.N., 2015. Counteracting the politicization of science. *Journal of Communication, 65*(5), pp. 745–769.

Bolsen, T. and Druckman, J.N., 2018a. Do partisanship and politicization undermine the impact of a scientific consensus message about climate change? *Group Processes & Intergroup Relations, 21*(3), pp. 389–402.

Bolsen, T. and Druckman, J.N., 2018b. Validating conspiracy beliefs and effectively communicating scientific consensus. *Weather, Climate, and Society, 10*(3), pp. 453–458.

Brady, W.J., Crockett, M. and Van Bavel, J.J., n.d., The MAD model of moral contagion: The role of motivation, attention and design in the spread of moralized content online. *Perspectives on Psychological Science*, Forthcoming.

Campbell, T.H. and Kay, A.C., 2014. Solution aversion: On the relation between ideology and motivated disbelief. *Journal of Personality and Social Psychology, 107*(5), p. 809.

Chan, M.P.S., Jones, C.R., Hall Jamieson, K. and Albarracín, D., 2017. Debunking: A meta-analysis of the psychological efficacy of messages countering misinformation. *Psychological Science, 28*(11), pp. 1531–1546.

Cook, J. and Lewandowsky, S., 2011. *The debunking handbook.* St. Lucia: University of Queensland.

Cook, J., Lewandowsky, S. and Ecker, U.K., 2017. Neutralizing misinformation through inoculation: Exposing misleading argumentation techniques reduces their influence. *PLoS One, 12*(5).

Crockett, M.J., 2017. Moral outrage in the digital age. *Nature Human Behaviour, 1*(11), pp. 769–771.

Dietz, T., 2013. Bringing values and deliberation to science communication. *Proceedings of the National Academy of Sciences, 110*(Supplement 3), pp. 14081–14087.

Druckman, J.N., 2015. Communicating policy-relevant science. *PS: Political Science & Politics, 48*(Supplement 1), pp. 58–69.

Druckman, J.N., 2017. The crisis of politicization within and beyond science. *Nature Human Behaviour, 1*(9), pp. 615–617.

Druckman, J.N. and Bolsen, T., 2011. Framing, motivated reasoning, and opinions about emergent technologies. *Journal of Communication*, *61*(4), pp. 659–688.

Druckman, J.N., Klar, S., Krupnikov, Y., Levendusky, M. and Ryan, J.B., 2020. *Affective polarization and COVID-19 attitudes*. Working Paper, Northwestern University. https://psyarxiv.com/ztgpn/

Druckman, J.N. and Lupia, A., 2017. Using frames to make scientific communication more effective. In *The Oxford handbook of the science of science communication*. Oxford: Oxford University Press, pp. 243–252.

Druckman, J.N. and McGrath, M.C., 2019. The evidence for motivated reasoning in climate change preference formation. *Nature Climate Change*, *9*(2), pp. 111–119.

Druckman, J.N., Peterson, E. and Slothuus, R., 2013. How elite partisan polarization affects public opinion formation. *American Political Science Review*, *107*(1), pp. 57–79.

Dunning, D. 2015. Motivational theories. In B. Gawronski and G. V. Bodenhausen, eds., *Theory and explanation in social psychology*. New York: Guilford.

Farrell, J., McConnell, K. and Brulle, R., 2019. Evidence-based strategies to combat scientific misinformation. *Nature Climate Change*, *9*(3), pp. 191–195.

Feinberg, M. and Willer, R., 2013. The moral roots of environmental attitudes. *Psychological Science*, *24*(1), pp. 56–62.

Flynn, D.J., Nyhan, B. and Reifler, J., 2017. The nature and origins of misperceptions: Understanding false and unsupported beliefs about politics. *Political Psychology*, *38*, pp. 127–150.

Goldfarb, J.L. and Kriner, D.L., 2017. Building public support for science spending: Misinformation, motivated reasoning, and the power of corrections. *Science Communication*, *39*(1), pp. 77–100.

Grinberg, N., Joseph, K., Friedland, L., Swire-Thompson, B. and Lazer, D., 2019. Fake news on Twitter during the 2016 US presidential election. *Science*, *363*(6425), pp. 374–378.

Guess, A.M., Nyhan, B. and Reifler, J., 2020. Exposure to untrustworthy websites in the 2016 US election. *Nature Human Behaviour*, pp. 1–9.

Iyengar, S. and Massey, D.S., 2019. Scientific communication in a post-truth society. *Proceedings of the National Academy of Sciences*, *116*(16), pp. 7656–7661.

Jerit, J., Paulsen, T. and Tucker, J.A., 2020. *Science misinformation: Lessons for the Covid-19 Pandemic*. Working Paper. New York: Stony Brook and New York University Press.

Jerit, J. and Zhao, Y., 2020. Political misinformation. *Annual Review of Political Science*, *23*.

Kahan, D.M., 2015. Climate-science communication and the measurement problem. *Political Psychology*, *36*, pp. 1–43.

Kahan, D.M., Jenkins-Smith, H. and Braman, D., 2011. Cultural cognition of scientific consensus. *Journal of Risk Research*, *14*(2), pp. 147–174.

Kuklinski, J.H., Quirk, P.J., Jerit, J., Schwieder, D. and Rich, R.F., 2000. Misinformation and the currency of democratic citizenship. *Journal of Politics*, *62*(3), pp. 790–816.

Kunda, Z., 1990. The case for motivated reasoning. *Psychological Bulletin*, *108*(3), p. 480.

Lazer, D.M., Baum, M.A., Benkler, Y., Berinsky, A.J., Greenhill, K.M., Menczer, F., Metzger, M.J., Nyhan, B., Pennycook, G., Rothschild, D. and Schudson, M., 2018. The science of fake news. *Science*, *359*(6380), pp. 1094–1096.

Levy, J. 2020., *Focusing on misinformation content: Comparing corrections for demonstrably false statements and ambiguous statements*. Working Paper, Northwestern University.

Lewandowsky, S., Ecker, U.K. and Cook, J., 2017. Beyond misinformation: Understanding and coping with the "post-truth" era. *Journal of Applied Research in Memory and Cognition*, *6*(4), pp. 353–369.

Lewandowsky, S., Ecker, U.K., Seifert, C.M., Schwarz, N. and Cook, J., 2012. Misinformation and its correction: Continued influence and successful debiasing. *Psychological Science in the Public Interest*, *13*(3), pp. 106–131.

Lewandowsky, S., Gignac, G.E. and Oberauer, K., 2013. The role of conspiracist ideation and worldviews in predicting rejection of science. *PLoS One*, *8*(10).

Li, J., 2020. Toward a research agenda on political misinformation and corrective information. *Political Communication*, *37*(1), pp. 125–135.

Lupia, A., 2013. Communicating science in politicized environments. *Proceedings of the National Academy of Sciences*, *110*(Supplement 3), pp. 14048–14054.

Ma, Y., Dixon, G. and Hmielowski, J.D. 2019. Psychological reactance from reading basic facts on climate change: The role of prior views and political identification. *Environmental Communication*, *13*(1), 71–86.

Mildenberger, M. and Tingley, D. 2019. Beliefs about climate beliefs: The importance of second-order opinions for climate politics. *British Journal of Political Science*, *49*(4), 1279–1307.

Nelson, J.L. and Taneja, H., 2018. The small, disloyal fake news audience: The role of audience availability in fake news consumption. *New Media & Society*, *20*(10), pp. 3720–3737.

Nyhan, B. and Reifler, J., 2010. When corrections fail: The persistence of political misperceptions. *Political Behavior*, *32*(2), pp. 303–330.

Nyhan, B. and Reifler, J., 2015. Displacing misinformation about events: An experimental test of causal corrections. *Journal of Experimental Political Science*, *2*(1), pp. 81–93.

Oliver, J.E. and Wood, T.J., 2018. *Enchanted America: How intuition & reason divide our politics*. Chicago: University of Chicago Press.

Oreskes, N. and Conway, E.M., 2010. Defeating the merchants of doubt. *Nature*, *465*(7299), pp. 686–687.

Osmundsen, M., Bor, A., Vahlstrup, P.B., Bechmann, A. and Petersen, M.B., 2020. *Partisan polarization is the primary psychological motivation behind "fake news" sharing on Twitter*. Working Paper. Aarhus: Aarhus University.

Pasek, J., 2018. It's not my consensus: Motivated reasoning and the sources of scientific illiteracy. *Public Understanding of Science*, *27*(7), pp. 787–806.

Pennycook, G., Epstein, Z., Mosleh, M., Arechar, A., Eckles, D. and Rand, D., 2019. *Understanding and reducing the spread of misinformation online. 2019*. Unpublished manuscript. https://psyarxiv. com/3n9u8

Roozenbeek, J. and van der Linden, S., 2019a. The fake news game: Actively inoculating against the risk of misinformation. *Journal of Risk Research*, *22*(5), pp. 570–580.

Roozenbeek, J. and van der Linden, S., 2019b. Fake news game confers psychological resistance against online misinformation. *Palgrave Communications*, *5*(1), pp. 1–10.

Scannell, L. and Gifford, R., 2013. Personally relevant climate change: The role of place attachment and local versus global message framing in engagement. *Environment and Behavior*, *45*(1), pp. 60–85.

Scheufele, D.A. and Krause, N.M., 2019. Science audiences, misinformation, and fake news. *Proceedings of the National Academy of Sciences*, *116*(16), pp. 7662–7669.

Schuldt, J.P., Yuan, Y.C., Song, Y. and Liu, K. (2019). Beliefs about whose beliefs? Second-order beliefs and support for China's coal-to-gas policy. *Journal of Environmental Psychology*, *66*, p. 101367.

Sunstein, C.R., 2001. *Republic. com*. Princeton, NJ: Princeton University Press.

Sunstein, C.R. and Vermeule, A., 2009. Conspiracy theories: Causes and cures. *Journal of Political Philosophy*, *17*(2), pp. 202–227.

Van Bavel, J.J., Boggio, P., Willer, R.et al., 2020. Using social and behavioural science to support COVID-19 pandemic response. *Nature Human Behavior*, *4*.

van der Linden, S., Leiserowitz, A. and Maibach, E., 2018. Scientific agreement can neutralize politicization of facts. *Nature Human Behaviour*, *2*(1), pp. 2–3.

van der Linden, S., Leiserowitz, A., Rosenthal, S. and Maibach, E., 2017. Inoculating the public against misinformation about climate change. *Global Challenges*, *1*(2), p. 1600008.

van der Linden, S., Maibach, E., Cook, J., Leiserowitz, A. and Lewandowsky, S., 2017. Inoculating against misinformation. *Science*, *358*(6367), pp. 1141–1142.

van Stekelenburg, A., Schaap, G., Veling, H. and Buijzen, M., 2020. Correcting misperceptions: The causal role of motivation in corrective science communication about vaccine and food safety. *Science Communication*, *42*(1), pp. 31–60.

Vraga, E.K., Kim, S.C. and Cook, J., 2019. Testing logic-based and humor-based corrections for science, health, and political misinformation on social media. *Journal of Broadcasting & Electronic Media*, *63*(3), pp. 393–414.

Walter, N. and Tukachinsky, R., 2020. A meta-analytic examination of the continued influence of misinformation in the face of correction: How powerful is it, why does it happen, and how to stop it? *Communication Research*, *47*(2), pp. 155–177.

Wang, Y., McKee, M., Torbica, A. and Stuckler, D., 2019. Systematic literature review on the spread of health-related misinformation on social media. *Social Science & Medicine*, *240*, p. 112552.

Wolsko, C., Ariceaga, H. and Seiden, J., 2016. Red, white, and blue enough to be green: Effects of moral framing on climate change attitudes and conservation behaviors. *Journal of Experimental Social Psychology*, *65*, pp. 7–19.

23
GOVERNMENT DISINFORMATION IN WAR AND CONFLICT

Rhys Crilley and Precious N. Chatterje-Doody

Introduction

'The first casualty when war comes', wrote US Senator Hiram Johnson in 1917, 'is truth' (Knightley 2004), and research has shown that through the ages, war and conflict have always been marked by the use of lies, propaganda, and what we now often refer to as mis- or disinformation (Taylor 2003).[1] The Trojan Horse is perhaps the most infamous early tale of deception during wartime, and regardless of its veracity, it suggests that disinformation was on the minds of those who lived and waged war in ancient times. From these early days of history through the city-states, empires, and countries that followed to the high-tech globalised societies of today, political authorities have sought to harness disinformation to win conflicts. With this in mind, this chapter provides an insight into government disinformation in war and conflict. We begin by setting out why government disinformation matters for the study of conflict and war, before introducing the concepts of propaganda, framing, strategic narrative, and discourse to help make sense of government disinformation in war. We then reflect on what exactly may be novel about contemporary practices of government disinformation in war and conflict. Finally, we explore the limitations of current research and suggest potential new directions for research.

Disinformation matters in war and conflict

In what is considered one of the foundational texts for understanding modern war and conflict, Clausewitz notes that a 'great part of the information obtained in war is contradictory, a still greater part is false, and by far the greatest part is of a doubtful character' (Clausewitz 2017, 46). Yet, despite claims like this in such influential texts and despite the prominent examples of disinformation in wars and conflicts throughout history, scholars have often treated information and communication as though they were peripheral to the study of conflict. In this line of 'realist' thinking, 'the supreme importance of the military instrument lies in the fact that the ultima ratio of power in international relations is war' (Carr 2016, 102). Power is viewed simply in terms of having the material resources and capabilities to wage war, win battles, and use threats of violence to get others to do what they otherwise would not (Schmidt 2005, 528). Despite having an appealing simplicity, such realist approaches are rarely useful for understanding the complexity of global politics (Ashley 1984; Cohn 1987; Enloe 2000), nor are they helpful in understanding how governments attempt to wield power by influencing perceptions – for example, through the use of disinformation. Given that traditional approaches to war do not provide us with sufficient conceptual and analytical tools to make sense of disinformation in war, we now introduce four (ultimately overlapping and interlinked) concepts and their associated bodies of scholarship that can help us understand government disinformation in war.

Propaganda

Following the world wars of the early twentieth century, a new field of study was built around the concept of propaganda (Bernays 2004 [1928]; Lasswell 2013 [1934]; Lippman 2010 [1922]). This was understood to be 'the technique of influencing human action through the manipulation of representations' (Lasswell 2013 [1934], 13). At the time it was recognised that this could involve lying, but optimists viewed it as something that would largely be grounded in the truth. Authors such as Bernays viewed it as a predominantly positive tool that could be used to help shape public opinion for the better, viewing propaganda as 'necessary to orderly life' (Bernays 2004 [1928], 39) in democracies. Despite Bernays's founding vision to be 'a propagandist for propaganda', the term *propaganda* is now widely regarded as something morally questionable, socially destructive, and politically negative. Even Bernays's contemporaries saw propaganda as 'the defilement of the human soul' (Ponsonby 2010 [1926], 18).

More recent scholarship defines propaganda as 'the deliberate manipulation of representations . . . with the intention of producing any effect in the audience . . . that is desired by the propagandist' (Briant 2014, 9). Such scholarship provides an important grounding for the study of government disinformation in war. In particular, it provides rich accounts of the history of propaganda (Taylor 2003), as well as insights into the contemporary disinformation practices of governments in the digital age (Bjola and Pamment 2018; Briant 2014). The research on propaganda demonstrates that government disinformation in war has a rich and bloody history and that governments have historically sought to lie and mislead their adversaries. The concept of propaganda then can be useful, but it is limited by normative 'baggage' (Taylor 2003, 2). Indeed, the negative connotations of propaganda are so strong as to immediately delegitimise those accused of engaging in it – even if proponents of the concept believe that 'what we really need is more propaganda not less. We need more attempts to influence our opinions and to arouse our active participation in social and political processes' (Taylor 1992).

Even when conceptualised as a positive addition to a state's wartime toolkit, the concept of propaganda is perhaps too broad to provide specific analytical utility to explain how and why government disinformation in war happens or is effective. It is intuitive, perhaps, that governments will lie during wars so that they may beat their adversaries and win victories, but what explains how that disinformation circulates widely in countries that now have free and fair media?

Various explanations have been offered. Some point towards the shared ideological views of government officials and media elites who are oriented around making profits from audiences who are more likely to accept patriotic coverage of wars than critical reporting (Herman and Chomsky 1995). Related to this is the role of national patriotism, in which journalists 'rally around the flag' as national populations have been found to support their leaders during times of national crisis such as wars and conflicts (Stahl 2010). Other factors include how journalists are reliant on official sources for their reporting (Bennett 1990) and are thereby faithful to governments so as to ensure their access to information. Further relevant factors in the digital age include the rapidity of information flows in the contemporary news environment, which commercially incentivises the production of high-speed, low-quality 'churnalism' that prioritises sensationalist social media trend reporting over investigative reporting (Chatterje-Doody and Crilley 2019, 84–85) or neglects due diligence in verifying the claims of state-backed sources (Ramsay and Robertshaw 2018, 10–11). In addition, digital factors enable governments to bypass traditional media gatekeepers, using social media to communicate directly with audiences (O'Hagan 2013). For these reasons, propaganda – or government disinformation in war – can circulate widely, even domestically in societies that are supposedly predisposed to valuing journalistic objectivity, facts, and the truth.

Framing and strategic narratives

Alongside propaganda, two other concepts – framing and strategic narrative – have recently gained traction in the study of political communication and may help us understand government disinformation during war. Both these analytical concepts provide a structured way of making sense of disinformation. Framing, for example, 'entails selecting and highlighting some facets of events or issues, and making connections among them so as to promote a particular interpretation, evaluation and/or solution' (Entman 2003, 417). In this way, framing is reliant 'on selection, exclusion and emphasis as a communicator chooses which information to include, which to omit and which to highlight through placement, repetition or association with culturally significant symbols' (Manor and Crilley 2018, 371). Studies suggest that frames consist of four key constituent parts. First, they involve a definition of a problem. Second, they identify the cause of that problem. Third, they provide a moral evaluation of those involved, and fourth, they offer a solution. To illustrate this with an example, consider how, throughout the war on terror, the Bush administration consistently framed the events of 9/11 as a problem of global terrorism caused by radical Islamists who were 'evil' and could only be stopped through a global 'war on terror'. This frame cascaded down from the Bush administration, played out in news coverage, and shaped how people understood what was happening and what should be done in response to it – such as the invasions of Afghanistan and Iraq (Entman 2003; Tumber and Palmer 2004).

The concept of strategic narrative has recently become popular as a way of understanding how political actors communicate and what effects these communications have in contemporary global politics. Strategic narratives are seen as 'a tool for political actors to extend their influence, manage expectations, and change the discursive environment in which they operate' (Miskimmon et al. 2013, 2). They are defined as

> representations of a sequence of events and identities, a communicative tool through which political actors – usually elites – attempt to give determined meaning to past, present, and future in order to achieve political objectives. . . . [T]hey articulate end states and suggest how to get there.
>
> (Miskimmon et al. 2013, 5)

Subsequently, proponents of strategic narrative theory focus on studying the component parts of narratives: actors, actions, agency, purpose, and scene. Studies to date have demonstrated the utility of using strategic narrative to understand disinformation during war, including how state governments use social media to deploy strategic narratives that provide overly simplistic dichotomies of conflicts that dehumanise other people (Manor and Crilley 2018) and may persist despite attempts to refute disinformation in the digital sphere (Khaldarova and Pantti 2016; Szostek 2018).

Strategic narrative approaches are distinct from framing theory as strategic narratives involve a focus on temporality – where narratives often have a beginning, middle, and end – and a sense of causality that links together the elements of the narrative in a coherent plot. Even so, the difference between the two approaches can be exaggerated. While both approaches provide a structured way of analysing government disinformation in war, they share similar limitations. Specifically, both suffer some limitations in making sense of the digital disinformation nowadays deployed by governments that is visual; involves the use of humour, memes, and multiple layers of interpretation and meaning; is personalised; and is directed at specific individuals and audiences through participatory social media platforms (Merrin 2018). This is even more significant given indications that disinformation that incorporates visual as well as textual components is more likely to be believed (Hameleers et al. 2020).

Discourse

A final concept that can help students of government disinformation during war is that of discourse. Discourse is a rather broad concept that it is no simple matter to concisely define. Some refer to discourse as 'systems of signification' (Milliken 1999, 229) that enable us to make sense of the world or as 'a cohesive ensemble of ideas, concepts, and categorizations about a specific object that frame that object in a certain way and, therefore, delimit the possibilities for action in relation to it' (Epstein 2005, 2). Influenced by poststructural philosophers like Foucault, discourse theorists explore how meanings are constructed through written and spoken language and other forms of communication, such as visual media and popular culture. In doing so, discourse analysis pays attention to the interconnectedness of power and knowledge, explores how identities are constructed and positioned in relation to each other (often through dichotomies such as us/them, good/evil, natural/unnatural), how meanings are naturalised as facts, and how these things make certain political outcomes (such as war and conflict) possible.

Discourse theorists often come under scrutiny given the supposed ways in which they have been seen to undermine claims about objectivity and truth – especially in the age of 'post-truth' politics, when post-modernism is seen as a harbinger of and foundation for fake news, lies, and disinformation. However, these claims are generally unwarranted and grounded in poor understandings of what post-modern philosophers were arguing. Post-modern approaches to discourse do not demand that we reject 'facts', and they do not advocate for politicians to lie. Rather, the aim of discourse analysis is 'to recognise how particular ideas and practices gain the status of "facts" or "common sense" knowledge as a result of the way in which they are represented, abstracted or interpreted' (Crilley and Chatterje-Doody 2018, 2). It is to understand the ways in which ' "truths" are mobilized and meted out' (Epstein 2005, 13).

An approach that places its attention not on the validity of truth claims but rather on the ways in which they are mobilised may seem like an odd approach for the study of disinformation – particularly in times of war when the stakes are high. But, on the contrary, attention to discourse can reveal important dynamics that may be overlooked by other approaches to propaganda, framing, or strategic narrative. This is best illustrated through an example. Jean Baudrillard's collection of essays about the first Gulf War – *The Gulf War Did Not Take Place* (1995) – are often ridiculed on the grounds that the Gulf War did, of course, take place. As war was waged, lives were lost, and so it may seem irresponsible – it may even seem like disinformation itself – to claim that it did not take place. However, this is not the point of Baudrillard's work at all, which does, indeed, recognise, and is astutely aware of, the human cost of the war. Instead, what Baudrillard is claiming with his provocatively titled analysis is that the overly sanitised representation of the Gulf War – with a focus on precision missiles affixed with cameras, war reporting in which no casualties were shown, and computer simulations of what was happening in the desert – served to limit how audiences comprehended the war and the armed violence being used against other people in far-away places.

Subsequently, approaches interested in propaganda, framing, or strategic narrative may be interested in looking at how specific instances of disinformation are deployed by governments at war or in evaluating the truthfulness of certain claims made by governments in conflicts. But attention to discourse can reveal how 'facts', accurate information, the ways in which they are communicated, and the representation of an entire war – such as Baudrilliard's analysis of Western coverage of the Gulf War or other studies of more recent conflicts (Butler 2010; Der Derian 2009; Stahl 2010) – can themselves approximate disinformation. Moreover, a broader approach to discourse can reveal aspects of disinformation that may be overlooked by studies of strategic narrative. For example, recent work on the Russian state-funded international broadcaster RT has found that its coverage of the Syrian conflict does not provide a clear strategic narrative that fits with the foreign policy goals of the Russian government – rather, it is much more reactionary and attempts to seize discourse and shape meanings as events unfold on the ground (Dajani et al. 2019). Ultimately, however, there are overlaps between the approaches identified here, and scholars often work with several of these concepts to understand government disinformation during war.

The novelty of today's government disinformation during war

While disinformation has always been a feature of war, its form and reach have evolved to best fit with prevailing conditions. Nowadays, the particularities of a saturated real-time interactive global media environment work to shape the nature of conflict disinformation, not least because long-standing institutional bulwarks against disinformation have been eroded in the internet age (Lazer et al. 2018). So, too, does the increasingly visible public debate about the threat that such disinformation poses: disinformation is now itself a securitised issue. The prevailing environment has been referred to variously in recent years as the 'post-truth age' and an 'age of political uncertainty' (Surowiec and Manor 2021). It is an age in which people are increasingly amenable to placing their trust in 'alternative' sources rather than in established sources of political and institutional authority (Coleman 2018). Add to this the vast number of commercial and state-funded 'alternative' news providers in operation, and the environment in which disinformation is circulated becomes exponentially more complex and multidirectional, with often unclear relationships between the different actors.

One of the most obvious results of this change is an instant ability to bypass the traditional gatekeepers of news and information. It is now the norm for states, defence ministries, embassies, and militaries to engage directly with publics via social media (Crilley 2016; Kuntsman and Stein 2015). Throughout the Syrian conflict, for example, many states and political actors sought to use social media to communicate with different audiences, and Russia's defence ministry has come under scrutiny for releasing many questionable statements. These included the sharing of a video ostensibly showing the 'undamaged and fully operational' marketplace of a town recently reported as being bombed. Russia's embassy in Syria followed this with a tweet subsequently alleging that the 'White Helmets' had faked the bombing, and its account was temporarily suspended by Twitter for violating their rules.

Sometimes, however, disinformation campaigns are more opportunistic. After a controversial US politician insinuated that the 2017 Khan Sheikhoun sarin attack may have been a 'false flag' operation, coordinated activity from sources previously linked to Russian information campaigns emerged around the #Syriahoax hashtag (Hindman and Barash 2018, 39–40). Similarly, disinformation is often articulated by actors at one remove: Russia's international broadcasters, RT and Sputnik, frequently repeat their scepticism of the White Helmets organisation across their broadcast content and multi-platform online outputs, often using 'independent' voices such as freelance journalists, academics, and high-profile celebrities to give legitimacy to the charges made (RT 2018b; Sputnik 2018). Such guests tend to disseminate their controversial claims across a particular range of fringe news outlets online, including Dissident Voice, 21st Century Wire, and Alternative View. When presenting their views to Russia's international broadcasters, it is not uncommon for these guests to engage in complex conspiracy theorising or to project the charge of 'disinformation' at the opposing side (RT 2018a, 2020; Sputnik 2018). For the media outlets concerned, this offers a degree of plausible deniability: a network that accurately reports what an external figure has said can be represented as fulfilling all its journalistic obligations. If the claim itself contains disinformation, the network can argue that it has merely reported it, rather than endorsing it.

However, this low–entry cost, fragmented media market is vital to understanding how disinformation operates online. This is because an individual's likelihood of believing a falsehood to which they have been exposed increases in line with repeated exposure (Pennycook et al. 2018), and news consumers are often unmotivated to critically assess the news that they are consuming (Pennycook and Rand 2018). As these processes demonstrate, it is not necessarily obvious whether the states involved generated particular claims or whether state-aligned actors merely reproduce externally circulating disinformation that suits their sponsors' preferred framing of a conflict. Either way, it appears that audiences having prior awareness of the affiliation and/or intentions of actors like RT does not influence whether the actors' specific claims have an impact on them (Fisher 2020). What is more, audiences no longer passively consume disinformation but play a role in its production and recirculation. Liking, sharing, or commenting on particular social media posts can disseminate them amongst social networks and also increase their effect due to the 'implicit endorsement that comes with sharing' (Lazer et al. 2018, 3).

Perhaps one of the clearest conclusions from this real-time feedback is how conducive affective and emotive representations are to the viral spread of particular stories and claims. That is to say, stories are most likely to spread rapidly when told from an immediate or urgent perspective, such as those of an eye-witness (Andén-Papadopoulos 2013). Furthermore, news markets are structured around the knowledge that users tend to share items presented in an emotive way (Bakir and McStay 2018), even though they may not have read beyond the headline (Dafonte-Gomez 2018), and the business model of most social networks is built upon complex statistical models that predict and maximise audience engagement in order to drive advertising revenue (Bakshy et al. 2015). When it comes to media content about war, it is precisely these affective and emotive stimuli – so easy to combine in online multimedia offerings – to which audiences are most likely to relate (Solomon 2014).

Aside from as eye-witnesses, the role of fellow individuals as media consumers and producers is also crucial in understanding the spread of disinformation about war and conflict today. For instance, fellow citizens are often perceived as more trustworthy or reliable than official sources, and their online comments can influence how subsequent viewers assess particular online artefacts. However, it is difficult to reliably ascertain whether particular sources are themselves state sponsored, independent, or operating in a grey space in between. For example, it is a relatively simple matter to use 'astroturfing' techniques to create the impression that comments deriving from managed groups of social media accounts represent 'ordinary citizens acting independently'. Such comments often disseminate and amplify disinformation. Their impact on political social media discussions beyond their own network of information operatives is debatable (Keller et al. 2020), but there is evidence that their discussions have the power to change individuals' opinions about some of the issues they discuss, as well as increasing uncertainty about them – even when those individuals are aware that commenters may not be genuine (Zerback et al. 2020).

Today, disinformation efforts in war need not necessarily be convincing in isolation nor stand up particularly well to scrutiny as media research has shown that at crucial times, false stories are more widely shared than accurate news (Silverman 2016) and are widely believed (Silverman and Singer-Vine 2016). What is more, it can be hard to reverse the overall impact of these rapid reactions, since the mere appearance of fake news and debates about it can set the media agenda (Vargo et al. 2018), yet repeated exposure to falsehoods (even as part of a retraction) has been associated with increased belief in them (Pennycook et al. 2018; Swire et al. 2017). Given these issues, we now turn to discussing new directions for research on government disinformation during war.

New directions for research

If the novelty of the contemporary disinformation environment lies primarily in the ways in which its structure influences the formation and spread of disinformation, then it is clear that any effective response to the contemporary challenge of disinformation about war requires genuine engagement with the mechanisms that govern this environment. Without an overarching vision of how contemporary disinformation operates, activities that may seem intuitively commendable (including some fact-checking) could have counterproductive consequences (Swire et al. 2017). That is not to say that detailed investigations into the spread of particular disinformation campaigns should not be undertaken. Whilst rigourous research into disinformation activities should be 'encouraged and improved, published and cited', their findings should not be blindly extrapolated from specific cases of disinformation campaigning to characterise network activity more generally or even to characterise particular information campaigns as a whole (Benkler et al. 2018, 265).

Interdisciplinary collaboration is crucial for addressing disinformation in the current age so that computational data about disinformation's spread can be contextualised within analyses of its wider dissemination and acceptance. After all, evidence of the volume of discussion alone is a poor indicator of spread because disinformation campaigners tend to self-amplify within their own networks (Keller et al. 2020), and even evidence of spread provides no evidence of any effect. So, for a better understanding of contemporary government disinformation in war, it is crucial to conduct further research into if and how disinformation appeals and to whom. It is not enough to investigate the prevalence of specific disinformation about war and conflict: significant levels of interdisciplinary collaboration are necessary to tease apart how media market dynamics, journalistic practice, individual and group psychology, and social media platform logics intersect.

The media systems of most developed democracies are as resilient to foreign disinformation, trolls, and bots as they are to other falsities (Benkler et al. 2018, 267). The problem is, however, that the prevailing context is one in which these safeguards as a whole have been eroded (Pennycook and Rand 2020). Time pressures and market trends reward the rapid reproduction of unverified information, and the dissemination of disinformation about war and military capacity can sometimes occur as a side effect of this process (Ramsay and Robertshaw 2018, 10–11). Confronting this kind of trend demands further research into industry expectations and the communities of journalistic practice that sustain them.

It is vital to conduct further study into the factors that make disinformation appeal to different audiences. When it comes to media content about war and conflict, the act of spectatorship can create a powerful link between the viewer and the viewed (Sylvester 2013, 13), and the stimulation of emotions is related to the reasoning process (Lisle 2017). This being the case, there is some evidence that it is the affective or emotive stimuli in representations of war and conflict to which audiences are most likely to relate, and the visual imagery of the online news environment encodes such stimuli in multiple sensory layers (Chatterje-Doody and Crilley 2019; Crilley and Chatterje-Doody 2020). The same research gives a preliminary indication of a potentially gendered, militaristic dimension to the acceptance of conflict disinformation, whilst other research has shown (ex-)military personnel networks being targeted by conspiratorial interest groups across multiple social networks (Gallacher et al. 2017). It would therefore seem prudent to expand the research agenda on the link between disinformation, emotions, and visual representations of war and conflict. For, if 'seeing is believing', then such imagery has the potential to convey rapid support for disinformation claims – as with the videos purporting that Syrian attacks have been faked.

Future research needs to be interdisciplinary. It will need to include technical analyses aimed at detecting the increasingly sophisticated 'deepfakes' in circulation online, which will have to be consistently updated in response to the refinement of faking techniques, artificial intelligence, and other technologies. Yet such research must be informed by research into audiences – for disinformation is only impactful if the audiences it is aimed at accept, believe, or feel emotionally attached to it. Only with such analyses can successful counter-disinformation strategies be developed (Swire et al. 2017). These are crucial matters demanding further investigation in order to build up a complex picture of the effects of disinformation over time. There is unlikely to be a one-size-fits-all solution.

The final area in which significant further research is necessary is the cyclical nature of the contemporary disinformation ecosystem. For, just as Western politicians and media highlight and criticise the circulation of contentious claims between Russian officials, media outlets, and fringe communities, so, too, do Russian politicians and media outlets seize upon the circulation of questionable claims in Western political and media spheres. These dynamics can entrench many of the problems – such as the fixing of identities, preconceptions, and prejudices, as well as dehumanisation through othering – that drive disinformation, reduce critical awareness of it, and decrease trust in establishment sources (Coleman 2018). Similarly, any attempts to identify, analyse, and counter disinformation must themselves be maximally transparent and accurate. If this is not the case, then they risk not only feeding into the mirroring of 'disinformation' activities and the further erosion of trust but also, from a practical perspective, impeding the effective countering of the disinformation with which they engage (Hutchings and Tolz 2020).

In sum, government disinformation in war has a long history and can be made sense of through a variety of perspectives and concepts. Whether studied through the lens of propaganda, framing, strategic narratives, or discourse, we now need to account for the contemporary dynamics of digital communication when studying disinformation during war. As the realm of information has itself become a battleground for states and other political actors (Merrin 2018; Singer and Brookings 2018), the study of disinformation in war is now more important than ever before.

Note

1 We understand the difference between mis- and dis-information to be largely one of intent; where misinformation is that which is inaccurate due to error, disinformation refers to purposefully deliberate falsehoods used to deceive others. For this purpose, we refer to disinformation throughout this chapter;

however, we recognise that there can be overlap between the two terms, not least because it is often impossible to infer someone's 'true' intentions.

References

Andén-Papadopoulos K (2013) Citizen Camera-Witnessing: Embodied Political Dissent in the Age of 'Mediated Mass Self-Communication'. *New Media & Society*. DOI: 10.1177/1461444813489863.

Ashley RK (1984) The Poverty of Neorealism. *International Organization*, 38 (2), pp. 225–286.

Bakir V and McStay A (2018) Fake News and the Economy of Emotions. *Digital Journalism*, 6 (2), pp. 154–175.

Bakshy E, Messing S and Adamic LA (2015) Exposure to Ideologically Diverse News and Opinion on Facebook. *Science*, 348 (6239), pp. 1130–1132.

Baudrillard J (1995) *The Gulf War Did Not Take Place*. Bloomington: Indiana University Press.

Benkler Y, Faris R and Roberts H (2018) *Network Propaganda: Manipulation, Disinformation, and Radicalization in American Politics*. Oxford: Oxford University Press.

Bennett WL (1990) Toward a Theory of Press-State Relations in the United States. *Journal of Communication*, 40 (2), pp. 103–127. Wiley Online Library.

Bernays E (2004 [1928]) *Propaganda*. Brooklyn, NY: IG Publishing.

Bjola C and Pamment J (eds) (2018) *Countering Online Propaganda and Extremism: The Dark Side of Digital Diplomacy*. 1 edition. Abingdon, Oxon and New York: Routledge.

Briant E (2014) *Propaganda and Counter-Terrorism: Strategies for Global Change*. Manchester: Manchester University Press.

Butler J (2010) *Frames of War: When Is Life Grievable?* London: Verso.

Carr EHH (2016) *The Twenty Years' Crisis, 1919–1939: Reissued with a New Preface from Michael Cox*. 1st edition. London: Palgrave Macmillan.

Clausewitz C von (2017) *On War*. North Charleston, SC: Jazzybee Verlag.

Cohn C (1987) Sex and Death in the Rational World of Defense Intellectuals. *Signs*, 12 (4), pp. 687–718.

Coleman S (2018) The Elusiveness of Political Truth: From the Conceit of Objectivity to Intersubjective Judgement. *European Journal of Communication*, 33 (2).

Crilley R (2016) Like and Share Forces: Making Sense of Military Social Media Sites. In: *Understanding Popular Culture and World Politics in the Digital Age*. London: Routledge, pp. 51–67.

Crilley R and Chatterje-Doody PN (2018) Security Studies in the Age of 'Post-Truth' Politics: In Defence of Poststructuralism. *Critical Studies on Security*, 6 (1).

Crilley R and Chatterje-Doody PN (2020) Emotions and War on YouTube: Affective Investments in RT's Visual Narratives of the Conflict in Syria. *Cambridge Review of International Affairs*, Online First, pp. 1–21.

Chatterje-Doody PN and Crilley R (2019) Populism and Contemporary Global Media: Populist Communication Logics and the Co-construction of Transnational Identities. In: Stengel F, MacDonald D and Nabers D (eds) *Populism and World Politics*. London: Palgrave Macmillan, pp. 73–99.

Dafonte-Gomez, A (2018) Audience as Medium: Motivations and Emotions in News Sharing. *International Journal of Communication*, 12, pp. 2133–2152.

Dajani D, Gillespie M and Crilley R (2019) Differentiated Visibilities: RT Arabic's Narration of Russia's Role in the Syrian War. *Media, War & Conflict*. DOI: 10.1177/1750635219889075.

Der Derian J (2009) *Virtuous War: Mapping the Military-Industrial-Media-Entertainment-Network*. 2nd edition. London: Routledge.

Enloe CH (2000) *Bananas, Beaches and Bases: Making Feminist Sense of International Politics*. Berkeley: University of California Press.

Entman RM (2003) Cascading Activation: Contesting the White House's Frame After 9/11. *Political Communication*, 20 (4), pp. 415–432. Taylor & Francis.

Epstein C (2005) *The Power of Words in International Relations: Birth of an Anti-Whaling Discourse*. Cambridge, MA: MIT Press.

Fisher A (2020) Demonizing the Enemy: The Influence of Russian State-Sponsored Media on American Audiences. *Post-Soviet Affairs*. DOI: 10.1080/1060586X.2020.1730121.

Gallacher, JD, Barash, V, Howard PN and Kelly J (2017) *Junk News on Military Affairs and National Security: Social Media Disinformation Campaigns Against US Military Personnel and Veterans*. COMPROP DATA MEMO. https://arxiv.org/ftp/arxiv/papers/1802/1802.03572.pdf

Hameleers M, Powell, TE, Van Der Meer TGLA and Bos L (2020) A Picture Paints a Thousand Lies? The Effects and Mechanisms of Multimodal Disinformation and Rebuttals Disseminated via Social Media. *Political Communication*, 37 (2), pp. 281–301. DOI: 10.1080/10584609.2019.1674979.

Herman ES and Chomsky N (1995) *Manufacturing Consent: The Political Economy of the Mass Media*. 1 edition. London: Vintage.

Hindman, M and Barash V (2018) *Disinformation, 'Fake News' and Influence Campaigns on Twitter, Knight Foundation*. www.issuelab.org/resources/33163/33163.pdf.

Hutchings S and Tolz V (2020) *COVID-19 Disinformation: Two Short Reports on the Russian Dimension, Reframing Russia*, April 6. https://reframingrussia.com/2020/04/06/covid-19-disinformation-two-short-reports-on-the-russian-dimension/.

Keller FB, Schoch D, Stier S and Yang JH (2020) Political Astroturfing on Twitter: How to Coordinate a Disinformation Campaign. *Political Communication*, 37 (2), pp. 256–280. DOI: 10.1080/10584609.2019.1661888.

Khaldarova I and Pantti M (2016) Fake News. *Journalism Practice*, 10 (7), pp. 891–901.

Knightley P (2004) *The First Casualty: The War Correspondent as Hero and Myth-Maker from the Crimea to Iraq*. 3rd edition. Baltimore, MD: The Johns Hopkins University Press.

Kuntsman A and Stein RL (2015) *Digital Militarism: Israel's Occupation in the Social Media Age*. Stanford, CA: Stanford University Press.

Lasswell HD (2013 [1934]) *Propaganda Technique in the World War*. Mansfield Centre, CT: Martino Fine Books.

Lazer D et al. (2018) The Science of Fake News. *Science* 359 (6380), pp. 1094–1096.

Lippman W (2010 [1922]) *Public Opinion*. New York: Greenbook Publications, LLC.

Lisle D (2017) Witnessing Violence Through Photography: A Reply. *Global Discourse*, 7 (2–3), pp. 282–284.

Manor I and Crilley R (2018) Visually Framing the Gaza War of 2014: The Israel Ministry of Foreign Affairs on Twitter. *Media, War & Conflict*, 11 (4), pp. 369–391.

Merrin W (2018) *Digital War: A Critical Introduction*. 1st edition. London and New York: Routledge.

Milliken J (1999) The Study of Discourse in International Relations: A Critique of Research and Methods. *European Journal of International Relations*, 5 (2), pp. 225–254.

Miskimmon A, O'Loughlin B and Roselle L (2013) *Strategic Narratives: Communication Power and the New World Order*. New York and London: Routledge.

O'Hagan J (2013) War 2.0: An Analytical Framework. *Australian Journal of International Affairs*, 67 (5), pp. 555–569.

Pennycook G, Cannon T and Rand DG (2018) Prior Exposure Increases Perceived Accuracy of Fake News. *Journal of Experimental Psychology: General*, 147 (12), pp. 1865–1880.

Pennycook G and Rand DG (2018) Lazy, Not Biased: Susceptibility to Partisan Fake News Is Better Explained by Lack of Reasoning Than by Motivated Reasoning. *Cognition*. DOI: 10.1016/j.cognition.2018.06.01.

Pennycook G and Rand DG (2020) Who Falls for Fake News? The Roles of Bullshit Receptivity, Overclaiming, Familiarity, and Analytic Thinking. *Journal of Personality*, 88 (2), pp. 185–200.

Ponsonby A (2010 [1926]) *Falsehood in War Time: Containing an Assortment of Lies Circulated Throughout the Nations During the Great War*. Uitgever: Kessinger Publishing.

Ramsay G and Robertshaw S (2018) *Weaponising News: RT, Sputnik and Targeted Disinformation*. London: Kings College London. https://www.kcl.ac.uk/policy-institute/assets/weaponising-news.pdf.

RT (2018a) *US Wants Terrorists to Stay in Idlib; Just Imagine What Pompeo Would Say if They Were in Oregon*. www.rt.com/news/437524-idlib-terrorists-pompeo-syria/.

RT (2018b) *Roger Waters: White Helmets Is a Deep Rabbit Hole*. www.rt.com/shows/sophieco/437840-pink-floyd-music-politics/.

RT (2020) *White Helmets Use Covid-19 Crisis to Further US Coalition Regime Change Agenda in Syria*. www.rt.com/op-ed/484185-white-helmets-coronavirus-syria/.

Schmidt BC (2005) Competing Realist Conceptions of Power. *Millennium*, 33 (3), pp. 523–549. Sage. DOI: 10.1177/03058298050330031401.

Silverman C (2016) This Analysis Shows How Viral Fake Election News Stories Outperformed Real News on Facebook. *BuzzFeed*. www.buzzfeednews.com/article/craigsilverman/viral-fake-election-news-outperformed-real-news-on-facebook#.rtj0KJJGp.

Silverman C and Singer-Vine J (2016) Most Americans Who See Fake News Believe It, New Survey Says. *BuzzFeed*. www.buzzfeednews.com/article/craigsilverman/fake-news-survey#.kuo0e6QdV.

Singer PW and Brookings ET (2018) *LikeWar: The Weaponization of Social Media*. New York: Houghton Mifflin Harcourt.

Solomon T (2014) The Affective Underpinnings of Soft Power. *European Journal of International Relations*, 20 (3), pp. 720–741.

Sputnik (2018) *During Syrian Conflict, Media "Cropped Images to Suit UK Regime" – Activist*. https://sputniknews.com/analysis/201804161063623847-mass-media-images-syria-uk/.

Stahl R (2010) *Militainment, Inc.: War, Media, and Popular Culture*. London: Routledge.

Surowiec P and Manor I (2021) *Public Diplomacy and the Politics of Uncertainty*. London: Palgrave Macmillan.

Swire B, Ecker UKH and Lewandowsky S (2017) The Role of Familiarity in Correcting Inaccurate Information. *Journal of Experimental Psychology: Learning, Memory, and Cognition*, 43 (12), pp. 1948–1961, December.

Sylvester C (2013) *War as Experience: Contributions from International Relations and Feminist Analysis*. London: Routledge.

Szostek J (2018) News Media Repertoires and Strategic Narrative Reception: A Paradox of Dis/Belief in Authoritarian Russia. *New Media & Society*, 20 (1), pp. 68–87. DOI: 10.1177/1461444816656638.

Taylor PM (1992) Propaganda from Thucydides to Thatcher: Some Problems, Perspectives and Pitfalls. *Opening Address to the annual conference of the Social History Society of Great Britain*. www. scribd. com/document/57111621/Propaganda-From-Thucydides-to-Thatcher.

Taylor PM (2003) *Munitions of the Mind: A History of Propaganda from the Ancient World to the Present Era*. 3rd edition. Manchester: Manchester University Press.

Tumber H and Palmer J (2004) *Media at War: The Iraq Crisis*. London: Sage.

Vargo CJ, Guo L and Amazeen MA (2018) The Agenda-Setting Power of Fake News: A Big Data Analysis of the Online Media Landscape from 2014 to 2016. *New Media & Society*, 20 (5), pp. 2028–2049.

Zerback T, Töpfl F and Knöpfle M (2020) The Disconcerting Potential of Online Disinformation. *New Media and Society*, online first. DOI: 10.1177/1461444820908530.

24

MILITARY DISINFORMATION

A bodyguard of lies

Kevin Foster

Disinformation and propaganda

On 30 April 1943, Spanish fishermen off the coast of Huelva plucked a uniformed corpse from the waters of the Atlantic. Identity discs and miscellaneous papers identified the body as Major William Martin of the Royal Marines, who had apparently perished in an air crash. Chained to Martin's waist was a black attaché case which contained a sealed military envelope. Over the following days, British authorities urgently sought the return of the briefcase. When the Spaniards copied and passed on the contents of the envelope to German intelligence, they caused a sensation. Martin had been carrying a personal letter from the vice chief of the Imperial General Staff, General Archibald Nye, to General Harold Alexander, commander of the 15th Army Group in Tunisia, detailing plans for the allies' forthcoming landings in Southern Europe. The letter confirmed that the allies would come ashore in the Balkans, German-held Greece, and Sardinia. In response, significant Axis personnel and materiel were redeployed from Western and Southern Europe to the Balkan flank:

> In March 1943, there were eight German divisions in the Balkans; by July there were eighteen, with the number in Greece having increased from a single division to eight; two divisions were sent to reinforce Sardinia and Corsica. That left just two for Sicily.
>
> (Fennell 2019, 340)

When the allies landed 160,000 troops in Sicily in early July, they overran the island's depleted defences in less than six weeks.

The allies had had no intention of invading the Balkans. The letter carried by Major Martin was a hoax – as was the major himself. The body was that of a mentally ill itinerant, Glyndwr Michael, who had been found dead in London. Military intelligence claimed the body, provided it with a new identity, and armed it with disinformation specifically targeted to mislead the Germans as to allied invasion plans for Southern Europe. Operation Mincemeat, described here, offers an exemplar of military disinformation: that is to say, the 'dissemination of deliberately false information, esp. when supplied by a government or its agent to a foreign power or the media with the intention of influencing the policies or opinions of those who receive it' (Simpson and Weiner 1991, 448).[1] Ironically, it would not have been possible to have described

253

it as a disinformation operation at the time as the first use of the term in English was not recorded until 1955. The *Oxford English Dictionary* traces the etymology of 'disinformation' to the Russian *dezinformatsiya*, first used in 1949.[2] By contrast, misinformation, the 'action of misinforming or condition of being misinformed', without any hint of calculation or purpose, has a far more venerable pedigree, with its first use recorded in 1547 (Simpson and Weiner 1991, 1092).

Misinformation and disinformation are entirely different in their purposes, if not their effects.[3] What distinguishes disinformation is its emphasis on deliberation and intent – it is purposefully misleading towards specific ends. This lays bare its close relationship with propaganda, which Philip Taylor defines as

> the *deliberate* attempt to persuade people to think and behave in a *desired way* . . . the conscious, methodical and planned decision to employ techniques of persuasion designed to achieve specific goals that are *intended to benefit those organising the process.*
>
> (Taylor 2003, 6, emphasis in original)[4]

The changed nature of conflict during the twentieth century, the introduction of conscription, the development of the long-range bomber, the targeting of civilian populations, and the total wars these brought meant that 'men, women and children formed the new armies and their morale, their will to fight and resist on a mass scale, accordingly became a significant military asset' (Taylor 2003, 173). In this context, propaganda and the disinformation it entailed became key weapons of war as nations set out to undermine their enemy's morale while shoring up their own. During the Tehran conference in late 1943, Churchill is reputed to have told Stalin that in wartime, truth is so precious that it should always be attended by 'a bodyguard of lies' (Gilbert 1988, 586).[5] In what follows I will detail why this bodyguard has grown into a mass, organised force and how (dis)information has become both an increasingly important weapon in and the dominant domain of modern conflict.[6]

'This will not be another Vietnam'

By March 1973, when US forces formally withdrew from Vietnam, the conviction that the nation's defeat was attributable to a sophisticated disinformation campaign, organised in Hanoi but executed by the Western media, was widespread. Communist North Vietnam had 'bombarded our domestic opinion with continuing propaganda' until the American public, wearied by the media's focus on blood and carnage, balked at further sacrifice, turned against its political proponents, and demanded peace (Tiffen 1983, 186). This oppositional media thesis regarded the free press as an active fifth column, 'instinctively "agin the Government" – and, at least reflexively, for Saigon's enemies'. As a result of their coverage, disinformation triumphed over force of arms, and 'For the first time in modern history the outcome of a war was determined not on the battlefield, but on the printed page and, above all, on the television screen' (Elegant 1981, 73). Many scholars, Daniel Hallin among them, have demonstrated the conviction that 'the media were adversaries to American policy in Vietnam or a decisive factor in the outcome of the war' to be false (Hallin 1989, x).[7] Indeed, many reporters regarded their coverage as a corrective to the Joint US Public Affairs Office (JUSPAO) briefings, whose cheery summaries of body counts, kill ratios, and pacified villages misrepresented the true state of the war. JUSPAO, Michael Herr observed, 'had been created to handle press relations and psychological warfare, and I never met anyone there who seemed to realize that there was a difference' (Herr 1977, 174).

Despite its demonstrable falsehood, the conviction that media coverage had lost the war in Vietnam bred a hostility to the fourth estate that 'soaked deep into the military's cultural tissue' (Rid 2007, 62).[8] In response, in the conflicts that followed, militaries and their political masters set out to corral the media, control the flow of information, and so shape the message. During Britain's re-conquest of the Falkland Islands (1982) and the US assaults on Grenada (1983) and Panama (1989), the military strictly regulated media access to, freedom of movement in, and content and transmission of copy from the area of operations. In each case, the military assault was coordinated with an official information offensive, which ensured positive coverage and promoted popular support for the operation. The inaccessibility of the Falklands and the monopoly this afforded the Ministry of Defence (MoD) over transportation to and information provision from the islands meant that 'hardly ever have circumstances been more propitious for a censor than they were for the British in the Falklands' (Mercer et al. 1987, 39). The task force included a number of MoD public affairs 'minders', whose role was to review reporters' copy at the source (Harris 1983, 27). Not that much censorship was required. A number of the correspondents 'decided before landing that our role was simply to report as sympathetically as possible what the British forces are doing here today' (Hastings 1982, 1). The military campaign may have been a close-run thing, but the information offensive was a walkover.

Though Grenada was more proximate, it was no more accessible to the US media. Excluded from the invasion, the few resourceful reporters who reached the islands independently were detained by US troops. Only when the shooting finished was a handpicked pool from the major broadcasters escorted around the conflict's key sites by a team of public affairs (PA) personnel. Once their material had been vetted, the reporters were cleared to travel to Barbados to transmit their copy, thus formally ending the news blackout. However, while they waited for their flight, the networks carried President Reagan's live broadcast from the Oval Office announcing victory in Grenada and the safe evacuation of all US citizens. Succeeding bulletins illustrated the story with the only visuals available, US Army footage of 'young American students making the "V" sign and smiling at the cameras as they walked up the ramp of the rescue aircraft' (Young and Jesser 1997, 132). A humiliation for the media, Grenada 'was a lovely war from the public information point of view' (Young and Jesser 1997, 133). The Sidle Commission, established in its wake to review future conflict reporting arrangements, made eight recommendations, among them the creation of a national media pool. Yet its insistence that 'The American people must be informed about United States military operations and this information can best be provided through both the news media and the government' ensured that information would continue to be released at the behest of and in the interests of the authorities and that the media would remain shackled (Young and Jesser 1997, 134).

This was clearly demonstrated in the first Gulf War when the military's strategy to positively shape public responses to the liberation of Kuwait centred on two of the Sidle Report's proposals: the creation of media pools for a few select reporters, which radically constrained the fourth estate's access to the war zone, and the live broadcast of military briefings to furnish the bulk of reporters and the public with a steady flow of upbeat, official information.[9] Not that the military needed to worry about the media's loyalty. Its patriotic purpose recharged by the celebratory nationalism of the Reagan years, the media clamoured to cover the war and became 'a vital conduit for mobilizing support for US policy'. During the build-up, 'hardly any dissenting voices were heard in the mainstream media', which became 'little more than public relations outlets for the White House and the Pentagon' (Kellner 1991).

If the principal purpose of US information was to underpin domestic support, the Iraqis also targeted US public opinion. The two countries' leaders were obsessed with Vietnam, each convinced that US public support for the war had buckled under graphic coverage of its costs.[10] Where Bush reassured the American public that 'this will not be another Vietnam', Hussein did his utmost to ensure that it would (Bush 1991). Iraq's Ministry of Information helped Western reporters who had remained in Baghdad during the coalition bombardment of January and February of 1991 cover stories where there was evidence of coalition mistargeting and Iraqi civilian casualties, most notably the coalition airstrike on the Amiriyah bomb shelter, which incinerated 400 Iraqi civilians. However, Hussein not only overrated the media's power in Vietnam, (as did Bush), he also failed to see that public distaste for him framed US responses to Iraqi information. Unlike Ho Chi Minh, whose determined pursuit of national self-determination had been grudgingly respected, Hussein 'had no constituency in the US' (Cumings 1992, 104). Though his information policies failed to dent US public support for the war, they persistently wrong-footed the coalition militaries and accelerated debate about the role and purpose of information on the battlefield.[11]

'The fifth dimension of war'

In the 30 years since the first Gulf War, the nature of war has radically transformed. The conflicts in Somalia (1993), Kosovo (1999), Afghanistan (2001–present) and Iraq (2003–2011) laid bare the limits of conventional military force. In each of these conflicts, the overwhelming advantage in firepower enjoyed by the US and its allies failed to subdue their adversaries, who took the fight to the information domain and triumphed. As a result, information moved from the periphery to the centre of military strategy.

Policy development on information as a strategic asset began with the collapse of the Soviet Union.[12] In 1992, planners at the Joint Chiefs of Staff produced DOD Directive TS3600.1 'Information Warfare', a policy on the use of information as a war-fighting tool. The secretary of defense at the time, Les Aspin, defined information warfare as

> the actions taken to preserve the integrity of one's own information systems from exploitation, corruption or destruction, whilst at the same time exploiting, corrupting, or destroying an adversary's information systems and, in the process, achieving an information advantage in the application of force.
>
> (Department of Defense 1994, 244)

From its outset, information warfare's focus on the corruption and destruction of adversary systems established disinformation as a perennial, shadow presence in all discussions about information operations.[13] That is to say, information operations are, by nature, disinformation operations.

In early 1993 Arquilla and Ronfeldt endorsed the new centrality of information when they proposed that 'Warfare is no longer primarily a function of who puts the most capital, labor and technology on the battlefield, but of who has the best information about the battlefield. What distinguishes the victors is their grasp of information' (Arquilla and Ronfeldt 1993, 141–142). Two years later, General Ronald Fogelman of the US Air Force formally identified information as 'the fifth dimension of war' while acknowledging that 'Dominating this information spectrum is going to be critical to military success in the future' (Fogelman 1995).

Just how critical was driven home during Operation Allied Force, the 1999 air force mission to halt Serb ethnic cleansing of Kosovo. NATO recognised that without boots on the ground and the information they could supply, it needed a convincing explanation for why it was bombing targets in the Balkans. To furnish this it organised

> dedicated IO [information operations] cells . . . at the command and joint task force levels, tasked to integrate – and employ – such diverse tools as civil affairs, electronic warfare, intelligence, and public information in an effort to control and dominate the 'information battle space'.
>
> (Pounder 2000, 58)

Yet their efforts were undermined by the Pentagon's refusal to release 'specific information on friendly force troop movements, tactical deployments, and dispositions' because they 'could jeopardize operations and endanger lives' (Pounder 2000, 66).

In the absence of information from the battlefront, NATO Public Affairs promoted its cause by launching an aggressive 'media saturation strategy' through which it controlled the news cycle by permanently occupying it (Combelles Siegel 2002, 191):

> [O]ur credo at NATO was just to be on the air the whole time, crowd out the opposition, give every interview, do every briefing. . . . We occupied the whole day with our information. And the more we did, the less the media put on talking heads and others who could nullify our briefings.
>
> (Shea 2002, 167–168)[14]

Thus, NATO's (dis)information crowded out the enemy's.

Yet despite the omnipresence of its spokesmen, NATO lost the information war. The Serbs controlled the ground, where they gathered and promoted, through their antagonists' own media channels, information tailored to advance their narrative of innocent victimhood. Their information campaign was a masterwork of strategic disinformation. The commander of allied forces in Southern Europe conceded that

> the enemy was much better at this than we were . . . and far more nimble. The enemy deliberately and criminally killed innocents by the thousands, but no one saw it. . . . We accidentally killed innocents, sometimes by the dozens, and the world watched on the evening news.
>
> (Pounder 2000, 58)

NATO's defeat in the information domain was not just due to a lack of news and images from the field. It was also attributable to its own organisational shortcomings, its failure to track how the weaponisation of information required adaptations in its own internal systems to optimise information effects. The conventional military's existing organisational structures produced 'a detailed institutional division of labor' between public affairs (PA) and information operations (IO) personnel. This underpinned the 'firewall' that notionally existed between information provision and influence operations: 'PA officers and IO officers receive separate educations and training, they follow diverging career paths, they work for specialized sub-organizations, they think in contrasting mindsets and philosophies of war, and they do not read the same publications and doctrines' (Rid 2007, 115). NATO's efforts 'to integrate public information into IO planning . . . came to naught' because military public affairs (PA) officers were reluctant to involve themselves in an information operations campaign (Pounder

2000, 60). They believed that putting public information at the service of information operations would damage the reputation for trustworthiness on which PA operations depended.[15] As a result, the military's own organisational systems militated against 'the implementation of IO initiatives based on public information' (Pounder 2000, 60). The deputy director of the USAF's Public Affairs Center of Excellence believed that this fine distinction between public information and information effects was an ethical luxury that militaries could no longer afford: 'Everyone – commanders, IO specialists, and public affairs officers – needs to understand public information is a battlespace that must be contested and controlled like any other' (Pounder 2000, 60). To exercise one's scruples and vacate the field was to surrender it to the enemy.

The digital battlefield

The principal lesson that Jamie Shea took from Operation Allied Force was that 'Winning the media campaign is just as important as winning the military campaign' (Shea 2002, 167). The experience in Afghanistan and Iraq demonstrated that militaries could not do one without the other. Yet the democratisation of the means of media production and distribution in the mid-2000s advantaged non-state actors and made the media campaign that bit more challenging for conventional militaries. If, in the 1960s and 70s, those seeking the liberation of Palestine needed to hijack an airliner or attack an OPEC meeting to attract the attention of the world's media, by the mid-2000s, the digital revolution in communications meant that Iraqi insurgents and the Taliban needed nothing more than a mobile phone and an internet connection to promote their causes: 'Never before in history have terrorists had such easy access to the minds and eyeballs of millions' (Koerner 2016).

When the US and its allies pursued the enemy leadership or their production and broadcasting facilities, they found that their targets had evaporated. Abandoning military hierarchy and disengaged from studios, transmission towers, and satellite dishes, their non-state adversaries communicated with, motivated, and directed their followers and the public via a decentralised network of semi-autonomous nodes: 'a collection of remote hubs, which are themselves points of centralized "transmission"'. (Jones and Holmes 2011, 161). The futility of bombing a virtual target that was concurrently everywhere and nowhere laid bare the extent to which the conduct of war had undergone a paradigm shift that brought (dis)information to its heart.

As they struggled to suppress the insurgencies in Afghanistan and Iraq, the US and its allies reappraised what force of arms could achieve, the weapons they needed to deploy, and the battlespaces they had to contest. Rid and Hecker describe this transformation in terms of a shift from War 1.0 to War 2.0: 'a predominantly military exercise', War 1.0

> focuses on enemy formations, aims to interrupt decision cycles, has short duration, progresses quickly, ends in clear victory, uses destructive methods . . . and is run by top-down initiatives with a clear chain of command. The media and the public in War 1.0, are a side problem, to be ignored. Information is protected, secret, and used primarily for internal purposes.

By contrast, War 2.0, is as much a political, social, and cultural exercise as it is a military venture:

> Its focus is on the population, its aims to establish alternative decision cycles, its duration long, its progress slow, its end a diffuse success at best, its methods productive (such as nation-building). . . . Its initiatives often come from the bottom up, with

decentralized structures of authority. The media and the public, in War 2.0, are the central battleground and they have the highest priority. Information is predominantly public, open-source, and intended for external consumption.

(Rid and Hecker 2009, 10)

As the conflicts in Afghanistan and Iraq settled into their insurgent phase and the struggle for the trust and loyalty of local and dispersed publics, it became clear to the US and its allies that the terrain they were contesting was human and cognitive, not topographical and inert. In their efforts to win the peoples' trust, the militaries increasingly turned to the strategies and tactics of War 2.0, in which the core battlefield and the key weapons in the struggle were information, disinformation, and influence activities. As a consequence, Maltby (2012) notes, the media not only played a more prominent role in conflict, but, increasingly, militaries also designed their presentation of war through and for the media.

Military disinformation in Afghanistan and Iraq was driven by close cooperation between the US and British governments. Together they maintained top-down control over the war's strategic narratives and the micro-messaging that supported them to ensure that information from the front lines both reflected and could be accommodated within the larger frames of disinformation through which the allies advanced their cause. The information arrangements for the second Gulf War offer a model disinformation campaign. Coordination began with the White House press secretary, Ari Fleischer, who 'set the day's message with an early-morning conference call to British counterpart Alastair Campbell, White House communications director Dan Bartlett, State Department spokesman Richard Boucher, Pentagon spokesperson Torie Clarke, and White House Office of Global Communication [OGC] director Tucker Eskew' (Quenqua 2003, 1).[16] Thus, the message 'cascaded down to the rest of the propaganda apparatus' from the White House (Miller 2004, 81).

The OGC's role was to keep 'all US spokespeople on message. Each night, US Embassies around the world, along with all federal departments in DC, will receive a "Global Messenger" email containing talking-points and ready-to-use quotes'. As a consequence, wherever they were in the world, US, British, and global publics received a consistent set of messages about the war, reinforced by saturation coverage throughout the news cycle:

When Americans wake up in the morning they will first hear from the (Persian Gulf) region, maybe from General Tommy Franks. . . . Then later in the day, they'll hear from the Pentagon, then the State Department, then later on the White House will brief.

(Quenqua 2003, 1)[17]

David Miller notes that this apparatus provided a constant flow of disinformation. The OGC, and through it, government departments across the US 'fed out the lies about the threat posed by the Hussein regime including the faked and spun intelligence information supplied by the UK and by the secret Pentagon intelligence operation, the Office of Special Plans'. In the UK, the Coalition Information Centre (CIC), led by the prime minister's press secretary, Alistair Campbell, directed

the campaign to mislead the media about the existence of weapons of mass destruction (WMD). . . . In particular it oversaw the September [2002] dossier on WMD and the second "dodgy" dossier of February 2003 which was quickly exposed as plagiarised and spun.

Beneath this upper-level coordination of messaging, Miller notes, the disinformation apparatus comprised four integrated elements that reached from the Cabinet and the foreign office right down to psychological operations (PsyOps) teams out in the field in Iraq:

> First was the external system of propaganda run by the Foreign Office and coordinated by the Public Diplomacy Policy Department. Second was internal propaganda focused on the alleged 'terrorist threat' coordinated out of the Cabinet Office by the newly established Civil Contingencies Secretariat. Third and very much subordinate to the command and control propaganda systems in Washington and London was the operation 'in theatre' – the stage for the crushing of Iraq. This was Centcom in Doha, Qatar; the Forward Press Information Centre in Kuwait; and the embedded reporters with their military minders. Lastly, there were the US and UK military psychological operations teams undertaking overt and covert operations in Iraq, which were said only to target enemy opinion to break resistance.
>
> (Miller 2004, 82)

Despite this top-down regulation, disinformation flows were increasingly deregulated as the capacity to isolate domestic consumers from foreign news sources, and vice versa, collapsed in the face of the digital communications revolution. By early 2003, just as defensive public information targeted at a domestic audience could be picked up by and influence foreign audiences, so information effects operations intended to manage the perceptions of adversary and foreign audiences could loop back to influence domestic audiences. Disinformation flowed in both directions.

'Psy-oping the home team'

Over this period, militaries struggled to ensure that doctrine kept abreast of technological advances, the new capabilities they made available, and their effects on the contemporary battlefield. When the USAF's *Basic Doctrine* (2003 [1997]) was revised in 2003, it reflected the air force's developing grasp of the battlespaces specific to information operations and the assets that had to be controlled to ensure information dominance. The revised doctrine proposed that the 'action taken to affect adversary information and information systems while defending one's own information and information systems' was not a single entity but the product of three integrated non-kinetic actions: 'Electronic Warfare Operations', 'Network Operations', and 'Influence Operations' (USAF 2003, 31). While the first two focus on control over radio frequencies, 'satellite links . . . telemetry . . . telecommunications; and wireless communications network systems', influence operations take place in the 'cognitive battlespace'.[18] Here, 'Influence operations . . . capabilities' are deployed to

> affect behaviors, protect operations, communicate commander's intent, and project accurate information to achieve desired effects across the cognitive battlespace. These effects should result in differing behaviors or a change in the adversary decision process, which aligns with the commander's objectives.
>
> (USAF 2003, 31)

Efforts to target enemy decision-making and influence foreign and domestic audiences were evident in an array of information operations undertaken in Afghanistan and Iraq. The Taliban's only radio transmitter in Kabul was destroyed by cruise missiles in October 2001 when US forces invaded, 'and the frequency was taken over by U.S. PSYOP'. Its broadcasts sought to 'explain to Afghanis what happened in the United States on September 11, 2001, and why our government had decided to invade their country'. To maximise the audience and the information effect, the air force dropped 'thousands of hand-cranked radios locked to U.S. PSYOP frequencies' (King 2011, 8). In an effort to bolster its 'source credibility' in Iraq, the US planted ghost-written, pro-US messages in local newspapers, falsely attributed to Iraqi authors (Marx 2006, 51–59). On the home front, the Department of Defense Digital Video Imagery Distribution System (DVIDS) supplied 'pre-packaged video, audio news stories, and images of U.S. military activity', gathered by military public affairs personnel, 'without charge, to any broadcast news organization in the world, including U.S. domestic channels'. Its 'up-to-the-minute images and broadcast-quality video of military activity' was supplemented by 'a huge, accessible electronic library of previously produced images, video, and stories'. Sara King notes that while 'all major U.S. networks, both over-the-air and cable, use DVIDS material', their viewers would have had no idea which material had been gathered by professional journalists and which by uniformed servants of the military, as 'Information provided by DVIDS is identified as "public" and users are not required to credit DVIDS when using the products that it provides' (King 2011, 11). Thus, military propaganda and the disinformation it entails is transformed into news.

British efforts to ensure an equivalent pipeline of military-sourced information coincided with and grew out of the drawdown in Afghanistan in 2014, which instigated 'the biggest shake-up to military reporting in a generation'. As the traffic of British reporters through Camp Bastion dwindled to near zero, news management teams in the MoD were thinned out, and their remaining staff were redeployed to the media operations group (MOG) to work on 'direct to audience communication'. Under these new arrangements, the gaps in information provision would be filled by uniformed 'media operators . . . filming and photographing [the army's] own operations, before posting the edited material online' (Hill 2014).

These reforms were led by Stephen Jolly, a former instructor with 15 (UK) Psychological Operations Group (15 PsyOps). Jolly was 'keen to see a greater emphasis on this kind of in-house news-gathering, in which material is channelled through the open gateway of digital communication and social media', free from oversight by the fourth estate. In 2014, when MOG and 15 PsyOps moved into neighbouring buildings at Denison Barracks in Berkshire to form the new security assistance group (SAG), their cohabitation laid bare the MoD's determination to lower the firewall between news provision and information operations:

> Traditionally, the two worlds of the MOG and Psyops have existed in separate universes, the former being expected to deal in the honest-to-goodness truth, the latter being more closely associated – fairly or unfairly – with the "dark arts", usually directing its material at an enemy's audience.
>
> (Hill 2014)

Two years earlier, 15 PsyOps had been awarded the Firmin Sword of Peace for setting up and supporting seven local radio stations across Helmand.[19] Research had revealed that, given the low rates of literacy among Afghans and negligible internet coverage, the most effective channel for psy-ops was radio.[20] The unit's CO, Commander Steve Tatham, insisted that the stations were committed to information provision, not covert influence:

> Psy-ops is all about communicating with people around and on the battlefield, who ordinarily might not hear what's going on. . . . Most of our work in Helmand is about

talking to Afghans, and explaining and encouraging them to engage in the debate about what's happening in their country.

(Wyatt 2012)[21]

Captain Kieron Lyons, who ran one of the stations and had previously 'spent a lot of time planning the "information effect" for large-scale military operations' in Afghanistan, acknowledged that while the broadcast material had to be truthful and attributable, its purpose was 'to create behavioural change' (Wyatt 2012).

To ensure that sufficient numbers of Afghans could tune in to the broadcasts from 15 Psy-Ops–sponsored Radio Tamadoun ('all the Afghans I ever met called it what it was, Radio ISAF'), psy-ops personnel handed out thousands of wind-up radios to locals. Chris Green, who monitored coalition influence effects in Helmand, claimed he 'never saw any of the locals actually using the radios or listening to Radio ISAF'. Despite claims that some DJs were attracting audiences of up to 50,000 for their shows, signal reception beyond the towns was 'patchy at best and non-existent in many areas'. Further, phone-in reports revealed that most of the calls to the station's much-vaunted talkback sessions 'came from the same half-dozen callers'. In Green's view, 'by overstating the role and value' of radio in the counter-insurgency, 15 Psy-Ops had been 'psy-oping the home team' (Green 2016).

Just a few months after its formation, SAG was absorbed into the newly formed 77th Brigade, where Tatham's view that information, disinformation, and influence were indistinguishable was a basic operating premise.[22] 'Inspired by the successes of Israel and the USA', the establishment of 77th Brigade was also a 'response to Russia's propaganda activities in the Crimea and the effective use of social media by the Islamic State' (Merrin 2019, 122). Named in honour of Orde Wingate's Chindit guerrilla force, 77th Brigade was tasked with bringing the same 'spirit of innovation' to the unorthodox environment of the online battlespace, where 'the actions of others . . . can be affected in ways that are not necessarily violent' (Beale 2015).

In July 2016, 77th Brigade established the organisation and command structure for both an overt online presence and its non-attributable covert systems. This resulted in the establishment of the digital operations group (Digi Ops), which is divided into two teams. Members of the production team 'design and create video, audio print and digital products that aim to influence behaviours for both Army and external audience. Additionally, they advise on campaign strategy and propose innovative behavioural change methods', while the Web Ops team 'collects information and understands audience sentiment in the virtual domain. Within the extant OSINT policy framework, they may engage with audiences in order to influence perceptions to support operational outcomes' (British Army 2020).[23] The COVID-19 crisis revealed that one of the key targets for perception and behaviour influence was the British public. In April 2020, the chief of the defence staff, General Sir Nick Carter, disclosed that members of 77th Brigade were 'helping to quash rumours about misinformation, but also to counter disinformation'. The information effects staff had been 'tackling a range of harmful narratives online – from purported "experts" issuing dangerous misinformation to criminal fraudsters running phishing scams' (D'Urso 2020).

While the Digi Ops team engaged in the open source environment with a range of actors, the delivery of covert strategic and tactical fires had passed to the task group, which provided 'the deployable framework to deliver Information Activity and Outreach (IA&O)' through one of its cells or teams (British Army 2020).[24] Carl Miller suggested that the work of GCHQ's Joint Threat Research Intelligence Group (JTRIG) provides a model for the sort of covert work undertaken by 77th Brigade. Our knowledge of JTRIG's work comes from a series of slides Edward Snowden passed on to Wikileaks in 2013:

> According to the slides, JTRIG was in the business of discrediting companies by passing 'confidential information to the press through blogs etc.' and by posting negative information on internet forums. They could change someone's social media photos ('can take "paranoia" to a whole new level', a slide read). They could use masquerade-type techniques – that is, placing 'secret' information on a compromised computer. They could bombard someone's phone with text messages or calls. JTRIG also boasted an arsenal of 200 info-weapons, ranging from in development to fully operational. A tool dubbed 'Badger' allowed the mass delivery of email. Another, called 'Burlesque', spoofed SMS messages. 'Clean Sweep' would impersonate Facebook wall posts for individuals or entire countries. 'Gateway' gave the ability to 'artificially increase traffic to a website'. 'Underpass' was a way to change the outcome of online polls.
>
> (Miller 2018)

Yet conventional militaries are still playing catch-up when it comes to the sophisticated deployment of disinformation. When ISIS forces seized Mosul in June 2014, their assault was spearheaded by a potent disinformation campaign. Employing Twitter, Snapchat, and other social media platforms, it publicised the gory fate that awaited those who defended Mosul. Over one 24-hour period, it issued almost 40,000 tweets, its output peaking at almost 200 per minute (Berger 2014). As a result, an attacking force of scarcely 1,500 ISIS fighters seized Iraq's second city, whose 60,000-strong military and police detachment fled, their morale shattered by a precisely targeted disinformation offensive. This triumph brought home to conventional militaries around the world that they could not hope to match the enemy's speed, agility, or virtual firepower.[25] They lacked the tools, the personnel, and above all else the organisational systems they needed to optimise and deploy the information assets they possessed.

Disinformation has become a key weapon on the information battlefields of modern conflict. For today's militaries and the governments that direct them, the question is not whether to deploy disinformation against their adversaries but how to do so to best effect while retaining their credibility with domestic audiences. Truth was never more precious than it is now, so much so that the bodyguard of lies that once protected it has grown to become an army.

Notes

1 For more on Operation Mincemeat, see MacIntyre 2010.

2 It appears to have arrived in English from the French *désinformation*, whose first use was in 1954 (see Simpson and Weiner, 448).

3 UNESCO defines disinformation as 'Information that is false and deliberately created to harm a person, social group, organisation or country', whereas misinformation describes 'Information that is false but not created with the intention of causing harm' (Ireton and Posetti 2018). Given that I am focused on the purposeful use of information to establish advantage over one's adversary, what follows will be focused on disinformation.

4 In their overview of its history and evolution, Jowett and O'Donnell define propaganda as 'the deliberate, systematic attempt to shape perceptions, manipulate cognitions, and direct behaviour to achieve a response that furthers the desired intent of the propagandist' (Jowett and O'Donnell 2015, 7). It has since accrued a diverse array of often highly specialised definitions, focused variously on its function as behaviour control, psychological manipulation, corporate persuasion, pleading and convincing, a

participatory co-production, the transmission of messages, and more. See Doob 1948; Qualter 1962; Ellul 1965; Bogart 1995; Pratkanis and Turner 1996; Carey 1997; Taithe and Thornton 2000; Parry-Giles 2002; O'Shaughnessy 2004.

5 Stalin would have approved. The Soviets ran a highly sophisticated deception operation, integrated into operations and strategy throughout World War II. See Glantz 1989.

6 There is a wealth of material on information warfare; for a useful overview see Taylor 2003; Rid and Hecker 2009; Merrin 2019.

7 For more on this, see Mandelbaum 1982; Braestrup 1986; Kimball 1988; Hammond 1989.

8 See also Trainor 1990; Shotwell 1991; Gole 1996.

9 For more details on these arrangements, see Rid 2007, 77–82; Carruthers 2011, 131–138; Taylor 2003, 290–291.

10 See Cumings 1992, 103–128.

11 See Taylor 2003, 294–295; Carruthers 2011, 138–140; Knightley 2004, 492–494.

12 See Armistead 2010, 47. The US administration's first official definition of information warfare was contained in Department of Defense 1994, in a section on 'C4I Cross-Functional Integration'.

13 The *Department of Defense Dictionary of Military Terms* defines information operations as 'The integrated employment, during military operations, of information-related capabilities in concert with other lines of operation to influence, disrupt, corrupt, or usurp the decision-making of adversaries and potential adversaries while protecting our own' (Department of Defense 2016, 110).

14 NATO's briefings offer an exemplary illustration of mediatisation in which the media assume 'an active performative involvement and constitutive role' in the conduct of war (Cottle 2006, 9).

15 Sergeant Marilee Philen, a former USAF Europe PAO, claimed that IO planners 'were more interested in "media manipulation" than dissemination of factual information' (quoted in Pounder 2000, 64).

16 Quenqua notes that this routine 'mirrors procedure during the conflict in Afghanistan' (Quenqua 2003, 1).

17 Robin Brown notes that the OGC in Washington was essentially a reincarnation of the Office of Strategic Influence (OSI), which had been established in the Department of Defense in the autumn of 2001 to '"roll up all the instruments within DoD to influence foreign audiences" including those in neutral and allied countries' (Brown 2003, 167). News of the OSI's existence and purposes was leaked to the press in February 2002 by DoD public affairs staff concerned about potential damage to their credibility and that of the information they disseminated. This resulted in 'a storm of criticism from the press, who feared that they were going to be the targets of false information. This, in turn, drew in the presidential communications staff who were concerned about the risk to their own credibility if the US was seen to be in the business of deceiving media organizations' (Brown 2003, 167). Disinformation was not only toxic; it was contagious. Within a week, Rumsfeld had closed the OSI, shifting its responsibilities and its influence activities to the OGC.

18 Alberts et al. define the cognitive domain as the 'domain of the mind of the warfighter and the warfighter's supporting populace' (Allen and Gilbert 2009, 135) while Kelton et al. describe it as 'a unified threat environment where both state and non-state actors' pursue 'a continual arms race to influence – and protect from influence – large groups of users online' (Kelton et al. 2019, 860).

19 This is an annual award presented to a unit of the British armed forces deemed to have made an outstanding contribution to improving civil-military relations in the UK or overseas.

20 See Wyatt 2012. For internet penetration rates in Afghanistan, see Rennie et al. 2009, 137–145.

21 The radio stations were set up using radio-in-a-box (RIAB), tape and CD decks, and recording and broadcasting equipment, all contained in a single, cumbersome box, which required only the addition of electricity, an antenna, and a DJ to set up a working radio station.

22 For more on 77th Brigade, see British Army 2020.

23 OSINT refers to open-source intelligence.

24 The two cells and four teams are Division IA&O (Information Activity and Outreach) Cell, Brigade IA&O Cell, IA&O Teams, Information Warfare Team (IWT), Tactical Engagement Team (TET), and IA Training and Advisory Team (TAT).

25 For more on this, see Brooking and Singer 2016.

References

Allen, Patrick D., and Dennis P. Gilbert, 'The Information Sphere Domain – Increasing Understanding and Cooperation', *The Virtual Battlefield: Perspectives on Cyberwar*, eds. Christian Czosseck and Kenneth Geers, Washington, DC: IOS Press, 2009, 132–142.

Armistead, Leigh, *Information Operations Matters: Best Practices*, Washington, DC: Potomac Books, 2010.

Arquilla, John, and David Ronfeldt, 'Cyberwar Is Coming!' *Comparative Strategy*, Vol. 12, No. 2 (1993), 141–165.

Beale, Jonathan, 'Army Sets Up New Brigade for "Information Age"', *BBC News*, 31 January 2015. www.bbc.com/news/uk-31070114 (Accessed 28 January 2017).

Berger, J.M., 'How ISIS Games Twitter,' *Atlantic*, 16 June 2014. www.theatlantic.com/international/archive/2014/06/isis-iraq-twitter-social-media-strategy/372856/ (Accessed 16 April 2020).

Bogart, L., *Cool Words, Cold War: A New Look at USIA's Premises for Propaganda*, Washington, DC: American University Press, 1995.

Braestrup, Peter, *Battle Lines*, New York: Priority Press, 1986.

British Army, *77th Brigade: Influence and Outreach*, 2020, www.army.mod.uk/who-we-are/formations-divisions-brigades/6th-united-kingdom-division/77-brigade/groups/ (Accessed 24 March 2020).

Brooking, Emerson T., and P.W. Singer, 'War Goes Viral', *The Atlantic*, November 2016. www.theatlantic.com/magazine/archive/2016/11/war-goes-viral/501125/ (Accessed 13 March 2020).

Brown, Robin, 'Spinning the War: Political Communications, Information Operations and Public Diplomacy in the War on Terrorism', *War and Media: Reporting Conflict 24/7*, eds. Daya Thussu and Des Freedman, London: Sage, 2003, 163–175.

Bush, President George H.W., 'Address to the Nation Announcing Allied Military Action in the Persian Gulf, 16 January 1991', *The American Presidency Project*, Santa Barbara: University of California-Santa Barbara, n.d. www.presidency.ucsb.edu/ws/?pid=19222.

Carey, A., *Taking the Risk Out of Democracy: Corporate Propaganda Versus Freedom and Liberty*, Urbana: University of Illinois Press, 1997.

Carruthers, Susan, *The Media at War*, second edition, New York: Palgrave, 2011.

Combelles Siegel, Pascale, 'Operation Allied Force: The Media and the Public', *Lessons from Kosovo: The KFOR Experience*, ed. Larry Wentz, Washington, DC: Department of Defence Command and Control Program, 2002, 175–203.

Cottle, Simon, *Mediatized Conflict: Developments in Media and Conflict Studies*, Maidenhead: Open University Press, 2006.

Cumings, Bruce, *War and Television*, London: Verso, 1992.

Department of Defense, *Annual Report to the President and Congress*, Washington, DC: Department of Defense, 1994.

Department of Defense, *Department of Defense Dictionary of Military and Associated Terms*, Joint Publication 1–2, Washington, DC: Department of Defense, 2016.

Doob, L.W., *Public Opinion and Propaganda*, New York: Henry Holt and Co., 1948.

D'Urso, Joey, 'The British Army's Information Warfare Unit Is Helping Combat Coronavirus Misinformation', *BuzzFeed News*, 23 April 2020. www.buzzfeed.com/joeydurso/coronavirus-british-army-information-warfare-77-brigade.

Elegant, Robert, 'How to Lose a War', *Encounter*, Vol. 57, No. 2 (1981), 73–90.

Ellul, Jacques, *Propaganda: The Formation of Men's Attitudes*, New York: Knopf, 1965.

Fennell, Jonathan, *Fighting the People's War: The British and Commonwealth Armies in the Second World War*, Cambridge: Cambridge University Press, 2019.

Fogelman, General Ronald R., 'Information Operations: The Fifth Dimension of Warfare', *IWS – The Information Warfare Site*, Vol. 10, No. 47 (1995). www.iwar.org.uk/iwar/resources/5th-dimension/iw.htm (Accessed 10 September 2018).

Gilbert, Martin, *Winston S. Churchill, Volume VII: Road to Victory 1941–1945*, London: Heinemann, 1988.

Glantz, David M., *Soviet Military Deception in the Second World War*, London: Routledge, 1989.

Gole, Henry, 'Don't Kill the Messenger: Vietnam War Reporting in Context', *Parameters*, Vol. 26, No. 4 (Winter 1996), 148–153.

Green, Chris, 'Radio-In-A-Box (RIAB)', *Spin Zhira: Old Man in Helmand*, 22 May 2016. https://spinzhira.com/2016/05/22/radio-in-a-box/ (Accessed 31 May 2020).

Hallin, Daniel, *The 'Uncensored War': The Media and Vietnam*, Berkeley: University of California Press, 1989.

Hammond, William, 'The Press in Vietnam as an Agent of Defeat: A Critical Examination', *Reviews in American History*, Vol. 17, No. 2 (June 1989), 312–323.

Harris, Robert, *Gotcha! The Media, the Government and the Falklands Crisis*, London: Faber and Faber, 1983.

Hastings, Max, 'Why None of Us Can Be Neutral in This War', *Daily Express*, 8 June 1982.

Herr, Michael, *Dispatches*, London: Picador, 1977.

Hill, Christian, 'Army's Press Team Locked in an Embrace with the "Dark Arts" Squad', *Guardian*, 11 September 2014. www.theguardian.com/media/greenslade/2014/sep/11/ministry-of-defence-war-reporting.

Ireton, Cherylin and Julie Posetti, *Journalism, Fake News and Disinformation: A Handbook for Journalism Education and Training*, Paris: UNESCO, 2018. https://en.unesco.org/fightfakenews.

Jones, Paul, and David Holmes, *Key Concepts in Media and Communications*, London: Sage, 2011.

Jowett, Garth S. and Victoria O'Donnell, *Propaganda and Persuasion*, sixth edition, London: Sage, 2015.

Kellner, Douglas, 'The "Crisis in the Gulf" and the Mainstream Media', *The Electronic Journal of Communication*, Vol. 2, No. 1 (1991). www.cios.org/EJCPUBLIC/002/1/00215.HTML.

Kelton, Maryanne, Michael Sullivan, Emily Benvenue and Zac Rogers, 'Australia, the Utility of Force and the Society-Centric Battlespace.' *International Affairs*, Vol. 95, No. 4 (2019), 859–876.

King, Sara B., 'Military Social Influence in the Global Information Environment: A Civilian Primer', *Analyses of Social Issues and Public Policy*, Vol. 11, No. 1 (2011), 1–26.

Kimball, Jeffrey P., 'The Stab-in-the-Back Legend and the Vietnam War', *Armed Forces and Society*, Vol. 14, No. 3 (Spring 1988), 433–457.

Knightley, Phillip, *The First Casualty: The War Correspondent as Hero and Myth Maker from the Crimea to Iraq*, third edition, Baltimore, MD: Johns Hopkins University Press, 2004.

Koerner, Brendan I., 'Why ISIS Is Winning the Social Media War', *Wired*, April 2016. www.wired.com/2016/03/isis-winning-social-media-war-heres-beat/.

MacIntyre, Ben, *Operation Mincemeat: How a Dead Man and a Bizarre Plan Fooled the Nazis and Assured Allied Victory*, New York: Harmony Books, 2010.

Maltby, Sarah, *Military Media Management: Negotiating the 'Front' Line in Mediatized War*, London: Routledge, 2012.

Mandelbaum, Michael, 'Vietnam: The Television War', *Daedalus*, Vol. 111, No. 4 (Fall 1982), 157–169.

Marx, Willem, 'Misinformation Intern: My Summer as a Military Propagandist in Iraq', *Harper's Magazine*, Vol. 313 (2006), 51–59.

Mercer, Derrik, Geoff Mungham, Kevin Williams, *The Fog of War: The Media on the Battlefield*, London: Heinemann, 1987.

Merrin, William, *Digital War: A Critical Introduction*. London: Routledge, 2019.

Miller, Carl, 'Inside the British Army's Secret Information Warfare Machine', *Wired*, 14 November 2018. www.wired.co.uk/article/inside-the-77th-brigade-britains-information-warfare-military.

Miller, David, 'The Propaganda Machine', *Tell Me Lies: Propaganda and Media Distortion in the Attack on Iraq*, ed. David Miller, London: Pluto Press, 2004, 80–99.

O'Shaughnessy, N.J., *Politics and Propaganda: Weapons of Mass Seduction*, Ann Arbor: University of Michigan Press, 2004.

Parry-Giles, S.J., *The Rhetorical Presidency, Propaganda and the Cold War: 1945–1955*, Westport, CT: Praeger, 2002.

Pounder, Major Gary, 'Opportunity Lost: Public Affairs, Information Operations, and the Air War Against Serbia', *Aerospace Power Journal*, Vol. 14, No. 2 (Summer 2000), 56–78.

Pratkanis, A. R., and M.E. Turner, 'Persuasion and Democracy: Strategies for Increasing Deliberative Participation and Social Change', *Journal of Social Issues*, Vol. 52 (1996), 187–205.

Qualter, T.H., *Propaganda and Psychological Warfare*, New York: Random House, 1962.

Quenqua, Douglas, 'White House Prepares to Feed 24-Hour News Cycle', *PR Week*, 24 March 2003.

Rennie, Ruth, Sudhindra Sharma, and Pawan Sen, *Afghanistan in 2009: A Survey of the Afghan People*, San Francisco: The Asia Foundation, 2009, 137–145. http://asiafoundation.org/resources/pdfs/Afghanistanin2009.pdf.

Rid, Thomas, *War and Media Operations: The US Military and the Press from Vietnam to Iraq*, New York: Routledge, 2007.

Rid, Thomas, and Mark Hecker, *War 2.0: Irregular Warfare in the Information Age*, Washington, DC: Praeger Security International, 2009.

Shea, Dr Jamie P., 'The Kosovo Crisis and the Media: Reflections of a NATO Spokesman', *Lessons from Kosovo: The KFOR Experience*, ed. Larry Wentz, Washington, DC: Department of Defense Command and Control Program, 2002, 153–174.

Shotwell, Colonel John, 'The Fourth Estate as a Force Multiplier', *Marine Corps Gazette*, Vol. 75, No. 7 (July 1991), 70–79.

Simpson, J.A. and E.S. Weiner, *The Compact Oxford English Dictionary*, second edition, Oxford: Clarendon Press, 1991.

Taithe, Bertrand, and Tim Thornton (eds.), *Propaganda: Political Rhetoric and Identity, 1300–2000*, Oxford: Sutton, 2000.

Taylor, Philip M., *Munitions of the Mind: A History of Propaganda from the Ancient World to the Present Day*, third edition, Manchester: Manchester University Press, 2003.

Tiffen, Rodney, 'News Coverage of Vietnam', *Australia's Vietnam: Australia in the Second Indo-China War*, ed. Peter King, Sydney: George Allen and Unwin, 1983, 165–187.

Trainor, Bernard, 'The Military and the Media: A Troubled Embrace', *Parameters*, Vol. 20, No. 4 (Winter 1990), 2–11.

United States Air Force, *Air Force Basic Doctrine: Air Force Doctrine Document 1*, Washington, DC: US Air Force, 2003 (1997).

Wyatt, Caroline, 'Psy-ops: Tuning the Afghans into Radio', *BBC News*, 27 October 2012. www.bbc.com/news/world-south-asia-20096416.

Young, Peter, and Peter Jesser, *The Media and the Military: From the Crimea to Desert Strike*, London: Palgrave Macmillan, 1997.

25

EXTREME RIGHT AND MIS/ DISINFORMATION

Thomas Frissen, Leen d'Haenens, and Michaël Opgenhaffen

Key concepts and a brief note on conceptual ambiguity

Before exploring how the extreme right and information disorders have mutually shaped one another, we need a clear definition of the notions of 'extreme right' (or far right) and 'information disorder'. Easier said than done. As with most social and political-scientific concepts, reducing complex and multi-faceted phenomena to a clear-cut definition is a tricky operation which depends on normative and politicised perspectives. What is 'extreme' (or 'fake', as in 'fake news') for one scholar may be viewed as 'alternative' by another and as a discursive signifier by yet another. Given such a conceptual ambiguity within the current literature, anyone intending to study such concepts faces a number of epistemological, ontological, methodological, and ideological challenges. It is therefore necessary to briefly outline the perspective from which this chapter approaches the concepts of extremism and information disorders.

Extreme right

In this chapter the definition of extremism is approached through two premises. The first one has to do with the envisioned end goal of extremists. In the *Ethica Nicomachea*, Aristotle developed the conception of 'extremes' in the context of his virtue theory (Aristotle, Ross and Brown 2009). He saw a virtue as a character trait – of a human being or of a community – and as the perfect common middle ground between two vices: that is, extremes (Frissen 2019). In contrast to 'virtue', the extremes are the margins where bad qualities prevail. While people or communities at those extremes can be diametrically opposed to one another, what defines them is a rejection of the virtue; 'the extremes reject a common middle ground' (Leman 2016, 4). This is the first premise through which this chapter approaches the definition of extremism: a rejection of the common ground. As a consequence, extremists are best defined as those who strive for the creation of a homogenous society based on an uncompromising, uniform, dogmatic ideology that 'tolerates no diversity' (Schmid 2013, 10). For the purposes of this chapter, the 'extreme right' is a phenomenon based on various ideologies (e.g. neo-Nazi, white supremacist, xenophobic, religious, homophobic, or gender related) that always legitimise violence against specific ethnic or cultural groups.

268

The second premise concerns the ways in which this end goal is achieved. While political change can be achieved through a wide variety of means, extremists favour the use of force/violence over debate and persuasion (Schmid 2013; Frissen 2019). On the basis of a historical analysis, Midlarsky (2011) argues that a willingness to kill massively for a cause or collective is what characterises all extremist groups, from fascists to communists and from separatists to nationalists. More explicitly, he states that '[p]olitical extremisms of all sorts share a propensity towards the mass murder of actual or potential opponents of their political programs' (Midlarsky 2011, 8). As a result, the second premise of this chapter's definition of extremism is that extremists turn to violence in the hope of arriving at a non-pluralistic, non-democratic, non-virtuous society. In the next section, we explore how the information ecosystem has helped in shaping such violence.

Information disorders

The production and dissemination of misleading information, myths, and propaganda are certainly nothing new. A brief peek into the twentieth century provides us with many examples, ranging from Orson Welles *War of the Worlds* to Joseph Goebbels' machinery of 'public enlightenment'. In recent years, however, these phenomena have spurred heightened scientific interest. This is a debate at whose epicentre lies the question of how to define whether information is true or false and intentional or unintentional. Scholars seem to have been mostly occupied with disentangling misinformation from disinformation. As a result, misinformation has been conceptualised as 'publishing wrong information without meaning to be wrong or having a political purpose in communicating false information' (Benkler, Faris and Roberts 2018, 24) while disinformation is 'defined as manipulating and misleading people intentionally to achieve political ends' (Benkler, Faris and Roberts 2018, 24). The locus of concern in these debates is on the issue of intentionality behind the production and circulation of false information (Farkas and Schou 2018). The problem is that this is often based on guesswork rather than well-grounded findings, leading to conceptual ambiguity in the literature.

Therefore, this chapter follows Benkler, Faris and Roberts's (2018) concept of information disorder(s). This concept is much more inclusive in the sense that its definition is not only based on the piece of information as such: it also encompasses the broader role of the technological drivers and architecture in the (online) information ecosystem, such as digital platforms and social media. In other words, the concept of information disorders also refers to environmental and infrastructural phenomena such as algorithmic filtering, filter bubbles, and micro-targeting (Benkler, Faris and Roberts 2018). Furthermore, the concept of information disorder(s) is meaningful because it is not just based on the (intention of the) sender. It instead considers the outcome as the leading defining principle. Indeed, the word *disorder* conveys the consequences – a 'disturbed order' in the information ecosystem – of intentionally or unintentionally misleading pieces of information. As will become clear in the next section, instead of just capitalising on the rise of misinformation/disinformation (such as 'fake news' or memes), it is this notion of disorder that a deeply mediatised extreme right has instrumentalised for their cause (Bennett and Livingston, 2018).

A deeply mediatised extreme right

On 15 March 2019, around 1:40 PM local time, a right-wing extremist embarked on a 'mission "against the invaders"' in Christchurch, New Zealand (Macklin 2019a, 18). In a little over half an hour, he entered two mosques and killed 51 people. What was unprecedented about this attack was the fundamental part played by digital technologies. This criminal announced his attack on the/pol/board on 8chan, an image board in the web's social outskirts on which extreme-right information circulates freely (Davey and Ebner 2019). He posted on numerous file-sharing web sites a manifesto titled 'The Great Replacement', and he broadcast the atrocity on Facebook Live, using a GoPro sports camera. By orchestrating his livestream as in a first-person shooter game, the attacker showed he understood the logic of the digital information ecosystem and how to use it to make sure his message would be heard. And heard it was. The video was shared a few million times on multiple social media platforms. It was celebrated with memes on 8chan, and it fuelled anti-Muslim hatred online (Macklin 2019a). But, what the Christchurch shooting mainly caused was a 'chain reaction' of near-identical right-wing extremist attacks against ethnic and cultural communities perceived as invaders or occupiers, such as in Halle (DE) and in El Paso (US) (Koehler 2019; Macklin 2019b). As a result, the Christchurch shooting ushered in a new era for the extreme right: one in which actions are increasingly shaped by digital media and their logic. This chapter therefore states that the extreme right has become deeply mediatised (see Hepp 2020). Deep mediatisation has been defined as 'an advanced stage of [mediatisation] in which all elements of our social world are intricately related to digital media and their underlying infrastructures' (Hepp 2020, 5). Indeed, the Christchurch scenario would never have been possible without digital technologies. In the next two sections, this notion is explored further by looking at two 'triggers' for the deep mediatisation of the extreme right: (1) the broader context of globalisation and immigration and (2) information disorders and the information ecosystem.

Broader context of globalisation, immigration, and trust in institutions

In order to understand how the current era of deeply mediatised right-wing extremism came into being, it is necessary to discuss the broader context first. Although it is impossible to conclusively point to specific antecedents and consequences, a series of circumstances (e.g. globalisation, the migration crisis, anti-Muslim sentiment) have been immensely influential. In our current societies, globalisation has triggered a shift from a 'solid' society based on control and concrete points of reference to a 'liquid' society whose key traits are perpetual change, insecurity, and hopelessness about the future (Bauman 1998). The change in intercommunity relations due to immigration has been associated with an increase in intergroup conflict due to discrimination against diverse minorities and the upsurge of different forms of radicalisation and (political, religious, and xenophobic) extremism across the world. Phenomena such as ideological polarisation, radicalisation, violent extremism, ethno-nationalism, and anti-Muslim sentiment are a 'minefield' and a threat to basic human rights, fundamental freedoms, and intergroup relations and tolerance (Sedgwick 2010). More concretely, in many countries, globalisation and immigration are exerting tremendous pressure on social cohesion (shared public values, communal and group values, guiding principles, and normative values). As a consequence, an increasingly recurring and prominent narrative – especially within extreme-right circles – is that of 'white genocide'. The idea behind this is 'that white populations are being replaced through immigration, integration, abortion and violence against white people' (Davey and Ebner 2019, 6). The 'white genocide' ideology was a driving factor behind the Christchurch attack, for example. Because this narrative is becoming more and more visible in society, it led to a divided public opinion that tends to be more overtly hostile towards migration (European Commission 2015).

This fragmentation in public opinion has been increased by a series of recent political developments and a worldwide decline of trust in democratic institutions such as the news media.

Indeed, in the wake of the 2016 US presidential election, the Brexit vote, and the European migration crisis, political and societal polarisation (i.e. a vast and growing gap between political ideologies and public opinion) have increased rapidly (Newton 2019). And each side of the polarised spectrum holds the same idea as truth: 'we are right, they are wrong, no matter what' (Pattyn 2014, 231). Together with the sudden rise of populist leaders and discourses across Europe, this has resulted in today's 'disaffected democracies' being trapped in an epistemic crisis in which citizens are increasingly unable to tell truths from falsehoods (Benkler, Faris and Roberts 2018). For instance, populist leaders all over the world – most notably President Trump – now routinely use the term 'fake news' to describe news that is critical of them or embarrassing. It is no surprise that such dominant discourses have gradually affected people's relation to news media in a negative way. In the last decade, scientific studies and polls have consistently pointed to a decline of citizens' trust in the conventional news media (Newman et al. 2019).

Audiences increasingly tend to rely on self-selection of online and social media sources ('my media') that they choose to trust for news, background, and information. This has raised concerns as people may get isolated intellectually if they are no longer seeking additional sources that convey diverse news (Newton 2019). In this regard, both mediated and interpersonal types of communication have been blamed for facilitating political and societal polarisation, which paved the way for right-wing extremism (Yadlin-Segal and Ramasubramanian 2017). Social media platforms also include contentious content such as extreme-right-inspired hate speech, offensive comments, misinformation and disinformation, blurred lines between fact and fiction, and propaganda – all of which result in a polarised society and in division between communities, some of which become ostracised. This brings us to the second issue related to this deeply mediatised extreme right, one which pertains to information disorders and the information ecosystem.

'*It's the information ecosystem, stupid*'

This part of the chapter discusses the umbilical role that information disorders and the information ecosystem at large have played in the deep mediatisation of the extreme right (Maly 2019). Rather than attempting to be complete or exhaustive, this section looks at the three most pervasive information disorders used by the extreme right: (1) 'fake news' and propaganda, (2) memes and memetic warfare, and (3) digital platforms.

On fake news and propaganda

The first information disorder that has boosted the mediatisation of the extreme right is 'fake news'.[1] Apart from its deceptiveness, the most prominent feature of fake news is probably its virality: the capacity to pollute the mediated public debate by spreading and transforming falsehoods and myths (see Venturini 2019). According to Mourão and Robertson (2019, 2077), fake news relies on 'genre blending combining elements of traditional news with features that are exogenous to normative professional journalism: misinformation, sensationalism, clickbait and bias'. However, the assumption that fake news demonstrably and significantly undermines democracy is not a matter of agreement (Marda and Milan 2018). Nevertheless, while the total volume of fake news in comparison with real news is rather limited, at least in some cases, and very dependent on the topic or the event, it definitely needs studying – its existence, its design, and the machinery behind it (see Bayer et al. 2019). Not least because right-wing-inspired fake news stories have been found to outperform real news in terms of user engagement and popularity (Silverman 2016).

In line with their anti-establishment stance, (violent) extreme-right activists demand absolute free speech, no matter how offensive this may be to specific individuals or groups of people. In this respect the following elements in Bayer et al.'s definition (2019) of disinformation and propaganda is important: this is content designed to be false, manipulated, or misleading (disinformation) disseminated using unethical persuasion techniques (propaganda) on a topic of public interest, with the intention of generating insecurity, inciting hostility, or disrupting democratic processes and often making use of automated dissemination techniques for amplifying purposes. In a context of growing international tensions, a critical challenge is to try to identify the sources of manipulation techniques such as lies, omission, exaggeration, and misdirection, used strategically to influence domestic and foreign population groups, governments, and news professionals.

On memes and memetic warfare

While memes may be viewed as trivial and mundane artefacts, they reflect deep social and cultural structures, and when used for subtle (or not-so-subtle) political purposes, they can be 'deadly serious'. The extreme-right has no use for complex arguments and nuanced language: to persuade mass audiences, it knows it needs a sledgehammer rather than a feather. In other words, it favours simple, emotional, and dramatic language, including humour, ironic memes, and jokes. 'Memes' are (often a set of) images, photographs, and text fragments, or a combination of these, which are posted online, shared, imitated, and transformed by users (Shifman 2013). Often shared and commented upon in online public spaces such as Facebook, Twitter, and Instagram, they are also very popular on more exclusive online forums such as cloaked Facebook groups, WhatsApp groups, and channels on Discord, Reddit, 4chan and 8chan. Memes often take the form of so-called remixes, in which visual and textual elements are combined to send out a multimodal message and are usually a combination of content and design (Dancygier and Vandelanotte 2017; Heikkilä 2017; Shifman 2013), which makes them an appropriate mode of communication for political-ideological purposes (e.g. Börzsei 2013; Shifman 2014).

One common characteristic of extreme-right memes is the 'anomalous juxtaposition', putting incongruous images together to make the message absurd or provocative. This is used for 'maximising the susceptibility of the idea being passed from mind to mind' (Knobel and Lankshear 2007, 215). The use of elements from visual and popular culture and the injection of humour helps the extreme-right internet memes appear innocent at first sight while they send a powerful message around the world through this 'racial humour' (Yoon 2016). According to Bogerts and Fielitz (2019), far-right actors are aware of this duality and use this 'wolf in sheepskin' strategy to make their message attractive to the wider public rather than just the already convinced: this boils down to 'mainstreaming' an extreme message (Davey and Ebner 2017).

Bogerts and Fielitz (2019) investigated memes used by the German far right. They found that memes are often based on elements of popular culture, such as cartoons and video games, but also historical images (see also Boudana et al. 2017). Such memes mostly pertain to immigration, foreign politics, and the media but are also about the so-called naive leftists. Although memes are shared and commented upon at the micro level, they are capable of influencing society at the macro level (Gal, Shifman and Kampf 2016; Shifman 2013). A good example of this is the Christchurch mosque attack described earlier. Both the livestream video and the manifesto were drenched in references to a broader extreme-right internet culture. As noted by Davey and Ebner (2019, 24), the amount of intertextuality with the web's extreme-right subculture gave the attack almost the character of one big 'inside joke'. For instance, the background music that the attacker played in the car while driving to the first mosque was the song called 'Remove

Kebab', which was recorded by Bosnian Serb soldiers in the context of the Yugoslav wars and genocide against Bosnian Muslims and then became popular within the extreme right at large.

When the creation and dissemination of memes via social media are conducted on a large scale with the strategic intention of propagating a specific message or ideology, this is called memetic warfare (see e.g. Wall and Mitew 2018). This happened on a large scale during and after the 2016 US presidential election: a pro-Trump campaign was organised via memes that were crafted and pushed into the mainstream discourse from various online fringe communities such as Twitter, Reddit and 4chan (see e.g. Zannettou et al. 2018). More recent examples of the implementation of memes in (mainstream) political communication are the meme campaigns by presidential candidates Bernie Sanders and Michael Bloomberg in the first months of 2020, with the latter also using Instagram influencers to disseminate the memes (see e.g. Lorenz 2020).

One of the better-known internet memes used by the extreme right (and mainstreamed regularly) is that of 'Pepe the Frog' (see e.g. Pelletier-Gagnon and Pérez Trujillo Diniz 2018). It is a 2005 creation by comic artist Matt Furie and was featured as a character in the popular comic series *Boy's Club*. Because of Pepe's popularity as an online meme, he was hijacked by extreme-right movements in order to disseminate hate speech by depicting Pepe with a Hitler moustache or a long nose and a Jewish star. This practice was offensive enough for the Anti-Defamation League to include Pepe the Frog on its 2017 list of hate symbols. Authors and remixers of these memes injected humour through the funny-looking figure (Pepe is a green frog with bright red lips) in combination with familiar or historical settings and a tantalising quote. There is also the 'clown world meme', a derivative of Pepe which the extreme right uses to indicate that we live in an absurd, 'left-wing' 'clown world'. The jocular use of a clown results in the meme being enthusiastically shared by both alt-right supporters and people who just like to provoke, gradually making more people familiar with far-right ideology.

On algorithms and (the Achilles heel of) platforms

Besides the contents and forms of the communicative artefacts such as fake news and memes, the concept of information disorders also refers to the broader role of the ecosystem. In particular, social media platforms have been highly useful channels for the dissemination of populist messages. These platforms make it possible to have direct contact with an audience, bypassing professional news media and providing infinite possibilities to personalise a message and target specific users or groups (Ernst et al. 2017). We have already noted that mainstreaming involves the demarginalisation of extreme points of view by bringing them from the extreme poles of public discourse to the centre, thus making them negotiable (see earlier). And while one can argue that there is a kind of 'media populism' (Krämer 2014) happening in traditional media (which mostly present the political debate in emotional terms and often frame political items as in-group versus out-group issues), the gatekeeping on social media is much more open than on more traditional media platforms, where the focus is still mainly on elite and mainstream sources (see, among others, Grabe et al. 1999; Schoemaker and Vos 2009). Even traditional news media covering news on social media platforms use a new form of gatekeeping induced by social media logic (see, e.g. Bruns and Highfield 2015; Tandoc and Vos 2016). It should therefore come as no surprise that extreme-right movements and actors have started to see social media as a rewarding and easy way to send their messages to both followers (as a form of 'activism') and non-followers (as a form of 'mainstreaming'). Studies in this domain have been focusing on extreme-right discourses and hate speech on social media platforms such as Facebook (e.g. Awan 2016; Ben-David and Matamoros-Fernández 2016; Farkas, Schou and Neumayer 2018); Twitter (e.g. O'Callaghan et al. 2012; Nguyen 2016); YouTube (Ekman 2014; O'Callaghan et al. 2015); and, to a lesser extent, Reddit (e.g. Topinka 2018) and Instagram (Ichau et al. 2019) or a combination of different platforms (e.g. Matamoros-Fernández 2017; Ernst et al. 2017). Most platforms' terms of agreement and so-called community standards forbid hate speech, but in practice hate speech flourishes on such platforms because of the often-thin line between hate speech and free speech or humour. The platforms must achieve a difficult balancing act between wanting to be an open platform (and attract users through sensationalistic content) on the one hand and being called on to delete offensive content on the other hand (see e.g. Gillespie 2018).

As described by Macklin (2019a), events such as the Christchurch shooting highlight the Achilles heel of many of these platforms when confronted with extreme violent content. In determining whether content should be removed or not, platforms tend to rely heavily on artificial intelligence and algorithms. As a result, when interrogated in terms of their responsibilities in disseminating extreme-right materials, platforms often hide behind a narrative of solutionism, or 'we have an algorithm for that' (Morozov 2013). However, these algorithms have been found to be problematic in their own right. Not every message posted on social media (the input) is equally likely to be shown to the general public (the output) since both editorial (by content moderators) and algorithmic filtering take place between input and output (Diakopoulos 2015; Napoli 2014; Wallace 2018). Poell and Van Dijck (2014) indicate how this selection is anything but neutral. They argue that platforms have a strong preference for breaking news and news in line with the users' prior search and click behaviour. As far as breaking news is concerned, they claim that items or hashtags that generate a sudden, steep peak in the volume of tweets are more likely to be selected as trending topics than items that may generate a larger total volume but for which there is no clear peak. And this focus on a peak may favour spectacular, sensational, and bizarre news over complex, nuanced, but socially relevant news. This is in line with previous research indicating that the algorithms give toxic messages extra attention (Massanari 2017). These insights can teach us how sensationalistic news but also fake news and extreme partisan messages can reach millions almost instantaneously – as epitomised by the success of #pizzagate, the hashtag that accompanied messages about an alleged paedophilia network headed by Hillary Clinton that was initially launched by a troll account that mainly tweeted pro-Nazi content (Metaxas and Finn 2019).

This logic of algorithmic filtering and entanglement with political actors could lead to the notorious filter bubble (see e.g. Pariser 2011) and 'information cocoons' or echo chambers (see, e.g. Sunstein 2007; Jamieson and Cappella 2008). In short, a filter bubble is the result of not being able to see deviating sources and content (due to the algorithms' filtering), and an echo chamber describes a virtual 'self-protective enclave' in which extreme right-wing users, for example, only consume sources and content that repeat their own thoughts over and over again and confirm their already-internalised convictions (Jamieson and Cappella 2008). There are a number of studies indicating the existence of filter bubbles and echo chambers (see, e.g. Barberá 2015; Colleoni et al. 2014; Walter et al. 2018; Sunstein 2004), but more and more studies indicate that the existence of this kind of insulate, virtual spaces in which users only come into contact with like-minded people and content must be nuanced (Flaxman et al. 2016; Zuiderveen Borgesius et al. 2016). Bruns (2019) even argued that we should abandon the dogma that platforms by definition lead to filter bubbles and echo chambers, which is probably triggered by a form of 'moral panic', and that it is more valuable to study what people do with the news and information once they are confronted with it. Consequently, more research is required.

Directions for future research

Both the earlier discussion and the Christchurch shooting show that the interplay between extremism and information disorders seems to be cyclic. Against a backdrop of globalisation and immigration, societal and political polarisation is on the increase. In turn, this climate of societal polarisation feeds into an increasing state of intergroup tensions, conflicts, and intolerance. Consecutively, these increased levels of intergroup conflict are a breeding ground for violent extremist attacks such as in Christchurch. These attacks set in motion a chain reaction of similar attacks everywhere around the world, leading in turn to increased societal polarisation. And the cycle starts over again. At the epicentre of this global cyclic movement is the information ecosystem and, specifically, the increasing spread of information disorders.

In that sense, this cyclic pattern is similar to the 'flywheel hypothesis' of extremism (see Frissen 2019, 89–93). This hypothesis states that such a cyclic chain of events is much like a mechanical flywheel, in as much as information disorders provide the initial energy supply to get the cycle in motion. At the same time, they provide additional kinetic energy to keep it going. The stronger the driving force, the more kinetic energy is built up in the cyclic process and the more inertia the flywheel possesses. This metaphor also implies that even if the driving force is briefly taken away, the flywheel will remain in motion for a while. As a result, it is through the driving forces of information disorders that the flywheel builds up kinetic energy and keeps turning.

A consequence of this hypothesis is that if we wish to study phenomena such as extremism – including the extreme right – we need to approach it from a 'bird's eye' perspective. Current research lacks a holistic approach enabling a deeper understanding of the creation, dissemination, and impact of information disorders, as well as the combined roles of interpersonal and mediated types of communication. Most research about the extreme right has taken either a theoretical approach (e.g. 'What is it like?') or a quantitative perspective mainly aimed at the sources (e.g. 'Who follows it, and how is it spread?'). However, we know very little about the way the target audiences – that is, the users of this contentious and socially unacceptable content – actually define and make sense of this kind of content. Since it has often been argued that fake news and disinformation are 'in the eye of the beholder', there is a crucial need for additional research on people's own understanding of contentious content. We need to better understand the social-psychological characteristics of vulnerable individuals (both as target audience and as subject of the contentious content) and set up initiatives able to make people more resistant to extreme-right disinformation. At the same time, increased scientific attention is needed vis-à-vis the role of digital platforms and the increasing dominance of algorithms in the information ecosystem. For this kind of research, scholars may want to include predictive modelling, forecasting, and computational methods (such as agent-based models).

Note

1 The actual scientific and analytical meaning of the term 'fake news' evaporated almost overnight after its introduction by Craig Silverman (2016) and its appropriation by US president Donald Trump, who rightly saw it as a powerful weapon against critical journalists and media. A thorough discursive analysis of what fake news exactly is goes beyond the scope of this chapter. For such an analysis, see Farkas and Schou (2018).

References

Aristotle, Ross, D. and Brown, L. (2009). *The Nicomachean ethics*. New York: Oxford University Press. doi: 10.1017/UPO9781844653584.004.
Awan, I. (2016). Islamophobia on social media: A qualitative analysis of the Facebook's walls of hate. *International Journal of Cyber Criminology*, 10(1).

Barberá, P. (2015). Birds of the same feather tweet together: Bayesian ideal point estimation using Twitter data. *Political Analysis*, 23, 76–91.

Bauman, Z. (1998). *Globalization: The human consequences.* Cambridge: Polity Press.

Bayer, J., Bitiukova, N., Bárd, P., Szakács, J., Alemanno, A. and Uszkiewicz, E. (2019). *Disinformation and propaganda – impact on the functioning of the rule of law in the EU and its member states.* Available at: www.europarl.europa.eu/supporting-analyses (Accessed: 30 April 2020).

Ben-David, A. and Matamoros-Fernández, A. (2016). Hate speech and covert discrimination on social media: Monitoring the Facebook pages of extreme-right political parties in Spain. *International Journal of Communication*, 10, 1167–1193.

Benkler, Y., Faris, R. and Roberts, H. (2018). *Network propanda: Manipulation, disinformation, and radicalization in American politics.* New York: Oxford University Press.

Bennett, W. L. and Livingston, S. (2018). The disinformation order: Disruptive communication and the decline of democratic institutions. *European Journal of Communication*, 33(2), 122–139. doi: 10.1177/0267323118760317.

Bogerts, L. and Fielitz, M. (2019). Do you want a meme war?”: Understanding the visual memes of the German far right. In Fielitz, M. and Thurston, N. (eds.), *Post-digital cultures of the far right: Online actions and offline consequences in Europe and the US.* Bielefeld: Transcript.

Börzsei, L. K. (2013). Makes a meme instead: A concise history of Internet memes. *New Media Studies Magazine*, 7, 1–25. Available at: https://works.bepress.com/linda_borzsei/2/.

Boudana, S., Frosh, P. and Cohen, A. A. (2017). Reviving icons to death: When historic photographs become digital memes. *Media, Culture & Society*, 39(8), 1210–1230.

Bruns, A. (2019). *Are filter bubbles real?* Hoboken, NJ: John Wiley & Sons.

Bruns, A. and Highfield, T. (2015). From news blogs to news on Twitter: Gatewatching and collaborative news curation. In *Handbook of digital politics.* Cheltenham: Edward Elgar Publishing.

Colleoni, E., Rozza, A. and Arvidsson, A. (2014). Echo chamber or public sphere? Predicting political orientation and measuring political homophily in twitter using big data. *Journal of Communication*, 64, 317–332.

Dancygier, B. and Vandelanotte, L. (2017). Internet memes as multimodal constructions. *Cognitive Linguistics*, 28(3), 565–598.

Davey, J. and Ebner, J. (2017). *The fringe insurgency: Connectivity, convergence and mainstreaming of the extreme right.* Available at: https://www.isdglobal.org/isd-publications/the-fringe-insurgency-connectivity-convergence-and-mainstreaming-of-the-extreme-right/.

Davey, J. and Ebner, J. (2019). *The great replacement: The violent consequences of mainstreamed extremism.* Available at: www.isdglobal.org/wp-content/uploads/2019/07/The-Great-Replacement-The-Violent-Consequences-of-Mainstreamed-Extremism-by-ISD.pdf.

Diakopoulos, N. (2015). Algorithmic accountability: Journalistic investigation of computational power structures. *Digital Journalism*, 3(3), 398–415.

Ekman, M. (2014). The dark side of online activism: Swedish right-wing extremist video activism on YouTube. *MedieKultur: Journal of Media and Communication Research*, 30(56), 21.

Ernst, N., Engesser, S., Büchel, F., Blassnig, S. and Esser, F. (2017). Extreme parties and populism: An analysis of Facebook and Twitter across six countries. *Information, Communication & Society*, 20(9), 1347–1364.

European Commission. (2015). *Eurobarometer 83: Public opinion in the European Union*, July. Available at: http://ec.europa.eu/commfrontoffice/publicopinion/archives/eb/eb83/eb83_first_en.pdf.

Farkas, J. and Schou, J. (2018). Fake news as a floating signifier: Hegemony, antagonism and the politics of falsehood. *Javnost*, 25(3), 298–314. doi: 10.1080/13183222.2018.1463047.

Farkas, J., Schou, J. and Neumayer, C. (2018). Cloaked Facebook pages: Exploring fake Islamist propaganda in social media. *New Media & Society*, 20(5), 1850–1867.

Flaxman, S., Goel, S. and Rao, J. M. (2016). Filter bubbles, echo chambers, and online news consumption. *Public Opinion Quarterly*, 80(S1), 298–320.

Frissen, T. (2019). *(Hard)wired for terror: Unraveling the mediatized routes and roots of radicalization.* KU Leuven. Available at: https://lirias.kuleuven.be/2790809?limo=0.

Gal, N., Shifman, L. and Kampf, Z. (2016). “It gets Better”: Internet memes and the construction of collective identity. *New Media & Society*, 18(8), 1698–1714.

Gillespie, T. (2018). *Custodians of the Internet: Platforms, content moderation, and the hidden decisions that shape social media.* New Haven, CT: Yale University Press.

Grabe, M. E., Zhou, S. and Barnett, B. (1999). Sourcing and reporting in news magazine programs: 60 minutes versus hard copy. *Journalism & Mass Communication Quarterly*, 76(2), 293–311.

Heikkilä, N. (2017). Online antagonism of the alt-right in the 2016 election. *European Journal of American Studies*, 12(2).

Hepp, A. (2020). *Deep mediatization, deep mediatization*. New York: Routledge. doi: 10.4324/97813510 64903.

Ichau, E., Frissen, T. and d'Haenens, L. (2019). From #selfie to #edgy: Hashtag networks and images associated with the hashtag #jews on Instagram. *Telematics and Informatics*, 44(September), 101275, Elsevier. doi: 10.1016/j.tele.2019.101275.

Jamieson, K. H. and Cappella, J. N. (2008). *Echo chamber: Rush Limbaugh and the conservative media establishment*. Oxford: Oxford University Press.

Knobel, M. and Lankshear, C. (2007). Online memes, affinities, and cultural production. *A New Literacies Sampler*, 29, 199–227.

Koehler, D. (2019). The Halle, Germany, Synagogue attack and the Evolution of the far-right terror threat. *CTC Sentinel*, 12(11), pp. 14–20. Available at: https://ctc.usma.edu/wp-content/uploads/2020/02/CTC-SENTINEL-112019.pdf.

Krämer, B. (2014). Media populism: A conceptual clarification and some theses on its effects. *Communication Theory*, 24(1), 42–60.

Leman, J. (2016). Socio-political dimensions of extremism. In *Countering Violent Extremism: Mujahada and Muslims' responsibility*. Brussels. Available at: https://soc.kuleuven.be/fsw/english/news/international-symposium-countering-violent-extremism-mujahada-and-muslims2019-responsibility-15-2013-16-march-2016-brussels.

Lorenz, T. (2020). *Michael Bloomberg's campaign suddenly drops memes everywhere*. Available at: www.nytimes.com/2020/02/13/style/michael-bloomberg-memes-jerry-media.html.

Macklin, G. (2019a). The Christchurch attacks: Livestream terror in the viral video age. *CTC Sentinel*, 18–30, July. Available at: https://ctc.usma.edu/july-2019/.

Macklin, G. (2019b). The El Paso terrorist attack: The chain reaction of global right-wing terror. *CTC Sentinel*, 12(11). Available at: https://ctc.usma.edu/wp-content/uploads/2020/02/CTC-SENTINEL-112019.pdf.

Maly, I. (2019). New right metapolitics and the algorithmic activism of Schild & Vrienden. *Social Media + Society*, 5(2). doi: 10.1177/2056305119856700.

Marda, V. and Milan, S. (2018). *Wisdom of the crowd: Multistakeholder perspectives on the fake news debate*. Internet Policy Review Series, Annenberg School of Communication. SSRN. Available at: https://ssrn.com/abstract=3184458.

Massanari, A. (2017). # Gamergate and the fappening: How Reddit's algorithm, governance, and culture support toxic technocultures. *New Media & Society*, 19(3), 329.

Matamoros-Fernández, A. (2017). Platformed racism: The mediation and circulation of an Australian race-based controversy on Twitter, Facebook and YouTube. *Information, Communication & Society*, 20(6), 930–946.

Metaxas, P. and Finn, S. (2019). Investigating the infamous# Pizzagate conspiracy theory. *Technology Science*. Available at: https://techscience.org/a/2019121802/.

Midlarsky, M. I. (2011). *Origins of political extremism: Mass violence in the twentieth century and beyond*. Cambridge: Cambridge University Press.

Morozov, E. (2013). *To save everything, click here*. New York: PublicAffairs.

Mourão, R. and Robertson, C. (2019). Fake news as discursive integration: An analysis of sites that publish false, misleading, hyperpartisan and sensational information. *Journalism Studies*, 20(14), 2077–2095. doi : 10.1080/1461670X.2019.1566871.

Napoli, P. M. (2014). Automated media: An institutional theory perspective on algorithmic media production and consumption. *Communication Theory*, 24(3), 340–360.

Newman, N., Fletcher, R., Kalogeropoulos, A. and Nielsen, R. K. (2019). *Reuters institute digital news report 2019*, June 12. SSRN. Available at: https://ssrn.com/abstract=3414941.

Newton, K. (2019). *Surprising news: How the media affect – and do not affect – politics*. Boulder: Lynne Rienner Publishers.

Nguyen, N. M. (2016). I tweet like a white person tbh!# whitewashed: Examining the language of internalized racism and the policing of ethnic identity on Twitter. *Social Semiotics*, 26(5), 505–523.

O'Callaghan, D., Greene, D., Conway, M., Carthy, J. and Cunningham, P. (2012). An analysis of interactions within and between extreme right communities in social media. In *Ubiquitous social media analysis* (pp. 88–107). Berlin and Heidelberg: Springer.

O'Callaghan, D., Greene, D., Conway, M., Carthy, J. and Cunningham, P. (2015). Down the (white) rabbit hole: The extreme right and online recommender systems. *Social Science Computer Review*, 33(4), 459–478.

Pariser, E. (2011). *The filter bubble: How the new personalized web is changing what we read and how we think.* New York: Penguin.

Pattyn, B. (2014). *Media en mentaliteit.* 3rd edn. Leuven: LannooCampus.

Pelletier-Gagnon, J. and Pérez Trujillo Diniz, A. (2018). Colonizing Pepe: Internet memes as cyber-places. *Space and Culture.* doi: 10.1177/1206331218776188.

Poell, T. and Van Dijck, J. (2014). Social media and journalistic independence. *Media Independence: Working with Freedom or Working for Free,* 1, 181–201.

Schmid, A. P. (2013) *Radicalisation, de-radicalisation, counter-radicalisation: A conceptual discussion and literature review.* ICCT Research Paper. The Hague. Available at: www.icct.nl/download/file/ICCT-Schmid-Radicalisation-De-Radicalisation-Counter-Radicalisation-March-2013.pdf.

Sedgwick, M. (2010). The concept of radicalization as a source of confusion. *Terrorism and Political Violence,* 22(4), 479–494. doi: 10.1080/09546553.2010.491009.

Shifman, L. (2013). Memes in a digital world: Reconciling with a conceptual troublemaker. *Journal of Computer-Mediated Communication,* 18(3), 362–377.

Shifman, L. (2014). *Memes in digital culture.* Cambridge, MA: MIT Press.

Shoemaker, P. J. and Vos, T. (2009). *Gatekeeping theory.* London: Routledge.

Silverman, C. (2016). This analysis shows how viral fake election news stories outperformed real news on Facebook. *Buzzfeed.com.* Available at: www.buzzfeednews.com/article/craigsilverman/viral-fake-election-news-outperformed-real-news-on-facebook#.emA15rzd0 (Accessed: 15 November 2018).

Sunstein, C. (2004). Democracy and filtering. *Communications of the ACM,* 47(12), 57–59.

Sunstein, C. R. (2007). *Republic.com 2.0.* Princeton, NJ: Princeton University Press.

Tandoc, E. C. and Vos, T. P. (2016). The journalist is marketing the news: Social media in the gatekeeping process. *Journalism Practice,* 10(8), 950–966.

Topinka, R. J. (2018). Politically incorrect participatory media: Racist nationalism on r/ImGoingToHellForThis. *New Media & Society,* 20(5), 2050–2069.

Venturini, T. (2019). From fake to junk news, the data politics of online virality. In D. Bigo, E. Isin and E. Ruppert (Eds.), *Data politics: Worlds, subjects, rights.* London: Routledge.

Wall, T. and Mitew, T. E. (2018). Swarm networks and the design process of a distributed meme warfare campaign. *First Monday,* 22, 1–33.

Wallace, J. (2018). Modelling contemporary gatekeeping: The rise of individuals, algorithms and platforms in digital news dissemination. *Digital Journalism,* 6(3), 274–293.

Walter, S., Brüggemann, M. and Engesser, S. (2018). Echo chambers of denial: Explaining user comments on climate change. *Environmental Communication,* 12(2), 204–217.

Yadlin-Segal, A. and Ramasubramanian, S. (2017). Media influence on stigma. In P. Rössler (Ed.), *The international encyclopedia of media effects.* Malden: Wiley-Blackwell.

Yoon, I. (2016). Why is it not just a joke? Analysis of Internet memes associated with racism and hidden ideology of colorblindness. *Journal of Cultural Research in Art Education,* 33.

Zannettou, S., Caulfield, T., Blackburn, J., De Cristofaro, E., Sirivianos, M., Stringhini, G. and Suarez-Tangil, G. (2018). On the origins of memes by means of fringe web communities. In *Proceedings of the Internet Measurement Conference 2018* (pp. 188–202), October. Available at: https://dl.acm.org/doi/10.1145/3278532.3278550.

Zuiderveen Borgesius, F., Trilling, D., Möller, J., Bodó, B., De Vreese, C. H. and Helberger, N. (2016). Should we worry about filter bubbles? *Internet Policy Review. Journal on Internet Regulation,* 5(1).

26

INFORMATION DISORDER PRACTICES IN/BY CONTEMPORARY RUSSIA

Svetlana S. Bodrunova

Introduction: the 'Russian trolls' and academic research

Research on modern 'Russian propaganda' has been rapidly growing in recent years. It has examined information disorder activities (Wardle and Derakhshan 2017) organised, allegedly, by actors formally or informally affiliated with the Russian state and mostly directed at foreign populations. The focus has been on the study of the activities of RT (formerly Russia Today), the state-owned corporation oriented to foreign audiences, and detecting and proving the existence (and, rarely, assessing the impact) of online computational propaganda tools (Woolley and Howard 2018), including hacking, bot activity, trolling, and mixed-media propagation of fake and misleading information.

The first line in this research comprises investigative reports by US and European defence institutions, parliamentary groups, and think tanks, as well as detailed accounts based on open sources (see Lysenko and Brooks 2018), within the framework of international cyberwar. The main goals are to identify and prove organised efforts, define the extent of threat to national security, and suggest counteraction strategies. Scholars have studied alleged Russian disinformation campaigns on social networking sites through a combination of social network analysis and textual methods, with varying degree of difference between trolls/bots and random users. Also, Twitter has released datasets of at least 3.800 accounts altogether (without, though, publishing the methodology for such identification); these datasets were used for machine learning and journalistic investigations by NBC News and CNN. Other platforms like Facebook and Tumblr also announced blockages of the accounts identified as trolls/bots linked to Russia.

Several research findings are echoed in government investigations such as the Report on the Investigation into Russian Interference in the 2016 Presidential Election, known as Mueller Report (2019), and the subsequent indictment by the grand jury of the Court of the District of Columbia (www.justice.gov/file/1035477/download). The indictment states that 13 people of Russian citizenship were engaged in activities that breached the US FECA and FARA Acts related to federal elections and registration of foreign agents. The described actions went further than pro-Russian or pro-Trump posting: they included, as was stated, using stolen identities and spending money on political advertising without registering. Unlike the Mueller report, the indictment did not openly relate these activities to the Russian authorities – who have also repeatedly denied any relation to them. Despite this, the indictment has led to widening the list of US sanctions against Russian individuals.

A second line of research has approached the subject by foregrounding questions about democratic communication. Karpan and co-authors (2019) closely examined the organisational routines of troll factories in Russia (better known as 'Olgino trolls'), China, and the Philippines, including an attempt aimed at 'finding an online army'. Other studies, instead, argue that there is no simple technique capable of detecting a troll (unlike a bot). Today's sophisticated work of potential trolls is often based on bias, spin (Linvill and Warren 2020), and subversive tactics of 'justifying their upsetting and threatening statements by characterization of reality as upsetting and threatening' (Wijermars and Lehtisaari 2019: 233). This makes trolls hardly distinguishable from ordinary users expressing discontent.

Within this line of research, here I follow a regretfully small number of works that offer a more nuanced view of the distortions of Russian-language communication. Kazakov and Hutchings (2019) intelligently point out the 'questionable assumption that information war is invariably a one-sided affair – Kremlin-initiated activities to be "countered" by Western democracies'. In their view, the argument about a line of transmission of misleading messages 'from "media outlets" through "force multipliers" to "reinforcing entities"' reconstructed "in the numerous intelligence-led reports" (ibid.) neglects the underlining instability and fluidity of the communities at which potential disinformation is targeted and genuine grassroots user participation in the ideological Russia-West clash. In his comprehensive reconstruction of contemporary studies of Russia-linked computational propaganda, Sanovich (2017) shows that disinformation directed both outside and inside the country has been, quite unexpectedly, linked to competition for influence within the political elite and has had a non-systemic, trial-and-error nature. Thus, the post-Soviet stereotypes that tell of wide-scale, monolithic, and well-coordinated state propagandistic efforts might be misleadingly simplistic when used to assess today's situation.

I would add further thoughts to reconsider the dominant cyberwar paradigm prone to focus on external dimensions of Russian propaganda that omits other important dimensions.

First, academic research does not aim to (dis)prove the linkages of disinformation activities, even if identified, to particular people or organisations; ultimately, that is done by courts and international organisations. But, on the other hand, without such proof within academic texts, the researchers' speculations on 'propaganda machines' remain allegations. Of the over 40 academic papers on Russian disinformation I have reviewed, none have contained airtight, solid proof of the linkage of disinformation efforts to particular government authorities in Russia. Actually, it would be surprising if we could find any: searching for proof would go against the research designs and, in general, turn science into investigation. It might endanger the domestic scholars as well, especially in countries with the regimes more restrictive than that in Russia.

Second, one needs to remember that it is way too easy to view pro-Russian information activity as organised and state-induced. One example comes from the same review by Sanovich (2017: 9). He states that Berkman Center at Harvard (Barash and Kelly 2012) detected the first large-scale use of pro-government bots and trolls in 2012 while the paper itself never mentions bots or trolls and states that 'committed set of users may use the pro-government hashtag . . . perhaps in an organizational or mobilizing capacity' as a possible *alternative* explanation of the density of pro-governmental clusters on Russian Twitter (ibid.: 10). Taken together, these considerations show that the scholarly community needs to better elaborate whether, and how exactly, we should incorporate data on disinformation into academic research.

Third, most of the reviewed research assumes but does not demonstrate that disinformation efforts had impact. Actual measurements of impact are rare. Just a handful of works set out to measure impact of trolling on Twitter, by analysing exposure to the discovered trolls/bots, be it by ordinary users with left/right leanings (Badawy, Ferrara, Lerman 2018; Spangher et al. 2018) or by journalists (Im et al. 2019), or the ability to disseminate links to various platforms (Zannettou et al. 2019). Exposure estimates may, indeed, be impressive: tweets plus retweets by spreaders of Russia-linked content could reach 12 million during the 2016 elections (Badawy, Ferrara, Lerman 2018: 262). However, the high impact of trolls/bots on behaviors such as voting and protesting remains largely undocumented. One exception (Zerback, Toepfl, Knoepfle 2020) found short-term impact of exposure on expressed views.

Fourth, there is not enough proof to attribute all misinformation in the 2016 US elections to Russia or to argue that it is widespread in Western public opinion. A widely cited technical report by the European Commission (EC) on selective exposure to fake news during the elections (Guess, Nyhan, Reifler 2018) does not link fake news websites to Russia, while it mentions US-based sites such as the ultra-right Breitbart and the satirical The Daily Currant. Figures on impact are uneven. Whereas the EC report claimed that approximately one in four Americans visited a fake news website during the 2016 elections, a study of electoral Twitter in Michigan by Howard and colleagues (2017) attributed only 1.8 percent of junk/bot news to Russian sources, and another study (Im et al. 2019) stated that a meagre 2.6 percent of US journalists on Twitter were reached by the suspect accounts. These findings may leave room for claiming that, even if the Russian effort existed, its impact was negligible and that 'the studies . . . do not add any substance to allegations of Kremlin culpability' (Martin 2017).

Fifth, research on Russian computational propaganda, as my colleagues and I have stated elsewhere (Koltsova and Bodrunova 2019), overshadows both the multi-faceted communication processes evolving in Russia since the early 2000s and their wider political, societal, and historical causes. Going beyond big data studies and 'engag[ing] with the forms of power and knowledge that produce' computational propaganda (Bolsover and Howard 2017) are not enough. We need to place the disinformation-oriented efforts into contexts that provide explanations and propose solutions. Shedding light on the communicative climate in the Russia of the 2010s would help expand the Russian disinformation studies by shifting the dominant focus from cyberwarfare to how disinformation and misinformation permeated domestic Russian communication, in which organised pro-establishment efforts only played a part. Next, we reconstruct the structural features of the Russian public sphere that have prevented efficient strategies for addressing the growing wave of disinformation practices.

Media in Russia after 2012: the structural impossibility of public debate and effervescence of Runet

Fragmentation of society and media

By 2011, Russian society and its media system were deeply fragmented. Toepfl (2011) described four clusters in the Russian media and political divisions between them, with social media being a separate cluster with yet undefined political stance. During the 2011–2012 'For fair elections' protests, public affairs media started to polarise politically, and soon impartiality and balance vanished. Even those media that sought to be impartial were labelled oppositional. A major problem was the absence of outlets that would bridge the worldviews of various populations such as cosmopolitan urban, post-Soviet town, depoliticised rural, and ethnic and immigrant social groups (Zubarevich 2011). The newspaper market largely consisted of business dailies that were hardly of interest to the general readership and post-Soviet (now tabloid) titles loyal to the elite and adhering to the 'traditional values' of post-Soviet conservatism, including the traditional family (in which, though, women work but prioritise housekeeping and children) and mistrust of capitalism and democratic rule. National television received 80 percent of the audience and featured public-affairs 'federal channels' (state-owned or state-affiliated) and non-political entertainment channels. Journalism experienced generational, political, and deontological divisions (Pasti, Chernysh, Svitich 2012), sometimes to the extent of 'non-handshakeability' between staff of liberal-oppositional and state-owned media (Bodrunova, Litvinenko, Nigmatullina 2020). It lacked legal protection and efficient self-regulation, and societal demand for strong independent journalism was weak.

The structural absence of substantial and inclusive public dialogue in the offline media left space for the internet to fill this gap. However, societal cleavages were mirrored by nationwide echo chambers in media and social networks. Russian Facebook was generally perceived as a liberal-oppositional filter bubble while Twitter was occupied by two opposite nationalistic discourses that diverged on seeing the elite as either those who 'stole the country' in the 1990s or those who 'made Russia rise from the knees' in the 2000s (Bodrunova et al. 2019). Facebook and 'alternative-agenda' media in a 'parallel' public sphere helped cultivate the 2011–2012 protest consensus (Bodrunova and Litvinenko 2013; Kiriya 2012). After the Crimea and Donbass conflicts erupted, the choice in online communication was between taking sides or self-silencing, which led to further divergence and even political battles between the uncritical (pro-government or silent) and leadership-critical online publics (Toepfl 2018). Simultaneously, Runet grew in popularity among younger audiences as their major source of news (Vendil Pallin 2017). A mirror for the still covertly boiling political antagonisms, Runet could not help becoming a focus of attention for pro-governmental forces.

'Services to the Fatherland': youth movements and attempts of state expansion online

In January 2012, a Twitter account @op_russia that called itself 'representatives of Anonymous in Russia' published a hacked email archive that, allegedly, contained letters by, among others, Vasily Yakemenko and Kristina Potupchik. The former was the chief of the Federal Agency for Youth Affairs and ex–federal commissar of the pro-governmental youth movements called '*Nashi*' ('Ours') and '*Iduschie vmeste*' ('Going together'). The movements were perceived as instruments of contentious politics that could be used against the 'orange revolution threat' and protest outbursts (Atwal and Bacon 2012). Potupchik was the press secretary of Nashi. The revealed emails contained information on payments to bloggers for postings on LiveJournal and major news portals. The letters also discussed 'creating unbearable conditions' for the national daily *Kommersant*, including organising DDOS attacks, buying out print copies, blockage of the print facilities, and 'physical and psychological attacks' on the staff (Karimova 2012); later, the *Kommersant* general director Demyan Kudryavtsev publicly blamed Nashi for the DDOS attacks, but no action followed. Neither Yakemenko nor Potupchik dismissed the letters as false. Moreover, in a recent interview, Potupchik debunked the organisational mechanics of troll work organised even before the Olgino trolls appeared onstage (Loshak 2019). In April 2019, Potupchik received a Medal of Order 'For Services to the Fatherland', Class I, when he was 33 years old.

After 2012, paid practices quickly spread along Runet. In Potupchik's opinion, the infestation of LiveJournal by 'youth activists who struggled in comments with oppositionists and were engaged in spamming' (Loshak 2019) in favour of various political actors contributed to bloggers' 'mass exodus' from LiveJournal (Bodrunova and Litvinenko 2015: 74). As Potupchik stated, the 'youth activists' followed the liberal community to Twitter and Facebook; on Twitter, their work was easy enough, while Facebook algorithmically prevented efficient automatisation of trolling. The strategy of trolling on Twitter differed from that on LiveJournal. Instead of active commenting and persuasion of individual users by 'small networks' of co-minded bloggers, interception ('hijacking') of popular hashtags and bot-based inflation of popularity were used (Loshak 2019). Bot activity as a crucial distortion in political talk on Russian Twitter was proved by Stukal and colleagues (2017), who detected that, within political topics, 'the proportion of tweets produced by bots exceed[ed] 50%' (p. 310). While bots discussed politics with other bots on Twitter, the 'youth activists' moved further on to YouTube and Telegram (see later in this chapter).

The early days of Nashi's internet crusade show two developments that have been largely unnoticed by scholars. First, disinformation that targeted domestic populations in Runet started earlier than in other countries. Second, it was more scattered, personal-project-like, and amateur than the orchestrated performance by the federal channels or the alleged actions abroad.

Activities of youth movements were early signs of what later became overwhelming: politicisation, political polarisation, and fakeisation of Runet. Bots and trolls helped heat it up, but they were not solely responsible. Next, I turn to discussing how changes in the legal regime, the blurring of journalistic standards, the mutual blaming by political actors, and anonymity shaped the polarised, post-truth atmosphere in Runet. Confrontation among polarised online publics prevailed over the decent core of public debate and the search for consensus.

A plague on both your houses: the rise of political Runet in the post-truth age

Tightening the screws in Runet regulation

If not for two factors, the political polarisation of Runet that brought along the growth of political debate could have been a sign of democratisation and growing online freedom.

First, the tightening of the internet legal regime created obstacles for open criticism of authorities and security services as criticism could be now interpreted as 'extremism'. Before 2012, Runet was relatively unregulated compared to offline media (Vendil Pallin 2017). Since 2012, the regulatory activity has grown dramatically in both quantity and toughness. From 2016 to 2019, there were 355 law initiatives, including the non-yet-implemented Yarovaya package and the so-called law on sovereign internet, and 143 cases of imprisonment for online activities (2019.runet.report/assets/files/Internet_Freedom%202019_The_Fortress.pdf). Regulatory control supported the practice of governmental 'gardening' of the leadership-critical segments of the public (Litvinenko and Toepfl 2019). This expression refers to, among other things, silencing radicals and cultivating moderate critics of the federal authorities. By regulating online expression, the authorities seemed to respond to popular demand: in 2014, a Levada Center poll found that 54 percent of the respondents believed internet censorship was necessary (Vendil Pallin 2017: 20). For Western observers, this would be incomprehensible or troubling. However, it is necessary to realise that a plea for censorship did not necessarily mean support for oppression but rather for clear and comprehensive rules (Bodrunova, Litvinenko, Nigmatullina 2020).

As Vendil Pallin (2017) discusses, another form of increased control was through direct ownership of technical facilities by the government and loyalty by domestic internet business. In dealing with global companies, though, this resulted in a change of legislation and blockage of platforms because they refused to store data in Russia. (The biggest victim of this policy was, ridiculously, apolitical LinkedIn.) The policy was framed as 'measures to increase national security and safeguard the individual security of Russian citizens' (ibid.: 29). However, amid low trust in public institutions, it has been impossible to distinguish between protection against malicious content or foreign attacks and politically motivated surveillance.

The second obstacle to democratisation was a rapidly growing atmosphere of fakes, debunking fakes, and mutual blaming by pro-establishment and oppositional/independent media. Projects like *Lapschesnimalochnaya* ('Wool-off-eyes-service') or the 'Fake news' programme on TV channel *Dozhd'* debunked misinformation (or, allegedly, purposeful disinformation) on federal TV and RT. Oppositional actors also provided repeated chances to be attacked, like Alexey Navalny's staff, who put a fake 'United Russia' manifesto party online and then denied the fake, giving birth to a meme: 'don't discuss, just spread and make them repulse'. Dozens of minor fake revelations from both sides have been a poor substitute for substantial political debate. The law package against fake news did not help and was soon used in ambiguous ways. It was introduced on 18 March 2019, the same day the law that prohibited offending civil servants was passed. It immediately prompted a political joke: 'don't speak of civil servants – criticizing them enacts the law on their offense while praising them enacts the one on fake news'.

The blurred meaning of independence: online media as 'state projects' and 'foreign agents'

Simultaneous to growing control, distrust of online sources increased for several reasons. Together with the trolling and botisation described earlier, news sources like FAN, Ridus, Pravda.ru, and Tsargrad were revealed as state affiliated. Also, in the early 2010s, several major media experienced editorial reshuffles, allegedly due to pressure on editors and owners. The reshuffles were perceived as 'units of one bloody chain' (Morev and Byhovskaya 2012) and led to changes in editorial positions. New online media were established by sacked editors, but the changes in several outlets that had gained trust across the political spectrum, like Lenta.ru or the state-owned but editorially independent RIA Novosti, were felt as a significant loss.

Also, as mentioned earlier, online audiences enjoyed the rise of 'alternative agenda' media, like online-only Openspace.ru or hybrid *Bolshoy gorod* ('Big city') during the 2000s. These media developed 'in parallel' to openly oppositional *Novaya gazeta*, or Echo of Moscow, and pursued alternative news topics such as urban life, public health, and high culture. Instead of direct political criticism, they employed social critique and described millennial mindsets and lifestyles, blending the Russian tradition of *publizistika* with Western values and philosophy. After the 'bloody chain', newly created media like *Meduza* by Galina Timchenko (ex-Lenta. ru) have made the 'alternative-agenda' media segment more distinctly anti-regime. However, although it is hard to disprove their revelations, the fact that outlets like *Meduza* or *Proekt* by Roman Badanin didn't disclose their funders made them vulnerable to legitimate criticism. In January 2019, RT published an investigation of the money behind these media, linking them to American and European funders such as the National Endowment for Democracy (US) and the European Endowment for Democracy, as well as to the exiled businessman Mikhail Khodorkovsky (russian.rt.com/world/article/593261-hodorkovskii-tsar-rassledovanie). While the investigation by RT was not impeccable, it supported the widely popularised claim that all activities of the Russian opposition were financed from abroad in order to weaken Russia's international standing. Also, it is important to acknowledge that the way *Meduza* or *Proekt* (do not) report on their sponsors blurs the understanding of independent journalism as one based on publicly scrutinised commercial income free from undisclosed donors, including foreign ones. If investigative media outlets in the US or Europe revealed they received financial aid from

Russian (or other foreign) NGOs or government agencies, this would immediately undermine their credibility as independent outlets; one needs to find a clear answer why similar opinions should not be legitimate in Russia.

Another group of new outlets blended information service with activism in a new approach to journalistic standards. Part of the foundation 'Help needed', *Takie dela* ('So it goes') successfully combined 'person-centered' reporting with fundraising. *Mediazona* merged reporting with protection of prisoners' rights. The 'No-drug city' foundation became the media project *Esli chestno* ('Frankly speaking'). Since 2014, *Baten'ka, da vy transformer* ('Dearest, you are a transformer, aren't you') has insistently employed personal gatekeeping by particular journalists, calling it *samizdat*. *Meduza* united investigations with 'Chapiteau', a rubric of fun and quizzes, to attract younger audience.

Given the polarised media market of lost trust described earlier, intentions to create 'new journalism' linked to advocacy for disadvantaged social groups and the struggle for human rights were indisputably humanist. The growing popularity of such projects only supported this claim. However, substantial professional discussion was missing on why the standards of objective journalism should be mixed with subjectivity and activism and whether the lack of domestic financing for independent investigative media meant a lack of social demand. The scarcity of debate on how healthy journalism should look like has left the experimental and investigative media unprotected from accusations that it represents undisclosed interests; this ultimately added to mistrust in Runet.

Rutube: fun and mimicry

With time, political YouTube became a sort of alternative television for a part of the Russian audience (Litvinenko forthcoming). By 2009, Vasily Yakemenko had realised that it provided wide possibilities for dissemination of viral content. Several projects on early Rutube, like 'My Duck's Vision' and 'Thank you Eva', allegedly received funding from the Nashi movement (Loshak 2019). Their content never directly praised the government; instead, it provided 'pure fun' while downgrading oppositional leaders or promoting senior authorities (ibid.). A new wave of attention to YouTube came in 2016: a young female vlogger was invited to give a speech to the State Duma, where an initiative to create 'a council of bloggers' appeared but quickly vanished.

By 2017, Rutube channels critical of the political establishment, such as Dmitry Ivanov's *kamikazedead*, had hundreds of millions of views. While the federal TV channels were biased in favour of 'system' voices, YouTube seemed tilted towards oppositional ones, even if Ivanov blamed YouTube for artificial downgrading critical videos and financial preferencing (bbc.com/russian/news-40674508). As the grassroots critical accounts were growing in power, a certain mimicry in pro-establishment video blogs was noticeable as they tried to look more amateurish to build trust (Litvinenko forthcoming).

Telegram: anonymity as a double-edged sword

After 2015, Telegram Messenger, a mobile application created by brothers Nikolai and Pavel Durov, gave a new flavor to the post-truth atmosphere of mistrust of information in Runet. Pavel Durov, the 'Russian Mark Zuckerberg' who earlier developed Vkontakte (now VK.com), the largest Russian-speaking social networking site, has struggled for years against surveillance capitalism – both in terms of surveillance and capitalism, like targeted-ad-based business models. However, his cyberlibertarian vision that demanded that the users and authorities trust

Telegram without public scrutiny led to conflicts with both Russian and American authorities. Durov left Russia in 2014, after he was coerced to sell his share of VK.com.

Initially, Telegram was developed as a part of the Telegram Open Network, a 'huge distributed. . . "superserver"' (Durov 2017: 1). The application allows anonymous postings and protects data by distributed key storage, which makes provision of the encryption code keys to the security services technically impossible. The application quickly became widely popular worldwide (with over 400 million accounts by May 2020), especially 'in Iran . . . and in Russia, where Telegram [was] popular among the urban dissenters' (Akbari and Gabdulhakov 2019: 223), including professionals and high-income groups (Salikov 2019). In various political contexts, Telegram gained diametrically different political reputations. Thus, external observers saw it as a tool for the liberation of online political talk in non-democracies (Akbari and Gabdulhakov 2019). Perhaps the Russian authorities shared this view, given that they attempted to block Telegram after the company refused to disclose the encryption keys in 2018. It almost failed as the app continued to function. Subsequently, a wave of urban protest ridiculed *Roskomnadzor*, the federal agency that observes communication. However, some Russian scholars noted that the protective anonymity of Telegram channels made the messenger a substitute for a public sphere for the elite, including politicians, civil servants, journalists, PR practitioners, businessmen, and intellectuals. In Indonesia and Israel, instead, the app gained a reputation of a safe space for ISIS terrorists (Fainberg 2017; Magdy 2016); the Russian police also claimed Telegram was used during the terrorist attack in St. Petersburg in April 2017.

Whatever anti-surveillance idea was behind Telegram, it worked in a twofold way in the Russian public sphere. On the one hand, it filled the niche of protecting anonymity after the amount of legal punishment for online posting grew (Loshak 2019); on the other hand, anonymity significantly boosted the climate of rumours and uncertainty. Also, in 2016, Telegram channels started to be used regularly for leaking political information as, for example, when speculations were rampant for a month on who would be a new chair of the presidential administration.

Since then, the number, popularity, and media impact of anonymous political channels on Telegram rose significantly, blurring the borders between fact and rumour on an unprecedented scale. Moreover, several top channels of political information, like tme_Nezygar' and tme_Mediatehnolog, raised doubts about their independent nature. Investigations of ownership/authorship linked at least ten of the most popular political channels to the ruling elite (proekt.media/narrative/telegram-kanaly/). The alleged owners either fiercely denied or made no comments about the accusations. However, the major issue was not even pro-state content but the ultimate impossibility of distinguishing between pro-Kremlin and oppositional bloggers as content was spun well enough to confuse. The role of Telegram in spreading fake news looks substantial, too, although no reliable research data is available. For example, in 2018, Maria Zaharova, the Ministry of Foreign Affairs chief press officer, officially responded to fake claims by Teresa May published in tme_Nezygar'. Between 2018 and 2020, Telegram channels were often used for so-called *vbrosy* – targeted leaks or information injections against particular politicians.

By way of a conclusion: the web that failed (again)?

Evidently, there were no solid structural elements in public communication to resist the rise of misinformation and disinformation in Russia in the 2010s, given that TV and mass-market print outlets were biased, business dailies were used by a small segment of the population, social networks had become 'echo chambered', and online news media and Telegram channels polarised opinions and remained partly anonymous. This went hand in hand with dramatically low levels of trust in public institutions and communication (Edelman 2020). Online political communities were divided in an unprecedented manner. On one side, there were infiltration networks, state-affiliated news portals, anonymous Telegram channels, RT reporting, and bots discussing politics; on the other side, there were other anonymous Telegram channels, investigative media with unknown donors, and news sites that claimed a moral ground but altered journalistic standards. The atmosphere of blurred information sources and mutual blaming has been more destructive for the Russian media sphere than scattered and non-systematic organised disinformation efforts.

However, the disruptiveness of the media system is only a consequence of the nature, mindset, and traditions of the public. Toepfl (2018) has suggested three types of (semi)authoritarian publics: uncritical, policy-critical, and leadership-critical publics. But, in contemporary Russia, criticism of the leader does not imply substantial policy debate while policy criticism does not challenge the political incumbents. What is lacking is policy-and-leadership-critical publics that would link discussions on policies to the flawed organisational patterns of government and particular policy makers. The causes of this deficiency are multiple, and they demand further analysis. The growth of such publics is further hampered by the lack of general awareness about healthy patterns of public debate based on bridging socioeconomic cleavages rather than on political and moral divisions between post-Soviet, liberal-oppositional, and new advocacy journalism and blogging. The Russian web once called 'failed' (Fossato and Lloyd 2008) showed its mobilisation capacity (Bodrunova and Litvinenko 2013). However, it is on the verge of failing again. This is not due to low mobilisation potential or the absence of creative forms of journalism; rather, it is because of polarisation, distrust, and the historical absence of actors who would be trustworthy and independent enough to resist post-truth and bridge the confronting groups of today's Russian society.

References

Akbari, A. and R. Gabdulhakov. 2019. Platform surveillance and resistance in Iran and Russia: The case of Telegram. *Surveillance and Society* 17(1/2): 223–231.

Atwal, M. and E. Bacon. 2012. The youth movement Nashi: Contentious politics, civil society, and party politics. *East European Politics* 28(3): 256–266.

Badawy, A., E. Ferrara and K. Lerman. 2018. Analyzing the digital traces of political manipulation: The 2016 Russian interference Twitter campaign. In *ASONAM Proceedings 2018*, 258–265. IEEE.

Barash, V. and J. Kelly. 2012. *Salience vs. commitment: Dynamics of political hashtags in Russian Twitter*. Berkman Center Research Publications, #2012–9. https://papers.ssrn.com/sol3/papers.cfm?abstract_id=2034506.

Bodrunova, S. S., I. Blekanov, A. Smoliarova and A. Litvinenko. 2019. Beyond left and right: Real-world political polarization in Twitter discussions on inter-ethnic conflicts. *Media and Communication* 7(3): 119–132.

Bodrunova, S. S. and A. A. Litvinenko. 2013. New media and political protest: The formation of a public counter-sphere in Russia, 2008–12. In *Russia's changing economic and political regimes: The Putin years and afterwards*, ed. Makarychev, A., and A. Mommen, 29–65. London: Routledge.

Bodrunova, S. S. and A. A. Litvinenko. 2015. Four Russias in communication: Fragmentation of the Russian public sphere in the 2010s. In *Democracy and Media in Central and Eastern Europe 25 Years On*, ed. Dobek-Ostrowska, B., and M. Glowacki, 63–79. Warsaw: Peter Lang.

Bodrunova, S. S., A. A. Litvinenko and K. R. Nigmatullina. 2020. Who Is the Censor? Self-Censorship of Russian Journalists in Professional Routines and Social Networking. *Journalism*, 1464884920941965.

Bolsover, G. and P. Howard, P. 2017. Computational Propaganda and Political Big Data: Moving Toward a More Critical Research Agenda. *Big Data* 5(4): 273–276.

Durov, N. 2017. *Telegram Open Network*. http://telegrammar.ru/wp-content/uploads/blockchain-ton-telegram-materials.pdf.

Edelman. 2020. *2020 Edelman Trust Barometer*. www.edelman.com/trustbarometer.

Fainberg, A. 2017. *Spread the Word: Russia Social Media on the Service of Jihad*. International Institute of Counter-Terrorism, Spring 2017. www.academia.edu/32680478/Russia_Social_Media_on_the_service_of_jihad.

Fossato, F. and J. Lloyd. 2008. *The Web that Failed*. Reuters Institute for the Study of Journalism, University of Oxford. ora.ox.ac.uk/objects/uuid:5ebe466e-9622–46d4-b374–87e94630a5cb/download_file?safe_filename=The%2BWeb%2Bthat%2BFailedandfile_format=application%2Fpdfandtype_of_work=Book.

Guess, A., B. Nyhan and J. Reifler. 2018. Selective exposure to misinformation: Evidence from the consumption of fake news during the 2016 US presidential campaign. *European Research Council* 9: 1–14.

Howard, P. N., G. Bolsover, B. Kollanyi, S. Bradshaw and L. M. Neudert. 2017. Junk news and bots during the US election: What were Michigan voters sharing over Twitter. *CompProp*, OII, Data Memo. http://blogs.oii.ox.ac.uk/politicalbots/wp-content/uploads/sites/89/2017/03/What-Were-Michigan-Voters-Sharing-Over-Twitter-v2.pdf.

Im, J., E. Chandrasekharan, J. Sargent, P. Lighthammer, T. Denby, A. Bhargava, L. Hemphill, D. Jurgens and E. Gilbert. 2020. Still out there: Modeling and Identifying Russian Troll Accounts on Twitter. In Proceedings of the 12th ACM Conference on Web Science. New York: ACM, pp. 1–10.

Karimova, A. 2012. Kremlyovskaya blogodel'nya [The Kremlin's almshouse for bloggers]. *Kommersant*. February 13, 2012. www.kommersant.ru/doc/1868022.

Karpan, A., ed. 2019. *Troll Factories: Russia's Web Brigades*. Farmington Hills, NY: Greenhaven Publishing.

Kazakov, V. and S. Hutchings. 2019. Challenging the 'information war' paradigm. In *Freedom of Expression in Russia's New Mediasphere*, ed. Wijermars, M. and K. Lehtisaari (pp. 135–158). London: Routledge.

Kiriya, I. 2012. The culture of subversion and Russian media landscape. *International Journal of Communication* 6: 446–466.

Koltsova, O. and S. S. Bodrunova. 2019. Public Discussion in Russian Social Media: An Introduction. *Media and Communication* 7(3): 114–118.

Linvill, D. L. and P. L. Warren. 2020. Troll factories: Manufacturing specialized disinformation on Twitter. *Political Communication* 37(4), 447–467.

Litvinenko, A. forthcoming. YouTube as alternative television in Russia: Political videos during the presidential election campaign 2018. *Social Media + Society* (accepted for publication in 2020).

Litvinenko, A. and F. Toepfl. 2019. The 'gardening' of an authoritarian public at large: How Russia's ruling elites transformed the country's media landscape after the 2011/12 protests 'for fair elections'. *Publizistik* 64(2): 225–240.

Loshak, A. 2019. Bolshoe intervyu c Kristinoy Potupchik [A big interview with Kristina Potupchik]. *Nastoyaschee vremya*. October 31, 2019. www.currenttime.tv/a/potupchik-interview/30232662.html.

Lysenko, V. and C. Brooks. 2018. Russian information troops, disinformation, and democracy. *First Monday* 23(5). journals.uic.edu/ojs/index.php/fm/article/download/8176/7201.

Magdy, S. 2016. A safe space for terrorists. *British Journalism Review* 27(4): 23–28.

Martin, A. J. 2017. Long read: Key evidence linking Kremlin to social media trolls is lacking. *SkyNews*. November 25, 2017. https://news.sky.com/story/long-read-key-evidence-linking-kremlin-to-social-media-trolls-is-lacking-11137255.

Morev, G. and P. Byhovskaya. 2012. Eto zvenya odnoy grebanoy tsepi [These are the elements of one bloody chain]. *Openspace.ru*. June 7, 2012. http://os.colta.ru/media/paper/details/37626/.

Mueller, R. S. and Man With A. Cat. 2019. *Report on the Investigation into Russian Interference in the 2016 Presidential Election* (Vol. 1). Washington, DC: US Department of Justice. relayto.com/cdn/media/files/6hE5LFPORw2TKnEf8TkK_mueller-report%20(2).pdf.

Pasti, S., M. Chernysh and L. Svitich. 2012. Russian Journalists and Their Profession. In *The global journalist in the 21st century*, ed. Weaver, D. H., and L. Willnat, 267–282. London: Routledge.

Salikov, A. 2019. Telegram as a means of political communication and its use by Russia's ruling elite. *Politologija* 3(95): 83–110.

Sanovich, S. 2017. Computational propaganda in Russia: The origins of digital misinformation. *OII Working Paper* 2017.3. https://ora.ox.ac.uk/objects/uuid:555c1e20-60d0-4a20-8837-c68868cc0c96/download_file?file_format=pdfandsafe_filename=Comprop-Russia.pdfandtype_of_work=Report.

Spangher, A., G. Ranade, B. Nushi, A. Fourney and E. Horvitz. 2018. *Analysis of Strategy and Spread of Russia-sponsored Content in the US in 2017*. arXiv:1810.10033.

Stukal, D., S. Sanovich, R. Bonneau and J. A. Tucker. 2017. Detecting bots on Russian political Twitter. *Big data* 5(4): 310–324.

Toepfl, F. 2011. Managing public outrage: Power, scandal, and new media in contemporary Russia. *New Media and Society* 13(8): 1301–1319.

Toepfl, F. 2018. Comparing authoritarian publics: The benefits and risks of three types of publics for autocrats. *Communication Theory*. 30(2), 105–125.

Vendil Pallin, C. 2017. Internet control through ownership: The case of Russia. *Post-Soviet Affairs* 33(1): 16–33.

Wardle, C. and H. Derakhshan. 2017. Information disorder: Toward an interdisciplinary framework for research and policy making. Council of Europe Report DGI(2017)09. https://rm.coe.int/information-disorder-report-november-2017/1680764666.

Wijermars, M. and K. Lehtisaari (eds). 2019. *Freedom of Expression in Russia's New Mediasphere*. London: Routledge.

Woolley, S. C. and P. N. Howard (eds). 2018. *Computational Propaganda: Political Parties, Politicians, and Political Manipulation on Social Media*. Oxford: Oxford University Press.

Zannettou, S., T. Caulfield, W. Setzer, M. Sirivianos, G. Stringhini and J. Blackburn. 2019. Who let the trolls out? Towards understanding state-sponsored trolls. In *Proceedings of the 10th ACM Conference on Web Science*, 353–362. ACM.

Zerback, T., F. Toepfl and M. Knoepfle. 2020. The disconcerting potential of online disinformation: Persuasive effects of astroturfing comments and three strategies for inoculation against them. *New Media and Society*, 1461444820908530.

Zubarevich, N. 2011. Chetyre Rossii [Four Russias]. *Vedomosti*. December 30, 2011. www.vedomosti.ru/opinion/articles/2011/12/30/chetyre_rossii.

27

PROTEST, ACTIVISM, AND FALSE INFORMATION

Jennifer Earl, Rina James, Elliot Ramo, and Sam Scovill

False information about and within social movements has a long history, from early conceptions of collective behavior as susceptible to irrational beliefs (Garner 1997) to government suppression of social movements through the spreading of false information (Cunningham 2004) to unintentional but nonetheless inaccurate reporting about social movements (Gitlin 1980). In recent years, though, the quality, quantity, range of producers and spreaders, and reach of false information has greatly expanded, aided by the pervasiveness of digital and social media (Anderson 2019), making the relationship between false information and social movements a pressing academic and practical concern.

In this chapter, we focus on disinformation, which we define as false information created and spread with knowledge of its inaccuracies, and misinformation, false information spread without knowledge of its inaccuracies (see Spies 2019 on definitional debates). Both are false information, which we use when finer distinctions are not useful. We also discuss propaganda, which involves government and/or corporate uses of true, false, and misleading information for political goals (Benkler et al. 2018).

Our fundamental argument is that false information and propaganda play different theoretical roles in social movements based on the producer and/or diffuser. We briefly review the history of scholarship on false information in social movements and then build on these insights to specify five different theoretical lenses – each connected to specific producers – for understanding false information in social movements.

False information in the history of social movement studies

Collective behavior research from the late nineteenth and early twentieth centuries, the scholastic progenitor to social movements research, offers the earliest view of false information, viewing crowds (including protests) as irrational and susceptible to rumour (Garner 1997). As populist-turned-authoritarian movements swept across Europe in the 1930s to the 1950s, students of collective behavior shifted towards analysing political movements, arguing that individual traits made some susceptible to the demagoguery and propaganda of authoritarian rulers (Adorno et al. 1950). In both views, false information drove collective action.

In the 1960s, contemporary social movement scholarship challenged negative understandings of protest and distinguished it from collective behavior (Garner 1997). Attention shifted

290

towards governments' usage of false information to suppress social movements (e.g. government agents misrepresenting social movements to the press and spreading false information through informants to generate internal conflict; see Marx 1974; Cunningham 2004), casting false information as a protest inhibitor.

The rise of populist and/or alt-right movements in the US and in Europe has swung the pendulum back to the catalysing view (Bennet and Livingston 2018). Both views are important, and we add three more theoretical relationships, discussing all five in the next section.

Five theoretical lenses for false information and social movements

Despite the ominous moniker of disinformation, it has multiple theoretical roles in social movements. We identify five relationships between false information and social movements: (1) false information as movement catalyst, (2) disinformation and propaganda as repressive tools, (3) false information as a weaponisation of free speech, (4) false information as a commodity, and (5) misinformation resulting from journalistic norms applied to protest. Each of these approaches varies in the amount of existing scholarship and is organised around different producers of false information.

False information as a movement catalyst

Resource mobilisation theory claims that social movements emerge when grievances are connected with resources, but grievances still must be perceived and interpreted (Earl 2009), allowing false information to serve as a catalyst. As a result, misinformation has contributed to the rise of movements internationally, including the Velvet Revolution in Czechoslovakia, in which false rumours served as a catalyst for protest (Hassanpour 2014), and the worldwide anti-vaccination movement. For modern vaccination objectors, who are carrying forward safety concerns that began in the mid-1800s (Ołpiński 2012), two pieces of misinformation are particularly impactful: a 1982 documentary claiming the diphtheria, pertussis, and tetanus vaccine caused brain damage, seizures, and developmental delays (Ołpiński 2012) and a 1995 journal article linking autism to the measles, mumps, and rubella vaccine (Kata 2010). Both claims were the result of poor science, but this misinformation contributed to enduring vaccine scepticism.

Disinformation can also catalyse movements. In 2014, a false claim about a CDC whistle-blower reinforced fears over a vaccine-autism link and was emphasised, along with other high-profile disinformation, in recent anti-vaccination converts' online discourse (Mitra et al. 2016). White supremacists spread false information covertly to grow their movement; 'cloaked websites' (i.e. websites that obscure their political agenda) spread racist viewpoints while deliberately misleading their audiences about the source and validity of their claims (Keener 2018).

Based on the anti-vaccination movement, some have suggested that disinformation spreads easily to those with a predisposition for conspiracy thinking (e.g. Mitra et al. 2016). But false information may spread easily simply because it resonates with pre-existing views: people are more willing to believe content that confirms their existing beliefs and disbelieve and/or see as biased information that contradicts pre-existing views (Earl and Garrett 2017). For instance, false information from right-wing sources like Breitbart, which is heavily implicated in the rise of the alt-right (Bennet and Livingston 2018), is believable due to readers' pre-existing right-wing leanings.

Some argue the alignment of pre-existing beliefs with false information especially benefits all populist movements, not just the alt-right, but many populist movements do not depend on false information. Populist movements vary broadly across time, and some emerge precisely because they surface accurate information obscured by elites (e.g. progressives who benefited from muckraking). Moreover, as Bennet and Livingston (2018) argue, the alt-right claims a populist mantel but is actually racist and xenophobic. However, it is very likely that pre-existing views make false information more believable in movements attacking expertise (e.g. climate denial and anti-vaccination movements).

No matter the movement, belief in false information may spiral. For instance, Lewis and Marwick (2017) postulate a vicious cycle in which acceptance of one alt-right talking point begets acceptance of another, with people becoming increasingly vulnerable to false information as acceptance increases, and trust in mainstream media is undermined. Thus, anti-vaccination or alt-right engagement may be the result of a vicious cycle of increasing false information, aided by biased consumption, rather than a broad acceptance of conspiracy theories.

The evolution of believing the increasingly unbelievable is important because it helps explain the rise of radical and potentially dangerous extremes in movements that thrive on false information. The rise of alt-right terrorism is a prime example, with many citing 'Pizzagate', an alt-right conspiracy theory that spread widely on social media and fake news websites including Infowars (e.g. Keener 2018), as a critical example. 'Pizzagate' proponents claimed Democratic Party members were involved in a pedophile sex-trafficking ring run from a pizza parlor. Based on these claims, an armed man entered the restaurant, attempting to rescue the (nonexistent) victims. Keener (2018) summarises this self-reinforcing cycle: 'Propelled by far-right populist rhetoric and the legitimation of alternative forms of "news", it became thinkable that this conspiracy. . . *could* be possible' (147).

This escalation may be further aided by fractures in movements in which moderates who are unprepared to believe increasingly unbelievable false information are separated from extremists who are. Zwerman et al. (2000) showed that when moderate and more extreme activists become socially and/or organisationally separated from one another, moderates cannot restrain a spiral towards extreme beliefs. Left in an echo chamber with only other extremists, extremists push further away from the mainstream and towards violence, even when false information is not involved.

In sum, false information can catalyse movement emergence and feed spirals towards extremism. But accurate information may drive initial support for other movements. The truth of both statements suggests that scholars need to understand the conditions under which accurate information, contested information (i.e. accurate information that may lead to many alternative conclusions), and false information prove consequential to the rise of movements and whether false information is unique in its ability to drive self-perpetuating shifts towards the extreme.

False information as a strategy of social movement repression

We identify three types of actors who may use false information to oppose or repress social movements (see Earl 2011 for a review on repression).

State-based domestic repression

When domestic authorities engage movements, larger propaganda repertoires – which mix accurate information, misrepresented information, and disinformation – are called upon. The most successful realisation of social movement repression is quiescence. Decades ago, propaganda and censorship achieved some modicum of quiescence in the USSR, China, and other authoritarian states. While Russia and China used propaganda and censorship somewhat differently (Zhao 2012), they both used state-controlled media to bolster their regimes and censorship to limit unfavourable information. For instance, Munger describes the Chinese approach to Tiananmen:

> Early in the occupation of the Square by student protesters, the Chinese regime used the media to promote the narrative that these students were agents of the United States, aiming to undermine China. The students were unable to broadcast their true goal and grievances, and the regime's narrative was unchallenged throughout much of China. Once the regime found it necessary to begin shooting, they switched their media strategy, banning all mention of the protest and its repression.
>
> (Munger et al. 2019, 820)

More generally, Hassanpour (2014) argues that state control over news media may prevent mass dissatisfaction from becoming widespread in times of political unrest. What amounts to state-run media may also exist in nations with democratic elections but authoritarian leanings (e.g. Turkey, Ecuador) and serve a similar function (Walker and Orttung 2014).

Widespread internet usage has complicated this approach. Deibert et al. (2010) posit a 'three generation' framework for online propaganda, which interestingly translates historical offline tendencies. First, governments may limit access to the internet entirely (e.g. North Korea) or only in moments of turmoil (e.g. Egypt during the Arab Spring) (Howard et al. 2011). But wholesale restrictions are difficult to maintain economically; targeted censorship represents a second-generation approach, as has occurred in Russia, with government-requested removals of anti-Putin social media posts (Sanovich et al. 2018). Chinese authorities allow criticisms of the state but heavily censor social media support for activism (King et al. 2013). Both first- and second-generation restrictions occur while traditional state-based or 'statist commercialized' media (Vartanova 2011) circulate pro-regime messages.

Third-generation strategies, which Deibert et al. (2010) refer to as 'active engagement', go on the information offensive (Gunitsky 2015). Unable to censor social movements entirely, governments hope to advance views favourable to the regime, promote seemingly grassroots opposition to social movements and distract from opponents' messages by offering alternatives. King et al. (2017) estimate the Chinese government uses the so-called '50ct army' to create 448 million social media comments per year that largely 'involve cheerleading for China, the revolutionary history of the Communist Party, or other symbols of the regime' (484). These posts do not engage with government sceptics or discuss controversial issues. Rather, 'the goal of this massive secretive operation is . . . to distract the public and change the subject' (King et al. 2017, 484). As with any state propaganda, these efforts may spread disinformation or contested information that is reported as uncontested.

This response can be found in many nations. Munger et al.'s study of the La Salida/anti-Maduro movement showed that governments may 'advance many competing narratives that [address] issues unrelated to the opposition's criticism' (2019, 815) in the hopes of flooding social media platforms and diverting attention from information they cannot suppress. In Mexico, so-called 'Peñabots' promote fake trends in order to distract and drown out government criticism (Porup 2015). Elections and social movements may cross over, as occurred when Peñabots tried to distract from the emergence of the #YoSoy132 movement around the 2012 Mexican elections (Treré 2016).

Governments may also drown out messages they oppose by flooding digital spaces with spam. In Mexico, Suárez-Serrato et al. (2016) reported on an influx of spam tweets in response to the #YaMeCanse hashtag protesting government complacency in the disappearance of more than 40 student activists.

Authorities may also directly attack or discredit opponents by 'mobilizing regime supports to disrupt planned rallies, plant false information, monitor opposition websites, and harass opposition members' (Gunitsky 2015, 45), drawing on age-old government false information tactics used even in nations with democratically elected governments (Cunningham 2004). During the 2009 Iranian protests, for instance, some Twitter accounts were suspected to be government-run in order to mislead the public about protest activities (Cohen 2009). YouTube and Twitter spread protest news, some of which came from inside Iran's governmental regime, in hopes of paving the way for arresting opposition leaders (Esfandiari 2010). Likewise, following the Gezi protests, the Turkish government hired social media experts to boost pro-Erdoğan accounts and spread disinformation (Medieros 2014).

Regime campaigns can be quite sophisticated. Keller et al. (2017) show a division of tasks amongst different state actors promoting propaganda, including groups that used their bots to amplify favoured news or social media posts (generated from within and from real external users) while others attacked opponents. State-orchestrated propaganda can also be designed to appear as if it is civic in origin (Keller et al. 2017). As with the astroturf movements discussed later in this chapter, even when information is not false, an element of deceit may come from making social media activity appear as if it is grassroots when it is not.

The effectiveness of these campaigns, though, is unclear (Gunitsky 2015). Fominaya (2011), studying protests in Spain that erupted when the Spanish government was thought to have spread disinformation about the 11-M terrorist bombings in Madrid, shows that disinformation can backfire. Moreover, movements can co-opt these tactics, as leaders of the Egyptian Uprising of 2011 did by posting disinformation about protests to evade Egyptian police (Kirkpatrick 2011).

Corporate repression

Although far less researched, private actors play important roles in repression (Earl 2004). So, too, is the case with false information within the repressive repertoire. Corporations have also used false information to create quiescence, attack critics, and misdirect attention. For instance, despite consensus on anthropogenic climate change among scientists, the fossil fuel industry has funded disinformation campaigns to limit the effectiveness of climate advocacy, increase public doubt about climate change, downplay the benefits of sustainable technologies, and overstate the risks of 'green' energy sources (e.g. Livesey 2002). Chemical companies attempt to reduce activism by challenging independent studies and producing and distributing misleading scientific information (e.g. Olsson 2011). The food and beverage industry has run misinformation campaigns to downplay the risks of high sugar consumption, targeting Black families, Hispanic youth, and people who are poor, and run false information campaigns about 'healthy' foods that contain deceptively high amounts of sugar to limit activism demanding change (e.g. Bailin et al. 2014).

Astroturf countermovements are designed to make it appear as though there is organic, civic opposition to movements when there may be none. The misrepresentation of the source is misleading, and these campaigns often also include false and/or misrepresented substantive information. As Walker (2014) notes, astroturf campaigns camouflage corporate interests as grassroots activism. Smokers' rights, for instance, was more boardroom strategy than grassroots concern (Derry and Waikar 2008), yet it has been key to limiting anti-smoking activism, undermining tobacco control policies, and deflecting responsibility for health effects (Wander and Malone 2006).

Countermovements

Countermovements can use disinformation to attack opponents. For instance, a prominent white supremacist spread disinformation about Black Lives Matter (BLM) in hopes that the government would classify BLM as a terrorist organisation (Lewis and Marwick 2017). False information can make movements defend the accuracy of their own claims and materials because of doubt sowed by countermovements and governments (Tufekci 2017). For instance, Project Veritas, an alt-right group, has a track record of attacking movements through misleading editing of videos and through fabricated 'sting' operations (Benkler et al. 2018). The Center for Medical Progress's leader lost a \$2 million lawsuit as the result of misleading videos aimed at reducing abortion access (Tavernise 2019), but not before the videos led to legislative action and rallied opponents of abortion access.

Larger complexes of opposition groups, including corporations, countermovements, and others, may collaborate in the supply and distribution of false information. For instance, where climate denial is concerned, Brown (2017) argues that the 'climate disinformation campaign can be understood as a movement of corporations, organizations, and individuals that have systematically attacked mainstream climate change science using tactics that are radically inconsistent with responsible scientific skepticism' (128). These actors operate independently of one another but are able to connect through the internet to develop a 'denial machine' (Brown 2017, 129) or through think tanks, which 'were key organizational components. . . [that] developed and promulgated scientific misinformation via a wide range of distribution channels, including mass media appearances, Web sites, publication of books, and providing testimony in congressional hearings' (Brulle 2019, 2).

Polarised (mis)perceptions create difficulty in studying movement-countermovement false information though. In abortion politics, rhetoric is so contested that the labelling of opponents is disputed. Groups that claim the label 'pro-life' refer to opponents as 'pro-abortion'. But their opponents disagree with that label, using terms like 'reproductive rights' or 'abortion rights' instead. Abortion rights activists disagree that their opponents are pro-life, preferring the term 'anti-choice'.

Divergent frames and rhetoric may lead actors to see misinformation as among opponents' tactics, but disinformation exists too. For example, Bryant et al. (2014) examined the websites of crisis pregnancy centres in states with abortion access waiting periods, finding that about 80 percent of websites included at least one piece of false information about abortions. Such false information serves to further rally support for countermovements and threatens to reduce resources and support for their opponents.

False information as a weaponisation of free speech

Nations often believe that domestic social movements are the result of foreign intervention. J. Edgar Hoover dedicated the FBI to the repression of communism and other movements, which Hoover saw as duped by communists into agitation (Cunningham 2004). Likewise, many regimes internationally see the US as responsible for instigating movements in their countries. Though the veracity of these claims historically varies, disinformation is a key ingredient. Furthermore, there is significant evidence that countries are intervening in the politics and social movements of other nations, with Russia as a leading perpetrator.

In the case of Russian intervention in the US, Russia appears to be trying to weaponise free speech by using it as the opening to sow disinformation, which increases political polarisation, reduces trust in institutions, and causes democratic turmoil. In this way, the freedoms that allow social movements to emerge and develop in democratic nations are weaponised to poison the political soil out of which these movements grow. Directly repressing or diminishing specific social movements is not the goal of these interventions, but rather the diminishment of democratic politics more generally. Indeed, Russian accounts have been linked to orchestration of both left- and right-wing protests (Benkler et al. 2018).

Efforts have included the coordination of campaign events alongside 'methods clearly intended to instigate street clashes' (Benkler et al. 2018, 241). So-called troll farms, often attributed to foreign powers, engage with activist hashtags to increase political polarisation (Nimmo et al. 2018), as they did with #BlackLivesMatter and #BlueLivesMatter.

Where Russian interference is concerned, there is no neat separation between interventions into elections and social movements. According to platform-provided data from Twitter, YouTube, Instagram, and Facebook, Russia leveraged social media to spread propaganda in the US, using a specific list of social issues to engage Americans. Posts documented protests and pushed people to attend or incite protests. In addition to BLM and various separatist movements, Russian operatives also targeted movements around gun rights, patriotism, police brutality, and LGBT issues to drive polarisation (Diresta et al. 2018).

For social movements, this weaponisation of free speech may have significant consequences. Tufekci (2017) claims disinformation campaigns so overwhelm people that they become disillusioned and give up trying to actually figure out the truth. We argue polarisation itself is also significant because of the kinds of vicious information cycles discussed earlier. Polarisation also increases group identity (Yardi and Boyd 2010) and motivates partisans while demobilising moderates (Wojcieszak 2011) so that people with more moderate views may become less likely to participate in social movements (Earl and Garrett 2017).

These collateral effects of disinformation and the assault on democracies that the weaponisation of free speech represents may be more important than the specific disinformation. Benkler et al. (2018), for instance, shows Russian accounts only successfully organised a few small protests, and social movements with substantial web presences can 'correct and challenge misinformation shared online and offline' (Anderson 2019, 203). But how quickly and how far those corrections can spread is uncertain (Starbird et al. 2014) and may vary by country (Applebaum et al. 2017).

False information as a commodity

For-profit actors create and/or distribute false information related to social movements to make money regardless of the impact false information has on activism. Three key actors profit from the spread of false information: disinformation producers, ad placement companies, and social media platforms.

Citizens of Eastern European countries such as Georgia and Macedonia have been identified as particularly prolific producers of false information due to high unemployment and few sanctions (Kshetri and Voas 2017), although organisations may also be involved (Figueira and Oliveira 2017). It is tempting to link for-profit actors to larger political motivations, but ideology likely only reflects profit: content aimed at right-wing audiences appears particularly lucrative (Kshetri and Voas 2017) while similar content aimed at leftist voters is not (Vojak 2018).

Ad placement companies enable the spread of for-profit false information by providing revenue to disinformation websites. These companies profit from linking businesses to disinformation websites and have little incentive to blacklist disinformation sites (Braun and Eklund 2019).

Social media platforms benefit from false information through the artificially inflated user growth created by fake accounts associated with false information (Dayen 2017). Companies such as Facebook and Twitter have economic models that rely heavily on user growth, creating little incentive to remove fake accounts and making them slow to do so (Dayen 2017; Matyus 2019).

Profit-motivated production of and brokering in false information means that when protest is an important topic of public discussion, injecting false information about protest will become even more profitable. For instance, in Hong Kong, for-profit false information producers discredited Hong Kong protestors as unrest grew (Matyus 2019). This implies that a consequence of growing public interest in a movement may be the growth of for-profit disinformation circulating about it. As with the weaponisation of free speech, false information about movements has negative consequences for targeted movements and democratic life.

Misinformation and journalistic norms in the coverage of protest

One critical difference between institutional political elites and social movement actors involves standing (Amenta et al. 2017), which refers to assumed newsworthiness or expertise. Social movements have to work to achieve standing and compete for scant coverage while institutional political elites face far fewer barriers in gaining coverage because of their assumed standing (Gamson 1998). The relative lack of standing for social movement actors means that when false information is shared about them, they face significant hurdles in correcting it. For instance, BLM has not been able to fully confront claims in reporting that were promoted by Russian trolls.

Journalists play a major role in publicly defining movements even though journalists may be selecting for extremity (Gitlin 1980), perceived authenticity (Sobieraj 2010), or other characteristics in deciding which movement issues and actors to cover and how (Gottlieb 2015). Scholars generally do not believe that professional journalists make conscious, calculated efforts to frame stories in derogatory, false, or misleading ways; however, informational biases can still lead to coverage that supports misperceptions (Boykoff 2006) and may be perceived as misinformation. Similarly, professional journalistic practices may hamper the efforts of countermovements to spread disinformation through the news (Benkler et al. 2018), implying that journalist practices may make misinformation more likely but disinformation less likely.

Conclusion

The research reviewed demonstrates the varied roles of false information (and its producers) in social movements. Public acceptance of misinformation and the intentional spread of disinformation may serve as movement catalysts. Disinformation may also serve as a tool for movement opponents, including state-based and corporate repression using false information to create quiescence, attack critics, and misdirect attention away from negative information, and for countermovements focused on discrediting their opponents.

Social movements are caught in the crossfire as foreign actors weaponise free speech, spreading movement-related disinformation to increase political polarisation, and for-profit actors profit from clicks on movement-related disinformation. In both cases, while social movements are the not the direct targets of false information, there are significant collateral consequences for social movements and democratic systems. Journalistic norms around standing may also unintentionally contribute to the misrepresentation of social movements, although these norms likely guard against disinformation about social movements.

The current technological and political contexts exacerbate the potential for false information to impact movements as social media facilitates rapid dissemination, and political polarisation makes combatting false information exponentially more difficult. Research examining the spread and effects of false information related to social movements is very important, with many areas needing more development (e.g. the use of false information by countermovements). It is important that scholarship consider how accepted-but-false beliefs have informed conventional and protest politics in the past as well. For instance, racist, xenophobic, and sexist social policies are often built around and justified by false information about group differences, rendering the relationship between politics and false information even older than many acknowledge.

References

Adorno, T.W., Frenkel-Brunswik, E., Levison, D.J. & Sanford, R.N., 1950. *The authoritarian personality.* New York: Harper & Brothers.

Amenta, E., Elliott, T.A., Shortt, N., Tierney, A.C., Türkoğlu, D. & Vann Jr., B., 2017. From bias to coverage: What explains how news organizations treat social movements. *Sociology Compass,* 11(3), pp. 1–12.

Anderson, P., 2019. 'Independence 2.0': Digital activism, social media, and the Catalan independence movement. *Catalan Journal of Communication & Cultural Studies,* 11(2), pp. 191–207.

Applebaum, A., Pomerantsev, P., Smith, M. & Colliver, C., 2017. *'Make Germany great again': Kremlin, alt-Right and international influences in the 2017 German elections.* [pdf] London: Institute for Strategic Dialogue & Institute for Global Affairs. Available at: <www.isdglobal.org/wp-content/uploads/2017/12/Make-Germany-Great-Again-ENG-061217.pdf> [Accessed 11 November 2019].

Bailin, D., Goldman, G. & Phartiyal, P., 2014. *Sugar-coating science: How the food industry misleads consumers on sugar.* [pdf] Cambridge: Union of Concerned Scientists. Available at: <www.ucsusa.org/resources/sugar-coating-science> [Accessed 25 February 2020].

Benkler, Y., Faris, R. & Roberts, H., 2018. *Network propaganda: Manipulation, disinformation, and radicalization in American politics.* New York: Oxford University Press.

Bennet, W.L. & Livingston, S., 2018. The disinformation order: Disruptive communication and the decline of democratic institutions. *European Journal of Communication,* 33(2), pp. 122–139.

Boykoff, J., 2006. Framing dissent: Mass-media coverage of the global justice movement. *New Political Science,* 28(2), pp. 201–228.

Braun, J.A. & Eklund, J.L., 2019. Fake news, real money: Ad tech platforms, profit-driven hoaxes, and the business of journalism. *Digital Journalism,* 7(1), pp. 1–21.

Brown, D.A., 2017. The enormity of the damage done by the climate change disinformation campaign as the world struggles to implement the Paris Agreement. *In:* Westra, L. & Gray, J. (eds.), *The Role of Integrity in the Governance of the Commons.* New York: Springer.

Brulle, R.J., 2019. Networks of opposition: A structural analysis of U.S. climate change countermovement coalitions 1989–2015. *Sociological Inquiry,* pp. 1–22.

Bryant, A.G., Narasimhan, S., Bryant-Comstock, K. & Levi, E.E., 2014. Crisis pregnancy center websites: Information, misinformation and disinformation. *Contraception,* 90(6), pp. 601–605.

Cohen, N. 2009. Twitter on the barricades: Six lessons learned. *The New York Times,* [online] June 20. Available at: <www.nytimes.com/2009/06/21/weekinreview/21cohenweb.html> [Accessed 17 January 2020].

Cunningham, D., 2004. *There's something happening here: The new left, the Klan, and FBI counterintelligence.* Berkeley: University of California Press.

Dayen, D. 2017. How Twitter secretly benefits from bots and fake accounts. *The Intercept,* [online] November 6. Available at: <https://theintercept.com/2017/11/06/how-twitter-secretly-benefits-from-bots-and-fake-accounts> [Accessed 3 March 2020].

Deibert, R., Palfrey, J., Rohozinski, R., Zittrain, J. & Haraszti, M., 2010. *Access controlled: The shaping of power, rights, and rule in cyberspace.* Cambridge, MA: MIT Press.

Derry, R. & Waikar, S.V., 2008. Frames and filters: Strategic distrust as a legitimation tool in the 50-year battle between public health activists and Big Tobacco. *Business and Society,* 47(1), pp. 102–139.

Diresta, R., Shaffer, K., Ruppel, B., Sullivan, D., Matney, R., Fox, R., Albright, J. & Johnson, B., 2018. *The tactics & tropes of the internet research agency.* [pdf] Washington, DC: United States Senate Select

Committee on Intelligence. Available at: <www.yonder.co/articles/the-disinformation-report/> [Accessed 20 December 2019].

Earl, J., 2004. Controlling protest: New directions for research on the social control of protest. *Research in Social Movements, Conflicts, and Change*, 25(3), pp. 55–83.

Earl, J., 2009. When bad things happen: Toward a sociology of trouble. *Sociology of Crime, Law, and Deviance*, 12, pp. 231–254.

Earl, J., 2011. Political repression: Iron fists, velvet gloves, and diffuse control. *Annual Review of Sociology*, 37, pp. 261–284.

Earl, J. & Garrett, R.K., 2017. The new information frontier: Toward a more nuanced view of social movement communication. *Social Movement Studies*, 16(4), pp. 479–493.

Esfandiari, G. 2010. The Twitter devolution. *Foreign Policy*, [online] June 8. Available at: <https://foreignpolicy.com/2010/06/08/the-twitter-devolution/> [Accessed 17 January 2020].

Figueira, Á. & Oliveira, L., 2017. The current state of fake news: Challenges and opportunities. *Procedia Computer Science*, 121, pp. 817–825.

Fominaya, C.F., 2011. The Madrid bombings and popular protest: Misinformation, counter-information, mobilisation and elections are'11-M'. *Contemporary Social Science*, 6(3), pp. 289–307.

Gamson, W.A., 1998. Social movements and cultural change. *In:* Giugni, M.G., McAdam, D. & Tilly, C. (eds.), *From contention to democracy*. Lanham, MD: Rowman and Littlefield Publishers, Inc.

Garner, R., 1997. Fifty years of social movement theory: An interpretation. *In:* Garner, R. & Tenuto, J. (eds.), *Social movement theory and research: An annotated bibliographical guide*. Lanham, MD: Magill Bibliographies, Scarecrow Press and Salem Press.

Gitlin, T., 1980. *The whole world is watching: Mass media in the making and unmaking of the new left*. Los Angeles: University of California Press.

Gottlieb, J., 2015. Protest news framing cycle: How the New York Times covered Occupy Wall Street. *International Journal of Communication*, 9, pp. 1–23.

Gunitsky, S., 2015. Corrupting the cyber-commons: Social media as a tool of autocratic stability. *Perspectives on Politics*, 13(1), pp. 42–54.

Hassanpour, N., 2014. Media disruption and revolutionary unrest: Evidence from Mubarak's quasi-experiment. *Political Communication*, 31(1), pp. 1–24.

Howard, P.N., Agarwal, S.D. & Hussain, M.M., 2011. When do states disconnect their digital networks? Regime responses and the political uses of social media. *The Communication Review*, 14(3), pp. 216–232.

Kata, A., 2010. A postmodern Pandora's box: Anti-vaccination misinformation on the internet. *Vaccine*, 28(7), pp. 1709–1716.

Keener, K., 2018. Alternative facts and fake news: Digital mediation and the affective spread of hate in the era of Trump. *Journal of Hate Studies*, 14(1), pp. 137–151.

Keller, F., Schoch, D., Stier, S. & Yang, J., 2017. How to manipulate social media: Analyzing political astroturfing using ground truth data from South Korea. *In:* (AAAI) Association for the Advancement of Artificial Intelligence, *Eleventh International AAAI Conference on Web and Social Media*. Montréal, Québec, Canada, 15–18 May 2017. Palo Alto, CA: The AAAI Press.

King, G., Pan, J. & Roberts, M.E., 2013. How censorship in China allows government criticism but silences collective expression. *American Political Science Review*, 107(2), pp. 326–343.

King, G., Pan, J. & Roberts, M.E., 2017. How the Chinese government fabricates social media posts for strategic distraction, not engaged argument. *American Political Science Review*, 111(3), pp. 484–501.

Kirkpatrick, D.D. 2011. Wired and shrewd, young Egyptians guide revolt. *The New York Times*, [online] February 9. Available at: <www.nytimes.com/2011/02/10/world/middleeast/10youth.html> [Accessed 17 January 2020].

Kshetri, N. & Voas, J., 2017. The economics of 'fake news'. *IT Professional*, 19(6), pp. 8–12.

Lewis, R. & Marwick, A., 2017. Taking the red pill: Ideological motivations for spreading online disinformation. *In: Understanding and Addressing the Disinformation Ecosystem*. University of Pennsylvania, 15–16 December 2017. Philadelphia, Pennsylvania: Annenberg School for Communication.

Livesey, S.M., 2002. Global warming wars: Rhetorical and discourse analytic approaches to ExxonMobil's corporate public discourse. *The Journal of Business Communication*, 39(1), pp. 117–146.

Marx, G.T., 1974. Thoughts on a Neglected Category of Social Movement Participant: The Agent-Provacateur and the Informant. *American Journal of Sociology*, 80(2), pp. 402–442.

Matyus, A. 2019. The real reason fake social media accounts will haunt us for years to come. *Digital Trends*, [online] August 22. Available at: <www.digitaltrends.com/social-media/why-fake-social-media-accounts-will-haunt-us/> [Accessed 3 March 2020].

Medieros, J.D., 2014. *Turkey's Twitter-bot army and the politics of social media.* [online] Entwickelr.de. Available at: <https://entwickler.de/online/webmagazin//turkeys-twitter-bot-army-and-the-politics-of-social-media-1153.html> [Accessed 15 January 2020].

Mitra, T., Counts, S. & Pennebaker, J.W., 2016. Understanding anti-vaccination attitudes in social media. *In:* (AAAI) Association for the Advancement of Artificial Intelligence, *The Tenth International AAAI Conference on Web and Social Media,* 17–20 May 2016. Palo Alto, CA: The AAAI Press.

Munger, K., Bonneau, R., Nagler, J. & Tucker, J.A., 2019. Elites tweet to get feet off the streets: Measuring regime social media strategies during protest. *Political Science Research and Methods*, 7(4), pp. 815–834.

Nimmo, B., Brookie, G. & Karan, K. 2018. #TrollTracker: Twitter troll farm archives. *Medium*, [online] October 17. Available at: <https://medium.com/dfrlab/trolltracker-twitters-troll-farm-archives-d1b4df880ec6> [Accessed 20 December 2019].

Ołpiński, M., 2012. Anti-vaccination movement and parental refusals of immunization of children in USA. *Pediatria Polska*, 87(4), pp. 381–385.

Olsson, T.C., 2011. The world according to Monsanto: Pollution, corruption, and the control of our food supply (Review). *Enterprise and Society*, 12(3), pp. 668–670.

Porup, J.M. 2015. How Mexican Twitter bots shut down dissent. *Vice News, Vice Media,* [online] August 24. Available at: <https://motherboard.vice.com/en_us/article/how-mexican-twitter-bots-shut-down-dissent> [Accessed 23 November 2019].

Sanovich, S., Stukal, D., Penfold-Brown, D. & Tucker, J., 2018. Turning the virtual tables: Government strategies for addressing online opposition with an application to Russia. *Comparative Politics*, 50(3), pp. 435–482.

Sobieraj, S., 2010. Reporting conventions: Journalists, activists, and the thorny struggle for political visibility. *Social Problems*, 57(4), pp. 505–528.

Spies, S., 2019. *Defining 'disinformation'.* [online] *MediaWell.* Available at: <https://mediawell.ssrc.org/literature-reviews/defining-disinformation/versions/1-0/> [Accessed 2 December 2019].

Starbird, K., Maddock, J., Orand, M., Achterman, P.P. & Mason, R., 2014. Rumors, false flags, and digital vigilantes: Misinformation on Twitter after the 2013 Boston marathon bombing. *In:* iSchools, *iConference 2014*, Berlin, Germany, 4–7 March 2014 University of Illinois at Urbana-Champaign: Illinois Digital Environment for Access to Learning and Scholarship.

Suárez-Serrato, P., Roberts, M.E., Davis, C.A. & Menczer, F., 2016. On the influence of social bots in online protests: Preliminary findings of a Mexican case study. *In:* SocInfo, *International Conference on Social Informatics.* Bellevue, Washington, 11–14 November 2016. Cham, Switzerland: Springer.

Tavernise, S. 2019. Planned parenthood awarded $2 Million in lawsuit over secret videos. *The New York Times,* [online] November 15. Available at: <www.nytimes.com/2019/11/15/us/planned-parenthood-lawsuit-secret-videos.html> [Accessed 11 March 2020].

Treré, E., 2016. The dark side of digital politics: Understanding the algorithmic manufacturing of consent and the hindering of online dissidence. *IDS Bulletin*, 47(1), pp. 127–138.

Tufekci, Z., 2017. *Twitter and tear gas: The power and fragility of networked protest.* New Haven, CT: Yale University Press.

Vartanova, E., 2011. The Russian media model in the context of post-Soviet dynamics. *In:* Hallin, D.C. & Mancini, P. (eds.), *Comparing media systems beyond the western world.* Cambridge: Cambridge University Press.

Vojak, B., 2018. Fake news: The commoditization of internet speech. *California Western International Law Journal*, 48(1), pp. 123–158.

Walker, C. & Orttung, R.W., 2014. Breaking the news: The role of state-run media. *Journal of Democracy*, 24(1), pp. 71–85.

Walker, E.T., 2014. *Grassroots for hire: Public affairs consultants in American democracy.* Cambridge: Cambridge University Press.

Wander, N. & Malone, R.E., 2006. Making big tobacco give in: You lose, they win. *American Journal of Public Health*, 96(11), pp. 2048–2054.

Wojcieszak, M., 2011. Pulling towards or pulling away: Deliberation, disagreement and opinion extremity in political participation. *Social Science Quarterly*, 92(1), pp. 207–225.

Yardi, S. & Boyd, D., 2010. Dynamic debates: An analysis of group polarization over time on Twitter. *Bulletin of Science Technology & Society*, 30(5), pp. 316–327.

Zhao, Y., 2012. Understanding China's media system in a world historical context. *In:* Hallin, D.C. & Mancini, P. (eds.), *Comparing media systems beyond the western world*. Cambridge: Cambridge University Press.

Zwerman, G., Steinhoff, P.G. & Della Porta, D., 2000. Disappearing social movements: Clandestinity in the cycle of new left protest in the U.S., Japan, Germany and Italy. *Mobilization*, 5(1), pp. 85–104.

28

CONSPIRACY THEORIES

Misinformed publics or wittingly believing false information?

Jaron Harambam

Introduction

The question of Truth – with a capital T – takes center stage today. Ever since the tumultuous year of 2016, when Trump rose to power in the US and the Brits decided to leave the European Union, academics and public commenters seriously started to worry about the rise of various forms of 'untruths' in our (online) public domain. In addition to fake news and mis/disinformation, much attention in such discussion is paid to the popularity of conspiracy theories in this so-called post-truth era. The idea that the world is not as it seems and that official explanations provided by mainstream epistemic institutions (media, politics, science) are untrustworthy has great resonance today. Both political elites and ordinary people in various countries in the world interpret current and historical affairs along conspiratorial schema and play with the tropes of collusion, deceit, and manipulation. But who are these people? What do they actually believe? Why are these ideas so popular nowadays? How do they circulate in today's complex information landscape? And should we do something about them? This chapter goes into more detail about all these questions by discussing the various ways conspiracy theories play a role in contemporary societies. Moving away from persistent stereotypifications, it draws on empirically grounded social-scientific analyses and aims to offer better insight into a politically contested and highly moralised cultural phenomenon. Conspiracy theories exist in various times and places, and such differences are relevant for their understanding (Butter and Knight 2020: Section V). The focus of this chapter is therefore on the contemporary situation in (Western) Europe and the United States.

Definitions: slippery concepts and rhetorical weapons

Misinformation and conspiracy theories are often mentioned in one breath, signifying the false or dubious content post-truth is all about, but what do these two concepts actually share? Misinformation is usually defined as 'false or inaccurate information', which seems pretty straightforward and often is: blatant lies and clear falsehoods are easily spotted. However, the history and sociology of fact-checking, societies' most established effort to identify misinformation, shows the complexity and the interpretative work involved in this business (Graves 2016). It is often not that easy and unequivocal to separate true from false information; truth knows many shades of grey, after all. Although institutionalised fact-checkers generally abide by professional standards and clear procedures to identify misinformation, their work remains human and is thus subject to social, cultural, and ideological influences. On a more abstract level, then, it can be argued that truth and its opposites are products of societal power (Fuller 2018). What misinformation *is* becomes what is defined as such, and this perspective highlights definitional power: who is capable of coining certain forms of information as false (Becker 1967; Schiappa 2003)?

This necessary move from an essentialist to a relational definition rings even more true for conspiracy theories (Harambam 2020b, 34–35). Again, at first glance, it may seem obvious what they mean: explanations of events that involve the nefarious covert actions of some people. Such literal definitions, however, do not adequately cover what is commonly meant by conspiracy theories. After all, the official explanation of what happened on 9/11 – the plot of 19 angry Arab men hijacking planes to attack the US – would then qualify, but that is generally not seen as a conspiracy theory. Instead, doubts about this official narrative and accusations that the CIA, Mossad, or high officials in the US government are behind the attacks are seen as conspiracy theories. It thus makes more sense to define conspiracy theories as those ideas challenging official narratives (Coady 2006, 2–3). Moreover, because 'a view becomes a conspiracy theory only because it has been dismissed as such' (Knight 2000, 11) and is thus defined 'by [its] discursive position in relation to a "regime of truth"' (Bratich 2008, 3), it is imperative to foreground the definitional practices, and their socio-political context, that discard certain forms of knowledge/thought as conspiracy theory (Harambam 2020b, 18). Obviously, there are some substantive qualities that most conspiracy theories share (Barkun 2006; Byford 2011; Douglas et al. 2019; Sunstein and Vermeule 2009), but these alone cannot account for what is commonly meant by them: delusional, irrational, paranoid, militant, dangerous, and mostly untrue explanations of reality (Dentith 2018; Thalmann 2019).

Both misinformation and conspiracy theories are slippery concepts and never neutral but intimately tied to cultural interpretations and societal power relations. What we regard as misinformation or conspiracy theories is thus never merely descriptive, but historically situated and performative. Because of the stigma associated with both terms, defining or calling something or someone that way has clear rhetorical effects. As Husting and Orr brilliantly show, using the conspiracy theory label allows the interlocutor to 'go meta', sidestepping the content and gaslighting the opponent, and works as a routinised strategy of exclusion (2007). Misinformation and conspiracy theories are thus powerful rhetorical weapons in public battles for truth and authority as they sweepingly discard both content and author from legitimate political debate (Bjerg and Presskorn-Thygesen 2017; Harambam and Aupers 2015). But these terms also have longer-lasting political consequences, since what becomes tainted with the conspiracy theory stigma will be off limits and subject to self-censorship by journalists and academic scholars alike (Hagen 2020; Hughes 2020; Pelkmans and Machold 2011).

Contents: from scapegoating an exotic Other to popular critiques of societal institutions

The previously mentioned politics of defining notwithstanding, there are important themes and topics to discern in the vast and diverse world of what are labelled conspiracy theories (Harambam 2020b, 58–101). Barkun highlights three central characteristics: 'nothing happens by accident', 'nothing is as it seems', and 'everything is connected' (2006, 3–4). He continues to distinguish conspiracy theories by scope: singular dramatic events, systemic ones of structural deceit, and 'superconspiracy theories' (Barkun 2006, 6). The first detail murders of key political figures (JFK) and pop-star celebrities (John Lennon, Tupac Shakur, or Michael Jackson), terrorist attacks (9/11, Charlie Hebdo), or various societal catastrophes (financial crises, wars, epidemics). The second category is about structural mechanisms of deceit: conspiracy theories about the way the pharmaceutical industries (inventing diseases and medications to keep people hooked on them instead of curing people) or monetary fiat systems (making money out thin air to enslave humanity with debt) work. The third are perhaps the most marvellous ones as they unite various singular conspiracy theories into one grand master narrative of deception. One popular propagator of such all-encompassing superconspiracies is flamboyant David Icke (Harambam and Aupers 2019). He is best known for his controversial reptilian thesis, in which our global elites are actually shapeshifting reptilian human–alien hybrids who secretly rule the world and combines New Age teachings with apocalyptic narratives about a coming totalitarian new world order (Barkun 2006; Ward and Voas 2011).

But what can we say about the substantive contents of conspiracy theories? Historically, conspiracy theories entailed allegations of societal subversion by three types of cabals that were seen as enemies of the dominant social order: secret societies (like the Illuminati or the Free-masons), powerful factions or interest groups (like the communists or the abolitionists), and the Jews (Harambam 2020b, 59–60). Such conspiracy theories advanced the notion that these societal outsiders were secretly plotting the demise of mainstream society and became objects of blame for societal misfortune (Pipes 1997). By scapegoating a concrete and identifiable enemy, this allegedly dangerous Other, such conspiracy theories bolstered collective in-group identities. This is what Knight calls 'secure paranoia' (2000, 3–4). They may engender a sense of peril, but as the cabal is made known and their sinister objectives made clear, such conspiracy theories paradoxically generate a state of reassurance, stability, and order. This type of conspiracy dis-course has often been deployed by those in power in various countries and of various political affiliations to unite a troubled people through the construction of a dangerous enemy (Pipes 1997; Robins and Post 1997).

While such conspiracy theories live on in the rhetoric of Islamophobic Eurabia theories and in Russian and Eastern European conspiratorial fears of a progressive West endangering tradi-tional values (Yablokov 2018), many contemporary conspiracy theories focus on the workings of our own societal institutions (Harambam 2020b, 66–81). Various scholars (Fenster 2008; Knight 2000; Melley 2000; Olmsted 2009) argue that conspiracy theories today are no longer about a demonised *Other* threatening a stable *us*, but rather, the enemy now comes from within. Indeed, most contemporary conspiracy theories advance radical suspicions about the workings of mainstream societal institutions (Aupers 2012). Based on a content analysis of popular con-spiracy websites, Harambam distinguishes six main categories of conspiracy narratives: finance, media, corporatism, science, government, and the supernatural (2020b, 66–81). Besides the last one, most conspiracy theories thus have a strong institutional focus: they do not so much assume the conspiracy of a malign and manipulative cabal as articulate suspicions and discontent about the very way mainstream operations, routines, procedures, and formal legislations are insti-tutionalised. More specifically, conspiracy theorists distrust, critique, and contest mainstream epistemic institutions and the knowledge they produce (Harambam and Aupers, 2015). As a result, conspiracy theories embody, par excellence, the unstable and contested nature of truth and knowledge in post-modern societies (Fuller 2018; Harambam 2020b).

Circulations: how conspiracy theories exist and travel in today's media ecosystem

Conspiracy theories have been around for many centuries. They were transmitted orally, in written and visual forms, and later also in various printed documents (flyers, newspapers, and books) as new technologies emerged (Butter 2014; Byford 2011; Pipes 1997; Thalmann 2019). While hard to precisely quantify, the internet proved a major game-changer in the form, quantity, speed of circulation, and general reach of conspiracy theories. The decline of traditional information gatekeepers accompanied a rise of various types of bulletin boards, independent and alternative news sites, and personal websites and blogs that published conspiracy theories online (Birchall 2006; Dean 1998; Knight 2000). This enormous democratisation of information was a key spearhead of the early internet utopians and similarly proved for many conspiracy theorists a great emancipatory force. For many people in the field, the internet was *the* information sanctuary to learn about facets of life that, in their eyes, had been hidden or obscured before but were now open for everybody to see (Harambam 2020b). In a typical 'prosumer culture' fashion, conspiracy theorists were producing, reading, sharing, editing, and bricolaging all kinds of textual and audiovisual information and (re)publishing it on their own websites. Much variety existed: from small individual do-it-yourself-style websites with simple text to professionally produced and sometimes cooperatively managed conspiracy theory websites boasting news articles and visually stunning documentaries attracting thousands of visitors per day (Harambam 2020b, 39–47).

The rise of social media and internet 2.0 radically changed again the way conspiracy theories are produced, transmitted, and consumed. Whereas older websites were rather static and unidirectional and people had to 'go' to conspiracy websites for information, the online media-ecosystem of today highlights hyper-connectivity, interactivity, and virality (Dijck et al. 2018). In addition to consulting articles and videos on conspiracy theory websites, people find such contents in their social media feeds and/or share them in closed messenger groups (Mortimer 2017). Conspiracy theories as such travel easily across different platforms, reaching different audiences. Given the different affordances of each platform, conspiracy theories take different forms now as well; next to mere text and video, we find today conspiratorial Twitter messages and playful memes as new conspiracy theory genres. At every step, people can frame, adjust, and contextualise conspiracy theory texts and visuals into new forms with which they change and recreate original meanings (Aupers 2020). However, powerful conspiracy theory actors remain influential, be they conspiracy theory entrepreneurs or social movements: for example, in the form of popular YouTube channels to which people subscribe or Twitter accounts they follow (Harambam 2020a; Starbird 2017).

In recent years it has become clear that the contemporary information landscape looks more like a complex war zone where various strategic actors fight for the minds and hearts of people with misinformation, troll factories, and invisible technological weapons such as bot(net)s and curating algorithms (Bennett and Livingston 2018; Wardle and Derakhshan 2017). Without actually knowing so, people would end up in 'echo chambers' of like-minded people due to the effects of 'filter bubbles' and 'recommendation algorithms' funneling people into extremist conspiracy theories (Flaxman et al. 2016; Sunstein 2018). While such understandings of people as gullible and passive recipients of misinformation are naïve and have been critiqued (Bruns 2019), much of the complex entanglement of human behavior, technology, platform business models, and (geo)politics that spurs the spread of conspiracy theories and misinformation online is still to be explored.

Motivations: paranoid militants, cultural dupes, or witting activists?

A central topic in studies on conspiracy theories and misinformation is the question of why people 'believe' them. One strand of scholars regards conspiracy theories as irrational behavior and thought and often discards them as such (Barkun 2006; Byford 2011; Pipes 1997; Sunstein and Vermeule 2009). They build on Hofstadter, who saw it as unreasonable paranoia, over-heated suspicion, and dangerous militancy (2012), and to Popper, who saw it as secularised remnants of an outdated religious worldview prioritising intent above chance (2013, 306). These two qualities of conspiracy theorists performing 'paranoid politics' and 'bad science' (Harambam 2020b, 12–17) live on in many contemporary discussions of contemporary populist leaders (Trump, Orban, Bolsonaro) and movements (Tea Party, 5 stars, AfD) that (allegedly) manipulate the public with inciting polarisations and false or alternative facts (Norris and Inglehart 2019).

A second group of scholars argue that it is neither fruitful nor possible to insist on the irrationality and falsity of conspiracy theories, especially if we want to understand their broad contemporary appeal and cultural significance. Such scholars take a more neutral stance to exploring the meaning conspiracy theories have for those engaging with them without condemning them as ludicrous and dangerous. Some argue that conspiracy theories bring back a sense of control as they explain inexplicable events and give meaning to complex, increasingly opaque and globalised systems (e.g. bureaucracies, capitalist systems, mass-communication technologies) (Aupers 2012; Dean 1998; Knight 2000; Melley 2000). From that perspective, conspiracy theories – half soothing, half unsettling – are a cultural coping mechanism to deal with a complex and uncertain world. Social psychologists make similar arguments by pointing to how conspiracy theories give back feelings of agency and control in disturbing or confusing situations in time (Douglas et al. 2017).

Others highlight the contested nature of truth and knowledge in post-modern societies and show how this 'epistemic instability' opens up a cultural space for conspiracy theories to thrive (Birchall 2006; Fenster 2008; Harambam 2020b). Mainstream societal institutions (media, religion, politics, and science) and the knowledge they produce are distrusted for they are (supposedly) corrupted by both dogma and material interests (Harambam and Aupers 2015) or because they don't allow for 'soft' epistemologies (emotions, feelings, experiences, testimonies, traditions) (Harambam and Aupers 2019). Various new religious movements deploy conspiracy theories in their teachings as they do provide existential meaning in contrast to 'cold' rational institutions by explaining societal injustices along larger spiritual narratives of good and evil (Dyrendal et al. 2018). Social relations are important drivers of conspiracy theories too: people may express them to foreground their ideological group affiliation (Lewandowsky et al. 2017), or they are cultivated and enforced in social contexts such as 'alternative' schools or community centers (Sobo 2015). But conspiracy theories also channel discontent with mainstream institutions and represent populist challenges to the existing order (Fenster 2008; Harambam 2020b). While conspiracy theories thus operate in a cultural climate where various societal groups contest the epistemic authority of mainstream authorities (Fuller 2018), the reasons and motivations they do so greatly differ.

People: suspicious minds or are we all conspiracy theorists now?

Traditionally, conspiracy theorists were seen as people on the extremist margins of society, those radical paranoids Hofstadter spoke about, but given the contemporary popularity of conspiracy theories, this assumption is hard to maintain. Different scholars and disciplines say something about what kind of people believing in conspiracy theories. Social psychological research maps key personality characteristics of people scoring high on a 'conspiracist scale' (Brotherton et al. 2013), who would display certain personality traits (e.g. authoritarian, narcissistic), cognitive biases (e.g. confirmation bias and illusory pattern recognition), and more general psychological afflictions (anxiety, stress, uncertainty, exclusion, victimisation, anomie, cynicism, distrust, etc.) (Prooijen and Douglas 2018). Coupled together, such scholars highlight epistemic (understanding one's environment), existential (being safe and in control of one's environment), and social (maintaining a positive image of the self and the social group) factors as core identity traits of conspiracy theorists (Douglas et al. 2017, 2019).

Quantitative studies in political science measure the distribution of conspiracy theory beliefs across societal groups (Uscinski 2018). While many agree on the percentage of people endorsing one or more conspiracy theories (from 20 percent to almost a half the population, depending on the framing of the questions), their findings are less conclusive regarding the social and demographic factors correlating with conspiracy theory beliefs. Some argue that they cuts across age, gender, ideological conviction, religion, income, education, and ethnicity, whereas others found that conspiracy theorists were more likely to be male, unmarried, less educated, in a lower-income household, outside the labour force, from an ethnic minority group, not attending religious services, and perceiving themselves as of lower social standing than others (Douglas et al. 2019). Not surprisingly, conspiracy theorists showed higher alienation from established politics and lower levels of political engagement and are found on the more extreme, often populist, end of the political spectrum (Uscinski 2018; van Prooijen et al. 2015).

Qualitative scholars take a different approach to understand who conspiracy theorists are. In contrast to the aforementioned deductive-quantitative research favouring *etic* categories, qualitative studies focus on the *emic*, or self-perceptions of conspiracy theorists. Inspired by symbolic-interactionism and social identity theory (Jenkins 2014), they focus not just on how conspiracy theorists' construct their own identities as 'reflexive projects', but also how they deal with their 'stigmatized identity' in everyday life (Harambam 2020b). For example, people actively resist their stigmatisation as 'conspiracy theorists' by distinguishing themselves from the gullible mainstream as 'critical freethinkers' (Harambam and Aupers 2017). Their ideas of self and other make three subcultural conspiracy groups apparent: activists, retreaters, and mediators. Harambam further distinguishes between conspiracy theory entrepreneurs, social movements, and individuals (Harambam 2020a). Other scholars follow marginalised or disenfranchised groups in society, such as African Americans, who deploy conspiracy theories to critique power, explain their marginal position, and garner momentum for resistance and uprising (Dean 1998; Fenster 2008; Knight 2000). Since conspiracy theorists cannot be seen as one of a kind, it is imperative to differentiate.

Mitigations: debunking, or what else to do with conspiracy theories?

Conspiracy theories are generally seen as a societal problem much in line with misinformation, fake news, and other forms of (allegedly) false information in our public domain (Waisbord 2018). This is because access to quality information regarding various aspects of life, from politics to health, is of utmost importance for people in liberal democracies to form opinions and participate in public debates (Fuchs 2014). However, conspiracy theories are said to have more adverse individual and societal effects. Scholars argue that they can erode trust in governments and mainstream institutions, deny and discard scientific evidence, increase depression and alienation, inform dangerous (public) health decisions, incite or stimulate hatred and prejudice, create a climate of distrust towards experts and truth, increase radical and extremists behaviour, and decrease political participation (Douglas et al. 2019; Lewandowsky et al. 2017). While (some) conspiracy theories can be productive challenges to dominant societal hierarchies, may hold powerful authorities accountable, and can be an impetus for institutional change (Dentith 2018; Harambam 2020b), the list of negative consequences is long and serious. It is thus imperative to be more specific about which conspiracy theories pose such dangers, when, and how (Hagen 2020).

Academics, NGO's, governments, and various other organisations initiate campaigns to combat conspiracy theories. Just as in the fight against misinformation, the most dominant mitigation strategy is debunking or fact-checking: showing the public that conspiracy theories are flawed understandings of reality would result in their no longer believing and trafficking in them (Krekó 2020). While it is obviously important to trace, highlight, and correct false information in our public sphere, the practical reality is more complex. First, it's not always clear which (parts of) conspiracy theories are actually false, and proving them wrong involves much interpretative and investigative work (Dentith 2018; Graves 2016). Second, conspiracy theories are said to be have a 'self-sealing quality': counterevidence is construed as part of the conspiracy (Barkun 2006; Sunstein and Vermeule 2009). Third, debunking strategies are rarely effective: people generally do not accept fact-checking corrections that go against their ideology or worldview or when they come from ideologically opposed societal groups (Harambam 2017). Paradoxically, debunking information may then even be counterproductive, strengthening original beliefs and increasing their reach (Lewandowsky et al. 2017). Other strategies, such as 'inoculating' or exposing the flawed rhetorical arguments and tropes of conspiracy theories, may be more effective (Krekó 2020).

An even bigger problem than the (un)truthfulness of conspiracy theories is perhaps their presence in today's technologically saturated (social) media ecosystem (Bennett and Livingston 2018; Wardle and Derakhshan 2017). Spurred by troll factories, bot(net)s, and recommendation algorithms alike, conspiracy theories rapidly spread over the internet, reaching great audiences (Bounegru et al. 2018). Of particular concern are the (business models of) Big Tech companies: these have created an opaque information landscape, in which they exploit and expand information asymmetries to target (and sell) specific audiences based on inferred psychometric profiles (Gary and Soltani 2019). Given the powerful role these allegedly neutral platforms play in the proliferation of contentious contents online (Dijck et al. 2018), they are called to take action (Harambam et al. 2018). While resisting external regulations, they have committed in Europe to a 'Code of Practice on Disinformation' and increased their efforts to limit the spread of conspiracy theories via content moderation and adjusting recommendation algorithms. However, given unchanged platform business models and the aforementioned paradoxes and complexities that only aggravate when automated at scale, it is to be seen what these efforts will achieve (Gillespie 2018; Graves 2018). The broader question of how not to throw the baby (free speech and legitimate societal critique) out with the bathwater (disinformation) will continue to haunt platforms, academics, and legislators.

Future research: exploring the affective and playful dimensions of conspiracy theories

Research on conspiracy theories is mostly rather serious business. It features the causes and consequences of a cultural phenomenon that is generally regarded a societal problem and hence focuses (too) much on its dangers (Harambam 2020b, 216). This obscures the affective and playful dimensions that are just as much part of conspiracy theories. To close this chapter, some suggestions are offered for future research in this direction. First, scholars can explore how conspiracy theorising and the practical search for truth offers effects such as excitement and satisfaction. Fenster made an important point years ago about how 'the rush and vertiginous feelings associated with discovering conspiracy' induce 'a sense of pleasure' (2008, 14). Future research can substantiate this claim further in all empirical details: how do different people take pleasure in the sifting of clues and the ferreting out of hidden truths, and how does this affective dimension of conspiracy theorising empirically manifest itself in different ways? Second, scholars can investigate how people engage with conspiracy theories in playful or ironic ways.

Pointing to the ludic online hype of the Area 51 raid that quickly gathered millions of interested people on Facebook, Sobo argues for looking at conspiracy theories through the lens of play as another way to understand their contemporary popularity (2019). When playing, people feel free to experiment with wild thinking, imagine 'what if?' possibilities, and oppose opaque power without serious ramifications (Harambam et al. 2011). Humour, irony, and play are similarly important ways to show cultural capital to peers and build social networks. Conspiracy culture is full of playful references to popular culture, and conspiracy memes are a staple ingredient of today's memetic culture online. It is about time that academics take seriously the playful sides of conspiracy theories as well.

References

Aupers S (2012) 'Trust No One': Modernization, Paranoia and Conspiracy Culture. *European Journal of Communication* 4(26), 22–34.

Aupers S (2020) Decoding Mass Media/Encoding Conspiracy Theory. In: Butter M and Knight P (eds) *Routledge Handbook of Conspiracy Theories*. London: Routledge.

Barkun M (2006) *A Culture of Conspiracy: Apocalyptic Visions in Contemporary America*. Berkeley: University of California Press.

Becker HS (1967) Whose Side Are We On? *Social Problems* 14(3), 239–247.

Bennett WL and Livingston S (2018) The Disinformation Order: Disruptive Communication and the Decline of Democratic Institutions. *European Journal of Communication* 33(2), 122–139.

Birchall C (2006) *Knowledge Goes Pop: From Conspiracy Theory to Gossip*. Oxford: Berg.

Bjerg O and Presskorn-Thygesen T (2017) Conspiracy Theory: Truth Claim or Language Game? *Theory, Culture & Society* 34(1), 137–159.

Bounegru L, Gray J, Venturini T, et al. (eds) (2018) *A Field Guide to 'Fake News' and Other Information Disorders*. Amsterdam: Public Data Lab.

Bratich JZ (2008) *Conspiracy Panics: Political Rationality and Popular Culture*. New York: SUNY Press.

Brotherton R, French CC and Pickering AD (2013) Measuring Belief in Conspiracy Theories: The Generic Conspiracist Beliefs Scale. *Frontiers in Psychology* 4 (279).

Bruns A (2019) *Are Filter Bubbles Real?* Cambridge: Polity Press.

Butter M (2014) *Plots, Designs, and Schemes: American Conspiracy Theories from the Puritans to the Present*. Berlin: Walter de Gruyter.

Butter M and Knight DP (eds) (2020) *Routledge Handbook of Conspiracy Theories*. London: Routledge.

Byford J (2011) *Conspiracy Theories: A Critical Introduction*. London: Palgrave Macmillan.

Coady D (2006) *Conspiracy Theories: The Philosophical Debate*. Aldershot: Ashgate Publishing.

Dean J (1998) *Aliens in America: Conspiracy Cultures from Outerspace to Cyberspace*. Ithaca, NY: Cornell University Press.

Dentith MRX (2018) *Taking Conspiracy Theories Seriously*. London: Rowman & Littlefield.

Dijck J van, Poell T and Waal M de (2018) *The Platform Society: Public Values in a Connective World*. Oxford: Oxford University Press.

Douglas KM, Sutton RM and Cichocka A (2017) The Psychology of Conspiracy Theories. *Current Directions in Psychological Science* 26(6), 538–542.

Douglas KM, Uscinski JE, Sutton RM, et al. (2019) Understanding Conspiracy Theories. *Political Psychology*. John Wiley & Sons, 3–35.

Dyrendal A, Robertson DG and Asprem E (eds) (2018) *Handbook of Conspiracy Theory and Contemporary Religion*. Leiden: Brill.

Fenster M (2008) *Conspiracy Theories: Secrecy and Power in American Culture*. Minneapolis: University of Minnesota Press.

Flaxman S, Goel S and Rao JM (2016) Filter Bubbles, Echo Chambers, and Online News Consumption. *Public Opinion Quarterly* 80(S1), 298–320.

Fuchs C (2014) Social Media and the Public Sphere. *TripleC: Communication, Capitalism & Critique* 12(1), 57–101.

Fuller S (2018) *Post-Truth: Knowledge As A Power Game*. London: Anthem Press.

Gary J and Soltani A (2019) First Things First: Online Advertising Practices and Their Effects on Platform Speech. *Knight First Amendment Institute at Columbia University*.

Gillespie T (2018) *Custodians of the Internet: Platforms, Content Moderation, and the Hidden Decisions That Shape Social Media*. New Haven, CT: Yale University Press.

Graves L (2016) *Deciding What's True: The Rise of Political Fact-Checking in American Journalism*. New York: Columbia University Press.

Graves L (2018) Understanding the Promise and Limits of Automated Fact-checking. *Reuters Institute for the Study of Journalism Factsheets*.

Hagen K (2020) Should Academics Debunk Conspiracy Theories? *Social Epistemology*, 1–17.

Harambam J (2017) De/politisering van de Waarheid. *Sociologie* 13(1), 73–92.

Harambam J (2020a) Conspiracy Theory Entrepreneurs, Movements and Individuals. In: Butter M and Knight P (eds) *Routledge Handbook of Conspiracy Theories*. London: Routledge, 278–291.

Harambam J (2020b) *Contemporary Conspiracy Culture : Truth and Knowledge in an Era of Epistemic Instability*. London: Routledge.

Harambam J and Aupers S (2015) Contesting Epistemic Authority: Conspiracy Theories on the Boundaries of Science. *Public Understanding of Science* 24(4), 466–480.

Harambam J and Aupers S (2017) 'I Am Not a Conspiracy Theorist': Relational Identifications in the Dutch Conspiracy Milieu. *Cultural Sociology* 11(1), 113–129.

Harambam J and Aupers S (2019) From the Unbelievable to the Undeniable: Epistemological Pluralism, or How Conspiracy Theorists Legitimate Their Extraordinary Truth Claims. *European Journal of Cultural Studies*. doi:10.1177/1367549419886045

Harambam J, Aupers S and Houtman D (2011) Game over? Negotiating modern capitalism in virtual game worlds. *European Journal of Cultural Studies* 14(3), 299–319.

Harambam J, Helberger N and van Hoboken J (2018) Democratizing Algorithmic News Recommenders: How to Materialize Voice in a Technologically Saturated Media Ecosystem. *Philosophical Transactions of the Royal Society A: Mathematical, Physical and Engineering Sciences* 376(2133), 20180088.

Hofstadter R (2012) *The Paranoid Style in American Politics*. New York: Knopf Doubleday Publishing Group.

Hughes DA (2020) 9/11 Truth and the Silence of the IR Discipline. *Alternatives: Global, Local, Political*. doi:10.1177/0304375419898334

Husting G and Orr M (2007) Dangerous Machinery: "Conspiracy Theorist" as a Transpersonal Strategy of Exclusion. *Symbolic Interaction* 30(2), 127–150.

Jenkins R (2014) *Social Identity*. London: Routledge.

Knight P (2000) *Conspiracy Culture: From Kennedy to The X Files*. London: Routledge.

Krekó P (2020) Countering Conspiracy Theories and Misinformation. In: Butter M and Knight P (eds) *Routledge Handbook of Conspiracy Theories*. London: Routledge, 242–255.

Lewandowsky S, Ecker UKH and Cook J (2017) Beyond Misinformation: Understanding and Coping with the "Post-Truth" Era. *Journal of Applied Research in Memory and Cognition* 6(4), 353–369.

Melley T (2000) *Empire of Conspiracy: The Culture of Paranoia in Postwar America*. Ithaca, NY: Cornell University Press.

Mortimer K (2017) Understanding Conspiracy Online: Social Media and the Spread of Suspicious Thinking. *Dalhousie Journal of Interdisciplinary Management* 13(1) 1.

Norris P and Inglehart R (2019) *Cultural Backlash: Trump, Brexit, and Authoritarian Populism*. Cambridge: Cambridge University Press.

Olmsted KS (2009) *Real Enemies: Conspiracy Theories and American Democracy, World War I to 9/11*. Oxford: Oxford University Press.

Pelkmans M and Machold R (2011) Conspiracy Theories and Their Truth Trajectories. *Focaal* 2011(59), 66–80.

Pipes D (1997) *Conspiracy: How the Paranoid Style Flourishes and Where It Comes From*. New York: The Free Press.

Popper K (2013) *The Open Society and Its Enemies*. Princeton, NJ: Princeton University Press.

Prooijen J-W van and Douglas KM (2018) Belief in Conspiracy Theories: Basic Principles of an Emerging Research Domain. *European Journal of Social Psychology* 48(7), 897–908.

Robins RS and Post JM (1997) *Political Paranoia: The Psychopolitics of Hatred*. New Haven, CT: Yale University Press.

Schiappa E (2003) *Defining Reality: Definitions and the Politics of Meaning*. Carbondale, IL: Southern Illinois University Press.

Sobo E (2019) Playing with Conspiracy Theories. *Anthropology News* 60(4).

Sobo EJ (2015) Social Cultivation of Vaccine Refusal and Delay among Waldorf (Steiner) School Parents. *Medical Anthropology Quarterly* 29(3), 381–399.

Starbird K (2017) Examining the Alternative Media Ecosystem Through the Production of Alternative Narratives of Mass Shooting Events on Twitter. *Eleventh International AAAI Conference on Web and Social Media*, 3 May 2017.

Sunstein CR (2018) *#Republic: Divided Democracy in the Age of Social Media*. Princeton, NJ: Princeton University Press.

Sunstein CR and Vermeule A (2009) Conspiracy Theories: Causes and Cures. *Journal of Political Philosophy* 17(2), 202–227.

Thalmann K (2019) *The Stigmatization of Conspiracy Theory since the 1950s: 'A Plot to Make Us Look Foolish'*. London: Routledge.

Uscinski JE (2018) *Conspiracy Theories and the People Who Believe Them*. Oxford: Oxford University Press.

van Prooijen J-W, Krouwel APM and Pollet TV (2015) Political Extremism Predicts Belief in Conspiracy Theories. *Social Psychological and Personality Science* 6(5), 570–578.

Waisbord S (2018) Truth is What Happens to News. *Journalism Studies* 19(13), 1866–1878.

Ward C and Voas PD (2011) The Emergence of Conspirituality. *Journal of Contemporary Religion* 26(1), 103–121.

Wardle C and Derakhshan H (2017) Information Disorder: Toward an interdisciplinary framework for research and policy making. *Council of Europe Report* 27.

Yablokov I (2018) *Fortress Russia: Conspiracy Theories in the Post-Soviet World*. Cambridge: Polity Press.

29
CORRUPTED INFRASTRUCTURES OF MEANING

Post-truth identities online

Catherine R. Baker and Andrew Chadwick

False and distorted beliefs are widespread in contemporary societies. In 2018, almost a third of the US population did not believe in the safety of vaccines (Wellcome Trust 2018). In stark contrast with earlier predictions that social media would enhance rationality in the public sphere, a troubling array of communities based on what we term post-truth identities have now set sail online, unmoored by fact-based discourse. From 'anti-vaxxers' to #MGTOW ('Men Going Their Own Way') supporters, from 'flat-Earthers' to Obama 'truthers', from 9/11, '#QAnon', and '#Pizzagate' conspiracy theorists to proponents of scientifically unproven 'miracle cures' for pandemics and terminal diseases – many such online communities have achieved remarkable levels of public prominence. In this chapter, we offer some explanations why.

Our overarching argument is that post-truth identities emerge from a confluence of individual-level and contextual factors. Cognitive biases that shape how individuals encounter and process information have recently been granted freer rein as a result of changes in the technological basis of media systems in the advanced democracies. Post-truth identities rely upon what we term corrupted, self-initiated infrastructures of meaning that are animated by emotional narratives and repositories of cherry-picked, misrepresented justifying 'evidence'. These infrastructures are, in part, enabled by the unique affordances of social media for decentralising, but also algorithmically organising, the production and circulation of socially consequential information. And yet much of the infrastructural scaffolding exists on the broader internet, away from social media platforms, in dedicated folksonomic settings. These infrastructures of meaning also provide ready-made materials that mainstream media organisations can use in their reporting, which further contributes to the spread of false and distorted beliefs and the formation of identity among both existing supporters and new recruits.

We adapt the term infrastructure of meaning from its fleeting appearance in Weinberger's optimistic web 2.0 prophecy *Everything Is Miscellaneous* (2007, 171–172). This is how he described it:

> For the first time, we have an infrastructure that allows us to hop over and around established categorizations with ease. We can make connections and relationships at a pace never before imagined. We are doing so together. We are doing so in public . . . Each connection tells us something about the connected things, about the person who

made the connection, about the culture in which a person could make such a connection, about the sorts of people who find that connection worth noticing. This is how meaning grows . . . This infrastructure of meaning is always present and available, so that we can contextualize the information we find and the ideas we encounter.

In this chapter, we jettison Weinberger's optimism and instead turn the concept of an infrastructure of meaning to critical use for making sense of post-truth identities. As we show, the ability to 'hop over' 'established categorizations' (in Weinberger's terminology) also enables the production of distorted systems of internally coherent classifications that are designed to enhance in-group coherence and systematically mislead. The culture and sense of belonging that derive from public connection can also enable signaling, legitimising, and giving license to false and distorted beliefs. Unaccountable modes of algorithmic prioritisation in search and social media platforms often bring such beliefs to audiences far beyond the core adherents. 'Always present' contextualisation also enables online post-truth communities to selectively attend to information that promotes falsehoods and bigotry while marginalising contradictory evidence.

Post-truth identities have developed in a long-term context of declining trust in established media and political institutions and growing cynicism towards authority and expertise among significant segments of the public. There has also been a generational shift in the transnational modes of connectivity available to those who hold conspiracy mentalities and extreme ideologies of hatred and who wish to build networks with like-minded others across the globe.

But in addition to these macro-structural changes, we suggest that attention ought to focus on how post-truth identities come to be formed and maintained at the micro level, in everyday life. Here, drawing upon the social identity theory tradition in social psychology, we assume that identity is inextricably bound up with group formation and group belonging (e.g. Tajfel 1982). All kinds of conspiracy theories are active at any given time – consider, for example, the false belief, widespread in the UK, that the coronavirus epidemic of 2020 was caused by the installation of 5G radio masts by Chinese telecom companies. But the fact of a conspiracy theory's existence does not automatically lead to the formation of post-truth identities. Instead, post-truth identities are distinguished by their remarkable and disturbing resilience over time, which makes them particularly important objects of study. Online, such groups build shared identities through the selective production of knowledge, norms, and values. In this context, we define 'knowledge' in neutral terms, as a process involving the justification of beliefs. The process of identity-building depends heavily upon self-initiated, online infrastructures of meaning, not least because such groups only fleetingly see themselves represented in mainstream media coverage. Identity-affirming knowledge, norms, and values are continuously and publicly constructed by those who congregate in post-truth communities on mainstream online platforms such as YouTube, Facebook, Twitter, and Reddit. Identity affirmation may, in turn, be reinforced by the major online platforms' commercially driven, personalised recommendation affordances, such as Google search's autosuggest, YouTube's autoplay, and Facebook's news feed. Such affordances contribute to shared experiences among believers but can also make it more likely that larger audiences will be exposed to falsehoods as part of everyday searching, reading, viewing, and sharing. At the same time, it ought to be recognised that much post-truth discursive identity work happens in online spaces away from social media platforms – in forums, wikis, email lists, podcasts, and alternative news sites. And finally, this identity work is itself also boosted from time to time by celebrity endorsements and news coverage by professional media organisations. We illustrate these themes with three examples: 'anti-vaxxers', 'flat-Earthers', and 'incels'.

The roots of post-truth identities: emotionality, cognitive biases, and changing media systems

Lying and deception are as old as human communication, but post-truth involves something more than these (D'Ancona 2017; Kalpokas 2019). McIntyre (2018), for example, defines post-truth as 'not the abandonment of facts, but a corruption of the process by which facts are credibly gathered and reliably used to shape . . . beliefs about reality'. Similarly, Kalpokas's account (2019, 5) suggests that post-truth implies a general erosion of the boundaries between truth and falsity: a 'condition of detachment of truth-claims from verifiable facts and the primacy of criteria other than verifiability'. Fears about propaganda and misinformation have often hinged on whether people will be directly deceived by falsehoods, but the lesson of the past is that people are just as likely to become uncertain about what to trust and believe (Chadwick 2019). This was an important strand of dissident critiques of the neo-Stalinist states in Eastern Europe. It has its origins in revisionist accounts of propaganda that focus not on mass deception but on how a spiral of distrust grows in conditions of chaos and indeterminacy. Post-truth identities are best situated in this overarching context.

Emotionality

In Kalpokas's account (2019, 5), chief among the 'criteria other than verifiability' for truth claims is 'affective investment' in emotional narratives: ways of understanding that people value, not because they offer 'better' understanding of the world but rather because they have utility for maintaining a sense of personal well-being and for influencing the attitudes and behaviour of others. Such narratives are also important for forming and maintaining a stable sense of self and collective identity.

The centrality of emotions, particularly fear and anxiety, to people's processing of information is a central theme in accounts of post-truth (Laybats and Tredinnick 2016). Social psychologists have long shown that affect is important in decision-making (Lerner, Li, Valdesolo, and Kassam 2015), but the literature on post-truth has stressed emotionality's heightened significance when individuals attempt to find order and coherence within a messy, complex, and overwhelming abundance of information and opinion (Metzger and Flanagin 2013). In a hypercompetitive media system, emotionally engaging media content is an important generator of individual attention, perhaps even more so than when broadcast media were the dominant means of communication (Papacharissi 2014).

Cognitive biases

Since the mid-twentieth century, strands of social science research, particularly in disciplines such as psychology, economics, management, communication, and political science, have challenged rationality-based accounts of human attitudes and behaviour. Studies of cognitive biases beginning in the 1950s drew attention to the prevalence of irrationality in decision-making, and their findings have had a significant impact on recent debates about post-truth (e.g. Asch 1955; Lerner, Li, Valdesolo, and Kassam 2015; Metzger and Flanagin 2013; Tversky and Kahneman 1974; Wason 1960). Understanding of the consistent susceptibility of individuals to false information has improved significantly since the turn of this century even if much (though not all) of the research has applied concepts that pre-date recent concerns.

Behavioural research has shown that people fall into predictable traps when making judgments (e.g. Asch 1955; Tversky and Kahneman 1974; Wason 1960). Two concepts with particular relevance are motivated reasoning and confirmation bias. Motivated reasoning is a state of being in which our decision-making and truth assessments are swayed by what we want to believe, even if what we want to believe is not in accordance with observable facts (Kunda 1990). Individuals strive to maintain a positive self-image and will often make irrational choices to reduce the conflict they experience when faced with information that contradicts this self-image (e.g. Elliot and Devine 1994; Festinger 1957). Confirmation bias (Nickerson 1998; Wason 1960) is a cognitive process through which people enact motivated reasoning and prioritise information that conforms with decisions they have already made, especially when such decisions have been guided by strongly held beliefs. People are often skilled in developing rationalisations that support their prior beliefs (Lodge and Taber 2013).

Motivated reasoning and confirmation bias have featured in much of the research on misperceptions. Some research has extended this approach to encompass ideological beliefs and group belonging. For example, Kahan (2013, 1) points to another type of motivated reasoning – identity-protective cognition – wherein individuals tend to process information in ways that help them develop beliefs that 'signify their loyalty to important affinity groups'. In a 'self-defence' strategy designed to maintain the status, social support, and sense of belonging that derive from group affinity, people tend to resist information that contradicts the dominant beliefs of the group whose membership they particularly value.

This resonates with another relevant cognitive bias from the early days of social psychology – social conformity. First demonstrated in laboratory experiments by Asch in the 1950s (e.g. Asch 1955) and replicated in several studies since then, people's bias towards social conformity means that they are more likely to adopt false beliefs if they observe belief in falsehoods among individuals who surround them. The effect is particularly strong when there appears to be a visible consensus among numerous others. Beliefs are profoundly relational. Many do not derive from direct observation but from our perception that others in our social networks exhibit them. We might also perceive that there is some degree of consensus among other believers, and, if we lack information that will counter that consensus, this gives information particular force based on what Kuran and Sunstein (1999) have termed 'availability cascades'. An availability cascade occurs when people who have poor or incomplete information take shortcuts by simply basing their beliefs on the beliefs of others. The result is that people join an emerging consensus because it is easier to do and more likely to help them fit in and advance their social status in that particular context.

Of course, most post-truth identities do not find genuinely mass support, so it is important to consider how individual dispositions can shape susceptibility to false beliefs. Media and social psychologists are starting to learn more about these dispositions. For example, 'conspiracy mentality' is linked to devout religious beliefs, low levels of science literacy, feelings of disempowerment, and cynicism towards experts and public institutions (Landrum, Olshansky, and Richards 2019; Landrum and Olshansky 2019).

A further key point here is that if the cognitive biases and mentalities that lead people to adopt false beliefs were observed by social psychologists before the recent debate about post-truth, what is special about the recent period? We now discuss how systemic change in the media environment over the last decade has contributed to a context in which these basic human frailties have become increasingly consequential for public communication.

Changing media systems

Research in this field is in its infancy, but there are aspects of mass social media use that have enabled the cognitive biases and mentalities we have outlined to become more readily activated, distributed, and, above all, visible.

This first point we want to make here is well known to researchers of online communication, even if there have often been disagreements about the overall implications. It is that many of the constraints that typically shape face-to-face communication apply only weakly in online settings. In social media interactions, anonymity or pseudonymity are widespread, or people use their real names but have weak or no social ties with many of those with whom they discuss issues. As a result, when interacting on social media, people are generally more likely to question authority and worry less about having to face reprisals for their behaviour (Suler 2004). The fact that many social media users feel less bounded by authority structures does not inevitably lead to problematic outcomes. Social media environments have encouraged the expression of legitimate but underrepresented views and the airing of grievances that have not been addressed by professional media. However, social media also afford a communication environment in which it is easier to circulate ideas and signal behavioural norms that may, depending on the specific context, undermine tolerance, social trust, and fact-based discourse.

Second, research in communication on selective exposure has shown that many individuals tend to seek out and disproportionately focus on media information congruent with their motivated reasoning (Sears and Freedman 1967). Social media have created historically unprecedented opportunities to encounter and share the beliefs of others. They have also made it relatively simple to create online communities in which emotionally charged narratives can work to sustain social solidarity and group belonging in the absence of direct, embodied relationships (Chadwick 2019; Papacharissi 2014). Online, identity based on affective ties seems to be curiously difficult to dislodge. There are plenty of opportunities to have our views reinforced by like-minded others; there are readily available, designed-in signals of other people's views, such as likes, upvotes, and shares; and there is much less friction involved in seeking out and connecting with others who hold beliefs that are usually marginalised from mainstream news and other traditionally authoritative sources of information.

The mass diffusion of social media is reshaping the broader epistemic landscape of societies. 'Counter-epistemic communities' (Waisbord 2018) may vary in scale from the large numbers who reject global warming to the smaller numbers who promote extreme misogyny, but the key point is that, for their adherents, these beliefs are not marginal at all but play a significant role in generating the affective ties that are essential precursors to identity formation and political agency. When combined with the algorithmic organisation of information, which can enhance a sense of commonality and thrust seemingly marginal ideas to the centre of the average user experience on platforms such as YouTube, such communities can, under certain conditions, play a more prominent role in the marketplace of ideas than would have been the case during the era of broadcast and print media.

At the same time, it is important to recognise that the ideas on which these post-truth identities rest often attract coverage by professional news organisations. User-generated forums and wikis function as strategically created semantic reservoirs whose meanings, however extreme and bizarre, can flow into mainstream news discourse, not least because professional journalists are now so dependent on online sources. This grants such ideas the imprimatur of elite media coverage and larger audiences. For example, there has been a relative absence of restraint by professional journalists when reporting the attention-grabbing actions of the so-called incels. Some professional journalists have remediated and amplified incel beliefs, using time-worn sensationalist framings, particularly when narrating the background stories behind terrorist events. The same applies to anti-vaxxer ideas.

Among editors and news audiences, there is an enduring enthusiasm for emotional resonance. But this has been granted freer rein now that personal choice has become so important in the consumption of information. Social media platforms' 'feeds' are the central organising experience of most people's online activity and can play a role in identity formation by heightening hostility towards political enemies (Settle 2018). The dominant business model of platform companies has been based on selling individuals' attention to advertisers. To this end, companies have designed user experiences sufficiently attractive to keep people interacting and sharing information. In practice, this has meant that users' feeds often (though not always) tend to reinforce what network scientists call homophily: humans' long-observed bias towards forming bonds with those who are similar to themselves. Those who share information to increase their sense of group belonging are less likely to see the media environment as an opportunity to learn from others. They are more likely to use their online communication to advance their own group's identity and are less likely to be interested in engaging with those they consider to be threats to that identity.

To illustrate these conceptual points, we now turn to a discussion of three examples of post-truth identities: anti-vaxxers, flat-Earthers, and incels.

Anti-vaxxers

The global scientific and policy consensus that vaccines are safe and effective in preventing the spread of infectious diseases dates back to the nineteenth century. Yet minorities of publics – and sometimes substantial minorities – are sceptical about vaccines' safety and refuse to have their children immunised. In some parts of Europe, such as Italy, vaccination rates have declined over the past two decades (Wilson 2019).

Anti-vaxx groups are highly visible online and were among the first post-truth communities to use the internet to disseminate information (Kata 2010; Wolfe, Sharp, and Lipsky 2002b). Over the last decade, the groups have shifted their focus to social media and online forums. Facebook (Schmidt et al. 2018; Smith and Graham 2019) and YouTube (Briones et al. 2012; Keelan et al. 2007) have been particularly important for the anti-vaxxer infrastructure of meaning, though there is emerging evidence that private encrypted platforms such as WhatsApp have become more significant in the spread of such attitudes in recent years (Darrach 2020). Bradshaw and colleagues (2020) show that anti-vaccine groups operate in highly social groups with shared group norms. This is congruent with the by-now-familiar argument that online identity construction is often influenced by the way in which one wants to be perceived by an imagined audience (Boyd and Marwick 2010).

Anti-vaxxer videos frequently appear in the top list of results on YouTube, even for searches using the neutral keyword 'vaccines'. This suggests the selective exposure that occurs when people purposively search for anti-vaccine material on YouTube is not the whole story: casual searchers are incidentally exposed to the material. More specific search queries, on the links between vaccines and autism, for example, or searches using ordinary language such as 'should I vaccinate my child?' return even greater quantities of anti-vaxxer material (Basch, Zybert, Reeves, and Basch 2017; Venkatraman, Garg, and Kumar 2015).

Common arguments found in anti-vaxxer groups are that vaccines harm immunity, spread the diseases they are meant to eradicate, and cause other conditions such as autism, sudden infant death syndrome, Parkinson's, and Alzheimer's (Kata 2010; Wolfe, Sharp, and Lipsky 2002b). Emotionally laden narratives are an important part of anti-vaxxer identity work. These often involve personal stories, particularly about children who have supposedly been harmed by vaccinations. Testimony by parents and images of children are common devices. Conspiracy theories often appear on anti-vaxx sites. The conflict is often framed as an 'us versus them' battle of anti-vaxxers versus the government, pharmaceutical companies, medical experts, and mainstream media. As with other conspiracy mentalities, criticism of vaccination stands in for meta-explanations of inequalities of power and influence across society (Van den Bulck and Hyzen 2020). Celebrity endorsements and sensationalist coverage have also been significant for bringing these ideas to wider audiences.[1]

A large-scale analysis of seven years of Facebook posts by 2.6 million users between 2010 and 2017 revealed that the pro- and anti-vaccine networks are polarised (Schmidt et al. 2018). A majority of users on each side of the debate only consumes or produces information that reinforces their own attitudes. More active members of the anti-vaccination network tend to consume greater numbers of posts on the subject than those in the pro-vaccination network. There is little evidence of interaction among the two networks. The divide between them widened over the seven-year period studied. These findings suggest that social conformity bias and availability cascades among participants in these networks can play a role in entrenching anti-vaccination attitudes (Kuran and Sunstein 1999). Anti-vaxx groups also operate using dedicated sites and forums, which are interconnected via hyperlinks, again amplifying the effects of social conformity and availability cascades. Individuals often seek out these groups as a form of social support (Smith and Graham 2019), and this leads to emotional investment in group membership, which leads members to resist information that contradicts the group's beliefs.

Flat-Earthers

Flat-Earthers are a self-described 'movement' united around the false belief that Earth is not a sphere but a flat disc. They exemplify many of the characteristics of post-truth identities we discussed earlier. Their official website, tfes.org, hosts a library of selected articles and writings on the topic, a discussion forum with almost 6,000 members, and the 'Flat Earth Wiki' – a user-generated database of terms and linked concepts that runs on the widely used MediaWiki platform (the same technology used to host Wikipedia). The Flat Earth wiki describes a flat-Earther as 'someone who believes in the Flat Earth theory'. This use of identity labelling is common in such online groups, as we will see again with incels later in the chapter.[2]

Much flat-Earth misinformation propagates on YouTube. Key to this is YouTube's autoplay personalised recommendation algorithm, which analyses past viewing and generates similar material in an ongoing stream of suggestions (Landrum, Olshansky, and Richards 2019). Videos on flat-Earth topics run into the tens of thousands and have collectively amassed many millions of views, with 2016 to 2018 showing a spike in video uploads that prompted public criticism of YouTube, which then modified its algorithm to down-rank the material in search and autoplay (Paolillo 2018). Celebrity endorsements from musician Bobby Ray Simmons Jr. (aka B.o.B.) among others have played a role in increasing the visibility of flat-Earth ideas, as has publicity in mainstream broadcast shows with large audiences, such UK ITV's *This Morning*. For example, in February 2020, while we were conducting research for this chapter, a *This Morning* feature about flat-Earth ideas appeared on YouTube and received 1.5 million viewings in just three weeks.[3]

Flat-Earthers' infrastructure of meaning employs the familiar signals of authority, legitimacy, and interactivity that are the staples of the post-web 2.0 internet. The wiki outlines various of the movement's beliefs, such as the 'space travel conspiracy' it claims was faked by NASA 'to further America's militaristic dominance of space'. The materials employ pseudo-scientific language and jargon. However, flat-Earth discourse also relies on emotive narratives of conspiracy, corruption, and cover-up, which appeal to fear and anxiety (Parker and Racz 2019). These conspiracy theories offer simple narrative explanations that seemingly produce order out of a complex and chaotic world (Van den Bulck and Hyzen 2020). Field research at flat-Earth gatherings has shown that conspiracy mentality is widespread among the supporters (Landrum,

Olshansky, and Richards 2019). Identity-protective cognition, in this case, appears to allow information congruent with the beliefs of the group to be prioritised over empirical evidence. Flat-Earth conspiracy theories often operate as ideological telescopes: belief in the conspiracy derives from the more totalising ideological position it represents, such as mistrust of the establishment or elites, rather than the specifics of the theory itself (Van den Bulck and Hyzen 2020).

Incels

Incels ('involuntary celibates') are an online subculture of heterosexual men who define themselves by their inability to obtain a sexual or romantic partner, due to what they claim is systematic social hostility by women towards men (Heritage and Koller 2019; Zimmerman, Ryan and Duriesmith 2018). In the incel community, the term *incel* has always been a clear identity label, with members self-identifying as incels (Maxwell, Robinson, Williams, and Keaton 2020). The main online incel forum restricts membership to incels and those interested in their ideology, with strict criteria for who qualifies as an incel and much infighting over the identity boundaries (Jaki et al. 2019). Identity groups often denigrate out-groups with negative identity labels (Jaki et al. 2019). For example, in the incel community, women are commonly referred to as 'foids' (a portmanteau of female humanoid).

The subculture revolves around a worldview known as the 'Black Pill', which sets out that physical attractiveness is the sole decisive factor in love and sex (Jaki et al. 2019). Incels have gained notoriety for a particularly violent strain of misogynist ideology and have been linked to several terrorist attacks (*The Guardian* 2017; The *New York Times* 2018). The identity rests on an emotional narrative of 'male victimhood' (Blommaert 2018), male supremacy, heteronormativity, white supremacy, and a desire to aggressively re-establish what they present as traditional gender norms (Zimmerman, Ryan, and Duriesmith 2018). Anger, sadness, and frustration are common themes on the incel forum, as are aggressively insulting sexual and physical descriptions (Jaki et al. 2019). They combine conspiracy mentality with reductive and simplistic explanations of complex social phenomena.

Incels' distorted infrastructure of meaning operates in ways similar to those of the anti-vaxxers and flat-Earthers. Having been banned from the online platform Reddit, they created their own site, incel.co, which hosts an active discussion forum, a FAQ and information page, and 'Inside incel', an elaborate wiki of specialised insider terminology. This user-generated material contains invented narratives, neologisms, and self-referential cultural memes, as well as a curated list of academic and pop culture articles that purportedly provide evidence for the ideology of the group, organised under the heading 'Scientific Blackpill'. This list features articles on gendered racial bias in dating, the importance of attractiveness in predicting positive dating outcomes, and studies supposedly showing that heterosexual women are more romantically interested in men with traditionally 'masculine' physical features. These studies are embedded in a narrative that men are unable to form romantic relationships due to the actions of women. Other articles listed include those purportedly showing that women initiate divorce more often than men, that women exhibit sexual fantasies about non-consensual sex, and that women are more likely to use the dating app Tinder for casual sex (the last being included on a list of articles under the heading 'sluts'), all of which are used to legitimise aggressive misogyny.

The use of curated lists of academics articles, pseudo-science, and highly selective findings from news reports and academic research is a common thread running through post-truth infrastructures of meaning. In the incel wiki, articles are decontextualised and re-embedded in misogynist narratives. We found that many of the articles listed were actually inconsistent with incel ideology or were stripped of their theoretical underpinnings and their authors' own conclusions. Incels selectively attend to information that upholds misogyny while ignoring alternative information and interpretations. Neologisms and specific in-group language function to police a boundary between incels and those outside the group (Blommaert 2018) but also create a ready-made system of ideas important for legitimising and maintaining the group's identity, attracting new recruits, and representing their cause to journalists (*The Guardian* 2017; The *New York Times* 2018).

Conclusion

In this chapter, we have sketched out a framework for understanding post-truth identities. We have argued that such identities rest on a confluence of cognitive biases, conspiracy mentalities, and systemic changes in media systems over the past decade that have generated new affordances for the production, circulation, and discovery of false and highly distorted beliefs. Post-truth identities rest upon corrupted, self-initiated infrastructures of meaning that play a role in generating distorted knowledge, norms, and values, where 'knowledge' refers to a process involving the justification of beliefs, even if the beliefs are false. Post-truth identities also rest upon affective solidarity among their participants while they also provide ready-made systems of ideas for new recruits and, on occasion, journalists in media organisations who report on these developments. The algorithmic organisation of material on social media platforms plays a role in reinforcing group identity and in bringing these ideas to wider audiences. We conclude with some broader reflections.

Some of the writing on post-truth has presented a false dichotomy between, on the one hand, the supposedly always-reliable and responsible traditional media organisations of the past, who are often portrayed as enlightened, truth-seeking editorial gatekeepers and, on the other hand, online spaces populated by partisans, trolls, and the ignorant who supposedly pollute the public sphere with falsehoods and conspiracy theories. The reality is much more complex. The broadcast- and print-dominated media systems of the twentieth century displayed many biases and distortions caused by the demands of commercial competition and advertisers. At the same time, these factors remain important today: mainstream media organisations can, and do, present the ideas of post-truth communities to broader audiences.

The decentralisation of public communication over the last decade has had many positive effects, including the diversification of voices in the public sphere and increased access to scientific information among mass publics. That being said, the proliferation of digital and social media has also provided many new opportunities for the distribution and consumption of mis- and disinformation. While cognitive biases, conspiracy mentalities, and the long-term decline of trust in institutions are important roots of post-truth identities, digital and social media have played a role in enabling the construction and visibility of these identities and have made it easier for their adherents to connect with each other and sustain their knowledge, norms, and values. Research in this field is now gathering momentum. Future research might pay attention to how the convergence of cognitive biases and affordances we outline here contributes to the spread of falsehoods and misrepresentations. Understanding how post-truth identities are formed and maintained will better equip societies to combat the spread of false and highly distorted beliefs.

Notes

1 One good example of celebrity and news values converging is a June 2019 article on *RollingStone.com*: A Guide to 17 Anti-Vaccination Celebrities. www.rollingstone.com/culture/culture-features/celebrities-anti-vaxxers-jessica-biel-847779/ (accessed March 9, 2020).

2 https://theflatearthsociety.org/tiki/tiki-index.php?page=Flat-Earther&highlight=flat%20earther (accessed April 29th, 2020).
3 www.youtube.com/watch?v=wClJlarfyhE (accessed March 6, 2020).

References

Asch, S. E. (1955). Opinions and Social Pressure. *Scientific American, 193*(5), 31–35.

Basch, C. H., Zybert, P., Reeves, R., & Basch, C. E. (2017). What Do Popular YouTube Videos Say About Vaccines? *Child: Care, Health and Development 43*(4), 499–503.

Blommaert, J. (2018). Online-offline Modes of Identity and Community: Elliot Rodger's Twisted World of Masculine Victimhood. In Hoondert, M., Mutsaers, P., & Arfman, W. (Eds.), *Cultural Practices of Victimhood* (pp. 55–80). London: Routledge.

Boyd, D., & Marwick, A. E. (2010). I Tweet Honestly, I Tweet Passionately: Twitter Users, Context Collapse, and the Imagined Audience. *New Media Society, 13*(1), 114–133.

Bradshaw, A. S., Shelton, S. S., Wollney, E., Treise, D., & Auguste, K. (2020). Pro-Vaxxers Get Out: Anti-Vaccination Advocates Influence Undecided First-Time, Pregnant, and New Mothers on Facebook. *Health Communication*, 1–10. Online First. doi:10.1080/10410236.2020.1712037

Briones, R., Nan, X., Madden, K., & Waks, L. (2012). When Vaccines Go Viral: An Analysis of HPV Vaccine Coverage on YouTube. *Health Communication, 27*(5), 478–485. https://doi.org/10.1080/104 10236.2011.610258

Chadwick, A. (2019). *The New Crisis of Public Communication: Challenges and Opportunities for Future Research on Digital Media and Politics*. Online Civic Culture Centre, Loughborough University. www. lboro.ac.uk/research/online-civic-culture-centre/news-events/articles/o3c-2-crisis/

D'Ancona, M. (2017). *Post-truth: The New War on Truth and How to Fight Back*. London: Ebury Press.

Darrach, A. (2020). It's Not Misinformation. It's Faith. *Columbia Journalism Review,* February 7. www.cjr. org/special_report/vaccination-whatsapp.php

Elliott, A. J., & Devine, P. G. (1994). On the Motivational Nature of Cognitive Dissonance: Dissonance as Psychological Discomfort. *Journal of Personality and Social Psychology, 67*(3), 382.

Festinger, L. (1957). *A Theory of Cognitive Dissonance*. Stanford, CA: Stanford University Press.

Heritage, F., & Koller, V. (2019). *Incels, In-groups, and Ideologies: The Representation of Gendered Social Actors in a Sexuality-based Online Community*. Paper presented to Lavender Languages 2 Conference, Gothenburg, Sweden, May. www.research.lancs.ac.uk/portal/en/publications/incels-ingroups-and-ideologies(b6b3ff7c-2223-4e1a-a4fc-0127e01a7952).html

Jaki, S., De Smedt, T., Gwóźdź, M., Panchal, R., Rossa, A., & De Pauw, G. (2019). Online Hatred of Women in the Incels.me Forum: Linguistic Analysis and Automatic Detection. *Journal of Language Aggression and Conflict, 7*(2), 240–268.

Kahan, D. M. (2013). Ideology, Motivated Reasoning, and Cognitive Reflection: An Experimental Study. *Judgment and Decision Making, 8*, 407–424.

Kalpokas, I. (2019). *A Political Theory of Post-Truth*. Cham: Springer.

Kata, A. (2010). A Postmodern Pandora's Box: Anti-Vaccination Misinformation on the Internet. *Vaccine, 28*(7), 1709–1716.

Keelan, J., Pavri-Garvia, V., Tomlinson, G., & Wilson, K. (2007). YouTube as a Source of Information on Immunization: A Content Analysis. *Journal of the American Medical Association, 298*(21), 2482–2484.

Kunda, Z. (1990). The Case for Motivated Reasoning. *Psychological Bulletin, 108*(3), 480–498.

Kuran, T., & Sunstein, C. R. (1999). Availability Cascades and Risk Regulation. *Stanford Law Review, 51*(4), 683–768.

Landrum, A. R., & Olshansky, A. (2019). The Role of Conspiracy Mentality in Denial of Science and Susceptibility to Viral Deception about Science. *Politics and the Life Sciences*. Online First. doi:10.1017/pls.2019.9

Landrum, A. R., Olshansky, A., & Richards, O. (2019). Differential Susceptibility to Misleading Flat Earth Arguments on YouTube. *Media Psychology*. Online First. doi:10.1080/15213269.2019.1669461

Laybats, C., & Tredinnick, L. (2016). Post truth, Information, and Emotion. *Business Information Review, 33*(4), 204–206.

Lerner, J. S., Li, Y., Valdesolo, P., & Kassam, K. S. (2015). Emotion and Decision Making. *Annual Review of Psychology, 66*, 799–823.

Lodge, M. & Taber, C. S. (2013). *The Rationalizing Voter.* New York: Cambridge University Press.

Maxwell, D., Robinson, S. R., Williams, J. R., & Keaton, C. (2020). "A Short Story of a Lonely Guy": A Qualitative Thematic Analysis of Involuntary Celibacy Using Reddit. *Sexuality & Culture*, 1–23.

McIntyre, L. (2018). *Post-Truth.* Cambridge, MA: MIT Press.

Metzger, M. J., & Flanagin, A. J. (2013). Credibility and Trust of Information in Online Environments: The Use of Cognitive Heuristics. *Journal of Pragmatics, 59*, 210–220.

Nickerson, R. S. (1998). Confirmation Bias: A Ubiquitous Phenomenon in Many Guises. *Review of General Psychology, 2*(2), 175–220.

Paolillo, J. C. (2018). The Flat Earth Phenomenon on YouTube. *First Monday, 23*(12).

Papacharissi (2014). *Affective Publics: Sentiment, Technology, and Politics.* New York: Oxford University Press.

Parker, S., & Racz, M. (2019). Affective and Effective Truths: Rhetoric, Normativity and Critical Management Studies. *Organization.* Online First. https://doi.org/10.1177%2F1350508419855717

Schmidt, A. L., Zollo, F., Scala, A., Betsch, C., & Quattrociocchi, W. (2018). Polarization of the Vaccination Debate on Facebook. *Vaccine, 36*(25), 3606–3612.

Sears, D. O., & Freedman, J. L. (1967). Selective Exposure to Information: A Critical Review. *Public Opinion Quarterly, 31*(2), 194–213.

Settle, J. E. (2018). *Frenemies: How Social Media Polarizes America.* New York: Cambridge University Press.

Smith, N., & Graham, T. (2019). Mapping the Anti-Vaccination Movement on Facebook. *Information, Communication & Society, 22*(9), 1310–1327.

Suler, J. (2004). The Online Disinhibition Effect. *Cyberpsychology & Behavior* 7(3), 321–326.

Tajfel, H. (1982). Social Psychology of Intergroup Relations. *Annual Review of Psychology, 33*(1), 1–39.

The Guardian (2017). 'Incel': Reddit Bans Misogynist Men's Group Blaming Women for Their Celibacy. www.theguardian.com/technology/2017/nov/08/reddit-incel-involuntary-celibate-men-ban

The New York Times (2018). What Is an Incel? A Term Used by the Toronto Van Attack Suspect, Explained. www.nytimes.com/2018/04/24/world/canada/incel-reddit-meaning-rebellion.html

Tversky, A., & Kahneman, D. (1974). Judgment Under Uncertainty: Heuristics and Biases. *Science, 185*(4157), 1124–1131.

Van den Bulck, H., & Hyzen, A. (2020). Of Lizards and Ideological Entrepreneurs: Alex Jones and Infowars in the Relationship Between Populist Nationalism and the Post-Global Media Ecology. *International Communication Gazette, 82*(1), 42–59.

Venkatraman, A., Garg, N., & Kumar, N. (2015). Greater Freedom of Speech on Web 2.0 Correlates with Dominance of Views Linking Vaccines to Autism. *Vaccine, 33*(12), 1422–1425.

Waisbord, S. (2018). Truth is What Happens to News: On Journalism, Fake News, and Post-Truth. *Journalism Studies, 19*(13), 1866–1878.

Wason, P. C. (1960). On the Failure to Eliminate Hypotheses in a Conceptual Task. *Quarterly Journal of Experimental Psychology, 12*, 129–140.

Weinberger, D. (2007). *Everything Is Miscellaneous: The Power of the New Digital Disorder.* New York: Times Books.

Wellcome Trust. (2018). *Wellcome Global Monitor 2018.* London: Wellcome Trust. https://wellcome.ac.uk/reports/wellcome-global-monitor/2018

Wilson, C. (2019). Italy Bans Unvaccinated Children from Schools After Measles Outbreaks. *New Scientist,* March 13. www.newscientist.com/article/2196534-italy-bans-unvaccinated-children-from-schools-after-measles-outbreaks/

Wolfe, R. M., Sharp, L. K., & Lipsky, M. S. (2002b). Content and Design Attributes of Antivaccination Websites. *JAMA, 287*(24), 3245–3248.

Zimmerman, S., Ryan, L., & Duriesmith, D. (2018). Recognizing the Violent Extremist Ideology of 'Incels'. *Women In International Security Policy Brief, 9.* www.wiisglobal.org/wp-content/uploads/2018/09/Policybrief-Violent-Extremists-Incels.pdf

30

CONSUMPTION OF MISINFORMATION AND DISINFORMATION

Sophie Lecheler and Jana Laura Egelhofer

While the relevance of incorrect or misleading information that is disseminated unintentionally (i.e. 'misinformation'), as well as of incorrect or misleading information that is disseminated deliberately (i.e. 'disinformation') has been widely discussed (Bennett and Livingston 2018; Waisbord 2018a, 2018b; Lewandowsky et al. 2017), there are only a relatively small number of studies that can help us understand how common the actual consumption of misinformation and disinformation is and what motivates this consumption.

What is more, because public worries and excessive news media coverage about a disinformation crisis have been so significant, there is likely also a certain level of perceived consumption of misinformation and disinformation among citizens (Egelhofer and Lecheler 2019). This means that citizens are so worried about being manipulated in a polarised political environment that they either believe that a media outlet intentionally disseminates disinformation once the label 'fake news' is applied to it (e.g. a populist politician labelling a news organisation), or they generally overestimate the ratio of misinformation and disinformation in their media diet. This perceived consumption might be harmful, in that it may demobilise and raise levels of distrust and cynicism among citizens (e.g. Van Duyn and Collier 2019). But it might also backfire against those who try to cause it. For example, exposure to 'fake news' labels against legacy news organisations may actually raise media trust (Tamul et al. 2020).

In this chapter, we summarise the available theoretical and empirical literature on both actual and perceived consumption of misinformation and disinformation.[1]

The dual consumption of misinformation and disinformation

We live in a digital age, when information may be created and spread more cost efficiently and quickly than ever before and in which audiences are now able to participate in news production and dissemination processes (e.g. Lazer et al. 2018; McNair 2017). As a result, classic selection mechanisms, such as trust in the gatekeeping function of professional journalism, are impaired (e.g. Nielsen and Graves 2017; Starr 2012), not only because it is increasingly challenging to differentiate between professional and unprofessional content but also because journalists themselves are now challenged in properly verifying digital information during the news production process (Lecheler and Kruikemeier 2016). This challenge puts the assessment of information credibility increasingly with an overwhelmed user (Metzger et al. 2003), and even so-called digital natives struggle with evaluating online information. In addition, digital advertising makes, in particular, disinformation or 'fake news' financially attractive as views or 'clicks', instead of the accuracy of the content, create business success (e.g. Allcott and Gentzkow 2017). This idea links disinformation to the emergence of clickbait, or the creation of news content solely aimed at generating attention through sensational and emotionally appealing headlines (Bakir and McStay 2018).

These technological developments are met by a number of social and political trends: most scholars connect the emergence of the so-called disinformation crisis to a larger crisis of trust in journalism (e.g. Lazer et al. 2018; McNair 2017; Nielsen and Graves 2017). While most prominently discussed in the US, where media trust has dropped to 'a new low' (Swift 2016), increasing mistrust towards news media is also a problem (in varying degrees) in other countries (Newman et al. 2017). Importantly, media trust is not decreasing for all citizens and rather has to be seen in the context of increasing political polarisation. In the US, media perceptions are divided by partisanship, with Democrats having more positive attitudes towards the media than Republicans (e.g. Gottfried et al. 2018; Guess et al. 2017). In (Western) Europe, citizens holding populist views are more likely to have negative opinions of news media than those holding non-populist views (Mitchell et al. 2018). However, for some, decreasing trust in traditional journalism might lead to a higher acceptance of other information sources, including disinformation. Furthermore, increasing opinion polarisation leads to homogeneous networks, where opposing views are rare, and the willingness to accept ideology-confirming news – true or false – is high (e.g. Allcott and Gentzkow 2017; Lazer et al. 2018; Mihailidis and Viotty 2017).

When considering all this, we can pinpoint two pathways to the consumption of misinformation and disinformation. First, there is, of course, the actual consumption of factually incorrect information, be it online or through other channels. Then there is a second pathway of perceived consumption, in which citizens overestimate the occurrence of false information in their media diets, ascribing the label 'fake news' to everything they do not believe in or that may even just feature opinions different from their own.

Actual consumption of misinformation and disinformation

The literature on the consumption of mis- and disinformation is a moving target, with new studies emerging at a fast pace (Ha et al. 2019). In the most general sense, citizens can be exposed to mis- and disinformation directly or indirectly. That means they may see or read it on a website or on other channels it originates from. What is also possible, however, is that they consume it indirectly: that is, they learn about it through other platforms or channels that have adapted and disseminated this information.

A direct form of consumption often discussed in the literature are websites dedicated to disseminating disinformation (e.g. Vargo et al. 2018). Egelhofer and Lecheler (2019) refer to these websites as the true form of 'fake news' because they are not only low in facticity but are also created with the intention to deceive using pseudojournalistic cues. For example, fake news websites often have names that imitate those of established news outlets (Allcott and Gentzkow 2017) (e.g. the Political Insider or the Denver Guardian). They are, however, also short lived as 'they do not attempt to build a long-term reputation for quality, but rather maximize the short-run profits from attracting clicks in an initial period' (Allcott and Gentzkow 2017, 218–219). This makes accumulating data on actual consumption rather tricky. The available research does, however, show that traffic to these websites is rather limited compared to the general media diet of an average citizen (Fletcher et al. 2018; Nelson and Taneja 2018).

A second way in which misinformation and disinformation may be directly consumed is through social media communication (Tucker et al. 2018). Initially, research suggested that Facebook plays a particularly important role when estimating the role of disinformation consumption in people's daily lives (e.g. Guess et al. 2018; Nelson and Taneja 2018). Research focusing on the 2016 US presidential election suggests that there were posts containing disinformation that received more shares and likes during the election campaign than many mainstream news stories (Silverman 2016). However, recent research shows that disinformation spreads across platforms (Wilson and Starbird 2020) and is driven by the affordances of different platforms, such as hashtags (Weber et al. 2020), algorithmic targeting (e.g. Hussain et al. 2018), and visual communication tools (Diakopoulos and Johnson 2020). Another aspect of social media communication that has received particular attention in research is bots – which are often discussed for their ability to 'amplify marginal voices and ideas by inflating the number of likes, shares and retweets they receive, creating an artificial sense of popularity, momentum or relevance' (Bradshaw and Howard 2017, 11). However, comparisons show that humans are the main drivers of falsity online (Vosoughi et al. 2018, 1146) and that 'effective disinformation campaigns involve diverse participants; they might even include a majority of "unwitting agents" who are unaware of their role, but who amplify and embellish messages that polarize communities and sow doubt about science, mainstream journalism and Western governments' (Starbird 2019). Given all this, it is still difficult to generalise on how far reaching consumption of misinformation and disinformation on social media really is. While a growing number of studies detect cases of disinformation campaigns during, for instance, election campaigns (e.g. Bossetta 2018), there is only limited contrasting knowledge on the role these disinformation campaigns play in daily media consumption patterns of citizens. For example, Grinberg et al. (2019, 374) argue that 'engagement with fake news sources was extremely concentrated [during the 2016 elections]. Only 1% of individuals accounted for 80% of fake news source exposures, and 0.1% accounted for nearly 80% of fake news sources shared'. The direct consumption of misinformation and disinformation also warrants a look at the relationship between social media communication and alternative and partisan media websites (Faris et al. 2017; Tucker et al. 2018). While this is a bit of an empirical grey area, raising questions about the relationship between false information and biased presentation of information, research suggests that consumption is tied to alternative news websites; new digital forms of populist party communication, such as YouTube channels; and new forms of party magazines (Bennett and Livingston 2018, 128).

'Indirect forms of consumption of disinformation and misinformation' most often describes the experience of information through legacy news media. News media play an important role in the disinformation crisis because they may spread misinformation either by mistake through lack of proper verification (Van Leuven et al. 2018) or even intentionally. Importantly, however, intentionality here is hard to measure and has so far not been covered empirically (Egelhofer and Lecheler 2019). Yet indirect consumption through news media is likely one of the most important aspects of the study of disinformation because even in a digital age, news journalists fulfil a disseminator function for many citizens, and misperceptions formed on the basis of false news are difficult to correct (Flynn et al. 2017; Tsfati et al. 2020). Bennett and Livingston (2018, 123) argue this importance of indirect consumption through news media:

> While the origins of much, and perhaps most, disinformation are obscure, it often passes through the gates of the legacy media, resulting in an 'amplifier effect' for stories that would be dismissed as absurd in earlier eras of more effective press gatekeeping.

Be it direct or indirect, the motivations for consumption are equally relevant, yet equally hard to pinpoint. First, many scholars assume that citizens consume false content simply because they lack the digital literacy to distinguish it from factually correct information (Vraga and Tully 2019). Here, heavy news users may be better in recognising and rejecting 'fake news', depending on what kind of news media they regularly use (Lewandowsky et al. 2017). Another proxy for digital literacy is age, and in the context of the 2016 US election, Grinberg et al. (2019, 374) showed that registered voters on Twitter were most likely to engage with fake news when they were 'conservative leaning, older, and highly engaged with political news'. Also, there is research showing that consumption of false information is related to media trust (Zimmermann and Kohring 2020).

Another important variable is political ideology. While some research shows that conservatives are more likely to consume disinformation (Guess et al. 2019), other studies do not find this connection. For example, Bossetta (2018) shows that one in five Twitter users are susceptible to spear phishing attacks, independent of their political ideology. Humprecht et al. (2020, 7) argue that consumption of disinformation is tied to populist communication because 'populism and partisan disinformation share a binary Manichaean worldview, anti-elitism, mistrust of expert knowledge, and conspiracy theories'. This relates consumption of disinformation to the confirmation bias and motivated reasoning literature, which shows that congruent information is more likely to be accepted than incongruent information (see Hameleers 2020).

Perceived consumption of misinformation and disinformation

In a growing literature across scientific fields, the impact misinformation and disinformation have on society is perceived to be extremely large (Manor 2019). This huge saliency of the role misinformation and disinformation should play in our lives has led to growing public anxieties about the prevalence of false information in our daily lives. For example, in a multi-country survey conducted by the Reuters Institute for the Study of Journalism at the University of Oxford, more than half the participants across 38 countries were gravely concerned about the amount of false information on the internet (Newman 2018, 2019). Also, a 2019 survey by the Pew Research Center showed that US citizens ranked fake news as a bigger threat to their country than climate change, racism, or terrorism (Mitchell et al. 2019). All this is hard to marry with empirical evidence carefully suggesting that the actual percentage of mis- and disinformation the 'average' citizen is exposed to may be relatively limited, particularly when these citizens also use legacy news sources (Fletcher et al. 2018; Nelson and Taneja 2018; see also Grinberg et al. 2019). Instead, large-scale public anxieties about disinformation may cause some sort of placebo effect.

Specifically, the salience of the threat of being exposed to misinformation and disinformation can lead to perceived consumption: that is, citizens' own estimation of how much misinformation and disinformation they themselves and others are exposed to. This estimation is likely only weakly related to actual consumption of inaccurate information. While we know that individuals generally have a hard time properly estimating their media consumption (Prior 2009), perceived consumption of misinformation and disinformation may be a political variable in its own right, connected to populist politics and rising media criticism in many Western democracies.

More precisely, attributions of inaccurate information are increasingly used as a strategy to discredit opposed information sources (Hameleers 2020). Most prominently, US president Donald Trump successfully generated a public debate about disinformation by labelling legacy outlets as 'fake news'. A growing number of studies suggest that mostly populist politicians around the world are involved in accusations of intentional falsehood (e.g. Hameleers 2020). This can be linked to the binary worldview of populism, distinguishing between 'the people' and 'the elite'. In that view, both groups 'hold their own version of truth', or, put more bluntly, 'the people' know and speak the truth while 'the elite institutions', such as journalism and science, are lying (Waisbord 2018a, 25). This is, for example, reflected in surveys that find that citizens holding populist attitudes are generally more distrustful towards news media (e.g. Fawzi 2019; Mitchell et al. 2018; Schulz et al. 2020).

This also suggests a polarisation of what is understood as 'true' and 'false', as well as a close connection of truth and facts with political ideology (Waisbord 2018a). As mentioned earlier, this is linked to confirmation bias, which explains how predispositions influence the processing of information (e.g. Casad 2007). For example, information that aligns with one's political attitudes is likely processed in an uncritical way while information that contradicts one's ideology is rejected. In the same vein, attributions of misinformation and disinformation (or 'fake news') to information sources are dependent on pre-existing attitudes (Hameleers 2020). For example, US president Trump frequently accuses liberal news outlets such as the *New York Times* and CNN of spreading fake news while he shares and supports the coverage of conservative outlets such as Fox News (Meeks 2020). Also, Australian politicians have been shown to use 'fake news' labels to discredit critical news media and political opponents (Farhall et al. 2019). Importantly for this chapter, this polarisation of perceptions of what constitutes disinformation is also mirrored in the public. For example, Van der Linden and colleagues (2020) asked US citizens to indicate which sources they associated with the term 'fake news'. While conservatives mainly identified CNN as fake news, liberals associate the term more often with Fox News. Similarly, research shows that citizens use the term in social media communication to discredit information provided by opposing political parties (Brummette et al. 2018).

In sum, the 'disinformation crisis' is one of the most salient topics in current political discourses, and citizens are increasingly worried about its consequences. While the proportion of actual consumption of false information is increasingly often studied, there is likely also a high level of perceived consumption in polarised democracies. Because of the increasing political divide in many Western democracies and the close current link between 'truth' and partisan ideology, we propose that any study on the consumption of misinformation and disinformation must focus on a dual model of consumption as described earlier.

Conclusion

Citizens consume misinformation and disinformation – be it online, where social media affordances such as bots, hashtags, and visuals distract them, or through traditional news media channels. This consumption is increasingly linked with research on polarisation and populist views: for example, because there is evidence that citizens consume alternative media with biased and one-sided content. Importantly, however, actual consumption goes hand in hand with the perceived consumption of disinformation and misinformation. This is the belief that a piece of news or information is 'fake', independent of its actual facticity or journalistic quality cues. Perceived consumption matters to us as scholars because media perceptions shape citizens' use of and trust in news media and how they are affected by such media. In addition, it helps explain a rising relativism of facts among citizens when mediated communication is concerned. Both the 'real' as well as the 'placebo' pill of misinformation and disinformation may thus have equally powerful effects.

Note

1 Parts of this chapter are based on Egelhofer and Lecheler (2019) and Egelhofer et al. (2020).

References

Allcott, H. and Gentzkow, M. (2017) 'Social media and fake news in the 2016 election', *Journal of Economic Perspectives*, 31(2), pp. 211–236. Doi: 10.1257/jep.31.2.211

Bakir, V. and McStay, A. (2018) 'Fake news and the economy of emotions: Problems, causes, solutions', *Digital Journalism*, 6(2), pp. 154–175. Doi: 10.1080/21670811.2017.1345645

Bennett, W. L. and Livingston, S. (2018) 'The disinformation order: Disruptive communication and the decline of democratic institutions', *European Journal of Communication*, 33(2), pp. 122–139. Doi: 10.1177/0267323118760317

Bossetta, M. (2018) 'A simulated cyberattack on Twitter: Assessing partisan vulnerability to spear phishing and disinformation ahead of the 2018 US midterm elections'. arXiv preprint arXiv:1811.05900

Bradshaw, S. and Howard, P. (2017) 'Troops, trolls and troublemakers: A global inventory of organized social media manipulation', Oxford Internet Institute, 12, pp. 1–37 [online]. Available at: https://ora.ox.ac.uk/objects/uuid:cef7e8d9-27bf-4ea5-9fd6-855209b3e1f6 (Accessed: 18 May 2020).

Brummette, J., DiStaso, M., Vafeiadis, M. and Messner, M. (2018) 'Read all about it: The politicization of "fake news" on Twitter', *Journalism & Mass Communication Quarterly*, 95(2), pp. 497–517. Doi: 10.1177/1077699018769906

Casad, B. (2007) 'Confirmation bias' in Baumeister, R. F. and Vohs, K. D. (eds), *Encyclopedia of social psychology*. Thousand Oaks, CA: SAGE Publications, Inc., pp. 163–164. Doi: 10.4135/9781412956253.n97

Diakopoulos, N. and Johnson, D. (2019) 'Anticipating and addressing the ethical implications of deepfakes in the context of elections', *New Media & Society* [online]. Available at: https://papers.ssrn.com/sol3/papers.cfm?abstract_id=3474183 (Accessed 18 May 2020).

Egelhofer, J. L., Aaldering, L., Eberl, J. M., Galyga, S. and Lecheler, S. (2020) 'From novelty to normalization? How journalists use the term "fake news" in their reporting', *Journalism Studies*, pp. 1–21. Doi: 10.1080/1461670X.2020.1745667

Egelhofer, J. L. and Lecheler, S. (2019) 'Fake news as a two-dimensional phenomenon: A framework and research agenda', *Annals of the International Communication Association*, 43(2), pp. 97–116. Doi: 10.1080/23808985.2019.1602782

Farhall, K., Carson, A., Wright, S., Gibbons, A. and Lukamto, W. (2019) 'Political elites use of fake news discourse across communications platforms', *International Journal of Communication*, 13, pp. 4353–4375 [online]. Available at: https://ijoc.org/index.php/ijoc/article/view/10677 (Accessed 18 May 2020).

Faris, R., Roberts, H., Etling, B., Bourassa, N., Zuckerman, E. and Benkler, Y. (2017) 'Partisanship, propaganda, and disinformation: Online media and the 2016 US presidential election', Berkman Klein Center Research Publication, 6 [online]. Available at: https://dash.harvard.edu/handle/1/33759251 (Accessed 18 May 2020).

Fawzi, N. (2019) 'Untrustworthy news and the media as "enemy of the people?" How a populist worldview shapes recipients' attitudes toward the media', *The International Journal of Press/Politics*, 24(2), pp. 146–164. Doi: 10.1177/1940161218811981

Fletcher, R., Cornia, A., Graves, L. and Nielsen, R. K. (2018) *Measuring the reach of "fake news" and online disinformation in Europe* [online]. Available at: https://reutersinstitute.politics.ox.ac.uk/our-research/measuring-reach-fake-news-and-online-disinformation-europe (Accessed 18 May 2020).

Flynn, D. J., Nyhan, B. and Reifler, J. (2017) 'The nature and origins of misperceptions: Understanding false and unsupported beliefs about politics', *Political Psychology*, 38(S1), pp. 127–150. Doi: 10.1111/pops.12394

Gottfried, J., Stocking, G., and Grieco, E. (2018) *Democrats and republicans Remain split on support for news media's watchdog role*. Pew Research Center [online]. Available at: www.journalism.org/2018/09/25/democrats-and-republicans-remain-split-on-support-for-news-medias-watchdog-role/ (Accessed 18 May 2020).

Grinberg, N., Joseph, K., Friedland, L., Swire-Thompson, B. and Lazer, D. (2019) 'Fake news on Twitter during the 2016 US presidential election', *Science*, 363(6425), pp. 374–378. Doi: 10.1126/science.aau2706

Guess, A., Nagler, J. and Tucker, J. (2019) 'Less than you think: Prevalence and predictors of fake news dissemination on Facebook', *Science Advances*, 5(1), eaau4586. Doi: 10.1126/sciadv.aau4586

Guess, A., Nyhan, B. and Reifler, J. (2017) *"You're fake news": The 2017 Poynter media trust survey* [online]. Available at: https://poyntercdn.blob.core.windows.net/files/PoynterMediaTrustSurvey2017.pdf (Accessed 18 May 2020).

Guess, A., Nyhan, B. and Reifler, J. (2018) 'Selective exposure to misinformation: Evidence from the consumption of fake news during the 2016 U. S. presidential campaign', *European Research Council*, 9, pp. 1–49 [online]. Available at: https://pdfs.semanticscholar.org/a795/b451b3d38ca1d22a6075dbb0be4fc94b4000.pdf?_ga=2.73893649.248815588.1589815717-1705645063.1585068054 (Accessed 18 May 2020).

Ha, L., Andreu Perez, L. and Ray, R. (2019) 'Mapping recent development in scholarship on fake news and misinformation, 2008 to 2017: Disciplinary contribution, topics, and impact', *American Behavioral Scientist*. Doi: 10.1177/0002764219869402

Hameleers, M. (2020) 'My Reality is more truthful than yours: Radical right-wing politicians' and citizens' construction of "fake" and "truthfulness" on social media – evidence from the United States and The Netherlands', *International Journal of Communication*, 14, pp. 1135–1152 [online]. Available at: https://ijoc.org/index.php/ijoc/article/view/12463/2981 (Accessed 18 May 2020).

Humprecht, E., Esser, F. and Van Aelst, P. (2020) 'Resilience to online disinformation: A framework for cross-national comparative research', *The International Journal of Press/Politics*. Doi: 10.1177/1940161219900126

Hussain, M. N., Tokdemir, S., Agarwal, N. and Al-Khateeb, S. (2018) 'August. Analyzing disinformation and crowd manipulation tactics on YouTube', *2018 IEEE/ACM International Conference on Advances in Social Networks Analysis and Mining* (ASONAM) Barcelona, pp. 1092–1095. Doi: 10.1109/ASONAM.2018.8508766

Lazer, D. M., Baum, M. A., Benkler, Y., Berinsky, A. J., Greenhill, K. M., Menczer, F., Metzger, M. J., Nyhan, B., Pennycook, G., Rothschild, D. and Schudson, M. (2018) 'The science of fake news', *Science*, 359(6380), pp. 1094–1096. Doi: 10.1126/science.aao2998

Lecheler, S. and Kruikemeier, S. (2016) 'Re-evaluating journalistic routines in a digital age: A review of research on the use of online sources', *New Media & Society*, 18(1), pp. 156–171. Doi: 10.1177/1461444815600412

Lewandowsky, S., Ecker, U. K. H. and Cook, J. (2017) 'Beyond misinformation: Understanding and coping with the "post-truth" era', *Journal of Applied Research in Memory and Cognition*, 6, pp. 353–369. Doi: 10.1016/j.jarmac.2017.07.008

Manor, I. (2019) 'The specter of echo chambers – public diplomacy in the age of disinformation' in Manor, I. (ed.) *The digitalization of public diplomacy*. Palgrave Macmillan Series in Global Public Diplomacy. Palgrave Macmillan, pp. 135–176. Doi: 10.1007/978-3-030-04405-3_5

McNair, B. (2017) *Fake news: Falsehood, fabrication and fantasy in journalism*. London: Routledge. Doi: 10.4324/9781315142036

Meeks, L. (2020) 'Defining the enemy: How Donald Trump frames the news media', *Journalism & Mass Communication Quarterly*, 97(1), 211–234. Doi: 10.1177/1077699019857676

Metzger, M. J., Flanagin, A. J., Eyal, K., Lemus, D. R. and McCann, R. M. (2003) 'Credibility for the 21st century: Integrating perspectives on source, message, and media credibility in the contemporary media environment' in Kalbfleisch, P. J. (ed.) *Communication yearbook 27*. Lawrence Erlbaum Associates Publishers. pp. 293–335. Doi: 10.1080/23808985.2003.11679029

Mihailidis, P. and Viotty, S. (2017) 'Spreadable spectacle in digital culture: Civic expression, fake news, and the role of media literacies in "post-fact" society', *American Behavioral Scientist*, 61(4), pp. 441–454. Doi: 10.1177/0002764217701217

Mitchell, A., Gottfried, J., Fedeli, S., Stocking, G. and Walker, M. (2019) 'Many Americans say made-up news is a critical problem that needs to be fixed', *Pew Research Center, Journalism and Media, June*, 5 [online]. Available at: www.journalism.org/2019/06/05/many-americans-say-made-up-news-is-a-critical-problem-that-needs-to-be-fixed/ (Accessed 18 May 2020).

Mitchell, A., Matsa, K. E., Shearer, E., Simmons, K., Silver, K., Johnson, C. and Taylor, K. (2018) 'Populist views, more than left-right identity, play a role in opinions of the news media in Western Europe', *Pew Research Center* [online]. Available at: www.journalism.org/2018/05/14/populist-views-more-than-left-right-identity-play-a-role-in-opinions-of-the-news-media-in-western-europe/#table (Accessed 18 May 2020).

Nelson, J. L. and Taneja, H. (2018) 'The small, disloyal fake news audience: The role of audience availability in fake news consumption', *New Media & Society*, 20(10), pp. 3720–3737. Doi: 10.1177/1461444818758715

Newman, N. (2018) Digital *News report overview and key findings of the 2018 report* [online]. Available at: www.digitalnewsreport.org/survey/2018/overview-key-findings-2018/ (Accessed 18 May 2020).

Newman, N. (2019) *Digital news report executive summary and key findings of the 2019 report* [online]. Available at: www.digitalnewsreport.org/survey/2019/overview-key-findings-2019/ (Accessed 18 May 2020).

Newman, N., Fletcher, R., Kalogeropoulos, A., Levy, D. A. L. and Nielsen, R. K. (2017) 'Reuters institute digital news report 2017', [online]. Available at: https://reutersinstitute.politics.ox.ac.uk/sites/default/files/Digital%20News%20Report%202017%20web_0.pdf (Accessed 18 May 2020).

Nielsen, R. K. and Graves, L. (2017) 'News you don't believe: Audience perspectives on fake news', [online]. Available at: https://reutersinstitute.politics.ox.ac.uk/sites/default/files/2017-10/Nielsen%26Graves_factsheet_1710v3_FINAL_download.pdf (Accessed 18 May 2020).

Prior, M. (2009) 'The immensely inflated news audience: Assessing bias in self-reported news exposure', *Public Opinion Quarterly*, 73(1), pp. 130–143. Doi: 10.1093/poq/nfp002

Schulz, A., Wirth, W. and Müller, P. (2020) 'We are the people and you are fake news: A social identity approach to populist citizens' false consensus and hostile media perceptions', *Communication Research*, 47(2), 201–226. Doi: 10.1177/0093650218794854

Silverman, C. (2016) 'This analysis shows how viral fake election news stories outperformed real news on Facebook', *BuzzFeed News* [online]. Available at: www.buzzfeed.com/craigsilverman/viral-fake-election-news-outperformed-real-news-on-facebook?utm_term=.df1X0G6eG#.joeLeg8xg (Accessed 18 May 2020).

Starbird, K. (2019) 'Disinformation's spread: Bots, trolls and all of us', *Nature*, 571(449) [online]. Available at: Doi: 10.1038/d41586–019–02235-x; www.nature.com/articles/d41586-019-02235-x (Accessed 18 May 2020).

Starr, P. (2012) 'An unexpected crisis: The news media in postindustrial democracies', *The International Journal of Press/Politics*, 17(2), pp. 234–242. Doi: 10.1177/1940161211434422

Swift, A. (2016) 'Americans' trust in mass media sinks to new low', *Gallup News*, 14(6) [online] Available at: http://news.gallup.com/poll/195542/americans-trust-mass-media-sinks-new-low.aspx (Accessed 18 May 2020).

Tamul, D. J., Ivory, A. H., Hotter, J. and Wolf, J. (2020) 'All the president's tweets: Effects of exposure to Trump's "fake news" accusations on perceptions of journalists, news stories, and issue evaluation', *Mass Communication and Society*, 23(3), pp. 301–330. Doi: 10.1080/15205436.2019.1652760

Tsfati, Y., Boomgaarden, H. G., Strömbäck, J., Vliegenthart, R., Damstra, A. and Lindgren, E. (2020) 'Causes and consequences of mainstream media dissemination of fake news: Literature review and synthesis', *Annals of the International Communication Association*, 44(2), pp. 157–173. Doi: 10.1080/23808985.2020.1759443

Tucker, J. A., Guess, A., Barberá, P., Vaccari, C., Siegel, A., Sanovich, S., Stukal, D. and Nyhan, B. (2018) *Social media, political polarization, and political disinformation: A review of the scientific literature. Political polarization, and political disinformation: A review of the scientific literature* [online]. Available at: https://papers.ssrn.com/sol3/papers.cfm?abstract_id=3144139 (Accessed 18 May 2020).

Van der Linden, S., Panagopoulos, C. and Roozenbeek, J. (2020) 'You are fake news: Political bias in perceptions of fake news', *Media, Culture & Society*, 42(3), pp. 460–470. Doi: 10.1177/0163443720906992

Van Duyn, E. and Collier, J. (2019) 'Priming and fake news: The effects of elite discourse on evaluations of news media', *Mass Communication and Society*, 22(1), pp. 29–48. Doi: 10.1080/15205436.2018.1511807

Van Leuven, S., Kruikemeier, S., Lecheler, S. and Hermans, L. (2018) 'Online and newsworthy: Have online sources changed journalism?', *Digital Journalism*, 6(7), pp. 798–806. Doi: 10.1080/21670811.2018.1498747

Vargo, C. J., Guo, L. and Amazeen, M. A. (2018) 'The agenda-setting power of fake news: A big data analysis of the online media landscape from 2014 to 2016', *New Media & Society*, 20(5), pp. 2028–2049. Doi: 10.1177/1461444817712086

Vosoughi, S., Roy, D. and Aral, S. (2018) 'The spread of true and false news online', *Science*, 359(6380), pp. 1146–1151. Doi: 10.1126/science.aap9559

Vraga, E. K. and Tully, M. (2019) 'News literacy, social media behaviors, and skepticism toward information on social media. Information', *Communication & Society*, pp. 1–17. Doi: 10.1080/1369118X.2019.1637445

Waisbord, S. (2018a) 'Truth is what happens to news: On journalism, fake news, and post-truth', *Journalism studies*, 19(13), pp. 1866–1878. Doi: 10.1080/1461670X.2018.1492881

Waisbord, S. (2018b) 'The elective affinity between post-truth communication and populist politics', *Communication Research and Practice*, 4(1), pp. 17–34. Doi: 10.1080/22041451.2018.142892

Weber, D., Nasim, M., Falzon, L. and Mitchell, L. (2020) '#ArsonEmergency and Australia's "Black Summer": Polarisation and misinformation on social media', *MISDOOM* 2020 [online]. Available at: https://arxiv.org/abs/2004.00742 (Accessed 18 May 202).

Wilson, T. and Starbird, K. (2020) 'Cross-platform disinformation campaigns: Lessons learned and next steps'. *Harvard Kennedy School Misinformation Review* [online]. Available at: https://misinforeview.hks.harvard.edu/article/cross-platform-disinformation-campaigns/ (Accessed 18 May 2020).

Zimmermann, F. and Kohring, M. (2020) 'Mistrust, disinforming news, and vote choice: A panel survey on the origins and consequences of believing disinformation in the 2017 German parliamentary election', *Political Communication*, 37(2), pp. 215–237. Doi: 10.1080/10584609.2019.1686095

PART IV

Media and populism

31

POPULISM IN AFRICA

Personalistic leaders and the illusion of representation

Bruce Mutsvairo and Susana Salgado

Introduction

From anti-colonial figureheads like the late Zimbabwean President Robert Mugabe to the emerging crop of politicians such as South Africa's Economic Freedom Fighters party's firebrand leader Julius Malema, known for his radically left-leaning yet unequivocal stance on black consciousness, Africa has had its share of populist politicians, and several of the features of what is considered populism in European and American countries have also been present in African politics over the last decades. In addition to strong personalistic leaders (Resnick 2017), there have also been political strategies aimed at strengthening a direct connection between the political leader and citizens, nationalism and nativism, as well as anti-immigration positions (e.g. Angola), or the 'us and them' divide of society (e.g. against ethnic and sexual minorities in Uganda). Such populist rhetoric is often mixed with illiberal and sometimes even despotic approaches to political power. The rise of populism in Africa, both historically and contemporarily, has been significantly aided by the presence of media outlets that take an uncompromising stance, especially when it comes to supporting their leader. In Southern Africa, the majority of political establishments that brought independence have lingered in power and are known for their uncompromising anti-colonialism stance. Their position is frequently supported by state media outlets that consider opposition parties as an extension of neo-colonialism or as the enemy of the people: for example, newspapers such as the state-owned *Herald* in Zimbabwe that steadfastly support the ruling ZANU PF party using both propaganda and innuendos to convince supporters and discredit foes.

The purpose of this chapter is to give an account of populism in Africa analysing extant literature and looking at four specific cases (Amin in Uganda, Machel in Mozambique, Mugabe in Zimbabwe, and Malema in South Africa), who were selected considering their varying features of populism and distinct generational differences. Our overall goal is to critically analyse and contribute to the understanding of the political and media populism that have persisted on the continent since the days of colonialism.

Some singularities of populism in Africa

They come in different shapes and sizes, but what binds them together seems to be their desire to represent the 'will of the people' (Mudde and Kaltwasser 2017, 90). Indeed, populism involves putting the 'people' (e.g. the common citizen, the worker, the poor) at the centre of speeches and decisions. Basically, it holds that state institutions should be first and foremost responsive to the needs and concerns of the people. The ideal of morality is often central in populist claims. In the form of liberation movements' leaders, and over time, several African political leaders have become known for their populist charisma or for having resorted to populist ideas and strategies to mobilise supporters. As Resnick (2017) posits, 'Africa represents an especially challenging case for delineating populism due to the predominance of personalistic leaders and the lack of policy ideology underlying many political parties'. In defining populism within a South African context, Vincent (2011) posits,

> what makes a politics 'populist' is not a particular, definable set of values or a particular social, political or economic programme but rather an antagonism to existing orthodoxies, to elite values and to the existing hierarchies governing the way in which power is organised and distributed.
>
> (2011, 4)

An African populist has to appeal 'directly to the masses for legitimacy' (Carbone 2005, 1), present an image of 'one of the people' ready to use their common sense and lived experience to defend the 'common man' against manipulative elites (Cheeseman and Larmer 2015, 5), or make an attempt to 'remake a connection between parties and voters whose livelihoods and communities are precarious' (Fraser 2017, 461). According to Vincent, the central theme that connects African populists with each other is 'the appeal to "the people" as the legitimizing authority for a particular set of ideas' (2011, 3).

While in many parts of the world, radical politicians lead from the front against established political elites, in Africa, history has been at the centre of emerging and evolving populist discourses. Across the continent, populists are often united by their unwavering anti-colonial rhetoric. Theirs is a message of hope, and they take no shame in delivering such a message, even if it catches them in blunt contradictions, including instances in which they would have privately benefited from the same system they staunchly oppose publicly. They delegitimise all opposition: basically any political leader other than themselves.

Yet populist political leaders in Africa are not usually short of admirers. They could be bound by their 'shared experience of violent struggle' (Levitsky and Way 2010, 3), or they could simply enjoy riding on their charm, dominance, and charisma (Tormey 2018). Populism in Africa, needless to say, 'legitimizes' former freedom fighters' quest to offer a message of hope in the light of perceived Western domination (Melber 2018, 679). Such a message instantly appeals to the multitudes, most of whom have come across some similar versions of colonial history at primary or secondary school. Facts are framed to fit a particular narrative, one in which the 'subaltern' is often portrayed as a victim of long-lasting colonial servitude (Spivak 1988, 271).

Extant research has conceptualised populism differently: it can be ideological, stressing the direct connection with the will of the people; a communication frame which purports to speak in the name of the people; a discursive or performative style, in which a populist adopts of political style that appeals to the people; or a form of political mobilisation (e.g. Gidron and Bonikowski 2013; Nai and Comma 2019). Equally, African populists adopt various tactics, including the use of simplified rhetoric, to present themselves as genuine representatives of the people and to establish a direct connection between them and the people. Key to their success is their claim to give voice (and thus power) to the people (Adeakin and Zirker 2017). But, as in other contexts, the word 'people' itself is problematic. It is difficult to tell how they measure which people whose interests they purport to represent. For example, it is not credible that the entire population of Uganda summarily supported Amin's decision to expel Asians from the East African country, yet he nevertheless claimed his decision was being made in the interest of his 'country folk'. Even when populist leaders claim to speak on behalf of the majority, it is unclear which yardstick is used to determine their claim of democratic superiority.

Although populism has often been associated with the erosion of freedom of expression and press freedom in other parts of the world, the media environment in African countries makes it difficult to evaluate the actual impact of populism on media freedom. The political instrumentalisation of mainstream media by ruling elites is a common characteristic of several governments in Africa, even in countries where democratic consolidation has found little obstacles to flourishing, such as Cape Verde (e.g. Salgado 2014). Most media outlets, particularly state-controlled news media with nationwide dissemination, are frequently used as tools to support the governments' decisions and influence the citizens' views. In the 1990s, changes in national laws allowed for the proliferation of privately owned media in many countries, but with few exceptions, these did not become fully independent from political and economic powers and often struggled to survive. More recently, the internet and social media have strengthened the forms of populism more dependent on the unmediated links between the political leader and the people.

Research focused on other parts of the world has already provided evidence of the key role that the media plays in supporting and mobilising for populist causes (e.g. Mazzoleni 2014; Mudde 2004). Even when media outlets do not openly support populist politicians, when politics is covered through oversimplified, negative, and sensationalist news reports, it tends to favour populist politicians by shaping favourable climates of opinion for populist leaders, thus improving their chances of getting elected. Media players can also help populist political leaders by generating user-friendly political news (Manucci 2017) or giving them the platform to prove their media savviness (Boczkowski and Papacharissi 2018), which is a key factor in maintaining their popularity.

For many populist leaders, some of whom could have their integrity questioned by the neoliberal private media (e.g. Malema in South Africa), the advent of social media has facilitated direct access to the people without journalistic interference. This type of media offers an opportunity not only to frame issues, but also to set a narrative that influences the agenda and consequently gain a favourable public opinion (e.g. Gainous and Wagner 2014; Blumler and Gurevitch 2001).

Some African cases of populism

Next, we look closely at four cases that represent different manifestations of populist politics and leadership in Africa. We analyse these four political leaders' rhetoric, tactics, strategies, and policies with the overall aim of contributing to the understanding of the origins and impact of populism in contemporary African societies.

Idi Amin in Uganda

Described by Hoberman (2017) as a 'populist demagogue', Amin come to power through a military coup and ruled Uganda with an iron fist for nearly a decade between 1971 and 1979. Keatley (2003) argues that the self-proclaimed Conqueror of the British Empire responded to all forms of dissent from both loyalists and political enemies with heavy-handed systematic brutality and repression. Even though he associated himself with local benevolence, he nevertheless unleashed an ethnically charged wave of repression against the same people he claimed to be representing (Munnion 1972; Tall 1982; Kyemba 1977).

In defining populism, Kyle and Gultchin (2018) propound that 'rather than seeing politics as a battleground between different policy positions, populists attribute a singular common good to the people: a policy goal that cannot be debated based on evidence but that derives from the common sense of the people'. By targeting the Asian community, consequently deporting them by the thousands, Amin saw no irony in claiming that dispatching Asians from Uganda was being done to protect the interests of ethnic Ugandans, who he had targeted (Jørgensen 1981). Chasing Asians away on a radical nationalist, nativist, and thus exclusionary populist platform was therefore justified by what he considered to be a pro-people agenda that was meant to benefit black Ugandans. Amin, who claimed 'God told him to order the expulsion' (Bhushan 2020), accused the Asians of 'milking Uganda's money' or 'sabotaging Uganda's economy' (Dawood 2016). In insisting that he was protecting the interests of locals by chasing out Asians, Amin turned to the "us versus them" rhetoric which is often used by populists to win the support of the native people (e.g. Henning 2018; Rice-Oxley and Kalia 2018).

The argument by Barber (2019) that 'populists are not tyrants or dictators' because they 'rely on the support of the people for their power' (2019, 129) appears to be not in tandem with African politics, in which, in the case of Amin and others, dictatorial tendencies are apparent, whereas appealing to the people seems to be equally significant. While protecting the interest of 'ethnic Ugandans' appealed to locals, many did not realise Amin only did this whenever it was handier for him to do so. Patel (1972) argues that African leaders, apart from Zambia's Kenneth Kaunda and Tanzania's Julius Nyerere, responded to Amin's persecution of Asians by adopting a non-interference policy, an approach that would prove to be instrumental in the successful implementation of populist agendas by the next generation of anti-colonial leaders, such as Zimbabwe's Mugabe. Religion was one of the reasons evoked by Amin to justify the expulsion of Asians from his country. This justification would also receive a tacit endorsement from future populist leaders (e.g. Mugabe in Zimbabwe, Yoweri Museveni in Uganda, and Jacob Zuma in South Africa) as they also turned to religion to rationalise their actions.

Samora Machel in Mozambique

Samora Machel, a guerrilla leader, became Mozambique's first president after independence from Portugal in June 1975 and until 1986, when he died in a plane crash. For several years, Machel held 'the country together largely by force of his own personality, traveling extensively, condemning corruption and inefficiency' (Krebs 1986). Even though the use of (populist) ideas and words always needs to be placed into the proper context, there are several elements that substantiate Machel's populist approach to politics and thus support the label of populist leader in his case: the use that he made of his own charisma and the way in which he framed his proposals are just a couple of examples. Machel's approach to politics was completely people centred; there are several references to the 'people's power' and to the priority that should always be given to the people: for example, in a speech he gave in Maputo on 7 February 1980, Machel's own words were, 'The State must be the first to be organized and totally committed to serving the interests of the people' (Machel 1987).

The anti-system narrative was also recurrent in his rhetoric (e.g. 'profound change of the country's society and politics'), even after Samora Machel formed his government and became part of the 'system'. The anti-system position was rooted in a dramatic change from the colonial system of politics and society, but it also pushed forward a socialist model of society. Not only was it against the Portuguese settlers ('imperial domination') and the Mozambicans who had supported the Portuguese rule (Machel referred often to 'the victory of the people over the forces of oppression and exploitation'), but it was also aimed at transforming social and economic relations (Lipschutz and Rasmussen 1986). The people would overthrow completely the inheritance of the colonial state that, after the country's independence, was being somehow maintained by the native bourgeoisie (Parry 2004, 85). For Machel it was necessary to break away from the bourgeois culture and enforce the culture of the people.

The idea of unity of the people was ever present in Machel's speeches (see e.g. Machel 1976; Sopa 2001). Because he was well aware of the dangers of tribalism in Mozambique and of the differences among the country's many ethnic groups, he always presented the people as unitary while he strived to unite them around common goals and especially against common enemies: first, against colonialism and then against those who were 'corrupt', 'opportunist', 'lazy', or 'recidivist'. It is interesting to note that cities were seen as places of corruption, in contrast to the correctness and purity of rural life.

In addition to the unitarian vision of the people, Machel targeted those who did not share his unitarian view of Mozambican society. After independence, when the 'enemy Portugal' was no longer relevant, Machel was not able to unite the entire country around his vision of establishing a socialist state in Mozambique; instead, he had to face a new opponent, the Mozambican National Resistance (RENAMO) and, ultimately, civil war. RENAMO started as a militant political organisation and guerrilla movement in Mozambique and was founded in 1975 in Rhodesia in opposition to Machel's FRELIMO (the Mozambique Liberation Front, which resulted from the merger of several nationalist groups into a single organisation and was founded in 1962 by Eduardo Mondlane as a nationalist independence movement) and its ideological stance. RENAMO was mostly an anti-Machel resistance movement. As Hanlon (1991) explains, 'when FRELIMO started losing control, the response was a complex mix of populism and authoritarianism' (1991, 27).

Context dictated that Machel would have to face different opponents throughout his political life. He commonly used the word *enemy* (see e.g. Lefanu 2012), which was a distinctive strategy employed in his speeches and in his specific framing of reality. Eduardo Mondlane (the first FRELIMO president assassinated in 1969) had already persuaded many to unite against a shared enemy (Salazar's Portugal), and Machel commonly interpreted events through this logic. But the enemy was not only Salazar's Portugal or RENAMO, which Machel often referred to as 'enemies of the people', but also several other enemies, vague or specific (e.g. the 'enemy of the nation', the 'enemy of women', etc.).

Robert Mugabe in Zimbabwe

Mugabe, known internationally for his bitterly anti-colonial stance, was one African leader who saw no shame in associating himself with 'populist nationalist rhetoric' (Woolf 2017). Examples of his populist interventions, argues Mhlanga (2017), included his resolution to publicly overrule his finance minister's decision to hold off bonus payments to civil servants due to a crippling economic downturn. Never the one to shy away from controversy and always eager to please 'his people', Mugabe declared in a national address that all government workers would receive their 13th cheque, to the utter disbelief and embarrassment of his minister. Buoyed by his uncompromising stance on the land reform, Mugabe's economic populism was notable. In taking land from the white farmers, he followed Amin by using the need to economically empower the native population as a way of justifying his policies. Yet, the white farmers' decision to financially back Mugabe's fiercest political opponent (Morgan Tsvangirai) was largely perceived to be the main motive of his retaliatory move (Mutsvairo and Muneri 2019). When the prices of foodstuffs sharply rose in 2007, Mugabe blamed the white business owners for using their businesses to effect a Western-backed regime change agenda. His response was to introduce price controls, which led to severe shortages. Some Western journalists, who Mugabe had long argued deliberately wrote false accounts to destroy his image, were also kicked out of the country.

Thus, in Mugabe's populist agenda, there was always someone to blame. The key targets were journalists, opposition leaders and their supporters, businessmen, and Western leaders, all of whom, he argued, were keen to oust him because of his pro-black policies. African leaders – apart from Botswana's Ian Khama, who Mugabe sharply rebuked at every given opportunity – did not interfere in Zimbabwe, arguing the Southern African country was a sovereign state that could deal with its own internal affairs. The non-interference of African leaders, just like with Amin in Uganda, gave Mugabe an unmatched conviction that he was indeed Africa's true anti-colonial champion. He was also accused, like Amin was before, of ethnically targeting those opposed to his rule. But his supporters saw him as a liberation icon, someone who had empowered his people by giving them land previously owned by white people.

Mugabe used his intellect and charisma to administer his anti-Western populist agenda. Even those who opposed his politics sometimes could not help but admire him. One of those was Tendai Biti, a known figurehead of opposition politics in Zimbabwe, who reacted to news of Mugabe's death by calling a man he said had tortured and jailed him the 'founding father of our struggle' (SABC 2019) while, contrastingly, a spokesman for the British government called Mugabe a 'barrier to a better future' (France24 2019). Tendai Biti had also praised Mugabe by suggesting he found 'counsel and wisdom in him' (Vava 2012).

Julius Malema in South Africa

Agenda-setting Malema, a vicious proponent of socialism, could represent Africa's young and modern-day populists. According to Karimi (2012), he is a 'populist, an opportunist, or both, depending on whom you ask'. Eloquent, confident, and tough-talking, the militant Malema rose to prominence in the African National Congress (ANC), South Africa's ruling party's youth wing. At first, nobody paid attention to his rise until he demanded, during ex-president Thambo Mbeki's rule, that mines be nationalised and, in keeping with Mugabe's acquisition of land for redistribution to black people, appealed for the confiscation of white farmland. In response, the media has sharply rebuked 'toxic, destructive populism' by Malema (Lincoln-Reader 2020). He does not try to hide radical, racially propelled, economic populism, which has been the face of his self-styled far-left Economic Freedom Fighters party. While he claims to have nothing against whites, he has issued racially charged statements on numerous occasions, recently declaring, 'We are not calling for the slaughtering of White people – at least for now' (York 2019).

His expulsion from the ANC came after he sang a song that openly called for the killing of a white farmer, but in 2013, he formed his own pan-Africanist party (Economic Freedom Fighters), which is now the third largest nationally in terms of parliamentary representation. Malema's critics, who accuse him of deliberately inciting racism and anti-white prejudice against his opponents, have warned he lacks the credibility and political willpower to preside over an already racially divided nation, but his supporters, especially the young unemployed blacks, see him as the perfect answer to South Africa's unequal society. This inequality seems to be at the centre of everything Malema and his party do, which is basically 'fighting for equality not for blacks to oppress whites' Cotterill (2019). Malema uses combative rhetoric to appeal to his supporters, especially the youths. He sees himself as the voice of the voiceless, particularly those who have failed to see the gains from the end of apartheid. He has also issued scathing attacks on global icon Nelson Mandela for what he considers to be his pro-white policies, suggesting for instance that Mandela made a mistake by not prioritising free education when he took over power in 1994. There are some who consider Malema an 'unapologetic fascist' or a 'dangerous politician'. Yet there are others who see him as a symbol of economic egalitarianism in an already deeply divided country.

Populism and representation in Africa

As Cheeseman (2018) notes, 'it is not surprising that populist appeals are commonplace, given the context within which African political leaders operate' (2018, 359). Weak party structures, the low political sophistication of most voters, and pervasive inequalities tend to emphasise the emergence of strong leaders with magnetic personalities and disruptive discourses. We examined four political leaders who have been successful in part because of these characteristics. Adding to these, they have also resorted to rhetorical strategies commonly known as populist, such as people-centrism, blame-shifting, or the 'us versus them' view of society. The populist, simplistic logic of the enemy is also prevalent in the discourse of all these political leaders. The identification of the 'enemies of the people', those who threaten the people's rights and space, and exclusionary stances (e.g. against foreigners, religious groups, etc.) have been, in these cases, directly anchored in plans to revitalise the country's economy.

The four cases described in this chapter also demonstrate how initially populism in Africa was mostly linked to anti-colonial politics and that later, it also emerged as a differentiation strategy and a response to governments that had become too detached from the population. The anti-elitism stance is thus consistently present, first against the colonisers and later against the 'self-interested' and 'corrupt' political leaders. The anti-colonial discursive appeal gave African populations promises of post-colonial glory in which racial tensions would cease to exist, and natives would have equal access to jobs and other opportunities. The belief that such promises have not been met has propelled a new brand of youthful political leaders, such as Malema, to prominence. But, as Sharra (2020) warns, the dominance of established mavericks like Malema has made it more difficult for many to come to terms with an emerging force of populist African political movements that are establishing themselves thanks to the advent of social media networks such as Facebook. These, he argues, need not be in the mainstream like Malema, but they use the internet to demand and sometimes secure change.

Notwithstanding existing prior identifications of populist political leaders in Africa (e.g. Resnick 2017; Cheeseman 2018), populism also has been used as an effective strategy for political mobilisation in different African countries (e.g. Thomson 2000; Resnick 2019). It is therefore useful to follow an approach that identifies the key characteristics of populist rhetoric and strategies and then investigate the extent to which different political actors make use of them (Stanyer et al. 2017), rather than just naming the examples of populist political actors who have been labelled as such. In Africa, where there is a tradition of strongmen leaders and instrumentalisation of the media is customary, elements that are deemed normal could be easily mistaken for populism if Western standards were applied.

As a belief-system influencing decision-making, populism can also be the idea that the people should be directly involved in political processes (e.g. the People's Defence Committees in Ghana or the revolutionary committees in Burkina Faso in Sankara's government). However, on the few occasions that such opportunity arose, governments held on to power and resisted the actual transfer of power to the people. Nationalist arguments have been used, too, but as excuses to strengthen national unity rather than to fragment the decision-making power, which could – in their view – jeopardise the country's development or even peace. In fact, so far, this type of African populist experiments have proved to be more useful as a method for the state to penetrate civil society than for civil society to penetrate the state (Thomson 2000, 43).

Although this is still an under-researched area of study in Africa, we can observe that similar ideological methods that have been reported in the West, such as engaging in pro-people rhetoric and proposing a Manichean view of society, have also been used by African political leaders. They may also cling to repressive media laws and policies because they fear dissent or alternative voices could threaten their power. Economy and exclusion are also relevant elements in their populist approach to politics. But there are also important singularities in the manifestations of populism in Africa, which are clearly related to the specificities of the context: the history of colonialism and how that legacy has affected political structures and identities. The varied ethnic composition of most of these countries also adds to the complexity, particularly in attempts to define the unitary 'the people' and determine who belongs to 'the people'. In view hereof, populist leaders have primarily framed 'the other' as an outsider, an immigrant, or from a different race or have applied morality standards pointing the finger at those considered 'lazy' or 'corrupt'.

While populist African leaders could display some similar tendencies among themselves, remarkable differences in approach can also been noted. For example, on a continent known for its long-time leaders, a populist leader in opposition has to adopt different tactics if he or she is to be elected because access to mainstream media is either limited or not available. As in other parts of the world, the development of social media has brought new opportunities for fringe politicians and for unmediated forms of political communication in Africa. Although attempts to censor online content and to control the internet by ruling politicians have been reported in several African countries, it is also expected that, in time, online media will function as important tools for other types of populist manifestations, this time from the grassroots and populations who feel poorly represented and not from personalistic, strong leaders.

References

Adeakin, I. and Zirker, D. (2017) Democracy vs. populism: The transformation of politics in Nigeria? *PRACS: Revista Eletrônica de Humanidades do Curso de Ciências Sociais da UNIFAP*, 10 (1): 169–189.

Barber, N.W. (2019) Populist leaders and political parties. *German Law Journal*, 20 (2): 129–140.

Bhushan, S.A.K. (2020) In his own words: Why Idi Amin expelled Indians from Uganda? *Coastweek*. Available at: www.coastweek.com/3734-Kul-Bhushan-In-his-own-words-Why-Idi-Amin-Expelled-Indians-from-Uganda.htm [Accessed on 22 May 2020].

Blumler, J.G. and Gurevitch, M. (2001) The new media and our political communication discontents: Democratizing cyberspace. *Information, Communication & Society*, 4 (3): 1–14.

Boczkowski, P.J. and Papacharissi, Z. (2018) *Trump and the Media*. Cambridge, MA and London: The MIT Press.

Carbone, G. (2005) Populism visits Africa: The case of Yoweri Museveni and no party 'populism' in Africa. *Working Paper Series*, 1 (73): 1–19.

Cheeseman, N. (2018) Populism in Africa and the potential for "ethnically blind" politics. In C. de la Torre (Ed.), *Routledge Handbook of Global Populism*. Oxon and New York: Routledge, 357–369.

Cheeseman, N. and Larmer, M. (2015) Ethnopopulism in Africa: Opposition mobilization in diverse and unequal societies. *Democratization*, 22 (1): 22–50.

Cotterill, J. (2019) Malema eyes South Africa election breakthrough against ANC. *Financial Times*. Available at: www.ft.com/content/4febe866-7010-11e9-bf5c-6eeb837566c5. [Accessed on 22 May 2020].

Dawood, F. (2016) Ugandan Asians dominate economy after exile. *BBC*. Available at: www.bbc.com/news/world-africa-36132151 [Accessed on 22 May 2020].

France24 (2019) African anti-colonial 'champion' who 'stayed too long': World reacts to Mugabe's death. Available at: www.france24.com/en/20190906-robert-mugabe-death-reactions-africa-champion-mixed. [Accessed on 22 May 2020].

Fraser, A. (2017) Post-populism in Zambia: Michael Sata's rise, demise and legacy. *International Political Science Review*, 38 (4): 456–472.

Gainous, J. and Wagner, K.M. (2014) *Tweeting to Power: The Social Media Revolution in American Politics*. New York: Oxford University Press.

Gidron, N. and Bonikowski, B. (2013) Varieties of populism: Literature review and research agenda. Weatherhead Centre for International Affairs, Harvard University, Working Paper Series, No. 13–0004.

Hanlon, J. (1991) *Mozambique: Who Calls the Shots?* London and Bloomington: James Currey Ltd. and Indiana University Press.

Henning, M. (2018) Populism in Southern Africa under liberation movements as governments, *Review of African Political Economy*, 45 (158): 678–686.

Hoberman, J. (2017) *Totalitarian Recall*. Book Forum. Available at: www.bookforum.com/print/2602/the-new-faces-of-fascism-populism-and-the-far-right-by-enzo-traverso-22009 [Accessed on 22 May 2020].

Jørgensen, J.J. (1981) *Uganda: A Modern History*. New York: Taylor & Francis.

Karimi, F. (2012) South Africa's Julius Malema: Populist or opportunist? *CNN*. Available at: https://edition.cnn.com/2012/09/16/world/africa/julius-malema-profile/index.html [Accessed on 22 May 2020].

Keatley, P. (2003) Idi Amin. *The Guardian*, August 17, 2003. Available at: from www.theguardian.com/news/2003/aug/18/guardianobituaries [Accessed on 22 May 2020].

Krebs, A. (1986) Samora M. Machel, Man of Charisma. *The New York Times*. [online] 21 October 1986 edition. Available at: www.nytimes.com/1986/10/21/obituaries/samora-m-machel-man-of-charisma.html [Accessed on 20 May 2020].

Kyemba, H. (1977) *A State of Blood: The Inside Story of Idi Amin*. New York: Paddington Press.

Kyle, J. and Gultchin, L. (2018) *Populism in Power Around the World*. Tony Blair Institute for Global Change. Available at: https://papers.ssrn.com/sol3/papers.cfm?abstract_id=3283962. [Accessed on 22 May 2020].

Lefanu, S. (2012) *S is for Samora: A Lexical Biography of Samora Machel and the Mozambican Dream*. London: Hurst and C. Ltd. Publishers.

Levitsky, S. and Way, L.A. (2010) *Beyond Patronage: Ruling Party Cohesion and Authoritarian Stability*. Paper prepared for the American Political Science Association Annual Meeting. Washington, DC, 2–5 September.

Lincoln-Reader, S. (2020) SLR: MI6, Malema and export of destructive populism. *BizNews*. Available at: www.biznews.com/global-citizen/2020/02/27/slr-mi6-malema-populism [Accessed on 22 May 2020].

Lipschutz, M.R. and Rasmussen, R.K. (1986) *Dictionary of African Historical Biography*. Berkeley: University of California Press.

Machel, S. (1976) *Establishing People's Power to Serve the Masses*. Dar es Salaam: Tanzania Publishing House.

Machel, S. (1987) *Samora Machel, an African Revolutionary: Selected Speeches and Writings*. Edited by Barry Munslow. Harare: College Press.

Manucci, L. (2017) Populism and the media. In C.R. Kaltwasser, P.A. Taggart, P.O. Espejo and P. Ostiguy (Eds.), *The Oxford Handbook of Populism*. Oxford: Oxford University Press.

Mazzoleni, G. (2014) Mediatization and political populism. In F. Esser and J. Strömbäck (Eds.), *Mediatization of Politics: Understanding the Transformation of Western Democracies*. Basingstoke: Palgrave Macmillan, 42–56.

Melber, H. (2018) Populism in Southern Africa under liberation movements as governments. *Review of African Political Economy*, 45 (158): 678–686.

Mhlanga, F. (2017) Mugabe's populism haunts govt. *The Zimbabwe Independent*. Available at: www.theindependent.co.zw/2017/03/10/mugabes-populism-haunts-govt/ [Accessed on 22 May 2020].

Mudde, C. (2004) The populist zeitgeist: *Government and Opposition*, 39 (4):541–563.

Mudde, C. and Kaltwasser, C.R. (2017) *Populism: A Very Short Introduction*. Oxford: Oxford University Press.

Munnion, C. (1972) The African who kicked out the Asians, who said Hitler was right, who has made his country a state sinister. *New York Times*. Available at: www.nytimes.com/1972/11/12/archives/if-idi-amin-of-uganda-is-a-madman-hes-a-ruthless-and-cunning-one.html [Accessed on 22 May 2020].

Mutsvairo, B. and Muneri, C. (2019) *Journalism, Democracy and Human Rights in Zimbabwe*. Lanham, MD: Lexington Books.

Nai, A. and Comma, F.M. (2019) The personality of populists: Provocateurs, charismatic leaders, or drunken dinner guests? *Western European Journal*, 42 (7): 1337–1367.

Parry, B. (2004) *Postcolonial Studies: A Materialist Critique.* London and New York: Routledge.

Patel, H.H. (1972) General Amin and the Indian Exodus from Uganda. *Journal of Opinion,* 2 (4): 12–22.

Resnick, D.E. (2017) Populism in Africa. In C.R. Kaltwasser, P. Taggart, P.O. Espejo, and P. Ostiguy (Eds.), *The Oxford Handbook of Populism.* Oxford: Oxford University Press, 101–120.

Resnick, D.E. (2019) Populist politics in Africa. In W. Thompson (Ed.), *The Oxford Research Encyclopedia of Politics.* Oxford: Oxford University Press. Available at: https://oxfordre.com/politics/view/10.1093/acrefore/9780190228637.001.0001/acrefore-9780190228637-e-699 [Accessed on 20 May 2020].

Rice-Oxley, M. and Kalia, A. (2018) How to spot a populist. *The Guardian.* Available at: www.theguardian.com/news/2018/dec/03/what-is-populism-trump-farage-orban-bolsonaro [Accessed on 22 May 2020].

SABC (2019) *Zimbabwe's Tendai Biti Remembers Robert Mugabe.* Available at: www.sabcnews.com/sabcnews/zimbabwes-tendai-biti-remembers-robert-mugabe/ [Accessed on 22 May 2020].

Salgado, S. (2014) *The Internet and Democracy Building in Lusophone African Countries.* London and New York: Routledge.

Sharra, A. (2020) *Creativity in Populism: New Faces, Ideas and Approaches in Africa.* Available at: https://politicsafterwar.com/2019/09/18/historical-and-contemporary-expressions-of-populism-in-africa-and-beyond-workshop/ [Accessed on 22 May 2020].

Sopa, A. (2001) (Ed.) *Samora: Man of the People.* Maputo: Maguezo Editores.

Spivak, G.C. (1988) Can the subaltern speak? In C. Nelson and L. Grossberg (Eds.), *Marxism and the Interpretation of Culture.* Urbana, IL: University of Illinois Press, 271–313.

Stanyer, J., Salgado, S. and Strömbäck, J. (2017) Populist Actors as Communicators or Political Actors as Populist Communicators: A Cross-National Findings and Perspectives. In T. Aalberg, F. Esser, C. Reinemann, J. Strömbäck and C. de Vreese (Eds.), *Populist Political Communication in Europe.* London and New York: Routledge, 353–364.

Tall, M. (1982) Notes on the civil and political strife in Uganda. *A Journal of Opinion,* 12 (1/2): 41–44.

Thomson, A. (2000) *An Introduction to African Politics.* London and New York: Routledge.

Tormey, S. (2018) Populism: Democracy's Pharmakon? *Policy Studies,* 39 (3): 260–273.

Vava, B. (2012) *MDC-T a Smaller ZANU PF in the Making.* Available at: http://archive.kubatana.net/html/archive/opin/120906bv.asp?sector=OPIN&year=0&range_start=331 [Accessed on 22 May 2020].

Vincent, L. (2011) Seducing the people: Populism and the challenge to democracy in South Africa. *Journal of Contemporary African Studies,* 29 (1): 1–14.

Woolf, C. (2017) How Mugabe became Zimbabwe's leader and clung on till now. *The World.* Available at: www.pri.org/stories/2017-11-15/how-robert-mugabe-became-zimbabwe-s-leader-and-clung-till-now. [Accessed on 22 May 2020].

York, G. (2019) South Africa's populist party EFF gains traction as country sees rise in apathy and alienation. *Globe and Mail.* Available at: www.theglobeandmail.com/world/article-south-africas-populist-party-eff-gains-traction-as-country-sees-rise/. [Accessed on 22 May 2020].

32

POPULISM AND MISINFORMATION FROM THE AMERICAN REVOLUTION TO THE TWENTY-FIRST-CENTURY UNITED STATES

Chris Wells and Alex Rochefort

Acknowledgement: The authors wish to thank Lewis A. Friedland for his helpful comments on the material presented in this chapter.

Introduction

Locating populism in the United States is a tricky business because American political culture is pervaded by populistic elements. Populism's foremost defining characteristic, its anti-elitism – its sense that some set of 'genuine' people are suffering at the hands of a (variously defined) set of economic, political, or cultural elites – is to be found throughout the country's history, across its political spectrum, and in every campaign season (Judis 2016; Kazin 1998).

Still, there are historical moments in which movements or individuals projecting more explicitly populist signals resonate with a sufficient base of citizen concerns to win public acclaim and even electoral success. Ours is quite clearly one of those moments, with Donald Trump, on the political right, and Bernie Sanders, on the left, regularly referred to as populists (e.g. Oliver and Rahn 2016).

We also are in the midst of a 'disinformation order' (Bennett and Livingston 2018), in which core societal institutions for describing and discussing reality are faltering (Waisbord 2018). 'Fake news', misinformation, and disinformation from a variety of sources are widely circulated in social media (and some news media).

What do these phenomena have to do with one another? In this chapter, we describe the political and informational logics of the contemporary 'populist zeitgeist' (Mudde 2004) as it exists in the United States. We begin with a brief historical review demonstrating that tendencies towards populism and susceptibility to misinformation are long-standing – even characteristic – aspects of American political culture. We then turn to the populism and misinformation of the current day, which we argue are well understood as extensions of those older patterns, shaped by the contemporary political-economic context and the twenty-first-century information environment.

A brief terminological note: we are wary of too prescriptively drawing the borders of populism (Judis 2016). Generally, our conception of populism is stylistic (cf. Moffitt 2016), understanding populism as a way of representing politics that emphasises 'the people' in opposition to elites, and that views the people as a repository of deep moral righteousness yet, in some way, under the subordination of self-serving elites. This rougher conception enables us to connect to several related themes in American political culture.

'Jealousies of power' in the founding of the republic

Discussions of populism have a tendency to view the American populist movement of the 1890s as populism's genesis moment. But populism's central concerns, its scepticism and hostility towards elites, and its suspicions about elites' efforts to subvert the people's will can be found even deeper in the American political psyche.

This becomes visible when we move away from the specific terminology of populism and consider related habits of thought. Looking back to the rhetorical heroes of the American Revolution, Jessen (2019) notes that 'an abiding suspicion of power was implanted in American political culture well in advance of the Revolution' (685). He adopts Alexander Hamilton's phrase 'jealousy of power' to capture this manner of instinctive scepticism, anti-elitism, and anti-authority thinking.

This innate anti-elitism was, early on, set against a vision associated with Jefferson, who imagined democracy to rest with citizens who are 'sensible, hard-working, independent folk secure in their possession of land, free of the corruptions of urban poverty and cynicism, free of dependence on a self-indulgent aristocracy of birth, responsible to the common good' (Bailyn 1993, 503). This notion of American democracy as grounded in the wisdom of common, productive folk set apart from, and often against, the corruptions of privilege and power has been an enduring contribution to our self-conception. It has made the central elements of the populist binary readily available to American political thinking. In some ways, the ideal's silence on the dependence of eighteenth-century agrarian economics on slavery, especially in the South, also has provided populism with a toxic racist undercurrent that has never fully resolved.

Inborn distrust of elites and authority also has a tendency to prompt speculations about what actually lies behind authorities' actions, distrust of authorities' explanations, and theorising about the hidden reality. Jessen notes that 'conspiracy theories are used to explain *why* governments fail to represent their people', and details their prolific invention and deployment in the pre-revolutionary period (Jessen 2019, 682, emphasis in original). And rather than delusions of clinical paranoiacs, Wood (1982) observes, the eighteenth-century conspiracy tradition might be better understood as the product of the emergent Enlightenment ideal that individuals can find the truth – independent of ordained experts – by reasoning through available evidence.

Deep suspicion of authority and conspiratorial habits of thought did not dissipate with the successful revolution; both continued to be prominent features of politics in the young republic as the former radicals became political competitors, weaving conspiratorial accusations into the original fabric of American democracy (Kazin 1998).

Developments in the nineteenth century

The movement that would give populism its name emerged in the last decades of the nineteenth century, most strongly among farmers and industrial workers in the American South and West. The movement's origins lay in a crisis of legitimacy resulting from the growing concentration of economic wealth and political power in the hands of large corporations and financiers, which were both remote (concentrated in the Northeast) and increasingly dominant in the lives of farmers, through lending practices and currency management. Crucial, as well, was the populists' disillusionment with both the Democratic and Republican Parties, which they perceived as ignoring their interests.

In response, in 1892, the populist movement coalesced into a third party, the People's Party, with a platform privileging agricultural issues, labor protections, regulation of the monopolistic railroad industry, and government intervention in the financial markets. The movement was strategically and discursively organised around the need to return power to the industrious people of the country. As one scholar notes, the populists wanted to 'restore the government of the Republic to the hands of "plain people"' (Federici 1991, 32).

This was a powerful expression of what Kazin (1998, 13) calls the 'producer ethic' – a belief in the virtue and moral value of productive, material labor, set against means of making money that involve no material creation. Rhetorical framers of the populist movement, such as Tom Watson and Ignatius Donnelly, explicitly interpreted the economic-political conditions of the 1890s as a perversion of Jefferson's dream. (Note that the populists' vision conceptualised hard-working producers in terms mainly of white citizens; segments of the movement excluded or actively denigrated, to varying degrees, Chinese immigrants, African Americans and newly arrived eastern Europeans; Judis 2016).

Populists used newspapers, newsletters, and books to communicate with and mobilise publics, and some of their content included conspiracy theories of various sorts (Ostler 1995). *Seven Financial Conspiracies Which Have Enslaved the American People* (1887) – a book argued to be one of the most circulated populist publications – figured prominently in the early populist movement. The work advanced specious reasons for a variety of contemporary economic problems while claiming that Wall Street moneymakers, the banking system (Jewish bankers in particular), and the deliberate manipulation of the press were complicit in the hardships of ordinary Americans. Most spectacular was the book's ultimate claim that US government officials were collaborating with a clique of British financiers intent on looting the states (Ostler 1995).

Populist firebrands in the 1930s

From the populists until Father Coughlin's anti-Semitic and anti–New Deal turn in the late 1930s, American populism was essentially a movement of agriculture and labor, fundamentally concerned with the power of unfettered, monopolistic capitalism in American life; the need for government intervention to remedy injustice; and, often, the reticence of the major parties to act in the interests of working people (Kazin 1998). Indeed, Judis (2016) credits Huey Long's left-populist pressure with substantially strengthening Roosevelt's New Deal.

Coughlin is notable here both for his later rightward turn and embrace of conspiratorial thinking and for his use of radio as a new communication medium. Coughlin's weekly radio programme began as a religion and politics broadcast in a Detroit suburb and was later syndicated around the country. His early politics were left leaning, inflected by his Catholic background: he aligned himself against 'money-changers', bankers, sometimes capitalism in general, and communists and sided with the citizens being harmed by the forces controlling the country (Kazin 1998). By the 1930s, CBS was airing Coughlin across the country to an estimated 30 million listeners (Modras 1989). His use of emotion and indignation and his nature of speaking 'around' centres of power articulated one of the first 'challenges to middlebrow journalism' then developing (Peck 2019, 65).

In the later 1930s, Coughlin espoused anti-Semitism and admiration for the Nazis and other fascist regimes. Anti-Semitic conspiracy theories in particular were integrated into Coughlin's populist style, 'carried out in the name of "the people", whose innate virtue is threatened by external, alien forces' (Cremoni 1998, 30). CBS cancelled Coughlin when the priest refused to allow the company to moderate his programme, but Coughlin quickly established his own autonomous radio network (Kay et al. 1998).

Populism's rightward turn in the post-war era

Following in Coughlin's steps, after the Second World War, American populism's foundation shifted from left-leaning critiques of the economic system to right-wing concerns over cultural elitism and governmental power (Kazin 1998). Factors shaping this evolution included the transformative New Deal, growing fears of communism, and economic growth that led growing numbers of Americans to identify as middle-class consumers and taxpayers.

It was in this period that the nonpareil of American conspiracy theorising, Joe McCarthy, appeared. McCarthy articulated a powerful blend of populist resentment, anger, and apocalyptic warnings of communist subversion. Tying elite politicians (Adlai Stevenson) and media (*New York Times*) to the communist cause, he presented himself as defending average Americans and traditional American culture.

The widespread fear of subversion – by foreign ideas but in the heart of American government – was ripe for conspiracy theorising, and McCarthy delivered. He found a conflicted partner in the news media, producing a tension that presages twenty-first-century populism. On one hand, McCarthy courted the media and relied on them not only for his own political self-aggrandisement but also to maintain regular communications with the public (Federici 1991). On the other, he waged a relentless war on the press, lambasting them for unfavourable coverage and accusing many outlets of communism. For their part, the media struggled in covering McCarthy. Despite his steady deluge of attacks, misinformation, and disinformation, wire services avoided negative reporting for fear of alienating publishers, and newspapers had trouble unwinding McCarthy's misrepresentations. As one scholar of the era wrote, 'It was no wonder that so many people were convinced that McCarthy was exposing Communists. The newspapers had said so' (Bayley 1981, 217).

The long 1960s and American populism

McCarthy is too often seen as an exceptional character, extracted from the wider political stream that produced him, including bipartisan anti-communist panic (Ribuffo 2017). In fact, he represented a form of right-wing political jealousy that long outlasted him. From the 1950s through the 1970s, several forms of conservative activism were taking shape in opposition to the New Deal, the civil rights movement, and cultural change. These included suburban citizen activists (McGirr 2015), media activists critical of the press and culture industries as purveyors of social liberalisation (Hemmer 2016), and Americans of moderate means who combined support for New Deal programmes such as Medicare and Social Security with culturally conservative attitudes and hostility to welfare and affirmative action (Warren's "Middle American Radicals"; 1976).

George Wallace, the most explicitly populist politician of the second half of the twentieth century, appealed strongly to this latter group (Warren 1976). Although a supporter of the New Deal, Wallace innovated a populist campaign that emphasised the resentment felt by white Americans uncomfortable with growing federal power and wider cultural change. In the cultural-political context of his time, this ultimately meant siding with the 'defense of the average (white) American against the tyranny of Washington bureaucrats. Big government was on its way to imposing its way on the average person' (Judis 2016, 34).

Growing anti-governmentalism

Wallace's pairing of anti-governmentalism with white backlash was simultaneously a manifestation of deep currents of American populism, reflective of the geo-political reality of the United States at the time, and an early step in what would become a defining feature of conservative (and Republican Party) thinking. It is worth digressing briefly into the profound implications that changing public attitudes towards government – basic ideas about what the nation's governing institutions could and should do – have had for American populism and American political culture.

Though a pan-cultural shift (Rodgers 2011), it was on the political right that anti-governmentalism took a particularly powerful form as Republican leaders, notably Nixon, Reagan, and Gingrich, largely adopted Wallace's populist formulation of a culturally conservative 'middle America' resenting 'big government's' intrusion into its wholesome way of life while eliding its (overt) racism (Kazin 1998). This was attractive to middle-American radicals and their descendants, including the Tea Party, whose mixed views on economic redistribution saw the middle class as squeezed between a hostile government elite and a sponging underclass (Skocpol and Williamson 2013). This resentment of government was married to a much smaller but extremely well-funded movement of billionaires and think tanks advocating laissez-faire economic policies that has pulled the Republican Party strongly to the economic right (Hacker and Pierson 2016). At their intersection, the Republican Party found a formula with the potential to appeal to diverse constituencies, including the white working class they increasingly courted, on its way to becoming, in Skocpol's (2020) words, a party of 'billionaire ultra-free-market fundamentalism and popularly rooted ethno-nationalist resentment' (4).

Lessons from American populist history

Several points from this (very brief) survey of the history of American populism through the twentieth century bear repeating. First, 'jealousy of power' represents a deep tendency in American political thought that is always present but tends to breach the surface during periods of democratic misrepresentation and crises of legitimacy (Judis 2016). Note that such crises often relate to objective circumstances but also are phenomena of perception, dependent on citizens' interpretive frameworks for understanding their conditions (e.g. Hochschild 2016).

The Jeffersonian tradition and related 'producer ethic' (Kazin 1998) have also contributed to the inborn populism of American political culture, telling a powerful moral story about hardworking people who contribute materially to society but are burdened by the predations of elites. As we have seen, however, this ethic has almost always been conceptualised in particular racial terms: at its most innocuous, simply conceptualising producerism in implicitly white terms and in other cases actively depicting members of non-white groups either as incapable of dignified productive work or as actively colluding with elites.

The chameleonic nature of populism means that it is heavily dependent on how the poles of 'people' and 'elite' are formulated, and this has varied across American political movements. Most significant for our remaining discussion is the shift that took place in the mid–twentieth century: prewar populism tended to understand the people as industrial workers and agrarian producers and the elite in economic and financial terms. Government, in this formulation, could serve to protect the working classes. The right-leaning populisms of the post-war period, by contrast, have seen elites more in cultural terms (Peck 2019) and emphasised their alliance with an undeserving underclass, forming a pincer threat to the hardworking middle class. Concordantly, the government, especially the federal government, became an enemy: bloated, captured by cultural elites, and now a threat to traditional (white) American culture. In this conceptualisation, economic elites blend to a surprising degree with the middle class – especially small business owners – all of whom can now fall under the frame of 'job creators' (Hacker and Pierson 2016).

Finally, since the eighteenth century, a certain logic has tied jealousy of power to the unmasking of machinations occurring behind the visible scenes of power; when a political order becomes highly suspect, especially when elite communicators are associated with that political order, the temptation to hypothesise elaborate conspiracies becomes intense.

There is a tendency to dismiss conspiracy theorists as clinically disturbed. But this is probably short sighted if our goal is to understand the appeal of this manner of thinking and its considerable resistance to factual correction. Hofstadter (1965) describes conspiracy theories as built on mountains of 'evidence': 313 footnotes in one of McCarthy's pamphlets and a 100-page bibliography in a book by Robert H. Welch, co-founder of the John Birch Society, concluding that far from being disinterested in facts, such theorists had an 'extravagant passion' for them (37). In this light, we might better think of conspiracy theories as attempts to knit together a coherent explanation of the world when centring institutions of social epistemology have been degraded or delegitimised.

Populism and misinformation in the twenty-first-century United States

These trends are actively visible today, now shaped by new developments across society, media, and technology.

Democratic crisis and polarisation

A multi-faceted crisis of democratic legitimacy now provides the backdrop to American politics. Post-industrialisation and years of neoliberal hegemony have transformed the economies of Western democracies, yielding levels of inequality not seen in the post-war period, stagnation of living standards for the middle and working classes, and the inflating precariousness of many aspects of life. Historically low levels of trust in governmental, social, and media institutions reflect the inability of these institutions to address these problems (Achen and Bartels 2016).

American life has also polarised along multiple dimensions. Divisions between young and old, college educated and not, non-white and white, urban and rural have all increased in their relevance for electoral politics, culture, and outlook on life – reducing Americans' opportunities for cross-cutting exposures and common ground (Mason 2016). Though to depict American polarisation as somehow non-partisan or symmetric is empirically dishonest: the Republican Party has transformed itself from a conventional political party into one with the rather singular vision that government itself is a problem to be dismantled (Hacker and Pierson 2016).

At the nexus of the legitimacy crisis and rampant polarisation are signs of democratic deconsolidation – the weakening of citizens' commitments to democratic practices and norms (Foa and Mounk 2017). This includes democratic norms of discourse and truth-telling: Trump's constant promotion of untruths is well known, though we would do well to remember that it was to describe the administration of George W. Bush that the neologism *truthiness* was coined. Still, it was startling how little Trump's flouting of speech norms cost him (Kreiss 2017); Republicans embraced his candidacy in full knowledge of his habitual lying.

Kreiss (2017) argues that Trump's success lays bare a rupture in the epistemology of the civic sphere: the general democratic commitments citizens hold to seek common understanding of political affairs. In the face of widespread delegitimisation, it appears that partisan identity – itself driven in great part by out-group animus – has overtaken civic solidarity in shaping political opinions, interactions with political information, and electoral choices.

Contemporary conditions of collapsing political legitimacy echo earlier eras in which populists have risen to prominence. And while there have been recent bursts of left-wing American populism, from Occupy Wall Street to Bernie Sanders, it has been on the right that a powerfully cohesive narrative of delegitimisation has taken hold. Scholars such as Cramer (2016) and Hochschild (2016) have documented how the experiences and perceptions of many (mostly white) Americans have informed their support for leaders sounding populist chords, from Wisconsin's Scott Walker to Trump. What they reveal is a profound sense among many such citizens that their society is being transformed economically and culturally and that their own lifestyles are mocked and disrecognised by cultural and political elites. Hochschild (2016) demonstrates that the people she studied tended to understand their experiences in reference to a 'deep story' that was surprisingly consistent from person to person, all across the country. This story conveyed resentment that despite working hard and playing by the rules, these communities had decayed because powers above them have allowed other, less deserving groups to cut ahead in line.

The conservative media system

Importantly, such a deep story is not only an organic set of perceptions citizens tell one another; it is also fed and validated by a media system that has fundamentally transformed in recent decades. Most significant here is the development of an alternative media system supporting conservative causes. Intensifying after Goldwater's 1964 loss, the conservative media movement has long seen itself as oppressed by a more powerful cultural, political, and media establishment (Hemmer 2016). This populist ethos has been a hallmark of the conservative talk radio of the 1980s and 1990s, and a mainstay of Fox News's identity.

The billionaire funding of much conservative media is, of course, not populist in any economic sense. And here we must be careful not to place the blame for our disinformation order too squarely on populism per se; because suspicion of government, scientific expertise, and the news media have been assiduously cultivated by very un-populist factions within the conservative movement, most of all those devoted to advancing laissez-faire economic ideology and policy (Hacker and Pierson 2016). When their opposition to the government's role in managing public problems has run up against scientific evidence, such as in the case of climate change, this movement has developed tactics to misinform and confuse the public and systematically undermine public faith in scientific and journalistic institutions (Oreskes and Conway 2011).

But many conservative media display a powerfully populist style, conveyed in tabloid aesthetics; deviations from and overt rejections of 'high modern', 'aspirational' mainstream journalism; and repeated claims to be the lone voices of reason in a liberal media system; they project cultural populism (Peck 2019). Headlined by Fox News but now stylistically joined by a wide array of both mainstream and marginal digital sources, this ecosystem provides a steady supply of stories that map onto, reinforce, and elaborate the deep story; they also dabble, to varying degrees and with varying levels of concern for fact, in apocalyptic warnings that American culture is being systematically undermined (Polletta and Callahan 2017). As Benkler and colleagues (2018) have shown, this is genuinely an alternative system of media outlets, significantly more detached from centrist journalistic organisations than partisan media on the left. On the left, we suspect, the lack of a widely held and coherent deep story, combined with the tighter coupling of left political conversations to the political-media centre, has prevented the development of a misinformation apparatus on a scale comparable to that of the right (Benkler et al. 2018).

Misinformation in the social sharing system

Today, the long legacy of American populism and 'hermeneutics of suspicion' (see Sedgwick 2003) and an explicitly oppositional partisan media apparatus recombine with social media. The new attention economics of the social sharing economy democratise individuals' opportunities to communicate and establish major financial incentives (alongside any political agenda) for outlets and individuals to accrue audiences – primarily accomplished by stimulating anger and indignation in order to induce sharing across social media networks (Pickard 2019). Here, the plentiful supply of mis-, dis-, and malinformation meets citizens feeling acute resentment and social deprivation.

The unprecedented speed and reach of messages in this system are having effects we are only beginning to contemplate. Unlike earlier conspiracy theories, which were necessarily conveyed in relatively scarce and infrequent pamphlets and books, today's misinformation is reproduced and circulated on a daily basis. And although the evidence of comprehensively walled-off "echo chambers" is thin, the products of a substantial sub-ecology of disinformation that runs from 4chan, 8chan and Reddit into Breitbart and more establishment media (including the President's Twitter feed) can provide sceptical citizens with a daily 'inoculation' against more mainstream interpretations of events (Stroud 2019).

Further, as Zuckerman (2019) points out, there are substantial social and entertainment dimensions to the games of interpretation that take place in online communities such as Reddit, 4chan, and QAnon; there, conspiracy theorising is actively peer produced (Starbird et al. 2019). Harkening back to the days of Father Coughlin or Joe McCarthy, the excitement is still in the assembly of innumerable clues and in fitting them to an interpretation that reveals the fissures in official narratives of events and buttresses a satisfying understanding of the world. But the activity is now massively distributed and prolific.

This reveals several important points about misinformation and its populist connections in our era. We might do well to distinguish fully fledged conspiracy theories (of the sort peddled by McCarthy, or, today, Alex Jones or QAnon) from other forms of more piecemeal misinformation that are invented by online entrepreneurs of disinformation and circulated by partisan networks through digital media. The latter mis- or disinformation is, as Muirhead and Rosenblum (2019) put it, 'conspiracy without the theory'. This is the sort of misinformation promoted by Trump and is driven by the need 'less to explain than to affirm'; examining its information content misses its purpose of conveying identity solidarity. Here, the authoritarianism of Trump's populism is clear: in his pronouncements of clear falsehoods, without even a coherent conspiratorial hypothesis, he announces his dismissal of any 'collective effort to produce agreed-upon facts and reach consensus on the correspondence between assertions and reality' (Waisbord 2018, 2–3) and his intent to exercise power without democratic constraint.

What Muirhead and Rosenblum may overlook, however, is the power of the deep story to serve as a meta-narrative device into which both elaborated conspiracy theories and everyday, mundane misinformation can be set. With a widespread underlying narrative describing the illegitimacy of political opponents, the government, and the press, variations on the theme (the "deep state" seeks to destroy Trump, Hillary Clinton leads a paedophilia ring in Washington) may seem plausible or, at the least, satisfyingly irritating to East Coast liberal snobs.

Conclusion

Our observations on American populism and misinformation dispel the notions that populism and misinformation are somehow novel and that populism is itself the primary explanation for our current era of 'post-truth'. Our reading of the case suggests that American political culture is especially susceptible to populism and, in fact, *always* carries deep populist currents, owing to a long-standing phobia of the exercise of power and easily accessible notions of an imagined hardworking but put-upon 'real' American. Moreover, our analysis shows that in the evolution of the Republican Party and conservative media over 50 years, wealthy ideologues have done more than their share to cultivate messaging organs – and widespread distrust of centrist information institutions – that now undergird 'post-truth' politics.

This analysis suggests that populism and misinformation share common origins more than a linear causal relationship. Populism assumes prominence in contexts in which democratic legitimacy is called into question as it clearly is in the United States' current period of economic precarity and political polarisation. Its contemporary details are shaped by socio-economic circumstances that led one major party, for strategic reasons, to disavow major institutions of governing and public deliberation. The combination of the collapse of centrist meaning-making institutions with the explosion of digital media and the attentional economics they have developed has proven a fertile culture for misinformation. The capacity of media sub-ecologies to relentlessly re-articulate underlying resentments and supply endless resentful interpretations of current events is a permutation of misinformation the US has not seen before and poses a grave threat to democratic culture.

What hope is there for the reconstruction of broadly shared commitments to a common project of truth-telling under these conditions (Waisbord 2018)? Unfortunately, the underlying democratic crisis is not easily remedied. How a crisis of legitimacy is constituted is fundamentally a question of perception and interpretation: of the stories citizens – and their media – tell about groups in society and whether each is treated fairly. Here we should extend the line of research Hochschild and Cramer have pioneered and further explore how our communication system facilitates certain understandings and not others. Similarly, the now well-developed disinformation networks in digital will not be easily unwound. What will remain critical is the correction of misinformation by our core media institutions (Bode and Vraga 2015) and greater public accountability of major social media platforms that house these networks.

Finally, we caution against condemning populism itself as the root of the problem; any given populism's tenor and its relationship to democracy depend greatly on its particular conceptualisation of people and elites. Clearly, populism contains the potential for terrible racism, division, disinformation, and anti-civic disruption, but is probably better to call out these problematic aspects directly, as in 'authoritarian populism', 'ethno-nationalist populism', or, when appropriate, fascism. Because condemning populism will not address, and may even obscure, the underlying, and to some degrees genuine, origins of the populist impulse: the sense of many Americans – on left and right – that the political system treats them unfairly, that they have marginal economic opportunity, and that they are scorned by their fellow citizens.

References

Achen, C.H. and Bartels, L.M. (2016) *Democracy for realists: Why elections do not produce responsive government.* Princeton, NJ: Princeton University Press.

Bailyn, B. (1993) 'Jefferson and the ambiguities of freedom', *Proceedings of the American Philosophical Society*, 137(4), pp. 498–515.

Bayley, E. (1981) *Joe McCarthy and the press.* Madison: University of Wisconsin Press.

Benkler, Y., Faris, R., and Roberts, H. (2018) *Network propaganda: Manipulation, disinformation, and radicalization in American politics.* Oxford: Oxford University Press.

Bennett, W.L. and Livingston, S. (2018) 'The disinformation order: Disruptive communication and the decline of democratic institutions', *European Journal of Communication*, 33(2), pp. 122–139.

Bode, L. and Vraga, E.K. (2015) 'In related news, that was wrong: The correction of misinformation through related stories functionality in social media', *Journal of Communication*, 65(4), pp. 619–638.

Cramer, K.J. (2016) *The politics of resentment: Rural consciousness in Wisconsin and the rise of Scott Walker.* Chicago: University of Chicago Press.

Cremoni, L. (1998) 'Antisemitism and populism in the United States in the 1930s: The case of father Coughlin', *Patterns of Prejudice*, 32(1), 25–37. DOI: 10.1080/0031322X.1998.9970245.

Federici, M. (1991) *The challenge of populism: The rise of right-wing democratism in postwar America.* New York: Praeger.

Foa, R.S. and Mounk, Y. (2017) 'The signs of deconsolidation', *Journal of Democracy*, 28, pp. 5–15. DOI: 10.1353/jod.2017.0000.

Hacker, J.S. and Pierson, P. (2016) *American amnesia: How the war on government led us to forget what made America prosper.* New York: Simon & Schuster.

Hemmer, N. (2016) *Messengers of the right: Conservative media and the transformation of American politics.* Philadelphia: University of Pennsylvania Press.

Hochschild, A. R. (2016) *Strangers in their own land: Anger and mourning on the American right.* New York: New Press.

Hofstadter, R. (1965) *The paranoid style in American politics and other essays.* New York: Knopf.

Jessen, N. (2019) 'Populism and conspiracy: A historical synthesis of American countersubversive narratives', *American Journal of Economics and Sociology*, 78(3), pp. 675–715.

Judis, J. (2016) *The populist explosion: How the great recession transformed American and European politics.* New York: Columbia Global Report.

Kay, J., Ziegelmueller, G. and Minch, K. (1998) 'From Coughlin to contemporary talk radio: Fallacies & propaganda in American populist radio', *Journal of Radio Studies*, 5(1), pp. 9–21. DOI: 10.1080/19376529809384526.

Kazin, M. (1998) *The populist persuasion: An American history.* 2nd edn. Ithaca, NY: Cornell University Press.

Kreiss, D. (2017) 'The fragmenting of the civil sphere: How partisan identity shapes the moral evaluation of candidates and epistemology', *American Journal of Cultural Sociology*, 5, pp. 443–459.

Mason, L. (2016) *Uncivil agreement: How politics became our identity.* Chicago: University of Chicago Press.

McGirr, L. (2015) *Suburban warriors: The origins of the new American right.* Princeton, NJ: Princeton University Press.

Modras, R. (1989) 'Father Coughlin and anti-Semitism: Fifty years later', *Journal of Church and State*, 31(2), pp. 231–247. DOI: 10.1093/jcs/31.2.231.

Moffitt, B. (2016) *The global rise of populism: Performance, political style and representation.* Palo Alto, CA: Stanford University Press.

Mudde, C. (2004) 'The populist zeitgeist', *Government and Opposition*, 39(4), pp. 541–563.

Muirhead, R. and Rosenblum, N.L. (2019) *A lot of people are saying: The new conspiracism and the assault on democracy.* Princeton, NJ: Princeton University Press.

Oliver, J.E. and Rahn, W.M. (2018) 'Rise of the Trumpenvolk: Populism in the 2016 election', *The ANNALS of the American Academy of Political and Social Science*, 667(1), pp. 189–206. DOI: 10.1177/0002716216662639.

Oreskes, N. and Conway, E.M., 2011. *Merchants of doubt: How a handful of scientists obscured the truth on issues from tobacco smoke to global warming.* New York: Bloomsbury.

Ostler, J. (1995) 'The rhetoric of conspiracy and the formation of Kansas populism', *Agricultural History*, 69(1), pp. 1–27. www.jstor.org/stable/3744023.

Peck, R. (2019) *Fox populism: Branding conservatism as working class.* Cambridge: Cambridge University Press.

Pickard, V. (2019) *Democracy without journalism? Confronting the misinformation society.* New York: Oxford University Press.

Polletta, F. and Callahan, J. (2017) 'Deep stories, nostalgia narratives, and fake news: Storytelling in the Trump era', *American Journal of Cultural Sociology*, 5, pp. 392–408.

Ribuffo, L.P. (2017) 'Donald Trump and the "paranoid style" in American (intellectual) politics', ISSF POLICY Series. https://issforum.org/roundtables/policy/1-5an-paranoid

Rodgers, D.T. (2011) *Age of fracture.* Cambridge, MA: Harvard University Press.

Sedgwick, E.K. (2003) 'Paranoid reading and reparative reading, or, you're so paranoid, you probably think this essay is about you', *Touching feeling: Affect, pedagogy, performativity*, pp 123–151, https://doi.org/10.1215/9780822384786-005.

Skocpol, T. (2020) 'The elite and popular roots of contemporary Republican extremism', in Skocpol, T. and Tervo, C. (eds.) *Upending American politics: Polarizing parties, ideological elites, and citizen activists from the Tea Party to the anti-Trump resistance.* New York: Oxford University Press, pp. 3–27.

Skocpol, T. and Williamson, V. (2013) *The Tea Party and the remaking of Republican conservatism.* New York: Oxford University Press.

Starbird, K., Arif, A. and Wilson, T. (2019) 'Disinformation as collaborative work: Surfacing the participatory nature of strategic information operations', *Proceedings of the ACM on Human-Computer Interaction,* 127.

Stroud, N.J. (2019) 'Inoculation and selective exposure'. International Communication Association, Washington, DC.

Waisbord, S. (2018) 'The elective affinity between post-truth communication and populist politics', *Communication Research and Practice,* 4(1), pp. 17–34, https://doi.org/10.1080/22041451.2018.1428928.

Warren, D.I. (1976) *The radical center: Middle Americans and the politics of alienation.* South Bend, IN: University of Notre Dame Press.

Wood, G. S. (1982) 'Conspiracy and the paranoid style: Causality and deceit in the eighteenth century', *The William and Mary Quarterly,* 39(3), pp. 402–441.

Zuckerman, E. (2019) 'QANON and the emergence of the unreal', *Journal of Design and Science,* 6. https://jods.mitpress.mit.edu/pub/tliexqdu/release/4.

33

POPULISM, MEDIA, AND MISINFORMATION IN LATIN AMERICA

Ignacio Siles, Larissa Tristán, and Carolina Carazo

Latin America has had a long, complex, and complicated relationship with populism. Political figures in the region are usually considered some of the very founders or most iconic representatives of populism (De la Torre, 2000), starting with classic forms of populism (Lázaro Cárdenas in Mexico, Juan Domingo Perón in Argentina, and Getúlio Vargas in Brazil), followed by so-called neo-populisms (Alberto Fujimori in Peru, Carlos Salinas de Gortari in Mexico, Fernando Collor de Melo in Brazil, and Carlos Menem in Argentina), and more recent populist figures of the twenty-first century, such as Hugo Chávez in Venezuela, Evo Morales in Bolivia, and Rafael Correa in Ecuador. There is even an entire subfield of studies devoted specifically to Latin American populism (Retamozo, 2006).

Historically, media systems have played a key role in shaping Latin American populism. As Weyland (2001) argued about the region, 'through television populist leaders reach[ed] their followers directly and establish[ed] quasi-personal contact with millions of people simultaneously. While radio played a similar role for classical populists, television [was] more powerful in projecting charismatic leadership' (16). This chapter discusses the particular relationship between populism, media, and misinformation in Latin America. We envision populism as a 'media and communication phenomenon' (Waisbord, 2019) and thus examine the role of social media platforms in shaping populism and issues of misinformation in the region. Our analysis proceeds in four steps.

First, we briefly situate the study of populism and media in Latin America within a broader history. To this end, we discuss the links between populism and specific styles of political communication that emerged at the turn of the century. Second, we focus on how scholars have analysed the significance of digital media in shaping populism in Latin America. We thus examine the regional specificities of what some scholars have labelled 'populism 2.0'. Third, we assess how researchers have analysed specifically the 'elective affinity' (Waisbord, 2018a) between post-truth (in the form of its most symptomatic expression, so-called fake news) and populism in academic literature. Our discussion draws on an analysis of the theoretical preferences, methodological approaches, and conclusions of this body of work. We also review major findings that come from regional surveys on media use, misinformation, and populism. We argue that a consideration of the 'elective affinity' between post-truth and populism in the case of Latin America requires assessing the significance of religion and its associated forms of polarisation and messianic authority. We conclude by summarising the main contributions of scholarly literature on these issues and by suggesting new avenues for research on this topic.

Media and populism at the turn of century

In the beginning of the new century, the relationship between populism and media in Latin America found an expression in two parallel processes, which Waisbord (2014) summarises with precision: on the one hand, 'the politization of the media' and, on the other, 'the mediatization of politics' (17).[1] The former process refers to important attempts to reform media systems in many countries of Latin America. Such attempts took place in at least 11 countries of the region during the 2000s (Guevara, 2012). Waisbord (2014) considers some of these reforms – typically anchored in the idea of rupture in prevailing media systems – as populist, in that they expressed 'a statist vision of media systems aimed at strengthening the communicational power of the presidency and based on the logic of "friend/enemy" as the organizing principle' (29). Some have not hesitated to label the disputes that surrounded these reforms 'media wars' (Guevara, 2012).

The latter process – the mediatisation of politics – centres instead on specific styles or forms of political communication that took shape throughout the decade. It focuses on populism as a rhetoric, a 'strategy and a discursive frame' (Waisbord, 2019, 222). Newly elected presidents in Latin American countries turned to the media to 'genuinely and "directly" connect with "the people"' (Moffitt, 2019, 30). Because of the centrality of media in their political projects, Rincón (2008) referred to these figures as '*los tele-presidentes*' (the tele-presidents). Examples were found at both ends of the political spectrum. Hugo Chávez launched his television show *Aló, Presidente* in 1999, arguably the most iconic piece of political communication of the next decade in the region; Álvaro Uribe aired his *Consejos Comunales* starting in 2002 and thus turned 'the people into his main communication weapon'(de Vengoechea, 2008, 135); and Luiz Inácio Lula offered hundreds of radio interviews on a variety of topics in *Café com o Presidente*, created in 2003. These shows blended specific audiovisual formats and certain forms of political communication. In many ways, they sought to overcome a crisis of political representation well seated in the region during the 1990s.

The trademark of *los tele-presidentes* was establishing a form of 'live' communication that Guevara (2012) summarises thusly: 'The aim [was] to involve all citizens in the government decision-making and problem-solving processes, thereby claiming to make communication a new tool for public management' (118). For Rincón (2008, 9), the 'communications kit' of politicians during the decade also included the need to perform a presidential posture (in addition to actually having being elected), to 'govern for a spectator/viewer rather than for a citizen', to convey an affective national project, to 'turn the people into an ideological and aesthetic guide and inspiration', and to always be present in the media. Implementing this 'kit' also required incorporating aesthetic and formal elements of various genres (including advertising, talk shows, reality television, and news broadcasting) (Guevara, 2012; Rincón, 2008).

The rise of this form of political communication gathered the attention of scholars from the region and abroad (Berjaud, 2016; Boas, 2005; De la Torre, 2017). References to populism in this body of work range from latent to explicit. Rincón (2008) is among those who linked populism and the communication styles of *los tele-presidentes* in the most straightforward way:

> Political parties were over and a formula was created that mixed the media hero (a charismatic personality) with populism (direct welfare and social redemption of the poor) and liberal economy elitism (unrestricted support for businessmen and new riches). This new system is based on the leader who governs through a form of light

and entertainment-like authoritarianism; which enacts a live (*en directo*) democracy, without means or intermediaries; which thinks in local perspective.

Rincón (2008), p. 6

Most of these television and radio programmes did not survive the end of the 2000s. With the arrival of a new decade, both the attempts to communicate 'directly' with 'the people' and the social concerns generated by such forms of communication translated to media platforms that were starting to gain traction in the region: social media. This process unfolded as new populist politicians took office. Compared to their predecessors, Latin American political leaders of the 2010s were relatively less charismatic. Despite the attempts, Nicolás Maduro and Dilma Rousseff had difficulties reproducing the media success of Hugo Chávez and Luiz Inácio Lula, respectively. Yet they sought to maintain a form of populist authority in which social media played a central role.

The 'social media-populism nexus'

Social media platforms became a favourite object of study in Latin America in the early years of the 2010s (Siles, Espinoza, & Méndez, 2019). In this context, scholars have focused on the significance of social media in shaping populist practices and discourses. Some authors have seen the rise of such platforms as an opportunity for reinvigorating the populist communications kit that prevailed in the previous decade in Latin America – notably 'top-down' styles of communication that hailed presidential figures (Waisbord, 2014). Scholars have coined terms such as *technopopulism* (De la Torre, 2013) and *populism 2.0* to refer to this "social media–populism nexus" (Moffitt, 2019, 30).

It is not uncommon to find mentions in scholarly literature of the role of social media in enabling a 'new populist era' (Mudde, 2016, 29). Several features of social media platforms are typically envisioned as opportunities (or, more precisely, 'affordances') for populist communication. In these accounts, social media would be ideal for exploiting and empowering populism's historical penchants. For example, Waisbord and Amado (2017) note that

> In principle, Twitter facilitates the kind of horizontal, interactive communication praised by populist rhetoric. It offers a flattened communication structure in contrast to the top – down structure of the legacy media. It is suitable for unmediated exchanges between politicians and citizens.

Waisbord and Amado (2017), p. 1332

As Moffitt (2019, 31) notes, these ideas rely on the premise that social media allow presidents to be 'in touch with the people' in a 'multi-directional' way. It could also be suggested that social media is ideal for 'reinforcing in-group mentality against outgroups. . . [and] cement[ing] homophilic communication and identity-centred communication' (Waisbord, 2019, 229). It is perhaps for all these reasons that presidents in Latin America typically associated with populism have tended to be more active on social media platforms like Twitter than those who are not (Waisbord & Amado, 2017).

Populist communications on social media are characterised by specific features. Using statistical analysis of Twitter use and content analysis of presidents' tweets in Latin America, Waisbord and Amado (2017) showed that presidents who have adopted this form of communication tend to use Twitter to gain visibility, reinforce presidential figures, comment on a range of issues in a fast manner, 'throw rhetorical punches at political rivals', and 'spread presidential messages without tough questions, dissident views, and open exchanges with citizens' (1342). Farias (2018) also employed content analysis to compare the discourse of both Nicolás Maduro and the Venezuelan opposition on Twitter. She argued that Maduro continued with his predecessor's style, using a 'discursive communications [discourse] predominantly populist [that reflects] an understanding of politics as a zero-sum game' (89).

The media has been a typical target of populist discourse. Here, social media is seen as an ideal communication outlet because of its independence from 'the system', which is typically opposed in populist discourse (De la Torre, 2017). As Waisbord (2019) noted, 'populism exhibits what communication scholars call 'the hostile media' phenomenon – the perception that the media are biased against one's convictions and ideological preferences' (224). (The rise of fake news can also be interpreted as an instance of this phenomenon). In the case of Latin America, this can be envisioned as part of the complicated attempts of media reform that unfolded at the turn of the century in the region and continued through the 2010s. Campos-Domínguez (2017) summarises findings of the particularities of populist communication on social media in Latin America: 'instead of engaging with citizens to exchange views and listen to their ideas, populists have used Twitter to criticize critics, conduct personal battles and get the attention of the media' (786). For this reason, she concluded that the populist communication style in Latin America is not unlike that in other parts of the world.

Based on these findings, most scholars who have conducted empirical research tend to be cautious about the alleged promises of social media for communicating 'directly' with 'the people'. Waisbord and Amado (2017) concluded that:

> The promises of Latin American populism to overhaul the structure and dynamics of public communication ring hollow. Not only populism's top-down use of Twitter does not fit its grand vision of transforming communicative practices. Also, the way populist presidents use Twitter is not essentially different from the 'hegemonic' political communication style they often criticize.
>
> Waisbord and Amado (2017), p.1342

In a similar manner, Moffitt (2019, 31) considered most ideas associated with the revolutionary potential of social media as analytical 'traps' and warned against turning these assumptions into 'common wisdom'. He argued that these traps operate under a series of confusions: '(1) mistaking directness for being "in touch" with "the people"; (2) fetishising the "unmediated" nature of populism; . . . (3) assuming that populist online communication is multi-directional and (4) assuming that populist use of social media is relatively uniform' (Moffitt, 2019, 31). A more generalised conclusion in this body of work is that additional comparative and longitudinal data are needed to establish causal relationships between social media and the rise or spread of populism (Waisbord, 2019).

'Fake news', populism, and religion

Studying fake news in Latin America

More recently, researchers have turned their attention to the links between populism and misinformation (in the form of fake news and other types of content). Compared to other regions in the world, relatively little has been written about fake news in Latin America. In a literature review on the topic, Blanco Alfonso, García Galera, and Tejedor Calvo (2019) found only 2 out of 172 publications between January 2012 and April 2019 about Latin American (specifically

Chile and Mexico). A search conducted for this chapter in several academic databases yielded more results. We found at least 30 articles published in Latin America between 2017 and 2019 containing the term '*noticias falsas*' (fake news). This body of work seems to be growing over the years: in our sample, only 2 publications were from 2017, 12 were published in 2018, and 16 in 2019. These studies were unequally distributed by country: 13 publications were about Brazil, 5 about Mexico, 4 about Venezuela, 3 each about Argentina and Chile, and 2 about Colombia.[2]

Researchers have covered a variety of issues in their writings about fake news. Several articles offer major reflections on the problem (Morales Campos, 2018). Many seek to find solutions to the spread of fake news, either through media literacy initiatives (Freire França, Furlan Costa & Oliviera dos Santos, 2019), by discussing overall trends in news consumption and distribution (Montero-Liberona & Halpern, 2019), or by emphasising the gains of fact-checking projects (Sánchez, 2019).

Because of their significance in regional studies about fake news, fact-checking initiatives deserve a closer look. Sánchez (2019) argued that data verification platforms in the region 'followed the steps of the Argentinian *Chequeado*, a founding model in the continent in 2010' (101). Since then, she noted, similar initiatives have emerged: *Detector de Mentiras* and *ColombiaCheck* in Colombia; *Truco, Agência Lupa, Aos Fatos*, and *Agência Pública* in Brazil; *El Sabueso* and *Checa-Datos.mx* in Mexico, and *Con pruebas* in Guatemala. For Sánchez (2019), the growth of such initiatives in Latin America has stabilised over the past years, considering that 'in February 2018, there were 15 [Latin American projects] out of 149 active initiatives worldwide, a significant increase given that in 2014 there were only three' (101). Sánchez examined the Mexican *Verificado18*, a collaborative initiative that was born in the wake of the July 2018 elections and which brought together more than 60 organisations, including media outlets, universities, and foundations from around the country.

The circulation of fake news has been linked to major social and political events in many countries of the region, notably presidential elections. Most articles have addressed country-specific cases, and, although populism is not their main focus, most examples are related to Latin American politicians who have typically been labelled populists. Thus, in the case of articles about Venezuela, some were specifically about Hugo Chávez (Kitzberger, 2018) and about issues of immigration between Venezuela and Colombia (Ordóñez & Ramírez Arcos, 2019). In the cases of Mexico and Brazil, articles dealt mostly with the controversial electoral processes of 2018 won by Manuel Andrés López Obrador (Álvarez Monsivais, 2018; Meyenberg Leycegui, 2018) and Jair Bolsonaro (e.g. Rezende, 2018; Stefanoni, 2018), respectively.

Although not strictly academic studies, surveys and public opinion polls also shed light on the broader socio-political context that surrounds the discussion of misinformation and fake news in Latin America. Data from the *Latinobarómetro* (2018) report warns about the fragility of democratic regimes in the region: although support for authoritarian governments remains relatively stable (15 percent), there is a growing dissatisfaction with and indifference towards politics. Data also show that party affiliations continue to decline. This partially facilitates the emergence of populist and anti-system candidates from both the right and the left (such as López Obrador in Mexico and Bolsonaro in Brazil) and is a breeding ground for the spread of the strongly emotional content that characterises fake news.

The Latin American Communication Monitor (2018–2019), which surveyed 1,229 communication managers in 19 countries in the region, found that most professionals in this field (62.5 percent) pay attention to fake news and are convinced that this shapes the public sphere at the national level (62.7 percent). In their view, fake news come mostly from social media (83.8 percent) and media outlets (37.8 percent). Furthermore, 61.6 percent of communication managers in government organisations and 45 percent of them in companies indicated that fake news had affected their organisation once or on several occasions, and the countries they felt were most affected by this were the Dominican Republic, Colombia, and Costa Rica.

Misinformation and messianic populism in Latin America

Only a few scholars have addressed specifically the link between populism and misinformation in the region. Waisbord (2018a) argued that present conditions in public communication are ideal for the proliferation of populist politics (which is intrinsically oriented towards post-truth). In his words, 'the upsurge of populist politics is symptomatic of the consolidation of post-truth communication as a distinctive feature of contemporary politics' (Waisbord, 2018a, 18).

Waisbord drew on Weber's notion of 'elective affinity' to suggest that there are key links between populism and post-truth, a relationship that 'should not be mechanistically viewed as straightforward causation, but rather in terms of similarities, analogies, convergence, and/or reinforcement between social facts such as culture, politics, religion, and economics'' (Waisbord, 2018a, 18). In his view, two processes have led to this particular situation: the breakdown of the legacy media order and the increasing fragmentation of mediated spheres. From this perspective, the spread of misinformation both results from and empowers populism.

Building on Waisbord's analysis, we argue that religion has become a third key component of the elective affinity between populism and post-truth in the particular case of Latin America. Laclau's (2005) approach to populism is a key to making this argument. According to Laclau (2005), populism is not best defined by its political or ideological contents, but rather by 'a particular logic of articulation' that builds on discourses that dichotomise social spaces and collective identities (32). As a result, populism emerges whenever social events are framed in terms of a dichotomous border that separates 'those above' (us) from 'those below' (them) (Laclau, 1987, 30).

The dichotomous nature of populism holds important affinities with the discourse of Western religions. In the particular context of Latin America, this has been the case since colonial times. To this day, Catholicism has privileged a discourse that separates it from 'the people' through a binary that overlaps with the political realm, causing a dichotomy that hinders pluralism and diversity while fostering social polarisation. In this context, certain political ideologies have acquired almost the status of religious doctrines, such as Peronism in Argentina (Mansilla, 2012).

Extending forms of authority that prevailed at the turn of the century (which emphasised the idea of the hero who came to rescue 'the people'), populism in Latin America has acquired a much more explicitly religious expression (which stresses the role of messiahs in saving 'the people' from certain threats). This allows the establishment of another link with the work of Weber, who studied the mechanisms of charismatic authority in ways that tied together the political and religious realms. According to Weber (2013), charismatic authority is messianic in nature. In his words,

> The turning point is always the same: charismatic men and [their] disciples become companions admitted to the Lord's table and endowed with special and distinctive rights. . . . The dominated of the charismatic structure . . . become 'subjects' submitted . . . to the coercion and discipline of a rule and an order, or even 'citizens' obeying the law. The charismatic message inevitably becomes . . . dogma, doctrine, theory, regulation, legal code or content of a tradition that gets petrified.
>
> (Weber, 2013, 465–466)

Although the articulation or elective affinity between populism and religion dates back to pre-democratic times, it prevails in many democratic systems in Latin America. The binary essence of this discourse remains, but it has also varied in two important ways: (1) the nature of its manifestations (given the prevalence of fake news and misinformation issues) and (2) the institutional source of religious discourse (given that Catholicism is no longer the sole religious denomination that fuels populist rhetoric in the region). In what follows, we discuss these two issues in their relationship to issues of misinformation.

Framing religion as part of the elective affinity between populism and post-truth helps explain some of the particular manifestations that this link has acquired in Latin America over the past years. Recent presidential campaigns in various countries of the region show how this tripartite affinity has manifested in the parallel dissemination of particular kinds of content, served as a platform for the rise of populist political/religious figures, and shaped the outcome of electoral processes. For example, Guevara (2020) and Siles, Carazo, and Tristán (2020) demonstrated that, during the presidential elections that took place in 2018 in Brazil, Costa Rica, and Mexico, social media fuelled a polarisation of the electorate regarding topics such as sexual orientation and social values.

The combination of misinformation, populist styles of communication, and religious discourses has been a fertile ground for the rise of political/religious candidates and politicians from neo-Pentecostal churches. The cases of Jair Bolsonaro in Brazil and Fabricio Alvarado in Costa Rica (not to be confused with Carlos Alvarado, the country's president) exemplify how the rise of the neo-Pentecostal and evangelical churches have added nuance and complexity to the fight between multiple actors and movements for the 'populist reason' in Latin America (c.f. Laclau, 2005). Key in this process is the construction of a discursive premise that separates us from them, which is framed around the distinction between traditional values and new threats. This elective affinity enacted a form of symbolic violence that was crucial for understanding not only the results of these elections but also how they unfolded (Guevara, 2020; Siles, 2020).

In this context, the Bible has become a key component of the populist communications kit in Latin America; along with Brazil national soccer team's jersey, it was the central symbol of Jair Bolsonaro's discursive fight against 'the red flag, "gender ideology", and corruption' (Stefanoni, 2018); El Salvador's Nayib Bukele carried it with him during his inauguration, and, like many other presidents in the region, Guatemala's Alejandro Giammattei cited it as the main weapon to stop the 'battle' against the COVID-19 'enemy'. It is not surprising that, after the resignation of Evo Morales in November of 2019, Jeanine Áñez, the self-proclaimed president who took over the country's government, declared, 'The Bible returns to the Palace' after entering the *Palacio de Gobierno* in La Paz, Bolivia, on November 12, 2019.

Social media platforms and apps such as Facebook, Twitter, and WhatsApp are crucial in the creation of an 'epistemic democracy', (Waisbord, 2018b, 1870), in which journalistic values and populist/messianic discourses compete for the attention of digital communities. These constitute 'communities of belief', as Waisbord (2018b) calls them, and are 'anchored by common allegiance to politics, ideology, and religion as well as socio-demographic variables' (1870). Both in form and in substance, Bukele's speech at the United Nations General Assembly – where he snapped a selfie and positioned himself as a model in the political use of social media platforms for connecting with 'the people' in El Salvador – illustrates this phenomenon.

The relationship between populism, misinformation, and religion in Latin America is a threat to democracy and human rights. This is because the separation between us and them that underlies the populist/religious reason, often exploited by and reinforced through fake news, creates political scenarios in which certain groups are banned from expanding their rights or, even worse, losing rights that they had already acquired. Human Rights Watch's (HRW) director, Kenneth Roth, warned that the government of Jair Bolsonaro attacks human rights by repeatedly using excessive force against civil society and the media. In a similar manner, in the past Costa Rican election, Fabricio Alvarado, a candidate from the neo-Pentecostal political party *Restauración Nacional,* helped define the central media event of the campaign around the issue of 'gay marriage'. This not only polarised the election but also excluded other relevant topics from the democratic debate (Siles, 2020; Siles, Carazo & Tristán, 2020).

Concluding remarks

This chapter examined how researchers have studied issues of populism, media, and misinformation in Latin America. Populism in the region shares important characteristics with other expressions of this phenomenon around the world. Both at present and in the past, populist figures have emerged at both ends of the political spectrum. Yet populism has also shown specific regional features, such as its historical relationship with religious discourses that privilege a binary form of thinking. We conclude this chapter by noting some opportunities for future research in order to make visible both the similarities and differences in the study of populism and misinformation in Latin America and other parts of the world.

As noted in the first part of this chapter, researchers have been interested in identifying the main features of the populist communications kit in Latin America. There has been a long-standing interest in understanding how political figures have variously used media and communications (from legacy media to internet technologies) to materialise populist discourses. This has resulted in valuable knowledge about how certain communication styles and techniques have emerged and evolved over time in the region. However, a discussion of the implications of the populist communications kit has not always accompanied these studies. There is still a dearth of research that discusses exactly why populist communication approaches are troubling for democracy and human rights in Latin America, given the region's history and political specificities.

Despite the interest in the production of populist discourses, issues of reception have not received comparable attention. Only a handful of studies have empirically investigated how audiences and publics relate to, incorporate, or resist populist messages (Berjaud, 2016). The same could be said about fake news. Not much is known about how people interpret this kind of information and how they seek to authenticate it (that is, if they do). Understanding how and why populist discourse interpellates specific communities (both online and offline) could help address this void and thus broaden our understanding of how 'epistemic democracies' function.

Waisbord's (2018a) argument about the 'elective affinity' between populism and post-truth offers a fruitful avenue for understanding the spread of fake news in the region. Further studies could empirically verify how this argument applies to the particular case of Latin America. Has this elective affinity shown signs of cultural specificity? For example, Waisbord (2018a) provided only a brief account of the similarities between Hugo Chávez's and Donald Trump's discourses. In this chapter, we argued that religion has become a major component of this elective affinity in many countries of the region. Research could elaborate how this argument compares to other parts of the world.

Finally, there is a lack of comparative research in the region that goes beyond the use of statistics for illustrative purposes. Although not specifically about populism, Guevara's (2020) study of the role of social media in the electoral processes in Brazil, Colombia, Costa Rica, and Mexico shows the promises of this form of analysis in that it helps identify the main patterns of similarity and difference that cut across the region. Guevara (2020) thus showed what polarisation looks like in these particular countries, and what theoretical and methodological challenges are involved in studies conducted at a regional level. In this way, comparative research provides fruitful analytical lenses through which to view the links between populism, misinformation, and religion in Latin America.

Acknowledgement

We thank Erica Guevara for her most helpful suggestions about previous versions of this chapter.

Notes

1 All translations from quotes in languages other than English are our own.
2 We refer to articles about cases in each country that were published in that country or published by academics associated with universities in that country.

References

Álvarez Monsiváis, E. (2018). ¿Quién ganó el debate en el Estado de México? Las encuestas en Twitter como síntoma de posverdad. *Virtualis, 8*(16), 4–29.

Berjaud, C. (2016). *Cinq sur cinq, mi Comandante! Contribution à l'étude des réceptions des discours politiques télévisés*. Paris: Éditions Dalloz.

Blanco Alfonso, I., García Galera, C., y Tejedor Calvo, S. (2019). El impacto de las fake news en la investigación en Ciencias Sociales. Revisión bibliográfica sistematizada. *Historia y Comunicación Social, 24*(2), 449–469.

Boas, T. C. (2005). Television and neopopulism in Latin America: Media effects in Brazil and Peru. *Latin American Research Review, 40*(2), 27–49.

Campos-Domínguez, E. (2017). Twitter y la comunicación política. *El Profesional de la Información, 26*(5), 785–793.

De la Torre, C. (2000). *Populist Seduction in Latin America: The Ecuadorian Experience*. Athens: Ohio University Press.

De la Torre, C. (2013). El tecnopopulismo de Rafael Correa: ¿Es compatible el carisma con la tecnocracia? *Latin American Research Review, 48*(1), 24–43.

De la Torre, C. (2017). Hugo Chávez and the diffusion of Bolivarianism. *Democratization, 24*(7), 1271–1288.

de Vengoechea, A. (2008). El misionero enviado de Dios y el finquero de Colombia. In O. Rincón (Ed.), *Los telepresidentes: cerca del pueblo, lejos de la democracia* (pp. 135–126). Bogotá: Friedrich Ebert Stiftung.

Farias, A. (2018). Twitter and institutional change: Insights from populist and pluralist discourses in Venezuela. *Potentia: Journal of International and Public Affairs, 9*, 79–96.

Freire França, F., Furlan Costa, M. L., & Oliviera dos Santos, R. (2019). As novas tecnologias de informação e comunicação no contexto educacional das políticas públicas. *ETD-Educação Temática Digital, 21*(3), 645–661.

Guevara, E. (2012). "Téléprésidents" ou "média-activistes" de gauche? Argentine, Brésil, Venezuela, Colombie. In O. Dabène (Ed.), *La Gauche en Amérique latine, 1998–2012* (pp. 105–144). Paris: Presses de Sciences Po.

Guevara, E. (2020). Comentario: Redes sociales y "polarización": una mirada comparada de las elecciones de 2018 en Brasil, Colombia, Costa Rica y México. In I. Siles (Ed.), *Democracia en digital: Facebook, comunicación y política en Costa Rica* (pp. 207–232). San José: CICOM.

Kitzberger, P. (2018). "Caimanes del mismo pozo". Populismo y representaciones de los medios y la prensa en la estabilización hegemónica del chavismo. *Revista Mexicana de Opinión Pública, 25*, 15–38.

Laclau, E. (1987). Populismo y transformación del imaginario político en América Latina. *Boletín de Estudios Latinoamericanos y del Caribe y Boletín de Estudios Latinoamericanos, 42*, 25–38.

Laclau, E. (2005). *On Populist Reason*. New York: Verso.

Latin American Communication Monitor (LCM 2018–2019). Retrieved from: http://latincommunicationmonitor.com/

Mansilla, H. C. F. (2012). La religiosidad popular, las corrientes maniqueístas y la cultura política latinoamericana. El caso de las oposiciones binarias excluyentes. *Reflexión Política, 14*(27), 2–15.

Meyenberg Leycegui, Y. (2018). Votar en tiempos de cólera. *Revista Mexicana de Sociología, 80*(4), 947–954.

Moffitt, B. (2019). Populism 2.0: Social media and the false allure of 'unmediated' representation. In G. Fitzi, J. Mackert, & B. S. Turner (Eds.), *Populism and the Crisis of Democracy* (Vol. 2, pp. 30–46). New York: Routledge.

Montero-Liberona, C., & Halpern, D. (2019). Factores que influyen en compartir noticias falsas de salud online. *El Profesional de la Información, 28*(3), 1–9.

Morales Campos, E. M. (2018). *La posverdad y las noticias falsas: el uso ético de la información.* México: UNAM.

Mudde, C. (2016). Europe's populist surge: A long time in the making. *Foreign Affairs, 95*(November/December), 25–30.

Ordóñez, J. T., & Ramírez Arcos, H. E.(2019). (Des) orden nacional: la construcción de la migración venezolana como una amenaza de salud y seguridad pública en Colombia. *Revista Ciencias de la Salud, 17*, 48–68.

Retamozo, Martín (2006). La razón populista. *Perfiles Latinoamericanos, 13*(27), 253–258.

Rezende, R. (2018). Jair Bolsonaro, populismo de derecha y fin de ciclo político. *Revista Política Latinoamericana, 7*, 1–15.

Rincón, O. (2008). Introducción: ¿La comunicación no tiene ideología? In O. Rincón (Ed.), *Los tele-presidentes: Cerca del pueblo, lejos de la democracia* (pp. 5–13). Bogotá: Friedrich Ebert Stiftung.

Sánchez, A. N. (2019). Periodismo de confirmación vs. desinformación: Verificado18 y las elecciones mexicanas de 2019. *Ámbitos. Revista Internacional de Comunicación, 43, 95–114.*

Siles, I. (Ed.). (2020). *Democracia en digital: Facebook, comunicación y política en Costa Rica.* San José: CICOM.

Siles, I., Carazo, C., & Tristán, L. (2020). El "matrimonio gay" como tema electoral en Costa Rica: eventos mediáticos en sistemas híbridos de comunicación. In I. Siles (Ed.), *Democracia en digital: Facebook, comunicación y política en Costa Rica* (pp. 207–232). San José: CICOM.

Siles, I., Espinoza, J., & Méndez, A. (2019). La investigación sobre tecnología de comunicación en América Latina: Un análisis crítico de la literatura (2005–2015). *Palabra Clave, 22*(1).

Stefanoni, P. (2018). Biblia, buey y bala . . . recargados: Jair Bolsonaro, la ola conservadora en Brasil y América Latina. *Nueva Sociedad, 278*, 4. Retrieved from: https://nuso.org/articulo/biblia-buey-y-bala-ola-conservadora-brasil-bolsonaro-stefanoni/

Waisbord, S. (2014). *Vox populista: Medios, periodismo, democracia.* Barcelona: Gedisa.

Waisbord, S. (2018a). The elective affinity between post-truth communication and populist politics. *Communication Research and Practice, 4*(1), 17–34.

Waisbord, S. (2018b). Truth is what happens to news: On journalism, fake news, and post-truth. *Journalism Studies, 19*(13), 1866–1878.

Waisbord, S. (2019). Populism as media and communication phenomenon. In C. De la Torre (Ed.), *Routledge handbook of global populism* (pp. 221–234). New York: Routledge.

Waisbord, S., & Amado, A. (2017). Populist communication by digital means: Presidential Twitter in Latin America. *Information, Communication & Society, 20*(9), 1330–1346.

Weber, M. (2013). La transformation du charisme et le charisme de fonction. *Revue Française de Science Politique, 63*(3), 463–486.

Weyland, K. (2001). Clarifying a contested concept: Populism in the study of Latin American politics. *Comparative Politics, 34*(1), 1–22.

34

PERCEIVED MIS- AND DISINFORMATION IN A POST-FACTUAL INFORMATION SETTING

A conceptualisation and evidence from ten European countries

Michael Hameleers and Claes de Vreese

Today's digital communication environments are increasingly seen as hosting phenomena that are problematic for deliberative democracy (e.g. Van Aelst et al., 2017). One of the most pressing issues in that regard is the alleged spread of false information – which refers to information that is either inaccurate without the intention to mislead (misinformation) or manipulated or fabricated to achieve a political goal (disinformation) (e.g. Hameleers et al., 2020; Tandoc Jr. et al., 2018; Wardle, 2017). Although scholars have started to map the dimensions of communicative untruthfulness and its political consequences (e.g. Marwick & Lewis, 2017; Wardle, 2017), we know little about how mis- and disinformation are actually perceived by citizens. Do the widespread concerns about communicative untruthfulness resonate with citizens' interpretations of their information environment, and do they actually perceive their information setting as (deliberately) misleading and dishonest? In this chapter, we aim to give an overview of mis- and disinformation through the eyes of news consumers, offering evidence of how salient these media evaluations are among European news consumers.

In a communication era that has been described as post-truth or post-factual (e.g. Lewandowsky et al., 2012; Van Aelst et al., 2017) – the factual status of reality and the honesty of the news media's worldviews are no longer taken at face value but rather are seen as relative or subject to distortion. This means that citizens may become more cynical and distrusting towards information presented to them as truthful. In line with this, they may use their ideological identities or prior attitudes to separate facts from fiction – rather than basing their judgment on the veracity of information (Hameleers & van der Meer, 2019). In this setting, it is crucial to look not only at the actual facticity, neutrality, and honesty of information, but also at the perceptions of unintended misinformation and intentional disinformation. Hence, as multiple accounts of the same external reality may reach citizens in (online) news environments, it is crucial to explore the extent to which news consumers actually trust the media – or whether they perceive a crisis of accuracy and honesty in the news they are exposed to. Mis- and disinformation may thus correspond to societal developments beyond the lack of facticity and honesty of information and can spill over into demand-side evaluations of the media's accuracy and honesty.

Relying on existing supply-side conceptualisations that regard mis- and disinformation as different phenomena (e.g. Tandoc Jr. et al., 2018; Wardle, 2017), we discern two main dimensions by which news consumers perceptions of mis- and disinformation are structured: (1) misinformation perceptions pertaining to inaccurate news reporting that deviates from reality and (2) disinformation perceptions that tap the perceived dishonesty of the news environment, which corresponds to perceived intentional misleading, deception, and dishonesty of the media (see Hameleers et al., 2020).

Perceptions of disinformation in particular correspond to an overall populist worldview. Hence, it has been argued that populist voters increasingly regard the media and mainstream sources of knowledge as biased, corrupt, and deceptive (e.g. Egelhofer & Lecheler, 2019; Krämer, 2018; Tambini, 2017). More specifically, right-wing populist actors are said to rely on a discourse in which not only the political elites, but also the mainstream media are targeted as enemies of the people (Tambini, 2017). Hence, when people perceive that the media betray the people and deliberately manipulate reality to serve their own interests, an inherently populist worldview is expressed (Fawzi, 2018). Specifically, disinformation perceptions juxtapose the honest ordinary people with corrupt elites in the media. In tandem with the increasing concern about the pervasiveness of populist sentiments throughout Europe, we thus also need to comprehend how such perceptions are expressed towards the media as a likely salient scapegoat for the people's problems.

In the next sections, this chapter will give an overview of how mis- and disinformation can be conceptualised as perceptions of the news media's accuracy and honesty. We will present evidence of the extent to which people in different European countries actually hold these perceptions when evaluating the media's performance, also offering insights into the role of national-level opportunity structures that may give rise to lower or higher levels of these perceptions. As mis- and disinformation perceptions may have different democratic implications, it is important to assess the extent to which news consumers in different countries evaluate the media according to these dimensions, and whether they can distinguish unintentional falsehoods (misinformation) from deliberative deception (disinformation).

Beyond distrust and hostility: perceived mis- and disinformation

In conceptualising mis- and disinformation, we follow extant literature that has distinguished different forms of mis- and disinformation (e.g. Tandoc Jr. et al., 2018; Wardle, 2017). Although conceptual consensus on the scope of mis- and disinformation has not yet been reached (see, for example, Weeks & Gil de Zúñiga, 2019), many scholars have argued that fake news as a concept is too vague to fully express the nature of untruthful communication (e.g. Freelon & Wells, 2020; Wardle, 2017). Most conceptualisations have in common that different forms of mis- or disinformation are distinguished based on facticity and intent (Tandoc Jr. et al., 2018). Based on this core distinction, two main types of communicative untruthfulness can be distinguished: misinformation and disinformation.

Misinformation can simply be defined as communication that is inaccurate or untrue but without the intention of misleading receivers (e.g. Wardle, 2017). Misinformation thus scores 'low' on the facticity dimension (Tandoc Jr. et al., 2018) and refers to statements that are untrue when scrutinised by empirical evidence and/or expert opinion (Nyhan & Reifler, 2010). Misinformation can be disseminated by many different actors, such as politicians, advertisers, and journalists, but also ordinary citizens who communicate their positions via social media. The level or severity of untruthfulness may vary, depending on the deviation from the external, objective reality. More specifically, misinformation can be 'completely false' or 'mostly true' and everything in between these extremes. Such degrees of untruthfulness are also captured by fact-checking platforms such as Snopes or PolitiFact.

Different from misinformation, disinformation refers to the intentional or goal-directed manipulation or fabrication of information (e.g. Jackson, 2017; Marwick & Lewis, 2017; Wardle, 2017). The goals of disinformation may vary, but cultivating distrust; increasing support for, for example, radical left- or right-wing issue positions; and strengthening polarisation may be some of the political goals targeted by agents of disinformation (Jackson, 2017; Marwick & Lewis, 2017). Disinformation is often partisan in nature: it is tailored to specific issue publics or ideological groups in society that should be most likely to accept the dishonest claims (Marwick & Lewis, 2017). The partisan or ideological underpinnings make disinformation potentially harmful in today's media settings: when citizens are exposed to disinformation that reassures their partisan identities or issue positions, they are less likely to cast doubts on its veracity. As disinformation is intended to make an impact and as it can be distributed in a systematic, goal-directed way to bring about societal change or disruption, it may be problematic for deliberative democracy.

Although the distinction between mis- and disinformation has been made in conceptual literature, we know very little about the actual occurrence of these types of communicative untruthfulness in the digital media landscape. Hence, in light of digital developments fostering fragmentation, personalisation, and micro-targeting, researchers face an enormous challenge in mapping the scope of mis- and disinformation on the supply side. In addition, mis- or disinformation cannot simply be equated with any type of communication that lacks objective, factual coverage and/or expert knowledge, which makes it difficult to identify the scope of mis- and disinformation. What we can actually map empirically is how news consumers themselves perceive mis- and disinformation (see Hameleers et al., 2020), which may have crucial ramifications for the effects of false information on society and the selection decisions of citizens in fragmented media environments. More specifically, the more people perceive the traditional information environment as characterised by mis- and disinformation, the less they trust the news media and the more likely they are to resort to alternative sources and platforms. Based on the premises of motivated reasoning resulting in confirmation biases and defensive motivations (e.g. Hart et al., 2009), information that resonates with people's ideologies and prior attitudes is least likely to be subject to doubt and scepticism, which also implies that the perception of mis- and disinformation may mostly be assigned to information that challenges the existing beliefs of citizens. In that sense, these perceptions can have far-reaching democratic implications: if citizens dismiss incongruent realities as untrue or misleading, they can avoid cognitive dissonance and stick to congruent accounts of reality, irrespective of the actual veracity of information. If the same mechanism operates at opposite fringes of the political spectrum, mis- and disinformation perceptions may augment polarisation and partisan or ideological divides in society. In that sense, mis- and disinformation may not only relate to people's actual beliefs in the accuracy and honesty of information, but also serve as cues to defend attitudinal positions and identities in a high-choice media environment in which congruent truths are widely available.

Shifting our focus to the demand side of mis- and disinformation, mis- and disinformation can be perceived as individual-level attitudes corresponding to news consumers' perceptions of inaccurate, untruthful, and/or dishonest communication in their media environments (Hameleers et al., 2020). As distrust and hostility towards information and the press has become more politicised and, arguably, subject to populist framing (Fawzi, 2018; Hameleers et al., 2020), traditional measures of media trust and hostile media perceptions fall short of accurately capturing citizens' media evaluations. Hence, some citizens not only hold negative evaluations of the media's performance or biases but may also regard the media as part of the established order that deliberately misleads the people. Citizens with less-pronounced populist worldviews may believe that the media at times fail to report on the facts as they happened, without assigning this failure to goal-directed manipulation and deception.

In terms of consequences for deliberative democracy, distinguishing between these different dimensions of the media's evaluation may also separate healthy sceptics from cynical and distrusting citizens: People with misinformation attitudes may still trust the institution and democratic function of the news media to inform citizens, although they feel that information is not always accurate. Disinformation attitudes, in contrast, correspond to institutional distrust and cynicism: people who perceive that the media are lying to the people have no faith in the functioning and neutrality of the institutions that govern the supply of information in society. Together, in an information ecology characterised by increasing relativism towards the objective status of facts, news consumers' perceptions of media honesty, trustworthiness, and accuracy should be measured using a multidimensional measure of mis- and disinformation and not simply by established measures of media trust and/or hostile media perceptions (see Hameleers et al., 2020).

The populist nature of perceived mis- and disinformation

More than conventional media trust measures, mis- and disinformation perceptions aim to map the people's opposition to mainstream media in times of a so-called populist zeitgeist (Mudde, 2004). Hence, it has been argued that populist ideas – which concern the expression of an antagonistic worldview or ideology in which the ordinary people are framed in opposition to the 'corrupt' elites (e.g. Aalberg et al., 2017; Canovan, 1999; Mudde, 2004) – increasingly manifests itself outside the realm of populist politicians. For example, populist ideas have been found to manifest as frames or organising ideas in news coverage (e.g. Hameleers & Vliegenthart, 2020) and as individual-level attitudes corresponding to the perceived divide between the ordinary people's in-group and the evil and corrupt elites (e.g. Schulz et al., 2017).

Perceptions of mis- and disinformation resonate with populist sentiments. The element of anti-elitism central to populism pertains not only to the people's opposition towards political elites but also to media elites (e.g. Egelhofer & Lecheler, 2019; Krämer, 2018; Tambini, 2017). Hence, voicing critique of the functioning and honesty of the established press has become a key element of populist communication tactics, which increasingly revolve around an epistemic crisis that separates the people's truth from the lies and deception of the media. On the demand side of voters, empirical research has, indeed, established an affinity between citizens' populist attitudes and anti-media sentiments (e.g. Fawzi, 2018; Schulz et al., 2017). This means that the more salient people's populist attitudes, the more likely they are to perceive the media as an enemy of the people. Populist worldviews thus not only refer to an antagonistic divide between the ordinary people and the corrupt elite but can also emphasise that the news media are to blame for distorting reality and for depriving the ordinary citizens of the truth.

The affinity between populist perceptions and anti-media attitudes (Fawzi, 2018; Schulz et al., 2017) is captured in perceptions of mis- and disinformation. Although extant conceptualisations of populist attitudes measure the ordinary people's opposition to the elites (e.g. Schulz et al., 2017), populist attitudes do not specify the elite actors they refer to beyond the political realm. As populist ideas juxtapose the people not only to established politicians but also to media elites and institutions, we need to understand populist perceptions of the media as an integral part of populist worldviews. As populist movements on the left and right that accuse the media of spreading fake news are gaining electoral terrain (e.g. Egelhofer & Lecheler, 2019), it is important to assess how these delegitimising perceptions of the media spill over into the electorate.

Hence, moving beyond distrust towards the media and populist perceptions as distinct constructs, it can be argued that the perceived divide between the ordinary people and the dishonest or corrupt elite may also be conceived on the level of media elites and institutions of the mainstream press. We therefore incorporate populist anti-media sentiments in our measure of perceived disinformation – such as the people's perception that the news media are an enemy of the ordinary people, that they only serve their own self-interest, and that the news media are deliberately lying to the people. By integrating the anti-media component of populist ideology into our conceptualisation of perceived disinformation, we empirically approach the affinity between anti-media sentiments and populist media critique that has been developed recently (e.g. Fawzi, 2018; Schulz et al., 2017).

Illustrating perceptions of mis- and disinformation

We report on the findings of a large-scale comparative survey in ten European countries in the period of the 2019 European parliamentary elections (see Hameleers et al., 2020, for documentation and background information). The ten included countries, which represent different regions in Europe, are the Czech Republic, Germany, Denmark, Spain, France Greece, Hungary, the Netherlands, Poland, and Sweden. We selected these European countries to achieve a maximum variety in contextual-level factors and regional differences that may resonate with perceptions of mis- and disinformation on the individual level.[1]

Measures for misinformation perceptions tapped the perceived veracity, accuracy, and truthfulness of traditional news reporting. These perceptions were measured with the following items (all measured on seven-point disagree-agree scales): (1) The news media do not report accurately on facts that happened; (2) To understand real-life events, you cannot rely on the news media; (3) The news media are an unreliable source of factual information; and (4) The news media insufficiently rely on expert sources. Disinformation perceptions were measured with the following items: (1) The news media are an enemy of the ordinary people; (2) The news media are deliberately lying to the people; and (3) The news media only serve their own interests. The items used for perceived misinformation and disinformation were theoretically informed by conceptualisations of fake news (e.g. Tandoc Jr. et al., 2018; Wardle, 2017), as a well as populist attitudes (for the disinformation dimension only) (e.g. Schulz et al., 2017).

Do citizens systematically distinguish between deliberately misleading and inaccurate reporting, and in what countries are the differences between mis- and disinformation strongest? Our findings indicate that citizens in most countries distinguish between mis- and disinformation perceptions, with the exception of Greece and Spain (see Figure 34.1). Hence, in these countries, average levels of misinformation perceptions are equally as high as disinformation perceptions.

In all other countries, misinformation perceptions are significantly lower than disinformation perceptions. Citizens are thus mostly capable of distinguishing their critical perspective on the news media's performance from cynical and populist interpretations of the media's dishonesty. Spain and Greece, two Southern European countries with high overall levels of media distrust and corruption, may provide a contextual backdrop in which citizens hold negative and cynical attitudes towards the press. Distrust in the media may be so severe that citizens do not distinguish between 'honest' mistakes and 'lying' and corrupt media elites. When news consumers have at least a basic level of trust in the institutions governing the media, as in most countries, a fine-grained distinction between critical media perceptions and cynical or populist media attitudes can be maintained.

Looking at the differences between the countries in more detail, it can be observed that the average levels of mis- and disinformation perceptions vary strongly across national settings (see Figure 34.1). Regarding the average level of misinformation, France (M = 4.91, SD = 1.19) and The Netherlands (M = 3.75, SD = 1.12) differ most strongly. Differences of one full scale point can also be observed for Southern and Eastern European countries versus Northern and Western European countries. Interestingly, many of these differences mirror contextual factors that differ across the ten European countries. In countries where media trust levels and press freedom indicators are low and corruption is high, misinformation perceptions are most salient.

Differences in disinformation perceptions are even stronger than national differences in perceived misinformation. Specifically, disinformation perceptions are strongest in Greece (M = 4.91, SD = 1.19) and lowest in Sweden (M = 3.20, SD = 1.54). Similar substantial between-country differences can be observed between Southern European countries (e.g. Greece) and other Western and Northern European countries (e.g. The Netherlands).

Differences in levels of disinformation perceptions can be connected to contextual-level factors. Specifically, in countries with less press freedom and stronger indicators of corruption, news consumers are more likely to distrust the honesty of the press and perceive the news media as the people's enemy (e.g. in Greece and Poland). Contrary to what may be expected, the presence of successful right-wing populist parties is not associated with stronger disinformation perceptions. Hence, although right-wing populist parties are successful in many Western European countries (e.g. The Netherlands, Sweden), disinformation perceptions are generally lowest in Western Europe.

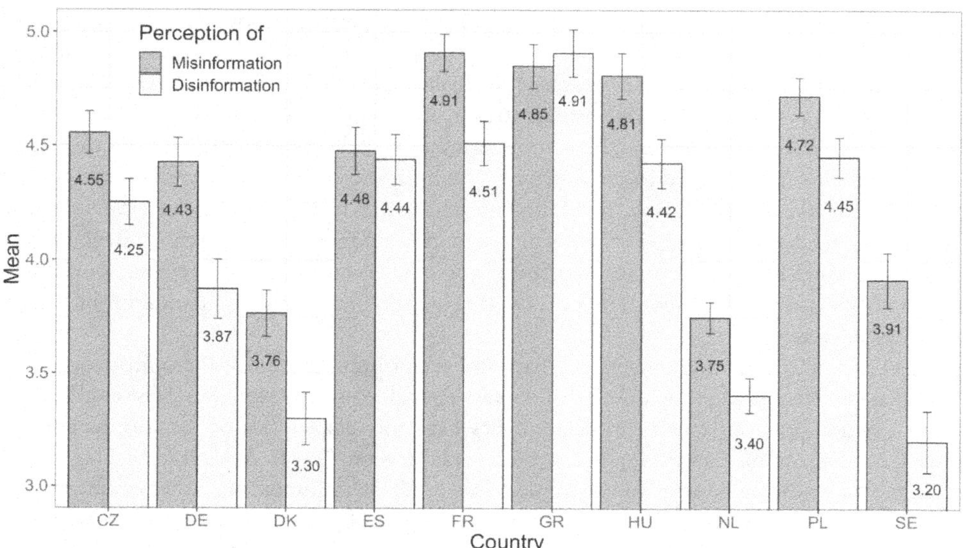

Figure 34.1 A depiction of the mean scores of mis- and disinformation perceptions in the ten countries under study

(See also Hameleers et al., 2020)

Discussion

In response to growing societal concerns about the honesty and accuracy of information in digital information settings, many scholars have attempted to conceptualise mis- or disinformation as a sender-side phenomenon (e.g. Tandoc Jr. et al., 2018; Wardle, 2017; Weeks & Gil de Zúñiga, 2019). Hence, (radical right-wing) politicians, ordinary citizens, journalists, and alternative media outlets are accused of spreading falsehoods, which are assumed to make an impact on public opinion and electoral outcomes (e.g. Bennett & Livingston, 2018; Marwick & Lewis, 2017). In an era where trust in mass media institutions is declining and citizens increasingly turn to non-journalistic alternative media outlets, we need to move beyond the dominant understanding of mis- and disinformation as supply-side phenomena that only have an effect by misleading and deceiving citizens. In a post-truth information era, facticity and expert knowledge are increasingly scrutinised or even counter-argued when they do not fit the perceptual screens of news consumers (Van Aelst et al., 2017). This debate on (un)truthfulness on its own may have far-reaching effects, as it can result in declining levels of trust in mainstream knowledge and the approach of alternative sources of information that are more prone to false information. For this reason, it is crucial to understand how news consumers themselves perceive mis- and disinformation. Do they distinguish healthy criticism of the veracity of information from cynical attitudes towards the deceptive intentions of the press?

Based on empirical data collected in ten diverse European nations, we can confirm that most citizens actually do distinguish between intentional disinformation and unintentional misinformation. Overall, perceptions of misinformation are significantly more salient than those of perceived disinformation. However, we observe strong between-country variation on the salience of mis- and disinformation perceptions. News consumers in Western and Northern European countries with higher levels of media trust and press freedom and lower levels of corruption are more likely to trust the accuracy of journalistic reporting and are less likely to doubt the honesty of the media elites. However, in national settings where press freedom is lower and corruption and distrust in media institutions is highest (Eastern and Southern European countries and France), citizens are more likely to have strong perceptions of mis- and disinformation. France may be regarded as a rather unique case. Even though it is a Western European country, disinformation perceptions are higher there than in all other countries. This can be explained by the political developments taking place at the time of data collection: the yellow vest movement gained visibility and managed to put distrust in the institutions of the press high on the political agenda. This means that real-life developments and contextual variations can have an impact on how the media are evaluated in terms of mis- and disinformation perceptions. Beyond more fixed contextual-level opportunity structures, mis- and disinformation perceptions may resonate with specific developments and crises that negatively impact the evaluation of the media's honesty and veracity.

Mis- and disinformation perceptions have important implications for the information ecology allegedly characterised by post-truth or post-factual relativism (e.g. Van Aelst et al., 2017). On a positive note, citizens in most countries have moderate levels of 'healthy scepticism', indicating that the media are seen as not being able to report on facts accurately. This may be an indicator of media literacy and more desirable levels of scepticism: in times of information overload and high choice, citizens should be able to critically navigate their information environment and should not uncritically accept all incoming political information. Citizens need to act as independent fact-checkers themselves as they cannot rely on their information environment to check the veracity of each and every claim they are exposed to. Importantly, these perceptions can be distinguished from disinformation perceptions. Disinformation perceptions align with populist worldviews in which the media are severely distrusted and seen as the people's enemy. In most countries, disinformation perceptions are lower than misinformation perceptions, indicating that scepticism in the accuracy of news reporting is more prominent that distrust in the honesty of the press. But how worrisome are such perceptions?

On average, disinformation perceptions are higher than the midpoint of the scale in most countries. This means that holding the media accountable for the supply of dishonest and misleading political information is a relatively salient attitude. In line with extant literature that has pointed to an affinity between anti-media perceptions and populist attitudes on the demand side of the electorate (e.g. Fawzi, 2018; Schulz et al., 2018), we found that many citizens regard traditional media as an elitist outsider that deprives the ordinary people of an honest worldview. The most important democratic implication is that although citizens with higher misinformation perceptions may still rely on the news media to be informed about the world around them, citizens with higher levels of disinformation may show a strong tendency to avoid traditional news media altogether. Hence, they do not simply distrust the content of information itself but cast severe doubts on the intentions underlying the production of news content: news producers are regarded as part of a corrupt established order that misleads news consumers as part of a scheme to hide the power discrepancy between the ordinary people and the corrupt elites.

As it reaches beyond the scope of this chapter to provide insights into the consequences of mis- and disinformation perceptions for media choices and political attitudes or behaviours, we recommend that future empirical endeavors further explore the extent to which mis- and disinformation perceptions correspond to specific (alternative and anti-establishment) media diets. Is it, indeed, the case that citizens with stronger disinformation perceptions avoid established media whilst approaching alternative outlets that mirror their populist, cynical, and anti-elitist worldviews? And if this the case, what are the consequences of exposure to these alternative media platforms? As increasing levels of disinformation perceptions may trigger selective exposure to anti-elitist content, which, in turn, intensifies negative perceptions and avoidance of the established political and media order, a vicious circle of distrust may become activated. To end on a more positive note, this chapter shows that perceived communicative untruthfulness is not a unidimensional construct – meaning that critical skills and distrust in the media's institutions are distinct perceptions used to interpret information from the media. As long as disinformation perceptions are less prevalent than perceived misinformation, the crisis of distrust and post-truth relativism may be less severe than is oftentimes assumed. An important task for journalists and established media platforms is to acknowledge the mis- and disinformation perceptions of society and respond with formats and reporting styles that restore trust in the fourth-estate function of the mainstream media.

Note

1 The levels of press freedom differ strongly in our sample – ranging from 8.3 in Sweden to 30.4 in Hungary on a 100-point scale (higher scores indicate less press freedom) (Reporters sans Frontières, 2019). Similarly, national levels of media trust differ across the sampled countries: only 24 percent of citizens in France trust the media, whereas these levels are much higher in Western and Northern European countries such as The Netherlands (53 percent) and Denmark (57 percent). Finally, our selected countries differ in terms of the electoral success of (radical) right-wing populist parties. Within the selected countries, data was collected by an external research agency (Kantar). To achieve a sample composition that approached national representativeness, light quotas were used for age, gender, education, and region. We achieved the following number of completes in the different countries: N_{CZ}=733, N_{DE}=518, N_{DK}=563, N_{ES}=557, N_{FR}=776, N_{GR}=494, N_{HU}= 588, N_{NL}=1067, N_{PL}=857, N_{SE}=497.

References

Aalberg, T., Esser, F., Reinemann, C., Strömbäck, J., & de Vreese, C. H. (2017). *Populist political communication in Europe*. London: Routledge.

Bennett, L. W., & Livingston, S. (2018). The disinformation order: Disruptive communication and the decline of democratic institutions. *European Journal of Communication*. doi: 10.1177/0267323118760317

Canovan, M. (1999). Trust the people! Populism and the two faces of democracy. *Political Studies, 47*, 2–16. doi: 10.1111/1467-9248.00184

Egelhofer, J. L., & Lecheler, S. (2019). Fake news as a two-dimensional phenomenon: A framework and research agenda. *Annals of the International Communication Association, 43*(2), 97–116. doi: 10.1080/23808985.2019.1602782

Fawzi, N. (2018). Untrustworthy news and the media as "enemy of the people?" How a populist worldview shapes recipients' attitudes towards the media. *International Journal of Press/Politics*. doi: 10.1177/1940161218811981

Freelon, D., & Wells, C. (2020). Disinformation as political communication. *Political Communication, 37*, 145–156. doi: 10.1080/10584609.2020.1723755

Hameleers, M., Brosius, A., Marquart, F., Goldberg, A., de Vreese, C. H., & Van Elsas, E. (2020). Mistake or manipulation? Conceptualizing perceived mis- and disinformation among news consumers in ten European countries. *Paper prepared for the annual meeting of the International Communication Association*.

Hameleers, M., & Van der Meer, G. L. A. (2019). Misinformation and polarization in a high-choice media environment: How effective are Political fact-checkers? *Communication Research*. doi: 10.1177/0093650218819671

Hameleers, M., & Vliegenthart, R. (2020). The rise of a populist zeitgeist? A content analysis of populist media coverage in newspapers published between 1990 and 2017. *Journalism Studies, 21*(1), 19–36. doi: 10.1080/1461670X.2019.1620114

Hart, W., Albarracín, D., Eagly, A. H., Brechan, I., Lindberg, M. J., & Merrill, L. (2009). Feeling validated versus being correct: A meta-analysis of selective exposure to information. *Psychological Bulletin, 135*(4), 555–588. doi: 10.1037/a0015701

Jackson, D. (2017, October 17). *Issue brief: Distinguishing disinformation from propaganda, misinformation, and "Fake News" – National endowment for democracy*. Retrieved September 18, 2018, from www.ned.org/issue-brief-distinguishing-disinformation-from-propaganda-misinformation-and-fake-news/

Krämer, B. (2018). How journalism responds to right-wing populist criticism. In K. Otto & A. Köhler (Eds.), *Trust in media and journalism* (pp. 137–154). Wiesbaden: Springer VS.

Lewandowsky, S., Ecker, U. K., Seifert, C. M., Schwarz, N., & Cook, J. (2012). Misinformation and its correction continued influence and successful debiasing. *Psychological Science in the Public Interest, 13*(3), 106–131. doi: 10.1177/1529100612451018

Marwick, A., & Lewis, R. (2017). Media manipulation and disinformation online (pp. 1–104). *Data and Society Research Institute*. Retrieved September 18, 2018, from https://datasociety.net/output/media-manipulation-and-disinfo-online/

Mudde, C. (2004). The populist zeitgeist. *Government and Opposition, 39*(4), 542–564. doi: 10.1111/j.1477-7053.2004.00135.x

Nyhan, B., & Reifler, J. (2010). When corrections fail: The persistence of political misperceptions. *Political Behavior, 32*(2), 303–330. doi: 10.1007/s11109-010-9112-2

Reporters sans Frontières (2019). *2019 world press freedom index*. Retrieved October 21, 2019, from rsf.org

Schulz, A., Müller, P., Schemer, C., Wirz, D. S., Wettstein, M., & Wirth, W. (2017). Measuring populist attitudes on three dimensions. *International Journal of Public Opinion Research*. doi: 10.1093/ijpor/edw037

Schulz, A., Wirth, W., & Müller, P. (2018). We are the people and you are fake news: A social identity approach to populist citizens' false consensus and hostile media perceptions. *Communication Research*. doi: 10.1177/0093650218794854

Tambini, D. (2017). *Fake news: Public policy responses. Media Policy Brief 20*. London: Media Policy Project, London School of Economics and Political Science. Retrieved from: http://eprints.lse.ac.uk/73015/

Tandoc Jr., E. C., Lim, Z. W., & Ling, R. (2018). Defining "fake news." *Digital Journalism, 6*(2), 137–153. doi: 10.1080/21670811.2017.1360143

Van Aelst, P., Strömbäck, J., Aalberg, T., Esser, F. de Vreese, C. H., Matthes, J., . . . Stanyer, J. (2017). Political communication in a high-choice media environment: A challenge for democracy? *Annals of the International Communication Association*, 4(1), 3–27. doi: 10.1080/23808985.2017.1288551

Wardle, C. (2017). Fake news. It's complicated. *First Draft*. Retrieved January 22, 2019 from https://medium.com/1st-draft/fake-news-its-complicated-d0f773766c79

Weeks, B. E., & Gil de Zúñiga, H. (2019). What's next? Six observations for the future of political misinformation research. *American Behavioral Scientist*. doi: 10.1177/0002764219878236

35

THE ROLE OF SOCIAL MEDIA IN THE RISE OF RIGHT-WING POPULISM IN FINLAND

Karina Horsti and Tuija Saresma

Introduction

Populism, although in itself an empty ideology, often attaches itself to other ideologies (Laclau 2005; Palonen & Saresma 2017; Ylä-Anttila 2017). Right-wing populism is typically entangled with xenophobic nationalism and neo-conservatism, which often usher in racism and misogyny (Palonen & Saresma 2019). A 'populist zeitgeist' is advancing across the globe across the ideological spectrum of populism (Suiter et al. 2018, 396); however, a particular right-wing populism has in the 2000s become a major political force in most European countries. In the Nordic countries that are characterised by multi-party systems, right-wing populist parties have been central in the political arena in the past decade.

Scholars have acknowledged that social media have become influential channels for spreading right-wing nationalist-populist messages (e.g. Mudde 2016, 28; Pettersson 2017; Suiter et al. 2018; Saresma 2020). However, we lack more detailed knowledge of how politicians of populist parties benefit from social media (Jacobs & Spierings 2019, 1692) and what other social processes, in conjunction with the emergence of social media, facilitate the spread of right-wing populism. In this chapter we take Finland as a case study to examine the role of media technology in the rise of right-wing populism. We argue that transformations in the mediascape that began in the 1990s – the internet, mobile technology, and market competition – crucially afforded the emergence of the right-wing populist movement and its transformation into a political force. However, we do not argue that the role of these shifts in the mediascape should be taken as a sign of technological determinism; rather, our analysis suggests a broader angle to the complex connections between different social processes: namely, racism, Islamophobia, and misogyny, together with changing technology, journalistic practice, and new forms of spreading and interpreting mediated contents.

The Finns party (*Perussuomalaiset*) in its current form is a populist radical right party that mixes traditional conservatism and anti-establishment sentiment with extreme nationalism. The party was established in 1995 on the grounds of the agrarian populist Finnish Rural Party (*Suomen maaseudun puolue*). It is an exceptional case among the right-wing populist parties as its agrarian populist political legacy is intertwined with a nationalist and socially conservative political agenda and, more recently, increasingly with ethnic nationalism (Keskinen, 2013, 2016; Mickelsson, 2011; Pyrhönen, 2015; Norocel et al., 2021). In the

2011 elections, the party took Finnish politics by storm, polling 19 percent of the votes. Again, in the 2015 elections, polling close to 18 percent, the party joined the right-wing governmental coalition (Kantola & Lombardo 2019, 1112). A significant ideological shift to right-wing nationalist populism, however, took place in 2017, when the party went through a dramatic leadership change. The moderate leader Timo Soini stepped aside, and his favourite candidate lost the election for the next chair of the party's right-wing fraction. Despite the break-up, in the 2019 elections, the party again polled 17.5 percent of the votes. The Finns Party was just one seat away from winning the general election, and it thus became the largest opposition party.

This transformation from centre-populist to far-right ideology in the party (Norocel et al., 2021) was enabled by the right-wing faction's popularity, gained gradually on social media, hidden from the sight of traditional media and political commentators. The party's new core element, the ethno-nationalism of Finnishness (Arter 2010, 485, 501–502), connects it to other right-wing parties in Europe. Ethno-nationalism refers to a belief that a nation is formed based on its ethnic and other uniform features, such as genetic heritage. Groups that come from different ethnic or cultural backgrounds are understood as fundamentally incompatible. Ethno-nationalism as an ideology produces a clear distinction between 'us' and 'the others', the latter being systematically excluded from 'our' nation (Ovaskainen 2019; Saresma & Tulonen, 2020).

In this chapter, we demonstrate the strengthening of the far-right ideology on and through social media from the beginning of 2010s. More specifically, we examine the rise of the present chair, Jussi Halla-aho, and his success in taking over the Finns Party as an example of how the transformation of the media environment from a centripetal phase of mass communication to a multi-platform and centrifugal phase facilitated the mainstreaming of Islamophobia and misogyny, ideologies that are at the core of right-wing populism throughout Europe.

In the first part of the chapter, we argue that analysis of present-day populism needs to examine the media environment as a system of connectivities by paying attention to two spheres: first, the structure and restructure of the media ecology in general, and second, the decentralised anonymous online spaces, the so-called echo chambers. Then we focus on the mediated construction of two entangled ideologies in the right-wing populist movement – racism (or, more specifically, Islamophobia) and misogyny. We argue that through these two intersecting ideologies, national and local right-wing populist movements connect to transnational flows of right-wing discourses and practices. Nevertheless, as our analysis shows, these developments are simultaneously deeply rooted in the particular social context.

Transforming media ecology and the Finnish case of right-wing populism

The mainstream public in Finland became aware of a right-wing populist movement with an outspoken anti-immigration and Islamophobic agenda in 2008 when a blogger, Jussi Halla-aho – the present chair of the Finns – gained electoral success as an independent candidate on the Finns (PS) list in the local elections in Helsinki.

Halla-aho's rise to the top in Finnish politics is intriguing for media research. Before his electoral success in 2008, he was unknown by the mainstream public as there was hardly any mention of him in the national media (Horsti 2015, 357). This counters the common argument in media research on right-wing populism that mainstream media attention, although critical and negative, is crucial for the success of new political populists (Ellinas 2010; Stewart et al. 2003). In the case of Jussi Halla-aho, while mainstream journalism did not recognise the movement around him before 2008, he succeeded in reaching a constituency in the online 'echo chambers'.

After his electoral success in 2008, traditional news values required the mainstream media to cover the political newcomer (see Norris 2009). Unlike in neighbouring Sweden, where the mainstream media categorically refused to include the right-wing populist Sweden Democrats among the regular political commentators, the Finnish media integrated Halla-aho into debates as the 'immigration critique' – a term the Finns Party preferred. The sudden rise of Halla-aho from 'nowhere' to electoral success – that is, his rise to politics through the unconventional path of blogging – illustrates the shift in the dynamics between the media and right-wing populism that began to take shape across Europe in late 2000s (Horsti & Nikunen 2013; Horsti 2015). However, it is also grounded in traditional news logic, such as the practice of covering a political newcomer and the practice of 'objective' journalism that seeks to 'balance' the treatment of controversial topics. Halla-aho figured as the 'immigration critique' who 'balanced' more liberal views on multiculturalism and migration.

Jussi Halla-aho's blog, *Scipta*, which he had started in 2005, began to attract a wide following and an active community of commentators who, in 2008, created a separate anti-immigration discussion forum named *Hommaforum*. Halla-aho introduced the Islamophobic narrative in Finland through his blog, and his message, combining nationalist and Islamophobic ideologies, was amplified in the internet echo chambers and with help of the 'digital foot soldiers' (Hatakka 2019). At the time, the practice of anonymous online discussion on news and discussion sites had become popular. Simultaneously, however, mainstream media providers' frustration over uncivil discussion on their anonymous discussion forums grew, and by about 2010, they began regulating online comments sections of news sites through pre-moderation, registration, and identification of commenters (Nikunen 2011, 71–73, 77). The tightening of anonymity and moderation in the Finnish mainstream media resulted in the number of comments in the threaded discussion spaces dropping (Pöyhtäri et al. 2013, 176). Debates among professional editors and journalists escalated, resulting in the self-governing body Council for Mass Media in Finland creating an annex to the journalists' guidelines for monitoring the content generated by users in 2011. These transformations in the mainstream news sites, which reduced hate speech and racism online, nevertheless increased the appeal of sites like *Hommaforum*, where anti-immigration opinions and misogynist jokes flourished. This development characterises the typical trans-platform circulation of content in online spaces. *Hommaforum* is a prime example of a folk-cultural production model (Benkler 2006) – a more reflexive and participatory cultural production than that of the mass cultural production. The site's architecture and structure invite participation and humour while allowing the members to be known only by their pseudonyms (Horsti 2015).

Halla-aho created his online presence at a time when politicians were not yet communicating directly with publics through social media platforms. Political blogs as a distinguished genre are often paradoxically positioned outside the traditional political sphere. Anyone is able to launch a blog as the technological equipment is easy to master. Like all social media, blogs as a medium are relatively uncontrolled and uncensored, so they enable publishing acrimonious criticism and adversarial opinions. For politicians it is valuable to be able to express opinions more freely than in traditional media (Saresma & Tulonen, 2020). Also, blogs as a medium are quicker and more flexible than the traditional media. As a genre, they allow the circulating of powerful, credible, and affective messages (Pettersson 2017, 6).

Halla-aho almost ceased his blogging after he took over the party leadership in 2017, reflecting a transformation from a political outsider into a political insider as the leader of the main opposition party. The recurring topics in his blog since 2005 connect to nationalism and severe opposition to immigration (particularly asylum seekers and refugees) and multiculturalism (Saresma & Tulonen, 2020). In a series of court cases, he gained public exposure for his writings from 2009 through 2012, and in 2012, he was convicted of blasphemy and ethnic agitation. Focus on clearly demarcated themes is an effective device in spreading propaganda, and repetition, which Halla-aho uses deliberately, is a typical means of populist communication (Taveira & Nyerges 2016).

Digitisation complicated the agenda-setting power of mainstream media, particularly by providing online spaces where news could be shared and discussed. It also contributed to a transformation of the media ecology. For instance, in Finland in 2009, the readership of the traditionally strong newspaper market dropped 10 percent compared to the previous year (Statistics Finland 2019). Digitisation and globalisation were forces that restructured journalism in Europe, including Finland. The boundary between journalistic content of edited opinions and non-edited contents became increasingly blurred, particularly because discussions around news shifted to echo chambers (Sunstein 2001): online spaces formed around web sites and blogs of nationalistic movements where like-minded individuals gather to exchange similar views.

However, this was only part of the story. Instead of dividing immigration debate into civil mainstream media spaces and aggressive online echo chambers, we suggest examining the media environment as a system of connectivities. This environment is a techno-cultural construct (van Dijck 2013), meaning that the connectivities and affordances emerge in the intersections of technology and human activity. The *Hommaforum* discussion space is an exemplary case in this respect. The architecture facilitated the construction of a community, creating a sense of belonging and commitment. This was particularly crucial for political mobilisation in the early phase of the movement before it gained electoral success and political power within the Finns Party.

The concept of a hybrid media system (Chadwick 2013) captures well the current situation, in which affordances of various media are utilised. This hybrid media system comprises traditional media, social media, and alternative or false media, and it enables various actors to participate in meaning making and knowledge production as well as dissemination and reframing of information (Hatakka 2019, 48). In the hybrid media system engendered by digital technologies, traditional news cycles are replaced by more dynamic information cycles (Suiter et al. 2018, 398), which may be an advantage for spreading misinformation, disinformation, and propaganda.

The case of the Finns Party public communication depicts the function of the hybrid media system and connectivity in an exemplary way. The Finns Party combined various media in their communication. They used traditional media, such as the party newspaper, which the older, agrarian conservatives trusted (Norocel et al., forthcoming) and paid campaign advertisement in legacy newspapers. The new radical right-wing anti-immigration faction, on the contrary, trusted much more communication on new social media platforms, such as blogs (Halla-aho's *Scripta*) and discussion forums (like *Hommaforum*). Halla-aho has also been active on Twitter and Facebook, and his comments spread to other media through these platforms.

Utilising the hybrid media system and the always alert 'digital foot soldiers', who willingly spread the message of their 'master', Halla-aho's message is circulated, repeated, and amplified through multiple social media channels through a media system of connectivities. His message is based on the entanglement of oppressive ideologies that are central for right-wing populist mobilisation – Islamophobia and misogyny. In what follows, we will demonstrate their mediated construction and their transnational connections – however, rooting them in the particular Finnish context.

Entangled ideologies of Islamophobia and misogyny

While being nationalist, Halla-aho's writing in his blog also connects to transnational radical right-wing ideologies circulating on social media and to populist networks that cross nation-state borders. The transnational Islamophobic movement divides the world into 'civilised Western culture' and 'primitive and dangerous Muslim culture'. It does so primarily through two discourses – racism (specifically Islamophobia) and misogyny (see, e.g. Horsti & Nikunen 2013; Nikunen 2015; Saresma 2017; Hatakka 2019; Saresma & Tulonen, 2020). It was, indeed, Halla-aho who mainstreamed Islamophobia into the Finnish public debate in the 2010s in his blog *Scripta – Kirjoituksia uppoavasta lännestä* [Writings from the sinking West]. As the title of the blog demonstrates, the key ideology in his writing is the alleged destruction of Western civilisation because of the intrusion of Muslims.

He emphasises cultural differences of certain groups of people, and these differences are a means of exclusion of the 'other'. An understanding of 'Finnishness' as a shared ethnic, linguistic, and cultural heritage is essential to the blog's message. However, he does not want to specify the common features, as if they were common knowledge:

> As I have written before, it is sophistic gimmickry to question 'Finnishness'. I admit that I cannot define a 'Finn'. I do, however, have a strong intuition, based on which I recognise who are Finns.
>
> (Halla-aho 2011)

An example of the blog's anti-immigration and anti-Muslim propaganda goes as follows:

> For every nine [immigrants] with attitude problems that we receive to be supported, there is one that is in some way useful. The reason is that those who accuse me of focusing too much on skin colour or religion do not see anything else in those who arrive. To them, the dark skin of the arrivals and the fact that they worship Allah are good enough criteria to enter the country. Because otherness is a fetish to them.
>
> (Halla-aho 2006a)

Here, mentioning Allah marks the unwanted immigrants as Muslims, a group framed throughout Halla-aho's blog as a threat to Western civilisation and the Finnish nation. This is Islamophobia in its purest form. Islamophobia is 'a form of culturalized racism that includes persistent Orientalist myths about Islam and Muslims' (Horsti 2017, 1442; see also Werbner, 2013; Taras, 2013). Islamophobia includes the beliefs that Islam creates a culture that is sexist, misogynistic, violent, and anti-democratic and that Muslims cannot think rationally (Kumar, 2012, 42–60). It is thus not only religion that is attacked, but the intersections of culture, ethnicity, modernity, class, and sexuality in relation to religion. Islamophobia is a form of cultural racism (Goldberg, 2009, 175), emphasising presumed differences in culture as the cause of certain incapability, instead of biology. However, characteristic to the Islamophobic discourse is the entanglement of biological racism with cultural arguments (Horsti 2017, 1442). The fragment of Halla-aho's blog cited earlier exemplifies this entanglement of cultural and biological racism as both religion ('worshipping Allah') and biology ('dark skin').

In Finland, as well as in the other Nordic countries, right-wing populists have utilised the common understanding of Nordic gender equality in their attack against Islam (Lähdesmäki & Saresma 2014; Horsti 2017), suggesting that Muslims 'are inherently patriarchal and backward' and thus a threat to liberal values such as the rights of women. Simultaneously, in other discussions, the same people are eager to narrow down these very rights: for example, by supporting anti-abortion mobilisation, gender-neutral marriage, or day care for all children in defence of conservative, even reactionary, gender politics (Poggio & Bélle 2018; Saresma 2018, about conservative gender ideology, see, e.g. Grönroos 2016).

The etymology of misogyny draws back to ancient Greek words *misogunía* and *misogúnēs*, 'woman hater'. Misogyny means the hatred of or prejudice against women and girls, or 'feelings of hating women, or the belief that men are much better than women', as *The Cambridge English Dictionary* defines it. It is important to note, however, that neither Islamophobia nor misogyny is a psychological state of a person; they are structural processes. Kate Manne (2018) suggests that misogyny should not be understood primarily in terms of the hatred or hostility some men feel towards all or most women. Instead, misogyny is 'hostile, demeaning, shaming, and punitive treatment of women'. In practice, it means controlling, policing, punishing, and exiling' 'bad' women, those who challenge male dominance. Misogyny is, thus, a cultural system and not just a matter of individual zealotry. It matches perfectly well with populist rhetoric where the homogenous 'us' is pitted against 'them' as the Other. In this scenario, creating an enemy functions as a means to strengthen the sense of 'us'.

Empirical analysis of Halla-aho's blog shows that the primary argument he makes repeatedly is based on gendering the immigrant Other (see, e.g. Saresma 2017; Saresma & Tulonen, 2020). For example, in a blog post titled '*Monikulttuurisuus ja nainen*' ('Multiculturalism and a woman'), Halla-aho (2006b) claims that multiculturalism (as a problematic phenomenon) is caused by women: unlike the majority of men who bravely stand against immigration, women and particularly 'green-leftist do-gooders' choose to defend immigrants, or 'barbaric rapists'. Halla-aho hopes that 'as rape will evidently increase', it will be these particular women who are raped by the foreign perpetrators. This violent misogynous fantasy of rape is channeled to target the 'suitable' victims: the women who do not share Halla-aho's Islamophobic ideology.

A more recent example of his social media communication through Twitter demonstrates how his gendered and racist views spread through the hybrid media system. In early spring 2020, the debate about Turkey opening its EU border to refugees made Jussi Halla-aho eagerly participate in this discussion in the parliament and on Twitter – now as the chairperson of the leading opposition party of Finland. On his Twitter page, he linked a mainstream media news article (MTV 2020) about Greece using tear gas against refugees who tried to enter the country at the border and tweeted: 'The [mainstream media] story claims there were women and children. On the video, there are bearded men who yell "*Allahu Akbar*". [These liberally minded people] say it is insulting to talk about invasion' (Halla-aho 2020). Again, refugees are racialised based on their religion and ethnicity and gendered, suggesting that there are no women among the refugees and that men would not be 'genuine' refugees. Halla-aho implies that the refugees are intruders – dangerous religious fanatics – invading the cradle of Western civilisation, but because of political correctness, it would be 'insulting' for him to explicitly say so. The tweet was liked by 1,700 people and retweeted 214 times, and so his message circulates and is amplified by the participatory labour of his followers.

His thinking follows the typical trajectory of transnational right-wing populist discourse that amalgamates Islamophobia and misogyny. The tropes of Muslim rape and Muslim invaders reappear in the transnational Islamophobic blogosphere (Fekete 2011; Horsti 2017). Muslim men are constructed both as infantile and emasculated and as violent, hypermasculine, animal-like, even beastly (Saresma & Tulonen, 2020; Puar 2007, xxv). Misogyny that intersects with Islamophobia is an example of Iris Marion Young's (2003) idea of masculine protection. In a patriarchal ideology, the white man is the protector of the Western society and the imagined white nation (signified by the white woman). He is the legitimate ruler, and women and children are expected to serve as his obedient and humble royal subjects. It is only this gendered power hierarchy that can save white women from brutal violence that is allegedly performed by racialised perpetrators. This politics of patriarchy has become a central frame for social media debates in the situation in which nationalistic, xenophobic, and racist rhetoric affect 'the social divides of nation, gender, and body', and people are either friends or enemies, either perpetrators or victims (Wodak 2015, 5).

In misogynist-Islamophobic ideology, the role of the white woman (and, in many cases, specifically the blonde Nordic woman) is, however, paradoxical (see Horsti 2017). On the one hand, the Nordic female represents the border of territory, family, race, culture, and identity that needs male protection. The woman embodies the nation and represents the threshold of what belongs to men. On the other hand, the (Nordic) white woman represents the civilised, independent, and emancipated modern woman (an opposite to the supposedly oppressed, primitive Muslim woman). However, while the role of an independent woman may be celebrated, her 'openness' and softness nevertheless are conceived as weaknesses; the female body is a boundary to which violation and infection from the outside are constant threats (on the feminist theory of the 'open body', see Jegerstedt 2012).

Conclusions

In this chapter, we have given examples of the relationship between social media and right-wing populism in a particular context, using as our case Finnish right-wing politician Jussi Halla-aho and his rise to political power. As we demonstrated, with the help of Halla-aho's online presence – through a blog and, more recently, Twitter – the emergence of transnationally widely spread right-wing populist ideologies of Islamophobia and misogyny has shaped political life and political practices. Social media appears to hold a significant role as a new political arena that shapes and structures public debates.

How are these particularly Finnish currents connected to transnational flows of right-wing discourses? It has been suggested that the women's rights movement and multiculturalism cause a need to re-imagine masculinity and whiteness in a turbulent societal setting, where both male privilege and white privilege are questioned. Nevertheless, the current atmosphere in many countries is characterised by hardened attitudes towards women's rights (such as abortion) and towards migration (particularly of Muslims), and they are interlinked with the rise of right-wing populism in the political sphere. The era of 'post-truth' and neo-conservatism and a backlash against women have made it possible for men such as Donald Trump in the United States and Viktor Orban in Hungary to gain major positions of power. Neither Trump nor Orban hides his disregard of women and women's rights. Perhaps on the contrary, Trump's blatant misogyny – besides his explicit racism and outspoken Islamophobia – could be interpreted as one of the reasons for his victory in the 2016 presidential election.

There are thus obvious similarities in the ways transnational right-wing populist movements amplify and gain significant affordances in the transformed media environment. Digitisation, social and participatory media practices, and the decline of legacy media structures (including public service media) have afforded the spread of racism and misogyny. The right-wing populist logic mobilises people transnationally by appealing to them emotionally and by creating a sense of community. The sense of 'us' is produced through feelings of resentment and hatred of others and through an unquestioned and ahistorical sense of entitlement that expresses itself as male privilege and white privilege. By bringing to the fore how Islamophobia and misogyny entwine in right-wing populist discourse and how the conjuncture of various transformations in the media environment tends to facilitate their appeal and spread in one specific case (Finland), this chapter has paved the way to allow scholars to analyse the similarities and differences of similar forces elsewhere in the world.

References

Arter, David 2010. "The breakthrough of another West European populist radical right party? The case of the True Finns", *Government and Opposition* 45(4), 484–504.

Benkler, Yochai 2006. *The Wealth of Networks: How Social Production Transforms Markets and Freedom*. New Haven, CT: Yale University Press.

Chadwick, Andrew 2013. *The Hybrid Media System: Politics and Power*. Oxford: Oxford University Press.

Ellinas, Antonis 2010. *The Media and the Far Right in Western Europe*. Cambridge: Cambridge University Press.

Fekete, Liz 2011. "The Muslim conspiracy theory and the Oslo massacre", *Race & Class* 53 (3), 30–47.

Goldberg, David 2009. *The Threat of Race: Reflections on Racial Neoliberalism*. Oxford: Blackwell.

Grönroos, Simon (ed.) 2016. *Epäneutraali sukupuolikirja. Puheenvuoroja sukupuolikysymyksistä*. Helsinki: Suomen Perusta.

Halla-aho, Jussi 2006a. "Valonpilkahduksia ja Mordorin yötä", *Scripta,* December 14, 2006. www.halla-aho.com/scripta/valonpilkahduksia_ja_mordorin_yota.html. Retrieved 9 May 2019.

Halla-aho, Jussi 2006b. "Monikulttuurisuus ja nainen", *Scripta,* December 20, 2006. www.halla-aho.com/scripta/monikulttuurisuus_ja_nainen.html. Retrieved 25 March 2020.

Halla-aho, Jussi 2011. "Tilastoista ja etnopositiivisuudesta", *Scripta,* October 26, 2011. www.halla-aho.com/scripta/tilastoista_ja_etnopostiivisuudesta.html. Retrieved 31 March 2020.

Halla-aho, Jussi 2020. "Tarinat kertovat naisista ja lapsista", *Twitter,* March 4, 2020. https://twitter.com/Halla_aho/status/1235272656540364802. Retrieved 2 November 2020.

Hatakka, Niko 2019. *Populism in the Hybrid Media System. Populist Radical Right Online Counterpublics Interacting with Journalism: Party Politics and Citizen Activism*. Turku: Turun yliopisto.

Horsti, Karina 2015. "Techno-cultural opportunities: The anti-immigration movement in the Finnish mediascape", *Patterns of Prejudice* 49 (4), 343–366.

Horsti, Karina 2017. "Digital Islamophobia: The Swedish woman as a figure of pure and dangerous whiteness", *New Media and Society* 19 (9), 1440–1457, https://doi.org/10.1177/1461444816642169.

Horsti, Karina & Nikunen, Kaarina 2013. "The ethics of hospitality in changing journalism: The response to the rise of the anti-immigrant movement in Finnish media publicity", *European Journal of Cultural Studies* 16(4), 480–504, https://doi.org/10.1177/1367549413491718.

Jacobs, Kristof & Spierings, Niels 2019. "A populist paradise? Examining populists' Twitter adoption and use", *Information, Communication & Society* 22 (12), 1681–1696.

Jegerstedt, Kari 2012. "Frykten for det feminine. Kjønnssymbolikk og misogyni i Behring Breiviks 'manifest'", in: Østerud, S. (ed.), *22. juli. Forstå – forklare – forebygge*. Oslo: Abstrakt forlag.

Kantola, Johanna & Lombardo, Emanuela 2019. "Populism and feminist politics: The cases of Finland and Spain", *European Journal of Political Research* 58(4), 1108–1128.

Keskinen, Suvi 2013. "Antifeminism and White identity politics. Political antagonisms in radical right-wing populist and anti-immigration rhetoric in Finland", *Nordic Journal of Migration Research* 3 (4), 225–232.

Keskinen, Suvi 2016. "From welfare nationalism to welfare chauvinism. Economic rhetoric, welfare state and the changing policies of asylum in Finland", *Critical Social Policy* 36 (3), 352–370.

Kumar, Deepa 2012. *Islamophobia and the Politics of Empire*. Chicago: Haymarket Books.

Laclau, Ernesto 2005. *On Populist Reason*. London: Verso.

Lähdesmäki, Tuuli & Saresma, Tuija 2014."Re-framing gender equality in Finnish online discussion on immigration", *NORA – Nordic Journal of Feminist and Gender Research* 22 (4), 299–313.

Manne, Kate 2018. *Down, Girl. The Logic of Misogyny*. Oxford: Oxford University Press.

Mickelsson, Rauli 2011. "Suomalaisten nationalistipopulistien ideologiat [The ideologies of Finnish national populists]", in: Matti Wiberg, M. (ed.), *Populismi. Kriittinen arvio*. Helsinki: Edita, 147–174.

MTV 2020. *Kreikan kiristyneet otteet Turkin rajalla jatkuvat.* www.mtvuutiset.fi/artikkeli/kreikan-kiristyneet-otteet-turkin-rajalla-jatkuvat-video-rajalta-nayttaa-turvallisuusjoukkojen-ampuvan-kyynelkaasulla-ja-vesitykeilla-maahan-pyrkivia-pakolaisia/7749708#gs.1j4ggl.

Mudde, Cas 2016. "Europe's populist surge: A long time in the making", *Foreign Affairs* 95, 25–30.

Nikunen, Kaarina 2011. *Enemmän vähemmällä.* Tampere: Tampereen yliopisto.

Nikunen, Kaarina 2015. "Politics of irony as the emerging sensibility of the anti-immigrant debate", in: Andreassen, Rikke & Vitus, Kathrine (eds.), *Affectivity and Race: Studies from Nordic Contexts.* Farnham: Ashgate, 21–42.

Norocel, Cristian, Saresma, Tuija, Lähdesmäki, Tuuli & Ruotsalainen, Maria 2021. Performing 'us' and 'them'. Intersectional analyses of populist right-wing media. *European Journal of Cultural Studies.*

Norris Pippa 2009. *Radical Right.* Cambridge: Cambridge University Press.

Ovaskainen, Teppo 2019. "PS-Nuorten johtohahmo ohjaisi 'ei-valkoiset' ulos maasta – Järjestö kieli keskellä suuta", *Uusi Suomi*, January 2, 2019. www.uusisuomi.fi/kotimaa/268214-ps-nuorten-johto hahmo-ohjaisi-ei-valkoiset-ulos-maasta-jarjesto-kieli-keskella-suuta. Retreived 28 August 2019.

Palonen, Emilia & Saresma, Tuija (eds.) 2017. *Jätkät ja jytkyt. Perussuomalaiset ja populistinen retoriikka.* Tampere: Vastapaino.

Palonen, Emilia & Saresma, Tuija 2019. "Kansallinen ja ylirajainen populismi: eliitinvastaisuutta, anti-intellektuellismia, EU-kriittisyyttä ja naisvihaa", in Ronkainen, Antti & Mykkänen, Juri (eds.), *Vapiseva Eurooppa: Mitä seuraa eurooppalaisen politiikan kaaoksesta.* Tampere: Vastapaino, 111–125.

Pettersson, Katarina 2017. *Save the Nation! A Social Psychological Study of Political Blogs as a Medium for Nationalist Communication and Persuasion.* Helsinki: Helsinki University.

Poggio, Barbara & Bélle, Elisa 2018. "New faces of populism: The Italian 'Anti-Gender' mobilization", in Kovala, Urpo, Palonen, Emilia, Ruotsalainen, Maria & Saresma, Tuija (eds.), *Populism on the loose.* http://urn.fi/URN:ISBN:978-951-39-7401-5.

Pöyhtäri, Reeta, Haara, Paula & Raittila, Pentti 2013. *Vihapuhe sananvapautta kaventamassa.* Tampere: Tampere University Press.

Puar, Jasbir 2007. *Terrorist Assemblages: Homonationalism in Queer Times.* Durham, NC: Duke University Press.

Pyrhönen, Niko 2015. *The True Colours of Finnish Welfare Nationalism: Consolidation of Neo-Populist Advocacy as a Resonant Collective Identity through Mobilization of Exclusionary Narratives of Blue-and-White Solidarity.* SSKH Skrifter 38. Helsinki: University of Helsinki.

Saresma, Tuija 2017. "Väkivaltafantasiat ja pelon politiikka. Sukupuolitetun ja sukupuolittavan verkkovihapuheen luentaa" [Fantasies of violence and Politics of Fear: Reading Gendered and Gendering Hate Speech], in: Karkulehto, Sanna & Rossi, Leena-Maija (eds.), *Sukupuoli ja väkivalta. Lukemisen etiikkaa ja politiikkaa.* Helsinki: SKS, 221–246.

Saresma, Tuija 2018. "Politics of fear and racialized rape: Intersectional reading of the Kempele rape case", in: Hervik, Peter (ed.), *Racialization, Racism, and Anti-Racism in the Nordic Countries.* London: Palgrave Macmillan. https://doi.org/10.1007/978-3-319-74630-2_3.

Saresma, Tuija 2020. "Vihan sfäärit. Valkoisten heteromiesten affektiivinen mobilisaatio sosiaalisessa mediassa" [The spheres of hatred. The affective mobilization of white heterosexual men on social media], in: Rinne, Jenni, Kajander, Anna, & Haanpää, Riina (eds.), *Affektit ja tunteet kulttuurien tutkimuksessa* [Affects and Emotions in Researching Culture]. Helsinki: Ethnos, 196–243.

Saresma, Tuija & Tulonen, Urho 2020. "Halla-ahon ahdistus ja ironia: Ulossulkeva suomalaisuus ja ahdas nationalismi *Scripta*-blogissa" [Halla-aho's anxiety and irony: exclusive Finnishness and narrow nationalism in the blog *Scripta*], in: Nykänen, Elise & Rossi, Riikka (eds.), *Suomalaiset ahdistukset [The Anxieties of the Finns].* Joutsen/Svanen – Erikoisjulkaisu. (In press.)

Statistics Finland 2019. *Joukkoviestinnän markkinatrendit ennallaan vuonna 2018.* www.stat.fi/til/jvie/2018/jvie_2018_2019-11-22_tie_001_fi.html.

Stewart, Julianne, Mazzoleni, Gianpietro & Horsfield, Bruce 2003. "Conclusions: Power to the media managers", in: Mazzoleni, Gianpietro, Stewart, Julianne & Horsfield, Bruce (eds.), *The Media and Neo-Populism: A Contemporary Comparative Analysis.* Westport, CT: Praeger, 217–237.

Suiter, Jane, Culloty, Eileen, Greena, Derek & Siapera, Eugenia 2018. "Hybrid media and populist currents in Ireland's 2016 general election", *European Journal of Communication* 33 (4), 396–412.

Sunstein, Cas 2001. *Echo Chambers. Bush v. Core. Impeachment and beyond.* Princeton, NJ: Princeton University Press.

Taras, Raymond 2013. "'Islamophobia Never Stands Still': Race, Religion, and Culture", *Ethnic and Racial Studies* 36(3), 417–433

Taveira, Rodney & Nyerges, Aaron 2016. "Populism and propaganda in the US culture industries", *Australasian Journal of American Studies* 35 (1), 3–10.

van Dijck, José 2013. *The Culture of Connectivity. A Critical History of Social Media.* Oxford: Oxford University Press.

Werbner, Pnina 2013. "Folk devils and racist imaginaries in a global prism: Islamophobia and anti-Semitism in the twenty-first century", *Ethnic and Racial Studies* 36(3), 450–467.

Wodak, Ruth 2015. *The Politics of Fear: What Right-Wing Populist Discourses Mean.* London: Sage.

Ylä-Anttila, Tuukka 2017. *The Populist Toolkit: Finnish Populism in Action 2007–2016.* Helsinki: Helsingin yliopisto.

Young, Iris Marion 2003. "The logic of masculinist protection: Reflections on the current security state", *Signs* 29 (1), 1–25.

36

SOCIAL MEDIA MANIPULATION IN TURKEY

Actors, tactics, targets

Bilge Yesil

Turkey has recently faced a number of domestic and international developments that range from an economic downturn to a coup attempt, from cross-border military operations to diplomatic crises. Despite the obvious differences in terms of their political, economic, military, and social contexts, these events can nonetheless be studied through a common denominator: the changing sets of tools pro-government actors employ to impose their narratives on social media as the events unfold. This frame provides a means to integrate the variety of social media users engaging in this dynamic: paid or unpaid, anonymous or identified, these users undertake online political messaging in order to suppress critical voices on social media and shore up support the AKP (Justice and Development Party) government and its leader, Recep Tayyip Erdogan. Moreover, these users not only serve a domestic political function but also, together with state actors, undertake information operations in English and other languages to influence global public opinion. For example, in July 2016, when a small group of insurgent military officers affiliated with Erdogan's arch enemy Fethullah Gulen orchestrated a coup to overthrow the government, social media activity on Turkish Twitter reached unprecedented levels. While users from all walks of life overwhelmed the site with news, information, and opinion, government-backed trolls and identifiable pro-AKP accounts carried out a sustained campaign to praise Erdogan and express support for the ongoing purge against putschists (Yildiz and Smets 2019). Meanwhile, news media outlets, already highly partisan and politicised, helped circulate the AKP narrative that Western powers might be using Gulen to destabilise Turkey and that Erdogan and his government could not be accused of human rights violations as they clamped down on the coup plotters. Last, but not least, a myriad of actors consisting of Turkish diplomats and representatives around the world, state agencies, and AKP supporters shared infographics and videos in English to communicate to foreign audiences that Gulen was a terrorist mastermind and that ordinary Turks fought bravely against his soldiers to safeguard democracy.

I begin with this example since it opens up a space for the discussion of information operations undertaken by pro-government users, the proliferation of pro-Erdogan and right-wing nationalist content on social media sites, and the structural conditions of the online sphere in Turkey. In fact, the coup attempt marked an important period in the socio-political, legal, and media processes, stretching over the last decade, that has allowed the AKP and its affiliates to develop tools for the control and manipulation of information online. During the AKP era (2002–present), the majority of news outlets have become vehicles of government propaganda, and journalistic autonomy and professionalism have sustained unprecedented damage. The social media environment is increasingly polarised as pro-AKP users, both paid operatives and average citizens, overwhelm Twitter and Facebook with government narratives and harass dissenters. Obviously, these problems are not specific to Turkey, yet the AKP's digital surveillance schemes and use of legal provisions to silence its critics make social media sites especially vulnerable to the effects of troll harassment and dis/misinformation campaigns.

In this chapter, I first provide an overview of the state of news media and the online public sphere in Turkey. After demonstrating how AKP's attempts to tame both realms over the past decade have made them highly vulnerable to polarisation and politicisation, I proceed to discuss AKP-backed social media operatives as well as other groups. Lastly, I point to some lines of inquiry that might remedy the gaps in literature concerning dis/misinformation campaigns in and from Turkey.

Turkey's news media and online public sphere

Turkey, a country of 80 million, boasts dozens of national newspapers and news channels and hundreds of local print and broadcast outlets. While these numbers might suggest a pluralistic ecosystem, one must keep in mind that news media in Turkey operates under conditions of clientelism, patrimonialism, and the predominance of informal arrangements in the sector. Although Turkey's news media have depended on their ties with the ruling elite for financial survival since at least the neoliberal restructuring of the country in the 1980s, party-press parallelism, marginalisation of critical voices, and the decline in journalistic professionalism reached unprecedented levels during the AKP era. Under the leadership of Erdogan, the AKP neutralised mainstream and oppositional media via legal and financial attacks, such as the prosecution of journalists, expropriation of critical outlets, and levying of tax penalties. In the meantime, it cultivated a number of partisan media conglomerates by distributing privatisation deals, public tenders, cheap credits, and government advertising to loyal businessmen (Kaya and Cakmur 2010; Akser and Baybars-Hawk 2012; Yesil 2016b, 2018; Somer 2016). The extent to which the media have become an integrated tool of the AKP government becomes especially clear during political, economic, and foreign policy crises that challenge the AKP's hegemony. Partisan newspapers use the same headlines and publish similarly worded op-eds, while pro-Erdogan news channels peddle conspiracy theories about myriad actors (the US, Europe, Israel, George Soros, IMF, etc.) supposedly preoccupied with destabilising Turkey. For example, during the nationwide Gezi protests in 2013, one newspaper published a fake interview with Christiane Amanpour in which she allegedly confessed that she and CNN were paid to overreport the Gezi protests in order to weaken Turkey (Fung 2013). Another pro-government newspaper fabricated (using Google Translate) parts of an interview with Noam Chomsky that seemingly defended Erdogan's policies during the Arab Spring (Peker 2013). After the failed coup in 2017, pro-AKP newspapers engaged in smear campaigns against the Open Society Foundation, Amnesty International, and foreign and Turkish academics and philanthropists, accusing them of having secret meetings to overthrow Erdogan and create chaos in Turkey (*Star* 2017).

The online sphere has not been immune to repression, polarisation, and manipulation either. The AKP's earliest attempts at imposing strict controls on online communications came in 2007, with the passage of the country's first Internet Law, which allowed the AKP to criminalise content that it deemed harmful to the youth (Akdeniz and Altiparmak 2008). Soon, government agencies and courts began to use this law and existing anti-terror laws and penal code provisions to ban websites with so-called harmful content, as well as to curb Kurdish political expression that allegedly threatened Turkish national unity. By the end of the 2000s, the number of blocked websites had reached tens of thousands, and users' access to information had been severely limited and freedom of speech violated (Kinikoglu 2014; Yesil 2016a). The AKP's attempts to control the online space intensified in the 2010s as politically engaged citizens, disenchanted with government interference in news media, came to rely on digital outlets to share news and information or to express critical opinions (Tunc 2014; Bulut 2016; Parks et al. 2017; Coskuntuncel 2018). Especially after the nationwide Gezi protests and the revelations of a massive corruption scandal in 2013, the AKP government imposed further restrictions to combat the alleged threats of online communications. The following year, it hastily amended the Internet Law and authorised the blocking of websites without a court order. It also amended the Law on State Intelligence Services and the National Intelligence Organization (MIT), expanding the online surveillance of citizens (Yesil et al. 2017).

After the botched coup in 2016, the AKP declared a state of emergency, under which it passed decree laws that facilitated the interception of digital communications and the collection of private data from state institutions and private companies. Perhaps more worryingly, law enforcement began to call on citizens to inform the authorities of social media users who posted anti-state and/or terrorist content. Since then, it has become customary for the AKP's 'informant network' in state bureaucracy and public institutions and its supporters to report critical voices to the authorities on charges of terrorism (Topak 2017).

Social media manipulation

In addition to creating strict new legal tools to control the digital realm by surveilling and prosecuting users, the AKP began to increase its user presence on social media sites in order to co-opt their information-sharing function, with the goal of suppressing critical news and disseminating government-friendly content. It was during the Gezi protests that the AKP officials came to recognise that social media, especially Twitter, served as a space for protest organisation and as a source of news and information. As the protests were underway and new forms of citizen journalism were beginning to take hold, the AKP hastily began to form its own social media team (Karatas and Saka 2017; Saka 2019). There is no publicly available information as to who put together this team and how, but there are a number of analyses that offer some clues. According to one explanation based on leaked emails, a pro-government NGO operative suggested to Erdogan's son-in-law that 'a team of professional graphic designers, coders, and former army officers with training in psychological warfare' could be formed in order to deliver pro-government messages on Twitter, 'counter critical narratives in foreign media outlets' and 'weaken the protest networks on social media' (Sozeri 2016a). According to Erkan Saka, an academic who conducted interviews with some of the leading pro-AKP Twitter users, private individuals with connections to higher echelons of the party wanted to 'seize the moment' and proposed to form a social media team and/or engaged in pro-government messaging themselves (2018: 165).

Despite the lack of clarity about its beginnings, the AKP's social media team is known to have grown and professionalised a few months after the Gezi protests. In September 2013, a team of 6,000 'volunteers' was formed in order to 'promote the party perspective and monitor online discussions' while 'correcting the [opposing camp] with valid information, always using positive language' (Albayrak and Parkinson 2016). However, in a few months, it became evident that 'hundreds of pro-government accounts mobilize[d] quickly, creating offensive hashtags and pouring on slurs' to intimidate journalists and academics who wrote critical pieces about Erdogan and the AKP (Kizilkaya 2013). These so-called volunteers thus came to be referred to as 'AK trolls', a designation used to draw attention to their aggressive tactics. To this day, the term refers to anonymous or identified, paid or unpaid social media users who engage in online harassment and doxing, as well as orchestrated information operations on behalf of Erdogan and the AKP.

AK trolls and lynch mobs

As Turkey's first 'Twitter army' and one deployed by an authoritarian regime, AK trolls have understandably become the nearly exclusive focus of scholarly analysis in this field (Karatas and Saka 2017; Bulut and Yoruk 2017; Saka 2018; Yesil et al. 2017; Yuksel 2018; Yildiz and Smets 2019; Saka 2019). Who are the AK trolls, then? A network analysis conducted in 2015 revealed that AK trolls comprise two major groups: identifiable users (e.g. party members, cabinet ministers, political consultants, pro-AKP pundits) and anonymous trolls. At the time of this analysis, the central node in the network connecting these two groups was Mustafa Varank, the chief advisor to Erdogan (Saka 2019: 55). As Saka notes, the composition of AK trolls has changed since 2013, tracking intra-party factions, and some prominent AK trolls have even closed their accounts and left the network (Saka 2018). In 2015, the AKP launched a new entity called the 'New Turkey Digital Office' to counter the negative connotations of the troll designation and to quell the internal strife amongst its social media team. The director of the office took pains to distance his 180 employees from AK trolls and noted that they functioned as the AKP's 'digital campaign office'. He also noted that this new entity was simply responsible for creating content about the AKP's and its local municipalities' accomplishments and for monitoring opposition parties' social media messages (Altuntas 2015). Since then, no information has been made available about the New Turkey Digital Office or its activities. However, in 2019, the Oxford Internet Institute, in its 'Global Disinformation Order' report, confirmed the existence of a 'medium capacity team' in Turkey that consists of an estimated 500 'cyber troops', a term used to refer to 'government or political party actors tasked with manipulating public opinion online'. The OII found that the Turkish team is affiliated with a government agency or agencies; its members are active on Facebook and Twitter; and they work primarily to suppress critical voices, amplify pro-government messages, and manipulate media content by creating memes and videos (Bradshaw and Howard 2019: 5, 6, 18, 19). It is unclear how many teams are backed by the AKP for purposes of social media manipulation and whether the AK trolls and the New Turkey Digital Office are the same individuals. However, there is ample information about who the AKP-backed team's targets are and what tactics they use. Among the most prominent targets are journalists and activists who are critical of the AKP, as well as politicians from opposition parties. A study conducted by the International Press Institute in 2016 found that journalists were among the prime targets of AK trolls. They are labelled 'traitors', 'terrorists', 'terrorist supporters', and 'infidels'; humiliated via offensive language, and attacked with sexual insults and threats (especially females) (2016). In their analysis, Karatas and Saka also revealed that AK trolls try to silence journalists, activists, and opposition party politicians as well as ordinary citizens through abusive language, label them 'terrorists' and 'traitors', and threaten them with arrest (2017).

AK trolls' attacks against these targets usually take the form of lynch mobs and unfold in a number of stages. First, prominent AK trolls tweet about an oppositional figure using non-threatening language or take a screenshot of their Twitter posts. Next, they mobilise anonymous trolls who then spam the user in question and/or create an incriminatory hashtag (Sozeri 2015; Saka 2019: 56). Finally, AKP officials and pro-government pundits retweet the incriminating tweets, which are then picked up by pro-Erdogan news media only to be reported as facts. In some cases, pro-AKP users and news outlets even call on the authorities to take action against the individual who's being attacked. For example, when a Turkish-Dutch journalist tweeted a picture of the Turkish flag with the hashtag #FuckErdogan, online vigilantes mobilised, and a prominent AK troll @tahaun (married to First Lady Emine Erdogan's private secretary) called on the police to 'detain this creature this evening'. Soon after, the journalist was arrested and released after a few days, but then blocked from leaving the country (*The Guardian* 2016).

AKP-backed operatives also rely heavily on bots, especially to push their hashtags to the top of trending topic lists (Saka 2019: 59–60). There is no research on the current number of bots used by AKP's teams, but in 2014, two researchers discovered 18,000 bots that were tweeting pro-AKP messages during the local election campaign (Poyrazlar 2014). Bots were used in another social media campaign in 2016 when the hashtag #WeLoveErdogan made it to the top of the trending topics list ahead of Erdogan's visit to the United States. When Twitter removed the hashtag on suspicions of bot activity, AKP officials accused the social media company of censorship and of being a part of a 'global [influence] operation' against Erdogan (*Hurriyet Daily News* 2016).

Pro-government messaging

AKP-backed social media operatives not only troll, dox, and harass critical voices; they also seek to mobilise the party's voter base by disseminating nationalist, religiously informed, and/or populist content. An example of such an information campaign occurred during the coup attempt in July 2016. The botched coup was the top-tweeted event in Turkey since the Gezi protests, especially by pro-government operatives, journalists, and pundits as part of their efforts to overwhelm Twitter with AKP narratives (Yesil et al. 2017: 22; Yildiz and Smets 2019). In their research, Yildiz and Smets describe the coup attempt as a moment of 'extraordinary, often religiously-framed mobilization on Twitter' wherein anonymous trolls, official AKP accounts, and identifiable pro-AKP accounts carried out a sustained campaign (Yildiz and Smets 2019: 350). Their thematic analysis of coup-related posts show that official AKP and identifiable pro-Erdogan accounts generally expressed devotion to Erdogan, asked citizens to attend anti-coup demonstrations, and accused the US and Israel of supporting the coup attempt. In contrast, anonymous trolls adopted threatening, humiliating, and intimidating tones in their posts. Their tweets were marked by binary oppositions such as 'us versus them', and 'the nation versus others' as they attacked journalists and academics and accused them of being 'foreign agents' (364). Such binaries are indeed central to AKP-backed information operations. As Bulut and Yoruk (2017) note, prominent AK trolls often deploy nationalist, populist themes in their Twitter campaigns to construct antagonisms between 'the nation' and 'its enemies'. They frame Turkey as the underdog victimised by the 'West' and Erdogan as the 'man of the people' who is under constant attack by internal and external enemies. In tweets that seek to praise Erdogan, they attribute Turkey's accomplishments to the 'will of the people', especially the pious segments of the population that comprise the backbone of AKP's voter base (4105).

Similar pro-government campaigns occurred during other politically charged episodes such as the constitutional referendum in 2017 and Turkey's military incursion in North Syria in 2019. In June 2020, Twitter announced that it took down a network of 7,340 accounts that consisted of fabricated users and pro-AKP retweet rings. In their analysis of the dataset, researchers at the Stanford Internet Observatory found that this 'influence operation' network was linked to the AKP's youth wing and that it carried out these operations and many others in order to circulate a pro-government narrative and criticize opposition parties (Grossman et al. 2020).

In my ongoing research, I also found that pro-AKP social media operations against the mayor of Istanbul, Ekrem Imamoglu, are laced with similar 'us versus them' and 'native versus other' antagonisms. AKP officials and their proxies in the media relentlessly criticise Imamoglu, an opposition politician who defeated the AKP candidate in local elections in 2019, effectively ending Erdogan and his allies' 25-year reign in Istanbul. On Facebook and Twitter, there are dozens of images of Imamoglu that have been photoshopped to show him as a cross-wearing Christian with a diploma from the masonic school who buys alcohol on trips to the grocery store. Designed to depict Imamoglu as a Western-oriented elite who espouses a foreign, non-Muslim lifestyle and is alienated from ordinary people's values, these social media posts stoke nationalist and religious sentiments. Needless to say, they are also circulated by the predominantly pro-government news media and used as fodder by the AKP as part of its populist politics.

Information operations in the international arena

As noted earlier, existing research on social media manipulation in Turkey has mostly focused on AK trolls and their domestic operations. Yet there are other actors that specifically target foreign audiences to propagandise on behalf of Erdogan and the AKP. In what follows, I provide an overview of these groups and their activities.

Bosphorus Global

Bosphorus Global is an entity founded in 2015 by a pro-Erdogan pundit Hilal Kaplan and her husband. Though they claim Bosphorus Global is an independent NGO, leaked emails have revealed that Kaplan and her husband received direct funding from Berat Albayrak, Erdogan's son-in-law and the minister of treasury and finance (Sozeri 2016b).

Bosphorus Global runs a number of websites and social media accounts to influence both domestic and international public opinion on behalf of Erdogan.[1] According to its website, Bosphorus Global is primarily concerned with Western media representations of Turkey and thus aims to create spaces in the international public sphere wherein 'subaltern groups', such as Turks and Muslims, can voice their viewpoints (Bosphorus Global, Mission n.d.). To this end, Bosphorus Global runs a number of information projects on the web and social media that target both domestic and foreign audiences. Domestic accounts in Turkish primarily involve narratives about exposing Gulen and the PKK, while international accounts aim to fact-check news items published in Western media about Turkey, highlight internal problems of the putative West, and, of course, inform foreign audiences about the Turkey's arch enemies, Gulen and the PKK.

One such account in English is Fact-Checking Turkey, which aims to monitor the 'factual accuracy of various news and claims about Turkey' (Bosphorus Global, Our Projects n.d.). Yet unlike genuine fact-checking initiatives, it relies on AKP officials' or anonymous sources' statements and unverified media reports instead of publicly available and verifiable information (Sozeri 2017). It also prioritises extraneous details over core issues and even engages in political offensives against Erdogan's so-called enemies. Other English-language accounts, Chronicles of Shame and Crackdown Chronicles, are exclusively concerned with the West. Chronicles of Shame seeks to present an 'archive' of various acts of racism and discrimination around the globe against Muslims and refugees and, to this end, publishes abridged versions of news stories from international media on Islamophobia, racism, and human rights violations in Europe and United States. Meanwhile, Crackdown Chronicles focuses on the 'inner political contradictions' of the West: that is, the tensions between Western ideals of democracy and human rights and actual practices of press censorship, police violence, and rights violations in Europe and the US (Crackdown Chronicles n.d.).

Anonymous groups

In addition to Bosphorus Global, there are anonymous accounts that promote pro-Erdogan arguments in the international arena. For example, in July 2016, a few days after the failed coup, a group of users began to circulate a narrative on 4chan that accused Hillary Clinton and the CIA of conspiring with Gulen to topple Erdogan. According to Buzzfeed, these users were 'extremely likely' to be AK trolls, although there is no evidence that confirms this claim. That question aside, the 4chan posts were ultimately picked up by American right-wing media outlets Breitbart and The Daily Caller, both of which published their own stories about so-called links between Gulen and the Clinton Global Initiative (Broderick 2019). Subsequent pieces on Breitbart and The Hill similarly claimed that 'Gulen's vast global network' was a 'cult' and a 'dangerous sleeper terror network'. These pieces were penned by Robert Amsterdam, an AKP attorney working on Gulen's extradition from the US, and Michael Flynn, who at the time received payments from an AKP-affiliated business-man (Amsterdam 2016; Flynn 2016). Shortly after the publication of these pieces, the same pro-Erdogan narrative was picked up by Rudy Giuliani, who began to call for the extradition of Gulen on cable news channels, thus lending the 4chan misinformation campaign a certain level of authority (Broderick 2019).

We do not know whether the anonymous 4chan users planned for American right-wing media and even Trump's personal attorney to pick up their allegations. Regardless, this episode shows how pro-Erdogan information operations can cross borders by leveraging the political salience of symbols foreign to Turkey's domestic context and allow operatives to influence pub-lic opinion internationally as well as in Turkey.

On various occasions, these international operations have also taken the form of hacking. For example, in March and April 2017, a number of German and Dutch state institutions, polit-ical parties and commercial organisations had their websites and social media accounts hijacked. The hackers posted swastikas and a message that read 'A little #OTTOMANSLAP for you, see you on #April16' under the hashtags #naziholland and #nazigermany. April 16 was the date of the referendum in Turkey that would greatly expand Erdogan's powers as president. Some AKP ministers had expressed their intention to hold rallies in Germany and the Netherlands in order to mobilise the Turkish diaspora in those countries. When the German and Dutch governments discouraged and/or rejected the ministers, tensions flared, and Erdogan accused the two coun-tries of being 'Nazi remnants' and said they would 'pay the price' for their treatment of Turkish officials (Jones 2017). To this day, it remains unknown which group(s) carried out the online attacks and whether they were contractors hired by the AKP.

Nationalist hacker groups

Similar nationalistic campaigns have been carried out by groups that openly take responsibility for breaking into foreign websites and social media accounts and are seemingly unaffiliated with the AKP. Amongst these groups is *AyYildiz Tim* (Star and Crescent Team), which self-identifies as 'a voluntary lobbying organisation to counteract cyberattacks against Turkey'. *AyYildiz Tim* hacked the Twitter accounts of former Fox News hosts and contributors and filled their feeds with pro-Erdogan content. The messages they posted in Turkish read, 'You are hacked by the

Turkish cyber army AyYildiz Tim! We got your DM correspondence! We will show you the power of the Turk!' and 'We love the Turks and Muslims in the world. We condemn those who persecute them, especially in the United States, and we share their suffering. We love Turkish soldiers, we love Erdogan, we love Turkey' (Russo 2018).

Another nationalistic hacker group, *Aslan Neferler Tim* (ANT) (Lion Soldiers Team) describes its mission as 'defending the homeland, Islam, nation, flag' and 'safeguarding our country in the cyber world' (Aslan Neferler, n.d.). Informed by ethnic Turkish nationalism, its operations target foreign countries that the group deems threatening to or critical of Turkey. For example, ANT has hacked the website of the Belgian Ministry of Defense, accusing the Belgian government of supporting the PKK, and the websites of Austrian parliament and several ministries and banks because of 'Austria's racism against Muslims' and the Austrian government's criticism of Turkey's human rights record (Souli 2018).[2]

Conclusion

As discussed in this chapter, the information landscape in contemporary Turkey is being polarised and manipulated by a deep-rooted and accelerating process of state intervention through new legislative tools as well as via informal or illegal collusion between state and non-state actors. Turkey's newspapers, news channels, and social media sites constitute fertile ground for dis/misinformation operations, especially given a prevailing political culture premised on 'us versus them' cleavages. Twitter has become the prime site of pro-government operations, especially those that exploit nationalist, populist, and/or conservative politics. Perhaps not as sophisticated or as far-reaching as their Russian and Chinese counterparts, AKP-backed operatives nonetheless troll, hack, and dox intra-party rivals and critical voices, such as journalists, academics, and activists. As discussed in preceding sections, different groups with organisational or ideological ties to the AKP have been working to manipulate the digital sphere by suppressing the opposition and amplifying pro-government content.

The proliferation of pro-AKP information operations present an opportunity for new lines of inquiry. Existing research has shown that AK trolls, pro-AKP accounts, and official AKP accounts participate in the co-production of nationalist, populist, and/or religiously framed information campaigns (Bulut and Yoruk 2017; Yildiz and Smets 2019). Future research can help us reveal how AKP's ideological perspectives shape such social media operations, both qualitatively and quantitatively. It would, for example, be interesting to map potential connections between specific moments of deterioration in the AKP's relations with Western governments, media, and policy circles and the deployment of social media operations to discredit them in the international public sphere. Researchers can also study citizen participation in these campaigns and the predominantly used discursive and visual themes.

As noted earlier, the literature on information operations in Turkey has been overwhelmingly concerned with pro-government actors. Yet there is definitely a need for more analyses of social media operatives who are affiliated with opposition parties, Gulenists, foreign actors, and other potential anti-AKP groups. Other than anecdotal evidence, there is no scientific research on whether and how opposition politicians, citizens, and activist groups critical of Erdogan initiate or participate in information operations. AKP officials and pro-AKP pundits often accuse mainstream secularist politicians, PKK-affiliated actors, Kurdish activists, and Gulenists of carrying out 'influence operations' against Erdogan, but there is no qualitative or quantitative data with which to assess this claim.

Last, but not least, there needs to be more research on social media operations (and their linkages to broadcast and print media) that are designed by the AKP and state organs to propagandise

Turkey's military operations and geopolitical initiatives. For example, when Turkey launched a cross-border military offensive in north Syria in 2019, there was a sustained Twitter campaign to communicate with international audiences. Likewise, when the AKP government carried out similar military operations in 2016 and 2018, it relied on various English language outlets (including the state-run TRT World and Anadolu News Agency, online news sites, NGOs and think tanks, paid social media teams, and volunteers) to amplify friendly content in the international public sphere. It would also be interesting to study whether there are any social media operations that the AKP undertakes in Africa, the Balkans, or the Middle East – all areas where Turkey has military and geopolitical objectives.

Notes

1 Access to Bosphorus Global's Twitter account (@BosphorusGlobal) has been restricted since June 2020 due to 'some unusual activity'.
2 Other nationalist hacker groups include *Akincilar* (Raiders) and the Turk Hack Team. For more information on these groups' hijacking of websites that belong to the Vatican, the Library of Congress and various Greek and Armenian entities, see *The National Herald* 2020.

References

Akdeniz, Y. and Altiparmak, K. (2008) *Internet restricted access: A critical assessment of Internet content regulation and censorship in Turkey*. Ankara, Turkey: Imaj Yayinevi.

Albayrak, A. and Parkinson, J. (2016, September 13) Turkey's government forms 6,000-member social media team. *The Wall Street Journal*. Available at: www.wsj.com/articles/SB100014241278873235270 04579079151479634742

Altuntas, O. (2015, May 18) AKP sosyal medya merkezinde bir gun. *BBC Turkce*. Available at: https://bbc.com/turkce/haberler/2015/05/150515_akp_sosyal_medya

Amsterdam, R. (2016, August 12) Gulen's Islamist cult buys off U.S. politicians in both parties to avoid investigations. *Breitbart*. Available at: www.breitbart.com/radio/2016/08/12/robert-amsterdam-gulens-islamist-cult-buys-off-u-s-politicians-in-both-parties-to-avoid-investigations/

Asker, M. and Baybars-Hawks, B. (2012) Media and democracy in Turkey: Toward a model of neo- liberal media autocracy. *Middle East Journal of Culture and Communication*, 5(3): 302–321.

Aslan Neferler (n.d.) *Hakkimizda kisaca*. Available at: www.aslanneferler.org/hakkimizda

Bosphorus Global (n.d.) *Our mission*. Available at: https://bosphorusglobal.org/en/mission

Bradshaw, S. and Howard, P. N (2019) *The global disinformation order: 2019 global inventory of organised social media manipulation*. Oxford Internet Institute, Oxford University. Available at: https://comprop.oii.ox.ac.uk/wp-content/uploads/sites/93 /2019/09/CyberTroop-Report19.pdf

Broderick, R. (2019, October 18) Turkish trolls working for Erdogan hijacked American right-wing media-and Rudy Giuliani's brain. *BuzzFeedNews*. Available at: www.buzzfeednews.com/article/ryanhatesthis/giuliani-turkey-gulen-erdogan-conspiracy-theory

Bulut, E. (2016) Social media and the nation state: Of revolution and collaboration. *Media, Culture & Society*, 38(4): 606–618.

Bulut, E. and Yoruk, E. (2017) Digital populism: Trolls and political polarisation of Twitter in Turkey. *International Journal of Communication*, 11: 4093–4117.

Coskuntuncel, A. (2018) Privatization of governance, delegated censorship, and hegemony in the digital era: The case of Turkey. *Journalism Studies*, 19(5): 690–708.

Flynn, M. (2016, August 11) Our ally Turkey is in crisis and needs our support. *The Hill*. Available at: https://thehill.com/blogs/pundits-blog/foreign-policy/305021-our-ally-turkey-is-in-crisis-and-needs-our-support

Fung, K. (2013, June 18) Turkish newspaper Takvim publishes fake Christiane Amanpour interview. *HuffPost*. Available at: www.huffpost.com/entry/christiane-amanpour-takvim-turkish-newspaper_n_3460023

Grossman, S., Akis, F. A., Alemdaroglu, A., Goldstein J. A. and Jonsson, K. (2020) *Political retweet rings and compromised accounts: A Twitter influence operation linked to the youth wing of Turkey's ruling party*. Stanford

Internet Observatory, Stanford University. Available at: https://fsi-live.s3.us-west-1.amazonaws.com/s3fs-public/20200611_turkey_report.pdf

Hurriyet Daily News (2016, March 30) Turkish ministers accuse Twitter of plotting against Erdogan. Available at: www.hurriyetdailynews.com/turkish-ministers-accuse-twitter-of-plotting-against-erdogan-97106

International Press Institute (2016, September 13) *Turkey trolls' use of insults stifling reporting.* Available at: www.freemedia.at/feature-turkey-trolls-use-of-insults-stifling-reporting/

Jones, M. (2017, March 15). Twitter accounts hijacked by Turkish hackers who tweet about Nazis. *ValueWalk.* Available at: www.valuewalk.com/2017/03/twitter-accounts-hijacked-turkish-hackers-tweet-nazis/

Karatas, D. and Saka, E. (2017) Online political trolling in the context of post- Gezi social media in Turkey. *International Journal of Digital Television,* 3(1): 383–401.

Kaya, R. and Cakmur, B. (2010) Politics and the mass media in Turkey. *Turkish Studies,* 11(4): 521–537.

Kinikoglu, B. (2014). Evaluating the regulation of access to online content in Turkey in the context of freedom of speech. *Journal of International Commercial Law and Technology,* 9(1): 36–52.

Kizilkaya, E. (2013, November 15) AKP's social media wars. *Al Monitor.* Available at: www.al-monitor.com/pulse/originals/2013/11/akp-social-media-twitter-facebook.html#ixzz6IT2U7dls

Parks, L., Goodwin, H. and Han, L. (2017) 'I have the government in my pocket': Social media users in Turkey, transmit-trap dynamics, and struggles over internet freedom. *Communication, Culture & Critique,* 10(4): 574–592.

Peker, E. (2013, September 5) Turkish newspaper's fake Chomsky interview lost in translation. *The Wall Street Journal.* Available at: https://blogs.wsj.com/emergingeurope/2013/09/05/turkish-newspapers-fake-chomsky-interview-lost-in-translation/

Poyrazlar, E. (2014, March 26) Turkey's leader bans his own Twitter bot army. *Vocativ.* Available at: www.vocativ.com/world/turkey-world/turkeys-leader-nearly-banned-twitter-bot-army/

Russo, C. (2018, January 17) Hackers messaged Donald Trump with former Fox News hosts' Twitter accounts. *HuffPost.* Available at: www.huffpost.com/entry/eric-bolling-greta-van-susteren-twitter-hacked_n_5a5eb17de4b096ecfca88729?ncid =txtlnkusaolp00000603%3B

Saka, E. (2018) Social media in Turkey as a space for political battles: AK trolls and other politically motivated trolling. *Middle East Critique,* 27(2): 161–177.

Saka, E. (2019) *Social media and politics in Turkey: A journey through citizen journalism, political trolling, and fake news.* Lanham, MD: Lexington Books.

Somer, M. (2016) Understanding Turkey's democratic breakdown: Old vs. new and indigenous vs. global authoritarianism. *Southeast European and Black Sea Studies,* 16(4): 481–503.

Souli, S. (2018, March 17) Turkey's band of pro-Erdogan hackers keep trolling Europe. *Vice.* Available at: www.vice.com/en_us/article/wj7enx/turkeys-band-of-pro-erdogan-hackers-keep-trolling-europe

Sozeri, E. K. (2015, October 22) Mapping Turkey's Twitter-troll lynch mobs. *Daily Dot.* Available at: www.dailydot.com/layer8/turkey-twitter-trolls/

Sozeri, E. K. (2016a) RedHack leaks reveal the rise of Turkey's pro-government Twitter trolls. *Daily Dot.* Available at: www.dailydot.com/debug/redhack-turkey-albayrak-censorship/

Sozeri, E. K. (2016b) Pelikan Dernegi: Berat Albayrak, Ahmet Davutoglu'nu neden devirdi? *Medium.* Available at: https://medium.com/@efekerem/pelikan-derneği-berat-albayrak-ahmet-davutoğlunu-neden-devirdi-5fabad6dc7de.

Sozeri, E. K. (2017, May 31) These fake 'fact-checkers' are peddling lies about genocide and censorship in Turkey. *Poynter.* Available at: https://www.poynter.org/fact-checking/2017/these-fake-fact-checkers-are-peddling-lies-about-genocide-and-censorship-in-turkey/

Star (2017, October 21) Kizil Soros Kavala yedi gun sorgulanacak. Available at: http://www.star.com.tr/politika/kizil-soros-kavala-7-gun-sorgulanacak- haber-1266524.

The Guardian (2016, April 24) Dutch journalist arrested in Turkey for criticising Erdogan. Available at: www.theguardian.com/world/2016/apr/24/dutch-journalist-ebru-umar-arrested-in-turkey-for-criticising-erdogan

The National Herald (2020, January 31) Hackers post Turkish flag on #Greece Instagram. Available at: www.thenationalherald.com/283409/hackers-post-turkish-flag-on-greece-instagram-cut-off-photos/

Topak, O. (2017) The making of a totalitarian surveillance machine: Surveillance in Turkey under AKP rule. *Surveillance & Society,* 15(3/4): 535–542.

Tunc, A. (2014) Can pomegranates replace penguins? Social media and the rise of citizen journalism in Turkey. In *Freedom house report: The struggle for Turkey's internet,* pp. 13–16. Available at: https://freedomhouse.org/sites/default/files/2020-02/The_Struggle_for_Turkeys_Internet_Report.pdf

Yesil, B. (2016a) State policy toward online communications and the internet regulatory regime in Turkey. In *Locating emerging media* (eds. Germaine Haleogua and Ben Aslinger), 44–58. London and New York: Routledge.

Yesil, B. (2016b) *Media in new Turkey: The origins of an authoritarian neoliberal state.* Urbana and Champaign, IL: University of Illinois Press.

Yesil, B. (2018) Authoritarian turn or continuity? Governance of media through capture and discipline in the AKP era. *South European Society and Politics,* 23(2): 239–257.

Yesil, B., Sozeri, E. K and Khazraee, E. (2017) *Turkey's internet policy after the coup attempt: The emergence of a distributed network of online suppression and surveillance.* University of Pennsylvania, Center for Global Communication Studies. Available at: https://repository.upenn.edu/cgi/viewcontent.cgi?article=102 1&context=internetpolicyobservatory

Yildiz, E. and Smets, K. (2019) Internet trolling in 'networked' authoritarianism: A qualitative content analysis of tweets by regime supporters and 'AK trolls' in July 2016. *Middle East Journal of Culture and Communication,* 12: 348–368.

Yuksel, H. (2018) Social media strategies of political power: An analysis of the ruling party in Turkey. In *Exploring the role of social media in transnational advocacy* (ed. F. P. Endong), 153–178. Hershey, PA: IGI Global.

37

POPULIST RHETORIC AND MEDIA MISINFORMATION IN THE 2016 UK BREXIT REFERENDUM

Glenda Cooper

On 23 June 2016, the United Kingdom voted narrowly to leave the European Union. The result was a shock for many onlookers after a succession of polls which had predicted a small victory for Remain – those who backed keeping the status quo (What UK Thinks 2016a). Even the primary figures involved in the Leave campaign – Nigel Farage, the leader of the right-wing populist UK Independence Party (UKIP) and Boris Johnson, the Conservative politician who, as prime minister, would eventually go on to facilitate Britain's exit – seemed surprised.

However, the Leave victory, narrow as it was, was not as surprising as politicians and pundits imagined. The debate over Europe followed decades of anti-European rhetoric from politicians on all sides, as well media organisations. The Leave campaign itself built on this and harnessed a message which incorporated classic populist tropes of appealing to ordinary people, criticising elites and 'othering' groups, most notably immigrants.

This chapter will look at the 2016 referendum through a populist and misinformation lens. While scholars agree that news media play a vital role in referendum campaigns, referendums are relatively underexamined compared to elections (Ridge-Newman 2018, 4). Yet referendums campaigns are often more important than election campaigns in determining outcome because of the short-term perceptions of the referendum question, the groups and individuals involved, and the public reaction to the campaign discourse (LeDuc 2002, 145). Populist approaches can therefore be very effective as the referendums are often outside traditional party issues. Research has commonly focused on whether the coverage of referendums is fair and balanced: for example, in the 2014 Scottish independence referendum (Robertson 2014; Tolson 2016). This chapter, however, argues that if news media follow the populist narrative, even while challenging and debunking misinformation, this can end up shaping public reaction.

Another problem is that if news media approach coverage of referendums and elections in the same way, the serious impact of the outcome can be lost. While elections have to be held at least every five years in the UK, for example, the 2016 Brexit[1] referendum could not be similarly rerun.[2] Yet many news media at least began by covering the referendum in the same way as they would an election – concentrating on inter-party strife and potential jockeying for power, particularly amongst the ruling Conservative party (so-called 'blue-on-blue' warfare) and treating many claims about the EU as they would promises made in party political manifestos.

The 2016 referendum was particularly unusual in that the result went contrary to the position that the three main parties (Conservative, Labour, and Liberal Democrat) officially backed. While David Cameron had called the referendum to allow 'the British people to have their say' (BBC 2013), the Remain campaign led by the government did not manage to convince the public. Unlike the Leave campaign, Remain failed to coalesce around a clear, populist slogan or persuade key swing voters. This was reflected in the news coverage, which found the soundbites of the Leave campaign easier to turn into a story or a broadcast package. Even when challenging the Leave campaign narrative, this still gave publicity to the assertions.

Finally, this chapter focuses mainly on news media coverage of the Leave campaign. The role that social media played in the Brexit referendum, particularly the questions around bots and trolls, has been widely debated elsewhere and was undoubtedly influential (Fuchs 2018; Hall et al. 2018; Gorodnichenko 2018; Hanska and Bauchowitz 2017). This chapter, however, seeks to examine the lessons of news coverage in referendums, examining misinformation and populism.

The background to Brexit

The UK's relationship with the EU, and Europe generally, had long been fractious. Anti-European discourse had been relatively unchallenged by the media and both main political parties for decades (Hensmans and van Bommel 2020), often as a balancing act to keep together the union of the four countries which make up the UK (Jones 1998). This led to a cultural anti-Europeanism – whether interpreted through nostalgia for the British Empire, the succession of wars dating back centuries against different European countries, or the idea of English exceptionalism (the narrative of Britain standing alone in the Second World War, for example). As the British empire crumbled and a globalised world advanced, an English populism hardened into Euroscepticism (Hensmans and van Bommel 2020).

The UK was not a founding member of the EU, or the European Communities as it was then called, but joined following a referendum held in 1975 in which 67.2 percent of the electorate voted in favour. Throughout the 1980s and 1990s, there were conflict and uncertainty about the UK's place in Europe. This encompassed both sides of the political divide – with Labour Party policy in 1983 being to leave the community, while rifts in the Conservative party deepened following the decision to join the Exchange Rate Mechanism (ERM) in October 1990 and Margaret Thatcher's resignation as prime minister the following month. The ratification of the Maastricht Treaty, which furthered European integration in 1993 without a referendum, led to increasing Euroscepticism in the Conservative party and the formation of the right-wing UK Independence Party in 1993.

This conflict over the UK's place in Europe was reflected in the media coverage. By the early 1990s, media coverage of the European Union was increasingly hostile in some quarters – for example, headlines such as *The Sun*'s 1990 'Up Yours, Delors', a blast against Jacques Delors, then president of the European Commission. A specific type of mythic storytelling also grew which relied on manipulation and distortion of tales about alleged EU regulation (Henkel 2018), a genre of reporting primarily created by *The Telegraph*'s Brussels correspondent at the time, Boris Johnson (Gimson 2012; Purnell 2011). While supposed bans on prawn cocktail crisps, bent bananas, and crooked cucumbers made for amusing reading, the EU was sufficiently concerned to set up a website to try to counter these 'Euromyths'[3] which were perpetuated.

In the aftermath of the Maastricht Treaty and the BSE crisis, which saw Europe ban imports of British beef,[4] Eurosceptic views on both left and right in the UK hardened and grew from 38 percent in 1993 to 63 percent in 2014 (Curtice and Evans 2015). Meanwhile, UKIP saw increasing success in European elections, moving from third place in the 2004 elections to first place in the 2014 elections with 27.5 percent of the vote (Deacon and Wring 2016) and then winning two national by-elections in 2014.

Faced with increased pressure within his own party and fears about the rise in UKIP's vote share, the Conservative prime minister David Cameron offered an in-out referendum on a renegotiated package with the EU if the party won the 2015 election. At the time, the Conservatives were in coalition with the pro-European Liberal Democrats. Cameron's surprise election victory in 2015 made the referendum inevitable, and he announced on 22 February 2016 that a referendum would be held on 23 June 2016.

Senior Conservative figures, in particular Boris Johnson, the MP and mayor of London, and Michael Gove, the justice secretary, chose to campaign aggressively for Leave, to Cameron's shock and dismay (Rayner 2019). On 24 June 2016, the electorate voted in favour of leaving[5] in England and Wales; Scotland and Northern Ireland's populations had voted to Remain.[6] But overall, the populist cry of 'take back control' had chimed with enough of the electorate for a Leave victory.

Linked to that slogan were three recurring messages, which were at best misleading and at worst disinformation and propaganda. But all three proved particularly potent in the run-up to the referendum and received widespread coverage via both legacy and social media. First was a battle bus slogan that linked £350 million sent to Brussels to funding for the UK's National Health Service (NHS), which was created by the official Vote Leave campaign. Second was the 'Breaking Point' poster, showing a long queue of migrants, which was created by the unofficial Leave.eu campaign. Third was messaging from both campaigns around the alleged imminent accession of Turkey to the EU. The success of all these tropes was embedded deeply in the history of UK populism, which had manifested itself as English exceptionalism and anti-European feeling for decades (Hensman and van Bommel 2020).

The power of this messaging was particularly important because of the volatility of referendum campaigns. Unlike election campaigns, in which party identification and ideological orientations characteristically play a large part, in referendums, some voters may be driven by strongly held beliefs while others may be more susceptible to change (LeDuc 2002). As Zaller (1992) puts it, opinion formation in elections is a combination of information and predisposition. With Brexit there had clearly been both media and political agendas going back decades which were anti-Europe, but polls suggested that this was not a clear-cut outcome. This situation becomes even more acute during referendums, as LeDuc puts it:

> When parties are internally divided, ideological alignments are unclear or an issue is new and unfamiliar to the mass public, voters might be expected to draw more of their information from the campaign discourse. Under these circumstances, the outcome of the contest becomes highly unpredictable.
>
> (LeDuc 2002, 713)

Dekavalla (2018), in her analysis of the 2014 Scottish referendum, refers to two common frames in which elections and referendums are constructed: the strategic game frame (politics as a competition focusing on opponents and win/lose metaphors) and the issue frame (policy issues). While in the Brexit referendum, there was clearly a strategic game frame, encouraged by Leave campaigners (who sought to portray the Conservative politicians Johnson and Gove as an alternative government), the issue frame was also a vital part because of the policies Leave chose to focus on: the economy, the NHS, and immigration, which were also the three most referenced in the media coverage (Moore and Ramsay 2017).

The information that was most successfully both communicated by politicians and replicated in the media appeared to be the Leave campaign's populist appeals. Jagers and Walgrave's 2007 typology of populism suggests that populist parties make appeals across three broad areas. While the Leave/Remain campaigners were not a political party (Vote Leave, for example, included Boris Johnson and Michael Gove from the right-wing Conservatives and Gisela Stuart from the left-wing Labour party, while the Remain coalition had David Cameron and George Osborne from the Conservative government and Alan Johnson from Labour), as populist movements, their appeals can be seen in this light.

The first trope Jagers and Walgrave suggest is appeals made to ordinary people – using language such as 'working people' and 'common sense'. The second is anti-elite appeals – most notoriously characterised in the Brexit campaign by Michael Gove's pronouncement on Sky News that the British public 'had had enough of experts'[7] but also by the way that Leave campaigners characterised the EU as unelected and unaccountable bureaucrats. The third is 'othering' – language which divides people into in-groups and out-groups – to illustrate the difference between the 'British' and the 'other'. In the case of Brexit, the appeal of the £350 million pledge was characterised as the first trope – an appeal to working families and common sense – but was also explicitly linked in Vote Leave messaging to fears of 'others' filling up NHS waiting rooms. The second two not only used 'othering' as a concept but suggested that the metropolitan elite had no idea of the problems caused by immigration.

Both official and unofficial Leave campaigns' use of such populist messages have been characterised as 'post-truth' (Marshall and Drieschova 2019). Dominic Cummings, the architect of Vote Leave and later chief advisor to Prime Minister Boris Johnson, wrote a 19,800-word account of the Leave campaign, in which he talked of creating a succession of 'simple and psychologically compelling stories' (Cummings 2017). The consumption of such narratives was not concerned with fact but with emotion. As Cummings himself pointed out, this approach was not only aimed at Leave voters but also Remainers:

> Almost none of these [graduates] know more about what a Customs Unions is than a bricky in Darlington. They did not vote on the basis of thinking hard about the dynamics of EMU or about how Brussels will cope with issues like gene drives. Millions thought – *there's two gangs and I know which one I'm in.*
>
> (Cummings 2017)

The emotional appeals by Leave, however, were helped by the particular idiosyncrasies of the British media system. According to Hallin and Mancini's (2004) definition of media systems, the UK falls into the North Atlantic/liberal model, categorised in particular by a professional model of broadcast governance and external pluralism: in the UK's case, in the press. This resulted in public service broadcasting adhering to an objectivity norm, in which broadcast news, particularly the BBC, presented contentious claims, particularly by Vote Leave, as one side of an argument rather than analysing them (Gaber 2018, 1020).

At the same time, the majority of the press coverage was firmly Eurosceptic. Startin (2015) divided portrayals of the EU in the British press into Europositive, Euroambivalent, and Eurosceptic. He concluded that tabloids and midmarkets were mainly Eurosceptic, with *The Mirror* being the only one categorised as Euroambivalent. As for the quality press, the majority were both Europositive and Euroambivalent, apart from *The Telegraph*, which was labelled Eurosceptic. The result was highly polarised coverage, with pro-Remain papers emphasising pro-Remain campaigners and arguments, and pro-Leave papers emphasising the pro-Leave equivalents. While the break between quality and tabloid might seem to establish a balanced amount of coverage, researchers at Loughborough University found that by the time of the referendum, in aggregate terms, this produced a 'coverage gap' of 59 percent – 41 percent in favour of Leave campaigners. However, when these differences were weighted by circulation, the difference extended to 82 percent versus 18 percent (Deacon et al. 2016).

The NHS, £350 million, and the battle bus

The UK's National Health Service (NHS) was created in 1948, and the country was the first place in the world where a free health service based on citizenship rather than payment of fees and insurance was implemented. It quickly became part of public life; it is a cliché to say is the closest thing the UK has to a national religion – although that has not stopped politicians or columnists reciting this very mantra (Spence 2017; Toynbee 2018). It has been praised as the 'most civilised achievement of modern government' (Webster 2002, 1). Certainly, the NHS is commonly framed as part of English 'exceptionalism', seen as the envy of the world, even if there are problems domestically as to how it operates. (As a side note, it is worth remembering that while much of English populism looks back to the events of the Second World War and the achievements of its wartime leader Winston Churchill, the creation of the NHS was the act of the post-war Labour government which unseated Churchill in 1945.)

So one of the most controversial claims that went straight to the heart of UK populism was Vote Leave's link between the money that the UK contributed to the EU budget and the suggestion that this could be funding the NHS instead. It was most plainly displayed on the bright red Vote Leave battle bus with the slogan 'We send the EU £350m each week. Let's fund the NHS instead' – a claim that, Vote Leave would later say, was a suggestion rather than a hard promise. The blogger Jon Worth, however, pointed out that early social media posts from Vote Leave's official Twitter account were more specific: 'Let's give the NHS the £350m the EU takes each week' (Worth 2017).

The level of NHS funding has been a constant political debate, and so the linking of the NHS to unaccountable Brussels budgets was a powerful populist trope – one of Cumming's 'compelling psychological stories' – which was articulated by Boris Johnson and Michael Gove in particular. And yet from the very beginning, there were problems with this claim. The £350 million was a gross figure that did not take into account the rebate that the UK received from the EU, as well as the money the UK itself received from the EU (Full Fact 2017). The UK Statistics Authority went on to call the £350 million figure 'misleading' (Dilnot 2016), and the UK fact-checking charity FullFact called it a 'clear misuse of official statistics' (FullFact 2017). Despite numerous complaints to the regulator, the Advertising Standards Authority, no action could be taken because political adverts are exempt from the advertising code (Sweney and Plunkett 2016). And many senior Leave campaigners, such as Iain Duncan Smith, David Davis, and Nigel Farage, went on to distance themselves from the claim in the aftermath of the election (Perraudin 2016; Riley-Smith 2016; Stone 2016).

It may be that the £350 million claim did sway fewer minds than thought. A YouGov poll just before the referendum found that 35 percent felt that leaving the EU would be good for the National Health Service (NHS), compared to 24 percent who thought it would be bad (What UK Thinks 2016b). The respective figures on 23 February (just after the referendum was announced) was 30 percent versus 11 percent, suggesting that there had been a far more rapid rise in those who thought it would be bad. But, as Reid (2019) points out, the main problem for Remainers was that the £350 million figure, even if incorrect, focused the overall debate beyond the NHS on the costs, not the benefits, of EU membership and 'problematis[ed] the epistemic authority of some bodies and figures, and in doing so erod[ed] the set of common factual reference points in the debate'. Without agreed 'facts' – or at least a common agreement on how to define such figures – the mutual justification necessary for democratic norms begins to fall apart.

Phillips, when talking about troll culture, notes that journalists are put in an invidious position, guided by the basic tenet to publish newsworthy information – the information imperative. However, while she is clear that this can serve a critical democratic function, this can also be 'harnessed as a tool of manipulation, a point exacerbated by the ubiquity of social media' (2018, 8). Between 20 February 2016, just before the referendum was announced, and 25 June 2016, after the referendum was held, there were 396 stories in the UK media which mentioned £350 million and the NHS within close proximity.[8] For example, *The Independent*, a left-leaning quality paper characterised as a Europositive/Euroambivalent newspaper (Startin 2015), carried fifty-five stories which referred to the £350 million and the NHS. Of these only six did not explicitly challenge the £350 million figure. Two of these were commentary on a referendum debate, two were election results pieces, and two were reviews of television coverage including the cancellation of the popular entertainment programme, *Loose Women*, on the day after the election. This meant, however, that the story, even if challenged, was part of the wider narrative Leave had set up.

The same was true of many of the other headlines about the £350 million claim which reported on the criticism, by people such as Sir Andrew Dilnot, chair of the UK Statistics Authority, and the MP Sarah Wollaston, a trained doctor herself, who left the Leave campaign over this figure; the sheer amplification of the story meant that it was a success for Leave.

The message was complicated further because of complications around public service broadcasters' need for 'due impartiality', particularly during electoral periods.[9] The broadcasting regulator Ofcom defines the concept as follows:

> 'Due' is an important qualification to the concept of impartiality. Impartiality itself means not favouring one side over another. 'Due' means adequate or appropriate to the subject and nature of the programme. So 'due impartiality' does not mean an equal division of time has to be given to every view, or that every argument and every facet of every argument has to be represented.

The BBC had previously been criticised for false equivalence over its coverage of climate change (Jones 2011), and there were concerns that it and other broadcasters failed to interrogate fully the claims made on both sides in the Brexit referendum (Suiter 2016), something that the BBC's director of news challenged in the aftermath (Harding 2016). But Gaber (2018) reported that BBC journalists said that they were being required to give great prominence to Leave because they had not reported unsubstantiated Leave assertions earlier in the campaign. As one BBC journalist put it:

> I was going back to 'Leave' to say that your press releases are rubbish. I would ask them to harden up the stories. I remember whilst working on a Sunday night package being told that I had to have more Leave clips than Remain. I was delivering unbalanced packages possibly to compensate for some earlier imbalance.
>
> (BBC Anonymous cited in Gaber 2018, 1022)

The continued debate around the bus with its £350 million slogan meant it became one of the most enduring images of Brexit – to the extent that when Boris Johnson, during his bid to become the Conservative party leader in 2019, said that he made model buses out of wine boxes to relax, there was immediate speculation that he was trying to game the Google algorithm to push references to the £350 million pledge further down the search page (Stokel-Walker 2019). The particular power of the bus pledge, however, was because of the close association that it created between the NHS and immigration, another of Cumming's 'compelling stories'.

A British Social Attitudes survey the year before revealed that 63 percent of respondents thought the NHS was being stretched by immigration (British Social Attitudes 2016). The Leave campaign repeatedly argued that migration from the EU put pressure on public services, resulting in longer queues for doctors' appointments and for surgery, rather than it being the responsibility of domestic government spending decisions. One of Vote Leave's most striking messages was their referendum broadcast, which contrasted the fate of a frail older woman and her health care both within and outside the EU.[10] After a graphic suggesting how many migrants might come to the UK if Turkey were to join the EU, the screen split,

> showing (staying in the EU) a surly foreign man elbowing a tearful elderly white woman out of the queue in A&E while (leaving the EU) the woman is contentedly treated without having to wait.
>
> (Shaw 2019)

Shaw sees the imagery in this broadcast as a clear homage to the Conservative politician Enoch Powell's 1968 'rivers of blood' speech, which described an elderly white woman living in a street taken over by immigrants.[11] The broadcast also employed another nostalgic trope included in the broadcast – the '*Dad's Army* style arrows swooping across the continent towards Britain'[12] (Wheeler 2016), indicating the possible numbers of Albanians, Turks, and others who could head to the UK if they were permitted to join the EU. As Cummings himself put it:

> Immigration was a baseball bat that just needed picking up at the right time and in the right way. . . . The right way was via the NHS (unifying) – not 'we want our country back' of Farage (divisive).
>
> (Cummings 2017)

This narrative was again picked up by the mainstream media whether it backed the Leave argument or not. A Nexis search of stories with immigration/immigrant in close proximity to the NHS retrieved 2,793 stories between 20 February 2016 and 25 June 2016.[13] Again, looking at *The Independent* – a Europositive/Euroambivalent publication, in which immigration was presented positively – there were still 100 stories in a 17.5-week period – on average more than 5 a week that linked these two things. For more Eurosceptic publications, such as *The Telegraph*, its online site had 214 stories, and *The Mail* online had 196 – 12 stories and 11 stories, respectively, a week. While the sheer weight of story numbers reflects that the limitless space online has, as opposed to print media, previous research has shown that online media tends to portray immigrants, refugees, and asylum seekers more often as threats than print media does (Blumell et al. 2020).

Breaking point and Turkey

Immigration generally was integral to both the official Vote Leave campaign and the unofficial Leave.eu campaign. It had been a salient issue for several years and covered widely in the media. After the accession of Central and East European states to the EU in 2004, many UK voters had become increasingly concerned about migration (Heath and Tilley 2005; McLaren and Johnson 2007). The 2015 refugee crisis, which had seen those fleeing Syria end up in different European countries, had seen an intensified anti-immigration narrative in the British press (Berry et al. 2016; Chouliaraki et al. 2017) and amongst political figures. This was seen even amongst Remainers in the referendum debate, complicating things for those who then tried to argue in favour of the EU. For example, Cameron had repeatedly pledged to bring down immigration figures and had referred to a 'a swarm of people coming across the Mediterranean, seeking a better life, wanting to come to Britain', phraseology he was condemned for (Taylor et al. 2015).

By the time of the 2016 referendum, immigration was ranked as the most important issue in the country – the highest level since 1999 and rising ten percentage points between May 2016 and June 2016 (Ipsos Mori 2016). Goodwin and Milazzo (2017) found that public support for leaving the EU was significantly stronger in areas where there had been high rates of ethnic demographic change before the referendum. The researchers also found that Remainers were also more likely to switch to Leave if they experienced rising levels of immigration. As a result, the decision of the Leave campaigns to focus on immigration issues, particularly towards the end of the campaign, was effective.

The oft-repeated mantra 'take back control' by Leavers was a deliberately ambiguous phrase (Gietel-Basten 2016, 673) and thus often a thinly veiled way of referencing immigration (Browning 2019). The number of articles referencing immigration reflected this, rising fourfold per week from mid-April until the referendum day (Moore and Ramsay 2017, 29). But this was a message that resonated. During the election campaign, the most unsubtle visualisation of this was UKIP's 'Breaking Point' poster.

The poster, unveiled by UKIP's leader Nigel Farage the week before the referendum, was widely condemned. It portrayed a long queue of (mostly) non-white men and the headline 'Breaking Point: The EU has failed us all'. It emerged that the picture was of Syrian migrants at the Croatian/Slovenian border – although Britain's refusal to sign the Schengen Agreement meant that such migrants would find it nearly impossible to enter the UK. But while the picture might have been factually inaccurate, the framing was clear. As Morrison (2016) suggests:

> This was UKIP's crystallisation of the fabled Cameron 'swarm'. Its malice lay in the fact that it simultaneously suggested a threefold untruth: that the inward migration encouraged by our EU membership is a non-white phenomenon; that it principally involves young, able-bodied males who can only be coming to steal our jobs and livelihoods; and that it is a Trojan horse for importing Islamist (ergo 'Middle Eastern-looking') terrorists.
>
> (Morrison 2016, 66)

The architects of Vote Leave distanced themselves from the poster – with Michael Gove saying that he 'shuddered' when he saw it (Simons 2016). It was compared to the aesthetics of 1930s propaganda (Wright 2016) and reported to the police for racial hatred (Stewart and Mason 2016). On the same day as the poster was launched, a man with far-right views fatally stabbed and shot Labour MP Jo Cox, shouting 'Britain first' as he attacked her and, when asked to give his name for the record in court, responded 'death to traitors, freedom for Britain' (Booth et al. 2016). Farage withdrew the poster after the death of Cox, although he said that it was only unfortunate timing and that it was wrong to link the MP's assassination to any arguments he or Gove might have made (ITV News 2016).

While the official Vote Leave campaign separated itself from such Leave.eu outputs, their focus also remained on immigration. The main Vote Leave communications via the website were clear: on the page titled Why Vote Leave? it stated that Turkey was joining the EU, along with Albania, Macedonia, Montenegro, and Serbia. The populations of each were given, with another big red arrow pointing from the region to the UK (Vote Leave 2016). This was followed by a poster stating that 'Turkey (population 76 million) is joining the EU' (Boffey and Helm 2016). But, although Turkey had begun accession talks in 2005, the pace of progress had been slow and stormy, and Turkey's record on human rights and the increasing authoritarianism of Recep Tayyip Erdogan's government had effectively put paid to any prospect of Turkey joining (Reuters 2019).

Yet in their study of UK media coverage of the referendum, Moore and Ramsay (2017) found that Turkey was most likely to be associated with immigration in the national press. Out of 461 articles that mentioned Turkey, 109 had a negative portrayal of Turkey or its citizens, in terms of criminality or the pressure that would be put on UK public services if Turkey joined the EU. Just 2 articles were positive – about statements Boris Johnson had made about his pride in his Turkish ancestry (2017, 107).

This was not surprising, given the common approach to immigration coverage and not just in the UK. Studies show that news media frequently portray those seeking asylum as an economic and security risk, for example (Caviedes 2015; Esses et al. 2013; KhosraviNik 2010; Parker 2015; Philo et al. 2013). In the UK news media, refugees, asylum seekers, immigrants, and migrants were often framed as 'dangerous criminals' and articles suggested 'that Britain is under attack from migrants, particularly asylum seekers and refugees' (International Policy Institute 2004, 42). This was aided by a long-standing approach by politicians on both sides of the political spectrum[14] to sound tough on immigration and raise issues of pressure on public services, rather than utilise other reports (e.g. Dustman and Frattini 2014, which found a positive contribution from immigrants).

Turkey became a useful conduit to combine EU migration and the refugee crisis in voters' minds, which allowed Vote Leave 'to play on the idea of the existential future of Europe . . . ageing, declining and weakening on the global stage . . . surrounded by hotbeds of population growth, poverty and fanaticism' (Gietel-Basten 2016, 676)

Conclusion

> Pundits and MPs kept saying 'why isn't Leave arguing about the economy and living standards'. They did not realise that for millions of people, £350m/NHS was about the economy and living standards – that's why it was so effective. It was clearly the most effective argument not only with the crucial swing fifth, but with almost every demographic. Even with UKIP voters it was level-pegging with immigration. Would we have won without immigration? No. Would we have won without £350m/NHS? All our research and the close result strongly suggests No. Would we have won by spending our time talking about trade and the Single Market? No way.
>
> *(Cummings 2017)*

In his influential work on populism, Mudde (2004) talked about the 'populist zeitgeist', which is facilitated by 'the media's preference for and receptivity to populist actors' (Aalberg and de Vreese 2017, 3). The success of the Leave campaigns in channelling populist messaging that had been utilised by politicians and media before the referendum meant that they managed to frame much of the debate.

Esser et al. (2017) distinguish between populism *by* and *through* the media. The first is the phenomenon by which media actively performs populism themselves – aligning themselves with or actively celebrating 'the people' (Moffit 2018). This was seen particularly strongly on referendum day, when front pages aligned themselves with their readers – whether *The Sun's* 'Independence Day' or *The Guardian's* 'Who do we want to be?' (Brady 2016) and *The Daily Mail's* headline the day after: 'Take a Bow Britain!' (Daily Mail 2016). The editorial – the voice of the paper, which is usually confined to inside pages – congratulated voters on withstanding 'hysterical threats and terrifying scares . . . insults and abuse' from 'self-serving elites'. Throughout the editorial, the pronoun *we* was used, the paper directly eliding itself with its readers.

As regards populism through the media, Moffit (2018, 242) defines this as the way media 'cover, promote and "set the stage"' for political populism. This may not necessarily be endorsing populist messages themselves, but by continually reporting on such actors, they inadvertently amplify them and their claims, resulting in the media becoming 'powerful mobilisation tools for populist causes' (Mazzoleni 2008, 50). This was the case with Brexit. Even though many of the arguments made by the Leave campaigns were often debated by journalists who reported on challenges to the £350 million figure, for example, or fact-checked claims themselves, the amplification of such arguments meant that the narrative was shaped by Leave.

Leave also benefited from an anti-European populist rhetoric articulated by both right-wing politicians and the right-wing media that had not been challenged for decades. This meant that it was complicated for those on the Remain side, now trying to make a positive case for staying in the EU. David Cameron himself had made a series of (unfulfilled) pledges on immigration, and the previous Labour government had employed a sustained discourse that constructed asylum seekers as threats and potential criminals (Innes 2010). It was therefore unsurprising that it proved difficult to overcome the arguments that Leave employed around criminality and border controls, when they were similar to ones that politicians had deployed earlier themselves.

Added to that, public service broadcasters who found themselves trying to negotiate a sense of balance combined with a mainly Eurosceptic press meant that misleading statements were either seen as one side of an argument or, even when they were rigourously pursued, sustained the narrative of cost rather than benefit of membership of the European Union in the public discourse. As LeDuc (2002) points out, the outcomes of referendums are often unpredictable, and short-term strategies and tactics can make a substantial difference, despite partisanship and ideology. The Leave campaigns' use of populist rhetoric combined with misinformation managed to overcome the supposed advantage of Remain, which had the main three parties backing it, along with business leaders, but which failed to encapsulate its message in a way that connected to the electorate.

Notes

1 An abbreviation for British exit from the EU.
2 The 2016 referendum was not binding legally as Parliament is sovereign in the UK but was seen as politically binding. For more discussion on this, see https://fullfact.org/europe/was-eu-referendum-advisory/.
3 The original EC website has now been archived post Brexit, but Euromyths can be found at www.europarl.europa.eu/unitedkingdom/en/media/euromyths.html.
4 BSE (bovine spongiform encephalopathy), otherwise known as mad cow disease, has mainly affected cattle in the UK, where millions of animals had to be destroyed in the 1990s. The ban on British exports was put in place after BSE was linked to Creutzfeldt-Jakob Disease (CJD), a disease that causes paralysis and death in humans.
5 Cameron resigned and was replaced by Theresa May. For the next three years, May struggled to facilitate an acceptable withdrawal from the EU; she resigned as prime minister on 24 July 2016 and was succeeded by Johnson, who finally succeeded in achieving withdrawal from the EU on 31 January 2020.
6 The UK would eventually leave the EU on 31 January 2020, under the premiership of Boris Johnson.

7 See www.youtube.com/watch?v=GGgiGtJk7MA.

8 Search was done on Lexis Nexis looking at £350m near/25 NHS (i.e. between 25 words, within the same paragraph) between 20 February 2016 and 25 June 2016. Search results included newspapers, web-based publications, video, news transcripts, audio, news, magazines, and journals based in the UK and Northern Ireland.

9 See www.ofcom.org.uk/tv-radio-and-on-demand/broadcast-codes/broadcast-code/section-five-due-impartiality-accuracy.

10 This has now been removed from the internet, although a description of it can be found at www.bbc.co.uk/news/uk-politics-eu-referendum-36367247.

11 The speech strongly criticising mass immigration was made in Birmingham on 20 April 1968, just before the second reading of the government's race relations bill. It caused an uproar, and Powell was dismissed from his role in the Shadow Cabinet by the Conservative leader Edward Heath.

12 *Dad's Army* was a popular BBC sitcom which ran from 1968 to 1977 and is still regularly repeated. It was based on the activities of the Home Guard in the Second World War. The Home Guard were local volunteers for a citizen militia comprising those too young, too old, or in reserved occupations, who would mobilise to delay any Nazi invasion. The opening graphics portrayed Nazi arrows advancing on Britain, only to be pushed back by union flag arrows representing the Home Guard.

13 A Lexis-Nexis search was done comprising 'immigra* near/25 NHS' between 20 February 2016 and 25 June 2016. Search results included newspapers, web-based publications, video, news transcripts, audio, news, magazines, and journals based in the UK and Northern Ireland,

14 For example, Labour prime minister Gordon Brown's 'British jobs for British workers', which caused controversy and was taken up by strikers.

References

Aalberg, T. & de Vreese, C., 2017. "Introduction: Comprehending populist political communication", in Aalberg, T., Esser, F., Reinemann, C., Stromback, J. & de Vreese, C. eds. *Populist political communication in Europe*. New York: Routledge, pp. 3–11.

BBC News, 2013, 23 January-last update. *David Cameron promises In-Out referendum on EU* [Homepage of BBC], [Online]. Available at: www.bbc.co.uk/news/uk-politics-21148282 [1 July 2020].

Berry, M., Garcia-Blanco, I. & Moore, K., 2016. *Press coverage of the refugee and migrant crisis in the EU: A content analysis of five European countries*. Cardiff: Cardiff School of Journalism, Media and Cultural Studies.

Blumell, L.E., Bunce, M., Cooper, G. & McDowell, C., 2020. "Refugee and asylum news coverage in UK print and online media", *Journalism Studies*, vol. 21, no. 2, pp. 162–179.

Boffey, D. & Helm, T., 2016, 22 May-last update. *Vote leave embroiled in race row over Turkey security threat claims* [Homepage of The Guardian], [Online]. Available at: www.theguardian.com/politics/2016/may/21/vote-leave-prejudice-turkey-eu-security-threat [28 June 2020].

Booth, R., Dodd, V., Rawlinson, K. & Slawson, N., 2016, 18 June-last update. *Jo Cox murder suspect tells court his name is 'death to traitors, freedom for Britain'* [Homepage of The Guardian], [Online]. Available at: www.theguardian.com/uk-news/2016/jun/18/thomas-mair-charged-with-of-mp-jo-cox [24 June 2020].

Brady, J., 2016, 23 May-last update. *Referendum front pages: UK and European newspapers make the case for and against as polls open* [Homepage of The Drum], [Online]. Available at: www.thedrum.com/news/2016/06/23/referendum-front-pages-uk-and-european-newspapers-make-case-and-against-eu-polls [29 June 2020].

British Social Attitudes, 2016. *Big majority believe immigration increases pressure on schools and hospitals* [Homepage of British Social Attitudes], [Online]. Available at: www.bsa.natcen.ac.uk/media-centre/archived-press-releases/bsa-33-big-majority-believe-immigration-increases-pressure-on-schools-and-hospitals.aspx [29 June 2020].

Browning, C.S., 2019. "Brexit populism and fantasies of fulfilment", *Cambridge Review of International Affairs*, vol. 32, no. 3, pp. 222–244.

Caviedes, A., 2015. "An emerging 'European' news portrayal of immigration?", *Journal of Ethnic and Migration Studies*, vol. 41, no. 6, pp. 897–917.

Chouliaraki, L., Georgiou, M., Zaborowski, R. & Oomen, W.A., 2017. *The European 'migration Crisis' and the media: A cross-European press content analysis*. London and Utrecht: London School of Economics and Utrecht University.

Cummings, D., 2017, 9 January-last update. *How the Brexit referendum was won* [Homepage of The Spectator], [Online]. Available at: www.spectator.co.uk/article/dominic-cummings-how-the-brexit-referendum-was-won [10 June 2020].

Curtice, J. & Evans, G., 2015. "Britain and Europe: Are we all Eurosceptics now?", *British Social Attitudes: The 32nd Report*. London: NatCen Social Research.

Daily Mail, 2016, 24 June-last update. *Take a bow Britain!* [Homepage of the Daily Mail], [Online.] Available at: www.dailymail.co.uk/debate/article-3659143/DAILY-MAIL-COMMENT-bow-Britain-quiet-people-country-rise-against-arrogant-touch-political-class-contemptuous-Brussels-elite.html[29 June 2020].

Deacon, D. & Wring, D., 2016, "The UK independence party, populism and the British news media: Competition, collaboration or containment?", *European Journal of Communication*, vol. 31, no. 2, pp. 169–184.

Deacon, D., Wring, D., Harmer, E., Downey, J. & Stanyer, J., 2016, "Hard evidence: Analysis shows extent of press bias towards Brexit", *The Conversation*, vol. 16.

Dekavalla, M., 2018. "Issue and game frames in the news: Frame-building factors in television coverage of the 2014 Scottish independence referendum", *Journalism*, vol. 19, no. 11, pp. 1588–1607.

Dilnot, A., 2016, 27 May-last update, *UK Statistics Authority statement on the use of official statistics on contributions to the European Union* [Homepage of UK Statistics Authority], [Online]. Available at: www.statisticsauthority.gov.uk/news/uk-statistics-authority-statement-on-the-use-of-official-statistics-on-contributions-to-the-european-union/ [24 June 2020].

Dustmann, C. & Frattini, T., 2014. "The fiscal effects of immigration to the UK", *The Economic Journal*, vol. 124, no. 580, pp. F593–F643.

Esser, F., Stępińska, A. & Hopmann, D.N., 2017. "Populism and the media. Cross-national findings and perspectives", in Aalberg, T., Esser, F., Reinemann, C., Stromback, J. & De Vreese, C. eds., 2016. *Populist political communication in Europe*. New York: Routledge, pp. 365–381.

Esses, V.M., Medianu, S. & Lawson, A.S., 2013. "Uncertainty, threat, and the role of the media in promoting the dehumanization of immigrants and refugees", *Journal of Social Issues*, vol. 69, no. 3, pp. 518–536.

Fuchs, C., 2018. *Nationalism 2.0: The making of Brexit on social media*. London: Pluto Press.

Full Fact, 2017, 19 September-last update. *£350 million EU claim "a clear misuse of official statistics"* [Homepage of Fullfact.org], [Online]. Available at: https://fullfact.org/europe/350-million-week-boris-johnson-statistics-authority-misuse/ [24 June 2020].

Gaber, I., 2018. "New challenges in the coverage of politics for UK broadcasters and regulators in the 'post-truth' environment", *Journalism Practice*, vol. 12, no. 8, pp. 1019–1028.

Gietel-Basten, S., 2016. "Why Brexit? The toxic mix of immigration and austerity", *Population and Development Review*, pp. 673–680.

Gimson, A., 2012. *Boris: The Adventures of Boris Johnson*. London: Simon and Schuster UK.

Goodwin, M. & Milazzo, C., 2017. "Taking back control? Investigating the role of immigration in the 2016 vote for Brexit", *The British Journal of Politics and International Relations*, vol. 19, no. 3, pp. 450–464.

Gorodnichenko, Y., Pham, T. & Talavera, O., 2018. *Social media, sentiment and public opinions: Evidence from# Brexit and# USElection* (No. w24631). National Bureau of Economic Research.

Hall, W., Tinati, R. & Jennings, W., 2018. "From Brexit to Trump: Social media's role in democracy", *Computer*, vol. 51, no. 1, pp. 18–27.

Hallin, D.C. & Mancini, P., 2004. *Comparing media systems: Three models of media and politics*. New York: Cambridge University Press.

Hänska, M. & Bauchowitz, S., 2017. "Tweeting for Brexit: How social media influenced the referendum", in Mair, J., Clark, T., Fowler, N., Snoddy, R. & Tait, R., eds., *Brexit, Trump and the media*. Bury St Edmunds: Abramis, pp. 31–35.

Harding, J., 2016, 24 September-last update. *A truly balanced view from the BBC: Don't blame us for Brexit* [Homepage of The Guardian], [Online]. Available at: www.theguardian.com/commentisfree/2016/sep/24/dont-blame-bbc-for-brexit-false-balance [22 June 2020].

Heath, A.F. & Tilley, J.R., 2005. "British national identity and attitudes towards immigration", *International Journal on Multicultural Societies*, vol. 7, no. 2, pp. 119–132.

Henkel, I., 2018. "How the laughing, irreverent Briton trumped fact-checking: A textual analysis of fake news in British newspaper stories about the EU", *Journalism Education*, vol. 6, no. 3, pp. 87–97.

Hensmans, M. & van Bommel, K., 2020. "Brexit, the NHS and the double-edged sword of populism: Contributor to agonistic democracy or vehicle of ressentiment?", *Organization*, vol. 27, no. 3, pp. 370–384.

Innes, A.J., 2010. "When the threatened become the threat: The construction of asylum seekers in British media narratives", *International Relations*, vol. 24, no. 4, pp. 456–477.

International Policy Institute, 2004. *Media image, community impact. Assessing the impact of media and political images of refugees and asylum seekers on community relations in London*. London: Kings College London.

Ipsos Mori, 2016, 23 June-last update. *Concern about immigration rises as EU vote approaches* [Homepage of Ipsos Mori], [Online]. Available at: www.ipsos.com/ipsos-mori/en-uk/concern-about-immigration-rises-eu-vote-approaches [24 June 2020].

ITV, 2016, 20 June-last update. *Nigel Farage: It's wrong to link motives behind Jo Cox death to Brexit campaign* [Homepage of ITV News], [Online]. Available at: www.itv.com/news/2016-06-20/nigel-farage-its-wrong-to-link-motives-behind-jo-cox-death-to-brexit-campaign/ [24 June 2020].

Jagers, J. & Walgrave, S., 2007. "Populism as political communication style: An empirical study of political parties' discourse in Belgium", *European Journal of Political Research*, vol. 46, no. 3, pp. 319–345.

Jones, E. 1998. *The English nation: The great myth*. Stroud, UK: Sutton Publishing.

Jones, S., 2011, July-last update. *BBC Trust review of impartiality and accuracy of the BBC's coverage of science* [Homepage of BBC], [Online]. Available at: http://downloads.bbc.co.uk/bbctrust/assets/files/pdf/our_work/science_impartiality/science_impartiality.pdf [24 June 2020].

KhosraviNik, M., 2010. "The representation of refugees, asylum seekers and immigrants in British newspapers: A critical discourse analysis", *Journal of Language and Politics*, vol. 9, no. 1, pp. 1–28.

LeDuc, L., 2002. "Referendums and elections: How do campaigns differ?", *Routledge ECPR Studies in European Political Science*, vol. 25, pp. 145–162.

Marshall, H. & Drieschova, A. 2019. "Post-truth politics in the UK's Brexit Referendum", *New Perspectives: Interdisciplinary Journal of CEE Politics and IR*, vol. 26, no. 3, pp. 89–105.

Mazzoleni, G., 2008. "Populism and the media", in Albertazzi, D. & McDonnell, D., eds., *Twenty-first century populism*. Basingstoke and New York: Springer, pp. 49–64.

McLaren, L. & Johnson, M., 2007. "Resources, group conflict and symbols: Explaining anti-immigration hostility in Britain", *Political Studies*, vol. 55, no. 4, pp. 709–732.

Moffitt, B., 2018. "Populism and media in Western Europe", in *Routledge handbook of global populism*. London: Routledge, pp. 235–248.

Moore, M. & Ramsay, G., 2017. *Acrimonious and divisive: The role the media played in Brexit*. Available at: https://blogs.lse.ac.uk/brexit/2017/05/16/acrimonious-and-divisive-the-role-the-media-played-in-brexit/ [29 October 2020].

Morrison, J, 2016. "Break-point for Brexit? How UKIP's image of 'hate' set race discourse reeling back decades", in Jackson, D., Thorsen, E. & Wring, D., eds., *EU referendum analysis 2016: Media, voters and the campaign*. Poole: Bournemouth University, pp. 66–67.

Mudde, C., 2004. "The populist zeitgeist", *Government and Opposition*, vol. 39, no. 4, pp. 541–563.

Parker, S., 2015. " 'Unwanted invaders': The representation of refugees and asylum seekers in the UK and Australian print media", *ESharp*, vol. 23, no. 1, pp. 1–21.

Perraudin, F., 2016, 26 June-last update. *Iain Duncan Smith backtracks on leave side's £350m NHS claim* [Homepage of The Guardian], [Online]. Available at: www.theguardian.com/politics/2016/jun/26/eu-referendum-brexit-vote-leave-iain-duncan-smith-nhs [25 June 2020].

Phillips, W. 2018. "The oxygen of amplification", *Data & Society*, vol. 22.

Philo, G., Briant, E. & Donald, P., 2013. *Bad news for refugees*. London: Pluto Press.

Purnell, S., 2011. *Just Boris: A tale of blond ambition-a biography of Boris Johnson*. London: Aurum Press Limited.

Rayner, G., 2019. *David Cameron: Boris Johnson asked if Michael Gove had 'cracked' following betrayal in 2016* [Homepage of The Telegraph], [Online]. Available at: www.telegraph.co.uk/politics/2019/09/15/boris-johnson-allies-jump-defence-david-cameron-claims-pm-chose/ [1 July 2020].

Reid, A., 2019. "Buses and breaking point: Freedom of expression and the 'Brexit' campaign", *Ethical Theory and Moral Practice*, vol. 22, no. 3, pp. 623–637.

Reuters, 2019, 21 February-last update. *Turkey condemns European parliament committee call to suspend accession* [Homepage of Reuters], [Online]. Available at: www.reuters.com/article/us-turkey-eu-idUSKCN1QA0MJ [28 June 2020].

Ridge-Newman, A., 2018. "Reporting the road to Brexit", in Ridge-Newman, A., León-Solís, F. & O'Donnell, H., eds., *Reporting the road to Brexit*. Basingstoke: Palgrave Macmillan, pp 3–21.

Riley-Smith, B., 2016, 13 September-last update. *David Davis distances himself from Vote Leave's pledge to spend £350m on NHS after Brexit* [Homepage of Telegraph Media Group], [Online]. Available at: www.telegraph.co.uk/news/2016/09/13/david-davis-distances-himself-from-vote-leaves-pledge-to-spend-3/ [24 June 2020].

Robertson, J., 2014. *Fairness in the first year? BBC and ITV coverage of the Scottish referendum campaign from September 2012 to September 2013*. Creative Futures Research Institute, University of the West of Scotland.

Shaw, M., 2019, 8 January-last update. *Vote Leave relied on racism. Brexit: The Uncivil War disguised that ugly truth* [Homepage of The Guardian], [Online]. Available at: www.theguardian.com/commentis free/2019/jan/08/vote-leave-racism-brexit-uncivil-war-channel-4 [24 June 2020].

Simons, N., 2016, 19 June-last update. *Nigel Farage Immigration Poster Made Me 'Shudder,' Says Michael Gove* [Homepage of Huffington Post], [Online]. Available at: www.huffingtonpost.co.uk/entry/nigel-farage-immigration-   poster-made-me-shudder-says-michael-gove_uk_57667022e4b01fb65863a316 [29 June 2020].

Spence, B., 2017, 7 February-last update. *The NHS is the closest thing we have to a religion – and that's why it must be privatised* [Homepage of The Independent], [Online]. Available at: www.independent. co.uk/voices/nhs-crisis-jeremy-hunt-health-service-religion-privatise-to-save-it-a7567056.html   [26 June 2020].

Startin, N., 2015. "Have we reached a tipping point? The mainstreaming of Euroscepticism in the UK", *International Political Science Review*, vol. 36, no. 3, pp. 311–323.

Stewart, H. & Mason, R. 2016, 16 June-last update, *Nigel Farage's anti-migrant poster reported to police* [Homepage of The Guardian], [Online]. Available at: www.theguardian.com/politics/2016/jun/16/ nigel-farage-defends-ukip-breaking-point-poster-queue-of-migrants [26 June 2020].

Stokel-Walker, C., 2019, 1 October-last update, *Is Boris Johnson really trying to game Google search results?* [Homepage of Wired], [Online]. Available at: https://www.wired.co.uk/article/boris-johnson-model-google-news [29 October 2020].

Stone, J., 2016, 24 June-last update. *Nigel Farage backtracks on Leave campaign's '£350m for the NHS' pledge hours after result* [Homepage of The Independent], [Online]. Available at: www.independent. co.uk/news/uk/politics/eu-referendum-result-nigel-farage-nhs-pledge-disowns-350-million-pounds-a7099906.html [1 June 2020].

Suiter, J., 2016. "Post-truth politics", *Political Insight*, vol. 7, no. 3, pp. 25–27.

Sweney, M. & Plunkett, J., 2016, 28 June-last update. *Ad watchdog powerless to act on controversial Brexit campaigns* [Homepage of The Guardian], [Online]. Available at: www.theguardian.com/media/2016/ jun/28/ad-watchdog-powerless-to-act-on-controversial-brexit-campaigns [24 June 2020].

Taylor, M., Wintour, P. & Elgot, J., 2015, 30 July-last update. *Calais crisis: Cameron pledges to deport more people to end 'swarm' of migrants* [Homepage of The Guardian], [Online]. Available at: www.theguardian. com/uk-news/2015/jul/30/calais-migrants-make-further-attempts-to-cross-channel-into-britain [29 June 2020].

Tolson, A., 2016. "English television news coverage of the Scottish referendum", *Scotland's Referendum and the Media: National and International Perspectives*, p. 97.

Toynbee, P., 2018, 3 July-last update. *The NHS is our religion: It's the only thing that saves it from the Tories* [Homepage of The Guardian], [Online]. Available at: www.theguardian.com/commentisfree/2018/ jul/03/nhs-religion-tories-health-service [23 June 2020].

Vote Leave, 2016. *Why vote leave* [Homepage of Vote Leave], [Online]. Available at: www.voteleavetake control.org/why_vote_leave.html [27 June 2020].

Webster, C., 2002. *The national health service: A political history*. Oxford: Oxford University Press.

What UK thinks EU, 2016a, 22 June-last update. *Eu referendum: Poll of polls* [Homepage of What UK thinks EU], [Online]. Available at: https://whatukthinks.org/eu/opinion-polls/poll-of-polls/ [1 July 2020].

What UK thinks EU, 2016b, 22 June-last update. *Do you think it would have a good or bad effect on the NHS if Britain left the EU?* [Homepage of What UK thinks EU], [Online]. Available at: https://whatuk thinks.org/eu/questions/do-you-think-it-would-have-a-good-or-bad-effect-on-the-nhs-if-we-left-the-european-union/ [20 June 2020].

Wheeler, B., 2016, 24 May-last update. *Ad breakdown: Vote Leave EU referendum broadcast* [Homepage of BBC], [Online]. Available at: https://www.bbc.co.uk/news/uk-politics-eu-referendum-36367247 [29 October 2020].

Worth, J., 2017. *The two versions of the £350m slogan for the NHS.* [Homepage of Jon Worth] [Online]. Available   at: https://jonworth.eu/the-two-versions-of-the-350-million-for-the-nhs-slogan/   [24 June 2020].

Wright, O., 2016, 19 June-last update. *EU referendum: Nigel Farage's anti-migrant poster like 1930s fascist propaganda, says George Osborne* [Homepage of The Independent], [Online]. Available at: www.inde pendent.co.uk/news/uk/politics/eu-referendum-poster-nigel-farage-polls-michael-gove-a7089946. html [24 June 2020].

Zaller, J.R., 1992. *The nature and origins of mass opinion*. Cambridge: Cambridge University Press.

38

MEDIA POLICY FAILURES AND THE EMERGENCE OF RIGHT-WING POPULISM

Des Freedman

Introduction: the structural conditions of mediated populism

Right-wing populist leaders across the globe reacted to the emergence of the COVID-19 pandemic in two main ways: by lashing out at 'foreigners' for spreading the virus and blaming the mainstream media for spreading 'bad news'. Donald Trump attacked journalists for downplaying his alleged policy successes in mitigating the 'Chinese virus' while Brazil's Jair Bolsanaro dubbed the pandemic a 'fantasy' and a 'media trick'. Hungary's prime minister, Viktor Orban, linked migration to the outbreak in Hungary and used COVID-19 as the pretext to cement his control of domestic media by passing a law that punishes anyone who publishes 'false' or 'distorted' facts. Matteo Salvini of Italy's Northern League pivoted from initial scepticism of the scale of the virus to circulating conspiracy videos indicating that coronavirus was engineered in a Chinese laboratory. Coronavirus is thus just the latest backdrop that allows populists to reproduce their binary worldview of a 'pure people' being infected by external forces; as a 'storytelling technique, a way of fitting things into a certain narrative about the world' (Cliffe 2020), populism depends on the ability both to communicate this frame and to govern according to its underlying logic.

One of the main explanations, therefore, for the rise in prominence of populist challenges to centrist political forces has focused on the former's effective use of the media: their ability to transmit 'sentiment' over 'fact', to use 'authentic' language, to make full use of social media, and to exploit the mainstream media's appetite for sensationalist stories. 'All neo-populist movements', argues Gianpetro Mazzoleni (2003, 6), 'rely heavily on some kind of indirect (and direct) complicity with the mass media, and all are led by politicians who, with few exceptions, are shrewd and capable "newsmakers" themselves'. In Europe and North America, this has worked to the advantage of iconoclastic far-right politicians like Trump, Orban, Bolsanaro, and Salvini – all of whom have received extensive airtime in which they have combined nativist rhetoric with outbursts against the political establishment (no matter how privileged they themselves may be). These leaders have been especially successful in winning coverage of their appeals to what Alvares and Dahlgren (2016, 49) describe as core populist tropes: 'an idealised sense of historical nation and (often ethnic) community – "the people", as well as a critical stance towards "the elites"'. Ruth Wodak argues that right-wing populist parties are actually dependent on 'performance strategies in modern media democracies' (Wodak 2013, 27) and insists that their growth is dependent on visibility generated by the media. A dangerous cocktail of tabloid values, falling levels of trust in the mainstream media, and unaccountable tech power (facilitating the spread of hyper-partisan news and disinformation) has therefore fuelled the marriage of a xenophobic populism with polarised media and political environments.

Yet insufficient attention has been paid in the literature on populism to the structural conditions which underlie what Victor Pickard calls the 'misinformation society' (Pickard 2020) and to the ideological and commercial imperatives that underpin the tendency of major news organisations to publicise and dramatise what they consider to be an 'illiberal' form of politics. In particular, there has been scant critical examination of the policy actions (and inactions) that have facilitated environments in which the coverage of populist leaders and narratives is not simply profitable but the logical outcome of media markets in liberal democracies that are wedded to ratings and controversy. Even the fiercest 'anti-populist' coverage is hardly likely to compensate for the systemic degeneration of communication systems in which power has been increasingly consolidated by oligopolistic digital intermediaries and media giants, in which mainstream news media have failed to appreciate sufficiently the roots of polarisation, in which public media have increasingly been identified not as monitors but as embodiments of elite power and, finally, in which highly partisan right-wing media have been emboldened and rewarded.

In this combustible context, this chapter reflects on the implication for media systems of conceptions of populism that see it not so much for its 'anti-pluralism' (Mueller 2016) or its appeal to a 'pure people' in opposition to a 'corrupt elite' (Mudde 2007, 23) but as a threat to 'reason' and social order, as well as to consensual and 'objective' journalism. This 'dismissal' of populism by mainstream political voices is, according to Ernesto Laclau, 'part of the discursive construction of a certain normality, of an ascetic political universe from which its dangerous logics had to be excluded' (2005, 19). For Laclau, this involves not simply the elite's fear of rowdy crowds and dissenting publics but also its denigration of populism's simplistic, binary operating system as 'irrational and undefinable' (2005, 16). For others on the left, who are attempting to restore progressive intent to populist projects, undifferentiated and apocalyptic attacks on populism by political centrists are part of a strategy to reassert their hegemony: 'Democracy, they say, is under threat from populism, and only a defense of [liberal] norms and institutions can exorcise the specter of a reckless citizenry' (Riofrancos 2017). Laura Grattan argues that this characterisation of populism as 'empty' and 'absurd', 'apolitical' and 'episodic' misses out on the potential of a 'grassroots populism' to engage in legitimate struggles to 'democratize power' (Grattan 2016, 3–4), as we have seen, in particular, with the 'pink tide' in Latin America (Guerrero and Marquez-Ramirez 2014).

From the perspective of traditional liberal democratic politics, however, populism and its mediated forms can be seen as examples of 'policy failure'. Yet the underlying reasons for this failure, and especially the idea that we might want to consider policy options that would foster resilient and tolerant political environments, are all too often ignored. The chapter seeks to correct this not by arguing that there is either a media policy or a legal 'solution' to populism – indeed, I am far from convinced that we need a 'solution' to all forms of populism – but that existing liberal democratic approaches to media policy have fostered highly unequal and distorted communication systems that have both been exploited by forces on the far right and helped to normalise far-right ideas through repeated exposure in mainstream media outlets (Mondon and Winter 2020). If populism is, indeed, at least in part a response to the failure of liberal politics to cater for all citizens, then to what extent has this failure been facilitated by contemporary media policy environments and with what consequences?

The chapter identifies four areas of 'policy failure' that have nurtured the highly skewed media environments prone to populist exploitation and concludes with a call to devise a new policy paradigm based around redistribution that aims that to reconstruct media systems in order both to resist both state and market capture and to undermine the appeal of populist forces on the far right. It focuses on examples from Europe and the US not because they epitomise some sort of undifferentiated 'global populism' (see Chakravartty and Roy 2017 for a fascinating account of 'mediatised populisms' across the Inter-Asian region; see also Artz 2017 for an equally interesting collection of essays on populist media policies across Latin America) but because, since the 1980s, they have provided some of the earliest and most visible examples of an emerging market-oriented communications policy paradigm characterised, according to Van Cuilenburg and McQuail (2003, 197), by a susceptibility to pragmatism and populism.

Media policy failures

Our communications systems are not in any sense 'natural' but created in the shape of the vested interests that dominate at any one time; communications policy is a highly political, value-laden, interest-driven field of decision-making. Since the 1980s, this has generally followed a market logic whereby decision makers have been in thrall to rhetorics concerning innovation, efficiency, and consumer sovereignty. Under the guide of neoliberalism (Freedman 2008) or 'corporate libertarianism' (Pickard 2014), communications markets have been restructured better to enhance capital accumulation and elite influence and to inscribe a commercial logic ever deeper into the cultural field.

Yet this policy restructuring is executed not simply through visible and identifiable legislative or regulatory acts but often through flawed decision-making processes that remove certain issues – notably those concerning concentrations of media power – from the policy agenda. Thus we have 'media policy silences' (Freedman 2014) and 'media policy failures' (Pickard 2014, 216) characterised by 'inaction' and 'invisibility' and often caused by the ideological affinity between and the mutual interests of policymakers, regulators, and industry voices. This underlies the 'regulatory failure' that Robert Horwitz (1989, 29, emphasis in original) describes as taking place when 'a captured agency *systematically* favors the private interests of regulated parties and *systematically* ignores the public interest'. I argue that a series of media policy failures and silences have taken place in Europe and North America that have further distorted our communications landscapes and worked to the advantage of parties and movements on the right.

Failure to tackle concentrated ownership

Traditional ownership controls in media markets that seek to prevent any single company from gaining undue dominance or any single voice from gaining undue prominence have long been a key part of a democratic toolkit. According to Ed Baker (2009), concentrated media ownership 'creates the possibility of an individual decision-maker exercising enormous unchecked, undemocratic, potentially demagogic power. . . . Even if this power is seldom exercised, no democracy should risk the danger'. This fear of 'demagogues' is at the heart of liberal opposition to all forms of populism – borne out by the warnings posed by the reign of former Italian prime minister Silvio Berlusconi, whose control of media outlets was essential to his populist success. Yet, as a result of pressure from lobbyists arguing that ownership rules are both a brake on innovation and an impediment to profitability at a time when traditional business models are under pressure, ownership rules in countries like the US, the UK, Australia, and New Zealand have been systematically relaxed since the 1980s. We have seen consolidation in terrestrial and satellite television markets, in the national and local press, in wholesale and retail radio, and online such that the top ten content companies in a study of 30 countries from across the globe account for an average 67 percent of national market share while the top four digital platforms account for a whopping 88 percent of their national media markets (Noam 2016, 9).

Concentrated media markets do not, of course, create populist movements out of thin air, but the desire of neoliberal policymakers to cement commercial values in, and to minimise regulatory controls on, accumulations of media power is hardly without consequence. First, this simply enhances the visibility, in particular, of far-right politicians who can be relied upon to generate the provocative speech and nativist appeals that play well with ratings. As Victor Pickard has argued in relation to Donald Trump's victory in 2016, 'the news media's excessive commercialism – driven by profit imperatives, especially the need to sell advertising – resulted in facile coverage of the election that emphasised entertainment over information' (Pickard 2020, 2). Second, size matters, especially in media landscapes where there is a fierce battle for attention and, therefore, strong incentives for political leaders to accommodate media power. The agenda-setting roles of Fox News in the US and of the tabloid *Daily Mail* and *The Sun* in whipping up anti-immigrant sentiment in the run-up to the Brexit vote were partly made possible by their status as dominant and very influential players in their respective news media markets. As long as liberal politicians and policymakers continue to exercise only a rhetorical commitment to plurality, the incentives for large news organisations to amplify the controversial – and often racist – content that far-right populists are only too pleased to provide will continue to exist.

Failure to regulate tech companies

The failure by policymakers to tackle monopolistic behaviour is particularly clear in the digital sphere, where a handful of giant intermediaries dominate their respective markets and where Facebook and Google alone account for such an overwhelming proportion of advertising revenue that, according to *The Financial Times*, they 'not only own the playing field but are able to set the rules of the game as well' (Garrahan 2016). Powered by ever-expanding piles of cash and the logic of network effects which rewards first-movers, these intermediaries are not simply expanding into associated fields but usurping some of the editorial and creative gatekeeping roles previously fulfilled by traditional content companies (Hesmondhalgh 2017). Yet this market power, combined with the specific ways in which their algorithms function, has created giant monopolistic machines for the circulation of misinformation and propaganda that some commentators have argued distorted recent ballots in the US and the UK (Cadwalladr 2017). Whether or not it can be proved that 'fake news' has changed the result of elections – and research suggests that its influence may well have been exaggerated (Allcott and Gentzkow 2016) – it is certainly the case that Google and Facebook have created both incentives and systems for low-cost, highly targeted transmission of clickbait posing as news. For Tim Berners-Lee, the founder of the web, the

> system is failing. . . . We have these dark ads that target and manipulate me and then vanish because I can't bookmark them. This is not democracy – this is putting who gets selected into the hands of the most manipulative companies out there.
>
> (quoted in Solon 2017)

The problem is that this is a situation generated not simply by the computational power of complex algorithms but by the reluctance of regulators to address intermediary dominance. True, the European Commission did impose a €2.4 billion fine on Google in 2017 for abusing its dominance by unduly prioritising its own price comparison service, but this is likely to be a mere inconvenience to its parent Alphabet as opposed to a structural challenge to its operating model. Regulators refuse to acknowledge Facebook and Google as media companies and instead continue to rely on the same liberal policy frameworks that were developed in the 1990s, which protected them from responsibility for the content they carry. US regulators like the Department of Justice and the Federal Trade Commission do have antitrust remits that would enable them to challenge intermediary power but, wedded to a neoliberal vision of market fundamentalism, prefer to remain silent. Indeed, according to Barry Lynn and Matt Stoller (2017), 'the FTC itself partially created the "fake news" problem by failing to use its existing authority to block previous acquisitions by these platforms such as Facebook's purchase of WhatsApp and Instagram'. Shackled by a worldview that still sees regulation as an impediment to innovation, neoliberal governments are happy to rely on industry self-regulation that is insufficiently strong to change corporate behaviour or to pre-empt hateful forms of speech that continue to circulate and that underpin the growth of far-right parties.

Failure to safeguard an effective fourth estate

First Amendment absolutism and libertarian conceptions of speech continue to undergird arguments against regulation of corporate interests. Yet this has not prevented attacks by the state on investigative journalism, one of the hallmarks of a functioning 'fourth estate' and one of the great traditional liberal defences against demagogues and tyrants. In the US, before 2008, a grand total of three cases had been brought against whistleblowers and leakers under the terms of the Espionage Act for helping journalists report on classified government programmes. The Obama administration, however, used the act to launch nine cases, leading the *New York Times* to comment that that if

> Donald J. Trump decides as president to throw a whistle-blower in jail for trying to talk to a reporter, or gets the F.B.I. to spy on a journalist, he will have one man to thank for bequeathing him such expansive power: Barack Obama'.
>
> (Risen 2016)

Similarly, the UK government passed the Investigatory Powers Act in 2016, which provides for unprecedented surveillance and hacking by the security services but fails to guarantee sufficient protection for journalists' sources. 'We do have to worry about a UK Donald Trump', commented one British lawmaker, Lord Strasburger. 'If we do end up with one, and that is not impossible, we have created the tools for repression' (quoted in MacAskill 2016). Politicians like Donald Trump have, therefore, inherited anti-democratic tools that can be used against legitimate journalistic inquiry in the context of the rise of surveillance states and anti-terror regimes.

Yet these authoritarian instincts − ones that have been successfully exploited by populist leaders like Orban in Hungary and Kaczynski in Poland − coincide with a reluctance in liberal democracies to create effective systems of fully independent press self-regulation. So, for example, in the UK, the government has refused to enforce the full recommendations of the Leveson Inquiry, which were designed to hold the press to account for the kinds of misrepresentation and distortion that were so evident, particularly in relation to coverage of immigration, in the run-up to the Brexit vote in some of the leading tabloids. This failure to ensure that there is low-cost access to justice for those individuals and groups who have been unfairly targeted by right-wing media, together with what Victor Pickard (2020, 4) calls the 'slow-but-sure structural collapse of professional journalism', both incentivises journalists to pursue stories that target and scapegoat minorities and undermines their ability to report on issues such as class, immigration, and wealth, which the far right are quick to sensationalise and simplify.

This is magnified by what Sarah Smarsh calls the 'economic trench between reporter and reported' (Smarsh 2016) – the fact that the highest levels of journalism are increasingly filled by those who can afford to go to journalism school and who are thus most likely to be drawn from the elites that are targeted by populist rage. 'That the term "populism" has become a pejorative among prominent liberal commentators should give us great pause', argues Smarsh. 'A journalism that embodies the plutocracy it's supposed to critique has failed its watchdog duty and lost the respect of people who call bullshit when they see it' (Smarsh 2016). One response to this would be to introduce new levies on digital intermediaries to fund outlets committed to public interest journalism, particularly those from the not-for-profit sector, in order to correct this imbalance. For many years, neoliberal administrations saw this kind of initiative as a tax-raising disincentive to innovation that has no part to play in a dynamic market economy. However, the sheer scale of government intervention into the world economy as a result of the coronavirus has changed the debate, and it is now incumbent on media reform advocates to make sure that subsidies are not ringfenced for the legacy press that helped normalise right-wing populism in the first place.

Failure to nurture independent public service media

One of the great fears of mainstream journalism is that partisan media environments fuel political polarisation (and vice versa) and destabilise democracy by shifting the political centre of gravity away from a 'moderate' consensus to 'extremes'. Media outlets in deregulated and highly commercial media systems gravitate towards wherever ratings and profits are to be found while media in authoritarian states are often 'captured' by business interests working closely with governments (Schiffrin 2017). In this context, one potential solution is regularly proposed: an independent public service news media that is strong enough to defy the pressure of both government and market and to serve citizens without fear or favour. According to this narrative, it is organisations like the British Broadcasting Corporation (BBC), the Norwegian NRK, and the Finnish YLE that are claimed to offer the best prospect of impartial, high-quality journalism that is insulated from the partisanship that feeds 'extremism'. According to the European Broadcasting Union (2016), countries with strong public service media traditions are likely to have greater press freedom, higher voter turnout, less corruption, and lower levels of right-wing extremism.

In reality, far from retaining independence from all vested interests and delivering a critical and robust public interest journalism, public service media are often far too implicated in and attached to existing elite networks of power to be able to offer an effective challenge to them. Indeed, public service media are likely to be intertwined – through funding arrangements, elite capture, and unaccountable modes of governance – with the specific configurations of political power in their 'home' states in the same ways as are commercial media. The BBC, for example, may lack the shrill tones of a Fox News or a Breitbart and is certainly publicly committed to impartial reporting, but by marginalising voices that are not part of the established liberal consensus and amplifying those closest to official sources (Mills 2016), it generates criticism from both left and right.

In Europe, public service media appears to be a particularly ineffective bulwark against extremism given the sizeable votes in recent years for far-right politicians in countries like Austria, Germany, France, and the Netherlands, all of which have high levels of consumption of public service content. These channels find it difficult either to transcend the tensions and polarisation that mark their wider political environments or to establish themselves as fully independent of power elites. In part, this is because public service media across the globe have been hollowed out – their funding has been cut, their staffing reduced, and their services suffused with a market logic – in ways that make it increasingly difficult for them to provide an authoritative centrist challenge to political polarisation. This is not to denigrate the need for a meaningfully independent form of public media that acts as a counterweight to vested interests but simply to note that existing institutions have all too often been identified with precisely the same power elites that populists claim they are seeking to challenge.

Conclusion: towards a new policy paradigm

Media policy failures did not cause the rise of Trump, Bolsanaro, Modi, the Alternative for Germany, the People's Party in Austria, or indeed Brexit. Those have other structural causes related to legacies of racism, experiences of insecurity and disenchantment with a political system that rewards people so unequally. In reality, populism is not a failure of a normally smoothly functioning political market but an inevitable, if volatile and contradictory, reaction to structural flaws in liberal democracy. Indeed, polarised political environments are not necessarily more illiberal than centrist political systems, which themselves police a narrow and unrepresentative consensus. However, in its predominant nativist and xenophobic orientations, populism poses a particular danger to minority populations and social justice more generally. If we want to see an end to reactionary and demagogic populist voices, then we will need to develop very different policy orientations from those that currently serve corporate and state elites and that have opened up spaces that have been exploited by the far right.

What is remarkable, however, is the extent to which those most contemptuous of populism's anti-elite narratives are so reluctant to acknowledge their own complicity in facilitating the discursive and material conditions they now seek to oppose. This is as true for media elites as it is for other areas of political life. Liberal media policies have been unable to lay the basis for independent, critical, and representative media systems that would articulate and respond to the very diverse sets of concerns that citizens have in their respective environments. Policy silences paved the way for the emergence of powerful and yet unaccountable digital intermediaries through whose channels travels the 'fake news' widely believed by mainstream politicians and commentators to have corrupted democratic politics. Policy silences smoothed the path for the implantation of commercial values throughout our communications systems, unshackling conceptions of the public interest from corporate responsibility so that poisonous coverage of refugees and other minorities is entirely legitimate and constitutionally protected while far-right populist figures litter news bulletins because a business logic demands it.

These policy silences are intensified by a regulatory failure to challenge the intimacy of governments and media executives – a familiarity which further contaminates democratic societies and simply hands ammunition to far-right populists who are then able to attack mainstream media as representatives of elite power. Liberal democratic media policy, with its commitment to market forces, its privileging of corporate speech rights, its complicity with the establishment, and its technocratic obsession for innovation ahead of the public interest, is therefore severely implicated in the growth of those reactionary movements that it is now affronted by. It has achieved this not by specifically tilting the policy framework towards populist parties but by failing to produce conditions which could sustain a robust and fearless media – one willing to stand up against populist bigotry while at the same time 'comforting the afflicted and afflicting the comfortable'. Instead, both commercial and public service media have all too often helped 'mainstream' populist ideas on race and immigration before, at least in some cases, turning their editorial ire onto precisely this kind of politics.

If centrist politicians and mainstream media really wished to remove the conditions in which anti-democratic forces are able to grow, they would acknowledge that is time for radically new communications policies – not solutions to populism per se so much as responses to degenerated media environments that have been captured by corporate and state elites. We need a new policy paradigm to supersede the market-oriented approach outlined by Van Cuilenburrg and McQuail (2003), one that is based not simply around notions of freedom, access, and accountability as they suggested, but on the redistribution that is necessary to confront the abuse of media power by states and corporations.

This is a paradigm designed to cater to the needs, above all, of disaffected citizens and depends on reversing the policy failures outlined in this chapter. Instead of allowing further concentrations of media power, a redistributive media policy will seek to break up existing oligopolies and tackle the corrupting influence that comes with market domination; instead of bowing down to the giant digital intermediaries whose algorithms increasingly structure patterns of everyday life, a redistributive model will seek to find ways to use these algorithms better to serve the public interest, in part by forcing private companies to share their proprietary models; a redistributive model will siphon cash from the giant stockpiles held by the largest intermediaries to support new, non-profit grassroots journalism start-ups with a mandate to serve diverse audiences; and, finally, a redistributive model will seek to construct vibrant public media systems that are independent of vested interests and meaningfully able to hold power to account; to cater to all audiences, irrespective of partisan affiliation and social background; and to cut the ground from underneath the poison of the far right.

References

Allcott H and Gentzkow M. (2016) Social Media and Fake News in the 2016 General Election. *Journal of Economic Perspectives* 31(2): 211–236.

Alvares C and Dahlgren P (2016) Populism, extremism and media: Mapping an uncertain terrain. *European Journal of Communication* 31(1): 46–57.

Artz L (ed) (2017) *The Pink Tide: Media Access and Political Power in Latin America*. London: Rowman & Littlefield.

Baker E (2009) Comments to FCC ownership workshop. Available at: https://transition.fcc.gov/ownership/workshop-110209/baker.pdf

Cadwalladr C (2017) The great British Brexit robbery: How our democracy was hijacked. The *Guardian*, 7 May. Available at: www.theguardian.com/technology/2017/may/07/the-great-british-brexit-robbery-hijacked-democracy

Chakravartty, P and Roy S (2017) Mediatized populisms: Inter-Asian lineages. *International Journal of Communication* 11: 4073–4092.

Cliffe, J (2020) How populist leaders exploit pandemics. *New Statesman*, 18 March. Available at: www.newstatesman.com/world/2020/03/how-populist-leaders-exploit-pandemics.

European Broadcasting Union (2016) EBU research shows strong public service media contributes to a healthy democracy. Press release, 8 August. Available at www.ebu.ch/news/2016/08/ebu-research-shows-strong-public-service-media-contributes-to-a-healthy-democracy

Freedman D (2008) *The Politics of Media Policy*. Cambridge: Polity.

Freedman D (2014) *The Contradictions of Media Power*. London: Bloomsbury.

Garrahan M (2016) Advertising: Facebook and Google build a duopoly. *Financial Times*, 23 June. Available at: www.ft.com/content/6c6b74a4-3920-11e6-9a05-82a9b15a8ee7

Grattan, L. (2016) *Populism's Power: Radical Grassroots Democracy in America*. Oxford: Oxford University Press.

Guerrero M and Marquez-Ramirez M (eds) (2014) *Media Systems and Communication Policies in Latin America*. Houndmills: Palgrave Macmillan.

Hesmondhalgh D (2017) Why it matters when big tech firms extend their power into media content. *The Conversation*, 15 November. Available at: https://theconversation.com/why-it-matters-when-big-tech-firms-extend-their-power-into-media-content-86876

Horwitz R (1989) *The Irony of Regulatory Reform*. Oxford: Oxford University Press.

Laclau E (2005) *On Populism*. London: Verso.

Lynn B and Stoller M (2017) How to stop Google and Facebook from becoming even more power-ful. The *Guardian*, 2 November, Available at: www.theguardian.com/commentisfree/2017/nov/02/facebook-google-monopoly-companies

MacAskill E (2016) 'Extreme surveillance' becomes UK law with barely a whimper. *The Guardian*, 19 November. Available at: www.theguardian.com/world/2016/nov/19/extreme-surveillance-becomes-uk-law-with-barely-a-whimper

Mazzoleni G (2003) The media and the growth of neo-populism in contemporary democracies. In Mazzoleni G, Stewart J and Horsfield B (eds) *The Media and Neo-Populism: A Contemporary Comparative Analysis*. Westport: Praeger, pp. 1–20.

Mills T (2016) *The BBC: Myth of a Public Service*. London: Verso.

Mondon, A and Winter, A (2020) *Reactionary Democracy: How Racism and the Populist Far Right Became Mainstream*. London: Verso.

Mudde C (2007) *Populist Radical Right Parties in Europe*. Cambridge: Cambridge University Press.

Mueller J-W (2016) *What is Populism?* Philadelphia: University of Pennsylvania Press.

Noam E (2016) *Who Owns the World's Media? Media Concentration and Ownership around the World*. Oxford: Oxford University Press.

Pickard V (2014) *Media Democracy: The Triumph of Corporate Libertarianism and the Future of Media Reform*. New York: Cambridge University Press.

Pickard V (2020) *Democracy Without Journalism? Confronting the Misinformation Society*. Oxford: Oxford University Press.

Riofrancos T (2017) Democracy without the People. *N+1*, 6 February. Available at: https://nplusonemag.com/online-only/online-only/democracy-without-the-people/

Risen J (2016) If Donald Trump targets journalists, thank Obama. *New York Times*, 30 December. Available at: www.nytimes.com/2016/12/30/opinion/sunday/if-donald-trump-targets-journalists-thank-obama.html

Schiffrin A (ed) (2017) *In the Service of Power: Media Capture and the Threat to Democracy*. Washington, DC: Centre for International Media Assistance.

Smarsh S (2016) Dangerous idiots: How the liberal media elite failed working-class Americans. The *Guardian*, 13 October. Available at: www.theguardian.com/media/2016/oct/13/liberal-media-bias-working-class-americans

Solon O (2017) Tim Berners-Lee on the future of the web: 'The system is failing'. The *Guardian*, 16 November. Available at: www.theguardian.com/technology/2017/nov/15/tim-berners-lee-world-wide-web-net-neutrality

Van Cuilenberg J and McQuail D (2003) Media policy paradigm shifts. *European Journal of Communication* 18(2): 181–207.

Wodak R (2013) *Right-Wing Populism in Europe: Politics and Discourse*. London: Bloomsbury.

39

DISENTANGLING POLARISATION AND CIVIC EMPOWERMENT IN THE DIGITAL AGE

The role of filter bubbles and echo chambers in the rise of populism

William H. Dutton and Craig T. Robertson[1]

Introduction

The outcomes of elections and referenda across the world, such as the election of Donald Trump as president of the United States and the Brexit vote for the United Kingdom to leave the European Union (EU), both in 2016, contributed to a growing sense that there was a rise in populist attitudes that would undermine liberal democratic institutions. This thesis has, in turn, fuelled internet-related theoretical perspectives on what is driving this populist resurgence. One prominent perspective is tied to the role of search engines and social media, along with the algorithms that govern them, to explain why internet users are being trapped in filter bubbles and echo chambers rather than being exposed to the diversity of information necessary for them to draw sound conclusions about what to believe and how to vote.

This chapter examines this explanatory thesis through the analysis of empirical data on internet users in seven developed nations. Gathered in early 2017, our surveys of internet users show that populism is, indeed, prominent as conventionally defined and, in fact, so prominent that it is difficult to view these beliefs and attitudes as extreme or radical in our contemporary digital age. Moreover, we find that those who hold populist beliefs and attitudes are no more likely to be trapped in filter bubbles or echo chambers than are other internet users. Quite the contrary: the opposite is the case. So-called populists are more politically engaged and more actively seek out sources of information about politics. In such ways our findings raise questions about the very meaning of populism and theories about its effects, leading us to speculate on alternative perspectives on populism, such as the rise of a sense of citizen empowerment and the polarisation of political communication in the digital age.

The following sections review key work on populism, including its operational definition, and how it is connected with dominant perspectives around filter bubbles and echo chambers. We then turn to the methodology of our survey research and the survey findings. The concluding sections briefly summarise the findings and speculate on alternative perspectives that are

420

suggested by the patterns of relationships emerging from our analysis. This study questions not only deterministic theories of access to political information but also the very conceptualisation and operational definition of populism in the digital age.

Conceptualising populism

Populism is a term with a number of different meanings and connotations (Kaltwasser 2015). These can range from anti-immigration right-wing populism in Europe (Kaltwasser 2015) to the progressive populism of Bernie Sanders in the United States (Gerbaudo 2018). Clearly, populism can be defined or viewed somewhat differently depending on the political context being considered, underscoring how populist sentiments cut across the political spectrum (Gerbaudo 2018; DeLuca et al. 2012).

To account for these variations in the manifestation of populism, scholars have argued that, at its core, populism is generally characterised by two features: anti-elitism and appeals to 'the people' as the just and ultimate authoritative force in a democracy (Canovan 1999; Mudde 2004). Canovan (1999), for instance, has argued for a structural understanding of populism, defining the concept not by its specific contents – e.g. the nationalism of right-wing populism or the anti-capitalism of left-wing populism – but by the structural relationship between its constituent actors: the people and elite (or dominant power structure). A structural definition reduces the concept of populism to its ethos or animus. Fundamentally, in this view, populist rhetoric involves 'some kind of revolt against the established structure of power in the name of the people' (Canovan 1999, 3). The populist ethos is anti-elitist and anti-establishment, one which seeks to wrestle power and authority away from a minority and give it to the majority, whether that majority is from the right or left of politics.

Generally, populists challenge the elite from the view that authority and sovereignty should not rest with a small number of individuals – whether they be political elites, economic elites, academics, or the media – but with the people as a whole. People are the core of a democracy, and the elite 'threaten the purity and unity of the sovereign people' (Akkerman et al. 2014, 1327). In light of this, populists often favour direct democracy (Canovan 1999) as an expression of the majority's preference. Mudde (2004, 543) follows a similar line of reasoning, albeit more pejoratively, arguing that populism is 'an ideology that considers society to be ultimately separated into two homogeneous and antagonistic groups, "the pure people" versus "the corrupt elite", and which argues that politics should be an expression of the *volonté générale* (general will) of the people'. Thus, while populism may be seen as a broad worldview with varying manifestations, its core has been characterised by a common feeling of distrust and antipathy towards elites.

Explaining populist impulses in Europe and the United States

From the election of Donald Trump in the Unites States to the Brexit vote in the United Kingdom to the National Front or National Rally in France, it has been argued that populism has been on the rise in recent years (Gerbaudo 2018). Here we touch on two key explanations for this apparent rise, tied to the internet and social media. Two overlapping perspectives are among the most prominent: the notions of filter bubbles and echo chambers.

Eli Pariser's (2011) notion of a filter bubble is the idea that the algorithms designed to personalise search and social media tend to feed users results that reflect the interests, location, and topics that internet users have searched for previously. From this perspective, individuals' past online behaviour shapes future results in ways that lead users to see a less diverse array of information which reinforces their existing views, rather than exposing them to countervailing information.

The idea of an echo chamber is that people have a confirmation bias that leads them to use social media and other sources of information in ways that confirm their pre-existing biases and which connect them with like-minded people (Nickerson 1998; Sunstein 2017). This bias could lead to the creation of relatively homogeneous groups of like-minded individuals with limited viewpoints and one-sided political information (Sunstein 2007, 2017). This social filtering of media choices by individuals, such as whom they follow and friend on social media, could reinforce algorithmic filtering to create a homogeneity bias among media users (Nikolov et al. 2015), populists in particular.

Populists, digital media, and echo chambers

Scholars have argued that the rise of populism cannot be explained by factors of economics, globalisation, or migration alone and that media technologies and systems have an important role to play (Schroeder 2018; Kaltwasser 2015; Postill 2018). In particular, digital media technologies may have provided opportunities for the formation of alternative counter-publics which seek to challenge dominant power structures (Schroeder 2018). Specifically, the idea that the internet has empowered individuals to hold institutions more accountable is a theme across research on the fifth estate (Dutton 2009; Dubois and Dutton 2014).

In a new media context where information flows have been democratised, Nichols (2017) argues that an increased sense of self-belief has been engendered in the public, who now feel better able to independently source news and political information, using it to challenge those in authority. The decline in media authority engendered by communication technologies (Waisbord 2018) and the apparent rise in populist sentiments may be seen as a positive in the sense of the public being empowered by their access to information and networks (Mudde 2004; Dubois and Dutton 2014).

On the other hand, these developments can be seen as a negative if populists find themselves in highly agreeable and potentially radical online echo chambers or filter bubbles (Nichols 2017; Schroeder 2018; Fawzi 2019). Gerbaudo (2018), for instance, argues that an 'elective affinity' between populists and social media may have come about because social media platforms suit populists' needs: they provide spaces where ordinary members of the public can come together to express their own views, support one another, and challenge elites. Once there, Gerbaudo (2018) argues that algorithmic features of social media may operate to provide populist users with content which matches their political dispositions while sheltering them from alternative views. Moreover, such technologies may also enhance connections between like-minded individuals, drawing them into online crowds. The risk here is that individuals may become more extreme within self-selected and algorithmically driven online echo chambers and filter bubbles.

Researchers have pointed out that digital media platforms appeal to populists because of two mutually reinforcing factors: (1) the exclusion of populists from the mainstream and (2) the negative attitude of many populists towards the mainstream media. First, scholars have noted the negative framing of both right- and left-wing populist movements in the mainstream media in Europe and the United States (Decker 2008; Jutel 2016; Esser et al. 2016; DeLuca et al. 2012). Such populist movements have been variously characterised as threats to liberal democracy, civil rights, and social order (Jutel 2016; Esser et al. 2016). In response to negative coverage and attitudes towards them, scholars observe that populist movements have used digital media (e.g. social media, online newspapers) to circumvent the mainstream media and spread their own messages (Krämer 2017; Schroeder 2018; Engesser et al. 2017).

As a tool, the internet 'provides platforms for both organized and ordinary populists to avoid not only journalistic gatekeeping, but also criticism and social control' (Krämer 2017, 1304). In particular, recent scholarship has noted how the affordances of social media have helped populist movements gain ground and sustain themselves by allowing them to easily communicate ideas, share information, organise, and build support (Schroeder 2018; Krämer 2017; Gerbaudo 2018; Engesser et al. 2017). For populist voters, social media spaces become places to rally and make their voices heard. And for populist politicians, being outside the mainstream media apparatus allows them to be stronger in their language, not having to comply with mass media logics (Engesser et al. 2017). Extreme political parties on both the left and right use social media to voice populist messages more than centrist parties do, attacking the political elite and advocating on behalf of the people (Ernst et al. 2017).

Second, and relatedly, populists tend to view the mainstream media as biased against them (Schroeder 2018; Schulz et al. 2020). Donald Trump, for instance, has railed against the mainstream media, accusing them of fabricating stories and trying to undermine him. In turn, he has made extensive use of his Twitter account to communicate messages to his supporters, often expressing his view that the mainstream press is 'fake'. Such opposition to the mainstream media may arise from the media's tendency to exclude or negatively frame populist movements but also because media outlets are seen as powerful influencers in democratic society that are part of an elite minority or political establishment that needs to be attacked or undermined (Gerbaudo 2018; Krämer 2017; Engesser et al. 2017; Schulz et al. 2020; Fawzi 2019).

Both these factors may drive individuals with populist attitudes away from mainstream news sources to alternative media and into politically agreeable online echo chambers (Schulz et al. 2020; Fawzi 2019). Moreover, the 'aggregation logics', 'filter-by-interest' dynamics, and network effects at play online may create populist filter bubbles whereby users are exposed to attitude-consistent content that is popular with dense networks of like-minded others (Gerbaudo 2018).

Methodological approach

In order to empirically examine the relationships between populist attitudes and media and information practices, our study draws on a larger study of how internet users access information about politics (Dutton et al. 2019). Supported by a grant from Google, internet users in seven nations were surveyed online in early 2017.[2]

The survey included a standard attitudinal scale of populism. One virtue of conceptualising populism in a structural way, with a focus on the people and the elite, is that it provides a definition which is able to 'travel' across contexts and the political spectrum (Akkerman et al. 2014, 1326). A structural definition allows for an appraisal of populism as an ideology, rather than being tied to specific political ideologies, policy platforms, types of organisation, or specific forms of communication (Mudde 2004). It also provides a way to measure the populist attitudes of the public by putting forth an operationalisable definition.

Based on this view of populism, scholars have formulated and tested survey items that tap into its core structural features (see Hawkins et al. 2012; Akkerman et al. 2014). The items in this measure are designed to capture a general populist attitude, including such statements as 'the people, not the politicians, should make the most important policy decisions', 'the political differences between the elite and the people are larger than the differences among the people', and 'politicians need to follow the will of the people', which speak to anti-elitist attitudes, views

Table 39.1 Populism scale items and percentage of respondents in each country who agreed or strongly agreed

	DE	ES	FR	IT	PL	UK	US
Elected politicians should follow the will of the people	75.3	79.5	72	76.4	77.7	70.4	73.9
Elected officials talk too much and take too little action	71.7	78.9	71.7	78.5	70.4	71.1	75.6
The people, not politicians, should participate in our most important policy decisions	50.5	65.6	65.3	59	65	54	61
The political differences between the people running this country and the people are larger than the differences among people in this country	50	65.9	56.7	56.8	61.7	49.4	55.9
What people call 'compromise' in politics is really just selling out on one's principles	45	47.2	50.9	55.5	52.5	47	43.7
% agreeing or strongly agreeing to all items	27.2	31.7	30.4	32.9	30.9	24.8	25.3
N =	2000	2007	2000	2000	2005	2000	2018
Scale reliability	α = .836	α = .791	α = .791	α = .822	α = .766	α = .811	α = .745
	M=2.76	M=2.97	M=2.89	M=2.89	M=2.86	M=2.77	M=2.82
	SD=.79	SD=.70	SD=.70	SD=.77	SD=.70	SD=.70	SD=.65

Note: Scale is 0=strongly disagree, 1=disagree, 2=neither agree nor disagree, 3=agree, 4=strongly agree

on differences between the people and the elite, and the idea of popular sovereignty (Hawkins et al. 2012; Akkerman et al. 2014; Schulz et al. 2018; Van Hauwaert et al. 2020). Agreement with these questions is considered an indicator of populist attitudes. The validity, reliability, distinctiveness, and predictive power of the measure has been supported by multiple studies in the US and Europe (e.g. Hawkins et al. 2012; Akkerman et al. 2014; Hawkins et al. 2020).

In line with these studies, our surveys asked respondents the extent to which they agreed with five populism scale items drawn from prior research (see Table 40.1). We found that the level of agreement with each of the items on the populism scale was sufficiently varied but relatively high, ranging from 45 percent to almost 80 percent, with a quarter to one-third of all respondents across the nations agreeing or strongly agreeing with all items.

Since these items are highly correlated, we created a single scale of populism by averaging across the five items with non-missing values. Cronbach's alphas ranged from .76 in the US to .84 in Germany, which is indicative of good scale reliability and in line with prior analyses (see Akkerman et al. 2014; Schulz 2019; Hameleers and de Vreese 2018; Tsatsanis et al. 2018; Spruyt et al. 2016).

Findings

Before focusing on how populist attitudes relate to patterns of internet use and access to political information, it is critical to note and discuss the items comprising the populism scale

(Table 40.1). We review our findings by describing the distribution of opinions, identifying who holds populist attitudes, and then looking at the relationship between populist attitudes and the information practices of internet users.

Support for populism

Most generally, the responses of internet users reinforce notions that populist attitudes are prominent in the US and EU. Nearly three-fourths of all respondents across all seven nations agree that 'elected politicians should follow the will of the people'. The weakest item in support of populism still has nearly half of respondents agreeing that 'what people call "compromise" in politics is really just selling out on one's principles' (Table 40.1). Populism is most often discussed as an outlier or offshoot of mainstream politics, but populist attitudes are found in nearly half or more of the general public of internet users across all seven nations.

That said, this finding is in line with prior studies in Europe and the US, which have found an affinity for populist attitudes among the public (Hawkins et al. 2012; Rico and Anduiza 2019; Tsatsanis et al. 2018; Spruyt et al. 2016; Hawkins et al. 2020). It is also further evidence that our indicators of populism are reliable. Rather than a small proportion of the public, our results echo Mudde's (2004) argument that populism has become mainstream in Western democracies. In this sense, the fact that a strong majority of respondents in our sample were classified as having populist attitudes might be surprising in light of the rhetoric surrounding recent elections but not surprising in light of other empirical research.

The populists

Who are the populists? We analysed variables that might explain or account for populist attitudes across the seven nations. Prior studies have found populist attitudes are shaped by demographic factors and political orientations. Major demographic correlates of populism have been older age and less education. Relevant political orientations have included a stronger political ideology and higher anti-immigrant (nationalist) sentiments (Hawkins et al. 2012; Bernhard and Hänggli 2018; Rico and Anduiza 2019; Tsatsanis et al. 2018; Spruyt et al. 2016).

Following this research, we looked at the multivariate relationships between populism, as indicated by our summary scale, and sets of demographic and political orientation variables. Populist attitudes were entered as the dependent variable in multiple regression analyses, with demographic and political antecedents entered as explanatory variables (see Table 40.2). The results of our multiple regression analyses show that populist attitudes tend to be most closely associated with older age and less education, in line with previous research, as well as higher levels of political participation and a stronger political ideology. Accounting for these associations, less education may be associated with populism due to a perceived elite/non-elite divide between those with greater and lesser education and stronger political attitudes due to populism's links to more radical politics (Hawkins et al. 2012; Bernhard and Hänggli 2018; Tsatsanis et al. 2018).

That populism is associated with greater levels of political participation may be reflective of the political discontent and desire for political action or change that populist rhetoric can stir. Scholars have also noted a relationships between political knowledge, political interest, and populism (Rico and Anduiza 2019; Bernhard and Hänggli 2018), associations which may emerge from a sense that citizens are in a better position now, due to higher levels of education, to pay attention to politics, judge politicians, and think for themselves (Mudde 2004).

Table 39.2 Multiple regressions predicting populist attitudes[1]

	DE	ES	FR	IT	PL	UK	US
	β	β	β	β	β	β	β
Demographic factors							
Age	.107***	.056*	.094**	.028	.094**	.050	.069**
Female	.007	.024	.021	.005	-.004	-.002	-.016
Education	-.121***	-.035	-.061*	-.145***	-.063*	-.153***	-.086**
Income	-.038	-.013	-.052	-.056*	.020	-.002	-.028
White (UK/US only)						.009	.014
Born in country	-.007	.066**	-.023	-.037	.038	-.038	.038
Political orientation							
Political interest	.070*	-.001	.015	.008	-.022	.005	.089**
Political participation	-.029	.104***	.113***	.068*	.045	.113***	.178***
Strength of ideology	.105***	.153***	.171***	.058*	-.016	.080**	.057*
R^2	.046***	.048***	.068***	.034***	.017*	.043***	.081***
N =	2000	2007	2000	2000	2005	2000	2018

Notes: Standardised coefficients displayed; * $p < .05$; ** $p < .01$; *** $p < .001$

1 Populism scale ranges from 0 (non-populist) to 4 (strong populist)
Models were also tested with marital status (single, married, lives with partner, divorced/separated, widowed) and life stage (student, employed, retired, unemployed), but these variables were non-significant and therefore excluded.

In short, while populists conform with some stereotypes, such as being older and less educated, they are more engaged and interested in politics than their non-populist counterparts. But are populists trapped in echo chambers or filter bubbles?

Populism, political engagement, and access to political information

We have two approaches to questions about the relationship between populism and online political echo chambers and filter bubbles (Gerbaudo 2018). First, our respondents were asked if 'most people you communicate with online tend to have political beliefs similar to yours, different political beliefs from you, or a mix of various political beliefs' and also how often they agreed with the political opinions or political content posted by friends on social media (1=almost never to 5=nearly aways). The relationships between these responses and populist attitudes are shown in Tables 40.3 and 40.4.

Generally, the results indicate that populist attitudes are not associated with higher levels of agreement with the political opinions or content posted by friends on social media or with a higher likelihood of communicating primarily with politically similar others online. Populist attitudes are positively associated with agreeing with content posted by friends on social media, but this relationship is not statistically significant except in Germany ($\beta = .072$, p < .01) and the United States ($\beta = .077$, p < .01). Meanwhile, among populists, there is only a higher likelihood of communicating with similar others in Germany (B = .268, p < .01). These findings go against arguments that online echo chambers foster populist sentiments but are in line with Groshek and Koc-Michalska (2017), who found that homogeneous online networks were not related to support for populist political candidates.

Agreement with the opinions or content posted by friends on social media is more closely associated with younger internet users and those most interested and involved in politics, as

Table 39.3 Multiple regressions predicting level of agreement with the political opinions or content posted by friends on social media

	DE	ES	FR	IT	PL	UK	US
	β	β	β	β	β	β	β
Demographic factors							
Age	-.286***	-.092**	-.219***	-.073*	-.046	-.215***	-.209***
Female	-.027	-.006	.005	.061*	.055	.007	-.051*
Education	-.057*	-.021	.031	.005	-.023	.028	.021
Income	-.021	.034	-.006	.044	.022	-.038	-.046
Online ability	.072*	.138***	.080**	.095**	.040	.093**	.089**
Political orientation							
Political interest	.083**	.113***	.110***	.020	.132***	.226***	.158***
Political participation	.266***	.188***	.305***	.266***	.281***	.210***	.203***
Strength of ideology	.022	.012	.015	.033	-.074*	.007	.022
Populist attitudes	.072**	.047	.013	.033	.037	-.026	.077**
R^2	.202***	.129***	.213***	.118***	.139***	.227***	.198***
N =	2000	2007	2000	2000	2005	2000	2018

Notes: Standardised coefficients displayed; * $p < .05$; ** $p < .01$; *** $p < .001$

Table 39.4 Logistic regressions predicting communication primarily with politically similar others online[1]

	DE	ES	FR	IT	PL	UK	US
	β	β	β	β	β	β	β
Demographic factors							
Age	-.008	-.003	-.003	.000	-.009	-023***	-.006
Female	.220	.145	-.050	.312	.513**	-.163	-.109
Education	-.030	-.069	.168	.106	-.090	-.053	.174
Income	-.057	.086	-.077	-.010	-.049	-.002	-.056
Online ability	.038	.294*	.288	.206	.170	.313*	.174
Political orientation							
Political interest	.104	.254*	.031	.280	.238	.606***	.385***
Political participation	.074*	.067*	.135***	.123***	.129***	081**	.056*
Strength of ideology	.197*	.208*	.342***	.360**	-.047	.437***	.455***
Populist attitudes	.268**	.049	.103	.158	.195	.063	.166
Nagelkerke R^2	.049	.070	.090	.096	.076	.197	.150
N =	2000	2007	2000	2000	2005	2000	2018

Notes: Standardised coefficients displayed; * $p < .05$; ** $p < .01$; *** $p < .001$

1 Outcome variable is binary 1 (communicates primarily with politically similar others) and 0 (communicates primarily with politically mixed or different others)

measured by participation (Table 40.3). Communicating primarily with similar others online is most closely associated with political participation and strength of ideology (Table 40.4). Thus, polarisation is more likely to be related to echo chambers than populism.

Secondly, we explored the diversity of populists' media use, assessing whether there is a risk of individuals with populist attitudes being trapped in online echo chambers or filter bubbles. If true, we might expect individuals with populist attitudes to visit fewer and less diverse sources of information. In this case as well, our findings counter the thesis of populists cocooned in echo chambers or filter bubbles.

We developed a number of indicators of the number and diversity of sources consulted online and offline. In all seven nations, respondents were asked how often they used seven different online sources of information about politics and public affairs, including social media sites, search engines, online-only news sites, legacy online news sites, email, political websites (e.g. for politicians or online political groups), and online video platforms (1=never to 5=very often). The more sources consulted frequently online, for example, the less likely it would be for them to be trapped in a filter bubble or echo chamber.

We then focused on the relationship between populist attitudes and this set of media use variables. We used multiple regressions, looking at the association between populism and source diversity, controlling for demographic and political variables that might moderate this relationship. We also included a measure of online ability as a control ('How would you rate your ability to do things online?' 1=bad to 5=excellent) as this may have been an obstacle to consulting more sources.

The results reported in Table 40.5 show that when controlling for demographic and political moderating variables, those with populist attitudes more often consult online news sources, contrary to what a populist narrative would suggest. Frequent consultation of more online sources is also associated with being younger, greater ability to use the internet, and more interest and participation in politics. In four of the countries, those with a strong ideological position were less likely to frequently consult more online sources.

Figure 40.1 shows the overall pattern of findings, indicating that as populist attitudes increase, the number of online political news sources consulted often or very often increases. Respondents were split into groups with high (+ 1 standard deviation above the mean), moderate, and

Table 39.5 Multiple regressions predicting number of online political news sources consulted often or very often[1]

	DE	ES	FR	IT	PL	UK	US
	β	β	β	β	β	β	β
Demographic factors							
Age	-.229***	-.101***	-.164***	-.096***	-.011	-.212***	-.269***
Female	-.024	.008	-.045	.006	.017	-.041	-.062**
Education	-.034	.013	-.014	.021	-.074**	.011	-.030
Income	.000	.050*	.013	-.026	.028	.017	-.008
Online ability	.180***	.184***	.160***	.179***	.105**	.173***	.117***
Political orientation							
Political interest	.154***	.193***	.134***	.137***	.210***	.189***	.154***
Political participation	.287***	.230***	.349***	.244***	.273***	.235***	.338***
Strength of ideology	-.048*	-.070**	-.039	.010	.041	-.052*	-.075***
Populist attitudes	.098***	.055*	.067**	.080**	.124***	.122***	.128***
R²	.264***	.226***	.279***	.200***	.217***	.287***	.345***
N =	2000	2007	2000	2000	2005	2000	2018

Notes: Standardised coefficients displayed; * $p < .05$; ** $p < .01$; *** $p < .001$

1 DE *M*=1.92, *SD*=1.92; ES *M*=2.82, *SD*=2.20; FR *M*=1.91, *SD*=2.05; IT *M*=2.32, *SD*=2.12; PL *M*=2.73, *SD*=2.18; UK *M*=1.80, *SD*=2.05; US *M*=2.18, *SD*=2.19
'White' and 'born in country' were removed from these analyses due to their lack of predictive power

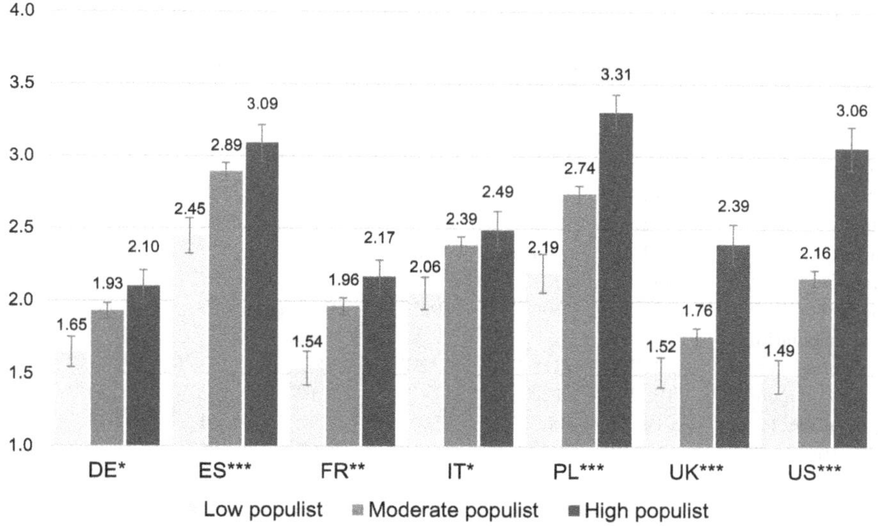

Figure 39.1 Average number of online political news sources consulted often or very often

Notes: Low populist = < populism mean score − 1 SD; high populist = > populism mean score + 1 SD

Means statistically different at * *p < .05;* ** *p < .01;* *** *p < .001*

One-way ANOVAs − DE: $F_{(2,1856)} = 3.80$, p = .022; ES: $F_{(2,1905)} = 8.05$, *p* < .001; FR: $F_{(2,1823)} = 7.37$, p = .01; IT: $F_{(2,1877)} = 3.83$, p = .022; PL: $F_{(2,1872)} = 20.10$, *p* < .001; UK: $F_{(2,1835)} = 16.37$, *p* < .001; US: $F_{(2,1897)} = 39.08$, *p* < .001

low (− 1 standard deviation below the mean) levels of populist attitudes, with these groupings becoming factors in one-way ANOVAs. The average number of online political news sources that strong populists used often or very often is significantly different than the number of sources consulted frequently by weak or non-populists in all nations.

This finding adds further evidence that populists may not be trapped in online echo chambers or filter bubbles. Instead, they seek out a greater range of political information from different sources. This finding is in line with that of Schulz (2019), who found that populists in Europe and the United States were also more likely to frequently consult multiple sources of news.

We also found that populist attitudes are significantly associated with more frequently reading disagreeable news or political information in all seven nations (Table 40.6). The pattern of results, represented graphically in Figure 40.2 (with one-way ANOVAs included), is the same as with diverse political news consumption: stronger populist attitudes are related to more frequent consumption of disagreeable political content. Also, those less likely to look at disagreeable news or information about politics are younger, less skilled in using the internet, and less interested and participative in political activity (Table 40.6).

While not reported in tables here, we also found that, when controlling for demographic and political orientation variables, in five of the nations surveyed, those with populist attitudes more frequently accessed a more diverse set of online and offline political news sources. In four nations, populist responders said they more frequently checked sources different from what they normally read. And in all nations surveyed, they indicated more frequent and diverse use of online searches as well as more frequent participation in a more diverse set of online activities. All these findings reinforce the basic theme of populism not being a determinant of individuals being trapped in filter bubbles or echo chambers.

Table 39.6 Multiple regressions predicting frequency of 'reading something you disagree with' when looking for news or political information[1]

	DE	ES	FR	IT	PL	UK	US
	β	β	β	β	β	β	β
Demographic factors							
Age	-.140***	-.115***	-.036	-.091**	-.107**	-.056*	-.078**
Female	.002	.008	-.074**	.016	-.001	.026	.008
Education	.022	.034	.006	.012	.017	.035	-.009
Income	.002	.007	-.005	-.009	.027	.029	.026
Online ability	.076**	.106***	.102***	.071*	.029	.085**	.031
Political orientation							
Political interest	.228***	.318***	.322***	.200***	.263***	.231***	.158***
Political participation	.192***	.122***	.174***	.161***	.133***	.184***	.213***
Strength of ideology	.014	-.083***	-.050*	-.007	-.001	-.015	-.045
Populist attitudes	.065**	.067**	.062*	.096***	.089**	.110***	.086***
R^2	.169***	.206***	.237***	.133***	.139***	.177***	.133***
N =	2000	2007	2000	2000	2005	2000	2018

Notes: Standardised coefficients displayed; * $p < .05$; ** $p < .01$; *** $p < .001$

1 DE M=3.11, SD=.98; ES M=3.20, SD=1.05; FR M=2.94, SD=1.09; IT M=3.27, SD=1.02; PL M=3.17, SD=.99; UK M=3.15, SD=1.05; US M=3.26, SD=1.10
'White' and 'born in country' were removed from these analyses due to their lack of predictive power

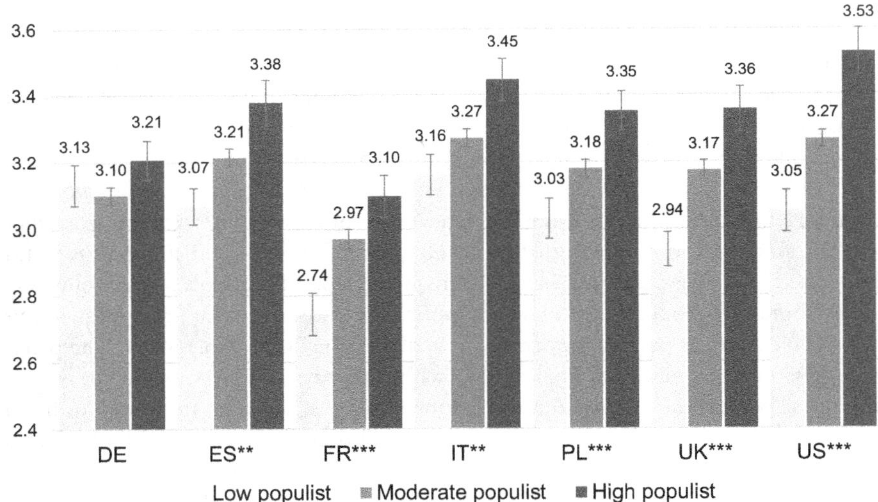

Figure 39.2 Average frequency of 'reading something you disagree with' when looking for news or political information

Notes: Scale is 1=never, 2=rarely, 3=sometimes, 4=often, 5=very often

Low populist = < populism mean score − 1 SD; high populist = > populism mean score + 1 SD

Means statistically different at * p < .05; **p < .01; *** p < .001

One-way ANOVAs − DE: F(2,1853) = 1.71, p = .180; ES: F(2,1903) = 7.39, p = .01; FR: F(2,1852) = 8.71, p < .001; IT: F(2,1886) = 6.18, p = .002; PL: F(2,1882) = 8.46, p < .001; UK: F(2,1839) = 13.94, p < .001; US: F(2,1905) = 17.07, p < .001

Conclusion: populism, empowerment, and political engagement?

Contrary to expectations, populists use a range of sources for political news and information more frequently than non-populists. This may be a positive finding, indicating that populists are unlikely to be trapped in echo chambers or filter bubbles (see also Groshek and Koc-Michalska 2017). Instead, they seek out political news and information from a variety of places on- and offline. This challenges the deterministic notion of digital media contributing to a rise in populism.

Schulz (2019, 105), however, has found that populists have a particular affinity for soft commercial television news and tabloid newspapers which may present an issue because they are 'the most sensationalist, scandalized, and dramatized news sources', which could stoke social divisions and promote populist sentiments (see also Fawzi 2019; Hameleers et al. 2017). Populists, Schulz (2019) reasons, may use such sources to reinforce their existing attitudes. In our study, it is possible that populists may be using online sources to reinforce their pre-existing attitudes, searching out agreeable information by visiting populist-friendly sources. Indeed, populists view the mainstream media negatively, seeing it as less trustworthy, and such attitudes may drive populists to alternative media (Fawzi 2019). Hameleers et al. (2017) found that populists are attracted to attitudinally congruent news content: that which supports their pre-existing attitudes. Unfortunately, our measure of political news use does not tap into what news outlets or sources populists are using online. But even if this were the case, sources of political information would have been chosen by internet users, rather than being the content filtered by a search algorithm or limited by an echo chamber. In this case, people have a confirmation bias and are the major deciders, not search engines or social media.

Nevertheless, Schulz (2019) also found that populists were just as likely to watch public television news, a finding which may indicate habitual news use or a need to stay up to date with content that is not aimed at populists. Also, again, it illustrates that users are not trapped in a filter bubble or echo chamber – they actively go to sources that are mainstream rather than right or left wing. While it may be argued that populists seek out quality news in order to learn and develop counter-arguments to elite media content (Schulz 2019), this is speculative and ignores the fact that the populists in our study went to more sources than non-populists. They may have greater interest in news and politics, period. Indeed, we also found that political participation was a predictor of populist attitudes. A potential reason for this and other findings may be that the measure of populist attitudes used in this study – and others – is reflective of an interest or engagement in public affairs.

It is plausible to hypothesise that the large number of people in Europe and the United States agreeing with the populism scale items suggests that the measure may be tapping into elements of citizen empowerment. In this sense, the level of populist attitudes may be a positive trend. As Mudde (2004, 554) argues, as a result of education and greater emancipation, 'citizens today expect more from politicians and feel more competent to judge their actions'. A 'cognitive mobilisation' has 'led citizens to stop accepting that the elites think for them and to no longer blindly swallow what the elites tell them'. This may also explain populists' more frequent use of political news sources: it represents a desire to find out for oneself. That said, Spruyt et al. (2016) have found opposite trends, with populist attitudes being related to lower interest in politics and political news in Belgium. But the direction of this relationship in Belgium is not consistent with our findings in seven other nations, including six European nations.

Perhaps, in light of the high level of agreement with populist sentiments, the measure of populist attitudes employed may be capturing more moderate populist attitudes, which are easier to agree with today than in earlier years (Van Hauwaert et al. 2020). Indeed, the items may well be agreeable to any follower of contemporary politics, particularly when politicians are so frequently criticised for not listening to public sentiments, for debating and stalling more than passing effective legislation, and for generally appearing out of touch with the people.

Alternatively, we did find some evidence of the strength of ideology tending to conform with a pattern of relationships connected with an echo chamber or filter bubble hypothesis. Those with more polarised opinions are more likely to communicate primarily with those politically similar to themselves (Table 40.4), less likely to often consult a range of online news sources (Table 40.5), and less likely to read something they disagree with, although that particular relationship is not statistically significant in five of the seven nations (Table 40.6).

Our findings therefore raise questions about whether the measure of populist attitudes used, which speaks largely to anti-establishment sentiments, appropriately taps into strong ideological sentiments, which are often exclusionary (nationalist, anti-immigrant) or extreme in nature (Hameleers and de Vreese 2018; Van Hauwaert et al. 2020). Such exclusionary ideologies might be better captured by our indicators of polarisation, tapping very left or very right of centre political orientations, and these are more line with an echo chamber thesis. These extreme forms of populism are not positive from a normative perspective, and an increase in such populist sentiments would be cause for alarm. But they are not captured by the standard operational definition of populism that we employed and might be better conceptualised as trends towards polarisation.

Overall, our findings problematise the very meaning and measurement of populism in a digital era of perceived citizen empowerment. It may be that those populist citizens who are anti-elitist and anti-establishment are actually politically interested individuals who express a desire to take back some control from political leaders, spurred on by their greater access to information and communication technologies. Are populist citizens simply more confident in thinking and finding out for themselves? Are they gaining a greater sense of empowerment through access to resources via the internet?

While we cannot definitively rule out populism being driven by digital media, the evidence we marshalled challenges this technologically deterministic view. For example, populists are more likely to be older, but younger internet users are more likely to avoid information they disagree with, consult fewer news sources online, and agree with the political opinions and content posted by their friends online. Our findings indicate that we need to disentangle citizen empowerment and polarisation from populist rhetoric. This chapter also shows why it is important for political researchers to examine the actual uses of search engines and social media more rigourously and rely less heavily on technologically deterministic perspectives.

Notes

1 This chapter is part of the Quello Search Project at Michigan State University, titled 'The Part Played by Search in Shaping Political Opinion', which was supported by Google Inc.
2 These nations and their sample size were Germany (N = 2000), Spain (N = 2007), France (N = 2000), Italy (N = 2000), Poland (N = 2005), the United Kingdom (N = 2000), and the United States (N = 2018).

References

Akkerman, A., Mudde, C. and Zaslove, A. (2014) How Populist Are the People? Measuring Populist Attitudes in Voters. *Comparative Political Studies* 47(9): 1324–1353.
Bernhard, L. and Hänggli, R. (2018) Who Holds Populist Attitudes? Evidence from Switzerland. *Swiss Political Science Review* 24(4): 510–524.

Canovan, M. (1999) Trust the People! Populism and the Two Faces of Democracy. *Political Studies* 47(1): 2–16.

Decker, F. (2008) Germany: Right-wing Populist Failures and Left-wing Successes. In Albertazzi, D. and McDonnell, D. (eds.), *Twenty-First Century Populism: The Spectre of Western European Democracy*. New York: Palgrave Macmillan.

DeLuca, K. M., Lawson, S. and Sun, Y. (2012) Occupy Wall Street on the Public Screens of Social Media: The Many Framings of the Birth of a Protest Movement. *Communication, Culture & Critique* 5(4): 483–509.

Dubois, E. and Dutton, W. H. (2014) Empowering Citizens of the Internet Age. In Graham, M., and Dutton, W. H. (eds.), *Society and the Internet*. Oxford: Oxford University Press, pp. 238–253.

Dutton, W. H. (2009) The Fifth Estate Emerging through the Network of Networks, *Prometheus* 27(1) (March): 1–15.

Dutton, W. H., Reisdorf, B. C., Blank, G., Dubois, E. and Fernandez, L. (2019) The Internet and Access to Information About Politics: Searching Through Filter Bubbles, Echo Chambers, and Disinformation. In Graham, M. and Dutton, W. H. (eds.), *Society and the Internet*, 2nd Edition. Oxford: Oxford University Press, pp. 228–247.

Engesser, S., Ernst, N., Esser, F., et al. (2017) Populism and social media: How politicians spread a fragmented ideology. *Information, Communication & Society* 20(8): 1109–1126.

Ernst, N., Engesser, S., Büchel, F., et al. (2017) Extreme Parties and Populism: An Analysis of Facebook and Twitter across Six Countries. *Information, Communication & Society* 20(9): 1347–1364.

Esser, F., Stępińska, A. and Hopmann, D. N. (2016) Populism and the Media: Cross-National Findings and Perspectives. In Aalberg, T., Esser, F., Reinemann, C., Stromback, J., and De Vreese, C (eds.), *Populist Political Communication in Europe*. New York: Routledge, pp. 365–380.

Fawzi, N. (2019) Untrustworthy News and the Media as "Enemy of the People?" How a Populist Worldview Shapes Recipients' Attitudes toward the Media. *The International Journal of Press/Politics* 24(2): 146–164.

Gerbaudo, P. (2018) Social Media and Populism: An Elective Affinity? *Media, Culture & Society* 40(5): 745–753.

Groshek, J. and Koc-Michalska, K. (2017) Helping Populism Win? Social Media Use, Filter Bubbles, and Support for Populist Presidential Candidates in the 2016 US Election Campaign. *Information, Communication & Society* 20(9): 1389–1407.

Hameleers, M., Bos, L. and de Vreese, C. H. (2017) The Appeal of Media Populism: The Media Preferences of Citizens with Populist Attitudes. *Mass Communication and Society* 20(4): 481–504.

Hameleers, M. and de Vreese, C. H. (2018) To Whom are "the People" Opposed? Conceptualizing and Measuring Citizens' Populist Attitudes as a Multidimensional Construct. *Journal of Elections, Public Opinion and Parties*, 1–20.

Hawkins, K. A., Riding, S. and Mudde, C. (2012). Measuring Populist Attitudes. *Political Concepts Committee on Concepts and Methods Working Paper Series* 55: 1–35.

Hawkins, K. A., Rovira Kaltwasser, C. and Andreadis, I. (2020) The Activation of Populist Attitudes. *Government and Opposition* 55(2): 283–307.

Jutel, O. (2016) The Liberal Field of Journalism and the Political – *The New York Times, Fox News* and the Tea Party. *Journalism: Theory, Practice & Criticism* 17(8): 1129–1145.

Kaltwasser, C. R. (2015) Explaining the Emergence of Populism in Europe and the Americas. In de la Torre, C. (ed.), *The Promise and Perils of Populism*. Lexington, Kentucky: University Press of Kentucky, pp. 189–228.

Krämer, B. (2017) Populist Online Practices: The Function of the Internet in Right-wing Populism. *Information, Communication & Society* 20(9): 1293–1309.

Mudde, C. (2004) The Populist Zeitgeist. *Government and Opposition* 39(4): 541–563.

Nichols, T. M. (2017) *The Death of Expertise: The Campaign against Established Knowledge and Why It Matters*. New York: Oxford University Press.

Nickerson, R. S. (1998) Confirmation Bias: A Ubiquitous Phenomenon in Many Guises. *Review of General Psychology* 2(2): 175–220.

Nikolov, D., Oliveira, D. F. M., Flammini, A., et al. (2015) Measuring Online Social Bubbles. *PeerJ Computer Science* 1: e38.

Pariser, E. (2011) *The Filter Bubble: What the Internet Is Hiding from You*. London: Viking.

Postill, J. (2018) Populism and Social Media: A Global Perspective. *Media, Culture & Society* 40(5): 754–765.

Rico, G. and Anduiza, E. (2019) Economic Correlates of Populist Attitudes: An Analysis of Nine European Countries in the Aftermath of the Great Recession. *Acta Politica* 54(3): 371–397.

Schroeder, R. (2018) *Social Theory after the Internet: Media, Technology, and Globalization.* London: UCL Press.

Schulz, A. (2019) Where Populist Citizens Get the News: An Investigation of News Audience Polarization along Populist Attitudes in 11 Countries. *Communication Monographs* 86(1): 88–111.

Schulz, A., Müller, P., Schemer, C., et al. (2018) Measuring Populist Attitudes on Three Dimensions. *International Journal of Public Opinion Research* 30(2): 316–326.

Schulz, A., Wirth, W. and Müller, P. (2020) We Are the People and You Are Fake News: A Social Identity Approach to Populist Citizens' False Consensus and Hostile Media Perceptions. *Communication Research* 47(2): 201–226.

Spruyt, B., Keppens, G. and Van Droogenbroeck, F. (2016) *Who* Supports Populism and *What* Attracts People to It? *Political Research Quarterly* 69(2): 335–346.

Sunstein, C. R. (2007) *Republic.com 2.0.* Princeton, NJ: Princeton University Press.

Sunstein, C. R. (2017) *#republic: Divided Democracy in the Age of Social Media.* Princeton, NJ: Princeton University Press.

Tsatsanis, E., Andreadis, I. and Teperoglou, E. (2018) Populism from Below: Socio-economic and Ideological Correlates of Mass Attitudes in Greece. *South European Society and Politics* 23(4): 429–450.

Van Hauwaert, S. M., Schimpf, C. H. and Azevedo, F. (2020) The Measurement of Populist Attitudes: Testing Cross-national Scales Using Item Response Theory. *Politics* 40(1): 3–21.

Waisbord, S. (2018) Truth is What Happens to News: On Journalism, Fake News, and Post-truth. *Journalism Studies* 19(13): 1866–1878.

PART V

Responses to misinformation, disinformation, and populism

40
LEGAL AND REGULATORY RESPONSES TO MISINFORMATION AND POPULISM

Alison Harcourt

Introduction

According to Google Trends, the frequency of misinformation has risen significantly since the 2016 US presidential elections (Figure 41.1). Disinformation and misinformation are not new phenomena but, as many authors explain, as old as time. However, distribution has been propagated by social media with most sharing taking place on Facebook (Marchal et al., 2019:2). This has been furthered by the practice of astroturfing and the creation of bots (Bernal, 2018:242; Marsden and Meyer, 2019). Bastos and Mercea found that a 'network of Twitterbots comprising 13,493 accounts that tweeted the United Kingdom European Union membership referendum, only to disappear from Twitter shortly after the ballot' (2017:1). Social media manipulation is on the increase globally, particularly in relation to state-engineered interference (Bradshaw and Howard, 2019). Many authors point to ownership structures and the lack of transparency and accountability in the media, coupled with a lack of sustainability of journalism and lack of trust in the media, for the exacerbation of disinformation and 'fake news' inquiry.

Stakeholders have called on governments and the European Union to take action. Two states, Germany and France, have introduced laws to tackle disinformation. Germany introduced its *Netzwerkdurchsetzungsgesetz*[1] law in 2017 (Deutscher Bundestag, 2017), which polices social media websites following a number of high-profile national court cases concerning fake news and the spread of racist material. It enables the reporting and take-down of online content. France passed a law on the manipulation of information[2] in 2018, which similarly obliges social media networks to take down content upon request by a judge. Candidates and political parties can also appeal to a judge to stem the spread of 'false information' under the control or influence of state foreign media during elections. The UK has taken a more self-regulative approach after a UK Commons committee investigation into fake news by the Digital, Culture, Media and Sport Committee concluded that Facebook's founder Mark Zuckerberg failed to show 'leadership or personal responsibility' over fake news (2017). The two-part inquiry focused on the business practices of Facebook, particularly in response to the Cambridge Analytica scandal. The UK's resulting 2019 Online Harms White Paper[3] proposes a self-regulatory framework under which firms should take responsibility for user safety under duty of care. The European Union (EU) has flanked national efforts with a 2016

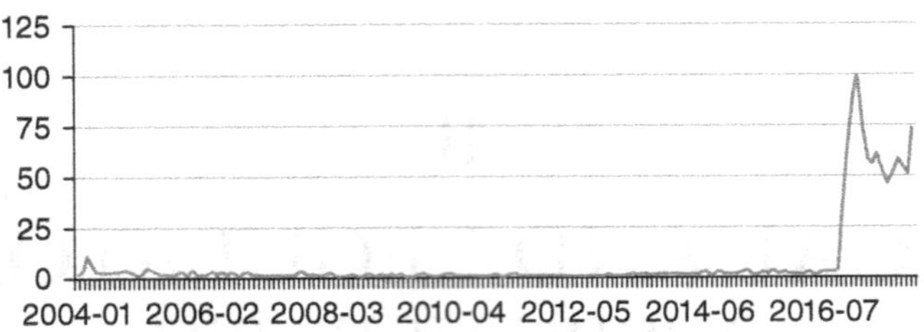

Figure 40.1   The Frequency of 'fake news' in Google Trends (2004–2018)

Source: Google Trends cited in Martens et al. (2018:8)

Conduct on Countering Illegal Hate Speech Online and 2018 action plan. This culminated in codes of practice in 2018 and 2019, which have been voluntarily adopted by social media platforms and news associations.

This chapter will outline different responses in case studies on Germany, France, and the UK. This is explained through existing legal instruments – namely, hate speech and strong privacy laws and right of reply in France and Germany (Richter, 2018; Heldt, 2019; Katsirea, 2019) – whereas the UK takes a more self-regulated approach as supported by recent case law (Craufurd-Smith, 2019; Woods, 2019).

National definitions

Misinformation is defined differently in different national contexts. The French law refers to '*nouvelles fausses*' (false information) in reference to Article 27 of the 1881 French Press Law[4] and French Electoral Code.[5] This was based upon recommendations from the *Conseil d'Etat* (Council of State)[6] for reasons of conformity with existing laws and judicial review (Craufurd-Smith, 2019:56). The German NetzDG refers to 'unlawful content' ('*Rechts-wichige Inhalte*') as defined under provisions in the German criminal code *Strafgesetzbuch* (StGB), which includes insult (§185), defamation (§186), intentional defamation (§187),[7] public incitement to crime (§111), incitement to hatred (§130), and dissemination of depictions of violence (§131). The law also stipulates that social networks define 'hate speech' within their terms of service.[8]

The UK 2019 Online Harms White Paper uses the word *disinformation*, which is defined as being 'created or disseminated with the deliberate intent to mislead; this could be to cause harm, or for personal, political or financial gain'. The white paper also refers to the Digital, Culture, Media and Sport (DCMS) Committee Commons Select Committee definition of *disinformation*: 'the deliberate creation and sharing of false and/or manipulated information that is intended to deceive and mislead audiences, either for the purposes of causing harm, or for political, personal or financial gain' (2018, 2019).[9]

The European Commission's 'high-level group on fake news and online disinformation' also uses the term *disinformation*, which is defined as 'all forms of false, inaccurate, or misleading information designed, presented and promoted to intentionally cause public harm or for profit' (European Commission, 2018:1). The term *disinformation* was adopted, in turn, by the United Nations, OSCE, OAS, and AU (OSCE, 2017) and also by the Council of Europe (Council of Europe, 2017). These efforts at avoiding the term *fake news* were aimed at disassociating it from the meaning of *news*. This is because 'disinformation' cannot be legally defined as 'news' as such.

Policy approaches within Europe

Germany

Germany's *Netzwerkdurchsetzungsgesetz* (NetzDG) (Law Improving Enforcement in Social Networks) was enacted in November 2017 and came into force in January 2018. It was introduced to the *Bundestag* by Heiki Maas, the minister of justice, and is largely based on hate speech provisions enshrined in the German Constitution. It obliges social networks with more than two million registered users in Germany, such as Facebook, Twitter and YouTube, to remove '*offensichtlich rechtswidrige Inhalte*' (manifestly unlawful content)[10] within 24 hours of receiving a complaint and within seven days if the content is not 'manifestly' illegal.

The NetzDG is based on subsection 1 of the *Strafgesetzbuch* (StGB) under sections 86, 86a, 89a, 91, 100a, 111, 126, 129 to 129b, 130, 131, 140, 166, 184b in relation to 184d, 185 to 187, 241 and also under 269 of the German Criminal Code. As translated by Article 19, these relate to Section 86, 'dissemination of propaganda material of unconstitutional organisations'; Section 86a, 'using symbols of unconstitutional organisations'; Section 89a, 'preparation of a serious violence offence endangering the state'; Section 91, 'encouraging the commission of a serious violence offence endangering the state'; Section 100(a), 'treasonous forgery'; Section 111, 'public incitement to crime'; Section 126, 'breach of the public peace by threatening to commit offences'; Section 129, 'forming criminal organisations'; Section 129a, 'forming terrorist organisations'; Section 129b, 'criminal and terrorist organisations abroad'; Section 130, 'incitement to hatred'; Section 131, 'dissemination of depictions of violence'; Section 140, 'rewarding and approving of offences'; Section 166, 'defamation of religions, religious and ideological associations'; Section 184b, 'distribution, acquisition and possession of child pornography' in conjunction with Section 184(d), 'distribution of pornographic performances by broadcasting, media services or telecommunications services'; Section 185, 'insult'; Section 186, 'defamation'; Section 187, 'intentional defamation'; Section 201(a). 'violation of intimate privacy by taking photographs'; Section 241, 'threatening the commission of a felony'; and Section 269, 'forgery of data intended to provide proof'.[11]

The law shifts primary responsibility for user-generated content to social media platforms. The minister cannot issue a take-down order, but content must be removed on a self-regulatory basis by platforms when faced with complaints.[12] A decision after seven days is referred to a self-regulatory body approved by the Ministry of Justice. Germany requires platforms to establish a clear complaints system for the reporting of unlawful content. The German law has more teeth than the French law, in the form of heavy fines which can be between €5 and €50 million. It is applicable to social media networks with over two million users. However, unlike in France, fines are only issued to platforms and not to their users.

Due to Germany's highly legalistic culture, laws are highly detailed with little flexibility as to implementation. As Theil explains, 'reporting obligations are quite detailed and include provisions that set out reviewer training and oversight requirements' (2019:46). For this reason, he reports a sharp rise in the hiring of content moderators by Facebook and Twitter due to the law, with German speakers accounting for one-sixth of Twitter's content team in 2018 (2019:49). The NetzDG obliges social media networks to produce biannual reports on content moderation for platforms with over 100 complaints per year (for analysis, see Heldt, 2019). Facebook was the first social media platform to be fined under the NetzDG in 2019, with a fine of €2 million.[13] A new bill was proposed to update the NetzDG in April 2020, which recommends increased transparency from social media networks and reference to the updated Audiomedia Services Directive.[14]

France

In 2018, the French National Assembly passed a law to combat the manipulation of information (National Assembly, 2018). The 2018 law is three pronged. Firstly, it enables citizens, regulatory bodies, and political parties to report misinformation, which permits a judge to issue take-down orders. Implicitly, as in Germany, the law obliges social media platforms to take responsibility for user content published on their pages. Secondly, it demands increased financial transparency from social media platforms on sponsored content and political advertising. Political sponsorship and the amount paid for it should be reported. Thirdly, the law grants powers to the *Conseil supérieur de l'audiovisuel* (CSA) to temporarily suspend licenses for television and radio channels which show evidence of disinformation propagated by foreign states. As Craufurd-Smith points out, the French approach has been focused on the threat of disinformation to democracy (2019:63).

France's Manipulation of Information law was adopted in December 2018 following scrutiny and approval by the *Conseil Constitutionnel* (Assembly Nationale, 2019).[15] The law is underpinned by existing measures, most significantly Article 27 of the 1881 French Press Law which. prohibits ' "false news" or "articles fabricated, falsified or falsely attributed to others", where this is done in bad faith and undermines, or could undermine, public order' (Craufurd-Smith, 2019:55). It also draws on applicable provisions on genocide denial and crimes against humanity (Article 24) and defamation (Articles 29–35 of the 1881 Press Law) and the Electoral Code,[16] under which (Article 97) 'false news, calumnies, or other fraudulent means' and commercial electoral advertising are prohibited (Dossier in Craufurd-Smith, 2019:55).

In addition to the laws mentioned previously, the 2018 law stipulated changes to the 1977 law on election to the European Parliament,[17] the 1986 law on the freedom of communication (Léotard Law),[18] the 2004 law on confidence in the digital economy,[19] the Electoral Code,[20] a decree from the Ministry of Culture on Article L111–7 of the Consumer Code,[21] the Education Code,[22] the 2018 law on filing candidacy for election,[23] and the public order code overseas.[24] Due to their different legal bases, implementation is conducted by judges for take-down orders, the *Conseil supérieur de l'audiovisuel* (CSA) for license suspension, and the *Autorité des Marchés Financiers* (AMF) for the issue of fines, respectively. Decisions are subject to judicial review.

The key target is political advertising and political party campaigning. Three months prior to an election, social media platforms are required to provide citizens access to 'fair, clear, and transparent' information on the purpose as well as the identity (natural persons or corporate name and registered office) of those paying to promote political debate, use of their personal data, and the amount paid (over a given threshold). This is made available to the public in an aggregated public register. Platforms are required to establish a notification mechanism for users to alert them to false information. There are also requirements for platforms regarding transparency on algorithms which organise content related to 'a debate of national interest' and publication on their functioning; the promotion of news publishers and agencies providing impartial, accurate information; and the deletion of disinformation accounts. Social media platforms must provide the CSA with annual reports. In particular, under Article 14 of the act, information on content, access to content (how often and when, based on platform recommendations), and the referencing by algorithms must be provided. In turn the CSA publishes regular reports on measures implemented by platforms.[25] During periods of election, fines of up to €75,000 and a possible prison sentence of one year can be imposed on social media platforms[26] and their users if content is not removed within 48 hours.

The UK

In the UK, inquiries into fake news began in 2017, firstly with a Digital, Culture, Media and Sport Committee commenced in January 2017 and finalised in June 2017, when the UK general election took place.[27] This was followed by a study of disinformation and 'fake news' conducted by the House of Commons Digital, Culture, Media and Sport Committee (DCMS) launched in September 2017.[28] This culminated in two reports on disinformation and 'fake news', the first an interim report in July 2018 with the final report published in February 2019.[29] After initial lukewarm government response to the interim report, the committee held three oral evidence sessions, received 23 written submissions from national stakeholders in July 2018, and conducted an 'international grand committee' in November 2018 with parliamentary representatives from nine different countries.[30] This fed into the UK government's 2019 Online Harms White Paper (OHWP), authored by the Department for Digital, Culture, Media and Sport and the Home Office. At the time of writing, the OHWP is still undergoing consultation with a Sub-Committee on Disinformation that was established by the Commons Select Committee in April 2020.

As in France, the key concern of both UK inquiries was inaccuracy and political bias in the news, particularly during election times. Fake news is identified in the report as a political problem as it creates a 'polarising effect and reduces the common ground on which reasoned debate polarising effect and reduces the common ground on which reasoned debate, based on objective facts, can take place' and thereby a threat to democracy. Both the interim and final reports highlight seven main legal issues relating to social media platforms.[31] Interestingly, as Craufurd-Smith points out, the UK approach differs from that of continental Europe in that English courts may be unwilling to take into consideration Article 10 of the European Convention on Human Rights, which grants the right to freedom of expression and information. Craufurd-Smith notes that 'the High Court in the judicial review case of Woolas held that the dishonest publication of false information prior to elections would not be protected by Article 10(1) ECHR' (Craufurd-Smith, 2019:80).

The UK approach focuses on enforcing greater transparency about the source of news, its funding, and how it is reaching citizens. In particular, the proposal addresses social media reach. As in France and Germany, the UK draws on existing regulatory instruments in application to the problem of disinformation. However, the basis is different. The main proposal resulting from the inquiries is the 2019 Online Harms White Paper (OHWP), which is, at the time of writing, undergoing consultation.[32] Unlike in Germany and France, the main statutory legal instruments are the obligation of duty of care, the adoption of technical measures, and codes of practice. Woods explains that this is based upon common-law practice (2019). 'Duty of care' derives from 'common law doctrine of negligence developed from *Donoghue v Stephenson*', which was initially developed within national case law but later implemented in statutory law, beginning with the 1974 Health and Safety at Work Act (Woods, 2019:7–9).

Lack of implementation of the Codes of Practice could meet with fines from the regulator. The government announced in February 2020 that the communication regulator OFCOM would be given responsibility for Online Harms implementation, but this proposal has met with a great deal of pushback to date.[33] One reason for the pushback is that OFCOM is funded by regulatees, and it is seen as a potential additional tax on social media platforms. The proposal innovates from the earlier French and German laws in that algorithmic measures are viewed as having a high level of potential to locate and identify content for take-down. A project has been established at the Turing Institute in London to 'use a mix of natural language processing techniques and qualitative analyses to create tools which identify and categorise different strengths and types of online hate speech'.[34]

According to the white paper, the UK regulator (yet to be created or assigned) will coordinate with social media platforms to create a code of practice to 'minimise the spread of misleading and harmful disinformation and to increase the accessibility of trustworthy and varied news content'. This includes making 'less visible' content which has been flagged by reputable fact-checking services; the promotion of 'authoritative news sources' and 'diverse news content'; improving the 'transparency of political advertising', enabling mechanisms for users to flag known false content; and transparency on company policies. Lastly, the white paper states that it seeks to maintain 'a news environment where accurate content can prevail and high quality news has a sustainable future'. Related to this, the white paper supports proposals of the 2019 Cairncross Review into the sustainability of high-quality journalism, which recommended that a 'news quality obligation' be required from social media companies, which would 'require these companies to improve how their users understand the origin of a news article and the trustworthiness of its source'.

There are other UK proposals which flank the Online Harms proposal, including changes to the Broadcasting Code, which is undergoing consultation by OFCOM in 2020;[35] potential changes to the Advertising Standards Authority (ASA)'s Code of Non-Broadcast Advertising and Direct and Promotional Marketing (CAP code); and the development of 'formal coordination mechanisms to ensure regulation is coherent, consistent, and avoids duplication' by the new regulator in coordination with the Competition and Markets Authority (CMA) and Information Commissioner's Office's (ICO).[36] Future changes to codes and practice in regulatory approach can be seen at the Financial Conduct Authority (FCA), the Gambling Commission the Electoral Commission, and the Equality and Human Rights Commission (EHRC). Similar to France and Germany, the UK assigns reasonability for users' content on social media platforms.

EU approach

The European Commission began tackling disinformation online with a Code of Conduct on Countering Illegal Hate Speech Online in 2016.[37] The Commission signed a 'code of conduct' with Facebook, Microsoft, Twitter, and YouTube to address hate speech online in 2016. This was followed by the establishment of a high level group of experts (HLEG) to address disinformation online in 2018. The HLEG produced a report identifying best practices in 2018.[38] The report requested that social media platforms adopt a number of measures by July 2018.

The 2018 measures were quite expansive, reflecting wider EU policy goals. They included enhancing the transparency of online news, including transparency on data sharing; promoting media and information literacy; developing tools for empowering users and journalists; safeguarding the diversity and sustainability of the European news media ecosystem; promoting research on disinformation; adapting social media advertising policies to a 'follow-the-money' principle based on clear, transparent, and non-discriminatory criteria; ensuring transparency in the processing of users' data for advertisement placements; and distinguishing sponsored content, including political advertising, from other content. There were also voluntary requirements on fact-checking. These included referencing 'cooperation with public and private European news outlets', making news suggestions and fact checking sites (where appropriate), and providing a role for press councils and the European level association, the Alliance of Independent Press Councils of Europe (AIPCE), in the creation of a code of conduct.

In 2018, the European Commission published its Communication on Tackling Online Disinformation: a European Approach.[39] This was followed by an updated Code of Practice on Disinformation,[40] published in September 2018. The code was signed in October 2018 by a number of social media platforms – Facebook, Twitter, Mozilla, and Google – and associations – the European Association of Communication Agencies, the Interactive Advertising Bureau, and the World Federation of Advertisers.[41] This was mostly in anticipation of the May 2019 European Parliament elections.

The 2019 code differs slightly from the 2018 code in that it no longer includes voluntary obligations to cooperate with European press councils and promote European publisher content. Its main focus is on fact-checking and disinformation. It commits signatories to 'improve the scrutiny of advertisement placements to reduce revenues of the purveyors of disinformation'; 'ensure transparency about political and issue-based advertising'; 'implement and promote reasonable policies against misrepresentation'; 'close fake accounts and establish clear marking systems and rules for bots to ensure their activities cannot be confused with human interactions'; 'communicate on the effectiveness of efforts'; 'invest in technological means to prioritize relevant, authentic, and accurate and authoritative information where appropriate in search, feeds, or other automatically ranked distribution channels'; 'not be compelled by governments . . . to delete or prevent access to otherwise lawful content'; enable 'users to understand why they have been targeted by a given political or issue-based advertisement'; 'dilute . . . disinformation by improving the findability of trustworthy content'; empower 'users with tools . . . to facilitate content discovery and access to different news sources representing alternative viewpoints'; provide 'tools to report Disinformation' by users; and enable 'factchecking and research activities . . . including data for independent investigation by academic researchers and general information on algorithms'. The UK decided to participate after Brexit in the 2019 initiative as the then–minister for digital, culture, media and sport, Margot James, decided that it was non-legislative and did not require implementation of EU law. As a result, the UK was 'broadly supportive of the EU's actions in this area' and did 'not believe that such action will prevent the UK taking action in this area'.[42]

From January 2019, signatories began to submit monthly reports on code implementation to the European Commission.[43] A number of initiatives to limit disinformation have been realised since this time, notably to handle the rise in disinformation during election periods. Google funded a $300 million project to support journalism in 2019 and introduced a database of stories with fact-checking tools.[44] Twitter decided to ban all political advertising from November 2019.[45] Google similarly limited political advertising by political affiliation or public voter records from December 2019 in the run-up to the US presentation election.[46] Political advertising is still permitted via Google but only by age, gender, and location (by post code). Facebook is coming under increasing pressure to implement more stringent measures, particularly after it removed a ban on advertising containing 'deceptive, false or misleading content' in October 2019, replacing it with a ban only on advertising that 'include[s] claims debunked by third-party fact-checkers, or, in certain circumstances, claims debunked by organisations with particular expertise'.[47]

As Marsden and Meyer point out, other EU initiatives have been promoting artificial intelligence for the removal of illegal content, including a 2020 proposal for the EU Regulation on the Prevention of Dissemination of Terrorist Content Online and Article 13 of the proposed Copyright in the Digital Single Market Directive (2020). Both initiatives recommend the use of algorithms and filtering technologies. However, as Marsden, Meyer, and Brown argue, 'Automated technologies such as AI are not a silver bullet for identifying illegal or "harmful" content.

They are limited in their accuracy, especially for expression where cultural or contextual cues are necessary' (2020:7).

Conclusion

There has been a clear shift in regulatory approach in all three states. All initiatives are self-regulatory in nature and move responsibility for content to the social network or platform carrying content and away from content providers and users. This is because platforms act as gateway providers for communication, whereas market provision for digital content (whether traditional or user generated) is increasingly fragmented and difficult to regulate. There are increasing technical solutions which enable the filtering of content. Search engines such as Google steer users towards content, whereas social networks can apply software to focus user attention. Post Brexit, greater EU coordination is expected once the UK is removed from the equation, given the greater appetite for more interventionist measures in France and Germany. Indeed, a May 2020 study released by the European Commission recommends the introduction of 'sanctions and redress mechanisms' under the EU's 2019 Code of Disinformation.[48]

Legal basis for statutory action within the EU (in the form of Directives or Regulations) is, however, tenuous. A mix of measures are emerging, thus far based on existing security and copyright legislation. Article 17(9) of the EU 2019 Copyright Directive, which is, at the time of writing, being implemented into national legislations, includes a complaint and redress mechanism which may be applied to social networks. Further action might arise out of competition law[49] and company law.[50] Indeed, the beginnings of this can be seen in the June 2020 proposal for a regulation on the ex ante regulatory instrument of very large online platforms acting as gatekeepers under the EU's Digital Services Act package.[51] This is flanked by court decisions such as the 2014 Google Spain case decided by the European Court of Justice,[52] which grants the 'right to be forgotten' to citizens requesting that result links relating their names be removed from public search engines upon request. More activity is expected on the self-regulatory front from ERGA. An ERGA sub-group is, at the time of writing, developing advice for the European Commission on the transposition of the Audiovisual Media Services Directive and the new Digital Services Act.

One marked problem with the introduction of any statute at national or European levels is the mismatch the between application of rules to traditional and online media. In the UK, television channels need to adhere to OFCOM's Broadcasting Code and newspapers to IPSO's Editors' Code of Practice or IMPRESS' standards code. However, as shown by the Leveson Inquiry, the imbalance between requirements on the different sectors and print media has largely gone unchallenged in the UK. The take-down of disinformation might, of course, be applied to articles appearing in online news media editions. Continental Europe has historically applied much stricter rules on the press, so disinformation in traditional media has been less prevalent. There has, however, been a rise in fake news stories in the German traditional press since their move online (Heldt, 2019).

Notes

1 *Gesetz zur Verbesserung der Rechtsdurchsetzung in sozialen Netzwerken (Netzwerkdurchsetzungsgesetz).*
2 Loi n° 2018–1202 *du 22 décembre* 2018 *relative à la lutte contre la manipulation de l'information.* www.legifrance.gouv.fr/affichLoiPreparation.do?idDocument=JORFDOLE000037151987&type=general&typeLoi=prop&legislature=15.
3 Online Harms White Paper" www.gov.uk/government/consultations/online-harms-white-paper.

4 *Loi du 29 juillet* 1881 *sur la liberté de la presse.* www.legifrance.gouv.fr/affichTexte.do?cidTexte=LEG ITEXT000006070722&dateTexte=vig Article 27 was last amended by Ordinance No. 2000–916 of September 19, 2000 – art. 3 (V) JORF September 22, 2000 effective January 1, 2002.

5 For English translation of the Electoral Code, see http://europam.eu/data/mechanisms/PF/PF%20 Laws/France/France_Electoral_Code_legislative_part_primary_leg_am2013_fr%20(1).pdf.

6 www.conseil-etat.fr.

7 Article 19 translates Sections 186 and 187 of the StGB as follows: Defamation – Section 186 of the Criminal Code reads: 'Whosoever intentionally and knowingly asserts or disseminates an untrue fact related to another person, which may defame him or negatively affect public opinion about him or endanger his creditworthiness shall be liable to imprisonment not exceeding two years or a fine, and, if the act was committed publicly, in a meeting 60 or through dissemination of written materials (section 11(3)) to imprisonment not exceeding five years or a fine'. Intentional defamation – Section 187 reads: '1) If an offence of defamation (section 186) is committed publicly, in a meeting or through dissemination of written materials (section 11(3)) against a person involved in the popular political life based on the position of that person in public life, and if the offence may make his public activities substantially more difficult the penalty shall be imprisonment from three months to five years. (2) An intentional defamation (section 187) under the same conditions shall entail imprisonment from six months to five years'. www.article19.org/wp-content/uploads/2018/07/Germany-Responding-to-%E2%80%98hate-speech%E2%80%99-v3-WEB.pdf.

8 See Facebook's definition of hate speech here: www.facebook.com/communitystandards/hate_speech.

9 Disinformation and 'fake news': Government Response to the Committee's Fifth Report of Session 2017–19, 23 October 2018, HC 1630 Government response to Interim Report, page 2.

10 Official translation can be found at www.bmjv.de/SharedDocs/Gesetzgebungsverfahren/Dokumente/ NetzDG_engl.pdf;jsessionid=D9F4B816F91A21413A3E9512204ED293.1_cid334?__ blob=publicationFile&v=2.

11 www.article19.org/wp-content/uploads/2018/07/Germany-Responding-to-%E2%80%98hate-speech%E2%80%99-v3-WEB.pdf.

12 'Das Bundesamt für Justiz kann rechtswidrige Inhalte (z. B. Hasskriminalität) nicht selbst löschen oder sperren bzw. die Löschung oder Sperrung anordnen. Es hat die Aufgabe, Verstöße gegen Pfl ichten, die nach dem Netzwerk durch setzungsgesetz zu beachten sind, im Wege eines Bußgeldverfahrens zu verfolgen, darunter den Umgang mit Beschwerden über rechtswidrige Inhalte. Bitte beschweren Sie sich daher in jedem Fall zunächst bei dem betreffenden sozialen Netzwerk über die unterlassene Lös-chung oder Sperrung von rechtswidrigen Inhalten'. www.bundesjustizamt.de/DE/Themen/Buergerdienste/NetzDG/Fragen/FAQ_node.html.

13 www.bundesjustizamt.de/DE/Presse/Archiv/ 2019/20190702_EN.html;jsessionid=AE3371DA35E5 EEFEEB5A8BFF7F52AFCA.1_cid392?nn=3449818.

14 https://dip21.bundestag.de/dip21/btd/19/187/1918792.pdf.

15 Decision no. 2018–773 DC of 20 December 2018. www.conseil-constitutionnel.fr/en/decision/2018/ 2018773DC.htm.

16 Electoral law in France consists of a series of acts: namely, Law No. 62–1292 of November 6, 1962, relating to the election of the President of the Republic by universal suffrage; Organic law n ° 2017–1338 of September 15, 2017 for confidence in political life; and the Electoral Code. The 2018 Law on the fight against the manipulation of information is also considered to be encompassed within electoral law, along with the Decision of the Constitutional Council n ° 2018–773 DC of December 20, 2018.

17 Article 26 of Law n ° 77–729 of July 7, 1977 relating to the election of representatives to the European Parliament. Consolidated version as of April 29, 2020. www.legifrance.gouv.fr/affichTexte.do?cidText e=LEGITEXT000006068600.

18 Law 86–1067 of September 30, 1986. www.legifrance.gouv.fr/affichTexteArticle.do?idArticle=LEGI ARTI000037855721&cidTexte=JORFTEXT000000512205&dateTexte=20181224.

19 Law n ° 2004–575 of June 21, 2004 for confidence in the digital economy. www.legifrance.gouv.fr/ affichTexte.do?cidTexte=JORFTEXT000000801164.

20 Electoral code, consolidated version, as of March 1, 2020. www.legifrance.gouv.fr/affichCode.do?cid Texte=LEGITEXT000006070239.

21 2000 Ministry decree Consumer Code. www.csa.fr/Arbitrer/Espace-juridique/Les-textes-reglemen taires-du-CSA/Les-deliberations-et-recommandations-du-CSA/Recommandations-et-deliberations-du-CSA-relatives-a-d-autres-sujets/Recommandation-n-2019-03-du-15-mai-2019-du-Conseil-superieur-de-l-audiovisuel-aux-operateurs-de-plateforme-en-ligne-dans-le-cadre-du-devoir-de-cooper

ation-en-matiere-de-lutte-contre-la-diffusion-de-fausses-informations. For translation, see: http://ec.europa.eu/growth/tools-databases/tris/en/index.cfm/search/?trisaction=search.detail&year=2019&num=2&dLang=EN.

22 Specifically, Articles 332–5, 771, 773 and 774 of the Code of Education have been updated. www.legifrance.gouv.fr/affichCode.do?cidTexte=LEGITEXT000006071191.

23 Law n ° 2018–51 of 31 January 2018 relating to the procedures for filing a candidacy for elections. www.legifrance.gouv.fr/affichTexte.do?cidTexte=JORFTEXT000036559728&categorieLien=id.

24 Overseas provisions, public order code. www.code-commande-publique.com/dispositions-relatives-a-loutre-mer/.

25 See also the 'Facebook experiment' Mission report by the French Secretary of State for Digital Affairs. www.numerique.gouv.fr/uploads/Regulation-of-social-networks_Mission-report_ENG.pdf.

26 The legal representative of a social media platforms can face a prison sentence.

27 www.parliament.uk/business/committees/committees-a-z/commons-select/culture-media-and-sport-committee/inquiries/parliament-2015/inquiry2/publications/.

28 www.parliament.uk/business/committees/committees-a-z/commons-select/digital-culture-media-and-sport-committee/inquiries/parliament-2017/fake-news-17–19/.

29 https://publications.parliament.uk/pa/cm201719/cmselect/cmcumeds/1791/1791.pdf.

30 Argentina, Belgium, Brazil, Canada, France, Ireland, Latvia, Singapore, and the UK.

31 These are the definitions, roles, and legal liabilities of social media platforms; data misuse and targeting; Facebook's knowledge of and participation in data-sharing; political campaigning; Russian influence in political campaigns; SCL influence in foreign elections; and digital literacy.

32 www.gov.uk/government/consultations/online-harms-white-paper%20www.gov.uk/government/consultations/online-harms-white-paper.

33 www.gov.uk/government/news/government-minded-to-appoint-ofcom-as-online-harms-regulator.

34 www.turing.ac.uk/research/research-projects/hate-speech-measures-and-counter-measures.

35 www.ofcom.org.uk/__data/assets/pdf_file/0025/192580/further-consultation-protecting-participants-tv-radio.pdf.

36 www.gov.uk/government/publications/cdei-review-of-online-targeting/online-targeting-final-report-and-recommendations.

37 https://ec.europpa.eu/justice/fundamental-rights/files/hate_speech_code_of_conduct_en.pdf.

38 A multi-dimensional approach to disinformation. Report of the independent high-level group on fake news and online disinformation. http://ec.europa.eu/newsroom/dae/document.cfm?doc_id=50271.

39 Communication from the Commission to the European Parliament, the Council, the European Economic and Social Committee, and the Committee of the Regions. Tackling online disinformation: a European approach COM(2018) 236 final. https://eur-lex.europa.eu/legal-content/EN/TXT/?uri=CELEX:52018DC0236.

40 https://ec.europa.eu/newsroom/dae/document.cfm?doc_id=54454.

41 https://ec.europa.eu/newsroom/dae/document.cfm?doc_id=54454.
ENT_19_6166.

42 Explanatory Memorandum from the Government (tackling online disinformation) (21 May 2018). http://europeanmemoranda.cabinetoffice.gov.uk/files/2018/07/Scan_Les_Saunders_20180709-141252_0465_001.pdf.

43 https://ec.europa.eu/digital-single-market/en/news/first-results-eu-code-practice-against-disinformation.

44 https://developers.google.com/fact-check/tools/api.

45 Twitter to ban all political advertising. www.bbc.co.uk/news/world-us-canada-50243306.

46 The UK has an existing ban on targeting by political affiliation.

47 See the Irish regulator BAI report on compliance with the EU Code of Practice on Disinformation. www.bai.ie/en/new-report-highlights-inconsistencies-across-digital-platforms-in-tackling-disinformation/.

48 Study for the assessment of the implementation of the Code of Practice on Disinformation. https://ec.europa.eu/digital-single-market/en/news/study-assessment-implementation-code-practice-disinformation https://ec.europa.eu/digital-single-market/en/news/study-assessment-implementation-code-practice-disinformation.

49 However, competition law stipulates subsidiarity the area of media pluralism protected by Article 21 (4) of the EU Merger.

50 The 5th Anti-Money Laundering Directive mandates that beneficial owners are registered, which is similar to requirements laid down in the French 2018 Disinformation Law during elections.
51 https://ec.europa.eu/info/law/better-regulation/have-your-say/initiatives/12418-Digital-Services-Act-package-ex-ante-regulatory-instrument-of-very-large-online-platforms-acting-as-gatekeepers.
52 Google Spain SL, *Google Inc. v Agencia Española de Protección de Datos, Mario Costeja González* (2014) http://curia.europa.eu/juris/liste.jsf?num=C-131/12.

References

Assembly Nationale (2019) "Lois relative à la lutte contre la manipulation de l'information". www.assemblee-nationale.fr/15/ta/tap0190.pdf

Bastos, M. T. and D. Mercea (2017) "The Brexit Botnet and User-Generated Hyperpartisan News". *Social Science Computer Review*.

Bernal, Paul (2018) *"Fighting Fakery" The Internet, Warts and All*. New York: Cambridge University Press.

Bradshaw, Samantha and Philip N. Howard (2019) "The Global Disinformation Order: 2019 Global Inventory of Organised Social Media Manipulation." Working Paper 2019.3. Oxford, UK: Project on Computational Propaganda. comprop.oii.ox.ac.uk

Council of Europe (2017) "Information Disorder: Toward an Interdisciplinary Framework for Research and Policy Making" commissioned report authored by Claire Wardle and Hossein Derakhshan DGI(2017)09 https://edoc.coe.int/en/media/7495-information-disorder-toward-an-interdisciplinary-framework-for-research-and-policy-making.html

Craufurd-Smith, Rachael (2019) "Fake News, French Law and Democratic Legitimacy: Lessons for the United Kingdom?". *Journal of Media Law* 11(1), pp. 52–81.

Department for Digital, Culture, Media and Sport, and the Home Office (2019) "Online Harms White Paper". April. Command Paper 57. https://assets.publishing.service.gov.uk/government/uploads/system/uploads/attachment_data/file/793360/Online_Harms_White_Paper.pdf

Department for Digital, Culture, Media and Sport (2018) "The 'Disinformation and 'fake news': Interim Report'" (HC 363). 29 July 2018. https://publications.parliament.uk/pa/cm201719/cmselect/cmcumeds/363/36302.htm

Deutscher Bundestag (2017) "Gesetz zur Verbesserung der Rechtsdurchsetzung in sozialen Netzwerken" (Netzwerkdurchsetzungsgesetz – NetzDG). Dokumentations- und Informationssystem für Parlamentarische Vorgänge (DIP). https://dipbt.bundestag.de/extrakt/ba/WP18/815/81582.html

European Commission (2018) "Final Report of the High Level Expert Group on Fake News and Online Disinformation". https://ec.europa.eu/digital-single-market/en/news/final-report-high-level-expert-group-fake-news-and-online-disinformation

Heldt, Amélie (2019) "Reading between the Lines and the Numbers: An Analysis of the First NetzDG Reports". *Internet Policy Review: Journal on Internet Regulation* 8(2), pp. 1–18.

Katsirea, I. (2019) "'Fake News': Reconsidering the Value of Untruthful Expression in the Face of Regulatory Uncertainty". *Journal of Media Law* 10(2), pp. 159–188.

Marchal, Nahema, Bence Kollanyi, Lisa-Maria Neudert and Philip N. Howard (2019) "Junk News During the EU Parliamentary Elections: Lessons from a Seven-Language Study of Twitter and Facebook". *Data Memo*. https://comprop.oii.ox.ac.uk/wp-content/uploads/sites/93/2019/05/EU-Data-Memo.pdf

Marsden, Chris and Trisha Meyer (2019) "How Can the Law Regulate Removal of Fake News?". *Society for Computers and Law*. www.scl.org/articles/10425-how-can-the-law-regulate-removal-of-fake-news

Marsden, Chris, Trisha Meyer and Ian Brown (2020) "How Can the Law Regulate Digital Disinformation?". *Computer Law & Security Review* 36.

Martens, Bertin, Luis Aguiar, Estrella Gomez-Herrera and Frank Mueller-Langer (2018) "The Digital Transformation of News Media and the Rise of Disinformation and Fake News". Seville. Joint Research Center, Digital Economy Unit, European Commission. https://ec.europa.eu/jrc/sites/jrcsh/files/jrc111529.pdf

National Assembly (2018) LOI n° 2018-1202 du 22 décembre 2018 relative à la lutte contre la manipulation de l'information www.legifrance.gouv.fr/affichLoiPreparation.do?idDocument=JORFDOLE000037151987&type=general&typeLoi=prop&legislature=15.

OSCE (2017) "Joint Declaration on Freedom of Expression and "Fake News," Disinformation and Propaganda". www.osce.org/fom/302796

Richter, Andrei (2018) "Fake News and Freedom of the Media". *Journal of International Media & Entertainment Law* 8(1), pp. 1–34.

Theil, Stefan (2019) "The Online Harms White Paper: Comparing the UK and German Approaches to Regulation". *Journal of Media Law* 11(2), pp. 41–51.

UK Digital, Culture, Media and Sport Committee (2017) "Inquiry into Fake News". www.parliament.uk/business/committees/committees-a-z/commons-select/digital-culture-media-and-sport-committee/inquiries/parliament-2017/fake-news-17–19/

Woods, Lorna (2019) "The Duty of Care in the Online Harms White Paper". *Journal of Media Law* 11(1), pp. 6–17.

41

GLOBAL RESPONSES TO MISINFORMATION AND POPULISM

Daniel Funke

Introduction: regulators take aim at misinformation

In November 2017, the European Commission announced that it was enlisting the help of experts across the continent to develop potential ways to curb the spread of false information online. The newly created High-Level Expert Group on Fake News and Online Disinformation was tasked with advising on 'policy initiatives to counter fake news and disinformation spread online' (EU Commission 2018). Beginning in January 2018, the experts, representing media companies, non-profit organisations, and academic institutions from around Europe, regularly travelled to Brussels to meet with EU officials, address their concerns about mis- and disinformation, and brainstorm how the commission could best combat the threat. The final result: a report of best practices and recommendations for the commission to consider when drafting any potential anti-misinformation legislation or communication.

That report, published in March 2018, advocates for an inclusive, collaborative approach to addressing misinformation around the world. Among its recommendations are additional financial support for news and fact-checking organisations, calls on technology platforms to share more data, and the creation of a network of research centres studying misinformation across the EU. The report also advises moderation in addressing the challenge of misinformation, recommending the abdication of the term *fake news*, and – crucially – not creating regulations that penalise the creation or dissemination of mis- and disinformation (Mantzarlis 2018).

While its multilateral effort is perhaps the most sweeping action that a governmental institution has taken against online misinformation in the past few years, it is far from the only one. Since the EU Commission first organised its high-level group on misinformation in early 2018, at least 50 countries around the world have taken legislative action against the spread of online falsehoods. Those actions span five continents and range from laws that criminalise the dissemination of false statements to state-run media literacy efforts (Flamini and Funke 2019). While the intention of each individual action is unique to the socio-political context in which it was crafted, nearly all of them are primarily concerned with how to slow the spread of political mis- and disinformation on the internet in an age when falsehoods could affect elections, international relations, and crisis response.

In this chapter, we will explore several state responses to misinformation around the world, how they've been implemented, and how they've affected free speech, press freedom, and

449

digital information sharing. We will analyse how the rise of widespread misinformation during the 2016 United States election sparked a global effort to contain the spread of political falsehoods in the form of hard and soft regulations. While some of these efforts are good natured, such a Nigerian initiative aimed at bolstering media literacy, others have co-opted the language of misinformation to persecute journalists. Take, for example, Egypt, where 21 journalists were imprisoned on false news charges in 2019 (Committee to Protect Journalists 2019). As some of these cases illustrate, the threat of online misinformation is big, but the threat of government abuse of power is just as, if not more, concerning.

This chapter will conclude by evaluating a few of the ways that governments have tried to regulate online deception. Ultimately, a successful approach to regulating mis- and disinformation might do something similar to the EU's 2018 high-level group: involve multiple stakeholders, place an emphasis on the role of the media in calling out falsehoods, teach media literacy, and – above all – adopt a modus operandi of caution and restraint when considering any regulations that tell people what's true and false.

2016: the rise of a global threat

While false news, conspiracy theories, rumours, hoaxes, and bad information have been around as long as humans have had language, the impact of misinformation on politics came to a head during the 2016 election in the US. And the outcome of that presidential contest inspired governments around the world, either directly or indirectly, to take a rash of actions aimed at countering the spread of political falsehoods online.

The popularisation of online falsehoods has its roots in the 1990s, when internet access became mainstream. The democratisation of information enabled more people to learn about and participate in politics and current events, but it also provided more room for the proliferation of bad information and misconceptions. The creation of Snopes in the mid-90s came at a time when urban legends and rumours were spreading like wildfire in chain emails, instant messages, and forums (Aspray and Cortada 2019). The abundance of online rumours grew quickly with the advent of social media platforms like Facebook and Twitter, which made it easier for people to share information with their friends and family. By the late 2000s, fact-checking outlets like FactCheck, The *Washington Post* Fact Checker, and PolitiFact were regularly debunking online hoaxes in addition to claims from politicians, media pundits, and advocacy groups (Graves 2016).

As social media platforms grew and new ones like Instagram were created, online misinformation expanded. Between the 2012 and 2016 elections, Facebook nearly doubled its number of monthly active users, reaching two billion by the second quarter of 2017 (Statista 2020). Twitter had a similar growth in monthly active users (Statista 2019). Meanwhile, trust in the mainstream media hit a record low in the fall of 2016 (Gallup 2016). Those conditions, as well as the combative rhetoric of presidential candidates Donald Trump and Hillary Clinton and growing partisan divides in the US, provided fertile ground for the proliferation of misinformation online. Falsehoods spread widely on platforms like Facebook and Twitter, partially due to the efforts of Russia's Internet Research Agency, which fabricated news, faked protests, and created memes aimed at dividing the American electorate and giving Trump a leg up in the election (Howard et al. 2018). Those tactics represented a departure from traditional campaigns, in which political action committees, advocacy organisations, and politicians themselves created most of the political spin (Persily 2017).

They were also effective. By the end of the election, political misinformation was so abundant on social media that it sometimes surpassed the reach of news organisations. A BuzzFeed

News analysis found that, in the final three months of the election, the top-performing fake news stories on Facebook generated more engagement than the top stories from news outlets like the *New York Times*, the *Washington Post* and NBC News combined (Silverman 2016). Researchers found that fake news sites disproportionately benefited from social media, with 65 domains getting three times as much traffic from social media as 690 mainstream news outlets (Allcott and Gentzkow 2017). Trump supporters and Facebook users were more likely to read fake news stories than Clinton supporters and people who didn't use Facebook (Guess et al. 2020).

Still, despite the fact that misinformation had a wide reach in 2016, later research indicated that relatively few Americans actually shared false news (Guess et al. 2019). And, while it's impossible to say for sure, it's unlikely that misinformation had a substantive role in electing Trump to the White House (Allcott and Gentzkow 2017). But the damage was done; a December 2016 poll indicated that 64 percent of Americans thought made-up news caused 'a great deal of confusion' about current events (Pew 2016). Mainstream news organisations published articles that claimed misinformation on Facebook helped propel Trump to the White House (The Guardian 2016). False news on social media was undoubtedly a problem in 2016; however, based on what we know now, the immediate response to the election seemed to be less about misinformation and more about who won.

Regardless, in the following year, at least five countries and the EU announced measures aimed at combatting the spread of online falsehoods. German prime minister Angela Merkel was among the first to sound the alarm about misinformation after the US election, saying in a November 2016 address to the Bundestag that 'Today we have fake sites, bots, trolls – things that regenerate themselves, reinforcing opinions with certain algorithms, and we have to learn to deal with them' (The *Washington Post* 2016). Merkel's concern later resulted in Germany's *Netzwerkdurchsetzungsgesetz* (NetzDG) legislation, which passed in June 2017. The measure forces technology platforms to remove 'obviously illegal' posts within 24 hours or risk fines of up to €50 million (Flamini and Funke 2019).

While NetzDG – one of the earliest actions taken after the 2016 US election to combat the spread of harmful content online – has more to do with hate speech rather than misinformation, it was widely covered by the press as Germany's answer to the rise of false information (BBC 2018). And it set the groundwork for a slate of global anti-misinformation regulations to come.

How states responded to misinformation

Since the 2016 US election, countries around the world have become increasingly concerned with how to restrict the flow of falsehoods on the internet. This concern is typically amplified during elections and other political events, when the threat of media manipulation and online disinformation is high (Ilves et al. 2020). Some authoritarian countries, such as China, have long had regulations that penalise citizens who share internet rumours, but the rise of widespread misinformation over the past few years has motivated a variety of different states to take similar steps. While some countries, such as Egypt and Russia, have opted to criminalise the dissemination of falsehoods online, others, such as Belgium and Nigeria, have favoured softer regulations, including initiatives aimed at bolstering media literacy (Flamini and Funke 2019).

In this section, we will analyse some of these different state actions and how they've affected information sharing online. The section draws heavily from the Poynter Institute's 'guide to anti-misinformation actions around the world', one of the most comprehensive sources of information about global state actions against misinformation. As of its August 2019 update, the guide had catalogued 98 individual anti-misinformation actions in 50 countries. The actions are

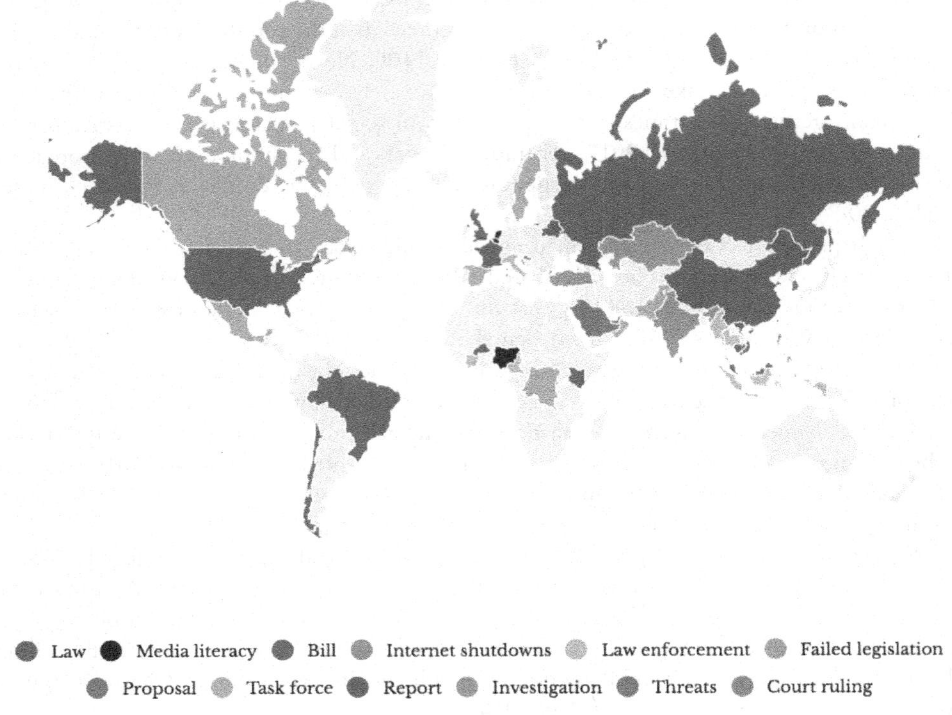

Figure 41.1 Countries that have taken action against online mis- and disinformation

Source: Poynter.org

divided into 12 different categories: laws, media literacy, bills, internet shutdowns, law enforcement, failed legislation, proposals, task forces, reports, investigations, threats, and court rulings (Flamini and Funke 2019).

This section will not cover each action in Poynter's guide but instead will analyse a few examples of each type of action that exemplify how different countries have approached regulating online mis- and disinformation. By applying the concepts of hard and soft power in international relations, these actions will be divided into hard regulations, those that necessitate state enforcement, and soft regulations, which are more focused on raising awareness, coalition building, or providing aid to citizens. The section will place these different kinds of actions in context, both chronological and geopolitical, to demonstrate how responses to online deception are rarely developed in a vacuum. Taken together, these responses present a clear picture of how some states could potentially address misinformation – and how others could use the problem to abuse their power and restrict free speech and the press.

Hard regulations

A great deal of news coverage about state responses to misinformation since 2016 has focused on legislation. And for good reason – bills and laws, as well as law enforcement and internet shutdowns, are among the most stringent actions that states can take. This subsection will discuss how some of these hard regulations have been aimed at restricting the spread of hate speech while others specifically criminalise the creation and dissemination of misinformation. Meanwhile, other countries have resorted to shutting off the internet altogether or detaining purveyors of false information, actions that press freedom groups have condemned (Flamini and Funke 2019).

One of the first pieces of legislation that followed Germany's NetzDG law came in December 2017 in Ireland. Lawmakers proposed a bill that would have criminalised the use of automated social media accounts to create 25 or more personas that spread political messages online, a tactic that Russian operatives employed during the 2016 US election (Howard et al. 2018). One month later, Croatian lawmakers introduced a bill aimed at limiting the spread of harmful content on Facebook. The legislation was similar to NetzDG in that it was more focused on restricting the spread of hate speech than sanctioning misinformation (Flamini and Funke 2019). Similarly, Ethiopian lawmakers passed a law in February 2020 that criminalises hate speech content that's published on social media to more than 5,000 followers. The move came months ahead of the country's August election and in the midst of ongoing ethnic violence (The Seattle Times 2020).

The blurring of lines between hate speech and mis- and disinformation is one of the many pitfalls of state responses to online falsehoods. While the former term is classified as malinformation since it is not necessarily false or misleading but rather intended to cause harm, the latter two must, by definition, describe content that is false, misleading, manipulated, or fabricated. While both hate speech and misinformation can cause harm on the internet, they are fundamentally different concepts (Derakhshan and Wardle 2017). However, lawmakers have tended to clump the two together in legislative proposals, leading to false expectations for laws like NetzDG. In general, passing regulation that criminalises the spread of false information online is more rare in democracies than in authoritarian states, perhaps because there are typically more legislative hoops to jump through and citizens have more agency to push back against restrictions on their free speech rights (Flamini and Funke 2019).

Still, there are plenty of examples of bills that do explicitly aim to regulate the spread of mis- and disinformation. In May 2018, there were 20 draft bills in the Brazilian Congress that focused on limiting the spread of online falsehoods ahead of the October election. The penalties ranged from fines starting around $400 to up to eight years in prison, and the bills covered everything from spreading fake news stories on social media to publishing inaccurate stories in the press (Flamini and Funke 2019). The bills attracted fierce criticism from press freedom groups like Freedom House and the Electronic Frontier Foundation, which said drafting legislation against misinformation is 'a risky path to address complex problems, especially when it involves deciding what is true or false' (Freedom House 2019b; Electronic Freedom Foundation 2019). Other countries pressed forward, with similar anti-misinformation bills proposed in Taiwan and the Philippines later in 2018. However, these kinds of bills tend to stall in democracies, with the exception of France. In November 2018, lawmakers passed legislation that gives officials the authority to remove fake content from social media and block the websites that spread it in the final three months of an election campaign (Flamini and Funke 2019). The law exemplifies how, when democratic countries do take legislative action against misinformation, the goal is usually to preserve the integrity of elections.

Nevertheless, such laws are more common in regimes classified as 'partly free' or 'not free' by Freedom House. In April 2018, Malaysia made it illegal to share online misinformation, becoming the first Southeast Asian country to do so (Flamini and Funke 2019). The law, which was repealed in December 2019, criminalised the publication and dissemination of false news, punishable by up to six years in jail and a fine of $128,000, and made online service providers responsible for third-party content on their platforms (The Star 2019). The next month,

Kenyan president Uhuru Kenyatta signed a bill that criminalises 17 different types of cyber-crimes, including misinformation. It also punishes those who share or create misinformation with fines and jail time. More recently, Singapore passed a law in May 2019 that makes it illegal to spread 'false statements of fact' that compromise security, 'public tranquility', public safety, or international relations. Singapore's legislation imposes fines and jail time for violators and increases sanctions for those who use an 'online account or a bot' to spread misinformation. Like Kenya's law, it also holds internet platforms liable for their role in spreading falsehoods (Flamini and Funke 2019).

Advocacy organisations have criticised those anti-misinformation laws for their potential to infringe on press freedom, but other laws more explicitly target the media (Committee to Protect Journalists, May 2019). In July 2018, Russian lawmakers introduced a bill, which passed in March 2019, that bans 'unreliable socially-important information' that could 'endanger lives and public health, raise the threat of massive violation of public security and order or impede functioning of transport and social infrastructure, energy and communication facilities and banks' (USA Today 2019). The law gives the government the power to block websites that prosecutors say are in violation of the rules, which includes those that publish information that 'disrespects' the state (The *Washington Post* 2019). While it's unclear to what extent that law has been implemented, a similar measure in Egypt has served as the foundation for the arrest of dozens of journalists since it was passed in July 2018. The law deems any account or blog with more than 5,000 followers a media outlet which can be prosecuted for publishing 'fake news'. Egypt has jailed the most journalists on false news charges since 2018, and media rights organisations say the state's law is being used to silence coverage that's critical of the government (Committee to Protect Journalists 2019). Other countries have fallen into a similar pattern, with countries like Cameroon, Indonesia, and Myanmar all arresting journalists on false news charges since early 2018. Kazakhstan and Turkey have also conducted investigations of news outlets that allegedly published false information (Flamini and Funke 2019).

Meanwhile, some anti-misinformation legislation focuses on punishing politicians instead of citizens, although this is comparatively rare. A bill proposed in February 2019 in Chile would have imposed penalties on politicians who participate in the 'dissemination, promotion or financing of false news'. While technically an example of a law enforcement action, not new legislation, a Côte d'Ivoire minister was imprisoned in January 2019 on 'false news' charges after tweeting about how a state prosecutor had arrested another MP. The arrest was made based on a state law that punishes the creation of 'false news', which has been used to jail journalists in the past (Flamini and Funke 2019). That kind of tactic, using anti–false news laws to justify the imprisonment of journalists, is common in regimes that Freedom House deems to be 'partly free' or 'not free'.

Legislation isn't the only kind of hard regulation that states have used to combat misinformation. Take India, for example, where the government regularly shuts off the internet to stem the spread of falsehoods during news events. In 2018, there were 134 internet shutdowns in the country – 47 percent of which took place in the politically tumultuous states of Jammu and Kashmir (Taye 2018; Rydzak 2019). In 2019, the number of internet shutdowns decreased slightly to 121, but India still led the world in incidents by far; Venezuela had the second-highest number of shutdowns with 12 (Taye 2019). One potential reason for India's proclivity for turning off the internet is the fact that the country has had a rash of misinformation-related killings over the past several years (Wired 2018). The trend has spread to neighbouring countries like Sri Lanka, where the government implemented internet shutdowns during the April 2019 terrorist attacks on Easter Sunday. But several media outlets cast doubt on whether it worked, reporting that misinformation still circulated in spite of the shutdown, partly due to the widespread use of virtual private networks (BuzzFeed News 2019). Those dispatches call into question the efficacy of hard regulations against online misinformation, even when they're enforced.

Soft regulations

While hard regulations are the most eye catching and the most common, they are not the only actions that states have taken to counter online mis- and disinformation in recent years. Several states, particularly those in Western Europe, have instead opted to adopt media literacy initiatives, publish reports, or create task forces aimed at improving public understanding of the threat posed by online falsehoods (Flamini and Funke 2019). While many countries have their own media literacy initiatives and proposals for dealing with misinformation, this subsection will focus on efforts launched since early 2018.

One of the most popular soft regulations states have initiated in recent years is the creation of task forces that address the threat of foreign disinformation campaigns. This chapter previously discussed how Russian influence operations promoted false content on social media in an attempt to affect the outcome of the 2016 US election. Many of the anti-disinformation task forces set up since early 2018 can be viewed as a reaction to that threat. Spain, for example, entered into a pact with Russia in November 2018 that explicitly prevents the two nations from using disinformation to affect each other's elections. The move came after Spanish ministers accused Russia of spreading disinformation about the Catalan referendum. In June 2018, Australia created a task force specifically charged with monitoring potential foreign influence operations ahead of elections. Lawmakers also announced a media literacy campaign called Stop and Consider, which encouraged voters to pay attention to the information they were sharing online. Meanwhile, some countries have set up task forces that are less focused on foreign interference, such as a state-run WhatsApp account in the Democratic Republic of the Congo that was created to field misinformation about Ebola. Similar mis- and disinformation monitoring systems have been created in Mexico, Oman, and Pakistan (Flamini and Funke 2019).

In democracies, media literacy provisions like Australia's have become especially popular. Take Canada, for example, which, in January 2019, announced a multi-pronged anti-misinformation effort ahead of its fall elections. The government gave $7 million to projects aimed at increasing public awareness of mis- and disinformation, ranging from awareness sessions and workshops to the development of learning materials for citizens (Department of Canadian Heritage 2019). Nigeria has taken a more direct approach by planning collaborations with media organisations and government agencies to teach citizens what's true and false on the internet – a move that has been met with praise from media literacy advocacy organisations (Flamini and Funke 2019; Media Literacy Now 2019). Media literacy initiatives are particularly popular in Western Europe, where Belgium, the Netherlands, and Sweden have published materials aimed at informing the public about misinformation. But such efforts have also taken place at local levels of government in countries like the US, where at least 24 states have tried to pass legislation aimed at funding or creating media literacy programmes. One example is Massachusetts, which passed a law in 2018 that mandates civic education with an emphasis on media literacy (Flamini and Funke 2019).

Meanwhile, other countries have taken a research-centric approach to developing anti-misinformation actions. In addition to creating an anti–foreign disinformation task force and public school curricula aimed at teaching students how to tell fact from fiction on the internet, a United Kingdom parliamentary committee published a report in July 2018 with several recommendations for government interventions. The recommendations include rejecting the term 'fake news', regulating online media like traditional media, and creating a working group to research the spread of misinformation. That's similar to the approach taken by the EU, which published a report about online misinformation based on the recommendations of a group of experts from across the continent (Flamini and Funke 2019). While those kinds of actions are less binding than task forces, and certainly less binding than hard regulations like laws or internet shutdowns, they are among the most multi-lateral, measured responses a state can take to combat online misinformation.

Conclusion: evaluating state anti-misinformation actions

Online mis- and disinformation is a threat to governments around the world. The rise of social media platforms like Facebook and Twitter has corresponded with the rapid growth of rumours, hoaxes, and false news stories on the internet. As the events leading up to the 2016 US election showed, misinformation can have tangible effects on democratic discourse and, in some circumstances, be wielded as political cudgel by foreign nations seeking to meddle in another country's affairs. If the governed cannot decide on basic facts, it becomes much harder to decide who should govern them.

What to do? As we've discussed in this chapter, at least 50 countries around the world have taken some sort of action against online mis- and disinformation. These actions range from hard regulations, such as laws and internet shutdowns, to soft regulations, such as media literacy initiatives and task forces. Since many of these responses have been made since late 2017, it's hard to tell how effective any of them have been at achieving their goals. While press freedom groups have criticised hard regulations for their potential to censor citizens, critics say there's little chance that soft regulations will elicit meaningful change in the digital sphere. One needn't look further than the misinformation that circulated about the COVID-19 pandemic to see how, years after 2016, falsehoods have only become more common online – especially during times of social and political change.

More research needs to be done on how state regulatory actions affect the spread of falsehoods on the internet. However, there are myriad theoretical benefits for states that use soft power instead of hard power – especially in the internet age. If a country's aim is to get people to stop sharing misinformation, it stands to reason that it would want to coerce its citizens into being more credulous media consumers. As political scientist Joseph S. Nye Jr. put it: 'Information is power, and today a much larger part of the world's population has access to that power' (Nye 2004). While their power can be used for good or ill, internet users are the future of our information ecosystem. Given the effects of recent anti-misinformation actions around the world, as well as literature on how people consume content online, soft regulations appear to present the best options for combatting falsehoods in the long run without infringing on the rights of internet users, as well as the press and politicians themselves.

References

Allcott, H. and Gentzkow, M. (2017) "Social Media and Fake News in the 2016 Election." *The Journal of Economic Perspectives*, Vol. 31, No. 2, pp. 211–236. Available at https://www.nber.org/papers/w23089.

Aspray, W. and Cortada, J.W. (2019) *From Debunking Urban Legends to Political Fact-Checking*. Basel, Switzerland: Springer. Available at https://doi.org/10.1007/978-3-030-22952-8_2.

BBC (January 1, 2018) "Germany Starts Enforcing Hate Speech Law." Available at www.bbc.com/news/technology-42510868.

BuzzFeed News (April 21, 2019) "Social Media Has Been Blocked for over 24 Hours In Sri Lanka After The Deadly Explosions." Available at www.buzzfeednews.com/article/janelytvynenko/sri-lanka-social-media-block.

Committee to Protect Journalists (2019) "250 Journalists Imprisoned in 2019." Available at https://cpj. org/data/reports.php?status=Imprisoned&start_year=2019&end_year=2019&group_by=location.

Committee to Protect Journalists (May 9, 2019) "Singapore Passes 'Fake News' Legislation that Threatens Press." Available at https://cpj.org/2019/05/singapore-passes-fake-news-legislation-that-threat.php.

Department of Canadian Heritage (July 2, 2019) "Helping Citizens Critically Assess and Become Resilient Against Harmful Online Disinformation." Available at www.canada.ca/en/canadian-heritage/news/2019/07/helping-citizens-critically-assess-and-become-resilient-against-harmful-online-disinformation.html.

Derakhshan, H. and Wardle, C. (September 27, 2017) "Information Disorder: Toward an Interdisciplinary Framework for Research and Policy Making." Strasbourg: Council of Europe. Available at https://rm.coe.int/information-disorder-report-november-2017/1680764666.

Electronic Freedom Foundation (January 31, 2019) "Brazil in 2019: Free Speech and Privacy in the Crosshairs. What Are the Threats?" Available at www.eff.org/deeplinks/2019/01/brazil-2019-free-speech-and-privacy-crosshairs-what-are-threats.

European Commission (March 12, 2018) "Final Report of the High Level Expert Group on Fake News and Online Disinformation." Available at https://ec.europa.eu/digital-single-market/en/news/final-report-high-level-expert-group-fake-news-and-online-disinformation.

Flamini, D. and Funke, D. (2019) "A Guide to Anti-misinformation Actions around the World." Available at www.poynter.org/ifcn/anti-misinformation-actions/.

Freedom House (2019a) "Freedom in the World 2019: Democracy in Retreat." Available at https://freedomhouse.org/report/freedom-world/2019/democracy-retreat.

Freedom House (2019b) "Freedom on the Net 2019: Brazil." Available at https://freedomhouse.org/country/brazil/freedom-net/2019#footnote4_gnr0o37.

Gallup (September 14, 2016) "Americans' Trust in Mass Media Sinks to New Low." Available at https://news.gallup.com/poll/195542/americans-trust-mass-media-sinks-new-low.aspx.

Graves, L. (2016) *Deciding What's True: The Rise of Political Fact-Checking in American Journalism.* New York: Columbia University Press.

Guess, A., Nagler, J., and Tucker, J. (January 2019) "Less than You Think: Prevalence and Predictors of Fake News Dissemination on Facebook." *Science Advances,* Vol. 5, No. 1. Available at https://doi.org/10.1126/sciadv.aau4586.

Guess, A., Nyhan, B., and Reifler, J. (March 2020) "Exposure to Untrustworthy Websites in the 2016 US Election." *Nature Human Behavior.* Available at https://doi.org/10.1038/s41562-020-0833-x.

Howard, P.N., Ganesh, B., Liotsiou, D., Kelly, J., and François, C. (2018) "The IRA, Social Media and Political Polarization in the United States, 2012–2018." Oxford: Project on Computational Propaganda. Available at https://comprop.oii.ox.ac.uk/research/ira-political-polarization/.

Ilves, T.H., Persily, N., Stamos, A., Stedman, S., Chinchilla, L., Leterme, Y., Heyzer, N., Okolloh, O., Sweeney, W., Smith, M., and Zedillo, E. (January 2020) "Protecting Electoral Integrity in the Digital Age." The Kofi Annan Commission on Elections and Democracy in the Digital Age. Available at https://fsi.stanford.edu/publication/protecting-electoral-integrity-digital-age.

Mantzarlis, A. (March 12, 2018) "Six Key Points from the EU Commission's New Report on Disinformation." Available at www.poynter.org/fact-checking/2018/six-key-points-from-the-eu-commission%c2%92s-new-report-on-disinformation/.

Media Literacy Now (September 29, 2019) "Media Literacy Center Created in Nigeria." Available at https://medialiteracynow.org/media-literacy-center-created-in-nigeria/.

Nye, J.S. Jr. Harvard Business School Working Knowledge (August 2, 2004) "The Benefits of Soft Power." Available at https://hbswk.hbs.edu/archive/the-benefits-of-soft-power.

Persily, N. (April 2017) "The 2016 U.S. Election: Can Democracy Survive the Internet?" *Journal of Democracy,* Vol. 28, No. 2. Available at https://muse.jhu.edu/article/653377/summary.

Pew Research Center (December 15, 2016) "Many Americans Believe Fake News Is Sowing Confusion." Available at www.journalism.org/2016/12/15/many-americans-believe-fake-news-is-sowing-confusion/.

Rydzak, J. (February 2019) "Of Blackouts and Bandhs: The Strategy and Structure of Disconnected Protest in India." Available at https://papers.ssrn.com/sol3/papers.cfm?abstract_id=3330413.

Silverman, C. (November 16, 2016) "This Analysis Shows How Viral Fake Election News Stories Outperformed Real News On Facebook." Available at www.buzzfeednews.com/article/craigsilverman/viral-fake-election-news-outperformed-real-news-on-facebook.

Statista (January 2020) "Number of Monthly Active Facebook Users Worldwide as of 4th Quarter 2019." Available at www.statista.com/statistics/264810/number-of-monthly-active-facebook-users-worldwide/.

Statista (April 2019) "Number of Monthly Active Twitter Users Worldwide from 1st Quarter 2010 to 1st Quarter 2019." Available at www.statista.com/statistics/282087/number-of-monthly-active-twitter-users/.

Taye, B. (2018) "The State of Internet Shutdowns Around the World." New York: Access Now. Available at www.accessnow.org/cms/assets/uploads/2019/07/KeepItOn-2018-Report.pdf.

Taye, B. (2019) "Targeted, Cut Off, and Left in the Dark." New York: Access Now. Available at www.accessnow.org/cms/assets/uploads/2020/02/KeepItOn-2019-report-1.pdf.

The Guardian (November 14, 2016) "Click and Elect: How Fake News Helped Donald Trump Win a Real Election." Available at www.theguardian.com/technology/2016/nov/10/facebook-fake-news-election-conspiracy-theories.

The Seattle Times (February 13, 2020) "Ethiopia Approves Controversial Law Curbing Hate Speech." Available at www.seattletimes.com/nation-world/nation/ethiopia-approves-controversial-law-curbing-hate-speech/.

The Star (December 19, 2019) "Finally, Dewan Negara Approves Repeal of Anti-Fake News Act." Available at www.thestar.com.my/news/nation/2019/12/19/finally-dewan-negara-approves-repeal-of-anti-fake-news-act.

The Washington Post (March 18, 2019) "With Putin's Signature, 'Fake News' Bill becomes Law." Available at www.washingtonpost.com/world/2019/03/18/with-putins-signature-fake-news-bill-becomes-law/.

The Washington Post (November 23, 2016) "'Fake News' Threatens Germany's Election, too, says Merkel." Available at www.washingtonpost.com/news/worldviews/wp/2016/11/23/fake-news-threatens-germanys-election-too-says-merkel/.

USA Today (March 7, 2019) "Russian Lawmakers Pass Bill to Punish Online Sites for Spreading 'Fake News'." Available at www.usatoday.com/story/news/world/2019/03/07/russian-lawmakers-pass-bill-punish-online-sites-fake-news/3090429002/.

Wired (December 12, 2018) "How WhatsApp Fuels Fake News and Violence in India." Available at www.wired.com/story/how-whatsapp-fuels-fake-news-and-violence-in-india/.

SINGAPORE'S FAKE NEWS LAW

Countering populists' falsehoods and truth-making

Shawn Goh and Carol Soon

Introduction

Framed as a growing threat to democracy, populism has become an increasingly unavoidable topic of discussion in both academic and popular discourses. While the concept of populism lacks a single coherent definition, its global rise is largely understood as a symptom of a crisis in democracy, underpinned by an erosion of democratic values like freedom of speech, acceptance of diversity and difference, and trust in government institutions and systems. As Momoc (2018, p. 68) highlighted, 'populism is the most seductive ideology when the institutional system is unable to resolve the imbalances caused by the change or the crisis in the political, economic, and social spheres'.

Scholars have also pointed out that it is not by chance that the surge of populism is happening alongside a scourge of misinformation, disinformation, and other forms of falsehoods. As will be discussed in this chapter, digital and social media have provided an ideal communication environment for populists to successfully mobilise propaganda, lies, and conspiracy theories to propagate populist narratives and augment populist truth-making in an era where emotions trump facts (Postill 2018).

Singapore has remained resilient against rising populism thus far. While experts previously highlighted the role that Singapore's strong authoritarian state plays in acting as a safeguard (Tan 2017), this chapter attempts to nuance the current picture. Using Singapore's Protection from Online Falsehoods and Manipulation Act (POFMA) as a case study, this chapter argues that the country's resilience against rising populism, in particular against populists' falsehoods and truth-making, stems from a combination of being calibrated in its design and use of a repressive tool like POFMA and remaining hyper-responsive to public reactions towards the use of the law. This has allowed the government to continue justifying strong-handed measures without implicating its credibility in a way that would allow populist opposition to challenge its legitimacy and make significant political gains in the long run.

From populism to populism 2.0

Populism can be characterised by two key features – 'anti-elitism' and 'people-centricism'. One of the best recognised definitions of 'populism' was proposed by political scientist Cas Mudde

(2004), who argued that populism is a 'thin' ideology with a few core beliefs. First, society is divided into 'the people' and 'the elite', where 'the people' are seen as good and virtuous while 'the elite' are regarded as corrupt and dangerous. This antagonistic relationship between 'the people' and 'the elite' is central to Mudde's concept of populism. Second, rather than representing the general will of the people, the current political establishment, together with its legal and public institutions, have instead infringed upon people's ability to exert collective power, depriving them of their rights, freedom, identity, values, and voice. Hence, populists often appeal to the masses by claiming to enjoy a close relationship with people on the ground and to embody their under-represented voices and professing to legitimately restore popular sovereignty to them (Mudde & Kaltwasser 2017).

Other scholars have focused on the exclusionary features of populism. For instance, Abts and Rummens (2007) argued that because populists appeal to the masses by challenging the legitimacy of and fuelling dissatisfaction towards the establishment, populism can also be understood as a form of 'vertical exclusion', with strong anti-elite (e.g. exclusion of the political elite), anti-establishment (e.g. exclusion of the media), and anti-system (e.g. exclusion of the capitalist system) characteristics. Furthermore, populism can also be understood as exclusion with a horizontal dimension. For instance, Taggart (2004) described populism as 'chameleon-like', adopting different 'ideological colours' depending on 'the other' against whom people are united. For example, right-wing populism often excludes migrants and ethnic minorities in the name of nationalism or protecting national culture, whereas left-wing populism often excludes foreign economic forces of globalisation such as wealthy economic elites or cheap foreign labour to protect people from economic inequality and instability (Müller 2016). This explains why politicians like Donald Trump and Bernie Sanders may both be labelled 'populist' despite occupying opposite ends of the political spectrum (Sullivan & Costa 2020). This protection of national economy and culture have also led some scholars to conceptualise populism as 'cultural backlash', in which features of economic insecurity and xenophobia indicate a fundamental rejection of pluralism (Norris & Inglehart 2016). In short, populists claim to advocate for the people by attacking the elite (vertical exclusion) and appeal to the masses by invoking the heartlander and by excluding 'others' (horizontal exclusion) (Brubaker 2017).

Scholars have also gone beyond the framing of populism as a political ideology, extending the concept to look at populism in practice, as a political strategy (Ware 2002), as political logic (Laclau 2005), and as political style (Moffitt & Tormey 2014). For instance, Jansen (2011) argued that populism serves as a means for political mobilisation, in which marginalised individuals occupying fringe spaces of society are brought into publicly visible arenas to be given a voice and supported by an anti-elite, nationalist rhetoric that valorises them. Communications scholars have also reconceptualised populism as a genre of political communication, focusing on the performative and communicative aspects of populist leaders. For example, Kho (2019) argued that President Duterte's form of populism in the Philippines involves a sophisticated social media machinery that mobilises fake news, bots, and trolls, exploiting behavioural biases to amplify identity-based rhetoric that resonates with groups of Filipino voters. In other words, populism is understood as a communicative repertoire that anyone willing to 'do populism' can employ (DeVreese et al. 2018).

Social media and the rise of digital populism

The utopian rhetoric surrounding the internet is a familiar one. Since its birth, the internet has been touted as embodying Habermas's (1989) idea of the public sphere, where citizens can come together to engage in critical discussion and deliberation through an open and democratic exchange of thoughts, ideas, and opinions. However, one major critique of Habermas's thesis was that it over-promised the democratising effects of the internet and overlooked its potential to polarise and fragment publics based on people's interests, ideologies, and values (Papacharissi 2002). Experts like Sunstein (2018) have argued that social media platforms have been occupied by disparate communities of people whose collective actions are driven by shared feelings and emotions. As Flew and Iosifidis (2020, p. 16) put it, on social media networks, 'rational persuasion is . . . weakened, while so-called "affective persuasion" becomes prevalent'.

Scholars exploring the relationship between digital media and populism have highlighted how innate affordances of social media platforms such as Facebook and Twitter provide a synergistic thrust to the populist agenda and populist communications in several ways.

First, social media platforms offer populists a direct and unmediated communication channel with their followers, bypassing information gatekeepers such as traditional media. Schroeder (2019) argued that while the use of digital media had different effects on right-wing populist movements in different countries, the ability of digital media to bypass traditional media gatekeepers itself had been a necessary precondition for the success of many populist movements. This rejection of traditional media further reinforces populists' anti-establishment narratives, in which traditional media is portrayed as part of the elite and accused of lying and manipulating public opinion (Engesser, Ernst, Esser & Büchel 2017). Social media also amplifies populist narratives at speed and scale by tapping into its logic of virality and network effect, thus boosting the reach and persuasiveness of populist appeals (Klinger & Svensson 2015; Vaccari & Valeriani 2015).

Second, the interactive and participatory features of social media augment this direct line to the people by allowing populists to feel the pulse of the people (Engesser, Fawzi & Larsson 2017), and lowering barriers of interaction to create a sense of social presence and closeness to the masses (Kruikemeier et al. 2013). Such characteristics have led to 'the rise of an interactive and participatory populism – a populism 2.0' (Gerbaudo 2014, p. 68). Furthermore, populists exploit the communicative architecture of social media platforms to craft personalised messages in a targeted fashion tailored to a heterogeneous audience of internet users, making populist appeals through digital technology more effective.

On top of leveraging social media affordances, populists are also adept at mobilising sympathisers by appealing to emotions like fear, anxiety, and a sense of insecurity and injustice. For example, Dittrich (2017) found that far-right populists like Marine Le Pen often enjoy a surge in social media engagement after national tragedies like terrorist attacks, suggesting that populists exploit such events to validate their rhetoric of fear and outrage. Focusing on the political relevance of emotions, Maldonado (2017) similarly sees populism as an 'affective performance' in which social media, an 'affective technology', is particularly conducive to populists' mobilising individual emotions to drive collective perceptions and actions. Furthermore, populists' emotional appeals concurrently discredit rational rhetoric while presenting their highly emotional and personalised communications as more authentic (Thompson 2017).

In short, the combination of populism and social media exacerbates the scourge of online falsehoods in today's post-truth age by undermining trust in experts, institutions, and rational debate while facilitating populists' truth-making by providing an environment in which the veracity of information is not assessed based on authenticity or credibility but on whether or not it feels right to people.

Singapore's fake news law: countering populists' falsehoods and truth-making

Singapore's authoritarian style of governance has often been the focus of criticism from the West, especially on issues relating to the freedom of speech. However, experts have also argued that features of Singapore's strong paternalistic state safeguard the country against the rise of populists and skillful demagogues. These include strong institutions that shape public moralities to protect values like diversity and inclusiveness, rigourously clean and meritocratic institutions, and a commitment to pragmatism and evidence-based policymaking instead of being guided by ideological positions (Tan 2017). The outcome is a high level of trust in the government that fortifies Singapore's resilience against populism.

Nonetheless, the government has been cautious to dismiss rising populism in Singapore as an unlikely scenario. With populist tides rising both globally and in Asia, the spectre of populism looms over the mindshare of Singapore's political leaders, and populists gaining a foothold in Singapore's political terrain is seen a plausible outcome if the existing governance system fails to continue engendering trust in its people. The government has, on several occasions in the past years, cautioned against the social impact of anti-foreigners and xenophobic rhetoric and taken action against websites (e.g. the now-defunct The Real Singapore website) and members of the opposition parties said to fan those sentiments (Lee 2016; Loh 2020).

In November 2019, Prime Minister Lee Hsien Loong spoke at the 65th People's Action Party (PAP)'s Conference-Convention about the importance of not letting a disconnect between the elite and the masses take root in Singapore. Citing Chile as an example where populist movements gained traction due to an entrenched split between the elite and the masses, Lee stressed the importance of maintaining the 'deep reservoir of trust' with Singaporeans by upholding high standards of honesty, transparency, and integrity in governance (Tee 2019). Similarly, Deputy Prime Minister Tharman Shanmugaratnam has also spoken about the importance of domestic policy responses in tackling issues such as increasing polarisation in politics and the media and an erosion of consensus and a sense of togetherness in society. He stressed that policy interventions such as greater redistribution, encouraging social mixing, and reinforcing social consensus in Singapore would serve as a strong safeguard for Singapore against populism (Yong 2017).

The Protection from Online Falsehoods and Manipulation Act (POFMA)

On 8 May 2019, Singapore passed the Protection from Online Falsehoods and Manipulation Act (POFMA), which provides the government with the legal power to swiftly act against perpetrators of online falsehoods.

During the second reading of the legislation in Parliament, Minister for Law K. Shanmugam cited populism as a serious consequence of online falsehoods and articulated the need for a law like POFMA. He highlighted how a lack of regulation of the online space resulted in fertile conditions for populist movements globally, where populists mobilise falsehoods to attack institutions, invoke divisive rhetoric, use conspiracy theories to oversimplify complex issues, and persuade people based on untruths. This has led people to lose faith in institutions, opening the doors to populism, which further exploits and deepens this trust deficit. He explained how legislation can help protect the foundations of a healthy democracy, which include trust, free speech, and the infrastructure of fact (Shanmugam 2019). In other words, POFMA can be understood as one example of Singapore's response to populism – particularly in the form of populism-fuelled falsehoods and populists' truth-making – to restore confidence in public institutions in the face of rising populism globally.

Singapore's ministers can invoke POFMA upon the fulfilment of two conditions – first, when there is digital dissemination of a 'false statement of fact', which excludes satire, opinion, or criticism and second, when a false statement of fact is deemed harmful to society, such as by undermining public interest in areas like security and public health, inciting ill will among communities, and the diminution of public confidence.

A false statement of fact can either be issued a 'correction direction' or a 'stop communication direction'. In the former, the falsehood will be allowed to remain online, but relevant actors must comply by putting up corrective information provided by the government alongside the falsehood. This will allow people to 'see both sides of the story' and make an informed decision for themselves. In contrast, a stop communication direction (or a 'take-down' direction) will be issued in egregious situations to promptly stem the spread of a falsehood by ensuring its removal so that it will no longer be available on the internet.

In both scenarios, the use of POFMA is subject to judicial review, and an appeal may be made to the high court to overturn the minister's order, which the government has argued prevents it from being the final arbiter of truth (Tham 2019).

Since coming into effect on 2 October 2019, POFMA has been invoked against falsehoods of a wide variety, including falsehoods about Singapore's education spending, population policies, and criminal justice system. As of December 2020, eight cases of falsehoods relating to the COVID-19 outbreak have also received correction orders.

The controversies surrounding POFMA

The controversial passing of POFMA was met with pushback from members of civil society, media practitioners, and academics, all of whom voiced concerns about the legislation in a few areas.

First, many felt that the language of the law was too broad and sweeping, giving the government too much discretionary power when using it. For example, although POFMA targets falsehoods that 'diminish public confidence in a state body', the definition of 'diminishing public confidence' remains vague, allowing ministers to have extremely broad latitude to decide what that entails (Vaswani 2019).

Second, critics argued that POFMA allows the government to decide what is factual as only ministers, but not opposition politicians or members of the public, can trigger corrections or take-down orders. With POFMA designed as a tool for exclusive use by the government, some feared that the law could be abused to clamp down on political dissent and to stifle the opposition. Since coming into force, POFMA has been used in multiple instances against opposition politicians and well-known critics of the state, reinforcing the perception that POFMA serves to strengthen the hegemony of the PAP government by monopolising the means of shaping public narratives, instead of cleaning up cyberspace (George 2019).

Third, media experts have pointed out that POFMA may have a chilling effect on speech, resulting in the worsening of a self-censorship culture. Research has found that self-censorship is already prevalent in Singapore. For example, the 2018 Reuters Institute Digital News Report found that 63 percent of Singaporeans were concerned that expressing their political views openly on the internet could get them into trouble with the authorities (Newman et al. 2018). With the addition of POFMA to the government's arsenal of speech laws, ordinary citizens may become even more hesitant to comment on socio-political issues online (Guest 2019).

Singapore's authoritarian conundrums in using POFMA

While the government laid out its rationale for enacting strong legislation to stem populists' falsehoods and truth-making, its approach to how POFMA has been designed and used signals the recognition of two conundrums that it has to contend with so that the use of POFMA would not paradoxically enable a populist opposition to make significant political gains.

First, although POFMA offers a strong and swift response against falsehoods that erode public trust, an over-reliance on this repressive and strong-handed response risks backfiring on the government's legitimacy if the law is not perceived to be used judiciously or is seen as unjustified legislative overreach. This may cause the government to lose credibility and trust, ironically making the Singapore electorate more susceptible to the appeals of a populist opposition, the very enemy it was fighting in the first place.

Second, an over-use of POFMA may have a serious chilling effect on speech, leading people to self-censor on the internet to avoid getting into trouble with the law. This may result in a counterproductive situation in which the government becomes less sentient of people's genuine sentiments, concerns, and dissatisfactions. One example of such a situation is China during its early stages of the COVID-19 outbreak, when the Chinese government's digital surveillance and censorship tactics for managing online dissent made citizens too afraid to talk about the virus for fear of being punished for spreading 'rumours', paradoxically stifling online conversations that would have offered signals about a potential viral outbreak (Tufecki 2020). In other words, the chilling effect of POFMA may lead to an inaccurate picture of public opinion, thus weakening the government's ability to anticipate challenges and adjust its strategies in response to shifts on the ground to bolster political support for the long run. This also gives populists political mileage to portray the government as 'not in touch' with the ground, reinforcing the populist narrative of a split between the elite and the masses.

The rest of this chapter highlights two approaches that the government has employed to solve the aforementioned dilemmas so that it may continue justifying the use of repressive tools without implicating its credibility in a manner that would allow a populist opposition to significantly challenge its legitimacy in the long run.

From repression to calibrated coercion

First, the government has been measured and calibrated in both its design and use of POFMA.

While the government had historically taken a heavy-handed approach to managing political dissent and criticism during the early stages of nation-building, its governance style has since strategically shifted to a light-touch approach. In his analysis of press controls in Singapore, George (2007) introduced the concept of 'calibrated coercion', in which the state is able to deploy repressive tools against dissenters yet incur minimum political cost. George argued that the advantages of calibrated coercion include reducing the prominence of coercive tactics in the public consciousness and minimising backlash and moral outrage from the public that may be strategically leveraged by a populist opposition to the government. Furthermore, calibrated coercion involves 'a dynamic process of creatively adapting regulations to suit recent experience and changed circumstances . . . quickly responding to news technologies. . . [that] pose a threat to [the government's] political control' (George 2007, p. 142).

In this respect, the calibrated design and use of POFMA can be understood as an extension of the government's strategy to discipline the online space in a way that uses just enough coercion to get the job done.

Firstly, the government has argued that the calibrated design of POFMA narrows its powers by allowing for more proportionate and measured responses (compared to existing legislation such as the Sedition Act and the Defamation Act, which are blunt and sweeping) (Mohktar 2019). For example, a correction direction against a falsehood, which the government has also said would be the primary response for most situations, allows the falsehood itself to remain accessible on the internet as long as the corrective information is published alongside it. Similarly, a stop communication direction would apply only to the content containing the falsehood – which must be made unavailable – but leaves the rest of the website available online. Heavier penalties, such as cutting off a website's revenue stream or shutting it down, would happen only if it received three directions within a period of six months. Hence, the calibrated design of POFMA grants room for the government to justify its use of the law in a manner that is synergistic with creating a public image of upholding free speech.

Secondly, on top of its calibrated design, the government's use of the law has also been calibrated thus far. Since the law came into effect, every instance of the government's use of POFMA has involved only the issue of correction directions, rather than its deploying the more extreme features of the law, such as take-downs. Tougher actions, such as compelling social media platforms to restrict access to certain websites, have only been taken when there has been noncompliance. Furthermore, the government has been cautious in ensuring that its use is targeted and narrow enough not to affect most Singaporeans directly, thus reducing the salience of its coercive tactics in Singaporeans' consciousness.

In other words, the government's calibrated design of POFMA and its measured use of the law (thus far) play a role in allowing the government to respond strongly against any populists' falsehoods that undermine public trust while not catching itself in a bind where the salience of its coercion backfires on its legitimacy and counterproductively give populists greater political mileage.

Hyper-responsiveness towards the public reactions of POFMA

Second, the government has been hyper-responsive in addressing concerns about and public reactions to the law. Borrowing from existing work on the concept of 'responsive authoritarianism', authoritarian regimes can demonstrate responsiveness in a few ways.

The first is through the formation of official avenues for civic and political participation by citizens, through which people's voices and opinions can be conveyed directly to the government (Means 1996; Qiaoan & Teets 2020). One example of this is the convening of the Select Committee on Deliberate Online Falsehoods in 2018, which sought to solicit public feedback on tackling online falsehoods, possibly through the use of legislation as a countermeasure. The public consultation exercise received a total of 170 submissions from academics, media and technology practitioners, members of civil society, and the public, of whom 65 appeared in front of the committee for oral hearing sessions that were widely reported by the local media. The committee eventually published a report that captured the public's feedback and proposed 22 policy recommendations that the government accepted in their entirety. On top of serving as a channel for gathering feedback, the select committee process also signaled a more consultative governance approach through its deliberative mode of communication (Marquis & Bird 2018; Teets 2013). This allowed the government to portray itself as less paternalistic, keen to work with citizens in partnership, and closely aware of public sentiments on the ground. This national display of a close relationship between the government and its people (which, in itself, could be argued as a populist strategy) may have had the effect of countering populist appeals claiming that the political elites were disconnected from everyday Singaporeans.

The second is through proactive sensing and monitoring of public concern about and opposition to policy decisions, which the government responds to when resistance is perceived to be widespread (Huerlin 2016). As mentioned earlier, the passing of POFMA saw significant opposition from civil society, academics, and free speech activists. Leaders in the government embarked on a series of public engagements that ranged from live interviews to closed-door discussions to explain the legislation, clarify misconceptions about it, and address concerns about its use. One of the most popular engagements was a video in which Minister Shanmugam was interviewed by internet personality Michelle Chong, who played her alter ego of an 'Ah Lian'[1] in an attempt to make the topic of POFMA (its rationale and what it sets out to do) more accessible to the working-class Singaporean. In the video, 'Ah Lian' conducted a light-hearted interview with the minister, who was himself more casual than his usual 'no-nonsense' public persona, using humour at times to diffuse the seriousness of the topic. The YouTube video has since received about 126,000 views. Such responses to public concerns by soft selling the legislation through light-hearted forms of communication may have moderated the public's perception of the law as chilling free speech and also signaled that the government is willing to respond to and engage with concerns on the ground as valid and understandable.

The third is by responding to criticisms about the law through frank debates in the public domain to signal openness and transparency. For example, the select committee provided a legitimate channel for critics to air their grievances, and a certain degree of dissent was tolerated. The government also candidly engaged with criticisms from foreign news media outlets, especially those from Western liberal democracies such as Bloomberg, *The Economist*, and the *Washington Post*, regarding its use of the law. This openness in responding to critics signals some tolerance of criticism and dissent in the public sphere, once again lending legitimacy to the government by giving the appearance that it upholds free speech to cushion the chilling effects of the law (Marquis & Bird 2018; Repnikova 2017).

In short, being hyper-responsive to public reactions towards the law allowed the government to portray itself as closely in touch with people and issues on the ground, dampening a populist opposition's ability to appeal to the masses by portraying the government as 'not in touch' with Singaporeans. Furthermore, the open engagement with criticisms produces a public image of upholding free speech and tolerance of dissent to moderate the chilling effect of the law that could, ironically, reduce its ability to accurately perform public opinion sensing in the long run.

Discussion and conclusion

In summary, this chapter has argued that understanding Singapore's resilience against populism – especially in the form of populists' falsehoods and truth-making – needs to go beyond looking at the role of Singapore's paternalistic state and strong institutions. While a top-down measure like POFMA indeed represents a manifest effort by the government to tackle falsehoods, erosion of trust, and populism through its conventionally authoritative approach, it is the latent qualities such its calibrated design and use of the law, its hyper-responsiveness to public reaction, and its engagement with criticisms that allow it to continue justifying its use of strong-handed measures at minimal political cost. This is crucial to solving the authoritarian dilemma in which an over-reliance on repression may instead backfire on the government's legitimacy, erode the deep reservoir of trust that it has built with Singaporeans, and ironically allow a populist opposition to gain traction in the country.

Moving forward, scholarly work exploring the relationship between populism, misinformation, and social media can afford to pay greater attention to two aspects.

First, many of the existing studies have been focused on explicating how digital and social media affordances have augmented populist appeals and uncovering how populists have coopted the digital space for their agenda, in order to explain the surge of populism around the world. However, Singapore's POFMA is but one example of a global move towards tighter regulation of the digital space to combat its online harms. Thus, future research should look into the effectiveness of state regulation of the online space in stemming populists' falsehoods and truth-making and how populists have been circumventing such controls or manipulating them to their advantage in response. This would give a more nuanced picture of rising populism in our age of digital media.

Second, as George (2007) pointed out in his concept of calibrated coercion, the process of introducing creative regulatory adaptions in response to new technologies is a key feature that determines the success of reducing the salience of coercive tactics. In other words, Singapore's ability to safeguard itself against populists' falsehoods and truth-making would depend not only on the government's continued balance of being calibrated in the use of POFMA and remaining responsive to public reaction but also on its ability to recognise when appropriate adjustments need to be made in order to maintain popular support. Hence, scholars focusing on media and politics in Singapore should analyse the specificities of new situations that arise in future on their own terms and explore new theoretical concepts as older ones lose their relevance and adequacy as the landscape continues to evolve.

Note

1 A colloquial term for a female who behaves in an uncouth manner, is loud, and is often seen as 'low-class'.

References

Abts, K & Rummens, S 2007. Populism versus democracy. *Political Studies*, *55*(2), pp. 405–424.

Brubaker, R 2017. Why populism? *Theory and Society*, *46*(5), pp. 357–385.

DeVreese, CH, Esser, F, Aalberg, T, Reinemann, C & Stanyer, J 2018. Populism as an expression of political communication content and style: A new perspective. *The International Journal of Press/Politics*, *23*(4), pp. 423–438.

Dittrich, PJ 2017. Social networks and populism in the EU. Available at www.delorscentre.eu/en/publica tions/detail/publication/social-networks-and-populism-in-the-eu-a-comparative-study/ (Accessed 27 January 2020).

Engesser, S, Ernst, N, Esser, F & Büchel, F 2017. Populism and social media: How politicians spread a fragmented ideology. *Information, Communication & Society*, *20*(8), pp. 1109–1126.

Engesser, S, Fawzi, N & Larsson, AO 2017. Populist online communication: Introduction to the special issue. *Information, Communication & Society*, *20*(9), pp. 1279–1292.

Flew, T & Iosifidis, P 2020. Populism, globalisation and social media. *International Communication Gazette*, *82*(1), pp. 7–25.

George, C 2007. Consolidating authoritarian rule: Calibrated coercion in Singapore. *The Pacific Review*, *20*(2), pp. 127–145.

George, C 2019. Disinformation: A debate that needs to be better informed. *Freedom from the Press blog*, blog post, 7 October. Available at: https://blog.freedomfromthepress.info/2019/10/07/disinforma tion-2/ (Accessed 1 March 2020).

Gerbaudo, P 2014. Populism 2.0: Social media activism, the generic Internet user and interactive direct democracy. In D Trottier & C Fuchs (eds), *Social media, politics and the state: Protests, revolutions, riots, crime and policing in the age of Facebook, Twitter and YouTube*, pp. 79–99. Routledge, London.

Guest, P 2019. Singapore says it's fighting fake news. Journalists see a ruse. *The Atlantic*, 19 July. Available at: www.theatlantic.com/international/archive/2019/07/singapore-press-freedom/592039/ (Accessed 1 March 2020).

Habermas, J 1989. *The structural transformation of the public sphere: An inquiry into a category of bourgeois society.* MIT Press, Cambridge, MA.

Heurlin, C 2016. *Responsive authoritarianism in China.* Cambridge University Press, Cambridge.

Jansen, RS 2011. Populist mobilization: A new theoretical approach to populism. *Sociological Theory, 29*(2), pp. 75–96.

Kho, KRG 2019. Behavioural biases and identity in social media: The case of Philippine populism, President Duterte's rise, and ways forward. Available at: https://scholarbank.nus.edu.sg/handle/10635/154272 (Accessed 17 February 2020).

Klinger, U & Svensson, J 2015. The emergence of network media logic in political communication: A theoretical approach. *New Media & Society, 17*(8), pp. 1241–1257.

Kruikemeier, S, Van Noort, G, Vliegenthart, R & DeVreese, CH 2013. Getting closer: The effects of personalized and interactive online political communication. *European Journal of Communication, 28*(1), pp. 53–66.

Laclau, E 2005. *On populist reason.* Verso Books, New York.

Lee, P 2016. The real Singapore trial: Co-founder Yang Kaiheng controlled bulk of ad revenue earnings. *The Straits Times*, 25 June. Available at: www.straitstimes.com/singapore/courts-crime/co-founder-controlled-bulk-of-the-ad-revenue-earnings (Accessed 27 January 2020).

Loh, D 2020. Singapore deputy PM warns opposition on exploiting social splits. *Nikkei Asian Review*, 20 January. Available at: https://asia.nikkei.com/Politics/Singapore-deputy-PM-warns-opposition-on-exploiting-social-splits (Accessed 27 January 2020).

Maldonado, MJ 2017. Rethinking populism in the digital age: Social networks, political affects and post-truth democracies. Available at: https://riuma.uma.es/xmlui/handle/10630/14500 (Accessed 27 January 2020).

Marquis, C & Bird Y 2018. The paradox of responsive authoritarianism: How civic activism spurs environmental penalties in China. *Organization Science, 29*(5), pp. 948–968.

Means, GP 1996. Soft authoritarianism in Malaysia and Singapore. *Journal of Democracy,* 7(4), pp. 103–117.

Moffitt, B & Tormey, S 2014. Rethinking populism: Politics, mediatisation and political style. *Political studies, 62*(2), pp. 381–397.

Mohktar, F 2019. Fake news laws narrow, rather than extend, Government's powers: Law ministry. *TODAY,* 2 May. Available at: www.todayonline.com/singapore/fake-news-laws-narrow-rather-extends-governments-powers-law-ministry (Accessed 1 March 2020).

Momoc, A 2018. Populism 2.0, digital democracy and the new 'enemies of the people'. *Communication Today, 9*(1), pp. 58–77.

Mudde, C 2004. The populist zeitgeist. *Government and Opposition, 39*(4), pp. 541–563.

Mudde, C & Kaltwasser, CR 2017. *Populism: A very short introduction.* Oxford University Press, Oxford.

Müller, JW 2016. *What is populism?* Penguin Books UK, London.

Newman, N, Fletcher, R, Kalogeropoulos, A & Nielsen, R 2018. Reuters institute digital news report 2018, Reuters institute for the study of journalism. Available at: www.digitalnewsreport.org/ (Accessed 6 March 2020).

Norris, P & Inglehart, R 2016. Trump, Brexit, and the rise of populism: Economic have-nots and cultural backlash. *Harvard JFK School of Government Faculty Working Papers Series*, pp. 1–52.

Papacharissi, Z 2002. The virtual sphere: The internet as a public sphere. *New Media & Society, 4*(1), pp. 9–27.

Postill, J 2018. Populism and social media: A global perspective. *Media, Culture & Society, 40*(5), pp. 754–765.

Qiaoan, R & Teets, JC 2020. Responsive authoritarianism in China: A review of responsiveness in Xi and Hu administrations. *Journal of Chinese Political Science, 25*(1), pp. 139–153.

Repnikova, M 2017. *Media politics in China: Improvising power under authoritarianism.* Cambridge University Press, Cambridge.

Schroeder, R 2019. Digital media and the entrenchment of right-wing populist agendas. *Social Media+ Society, 5*(4), pp. 1–11.

Shanmugam, K 2019. Second reading speech by Minister for Law, K Shanmugam on The Protection from Online Falsehoods and Manipulation Bill. Available at: www.mlaw.gov.sg/news/parliamentary-speeches/second-reading-speech-by-minister-for-law-k-shanmugam-on-the-protection-from-online-falsehoods-and-manipulation-bill (Accessed 27 January 2020).

Sullivan, S & Costa, R 2020. Trump and Sanders leading competing populist movements, reshaping American politics. *The Washington Post*, 2 March. Available at: www.washingtonpost.com/politics/2020/03/02/two-populist-movements-sanders-trump (Accessed 13 March 2020).

Sunstein, CR 2018. *# Republic: Divided democracy in the age of social media*. Princeton University Press, Princeton, NJ.

Taggart, P 2004. Populism and representative politics in contemporary Europe. *Journal of Political Ideologies*, *9*(3), pp. 269–288.

Tan, K P 2017. Resisting authoritarian populism: Lessons from and for Singapore. *TODAY*, 22 May. Available at: www.todayonline.com/commentary/resisting-authoritarian-populism-lessons-and-singapore (Accessed 28 February 2020).

Tee, Z 2019. PAP must not allow split between masses and elite to take root, says PM Lee Hsien Loong. *The Straits Times*, 10 November. Available at: www.straitstimes.com/politics/pap-convention-pap-must-not-allow-split-between-masses-and-elite-to-take-root-says-pm-lee (Access 27 January 2020).

Teets, JC 2013. Let many civil societies bloom: The rise of consultative authoritarianism in China. *The China Quarterly*, 213, pp. 19–38.

Tham, YC 2019. Government makes initial decision on falsehood but courts are final arbiter of truth: Shanmugam. *The Straits Times*, 2 April. Available at: www.straitstimes.com/politics/govt-makes-initial-decision-on-falsehood-but-courts-are-final-arbiter-of-truth-k-shanmugam (Accessed 27 January 2020).

Thompson, M 2017. *Enough said: What's gone wrong with the language of politics?* St. Martin's Press, New York.

Tufekci, Z 2020. How the coronavirus revealed authoritarianism's fatal flaw. *The Atlantic*, 22 February. Available at: www.theatlantic.com/technology/archive/2020/02/coronavirus-and-blindness-authoritarianism/606922/ (Accessed 6 March 2020).

Vaccari, C & Valeriani, A 2015. Follow the leader! Direct and indirect flows of political communication during the 2013 Italian general election campaign. *New Media & Society*, *17*(7), pp. 1025–1042.

Vaswani, K 2019. Concern over Singapore's anti-fake news law. *BBC*, 4 April. Available at: www.bbc.com/news/business-47782470 (Accessed 6 March 2020).

Ware, A 2002. The United States: Populism as political strategy. In Y Mény & Y Surel (eds), *Democracies and the populist challenge*, pp. 101–119. Palgrave Macmillan, London.

Yong, C 2017. 'Drift towards populism 'not inevitable': DPM Tharman. *The Straits Times,* 8 January. Available at: www.straitstimes.com/singapore/drift-towards-populism-not-inevitable (Accessed 27 January 2020).

43

DEBUNKING MISINFORMATION

Eun-Ju Lee and Soo Yun Shin

About midnight on the Christmas Eve of 2016, one of us got caught by her then-six-year-old son while secretly (and frantically) gift-wrapping his Christmas present. 'So *you* bought our Christmas presents!' Panic-stricken, she was fast searching for words to cover up, soon realising there was no need. 'You give Santa our gifts so he can deliver them to us!'

Misbeliefs are hard to correct. Even when inaccurate beliefs are corrected, their influence may linger on (Johnson and Seifert 1994). In this chapter, we aim to evaluate the literature on the debunking of misinformation in light of the following questions. First, what do we mean when we say corrective information is (not) effective? A range of outcome variables has been adopted to assess how 'effective' debunking efforts are, with varying success rates. Second, under what conditions is correction more and less effective? What source-, message-, receiver-, and context-related variables moderate the effectiveness of correction? Lastly, what psychological processes account for the successes and failures of debunking efforts? Understanding the cognitive mechanisms and potential biases that shape the correction process would help better counter misinformation. After addressing these questions, suggestions for future research are proposed with a view to developing theory-based recommendations for how to combat misinformation.

What does debunking misinformation do?

At its core, debunking misinformation entails exposing falsehood and inaccuracies in verifiable information, thereby correcting misbeliefs. Beyond the immediate and primary consequence of belief changes, researchers have examined the secondary effects of corrective information as well, such as attitudes and behavioural intention.

Factual belief

First and foremost, studies have examined how successful debunking messages are in rectifying individuals' faulty knowledge and misbeliefs. For instance, people who received a corrective message to US president Trump's misstatements regarding climate change showed better factual knowledge about climate change and the role of Paris Climate Accord than those who did not receive the correction (Porter et al. 2019). Similarly, corrective information concerning a new tobacco product led people to realise the health risks associated with it (Biener et al. 2007). Moreover, belief changes that followed the exposure to corrective information on the immigration issue in the US persisted up to four weeks (Carnahan et al. 2020).

Quite contrarily, attempts to correct misperceptions about vaccines were largely ineffective and often backfired, reinforcing rather than countering misbeliefs (e.g. 'Some vaccines cause autism in healthy children') (Pluviano et al. 2017; Pluviano et al. 2019). For political misbeliefs such as the existence of Iraqi WMD, a correction message increased misbeliefs, albeit only among conservatives (Nyhan and Reifler 2010). As a result, although a meta-analysis of 65 studies (N = 23,604) (Walter and Murphy 2018) confirmed that corrective messages, on average, significantly reduced misbeliefs (r = .35, p = .0005), it deserves attention when corrective information fails to overwrite previously acquired misinformation, leading to belief update.

Affective evaluation

Although attitudes towards an object are closely associated with the beliefs people hold about it, belief correction does not always incur corresponding attitude changes. In the aforementioned study, corrective messages about Trump's misstatements changed people's factual beliefs about climate change but did not alter their policy preferences (Porter et al. 2019). Likewise, exposure to journalistic fact-checks of Trump's campaign messages only improved people's belief accuracy, with no significant change in their attitudes towards him (Nyhan et al. 2019). Such persistent influence of corrected information on attitudes is referred to as belief echoes (Thorson 2016). However, evidence to the contrary also exists. After estimating federal spending on scientific research and then learning that the actual spending fell short of their estimates, participants showed higher levels of support for increased spending in science (Goldfarb and Kriner 2017). Likewise, the provision of accurate information about Chinese investment and regulations over foreign investment induced a stronger preference for a Chinese investment proposal in Canada (Li *et al.* 2019).

One possible explanation for the inconsistency concerns the strength of prior attitudes – the stronger the existing attitudes, like those towards a celebrity politician (versus government spending), the less likely a mere correction of certain facts is to alter them. Similarly, when the overall attitude is based on a complex, multi-faceted belief repertoire (and the evaluations of each belief component), correcting a part of the repertoire might not be sufficient to induce attitude changes.

Behavioural intention

Harms of misinformation go well beyond ill-advised opinions and misperceptions. Amid the COVID-19 pandemic, fake remedies were spread fast and wide over social media, and the mistaken belief that toxic methanol protects against the virus killed nearly 300 people in Iran (Karimi and Gambrell 2020). Relatively few studies examined how debunking messages affect individuals' behavioural intentions, either to follow the debunking message's recommendation or to refrain from the action advocated in the corrected misinformation, and self-reported intentions might not predict their actual behavior with as much precision as we would like. Still, corrective ads for a suspicious weight-loss drug weakened consumers' intention to try out the drug (Aikin et al. 2017), and providing facts against science denialism increased people's willingness to perform behaviors supported by science, such as vaccination or taking actions against climate change (Schmid and Betsch 2019).

In addition to factual beliefs, attitudes, and behavioural intentions directly related to the specific content of misinformation, exposure to debunking messages may affect more generalised, higher-order cognitions. For people with low interest in a political issue, reading a news article containing fact-checks lowered their confidence in the ability to find the truth in politics (i.e. epistemic political efficacy) (Pingree et al. 2014). Similarly, frequent exposure to debunking information might cultivate chronic scepticism and make 'false until proven true' the default mode of processing any information. Alternatively, as people get used to seeing false information being tagged as such, they might come to assume that information with no tag is truthful (i.e. implied truth effect) (Pennycook et al. 2020). Rather than treating these effects as unintended by-products, future research should look beyond the immediate correction of misbeliefs and attitude changes and explore second-order effects that can have longer-lasting impacts on how people interpret and respond to mediated information.

When is correction more and less effective?

Debunking misinformation is an inherently persuasive attempt whose objective is to undo or override the influence of false information. As a result, research has examined how factors known to affect persuasion in general, such as source credibility and message congruency, account for the (in)effectiveness of corrective information.

Attributes of misinformation

The stronger the misbeliefs are, the more resistant they are to the correction attempts. Thus, what makes misinformation more persuasive renders the correction less effective. For example, misbeliefs are more likely to persist when the misinformation is from a credible (versus a less credible) source and when repeated (versus not) (Walter and Tukachinsky 2020). Misinformation is also more difficult to correct when it offers causal explanations about the focal event than when it is only topically related. For instance, participants were more likely to believe the misinformation regarding the effect of kombucha, even after retraction, when it explained a story character's action that they had read than when it did not (Hamby et al. 2019). Just as the provision of a 'reason,' even a placebic one, was effective in eliciting compliance (Langer et al. 1978), misinformation that enables people to understand why something happens is better integrated into their knowledge structure, hence more persistent (Johnson and Seifert 1994).

Attributes of corrective information

More research has examined how various attributes of corrective information predict its effectiveness. Not surprisingly, expert sources such as a government agency (e.g. Centers for Disease Control and Prevention) (Vraga and Bode 2017) or news media (van der Meer and Jin 2019) are more effective in increasing belief accuracy than peer sources. Interestingly, algorithmic correction and peer correction (by other Facebook users) were not significantly different in reducing people's misbeliefs (Bode and Vraga 2018).

Self-interest is another source-related factor that affects how likely people are to accept corrective information. When the corrective message is against the communicator's (presumed) self-interest, like when Republicans (versus Democrats) endorse corrections supporting scientific consensus on climate change, people are more likely to accept it and modify their beliefs (Benegal and Scruggs 2018). Similarly, self-correction can be seen as a special case of self-defeating messages, for retracting one's own message potentially hurts the communicator's credibility. A meta-analysis indeed confirmed that self-corrections are more effective than third-party corrections (Walter and Tukachinsky 2020).

Why, then, are self-defeating corrections more persuasive? First, according to Fiske (1980), negative aspects of stimuli are more influential in the formation of judgments than positive ones (i.e. negativity effect) because negative information is less typical and thus deemed more informative. If (perceived) typicality determines the value of information, corrections against self-interest would be considered more informative and thus taken seriously, for they are uncommon and atypical. Second, self-defeating messages are unlikely to raise suspicions about the communicator's ulterior motives. Considering that the suspicion of ulterior motives heightens concerns about deception, which subsequently trigger resistance to persuasion (Fransen et al. 2015), corrections against self-interest are probably more effective because people are less likely to infer ulterior motives. The meta-analytic finding that corrections involving health are more successful than those concerning politics and marketing (Walter and Murphy 2018) might be due to lower levels of ulterior motives attributed to the former.

As for message characteristics, counter-attitudinal corrections are less effective than pro-attitudinal corrections (Walter and Tukachinsky 2020). Also, debunking messages are more effective when they explicitly state what to believe and what not to, rather than merely questioning the truth of the misinformation (Pingree *et al.* 2014). For example, applying a 'rated false' tag to a false news headline, rather than a 'disputed' tag, improved the accuracy of perceptions (Clayton et al. 2019). Similarly, correction was more effective when it refuted the false information completely rather than partially, leaving no room for the falsified misbeliefs (Walter et al. 2019).

Quality of message also matters. As shown in a meta-analysis (Walter and Tukachinsky 2020), appeals to coherence (e.g. providing alternative explanations for misinformation) were found more effective than appeals to source credibility. Although such results might seem indicative of systematic (versus heuristic) processing of corrective information, evidence also suggests that simple peripheral cues interfere with the correction of misbeliefs. For example, a message debunking people's misbelief that an Imam backing an Islamic cultural centre in NYC is a terrorist sympathizer was less successful in correcting the misbelief when it included his photo dressed in Middle-Eastern-style attire, as opposed to Western-style clothing (Garrett et al. 2013). Likewise, participants were less likely to accept the debunking message when it contained the Imam's previous controversial, yet unrelated, statements (Garrett et al. 2013). Thus, more research is needed to conclude whether such findings stem from unwarranted reliance on peripheral cues or biased systematic processing guided by prior beliefs or attitudes.

Findings are also mixed as to how emotionality of misinformation or corrective information influences the continuation of misperceptions. Although the intensity of emotion arising from misinformation (e.g. a report attributing a plane crash to terrorist attack versus bad weather) did not moderate the effectiveness of correction (Ecker et al. 2011), corrections containing negative emotional feedback from the victim of misinformation were more effective than corrections with no emotional feedback (Sangalang et al. 2019).

In addition to the source- and message-related factors, context can play a role too. Most researched is the time lag between the exposure to the initial misinformation and the correction. Generally, immediate corrections, such as presenting corrective 'related articles' right after fake news on social media (Smith and Seitz 2019), work better than delayed corrections (Walter and Tukachinsky 2020), for misinformation is less likely integrated firmly into individuals' knowledge structure if refuted immediately. However, such real-time corrections were more effective for those who found corrections favourable, rather than unfavourable, to their pre-existing attitudes (Garrett and Weeks 2013), suggesting potential contingencies.

Why is correction ineffective? Cognitive and motivational processes

Misbeliefs won't be corrected (1) if people deliberately avoid debunking messages (selective avoidance), (2) if misinformation has been well integrated into the recipient's mental model (proactive interference), and/or (3) if corrective messages are processed in a biased manner (motivated reasoning).

First, getting a message across to the target audience in this high-choice environment is an increasingly arduous task. Research on cognitive dissonance (Festinger 1957) and confirmation bias (Nickerson 1998) suggests that people are inherently motivated to avoid information incongruent with their existing beliefs and attitudes. Consequently, when a debunking message is expected to cause psychological discomfort by challenging their current understanding of the world, people actively avoid it. Hameleers and van der Meer's (2020) finding that people who opposed immigration were more likely than those who supported immigration to choose the fact-check that refuted pro-immigration news supports this notion.

Second, even when people are exposed to corrections, processing of corrective messages may be hampered by proactive interference as previously obtained misinformation impedes 'the acquisition and retrieval of newer materials' (Teague et al. 2011: 2028). It is challenging to update the mental associations established around the old (mis)information with new facts, like memorising a friend's new phone number. Proactive interference naturally transpires because of the way our memory works, so it presents inherent challenges with any correction attempts, especially when the previous misinformation plays a central role in explaining the focal event. Unless the correction provides a better alternative explanation, people will still fall back on old misinformation rather than the recent corrections (Wilkes and Leatherbarrow 1988).

Third, message recipients' existing attitudes and beliefs may bias how they process corrective messages. Research on motivated reasoning in general, and disconfirmation bias in particular, suggests that people 'spend time and cognitive resources denigrating and counter-arguing attitudinally incongruent arguments' (Taber et al. 2009: 139). In the face of corrective information, people may engage in motivated reasoning, discounting the validity of arguments and evidence that counter their misbeliefs while selectively heeding and summarily accepting attitudinally coherent facts. The meta-analysis finding that counter-attitudinal correction is less effective than pro-attitudinal correction (Walter and Tukachinsky 2020) suggests the robust operation of biased information processing.

What next? Future directions

The extant literature offers useful insights into what makes correction efforts more and less effective and why, but the empirical evidence and theoretical explanations are far from conclusive. Next, we identify several limitations in previous scholarship and suggest directions for future research.

Search for theory-grounded explanations

With research on misinformation amassed quickly, inconsistencies are also noted. For example, does repetition of misinformation in the corrective message, most notably in the myth-versus-fact form, lower its effectiveness or even backfire? Some have warned against the familiarity backfire effect, arguing that misinformation included in the corrective message may become more familiar, hence believed (e.g. Chan et al. 2017). Others have shown that false information should be explicitly negated for correction to occur (e.g. Weil et al. 2020). Although meta-analyses may provide an answer relatively immune to the idiosyncratic biases of individual studies, merely counting which side gets more empirical support falls short of elucidating why repetition matters. Instead, theory-based explanations need to be developed and tested to reconcile the seemingly inconsistent or even contradictory findings. If the detection of incompatibility is the key to explaining why repetition of misinformation enhances correction efficacy (Ecker et al. 2017), for example, one may systematically vary the salience of incompatibility between misinformation and corrective information and examine how it moderates the efficacy of correction.

Need for deeper theoretical grounding is also found with studies comparing diverse forms of correction for their relative effectiveness: rating scale plus contextual correction versus contextual correction (Amazeen et al. 2018) and visual truth scale (fact-o-meter) versus simple retraction versus short-form refutation (Ecker et al. 2020). While it is certainly useful to evaluate which correction method works better, without sufficient theorising, one cannot explain why one message format outperforms the other(s), which lowers confidence in observed findings. For example, why does the inclusion of graphical elements, such as a truth scale, reduce the effectiveness of correction messages (Walter et al. 2019)? Is it because an extra visual element distracts people from key facts and core arguments? Or is it because the truth scale makes the discrepancy between one's own beliefs/opinions and the correction message clearer that people downright reject the message without even reading it? To offer reliable practical recommendations for effective debunking strategies, more theoretical explorations are in order.

The search for theoretical explanations also involves identifying potential confounds in previous works. As Thorson (2016) suggested, corrections might have been ineffective because they were phrased as negations, rather than affirmations. Given that 'what is' is easier to process than 'what is not' (i.e. the affirmative-representation principle) (Pacini and Epstein 1999), the efficacy of corrective information might have been suppressed due to the use of negations in corrective messages (e.g. 'Vaccines do not cause autism'). Another potential confound is the valence of misinformation (and correction). If negative information tends to be considered more informative and thus more influential in social judgments (Fiske 1980), debunking misinformation might be less effective when the misinformation is negative than when it is positive. Misinformation, however, needs not be negative. Amid the coronavirus pandemic, the widely shared news about an Italian priest who allegedly died from coronavirus after giving up a respirator to a younger patient was invalidated later (Pleasance 2020). Potential methodological confounds, including syntactic and semantic features of misinformation, should be assessed thoroughly before any theoretical explaining is attempted.

User engagement at the core of conceptual framework

Most research has thus far focused on how people respond to misinformation and corrective information, once exposed. To make causal claims not contaminated by self-selection, participants were typically forced to read what was randomly assigned to them. However, not only do individual traits, such as processing style, affect how people respond to corrective information (Carnahan and Garrett 2019), but they also affect how likely people are to engage with it in the first place. Moreover, just as 'forced' exposure to partisan news yields different outcomes than 'selected' exposure (Stroud et al. 2019), those who willingly choose to read corrective information process and evaluate the information differently than those incidentally exposed to it. Therefore, research should start with questions such as what dispositional (e.g. need for closure, need for orientation) and situational (e.g. accuracy motivation, issue involvement) factors predict volitional exposure to corrective information like fact-checks.

User engagement also deserves more attention as an outcome variable. Possibly due to the legacy of the media effects paradigm, message acceptance is often positioned as the end result of the communication process. However, communication begets more communication. Especially considering that social media platforms and news aggregation sites are where people encounter misinformation most frequently, the specific patterns and consequences of user engagement like commenting and sharing demand empirical investigations. After all, it is how fast and far misinformation travels in the networked society that makes misinformation a real threat, which cannot happen without the voluntary engagement of countless individuals in the process.

Beyond controlled experiment

Much research reviewed herein relies on controlled experiments, whose known limitations include demand characteristics. Measuring the participants' factual knowledge or the perceived accuracy of misinformation immediately after presenting corrective information, for example, seems fairly close to a manipulation check. Similarly, to examine if participants' support for more investment in scientific research changes after they are informed that the current budget is less than what most people believe (Goldfarb and Kriner 2017) might have rendered the research objective all too transparent.

Another reason why researchers should look beyond a controlled setting is the paucity of research on the context. Amid a global pandemic, for instance, overwhelmed by the sheer amount of (mis)information, people might become even more susceptible to confirmation biases in the form of selective exposure and motivated reasoning. Alternatively, heightened accuracy motivation might lead people to seek information from more diverse sources than they normally prefer. By actively incorporating information environment as a variable and keeping track of how people seek, process, and share information over time, researchers can offer ecologically valid accounts of how the debunking of misinformation works in real life.

Conclusion

Challenges associated with the debunking of misinformation are well documented. Although the term *post-truth* may be new, the very human tendency it captures is not – our undue reliance on existing beliefs and attitudes in social judgments and decision-making is age old. At the same time, the conditions in which our mind operates seem to be undergoing drastic changes. Due to the unprecedentedly high volume, variety, and velocity of misinformation inundating people's daily news feed, public awareness of the perils and dangers of misinformation is more heightened than ever. Such changes might render the truth bias no longer a default mode of information processing, eventually altering the way human mind works. Potential changes such as this present interesting challenges and opportunities to communication scholars who are tasked with explaining how we make sense of the world we live in, among others.

References

Aikin, K. J., Southwell, B. G., Paquin, R. S., Rupert, D. J., O'Donoghue, A. C., Betts, K. R. and Lee, P. K. (2017) 'Correction of misleading information in prescription drug television advertising: The roles of advertisement similarity and time delay', *Research in Social and Administrative Pharmacy*, 13(2), pp. 378–388.

Amazeen, M. A., Thorson, E., Muddiman, A. and Graves, L. (2018) 'Correcting political and consumer misperceptions: The effectiveness and effects of rating scale versus contextual correction formats', *Journalism & Mass Communication Quarterly*, 95(1), pp. 28–48.

Benegal, S. D. and Scruggs, L. A. (2018) 'Correcting misinformation about climate change: The impact of partisanship in an experimental setting', *Climatic Change*, 148(1–2), pp. 61–80.

Biener, L., Bogen, K. and Connolly, G. (2007) 'Impact of corrective health information on consumers' perceptions of "reduced exposure" tobacco products', *Tobacco Control*, 16(5), pp. 306–311.

Bode, L. and Vraga, E. K. (2018) 'See something, say something: Correction of global health misinformation on social media', *Health Communication*, 33(9), pp. 1131–1140.

Carnahan, D., Bergan, D. E. and Lee, S. (2020) 'Do corrective effects last? Results from a longitudinal experiment on beliefs toward immigration in the U.S.', *Political Behavior*. Online advance publication.

Carnahan, D. and Garrett, R. K. (2019) 'Processing style and responsiveness to corrective information', *International Journal of Public Opinion Research*. Online advance publication.

Chan, M. S., Jones, C. R., Jamieson, K. H. and Albarracín, D. (2017) 'Debunking: A meta-analysis of the psychological efficacy of messages countering misinformation', *Psychological Science*, 28(11), pp. 1531–1546.

Clayton, K., Blair, S., Busam, J. A., Forstner, S., Glance, J., Green, G., Kawata, A., Kovvuri, A., Martin, J., Morgan, E., Sandhu, M., Sang, R., Scholz-Bright, R., Welch, A. T., Wolff, A. G., Zhou, A. and Nyhan, B. (2019) 'Real solutions for fake news? Measuring the effectiveness of general warnings and fact-check tags in reducing belief in false stories on social media', *Political Behavior*. Online advance publication.

Ecker, U. K. H., Hogan, J. L. and Lewandowsky, S. (2017) 'Reminders and repetition of misinformation: Helping or hindering its retraction?', *Journal of Applied Research in Memory and Cognition*, 6(2), pp. 185–192.

Ecker, U. K. H., Lewandowsky, S. and Apai, J. (2011) 'Terrorists brought down the plane! – No, actually it was a technical fault: Processing corrections of emotive information', *The Quarterly Journal of Experimental Psychology*, 64(2), pp. 283–310.

Ecker, U. K. H., O'Reilly, Z., Reid, J. S. and Chang, E. P. (2020) 'The effectiveness of short-format refutational fact-checks', *British Journal of Psychology*, 111(1), pp. 36–54.

Festinger, L. (1957) *A theory of cognitive dissonance*. Evanston, IL: Row, Peterson.

Fiske, S. T. (1980) 'Attention and weight in person perception: The impact of negative and extreme behavior', *Journal of Personality and Social Psychology*, 38(6), pp. 889–906.

Fransen, M. L., Smit, E. G. and Verlegh, P. W. J. (2015) 'Strategies and motives for resistance to persuasion: An integrative framework', *Frontiers in Psychology*, 6, p. 1201.

Garrett, R. K., Nisbet, E. C. and Lynch, E. K. (2013) 'Undermining the corrective effects of media-based political fact checking? The role of contextual cues and naïve theory', *Journal of Communication*, 63(4), pp. 617–637.

Garrett, R. K. and Weeks, B. E. (2013) 'The promise and peril of real-time corrections to political misperceptions', in *Proceedings of the 2013 conference on Computer supported cooperative work*. San Antonio, TX: Association for Computing Machinery (CSCW'13), pp. 1047–1058.

Goldfarb, J. L. and Kriner, D. L. (2017) 'Building public support for science spending: Misinformation, motivated reasoning, and the power of corrections', *Science Communication*, 39(1), pp. 77–100.

Hamby, A., Ecker, U. and Brinberg, D. (2019) 'How stories in memory perpetuate the continued influence of false information', *Journal of Consumer Psychology*. Online advance publication.

Hameleers, M. and van der Meer, T. G. L. A. (2020) 'Misinformation and polarization in a high-choice media environment: How effective are political fact-checkers?', *Communication Research*, 47(2), pp. 227–250.

Johnson, H. M. and Seifert, C. M. (1994) 'Sources of the continued influence effect: When misinformation in memory affects later inferences', *Journal of Experimental Psychology: Learning, Memory, and Cognition*, 20(6), pp. 1420–1436.

Karimi, N. and Gambrell, J. (2020) 'In Iran, false belief a poison fights virus kills hundreds', *AP News*, 26 March. Available at: https://apnews.com/6e04783f95139b5f87a5febe28d72015 (Accessed: 13 April 2020).

Langer, E. J., Blank, A. and Chanowitz, B. (1978) 'The mindlessness of ostensibly thoughtful action: The role of "placebic" information in interpersonal interaction', *Journal of Personality and Social Psychology*, 36(6), pp. 635–642.

Li, X., Kuang, Y. and Zhang, L. (2019) 'Misperceptions of Chinese investments in Canada and their correction: Evidence from a survey experiment', *Canadian Journal of Political Science*, 52(2), pp. 285–302.

Nickerson, R. S. (1998) 'Confirmation bias: A ubiquitous phenomenon in many guises.', *Review of General Psychology*, 2(2), pp. 175–220.

Nyhan, B., Porter, E., Reifler, J. and Wood, T. J. (2019) 'Taking fact-checks literally but not seriously? The effects of journalistic fact-checking on factual beliefs and candidate favorability', *Political Behavior*. Online advance publication.

Nyhan, B. and Reifler, J. (2010) 'When corrections fail: The persistence of political misperceptions', *Political Behavior*, 32(2), pp. 303–330.

Pacini, R. and Epstein, S. (1999) 'The interaction of three facets of concrete thinking in a game of chance', *Thinking & Reasoning*, 5(4), pp. 303–325.

Pennycook, G., Bear, A., Collins, E. T. and Rand, D. G. (2020) 'The implied truth effect: Attaching warnings to a subset of fake news headlines increases perceived accuracy of headlines without warnings', *Management Science*. Online advance publication.

Pingree, R. J., Brossard, D. and McLeod, D. M. (2014) 'Effects of journalistic adjudication on factual beliefs, news evaluations, information seeking, and epistemic political efficacy', *Mass Communication and Society*, 17(5), pp. 615–638.

Pleasance, C. (2020) 'Italian priest, 72, dies from coronavirus but did not give up a respirator', *Daily Mail*, 24 March. Available at: www.dailymail.co.uk/news/article-8145967/Italian-priest-72-dies-coronavirus-giving-away-respirator.html (Accessed: 19 April 2020).

Pluviano, S., Watt, C. and Della Sala, S. (2017) 'Misinformation lingers in memory: Failure of three pro-vaccination strategies', *PLOS ONE*, 12(7), p. e0181640.

Pluviano, S., Watt, C., Ragazzini, G. and Della Sala, S. (2019) 'Parents' beliefs in misinformation about vaccines are strengthened by pro-vaccine campaigns', *Cognitive Processing*, 20(3), pp. 325–331.

Porter, E., Wood, T. J. and Bahador, B. (2019) 'Can presidential misinformation on climate change be corrected? Evidence from Internet and phone experiments', *Research & Politics*. Online advance publication.

Sangalang, A., Ophir, Y. and Cappella, J. N. (2019) 'The potential for narrative correctives to combat misinformation', *Journal of Communication*, 69(3), pp. 298–319.

Schmid, P. and Betsch, C. (2019) 'Effective strategies for rebutting science denialism in public discussions', *Nature Human Behavior*, 3(9), pp. 931–939.

Smith, C. N. and Seitz, H. H. (2019) 'Correcting misinformation about neuroscience via social media', *Science Communication*, 41(6), pp. 790–819.

Stroud, N. J., Feldman, L., Wojcieszak, M. and Bimber, B. (2019) 'The consequences of forced versus selected political media exposure', *Human Communication Research*, 45(1), pp. 27–51.

Taber, C. S., Cann, D., & Kucsova, S. (2009) 'The motivated processing of political arguments', *Political Behavior*, 31(2), pp. 137–155.

Teague, E. B., Langer, K. G., Borod, J. C. and Bender, H. A. (2011) 'Proactive interference', in Kreutzer, J. S., DeLuca, J., and Caplan, B. (eds) *Encyclopedia of Clinical Neuropsychology*. New York: Springer, pp. 2028–2031.

Thorson, E. (2016) 'Belief echoes: The persistent effects of corrected misinformation', *Political Communication*, 33(3), pp. 460–480.

van der Meer, T. G. L. A. and Jin, Y. (2019) 'Seeking formula for misinformation treatment in public health crises: The effects of corrective information type and source', *Health Communication*, 35(5), pp. 560–575.

Vraga, E. K. and Bode, L. (2017) 'Using expert sources to correct health misinformation in social media', *Science Communication*, 39(5), pp. 621–645.

Walter, N., Cohen, J., Holbert, R. L. and Morag, Y. (2019) 'Fact-checking: A meta-analysis of what works and for whom', *Political Communication*. Online advance publication.

Walter, N. and Murphy, S. T. (2018) 'How to unring the bell: A meta-analytic approach to correction of misinformation', *Communication Monographs*, 85(3), pp. 423–441.

Walter, N. and Tukachinsky, R. (2020) 'A meta-analytic examination of the continued influence of misinformation in the face of correction: How powerful is it, why does it happen, and how to stop it', *Communication Research*, 47(2), pp. 155–177.

Weil, R., Schul, Y. and Mayo, R. (2020) 'Correction of evident falsehood requires explicit negation.', *Journal of Experimental Psychology: General*, 149(2), pp. 290–310.

Wilkes, A. L. and Leatherbarrow, M. (1988) 'Editing episodic memory following the identification of error', *The Quarterly Journal of Experimental Psychology Section A*, 40(2), pp. 361–387.

44

NEWS LITERACY AND MISINFORMATION

Melissa Tully

As high-profile examples of misinformation circulating on social media have come to public attention in recent years, calls for improving media literacy as a response have become commonplace. Educators and scholars have heeded this call by developing courses and research programmes to address both improved literacy and responses to misinformation. These approaches often focus on ways of developing knowledge and skills to navigate contemporary news environments where misinformation circulates and competes with news and information and testing and evaluating these approaches. With this backdrop in mind, this chapter addresses news literacy as a response to misinformation by providing a definition of news literacy and offering a framework for how equipping citizens with news literacy could be part of a solution to tackling misinformation while also addressing its shortcomings. The chapter also provides an overview of relevant studies that have looked at the relationship between news literacy and misinformation, highlighting consistencies and contradictions in this work. It will conclude with some takeaways for scholars interested in this area of research.

Defining news literacy

Defining and distinguishing various literacies – media, information, digital, and news – has always been a challenge for researchers and educators who work in these interdisciplinary domains (Aufderheide and Firestone 1993; Bulger and Davidson 2018; Potter and Thai 2019; Vraga, Tully et al. 2020). This challenge has led to a plethora of definitions and disagreements (Hobbs 2011; Potter 2010), which has made both research and educational efforts challenging, particularly in regards to isolating and measuring effects (which is often the goal of researchers) and impacts (which is often the goal of educators seeking to evaluate their curricula and programs) and developing theoretically robust research in this area (Hobbs and Frost 2003; Vraga, Tully et al. 2020).

News literacy has often been characterised as a type or subset of media literacy that focuses on news production, consumption, and contexts (Vraga and Tully 2015, 2016). Putting it under this broad umbrella has meant that its definition is often tied to a popular media literacy definition which emerged in the 1990s and describes media literacy as the ability to access, analyse, evaluate, create, and act using mediated messages (Aufderheide and Firestone 1993). Although this definition is useful for capturing a broad range of media and behaviors, it is less useful when

480

we think about how to operationalise it and measure it across different domains with media that serve very different purposes in our lives (Tully et al. 2019; Vraga, Tully et al. 2020). For example, the knowledge and skills needed to access, analyse, and evaluate video game content are undoubtedly different than the knowledge and skills needed to access, analyse, and evaluate news. Similarly, creating a persuasive social media post or shooting compelling images requires a different set of skills than writing a news story.

Given the differences in media and their roles in our lives, my colleagues and I have argued that news literacy requires its own definition and should be separated from other related literacies, which deserve their own definitions and scholarly attention (Vraga, Tully et al. 2020). We argue that news literacy is particularly relevant to identifying and rejecting misinformation, given the unique relationship between news and misinformation, which is either deliberately intended to look like news or is often perceived as news by audiences (Tandoc 2019). In other words, the knowledge and skills needed to identify news are the same as those needed to identify misinformation, and the resulting behaviors – sharing, fact-checking, verifying, and correcting, for example – are also arguably built on the same knowledge and skills.

We argue that developing news literacy means building knowledge and skills related to news processes and the role of news in society. If we understand what knowledge and skills contribute to news literacy, then we can measure and evaluate it and determine when and how individuals apply their news literacy. With this in mind, we define news literacy as 'knowledge of the personal and social processes by which news is produced, distributed, and consumed, and skills that allow users some control over these processes' (Vraga, Tully et al., 2020, p. 5). To develop news literacy, then, requires building relevant knowledge and skills in areas related to the news process from production to consumption (Tully et al. 2019). Therefore, we propose and define five domains – context, creation, content, circulation, and consumption – that make up news literacy building on existing research in this area (Ashley, Maksl and Craft 2017; Vraga and Tully 2016).

By narrowing the definition and scope of news literacy, we are able to develop measures to empirically test and evaluate news literacy efforts, which is essential to see what works for addressing the spread of misinformation. With this conceptual clarity, then, we can measure individuals' news literacy to see if and how it influences news choices, analysis, and evaluation with the goal of improving the knowledge and skills that matter for recognising and responding to misinformation (Amazeen and Bucy 2019; Craft, Ashley and Maksl 2017; Vraga and Tully 2019).

Knowledge about news contexts or the 'social, legal, and economic environment in which news is produced' would contribute to a greater understanding of the constraints on news processes, the ethics that guide news production and distribution, and the role of outside entities like technology firms in these processes. Research suggests that understanding this context contributes to valuing news more (Newman et al. 2018). As it relates to misinformation, this contextual knowledge should also contribute to an understanding of speech laws and regulations and the role of technology companies and governments in platform governance.

Knowledge about news creation, the 'process in which journalists and others engage in conceiving, reporting, and creating news stories and other journalistic content', should provide audiences with an understanding of the journalistic process and how it differs from other media creation. This should help audiences evaluate newsworthiness and other elements that separate news from misinformation. And, although most audiences will not regularly create news, they do post and share news, which contributes to its spread. Using journalistic skills like verification could ensure that they are sharing quality news and information, not misinformation.

Knowledge about news content or the 'characteristics of a news story or piece of news that distinguishes it from other types of media content' seems particularly relevant to recognising misinformation and differentiating it from news. This is an area that has been explored in news and media literacy research, education, and practice, which often focuses on identifying content characteristics that distinguish news from other media (Fleming 2014; Malik, Cortesi and Gasser 2013). Skills related to identifying news and distinguishing it from misinformation include evaluating the quality and credibility of sources in a story, recognising how claims are reported and supported, and differentiating between facts and opinions in stories.

News circulation or the 'process through which news is distributed and spread to potential audiences' is particularly important in a media environment where news and misinformation are circulated on social media. Understanding the role of various actors – organisations, humans, and computers – in circulation is becoming increasingly important as we turn to social media for much of our news and information (Thorson and Wells 2015). Newman et al. (2018) found that only 29 percent of survey respondents knew that the news they see on Facebook is determined by an algorithm, and many responded that they did not know how these decisions were made. Being able to customise settings on social media or curate feeds with high-quality news and information should contribute to news diets that are relatively free from misinformation, thus cutting down exposure to (and the likelihood of sharing) this kind of content (Newman et al. 2018; Vraga and Tully 2019).

Finally, knowledge about consumption or the 'personal factors that contribute to news exposure, attention, and evaluation' means that audiences recognise how their biases and predispositions influence news choices and interpretations. Research suggests that news literacy interventions can prompt people to more fairly evaluate news and to make choices that could lead to more diverse news diets (Vraga and Tully 2015). Skills related to consumption should prompt news consumers to seek out news and information, dedicate time to news, and evaluate it critically but fairly. This recognition and 'mindful processing' should prompt audiences to avoid being misled by misinformation as they evaluate it more critically (Craft, et al. 2017; Maksl, Ashley and Craft 2015).

This definition of news literacy does not determine how or if this literacy is put to use and intentionally separates knowledge and skills from attitudes, motivations, and other factors that may relate to news literacy but are distinct from it. Putting news literacy to use or applying news literacy would mean that audiences make news and information decisions that are informed by their news literacy, which should influence their exposure to and engagement with misinformation (Amazeen and Bucy 2019; Vraga, Tully et al. 2020). Therefore, we propose a model for predicting relevant behaviors that builds on our definition of news literacy and the theory

Table 44.1 Defining news literacy: 5 Cs

Domain	Definition
Context	Social, legal, and economic environment in which news is produced
Creation	Process in which journalists and others engage in conceiving, reporting, and creating news stories and other journalistic content
Content	Characteristics of a news story or piece of news that distinguish it from other types of media content
Circulation	Process through which news is distributed and spread to potential audiences
Consumption	Personal factors that contribute to news exposure, attention, and evaluation

Source: Adapted from Vraga, Tully et al. 2020

of planned behavior (TPB), building on a framework that has been rigourously tested in communication and related disciplines (Ajzen 2011; Vraga, Tully et al. 2020).

In this model, we can look at other factors like motivation, attitudes, and perceived efficacy that have been tested in the TPB to determine what is needed to apply our news literacy to a range of relevant behaviors, including being able to recognise and respond to misinformation by correcting it and providing quality evidence and curating a news diet that consists of quality sources of information and is generally free of misinformation (Tully, Vraga, and Bode 2020; Vraga, Tully et al. 2020). In this model, we suggest that news literacy is one factor that determines if and how people respond to misinformation and argue that accounting for news literacy, attitudes, social norms, and perceived behavioral control (factors from the TPB) offers a framework for predicting relevant behaviors, including recognising misinformation (Ajzen 2011; Vraga, Tully et al. 2020).

News literacy and misinformation

The role of news literacy in identifying misinformation has been the subject scholarly debate and disagreement. In some studies, news literacy is shown to have a powerful effect on distinguishing high- and low-quality information and misinformation (Amazeen and Bucy, 2019; Craft, et al. 2017) but produces no relationship or a negative relationship for others (Jones-Jang, Mortensen and Liu 2019). Some of these differences are perhaps a result in how news literacy has been defined and operationalised and what other characteristics, attitudes, and behaviours are also considered. Resolving the definitional issues explored in the first part of this chapter is a necessary first step to addressing some of the contradictions in existing research. However, reviewing this research offers some key contributions that can be used to continue to build the research in this area. First, a number of survey studies have shown that news knowledge does predict rejection of or scepticism towards misinformation, offering a starting point for building the knowledge and skills that make up news literacy. Second, experimental studies on interventions and messages have shown that specific messages with actionable steps are more effective at addressing misinformation than general warnings or messages about news literacy broadly. These studies suggest that tapping into different news literacy constructs *and* drawing on existing attitudes and perceived norms (from the TBP) may be effective, a proposition that needs to be further developed and tested. As a result, we propose a model of news literacy behaviours that will allow for just this kind of empirical work.

A number of survey studies have examined the relationship between news literacy and misinformation in various forms – conspiracy theories, false news, native advertisements, and information posted on social media. In three studies that relied on surveys of Americans, news knowledge was found to be positively related to rejecting misinformation. In a study that looked at the relationship between news literacy and conspiracy theory endorsement, Craft, Ashley and Maksl (2017) found that greater knowledge about the news media predicted a lower likelihood of supporting conspiracy theories, even those that aligned with participants' political predispositions. Importantly, this study found that news knowledge, specifically, predicted lower conspiracy theory endorsement:

> the greater one's knowledge about the news media – from the kinds of news covered, to the commercial context in which news is produced, to the effects on public opinion news can have – the less likely one will fall prey to conspiracy theories.
>
> (Craft, et al. 2017: 9)

Relatedly, Amazeen and Bucy (2019) found that knowledge of how the news operates contributed to a greater ability to identify false news and native advertising (ads designed to look like news). In their study, Amazeen and Bucy (2019) built on existing news literacy research to focus on knowledge of news industries and editorial practices (and not effects, which have been included in other research).

Using a nationally representative sample of US adults, Vraga and Tully (2019) looked at news literacy and misinformation on social media and found that those with higher news knowledge see and share less misinformation and are more sceptical of the information they see on social media, suggesting that news literacy shapes perceptions of information on social media. We measured news literacy using ten items from Maksl, Ashley, and Craft (2015) that capture news knowledge. In addition, we measured two related constructs – self-perceived media literacy (SPML) and value of media literacy (VML) – which tap into perceived efficacy and perceived democratic value of news literacy. Importantly, both news literacy (knowledge) and VML produced less social media engagement; SPML produced more exposure to news and information on social media and less scepticism. These results reiterate the importance of news literacy and suggest that related orientations warrant additional exploration as these perceptions and values may contribute to how and when individuals apply their news literacy, a proposition supported by the TBP and put forth in our model of news literacy behaviors (Ajzen 2011; Vraga, Tully et al. 2020).

However, Jones-Jang, Mortensen, and Liu (2019) found that higher news literacy did not increase the likelihood of identifying false news stories. In their study, only information literacy increased the likelihood of identifying false news posts. Importantly, however, Jones-Jang, Mortensen, and Liu (2019) did not measure news knowledge (questions with correct or incorrect answers), but rather used a different set of news literacy measures (from Ashley, Maksl and Craft 2013) that measure agreement-disagreement with a number of statements about the news media. Their findings could be attributed, in part, to this difference in measurement, which, again, reinforces the need for stronger theory and measurement in this area (Vraga, Tully et al. 2020).

In perhaps the only large-scale, multicountry assessment of news literacy, Newman and colleagues (2018) measured respondents' news literacy using three news knowledge questions adapted from Maksl, Ashley, and Craft (2015), offering a comparative perspective on differing levels of news literacy. Most relevant to the study of misinformation are findings that show that respondents with higher news literacy rely less on social media for news and are more discerning when using social media for this purpose. They look for credibility cues like news outlet and headline to help make decisions and are less likely to rely on popularity cues (e.g. comments and likes on social media) than those with lower news literacy, although all groups do use these cues. In addition, news literacy is also associated with sharing news and news diets. Respondents with higher news literacy share less and have more diverse news diets. This finding aligns with Vraga and Tully's (2019) findings regarding who sees and shares misinformation, suggesting that the less informed are perhaps sharing more news and information and may be contributing to the spread of misinformation. Finally, those with higher news literacy are most concerned about misinformation and believe that media and technology companies should do more to curb its spread (Newman et al. 2018).

A body of research has specifically examined the effects of exposure to news literacy interventions or messages on a number of outcomes related to misinformation using experimental studies. This work has looked at the effectiveness of messages on social media that attempt to warn participants about potential exposure to misinformation, provide steps or guidance for how to identify misinformation and to differentiate it from news and high-quality information, or encourage users to be responsible and critical news consumers (e.g. Clayton et al. 2020; Tully, Vraga and Bode 2020; Vraga, Bode and Tully 2020; Wojdynski, Binford and Jefferson 2019). This research has found mixed results in the effectiveness of these messages on a number of outcomes, including perceptions of misinformation and bolstering corrections of misinformation.

A strand of research has looked at 'warning' messages and reception of false news and misinformation (Clayton et al. 2020; Wojdynski, Binford and Jefferson 2019). Some research has found that warning people about misleading tactics can neutralise the effects of misinformation messages (Cook, Lewandowsky and Ecker 2017; van der Linden, Leiserowitz, Rosenthal and Maibach 2017). Wojdynski, Binford, and Jefferson (2019) found that warning participants about the presence of false news stories significantly increased their likelihood of detecting subsequent false stories and decreased the likelihood of misclassifying stories as fake when they were real. In addition, the warnings had no effect on subjects' ability to detect real stories but did make them more likely to misclassify these stories as false. In another experimental study, Clayton and colleagues (2020) found that a general warning message led to lower accuracy ratings for both misinformation and accurate information, suggesting an unintended spillover effect in which participants were more sceptical of all content after being warned. In addition, although a general warning message did reduce accuracy ratings for a false post, a specific warning was more effective at reducing accuracy perceptions of false information. Seeing a general warning in addition to the specific warning did not bolster the effectiveness of the specific warning. Importantly, neither of these studies situate their work in the realm of news literacy despite using messages that resonate with news literacy concepts, an issue that could be addressed by a stronger definition, explication, and operationalisation of news literacy that appeals to scholars across disciplines and offers much-needed clarity to the field (Tully et al. 2019; Vraga, Tully et al. 2020).

In a series of studies that specifically examined news literacy tweets, findings suggest that the effectiveness of these messages depends on both message characteristics and misinformation context (Tully et al. 2020; Vraga, Bode et al. 2020). First, in one experimental study, we found that a news literacy tweet that encouraged audiences to recognise how their viewpoints affected their news choices did not increase scepticism towards a misinformation tweet about genetically modified foods. Although the message in this tweet was developed from a review of relevant literature and from previous research that validated the message (Vraga and Tully 2016), it was not tailored for Twitter or social media specifically and did not provide actionable steps for users to take when evaluating news and information. Therefore, we designed a second study to test another news literacy message that specifically addressed misinformation and offered guidance on how to spot 'fake news'.

In this study, the news literacy tweet was able to affect perceptions of misinformation about the seasonal flu vaccine (Tully et al. 2020). In this case, the news literacy message and the misinformation post were more aligned: the news literacy tweet specifically mentioned 'fake news' and how to spot it, and the misinformation tweet featured a false story about the flu vaccine from an unreliable source known for circulating false stories. This finding suggests that messages need to be tailored for social media environments and that the messages must resonate with the kinds of content that audiences are seeing online, which is a challenge given the networked nature of social media and the algorithmic filtering that occurs on these platforms (Thorson and Wells 2015).

In addition, across two experiments, three different news literacy tweets did not enhance the effectiveness of user correction of misinformation, which were effective at correcting misperceptions on their own (Vraga, Bode et al. 2020). Furthermore, these tweets were not always noticed as they competed with other posts on the page. In fact, they were noticed less often than other content on the simulated Twitter feed. In part, taken together, these studies found that a single message cannot be expected to achieve multiple goals, a finding that suggests that campaigns need to be multipronged and messages repeated to be effective. Our findings echo Clayton and colleagues' (2020) findings that general warnings (like the tweets used in our experiments and the warning posts used in theirs) are not as effective as corrections or specific messages to debunk claims. In short, the findings from this body of work are inconclusive as to the effectiveness of these messages, and more work is needed to refine and test these messages in a variety of topical and social media contexts.

A one-size-fits-all approach will clearly not work when it comes to designing effective news literacy interventions and messages, but continued research could offer insights into characteristics or factors that contribute to the effectiveness of these messages and that do not produce spillover effects that make audiences sceptical of all news and information they encounter, a challenge that has beguiled news literacy educators and researchers who want to promote healthy scepticism without leading to cynicism or distrust towards all news (Craft, Ashley and Maksl 2016; Mihailidis 2008).

If, as the current body of research suggests, news knowledge does contribute to rejecting misinformation, then this seems like an area that warrants additional exploration. What knowledge, in particular, is most relevant to and effective at addressing misinformation? How can we ensure that audiences are exposed to the information they need to develop this knowledge and a set of related skills to respond to misinformation? Addressing these key questions will not only contribute to stronger news literacy curricula in K–12 and college classrooms but can also help researchers interested in isolating effects and building theory and practitioners who develop interventions and messages targeted to audiences on social media platforms where audiences get their news and where misinformation circulates.

Next steps

The current state of the field suggests that building news literacy – knowledge and skills – should be part of a solution to addressing misinformation. Focusing on news consumers, of course, does not take the onus off news outlets, technology companies, and governments to respond to misinformation (Marwick 2019; Newman et al. 2018). In fact, the misinformation landscape is so complex that it requires a multipronged solution, including changes to how technology companies operate, how governments regulate, how news outlets do their business, and how audiences interact with news and information, something that news literacy education, interventions, and research can and should address (Bulger and Davidson 2018). Acknowledging that user response to misinformation is just one piece of the puzzle and that empowering users is a moot point if we do not have better regulations and responses from tech companies is necessary if news literacy research is going to be leveraged as part of a solution. Additionally, ensuring that news literacy encompasses knowledge and skills related to technology companies, regulations, and legal frameworks is essential if audiences are going to be equipped with the necessary knowledge and skills to navigate contemporary media environments and to have some control over their experiences.

Finally, as interest in news (and other related) literacies has grown, it has become clear that consistency in definitions and measures is key to theory building and empirical studies to understand the relationship between news literacy and experiences with misinformation, including exposure, sharing, and correcting (Amazeen and Bucy 2019; Tully et al. 2020; Vraga and Tully 2019). Given inconsistencies in theoretical grounding and measurement, we cannot fully articulate, at this point, the relationship between news literacy and misinformation, although research is consistently showing that news literacy – defined as knowledge – is a predictor worthy of increased scholarly attention. Continuing to refine these knowledge measures by building on the existing literature and adding the necessary skills measures, which build from this knowledge, are much needed as they are sorely lacking in most research. This approach should provide a robust agenda for researchers and should result in valuable insights for educators and practitioners looking to develop curricula, interventions, and messages to improve news literacy that can be applied to evaluating news and (mis)information.

References

Ajzen, I. (2011). The theory of planned behavior: Reactions and reflections. *Psychology & Health*, 26, pp. 1113–1127.

Amazeen, M. A. and Bucy, E. P. (2019). Conferring resistance to digital disinformation: The inoculating influence of procedural news knowledge. *Journal of Broadcasting and Electronic Media*, 63, pp. 415–432.

Ashley, S., Maksl, A. and Craft, S. (2013). Developing a news media literacy scale. *Journalism and Mass Communication Educator*, 68, pp. 7–21.

Ashley, S., Maksl, A. and Craft, S. (2017). News media literacy and political engagement: What's the connection. *Journal of Media Literacy Education*, 9(1), pp. 79–98.

Aufderheide, P. and Firestone, C. F. (1993). *Media literacy: A report of the national leadership conference on media literacy*. Queenstown, MD: Aspen Institute. Retrieved from https://files.eric.ed.gov/fulltext/ED365294.pdf

Bulger, M. and Davidson, P. (2018). *The promises, challenges, and futures of media literacy*. Data & Society Research Institute. Retrieved from datasociety.net

Clayton, K., Blair, S., Busam, J. A., Forstner, S., Glance, J., Green, G., . . . Nyhan, B. (2020). Real solutions for fake news? Measuring the effectiveness of general warnings and fact-check tags in reducing belief in false stories on social media. *Political Behavior*, 42, pp. 1073–1095.

Cook, J., Lewandowsky, S. and Ecker, U. K. (2017). Neutralizing misinformation through inoculation: Exposing misleading argumentation techniques reduces their influence. *PLoS One*, 12(5), p. e0175799.

Craft, S., Ashley, S. and Maksl, A. (2016). Elements of news literacy: A focus group study of how teenagers define news and why they consume it. *Electronic News*, 10, pp. 143–160.

Craft, S., Ashley, S. and Maksl, A. (2017). News media literacy and conspiracy theory endorsement. *Communication and the Public*, 2(4), pp. 388–401.

Fleming, J. (2014). Media literacy, news literacy, or news appreciation? A case study of the news literacy program at stony brook university. *Journalism & Mass Communication Educator*, 69(2), pp. 146–165.

Hobbs, R. (2011). The state of media literacy: A response to Potter. *Journal of Broadcasting & Electronic Media*, 55(3), pp. 419–430,

Hobbs, R. and Frost, R. (2003). Measuring the acquisition of media-literacy skills. *Reading Research Quarterly*, 38(3), pp. 330–355.

Jones-Jang, S. M., Mortensen, T. and Liu, J. (2019). Does media literacy help identification of fake news? Information literacy helps but other literacies don't. *American Behavioral Scientist*. Online first.

Maksl, A., Ashley, S. and Craft, S. (2015). Measuring news media literacy. *Journal of Media Literacy Education*, 6(3), pp. 29–45.

Malik, M. M., Cortesi, S. and Gasser, U. (2013). The challenges of defining 'news literacy.' Berkman Center for Internet & Society.

Marwick, A. E. (2019). Why do people share fake news? A sociotechnical model of media effects. *Georgetown Law Technology Review*, 474(2), pp. 474–512.

Mihailidis, P. (2008). *Beyond cynicism: How media literacy can make students more engaged citizens*. Doctoral Dissertation, University of Maryland, College Park, MD.

Newman, N. R., Fletcher, R., Kalogeropoulos, A., Levy, D. A. L. and Nielsen, R. K. (2018). *Reuters institute digital news report 2018*. Retrieved from http://media.digitalnewsreport.org/wp-content/uploads/2018/06/digital-news-report-2018.pdf

Potter, W. J. (2010). The state of media literacy. *Journal of Broadcasting & Electronic Media*, 54, pp. 675–696.

Potter, W. J. and Thai, C. L. (2019). Reviewing media literacy intervention studies for validity. *Review of Communication Research*, 7, pp. 38–66.

Tandoc, Jr., E. (2019). The facts of fake news: A research review. *Sociology Compass*, pp. 1–9.

Thorson, K. and Wells, C. (2015). Curated flows: A framework for mapping media exposure in the digital age. *Communication Theory*, 26(3), pp. 309–328.

Tully, M., Maksl, A., Ashley, S., Vraga, E. K. and Craft, S. (2019, September). *Defining and measuring news literacy*. Future of Journalism Conference, Cardiff, UK.

Tully, M., Vraga, E. K. and Bode, L. (2020). Designing and testing news literacy messages for social media. *Mass Communication and Society*, 6, pp. 22–46.

van der Linden, S., Leiserowitz, A., Rosenthal, S. and Maibach, E. (2017). Inoculating the public against misinformation about climate change. *Global Challenges*, 1, pp. 1–7.

Vraga, E K., Bode, L. and Tully, M. (2020). Creating news literacy messages to enhance expert corrections of misinformation on social media. *Communication Research*. Online first.

Vraga, E. K. and Tully, M. (2015). Media literacy messages and hostile media perceptions: Processing of nonpartisan versus partisan political information. *Mass Communication and Society*, 18, pp. 422–448.

Vraga, E. K. and Tully, M. (2016). Effective messaging to communicate news media literacy concepts to diverse publics. *Communication and the Public*, 1, pp. 305–322.

Vraga, E. K. and Tully, M. (2019). News literacy, social media behaviors, and skepticism toward information on social media. *Information, Communication & Society*. Online first.

Vraga, E. K., Tully, M., Maksl, A., Craft, S. and Ashley, S. (2020). Theorizing news literacy behaviors. *Communication Theory*. Online first.

Wojdynski, B. W., Binford, M. T. and Jefferson, B. N. (2019). Looks real, or really fake? Warnings, visual attention and detection of false news articles. *Open Information Science*, 3, pp. 166–180.

45

MEDIA AND INFORMATION LITERACIES AS A RESPONSE TO MISINFORMATION AND POPULISM

Nicole A. Cooke

At the time of this writing, we are in a renewed and intensified period of disinformation fuelled in part by the political landscape (which saw an uptick in confusion and maliciousness during the 2016 US presidential election), a global pandemic of unknown origins (COVID-19), a crisis of racial injustice after the death of George Floyd and others at the hands of police, and unprecedented access to information, particularly online information. However, fake news, misinformation, and disinformation are not new phenomena, nor are information and media literacies. Indeed, as populism directs our attention to 'the people' versus 'the elite', information and media literacies have long been concerned with bridging the divide between the 'haves and have nots' in regard to information access and use. In this way, it is quite appropriate to view these literacies as a way to combat misinformation and disinformation. There are similarities and differences between information, media, and other literacies; however, they all have great pertinence and utility in the fight against misinformation, disinformation, and malinformation.

The problem: misinformation, disinformation, and malinformation

The concepts of misinformation and disinformation are increasingly discussed in the field of information science and many other disciplines and can be thought of as two sides of the same coin. Misinformation is simply defined as information that is incomplete (Fox 1983; Losee 1997; Zhou & Zhang 2007), but it can also be defined as information that is uncertain, vague, or ambiguous. Disinformation, on the other hand, is information that is deliberately false and designed to mislead and sow confusion. Disinformation is considered born of maliciousness or ill intent. Fallis (2009, pp. 1–3) provides additional perspective by suggesting that disinformation is carefully planned, can come from individuals or groups, and can be disseminated by entities other than the originators. Similarly, malinformation is 'genuine information that is shared to cause harm. This includes private or revealing information that is spread to harm a person or reputation' (Wardle 2018). Examples of malinformation include revenge porn and doxxing, which can be devastating and traumatic for the person(s) targeted. The scientific community defines disinformation as the 'cultural production of ignorance', and instead of using the term disinformation, they call it agnotology (Proctor & Schiebinger 2008, p. 1).

Misinformation, disinformation, and malinformation are much harder to discern in the online environment where there are 24-7 news cycles of information and media (both accurate and inaccurate) that often lack visual and aural clues, clues that in real life might alert an information consumer that something was faulty, misleading, or just incorrect. Because of the pervasiveness of addictive technologies in today's world (the latest of which are deepfakes and shallow fakes (Solsman 2020), technological biases (Benjamin 2019), extreme political partisanship (Chadwick 2017), and people's personal beliefs and emotional reactions to information and its sources (Cooke 2018a), it is especially important to be tuned in to misinformation, disinformation, and malinformation as they preclude understanding and informed action, both individually and collectively. Misinformation could ruin someone's dinner plans because there is an error in a printed recipe; misinformation could prevent someone from voting because precinct information was omitted or the precinct number transposed. If deliberately erroneous, this incorrect information could contribute to a severe allergic reaction or voter suppression, which are much more serious. Malinformation such as illegally captured and distributed personal information like intimate photos or social security numbers could lead to job loss, identity theft, and a host of other detrimental outcomes from which the victim may not be able to recover.

Additionally, misinformation, disinformation, and malinformation actually cause harm by deliberately and ferociously reinforcing racist and culturally insensitive images and messages. Zhou and Zhang (2007, p. 804) state, 'with the growing use of Internet and ubiquitous information access, misinformation is pervasive on the Internet and disseminated through online communication media, which could lead to serious consequences for individuals, organisations, and/or the entire society at large'. There is no shortage of examples of information and media that not only publicise stereotypes about racial, ethnic, religious, sexual, and other minority or marginalised communities, but also literally cause lasting harm to these populations. These stereotypes are so persistent that they can embolden people's implicit biases and cause them to grow out of control like a cancer, and these biases influence behaviour and thoughts, whether people are cognisant of that impact or not (Banaji & Greenwald 2016). A stunning example of this began in 2020 with the rapid onset of COVID-19, which killed hundreds of thousands of people. It was widely thought that the virus originated in the Wuhan province of China (other disinformation claimed that the virus was man made), and as a result, rampant and hateful physical attacks were showered upon Asian and Asian American people, whether they were Chinese or not. Malinformation and the recalcitrant calling the virus by racist names such as the 'China virus', the 'Chinese virus', or the 'kung flu' incited ignorant people (or, for the purposes of this chapter, information and media illiterate people) around the world to hit, kick, stab, and spit on anyone with Asian features (Rogers et al. 2020). This is an example of information being repeated over and over again in the media until it became accepted and almost normalised and, as a result, significantly marred and exacerbated an already-difficult global pandemic with xenophobia, racism, hatred, and violence.

Media and information literacy responses to misinformation

Media and information literacies have long been taught in libraries and classrooms, and with the recent uptick in fake news and discussions about misinformation and disinformation, there have been innumerable articles, books, and games designed to educate consumers about the perils of false information (e.g. the News Literacy Project's Checkology game). The News Literacy Project (https://newslit.org/), PEN America (https://pen.org/advocacy-campaign/fraudulent-news/), First Draft (https://firstdraftnews.org/), the Factual (www.thefactual.com/

about.html), the Misinformation Review Journal (https://misinforeview.hks.harvard.edu/), the Center for News Literacy (www.centerfornewsliteracy.org/), the American Library Association (www.ala.org/), and Project Navigate (www.navigateproject.eu/) are but a few consortia of educators, librarians, and journalists working diligently to combat misinformation and disinformation, and they have provided quality tools and strategies to enable teachers to better relay this content to enable students of all ages so they can better discern the information they consume.

For all of the good that the aforementioned groups do with their research and carefully vetted resources and curricula, there are gaps they currently do not fill and audiences they do not reach. Current efforts and responses around fake news, misinformation, and disinformation are seen as academic and are not widely available to the general public and to those who secure their information and 'news' on social media platforms. Even those who have had literacy instruction and acquired some level of formal education about misinformation and disinformation do not or cannot always automatically transfer their evaluation skills to popular information. Literacy efforts are also lost on those who are willfully ignorant and remain committed to their echo chambers and filter bubbles; no matter the factual information presented, they will not depart from their emotional attachments and beliefs. There are also people who believe that they are immune to false information and/or feel that interventions to the contrary do not apply to them (e.g. the coronavirus pandemic has revealed any number of people and communities that have said that they didn't believe they could catch the virus, and if they did it, wouldn't be worse than getting a cold).

These are the gaps that information and media literacies currently do not meet and need to bridge. Instruction and education need to be less academic and more relevant, and they need to meet their intended audiences where they are, which is outside formal classrooms, libraries, and research settings. Educators, librarians, and journalists need to continue developing information and appropriate platforms and pedagogies for non-academic information seekers and users.

Part of the solution: critical media consumption through multiple literacies

The romanticised lens of populism as a tool of empowerment and democracy provides a vital moment for a brief discussion of media and information literacies as combatants of misinformation, disinformation, and malinformation; these literacies, and others, are by design intended to empower people to become savvy information consumers and informed, proactive citizens. This is especially important with the type and amount of information humans regularly face. No one can absorb and utilise all the information that presents itself in the course of a day. As a result, people have implicit and explicit ways of filtering and prioritising information for use. Information and media literacies aim to strengthen and make inherent mental schemas more critical.

Media and information literacies aspire to impart a sense of 'civic agency' in students and information consumers. These literacies want to advance 'the power of "the people" to shape their destiny' (Boyte 2012, p. 173), and they rely on organising and civic education efforts (p. 174) to empower citizens. However, where these literacies tend to fall short, at least in the library and information science and related disciplines, is in the areas of diversity, equity, and inclusion. Information and media literacies encourage students to think critically about the quality and origin of information sources, but they don't always go further and deeper to encourage the examination of the sociocultural and socioinstitutional structures that create and shape said information and media. This gap can prohibit information consumers from recognising xenophobia, racism, sexism, classism, ableism, homophobia, transphobia, and other oppressions as constructs created and perpetuated by information and media. Subsequently, it is not uncommon for people to share problematic jokes, memes, and other content and think that it is not a big deal or not harmful because the inherent context is not the focus of traditional literacy education. Identifying problematic content is often addressed as a separate skillset, distinct from literacy education, that is taught in the social sciences (as opposed to communication studies, education, library and information science, and other applied disciplines).

The apotheosised version of populism values and combines equity, diversity, inclusion, and social justice 'with a deep commitment to people's agency and appreciation of the immense particularity of American communities' (Boyte 2012, p. 175). In order to fully match the tenets of populism, media and information literacies need to do better, they need to go deeper, and they need to be more current, candid, and contextual.

Information Literacy

Information literacy is an area of pedagogy and study most closely associated with library and information science. It is used prolifically in libraries and refers to the ability to read, decipher, evaluate, and use information in everyday life (Kulthau 1987). Information literacy is not the same as traditional reading-based literacy; rather, it refers to a frame of reference for consuming information and is a type of critical thinking. Information literacy considers the local context in which information is found and consumed (i.e. the who, what, where, when, and why of the source), and it seeks information that is relevant to a task and has long-term potential to be useful. Information literacy is widely taught in libraries with the goal of enabling students and patrons to locate and utilise quality information.

Critical information literacy

More recent literature and information literacy practices focus on critical information literacy (Accardi et al. 2010; Bawden, 2008; Bawden & Robinson, 2002; Elmborg 2006; Tisdell 2008), which extends information literacy by setting forth the expectation that in addition to looking at information in situ, people should recognise and understand the underlying power structures that shape information and media and subsequently grant agency to those acquiring quality information (or deny agency to those lacking quality information or to those who are unable to acquire any needed information). As the old adage goes, information is power, and this is played out in the proverbial 'haves and have nots' and in the digital divide. The digital divide was again put under a harsh spotlight during the COVID-19 crisis when students of all ages were sent home to learn online. It is a privilege to have the time, infrastructure, hardware, software, and funds to learn online, and not everyone has such privilege.

Critical information literacy is useful when understanding that cultural messages in particular are prone to misinformation, disinformation, and malinformation because it suggests examining information and media in context and outside the vacuums in which they are often found (Cooke 2018b). However, it does not go far enough in terms of explaining why cultural messages in particular are prone to misinformation, disinformation, and malinformation. The why requires recentring people and information from other cultures and intentionally examining media and information through a populist lens (please see the final section on critical cultural literacy).

Media literacy

Scholar Belinha De Abreu defines media literacy as follows:

> Media literacy is defined as the ability to access, understand, analyze, evaluate, and create media in a variety of forms. But what are 'media'? In the broadest sense, media are the tools and systems that are used to store and deliver information and data to large numbers of people. Media are thus the pathways of communication that are used to reach, inform, entertain, or influence people on a wide scale. That media include television and radio, newspapers and magazines, advertising, movies and videos, book publishing and photography, as well as various networks, platforms, outlets, and forums on the Internet. To put it briefly, the media are vehicles for mass communication.
>
> (De Abreu 2019, p. 3)

De Abreu goes on to detail the further distinctions and complexities contained within the umbrella term 'media'. Because media and information are indeed nuanced, she goes on to say:

> Media literacy involves critical thinking. To think that it does not would make the study of media literacy a passive undertaking, rather than an engaged dynamic. In truth, much of the media is consumed without a critical lens. The idea of media literacy is that we are actively involved in how we perceive, discuss, or consider the media we consume and the media we use in our lives.
>
> (De Abreu 2019, p. 3)

Key to De Abreu's definition are the ideas that media (and information) should be engaged with actively and through a critical lens. This is where current information and media literacies often fall short.

Because so much media and information are sought and consumed online, digital, media, and visual literacy skills are also important to consider and incorporate. These related concepts of digital, media, and visual literacies are essentially about being 'deeply literate in the digital world' and being 'skilled at deciphering complex images and sounds as well as the syntactical subtleties of words' (Lanham 1995, p. 198). Glister (1997) describes digital literacy as a mastery of ideas and not the mastery of keystrokes. Media literacy narrows the focus a bit by focusing on mass media such as television and radio, and it can also encompass video games and print products such as comic books and graphic novels. Visual literacy (also known as graphic literacy) is not limited only to electronically accessed images; it asks information and media consumers to decipher visual imagery and the intentional and unintentional messages contained within. This trio of literacies complement media and information literacies, and they are particularly important to understanding misinformation, disinformation, and malinformation that are transmitted through memes, videos, infographics, and other forms of non-print information.

Cultural literacy (cultural competence)

In some disciplines, cultural literacy is equated to being well versed in current events and historical and pop culture. But in the context of this discussion, cultural literacy is synonymous with cultural competence. Cultural competence is defined as 'a highly developed ability to understand and respect cultural differences and to address issues of disparity among diverse populations competently' (Overall 2009, p. 176). Cultural competence is an ongoing and dynamic cyclical process that celebrates and incorporates the differences that exist within various populations and communities (Cooke 2016, chapter 2). Cultural competence came out of the applied health sciences and is also discussed in the education, nursing, psychology, counseling, and business management literatures (also known as cultural intelligence).

With this background in mind, cultural literacy can be thought of as information that is reflective of and centred on diverse and marginalised communities and their cultural backgrounds (Ladson-Billings 1995). A strong understanding of cultural literacy is particularly useful when battling misinformation, disinformation, and malinformation as they pertain to cultural messages and the perpetuation of stereotypes, racism, and implicit biases. Cultural literacy facilitates the understanding of why cultural messages are particularly prone to misinformation, disinformation, and malinformation.

Critical cultural literacy

In order to fully understand the aforementioned *why*; to clearly recognise how misinformation, disinformation, and malinformation are so frequently racialised; and to really see how information devoid of context perpetuates that same racialised information and media, critical cultural literacy is required. Combining the foundational characteristics and purpose of traditional information and media literacies and reinforcing them with the best components of critical literacy and cultural literacy gives us critical cultural literacy. Critical cultural literacy is a strengthened literacy that best lives up to an idealised concept of populism. This is how media and information literacies do better, go deeper, and become more current, candid, and contextual.

Critical cultural literacy recentres marginalised and oppressed groups or content, allowing the information/media consumer to view what's relevant and useful from another and more robust vantage point. Critical cultural literacy situates information and media in such a way that diverse messages are purposefully incorporated, highlighted, and valued and not relegated to an afterthought or ignored all together.

As previously mentioned, there is no shortage of misinformation, disinformation, or malinformation on the internet. And despite their swift dissemination and staying power, critical cultural literacy can aid in verifying and refuting false, misleading, and harmful media and information. In order to be critical consumers of media and information, users should, of course, question the currency of the information (or lack thereof), consider where it's been published (or not published), consider the plausibility of the information, and consider the reputation and biases of the platform providing the information. But they should also be questioning and investigating the larger and cultural contexts of the information being presented and consider the bigger picture of what the message is trying to accomplish. Critical information consumption is not automatic, and information and media consumers need to be taught to evaluate, sort, and effectively use the overabundance of information available online, and they need to be versed in multiple forms of literacy (Daniels 2009, pp. 192–194).

Concluding critical cultural thoughts

Critical cultural literacy is not all that radical; rather, it requires thought and recognition that are decolonised and culturally competent. Put simply, decoloninsation asks that ideas and communities outside the heteronormative norm be sought out and accepted (i.e. accepting more than just what is white, wealthy, Christian, heterosexual, thin, male, etc.); cultural competence asks that these differences be valued and incorporated into a new normative schema.

For example, please consider these examples of topics that might be addressed by media and information literacy education and notice the changes between 'regular' literacy, critical literacy, and critical cultural literacy.

Topic 1: African Americans and COVID-19

> Traditional literacy: after refuting the misinformation that African Americans cannot contract the coronavirus that results in COVID-19, it is further revealed that African Americans and other minority communities are actually suffering disproportionately from the virus.
>
> Critical literacy: Minority communities routinely suffer more severely from illnesses, so it stands to reason that the same would be the case with COVID-19.
>
> Critical cultural literacy: Minority communities have long been predisposed to underlying conditions such as hypertension and diabetes that make them more susceptible to illnesses like COVID-19. Also, minority groups, especially African Americans, have long-term trust issues with traditional medicine because of a systemic lack of access to treatment, medical biases that preclude them from getting the same treatment as non-minorities (e.g. the maternal death rate is significantly higher for African American women), and the legacy of experimentation by and maltreatment from the medical establishment (e.g. the Tuskegee experiments).

Topic 2: Remote learning and COVID-19

> Traditional literacy: Remote learning is the solution during crises like COVID-19. With instruction, students can use their computers to complete coursework.
>
> Critical literacy: Not all communities/families are able to work at home because they lack the infrastructure and hardware to do so (i.e. the digital divide).
>
> Critical cultural literacy: Not all communities/families are able to work at home because, in addition to a lack of infrastructure and hardware, they are facing job loss, a lack of income, a lack of child care, and even a lack of technological capabilities from prior inadequate educational experiences.

Critical cultural literacy breaks open the vacuum that often contains information and media people consume and provides additional worlds of context that facilitate new perspectives and increased understanding. It takes a little extra legwork and openness to being uncomfortable with said context, but the rewards of amplified insight far surpass that discomfort.

Scholar Arundhati Roy provides another example of how to view a current event (COVID-19) through a critical cultural lens. She writes:

> The virus has moved freely along the pathways of trade and international capital, and the terrible illness it has brought in its wake has locked humans down in their countries, their cities and their homes. But unlike the flow of capital, this virus seeks proliferation, not profit, and has, therefore, inadvertently, to some extent, reversed the direction of the flow. It has mocked immigration controls, biometrics, digital surveillance and every other kind of data analytics, and struck hardest – thus far – in the richest, most powerful nations of the world, bringing the engine of capitalism to a juddering halt. Temporarily perhaps, but at least long enough for us to examine its parts, make an assessment and decide whether we want to help fix it, or look for a better engine.
>
> (Roy 2020, para. 4–5)

Critical cultural (populist) literacy enables information and media consumers to look beyond the problem at hand and instead incorporate context and new perspectives in order to seek community-empowered solutions and change.

Conclusion: going beyond academia

Literacy education, particularly in the populist sense, is about sharing information and building equitable, knowledgeable, engaged, and empowered communities. Part of this mission is to make sure that constituents are literate in a multitude of areas and are able to seek, differentiate, and select quality, culturally relevant information and media and subsequently apply them to their daily lives. The goal of literacy as an emancipatory social force through which marginalised groups challenge dominant power structures is precisely the stance and meaning behind critical cultural literacy. Communities can be taught and be empowered (especially communities that are disenfranchised, marginalised, and discriminated against) with critical cultural literacy skills to fight media misinformation, disinformation, and malinformation. However, it takes work (on the part of the educators and community members), a shift in the paradigm of what literacy education is, and a commitment to disrupting the status quo. Critical cultural information and media literacies 'cannot be treated as a panacea' (Bulger & Davison 2018, p. 3), especially in this age of rampant fake news, but they are certainly strong and substantial players in this landscape and benefit a 'diverse array of stakeholders' (p. 3).

References

Accardi, MT, Drabinski, E and Kumbier, A, eds., 2010, *Critical library instruction: Theories and methods.* Sacramento, CA: Library Juice Press, LLC.

Banaji, MR and Greenwald, AG, 2016, *Blindspot: Hidden biases of good people.* London: Bantam.

Bawden, D, 2008, Origins and concepts of digital literacy. *Digital literacies: Concepts, Policies and Practices*, vol. 30, pp. 17–32.

Bawden, D and Robinson, L, 2002, Promoting literacy in a digital age: Approaches to training for information literacy. *Learned Publishing*, vol. 15, no. 4, pp. 297–301.

Benjamin, R, 2019, *Race after technology: Abolitionist tools for the new Jim code.* Hoboken, NJ: John Wiley & Sons.

Boyte, HC, 2012, Introduction: Reclaiming populism as a different kind of politics. *The Good Society*, vol. 21, no. 2, pp. 173–176.

Bulger, M and Davison, P, 2018, *The promises, challenges, and futures of media literacy.* Data & Society Research Institute. Available at: https://datasociety.net/pubs/oh/DataAndSociety_Media_Literacy_2018.pdf

Chadwick, A, 2017. *The hybrid media system: Politics and power.* Oxford, UK: Oxford University Press.

Cooke, NA, 2016, *Information services to diverse populations: Developing culturally competent library professionals.* Santa Barbara, CA: ABC-CLIO.

Cooke, NA, 2018a, *Fake news and alternative facts: Information literacy in a post-truth era.* Chicago, IL: American Library Association.

Cooke, NA, 2018b, Critical literacy as an approach to combating cultural misinformation/disinformation on the Internet. *Information literacy and libraries in the age of fake news*, pp. 36–51. Santa Barbara, CA: ABC-CLIO.

Daniels, J, 2009, *Cyber racism: White supremacy online and the new attack on civil rights.* Lanham, MD: Rowman & Littlefield Publishers.

De Abreu, BS, 2019, *Teaching media literacy.* Chicago, IL: American Library Association.

Elmborg, J, 2006, Critical information literacy: Implications for instructional practice. *The Journal of Academic Librarianship*, vol. 32, no. 2, pp. 192–199.

Fallis, D, 2009, *A conceptual analysis of disinformation.* iConference. Chapel Hill, NC.

Fox, C, 1983, *Information and misinformation: An investigation of the notions of information, misinformation, informing, and misinforming.* Santa Barbara, CA: Greenwood Publishing Group.

Gilster, P, 1997, *Digital literacy.* Hoboken, NJ: Wiley Computer Publications.

Kulthau, CC, 1987, *Information skills for an information society* (Report ED 297740). ERIC Clearinghouse on Educational Resources.

Ladson-Billings, G, 1995, Toward a theory of culturally relevant pedagogy. *American Educational Research Journal*, vol. 32, no. 3, pp. 465–491.

Lanham, RA, 1995, Digital literacy. *Scientific American*, vol. *273*, no. 3, pp. 198–199.

Losee, RM, 1997, A discipline independent definition of information. *Journal of the American Society for Information Science*, vol. 48, no. 3, pp. 254–269.

Overall, PM, 2009, Cultural competence: A conceptual framework for library and information science professionals. *The Library Quarterly*, vol. 79, no. 2, pp. 175–204.

Proctor, RN and Schiebinger, L, 2008, *Agnotology: The making and unmaking of ignorance*. Stanford, CA: Stanford University Press.

Rogers, K, Jakes, L and Swanson, A, 2020, Trump defends using 'Chinese virus' label, ignoring growing criticism. *The New York Times*. Available at: www.nytimes.com/2020/03/18/us/politics/china-virus.html [Accessed April 17, 2020]

Roy, A, 2020, Arundhati Roy: 'The pandemic is a portal'. *Financial Times*, 3 April. Available at: www.ft.com/content/10d8f5e8-74eb-11ea-95fe-fcd274e920ca [Accessed April 7, 2020]

Solsman, JE, 2020, Deepfakes' threat to 2020 US election isn't what you'd think. *Elections 2020*. Available at: www.cnet.com/features/deepfakes-threat-to-the-2020-us-election-isnt-what-youd-think/ [Accessed May 7, 2020]

Tisdell, EJ, 2008, Critical media literacy and transformative learning: Drawing on pop culture and entertainment media in teaching for diversity in adult higher education. *Journal of Transformative Education*, vol. 6, no. 1, pp. 48–67.

Wardle, C, 2018, *Information disorder: The definitional toolbox*. Available at: https://firstdraftnews.org/latest/infodisorder-definitional-toolbox/ [Accessed May 1, 2020]

Zhou, L and Zhang, D, 2007, An ontology-supported misinformation model: Toward a digital misinformation library. *IEEE Transactions on Systems, Man, and Cybernetics-Part A: Systems and Humans*, vol. 37, no. 5, pp. 804–813.

46

PEOPLE-POWERED CORRECTION

Fixing misinformation on social media

Leticia Bode and Emily K. Vraga

Reviewing the misinformation problem and how to solve it

Although misinformation is not new (Lewandowsky et al. 2012; Nyhan & Reifler 2010; Porter & Wood 2019), its visibility as a problem and general concern about its prevalence have both increased in recent years (Mitchell et al. 2019). The rise of social media partially explains this renewed emphasis on the problem that misinformation presents.

We define *misinformation* as information 'considered incorrect based on the best available evidence from relevant experts at the time' (Vraga & Bode 2020, 138). Notably, this includes both misinformation (incorrect information created or shared as truth) and disinformation (incorrect information created or shared nefariously) as our definition focuses on the information itself rather than the intent of the person creating or sharing the misinformation.

Moreover, misinformation (the information itself) is distinct from the misperceptions (or individual beliefs on the topic) that it can spur (Nyhan & Reifler 2010) – and these misperceptions can lead to problematic behaviors based on mistaken beliefs about what is safe, appropriate, or normative. There are numerous examples of the deleterious effects of misperceptions: for example, belief in conspiracy theories can reduce intentions to vaccinate (Jolley & Douglas 2014; Schmid & Betsch 2019), mistaken beliefs that indoor tanning or e-cigarettes are safe promotes intentions to engage in these behaviors (Tan et al. 2015), and hearing false candidate rumours can shift preferences and voting intentions (Weeks & Garrett 2014: Thorson 2016).

Although misinformation is not unique to social media, social media is often blamed for promoting its spread. One noteworthy study found that 'falsehood diffused significantly farther, faster, deeper, and more broadly than the truth in all categories of information' (Vosoughi et al. 2018, 1147). Many have pointed to the qualities of social media that could explain why misinformation is so powerful online: the lack of established gatekeepers, less prominent signals for high-quality information, monetary incentives to promote viral spread, and malicious actors, to name a few (Broniatowski et al. 2018; Southwell et al. 2019). These features play on individuals' blind spots, including motivated reasoning, a preference for novel and emotional content, and growing distrust of elite institutions or groups (Edelman 2020; Lewandowsky et al. 2017; Vosoughi et al. 2018).

To combat this problem, a variety of solutions have been proposed. A non-exhaustive list of these includes bolstering public education and news literacy efforts (Lewandowsky et al. 2017),

498

encouraging users to think about information's accuracy (Fazio 2020; Pennycook et al. 2019), promoting reliable and credible information (Chadwick 2020), decreasing the ability to spread information in general (whether it's true or false; see Porter 2020), and government regulation of misinformation or of the platforms used to spread it (Kim 2020). While each of these solutions holds promise, each has limitations that prevent it from being a silver bullet.

For example, many have proposed that public education can play a significant role in mitigating the problem with sustained media literacy campaigns. Familiarity with and knowledge of media literacy has shown some positive effects, helping people identify misinformation, resist conspiracy theories, and express scepticism of online information (Amazeen & Bucy 2019; Craft et al. 2017; Kahne & Bowyer 2017; Vraga & Tully 2019). Indeed, Finland's K–12 emphasis on media literacy, in which students are consistently encouraged to read information critically across all aspects of their curriculum, is often touted as a prominent success story (Henley 2020). It is worth noting, however, that Finland may be the exception to the rule. In addition to investing significantly in these efforts, Finland is a highly literate and homogenous society (Mackintosh 2019) and top in the world in media trust (Newman et al. 2019). Similar efforts in other contexts may, therefore, be less successful. Moreover, because most media literacy efforts occur in the classroom, they fail to reach most of the population, especially older adults who may be most at risk of seeing and sharing misinformation (Guess et al. 2019). Media literacy campaigns can take place outside an educational environment, but attempts to design media literacy messages to appear on social media platforms have had only mixed success in helping people recognise misinformation (Tully et al. 2020a) or promoting reception of expert corrections (Vraga, Bode, et al. 2020) and may potentially spill over to harm evaluations of credible news (Clayton et al. 2019).

Closely related to media literacy interventions are attempts to inoculate people to misinformation. Theoretically, explaining the logical flaws in misinformation may help people recognise those same techniques in other spaces. There is some empirical evidence that logical corrections of misinformation are effective both before people see misinformation and in response to misinformation (Cook et al. 2017; Schmid & Betsch 2019; Vraga, Kim, et al. 2020). Promisingly, a game that teaches people misinformation techniques has shown promise in creating resistance to misinformation online without harming credible information (Roozenbeek et al. 2020). However, more work is needed to consider how to make these interventions scalable, as well as to consider their longevity.

At the other end of the spectrum, many people point to social media (rather than individuals or societal structures) as being responsible for addressing misinformation. Suggestions in this category include platforms detecting misinformation and then taking action to mitigate it – either by removing it from the platform entirely, de-amplifying it so fewer people see it, or providing educational efforts to platform users to lessen the effects of misinformation (Pennycook & Rand 2019). Platforms have begun taking concrete steps to address misinformation in their spaces, especially on health issues like vaccination, where there is clear scientific consensus and the potential for public harm. Pinterest announced that they would populate searches for vaccine information with links to highly credible health organisations (Ozoma 2019), while Facebook announced that it would reduce the ranking of groups that share vaccine misinformation, reject advertisements that contain vaccine misinformation, and connect people searching for vaccine information to 'authoritative information' (Facebook 2019), although others have questioned the success of these efforts for advertisements (Haskins 2020). However, it is effectively impossible for social media platforms to identify every piece of false content, and it risks ethical overreach for them to decide how to address such content (Bode 2020).

Observational correction

Partly as a consequence of the limitations of these strategies to correct misinformation, we propose one more: that of observational correction. Observational correction occurs whenever people update their own attitudes after seeing someone else being corrected on social media (Vraga & Bode 2017).

There are several key features of this definition that set it apart from other types of correction and may make it more successful than traditional formats for correction. First, it focuses on the community seeing an interaction on social media in which both misinformation and correction are offered, rather than considering the individuals (or organisations) sharing misinformation. Second, the community observes the correction simultaneously with or immediately after the misinformation (we therefore cannot speak to whether observational correction can occur when someone was exposed to the misinformation absent correction initially and only later sees a corrective response).

Most importantly, observational correction is not limited to one particular source. Our previous research outlines three potential ways in which observational correction can occur. First, corrections can come from algorithms driven by the platforms themselves – most notably, through Facebook's related stories algorithm (e.g. Bode & Vraga 2015, 2018; Smith & Seitz 2019). Newer examples of platforms responses – like showing messages to people who liked, reacted to, or commented on COVID-19 misinformation on Facebook (Rosen 2020) or adding fact-checks to manipulated information on Twitter (Roth & Achuthan 2020) – would fall under this domain of algorithmic correction. Future research should explore which of these mechanisms are most successful in responding to misinformation on the platform, but theoretically, these approaches may have merit when applied correctly.

Second, corrections can come directly from expert organisations. Our research shows that corrective responses by expert organisations reduce misperceptions, and engaging in these types of corrections do not hurt, and may in fact help, organisational credibility (Bode et al. n.d.; Vraga & Bode 2017; Vraga, Bode, et al. 2020). More research, however, is needed to understand the boundaries of who is considered an expert on a topic. For example, does simply including the title 'professor' in a social media handle imbue that user with sufficient credibility to function as an expert when offering a correction (e.g. Vraga, Kim, et al. 2020)? What level of existing organisational prominence or trust can be leveraged when offering corrections? And to what extent does a perception of expertise depend on the individual characteristics of the person viewing the correction?

Third, corrections can come from other social media users. This is where the true populist power of social media comes into play. Although user correction does reduce misperceptions, multiple corrections are sometimes necessary to have an impact, and corrections should provide links to expert information (for example, from the Centers for Disease Control, the American Medical Association, or a fact-check) on the topic to be effective (Vraga & Bode 2017, 2018). In other words, to mitigate misinformation, social media users should indicate the information is false, even if someone else has already done so, backing up their arguments with links to an expert organisation.

One might think the tone of the correction would affect its persuasiveness. However, the tone of user corrections does not appear to affect their effectiveness – at least on those observing the correction, rather than those being corrected (Bode et al. 2020). When users are uncivil in their responses, they are equally effective as when they are civil; likewise, expressing empathy and affirmation for why a user may be confused or sharing misinformation does not increase or limit the efficacy of such a response for the social media audience. Given that incivility can have numerous other deleterious effects on democratic society (Mutz 2006), a civil or understanding tone is still likely the best approach when offering corrective responses.

So why does observational correction work when other corrective responses often fail? One explanation relates to the distance between the person updating their attitudes and the correction. Observational correction is about people who *see* an interaction, rather than those who take part in it directly. People merely observing a correction may not be as determined to engage in motivated reasoning to protect their identity and are therefore more flexible in updating their beliefs (although there is at least some evidence to the contrary; see Bode & Vraga 2015).

Second, people are particularly sceptical of information shared on social media and thus may be more receptive to corrections that leverage expert sources. Indeed, 89 percent of Americans say they at least 'sometimes' come across made-up news and information (with 38 percent saying 'often'), and these numbers are higher among those who prefer social media for news (Mitchell et al. 2019). This scepticism may increase reliance on expertise, either from user corrections that highlight expert sources or from experts themselves. When facing information overload – as is common on social media – heuristic processing and relying on source cues regarding credibility may become even more important in shaping processing (Metzger et al. 2010; Tandoc 2019). Moreover, the fact that these corrections occur on social media – where exposure to news and information is often incidental to social purposes motivating online exposure (Bode 2016) – may also facilitate correction.

Third, the immediacy of the correction likely contributes to the success of observational correction on social media. In tests of observational correction, exposure to the misinformation occurs simultaneously with or immediately after exposure to the corrective information. Therefore, the misinformation is not able to linger and impact attitudes, reducing motivated reasoning in the face of corrective information and belief echoes of the misinformation (Thorson, 2016). Future research could use eye tracking to determine attention patterns – for example, whether people first look at the misinformation or the correction, their relative attention to the misinformation versus the correction, or how often they shift their attention between the misinformation and correction posts. The size, position, and memorable content attached to each are also likely to play a role.

Fourth, although this is outside the realm of what we have tested directly, correction imposes an indirect cost for sharing misinformation. Through observational correction, people see this cost – it may be embarrassing or harmful to one's reputation to share information that is then called out as false. If people believe sharing misinformation will have negative consequences such as these, it should theoretically produce disincentives for sharing misinformation in the first place. Because even small nudges to encourage people to think twice about sharing false information can have important impacts (Fazio 2020; Pennycook et al. 2019), this is a useful potential consequence of observational correction.

How is observational correction populist?

Therefore, there are several reasons why observational correction might work. But the biggest potential benefit of observational correction is that it presents not only a scalable way to address misinformation on social media but also one that is populist in its reliance on ordinary users. Observational correction does not rely on elite external actors – experts, platforms, fact-checking journalists, or others – but can occur from people in the communities being impacted by misinformation themselves. This means that social media users – everyday people – can play a major role in shaping the information environment of which they are a part. While this arguably has value in and of itself, it may also result in greater receptivity to user corrections than other actions designed to address misinformation.

Identifying and removing inaccurate content from social media is also virtually impossible at scale, given the massive quantity of information that passes through such platforms on a daily basis. Even successfully identifying a very high percentage of misinformation would still result in many thousands of pieces of inaccurate content persisting on social media (Bode 2020). While the scale is not 'fixed' with observational correction, it can be more effectively addressed, at least hypothetically. Given that one in three people around the world use social media (Ortiz-Ospina 2019), a virtual army of correctors exists to launch into action upon seeing misinformation posted.

Of course, user correction is only populist – and effective and scalable – if a wide range of people on social media platforms participate. Notably, observational correction is not as uncommon as people may assume. A recent study we conducted found that 23 percent of Americans report having corrected someone else on social media in the past week with regards to COVID-19, and 34 percent report having seen these corrections occur (Bode & Vraga 2020), which aligns with earlier work suggesting that 32 percent of Americans reported publicly flagging or reporting made-up news (Mitchell et al. 2019). Importantly, both those engaging in correction and those observing the correction are from a wide variety of backgrounds – including those from both sides of the partisan aisle. This is important: correction is not siloed within specific groups of people but can be found across broad swaths of the public. Moreover, corrections coming from others 'like us' are more likely to be trusted (Margolin et al. 2018; Tandoc 2019), meaning that anyone can experience correction, and such corrections are likely to be effective.

Likewise, our study found people generally endorsed correction as a valuable practice on social media. Not only do 68 percent of people agree that people should respond when they see someone sharing misinformation, 56 percent of people say they personally like seeing such corrections. While majorities of the public may believe that the news media hold primary responsibility for reducing made-up news and information broadly (Mitchell et al. 2019), this does not negate public support for a community solution to the problem on social media. Nascent social norms promoting user correction on social media may be emerging, which could make it even more populist in nature. If the public increasingly believes such corrections are appropriate or valued, and perceives that other people are engaging in correction, it lays the groundwork for injunctive and descriptive norms that may powerfully affect behaviors (Ajzen 1985, 2011; Cialdini et al. 2006), allowing more people to feel comfortable correcting others on social media.

Areas for future exploration

While existing research provides the groundwork for a populist solution to misinformation on social media, much work remains to be done in the space. First, more research is needed to examine the sources of misinformation and correction and how their credibility, proximity, relevance, and expertise affect how people perceive the information they share. User corrections, for example, may be more effective when they come from people we know personally or have close ties with (e.g. Margolin et al. 2018) or may be more effective from users with credibility or expertise cues in their name or post (for example, someone who claims they are a doctor, a scientist, or a professor) (Vraga, Kim, et al. 2020).

Likewise, user corrections may be more effective for some groups of people than for others. Given rising levels of scepticism towards elite institutions, news organisations, politicians, and scientists (Edelman 2020), user corrections from ordinary people may reach audiences who are sceptical of authority. Some evidence for this claim comes from research suggesting that user corrections were seen as equally credible to algorithmic corrections on Facebook among those higher in conspiracy ideation (Bode & Vraga 2018). Given the extensive research highlighting the importance of source cues in credibility and persuasion (Metzger et al. 2010; Petty & Cacioppo 1986), more research is needed into how myriad sources intersect (i.e. the source of the misinformation, the source of the correction, any additional links within the posts) when people see misinformation and correction online.

Second, more research is needed to understand who is most likely to engage in observational correction. As noted earlier, more people tend to ignore misinformation on social media than to respond to it (Bode & Vraga 2020; Tandoc et al. 2020), meaning that even user correction is not truly populist. Yet not enough is known about why some people respond to misinformation while others do not. Our initial research suggests that more educated people were more likely to say they had corrected others with regards to COVID-19, whereas older adults were less likely to say they had done so (Bode & Vraga 2020), although previous research had not found differences by education or age in terms of responding to 'fake news' on social media (Tandoc et al. 2020). In other research, we found that people who were misinformed about a topic were more likely to say they would respond to a misinformation post on the subject, suggesting that those who are most willing to respond may be the least equipped to reduce misperceptions (Tully, Vraga, & Bode 2020b, working paper). Clearly, much more research is needed to discover who is willing to correct others and the circumstances that may facilitate or deter correction.

Research is also urgently needed into what can be done to motivate people to correct others. Our research suggests user correction can be effective, but it requires people to be willing and able to engage with one another on social media. While research has not yet examined how to motivate corrections on social media specifically, several behavioral theories offer promising avenues to pursue. Notably, the theory of planned behavior highlights the importance of social norms – in conjunction with attitudes and perceived behavioral control – in spurring behavior (Ajzen 1985, 2011). Therefore, interventions that highlight public support for and engagement in correction represent a promising technique for encouraging more people to consider engaging in such corrections themselves (e.g. Cialdini et al. 2006). Likewise, user correction may be facilitated if combined with algorithmic correction; social media companies might consider prioritising user comments that include links to expert sources, elevating the visibility of such corrections.

In addition, most work has focused on either Facebook or Twitter, although other platforms like Instagram, Pinterest, and YouTube are also significant disseminators of misinformation. Indeed, initial studies suggest that incorporating video correction (Young et al. 2018) and graphics (Amazeen et al. 2018) enhances debunking efforts. Understanding what elements of observational correction successfully transfer between platforms and how corrections may need to be adopted to better fit the affordances of a given platform are essential.

Conclusion

Therefore, observational correction represents a flexible, robust, and community solution to misinformation on social media that appeals to populist ideals. Rather than depending on elites to combat the problem of misinformation, motivating ordinary users to respond to misinformation as they see it provides not only the scalable response needed but also one that can appeal to people regardless of their position or beliefs.

References

Ajzen, I. (1985). From intentions to actions: A theory of planned behavior. In *Action control* (pp.11–39). Springer, Berlin, Heidelberg.

Ajzen, I. (2011). The theory of planned behaviour: Reactions and reflections, 1113–1127.

Amazeen, M. A., & Bucy, E. P. (2019). Conferring resistance to digital disinformation: The inoculating influence of procedural news knowledge. *Journal of Broadcasting & Electronic Media, 63*(3), 415–432.

Amazeen, M. A., Thorson, E., Muddiman, A., & Graves, L. (2018). Correcting political and consumer misperceptions: The effectiveness and effects of rating scale versus contextual correction formats. *Journalism & Mass Communication Quarterly, 95*(1), 28–48.

Bode, L. (2016). Political news in the news feed: Learning politics from social media. *Mass communication and society, 19*(1), 24–48.

Bode, L. (2020). User correction as a tool in the battle against social media misinformation. *Georgetown Law and Technology Review*, forthcoming.

Bode, L., & Vraga, E. K. (2015). In related news, that was wrong: The correction of misinformation through related stories functionality in social media. *Journal of Communication, 65*(4), 619–638.

Bode, L., & Vraga, E. K. (2018). See something, say something: Correction of global health misinformation on social media. *Health Communication, 33*(9), 1131–1140.

Bode, L., & Vraga, E. K. (2020, May 7). Americans are fighting coronavirus misinformation on social media. *The Washington Post, Monkey Cage*. Retrieved from: www.washingtonpost.com/politics/2020/05/07/americans-are-fighting-coronavirus-misinformation-social-media/

Bode, L., Vraga, E.K., & Tully, M. (n.d.). *Correcting misperceptions about genetically modified food on social media*. Working paper.

Bode, L., Vraga, E. K., & Tully, M. (2020). Do the right thing: Tone may not affect correction of misinformation on social media. *The Harvard Kennedy School (HKS) Misinformation Review. https://doi.org/10.37016/mr-2020-026.*

Broniatowski, D. A., Jamison, A. M., Qi, S., AlKulaib, L., Chen, T., Benton, A., . . . & Dredze, M. (2018). Weaponized health communication: Twitter bots and Russian trolls amplify the vaccine debate. *American Journal of Public Health, 108*(10), 1378–1384.

Chadwick, J. (2020). Google launches 'SOS Alert' for coronavirus in search results to provide users with tips and information from the World Health Organisation on how to stay safe. *The Daily Mail*. Retrieved from: www.dailymail.co.uk/sciencetech/article-7951707/Google-launches-SOS-Alert-coronavirus-search-results.html

Cialdini, R. B., Demaine, L. J., Sagarin, B. J., Barrett, D. W., Rhoads, K., & Winter, P. L. (2006). Managing social norms for persuasive impact. *Social influence, 1*(1), 3–15.

Clayton, K., Blair, S., Busam, J. A., Forstner, S., Glance, J., Green, G., . . . & Sandhu, M. (2019). Real solutions for fake news? Measuring the effectiveness of general warnings and fact-check tags in reducing belief in false stories on social media. *Political Behavior*, online first.

Cook, J., Lewandowsky, S., & Ecker, U. K. (2017). Neutralizing misinformation through inoculation: Exposing misleading argumentation techniques reduces their influence. *PLoS One, 12*(5).

Craft, S., Ashley, S., & Maksl, A. (2017). News media literacy and conspiracy theory endorsement. *Communication and the Public, 2*(4), 388–401.

Edelman. (2020). *Edelman trust barometer 2020*. Retrieved from: www.edelman.com/sites/g/files/aatuss191/files/2020-01/2020%20Edelman%20Trust%20Barometer%20Executive%20Summary_Single%20Spread%20without%20Crops.pdf

Facebook. (2019). *Combatting vaccine misinformation*. Retrieved from: https://about.fb.com/news/2019/03/combatting-vaccine-misinformation/

Fazio, L. (2020). Pausing to consider why a headline is true or false can help reduce the sharing of false news. *Harvard Kennedy School Misinformation Review, 1*(2).

Guess, A., Nagler, J., & Tucker, J. (2019). Less than you think: Prevalence and predictors of fake news dissemination on Facebook. *Science Advances, 5*(1), eaau4586.

Haskins, C. (2020). Facebook is running anti-vax ads, despite its ban on vaccine misinformation. *Buzzfeed News*. Retrieved from: www.buzzfeednews.com/article/carolinehaskins1/facebook-running-anti-vax-ads-despite-ban-anti

Henley, J. (2020). How Finland starts its fight against fake news in primary schools. *The Guardian*. Retrieved from: www.theguardian.com/world/2020/jan/28/fact-from-fiction-finlands-new-lessons-in-combating-fake-news

Jolley, D., & Douglas, K. M. (2014). The effects of anti-vaccine conspiracy theories on vaccination intentions. *PloS One, 9*(2).

Kahne, J., & Bowyer, B. (2017). Educating for democracy in a partisan age: Confronting the challenges of motivated reasoning and misinformation. *American Educational Research Journal, 54*(1), 3–34.

Kim, S. (2020). Elizabeth Warren proposes criminal penalties for spreading voting disinformation online. *CNBC.* Retrieved from: www.cnbc.com/2020/01/29/warren-proposes-criminal-penalties-for-spreading-disinformation-online.html

Lewandowsky, S., Ecker, U. K., & Cook, J. (2017). Beyond misinformation: Understanding and coping with the "post-truth" era. *Journal of Applied Research in Memory and Cognition, 6*(4), 353–369.

Lewandowsky, S., Ecker, U. K., Seifert, C. M., Schwarz, N., & Cook, J. (2012). Misinformation and its correction: Continued influence and successful debiasing. *Psychological Science in the Public Interest, 13*(3), 106–131.

Mackintosh, E. (2019). Finland is winning the war on fake news. What it's learned may be crucial to Western democracy. *CNN.* Retrieved from: https://edition.cnn.com/interactive/2019/05/europe/finland-fake-news-intl/

Margolin, D. B., Hannak, A., & Weber, I. (2018). Political fact-checking on Twitter: When do corrections have an effect? *Political Communication, 35*(2), 196–219.

Metzger, M. J., Flanagin, A. J., & Medders, R. B. (2010). Social and heuristic approaches to credibility evaluation online. *Journal of Communication, 60*(3), 413–439.

Mitchell, A., Gottfried, J., Stocking, G., Walker, M., & Fedeli, S. (2019). Many Americans say made-up news is a critical problem that needs to be fixed. *Pew Research Center.* Retrieved from: www.journalism.org/2019/06/05/many-americans-say-made-up-news-is-a-critical-problem-that-needs-to-be-fixed/

Mutz, D. C. (2006). *Hearing the other side: Deliberative versus participatory democracy.* Cambridge: Cambridge University Press.

Newman, N., Fletcher, R., Kalogeropoulos, A., & Nielsen, R. (2019). *Reuters institute digital news report 2019* (Vol. 2019). Reuters Institute for the Study of Journalism. Retrieved from: https://reutersinstitute.politics.ox.ac.uk/sites/default/files/2019-06/DNR_2019_FINAL_0.pdf

Nyhan, B., & Reifler, J. (2010). When corrections fail: The persistence of political misperceptions. *Political Behavior, 32*(2), 303–330.

Ortiz-Ospina, E. (2019). *The rise of social media. Our world in data.* Retrieved from: https://ourworldindata.org/rise-of-social-media

Ozoma, I. (2019). *Bringing authoritative vaccine results to Pinterest search.* Retrieved from: https://newsroom.pinterest.com/en/post/bringing-authoritative-vaccine-results-to-pinterest-search

Pennycook, G., Epstein, Z., Mosleh, M., Arechar, A. A., Eckles, D., & Rand, D. G. (2019). *Understanding and reducing the spread of misinformation online* (preprint). Retrieved from: https://psyarxiv.com/3n9u8

Pennycook, G., & Rand, D. G. (2019). Fighting misinformation on social media using crowdsourced judgments of news source quality. *Proceedings of the National Academy of Sciences, 116*(7), 2521–2526.

Petty, R. E., & Cacioppo, J. T. (1986). The elaboration likelihood model of persuasion. In *Communication and persuasion* (pp. 1–24). Springer, New York.

Porter, E., & Wood, T. J. (2019). *False alarm: The truth about political mistruths in the trump era.* Cambridge: Cambridge University Press.

Porter, J. (2020). WhatsApp says its forwarding limits have cut the spread of viral messages by 70 percent. *The Verge.* Retrieved from: www.theverge.com/2020/4/27/21238082/whatsapp-forward-message-limits-viral-misinformation-decline

Roozenbeek, J., van der Linden, S., & Nygren, T. (2020). Prebunking interventions based on "inoculation" theory can reduce susceptibility to misinformation across cultures. *The Harvard Kennedy School (HKS) Misinformation Review.* https://doi.org/10.37016//mr-2020-008

Rosen, G. (2020, April 16). An update on our work to keep people informed and limit misinformation about COVID-19. *Facebook Newsroom.* Retrieved from: https://about.fb.com/news/2020/04/covid-19-misinfo-update/

Roth, Y., & Achuthan, A. (2020, February 4). Building rules in public: Our approach to synthetic and manipulated media. *Twitter.* Retrieved from: https://blog.twitter.com/en_us/topics/company/2020/new-approach-to-synthetic-and-manipulated-media.html

Schmid, P., & Betsch, C. (2019). Effective strategies for rebutting science denialism in public discussions. *Nature Human Behaviour, 3*(9), 931–939.

Smith, C. N., & Seitz, H. H. (2019). Correcting misinformation about neuroscience via social media. *Science Communication, 41*(6), 790–819.

Southwell, B. G., Niederdeppe, J., Cappella, J. N., Gaysynsky, A., Kelley, D. E., Oh, A., . . . & Chou, W. Y. S. (2019). Misinformation as a misunderstood challenge to public health. *American Journal of Preventive Medicine, 57*(2), 282–285.

Tan, A. S., Lee, C. J., & Chae, J. (2015). Exposure to health (mis) information: Lagged effects on young adults' health behaviors and potential pathways. *Journal of Communication, 65*, 674–698.

Tandoc Jr, E. C. (2019). Tell me who your sources are: Perceptions of news credibility on social media. *Journalism Practice, 13*, 178–190.

Tandoc Jr, E. C., Lim, D., & Ling, R. (2020). Diffusion of disinformation: How social media users respond to fake news and why. *Journalism, 21*(3), 381–398.

Thorson, E. (2016). Belief echoes: The persistent effects of corrected misinformation. *Political Communication, 33*, 460–480.

Tully, M., Vraga, E. K., & Bode, L. (2020a). Designing and testing news literacy messages for social media. *Mass Communication and Society, 23*(1), 22–46.

Tully, M., Vraga, E. K., & Bode, L. (2020b). *Who replies to misinformation on Twitter?* Working paper.

Vosoughi, S., Roy, D., & Aral, S. (2018). The spread of true and false news online. *Science, 359*, 1146–1151.

Vraga, E. K., & Bode, L. (2017). Using expert sources to correct health misinformation in social media. *Science Communication, 39*(5), 621–645.

Vraga, E. K., & Bode, L. (2018). I do not believe you: How providing a source corrects health misperceptions across social media platforms. *Information, Communication & Society, 21*(10), 1337–1353.

Vraga, E. K., & Bode, L. (2020). Defining misinformation and understanding its bounded nature: Using expertise and evidence for describing misinformation. *Political Communication, 37*(1), 136–144.

Vraga, E. K., Bode, L., & Tully, M. (2020). Creating news literacy messages to enhance expert corrections of misinformation on Twitter. *Communication Research*, 0093650219898094.

Vraga, E.K., Kim, S.C., Cook, J., & Bode, L. (2020). Testing the effectiveness of correction placement and type on Instagram. *International Journal of Press and Politics*, online first.

Vraga, E. K., & Tully, M. (2019). News literacy, social media behaviors, and skepticism toward information on social media. *Information, Communication & Society*, 1–17.

Weeks, B. E., & Garrett, R. K. (2014). Electoral consequences of political rumors: Motivated reasoning, candidate rumors, and vote choice during the 2008 US presidential election. *International Journal of Public Opinion Research, 26*(4), 401–422.

Young, D. G., Jamieson, K. H., Poulsen, S., & Goldring, A. (2018). Fact-checking effectiveness as a function of format and tone: Evaluating FactCheck. org and FlackCheck. org. *Journalism & Mass Communication Quarterly, 95*(1), 49–75.

47

COUNTERING HATE SPEECH

Babak Bahador

Counterspeech refers to communication that responds to hate speech in order to reduce it and negate its harmful potential effects. This chapter begins by defining hate speech and examining some of its negative impacts. It then defines and disaggregates the concept of counterspeech, differentiating five of its dimensions – audiences, goals, tactics, messages, and effects. This is presented in two sections. The first examines audiences, goals, and tactics. Audiences refers to the groups exposed to counterspeech, including hate groups, violent extremists, the vulnerable, and the public. Goals are the aims of those engaging in counterspeech efforts, which often vary by audience. Tactics assesses the different means and mediums used to reach these audiences. The second section examines messaging and effects. Messaging refers to the content typologies used to try and influence audiences. Effects analyses how the audiences exposed to counterspeech are influenced based on a review of recent studies in which the approach has been tested. In this section, five key findings from the counterspeech research literature are presented.

Defining hate speech

In its narrow definition, hate speech is based on the assumption that the emotion of hate can be triggered or increased towards certain targets through exposure to particular types of information. The emotion of hate involves an enduring dislike, loss of empathy, and possible desire for harm against those targets (Waltman and Mattheis 2017). Hate speech, however, is usually defined more broadly to include any speech that insults, discriminates, or incites violence against groups that hold immutable commonalities such as a particular ethnicity, nationality, religion, gender, age bracket, or sexual orientation. While hate speech refers to the expression of thoughts in spoken words, it can be over any form of communication, including text, images, videos, and even gestures. The term *hate speech* is widely used today in legal, political, and popular discourse. However, it has been criticised for its connection to the human emotion of hate and other conceptual ambiguities (Gagliardone et al. 2015; Howard, 2019). This has led to proposals for more precise terms such as *dangerous* (Benesch 2014; Brown 2016), *fear* (Buyse 2014) and *ignorant speech* (Lepoutre 2019).

While jurisdictions differ in the way they define and attempt to remedy the negative consequences of hate speech (Howard 2019), there is some international consensus through institutions such as the United Nations about what constitutes hate speech. According to Article 20 of

507

the International Covenant on Civil and Political Rights (United Nations n.d.), '[a]ny advocacy of national, racial or religious hatred that constitutes incitement to discrimination, hostility or violence shall be prohibited by law'. Other international legal instruments that address hate speech include the Genocide Convention on the Prevention and Punishment of the Crime of Genocide (1951), the International Convention on the Elimination of All Forms of Racial Discrimination or ICERD (1969) and the Convention on the Elimination of All Forms of Discrimination Against Women or CEDAW (1981).

While these international agreements are important representations of broadly recognised principles on the topic, in practice, much of hate speech today occurs on private social media platforms such as Facebook, Twitter, and Google. It can be argued that, as a result, a new type of jurisdiction has emerged in which the policies or 'community standards' of these organisations ultimately set the boundaries between free speech and hate speech (Gagliardone et al. 2015). These policies are ever evolving and are largely modelled on the same core principles enshrined in more traditional national laws and international treaties, with sanctions ranging from flagging hateful posts to removing such posts and closing associated accounts. However, many criticise the notion of relying on profit-making corporations to set such policies for a myriad of reasons including their slow response, inconsistent policy application, inappropriate enforcements (e.g. banning journalists or activists), and favouritism towards the powerful (Laub 2019).

Research on media effects and persuasion demonstrate that hateful messages are likely to have different effects on different members of in-group audiences, often determined by their predispositions. Hate speech, therefore, should be understood as speech that only has the potential to increase hate. Even when hate increases, however, other moral, cultural, political, and legal inhibitions can prevent hateful views from manifesting into behavioural responses such as violence and crime. Factors that can increase the risk of speech leading to violence include the speaker's influence, audience susceptibility, the medium, and the social/historical context (Benesch 2013; Brown 2016).

While hate speech can target individuals, it is much more concerning when groups are targeted. This is because, in such scenarios, all members of the group can become 'guilty by association' and the focus on collective blame and vicarious retribution, even if few were responsible for the purported negative actions (Lickel et al. 2006; Bahador 2012; Bruneau 2018). Hate speech targeting groups is almost always a form of disinformation because rarely is an entire group guilty of the negative actions and characteristics allocated to them. In the vast majority of cases, such allegations are either outright false or exaggerated or conflate the actions of a minority associated with the group to the entire group.

Hate speech is often used by populist leaders and politicians to shift blame for real or perceived societal problems or threats on domestic minorities within societies who have historically been the victims of prejudice and past hate. While one aspect of hate speech involves calls to dehumanise and demonise such groups, another involves incitement to exclude, discriminate, and commit violence against such groups as a solution to overcoming the social problems and threats. This type of speech is also used between nation-states and is a well-known precursor to international conflict to prepare and socially mobilise societies for war and the normalisation of mass violence (Dower 1986; Keen 1991; Carruthers 2011).

To offset the potential negative impacts of hate speech, governments, technology companies, non- and intergovernmental organisations, and experts have often proposed content removal (or take-downs) and other forms of punishment. While there is much criticism of the interpretation and implementation of such sanctions, as mentioned, there is a larger ethical issue at stake as such actions violate the human right to free speech, which is widely considered to be fundamental to a properly functioning democracy. Free speech is protected in the

Universal Declaration of Human Rights and within the constitutions of a number of countries, including the First Amendment to the United States Constitution. Within a US context, almost all speech is protected, with limitations only in very rare cases when 'imminent lawless action' is advocated (Tucker 2015). Furthermore, there is also the unintended risk of the Streisand effect, in which attempts to hide or censor something inadvertently increase its publicity (Lepoutre 2019).

Counterspeech

To reduce the harmful effects of hate speech without infringing on the freedom of speech, counterspeech is often evoked as a non-regulatory and morally permissible solution (Engida 2015; Strossen 2018; Howard 2019; Lepoutre 2019). Counterspeech is, by definition, communication that directly responds to the creation and dissemination of hate speech with the goal of reducing its harmful effects. Bartlett and Krasodomski-Jones define counterspeech as speech that argues, disagrees with, and presents an opposing view to offensive and extreme online content (2015). However, in practice, efforts under the counterspeech umbrella are sometimes much broader and include communication that is not directly responsive but rather aims to prevent or create the conditions to reduce hate speech and its negative effects (Benesch 2014; Lepoutre 2019). For the purposes of this chapter, analysis will primarily focus on attempts to counter hate speech directly. Furthermore, while counterspeech can occur across a range of online and offline mediums, especially when it is more broadly understood, the focus in this chapter will largely be on counterspeech in an online digital setting.

Before examining the concept of counterspeech more directly, it is important to understand that counterspeech is based on a set of assumptions. The first of these involves an underlying conviction in persuasion and media effects, especially at the individual psychological level. By exposing audiences to particular messaging, counterspeakers hope to achieve attitudinal and behavioural outcomes that will either reduce hate speech or negate its harmful effect. This approach, focused on change at the individual level, is in contrast to structuralists who view concepts like hate and its negative manifestations, such as violence, as functions of social and political structures that enable them to exist (Waltz 1959). For structuralists, hate speech only becomes more widely prevalent and dangerous under particular societal circumstances, so to solve the problem, the structures much be changed, not the speech itself. Structural solutions often focus on the importance of systemic change and often see media literacy and education as enabling 'digital citizens' to both identify hate speech and react to it through critical engagement that respects human rights and incorporates a broad set of ethical principles (Gagliardone et al. 2015; Porten-Cheé 2020).

Counterspeech, at its core, is rooted in a set of classical liberal values that assume a public that is both moral and rational in its decision-making, capable of deciphering truth from falsehood with sufficient information in the so-called marketplace of ideas (Schauer 1982; Ingber 1984; Carr 2001; Lombardi 2019). Hatred and prejudice, from this perspective, derive from ignorance and a lack of accurate information about others. This assumption is built into UNESCO's charter, which blames 'ignorance of each other's ways and lives' as the reason 'wars begin in the minds of men' (UNESCO, n.d.). However, through various means including education and communication, this same approach assumes that 'it is in the minds of men that the defences of peace must be constructed'. Inherent in this remedy is belief in the power of speech and deliberation to have almost therapeutic powers to correct errors and find solutions. They can also be seen as a way to enhance democracy and enable a new form of political participation and even civic duty (Porten-Cheé 2020).

From this perspective, counterspeech represents rational, accurate, and corrective information while hate speech represents irrationality based on falsehoods. These assumptions, of course, are problematic for a range of reasons, including the research findings that show humans to be driven less by rationality and more by emotion and bias in their decision-making. In addition, the so-called marketplace of ideas assumes that the public, and especially those holding opposing views, can meet in open public forums in which ideas can be readily exchanged. But communication in the online world is often marked by echo chambers of like-minded views that reinforce and radicalise polarised positions (Langton 2018).

There is a relatively limited body of research and literature on counterspeech specifically and, compared to the large body of work on hate speech, it can be considered under-researched, undertheorised and underdeveloped, and what is written is often by practitioners who have worked in various ways to operationalise the concept (Howard 2019). However, it is important to note that a number of parallel literatures overlap with it. Three that are particularly significant are the countering violent extremism (CVE)/deradicalisation literature, which aims to examine and/or counter the online and offline efforts of terrorist and extremist groups (Berger and Strathearn 2013; Koehler 2017; Bjola and Pamment 2018); the countering online incivility literature, which aims to understand and/or improve the tone or 'health' of communication online (Munger 2017; Tromble n.d.; Rossini 2019; Porten-Cheé 2020); and the countering dis/misinformation literature, which aims to examine and/or reduce and correct false or fake information online (Chan et al. 2017; Porter and Wood 2019).

To deconstruct counterspeech, it is important to examine it from at least five dimensions. While at its core, counterspeech is about messaging and content, there are at least four other dimensions that need examination to fully appreciate the contours of the concept and the effort to operationalise it. These are the audiences receiving it, the goals of practitioners who employ it in relation to these audiences, the tactics used to reach these audiences, and the effects it has in relation to its audiences. The following sections first examine the audiences, goals, and tactics of counterspeech and then its messaging and effects.

Audiences, goals, and tactics

Audiences are the different groups who are exposed to hate speech and counterspeech messages but with clear differences in their relationship to these messages. Understanding the differences between audiences is critical for the effectiveness of counterspeech in achieving its goals. In general, counterspeech aims to reduce the likelihood of audiences accepting and spreading hate speech and increase the willingness of audiences to challenge and speak out against such speech (Brown 2016). In this section, four different audiences and associated counterspeech goals are considered. The audiences examined are hate groups, violent extremists, the vulnerable, and the public. Individuals can potentially transition between these groups as a result of exposure to both hate speech and counterspeech, although such shifts often involve other factors beyond message exposure.

While those creating and sharing hateful messages are likely to hold a variety of motivations for their actions, a core goal of such groups is often to grow and strengthen their in-group. The first audience that can be distinguished in this analysis, therefore, is hate groups. In the United States, the Southern Poverty Law Center (n.d.) defines hate groups as organisations with 'beliefs and practices that attack or malign an entire class of people, typically for their immutable characteristics'. Hate groups are often voluntary social groups that vary in size, strength, and organisation. While some prominent groups, such as the Ku Klux Klan, have had organised and formal structures with thousands of members (at their peak), many other hate groups are diffuse and informally organised around a common ideology. Many white supremacist hate groups in recent years, for example, can be characterised as leaderless, without formal structure, and loosely organised around a common ideology (Berger 2019; Allen 2020). In such cases, there is often no official membership, and other terms indicating affiliation, such as *supporters* and *followers*, may be more accurate. The central goal of counterspeakers and counterspeech is to reduce the size and strength of hate groups collectively and to shift the discourse and ultimately the beliefs of the individuals producing hate speech (Benesch 2014).

The internet and social media create affordances to connect individuals with similar grievances to organise much more efficiently, leading many to link the growth in hate groups to the new media ecology. Furthermore, as digital media is increasingly adopted earlier in life and consumes a greater proportion of one's time, messages received in the digital media ecosystem can begin to penetrate young people at an early age when their core beliefs and identities are forming. Within this context, hate groups use a variety of forums to reach disaffected youth and offer them kinship and a sense of belonging they may lack (Kamenetz 2018).

In recent decades, hateful ideology and state power have merged at different times and places to implement discriminatory and violent policies against perceived enemies, leading to mass atrocities and even genocide in worst-case scenarios. Hateful policy against the Tutsi and moderate Hutu in Rwanda in 1994 and against the Rohingya in Myanmar in 2017, for example, led to the extermination of 800,000 in the former case and the ethnic cleansing of 700,000 in the latter. But even outside official power, hate groups often have members willing to operationalise their beliefs with acts of violence against target groups. Hate-driven massacres in 2019 against Muslims in Christchurch, New Zealand, and against Latinos in El Paso, Texas (United States), were, for example, conducted by 'lone wolves' who carried out hate-induced acts of terror. This leads to the second audience – violent extremists – who are often sub-groups within hate groups willing to carry out violence in the name of their cause. What turns or radicalises a member or supporter of a hate group to turn into a violent extremist is a matter of much concern and research. A key goal of counterspeech is to understand these triggers and use communication to offset them as much as possible so that hate does not turn into violence.

The final group in this analysis includes everyone else who may inadvertently or intentionally come across hateful rhetoric online. This audience is called the public in this chapter. For this analysis, we exclude members of the group targeted by hate speech and counterspeakers as part of the public and instead only focus on third-party individuals who are otherwise unaffiliated with any group or audience already mentioned. The public will usually be much larger than any of the other audiences. The goal of counterspeakers is to get this audience to pay attention and ideally to engage in constructive interventions as a civic duty to assist counterspeakers in their goals. It is important to note that hate groups are not just a random set of individuals but often claim to represent a larger community with common grievances. These commonalities can be based on immutable factors like the groups targeted for hate speech, creating an 'us versus them' dynamic. By highlighting common grievances and identifying targets to blame, hate groups hope to attract support from the larger group they claim to represent. The third audience, therefore, are referred to as the vulnerable – those who have immutable similarities with hate groups and are potential future supporters. Counterspeech aims to prevent this vulnerable audience from joining or supporting hate groups through a number of different messaging strategies that try and limit them to fringe movement within the larger group they hope to represent. When discussing tactics, this chapter refers to the types of observations in which researchers or practitioners are intentionally attempting to employ counterspeech to understand its effects and prevent harm from hate speech, respectively.

To reach these audiences online, Wright et al. suggest four tactics or vectors of counterspeech: one-to-one, in which a single counterspeaker converses with another person sharing hateful messages; one-to-many, in which an individual counterspeaker reaches out to a group that is using a particular hateful term or phrase through, for example, using a hateful hashtag; many-to-one, in which many respond to a particular hateful message that may have gone viral; and finally, many-to-many, in which a conversation involving many breaks out, often over a timely or controversial topic (2017). One example of many-on-many involved the hashtag #KillAllMuslims, which trended on Twitter but was then taken over by counterspeakers who reacted on mass to challenge it, with one particular countermessage shared over 10,000 times (Wright et al. 2017).

When examining counterspeech research, it is important to distinguish amongst the different means by which such activity is observed and understood and the degree of intervention. At the one end of the spectrum are naturalist studies that involve no direct intervention. In these studies, researchers observe organic conversations between hateful speakers and counterspeakers (neither of whom may identify themselves by these labels) through gathering data on real conversations from social media feeds. At the other end of the spectrum are full experimental research studies in which one or both sides are recruited and observed communicating in an artificial environment. However, between these spaces, activists and NGOs sometimes engage in coordinated counterspeech interventions to try and reduce the perceived negative impacts of hate speech. One notable example of this type of work is the activist group *#ichbinhier* and *#jagärhär* (German and Swedish for #Iamhere). This group, which operates in a number of countries, engage in a series of activities in this regard, including counterarguing against hateful posts (Porten-Cheé 2020).

The tactical choices for reaching hateful speakers online depend to some degree on which audiences counterspeakers want to influence. In this regard, there are at least three choices. If the goal is to reach hate group members and potential violent extremists in order to change their views and behavior, going into the 'hornet's nest' and finding the spaces where they congregate is an obvious option. This can involve particular website such as 8kun (formerly 8chan) or hate groups on social media platforms, although many have been removed based on recently updated community standard guidelines (Facebook, n.d.). The second tactic involves going to mainstream news websites and social media pages and monitoring these prominent locations for hateful comments, with the goal of catching them early and limiting influence and possible recruitment of vulnerable audiences and the broader public. The third approach involves countering event-driven hate, which can surge during planned events such as elections or unexpectedly after high-profile crimes or acts of terrorism. In such scenarios, emotions can be particularly elevated as the political stakes are high, so hateful rhetoric can spread rapidly amongst not just hate groups but also vulnerable audiences who might share common grievances or prejudices. In such scenarios, counterspeakers can play a calming role and try and prevent hateful rhetoric from turning into violence. This can involve countering hateful hashtags as they emerge following critical events (Wright et al. 2017) or sending preventive 'peace text' messages promoting calm during key events or responding to false rumours. These latter activities were employed by the NGO Sisi Ni Amani Kenya during the 2013 Kenyan elections to try and prevent a repeat of the violence that marred the 2007–2008 election (Shah and Brown 2014).

Messages and effects

So far, this chapter has examined the differences between four audiences and the goals of counterspeakers for each. It has also described some tactical issues faced by counterspeakers. This section now turns to the limited counterspeech research literature and highlights some key findings. It presents these through the lens of the final two counterspeech dimensions – the messaging or content employed by counterspeaker and the effects on audiences, which are presented as five key findings.

1 Changing online norms

As scholars of media and persuasion studies have found over decades of research, it is difficult to change opinions on core beliefs through communication. This is also true for those holding prejudiced and hateful attitudes. Those who are members or supporters of hate groups, and especially those willing to share their views online, are often deeply committed to their positions. As a result, responding with views that challenge their message is unlikely to change their views. But what counterspeech appears to do, especially when it gains momentum through growing numbers of counterspeakers, is to change the online norm and reduce the tendency of people espousing hate to continue the practice in forums with less support and more opposition (Miškolci et al. 2020). For those creating and sharing hateful messages, one attraction of going online and especially of participating in forums with like-minded views, is the support, reinforcement, and sense of community. When this changes, the new environment can become uncomfortable and confrontational and more akin to the offline world in which prejudicial views are largely unpopular. In the offline world, the 'spiral of silence' theory posits that people tend to avoid sharing their opinions when such views are perceived to be unpopular due to fear of social isolation (Noelle-Neumann 1974). In a similar manner, it appears that some notable percentage of those engaging in hate speech online disengage when they sense a change in general sentiment in the online forum in which they were participating (Miškolci et al. 2020).

Furthermore, when counterspeech is introduced, others who were not part of the counterspeech efforts but are likely to oppose bigotry and hate are more likely to engage and post comment in line with the counterspeakers (Foxman and Wolf 2013; Miškolci et al. 2020; Costello et al. 2017). This may include members of the public who come across online forums with a mix of hate speech and counterspeech. It may also include vulnerable audiences who may be on the fence but ultimately swayed in the direction of what appears to be the more popular sentiment. Various studies show that those entering online spaces are influenced by the norms already present (Kramer et al. 2014; Cheng et al. 2017; Kwon and Gruzd 2017; Molina and Jennings 2018). This has been described as 'emotional contagion' in which exposure to the volume of positive or negative expression results in posts in the same emotive direction (Kramer et al. 2014).

While counterspeech, as mentioned earlier, generally involves a response to existing hate speech, there is some concern that reacting to hate speech through counterspeech might draw attention to the original message and inadvertently amplify it. To prevent this, pre-emptive counterspeech has been proposed to condition the conversation context in a way that disables possible future hate speech (Lepoutre 2019). This could involve interventions before critical events such as forums known to draw hate speech.

2 Constructive approaches are more effective

Research on the nature of counterspeech finds that 'constructive' communication is more effective at garnering engagement than disparaging responses that involve name calling and insulting hateful speakers (Benesch et al. 2016) and attempting to invoke shame or combativeness (Bruneau et al. 2018). On the one hand, a constructive approach is about tone, so casual and sentimental tone and the use of humour when appropriate can disarm the serious nature of hateful rhetoric, making those espousing it open up and feel more comfortable engaging. On the other hand, constructive approaches include particular types of content such as personal stories and calling attention to the negative consequences of hate speech (Bartlett and Krasodomski-Jones 2015; Frenett and Dow 2015; Benesch et al. 2016). A constructive approach requires a combination of critical thinking and ethical reflexivity to understand the context and underlying assumptions, biases, and prejudices of hateful speakers in formulating effective responses (Gagliardone et al. 2015).

3 Self-reflective and hypocrisy messaging are particularly effective

When it comes to counterspeech content, it is often assumed that messages that rehumanise targeted groups are most effective (Bahador 2015). This can involve individualising the target group members by challenging assumptions of homogeneity or countering stereotypes by showing, for example, that out-groups thought to 'hate us' actually have affection for our side (Bruneau et al. 2018). However, research by Bruneau et al. finds that the most effective messaging for reducing collective blame and hostility towards an out-group, in their study looking at anti-Muslim sentiment in the US, involved messaging that exposed the in-group's hypocrisy (Bruneau et al. 2018). This was done through an 'intervention tournament' in which subjects were randomly assigned to ten groups (with nine treatments involving watching a video with different messages and one control group). The 'winning' intervention involved collective blame hypocrisy messaging, which highlighted hypocrisy as individuals blamed Muslims collectively for terrorist acts committed by individual group members but not white Americans/Christians for similar acts committed by individual members. Exposure to this type of messaging resulted in reductions in collective blame of Muslims and anti-Muslim attitudes and behavior (Bruneau et al. 2018). This finding appears to lead to change because it triggers cognitive dissonance, in which individuals first support a position and then are made aware that they advocate for action that contradicts that position. One way to redress this dissonance, therefore, is to change one's prejudiced position to create cognitive consistency (Festinger 1962; Aronson et al. 1991; Bruneau et al. 2018).

4 Source credibility matters

The importance of source credibility in persuasion is not unique to counterspeech and has been advocated as far back as at least Aristotle, who saw the credibility of the speaker to the audience ('ethos') as a central component of effective rhetoric. A key part of the critical thinking needed to construct an effective counterspeech message campaign, therefore, involves having messengers who are credible to the targeted audiences one seeks to influence (Briggs and Feve 2013; Brown 2016; Munger 2017). In many cases, this requires a deep understanding of the local context as hate speech is only impactful and dangerous within particular contexts, and different speakers also hold different levels of credibility in different locations. In one study of white nationalists, for example, it was found that more response was garnered when the speaker was conservative, suggesting it was someone with some similarities to them (Briggs and Feve 2013).

5 Fact-checking can moderate views

As mentioned earlier in this chapter, hate speech against groups is almost always based on dis- or misinformation. That is because the entire groups targeted for hate are almost never wholly guilty of the purported negative actions or characteristics allocated to them. To remedy various types of misinformation, including hate speech, counterspeech based on fact-checking appears to be an obvious solution. While there is some concern that under some circumstances, challenging the views of those holding misinformed hateful views can bring more salience to them (Lepoutre 2019) or even backfire and strengthen them, there is growing evidence that such cases are rare, and fact-checking, in fact, makes people's beliefs more specific and factually accurate (Porter and Wood 2019; Nyhan et al. 2019). As a result, fact-checking could be helpful amongst the arsenal of other tools used in crafting counterspeech messages. More than likely, as other research has shown, those with deeply held beliefs will be less likely to moderate their views based on fact-based corrections. However, others who are not as deeply committed, or who hold other values that contradict the underlying values of hate speech, may be susceptible to being affected by such counter-messages.

Conclusion

This chapter has defined hate speech and counterspeech and examined the latter concept through a review of five factors that help disaggregate it – audiences, goals, tactics, messaging, and effects. Through an examination of emerging counterspeech research and practice, the chapter identifies five key findings that show that counterspeech can have some effect on audiences under particular circumstances. While these findings are novel within this context, they tap into research findings on media effects and persuasion that are already well established, such as the spiral of silence theory and cognitive dissonance. These findings are particularly relevant today as there is growing social and political concern over the role of hate speech in individual and collective acts of violence from New Zealand to Myanmar. For practitioners seeking to develop new programmes to counter hate speech without infringing on free speech rights, engaging with this new body of research can be particularly helpful, and this chapter has aimed to highlight some of the latest findings in this regard.

References

Allen, J.R. (2020) White-Supremacist Violence is Terrorism. *The Atlantic*. February 24. www.theatlantic.com/ideas/archive/2020/02/white-supremacist-violence-terrorism/606964/ (accessed April 9, 2020).

Aronson, E., Fried, C., and Stone, J. (1991) Overcoming Denial and Increasing the Intention to Use Condoms through the Induction of Hypocrisy. *American Journal of Public Health* (81): 1636–1638.

Bahador, B. (2012) Rehumanizing Enemy Images: Media Framing from War to Peace. In K.V. Korostelina (Ed.), *Forming a Culture of Peace: Reframing Narratives of Intergroup Relations, Equity and Justice*: 195–211. New York: Palgrave Macmillan.

Bahador, B. (2015) The Media and Deconstruction of the Enemy Image. In V. Hawkins and L. Hoffmann (Eds.), *Communication and Peace: Mapping an Emerging Field*: 120–132. New York: Routledge.

Bartlett, J., and Krasodomski-Jones, A. (2015) Counter-speech: Examining Content that Challenges Extremism Online. *Demos*. At: https://counterspeech.fb.com/de/wp-content/uploads/sites/4/2017/05/2015-demos-counter-speech-report-part-i-english.pdf (accessed April 1, 2020).

Benesch, S. (2013). Dangerous Speech: A Proposal to Prevent Group Violence. *Dangerous Speech Project*. At: https://dangerousspeech.org/wp-content/uploads/2018/01/Dangerous-Speech-Guidelines-2013.pdf (accessed December 18, 2018).

Benesch, S. (2014). *Defining and diminishing hate speech*. State of the World's Minorities and Indigenous Peoples 2014. Minority Rights International: 18–25. At: https://minorityrights.org/wp-content/uploads/old-site-downloads/mrg-state-of-the-worlds-minorities-2014-chapter02.pdf (accessed November 1, 2018).

Benesch, S., Ruths, D., Dillion, K.P., Saleem, H.M., and Wright, L. (2016) Considerations for Successful Counterspeech. Dangerous Speech Project. At: https://dangerousspeech.org/considerations-for-successful-counterspeech/ (accessed November 29, 2019).

Berger, J.M. (2019) *The Strategy of Violent White Supremacy Is Evolving*. August 7. www.theatlantic.com/ideas/archive/2019/08/the-new-strategy-of-violent-white-supremacy/595648/ (accessed April 1, 2020).

Berger, J.M., and Strathearn, B. (2013). Who Matters Online: Measuring Influence, Evaluating Content and Countering Violent Extremism in Online Social Networks. *The International Centre for the Study of Radicalisation and Political Violence*. At: https://icsr.info/wp-content/uploads/2013/03/ICSR-Report-Who-Matters-Online-Measuring-influence-Evaluating-Content-and-Countering-Violent-Extremism-in-Online-Social-Networks.pdf (accessed April 1, 2020).

Bjola, C., and Pamment, J. (2018) *Countering Online Propaganda and Extremism: The Dark Side of Digital Diplomacy*. London: Routledge.

Briggs, R., and Feve, S. (2013) *Countering the Appeal of Online Extremism*. Institute of Strategic Dialogue. *Policy Briefing*. At: https://www.dhs.gov/sites/default/files/publications/Countering%20the%20Appeal%20of%20Extremism%20Online-ISD%20Report.pdf (accessed November 4, 2020).

Brown, R. (2016) *Defusing Hate: A Strategic Communication Guide to Counteract Dangerous Speech*. At: www.ushmm.org/m/pdfs/20160229-Defusing-Hate-Guide.pdf (accessed April 1, 2020).

Bruneau, E., Kteily, N., and Falk, E. (2018) Interventions Highlighting Hypocrisy Reduce Collective Blame of Muslims for Individual Acts of Violence and Assuage Anti-Muslim Hostility. *Personality and Social Psychology Bulletin* 44(3): 430–448.

Buyse, A. (2014) Words of Violence: "Fear Speech," or How Violent Conflict Escalation Relates to the Freedom of Expression. *Human Rights Quarterly* 36(4): 779–797.

Carr, E.H. (2001) *The Twenty Years' Crisis*. Basingstoke: Palgrave MacMillan.

Carruthers, S. (2011) *The Media and War*. Basingstoke: Palgrave MacMillan.

Chan, M.S., Jones, C.R., Jamieson, K.H. and Albarracin, D. (2017) Debunking: A Meta-Analysis of the Psychological Efficacy of Messages Countering Misinformation. *Psychology Science* 28(11): 1531–1546.

Cheng, J., Bernstein, M. Danescu-Niculescu-Mizil, C. and Leskovec, J. (2017). Anyone Can Become a Troll: Causes of Trolling Behavior in Online Discussions. *Proceedings of the 2017 ACM Conference on Computer Supported Cooperative Work and Social Computing – CSCW'17*, 1217–1230.

Costello, M., Hawdon, J., and Cross, A. (2017). Virtually Standing Up or Standing By? Correlates of Enacting Social Control Online. *International Journal of Criminology and Sociology* (6): 16–28.

Dower, J.W. (1986) *War Without Mercy: Race and Power in the Pacific War*. New York: Pantheon Books.

Engida, G. (2015) Forward. In I. Gagliardone, D. Gal, T. Alves, and G. Martinez (Eds.), *Countering Online Hate Speech*. UNESCO Series on Internet Freedom. Paris: France. At: https://unesdoc.unesco.org/ark:/48223/pf0000233231 (accessed April 1, 2020).

Facebook (n.d.) Dangerous Individuals and Groups. *Community Standards*. At: www.facebook.com/communitystandards/dangerous_individuals_organizations (accessed April 1, 2020).

Festinger, L. (1962) *A Theory of Cognitive Dissonance* (Vol. 2). Stanford, CA: Stanford University Press.

Foxman, A.H., and Wolf, C. (2013) *Viral Hate: Containing its Spread on the Internet*. New York: Palgrave Macmillan.

Frenett, R. and Down, M. (2015) One to One Online Interventions: A Pilot CVE Methodology. *Institute for Strategic Dialogue*. At: www.isdglobal.org/wp-content/uploads/2016/04/One2One_Web_v9.pdf (accessed April 1, 2020).

Gagliardone, I., Gal, D., Alves, T., and Martinez, G. (2015) *Countering Online Hate Speech*. UNESCO Series on Internet Freedom. Paris: France. At: https://unesdoc.unesco.org/ark:/48223/pf0000233231 (accessed April 1, 2020).

Howard, J. (2019) Free Speech and Hate Speech. *Annual Review of Political Science* 22: 93–109.

Ingber, S. (1984) The Marketplace of Ideas: A Legitimizing Myth. *Duke Law Review* 1984(1): 1–91.

Kamenetz, A. (2018) Right-Wing Hate Groups are Recruiting Video Gamers. *NPR*. November 5. At: www.npr.org/2018/11/05/660642531/right-wing-hate-groups-are-recruiting-video-gamers (accessed April 1, 2020).

Keen, S. (1991) *Faces of the Enemy: Reflections on the Hostile Imagination*. San Francisco: Harper & Row.

Koehler, D. (2017) *Understanding Deradicalization: Methods, Tools and Programs for Countering Violent Extremism*. London: Routledge.

Kramer, A. D. I., Guillory, J. E., and Hancock, J. T. (2014) Experimental Evidence of Massive-Scale Emotional Contagion through Social Networks. *Proceedings of the National Academy of Sciences*, 111: 8788–8790.

Kwon, K. H., and Gruzd, A. (2017) Is Offensive Commenting Contagious Online? Examining Public vs Interpersonal Swearing in Response to Donald Trump's YouTube Campaign Videos. *Internet Research*, 27(4): 991–1010.

Langton, R. (2018) Blocking as Counter-Speech. In D. Fogal, D.W. Harris, and M. Moss (Eds.), *New Works in Speech Acts*: 144–164. Oxford: Oxford University Press.

Laub, Z. (2019). Hate Speech on Social Media: Global Comparisons. *Council on Foreign Relations*. June 7. At: www.cfr.org/backgrounder/hate-speech-social-media-global-comparisons. (accessed April 1, 2020).

Lepoutre, M. (2019) Can "More Speech" Counter Ignorant Speech? *Journal of Ethics and Social Philosophy* 16(3): 155–191.

Lickel, B., Miller, N., Stenstrom, D.M., Denson, T.F. and Schmader, T. (2006) Vicarious Retribution: The Role of Collective Blame in Intergroup Aggression. *Personality and Social Psychology Review* 10(4): 372–390.

Lombardi, C. (2019) The Illusion of the "Marketplace of Ideas" and the Right to Truth. *American Affairs* 3(1). Spring. At: https://americanaffairsjournal.org/2019/02/the-illusion-of-a-marketplace-of-ideas-and-the-right-to-truth/ (accessed April 1, 2020).

Miškolci, J., Kováčová, L., and Rigová, E. (2020) Countering Hate Speech on Facebook: The Case of the Roma minority in Slovakia. *Social Science Computer Review* 38(2): 128–146.

Molina, R.G., and Jennings, F.J. (2018) The Role of Civility and Metacommunication in Facebook Discussions. *Communication Studies* 69(1): 42–66.

Munger, K. (2017) Tweetment Effects on the Tweeted: Experimentally Reducing Racist Harassment. *Political Behavior* 39(3): 629–649.

Noelle-Neumann, E. (1974) The Spiral of Silence A Theory of Public Opinion. *Journal of Communication* 24(2): 43–51.

Nyhan, B., Porter, E., Reifler, J., and Wood, T. (2019) Taking Fact-Checks Literally But Not Seriously? The Effects of Journalistic Fact-Checking on Factual Beliefs and Candidate Favorability. *Political Behavior* (21): 1–22.

Porten-Cheé, P., Kunst, M., and Emmer, M. (2020) Online Civil Intervention: A New Form of Political Participation Under Conditions of a Disruptive Online Discourse. *International Journal of Communication* (14): 514–534.

Porter, E., and Wood, T. (2019) *False Alarm: The Truth about Political Mistruths in the Trump Era*. Cambridge: Cambridge University Press.

Rossini, P. (2019) Disentangling Uncivil and Intolerant Discourse in Online Political Talk. In R.G. Boatright, T.J. Shaffer, S. Sobieraj, and D.G. Young (Eds.), *A Crisis in Civility: Political Discourse and its Discontents*: 142–158. New York: Routledge.

Schauer, F.F. (1982) *Free Speech: A Philosophical Enquiry*. Cambridge: Cambridge University Press.

Shah, S. and Brown, R. (2014) Programming for Peace: Sisi Ni Amani Kenya and the 2013 Elections. *CGCS Occasional Paper Series on ICTs, Statebuilding, and Peacebuilding in Africa*. No. 3. December. Center for Global Communication Studies. Annenberg School of Communication. University of Pennsylvania. At: https://global.asc.upenn.edu/app/uploads/2014/12/SisiNiAmaniReport.pdf (accessed April 1, 2020).

Southern Poverty Law Center (n.d.) *What is a Hate Group?* At: www.splcenter.org/20200318/frequently-asked-questions-about-hate-groups#hate%20group (accessed April 1, 2020).

Strossen, N. (2018) *HATE: Why We Should Resist it With Free Speech, Not Censorship*. Oxford: Oxford University Press.

Tromble, R. (n.d.) *Social Media and Digital Conversations*. At: www.rebekahtromble.net/political-communication (accessed April 1, 2020).

Tucker, E. (2015) How Federal Law Draws a Line between Freedom of Speech and Hate Crimes. *PBS News Hour*. December 31. At: www.pbs.org/newshour/nation/how-federal-law-draws-a-line-between-free-speech-and-hate-crimes (accessed November 2, 2018).

United Nations (n.d.) *International Covenant on Civil and Political Rights*. At: www.ohchr.org/en/professionalinterest/pages/ccpr.aspx (accessed April 1, 2020).

United Nations Educational, Scientific and Cultural Organization (UNESCO) Constitution (n.d.) At: http://portal.unesco.org/en/ev.php-URL_ID=15244&URL_DO=DO_TOPIC&URL_SECTION=201.html (accessed April 1, 2020).

Waltman, M. S., and Mattheis, A. (2017) Understanding Hate Speech. In *Oxford Encyclopedia of Communication*. Oxford: Oxford University Press. At: https://oxfordre.com/communication/view/10.1093/acrefore/9780190228613.001.0001/acrefore-9780190228613-e-422 (accessed April 1, 2020).
Waltz, K. (1959) *Man, the State and War*. New York: Columbia University Press.
Wright, L., Ruths, D., Dillon, K.P., Saleem, H.M., and Benesch, S. (2017) *Vectors of Counterspeech on Twitter*. At: www.aclweb.org/anthology/W17-3009.pdf (accessed April 1, 2020).

48

CONSTRUCTING DIGITAL COUNTER-NARRATIVES AS A RESPONSE TO DISINFORMATION AND POPULISM

Eva Giraud and Elizabeth Poole

Over the past three decades, the relationship between digital media and activism has been subject to fraught debate. Though early promise was attached to the capacity of new media technologies to support protest (Kahn and Kellner 2004), there has also always been concern that particular forms of software and hardware can simultaneously undermine the aims of activist groups who use them. Environmental groups, for instance, have long struggled to ameliorate the carbon footprint and e-waste generated by the media they use (Pickerill 2003) while anti-capitalist movements have faced well-documented challenges in articulating their ideals in a commercial media system that can cut against their values (Barassi 2015). That said, the promise of digital media was often seen to outweigh any problems. With the rise of social media and its alleged displacement of the alternative and activist media that flourished in the 1990s and early 2000s (Juris 2008; Lievrouw 2011; Gerbaudo 2017), however, critique of mediated activism has gathered force (see Curran et al. 2016; Fuchs 2017).

A growing body of research has suggested that social media are intrinsically problematic for radical or even progressivist forms of politics, lending themselves instead to the tactics of populist and conservative groups (e.g. Schradie 2019). Yet such criticisms are not all pervasive, and other research has shown cautious optimism, pointing to ongoing potentials for digital media in general, and social media in particular, for supporting counter-public and counter-narrative formation that can challenge authoritarian populism (Jackson and Foucault Welles 2015, 2016). Though not uncritical of social media, this work has pointed to contexts in which activists have successfully negotiated tensions associated with the platforms their work is entangled with, in order to push for social change, particularly in the context of anti-racist and feminist activism (Rambukanna 2015; Kuo 2018; Clark-Parsons 2019).

In the first half of this chapter, we trace the contours of these debates, touching on broader questions of de-politicisation, counter-publics, and frictions between activism and digital media technologies. The second half of the chapter then draws together a series of case studies that drill more specifically into the relationship between populism and the mediated activism that is trying to contest it. Before we begin this overview, however, it is important to add a brief clarification; we use populism here as shorthand for a constellation of movements that have emerged in the wake of events including the election of Trump, Brexit, and the rise of the far right in European (notably Hungary and Poland), as well as other contexts (e.g. India and Brazil). What unites these disparate events and contexts is the vitriol targeted at perceived 'shared enemies' of particular (xenophobic) imaginaries of the nation-state, as manifested in the rise of racialised hate speech targeted at ethnic and religious minorities. Our overall argument is that although social media do create opportunities to contest hegemonic discourses that perpetuate the marginalisation and exclusion of those who are often the target of hate, these platforms also lend themselves to populist sentiment itself and are often used more effectively by those (broadly speaking) on the right.

Shifting narratives of mediated activism

In the 1990s a number of optimistic claims were attached to the internet in the wake of high-profile instances of its use to both critique and materially resist specific instances of neoliberal economic policy and governance. A number of political developments have resulted in digital media technologies being framed as lending themselves to anti-authoritarian, non-hierarchical politics, in part due to the flourishing of online alternative media in support of the alter-globalisation movement's push for a more just 'other' or 'alter-' globalisation (see Juris 2008).

Perhaps the most influential instance of the radical potential of digital media was found in the tactics of the Zapatista National Army of Liberation. The Zapatistas' 1994 uprising against the Mexican state garnered international awareness and solidarity after their communiqués, which connected the marginalisation and poverty of indigenous communities in Chiapas to specific transnational trade agreements such as NAFTA, were circulated via online networks such as Peacenet and Usenet (Cleaver 1997). Though the role of digital media has perhaps been overstated in ways that obscure other, more significant, aspects of the Zapatistas' tactics, they have nonetheless been hugely influential on other mediated social movements themselves and scholarship about mediated activism (e.g. Castells 1997; Hands 2011; cf Wolfson 2012).

The Zapatistas were not alone in their political aims and for the alter-globalisation movement(s) that gathered force in the 1990s and early 2000s, the internet was seen as a counter-cultural space where activists could formulate ideologies and practices that offered alternatives to dominant-socioeconomic systems (Gerbaudo 2017). The emergence of the transnational alternative news network Indymedia, for instance, was an experiment in developing a publishing infrastructure that not only documented anti-capitalist actions but was also organised in accordance with the principles of direct democracy that were central to the alter-globalisation movement (Garcelon 2006; Pickard 2006).

At the same time that Indymedia was rising in prominence, however, early forms of social media were also emerging throughout the first decade of the 2000s. These platforms grew to prominence to the extent that they were seen as displacing grassroots activist-led media. In academic contexts activist media initiatives were often declared 'failures' (Ippolita et al. 2009) in the wake of the ascendancy of 'platform capitalism' (Srnicek 2017). These socio-technical and conceptual developments have resulted in dominant academic narratives about mediated activism effectively flipping, so the internet is no longer seen as lending itself to anti-authoritarian and progressivist narratives but instead is seen as the opposite. As Jen Schradie's (2019) work on conservative US-based activism or Emiliano Treré's (2018) analysis of the authoritarian populism of Italy's Five Star movement suggests, the contemporary media environment means that those with money and power – often groups on the right – often have the necessary resources to use digital media to broadcast their views more successfully than those on the left.

The evolution of mediated counter-publics

Perhaps one of the most prominent frameworks for conceptualising these shifts has been Habermasian theories of counter-publics. Following Nancy Fraser's definition (1990), counter-publics operate as a separate (counter) public sphere, constructing alternative narratives that may not be in line with mainstream debate. While early online activism was seen as holding potential to support the formation and spread of counter-public opinion (Ruiz 2014) – even though this process was complex (Downey and Fenton 2003) – today opportunities for exerting this influence are perceived as increasingly fleeting (particularly for the left). Since the early 2000s, these issues have only intensified, and it is not just the efficacy of progressivist counter-publics that has been called into question or even their capacity to form – though these concerns have indeed been raised – but the ongoing pertinence of Habermasian theory itself.

As activism has shifted from alternative media infrastructures (developed by the activists who use them) to social media, protest is argued to have become more ephemeral. Unlike the close-knit relationship between alternative media and activist identity formation that characterised initiatives such as Indymedia and McSpotlight, social media like Twitter have served as platforms for more instantaneous forms of mobilisation in relation to specific issues. Bruns and Burgess (2011), for instance, describe how 'ad hoc' publics regularly emerge on Twitter and form collective responses to specific social and political developments (see also Dawes 2017). Rather than the collective identity-building that is necessary to sustain counter-publics, what emerges is much looser networks of individuals who coalesce temporarily around specific issues before dissipating. These dynamics are not wholly negative and have potentials as well as drawbacks (as discussed next; see also Jackson et al. 2020).

Two particular issues, however, complicate wholly positive appraisals of these tactics. Firstly, as we elucidate shortly, such approaches lend themselves to authoritarian populism as much as progressivist critiques of contemporary political development. The second complicating issue relates more to the implications of Habermasian speech ideals. Despite well-documented concerns, social media platforms still often present themselves as contributors to 'public conversation' (Poole et al. 2020); such narratives evoke a Habermasian ideal that more speech equates to good speech and that if the fragmentation created by social media could be overcome – and different voices brought together – then a healthier public sphere would emerge. What is missing from such arguments is the fact that on platforms such as Twitter, different publics are often already brought together, converging on particular hashtags to engage in debate (Siapera et al. 2018; Poole et al. 2019). Yet these engagements rarely result in dialogue and mutual understanding but instead lead to what Karlsen et al. (2017) describe as a 'trench warfare' dynamic in which pre-existing standpoints are reinforced through argumentation. Before engaging with examples that can be used to conceptualise these problems in more depth, however, it is useful to turn to a slightly different body of work that can be used to point to some more hopeful political and theoretical trajectories.

Frictions and entanglements

For all the concern about social media, as internet use has shifted from being counter-cultural to everyday (Gerbaudo 2017), there has been a growing sense that contemporary activism is necessarily entangled with technologies that might create tensions but whose use is difficult to avoid. For this reason, a growing body of work has departed from deterministic narratives about how particular media constrain or enable activism. Instead, the focus is placed on how activists navigate tensions – or 'frictions' – associated with the communications platforms their work is necessarily entangled with (Shea et al. 2015; Treré 2018; Giraud 2019).

Shea et al.'s 2015 edition of *Fibreculture*, for instance, contains a range of articles that examine moments when particular media platforms clash with the needs of activists, who are then forced to develop workarounds for these problems. Here friction is not merely a problem to be overcome but a site of agency; when confronted with tensions generated by their media use, activists are often forced to reflect critically on their practice and craft alternative ways of doing things. Commonplace tactics, for instance, included juxtaposing public-facing social media with alternative activist media or limiting how and why commercial platforms are used. These approaches have often created space for activist perspectives to be propelled to wider audiences. Others in the special edition use the concept of productive friction in a slightly different sense, in reference to discursive frictions that arise when hegemonic social norms conflict with online counter-narratives on social media (Rambukkana 2015). As with frictions associated with technologies themselves, here, too, space is often created for more critical voices to gain visibility beyond the communities from which they originate.

Although social media activism is seemingly less radical than the grassroots, participatory alternatives that inspired so much hope at the end of the millennium, therefore, perhaps it offers a slightly different hope for narratives against populism to reach beyond the activist communities in which they originate and make incursions in the public sphere. Indeed, in the examples we focus on next, these potentials have been borne out. At the same time, these platforms' concurrent use in spreading hate speech offers a reminder that any such hopes should remain modest.

Networked publics

Our own research into digital activism followed the hashtag #StopIslam on Twitter for 40 days after the Brussels terrorist attack on 22 March 2016 (resulting in a final dataset of 302,342 tweets) (Poole et al. 2019, 2020). We became interested in this hashtag after a large number of mainstream news sources (CNN, *Washington Post,* and *Nigeria News*, amongst others) reported that it was trending because people were posting counter-narratives on Twitter *against* the intention of the hashtag, which was originally formed to spread Islamophobic hate speech. Common examples of counter-narrative tweets included attempts to negate the relationship between Islam and terrorism and using memes to demonstrate peaceful messages in the Quran. We found a prevalence of these counter-narratives, particularly in the 24 hours following the terrorist attack, in terms of the most shared (or retweeted) posts using the hashtag. For example, nine out of the top ten retweets contained counter-narratives; one of these, the post that was shared the most, was retweeted 6,643 times, compared to the most shared dominant narrative (attacking Islam), which was retweeted 1,500 times.

These findings resonated with other studies, which have demonstrated how digital media platforms such as Twitter have 'technical architecture' that offers democratic potential, allowing groups who were previously marginalised from the mainstream media to form counter-publics. Jackson and Foucault-Wells's (2015, 3) study of the hashtag #myNYPD, for example, extends Fraser's (1990) work arguing that not only do online publics play a role in 'legitimising and sustaining marginalised communities', but they also 'explicitly and strategically seek to challenge the "dominant knowledge" inherent to the mainstream public sphere'.

The hashtag #myNYPD was initiated by the New York Police Department as a publicity campaign in 2014 but was quickly co-opted by online publics to highlight police misconduct against African American communities. A significant finding of this study was the importance of 'crowdsourced elites' (Papacharissi and de Fatima Oliveira 2012) in counter-public activism.

The platform's features, such as retweeting, allow for the emergence of these non-traditional leaders, who are then able to expose wider publics to alternative narratives (a dynamic they also observed in the case of #Ferguson; Jackson and Foucault Welles 2016). While Jackson and Foucault Welles found a traditional broadcast structure with a few influential individuals in their study (whom they later conceptualised as 'brokers'; 2019), these were a diverse range of actors who had previously had relatively low profiles. The hashtag therefore worked to connect disparate messages and actors, raising its visibility and meaning overall (and into the mainstream media, as explored next).

Other studies, in contrast, have shown how right-wing groups have harnessed the affordances of social media in a more structured, instrumental way than those participating in counter-narratives (Siapera et al. 2018). Our own project demonstrated how the networks of (mostly US) right-wing actors tweeting the dominant narrative of #stopIslam were much more tightly clustered around significant nodes and, through persistent and consistent use of 'flak', or what has also been known as social media mobbing (Blevins et al. 2019), were able to close down counter-narratives and afford their messages more longevity.

Likewise, Siapera et al.'s (2018, 207) work on refugees and voice on Twitter demonstrates how 'power is exercised by those who are successfully able to create, tap and steer information flows in ways to suit their goals', illustrating that right-wing groups have become particular adept at such tactics. Although the affordances of Twitter allow for the emergence of grassroots activism, this power is 'liminal', they suggest, because of the structural dynamics of Twitter, where publics coalesce around established actors and narratives. The refugee crisis, for instance, could be easily politicised by 'densely connected' US Trump supporters to garner support in the presidential race, due to its resonating with existing (negative) tropes and discourses about refugees in the mainstream media (see also Holohan 2019). Echoing these tactics, a growing body of work has pointed to the way that 'trigger events' (Copsey et al. 2013), such as terrorist attacks, are regularly used to gain visibility for extreme right views, with white supremacist groups explicitly offering guidelines about how to use news events as a means of disseminating and normalising xenophobia via social media (Siapera 2019). In addition to activists working to contest populist rhetoric on uneven discursive terrain in comparison to those perpetuating it, a number of studies have also pointed to the role of uneven levels of affective investment.

Affective labour

According to Siapera et al. (2015), the information flows that characterise online narrative and counter-narrative formation are propelled by affective investment. There has been a growth of interest in 'digital affect culture' (Evolvi 2019, 4; Wahl-Jorgensen 2019; Papacharissi 2015) and, in particular, the relationship between mediated emotional politics and the rise of populism and nationalism, evidenced by political shocks such as Brexit and the election of Donald Trump.

Multiple studies show how hashtags can be used as an ideological and organising tool for harnessing collective power (#BlackLivesMatter, #Ferguson, #Baltimoreuprising, and #myN-YPD) to raise the visibility of alternative narratives in relation to marginalised groups. However, again, the combination of affective engagement – or 'collective affect' (Abdel-Fadil 2019) – and the tightly clustered networks described earlier have also advantaged right-wing groups. Several studies note how the emotional tenor of Twitter is dominated by 'rage' (Sills 2017; Evolvi 2019). According to Wahl-Jorgensen (2019), for instance, right-wing populist groups use anger strategically (and performatively) to mobilise support through discursively constructed grievances as well as enemies, forming 'affective frames' for their arguments (Jackson and Foucault-Wells 2019). Some individuals, defined as 'stokers' by Jackson and Foucault-Wells (2019) in their analysis of the networked publics circulating #Baltimoreriots, are especially influential in this respect.

Muslims have been a particular target for this kind of hostility (see Poole 2016) and while, as outlined earlier, Twitter has opened a degree of space for anti-Islamophobic counter-narratives, it has also enabled the spread of hate speech. Drawing on Mouffe (2013), for instance, Evolvi (2019) argues that Twitter engenders 'antagonistic' interactions that limit democratic participation by seeking to exclude Muslims rather than include them in debate. Her studies of #Islamexit (Evolvi 2018) and #Brexit (2019) demonstrate how Muslims avoid confrontation with Islamophobic users.[1] This was also evident in our analysis of #stopIslam, in which any attempts at rational debate or even defensive communications by Muslims or 'would-be allies' were worn down by the tactical interventions of the right.

Discursive strategies and tactical interventions

Providing alternative frames is a key strategy for digital activists, as a number of studies have found, notably Jackson and Foucault-Welles's work on racial justice hashtags (2015, 2016, 2019; see also Jackson with Freelon et al. 2018). In the case of #Baltimoreuprising, #Ferguson, and #myNYPD, they argue that a key strategy of networked counter-publics is to shift mainstream debates about racial politics using collective power (i.e. 'network framing'). In their case studies, some of the discursive strategies used by activists (from different political positions) in the face of conflict included retweeting posts in line with their own ideologies to 'crowd out' alternative views, engagement to reconcile difference (though this was more limited), and appropriation, particularly in the case of #myNYPD.

In our own work, we suggest that the approaches used by key actors in mediated activism often serve as 'tactical interventions' (Giraud 2018; Poole et al. 2020), wherein users attempt 'to interfere in complex communication ecologies by modulating the affordances of particular media, a sort of digital weapon of the weak intended to counteract the growing power differentials in this realm' (Lezaun 2018, 224). In the case of #stopIslam, for example, activists were able to circumvent power-law effects that tend to give prominence to already well-connected actors and hegemonic opinions, but, again, populist groups used similar tactics and, indeed, were often more successful. Schradie (2019) argues that having a single message about freedom, along with more hierarchical structures, enables the right to be more effective and consolidate power (whereas we found that the topics of counter-narratives tended to be somewhat more diverse).

In the case of #stopIslam, for instance, although the most prominent retweets circulating with this hashtag were counter-narratives (supporting Muslims), the way they were framed generated tensions that undermined their aims (Poole et al. 2020). Most of the counter-narratives used generalised criticisms of hate speech to contest #stopIslam, defending Muslims and Islam and criticising Islamophobia, often using memes to underline their points, including quotes from the Quran. However, this approach left openings for self-identified right-wing Twitter users to undermine them with more specific counter-evidence. This approach (using 'alternative facts' often sourced from influential right-wing websites) and the frequency with which the right responded to the counter-narratives had the paradoxical effect of the counter-narratives contributing to the greater circulation of the hate speech they sought to contest. In this case attempts to appropriate right-wing propaganda (#stopIslam) were, in turn, 'hijacked' by the right to reinscribe representational inequalities.

It is also important to note that participation in counter-narratives was not equally open to all; some of these counter-narratives were circulated by (self-identified) Muslims, although they were less visible than other voices (15.8 percent of 4,263 retweets examined through manual quantitative analysis). This could be strategic, given the hazards attached to making identity claims online; these tweets received more flak than others, and so most Muslims did not attempt to engage with any Islamophobic responses (also, potentially, to curtail further circulation). However, there was evident of *support* from Muslims for some counter-narratives, particularly to those posted on celebrity accounts, with many Muslims offering thanks for this. Eckert et al. (2019) suggest that Muslims constitute 'hyper differential counter-publics' precisely because they have to navigate difficult and shifting environments, creating 'hyper-situational responses'.

Responses to counter-narratives (in the form of comments) were much more likely to be in line with the original intention of the hashtag, with minimal interaction from more progressive voices. Right-wing actors used tactics that included disputing, dismissing, and refuting the claims of counter-narrative tweets, as well as defending their own ideological positions. Additional tactics included appropriation, affirmation, and sarcasm to disrupt the counter-narrative hijacking of their hashtag. Affirmation through volume was a typical response; sharing memes using sarcasm and humour is a well-documented characteristic of Twitter content and often functions to complicate and legitimise racist discourse (Brock and Brooker cited in Sharma and Brooker 2016). The appropriation of international news items to reinforce agendas also contributes authority to the right's 'evidence-based' approach. The dynamics of this hashtag demonstrate the tensions generated in trying to counter right-wing activism online without further reproducing existing inequalities by opening up avenues for further disinformation to be propagated.

Conclusion: understanding populist media ecologies

Despite tensions generated by social media, existing studies show how the collective labour and contestation that gives alternative narratives visibility online also translates to mainstream media. The newsworthy element of hashtag campaigns being 'hijacked' has led to prominent media organisations reporting on this trend in the case of #stopIslam, #Muslimrage, #GazaUnderAttack, #Ferguson, #myNYPD, #Baltimoreuprising, and, in particular, #BlackLivesMatter. Far from operating in echo chambers, then, these studies show how Twitter debates can cut across a range of social issues, intersectional identities, geographical localities, and media platforms.

However, once noticed in the mainstream public sphere, counter-narratives can be subject to criticism. Even online, dominant publics monopolise (with whiteness at the centre of internet use; Nakamura 2002) and re-establish hegemonies through strategies such as social media mobbing. Populism itself has been successful in taking advantage of a 'hybrid media system', circulating material from extreme right sources on social media with the aim of normalising these values (Siapera 2019). In the case of #stopIslam, the tightly structured networks of the right combined with the structural constraints of the platform not only undermined the longevity and coherence of counter-narratives but also subtly modulated the affordances of Twitter in ways that enabled these users to extend their voice outwards (by navigating Twitter's policies on hate speech through the appropriation of mainstream media stories, for example). A further issue with counter-narratives is that they remain reactionary and so can sometimes be counterproductive in contributing to the continued circulation of stereotypical tropes, reinforcing them by seeking to prove otherwise and thus inadvertently opening up spaces where racism is presented as something that can be 'debated' (Titley 2019). For example, encouraging Muslims to condemn actions of political violence also allows dominant groups to frame the discourse around their representation (Law et al. 2018). Hence, we should be considering how progressive groups might be instrumental in constructing alternative narratives rather than seeking to contest hate speech.

Overall, the studies touched on here demonstrate how the digital and mainstream media are not separate discursive spheres but critically intersect, and therefore, it is necessary to study the relations within these media ecologies. While digital spaces offer marginalised communities some opportunities to claim social power, we should remember that they are located in socio-political systems where the distribution of power is unequal; hence, structural inequalities tend to be reproduced online. Due to its organisational power, black Twitter has been somewhat successful in being able to reframe media discourse about specific events; for counter-narratives about Muslims to succeed, however, according to Law et al. (2018, 14), these networks must be mobilised to ensure that the 'core political, media and populist value that Islamophobia is . . . exposed, denigrated, dismantled and de-normalised'.

Note

1 This is not to suggest Muslims are a homogenous group but that they often share similar political positions in the face of Islamophobic attacks.

References

Abdel-Fadil, M. (2019). The politics of affect: The glue of religious and identity conflicts in social media. *Journal of Religion, Media and Digital Culture*, 8(1), 11–34.

Barassi, V. (2015). *Activism on the web: Everyday struggles against digital capitalism*. London: Routledge.

Blevins, J.L., Lee, J.J., McCabe, E.E. and Edgerton, E. (2019). Tweeting for social justice in #Ferguson: Affective discourse in Twitter hashtags. *New Media and Society*, 1–18. DOI: 10.1177/1461444819827030

Bruns, A and Burgess, J. (2011). The use of Twitter hashtags in the formation of Ad hoc publics. In *Proceedings of the 6th European Consortium for Political Research (ECPR) General Conference 2011*, University of Iceland, Reykjavik. Available from: https://eprints.qut.edu.au/46515/

Castells, M. (1997). *The information age: The power of identity*. Oxford: Blackwell Publishing.

Clark-Parsons, R. (2019). "I SEE YOU, I BELIEVE YOU, I STAND WITH YOU": # MeToo and the performance of networked feminist visibility. *Feminist Media Studies*, 1–19. DOI: 10.1080/14680777.2019.1628797

Cleaver, H. (1997). The Zapatistas and the electronic fabric of struggle. Available from: www.schoolsforchiapas.org/wp-content/uploads/2014/07/HarryCleaver.pdf

Copsey, N., Dack, J., Littler, M. and Feldman, M. (2013). *Anti-Muslim hate crime and the far right*. Middlesbrough: Teeside University.

Curran, J., Fenton, N. and Freedman, D. (2016). *Misunderstanding the internet*. London: Routledge.

Dawes, S. (2017). #JeSuisCharlie, #JeNeSuisPasCharlie and ad hoc publics. In G. Titley., D. Freedman., G. Khiabany, and A. Mondon (Eds.), *After Charlie Hebdo* (pp. 180–191). London: Zed Books.

Downey, J. and Fenton, N. (2003). New media, counter publicity and the public sphere. *New Media & Society*, 5(2), 185–202.

Eckert, S., Metzger-Riftkin, J., Kolhoff, S. and O'Shay-Wallace, S. (2019). A *hyper differential counterpublic*: Muslim social media users and Islamophobia during the 2016 US presidential election. *New Media and Society*. DOI: 10.1177/1461444819892283

Evolvi, G. (2018). #Islamexit: Inter-group antagonism on Twitter. *Information, Communication & Society*, 22(3), 386–401.

Evolvi, G. (2019). Emotional politics, Islamophobic Tweets: The Hashtags #Brexit and #chiudiamoiporti. *PArtecipazione eCOnflitto: The Open Journal of Sociopolitical Studies*, 12(3). DOI: 10.1285/i20356609v12i3p871

Fraser, N. (1990). Rethinking the public sphere: A contribution to the critique of actually existing democracy. *Social Text*, 25/26, 56–80.

Freelon, D., Clark, M., Jackson, S.J. and Lopez, L. (2018). *How Black Twitter and other social media communities interact with mainstream news*. Knight Foundation. Available from: https://knightfoundation.org/features/twittermedia/

Fuchs, C. (2017). *Social media: A critical introduction*, 2nd edition. London: Sage.

Garcelon, M. (2006). The Indymedia 'experiment': The Internet as movement facilitator against institutional control. *Convergence*, 12(1), 55–82.

Gerbaudo, P. (2017). From Cyber-Autonomism to Cyber-Populism: An ideological analysis of the evolution of digital activism. *TripleC: Communication, Capitalism & Critique*. 15(2), 477–489.

Giraud, E. (2018). Displacement, 'failure' and friction: Tactical interventions in the communication ecologies of anti-capitalist food activism. In T. Schneider., K. Eli., C. Dolan, and S. Ulijaszek (Eds.), *Digital food activism* (pp. 48–68). New York and London: Routledge.

Giraud, E. (2019). *What comes after entanglement? Activism, anthropocentrism and an ethics of exclusion.* Durham, NC: Duke University Press.

Hands, J. (2011). *@ is for activism: Dissent, resistance and rebellion in a digital culture.* London: Pluto Press.

Holohan, S. (2019). Some human's rights: Neocolonial discourses of Otherness in the Mediterranean refugee crisis. *Open Library of Humanities*, 5(1). Available from: https://olh.openlibhums.org/articles/10.16995/olh.423/

Ippolita, Lovink, G. and Rossiter, N. (2009). The digital given: 10 web 2.0 theses. *The Fibreculture Journal*, 14. Available from: http://journal.fibreculture.org/issue14/issue14_ippolita_et_al_print.html

Jackson, S.J., Bailey, M. and Foucault Welles, B. (2020). *#HashtagActivism: Networks of race and gender justice.* Cambridge, MA: MIT Press.

Jackson, S.J. and Foucault Welles, B. (2015). Hijacking #myNYPD: Social media dissent and networked counterpublics. *Journal of Communication*, 65(6), 932–952.

Jackson, S.J. and Foucault Welles, B. (2016). #Ferguson is everywhere: Initiators in emerging counterpublic networks. *Information, Communication & Society*, 19(3), 397–418.

Jackson, S.J. and Foucault Welles, B. (2019). The battle for #Baltimore: Networked publics and the contested framing of urban unrest. *Journal of Communication*, 13, 1–21.

Juris, J.S. (2008). *Networking futures: The movements against corporate globalization.* Durham, NC: Duke University Press.

Kahn, R. and Kellner, D. (2004). New media and internet activism: From the 'Battle of Seattle' to blogging. *New Media & Society*, 6(1), 87–95.

Karlsen, R., Steen-Johnsen, K., Wollebæk, D. and Enjolras, B. (2017). Echo chamber and trench warfare dynamics in online debates. *European Journal of Communication*, 32(3), 257–273.

Kuo, R. (2018). Racial justice activist hashtags: Counterpublics and discourse circulation. *New Media & Society*, 20(2), 495–514.

Law, I., Easat-Daas, A. and Sayyid, S. (2018). *Counter-Islamophobia kit: Briefing paper and toolkit of counternarratives to Islamophobia.* Available from: https://cik.leeds.ac.uk/wp-content/uploads/sites/36/2018/09/2018.09.17-Job-44240.01-CIK-Final-Booklet.pdf

Lezaun, J. (2018). The public's two bodies: Food activism in digital media. In T. Schneider., K. Eli., C. Dolan, and S. Ulijaszek (Eds.), *Digital food activism* (pp. 220–227). London: Routledge.

Lievrouw, L. (2011). *Alternative and activist new media.* Cambridge: Polity Press.

Mouffe, C. (2013). Agonistics: Thinking the world politically. London and New York: Verso.

Nakamura, L. (2002). *Cybertypes: Race, ethnicity and identity on the internet.* New York: Routledge.

Papacharissi, Z. (2015). *Affective publics: Sentiment, technology, and politics.* Oxford: Oxford University Press.

Papacharissi, Z. and de Fatima Oliveira, M. (2012). Affective news and networked publics: The rhythms of news storytelling on #Egypt. *Journal of Communication*, 62(2), 266–282.

Pickard, V.W. (2006). United yet autonomous: Indymedia and the struggle to sustain a radical democratic network. *Media, Culture & Society*, 28(3), 315–336.

Pickerill, J. (2003). *Cyberprotest: Environmental activism online.* Manchester: Manchester University Press.

Poole, E. (2016). The United Kingdom's reporting of Islam and Muslims: Reviewing the Field. In S. Mertens and H. de Smaele (Eds.), *Representations of Islam in the news* (pp. 21–36). London: Lexington Books.

Poole, E., Giraud, E. and de Quincey, E. (2019). Contesting #stopIslam: The dynamics of a counternarrative against hate speech. *Open Library of Humanities*, 5(1), 1–39.

Poole, E., Giraud, E. and de Quincey, E. (2020). Tactical interventions in online hate speech: The case of #stopIslam. *New Media and Society*. DOI: 10.1177/1461444820903319

Rambukanna, N. (2015). From #racefail to #Ferguson: The digital intimacies of race-activist hashtag publics. *The Fibreculture Journal*, 26. Available from: http://twentysix.fibreculturejournal.org/fcj-194-from-racefail-to-ferguson-the-digital-intimacies-of-race-activist-hashtag-publics/

Ruiz, P. (2014). *Articulating dissent: Protest and the public sphere.* London: Pluto Press.

Schradie, J. (2019). *The revolution that wasn't: How digital activism favors Conservatives*. Cambridge, MA: Harvard University Press.

Sharma, S. and Brooker, P. (2016). #notracist: Exploring racism denial talk on Twitter. In J. Daniels, K. Gregory, and T. McMillan Cottom (Eds.), *Digital sociologies* (pp. 459–481). Bristol: Policy Press.

Shea, P., Notley., T. and Burgess, J. (2015). Entanglements – activism and technology: Editors' introduction. *Fibreculture Journal*, 26, 1–6. Available from: http://twentysix.fibreculturejournal.org/

Siapera, E. (2019). Organised and ambient digital racism: Multidirectional flows in the Irish digital sphere. *Open Library of Humanities*, 5(1), 13.

Siapera, E., Boudourides, M., Lenis, S. and Suiter, J. (2018). Refugees and network publics on Twitter: Networked framing, affect, and capture. *Social Media and Society*, 1, 1–21. DOI: 10.1177/2056305118764437

Siapera, E., Hunt, G. and Lynn, T. (2015). #GazaUnderAttack: Twitter, Palestine and diffused war. *Information, Communication & Society*, 18(11), 1217–1319.

Sills, L. (2017). Hashtag comedy: From Muslim rage to #Muslimrage. *ReOrient*, 2(2), 160–174.

Srnicek, N. (2017). *Platform capitalism*. Cambridge: Polity Press.

Titley, G. (2019). *Racism and the media*. London: Sage.

Treré, E. (2018). *Hybrid media activism: Ecologies, imaginaries, algorithms*. London: Routledge.

Wahl-Jorgensen, K. (2019). *Emotions, media and politics*. London: Polity Press.

Wolfson, T. (2012). From the Zapatistas to Indymedia: Dialectics and orthodoxy in contemporary social movements. *Communication, Culture & Critique*, 5(2), 149–170.

49

JOURNALISTIC RESPONSES TO MISINFORMATION

Maria Kyriakidou and Stephen Cushion

Asking how journalists respond to misinformation might, in theory, appear unnecessary. After all, the 'discipline of verification' is widely viewed as being the essence of journalism (Kovach & Rosenstiel 2007, 71). Establishing the veracity of an event or issue and accurately informing the public about it are ultimately the basic principles of journalism. They are deeply ingrained in the 'fourth estate role' the news media play in holding power to account and exposing abuses of authority. However, over recent decades, attempts to manipulate information and deceive the public have become ever more sophisticated, renewing the urgency of the demands placed on journalists to respond to and counter misinformation and disinformation.

False or misleading information circulates on social media, creating misconceptions and undermining public understanding of a wide range of issues. In the early months of the COVID-19 pandemic, for example, false news spread as quickly as the pandemic itself on social media, notably in closed private platforms such as WhatsApp (Brennen et al. 2020). Such fake news, irrespective of its absurdity or source, is hard for journalists to ignore as it is reproduced by partisan and online news media, infiltrating and influencing public discourse (Vargo et al. 2018). At the same time, disinformation is also produced and circulated by politicians and other public figures at the forefront of political reporting (Satariano & Tsang 2019). Failing to challenge these tactics of manipulation can turn journalists into amplifiers of political propaganda. Meanwhile, the distraction of public agendas by false and misleading stories, attacks on established media by populist leaders as 'fake news', and increasing political polarisation contribute to the slow erosion of public trust in the media (IPSOS 2019). It is against this backdrop that journalists are called upon not only to report 'the truth' about current affairs but also to report on and challenge any misinformation or disinformation they encounter. This is necessary for the protection of both civic discourse and journalistic legitimacy.

In this context, academic attention has turned to exploring the ways journalism can be renewed for public good, identifying how and where disinformation or misinformation can be countered by journalists. In this chapter we review the arguments made for the evolution of journalistic practices in the face of these challenges. Although we mostly use the term *misinformation* throughout the chapter to refer to the spreading of false or inaccurate information, we understand the concept as being distinct from disinformation, which describes the dissemination of deliberately false information (Wardle 2018). Despite their significant differences, both types of 'information disorder' (Wardle 2018) potentially mislead and influence people, as well as shape media agendas, undermining public debate. The news media, in this context, have an important role to play in establishing the facts and identifying and challenging misinformation, in order to safeguard the quality of information and maintain journalistic standards in the face of public mistrust.

Although the issues and developments addressed in this chapter are affecting journalists at the global level, we primarily focus in this chapter on the UK context and, in particular, the challenges of reporting misinformation in public service media, defined by obligations to report accurately and impartially. After first introducing how journalism has attempted to address the challenges of misinformation, the second section turns to the British context and examines the ways UK journalists have dealt with contemporary mis/disinformation campaigns. The final section will address the challenges associated with effectively countering and communicating misinformation in ways that might, we argue, reinforce and promote public legitimacy in journalism.

Changing journalistic practices

The acknowledgement of disinformation as a new challenge for journalism is reflected in recently updated training and educational initiatives. UNESCO (2018), for example, published its 'Journalism, Fake News and Disinformation' handbook on the assumption that misinformation has constructed new conditions for journalism, requiring new skills and training. Besides the development of digital skills, in order to verify social media sources and content' and fact check and combat online abuse, the handbook also focuses on definitions of *truth, disinformation, misinformation,* and *fake news* inviting journalists to rethink these concepts in the context of new technological, sociocultural, and normative developments. The need for this renewal and re-focus of journalistic attention stems from the fear that mis/disinformation not only renders news journalism malleable to hoaxes and political manipulation but also contributes to the weakening of public trust in the media. In this context, it is argued that journalism needs to take up a new mission to 'proactively detect and uncover new cases and forms of disinformation' (UNESCO 2018, 11).

This call to take proactive action entails a number of suggestions for the improvement of journalistic practices. Transparency takes a central place in such debates as a tool for increasing accountability and, by extension, public trust in journalism. Understood as openness in how journalists work, both by providing explanations about how news is made and inviting the public to partake in news-making (Karlsson & Clerwall 2018, 1923–1924), transparency has been approached with renewed interest by academics and journalists as a way of tackling misinformation and its challenges. Relevant initiatives include publicly verifying sources and facts, asking news readers to help with fact-checking, and explaining and showing audiences the processes of fact-checking. This openness about how news media deal with misinformation can allow journalists to either 'publicly and swiftly respond to valid critiques of their work' (UNESCO 2018, 60) or pre-emptively address any criticisms. However, although such initiatives are on the rise and have been recommended as part of an effort to regain public trust, recent research has suggested that news audiences are indifferent to journalistic transparency and even evaluate negatively user participation in the news (Karlsson & Clerwall 2018).

One long-standing practice that has been criticised in light of debates about journalists effectively countering disinformation is the 'he said, she said' approach to reporting, which has long been employed as a way of constructing balanced reporting, allowing for at least two sides of a story to be heard. Such a way of approaching every issue, however, can lead to false equivalence by framing the debate in misleading ways that can undermine the evidence or scientific basis of an issue. The convention of the 'he said, she said' reporting style has been criticised for enabling the spread of mis/disinformation in debates about vaccines (Nyhan 2013), climate change (Boykoff & Boykoff 2007), and the Brexit referendum (Damazer 2019). Even when journalists point out the facts that discredit fringe claims, the framing of the issue as a genuine debate has long-term consequences, legitimising falsehoods as valid opinions. Attempts to balance reporting in the style of 'he said, she said' can help inoculate journalists from accusations of bias, but it can also add to public confusion.

Actively resisting the practice of false balance (Amazeen 2019), the use of fact-checking has become a significant journalistic weapon in the fight against mis/disinformation. Of course, journalists have always sought to verify facts. But it is the concerted focus on determining the accuracy and truthfulness of claims, notably from political elites, that characterises fact-checking initiatives (Amazeen 2019, 543). The essence of fact-checking is the reporting of mis/disinformation itself; it aims to proactively detect and uncover it. This distinguishes it from traditional internal fact-checking in news organisations, which aims to verify reporters' sources in order to correct mistakes and falsehoods before the publication of a story (Graves 2016, 7). Fact-checking has been broadly celebrated as a professional movement of a 'new style of political news' that revitalises traditional journalism by holding public figures accountable for spreading disinformation and falsehoods (Graves 2016, 6). Not only can it act as a journalistic mechanism of accountability; it also constitutes a tool to help the public navigate through misinformation and falsehoods circulating in high-choice media environments. It is viewed as a central development in restoring public trust in journalism and enhancing the quality of public debate.

This turn to a proactive style of exposing falsehoods is not new as the first fact-checking organisations emerged in the US in the early 2000s, with the website FactCheck launching in 2003 and PolitiFact and Fact Checker following four years later (Graves 2016). What has been renewed in recent years, as sources of misinformation multiply in numbers and expand in reach, is the interest in fact-checking as a tool for countering disinformation in routine news reporting. This entails the move of fact-checking from the margins of independent initiatives to established media organisations. However, fact-checking is still largely discussed separately from the conventions and practices of mainstream journalism, considered to overlap with, but distinctive from, the day-to-day role of being a professional journalist. This discussion is arguably skewed by US-centric research on fact-checking (Nieminen & Rapeli 2019, 306) as American fact-checking is characterised by a distinction between professional and partisan fact-checkers, as well as the proximity of the field to academic and non-profit organisations (Graves 2016). As fact-checking initiatives soar around the world, they also display wide variations, expressive of the journalistic and political cultures within which they are embedded.

As of April 2020, according to the Duke Reporters' Lab, there are 237 fact-checking organisations in nearly 80 countries (Stencel & Luther 2020). The differences among these organisations vary from their form and style of reporting – such as the use of rating systems to rank false claims – to substantial institutional characteristics, including levels of professionalism and funding sources. In some countries, fact-checking is conducted by the 'fifth estate' of bloggers, activists, academics, and NGOs (UNESCO 2018, 10). In others, fact-checking initiatives are embedded within and operated by legacy media (Graves & Cherubini 2016). This is the case in the UK, with some of the most prominent fact-checking produced by public service broadcasters. It is this journalistic context that the next section focuses on.

Reporting misinformation and journalism in the UK

If the election of Donald Trump in 2016 was a key moment in the US for alerting the public to the consequences of disinformation and fake news on democracy, the EU referendum campaign a few months later had similar repercussions in the UK. The now-infamous claim of the Leave campaign that the UK sends the EU £350 million per week has become emblematic of a campaign rife with mis/disinformation. Tabloid newspapers actively participated in the spread of such misinformation (Bennhold 2017), continuing a long-held tradition of hyperbolic and misleading reporting. Other media, however, have taken active steps against misinformation. Having already launched a Reality Check section in 2011, *The Guardian*, for example, introduced a regular 'Factcheck' feature assessing all political claims during the 2019 election campaign. Sky News introduced a similar 'Campaign Check' section on its website, which often featured on their television news coverage. The news channel also launched the 'Under the Radar' project with the aim of tracking political activity, advertising on social media during the campaign, and identifying possible disinformation (Manthorpe 2019). The broadcaster, as well as other major news media in the UK, such as *The Independent* and *The Telegraph*, have also cooperated with Full Fact, an independent fact-checking service, to check the validity of stories and report on misinformation during the election campaign and beyond (Graves & Cherubini 2016). Full Fact, the UK's largest fact-checker, launched in 2010 and is a registered charity with trustees who include journalists as well as members of the main political parties (Graves & Cherubini 2016, 11).

The most evidently active position against misinformation and disinformation, however, has been taken by the two main public service broadcasters: the BBC and Channel 4, which have established their own fact-checking services. BBC Reality Check started with somewhat limited resources in 2015, only to be reinvigorated during the run-up to the Brexit referendum in 2016 (Graves & Cherubini 2016, 9). Since then, and in the aftermath of the Brexit vote and its preceding campaign, a permanent BBC editorial team was allocated to Reality Check in 2017 (Samuels 2017). Channel 4 launched FactCheck, the first initiative of political fact-checking in Europe, as a blog covering the 2005 general election and turned it into a permanent feature in 2010 (Graves & Cherubini 2016, 6). Both fact-checking initiatives position themselves as watchdogs of political actors and their claims, with BBC Reality Check describing its mission as 'cut[ting] through the spin and concentrat[ing] on the facts' (BBC RealityCheck n.d.), whereas FactCheck is 'testing the claims of people in power' (FactCheck n.d.). They are, together with Full Fact, the main fact-checkers in the UK and the only ones bound to impartiality due to their public service status.

As their relatively short and rather fragmented history illustrates, Reality Check and FactCheck gain significance during election periods and moments of crisis. Both fact-checkers extensively challenged the Leave campaign's 'bus claim' of the UK saving £350 million per week both before and after the referendum. These fact-checks were further broadcast and discussed in the main news bulletins of the respective channels (Goss & Renwick 2016). During the 2016 election campaign, despite accusations and perceptions of political bias by mainstream media against the Labour leadership (Cammaerts 2016), the evidence suggests fact-checkers paid fairly even-handed attention to both Labour's and Conservatives' claims (Birks 2019b, 52) and effectively questioned official claims and reports on crucial campaign issues (Birks 2019b, 77). In the 2019 snap election, Reality Check and FactCheck were given regular slots on flagship news programmes (Birks 2019a). During the COVID-19 pandemic, both Reality Check and Channel 4 focused almost exclusively on the health crisis, regularly updating their content and challenging misinformation (Cushion 2020).

Allocating resources and attention to fact-checking during periods of crisis can be seen as part of the public service mission of BBC and Channel 4 and their commitment to providing citizens with facts, set apart from misinformation and spin (Jackson 2017). Both Reality Check and FactCheck, however, are mostly online operations at present, with dedicated websites and Twitter accounts. When Reality Check was set up as a permanent feature, the then-director of BBC News, James Harding, committed to turning the fact-checking service to 'more than a public service, we want it to be hugely popular. We will aim to use styles and formats – online, on TV and on radio – that ensure the facts are more fascinating and grabby than the falsehoods' (Jackson 2017). Despite informing some broadcast news programming, especially during election campaigns, how extensively and effectively television news draw upon their fact-checkers remains open to question. This relationship is not necessarily straightforward, no less because online content does not easily translate into broadcasting, which does not favour contextual information or hyperlinks (Mantzarlis 2016). For fact-checking to reach mass audiences, broadcasting will need to find more creative ways to embed it in its routine conventions and practices. At the same time, fact-checkers have sought to make their presence stronger on social media platforms so that they reach and appeal to younger generations. Channel 4, for example, has a series of YouTube videos titled 'FactCheck Explains', while Chris Morris, the main Reality Check presenter, makes occasional appearances on BBC News's Instagram account with short videos and explainers.

The growth of fact-checking journalism within public service broadcasters represents an important development. Unless reported by the media, independent fact-checking remains significant only for an engaged and, most likely, educated minority. In their mission to influence public discourse and increase their reach and impact, fact-checking organisations depend on their relationship with established news media (Graves & Cherubini 2016, 25). At the same time, fact-checkers try to avoid having their material used by partisan media for political purposes (Graves & Cherubini 2016, 25–26). In this context, public service media and fact-checking are ideal partners, due to their commitment to impartiality. In contrast to many independent fact-checkers, public service broadcasters, such as the BBC and Channel 4, have more resources and a bigger platform to communicate their challenging of misleading claims and disinformation. They are well placed to move fact-checking from the margins to a mainstream source of information, news, and analysis.

Such developments represent a way of enhancing journalistic legitimacy and reinvigorating trust in public service broadcasters. While ostensibly criticising public actors for their misleading or false claims, independent fact-checkers also constitute a thinly veiled, if not explicit, critique of mainstream media and their assumed failure to directly engage with such claims and point out their falsehood. If fact-checking is only referred to as external to mainstream journalists, this can further undermine trust in established media institutions (UNESCO 2018, 11). The adoption of fact-checking services and practices by public service broadcasters can be seen as an indication of legacy media utilising this critique by bringing fact-checking where 'it has always belonged, at the heart of good journalism' (Full Fact 2019).

Despite high levels of trust in public service broadcasting in the UK (Nielsen et al. 2020), recent political developments have left a bitter aftertaste about the role of broadcasting in reporting politics in a 'post-truth' era. In the aftermath of the Brexit vote, in particular, and despite the work of fact-checkers before the referendum (Goss & Renwick 2016; Mantzarlis 2016), debates often focused on mainstream media not doing enough to rigorously challenge disinformation during election campaigns (Sambrook 2016). In strengthening their fact-checking services and placing them centrally in their news reporting, public service broadcasters appear to be taking the countering of misinformation more seriously.

Challenges in reporting misinformation

Public service broadcasters, however, face a number of challenges in reporting misinformation. The first has to do with maintaining a balanced and impartial news service while also making clear judgments about the veracity of claims and counter-claims. Analysis of the 2017 general election coverage discovered that 67 percent of fact-checks included a clear verdict about the validity of the claims examined; the rest were mostly 'explainers', 'similar to news analysis articles in mainstream journalism' (Birks 2019b, 41). When the analysis was undertaken again during the 2019 election campaign, the decisiveness of fact-checking verdicts increased (Birks 2019c). But the research revealed both the difficulties in unpacking non-factual claims that are part of an election campaign and the reluctance of public service media to 'label' politicians 'as liars', leaving that 'judgement for audiences to make about an individual's motives' (Jordan 2019). Without explaining the reasoning behind claims, however, and being limited to narrow empirical clarifications, fact-checking can do little to improve the quality of public debate (Birks 2019b, 83). Furthermore, in attempting to treat political parties impartially and pay equal attention to dubious statements, journalists risk constructing a false equivalence between competing claims. Such an approach can contribute to the public's feeling of mistrust and helplessness about understanding which political actors and parties lie to them the most (Rosen 2009).

A second challenge has to do with the choice of claims being fact-checked. This is a difficulty intrinsic in fact-checking as a journalistic practice. Narrow empirical facts, such as the numbers of hospitals being built by the government (Hutchison & Murray 2019), are far easier to fact-check than broad promises such as 'getting Brexit done' (Morris 2019). While fact-checking empirical facts is important, it does sometimes overlook the ways these facts are being employed in political argumentation. The political significance of facts is defined by the political context within which they are instrumentalised. In our view, fact-checking could do more to engage with both in order to help the public understand competing political claims. Furthermore, research suggests broadcasters focus largely on fact-checking political claims, especially during election campaigns, which is of limited scope. Moreover, this focus can reproduce elite discourses (Birks 2019b, 92) while ignoring the politics of everyday life. Political misinformation is not restricted to campaign promises or statements of the most prominent politicians. Furthermore, misinformation and fake news are proliferating in social media and online partisan media (Vargo et al. 2018) and play an important role in public understandings of politics. Neglecting this type of misinformation dismisses the diversity of ways media users become informed about the world and risks further alienating the public from legacy media. Identifying and challenging such types of misinformation, however, is a difficult task for public service broadcasters.

The call for a more alert approach to journalism, exemplified by but not restricted to fact-checking, rests, of course, on the assumption that such a development will have a positive impact on public knowledge and engagement with politics. Research on the efficacy of such journalistic practices, however, is inconclusive. Public misperceptions do not seem to always be the result of misinformation. Experiments have shown that people engage with motivated reasoning when confronted with misinformation (Schaffner & Roche 2017) and are, therefore, prone to reject corrective messages that challenge their worldview (Lewandowsky et al. 2012). Exposure to misinformation may cause 'belief echoes' that remain, even when misinformation is corrected, because of the reasoning that 'where there's smoke, there's fire' (Thorson 2016, 461). Despite, for example, fact-checkers' producing clear-cut judgments that the UK does not send £350 million per week to the EU, nearly half the British public still believed the claim days before the EU referendum vote (Stone 2016). Birks has shown how, during the 2017 general election campaign, accusations of bias against @BBCRealityCheck by Twitter users were expressive of motivated reasoning and a broader mistrust of the BBC overall as, in some cases, it was evident that these users had not even read the tweets they were attacking (Birks 2019b, 56).

At the same time, however, evidence shows that people tend to have more favourable attitudes towards the media when fact-checking is employed (Amazeen 2019, 543). Research also suggests people have generally positive views of fact-checking and that randomised exposure to it helps them become better informed (Nyhan & Reifler 2015). Despite the inconsistencies of the findings and the mostly experimental nature of the research, there is evidence that particular forms of fact-checking can be more effective than others (Thorson 2016). Adopting a more forensic approach to fact-checking in day-to-day news reporting represents a longer-term process of change in journalism. As a consequence, how audiences respond to new conventions and practices will be understood in the longer term, rather than in relation to short-term effects that many fact-checking studies measure.

Conclusion

The challenges described in this chapter are not unique to public service broadcasting nor should they be approached as being confined to fact-checking. In the critical juncture of the current disinformation order, the reporting of disinformation and misinformation should take centre stage in all types of professional journalism. This is not only necessary for holding the powerful to account but also essential in safeguarding journalistic legitimacy. The circulation of misleading information in the public sphere has grave consequences not only for manipulating public opinion and influencing political choices but also for corroding over time public trust in news media, reproducing a culture of cynicism and mistrust. In high-choice and polyphonic media environments, journalists need to convince the public that they hold the cultural authority to identify and challenge falsehoods in order to help them understand contemporary politics.

The role of research is also central in this endeavour. In this chapter we focused on the UK context and, in particular, the ways public service broadcasters have attempted to tackle misinformation. We discussed BBC Reality Check and Channel 4's FactCheck as illustrations of these attempts, which represent, in our view, positive steps towards a journalism that challenges falsehoods and misinformation in a direct way for audiences. More research, however, is necessary to explore the diversity and effectiveness of these practices not just in the UK but globally. Such research should investigate good practice in terms of fact-checking in different political and journalistic contexts. It should also move beyond fact-checking in order to identify alternative ways journalists can tackle misinformation in their routine reporting. Similarly, more research is necessary to understand the effectiveness of these practices in relation to news audiences and users. Most research so far has been experimental and episodic, focusing on elections and campaign misinformation. Different approaches are needed to help understand how news audiences encounter and deal with misinformation in the context of their everyday lives, as well as how they understand what constitutes misinformation. Such insights can further promote public and academic debates on misinformation and form the basis for transformative changes in journalism. For journalists to enhance their legitimacy, we argue, they need to not only report accurately and authoritatively but also play a leading role in tackling misinformation and disinformation both in routine instances and high-profile events and campaigns.

References

Amazeen, M. A. (2019). Practitioner perceptions: Critical junctures and the global emergence and challenges of fact-checking. *International Communication Gazette, 81*(6–8), 541–561.

BBC RealityCheck (n.d.). Twitter profile. *Twitter.* Retrieved 30 April 2020, from https://twitter.com/BBCRealityCheck

Bennhold, K. (2017, May 2). To understand 'Brexit,' look to Britain's tabloids. *The New York Times.* www.nytimes.com/2017/05/02/world/europe/london-tabloids-brexit.html

Birks, J. (2019a). UK election 2019: Public resistance to factchecking. *The Conversation.* http://theconversation.com/uk-election-2019-public-resistance-to-factchecking-128565

Birks, J. (2019b). *Fact-Checking Journalism and Political Argumentation: A British Perspective.* Cham: Palgrave MacMillan.

Birks, J. (2019c). Fact-checking GE2019 compared to fact-checking GE2017. *British Politics and Policy at LSE.* https://blogs.lse.ac.uk/politicsandpolicy/fact-checking-ge2019/

Boykoff, M. T., & Boykoff, J. M. (2007). Climate change and journalistic norms: A case-study of US mass-media coverage. *Geoforum, 38*(6), 1190–1204.

Brennen, J. S., Simon, F. M., Howard, P. N., & Nielsen, R. K. (2020). *Types, Sources, and Claims of COVID-19 Misinformation.* Oxford: Reuters Institute for the Study of Journalism.

Cammaerts, B. (2016). *Journalistic Representations of Jeremy Corbyn in the British Press: From Watchdog to Attackdog.* London: Media @LSE.

Cushion, S. (2020). COVID-19: To counter misinformation, journalists need to embrace a public service mission. *The Conversation.* http://theconversation.com/covid-19-to-counter-misinformation-journalists-need-to-embrace-a-public-service-mission-133829

Damazer, M. (2019). Could Brexit break the BBC? The tensions, the bewildering question of 'balance'–and how to get it right. *Prospect Magazine.* www.prospectmagazine.co.uk/magazine/mark-damazer-bbc-brexit-coverage-bias

FactCheck. (n.d.). FactCheck Twitter profile. *Twitter.* Retrieved 30 April 2020, from https://twitter.com/FactCheck

Full Fact. (2019). Fact checking doesn't work (the way you think it does). *Full Fact.* https://fullfact.org/blog/2019/jun/how-fact-checking-works/

Goss, Z., & Renwick. (2016). Fact-checking and the EU referendum. *The Constitution Unit Blog.* https://constitution-unit.com/2016/08/23/fact-checking-and-the-eu-referendum/

Graves, L. (2016). *Deciding What's True: The Rise of Political Fact-Checking in American Journalism.* New York: Columbia University Press.

Graves, L., & Cherubini, F. (2016). *The Rise of Fact-Checking Sites in Europe.* Oxford: Reuters Institute for the Study of Journalism.

Hutchison, S., & Murray, A. (2019, December 4). Are these 'new' hospitals actually new? *BBC News.* www.bbc.com/news/50579557

IPSOS. (2019). *Trust in the media.* IPSOS. https://www.ipsos.com/sites/default/files/ct/news/documents/2019-06/global-advisor-trust-in-media-2019.pdf

Jackson, J. (2017, January 12). BBC sets up team to debunk fake news. *The Guardian.* www.theguardian.com/media/2017/jan/12/bbc-sets-up-team-to-debunk-fake-news

Jordan, D. (2019, November 21). Letter to the Guardian. *The Guardian.* www.theguardian.com/politics/2019/nov/21/deceit-is-at-the-heart-of-tory-election-campaign

Karlsson, M., & Clerwall, C. (2018). Transparency to the rescue? *Journalism Studies, 19*(13), 1923–1933.

Kovach, B., & Rosenstiel, T. (2007). *The Elements of Journalism: What Newspeople Should Know and the Public Should Expect.* New York: Three Rivers Press.

Lewandowsky, S., Ecker, U. K. H., Seifert, C. M., Schwarz, N., & Cook, J. (2012). Misinformation and Its correction: Continued influence and successful debiasing. *Psychological Science in the Public Interest, 13*(3), 106–131.

Manthorpe, R. (2019). Sky news to investigate how tech is used and misused through the election with under the radar project. *Sky News.* https://news.sky.com/story/sky-news-to-investigate-how-tech-is-used-and-misused-through-the-election-with-under-the-radar-project-11850473

Mantzarlis, A. (2016). Can the worldwide boom in digital fact-checking make the leap to TV? *Poynter.* www.poynter.org/fact-checking/2016/can-the-worldwide-boom-in-digital-fact-checking-make-the-leap-to-tv/

Morris, C. (2019, November 6). What does 'Get Brexit done' mean? *BBC News.* www.bbc.com/news/uk-50222315

Nielsen, R., Schulz, A., & Fletcher, R. (2020). *The BBC is under scrutiny. Here's what research tells about its role in the UK.* Oxford: Reuters Institute for the Study of Journalism.

Nieminen, S., & Rapeli, L. (2019). Fighting misperceptions and doubting journalists' objectivity: A review of fact-checking literature. *Political Studies Review, 17*(3), 296–309.

Nyhan, B. (2013). When 'he said,' 'she said' is dangerous. *Columbia Journalism Review.* www.cjr.org/united_states_project/media_errs_giving_balanced_coverage_to_jenny_mccarthys_discredited_views.php

Nyhan, B., & Reifler, J. (2015). Estimating fact-checking's effects: Evidence from a long term experiment during campaign 2014. *American Press Institute.* www.americanpressinstitute.org/wp-content/uploads/2015/04/Estimating-Fact-Checkings-Effect.pdf

Rosen, J. (2009). *PressThink: He Said, She Said Journalism: Lame Formula in the Land of the Active User.* http://archive.pressthink.org/2009/04/12/hesaid_shesaid.html

Sambrook, R. (2016) Why the media got it so wrong on Trump and Brexit. *The Conversation.* http://theconversation.com/why-the-media-got-it-so-wrong-on-trump-and-brexit-68542

Samuels. (2017, January 13). BBC has started a team to take down 'fake news'. *The Independent.* www.independent.co.uk/news/media/bbc-team-debunk-fake-news-stories-media-james-harding-a7525686.html

Satariano, A., & Tsang, A. (2019, December 10). Who's spreading disinformation in U.K. election? You might be surprised. *The New York Times.* www.nytimes.com/2019/12/10/world/europe/elections-disinformation-social-media.html

Schaffner, B. F., & Roche, C. (2017). Misinformation and motivated reasoning responses to economic news in a politicized environment. *Public Opinion Quarterly, 81*(1), 86–110.

Stencel, M., & Luther, J. (2020). Update: 237 fact-checkers in nearly 80 countries…and counting. *Duke Reporters' Lab.* https://reporterslab.org/update-237-fact-checkers-in-nearly-80-countries-and-counting/

Stone, J. (2016, June 16). Nearly half of Britons believe vote leave's false '£350 million a week to the EU' claim. *The Independent.* www.independent.co.uk/news/uk/politics/nearly-half-of-britons-believe-vote-leaves-false-350-million-a-week-to-the-eu-claim-a7085016.html

Thorson, E. (2016). Belief echoes: The persistent effects of corrected misinformation. *Political Communication, 33*(3), 460–480.

UNESCO (2018). *Journalism, fake news & disinformation: Handbook for journalism education and training – UNESCO Digital Library.* UNESCO. https://unesdoc.unesco.org/ark:/48223/pf0000265552

Vargo, C. J., Guo, L., & Amazeen, M. A. (2018). The agenda-setting power of fake news: A big data analysis of the online media landscape from 2014 to 2016. *New Media & Society, 20*(5), 2028–2049.

Wardle, C. (2018). The need for smarter definitions and practical, timely empirical research on information disorder. *Digital Journalism, 6*(8), 951–963.

50

RESPONSES TO MIS/ DISINFORMATION

Practitioner experiences and approaches in low income settings

James Deane

Introduction

This chapter is informed by the experience and response to mis and disinformation by BBC Media Action, the BBC's international media support charity. It draws on the work and analysis of numerous colleagues and country offices. BBC Media Action works in 26 mostly low-income and fragile countries, and this experience heavily informs this chapter. The chapter is not intended to reflect the perspective of the BBC itself, although it does incorporate some of the lessons and experiences of the wider BBC.

In this chapter I summarise some of the strategies and approaches that a media support organisation is using to combat mis- and disinformation. The diversity of approaches and contexts that are described makes it difficult to provide a single theoretical framework or reference a particular body of literature as these are now vast. Programmes draw on particular theoretical reference points and literature according to context and objective.

The approaches outlined here are highly specific to different political, social, and economic contexts, but populism is not necessarily a key factor in shaping the strategies and approaches outlined here. Populism is often a product of particular information and communication environments of the type that are now the norm. If information and communication environments privilege misinformation and disinformation, diminish access to trustworthy information, enable patterns of communication that drive societal fragmentation and polarisation, and create a hostile environment for dialogue and debate across societal divides, we argue that they provide fertile ground for populism and authoritarianism to gain ground. BBC Media Action believes that improving the character and quality of the information and communication environment – privileging the availability of and access to trustworthy information, increasing societal capacity for debate and dialogue across societal divides, enabling a diversity of voices to be heard – makes societies more resilient to (although certainly not immune to) populism as well as authoritarianism. The evidence for the practical efficacy for this approach is fragmented, not only from our own experience but more broadly, and towards the end of this chapter, we suggest better ways through which learning and evidence can draw on practitioner experience. However, it should be said at the outset that our analysis tends to focus on populism less as a driver than as a consequence of dysfunctional information and communication environments.

538

Definitions

We use the following definitions.

Misinformation is untrue information spread by a source who believes it to be true.

Disinformation is untrue information spread by a source who knows it is untrue (i.e. it is a deliberate lie).

Our projects generally seek to identify the principal problem to be addressed and design accordingly, but it is rare that they tackle only one of these challenges. In other words they take a blended approach to tackling both misinformation and disinformation.

Fake news is understood by most people to mean anything that is not true, covering all types of mis/disinformation. Academic papers and institutions such as the European Commission reject the use of the phrase 'fake news', although the BBC does continue to use the phrase principally because it is one which their audiences use and recognise (EU 2018). BBC Media Action tends to avoid this term unless it remains the most effective way of engaging people.

We also recognise that the terms *misinformation* and *disinformation* are used in civic discourse interchangeably. It is sometimes helpful to think of the phenomena as the spread of untrue information in a world where trust in reliable sources is in decline, where there are solutions on the demand side (e.g. building trust and media literacy) and the supply side (e.g. reducing the amount of untrue information being spread).

Our projects may seek to address two different perceived problems: the organised sharing of disinformation and the organic spread of misinformation.

Principles and foundations

In the following sections, we outline some of the strategies and approaches that BBC Media Action is taking to respond to misinformation and disinformation, but at the outset, some of the principles and foundational components that inform our approach should be spelled out.

Research and context

There are few if any template approaches to tackling misinformation and disinformation. Effective strategies need to be rooted in thorough research and understanding of context. This means:

- Audience research focused on understanding, for example, how people access information, how they communicate, who they trust, and which information sources they most value. Patterns of access will look very different within countries as well as between them. For example, in Myanmar, where BBC Media Action has devised a major programme combatting rumour and misinformation, almost one-third of the population use Facebook daily, but almost half never use it, according to our research.[1] Those who do use it tend not to trust it, with just 44 percent of people saying they trust what they access on social media. Effective strategies cannot be devised unless they are rooted in this kind of detailed, contextual knowledge. Research approaches are also tailored to context ranging from traditional nationally representative surveys and qualitative research to artificial intelligence techniques focused on discourse analysis, influencer maps, audience segmentation, and other approaches.
- Political economy analysis and media mapping focused on understanding ownership and power structures in the media and communication space; who is generating information content with what purpose; the conditions and potential for public interest media to

survive and thrive; and the influence over media of government, oligarchs, and political actors, as well as the incentives and objectives of organised efforts to subvert or confuse the information and communication space.

- Real-time learning of what works. There are few tried and trusted solutions to tackling misinformation and disinformation, and those solutions that are proving effective now in one context are unlikely to do so at another time in another. Learning within organisations and across organisations is vital in developing an effective knowledge based of what works and what does not. So, too, are investing in and respecting practitioner research. While there is substantial research informing policy responses, there are currently quite poorly developed learning systems capable of sharing insights between those organisations designing and implementing strategies to address these challenges (further analysis of this issue is focused on later in this chapter).

Theories of change

Developing project-specific theories of change is vital to ensuring complete clarity of what change is expected to come about and understanding the logic of how and why that intervention is likely to achieve the change required. At its most basic, for example, it encourages assessment and challenge of why logical responses (such as the provision of factual information) are expected to provide an effective response to the often emotionally driven behavioural drivers of misinformation.

A mix of responses and a multidisciplinary approach

Misinformation is complex and multi-faceted, and effective responses are likely to involve a mix of strategies. Some of these are outlined later in this chapter. Misinformation is organic, generated virally, amplified by a multiplicity of actors and forces, and rooted in the social reality of human nature. No one strategy is likely to be effective in this context; a range of responses is required, and a high degree of collaboration between different organisations designing and implementing those responses is likely to be required.

BBC Media Action has strong skills and networks in the field of working with media and journalism, in research, in editorial and digital capacities, and in a long history of working in partnership to shift social and behavioural norms. A truly multidisciplinary response requires many more skills than this, especially from the behavioural sciences, data analytics, and political economy, among other areas. Similarly, effective research into impact assessment is likely to draw on similar approaches.

Informed by BBC values

Our approach is heavily informed by BBC values.[2] These are particularly:

- Public service, placing the public interest above all others, and putting audiences or people at the heart of any strategy.
- Universality, with a particular focus on engaging those who cannot afford to pay for accurate information as well as encouraging fact-based dialogue across divides in society.
- Due impartiality, with a focus on improving access to factual information as well as exposure to a diversity of perspectives, whilst not amplifying perspectives which are factually untrue or not supported by science.[3]

- Trust and ensuring that all activities work towards the creation of more trusted information and communication environments and ensuring that information provision, platforms for public debate, and other forms of citizen engagement are underpinned by fact.
- Putting people at the heart of what we do. Our research and programming are focused on understanding, engaging, and listening to people, and we argue that media support strategies are unlikely to succeed unless they are rooted in meeting the information and communication needs of people. In supporting media we recognise that the principal challenge is in finding systems capable of supporting journalists, programme makers, and other media professionals. Our investments in technological solutions and platforms are substantial and growing, but technology is not our first point of entry to addressing the challenges of media development. People and politics are.
- Creativity and innovation. Rooted in the research process, BBC Media Action prizes highly the creativity of its approach. This means that the organisation is consistently experimenting with new approaches, platforms, technologies, and partnerships.
- Scale. Our partnerships are designed to engage everyone in society, especially those who are economically and politically marginalised. Our programmes, implemented with our partners, are successful in engaging a representative cross section of society, both economically and demographically, with a particularly strong track record of engaging young audiences.
- The BBC. At the heart of the twenty-first-century media development challenge is addressing the challenge of how to attract audiences across demographic, political, and other areas whilst also maintaining trust. The BBC is itself engaged in a major process of change and reinvigoration in order to ensure it remains the most trusted information source in the world and one capable of continuing to engage all sections of society, including young people. BBC Media Action also draws on this expertise and experience whilst designing its own programmes to meet these objectives.

Working at scale

Misinformation works at scale. Responses need to work at similar scale to be effective. However, scale is achieved by misinformation by appealing to emotional triggers that encourage people to share information even if they know it to be untrue. Sharing factual information cannot easily tap into the same emotional drivers and faces huge challenges in achieving the same virality as misinformation. Working at scale can therefore involve maximising the continuing capacity to reach broadcast and online audiences through our partnerships and networks; BBC Media Action seeks to work at large scale. Through its capacity building and broadcast partnerships, it reaches more than 100 million. The bulk of this is achieved through national and local partnerships with broadcast, digital, and other media institutions. Some of it is achieved through partnerships with the language services of the BBC World Service.

Investing in local/national media

BBC Media Action focuses heavily on working to support the capacity, capability, and sustainability of in-country media and other trustworthy institutions and entities. Tackling misinformation cannot be restricted to a set of tactical interventions or externally supported projects. It ultimately depends on the existence of an information ecosystem capable of making trustworthy, credible information accessible and appealing across all of society. These media development activities can range from a 15-year support programme to the most the trusted independent media institution in Iraq, called Al Mirbad, to support to networks of community broadcasters in countries as diverse as Nepal, Tanzania, and Zambia to working to establish public interest media systems in contexts as diverse as Libya, Myanmar, and Tunisia. Some of this work is rooted in a broad strategic effort to support public interest media systems which can be commercial, community, or publicly subsidised. Some of it is specifically contextualised to counter misinformation or disinformation. For example, we have worked with public service broadcasters in the Baltic states of Estonia and Latvia, which have large minority Russian-speaking populations but where the provision of independent information from within these states in the Russian language has been extremely limited.[4] As a consequence, these populations largely access content produced from within Russia itself, including disinformation. Support has focused on working with national public service broadcasters and others to develop strategies better able to improve independent reporting and information provision (including entertainment) in the Russian language. In addition to this, substantial training, business mentoring, and other strategies are adopted to strengthen independent media in the countries in which BBC Media Action operates.

Local ownership and agency

A key principle of our work is that misinformation efforts should be locally owned and directed. Almost all implementing staff are drawn from the country concerned, and from research to programme development, strong efforts are made to ensure that programmatic strategies and content are driven by partners, people, and realities on the ground. It should be acknowledged, however, that this is not always easy. BBC Media Action receives almost no institutional funding, with 96 percent of its income tied to specific project deliverables. This means having a strong focus on programmatic impact, which requires careful consideration if it is to support, rather than override, local or national interests. Similar consideration is required to ensure adherence to BBC values, which stress a commitment to values such as due impartiality and constrain programmatic advocacy or campaigning.

Acute or chronic disinformation

Designing effective responses also needs to be rooted in understanding whether disinformation is acute or chronic. The distinction is most obviously seen in humanitarian, health, and similar responses. At a time of disaster – conflict, epidemic, or natural disaster, for example – rumour and disinformation can complicate the response. Combatting rumours of acute disinformation – for example, falsely claiming that a cure exists for a particular disease, which can lead to people dying by taking that treatment, and false claims that people or groups are carriers of a particular disease – are examples of acute disinformation. Disinformation around the efficacy of vaccines – part of a sustained narrative over time and multiple geographies and often linked to populist politics – is an example of chronic disinformation (more obviously disinformation than misinformation). Strategies to combat the latter needed to be rooted in the overall public health (or equivalent response) involving building the trust and legitimacy of any effort designed to encourage people to adopt (in this case) a particular behaviour, such as getting their children vaccinated.

Working in partnership and coordination

Huge numbers of organisations and agencies are increasingly tackling mis- and disinformation. Coordinating efforts with others is a key component of any effective response, although the architecture for doing this effectively in many settings is very weak. BBC Media Action works with a broad constellation of actors, depending on the media context. These range from national online platform partnerships to large-scale community radio networks, partnerships with commercial media networks (working with 200 broadcast partners across Nigeria, for example) to national commercial and public service or state broadcasters capable of engaging more than a third of a country's adult population. Internationally, we work with academic, policy, and other media development partners both in generating learning of what works and does not work and applying and communicating that learning across the development and media development communities.

Strategies

The key strategies that are used fall into the following categories. As outlined earlier, they rarely stand alone and involve a mix of approaches:

Rational-based responses

Rational-based responses are aimed at helping ensure that public debate is underpinned by factual information, which enables citizens to sift trustworthy from untrustworthy sources of information and increases the availability of, access to, and predominance of trustworthy information.[5] It is recognised that the emotional triggers that drive misinformation are not necessarily effectively countered by rational-based responses, but we consider them an essential component of any response.

These include:

- Providing factual information. While this may be obvious, the more factual information populating the public sphere and the more that information reaches across society, the more difficult it is for misinformation and disinformation to take hold. BBC Media Action and its partners reach more than 100 million people worldwide, and it often works with the BBC World Service, which itself reaches more than 400 million people worldwide. Public demand for information that people can trust tends to grow markedly in times of crisis, such as during epidemics, social unrest, or other emergencies. BBC audiences both nationally and internationally tend to spike sharply at times of crisis as people turn to information they can trust. Factual information also needs to be engaging and relevant to people across society and is more likely to take the format of an interactive youth-produced digital and broadcast programme than any conventional news reporting format. Misinformation that reflects the lived reality of people is likely to be shared and believed more than factual information, however accurate or trustworthy, that does not reflect that lived reality. Factual information needs to be rooted the reality of people's lives if it is to have salience.
- Fact-checking. We support media partners, especially during elections or at other times of high political tension, to carry out fact-checking. The BBC itself now has a well-established process, Reality Check, which some of these activities are often modelled on, although it is key that strategies are context specific.[6] To be effective, fact-checking needs to have the ability to reach a similar number of people as are exposed to disinformation. It also has to have a way of cutting through to people in ways that resonate with them. Highly creative, context-specific approaches are often required. This is just one of a range of interventions that link to the BBC. The BBC World Service has mounted a major 'fake

news' season, and BBC Monitoring is a preeminent source of monitoring and analysis of how misinformation is manifested in different contexts around the world.

- Media literacy. We carry out school- and high school–based media training, often adapted from the BBC's own School Report Programme. Media and digital literacy programmes are also developed, aimed at the broader general public, although there are few of these. A key challenge with media literacy is how to achieve sustained impact at scale, and this is an area where special focus on collaborative research and learning is required to discern what works and what doesn't.
- Systemic interventions, including an international fund for public interest media. Misinformation cannot ultimately be tackled without building a healthy public interest information ecosystem. The pressures on independent media and other mechanisms and institutions vital to such an ecosystem extend well beyond what any project or set of interventions can address. Ultimately, they depend on a political economy that can support and encourage public interest media in all its forms. BBC Media Action has been documenting the political economy of the media in different countries for many years, highlighting both the increasing levels of political co-option of independent media and the rapidly intensifying economic pressures that are collapsing business media models around the world (Bhandari et al. 2016; Deane 2013). The most intense pressures, and often the most acute democratic and societal effects, are in resource-poor states. This has led us to recommend the creation of a new international fund for public interest media (Deane and Taki 2020). It would raise funds from bilateral donors, who currently only allocate 0.3 percent of development funding to international media support, as well as technology companies and others with resources and an interest in supporting public interest media. A major feasibility study, supported by the Luminate Group, has been developed, outlining how such a fund could be operationalised, including recommendations around its governance, structures, and measurement and learning processes.

Emotion-based responses

Sharing misinformation and disinformation is widely acknowledged to be effective because it appeals to issues of emotion, of identity, and of lived reality. No purely rational response to misinformation can be expected to succeed. While the evidence of the efficacy of emotion-based responses in tackling misinformation is not yet strong, our experience suggests that substantial impact can be achieved. Narrative-based strategies have been deployed for years to shift social norms,[7] to tap into and sometimes positively challenge negative norms deep rooted in group identities and to improve social cohesion, including among groups with histories of devastating conflict (Staub 2014).[8]

An example is provided by a programme in Myanmar designed to counter rumour and misinformation. These interventions take the form of televised public service announcements, a YouTube miniseries and working with a v-logger/influencer. Its central emphasis is focused on appealing to people's social responsibility with a punchline asking the audience to consider three questions: 'Is it true? Is it kind? Is it necessary?' Audience research carried out around the programmes suggest they are effective at encouraging people to pause and think before sharing information they cannot be sure of. The communication content uses images of modernity, lifestyle, and fashion, with traditional deities. Another example is a drama produced in response to the Ebola emergency, which dramatised real-life scenarios illustrating how people within families dealt with fear often arising from misinformation. According to Yvonne Macpherson, who designed it, 'drama can tap in to observational or social learning – by listening to or watching the consequences of characters' decisions, people will draw parallels and practice what others do'.

BBC Media Action supports multiple dramas, soap operas, and other narrative formats using a broad range of traditional and other platforms and focused on diverse objectives, ranging from improving social cohesion, shifting social norms, and changing behaviour to improving health and building political participation. The evidence of impact in these areas suggests significant impact could be achieved in tackling misinformation.

When and how to respond

Responding to misinformation and disinformation is often focused on contexts and times when it can be most effective and when misinformation and disinformation are either most prevalent or most damaging. These examples include:

Elections. Misinformation tends to spike around moments of political intensity or crisis, most predictably during elections. BBC Media Action carries out specific programmes drawing on the strategies and approaches described earlier. However, tackling misinformation during elections is usually embedded in broader programmes of activities designed to work with national or local partners to improve public debate and coverage or foster political participation. Examples of programmes include broadcasting electoral debates with presidential or other electoral candidates in partnership with national or local media, voter education (for example, how to get registered), media training, and programmes to defuse social tension or reduce the risk of electoral violence. During the 2018 presidential election in Sierra Leone, a set of interventions was designed, building on a long-standing programme of media support in the country which, among other networks, had established the most popular Facebook page in the country with 500,000 followers. This involved designing and delivering in-depth training sessions on responsible use of social media to three key groups – journalists, election management bodies, and young people who are active on social media – and producing a range of media content (films and graphics) to inform wider audiences about more responsible use of social media (Ferguson 2018). Internationally, there are also efforts to encourage a much greater prioritisation of media engagement and media support by electoral assistance organisations, electoral commissioners, and others. Media support conventionally involves short programmes of media training, but our experience is that supporting provision of and access to trustworthy information and platforms for public debate and mitigating misinformation requires a long-term approach across the electoral cycle. Misinformation and disinformation around elections have intensified in recent years, with the use and abuse of data analytics services offered by international actors to specific political actors who can afford to pay for them becoming an especially acute challenge. Multiple strategies are required to respond to these challenges – technological and regulatory as well as informational – and from multiple actors (governments, international regulatory bodies, technology companies, and the media themselves), but an organised response to support access to trustworthy information and platforms for public debate is key.

Emergencies, Some of the most damaging effects of misinformation are manifested at times of disaster, humanitarian crisis, conflict, or other emergency situations. Challenging rumours and providing accurate information have been key in, for example, responses to the Ebola epidemic, the Rohingya response, Nepal's 2015 earthquake, and civil war in Libya. At the time of writing, the COVID-19 pandemic is just beginning to materialise in terms of scale and crisis, and the informational characteristics of that – what the secretary general of the World Health Organization dubbed an 'infodemic' – are emerging in what will be seen as its infancy. The value, importance, and public appreciation of trustworthy information accessible via public interest media tends to intensify at such moments.

The need for fresh approaches to learning

The evidence base supporting the efficacy of different strategies to address misinformation is, we believe, weak. This applies globally but is especially the case in low-income settings. There is an extraordinary proliferation of energy, imagination, and expertise being brought to bear to tackle the challenges in all their diversity and complexity. The fact remains that proven strategies are scarce. To the extent that clear strategies are identified and evidence built, the information and communication landscape is so fast moving that these strategies may quickly prove redundant.

Outlined here is just a sample of the kinds of strategies that BBC Media Action adopts, but throughout, the emphasis has been on designing strategies through strong research, adapting them to context, and learning from implementation and from the work of others.

There remains a structural problem, however, in that there are few effective and sufficiently well-structured spaces for learning what works and what does not work in tackling misinformation and disinformation, especially among practitioners focused on addressing these challenges. There are multiple conferences and convenings, but these are poor at building a collective and cumulative evidence base capable of enabling rapid adaptation of strategy.

BBC Media Action has proposed the creation of a collaborative Media Development Lab designed to turbocharge learning of what works (and what doesn't) in tackling misinformation and supporting independent public interest media. The lab would be designed to focus on geographic and political contexts where access to trustworthy information and debate often matter most – where media markets are weakest, resources most scarce, conflict most likely and most devastating, and democracy and the prospects for democracy most fragile. It would be designed to blend and provide an organising framework for practitioner experience, practitioner research, and academic research and expertise to best enable strategic adaptation and impact of efforts to tackle misinformation. Currently, there is little in the way of rigourous collective lesson learning and investigation into what works and what does not work in these approaches and often not a great deal of collective confidence that some of the most commonly established strategies (such as media literacy) will prove impactful at scale.

BBC Media Action has an extensive network of researchers on the ground from the countries in which it works, generating real-time analysis and learning of what works and what does not work, and some other organisations have similar capacities. There is a strong appetite to share learning and certainly also to learn from the best of what others are doing. A media development lab would be a useful and effective way of generating such learning.

Notes

1 BBC Media Action Nationally Representative Survey, December 2019, asked of social media users (n=1,181). While as much data as possible is published externally on BBC Media Action's data portal (bbcmediaaction.org/dataportal), the research is principally focused on ensuring maximum possible project impact and, for resourcing reasons, is not always externally available.
2 SBBC Editorial Guidelines, www.bbc.co.uk/editorialguidelines/guidelines.
3 For example, due impartiality does not mean giving credence to voices that deny man made climate change.

4 'Understanding media habits and information needs of Russian speakers in the Baltics', BBC Media Action Research Summary, April 2018.

5 We are conscious that the term *trustworthy* is contentious, difficult to define, and challenging to measure. We are guided by BBC editorial guidelines in supporting trustworthy content but realise that trustworthy content can be produced that is partisan or is inconsistent with these guidelines in other ways. For the purposes of this chapter, the focus is on news, information, and platforms for public debate that are fact based, serve the public interest, and are found trustworthy by a cross section of the public.

6 www.bbc.co.uk/news/reality_check.

7 See, for example, Soul City Evaluation Impact Evaluation, Series 4, Violence Against Women, 2001.

8 See, for example, Staub E, 'The challenging road to reconciliation in Rwanda: societal processes, interventions and their evaluation', *Journal of Social and Political Psychology* 2(1):505–517 October 2014.

References

'A multidimensional approach to disinformation: Report of the independent high-level group on fake news and online disinformation', EU Directorate General for Communication Networks, Content and Technology 2018.

Bhandari K, Bhattarai D and Deane J (2016) 'Accountability, nation and society: the role of media in the remaking of Nepal', BBC Media Action Policy Briefing.

Ferguson G (27 July 2018), 'Helping people spot fake news in Sierra Leone', BBC Media Action blog.

Deane J (2013) 'Fragile states: the role of information and communication', BBC Media Action Policy Briefing.

Deane J and Taki M (2020) 'Enabling media markets to work for democracy: Feasibility study for an international fund for public interest media', BBC Media Action.

Staub E (October 2014) 'The challenging road to reconciliation in Rwanda: societal processes, interventions and their evaluation', *Journal of Social and Political Psychology* 2(1): 505–517.

51

THE EFFECT OF CORRECTIONS AND CORRECTED MISINFORMATION

Emily Thorson and Jianing Li

Introduction

Misinformation poses a normative problem because it has the potential to distort both beliefs and attitudes, causing people to believe things that are not true as well as to hold attitudes that differ from those that they would have held if they had been correctly informed. Ideally, then, a successful correction will alter both beliefs and attitudes, reverting both to the same state as prior to receiving the misinformation. However, not all corrections achieve both goals. Sometimes, a correction fails to alter beliefs at all. And sometimes, it successfully changes beliefs but has no effect on attitudes.

A large body of work, including some discussed in this volume, has taken on the question of how to ensure that corrections reach the people who need them most. This chapter focuses on different questions: what happens after a person receives a correction to a piece of misinformation? When are corrections successful, and when do they fail? Can misinformation continue to affect attitudes even after it is successfully corrected? This chapter begins by outlining why some corrections are more effective than others. Then, we discuss the ways in which even misinformation that is successfully corrected can shape beliefs and attitudes.

When are corrections successful at debunking misinformation?

This section discusses factors that contribute to a correction's success at debunking misinformation. On aggregate, people do tend to move their beliefs in the expected direction when given a correction. A much-publicised 2010 study by Brendan Nyhan and Jason Reifler suggested that under certain circumstances, a correction might 'backfire', leading people to double down on their incorrect beliefs. However, more recent attempts to replicate and expand on those findings have demonstrated that in practice, the backfire effect is extremely rare. Wood and Porter (2019) conducted five separate experiments in which respondents were exposed to corrections of 52 different misperceptions. In the substantial majority of cases, corrections moved people closer to the truth. A similar study, conducted in the context of the 2016 US presidential election, showed that exposing people to journalistic fact-checks of false claims made by Donald Trump

548

led them to hold more accurate beliefs. This was true for Trump supporters as well as for the sample as a whole (Nyhan et al. 2019).

However, while corrections may on aggregate move people closer to the truth, they are by no means a panacea. First, while it is not the focus of this chapter, the people most likely to need corrections are often the ones least likely to see them (Guess et al. 2020). And second, not everyone is equally likely to accept a correction. The following section details several factors that affect the likelihood of a correction being accepted. These factors include individual-level characteristics (for example, partisanship) as well as aspects of the correction (for example, whether it includes an image).

Individual-level characteristics

Identity and motivated reasoning

When people process a new piece of information (including corrections), they are rarely objective. Rather, their pre-existing beliefs and attitudes shape the extent to which they attend to, process, and believe the new information. This tendency is called motivated reasoning (Kunda 1990; Kraft et al. 2015). The term *motivation* refers the human tendency to be motivated by two different end goals. The first goal is accuracy – people generally want to hold accurate beliefs and make 'correct' decisions. The second goal is directional: people want to defend pre-existing identities and attitudes. The existence of motivated reasoning means that when a piece of misinformation reflects directly on someone's identity (for example, if it concerns a controversial political issue), it will be more difficult to correct.

Political misinformation can be especially difficult to correct because it is closely tied to people's political identities. When a piece of misinformation reinforces a person's partisanship, they are less likely to accept a correction. For example, Ecker and Ang (2019) found that people were less likely to accept corrections of fictitious misconduct of Australian politicians if the corrections were incongruent with their partisanship. The impact of political identity on the effectiveness of corrections has also been found in comparative political settings. In a study conducted shortly after major combat in the Iraq War ended, Lewandowsky et al. (2005) found that participants in countries that supported the war were less likely to accept corrections of Iraq-related misinformation than were participants in countries that were more sceptical of the war.

Beyond political identity, social categories and cultural identities also contribute to biased processing of corrections. Recent research on 'cultural cognition' sheds light on the importance of underlying cultural values in orienting opinion formation and change through social and cognitive processes (Kahan and Braman 2006; Kahan et al. 2007). Motivated reasoning of corrective information not only stems from partisan biases but also results from self-serving biases fuelled by any important identities, core values, or attitudes that people hold strongly. For example, among people with strong anti-vaccine attitudes, debunking false claims on the risks of flu and MMR vaccines can result in decreased intentions to vaccinate themselves or a future child (Nyhan et al. 2014; Nyhan and Reifler 2015). Similarly, when highlighting the Muslim American identity of a religious leader, people are less likely to accept corrections of false news coverage of his claims. This tendency is heightened among those with unfavourable opinions of Islam and high social-dominance orientation (Garrett et al. 2013).

Cognitive reflection and curiosity

Individuals who are better at engaging in analytical thinking may be more capable of accepting corrections, including counter-attitudinal ones. Analytical thinking is often measured by the cognitive reflection test (CRT), on which individuals perform better if they are able to 'reflect on a question and resist reporting the first response that comes to mind' (Frederick 2005). There are two competing arguments on whether cognitive reflection mitigates or exacerbates the propensity to engage in biased processing of corrections (Pennycook and Rand 2019). First, 'classical reasoning approaches', including dual-process theory, usually expect that more deliberative or analytical processing can lead to better judgments: for example, studies have shown that people who score high in analytical thinking are less likely to believe in paranormal and conspiracy concepts (Pennycook et al. 2015) and more likely to endorse scientific conclusions on evolution (Gervais 2015). On the other hand, research on motivated reasoning has offered evidence that cognitive reflection actually promotes the formation and maintenance of beliefs congruent with one's identity and leads to a higher chance of 'System 2 motivated reasoning' (Kahan 2013) or opinion polarisation (Kahan et al. 2012).

Research that directly tests these competitive mechanisms in processing corrections is still scarce. Some initial evidence comes from Pennycook and Rand (2019), who found that better performance in analytical thinking was associated with more accurate judgment on whether a news headline was real or fake. Further, such relationship between analytical thinking and misinformation detection was unrelated to how closely the news headline aligned with one's political ideology – which suggests that the reason for susceptibility to misinformation is 'lazy, not biased' (Pennycook and Rand 2019).

Personal interest in or curiosity about a particular topic may also mitigate motivated reasoning. Kahan et al. (2017) developed a scale of science curiosity and found that while more science comprehension led to a partisan-motivated perception of global warming and fracking (in line with 'System 2 motivated reasoning' argument), science curiosity counteracted the tendency to engage in motivated reasoning. Further, those who had low to modest science curiosity actively sought out unsurprising, congruent information, and those who had high science curiosity showed a high preference for surprising information, even when it was identity incongruent.

News literacy

People who are less able to navigate the changing media environment may also be more susceptible to misinformation as well as less able to understand and process corrections. In an observational study of sharing behavior during the 2016 election, Guess et al. (2019a) found that people over 65 years old, so-called digital immigrants, shared nearly seven times as much online misinformation as 'digital natives' aged 18 to 29. Vraga and Tully (2019) also found that those who with higher 'news literacy' (i.e. those with more knowledge about media industries, systems, and effects) shared less news and political content on social media and were more sceptical of information quality on social media.

Recent attempts to improve news literacy among the public have generated both hope and caveats. Simple intervention such as a general warning of online misinformation (Clayton et al. 2019) and news literacy intervention with more detailed tips on spotting misinformation (Guess et al. 2019b) can help people perceive false headlines as less accurate, even when the false headlines are congenial to their political identity. However, the increased scepticism of false headlines also had a spillover effect, leading people to become more sceptical of true news headlines (Clayton et al. 2019; Guess et al. 2019b). While research has not specifically examined whether this spillover effect extends to corrections, it is plausible that by increasing scepticism of all information, news literacy interventions may also make people less inclined to believe corrections.

Further, the effects of news literacy interventions may not last over time (Guess et al. 2019b). Another concern is the practicality of these interventions in the real-world media environment as, in most studies, participants were exposed to a message provided by researchers in an experimental setting. Tully et al. (2019) found evidence that a 'promoted tweet' (Twitter's paid post) encouraging users to be critical news consumers can mitigate the effect of exposure to misinformation on GMOs and flu vaccines. However, the effect was not consistent across experiments. In addition, most experimental interventions designed to increase news literacy are focused on changing how people process misinformation. More research is needed to understand how news literacy interventions might also affect how they process corrections.

Characteristics of the correction

Source

A long literature in communication has examined the power of source credibility, including both perceived expertise and trustworthiness, in shaping whether or not a given piece of information is accepted (Page et al. 1987; Eagly and Chaiken 1993; Gilbert et al. 1998). This literature has direct implications for how people process both misinformation and corrections. The source of a piece of information – whether it is a politician, a fact-checking organisation, or a friend – affects whether people believe it. The more credible they deem the source, the more likely they are to accept the information.

Perceptions of source credibility are shaped by a person's pre-existing attitudes and beliefs, with congenial sources deemed more credible and thus more persuasive. For example, people may find a person who shares more cultural values with them (e.g. hierarchy-egalitarianism, individualism-communitarianism) more credible and more persuasive in their arguments, either pro- or anti-vaccination (Kahan et al. 2010). Guillory and Geraci (2013) offered direct evidence for how source congeniality shaped the effectiveness of corrections. They found that corrections of fictitious misinformation about political bribery were more effective when coming from sources that participants had previously deemed credible. In particular, the perceived trustworthiness of the source sufficiently reduced reliance on misinformation while perceived expertise was less powerful (Guillory and Geraci 2013).

The effect of source congeniality transfers to real-world social contexts too: Twitter users are more likely to accept corrections coming from users with whom they have a mutual follower-following relationship than corrections coming from strangers (Margolin et al. 2018). However, while congeniality matters, people may also take into account the motives of the corrector: for example, a Republican correcting a fellow Republican may be seen as an especially credible source because she appears to be acting in a way that runs counter to her own interests (Berinsky 2017). Finally, while this chapter is focused mainly on corrections, it is worth noting that the original source of the misinformation can be as important, if not more important, than the source of the correction. In an experiment examining false statements made by American presidential candidate Donald Trump, Swire et al. (2017) found that while the source of the correction had little impact on the correction's effectiveness, the source of the misinformation mattered more.

Since one of the major sources of corrections is fact-checking organisations, it is important to understand both when and why these organisations are deemed credible. Whether or not the practices of fact-checking organisations are reliable and unbiased has been questioned in academic research and public discourse (Nieminen and Rapeli 2019). Shin and Thorson (2017) used a unique dataset to examine public reactions to fact-checkers: how Twitter users share and comment on fact-checks from PolitiFact. They found that fact-checks of politicians spurred users who shared that politician's party to criticise fact-checking organisations, including accusing them of bias. These critiques may have downstream effects, reducing the perceived credibility of these organisations (Thorson et al. 2010). Finally, at least in the American context, partisanship also shapes the perceived credibility of fact-checkers. In surveys, Republicans are substantially more likely than Democrats to say that fact-checkers tend to favour one side (Walker and Gottfried 2019). Republicans are also more likely to criticise fact-checking organisations on social media (Shin and Thorson 2017).

Some corrections come not from fact-checks but directly from journalists. In the US, fact-checking practices are adopted by several mainstream news outlets such as AP and *USA Today* and also occupy a notable, although non-primary, role in journalists' own use of Twitter (Coddington et al. 2014). The practice of directly correcting a politician's false statement, often termed 'journalistic adjudication', is controversial as it runs counter to the traditional 'he said, she said' model of reporting disputed factual claims (Pingree et al. 2014). However, journalistic adjudication can be an effective approach to fact-checking, even when a correction runs counter to pre-existing political attitudes (Lyons 2018). Finally, experts can be an effective source of corrections. In the social media context, corrections of health misinformation that come from expert sources like the Centers for Disease Control (CDC) are more successful than those that come from social media users (Vraga and Bode 2018; van der Meer and Jin 2020)

Context

How people encounter a correction – be it on social media, in a news article, or passed on by a friend – can shape its effectiveness. Social media can enable the spread of not only misinformation but also corrections, although people are more likely to share corrective information that is relatively advantageous to their own side (Shin and Thorson 2017). Such 'social correction' of misinformation is most effective when users have a mutual following-follower relationship (Margolin et al. 2018) or when an expert source is attached to the information (Vraga and Bode 2018).

Platforms can also play a role in facilitating the correction of misinformation. When a correction was recommended by Facebook as a 'related story' presented under a post containing misinformation about GMOs, it substantially reduced users' misperceptions about GMOs (Bode and Vraga 2015). The effectiveness of this 'related story' function, however, was not seen in the context of vaccine-autism misperception, in which people's attitudes were held much more strongly (Bode and Vraga 2015). Further, flagging a false story's publisher as an 'self-identified source of humor' can reduce misperceptions even more effectively than flags generated by fact-checkers or other social media users, especially among those most predisposed to believe the misinformation (Garrett and Poulsen 2019). One reason for the effectiveness of this strategy may be that it not only corrects the misinformation but also provides an 'alternative narrative' to explain why it exists in the first place (Hamby et al. 2020).

Format

In some circumstances, visuals can increase the effectiveness of corrections. Dixon et al. (2015) found that when correcting vaccine misinformation with messages about scientific consensus, providing a visual exemplar of such consensus, such as a photo of a group of scientists, was more effective in refuting the vaccine-autism link than text-only corrections, especially among those who had pre-existing unfavourable views of science. Figures that present numeric information (e.g. the number of attacks in the Iraq War, the growth in jobs, the change in global average temperature) can also reduce misperceptions more effectively than equivalent texts (Nyhan and Reifler 2019). In addition, 'truth scales' that visualise the ruling on the veracity of the claim can also be more effective than a text-only correction (Amazeen et al. 2018). Finally, putting fact-checks in a video format increases the likelihood that viewers will pay attention, understand the issue, and accept the correction (Young et al. 2018).

Not all images are equally effective. Hameleers et al. (2020) found that 'multimodal' fact-checks on social media (i.e. those that include images) were no better than text-only ones at reducing misperceptions. However, the images used in their experimental manipulation were not directly relevant to the content of the fact-check. This finding suggests that in order for an image or video to increase a fact-check's effectiveness, it should directly reinforce the central message of the correction.

Wording

Researchers have studied several different aspects of how wording might shape effectiveness. We focus here on two central questions. The first is whether it helps or hurts to repeat the initial misinformation as part of the correction. The second is whether it is useful to provide an 'alternative narrative' as part of the correction that provides more detail about the true story.

When a piece of misinformation is repeated, it starts to take on the 'illusion of truth', seeming more familiar and thus more true (Berinsky 2017). For example, people who are exposed to 'fake news' articles even once are more likely to later say that they are accurate (Pennycook et al. 2018). The worry, then, is that if corrections repeat the initial misinformation, they may have the unintended effect of making the misinformation seem more plausible. However, the empirical evidence for this effect is limited: while corrections that repeat the initial misinformation are slightly less effective than those that do not, they do not fully backfire (Swire, Ecker, et al. 2017). Indeed, recent evidence has even shown that corrections that explicitly repeated the misinformation can be more effective in improving belief accuracy than corrections that avoided repeating the misinformation, possibly due to the increased salience of the falsity of the misinformation (Ecker et al. 2017).

The amount of detail provided in the correction also matters for its success. A full explanation of why a piece of misinformation is wrong (a refutation) is more effective than a simple statement that a piece of misinformation is wrong (a retraction), and these effects persist for weeks after seeing the initial misinformation and correction (Swire, Ecker, et al. 2017). Similarly, Sangalang et al. (2019) found that corrections embedded within a narrative story were effective in correcting misperceptions about tobacco products and changing related behavior intentions, potentially because they increased involvement in and attention to the content of the correction.

The correction worked – what next?

Even when a correction is fully accepted – in other words, when a person believes the correction and understands that the misinformation is false – its effects can linger. This section focuses on how successfully corrected misinformation can shape beliefs, attitudes, and trust.

The effect of misinformation on attitudes can persist

Even when corrective information successfully updates people's beliefs, it may not be equally effective at influencing attitudes that were influenced by the misinformation. Thorson (2016) refers to these lingering attitudinal effects as 'belief echoes', presenting experimental evidence that even when a correction successfully reverts beliefs back to pre-misinformation levels, attitudes are still swayed by the retracted misinformation (Thorson 2016). The 'belief echoes' effect has also been replicated in contexts where accurate belief updating failed to produce downstream effects on favourability towards Donald Trump (Nyhan et al. 2019) or attitudes towards immigration (Hopkins et al. 2019).

Corrected misinformation also continues to shape attitudes and opinions in non-political contexts. It affects behavior, memory, and opinion through a process sometimes called the 'continued influence effect' (Ecker, Lewandowsky, and Apai 2011; Ecker, Lewandowsky, Swire, et al. 2011). Across a wide range of topics and outcomes, the results are consistent: even when someone accepts a correction, it does not always fully 'un-ring the bell' of misinformation.

There are several mechanisms for this continued influence effect. First, people sometimes engage in attitude-congruent motivated reasoning. Even when their misperceptions are corrected, they 'explain away' this new information by looking for other arguments that help align the uncongenial information with their preferred worldview. One such strategy is biased attribution of blame: even when partisans accept facts about the changes in economic conditions, they rationalise the information by blaming the opposing party for the worsening conditions and praise their own party for the improvements (Bisgaard 2019). People may also explain away the uncongenial information with biased credibility judgments, expressing their displeasure by concluding that the source of the uncongenial information is not credible after all (Khanna and Sood 2018).

Second, sometimes the misinformation becomes part of a person's 'mental model' of a particular event and thus becomes more difficult to dislodge (Ecker et al. 2015). For example, when retracting misinformation about a fictitious warehouse fire (that it was due to negligence with volatile materials), the retraction was not effective in reducing reliance on the misinformation unless it offered an alternative explanation (evidence of arson was found elsewhere) (Johnson and Seifert 1994). Because alternative explanations help people to revise their mental models, they can be more effective than simple retractions at reducing the continued influence effect (Walter and Murphy 2018).

Finally, a piece of misinformation can carry an 'affective charge' that shapes a person's emotional reactions to the object of the misinformation in a way that even a successful correction cannot fully eliminate (Sherman and Kim 2002). Lodge and Taber (2005) call this 'hot cognition' and found that the affective charge attached to a socio-political concept can be activated within milliseconds of exposure, much faster than the cognitive evaluation of the concept. Further, people had a more difficult time processing affectively incongruent information (e.g. cockroach – delightful) than affectively congruent information (e.g. cockroach – disgusting), which implies that corrections that run counter to one's automatic affective responses may be less effective.

Unintended consequences of the media's focus on corrections

Finally, it is worth noting that the intense media focus on fact-checking and misinformation may have additional unintended consequences. When people are repeatedly exposed to corrected misinformation, they may infer a larger lesson: that the information environment is a dangerous and difficult to navigate place (Wenzel 2019). Some empirical evidence gives credence to this concern. For example, an intervention such as a general warning about misinformation on social media, despite reducing people's beliefs in false news headlines, also reduced their beliefs in true headlines (Clayton et al. 2019). This spillover effect can be also seen in similar interventions such as providing tips on detecting misinformation (Guess et al. 2019b), although in both types of interventions, the effect size of reducing beliefs in true headlines is substantially smaller than the effect size of reducing beliefs in false ones. Further, reading corrections in which journalists adjudicate factual disputes can also reduce the confidence in one's ability to find truth in politics among those who are less interested in the topic under dispute, raising normative concerns over the unintended effect on political efficacy (Pingree et al. 2014).

Conclusion

On average, corrections are successful at moving people closer to the truth. When confronted with a piece of corrective information, at least some people will change their beliefs in the direction of the correction. However, 'some' is often not good enough, especially when it comes to misinformation with direct health consequences (for example, vaccines). The literature reviewed in this chapter offers a larger framework for how to think about what makes a correction successful, as well as specific, evidence-based advice for those looking to design corrections that work.

When evaluating whether a correction is successful, it is important to first offer a clear definition of success. Even when a correction is fully accepted, it may not have downstream effects on related attitudes. Normatively, this is not always a problem. To give a specific example, we would neither expect nor want a single correction of a politician's falsehood to turns someone from an ardent supporter to a fierce opponent. Attitudes, especially central ones like those related to politics and health, are not so easily changed by a single piece of information (or its correction) – nor should they be.

Many of the empirical findings about what makes corrections successful are to some extent common sense. Most importantly, corrections are more successful when a person is inclined to believe them anyway (i.e. when a correction confirms what they already wish was true). However, much of the time, we are concerned about how to make corrections work for people who are not inclined to believe them. A decade ago, to answer this question we would have had to rely on intuition and/or theories imported from other contexts. Today, we can draw on hundreds of empirical investigations of how to correct misinformation across a range of contexts. While these investigations offer a nuanced view of how and when corrections succeed, a few major lessons stand out. Corrections work better when they come from a trusted source. Corrections work better when they offer the reader (either with visuals or with narrative) a clear, compelling story. And finally, they work better when are met with curiosity, desire for accuracy, and the ability to navigate the increasingly complex media environment.

References

Amazeen, M.A., Thorson, E., Muddiman, A., and Graves, L., 2018. Correcting Political and Consumer Misperceptions: The Effectiveness and Effects of Rating Scale Versus Contextual Correction Formats. *Journalism & Mass Communication Quarterly*, 95 (1), 28–48.

Berinsky, A.J., 2017. Rumors and Health Care Reform: Experiments in Political Misinformation. *British Journal of Political Science*, 47 (2), 241–262.

Bisgaard, M., 2019. How Getting the Facts Right Can Fuel Partisan-Motivated Reasoning. *American Journal of Political Science*, ajps.12432.

Bode, L., and Vraga, E.K., 2015. In Related News, That was Wrong: The Correction of Misinformation Through Related Stories Functionality in Social Media. *Journal of Communication*, 65 (4), 619–638.

Clayton, K., Blair, S., Busam, J.A., Forstner, S., Glance, J., Green, G., Kawata, A., Kovvuri, A., Martin, J., Morgan, E., Sandhu, M., Sang, R., Scholz-Bright, R., Welch, A.T., Wolff, A.G., Zhou, A., and Nyhan, B., 2019. Real Solutions for Fake News? Measuring the Effectiveness of General Warnings and Fact-Check Tags in Reducing Belief in False Stories on Social Media. *Political Behavior*, retrieved from <https://doi.org/10.1007/s11109-019-09533-0>.

Coddington, M., Molyneux, L., and Lawrence, R.G., 2014. Fact Checking the Campaign: How Political Reporters Use Twitter to Set the Record Straight (or Not). *The International Journal of Press/Politics*, 19 (4), 391–409.

Dixon, G.N., McKeever, B.W., Holton, A.E., Clarke, C., and Eosco, G., 2015. The Power of a Picture: Overcoming Scientific Misinformation by Communicating Weight-of-Evidence Information with Visual Exemplars: The Power of a Picture. *Journal of Communication*, 65 (4), 639–659.

Eagly, A.H., and Chaiken, S., 1993. *The Psychology of Attitudes*. Orlando, FL: Harcourt Brace Jovanovich College Publishers.

Ecker, U.K.H., and Ang, L.C., 2019. Political Attitudes and the Processing of Misinformation Corrections. *Political Psychology*, 40 (2), 241–260.

Ecker, U.K.H., Hogan, J.L., and Lewandowsky, S., 2017. Reminders and Repetition of Misinformation: Helping or Hindering Its Retraction? *Journal of Applied Research in Memory and Cognition*, 6 (2), 185–192.

Ecker, U.K.H., Lewandowsky, S., and Apai, J., 2011. Terrorists Brought Down the Plane! – No, Actually it was a Technical Fault: Processing Corrections of Emotive Information. *Quarterly Journal of Experimental Psychology*, 64 (2), 283–310.

Ecker, U.K.H., Lewandowsky, S., Cheung, C.S.C., and Maybery, M.T., 2015. He did it! She did it! No, She did not! Multiple Causal Explanations and the Continued Influence of Misinformation. *Journal of Memory and Language*, 85, 101–115.

Ecker, U.K.H., Lewandowsky, S., Swire, B., and Chang, D., 2011. Correcting false information in memory: Manipulating the strength of misinformation encoding and its retraction. *Psychonomic Bulletin & Review*, 18 (3), 570–578.

Frederick, S., 2005. Cognitive Reflection and Decision Making. *Journal of Economic Perspectives*, 19 (4), 25–42.

Garrett, R.K., Nisbet, E.C., and Lynch, E.K., 2013. Undermining the Corrective Effects of Media-Based Political Fact Checking? The Role of Contextual Cues and Naïve Theory. *Journal of Communication*, 63 (4), 617–637.

Garrett, R.K. and Poulsen, S., 2019. Flagging Facebook Falsehoods: Self-Identified Humor Warnings Outperform Fact Checker and Peer Warnings. *Journal of Computer-Mediated Communication*, 24 (5), 240–258.

Gervais, W.M., 2015. Override the Controversy: Analytic Thinking Predicts Endorsement of Evolution. *Cognition*, 142, 312–321.

Gilbert, D.T., Fiske, S.T., and Lindzey, G., 1998. *The Handbook of Social Psychology*, Vols. 1–2, 4th ed. New York: McGraw-Hill.

Guess, A.M., Lerner, M., Lyons, B., Montgomery, J. M., Nyhan, B., Reifler, J., and Sircar, N. 2019b. A Digital Media Literacy Intervention Increases Discernment between Mainstream and False News in the United States and India. *Working Paper*.

Guess, A.M., Nagler, J., and Tucker, J., 2019a. Less than You Think: Prevalence and Predictors of Fake News Dissemination on Facebook. *Science Advances*, 5 (1), eaau4586.

Guess, A.M., Nyhan, B., and Reifler, J., 2020. Exposure to Untrustworthy Websites in the 2016 US Election. *Nature Human Behaviour*, 1–9.

Guillory, J.J. and Geraci, L., 2013. Correcting Erroneous Inferences in Memory: The Role of Source Credibility. *Journal of Applied Research in Memory and Cognition*, 2 (4), 201–209.

Hamby, A., Ecker, U., and Brinberg, D., 2020. How Stories in Memory Perpetuate the Continued Influence of False Information. *Journal of Consumer Psychology*, 30 (2), 240–259.

Hameleers, M., Powell, T.E., Meer, T.G.L.A.V.D., and Bos, L., 2020. A Picture Paints a Thousand Lies? The Effects and Mechanisms of Multimodal Disinformation and Rebuttals Disseminated via Social Media. *Political Communication*, 37 (2), 281–301.

Hopkins, D.J., Sides, J., and Citrin, J., 2019. The Muted Consequences of Correct Information about Immigration. *The Journal of Politics*, 81 (1), 315–320.

Johnson, H.M. and Seifert, C.M., 1994. Sources of the Continued Influence Effect: When Misinformation in Memory Affects Later Inferences. *Journal of Experimental Psychology: Learning, Memory, and Cognition*, 20 (6), 1420–1436.

Kahan, D.M., 2013. Ideology, Motivated Reasoning, and Cognitive Reflection. *Judgment and Decision Making*, 8 (4), 407–424.

Kahan, D.M. and Braman, D., 2006. Cultural Cognition and Public Policy. *Yale Law & Policy Review*, 24, 147–170.

Kahan, D.M., Braman, D., Cohen, G.L., Gastil, J., and Slovic, P., 2010. Who Fears the HPV Vaccine, Who Doesn't, and Why? An Experimental Study of the Mechanisms of Cultural Cognition. *Law and Human Behavior*, 34 (6), 501–516.

Kahan, D.M., Braman, D., Gastil, J., Slovic, P., and Mertz, C.K., 2007. Culture and Identity-Protective Cognition: Explaining the White-Male Effect in Risk Perception. *Journal of Empirical Legal Studies*, 4 (3), 465–505.

Kahan, D.M., Landrum, A., Carpenter, K., Helft, L., and Jamieson, K.H., 2017. Science Curiosity and Political Information Processing. *Political Psychology*, 38 (S1), 179–199.

Kahan, D.M., Peters, E., Wittlin, M., Slovic, P., Ouellette, L.L., Braman, D., and Mandel, G., 2012. The Polarizing Impact of Science Literacy and Numeracy on Perceived Climate Change Risks. *Nature Climate Change*, 2 (10), 732–735.

Khanna, K. and Sood, G., 2018. Motivated Responding in Studies of Factual Learning. *Political Behavior*, 40 (1), 79–101.

Kraft, P.W., Lodge, M., and Taber, C.S., 2015. Why People "Don't Trust the Evidence": Motivated Reasoning and Scientific Beliefs. *The ANNALS of the American Academy of Political and Social Science*, 658 (1), 121–133.

Kunda, Z., 1990. The Case for Motivated Reasoning. *Psychological Bulletin*, 108 (3), 480–498.

Lewandowsky, S., Stritzke, W.G.K., Oberauer, K., and Morales, M., 2005. Memory for Fact, Fiction, and Misinformation: The Iraq War 2003. *Psychological Science*, 16 (3), 190–195.

Lodge, M., and Taber, C.S., 2005. The Automaticity of Affect for Political Leaders, Groups, and Issues: An Experimental Test of the Hot Cognition Hypothesis. *Political Psychology*, 26 (3), 455–482.

Lyons, B.A., 2018. When Readers Believe Journalists: Effects of Adjudication in Varied Dispute Contexts. *International Journal of Public Opinion Research*, 30 (4), 583–606.

Margolin, D.B., Hannak, A., and Weber, I., 2018. Political Fact-Checking on Twitter: When Do Corrections Have an Effect? *Political Communication*, 35 (2), 196–219.

Nieminen, S., and Rapeli, L., 2019. Fighting Misperceptions and Doubting Journalists' Objectivity: A Review of Fact-checking Literature. *Political Studies Review*, 17 (3), 296–309.

Nyhan, B., Porter, E., Reifler, J., and Wood, T.J., 2019. Taking Fact-Checks Literally But Not Seriously? The Effects of Journalistic Fact-Checking on Factual Beliefs and Candidate Favorability. *Political Behavior*, 42, 939–960.

Nyhan, B. and Reifler, J., 2015. Does Correcting Myths about the Flu Vaccine Work? An Experimental Evaluation of the Effects of Corrective Information. *Vaccine*, 33 (3), 459–464.

Nyhan, B. and Reifler, J., 2019. The Roles of Information Deficits and Identity Threat in the Prevalence of Misperceptions. *Journal of Elections, Public Opinion and Parties*, 29 (2), 222–244.

Nyhan, B., Reifler, J., Richey, S., and Freed, G.L., 2014. Effective Messages in Vaccine Promotion: A Randomized Trial. *PEDIATRICS*, 133 (4), e835– e842.

Page, B.I., Shapiro, R.Y., and Dempsey, G.R., 1987. What Moves Public Opinion? *American Political Science Review*, 81 (1), 23–43.

Pennycook, G., Cannon, T.D., and Rand, D.G., 2018. Prior exposure increases perceived accuracy of fake news. *Journal of Experimental Psychology: General*, 147 (12), 1865–1880.

Pennycook, G., Fugelsang, J.A., and Koehler, D.J., 2015. Everyday Consequences of Analytic Thinking. *Current Directions in Psychological Science*, 24 (6), 425–432.

Pennycook, G., and Rand, D.G., 2019. Lazy, Not Biased: Susceptibility to Partisan Fake News is Better Explained by Lack of Reasoning than by Motivated Reasoning. *Cognition*, 188, 39–50.

Pingree, R.J., Brossard, D., and McLeod, D.M., 2014. Effects of Journalistic Adjudication on Factual Beliefs, News Evaluations, Information Seeking, and Epistemic Political Efficacy. *Mass Communication and Society*, 17 (5), 615–638.

Sangalang, A., Ophir, Y., and Cappella, J.N., 2019. The Potential for Narrative Correctives to Combat Misinformation. *Journal of Communication*, 69 (3), 298–319.

Sherman, D.K. and Kim, H.S., 2002. Affective Perseverance: The Resistance of Affect to Cognitive Invalidation. *Personality and Social Psychology Bulletin*, 28 (2), 224–237.

Shin, J. and Thorson, K., 2017. Partisan Selective Sharing: The Biased Diffusion of Fact-Checking Messages on Social Media: Sharing Fact-Checking Messages on Social Media. *Journal of Communication*, 67 (2), 233–255.

Swire, B., Berinsky, A.J., Lewandowsky, S., and Ecker, U.K.H., 2017. Processing Political Misinformation: Comprehending the Trump Phenomenon. *Royal Society Open Science*, 4, 160802.

Swire, B., Ecker, U.K.H., and Lewandowsky, S., 2017. The Role of Familiarity in Correcting Inaccurate Information. *Journal of Experimental Psychology: Learning, Memory, and Cognition*, 43 (12), 1948–1961.

Thorson, E., 2016. Belief Echoes: The Persistent Effects of Corrected Misinformation. *Political Communication*, 33 (3), 460–480.

Thorson, K., Vraga, E., and Ekdale, B., 2010. Credibility in Context: How Uncivil Online Commentary Affects News Credibility. *Mass Communication and Society*, 13 (3), 289–313.

Tully, M., Vraga, E.K., and Bode, L., 2019. Designing and Testing News Literacy Messages for Social Media. *Mass Communication and Society*, 0 (0), 1–25.

van der Meer, T.G.L.A., and Jin, Y., 2020. Seeking Formula for Misinformation Treatment in Public Health Crises: The Effects of Corrective Information Type and Source. *Health Communication*, 35 (5), 560–575.

Vraga, E.K. and Bode, L., 2018. I Do Not Believe You: How Providing a Source Corrects Health Misperceptions across Social Media Platforms. *Information, Communication & Society*, 21 (10), 1337–1353.

Vraga, E.K. and Tully, M., 2019. News Literacy, Social Media Behaviors, and Skepticism Toward Information on Social Media. *Information, Communication & Society*, 0 (0), 1–17.

Walker, M. and Gottfried, J. 2019. *Republicans Far More Likely than Democrats to Say Fact-checkers Tend to Favor One Side*. Pew Research Center, viewed 23 April 2020, <www.pewresearch.org/fact-tank/2019/06/27/republicans-far-more-likely-than-democrats-to-say-fact-checkers-tend-to-favor-one-side/>

Walter, N. and Murphy, S.T., 2018. How to Unring the Bell: A Meta-analytic Approach to Correction of Misinformation. *Communication Monographs*, 85 (3), 423–441.

Wenzel, A., 2019. To Verify or to Disengage: Coping with "Fake News" and Ambiguity. *International Journal of Communication*, 13 (0), 19.

Wood, T. and Porter, E., 2019. The Elusive Backfire Effect: Mass Attitudes' Steadfast Factual Adherence. *Political Behavior*, 41 (1), 135–163.

Young, D.G., Jamieson, K.H., Poulsen, S., and Goldring, A., 2018. Fact-Checking Effectiveness as a Function of Format and Tone: Evaluating FactCheck.org and FlackCheck.org. *Journalism & Mass Communication Quarterly*, 95 (1), 49–75.

BUILDING CONNECTIVE DEMOCRACY

Interdisciplinary solutions to the problem of polarisation

Christian Staal Bruun Overgaard, Anthony Dudo, Matthew Lease, Gina M. Masullo, Natalie Jomini Stroud, Scott R. Stroud, and Samuel C. Woolley

Polarisation and its consequences

Recent decades have seen an increase in polarisation, or the extremisation of beliefs, in several contexts and a surge in research on the topic. The vast majority of this research has focused on the nature, origins, and outcomes of polarisation; scholars have paid relatively little attention to how the negative consequences of polarisation can be mitigated. In this chapter, we use connective democracy – a new approach that seeks to reduce divisiveness and promote constructive discursive spaces – as a lens for understanding the problem, with an orientation towards bridging societal and political divides. To this end, we review recent advances from a variety of disciplines in search of practical and feasible solutions to the harmful consequences of polarisation.

There are different forms of polarisation, and they have been documented in democracies across the world, including countries in Africa (Michelitch 2015; Southall 2018), East Asia (Dalton and Tanaka 2007), Europe (Westwood et al. 2018; Hobolt, Leeper and Tilley in press), Latin America (Singer 2016), and the United States (Iyengar et al. 2019). One type of polarisation relates to specific issues. For example, during the last three decades, the American public has become increasingly polarised on a wide range of political issues, such as environmental laws, immigration, and governmental regulation of business (Pew Research Center 2014). Polarisation is also evident on scientific topics, such as climate change, nuclear power, and childhood vaccinations (Nisbet, Cooper and Garrett 2015; Pew Research Center 2015). Another type, affective polarisation, involves dislike and distrust of those holding opposing views (Iyengar, Sood and Lelkes 2012). The rise of affective polarisation is particularly evident in the US (Iyengar et al. 2019), but similar trends have been found in Europe, notably in the UK, following the 2016 Brexit vote (Hobolt, Leeper and Tilley in press). Yet another definition of polarisation, the percentage of Americans identifying as Republicans or Democrats, or the extremism of self-reported ideologies (on the liberal-conservative spectrum), shows little change over time (Gentzkow 2016). For our purposes, we focus on issue and affective polarisation and review solutions for combatting their detrimental consequences.

Scholars have offered several explanations for rising polarisation, including negative political campaigning (Iyengar et al. 2019), polarising cues from political elites (Bisgaard and Slothuus 2018), media coverage and framing of polarisation (Levendusky and Malhotra 2016), the use of politically like-minded media (Stroud 2011), the proliferation of social media (Settle 2018), and the increasing salience of partisanship as a social identity (Iyengar, Sood and Lelkes 2012). These explanations make clear that interpersonal connections and mediated experiences contribute to polarisation.

Polarisation is worrisome because it strikes at central components of democracy. Well-functioning democracies depend on effective and equitable citizen participation, openness to persuasion, news media that hold powerful entities accountable, and citizen input into the political agenda (Dahl 1998). Polarisation can stymie each of these factors. This is not to say that all aspects of polarisation are democratically harmful; partisanship can have positive demo-cratic effects, such as increased political participation (Rosenblum 2008). It becomes a threat to democracy, however, when it undermines free flows of information, respect for individuals, and open decision-making (Dewey 1984; Habermas 1984). When this occurs, the institutions of government function poorly. Polarisation incentivises political leaders to avoid collaboration because voters become dismissive of compromise on important issues, which can lead to politi-cal gridlock in formal decision-making institutions such as the US Congress (Hetherington and Rudolph 2015; Jacobson 2016). Polarisation can also harm social relationships; Americans, for example, discriminate against out-party members in both professional and everyday situations (see Iyengar et al. 2019).

Global polarisation is tied to the spread of mis/disinformation (the unintentional and inten-tional, respectively, spread of false and misleading content) (Jack 2017). Polarisation exacerbates the spread of false content, and the spread of misinformation can lead to polarisation.

A polarised electorate is more susceptible to misinformation. This is because people with more extreme attitudes are more likely to engage in motivated reasoning (Kunda, 1990), which, in turn, can make people more likely to believe congenial misinformation. Van Prooijen, Krou-wel, and Pollet (2015) find that people with extreme opinions are more likely to believe in conspiracy theories. Tucker et al. (2018), similarly, argue that partisanship predicts the types of information that people tend to believe. The outcome is that partisans not only disagree on political issues but also even perceive objective facts about the world differently – a tendency that has increased in the US in recent decades (Jones 2019).

The spread of misinformation also can exacerbate polarisation. For example, Cook (2016) argues that, beginning in the 1990s, politically motivated disinformation about the causes of cli-mate change began to make many people doubt the scientific consensus on the issue. This led to a polarisation of views on the topic. Even a little misinformation can have real effects. Corner, Whitmarch, and Xenias (2012) show increases in climate change scepticism after reading one editorial undermining scientific consensus on the issue alongside one that took the issue more seriously. In fact, Woolley and Howard (2018) find that digital propagandists often specifically target already-polarised parties to inflame their polarisation. Given the negative consequences of polarisation and their connection to misinformation, finding ways of reducing polarisation is paramount. We turn to these strategies next.

Solutions to the problem of polarisation

Connective democracy is a new way of thinking about the problem of polarisation. Rather than focusing on the nature and consequences of the problem, connective democracy asks scholars to think about solutions that bridge societal and political divides. Pragmatic solutions to these problems could scale by, for example, being incorporated into existing and new forms of digital technology that facilitate connectivity. In the next section, we identify several potential solutions to the problem of polarisation.

Encouraging intergroup contact

A central finding in social psychology is that people tend to be prejudiced against members of their social out-groups (Allport 1954; Turner and Tajfel 1986). Such biases have led to discrimination against both racial and sexual minorities and, more recently, out-parties (Iyengar et al. 2019). Out-group biases are an ingrained part of human nature; in experiments, subjects discriminate against those in other groups even when they are aware of the group assignment being random and meaningless (Turner and Tajfel 1986). As a possible solution to the problem of out-group prejudice, a long line of psychology research, going back to Gordon Allport's (1954) seminal book *The Nature of Prejudice*, documents that intergroup contact can reduce out-group biases and intergroup hostility (for a review, see Pettigrew and Tropp 2013). Various forms of intergroup contact have been shown to reduce many types of prejudice, such as discrimination against the LGBT community (Rössler and Brosius 2001; Schiappa, Gregg and Hewes 2005) and Muslims (Bruneau, Kteily and Urbiola 2019). Intergroup contact has also been found to decrease racial discrimination (Goldman 2012; Harwood, Qadar and Chen 2016).

In its most basic form, intergroup contact occurs when people meet and interact with someone from their out-group. The positive effects of such contact are contingent on the contact being positive and on the people involved having shared goals. Also, the people involved must perceive each other as realistic representations of the social groups they are representing, and this group membership must be salient (Allport 1954; Goldman 2012). There are several explanations for why such contact can reduce biases: meeting an out-group member can demystify the out-group and increase familiarity, make people less afraid of future contact with out-group members, and enhance people's empathy for the out-group. In a meta-analysis of more than 500 studies, Pettigrew and Tropp (2008) find evidence of all these pathways, with strongest effects for fear and empathy. Similarly beneficial effects may arise from awareness of intergroup friendships (for a meta-analysis, see Zhou et al. 2019) and imagined contact with out-group members (for a meta-analysis, see Miles and Crisp 2014).

In the context of affective polarisation, however, the most promising type of intergroup contact may be mediated intergroup contact, which, for example, happens when people see sympathetic out-group members on TV or hear positive intergroup interactions on the radio. Survey data suggest that people who experience more mediated intergroup contact with a given out-group are less prejudiced towards that out-group (Goldman 2012; Schwab, Sagioglou and Greitemeyer 2019). Experimental work in which some subjects experience mediated intergroup contact with their out-group and others do not confirms this result. People who experience mediated intergroup contact tend to become less prejudiced against their out-group members. This has been shown in a wide range of contexts, including prejudice towards people with different racial backgrounds (Ramasubramanian 2015; Harwood, Qadar and Chen 2016; Kim and Harwood 2020), the LGBT community (Rössler and Brosius 2001; Schiappa, Sagioglou and Greitemeyer 2005), and people with tattoos (Rössler and Brosius 2001). What has received less scholarly attention is how mediated contact may influence affective polarisation. An exception to this is Huddy and Yair (2019), who find that subjects reading a news article about a friendly social encounter between two opposing party leaders feel less hostile towards members of the out-party than those reading about an unfriendly social encounter between the two leaders. Although more research is needed to understand how mediated intergroup contact works in a political context, it constitutes a promising solution to the problem of polarisation.

Correcting misperceptions

Given the linkages between mis/disinformation and polarisation, tactics that help reduce misperceptions also may have the benefit of reducing polarisation. Corrective messaging refers to tactics that, in various ways, present accurate information to mitigate the impact of misinformation or misperceptions. We review three such tactics next.

Immediate corrective messaging refers to the practice of providing accurate information immediately following exposure to misinformation. Several scholars find that this tactic can effectively reduce false beliefs (e.g. Goldfarb and Kriner 2017; Vraga and Bode 2017; although see Garrett and Weeks 2013). A recent meta-analysis by Walter and Tukachinsky (2020) shows that corrective messaging is most effective when done immediately after exposure to misinformation rather than later. Corrective messaging may be a way to reduce polarisation by reducing the misperceptions that undergird it.

A related tactic, prebunking, refers to pre-emptively refuting misinformation before people encounter it. As Cook (2016) points out, research suggests this approach is more effective than correcting misinformation after the fact. Likewise, Bolsen and Druckman (2015) find evidence of prebunking's ability to reduce the influence of misinformation. Their research suggests that prebunking is more effective than debunking. Many studies have demonstrated the ability of prebunking to reduce the impact of misinformation (for a meta-analysis, see Banas and Rains 2010).

A third tactic involves making people aware of misperceptions relating to polarisation. Although some forms of polarisation have increased in recent decades, many people think that the problem is worse than it is. The American public, for example, tends to overestimate how divided the country is (Ahler 2014; Westfall et al. 2015). Such exaggerations are not without consequences. Yudkin and colleagues (2019) find that people who have more extreme perceptions of how divided the country is view their political opponents more negatively. Perceptions of extreme polarisation can, as Ahler (2014) points out, become a self-fulfilling prophecy. If this is the case – and, as described later in this chapter, there is reason to believe that it is – one way of mitigating inter-party hostility may be to correct the public's misperceptions regarding polarisation.

Experimental work indeed finds that correcting people's misperceptions about polarisation can be a way to bridge divides. Ahler (2014) randomly assigned subjects to learn about the actual political positions of most Americans, which tend to be less extreme than people assume. This led the study participants to adopt more moderate political opinions (although, for a conflicting finding, see Levendusky and Malhotra 2016). Similarly, Ahler and Sood (2018) found that Americans overestimate the proportions of partisans belonging to party-stereotypical groups (for example, Democrats who are LGBT or Republicans who are wealthy) and that these misperceptions exacerbate affective polarisation. What's more, in two follow-up experiments, correcting these misperceptions improved the subjects' attitudes towards out-party members. Other recent experimental work documents that correcting misperceptions can be a way to bridge political divides (see van Boven, Ehret and Sherman 2018; Freeder 2018). Research on the effects of correcting misperceptions is still developing; nevertheless, it is a potentially effective solution to the problem of polarisation – and a fruitful avenue for future research.

Priming superordinate identities

Another possible solution is making people think of themselves less in terms of their issue, group, and partisan affiliations and more in terms of other social identities. As Iyengar and Krupenkin (2018) show, partisanship has become one of the most salient social identities in America; this, in turn, may make Americans more hostile towards their out-party. Further, recent studies suggest that decreasing the salience of people's partisan identities can decrease affective polarisation. Levendusky (2018a) demonstrates that priming Americans' national identity reduces affective polarisation – likely because it reduces the salience of their partisan identities. The same result emerged in a follow-up natural experiment, in which affective polarisation among survey respondents was lower among those who responded close to the Fourth of July – most likely because this day primed their national identity vis-à-vis their partisan identities. Similarly, in another natural experiment, Carlin and Love (2018) illustrate that Americans' 'trust gap' (i.e. their tendency to trust co-partisans more than rival partisans) narrowed during the time of Osama bin Laden's assassination in 2011.

Priming people's national identity may, however, have harmful consequences. Wojcieszak and Garrett (2018) uncover, across three experiments, that priming national identity makes American immigration opponents more affectively polarised. A way to overcome this limitation may be to make people think of their shared humanity rather than their national identity. Work on dehumanisation lends credence to this idea. In an experiment, Albarello and Rubini (2012) primed the superordinate identities of white Italian undergraduates (i.e. made their human identities salient) and used 'multiple categorisation' (by providing additional information about people besides skin colour – such as age, gender, and religion). These two interventions decreased subjects' dehumanisation of the person being described. Priming the salience of certain identities may help alleviate the discrimination that can result from polarisation; however, further research is needed to fully understand these effects.

Possible solutions that need refinement

Although it is useful to learn about solutions that seem to address polarisation, it is also worthwhile to review solutions with inconsistent evidence about their ability to reduce polarisation and solutions that seem to inflame, rather than reduce, polarisation. We review several such solutions next.

One proposed solution, with several studies providing preliminary support, draws from self-affirmation theory. Self-affirmation occurs when people see themselves positively (Steele and Liu 1983), such as when people think about their talents or aspects of their lives in which they excel. Applied to polarisation, people who have been self-affirmed are more likely to engage thoughtfully with views unlike their own (e.g. Binning et al. 2010), which can reduce polarisation. Yet subsequent evidence is less optimistic about the efficacy of self-affirmation for curbing polarisation; self-affirmation can increase polarisation under some circumstances (van Prooijen, Sparks and Jessop 2012) and fail to make any difference in others (Levendusky 2018b). Despite initial promise, there is a need for caution in seeing self-affirmation as a solution to polarisation.

Another proposed solution is to prime partisan ambivalence and encourage people to think about the desirable attributes of an opposing political party. Recognising the positive attributes of undesirable policies or polities might make people's attitudes less polarised. Efforts to prime partisan ambivalence, however, have not found any such effects on those with stronger partisan attitudes, although there appear to be some effects among moderates (Levendusky 2018b). This is explained by the difficulty that stronger partisans have in articulating desirable aspects of an opposing party.

A third solution involves encouraging people to recognise their lack of in-depth knowledge. People overestimate their understanding of how things work, which is known as the illusion of explanatory depth. Some research suggests that awareness of this overconfidence can lead to more moderate attitudes (Fernbach et al. 2013), yet additional research did not find evidence that prejudice towards those with different views was affected by a similar manipulation (Voelkel, MJ and Colombo 2018).

A fourth potential solution with particular relevance to science communication, consensus messaging, warrants additional examination. Especially relevant to the issue of climate change (Cook 2016), consensus messaging conveys the degree of agreement among experts about a scientific topic. Some studies suggest that consensus messaging can significantly increase perceived consensus and acceptance of anthropogenic climate change (Bolsen, Leeper and Shapiro 2014; Myers et al. 2015), as well as support for vaccinations (van der Linden, Clarke and Maibach 2015). Other research, however, has cast doubt on the efficacy of this approach (e.g. Dixon and Hubner 2018). More research on consensus messaging is needed and should be designed to reflect real-world conditions where accurate and misinformation co-exist (Cook 2016). Telling people the conclusions of experts, it seems, is not always sufficient to curb polarised beliefs and attitudes.

A final, often-discussed solution is education in critical reading and thinking skills and the importance of getting information from multiple sources. Education remains essential so that people can be savvy information consumers and effectively use new technologies with an appreciation for their capabilities and limitations. Yet identifying effective media literacy messaging to curb the spread of misinformation and combat polarisation is not always straightforward, with several projects turning up null results (e.g. Stroud 2011; Vraga, Bode and Tully 2020). More research on these proposed solutions may turn up more encouraging evidence, but to date, they do not seem to be viable solutions to polarisation.

Scalable solutions

The theories discussed earlier are rooted in psychology and offer theoretical rationales for and empirical evidence of their ability to reduce the harmful consequences of polarisation. Yet another important criterion for thinking of solutions is scalability. A successful in-person intervention building on interpersonal contact theory may work for the 40 people involved, but the extent of polarisation requires more far-reaching ideas.

The limitations of scale can easily be seen when evaluating approaches that ask people to fact-check information for themselves. These types of interventions quickly run afoul of the reality that information tracking and sense-making have become increasingly difficult. Effective information technologies can help us manage this information deluge. Social media platforms are estimated to employ over 100,000 human moderators to help filter objectionable content, and new programmes have been announced to figure out how to scale up misinformation efforts (Facebook 2019). In addition to human efforts, algorithms can be created to automatically remove content and to select and prioritise what content human moderators should review next. These efforts can be, and are being, employed at scale to try to reduce mis/disinformation and, in turn, polarisation. Other ideas offer similar potential to scale. Mediated interpersonal contact, for example, doesn't require people to meet in person, and even relatively small effects can be more cost effective than more in-depth interventions.

Conclusion

This chapter has laid out the problem of polarisation, its democratic consequences, and its intertwinement with the spread of misinformation. Using the perspective of connective democracy, we have reviewed possible solutions to these problems. Some solutions seem to have more promise than others. Ensuring that solutions can scale, whether through algorithmic approaches or using the media, is an important criterion when sorting through possible solutions.

The reviewed solutions all have limitations, and the research in this area is still in its infancy. Even the more promising approaches, such as intergroup contact, do not work in all circumstances and have not been thoroughly tested in political contexts. Priming superordinate identities is promising, but if national identity is primed, it can exacerbate the polarisation of attitudes towards people of other nationalities (Wojcieszak and Garrett 2018). Algorithms and machine-learning efforts are nascent in understanding the idiosyncrasies of human speech. Some strategies, such as fact-checking, can backfire and reinforce misinformation (Nyhan and Reifler 2010).

Our review of the literature suggests we need more – much more – research to fully understand how to solve the problems posed by polarisation. Research is needed to parse how intergroup contact works in a political context, how misperceptions can be corrected to ease polarisation, and which specific social identities can be primed to curb polarisation without causing other problems. These approaches also have been studied more frequently in an American context; future research should explore if and how they work in other cultures. In sum, we need more research that focuses on solving the problem of polarisation – rather than merely describing it – to build a connective democracy that breaks down barriers between opposing groups.

References

Ahler, DJ 2014, 'Self-fulfilling misperceptions of public polarization', *The Journal of Politics*, vol. 76, no. 3, pp. 607–620.

Ahler, DJ & Sood, G 2018, 'The parties in our heads: Misperceptions about party composition and their consequences', *The Journal of Politics*, vol. 80, no. 3, pp. 964–981.

Albarello, F & Rubini, M 2012, 'Reducing dehumanisation outcomes towards Blacks: The role of multiple categorisation and of human identity', *European Journal of Social Psychology*, vol. 42, no. 7, pp. 875–882.

Allport, GW 1954, *The nature of prejudice*, Doubleday, New York.

Banas, JA & Rains, SA 2010, 'A meta-analysis of research on inoculation theory', *Communication Monographs*, vol. 77, no. 3, pp. 281–311.

Binning, KR, Sherman, DK, Cohen, GL & Heitland, K 2010, 'Seeing the other side: Reducing political partisanship via self-affirmation in the 2008 presidential election', *Analyses of Social Issues and Public Policy*, vol. 10, pp. 276–292.

Bisgaard, M & Slothuus, R 2018, 'Partisan elites as culprits? How party cues shape partisan perceptual gaps', *American Journal of Political Science*, vol. 62, no. 2, pp. 456–469.

Bolsen, T & Druckman, JN 2015, 'Counteracting the politicization of science', *Journal of Communication*, vol. 65, no. 5, pp. 745–769.

Bolsen, T, Leeper, TJ & Shapiro, MA 2014, 'Doing what others do: Norms, science, and collective action on global warming', *American Politics Research*, vol. 42, no. 1, pp. 65–89.

Bruneau, EG, Kteily, NS & Urbiola, A 2019, 'A collective blame hypocrisy intervention enduringly reduces hostility towards Muslims', *Nature Human Behaviour*, pp. 1–10.

Carlin, RE & Love, GJ 2018, 'Political competition, partisanship and interpersonal trust in electoral democracies', *British Journal of Political Science*, vol. 48, no. 1, pp. 115–139.

Cook, J 2016, 'Countering climate science denial and communicating scientific consensus', in *Oxford Research Encyclopedia of Climate Science,* Oxford University Press, Oxford, UK.

Corner, A, Whitmarsh, L & Xenias, D 2012, 'Uncertainty, scepticism and attitudes towards climate change: Biased assimilation and attitude polarisation', *Climatic Change*, vol. 114, no. 3, pp. 463–478.

Dahl, RA 1998, *On Democracy*, second edition, Yale University Press, New Haven, CT.

Dalton, RJ & Tanaka, A 2007, 'The patterns of party polarization in East Asia', *Journal of East Asian Studies*, vol. 7, no. 2, pp. 203–223.

Dewey, J 1984, *The public and its problems. The later works of John Dewey*, JA Boydston (ed), Southern Illinois University Press, Carbondale.

Dixon, G & Hubner, A 2018, 'Neutralizing the effect of political worldviews by communicating scientific agreement: A thought-listing study', *Science Communication*, vol. 40, no. 3, pp. 393–415.

Facebook 2019, *Helping fact-checkers identify false claims faster*, retrieved from <https://about.fb.com/news/2019/12/helping-fact-checkers/>.

Fernbach, PM, Rogers, T, Fox, CR & Sloman, SA 2013, 'Political extremism is supported by an illusion of understanding', *Psychological Science*, vol. 24, no. 6, pp. 939–946.

Freeder, S 2018, 'Malice and stupidity: Outgroup motive attribution and affective polarization', Unpublished manuscript, Department of Political Science, University of California, Berkeley.

Garrett, RK, and Weeks, BE 2013, 'The promise and peril of real-time corrections to political misperceptions', CSCW'13, February 23–27, 2013, San Antonio, Texas, USA, viewed 24 April 2020, retrieved from <https://rkellygarrett.com/wp-content/uploads/2014/05/Garrett-and-Weeks-Promise-and-peril-of-real-time-corrections.pdf>.

Gentzkow, M 2016, *Polarization in 2016. Toulouse network for information technology whitepaper*, viewed 4 April 2020, retrieved from <www.researchgate.net/file.PostFileLoader.html?id=598f9eaded99e164d43cee91&assetKey=AS%3A526691693219840%401502584493637>.

Goldfarb, JL & Kriner, DL 2017, 'Building public support for science spending: Misinformation, motivated reasoning, and the power of corrections', *Science Communication*, vol. 39, no. 1, pp. 77–100.

Goldman, SK 2012, 'Effects of the 2008 Obama presidential campaign on White racial prejudice', *Public Opinion Quarterly*, vol. 76, no. 4, pp. 663–687.

Habermas, J 1984, *The theory of communicative action: Reason and the rationalization of society, volume 1*, Beacon, Boston.

Harwood, J, Qadar, F & Chen, C-Y 2016, 'Harmonious contact: Stories about intergroup musical collaboration improve intergroup attitudes', *Journal of Communication*, vol. 66, no. 6, pp. 937–959.

Hetherington, MJ & Rudolph, TJ 2015, *Why Washington won't work: Polarization, political trust, and the governing crisis*, University of Chicago Press, Chicago, IL.

Hobolt, S, Leeper, TJ & Tilley, J In press, 'Divided by the vote: Affective polarization in the wake of the Brexit referendum', *British Journal of Political Science*, retrieved April 24, 2020, from <www.cambridge.org/core/journals/british-journal-of-political-science>.

Huddy, L & Yair, O 2019, 'Reducing affective partisan polarization: Warm group relations or policy compromise?', viewed 4 April 2020, retrieved from <www.wpsanet.org/papers/docs/HuddyYair%20_WPSA%202019.pdf>.

Iyengar, S & Krupenkin, M 2018, 'Partisanship as social identity; Implications for the study of party polarization', *The Forum*, vol. 16, no. 1, pp. 23–45.

Iyengar, S, Lelkes, Y, Levendusky, M, Malhotra, N & Westwood, SJ 2019, 'The origins and consequences of affective polarization in the United States', *Annual Review of Political Science*, vol. 22, pp. 129–146.

Iyengar, S, Sood, G & Lelkes, Y 2012, 'Affect, not ideology: A social identity perspective on polarization', *Public Opinion Quarterly*, vol. 76, no. 3, pp. 405–431.

Jack, C 2017, 'Lexicon of lies: Terms for problematic information', *Data & Society*, vol. 3.

Jacobson, GC 2016, 'Polarization, gridlock, and presidential campaign politics in 2016', *The ANNALS of the American Academy of Political and Social Science*, vol. 667, no. 1, pp. 226–246.

Jones, PE 2019, 'Partisanship, political awareness, and retrospective evaluations, 1956–2016', *Political Behavior. Advance online publication*, retrieved from <https://doi.org/10.1007/s11109-019-09543-y>.

Kim, C & Harwood, J 2020, 'Parasocial contact's effects on relations between minority groups in a multiracial context', *International Journal of Communication*, vol. 14, p. 22.

Kunda, Z 1990, 'The case for motivated reasoning', *Psychological Bulletin*, vol. 108, no. 3, pp. 480–498.

Levendusky, MS 2018a, 'Americans, not partisans: Can priming American national identity reduce affective polarization?', *The Journal of Politics*, vol. 80, no. 1, pp. 59–70.

Levendusky, MS 2018b 'When efforts to depolarize the electorate fail', *Public Opinion Quarterly*, vol. 82, no. 3, pp. 583–592, doi: 10.1093/poq/nfy036.

Levendusky, MS & Malhotra, N 2016, 'Does media coverage of partisan polarization affect political attitudes?', *Political Communication*, vol. 33, no. 2, pp. 283–301.

Michelitch, K 2015, 'Does electoral competition exacerbate interethnic or interpartisan economic discrimination? Evidence from a field experiment in market price bargaining', *American Political Science Review*, vol. 109, no. 1, pp. 43–61.

Miles, E & Crisp, RJ 2014, 'A meta-analytic test of the imagined contact hypothesis', *Group Processes & Intergroup Relations*, vol. 17, no. 1, pp. 3–26.

Myers, TA, Maibach, E, Peters, E & Leiserowitz, A 2015, 'Simple messages help set the record straight about scientific agreement on human-caused cli- mate change: The results of two experiments', *PLoS ONE*, vol. 10, no. 3, p. 0120985.

Nisbet, EC, Cooper, KE & Garrett, RK 2015, 'The partisan brain: How dissonant science messages lead conservatives and liberals to (dis) trust science', *The ANNALS of the American Academy of Political and Social Science*, vol. 658, no. 1, pp. 36–66.

Nyhan, B & Reifler, J 2010, 'When corrections fail: The persistence of political misperceptions', *Political Behavior*, vol. 32, pp. 303–330.

Pettigrew, TF & Tropp, LR 2008, 'How does intergroup contact reduce prejudice? Meta-analytic tests of three mediators', *European Journal of Social Psychology*, vol. 38, no. 6, pp. 922–934.

Pettigrew, TF & Tropp, LR 2013, *When groups meet: The dynamics of intergroup contact*, Psychology Press, London.

Pew Research Center 2014, *Political polarization in the American public*, viewed 4 April 2020, retrieved from <www.people-press.org/2014/06/12/political-polarization-in-the-american-public/>.

Pew Research Center 2015, *Americans, politics and science issues*, viewed 18 April 2020, retrieved from <www.pewresearch.org/science/2015/07/01/americans-politics-and-science-issues/>.

Ramasubramanian, S 2015, 'Using celebrity news stories to effectively reduce racial/ethnic prejudice', *Journal of Social Issues*, vol. 71, no. 1, pp. 123–138.

Rosenblum, NL 2008, *On the side of the angels: An appreciation of parties and partisanship*, Princeton University Press, Princeton, NJ.

Rössler, P & Brosius, H-B 2001, 'Do talk shows cultivate adolescents' views of the world? A prolonged-exposure experiment', *Journal of Communication*, vol. 51, no. 1, pp. 143–163.

Schiappa, E, Gregg, PB & Hewes, DE 2005, 'The parasocial contact hypothesis', *Communication monographs*, vol. 72, no. 1, pp. 92–115.

Schwab, AK, Sagioglou, C & Greitemeyer, T 2019, 'Getting connected: Intergroup contact on Facebook', *The Journal of social psychology*, vol. 159, no. 3, pp. 344–348.

Settle, JE 2018, *Frenemies: How social media polarizes America*, Cambridge University Press, Cambridge, UK.

Singer, M 2016, 'Elite polarization and the electoral impact of left–right placements: Evidence from Latin America, 1995–2009', *Latin American Research Review*, vol. 51, no. 2, pp. 174–194.

Southall, R 2018, 'Polarization in South Africa: Toward democratic deepening or democratic decay?', *The ANNALS of the American Academy of Political and Social Science*, vol. 681, no. 1, pp. 194–208.

Steele, CM & Liu, TJ 1983, 'Dissonance processes as self-affirmation', *Journal of Personality and Social Psychology*, vol. 45, no. 1, pp. 5–19.

Stroud, NJ 2011, *Niche news: The politics of news choice*, Oxford University Press, New York.

Tucker, JA, Guess, A, Barberá, P, Vaccari, C, Siegel, A, Sanovich, S, Stukal, D & Nyhan, B 2018, 'Social media, political polarization, and political disinformation: A review of the scientific literature', *Political Polarization, and Political Disinformation: A Review of the Scientific Literature*, 1–95.

Turner, JC & Tajfel, H 1986, 'The social identity theory of intergroup behavior', *Psychology of intergroup relations*, vol. 5, pp. 7–24.

van Boven, L, Ehret, PJ & Sherman, DK 2018, 'Psychological barriers to bipartisan public support for climate policy', *Perspectives on Psychological Science*, vol. 13, no. 4, pp. 492–507.

van der Linden, SL, Clarke, CE & Maibach, EW 2015, 'Highlighting consensus among medical scientists increases public support for vaccines: Evidence from a randomized experiment', *BMC Public Health*, vol. 15, no. 1, pp. 1–5.

van Prooijen, A, Sparks, P & Jessop, DC 2012, 'Promoting or jeopardizing lighter carbon footprints? Self-affirmation can polarize environmental orientations', *Social Psychology and Personality Science*, vol. 4 no. 2, pp. 238–243. doi:10.1177/1948550612450465.

van Prooijen, JW, Krouwel, AP & Pollet, TV 2015, 'Political extremism predicts belief in conspiracy theories', *Social Psychological and Personality Science*, vol. 6, no. 5, pp. 570–578.

Voelkel, JG, MJ, B & Colombo, M 2018, 'I know that I know nothing: Can puncturing the illusion of explanatory depth overcome the relationship between attitudinal dissimilarity and prejudice?', *Comprehensive Results in Social Psychology*, vol. 3, no. 1, pp. 56–78.

Vraga, EK & Bode, L 2017, 'Using expert sources to correct health misinformation in social media', *Science Communication*, vol. 39, no. 5, pp. 621–645.

Vraga, EK, Bode, L & Tully, M 2020, 'Creating news literacy messages to enhance expert corrections of misinformation on Twitter', *Communication Research*, retrieved April 24, 2020, from <https://journals.sagepub.com/doi/10.1177/0093650219898094>.

Walter, N & Tukachinsky, R 2020, 'A meta-analytic examination of the continued influence of misinformation in the face of correction: How powerful is it, why does it happen, and how to stop it?', *Communication Research*, vol. 47, no. 2, pp. 155–177.

Westfall, J, van Boven, L, Chambers, JR & Judd, CM 2015, 'Perceiving political polarization in the United States: Party identity strength and attitude extremity exacerbate the perceived partisan divide', *Perspectives on Psychological Science*, vol. 10, no. 2, pp. 145–158.

Westwood, SJ, Iyengar, S, Walgrave, S, Leonisio, R, Miller, L & Strijbis, O 2018, 'The tie that divides: Cross-national evidence of the primacy of partyism', *European Journal of Political Research*, vol. 57, no. 2, pp. 333–354.

Wojcieszak, M & Garrett, RK 2018, 'Social identity, selective exposure, and affective polarization: How priming national identity shapes attitudes toward immigrants via news selection', *Human Communication Research*, vol. 44, no. 3, pp. 247–273.

Woolley, SC & Howard, PN 2018, *Computational propaganda: Political parties, politicians, and political manipulation on social media*, Oxford University Press, Oxford, UK.

Yudkin, DA, Hawkins, S & Dixon, T 2019, *The perception gap: How false impressions are pulling Americans apart*, viewed 4 April 2020, retrieved from <https://psyarxiv.com/r3h5q/download/?format=pdf>.

Zhou, S, Page-Gould, E, Aron, A, Moyer, A & Hewstone, M 2019, 'The extended contact hypothesis: A meta-analysis on 20 years of research', *Personality and Social Psychology Review*, vol. 23, no. 2, pp. 132–160.

INDEX

Saka, E. 389
Salvini, M. 411
Sánchez, A. N. 360
Sanders, B. 35, 74, 273, 345, 351, 421, 460
Sangalang, A, 553
Sanovich, S. 280
Sarkar, A. 170
Sarkeesian, A. 214
Scala, A. 96
Scheufele, D. A. 234
Schradie, J. 520, 524
Schroeder, R. 461
Schulz, A. 431
Schwartz, A. 111
science misinformation 231–232, 238–239; antidotes to 236–238; definitions and nomenclature in 232; framing and 238; individual ability and motivation to evaluate science and 233–234; inoculation messages and 236; institutional and techno-cognitive strategies and 238; as public problem 232–233; reasons for 233–235; shifting motivations and 237–238; systemic factors that encourage misperceptions and 235
selective attention 107
selective exposure 93
self-affirmation theory 563
self-perceived media literacy (SPML) 484
self-serving biases 550
Selva, M. 184
Sen, A. 67
Seven Financial Conspiracies Which Have Enslaved the American People 347
shallow fakes 490
Shanmugam, K. 462, 466
Shanmugaratnam, T. 462
Shapiro, B. 170
shared sensemaking 40
Sharra, A. 341
Shaw, M. 403
Shea, J. 257, 258
Shea, P. 522
Shin, J. 552
Siapera, E. 523
Siebert, F. S. 59, 72, 74
Siles, I. 362
Silverman, C. 61
Singapore: authoritarian conundrums in using POFMA in 464; discussion and conclusion on 466–467; growth of populism in 459–461; hyper-responsiveness towards public reactions of POFMA in 465–466; introduction to 459; passage of Protection from Online Falsehoods and Manipuliation Act (POFMA) in 462–463; from repression to calibrated coercion in 464–465
Skocpol, T. 349

Smarsh, S. 416
Smith, N. 96
Smith, S. 161
Snapchat 39
Snow, R. P. 54
Snowden, E. 263
social conformity 315
social correction 552
social media 19; activism 522; alternative online political media (AOPM) and 169–175; American populism and 352; anti-vaxxers and 318; circulation of conspiracy theories and 305; corrections on 500; epistemic democracy and 362; Europeans' use of American 85; failures to regulate 414–415; fake news and (*see* fake news); fake news in 503; false information in social movements and 290–298; hate speech and 82–84, 86; in India; mediatisation of politics and 52; memes and memetic warfare and 272–273; misinformation in 498, 529; online harassment of journalists and 178–185; polarisation and 131–138; and populism nexus in Latin America 358–359; post-truth and 21, 102–108; post-truth identities and 315–317; proliferation of 560; proliferation of mis/disinformation by 39; public-facing 522; resilience to mis/disinformation and 42; responses to 23; rise of digital populism and 460–461; state-based repression and 292–294; Telegram Messenger and 285–286; in Turkey 386–394; youth movements in Russia and 282–283; *see also* computational propaganda; filter bubbles and echo chambers
social movements, false information in: as commodity 296–297; conclusions on 297–298; five theoretical lenses for 291–297; history of 290–291; misinformation and journalistic norms in coverage of protest and 297; as movement catalyst 291–292; as strategy of social movement repression 292–295; as weaponisation of free speech 295–296
social psychology 561
societal fragmentation 538
soft regulations 455–456
Solon, O. 414
sorting 134–135
South Africa 335, 340–341
Spencer, R. 87, 154–155
Spruyt, B. 431
Stalin, J. 254
Starbird, K. 172
Startin, N. 400
state-based domestic repression 292–294
Steiner, A. 55
Steininger, R. 93
Stoller, M. 415
#StopIslam 522, 523, 524, 525